What's New in *Delphi 2 Unleashed*

This edition of Delphi 2.0 contains a vast amount of new material. Here are some of the major new subjects covered in this edition of the book:

- **Win32 Programming:** An in-depth discussion of threads, multitasking, Win32 memory management, critical sections, mutexes, and memory-mapped files. The text helps you understand how the Windows 95 and Windows NT 32-bit architectures impact Delphi programming.

- **Windows API Programming:** How does the Windows API fit into a Delphi program? Examples show how to construct DLLs and executables entirely out of Windows API calls, without using the VCL. This section gives you a close look at the API that forms the basis for all Windows programming, and which underlies the structures at the heart of the VCL.

- **Internet Programming:** This part show how to write CGI applications using Delphi objects, and gives other techniques for tapping into the full power of the Web. This part of the book explains how you can create database programs that interact with users while they are signed on to your Web site.

- **Using the Component Object Model (COM):** This section shows how to construct objects that can be used by C++ programs, as well as how to access C++ objects inside Delphi programs. You can share these same objects with Visual Basic and other programming environments.

- **Using the Games SDK:** The Games SDK is written using COM, so its objects are fully accessible from inside a Delphi program. This book includes Mike Scott's interface files that enable you to access all the features of the DirectDraw API. Also included is a sample 3-D maze built into Delphi 2.0 using the Games SDK.

- **OLE Automation:** This part of the book shows how to write Automation clients and servers using the built-in Delphi objects, and how to write IDispatch interfaces so that you can access Ole Automation on your own terms. This text shows how you can control other programs from inside Delphi, and how you can write Automation servers that can be controlled by other programs.

- **Delphi Under Win32:** A lengthy chapter explains the new Delphi long strings and shows how they differ from PChars and from the 256-character short strings used in Delphi 16. The text also covers variants, variant arrays, and the impact that 32-bit programming has had on fundamental Delphi types such as integers and pointers.

- **The New Database Features:** Delphi 2.0 includes multi-record objects, a TDataModule object for storing nonvisual components such as TTable and TQuery, a Database Explorer, a Data Dictionary, new lookup combo boxes and list boxes, new grids that support colors and embedded combo boxes, a new filter and searching technology, as well as the new 32-bit Borland Database Engine. All of these features are explored in easy-to-use sample programs.

- **Much more:** There are many other new features in this edition of *Delphi Unleashed*. Sample programs on the CD show how to use form inheritance, the Delphi memory manager, the DllEntryPoint, cached updates, the TThread object, the new and improved TOleContainer object, and hundreds of other examples that show the right way to construct robust 32-bit programs.

Delphi 2.0 is an almost unbelievably powerful programming environment. In this book I try to look beneath the surface of Delphi to see how it works. You can use this knowledge to help you construct robust programs that take advantage of the full power of Windows NT and Windows 95.

On the CD are 15 chapters that were dropped from the text in the second edition of this book. These chapters include much of the information you need to get started using Delphi. All of the sample programs from the first edition of the book are also included on the CD.

This is a big book crammed with lots of information and hundreds of sample programs. I've tried to include the information you need to access the most powerful and advanced features of Delphi 2.0.

Delphi® 2
UNLEASHED

Charles Calvert

PUBLISHING

201 West 103rd Street
Indianapolis, IN 46290

This book is dedicated to the hard-core Pascal developers and team members who stayed with the product all these years and made the transition from BP7 to Delphi. In particular, I'm thinking of Jason Sprenger, Xavier Pacheco, Pat Ritchey, Anders Hejlsberg, Bill Weber, Ramin Halvietti, Steve Teixeira, Chuck Jazdzewski, Steve Trefethen, Richard Nelson, Allen Bauer, Zack Urlocker, Gary Whizin, Neil Rubenking, Jeff Duntemann, Danny Thorpe, Mark Edington, Gary Bennar, Kim, Julian, Gary, Lee and the other folks at Turbo Power, Nick Hodges, Scott Bussinger, Bob Ainsbury, David Intersimone, Art Hill, Rich Jones, Karl Loblein, Lar Mader, Dave McDermitt, J. W. Rider, Christine Sherman, Luk Vermeulen, Blake Watson, and many others.

Copyright © 1996 by Sams Publishing

Overview

Contents

Part VII   Multimedia and Games

Foreword

Delphi 2 Unleashed is a great way to learn all of the programming techniques that Delphi offers. Whether you're a seasoned Delphi programmer looking to get the latest tips and techniques of OLE for Delphi 2.0 or a newcomer learning database fundamentals, this book offers what you need to be productive, because it's written by someone who's worked with Delphi from the start.

I remember back in early 1993, Charlie came to see me because he was concerned about what was going on in Borland's languages group. Charlie was manning the tech support phones and had written two very successful books, *Turbo Pascal 101* and *Teach Yourself Windows Programming in 21 days* (published by Sams).

He wanted to know where we were going to take the technology in the future. "We've got to make it easier, Zack. It's too hard to program for Windows."

So I took Charlie aside and told him about a new product under development. It was so top-secret it didn't really have a name, and no one outside of a core group of developers knew about it. Sometimes we called it "Visual Foo" since we didn't have a name; a few months later we came up with the codename "Delphi," and it stuck.

Although Delphi 1.0 was still under development, Charlie joined the Developer Relations group at Borland to become a Delphi evangelist and guru. One of his goals was to make sure that we had a large number of third-party consultants, system integrators, and developers supporting Delphi when it was released. As a result, Charlie was involved with Delphi since its earliest incarnations and has breadth and depth of knowledge that puts him in a unique position as an instructor.

Before we shipped Delphi 1.0, preliminary versions of this book were used to train thousands of consultants, system integrators, and third-party developers worldwide. Charlie refined the material in a three-day seminar that he taught to audiences of programmers in Scotts Valley, Amsterdam, and Munich.

Charlie is also known to many developers from his Delphi technical presentations and tutorials at dozens of user groups and industry conferences such as Software Development and Comdex.

One of the things you'll notice as you read this book is that Charlie has a friendly style that is open and accessible. Charlie explains the fundamentals of Delphi programming as well as advanced topics without ever sounding condescending. Maybe it's all the time he's spent on the phones helping customers find and fix bugs in their code, or perhaps its the live experience of teaching audiences, but the end result is that throughout this book Charlie conveys a feeling of a one-on-one tutorial.

Charlie has worked closely with the development, quality assurance, and documentation teams responsible for creating Delphi. In the final months before Delphi 1.0 shipped, we called on Charlie to help write material that would be part of the database manual. He came through with information that has helped hundreds of thousands of customers understand how to build PC LAN and client/server database applications in Delphi. And just a few months prior to the release of Delphi 2.0, I called on Charlie again, this time begging for some material on OLE Automation. Charlie worked closely with Anders Hejlsberg, the chief architect of Delphi, to explain the inner workings of OLE automation. Charlie took a complex topic and made it approachable. He tells what you need to know to make it work using practical tips and clear examples. You'll find additional expanded material on OLE automation in this book.

Even if you have the first edition of this book, you'll find plenty of new material explaining how to take advantage of new Windows 95 and NT features such as OCXs and OLE automation, multi-threading, the Direct Draw API, COM (Common Object Model) objects, and new advanced data controls.

You'll enjoy learning to use Delphi 2.0 to create high-performance desktop and client/server applications. With Charlie's book you've got a guide to take you there.

–Zack Urlocker, Director of Delphi Product Management at Borland International, January 1996

Acknowledgments

Several Borland employees answered many questions for me while I was working on this book. My thanks to Steve Trefethen, Nimish Vora, Dan Daley, Jason Sprenger, Steve Teixeira, David Intersimone, Gary Whizin, Allen Bauer, Zack Urlocker, Scott Clinton, Lar Mader, Scott Frolich, and Bruneau Babet. In particular, I want to thank Danny Thorpe for several lengthy conversations in which he provided remarkable insights into complex subjects.

There are others who I work with day to day who were a big help to me. They include Karen Giles, Nan Borreson, CJ Martin, Lisa Coenen, Yolanda Davis, Nancy Collins, and Christine Sherman.

At Sams, Chris Denny, Angelique Brittingham, and Mary Inderstrodt were, as always, a tremendous help. Chris, Angelique, Mary, and I have worked together on several projects, and I owe them all a big debt of gratitude for their good work, patience, and perseverance.

My deepest and most heartfelt thanks, however, are reserved for my wife Margie, who has cheerfully endured a rather hectic year and a half in which I got way, way, way too much writing done. Talk about the man who went too far! I should perhaps also add a note of thanks to my cats Valentine and Rupert. As is often the case, Rupert is here, literally in my lap, as I write this, and Valentine (incredibly enough) chose this very moment to run across the keyboard, leaving his own cryptic message on the screen. And after I summarily deleted it, who can blame him if he's now waiting patiently at the door to be let out?

About the Author

Charles Calvert is the author of *Delphi Unleashed, Teach Yourself Windows 95 Programming in 21 Days* and *Turbo Pascal Programming 101* (published by Sams). He has worked as a journalist for *The Morton Journal* and as an English teacher at an extension of Centralia College in Washington. For the last several years, Charlie has worked at Borland International, where he is now manager in Developer Relations. He lives with his wife, Marjorie, in Santa Cruz, California.

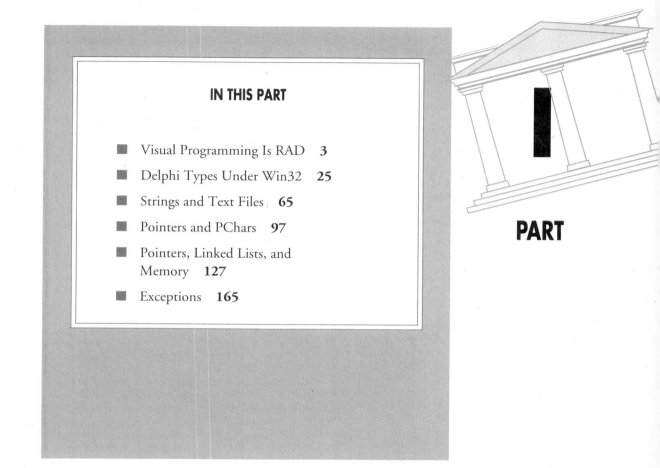

IN THIS PART

PART

Object Pascal

This section of the book covers several fundamental Object Pascal programming issues. It looks into some reasonably technical subject matter regarding arrays, pointers, strings, and files. Other matters covered in this section include new Delphi types and how some of the old types made the port to 32 bits.

Visual Programming Is RAD

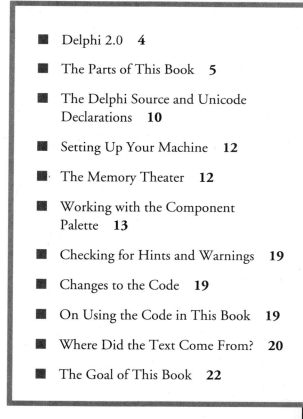

IN THIS CHAPTER

Welcome to the second edition of Delphi Unleashed. Over fifty percent of the material in this book is new, including new chapters on the Internet, the Windows API, database tools, COM objects, the Microsoft Games SDK, and Win32 programming.

Not all the material that comes with this package is evident from the pages you hold in your hands. There is also a CD loaded with megabytes of code and 15 chapters of text explaining the fundamentals of Object Pascal. These chapters were removed from the first edition of the book to make room for more advanced and up-to-date material. However, some of the chapters were favorites with readers, so they are included on the CD.

You will find that the text of the book is all about Windows 95 and Windows NT programming, whereas some of the chapters on disk address Windows 3.1 programming. Almost all the chapters on Delphi 2.0 cover intermediate or advanced material, whereas some of the chapters included only on the CD, cover material of interest to newcomers. As a result, many facets of the Delphi programming world are available to you in one large package that is loaded with information.

I have also called on three experts to write about the Internet, ReportSmith, and the Games SDK. These are subjects that interest me, but that I didn't have time to write about in my own words. As a result, you get four bonus chapters in this book from people who make their living working full-time in these cutting edge fields. I'll talk more about Ann Lynnworth, Mike Scott, and Andy Fearns later in this chapter, but their expert opinions and long professional experience should prove useful to most readers.

Delphi 2.0

Before beginning a discussion of the contents of this book, it is perhaps worth taking a moment to talk about Delphi 2.0. I will make this portion of the chapter very brief, as I'm sure you are already impressed with Delphi, or you wouldn't be interested in this text.

What's important to me about Delphi is not the fact that it has won so many awards, garnered so many kudos, or sold hundreds of thousands of copies. These things are nice, and they are part of what makes a product successful. However, Delphi's strongest features become apparent when one sees the way programmers react to daily use of a true object-oriented compiler. Serious programmers love Delphi because of its powerful, high performance compiler. It's a tool for professionals, for those who care about the quality of the products they use and make.

Once again, I don't want to simply list off all the great features of Delphi 2.0 because I don't think they are what's really important. You might be impressed by the Database Explorer, by Visual Form Inheritance, by the OCX support, and indeed these features are important. But they aren't the core of what makes Delphi great.

The best things about Delphi are its compiler, its superb object-oriented architecture, and its support for native components. Its key features are the simple elegance of Object Pascal itself; the power, size, and speed of its compiled code; and its ability to support every last nook and cranny of the Windows API.

The closer I get to the core of Delphi, the more impressed I am by its features. It's not the flashy things that you notice at first blush that make this product great, nor is it the esoteric features we show off at demos and trade shows. It's the core of the product that's important. The key elements are the 32-bit Windows API friendly compiler, the support for inheritance and polymorphism, and the support for reusable native components with their easy-to-use properties. These are the features that make Delphi great, and they are the ones that will be pushed to the fore, most often in this book.

The Parts of This Book

Delphi Unleashed is divided into eight parts:

- **Part I, "Object Pascal:"** The first part of this book is taken from the first edition of *Delphi Unleashed*. It is also probably the most pedestrian section in a wide-ranging and eclectic book. The first version of *Delphi Unleashed* painstakingly took you through all the elements of programming Object Pascal. I talked about types, about loops, about data structures—all the fundamental issues. The last few chapters of that section got into some fairly technical subject matter regarding arrays, pointers, strings, and files. These later, more technical chapters, are included in the first section of this book, along with some in-depth discussion of new Delphi types, and of how the old types made the port to 32 bits. An updated version of the original chapter on exceptions is also included in this section. All the old chapters that were cut appear in their original 16-bit form on the CD for this book. That way you don't miss anything, but you have printed copies of only the most challenging material from the original book.

- **Part II, "Win32:"** The second part of this book is about the Win32 operating systems. This includes a long look at multitasking, threading, and memory management. Specific information about mutexes, critical sections, virtual memory, heaps, memory-mapped files, and other Win32 programming issues are looked at both in the text and in sample programs.

- **Part III, "Windows API:"** The third part of the book delves into the Windows API. These chapters show you how to go beyond the VCL and construct executables and DLLs out of nothing but Windows API calls. The text also shows how the Windows API is used in the VCL, and how you can enhance VCL programs with the Windows API.

- **Part IV, "Databases:"** The fourth part of the book is about databases. After the theoretical issues explored in Parts II and III, these chapters help to ground the book with more concrete examples of how to perform specific tasks. This is the most "how-to" section of the book. It explores new features of Delphi, such as data modules, data dictionaries, lookups, filters, cached updates, and the new grids and multirecord objects. On a more theoretical note, the database material also explores what it means to create a relational database, and how Delphi's tools can be used to present relational databases to the user. The last chapter in this section is written by Andy Fearns. It gives you a highly professional, in-depth look at ReportSmith.

- ■ **Part V, "Objects:"** The fifth section of the text plunges into the heart of object-oriented programming. It includes chapters on inheritance, encapsulation, and polymorphism, as well as a description of how to create both visual and nonvisual components. This section, and the chapters on the Windows API, contain much of my favorite material.

- ■ **Part VI, "OLE and COM:"** The sixth section explores OLE and the COM object model. There are chapters on DDE, object linking and embedding, OLE automation, the method for implementing the Component Object Model in Delphi, and the Microsoft Games SDK. There is also some general discussion of OCXs, although this topic is not explored in depth.

- ■ **Part VII, "Multimedia and Games:"** The chapter on the Games SDK was written by multimedia expert Mike Scott. He was one of Delphi's earliest adopters, and he has proven his expertise in a number of settings, including construction of a popular Delphi WinG add-on.Creating multimedia programs with visual tools is the subject matter of the two chapters in this section of the book. The first multimedia chapter probably contains the easiest to understand material in this text. The second chapter in this section, on advanced multimedia, takes an in-depth look at the MCI interface to the Windows multimedia services. This chapter can be viewed as either a behind the scenes look at the code for the Delphi TMediaPlayer component, or an introduction to the techniques you need to write directly to the the most important Windows multimedia interface.

- ■ **Part VIII, "The Internet:"** The final section of the book, by guest author Ann Lynnworth, explores the Internet. Ann and business partner Michael Ax have used Delphi to create a series of Web-based tools that give you powerful access to some of the most advanced features in contemporary programming. Ann shares many of her technical secrets with you and gives you a working copy of her code so you can see how to program the Internet.

You might notice that this book is loaded toward the middle and the end, rather than toward the front. A lot of programming books put their best chapters up front, which is not the case with this particular book. Instead, I start with some general chapters on Object Pascal and then plunge into some of the more interesting chapters as the book wears on. The book is arranged this way on purpose, and it is best to read it from beginning to end. You should remember, however, that some of the most interesting material is found in the last third of the book.

Overall, this text is aimed at readers who are looking for insight into how Delphi and Windows are constructed and who want to know something of the theory behind this architecture. There are sections of the book that have a "how-to" structure to them, but this is not the main thrust of the book. As a rule, I have tried to stick to subjects that I feel are of general interest to a broad range of Delphi programmers.

I'm primarily interested in teaching deep-rooted knowledge that applies to a broad range of situations, rather than specific techniques for resolving particular problems. My feeling is that if you understand how and why Delphi works, you will always be able to find the solution to your current programming challenge. It's a little like the old saying about it being better to teach someone how to fish, than to merely give them a fish. I want this book to be more than a list of tips and tricks—I want it to show how to think about, design, and construct Delphi programs.

> **NOTE**
>
> You should also look on the CD for additional programs that might not be included in the text. As a rule, I try to organize all the related code in the appropriate chapters. For instance, if I have code on COM programming that I never got a chance to write up, I put it in the same place on the CD where I store the standard COM programs mentioned in the text. Check the ReadMe file on the CD for additional information.
>
> Some readers may have a legitimate need to get in touch with me. If you have pressing questions about this text or its accompanying code, you can reach me on CompuServe at 76711,533, on AOL at CHARLIECAL, and on the Internet at ccalvert@wpo.borland.com. Additional information might appear at www.borland.com or at the Sams Web site, http://www.mcp.com. On CompuServe, type GO SAMS to reach a site where information related to this book might appear. I can supply updates and bug fixes if you write me directly. If key updates or fixes need to be published, I will put them in a file called UNL2UP.ZIP and place them online at the various sites.
>
> If you have general technical questions about Delphi, you can get support online at:
>
> **Compuserve:**
> ```
> GO DELPHI
> ```
> **Internet:**
> ```
> comp.lang.pascal.delphi.misc
> comp.lang.pascal.delphi.components
> comp.lang.pascal.delphi.databases
> comp.lang.pascal
> comp.lang.pascal.borland
> alt.lang.delphi
> alt.comp.lang.borland-delphi
> ```
> There is also support in various sections on AOL.

The Windows API Chapters

One of the great ironies of an environment like Delphi is that it is a great boon to beginners but can occasionally confuse experienced programmers. In particular, Delphi makes some kinds of programming so easy that it can appear to put roadblocks in the way of those who want to see beneath the surface of the environment.

In particular, the VCL has a tendency to hide the exact implementation of certain objects, thereby preventing people from changing the code's default behavior. For instance, Delphi makes it so easy to put up a list box that it's hard to see how you can use some of the fancy Windows API messages that enable you to create columns in a list box or access other advanced features.

The point isn't that Delphi's tools don't work. The issue is that sometimes they work all too well! Delphi presents such a smooth, powerful, interface that it's hard to see that right beneath the surface is the key to Delphi programming excellence: the Windows API!

One of the goals of this book is to look beyond the VCL to the underlying API code. The VCL is built on the Windows API; and if you want to understand the VCL, you also have to understand the Windows API.

There is only one Windows API function that you cannot call from Delphi, and that routine's functionality is duplicated both in the Windows API itself and also internally in Delphi. In other words, there is nothing involving Windows programming that you can't do with Delphi. But to know how to do it, you have to know the Windows API.

> **NOTE**
>
> The Windows API function you can't call from Delphi is called `wvsprintf`. The Windows API function that duplicates its functionality is called `wsprintf`, and the internal Object Pascal call that duplicates its functionality is called `Format`. There are no other Windows API functions you can't call from Delphi. You can, of course, handle all the Windows API messages from inside Delphi.

The point here is that besides Delphi's wonderful strengths as a RAD tool and as a database tool, it also gives you full access to the Windows API. It can do this while producing code that is similar in quality to the code produced by the Borland C++ compiler and yet sometimes smaller and more compact. In fact, Delphi and C++ use the same compiler. Each language parses the syntactical elements of the code and then passes a series of tokens on to the same 32-bit optimizing compiler.

In short, Delphi is an excellent tool to use if you want to make full use of the Windows API. The only problem with this scenario is that many Delphi programmers don't know how to dig beneath the surface of the Delphi RAD tools to use the full power of the Windows API. One of the major goals of this book is to remedy that situation.

There is an entire section of this book, six chapters long, that digs into the Windows API. The section on Win32 also presents many of the key features that need to be understood by Windows programmers. After reading these eight chapters, you will understand how to use Delphi to create tiny executables that contain nothing but Windows API code. These programs are about one-tenth the size of a standard Delphi RAD program. You will also see how to create tiny DLLs using the Windows API.

Most importantly, however, the emphasis on the Windows API in this book enables you to dig beneath the surface of Delphi and tap into its real power. If you want to create sophisticated Delphi components, you have to know the Windows API. If you want to stretch Delphi to its limits, using the full capability of both the RAD tools and the powerful Windows 95 and Windows NT operating systems, you have to know the Windows API.

If you understand the Windows API, everything else is possible for you. If you don't understand the Windows API, you will keep running into brick walls.

Making the Best of This Book

One of the key things you need to understand when reading this text is that it is not a cookbook for creating Delphi executables in the fastest, simplest manner. There are plenty of examples of that sort of thing in this book, but there are also many long examples where I do things the hard way, rather than the easy way.

Why make things harder than they have to be?

Well, the goal here is to dig beneath the surface and show you how Delphi works and, sometimes, how the Windows API works. Rather than showing you the simplest way to do something, I often go to great lengths to rip back the surface of Delphi and show you the complicated machinery that lies beneath the surface of this smooth and well-designed machine.

The theory is that if you learn the basis on which Delphi is built, you can take the best possible advantage of Delphi's high-level tools. At first, this technique is bound to make you feel as though you are getting farther from your goal, rather than closer. However, once you begin to mine the book's ore, you will find that you can apply your knowledge to daily programming tasks and complete them faster and more artfully.

It's a little like getting in shape before a sport's season starts. What you want to do is go out there and play ball. It's frustrating when you're told that you need to run laps or perform repetitive drills first. However, if you take the time to learn some key skills, you find that you play ball much better than your competitors who never took the time to analyze the nature of their game.

The problem with the sporting analogy, of course, is that it's often boring to run drills. Digging into the heart of the Windows API, however, is anything but boring. Delphi and Windows are two of the most fascinating binary constructions currently available for exploration. The more you sift through these subjects, the more interesting they become. Many parts of this book plunge relentlessly into the heart of these complex topics, enabling you to mine rich ores of knowledge that are both fascinating and useful.

Other passages of this book are stocked with simple, useful techniques for building Delphi applications. That is not, however, the core intent of this text. My main goal is not so much to write an advanced book, and certainly not to write a difficult book. Instead, I want to write a revealing book. I want to bore beneath the surface of Windows and Delphi and show you how and why they work. Armed with that wealth of knowledge, you will find that tasks that previously seemed complicated or beyond your reach are suddenly easy to accomplish.

In particular, you will find that there are many fewer occasions when you simply can't accomplish a goal. Whereas before you might have hit a brick wall, after reading this book you should have enough theoretical knowledge to know how to solve many problems that used to present an opaque and confusing surface to you. If you understand the theory behind the tools, you will understand what they can and can't do, and how to go about reaching your goal.

On Reading the Rest of This Chapter

Except for some closing paragraphs at the end of this chapter, I'm finished with the overview sections that introduce you to the material in this book. The rest of this chapter is divided into three sections that cover the following material:

- Some general, nontechnical issues that I want all readers to be aware of before tackling the core technical chapters.
- A little hands-on work with the Component Palette. Everyone who works with Delphi needs to understand the Component Palette, and the best way to get up to speed is to take the thing apart and see how it's put together.
- A return to some relatively trivial technical and nontechnical issues that are still significant enough to be of general interest to readers of this book.

The last section of the chapter returns to the general introductory tone found in the preceding sections, and then you will be ready to plunge into the main part of the book. In general, you should view Chapter 1 as something of an introductory chapter with only one technical section in it. Nevertheless, there is material here that everyone ought to know, so I get it out right at the start so that no one will miss it when reading the technical chapters.

The Delphi Source and Unicode Declarations

It's now time to narrow the focus ever so slightly and start talking about some particulars.

Delphi Unleashed makes many references to the source code to the VCL. I strongly recommend that you buy a copy of the VCL if one did not ship with your copy of Delphi. Almost the entire source to the VCL is available to you from Borland for a very reasonable price. If you want to do serious work with Delphi, you have to have a copy of the source code.

You can buy the source code directly from Borland, or you can probably also obtain it from the Programmers Shop (1-800-421-8006) or Programmer's Paradise (1-908-389-9228). Be sure to check that the source did not already come with your copy of Delphi. In particular, if you have FORMS.PAS, CLASSES.PAS, WINDOWS.PAS, GRAPHICS.PAS, DB.PAS, SYSTEM.PAS, SYSUTILS.PAS, or other related files, you either have the source to Delphi or some portion of the source.

It is also possible that you have some files that have an INT extension on your system. Look for CLASSES.INT, for instance. This file would have the interface to CLASSES.PAS, but not the implementation. Having the INT files is useful, but not as good as having the full source.

Before I came to work for Borland I went through a period where I learned how to use Turbo Vision without ever getting a copy of the source to that object-oriented library. If I had bothered to get the source, I would have saved myself endless hours of trouble. Many of the answers I sought were right there in the source code. All I needed to do was spend a relatively small amount of money, and endless hours of frustrating (but rather entertaining) hacking could have been avoided.

Of course, it is possible that you literally cannot afford to buy the VCL. If that's the case, then okay, you can't afford to buy it. You will survive. In that situation, look hard for all the INT files on your system, and spend the time to learn what they mean. It's not as good as having the source, but it's better than having nothing.

In general, however, I expect the readers of this book to have access to the VCL source. I'm going to dig into some issues fairly deeply, and the conversation is much easier to follow if you have the source!

When reading the Delphi source code, and particularly the Delphi units that list functions imported from the operating system, remember that many declarations have to be made twice, once for ANSI and once for Unicode:

```
function mciGetDeviceIDA(pszDevice: PAnsiChar): MCIDEVICEID; stdcall;
function mciGetDeviceIDW(pszDevice: PWideChar): MCIDEVICEID; stdcall;
function mciGetDeviceID(pszDevice: PChar): MCIDEVICEID; stdcall;
```

The calls shown here are from MMSYSTEM.PAS. Notice that the `mciGetDeviceID` function is declared three times. Once it is declared as used in ANSI code, once as used in Unicode, and the third time as used in standard Delphi applications. The first and third declarations are syntactically identical in this case, the only difference being that the first has an A appended to its name. You should get used to seeing declarations that have an A appended to them in ANSI form and a W appended to them to show that they are the Wide, Unicode declarations.

The important point to remember in this regard is that Unicode takes double-wide characters where ANSI takes only single-byte characters. In particular, Unicode uses a 16-bit value where ANSI uses only an 8-bit value. This allows Unicode to use a much wider range of characters—65,000 in all. ANSI characters, on the other hand, are limited to only 256 possible elements.

In general, the only time you want to use Unicode is when you are working with COM or OLE programs. The Delphi VCL is not Unicode-aware at this time.

Despite the brief discussion of Unicode that appears here, the main thing I want to communicate in this section is that readers of this book will be better off if they have a copy of the VCL source. It is available from Borland or from third-party venders such as the Programmer's Shop or Programmer's Paradise.

Setting Up Your Machine

The code in this book relies on several units that ship on the accompanying CD. In particular, you will find that STRBOX.PAS and MATHBOX.PAS are referenced frequently in the programs used in this book. These units are kept in the UNITS subdirectory found on the CD. You should copy all these files onto you hard disk and then reference their location in the Tools | Options | Library | Library Path entry found from the Delphi main menu. For instance, on my system I appended the following path on the already existing entries in the Library Path edit control: C:\UNLEASH2\UNITS. I then made sure that all the units from the UNITS subdirectory on the CD were copied to this directory. The path to this directory will almost certainly differ on your machine.

Please note that I am not the person who writes the install program that places these files on your disk. I do not have a CD burner at home, so I am not responsible for the exact way the CD is organized, nor for the way its install program works. As a result, I do not know the root directory that is created for the programs accompanying this book by the install program found on your CD. In other words, the path on your system might be c:\delun\units, or c:\delphiun\units, or c:\delphi unleashed\units, or perhaps something else altogether. The people who work on the install program for the CD are experts who do a wonderful job, but they work independently from me. All the code on the CD is, with one or two exceptions, written by me or the other authors mentioned earlier.

The Memory Theater

Throughout this book I often refer to something called the Memory Theater. This is a metaphor I use for describing RAM and certain other aspects of the computer. The memory theater is not a perfect metaphor by any means, but it can help give you a way of visualizing what goes on inside a computer.

The basic idea behind the Memory Theater is that the CPU sits on a stage in front of a huge amphitheater. The amphitheater contains many seats, which are analogous to the RAM inside a computer. Each byte in RAM is analogous to one member of the audience.

This is an audience participation theater, and the CPU is constantly asking the members of the audience to remember certain facts. If the CPU wants to work with an Integer value, it asks four members of the audience to remember the Integer for a while. Four members of the audience are required because there are four bytes in an Integer. If the CPU wants to work with a Word value, only two members of the audience are required. For working with ShortStrings, the number of participants is 256, and so on.

Once again, the memory theater is not a perfect analogy, but it takes the events that go on inside a computer out of the realm of the abstract and makes them tangible. It's easy to imagine people sitting in the seats of a theater. Everyone can grasp that concept. It's harder, however, to understand what it means to manipulate a byte of memory in RAM. Therefore, for the sake of making the concepts introduced in this book as clear and simple as possible, I introduce a small conceit called the Memory Theater. If you want a detailed look at this analogy, view the basic chapters on types that come on the CD.

Working with the Component Palette

The text now turns a bit more technical, as I take a quick look at the Component Palette. This is the only hands-on section of this chapter. After you complete it, I return to the kind of material shown in the last few sections. That is, I review relatively nontechnical matters that I deem of general interest to the reader.

The Component Palette lies very much at the heart of Delphi. It's only reasonable to ask, then, what exactly does it do?

NOTE

The Component Palette is the place on the upper-right side of the Delphi IDE where you can snag TEdit, TButton, TTable and other controls before dragging them onto the main form. If this concept doesn't make sense to you, you might want to consider backing away from this book for a bit and reading a more introductory text. There are, in fact, many more introductory chapters on the CD of this book, and also at your local computer book store.

In general, I don't regard this as a particularly difficult book. Almost all the key technologies in Delphi are made readily available to you. As a result, there is no code in this book that is brutally difficult to understand. However, the text does assume that you are already up and running with Delphi and that you know some programming basics.

By the way, the word IDE stands for Integrated Development Environment, and it is the term I use to refer to the complex of Windows you see when you load Delphi into memory. The IDE includes the toolbar, Component Palette, Object Inspector, editor, integrated debugger, the watch window, and anything else you access from Delphi proper. The Delphi IDE stands in contrast to the Delphi command-line tools such as DCC32.EXE or BRCC32.EXE.

One good way to come to terms with the Component Palette is to take it out of the environment and see what you have left once it's gone. To do this, first make sure Delphi is shut down, then open up the Windows Explorer and find the CMPLIB32.DCL file in the `..\DELPHI 2.0\BIN` subdirectory. Use the Explorer to move this file out of the BIN subdirectory and into a subdirectory you create called BAK.

> **NOTE**
>
> I caution you to proceed with extreme care whenever you work with CMPLIB32.DCL. This file is vital to Delphi, and you should always keep at least one good copy of the file in a subdirectory on your hard drive. This is a large file, so you might not be able to put it on a floppy without first zipping it up. If you work on a laptop, you should be absolutely certain that you keep a backup of this file on your hard drive. If worst comes to worst, you can always reinstall Delphi, or simply copy CMPLIB32.DCL off the install CD.
>
> There is some chance that this file is not called CMPLIB32.DCL on your system. To check this, first open Delphi, then choose Component | Install from the menu. The Library filename is listed at the top of the Install Components dialog box.

After shutting down Delphi and moving CMPLIB32.DCL into the BAK subdirectory, you should then launch Delphi. You will get an error message saying that Delphi can't find or load CMPLIB32.DCL. Don't let this worry you. Just click the OK button and proceed.

If you try to compile a default Delphi project under these circumstances, you will get an error of one kind or another, probably one reading: `File Not Found: 'Unit1.DFM'`. To remedy this situation, bring up the Project Manager and remove, without saving, UNIT1.PAS from your project. Go to Tools | Options | Preferences and make sure you have not chosen to Autosave your projects. You don't want to try to save this file. Select View | Project Source so you can take a look at the DPR file for the program.

Now modify the DPR file for your program so it looks like this:

```
program Project1;

uses
  SysUtils;

begin
  WriteLn('Creeds and schools in abeyance');
  ReadLn;
end.
```

Go to the Project | Options | Linker menu choice and select Generate Console Application. Now close the Project Options dialog box and, if you like, you can also remove the uses clause from your program. (My copy of the Delphi IDE gets flustered if my main file doesn't have a uses clause.)

Now compile and run your application. You will see that it pops up a small console application in a DOS box. In the box you see a brief quotation from Walt Whitman's "Song of Myself." If you want, you can open up a stand-alone DOS box and run this program from the command prompt.

Don't let the appearance of this program deceive you. It's not a DOS program; it's a full 32-bit Windows program that runs from the command prompt. If you want, you can add Windows to the uses clause and call MessageBox from this application:

```
program Project1;

uses
  Windows;

begin
  MessageBox(0, 'Test balloon!', 'Hello from the command line!', mb_ok);
end.
```

You can also allocate huge arrays of over 64 KB in applications of this type. It is true 32-bit code.

What has this tiny example demonstrated? Two key things:

- You can't do any visual programming without the Component Palette.
- You can, however, compile and run an application.

In particular, you can see that the Component Palette has nothing to do with Delphi's compiler. This is a good thing. It's a sign of integrity. I would have a hard time trusting a programming environment that was so intimately wedded to its visual tools that it could not run without them. You want the sense that something solid lies at the heart of your programming tool, and, in this case, you can see that Delphi's world class compiler is still there even if the visual tools are absent. This is the same compiler that drives Borland C++ 4.52 and Borland C++ 5.0. It's as good a compiler as you will find anywhere on the market, and it was designed by one of the best minds in the computer industry.

Re-Creating CMPLIB32.DCL

Now that you have seen how to remove CMPLIB32.DCL from the environment, the next step is to see how to put it back in place. One simple way to do this is to simply copy CMPLIB32.DCL from the BAK subdirectory you created earlier into the BIN subdirectory. Now choose Component | Open Library from the menu and select the CMPLIB32.DCL file. Click the OK button and everything is back to normal. This is how you should proceed if anything ever causes any damage to your CMPLIB32.DCL file. (Remember that if you don't have the file in a BAK subdirectory, you can still retrieve it from the install CD.)

In this particular case, however, it might be more educational to re-create CMPLIB32.DCL from scratch, rather than simply recopying the file onto your hard drive. There are several reasons why it is a good thing to know how to do this, not the least of which is that it can help you if you are working off a laptop and get in a fix miles away from your install disk. (Actually, this has never happened to me, but I live in such healthy fear of it happening that I made sure I knew how to proceed if the worst should occur! I'm showing this to you now, however, not as an emergency measure, but as an insight into how Delphi works.)

To get started, choose Component | Install from the menu. Make sure the search path points to your LIB subdirectory:

```
C:\Program Files\Borland\Delphi 2.0\lib
```

Set the Library filename equal to the name you want to assign to your new library:

```
c:\Program Files\Borland\Delphi 2.0\bin\mylib.dcl
```

You can call it CMPLIB32.DCL if you like, or give it a new filename if you think you might want to keep it around. It is, in fact, possible that you will want to keep the file because Delphi lets you custom craft Library files that have special uses.

> **NOTE**
>
> I don't really recommend installing Delphi into the preceding path, but my version of the product installed itself there by default. On my main machine, I moved Delphi into the C:\DELPHI32 subdirectory. To move the product, it's best to uninstall first from the Control Panel, then reinstall into the new subdirectory. This is not a pressing issue, however, and you probably shouldn't bother moving Delphi at this particular stage of the game.

Click the Add button and browse into the `..\DELPHI 2.0\LIB` subdirectory and add STDREG.PAS, or STDREG.DCU, to your library. The Install Components dialog box should now look as it does in Figure 1.1.

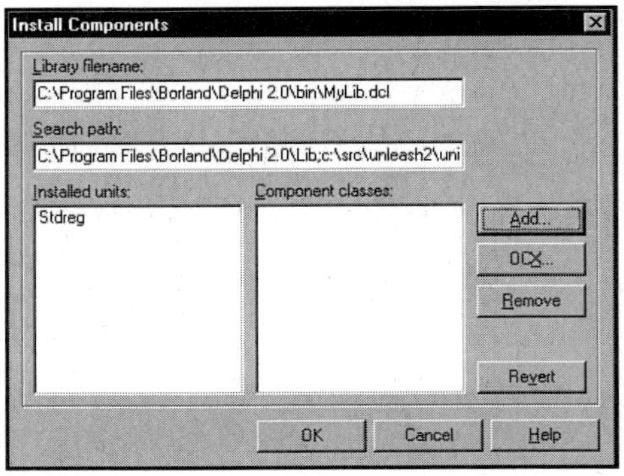

FIGURE 1.1.

The Install Components dialog box as it appears when you are first creating a library from scratch.

After you click the OK button, Delphi huffs and puffs in the background for a while as it works on compiling your library. When it's finished, you should see the Standard, Additional, and Win95 pages of the Component Palette back in place and more or less in working order. (It's not important if your version of Delphi has different pages in STDREG.PAS—all that matters is that you are seeing some of the core pages from the Component Palette. See Figure 1.2 to see how this looks on my system.)

FIGURE 1.2.

The Component Palette when only a few of the standard components are installed.

Go back to the Windows Explorer now, and take a look at MYLIB.DCL, or whatever file you have created. On my system, it's about 654 KB in size, which is considerably less than half the size of the standard CMPLIB32.DCL file that ships with Delphi.

Go ahead and drop a few components on the form designer and then compile and run your application. Does it compile any faster when the library file is smaller? On my system, there is a bit less swapping and a little faster response, but the result might be more significant if you are working on a system where memory is particularly tight.

Feel free to experiment at this point. You could, for instance, add the SYSREG.PAS file and see what new components are registered by that module. Next, you might want to add the DBREGS.PAS file, which contains the database tools.

At this point, you might be curious about what's to be found inside each of these *XXX*REG.PAS files. If you have the source, open them up, and you will find that they each contain one key method called Register. Here is an excerpt from STDREG.PAS:

```
RegisterComponents(LoadStr(srStandard), [TMainMenu, TPopupMenu, TLabel,
   TEdit, TMemo, TButton, TCheckBox, TRadioButton, TListBox, TComboBox,
   TScrollBar, TGroupBox, TRadioGroup, TPanel]);
```

This line of code registers most of the controls found on the Standard page of the Component Palette. If you want, you might try experimenting a little here and commenting out all but this one set of lines from the Register Procedure. Now choose Component | Install, and remove every other unit from the library except for STDREG.PAS. When you are done, you will have a very stripped-down library file, but it is still fairly large because a good chunk of VCL just sits in the background doing grunt work.

The point here is simply that CMPLIB32.DCL is not a mysterious entity. It's a relatively comprehensible chunk of code over which you have complete control, down to almost the lowest level. If you think your development process will benefit from it, you should go ahead and create a series of custom Component Palettes for use in different circumstances, or for use by different teams in your company. Customize these palettes to your heart's content. The developers of Delphi want you to be able to do this; they went to considerable effort to make it easy for you to gain control over the Component Palette.

> **NOTE**
>
> Before leaving this section, don't forget to restore the original CMPLIB32.DCL file, if you so desire, and to remove any comments that you don't want lingering in the STDREG.PAS file. If all else fails, simply reinstall Delphi.
>
> In truly desperate situations you can use the Add / Remove programs applet from the Control Panel to remove Delphi, making sure that all Delphi-related files are taken off your system. Check the Software section of HKEY_LOCAL_MACHINE in the registry. Make sure no references to Delphi are left. Then try a reinstall.
>
> I have found it's best never to save any of my own source files in the Delphi 2.0 directory. That area is for Delphi, and you should create a separate area for your own files. That way you can totally delete the Delphi 2.0 directory without affecting your own files.
>
> If you have a CD, it's relatively painless to let the install program churn away in the background while you go take a break. There is no reason why anything I have outlined in this section should damage your system, but just in case the worst happens, I want to be sure you know how to put things back together. The number one safety tip when working with Delphi, however, is to be sure to back up your library file!

Remember that the Component Palette is the place to turn if you need to add third-party tools to Delphi. Mike Scott's work with the Games SDK requires that you do this, and at one point in the book I have you add a few components to the environment. One of them, called TFileIterator, plays an especially important role in some key programs found in this book. The salient point here is that if you understand how the Component Palette works, you can always add a few new third-party components when needed.

That's all I want to say about the Component Palette. As with many portions of this book, I have dealt more with the theory behind this tool than with specific implementations. Some readers might want to now construct component libraries that are tailored to database work, or to graphics work, or maybe one library for each chore. Or perhaps you will never want to play with the Component Palette again. The point is to understand the tool and to dig in and see what it can do for you.

Checking for Hints and Warnings

I am now returning to the series of general interest points that I want all readers of this book to know about before they hit the hard core material. Some of these points are not particularly earth shattering, but I want to be sure everyone knows these facts before attempting the more complex subjects.

Delphi enables you to compile code that checks for minor programming errors that are not fatal, but that might cause trouble or waste clock cycles. To get this kind of error checking, you should select the Project | Options | Compiler menu item and select both Show Hints and Show Warnings. There is no necessity that you do this, but it is very good programming practice.

> **NOTE**
>
> While I'm talking about important aspects of the IDE, I might mention that on the Run menu is a choice called Program Reset. You can often use this option when you accidentally create a program that locks up on you. This terminates the errant program.

Changes to the Code

One of the most looked-for changes to the Object Pascal language is the introduction of a new type of comment. You can now comment single lines of code by inserting two forward slashes:

```
j := SecretOfUniverse;   // Call very high level function
```

For many programmers this might not be of great account, but it's one of my favorite new features in the compiler. Perhaps it's my background in C/C++, but I find these kinds of comments handsome, easy to write, and easy to read. Old hands at Object Pascal might be surprised when they find this syntax in my code, so I mention it here to prepare the unwary!

On Using the Code in This Book

You should always feel free to use any of the code in this book in your own programs. The book is published so that you can learn from it and reuse it if you want. What you can't do is use the code as the basis for an article or a book. If you want to show other people how some feature in Delphi works, then you need, within reason, to create your own examples and explain them in your own words. The point is that you can use the code in this book as the primary, or central, element in your own products.

Of course, some general-purpose routines get passed around from programmer to programmer and don't really belong to anyone anymore. Almost all the routines in STRBOX.PAS, MATHBOX.PAS, UTILBOX.PAS, and so forth, belong in this category. Feel free to use any of these routines as you see fit. It would not be right, however, to take one of these units wholesale, or in large part, and include it in a book on Delphi.

If you want to use this book in an academic or corporate setting, you should feel free to do so, as long as you are buying copies of the book for the people you are teaching. Don't just copy chapters from the book and hand the copied pages out to your classes.

This might seem like an unusual section to include in an opening chapter of a book, but I get a surprisingly large number of questions along these lines. The key point to remember is that if you are writing your own programs, you can use any of the code from this book as you see fit. I wouldn't want you to release one of the programs unmodified under your own name, but you can use the code in your programs without concern for copyright issues, as long as you are not another author selling the same wares that I sell. I publish the code because I want other programmers, professional and hobbyists, to use it. That's why it's there. I'm in the business of supplying information. It's both avocation and vocation.

Where Did the Text Come From?

This is the second edition of *Delphi Unleashed*. However, this is a somewhat unusual second edition for several reasons.

Considerably less than half the material in this book is from the first version of *Delphi Unleashed*. That's unusual for a second edition. Usually a second edition keeps most of the material from the first edition, updates it a little, and maybe adds a few new chapters. This is especially true of books that were as successful in their first edition as this one. Why change a book if it is already a success?

This book was very heavily rewritten. This is due not so much to the fact that Delphi 2.0 is so different from Delphi 1.0 as that there was a need to include more advanced material under this particular title. You will find many new chapters in this book, most written by me, but a few written by other authors. These additional authors were brought in to lend their expertise to this venture. There was no problem finding enough text of my own to fill the book— I simply thought it would be a good idea to bring in additional material. It makes the book stronger.

A few of the chapters in this book are rewritten versions of chapters that appeared in my book about C Windows API programming called *Teach Yourself Windows 95 Programming in 21 Days*. Needless to say, most of those chapters had to be heavily rewritten before they could be included in a book about Object Pascal.

Overall, this book contains an unusually large amount of totally new material for a second edition. As I said earlier, the reason for including this new material was simply to raise the bar, to provide material for those readers who are interested in advanced programming issues. It's not my way, however, to write a book that focuses solely on the most advanced, most obscure material. I tried to find subject matter that is of general interest to all readers but that is not likely to be covered in books aimed at beginning or intermediate programmers.

For those who miss the material that was cut, and for those who wish for more fundamental information about the basics of Delphi programming, I have put all the chapters that were cut from this edition on the CD. There are probably about 400–500 of these pages. The material is in Word 6.0 format, which can be read inside the WordPad program that ships with Windows 95.

As a rule, the chapters on disk have not been updated for Windows 95 or NT, but nearly all the programs discussed in those chapters should compile fine in Delphi 2.0. Delphi 2.0 is completely backwards-compatible with Delphi 1.0, so there is no reason why the code from the first edition wouldn't work under Delphi 2.0. Some of the discussion about types is a little outdated, but the second chatper of this book, "Delphi Types Under Win32," talks about how the types changed from Delphi 1.0 to Delphi 2.0.

For many readers of the first edition, the early chapters of *Delphi Unleashed*, the ones that are now on the CD, were the best parts of this book. As a result, I think the quality of the material on the CD is every bit as good as the material between the covers of the book.

Perhaps you should really think of this book as having overflowed onto the CD. If it were possible to bind that much material into one volume, the publishers would have done so, and the scope of this book would have been simply enormous. Indeed, there is a tremendous amount of material in this package, ranging from relatively easy-to-understand material for beginners, all the way through advanced material on the Windows API and COM objects. In fact, if you include the material on the CD, this might be the largest single volume computer book on your shelves.

The Other Authors

The scope of this book is considerably improved by the addition of other writers who have areas of expertise different from my own, or who were able to bring their considerable intelligence to bear on subjects that I never would have had time to tackle.

I'm delighted with the work that all the authors have done for this volume. Andy Fearns did great work with ReportSmith, a subject on which I am definitely not an expert. It's clear from early on in his chapter that he knows the material cold, and that his professional experience has taught him to explore some of the most powerful and interesting aspects of this great product.

ReportSmith is a great tool, especially if you are working in a large corporation that processes vast quantities of data. ReportSmith is not tailored for small tables or small chores, although it performs them with excellence. Its real area of expertise is as an industrial-strength tool that can tackle huge jobs with relative ease. If you have a smaller program that works with relatively small data sets, then you might use the TQuickReports object that ships with Delphi. However, if you have a big job to do, and need a powerful and easy-to-use tool to complete the job, you should read Andy's excellent chapter on ReportSmith. Andy Fearns has the experience and technical expertise to lead you through some fairly grueling projects, and I'm deeply indebted to him for bringing his expertise to this book.

Ann Lynnworth is one of the more talented, and if she'll forgive me, unusual people I have met in the computer industry. No one who meets her is ever likely to forget her. She has the power to hold large audiences in the palm of her hand, and to bring laughter and goodwill everywhere she goes. She was a very early adopter of both Delphi and the Internet, and she managed to leverage both technologies into a thriving business called HREF tools. She and her business partner, Michael Ax, have a considerable store of technological tips that they share with you.

Mike Scott is from Scotland. He has become a well-known expert on graphics and multimedia technology. His enthusiasm shows through in his chapter, and his technical expertise is beyond question. In fact, Mike is one of those programmers whose code has formed the basis for many other professional programming projects. There are just a few people in the industry with his level of expertise, and he fortunately is generous enough to share his knowledge with all of us. I have learned a lot from his code over the years, and so have many other programmers. He's an expert that the experts turn to when they need advice.

The Goal of This Book

Let me emphasize one last time that the goal of this book is not just to show you how to do a particular job as quickly and easily as possible, but to help you become a better programmer. To get the most out of this text, you have to be interested in the theory behind Windows and behind Delphi. I aim to look beyond the surface of these tools to see how they were made and why they were made that way.

Programming is an exciting profession, but it is also a confusing one. Here's a list of questions I find myself asking on my worst days:

- Why didn't that work?
- Why can't I do this? Isn't it allowed?
- Why do I have to do things this way?
- Isn't there a better way to do this?
- Is this possible? Can it be done at all?

- Why did this technique work under one set of circumstances but not under the current set of circumstances?
- Is it really legal to do this, or am I just getting away with something?

These are the kinds of questions I ask when I don't understand the way a technology works. The only way to get these kinds of questions answered is to dig beneath the surface and find out how the tools I'm using are put together! Only then can I unleash the full potential inside both the product and myself.

Some programmers are born with phenomenal skills. They have brains that work like finely tuned clocks. Most of us will never be as good as these extremely gifted men and women. However, there is a second way to become a very good programmer, and that is to learn how the system works and why it works.

If you know how to do a particular programming chore, you can get a particular job done. If you understand why Windows and Delphi work, and the principles upon which they are based, then you can figure out how to do anything that involves Delphi and Windows. One approach teaches you how to perform a particular list of actions; the second approach teaches you the skills you need to figure out how to do anything.

This book is in the second school of thought. Much of it is about the theory behind Windows and the theory behind Delphi. I have written this kind of book because I believe the most practical way to become a good programmer is to understand how the operating system itself works, and how Delphi is put together.

Maybe a short story from my life will help illustrate this point. When I first came to work at Borland's technical support department, I knew a lot about how to program in Turbo Pascal. I quickly learned, however, that simply memorizing a list of facts or techniques was not enough. The phone was going to ring, and someone was going to ask me a question about a tool that could manipulate the entire PC. There were too many facts to hope to memorize. I had to know how Windows worked, how DOS worked, how protected mode worked, how Turbo Vision worked, how OWL worked, how assembly language programming worked, and so forth. There was no way to memorize that much information.

I survived because I learned from the best programmers at Borland, from people who are now almost all on Object Pascal or C/C++ research and development. What they taught me was not how to perform a particular action, but why the computer worked as it did. Once I understood how memory was constructed, and why it was constructed that way, I could answer any question about memory and pointers. Sometimes I had to do a little work first and then call the person back, but I was never clueless about memory issues because I understood how the system worked.

The same applied to object-oriented programming. The key was not to memorize a list of commands, but to understand the theory behind objects. Once I knew what a VMT was and how virtual methods are called, OOP ceased to be a mystery, and I could simply think in terms of how things had to be implemented if they were going to work.

Understanding the theory behind objects, components, memory, the GDI, or any other topic does not mean that all your problems magically disappear. But it is the most practical way to get to be a good all-around programmer.

As you spend more and more time working with computers, you get to be a better programmer. Experience helps to shorten the learning curve that plagues new programmers. Because you keep learning more about computers, it takes you less time to learn new skills.

With experience you learn not only a list of techniques, but also an understanding of the theory behind the machines and tools that you work with day in and day out. This theoretical knowledge is the most practical knowledge in the world because it helps you get each individual task done in the shortest period of time.

Really talented programmers have a vision of how the system works, and they use that vision every time they sit down to code. This book is about that vision of how the system works.

Delphi Types Under Win32

2

IN THIS CHAPTER

In this chapter you get a look at the new types associated with Delphi 32-bit programming. There is also a short overview of the old types, and the names and values they have under Win32.

In particular, you look at the following subjects:

- The new long Pascal strings that have no significant limitation on their length.
- The Variant type, which can be used anywhere in your programs, but which is designed for use with OLE Automation. It is also a big help when you are working with databases.
- All the standard integer types and their values in the Win32 programming environment.
- A discussion of generic and fundamental integer types. Generic types (Integer, Cardinal) differ in kind between Win16 and Win32 implementations. The fundamental types (ShortInt, SmallInt, LongInt, Byte, Word) are the same in both 16- and 32-bit Delphi. The Currency type will also be discussed in this chapter.
- A brief discussion of WideChars and AnsiChars, as well as related types such as Chars, and the pointers PChars, PWideChar, and PAnsiChar.

This chapter is not designed to teach you about typed variables and how to use them in an Object Pascal program. If you are interested in that kind of information, see the chapters on that subject which appear only on the CD. The goal of this chapter is to give you an overview of the standard types found in Win32. In other words, this chapter highlights the differences between Object Pascal types under Win32 and Object Pascal types under Windows 3.1. See the DOC files on the CD-ROM for general information about types.

Old Strings and New Strings

Borland Pascal has long been known for its 255-character limitation on strings. As Delphi 2.0 was being developed there was some talk that this tradition was going to continue in the 32-bit versions of Delphi. However, the developers decided that it was not appropriate to continue burdening developers with a prohibitively short string type. As a result, the days of 255-character limits are behind us, and Delphi programmers can now create strings of virtually any length.

> **NOTE**
>
> These changes have nothing to do with the C-style PChar strings found in Borland Pascal 7 (BP7), in Delphi 16, and still found in this version of Delphi. PChars are very different animals than either the old-style Pascal strings or the new long strings. The long strings act very much like standard Pascal strings, only they are null-terminated and no longer have a length limitation.

I should perhaps add some additional information here for readers who might be interested in knowing how changes to the Delphi language come about. If you are used to programming in C, you know that a change to the language definition would have to be approved by the ANSI committee before it could appear in a major compiler. Fortunately, Object Pascal is not controlled by a committee, and is therefore not bound by restrictions that prevent it from growing or that force it to adhere to standards that might make little sense in the light of rapidly changing computer technologies. (There is an ANSI committee for Pascal, but the Borland Pascal compilers have never attempted to align themselves with it.)

As a result, the quality of the product, and of the language on which it relies, is very much a direct outgrowth of the talents of the men and women on the Delphi team. You will have to judge for yourself what you think of this scheme, but certainly there are some advantages to the arrangement as long as the caliber of the people working on the team remains high.

Pascal strings have very few limitations and can be of virtually any length. For a more precise explanation of exactly what I mean by "virtually any length," see Part II of this book, which is entitled simply, "Win32." For now, I can state briefly that whatever limitations you do encounter will be dictated not by limitations in Object Pascal, but by the amount of memory on your target machines and the size of memory allocated to your program by the system. The amount of memory on your machine is unlikely to exceed 64 MB plus what ever free disk space is available on your hard drive, and the Win32 operating system would probably prevent you from allocating much over 2 GB for the structures inside your program.

The old style of strings can still be used in Delphi. They are called ShortStrings and they have, naturally enough, a 255-character limitation. For instance, the following is the correct way to declare and use an old-style string:

```
procedure TForm1.Button1Click(Sender: TObject);
var
  S: ShortString;
begin
  Edit1.Text := IntToStr(High(S));
end;
```

Note that this code uses the High function, which at the time of this writing is associated with old strings but not with the new strings. The High function returns the maximum number of characters that can be stored in a string. In the preceding example, High will return 255.

The new strings are referred to as *long strings*, or more technically, AnsiStrings. The following function explicitly uses new strings:

```
procedure TForm1.Button2Click(Sender: TObject);
var
  S: AnsiString;
begin
```

```
  SetLength(S, 35);
end;
```

Note that this procedure uses the SetLength function, which is used to explicitly designate the length of a string. This function works only in Delphi 2.0 and will not work in Delphi 1.0. Here is how to issue the same command with a short string from Delphi 1.0, or an explicitly declared ShortString in Delphi 2.0:

```
S[0] := #35;
```

The preceding code would be an error if you were working with long strings because long strings have no 0th element. The first character in a long string is the first letter of the actual string you want to reference. Consider the following code fragment:

```
var
  S: string
  Ch: Char;
begin
  S := 'Delphi';
  Ch := S[1];
end;
```

This code would have the same result if S were a long string or a ShortString. In cases like this, S[1] always references the first letter of the string, which in this case is D. However, if S were a ShortString, then you could also reference S[0], which is the length byte. Referencing S[0] with a long string would be an error, and the length byte is stored at a negative offset, along with the size of the allocation and its reference count.

NOTE

Let me reiterate that the SetLength function will not work with ShortStrings in 16-bit Delphi, although it will work with them in 32-bit Delphi. If you need to implement the SetLength code in Delphi 16, then the following routine will do the trick:

```
procedure SetLength(var S: string; i: Integer);
begin
  S[0] := Chr(i);
end;
```

This function takes a string and an integer as parameters. If you want to set the string to a certain length, say 10 bytes, then you can pass in the value 10 in the second parameter. The function will then automatically set to 10 the length byte of the string in the first parameter. The Chr function translates integer values to character type values. Unlike the SetLength function used with long strings, the Chr function does not allocate or deallocate any memory. It does, however, provide a reasonable method for reusing code in the 16- and 32-bit versions of Delphi. Note that you can use the built-in Win32 conditional definition to tell if you are in 16- or 32-bit Delphi:

```
{$ifdef WIN32}.
```

Although the developers tried to make both types of strings work the same in Delphi 2.0, clearly it matters whether you use AnsiStrings or ShortStrings. Some commands work with one type of string, others don't, and some commands work with both types. Given these circumstances, one wonders about the implications of making the following declaration:

```
var
  S: string
```

Declaring code in this way is legal, but does it result in a long string or a ShortString?

It turns out that two different factors determine how the compiler views the preceding code. If you turn to the Project | Options | Compiler page you will find that there is a compiler option called Huge Strings. If this option is checked, then the preceding declaration will be considered an AnsiString. If the option is unchecked, then it will be a ShortString. By default, the option is turned on.

The next question, of course, is why the compiler option is called Huge Strings rather than AnsiStrings or long strings? The issue here is that you can turn on Huge Strings by writing the following compiler option in your code:

```
{$H+}
```

When they created the compiler option codes, there were only so many letters in the alphabet available to the developers of Delphi. Therefore, it's a safe bet that the developers chose $H because options such as $A (AnsiStrings) and $L (long strings) were not available to them. H is a good choice because Huge Strings forms at least a reasonable mnemonic to help you keep track of your options in this alphabet soup.

If you have the $H+ directive turned on, you can still use ShortStrings if you declare your string variables in one of two ways:

```
{$H+}
var
  S1: ShortString;  // Declaration One
  S2: string[50];   // Declaration Two
```

Both of these declarations produce ShortStrings. The first because it explicitly declares the S1 variable as a ShortString, and the second because it explicitly declares S2 as being less than 256 characters in length.

In this section of the chapter you have been introduced to the AnsiString and ShortString types. Here are the key points covered in this section:

- ShortStrings are identical to the old Pascal strings used in Delphi 1.0 and in the Turbo Pascal products.
- AnsiStrings are a new type of string that act very much like ShortStrings except when you try to treat them as an array.
- When treated as an array, an old style string has the length byte of the string in its 0th element, but AnsiStrings have no element 0, and instead start with element 1, which is the first character of the string.

■ By default, Delphi has the Huge Strings ($H+) compiler directive turned on. This means that all strings that are not explicitly declared as ShortStrings will be considered to be long strings.

■ There are two ways to explicitly declare a ShortString even when the Huge Strings compiler directive is turned on. One is to declare the variable to be of type ShortString, and the second is to give it a length of less than 256 characters: MyString[255].

Long Strings and the Stand-Alone Debugger

It's very important for you to understand that there is a big difference between ShortStrings and long strings. A ShortString is just an array that has a few additional properties, as explained in Chapter 3, "Strings and Text Files." A long string, on the other hand, is a pointer to a null-terminated string. It also is an unusual pointer in that it has data at a negative offset.

To learn more about long strings, create a project called StrMem, which will be used as a starting point for seeing how Delphi handles long strings. The StrMem program is found on the *Unleashed* CD-ROM, and is shown in Listing 2.1.

NOTE

The analysis of the StrMem program in Listing 2.1 gives you a look inside the current implementation of long strings. It is important to understand that in the shipping version of Delphi, long strings might be defined to have a certain behavior, not a certain implementation. In other words, it's possible that the developers of Delphi will never document the internal methods they use to represent long strings. They will, however, document the way in which long strings are expected to behave.

Good programmers almost always attempt to learn the way a particular feature in the compiler is implemented. This can help them write better code. However, the implementation of a feature is not always as important as the documented description of its behavior. Having said this, I have to add that I can rarely do anything useful with a programming feature until I have some conception of how it is implemented. If you always rely on the documentation for a feature, then you are forced to memorize a list of possible behaviors. If you understand how a feature works, then you don't have to memorize anything, but can instead rely on your understanding of how the object's implementation dictates its possible behaviors.

The point here is that you must be careful to understand the potential consequences of building your code around undocumented features of the product. In particular, using undocumented code might force you to make changes to your code when the compiler is updated.

Listing 3.1. The StrMem program is used to illustrate some of the low-level technical differences between `AnsiStrings` and `ShortStrings`.

```
unit main;

interface

uses
    SysUtils, Windows, Messages,
    Classes, Graphics, Controls,
    Forms, Dialogs,  StdCtrls;

type
  TForm1 = class(TForm)
    Button1: TButton;
    Button2: TButton;
    procedure Button1Click(Sender: TObject);
    procedure Button2Click(Sender: TObject);
  private
    { Private declarations }
  public
    { Public declarations }
  end;

var
  Form1: TForm1;

implementation

{$R *.DFM}

procedure TForm1.Button1Click(Sender: TObject);
var
  S: AnsiString;
begin
  S := '5';
  Caption := S;
  S := 'Fred';
  Caption := S;
end;

procedure TForm1.Button2Click(Sender: TObject);
var
  S: ShortString;
begin
  S := '5';
  Caption := S;
  S := 'Fred';
  Caption := S;
end;

end.
```

A quick look at the source code for this program shows that it does nothing more than assign some values to a string, and then display that string in the main caption of the program. The reason for this paucity of creativity is that the program is meant to be used as a testing ground in which you can learn about long and short strings. It's valuable as a testbed, not as an example.

To me, looking at a data type in the debugger is always very helpful. If I can actually see the way it is structured, then I feel as though I have a better grasp of how it operates. To get a good look at a long string, you need to load the StrMem program in the stand-alone debugger.

> **NOTE**
>
> Your version of Delphi 2.0 might not come with the stand-alone debugger. The debugger is called TD32.EXE, and is valuable for its capability to peer deep into memory.
>
> To examine a program in TD32, you must compile it with debug information. In particular, you should open up the Project | Options menu item in Delphi 2.0, and turn to the linker page. There you will see an option to "Include TDW debug Information." Make sure this is checked, and then close the Options dialog box and select Project | Build All.
>
> You should now launch TD32 from the subdirectory in which your program resides, passing it the name of your executable as a parameter. (If this fails, use the debugger's File menu to change to the directory where the executable is stored, and then explicitly load the program into TD32.) If you have done everything correctly, the Object Pascal source for your program will appear in the stand-alone debugger. If you find yourself looking at machine code rather than Pascal code, then you probably forgot to turn on debug information in Delphi before rebuilding.
>
> Note that the stand-alone debugger does not run in a normal window. Instead, it runs in a DOS box. You can maximize the DOS box if you want to get a clearer view of your code. When you run the stand-alone debugger with certain settings, you might find that you have to use the Alt+Tab key to switch back and forth between the debugger and your program. If you think the debugger or your program has locked up, trying switching back and forth to see if
>
> 1. Your program is active but the debugger is not
> 2. The debugger is active but your program is not
>
> In other words, under normal operating situations, there are times when you can use the debugger but not your program, or you can use your program but not the debugger. At other times you can use both. This is not a flaw in the debugger, but a natural consequence of the act of debugging, and one that also occurs in the integrated debugger.

When you first load the program into the stand-alone debugger, you will be looking at the first page of code in your program, which is the DPR file. Right-click the screen to bring up a local menu, and choose Module. A dialog box will appear listing the modules in your project. Select

MAIN.PAS. Now you will be able to see the code for the main module of the StrMem program, as shown in Figure 2.1.

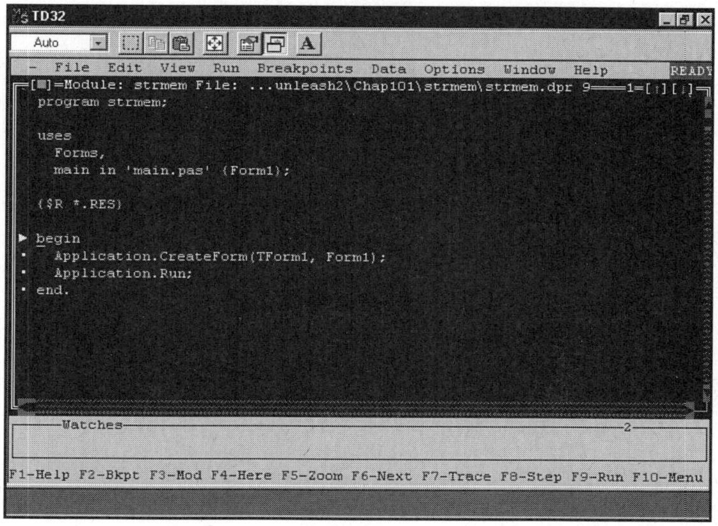

FIGURE 2.1.

A Windows 95 session with Turbo Debugger loaded in a window on the desktop.

In the stand-alone debugger, use the F2 key to set a break point at the beginning of the `Button1Click` procedure.

```
procedure TForm1.Button1Click(Sender: TObject);
var
  S: AnsiString;
begin
  S := '5';          // Set breakpoint here
  Caption := S;
  S := 'Fred';
  Caption := S;
end;
```

From the View menu, choose CPU. A window will appear in your program; it can be used to see the machine code that is generated for your program. The general scene should look like the one depicted in Figure 2.2.

Run StrMem from inside the debugger by pressing F9 or by selecting the appropriate option from the Run menu. Once your program is launched, press the button on the program's main form. Pause for a moment when the code reaches the first line in the assignment statement, the one with the `lea` command in it.

```
MAIN.32:  S := '5';
:0041F14C 8D45FC           lea    eax,[ebp-04]   ; Pause here
:0041F14F BAA8F14100       mov    edx,0041F1A8
:0041F154E84F2DFEFF        call   @LStrLAsg
```

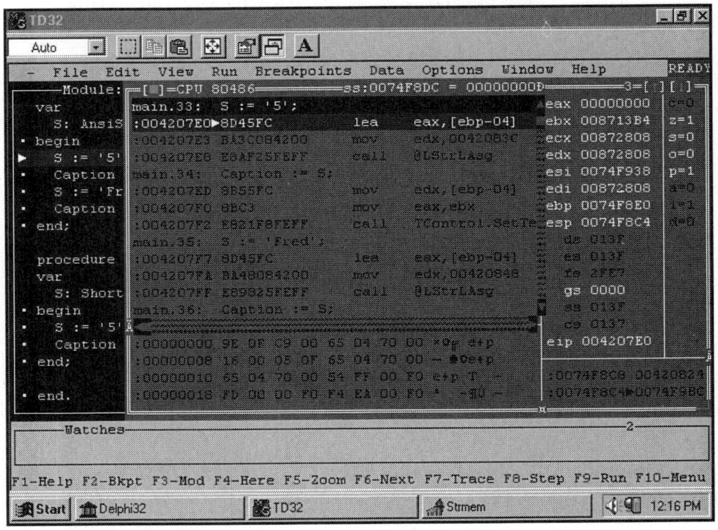

FIGURE 2.2.

The stand-alone debugger as you start stepping through your code.

Remember that the code won't look exactly like the code shown here, but it will have the same general structure. In particular, it is unlikely that any of your addresses will be identical to mine, but the assembly code will have the same format.

In the watch window at the bottom of the stand-alone debugger, enter the expression @S, and take a look at its contents.

```
@S                      :0073F8DC : POINTER
```

Move over to the dump window at the bottom left of the CPU window. Right-click the window to pop up a local menu, and then select Goto. A dialog box called Enter Address to Goto appears. Enter the variable S in this window.

When you first start stepping through your code, you will see something like the following values for S:

```
:0073F8DC 00 00 00 00 48 F9 73 00      H·s
```

Notice that the address on the left side of the display is the same as the address of the variable S as displayed in the Watch List window. On my machine, the address of the variable is $0073F8DC. The first four bytes, that is, the 32-bit value of the pointer, is currently nil: 00 00 00 00.

Step through your code two lines, until the code pointer is past the call to LStrLAsg.

```
MAIN.32:  S := '5';
:0041F14C 8D45FC          lea     eax,[ebp-04]
:0041F14F BAA8F14100      mov     edx,0041F1A8
:0041F154E84F2DFEFF      call    @LStrLAsg      ; Go past this line.
```

After you call the LStrLAsg function, you will see that the four bytes of data in your string pointer contain an address. This address might look something like this:

```
:0073F8DC A8 F1 41 00 48 F9 73 00     H·s
```

The first four bytes, A8 F1 41 00, is the relevant data in this example. This is the address in memory where your string can be found. Pop up the Goto menu by clicking the right mouse button in the Dump window. Enter the address shown in the first four bytes of your string variable. Remember that the Intel architecture places its bytes in reverse order. Therefore, if your string variable is at the address shown in the preceding line of code, then you should enter $0041F1A8 and then press OK. The result will be that you can view your string in memory.

```
:0041F1A8 35 00 00 00 FF FF FF FF 5     ____
```

In this case you set the string equal to the number 5. The number 5 is character $35 in the ANSI character set, and that value is displayed as the first byte of your string. The second byte of your string is a null character designating the end of your string. On the far right of the display is the number five written out in standard characters, and then followed by some garbage characters, which in my case happen to be displayed as underlines.

So far, you have learned two things by peering into the debugger:

- Long strings are pointers. If you go to the address of the string, there is nothing there but a pointer to another location in memory.
- You can find the string contained in your AnsiString variable by going to the address referenced by your long string variable.

It surprised me when I first saw this implementation because I didn't necessarily feel as though I were working with a pointer when I worked with a long string. The compiler conceals from you the true nature of the type. Nevertheless, if you want to get good at handling these little puppies, then you need to understand that they are really pointer variables.

As mentioned earlier, one of the interesting traits of long strings is that you cannot assign or read values from element zero in the string, which is where the length byte appeared in Delphi 16. By looking at the memory dumps shown earlier, you can see how Delphi's string architecture has changed. In particular, the first character of each string is no longer a length byte, but is now the first character of the actual string. In other words, element zero of the string has disappeared. It no longer exists.

This does not mean, however, that the length byte has actually disappeared. To see it, move the dump window back one line so that you can see the line above the one where your string starts. This string might look something like this:

```
:0041F1A0 FF FF FF FF 01 00 00 00 ____
```

If your string had the word Fred in it, instead of the string 5, then it would look like this:

```
:0041F1AC FF FF FF FF 04 00 00 00 ____
```

Notice that in the first case, the last 32-bit chunk of the string has the number 1 in it, while in the second case it has the number 4. This is because the string 5 has one character in it, whereas the string Fred has four characters in it.

Obviously, the length byte of long strings is kept at a negative offset from the beginning of the string. Furthermore, the value is no longer an eight-bit byte capable of addressing only 255 characters. Now it is a 32-bit value, which would have a limit of 4GB. As such, it would probably be appropriate to call it a length value, or length code.

For strings that are allocated on the heap, the next two 32-bit values going backward from the length value are also part of the string variable. One of these 4-byte values designates the allocated length of the string, while the other designates the reference count. For string constants there is no allocated length value, and the reference count is always -1. (Once again, remember to check the documentation on the shipping version of Delphi to see if these facts are documented. If they are not documented, then they might change in future versions of the product.)

In this section you had an overview of long strings. You have seen that they are not the same as the standard Pascal strings. Instead of being represented by an array, they are actually null-terminated strings referenced by a pointer. These null-terminated strings are unusual, in that they are preceded by a 32-bit value that references the length of the string.

A Close Look at *ShortStrings*

Now that you've had a close look at long strings, take a moment to do the same thing with ShortStrings. Put a breakpoint at the beginning of the Button2Click method from the StrMem program:

```
procedure TForm1.Button2Click(Sender: TObject);
var
  S: ShortString;
begin
  S := '5';   // Put the breakpoint here
  Caption := S;
  S := 'Fred';
  Caption := S;
end;
```

Run to the breakpoint and then examine the address of S in the watch window:

```
@S                            :0074FB60 : POINTER
```

Once again, your machine is unlikely to show the exact same address, but the general format of the display will be similar. Choose View | CPU from the menu, and move to the dump window and right-click it to bring up a local menu (pressing Alt+F10 has the same effect). Choose Goto, and enter S in the Enter Address to Position to dialog box. When you first look at the memory associated with the variable S it will be full of garbage.

```
0074FB60 3F 01 02 00 44 16 F7 BF ? D_+
```

Notice that the address of s is the same in the dump window as in the watch window. Although the number will almost surely differ on your system, at the time of this writing it was $0074FB60 on my system. In the preceding line, everything to the right of the address is random garbage, and will almost certainly differ on your system.

Step through the line of code that assigns the value 5 to the variable s.

```
:00420704 66C78500FFFFFF+mov    word ptr [ebp-00000100],3501
```

Once again, only the general format of this statement will look the same on your machine. Now, look back down at the dump window.

```
:0074FB60 01 35 02 00 44 16 F7 BF 5 D_+
```

Notice that the first byte of the string variable is set to 1, and the second byte is set to $35, which is the ASCII value for 5.

```
01 35
```

The rest of the string is full of garbage characters and will probably look different on your system. The first two bytes, however, will be identical. The key point here is that the first byte shown is the length byte, which is set to 1 because the string 5 has only one character in it. The second byte is 35, which is the offset of the ASCII character representing the number 5.

In the last two sections you have had a close look at long strings and ShortStrings. By now you should have a very well-grounded understanding of the difference in structure between these two string types. It should be obvious, for instance, that these two types are radically different. The developers of Delphi have gone to great lengths to enable you to treat the two types of strings in a very similar manner. However, underneath this area of similarity, you have seen that AnsiStrings and ShortStrings are two extremely different beasts.

Facts About AnsiStrings

In this section you learn some of the basic functionality associated with Pascal strings. This information is not necessarily new in the 32-bit version of Delphi, but it will help you to understand the types of things you can do with long strings. This section is a general overview of the subject and could perhaps safely be skimmed by experienced Delphi programmers.

Table 2.1 shows a set of functions that all work with both AnsiString and ShortStrings. Additional information about these routines can be found in the online help.

Table 2.1. These routines can be used with both `AnsiStrings` and `ShortStrings`.

Routine	Description
Delete	Deletes a substring from a string
DisposeStr	Deallocates a string from the heap
FmtLoadStr	Loads a string from a program's resource string table
Insert	Inserts a substring into a string
IntToHex	Converts an integer to a hexadecimal
IntToStr	Converts an integer to a string
IsValidIdent	Returns TRUE if the given string is a valid identifier
Length	Returns the dynamic length of a string
LoadStr	Loads the string resource from the application's executable file
LowerCase	Lowercases the given string
NewStr	Allocates a new string on the heap
Pos	Searches for a substring in a string
SetLength	Sets the length of a string
Str	Converts a numeric value to a string
StrToInt	Converts a string to an integer
StrToIntDef	Converts a string to an integer or default value
UpperCase	Uppercases the given string
Val	Converts a string value to its numeric representation

Two very important routines not listed in Table 2.1 are called `Format` and `FmtStr`. Both routines are nearly identical, but the former returns the result from a function call, whereas the latter returns the result as a parameter. The following pseudocode focuses on the differences between the two calls:

```
Result := Format(...)
FmtStr(Result, ...);
```

As you can see, the `FmtStr` procedure takes the result as a parameter, and the `Format` function returns the result. I tend to use the `Format` function more than the `FmtStr` function, so I will use that routine in the following discussion. However, both routines are based on similar principles, and if you understand one then you understand the other.

In Listing 2.2 you will find the main unit from the Formats program. This program shows several simple examples of how to use the `Format` function.

Listing 2.2. The Formats program shows how to use the `Format` function.

```
unit main;

interface

uses
  SysUtils, Windows, Messages,
  Classes, Graphics, Controls,
  Forms, Dialogs, StdCtrls, Buttons;

type
  TForm1 = class(TForm)
    ListBox1: TListBox;
    StrInput: TButton;
    IntHex: TButton;
    AllThree: TButton;
    DiskAvail: TButton;
    IntInput: TButton;
    bFloat: TBitBtn;
    bCommas: TBitBtn;
    bScience: TBitBtn;
    procedure IntInputClick(Sender: TObject);
    procedure StrInputClick(Sender: TObject);
    procedure IntHexClick(Sender: TObject);
    procedure AllThreeClick(Sender: TObject);
    procedure DiskAvailClick(Sender: TObject);
    procedure bFloatClick(Sender: TObject);
    procedure bCommasClick(Sender: TObject);
    procedure bScienceClick(Sender: TObject);
  end;

var
  Form1: TForm1;

implementation

uses
  UtilBox;

{$R *.DFM}

procedure TForm1.IntInputClick(Sender: TObject);
var
  i: Integer;
  S: string;
begin
  GetInteger('Enter integer: ', i);
  S := Format('This is a number: %d', [i]);
  ListBox1.Items.Add(S);
end;

procedure TForm1.StrInputClick(Sender: TObject);
var
  S: string;
begin
  S := GetInput;
  S := Format('You entered: %s', [S]);
```

continues

Listing 2.2. continued

```
  ListBox1.Items.Add(S);
end;

procedure TForm1.IntHexClick(Sender: TObject);
var
  i: Integer;
  S: string;
begin
  GetInteger('Convert Integer to Hex', i);
  S := Format('$%x', [i]);
  ListBox1.Items.Add(S);
end;

procedure TForm1.AllThreeClick(Sender: TObject);
var
  i, j: Integer;
  S: string;
begin
  GetInteger('Enter integer value', i);
  GetInteger('Convert Integer to Hex', j);
  S := GetInput;
  S := Format('Integer: %d, Hex: $%x, String: %s', [i, j, S]);
  ListBox1.Items.Add(S);
end;

procedure TForm1.DiskAvailClick(Sender: TObject);
var
  Free, Size: Integer;
  S: string;
begin
  Free := DiskFree(3);
  Size := DiskSize(3);
  S := Format('DiskSize: %d. DiskFree: %d', [Size, Free]);
  ListBox1.Items.Add(S);
end;

procedure TForm1.bFloatClick(Sender: TObject);
var
  i: Integer;
  f: Double;
  S: string;
begin
  GetInteger('Enter a number and I will find its square root: ', i);
  f := Sqrt(i);
  S := Format('The result: %f, To 5 decimal places: %12.5f, and as money: %m',
              [f, f, f]);
  ListBox1.Items.Add(S);
end;

procedure TForm1.bCommasClick(Sender: TObject);
var
  i: Integer;
  f: Double;
  S: string;
begin
  GetInteger('Enter a number between 1000 and 2000 (no commas)', i);
  f := i * 10000.45;
```

```
  S := Format('%d times 1000.45 equals %n', [i, f]);
  ListBox1.items.Add(S);
end;

procedure TForm1.bScienceClick(Sender: TObject);
var
  S: string;
begin
  ShowMessage('Press okay to see the value of pi in scientific notation');
  S := Format('Pi in scientific notation: %e', [pi]);
  ListBox1.Items.Add(S);
end;

end.
```

This program, shown in Figure 2.3, enables you to press various buttons that prompt the user for input. The data entered by the user is then run through the Format function for processing, and the resulting string is displayed in the list box at the top of the program. Many of the buttons in the program don't do anything very useful because this program is designed for programmers, not end users. Its purpose is just to show you how the Format function works.

FIGURE 2.3.

The Formats program prompts a user for input, which is processed and displayed in a list box.

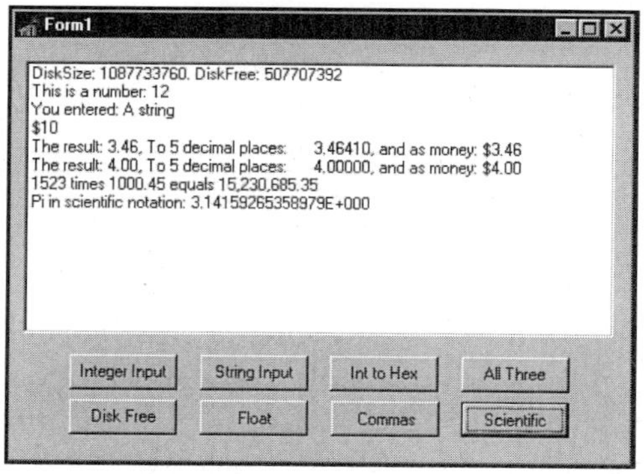

The Format function is a lot like the printf series of functions in C. In particular, it takes two parameters.

```
function Format(
  const Format: string;        // String plus format specifiers
  const Args: array of const   // Arguments to embed in first paramter
  ): string;                   // Function returns the formated string
```

The first parameter, called Format, is a string in which you can embed various specifiers. Each of these specifiers can hold the place of an argument that will be embedded in the string.

Consider the following example:

```
S := Format('This is an integer: %d', [23]);
```

This code fragment sets S to read: This is an integer: 23. In this example, %d is a format specifier and 23 is an argument. Notice that the arguments are placed inside brackets that delineate an array of const.

NOTE

An array of const is a special construction in Object Pascal that enables you to work with a variable number of arguments. The classic use of an array of const is to pass a variable number of arguments as parameters to a procedure. The following code demonstrates how that works:

```
procedure Foo(A: array of const);
var
  i: Integer;
  S: string;
begin
  i := High(A) + 1;
  S := Format('Num arguments passed: %d', [i]);
  ShowMessage(S);
end;

procedure TForm1.Button1Click(Sender: TObject);
begin
  Foo([5,3,2,1]);
  Foo([1,2,3]);
  Foo([1,2]);
end;
```

As you can see, the function foo is called first with four, then three, and then two "arguments." This is made possible by the structure of an array of const. If you want to see the preceding code fragment in action, see the AryConst program on the *Unleashed* CD-ROM.

There are a number of different format specifiers used with the Format function. Each of the specifiers is preceded by a percentage sign, and a variable number of internal arguments, as shown in the following list:

```
d: integer
e: scientific
f: fixed
g: general
n: number
m: Money
p: Pointer
s: string
x: Hex
```

Most of these arguments can be used to translate a numerical value into a string value. For instance, the p specifier will translate a computer address into a string value, as shown in the following code:

```
procedure TForm1.Button2Click(Sender: TObject);
var
```

```
  S: string;
begin
  S := Format('$%p', [@S]);
  ShowMessage(S);
end;
```

The preceding example prints out the address of the variable S in string format. For example, when I run the function on my computer it displays the value $0065F8DC in a message box. The actual result will probably differ on your machine.

Because the Args parameter to the Format function is an array of const, you can use it to pass in multiple arguments to the first parameter, as shown in the following code:

```
procedure TForm1.DiskAvailClick(Sender: TObject);
var
  Free, Size: Integer;
  S: string;
begin
  Free := DiskFree(3);
  Size := DiskSize(3);
  S := Format('DiskSize: %d. DiskFree: %d', [Size, Free]);
  ListBox1.Items.Add(S);
end;
```

In this example, the integer values Size and Free are passed in as arguments to the first parameter. The format specifiers in that parameter enable Delphi to convert the integer values into string format and properly imbed them in a string. The result is a string that might look something like this:

```
DiskSize: 523526144, DiskFree: 28868834
```

Sometimes, you might want to display floating-point numbers, and in particular, you might want to control the way the decimal portion of these numbers is displayed. There are a number of ways to do this, but the following fragment shows one common way to handle the problem:

```
procedure TForm1.bFloatClick(Sender: TObject);
var
  i: Integer;
  f: Double;
  S: string;
begin
  GetInteger('Enter a number and I will find its square root: ', i);
  f := Sqrt(i);
  S := Format('The result: %f, To 5 decimal places: %12.5f, and as money: %m',
              [f, f, f]);
  ListBox1.Items.Add(S);
end;
```

This code asks the user to enter an integer value. The square root of the number entered is then calculated and displayed to the user in three different ways. The first way simply displays the number with some default formatting. The second method specifies that the resulting string will be at least 12 characters in length, and that 5 digits will appear after the decimal point. The third specifier translates a floating-point number into a monetary value. For instance, it converts 35.3 into $35.30.

The Formats program shown in Listing 2.2 gives the Format function a reasonable workout. If you've never played with this type of function before, you should run the program so you have a general feeling for what it can do for you. In general, you will find that it solves a particular class of problem quickly and easily. For further information on the format specifiers used with this function, see the "Format Strings" entry in the online help.

The Trim Functions

One common problem that developers have involves the need to get clean string input from a user. In particular, users will often enter a string and then accidentally either append or prepend a certain number of spaces to it. Later, you might need to work with this string, and in particular you might want to compare it with other strings. If you try to compare the string "Mighty Morph " with the string "Mighty Morph", they will not prove identical because the first has a few spaces appended to it. To remedy this situation, Delphi provides three functions called Trim, TrimLeft, and TrimRight.

Delphi provides three trim functions rather than just one in order to optimize your use of these functions. For instance, there is no need to expend clock cycles removing spaces from both ends of a string if it is unlikely that the spaces appear in more than one position.

The Trims program found on the *Unleashed* CD-ROM provides some quick examples of how to use the new trim functions. For instance, the following is the Trim function in action:

```
procedure TForm1.Button1Click(Sender: TObject);
var
  S, Temp: string;
begin
  S := '   Sam   ';
  Temp := S;
  S := Trim(S);
  S := ReplaceChars(S, #32, '*');
  Temp := ReplaceChars(Temp, #32, '*');
  ListBox1.Items.Add(S);
  ListBox1.Items.Add(Temp);
end;
```

A string constant with preceding and succeeding spaces is assigned to the variable S. It then assigns S to another string variable called Temp. The third step in the procedure is to remove the spaces from the beginning and end of the string by calling Trim. At this point, the variable S is equal to the word "Sam" with no spaces on either end. The variable Temp still has spaces in it. To make this difference visible to you, the code replaces all the spaces in the Temp string with asterisks and then shows you the string in a list box. The ReplaceChars function is a custom routine found in the StrBox unit found on the *Unleashed* CD-ROM. You learn more about ReplaceChars in the next chapter, "Strings and Text Files." For now, just include the StrBox unit, which ships with this book, in your uses clause.

NOTE

STRBOX.PAS is kept in a directory called UNITS on the CD-ROM. If it's not already there, you should go to the Tools | Options | Library menu choice and make sure that the UNITS directory is listed in your library path. It's best if you copy the UNITS directory onto your hard drive before you try to reference it.

The following is the output from the `Button1Click` function shown above:

```
Sam
***Sam***
```

The `TrimRight` function is demonstrated in the following method from the Trims program:

```
procedure TForm1.Button2Click(Sender: TObject);
var
  S, Temp: AnsiString;
begin
  S := '   Sam   ';
  Temp := S;
  s := TrimRight(S);
  S := ReplaceChars(S, #32, '*');
  Temp := ReplaceChars(Temp, #32, '*');
  ListBox1.Items.Add(S);
  ListBox1.Items.Add(Temp);
end;
```

This code strips the spaces from the right part of the string S, but not from the left. The output in the list box therefore looks like this:

```
***Sam
***Sam***
```

The `Trim`, `TrimRight`, and `TrimLeft` functions are easy to use. They are mentioned here only so you will know that they are available. Readers of the previous versions of this book should note that these functions replace or have similar functionality to the `CleanString`, `StripBlanks`, and `StripFromFront` functions in the `StrBox` unit. I have kept all three functions in the `StrBox` unit, however, in part for compatibility with old code, and in part because the routines might still be useful under particular circumstances.

AnsiStrings and PChars

One of the great advantages of `AnsiStrings` is that they work very well with `PChars`. In particular, you can translate an `AnsiString` into a `PChar` just by typecasting it.

```
var
  S: string;
  Ch: Char;
begin
  Ch := 'C';
```

```
S := Format('Formatting drive %s', [Ch]);
MessageBox(Handle, PChar(S), nil, mb_Ok);
end;
```

The preceding example is interesting because MessageBox is a Windows API function that takes a PChar in the second parameter. In this particular rather contrived case, it was more convenient to use a string than a PChar. In the past, a decision of this type forced the programmer to call StrPCopy, which would translate a Pascal string into a PChar. The new long strings, however, enable you to perform this translation by making a simple typecast. This is possible, of course, because long strings are really just pointers to null-terminated strings with a few extra traits thrown in for good measure.

If you want to move in the other direction, from a PChar to string, then you can simply make a direct assignment. Consider the following declarations:

```
var
  P: PChar;
  S: AnsiString;
```

If you have two variables of these types, then you can write

```
S := P;
```

In short, you can directly assign a PChar to a long string.

Typecasting a long string to a PChar is not really a "simple" operation, in that the long string may be copied into a new allocation if the reference count in the original string is not 1. Recall that the compiler has no idea what the PChar is going to be used for and hence will make sure that everything is okay by ensuring that the string that is being typecast is a unique copy (with reference count 1).

Reference Counting

Delphi performs reference counting on the long strings you create. This means that if you assign one AnsiString to another, then Delphi does not necessarily copy the string over into a new place in memory. Instead, it simply increments a variable that keeps track of the number of users of a string. If one of the users of the string then goes out of scope, the memory associated with the string is not deallocated. Instead, the reference count is merely decremented by one. If the total number of users of the string goes down to zero, then the memory associated with the string is deallocated.

If you assign two variables to the same long string, and then change the value of the string associated with one of the string variables, the data associated with the changed string will be copied over to its own area of memory; the reference count of the other string will then be decremented by one. The new string, of course, will have a count of one.

Let me repeat the concepts outlined in the last paragraph just to be sure that what I am saying is clear. Consider the following example:

```
var
  S1, S2: string;
begin
  S1 := 'Sam';  // One string in memory.
  S2 := S1;     // Still one string in memory.
  S2[3] := 'p'; // Copy on change! Now there two strings in memory!
end;
```

After assigning the string "Sam" to S1, you have one AnsiString variable that points at an area in memory that contains a string. If you assign a second Delphi AnsiString variable to the first variable, then Delphi does not make a copy of the string for either the first or second variable. Instead, both variables will point at the same area in memory. Thus you have two variables, but only one string. As a result, the string's reference count will be set to two. If you then change the string associated with one of the variables, Delphi will proceed to make a copy of the string associated with the variable referenced at the time of the change. At this point there will be two variables and two strings. The reference count of each string will then be set to one. This concept is called "copy on change."

WideChars and Unicode

Delphi supports Unicode because it is accessible from the Windows API. However, Delphi 2.0 will not attempt to make all its controls Unicode-compliant. In other words, you can access WideChars and pointers to WideChars in Delphi applications, but you cannot display Unicode strings in Delphi controls such as the TEdit control or TListBox.

NOTE

Traditional Delphi characters are represented by 8-bit characters called Chars. In fact, 8-bit characters have been the standard in all Intel-based computer languages for years. The problem with 8-bit values, however, is that they can represent only 256 possible characters, which is not nearly enough for Asian languages or for many of the mathematical or other types of symbols that you might want to store.

Because 8-bit characters have limitations, the industry has decided to support a new 16-bit standard that will have not 256 possible characters, but 64KB worth of possible characters.

The new 16-bit characters used in Unicode applications are called WideChars. If you are working with a string of these characters, then you are working with a variable of type PWideChar. A WideChar has two bytes per character, whereas a standard old-style character, called an AnsiChar, has one byte per character. If you declare a variable of type Char, then it will be an AnsiChar by default in Delphi 2.0. You cannot count on the fact that Chars will always be considered 8-bit characters, and in future versions of Delphi, 16-bit Chars will probably become the default.

So far you have seen that Delphi provides support for Unicode, but that it is not yet hosted fully by all of Delphi's visual controls. Given these circumstances, the thing you want to be able to do is convert into AnsiStrings any Unicode strings that you get, so that you can use them in your controls. You will also need a routine to convert the strings back the other way. The program in Listing 2.3, WIDECHAR.DPR, shows you how to perform these conversions.

Listing 2.3. How to convert a Unicode string to an AnsiString, and vice versa.

```
unit main;

{
-- WideChar functions from SYSTEM.PAS:

function WideCharToString(Source: PWideChar): string;
function WideCharLenToString(Source: PWideChar; SourceLen: Integer): string;
procedure WideCharToStrVar(Source: PWideChar; var Dest: string);
procedure WideCharLenToStrVar(Source: PWideChar; SourceLen: Integer;
  var Dest: string);
function StringToWideChar(const Source: string; Dest: PWideChar;
  DestSize: Integer): PWideChar;

-- OLE string support procedures and functions

function OleStrToString(Source: PWideChar): string;
procedure OleStrToStrVar(Source: PWideChar; var Dest: string);
function StringToOleStr(const Source: string): PWideChar; }

interface

uses
  Windows, Messages, SysUtils,
  Classes, Graphics, Controls,
  Forms, Dialogs, StdCtrls,
  Ole2, ExtCtrls;

type
  TForm1 = class(TForm)
    BCLSID: TButton;
    bWideString: TButton;
    Edit1: TEdit;
    Panel1: TPanel;
    bDelCLSID: TButton;
    bDelphiWideString: TButton;
    Edit2: TEdit;
    procedure BCLSIDClick(Sender: TObject);
    procedure bWideStringClick(Sender: TObject);
    procedure bDelphiWideStringClick(Sender: TObject);
    procedure bDelCLSIDClick(Sender: TObject);
  end;

var
  Form1: TForm1;

implementation
```

```
uses
  OleAuto;

{$R *.DFM}

function AnsiToUnicode(S: string; var NewSize: Integer): PWideChar;
var
  Size: Integer;
  P: PWideChar;
begin
  Size := Length(S);
  NewSize := MultiByteToWideChar(CP_ACP, 0, PChar(S), Size, P, 0);
  P := VirtualAlloc(nil, Size, Mem_Commit, Page_ReadWrite);
  MultiByteToWideChar(CP_ACP, 0, PChar(S), Size, P, NewSize);
  Result := P;
end;

function UnicodeToAnsi(S: PWideChar): string;
var
  S1: PChar;
  i: Integer;
begin
  i := lstrlenw(S) + 1;
  GetMem(S1, i);
  i := WideCharToMultiByte(CP_ACP, 0, S, i, S1, i * 2, nil, nil);
  Result := S1;
  FreeMem(S1, i);
end;

procedure TForm1.BCLSIDClick(Sender: TObject);
const
  Size = 200;
var
  S: POleStr;
  hr: HResult;
begin
  S := VirtualAlloc(nil, Size, Mem_Commit, Page_ReadWrite);
  Hr := StringFromClsID(IID_IUnknown, S);
  if Succeeded(hr) then
    Edit1.Text := UnicodeToAnsi(S);
  VirtualFree(S, Size, Mem_Release);
end;

procedure TForm1.bWideStringClick(Sender: TObject);
var
  S: string;
  P: PWideChar;
  Size: Integer;
begin
  S := 'Wide Strings handled with raw API calls.';
  P := AnsiToUnicode(S, Size);
  S := UnicodeToAnsi(P);
  VirtualFree(P, Size, Mem_Release);
  Edit1.Text := S;
end;

// StringToWideChar and WideCharToString are in SYSTEM.PAS
procedure TForm1.bDelphiWideStringClick(Sender: TObject);
```

continues

Listing 2.3. continued

```
var
  S: string;
  P: array[0..127] of WideChar;
begin
  S := 'Wide Strings handled with native Delphi calls.';
  StringToWideChar(S, P, SizeOf(P) div 2);
  S := WideCharToString(P);
  Edit2.Text := S;
end;

// ClassIDToString is in OLEAUTO.PAS
procedure TForm1.bDelCLSIDClick(Sender: TObject);
begin
  Edit2.Text := ClassIDToString(IID_ICLASSFACTORY);
end;

end.
```

The Wides program has two buttons on it. One button can be used to convert a Unicode string into an AnsiString, and the other button shows how to move in the opposite direction. In particular, one button calls an OLE function that converts an OLE CLSID from the registry into a string. Unfortunately, the OLE functions usually work with Unicode strings, in part because OLE is a technology that looks toward the future.

When you call OLE string functions, you will often need to convert the Unicode strings used by OLE into AnsiStrings used by the Delphi visual controls. The Wides program shows you how to proceed. The other button on the form has a more contrived functionality: it simply converts from ANSI to Unicode and back, with no claim to real-world functionality.

The most useful function in the preceding program is probably UnicodeToAnsi:

```
function UnicodeToAnsi(S: PWideChar): string;
var
  S1: PChar;
  i: Integer;
begin
  i := lstrlenw(S) + 1;
  GetMem(S1, i);
  i := WideCharToMultiByte(CP_ACP, 0, S, i, S1, i * 2, nil, nil);
  Result := S1;
  FreeMem(S1, i);
end;
```

This function calls the WideCharToMultiByte Windows API function. I'm wrapping this function in a Delphi routine because it becomes a bit complex to call, due primarily to the number of parameters it takes. Here is the declaration for WideCharToMultiByte:

```
int WideCharToMultiByte(
    CodePage: Cardinal;         // code page
    dwFlags: Integer;           // performance and mapping flags
    lpWideCharStr: PWideChar;   // address of wide-character string
```

```
    cchWideChar: Integer;         // number of characters in string
    lpMultiByteStr: PChar;        // address of buffer for new string
    cchMultiByte: Integer;        // size of buffer
    lpDefaultChar: PChar;         // address of default for unmappable characters
    lpUsedDefaultChar: PBool;     // address of flag set when default char used
    );
```

To call WideCharToMultiByte, all you usually have to do is pass a PWideChar and its size, as well as a preallocated PChar and the size of the memory allocated for it. The specific amount of memory allocated for the PChar should be included in the call. The rest of the parameters can usually be set to zero, or to nil. The first parameter can receive a constant named CP_ACP, which designates the code page you want to work with. In short, the WideCharToMultiByte function is more powerful than anything you will need under normal circumstances. As a result, I have wrapped it in a Delphi function that will simplify its use. For more information, see the online help.

When you want to go the opposite way, from an AnsiString to a Unicode string, then you can call the following function from the Wides program:

```
function AnsiToUnicode(S: string; var NewSize: Integer): PWideChar;
var
  Size: Integer;
  P: PWideChar;
begin
  Size := Length(S);
  NewSize := MultiByteToWideChar(CP_ACP, 0, PChar(S), Size, P, 0);
  P := VirtualAlloc(nil, Size, Mem_Commit, Page_ReadWrite);
  MultiByteToWideChar(CP_ACP, 0, PChar(S), Size, P, NewSize);
  Result := P;
end;
```

This function allocates memory for the PWideChar that it returns. This means that you will be responsible for destroying the memory associated with the routine. The routine returns the size of the allocation in the NewSize parameter so that you will know how much memory to destroy.

AnsiToUnicode calls the MultiByteToWideChar function, which performs the opposite task from WideCharToMultiByte. Here is the declaration for MultiByteToWideChar:

```
function MultiByteToWideChar(
  CodePage: UINT;                  // Code Page
  dwFlags: DWORD;                  // Character-type Options
  const lpMultiByteStr: LPCSTR;   // Address of string to map
  cchMultiByte: Integer;          // Number of characters in string
  lpWideCharStr: LPWSTR;          // Address of WideChar buffer
  cchWideChar: Integer):          // Size of WideChar bugger.
    Integer; stdcall;             // Number of characters written to WideChar
```

The function MultiByteToWideChar can also return the number of bytes that need to be allocated for the PWideChar variable. To get the routine to perform this function, pass zero in the cchWideChar variable. Because the routine performs two functions, I call it twice in the AnsiToUnicode routine. The first time I am just getting the length of the PWideChar, and the second time I am getting the actual string.

That's all you will learn about long strings in this chapter. Hopefully, these pages have given you an introduction to the topic and will help you use them effectively in your own programs. Take special note of the built-in Delphi calls to `StringToWideChar`, `WideCharToString`, and `ClassIDToString` that are referenced in the code. These are the easiest ways to convert `WideChars` to `AnsiStrings`, and vice versa.

Variants

Variants are a new type in Delphi that can be assigned to a wide range of variable types. Some people jokingly refer to variants as a typeless type, because it can be used to represent a string, an integer, an object, or several other types.

The following is a simple procedure that illustrates the flexible nature of variants:

```
procedure TForm1.Button2Click(Sender: TObject);
var
  V:Variant;
begin
  V := 1;
  V := 'Sam';
end;
```

This procedure compiles fine under Delphi 2.0. As you can see, you are allowed to assign both a string and an integer to the same variant variable.

The following procedure, however, is not legal:

```
procedure TForm1.Button1Click(Sender: TObject);
var
  V: Variant;
begin
  V := 1;
  Caption := 'Sam' + V;
end;
```

The attempt to assign `Edit1.Text` to a variant concatinated with a string will be flagged as a type mismatch by the compiler because a variant takes on some of the attributes of an integer after being assigned to that type.

Underneath the surface, `Variant` types are represented by a 16-byte structure found in SYSTEM.PAS. At the time of this writing, that structure looks like this:

```
PVarData = ^TVarData;
TVarData = record
  VType: Word;
  Reserved1, Reserved2, Reserved3: Word;
  case Integer of
    varSmallint: (VSmallint: Smallint);
    varInteger:  (VInteger: Integer);
    varSingle:   (VSingle: Single);
    varDouble:   (VDouble: Double);
    varCurrency: (VCurrency: Currency);
```

```
    varDate:      (VDate: Double);
    varOleStr:    (VOleStr: PWideChar);
    varDispatch:  (VDispatch: Pointer);
    varError:     (VError: Integer);
    varBoolean:   (VBoolean: WordBool);
    varUnknown:   (VUnknown: Pointer);
    varByte:      (VByte: Byte);
    varString:    (VString: Pointer);
    varArray:     (VArray: PVarArray);
    varByRef:     (VPointer: Pointer);
end;
```

Notice that this is a variant record; that is, the various types represented in the case statement are overlaid in memory. (Variant records have nothing to do with the Variant type. The occurrence of the two names in the same context is just a coincidence.) The structure ends up being 16 bytes in size because the VType field is two bytes, the three reserved fields total six bytes, and the largest of the types in the variant section is the double, which is eight bytes in size (2 + 6 + 8 = 16). Once again, the case statement in the declaration is not a list of separate fields, but a list of different ways to interpret the eight bytes of data contained in the second half of the space allocated for the record.

The following are the declarations for the values used with variants:

```
varEmpty     = $0000;
  varNull    = $0001;
  varSmallint = $0002;
  varInteger = $0003;
  varSingle  = $0004;
  varDouble  = $0005;
  varCurrency = $0006;
  varDate    = $0007;
  varOleStr  = $0008;
  varDispatch = $0009;
  varError   = $000A;
  varBoolean = $000B;
  varVariant = $000C;
  varUnknown = $000D;
  varByte    = $0011;
  varString  = $0100;
  varTypeMask = $0FFF;
  varArray   = $2000;
  varByRef   = $4000;
```

NOTE

When you study these declarations, it's important to understand that Delphi defines a certain set of behaviors to be associated with variants, but might not guarantee that the implementation will remain the same from version to version. In other words, you can almost surely count on the fact that assigning both a string and an integer to the same variant will always be safe. However, you might not necessarily be sure that variants will always be represented by the same constants and record shown above. To check whether these implementations have been blessed as being permanent, refer to your Delphi documentation.

If I were writing the documentation for Delphi, I might decide not to show you the specific record shown previously because these kinds of details might change in later versions of the product, just as the internal representation for long strings might change. However, in this book I do not claim to be defining the language in a set of official documents. Instead, I am explaining the product to you, using the techniques that seem most useful. In this particular case, I think it helps to see behind the scenes and into the particulars of this implementation of the `Variant` type. Whether or not this will become a documented fact or an undocumented trick is not clear at the time of this writing.

It should be clear from the preceding code examples that knowing what type is represented by a variant at a particular moment can be important. To check the variant's type, you can use the `VarType` function, as shown here:

```
var
  Atype: Integer;
  V: Variant;
begin
  Atype := VarType(V);
  ...
end;
```

In this example, the `Integer` variable `AType` will be set to one of the constants shown above. In particular, it will probably be assigned to `varEmpty`, because in the preceding example this variable has not yet been assigned to another type.

If you want to get a closer look at a variant, you can typecast it to learn more about it, as shown in the following example:

```
procedure TForm1.Button1Click(Sender: TObject);
var
  V: Variant;
  VarData: TVarData;
begin
  V := 1;
  VarData := TVarData(V);
  Atype := VarData.vType;
end;
```

In this particular case, `AType` will be set to the same value that would be returned from a call to `VarType`.

To understand more about how all this works, see Listing 2.4, in which you can find the code for the VarDatas program. This code sets a single variant to a series of different values, and then examines the variant to discover the current value of its `VType` field.

Listing 2.4. The VarDatas program lets you examine variant types.

```
unit main;

interface

uses
  Windows, Messages, SysUtils,
  Classes, Graphics, Controls,
  Forms, Dialogs, StdCtrls;

type
  TForm1 = class(TForm)
    Button1: TButton;
    ListBox1: TListBox;
    procedure Button1Click(Sender: TObject);
  public
    procedure ShowVariant(V: Variant);
  end;

var
  Form1: TForm1;

implementation

{$R *.DFM}

function GetVariantType(V: Variant): string;
var
  VarData: TVarData;
  S: string;
begin
  VarData := TVarData(V);
  case VarData.vType of
    varEmpty: S := 'varEmpty';
    varNull:  S := 'varNull';
    varSmallint: S := 'varSmallInt';
    varInteger: S := 'varInteger';
    varSingle: S := 'varSingle';
    varDouble: S:= 'varDouble';
    varCurrency: S := 'varCurrency';
    varDate: S := 'varDate';
    varOleStr: S := 'varOleStr';
    varDispatch: S := 'varDispatch';
    varError: S := 'varError';
    varBoolean: S := 'varBoolean';
    varVariant: S := 'varVariant';
    varUnknown: S := 'varUnknown';
    varString: S := 'varString';
    varTypeMask: S := 'varTypeMask';
    varByRef: S := 'varByRef';
    varByte: S := 'varByte';
    varArray: S := 'varArray';
  end;
  Result := S;
end;

procedure TForm1.ShowVariant(V: Variant);
```

continues

56

Listing 2.4. continued

```
var
  S, Temp: string;
begin
  if VarIsNull(V) then begin
    Temp := 'Null';
    S := Format('Value: %-15s  Type: Null', [Temp]);
  end else begin
    Temp := V;
    S := Format('Value: %-15s  Type: %s', [Temp, GetVariantType(V)]);
  end;
  ListBox1.Items.Add(S);
end;

procedure TForm1.Button1Click(Sender: TObject);
var
  V: Variant;
  S: TObject;
begin
  ShowVariant(V);
  V := Null;
  ShowVariant(V);
  V := 1;
  ShowVariant(V);
  V := 'Sam';
  ShowVariant(V);
  V := 1.25;
  ShowVariant(V);
end;

end.
```

A typical run of this program is shown in Figure 2.4.

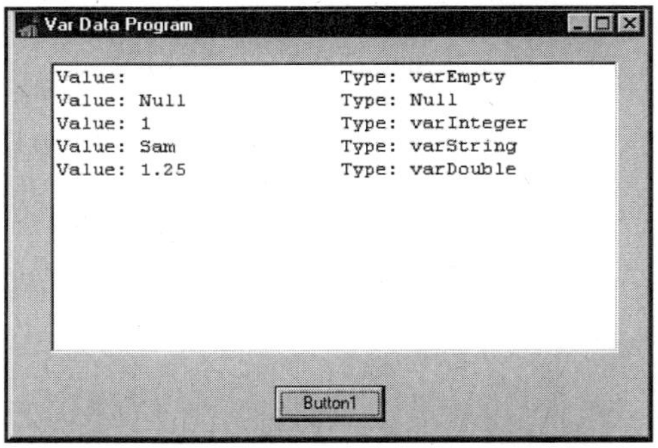

FIGURE 2.4.

The VarDatas program uses the TVarData structure to examine how variants are put together.

The data shown in the list box in Figure 2.4 represents the value and internal representation of a single variant that is assigned a series of different types. It's important to understand that Variant can't simultaneously represent all types, and can instead at any one moment take on the characteristics of only one particular type.

The code that assigns different types to a variant is easy to understand, as is shown here:

```
procedure TForm1.Button1Click(Sender: TObject);
var
  V: Variant;
  S: TObject;
begin
  ShowVariant(V);
  V := Null;
  ShowVariant(V);
  V := 1;
  ShowVariant(V);
  V := 'Sam';
  ShowVariant(V);
  V := 1.25;
  ShowVariant(V);
end;
```

The code that reports on the current type of a variant is somewhat more complex, but still relatively straightforward, as shown next:

```
function GetVariantType(V: Variant): string;
var
  VarData: TVarData;
  S: string;
begin
  VarData := TVarData(V);
  case VarData.VType of
    varEmpty: S := 'varEmpty';
    varNull:  S := 'varNull';
    varSmallint: S := 'varSmallInt';
    varInteger: S := 'varInteger';
    varSingle: S := 'varSingle';
    varDouble: S:= 'varDouble';
    varCurrency: S := 'varCurrency';
    varDate: S := 'varDate';
    varOleStr: S := 'varOleStr';
    varDispatch: S := 'varDispatch';
    varError: S := 'varError';
    varBoolean: S := 'varBoolean';
    varVariant: S := 'varVariant';
    varUnknown: S := 'varUnknown';
    varString: S := 'varString';
    varTypeMask: S := 'varTypeMask';
    varByRef: S := 'varByRef';
  end;
  Result := S;
end;
```

This code first converts a variant into a variable of type TVarData. In doing so, it is merely surfacing the true underlying type of the variant. However, a variable of type TVarData will not act the same as a variable of type Variant. This is because the compiler provides special services for variants that it would not provide for a simple record type such as TVarData.

It's important to note that there are at least two ways to write the first lines of code in this function. For instance, I could have written

```
function GetVariantType(V: Variant): string;
var
  I: Integer;
  S: string;
begin
  i := VarType(V);
  case i of
    varEmpty: S := 'varEmpty';
    varNull:  S := 'varNull';
    ...
  end;
end;
```

This code works the same as the code shown in the actual program found on the *Unleashed* CD-ROM.

However you decide to implement the function, the key point is that variants can take on the appearance of being of a certain type. The chameleon-like behavior of Variant is sparked by the type of variable to which it is assigned. If you want, you can think of a variant as being a chameleon that hides itself from view by assuming the coloration of the variable to which it is assigned. A variant is never of type Variant, it's always either empty, NULL, or the type of the variable to which it is assigned. In the same way, a chameleon has no color of its own, but is always changing to adapt its color to the environment around it. Either that or it is unborn, dead, non-existent, or has no color at all!

The following routines can all be used with variants. To learn more about these routines, look in the online help.

```
procedure VarClear(var V: Variant);
procedure VarCopy(var Dest: Variant; const Source: Variant);
procedure VarCast(var Dest: Variant; const Source: Variant; VarType: Integer);
function VarType(const V: Variant): Integer;
function VarAsType(const V: Variant; VarType: Integer): Variant;
function VarIsEmpty(const V: Variant): Boolean;
function VarIsNull(const V: Variant): Boolean;
function VarFromDateTime(DateTime: TDateTime): Variant;
function VarToDateTime(const V: Variant): TDateTime;
```

Here are some routines to use with Variant arrays, which are discussed in Chapter 29, "OLE Automation Basics."

```
function VarArrayCreate(const Bounds: array of Integer;
  VarType: Integer): Variant;
function VarArrayOf(const Values: array of Variant): Variant;
procedure VarArrayRedim(var A: Variant; HighBound: Integer);
function VarArrayDimCount(const A: Variant): Integer;
function VarArrayLowBound(const A: Variant; Dim: Integer): Integer;
function VarArrayHighBound(const A: Variant; Dim: Integer): Integer;
function VarArrayLock(const A: Variant): Pointer;
procedure VarArrayUnlock(const A: Variant);
function VarIsArray(const A: Variant): Boolean;
```

Before closing this section I want to make it clear that variants are not meant to be used broadly in your program whenever you need to work with a variable. I have no doubt that many people will in fact program that way, but I want to emphasize that the developers didn't really want variants to be used that way, mainly because they have some overhead associated with them that can slow down the compiler. (Some tricks performed by variants, such as string manipulation, happen to be very highly optimized. However, you should never consider a variant to be as fast or efficient as a standard Object Pascal type such as an Integer, Cardinal, or string.)

Variants are almost certainly best used in OLE and database applications. In particular, variants were brought into the language because they play a role in OLE automation. Furthermore, much of the structure and behavior of variants are defined by the rules of OLE. These unusual types also prove to be useful in database applications. As a rule, there is so much overhead involved in referencing any value from a database that a little additional variant manipulation code is not going to make a significant difference.

Generic and Fundamental Integer Types

When you are moving your code from 16 to 32 bits, there are no significant changes in regard to the way the compiler handles floating-point types. A Double in 16-bit Delphi is the same as a Double in 32-bit Delphi. Integers, however, are a different story. In particular, an integer in Delphi 16 is not the same as an integer in 32-bit Delphi.

> **NOTE**
>
> The word *integer* has two related meanings in Object Pascal. There is the Integer type, which is used in declarations. It is a 16-bit unsigned value in Delphi 16, and a 32-bit unsigned value in Delphi 32. There are also the integer types, which represent a generic way of referring to all ordinal, scalar types used in Delphi. In particular, Integer, Word, ShortInt, LongInt and Byte are all integer types. I will capitalize the word "integer" when I am referring to a specific type, and I will leave the word in small letters when I am referring to the whole family of integer types.

There are two types of integers in Delphi 2.0. The fundamental types remain the same in all versions of Object Pascal. Here is a short table showing the fundamental types:

```
ShortInt    -128 .. 127              Signed 8-bit
Byte         0  ..  255              Unsigned 8-bit
SmallInt    -32768 .. 32767          Signed 16-bit
Word         0  ..  65535            Unsigned 16-bit
LongInt      -2147483648 .. 2147483647      Signed 32-bit
```

If you are in Delphi 16 and use a ShortInt, then it will be an 8-bit signed value. If you are in Delphi 32 and use a ShortInt, then it will still be an 8-bit signed value.

The generic integer types are not the same in each version of Delphi. Here is a table showing the generic types:

```
Integer    -32768 .. 32767              Signed 16-bit
Integer    -2147483648 .. 2147483647    Signed 32-bit
Cardinal   0 .. 65535                   Unsigned 16-bit
Cardinal   0 .. 2147483647              Unsigned 32-bit
```

Generic types will have a 16-bit value in Delphi 16, and a 32-bit value in Delphi 32. There are two kinds of generic integers: signed and unsigned.

You should note that Cardinals in 32-bit land use only 31 of the 32 bits available to them. That is, the top number they store is 2GB, rather than the expected 4GB. The Delphi compiler assumes that all integer operations are going to fit into 32 bits. If the developers allowed Cardinals to use all 32 bits, there would be a good chance that you could add two numbers together to create a sum larger than what can be fit into 32 bits. This would create an overflow condition that would be difficult for the compiler to detect. As a result, you are limited to 31 bits in Cardinals and LongInts. You can still store 32 bits of information in a Cardinal and reliably perform bitwise operations on all 32 bits, but you could not safely use the number in a mathematical expression such as addition or multiplication. This is a limitation in the compiler that will hopefully be overcome in later editions of Delphi. The Delphi Comp type can be used if you need to perform integer math on values up to 64 bits in size.

Generic integers have the habit of changing their size to adapt to the current operating system. A 16-bit operating system is going to be very efficient when working with 16-bit values, and a 32-bit operating system will be very efficient when working with 32-bit values. Therefore, it can be convenient to have a type that switches back and forth between 16- and 32-bit values in order to adapt itself to the operating system or the current machine.

> **NOTE**
>
> The fact that 16-bit operating systems work best with 16-bit numbers means that it is sometimes more efficient to use a Word or an Integer under Delphi 16 than it is to use a Byte or ShortInt. In other words, smaller isn't necessarily better when it comes to producing fast integer math. The Holy Grail is usually not size, but matching the type to the CPU and the operating system.
>
> Having said this, I have to admit that I rarely give such matters much consideration when I program. I try to never use a type that might prove too small for the values I wish to store in it, and otherwise I don't tend to give the matter much thought. Still, there is some value in the idea that it's best to always use the Integer or Cardinal generic types, unless you have a specific reason for using the other types.

When you are dealing with simple integer types—and indeed with all Delphi types—it is worthwhile to spend some time browsing the WINDOWS.PAS unit, and in particular, the top few pages of it. There you will find a number of interesting declarations that might prove useful to you when you work with Windows API functions. Here is a sample selection of declarations:

```
WPARAM = Longint;
  LPARAM = Longint;
  LRESULT = Longint;

  LPSTR = PAnsiChar;
  LPCSTR = PAnsiChar;
  LPWSTR = PWideChar;
  LPCWSTR = PWideChar;

  DWORD = Integer;
  BOOL = LongBool;
  PBOOL = ^BOOL;
  PByte = ^Byte;
  PINT = ^Integer;
  PSingle = ^Single;
  PWORD = ^Word;
  PDWORD = ^DWORD;
  LPDWORD = PDWORD;

  UCHAR = Byte;
  PUCHAR = ^Byte;
  SHORT = Smallint;
  UINT = Cardinal;
  PUINT = ^UINT;
  ULONG = Cardinal;
  PULONG = ^ULONG;

  LCID = DWORD;
  LANGID = Word;

  THandle = Integer;
  PHandle = ^Thandle;
```

When you see Windows API books written about the C/C++ programming language, you will find many of the types just shown. For example, the UINT, DWORD, and LPSTR types are among the most frequently used types in Windows code. It is also interesting to note that commonly used Pascal types such as THandle simply resolve into an Integer.

Many Object Pascal programmers spend a good deal of time browsing Windows API books written about the C/C++ programming language. As a result, it is often useful for programmers to refer function parameters by the same names as they are given in C/C++ reference books. Therefore, it's tempting, under certain circumstances, to refer to a DWORD rather than an Integer, and a UINT rather than a Cardinal.

Despite the usefulness of these C/C++ -like declarations, I have to confess that I don't like the game of creating a type that is, in effect, little more than an alias for another type. I know that there are times when this technique is very useful, and indeed, sometimes it can save hours of work when you need to move back and forth between different platforms. In such cases, you probably should use these kinds of declarations. However, I prefer to keep my code as simple and lucid as possible. Everyone who understands the rudiments of Object Pascal will immediately understand the following declaration:

```
var
  I: Integer;
  S: string;
```

It is simple in the extreme, and its simplicity is an enormous virtue. The following declarations, on the other hand, are a bit confusing:

```
var
  i:  LCID;
  s: LPCSTR;
```

An LCID, for instance, translates into a DWORD, which in turn translates into an Integer. This whole business of having a type that is really an alias for another alias is the kind of thing on which C/C++ is built. Macros in C++ are frequently layered three or four levels deep, and this is indeed fine under certain circumstances. Object Pascal, however, typically draws a line in the sand around these types of issues. If you want the syntactical convenience and complexity of multiple inheritance, then you should use C/C++. If you want the sometimes artful ambiguity of operating overloading, then you should use C/C++. If you want to create multiple layers of aliases in order to achieve certain syntactical effects, then you probably ought to use C/C++.

Object Pascal, on the other hand, tends to be about simplicity and elegance. Indeed, well-written Object Pascal code comes close to being self-documenting. It says what it means. It's the opposite of a language such as C/C++, where even relatively simple functions are usually burdened under the weight of numerous, very necessary, comments.

Obviously, matters of this type are strictly matters of opinion, and perhaps it is objectionable for a writer to abuse the privileges of authorship by promoting a particular, possibly prejudiced, viewpoint. Nevertheless, I would still assert that it is in the nature of Object Pascal to attempt to be as simple, sparce, and elegant as possible. The classic Object Pascal method is about six lines long, takes only one simple parameter, and has only one local variable. It goes against the general tenor of the language to introduce complex syntactical conceits such as multiple inheritance, macros, or variable declarations that end up resolving into multiple layers of aliases. There is, in my opinion, a place for this kind of thing, but it's in C/C++, not in Object Pascal.

Currency Type

The Currency type represents the resolution to a long-term problem in Object Pascal. The issue here is that the binary representation of a decimal floating-point value is approximate in the majority of cases. As a result, they are not a good way to keep track of monetary values. Integer numbers, on the other hand, are always accurate. However, integer values are not a good way to track money because they don't have a convenient system for tracking dollars and cents; that is, there is no way to use them with decimal points or fractional parts of a dollar.

The Currency type resolves this problem because it is simultaneously an integer type and a floating-point type. Beneath the surface, Currency types are really integer values similar to the Comp type. However, they also support the concept of a decimal place. In particular, they have an implied decimal point that assumes 4 decimal places.

Consider the following example:

```
procedure TForm1.Button1Click(Sender: TObject);
var
  B: Currency;
begin
  B := 2.1 + 12;
  Panel1.Caption = Format('Money: %m', [b]);
end;
```

This function uses the Currency type to add two numbers together and display them in the caption of Panel. The output will be Money: $14.10, as shown in Figure 2.5.

FIGURE 2.5.

The output from the Money program.

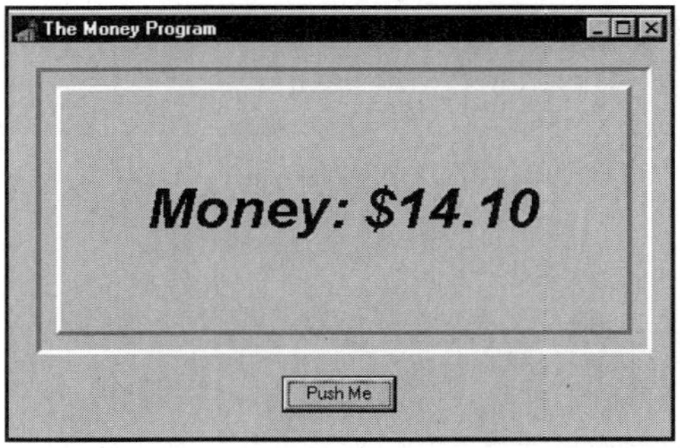

Because the Currency type will not become inaccurate when you are performing math on basic monetary transactions, it is the preferred type to use when you need to keep track of dollars and cents.

Summary

In this chapter, you learned about some of the new types found in Delphi 2.0. You also learned the changes made to some of the old types, and briefly learned a few of the issues you might want to keep in mind when you use Delphi variables.

On the whole, Delphi makes porting from 16 to 32 bits almost ridiculously easy. Most of the time you don't need to think about the port at all; it just happens automatically. However, there are some underlying issues that you need to consider if you want to delve deeply into the new compiler and into portability-related issues. As a result, I have tried to introduce some of the main topics in this chapter.

The following are the key points to remember from this chapter:

- Delphi has a new string type that no longer has a 255-character limitation. The new Delphi long strings are implemented as pointers to zero-terminated strings. They do not, however, act like pointers when you use them in your programs. They travel incognito, masquerading as normal strings.

- The `Variant` type is useful in OLE automation and database applications. It is unique in that it can be assigned several different types of data, although it is limited to containing only one type of data at a time. In other words, you can assign it to multiple types over time, but at any one time it is limited to only one type. This strange behavior has led to it jokingly being called a "typeless type." You should not use variants in standard Pascal routines because of the overhead associated with them. Use them only in OLE-based applications. They will also be used in database routines, but most `Variant`-based database code is implemented by the developers of Delphi, and you should usually just use regular variables in your database code.

- The generic `Cardinal` and `Integer` types vary in their definition depending on whether you are in the 16- or 32-bit version of the product. As a result, they tend to help you optimize your code if you need to switch back and forth between these two environments. The fundamental types remain the same in both 16- and 32-bit Delphi. The fundamental types are `ShortInts`, `SmallInts`, `LongInts`, `Bytes`, and `Words`.

Strings and Text Files

3

This chapter takes an in-depth look at strings. You have already worked with strings in this book, but there are a number of features associated with them that you haven't yet had a chance to explore. This chapter also explores text files, which provide a simple mechanism for storing strings in a file.

The first part of the chapter demonstrates that strings, even the new long strings, are really only a form of array. However, a number of interesting rules specific to strings do not apply to arrays, and my goal is to explain the most important of them in very explicit detail. In particular, you will see how to search for a substring in a string and how to parse a lengthy string.

Once you understand how strings work, the next subject to approach is how to store them in text files, and how to retrieve them again from those text files. While pursuing this subject, you get a chance to see how one goes about storing numbers in a text file.

A String Is Just a Form of an Array

A Pascal `ShortString` or `AnsiString` is very similar to, but not identical to, an array of characters. Consider the following declarations:

```
type
  TNearString = array[0..255] of Char;

var
  NearString: TNearString;
  MyString: string;
```

In this code fragment, `MyString` has nearly all the traits of `NearString`, plus a few special qualities. In other words, a string is a superset of an array of char, except that you can't access element zero in a long string. The first section of this chapter delineates exactly what special qualities belong to a string that do not belong to an array of char.

> **NOTE**
>
> This subject is complicated by the fact that `AnsiStrings` and `ShortStrings` have a very different internal structure. From reading Chapter 2, "Delphi Types Under Win32," you know that `AnsiStrings` are not simple arrays, but pointers to arrays. However, in this chapter, I discuss `AnsiStrings` as if they were simple arrays of `Char`, except when I absolutely need to clarify the situation for some particular reason.

All characters in an array of Char are equal. No one character has any special properties. In a `ShortString`, however, the first character is called a *length byte*. The length byte designates how many significant characters exist inside the string. Because the first character has this special task, the first meaningful letter is always offset one in the string. In an AnsiString, there is no character at element zero in the string. Instead, the length "byte," which might now be more appropriately called a length value, is stored in the first 4 bytes at a negative offset. Beyond that is another 4 bytes that tells you the memory allocated for the string, as well as another 4 that track the reference count.

> **NOTE**
>
> In the paragraphs that follow, you need to remember that most Chars can be represented in two different ways. For instance, the letter A can be printed verbatim or it can be represented by the 65th member in certain character sets. If you want to refer to the letter A by its place in a character set, you can write #65. The # in this example designates that the item in question is a char, not a simple numerical value. Therefore, the number 5 is represented as 5, but the fifth character in a character set is represented by #5. If you are having trouble grasping these concepts, you might want to refer to the chapter stored on the CD called, "Integer Types in Detail." Note also that not all character sets are identical. For instance, you can run the CharSet program that comes with Windows 3.1 to confirm that the 65th character in the WingDings character set is not an A.

Consider a string containing the word Hello. This string is five characters long, so the Length function will return the number 5:

```
Len := Length(NearString);
```

In this case, Len is set to the number 5. The next character in the array would be an H:

```
NearString[1] := 'H';   { H = #72 }
```

The rest of the letters would follow immediately after:

```
NearString[2] := 'e';
NearString[3] := 'l';
NearString[4] := 'l';
NearString[5] := 'o';
```

If you are working with a ShortString, the end result is an array of six characters that look like this:

```
#5,'H','e','l','l','o'
```

If you are working with a long string, the end result looks like this:

```
'H', 'e', 'l', 'l', 'o',#0
```

In this case, the string is null-terminated. All AnsiStrings are null-terminated, and their length byte is stored at a negative offset.

If the length byte of the ShortString in the preceding example was accidentally set to #6 instead of to #5, then whatever letter happened to be in memory at position 7 would automatically become part of the string, usually with disastrous results. The same thing would happen if you used the SetLength function to set the length of the AnsiString (in the previous example) to 6. For instance, the string Hello might suddenly become any of the following:

```
Hello1
Hellob
Hello#
Hello+
```

In short, the behavior you can expect to see is entirely undefined in such situations.

The code shown here will compile and run without error:

```
var
  S: ShortString;
begin
  SetLength(S, 5);   // OldStyle: S[0] = #5;
  S[1] := 'H';
  S[2] := 'e';
  S[3] := 'l';
  S[4] := 'l';
  S[5] := 'o';
  Edit1.Text := S;
end;
```

This code prints the word Hello inside an edit control. You can view this code fragment as the anatomy of a ShortString. It shows explicitly the various parts that go into making up the elements of this type.

The following code behaves in a manner identical to the code shown earlier:

```
var
  S: string;
begin
  S := 'Hello';
  Edit1.Text := S;
end;
```

This fragment is easier to write than the code shown previously. However, the fact that you can write code like this is really a special feature of the compiler. What it actually does is shown in the first example. However, it would be too much trouble to have you go through that lengthy process every time you wanted to assign a value to a string. Therefore, the compiler lets you write code like that in the second example.

The following short sample program, called EASYSTR, demonstrates the ideas presented in this section. (See Listing 3.1.) Specifically, EASYSTR shows what happens if you don't treat the length byte in a string with care.

The form for the EASYSTR program includes two buttons and an edit control, as shown in Figure 3.1.

FIGURE 3.1.

*To create the form for the
EASYSTR program, simply
drop two buttons, a panel,
and a label onto a form.*

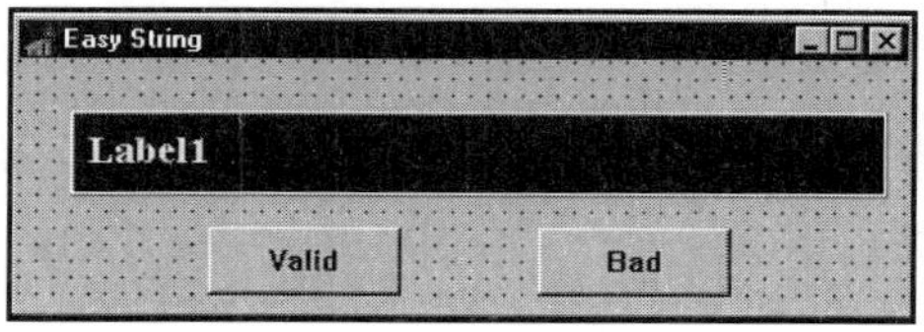

Listing 3.1. The main module for the EASYSTR program.

```
unit Main;

{ Program copyright (c) 1995 by Charles Calvert }
{ Project Name: EASYSTR }

{ This program demonstrates some basic facts
  about the way strings are structured. In particular,
  it gives you a look at the length byte, which is the
  zeroth element in all Pascal based ShortStrings. The length
  byte determines the length of a string. If the
  length byte is too large, then garbage characters can
  appear in your strings.
}

interface

uses
  SysUtils, WinTypes, WinProcs,
  Messages, Classes, Graphics,
  Controls, Forms, Dialogs,
  StdCtrls, ExtCtrls;

type
  TEasyString = class(TForm)
    Panel1: TPanel;
    Label1: TLabel;
    Valid: TButton;
    Bad: TButton;
    procedure BValidClick(Sender: TObject);
    procedure BBadClick(Sender: TObject);
  private
    { Private declarations }
  public
    { Public declarations }
  end;

var
  EasyString: TEasyString;

implementation

{$R *.DFM}

procedure ScrambleString(var S: ShortString);
var
  i: Integer;
begin
```

continues

Listing 3.1. continued

```
  for i := 0 to 255 do
    S[i] := Chr(Random(255 + 1));
end;

procedure TEasyString.BValidClick(Sender: TObject);
var
  S: ShortString;
begin
  ScrambleString(S);
  SetLength(S, 5);     // OldStyle: S[0] = #5
  S[1] := 'H';
  S[2] := 'e';
  S[3] := 'l';
  S[4] := 'l';
  S[5] := 'o';
  Label1.Caption := S;
end;


procedure TEasyString.BBadClick(Sender: TObject);
var
  S: ShortString;
begin
  ScrambleString(S);
  SetLength(S, 150); // OldStyle: S[0] = #150
  S[1] := 'H';
  S[2] := 'e';
  S[3] := 'l';
  S[4] := 'l';
  S[5] := 'o';
  Label1.Caption := S;
end;

end.
```

The EASYSTR program enables you to print a valid string and an invalid string inside an edit control. The invalid string is flawed because it has an incorrect length byte. In particular, it sets the length byte to 150, although the string you want to print is only five characters long.

This simple mistake would cause trouble in your program. However, I want to make sure you get a sense of what is going wrong, so I have added another procedure to the function that ensures that all the characters in a string get set to random values:

```
procedure ScrambleString(var S: ShortString);
var
  i: Integer;
begin
  for i := 1 to 255 do
    S[I] := Chr(Random(255) + 1)
end;
```

This function sets all the characters in a string to random values between 1 and 255. It does this by using the Random function, which returns a random number between zero and the value passed in its sole parameter. In this case, however, the goal is not to produce a random number, but a random character. To achieve this end, the Chr function is used. Chr is used to convert a numerical value into a character.

NOTE

There is no significant difference between using the Chr function and just typecasting the value returned from the random function

```
S[i] := Char(Random(255));
```

This code produces the same result as when the Chr function is used.

Note also that this program works with ShortStrings. You would have to modify the program slightly to get the same effects with long strings. In particular, you could not start writing random values to a long string without first allocating memory for the string! Or, to put the matter slightly differently, declaring a ShortString automatically allocates 256 bytes for your string.

Because I'm using ShortStrings, I could have the ScrambleString function iterate from 0 to 255, but I think Delphi programmers should now always be in the habit of not referencing element zero in a string.

Figure 3.2 depicts what can happen when you try to write a string to an edit control with the length byte set to an arbitrarily large value. Clearly the result is less than optimal. Random characters are scattered across the component like a series of strange hieroglyphics, and the word Hello is discernible only after you study the output in some depth.

FIGURE 3.2.

If the length byte of a string is set to the wrong value, the results can be fairly chaotic.

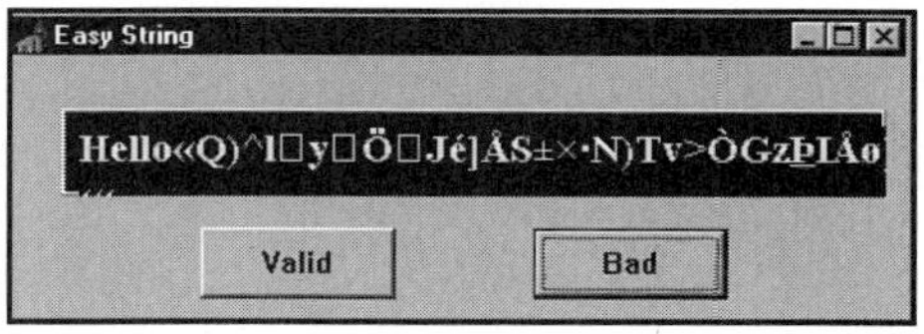

You can compare the general fiasco shown in Figure 3.2 with the orderly results shown in Figure 3.3. In this second case, the compiler is passed a valid length byte and the results are precisely defined and readily understandable.

FIGURE 3.3.

No matter how you scramble the extra characters in a string, the result shown to the screen will be fine as long as the length byte is assigned a valid value.

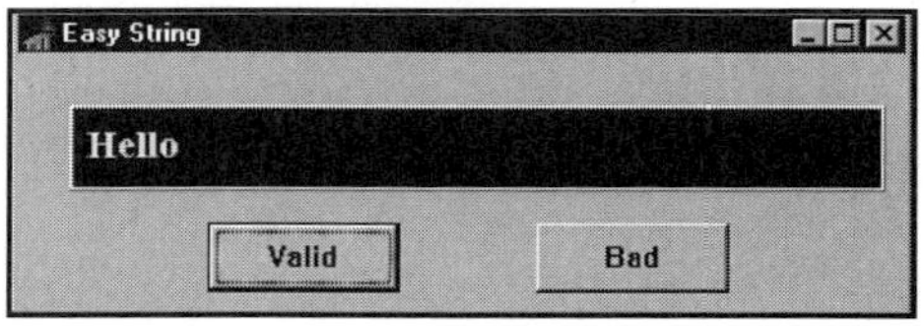

Remember that AnsiStrings differ from ShortStrings in that you can only manipulate the length of the string through the use of the SetLength function. Because of this limitation, it is probably best to always use SetLength, and to never reference element zero in a string directly.

PChars: Another Kind of Zero-Terminated String

Before going on to discuss strings in more depth, I'll spend a moment talking about PChars, which are zero-terminated strings, and the correct way to use an array of char as a string.

Like an AnsiString, a PChar has no length byte. PChars, however, do not have any data stored at negative offsets. Instead, the processor searches for a #0 character and assumes that this marks the end of a string. Specifically, if you go back to the examples shown in the last section, you can easily modify the functions so that they will print out a properly formatted zero-terminated string:

```
procedure TForm1.BCharsClick(Sender: TObject);
var
  S: array[0..25] of Char;
begin
  S[0] := 'H';
  S[1] := 'e';
  S[2] := 'l';
  S[3] := 'l';
  S[4] := 'o';
  S[5] := #0;
  Edit1.Text := S;
end;
```

This code prints the word Hello in a neat and orderly fashion. To do this, it sets the first character of a PChar to the letter H and sets the sixth character to the value of the first member of the currently selected character set. It is important to remember that you don't end zero-terminated strings with the number zero; you end them with #0. If you refer to the chapter on the Unleashed CD called "Integer Types in Detail," you will see that the number zero is usually the 48th member of a standard character set. It is entirely distinct from the first member of that character set.

PChars are pointers to arrays of char, and as a result you must allocate memory for them before you try to use them. For instance, in the following code I explicitly allocate 26 bytes of memory for a PChar before filling it in with characters and displaying it on the screen. When I am finished, I then deallocate that memory.

```
procedure TForm1.BCharsClick(Sender: TObject);
var
  S: PChar;
begin
  GetMem(S, 26);
  StrCopy(S, 'Hello');
```

```
  Edit1.Text := S;
  FreeMem(S, 26);
end;
```

When you allocate memory for a pointer, it is as if someone goes out into the memory theater and specifically tells a certain number of people that they are now part of a particular allocation. In this example, for instance, 26 members of the audience are grouped together under the aegis of a single PChar.

NOTE

If you don't want to call GetMem and FreeMem, you can also allocate memory for a PChar by writing the following type of code:

```
var
  S: array[0..25] of Char;
```

In most situations, the preceding declaration would be equivalent to a PChar and would be treated the same as a PChar. If you declared the array as being 1..26, instead of 0..25, the compiler would not treat the array as a PChar.

Devotees of the C/C++ language will notice that Delphi has a function called StrCopy that mirrors the job performed by strcpy in the land that AT&T made. That is, it copies one string into another. There are also functions called StrCat, StrPos, StrCmp, and so on. The StrPas function was used in Delphi 1.0 to convert a PChar into a string, but it is no longer needed. The developers were able to free us from the need to use that function perhaps in part because PChars and long strings have a very similar structure.

If you want to learn a little more about PChars, take a look at the EASYSTR2 program, which is on the Unleashed CD. It enables you to use the two functions shown previously.

For now, however, I'm going to back away from the subject of PChars and arrays of Char, content to have done little more than introduce the subject. My goal here is not yet to explain this second type of string in any detail, but to introduce the topic so that no one is taken by surprise when seeing these types of strings in day-to-day work.

In earlier versions of Delphi and Turbo Pascal, PChars were needed when you worked directly with Windows API functions. In fact, they are still used in these functions, but the chore of managing them is simplified because you can typecast an AnsiString as a PChar and assign a PChar to an AnsiString:

```
var
  P: PChar;
  S: String;
begin
  S := P;
  P := PChar(S);
end;
```

Because PChars are native to many Windows API functions, sooner or later you will meet them face to face in some dark coding alley. As a nod to their prominence in the language, I discuss them in depth in the next chapter, "Pointers and PChars."

Working with Strings

It is time to explore some real-world examples of the kind of challenges you might face when working with strings. One classic problem that comes up fairly frequently is that you might need to strip blanks off the end of a string. Consider the following code fragment:

```
uses
  MathBox;

procedure TForm1.Button1Click(Sender: TObject);
var
  S: String;
  R: Double;
begin
  S := '2.03      ';
  R := Str2Real(S);
  WriteLn(R:2:2);
end;
```

At first glance you might expect this code to print the number 2.03 to the screen. However, it will not because Str2Real is unable to handle the extra spaces appended after the characters 2.03.

It is likely that a problem similar to this could occur in a real-world program. For instance, a programmer might ask the user to enter a string, and the user might accidentally append a series of blanks to it, or perhaps the extra characters were added by some other means. To be sure that your program will run correctly, you have to strip those extra blank characters off the end of your string.

You, can, of course, use the Trim function to resolve this problem. However, it's also useful to have a more general-purpose routine that will strip off *any* specified character from the end of a string. The following function, called StripEndChars, can be used to remove not only blanks, but any other specified character from the end of a string:

```
function StripEndChars(S: string; Ch: Char): string;
var
  i: Integer;
begin
  i := Length(S);

  while (length(S) > 0) and (S[i] = Ch) do begin
    Delete(S,i,1);
    Dec(i);
  end;
  StripEndChars := S;
end;
```

This function does not change the string that you pass into it, but creates a second string that it passes back to you as the function result. This means you must use this function in the following manner:

```
S2 := StripEndChars(S1);
```

where S1 and S2 are both strings. You also can write code that looks like this:

```
S1 := StripEndChars(S1);
```

StripEndChars has one local variable, i, which is an integer:

```
var
  i: Integer;
```

This variable is set to the length of the string passed to the function:

```
  i := Length(S);
```

The Length function is one of the simplest and fastest executing routines in the Object Pascal language. In effect, it does nothing more than this, at least when working with ShortStrings:

```
function Length(S: ShortString): Integer;
begin
  Length := Ord(S[0]);
end;
```

Of course, the actual routine in the runtime library is almost certainly written in assembler, and it works with both ShortStrings and long strings. Nevertheless, like the one above, it returns the value of the length byte that is the first character of a ShortString, or that resides at a negative offset in a long string.

The next line in the function checks the value of the last character in the string under investigation:

```
  while S[i] = Ch do begin
```

More explicitly, it checks to see whether it is equal to the type of character you want to remove. If it is, then the following code is executed:

```
    Delete(S,i,1);
    Dec(i);
```

The built-in Delete function takes three parameters. The first is a string, the second is an offset into the string, and the third is the number of characters you want to delete from the first parameter. In this case, if you passed in the string 'Sam   ', which is the word Sam followed by three spaces; the last space would be lopped off so that the string would become 'Sam   ', where Sam is followed by two spaces.

The Delete function decrements the value of i and then returns to the top of the loop to see if the next character is equal to the value passed in:

```
while S[i] = Ch do begin
```

If it is, that character is also deleted from the end of the string.

The entire process is repeated until the last character in the string is no longer a space. At that point, the function ends, and a string is returned that is guaranteed not to have any spaces appended on the end of it.

The StripEndChars function itself is not crucial to most programming endeavors, but becoming familiar with functions of its type is essential. It isn't really that this one particular function is so important, although I do end up using it fairly often. What is crucial here is that StripEndChars is the kind of function that solves a common problem likely to be encountered by programmers, and furthermore, it does so by bearing down and manipulating a chunk of data on a byte-by-byte basis.

Date-Based Filenames

This section presents another function for manipulating strings. This function is not likely to be used every day by most programmers, but when you need it, it comes in very handy indeed. The primary reason for showing it, however, is just to give an example of working with strings.

Programmers often end up making reports or gathering data on a daily basis. For instance, I sign onto an online service nearly every day, and frequently I want to store the information I glean from cyberspace inside a file that contains the current date. In other words, if I sign onto CompuServe and download the current messages from the Delphi forum, I don't want to store that information in a file called DELPHI.CIS. I want a filename that includes the current date, so that I can easily tell what files were downloaded on a particular day. In short, I want to automatically generate filenames that look like this: DE022595.TXT, PA022695.TXT, DE022795.TXT, and so on, where 022795 is a date of the type *MMDDYY*.

> **NOTE**
>
> Given the long filename support in Windows 95, names such as those shown above are becoming less common. However, I still use them heavily, in part because the networks, command-line processors, and compression programs that I most often use do not yet support long filenames.

Here is a function that fits the bill:

```
{- - - - - - - - - - - - - - - - - - - - - - - - - - - - - - - - - - - - - -
        Name: GetTodayName function
 Declaration: GetTodayName(Pre, Ext: String): String;
        Unit: StrBox
        Code: S
        Date: 03/01/94
 Description: Return a filename of type PRE0101.EXT,
              where PRE and EXT are user supplied strings,
```

```
                and 0101 is today's date. PRE must not be
                longer than 2 letters.
-----------------------------------------------------}
function GetTodayName(Pre, Ext: string): string;
var
  y, m, d : Word;
  Year: String;
begin
  DecodeDate(Date,y,m,d);
  Year := Int2StrPad0(y, 4);
  Delete(Year, 1, 2);
  GetTodayName := Pre + Int2StrPad0(m, 2) + Int2StrPad0(d, 2) +
                  Year + '.' + Ext;
end;
```

This function, demonstrated online in EASYFILE.DPR, takes a two-letter prefix and a three-letter extension, and creates a filename of the type shown previously. The function begins by calling the built-in Delphi function Date, which returns a TDateTime structure. This, in turn, is passed to the DecodeDate function from SysUtils unit, which returns the current year, month, and day as Word values. If the date were Tuesday, March 25, 1994, the function would return the following:

```
Year       := 1994
  Month      := 3
  Day        := 25
```

Assuming that the user of this function passed in DE in the PRE parameter, and TXT in the EXT parameter, it would be fairly easy to use the IntToStr function to create something like this:

DE3251994.TXT

There are several problems with this result, the biggest being that it is 12 characters in length, which is too long for a legal filename that's compatible with the old 16-bit filenaming conventions. To solve the problem, it would be nice to be able to change the month to a number such as 03, to keep the day as 25, and to strip the 19 from the year:

DE032594.TXT

To achieve that end, GetTodayName needs a special function that will not only convert a number to a string, but also pad it with an appropriate quantity of zeros. The following function fits the bill:

```
{----------------------------------------------------
        Name: Int2StrPad0 function
 Declaration: Int2StrPad0(N: LongInt; Len: Integer): String;
        Unit: MathBox
        Code: N
        Date: 03/01/94
 Description: Converts a number into a string and pads
             the string with zeros if it is less than
             Len characters long.
-----------------------------------------------------}

function Int2StrPad0(N: LongInt; Len: Integer): string;
```

```
begin
  FmtStr(Result, '%d', [N]);
  while Length(Result) < Len do
    Result := '0' + Result;
end;
```

This function first uses the built-in Pascal routine called FmtStr to convert a LongInt into a string. If the string that results is longer than Len bytes in length, the function simply exits and returns the string. However, if the string is less than Len bytes, the function appends zeros in front of it until it is Len characters long. Here is the transformation caused by each successive iteration of the while loop if N equals 2 and Len equals 4:

```
2     { First iteration }
02    { Second iteration }
002   { Third iteration }
0002  { Fourth iteration }
```

The point here is that the function checks to see if the string is four characters long. If it isn't, the function prepends a zero to the string with the following code:

```
S := '0' + S;
```

In the case of the GetTodayName function, the value passed in the Len parameter is 2, because the need is to translate a number such as 3 or 7 into a number such as 03 or 07.

The final trick in the GetTodayName function is to convert a year such as 1994 into a two-digit number such as 94. Clearly, this can be easily achieved by merely subtracting 1900 from the date. However, that sound of hoofbeats in the distance is the rapid approach of the year 2000. Subtracting 1900 from 2001 would not achieve the desired result. The code therefore first converts the year into a string and then simply lops off the first two characters with the Delete function:

```
Year := Int2StrPad0(y, 4);
Delete(Year, 1, 2);
```

In this case, a 4 is passed to Int2StrPad0, because the year is originally a four-digit number.

As mentioned earlier, the Delete function is built into the Delphi language. It deletes characters from a string, starting at the offset specified in the second parameter. The number of characters to be deleted is specified in the third parameter. See the online help for more details.

ReplaceChars

It might be helpful if you take a look at one more function that performs basic string manipulation. The ReplaceChars function substitutes all instances of one character in a string with a second character:

```
function ReplaceChars(S: string; OldCh, NewCh: Char): string;
var
  Len: Integer;
  i: Integer;
```

```
begin
  Len := Length(S);

  for i := 1 to Len do
    if S[i] = OldCh then
      S[i] := NewCh;
  Result := S;
end;
```

The code first checks the length of the string. If it is zero, the function exits immediately; otherwise, the routine iterates through the string, character by character, looking for the character you want to replace. If the character is found, the new character is immediately written on top of it. Note that the routine starts with offset one, not offset zero.

Using the *Move* and *FillChar* Functions

The two built-in Delphi methods examined in this section are both very fast and very powerful. Speed of this sort is a luxury, but it comes replete with some dangers that you need to be sure to sidestep. In particular, neither the FillChar nor the Move function has much in the way of built-in error-checking.

As you can see in the chapter on the *Unleashed* CD called "Working with Arrays," the usual reason for using FillChar is to zero-out an array, record, or string. It will, however, fill a structure not only with zeros but with whatever character you specify.

FillChar takes three parameters. The first is the variable you want to copy bytes into, the second is the number of bytes you want to fill, and the third is the character you want placed in those bytes:

```
procedure FillChar(var X; Count: Word; value);
```

Consider the following array:

```
var
   MyArray: array[0..10] of Char;
```

Given this array, the following command will set all the members of this array to #0:

```
FillChar(MyArray, SizeOf(MyArray), #0);
```

If you want to fill the array with spaces, you could use the following syntax:

```
FillChar(MyArray, SizeOf(MyArray), #32);
```

This code would fill the array with the letter A:

```
FillChar(MyArray, SizeOf(MyArray), 'A');
```

The key thing to remember when using FillChar is that the SizeOf function can help you be sure that you are writing the correct number of bytes to the array. The big mistake you can make is to write too many bytes to the array. That is much worse than writing too few. If you think of memory as a theater with people, rather than 8-bit values in each seat, you can imagine 10 members of the audience sitting together, all considering themselves part of MyArray. Right next to them are two people who make up an integer. They are busy remembering the number 25. Now you issue the following command:

```
FillChar(MyArray, 12, #0);
```

All the people who are part of the array will start remembering #0, which is fine. But the command will keep right on going past the members of MyArray and tell the two folks remembering the number 25 that they should both now remember #0. In other words, the integer value will also be zeroed out and a bug will be introduced into your program. The result described here, you should understand, is a best-case scenario. Worst case is that the extra 2 bytes belong to another program, which means that your program will generate a General Protection Fault. The moral is that you should always use the FillChar procedure with care.

A function similar to FillChar is called Move. Its purpose is to move a block of data from one place to another. A typical use of this function might be to move one portion of a string to a second string, or to move part of an array into a string. The Copy function can also be used for a similar purpose. The advantage of the Copy function is that it is relatively safe. The disadvantages are that it is less flexible and can be somewhat slower under some circumstances.

Move takes three parameters. The first is the variable you want to copy data from, the second is the variable you want to move data to, and the third is the number of bytes you want to move:

```
procedure Move(var  Source, Dest; Count: Word);
```

Below you will find an example of a typical way to use the function. If you enjoy puzzles, you might want to take a moment to see if you can figure out what it does:

```
procedure TForm1.Button1Click(Sender: TObject);
var
 S1,S2: ShortString;
begin
  S1 := 'Heebee Gee Bees';
  Move(S1[12], S2[1], 4);
  SetLength(S2, 4);
  Edit1.Text := S2;
end;
```

The code shown here first sets S1 to a string value. It then indexes 12 bytes into that string and moves the next 4 bytes into a second string. (Don't forget to count the spaces when you are adding up the characters in a string!) Finally, it sets the length of the string to 4, which is the number of bytes that were moved into it. After executing this code, the final assignment statement will write out the word Bees in Edit1.Text. Here is how to accomplish the same task using the Pascal Copy function:

```
S1 := 'Heebee Gee Bees';
S2 := Copy(S1, 12, 4);
Edit1.Text := S2;
```

The first parameter to Copy is the string you want to get data from, the second is an offset into that string, and the third is the number of bytes you want to use. The function returns a substring taken from the string in the first parameter.

The Copy function is easier to use and safer than the Move function, but it is not as powerful. If at all possible, you should use the Copy function. However, there are times when you can't use the Copy function, particularly if you need to move data in or out of at least one variable that is not a string. Also, it is worth remembering that Move is very fast. If you have to perform an action over and over again in a loop, you should consider using Move instead of Copy.

It's interesting to note that the above function will not work if you are working with AnsiStrings. Instead, you would have to write code that looks like this:

```
procedure TForm1.Button1Click(Sender: TObject);
const
  Size = 4;
var
  S1, S2: string;
begin
  S1 := 'Heebee Gee Bees';
  SetLength(S2, Size);
  Move(S1[12], S2[1], Size);
  Edit1.Text := S2;;
end;
```

The issue here is that you cannot move memory into S2 without first allocating memory for it. In particular, recall that S2 is really a pointer to a string, and so you will generate an access violation if you try to just move memory into it.

As easy as it is to write data to the wrong place using the FillChar statement, you will find that the Move statement can lead you even further astray in considerably less time. It will, however, get you out of all manner of difficult corners—as long as you know how to use it.

The following function puts the Move procedure to practical use. As its name implies, the StripFirstWord function is used to remove the first word from a string. For instance, it would change the following string

```
'One Two Three'
```

into this string

```
'Two Three'
```

Here is the StripFirstWord function:

```
{ - - - - - - - - - - - - - - - - - - - - - - - - - - - - - - - - - - - - - - -
      Name: StripFirstWord function
Declaration: StripFirstWord(S : string) : string;
      Unit: StrBox
      Code: S
      Date: 03/02/94
Description: Strip the first word from a sentence,
            return the shortened sentence. Return original
```

```
                  string if there is no first word.
----------------------------------------------------}
function StripFirstWord(S : string) : string;
var
  i, Size: Integer;
begin
  i := Pos(#32, S);
  if i = 0 then begin
    StripFirstWord := S;
    Exit;
  end;
  Size := (Length(S) - i);
  Move(S[i + 1], S[1], Size);
  SetLength(S, Size);
  StripFirstWord := S;
end;
```

The first line in this function introduces you to the built-in Pos function, which locates a substring in a longer string. For instance, in this case, the Pos function is used to find the first instance of the space character in the string passed to the StripFirstWord function. The function returns the offset of the character it is looking for.

More specifically, the Pos function takes two parameters. The first is the string to search for, and the second is the string you want to search. Therefore the statement Pos(#32, S) looks for the space character inside a string, where the string is represented by the variable S.

If you passed in the following line of poetry: The pure products of America go crazy, the Pos function would return the number 4, which is the offset of the first space character in the preceding sentence. However, if you passed in a simpler string such as Williams, Pos would return 0 because there is no space character in the string. If the function does not find a space character in the string, it returns the original string:

```
if i = 0 then begin
  StripFirstWord := S;
  Exit;
end;
```

The built-in Exit procedure shown here simply exits the function without executing another line of code. This is the StripFirstWord function's sole, and rather limited, exercise in error-checking.

If the offset of a space character is returned by the Pos function, the Move function transfers "length - offset" number of characters from the string that is passed in to a different location in the same string:

```
i := Pos(#32, S);
...
Size := (Length(S) - i);
Move(S[i + 1], S[1], Size);
SetLength(S, Size);
```

The next line of code sets the length byte for the newly created string, which no longer contains the first word in the sentence.

The first step is to determine the number of characters in the sentence after the first word is removed. This is found by subtracting the number returned by `Pos` from the total length of the sentence. `StripFirstWord` then moves the remaining portion of the string from a position "offset" characters deep in the following string:

```
She was a child and I was a child, In a kingdom by the sea
```

to the very first spot in the string:

```
was a child and I was a child, In a kingdom by the sea sea
```

The extra characters, represented in this case by the second occurrence of `sea`, are then lopped off by setting the length byte to the appropriate number of characters:

```
was a child and I was a child, In a kingdom by the sea
```

The function then returns the shortened sentence.

The `StripFirstWord` function is not perfect. For instance, some readers may have noticed that the function would not perform as advertised if the first characters of the string passed to it were spaces. However, overall, it does the job required of it. Of course, you could call `TrimLeft` to strip spaces from the beginning of a string before calling `StripFirstWord`, or from inside a second version of `StripFirstWord` called `StripFirstWordEx`.

If you have been working with a computer language for a few years, a function such as `StripFirstWord` is probably not very hard for you to grasp. However, newcomers are likely to find it rather challenging. This brings up two major points:

- You need to become as familiar with the available debuggers as possible. Without a debugger, I would find a function such as `StripFirstWord` so unpleasant to write that I would probably throw up my hands in disgust and start looking around to see if a third-party tool vendor has already written it. As it is, I just spend a few minutes with the debugger and I have something I can use in my own programs. If you are having trouble understanding this procedure, do what I did when I created it: look at it in the debugger.

- Anyone who sees the code I have written in the last few sections of this chapter must realize that Delphi does not necessarily remove all the possible challenges from a programming job. Visual programming makes life much easier for most programmers, but it does not eliminate the need to write real code. If the act of writing code bores you or frustrates you, you should probably move along to one of the many walks of life that offers more excitement for someone like you. If you are determined to persevere, despite a growing sense of mordant depression, you should get to know the people who produce programmers' libraries. A good knowledge of TurboPower's tools, for instance, can do much to help alleviate your sense of frustration. (TurboPower is located in Colorado Springs, CO. Reach them by typing `GO TURBOPOWER` on CompuServe.)

Most of the routines you have seen in this chapter are useful enough for you to want to save for future use. With this thought in mind, I have placed them in the STRBOX unit, which is a companion unit to the MATHBOX unit found on the *Unleashed* CD-ROM, and discussed in the CD-based chapter "Units, Real Numbers, and Functions."

The following program, called TESTSTR, gives you a chance to work with the StripFirstWord function. This program takes any sentence you enter and separates it into a series of individual words that are displayed in a listbox.

To avoid any problems that might arise from accidentally prepending spaces before a string, the TESTSTR program makes use of the following function:

```
{- - - - - - - - - - - - - - - - - - - - - - - - - - - - - - - - - - - - -
       Name: StripFrontChars function
Declaration: StripFrontChars(S: string; Ch: Char) : String;
       Unit: StrBox
       Code: S
       Date: 03/02/94
Description: Strips any occurances of charact Ch that
            might precede a string.
- - - - - - - - - - - - - - - - - - - - - - - - - - - - - - - - - - - - -}
function StripFrontChars(S: string; Ch: Char): string;
var
  S1: string;
begin
  while (S[1] = Ch) and (Length(S) > 0) do
    S := Copy(S,2,Length(S) - 1);
  StripFrontChars := S;
end;
```

This routine removes a particular character from the start of a string until there are no more instances of the character prepended to the string, or until the string is completely empty. If you pass it a string and #32, it will make sure there are no spaces preceding the string. (If you want to remove only spaces from the front of a string, you can call TrimLeft.)

StripFrontChars works its magic by first checking to see if the initial character in the string has the same value as Ch. If it does, it finds the second character in the string and copies it and the remainder of the string back over the first character of the string, thereby accomplishing a task similar to that undertaken by the second Move statement in StripFirstWord.

> **NOTE**
>
> Several places in this chapter I have shown you two ways of accomplishing the same task. Experienced programmers know that writing code is a bit like writing prose: There are always several different ways to say the same thing. Some people believe that there are quantifiable ways of finding the best way to accomplish a particular task. To my mind, there is no objective way to determine the best course of action in many programming dilemmas. For instance, it is often true that one method is faster than

another, but it might also be more difficult to maintain. Which is better, the faster code or the more maintainable code? It depends.

There are few objective means of determining the best way to write a block of code; there are certain programmers who consistently write excellent code. Programming is one field in which there is little substitute for raw talent. However, average programmers can accomplish a lot if they have patience, good toolboxes, and good compilers.

The TESTSTR program uses an edit control, a button labeled Parse, and a listbox. The form for the program is shown in Figure 3.4, and the code in Listing 3.2.

FIGURE 3.4.

The form for the TESTSTR program.

Listing 3.2. The code for the TESTSTR program.

```
unit Main;

{ Program copyright (c) 1995 by Charles Calvert }
{ Project Name: TESTSTR }

{ This program demonstrates some routines from
  the STRBOX unit that can be used when you want
  to manipulate strings. The STRBOX unit is stored
  in the UTILS subdirectory, which should be on
  your Library Path. }

interface

uses
  WinTypes, WinProcs, Classes,
  Graphics, StdCtrls,  Controls,
  Forms;

type
  TForm1 = class(TForm)
    BParse: TButton;
    Edit1: TEdit;
    ListBox1: TListBox;
    procedure BParseClick(Sender: TObject);
```

continues

Listing 3.2. continued

```
  procedure FormCreate(Sender: TObject);
private
  TestStr: string;
end;

var
  Form1: TForm1;

implementation

uses
  StrBox;

{$R *.DFM}

procedure TForm1.BParseClick(Sender: TObject);
var
  S: string;
begin
  ListBox1.Clear;
  TestStr := Edit1.Text;
  repeat
    TestStr := StripFrontChars(TestStr, #32);
    S := RemoveFirstWord(TestStr);
    if S <> '' then
      ListBox1.Items.Add(S);
  until S = '';
  if TestStr <> #32 then
    ListBox1.Items.Add(TestStr);
end;

procedure TForm1.FormCreate(Sender: TObject);
begin
  TestStr := 'In the long sleepless watches of the night';
  Edit1.Text := TestStr;
end;

end.
```

The TESTSTR program uses the OnCreate event to specify a string and to pass it to the BParseClick function. This function uses RemoveFirstWord to break the sentence into individual words and to display each word in a listbox. One of the interesting aspects of the program is that it shows how you can place routines in a unit such as STRBOX and then call them in a neat and easily readable fashion.

There are hundreds of different functions you could write to help you perform certain string-oriented tasks. The ones in this chapter should help you get started creating a library of your own that you can turn to when you need a quick solution for a problem involving a string. The final version of the STRBOX program that ships with this book contains a number of additional string manipulation routines that I have built up over the years. Readers of the first edition of this book should note that the implementation for this unit has been changed rather heavily, in part because of the impact of long strings. The interface, however, is pretty much the same as in the first version of this book, except for the fact that there are a few new routines.

Limiting the Length of *ShortStrings*

At times it seems foolish to allocate an entire 256-byte block to deal with a very short string. For instance, your input routines may limit the length of the name the user can enter to 30 characters. If by some strange chance your name is longer than that limitation, you are out of luck. The key point, however, is that the string that holds the user's name need never be longer than 31 bytes (30 plus one for the length byte). Any more bytes would be wasted.

In situations like this, you can limit the length of the string you declare:

```
Name: string[30];
```

This syntax tells the compiler that it needs to set aside only 31 seats for this particular string. Thirty will hold the string itself, and the thirty-first holds the length byte. By declaring a string this way, you save 256–31, or 225 bytes.

Delphi enables you to declare ShortStrings of any length between 1 and 255. For instance, all of the following are valid ShortString declarations:

```
S: string[1];
S1: string[255];
S2: string[100];
S3: string[25];
```

Strings of certain lengths are declared so often that you might want to create special types for them:

```
type
  TStr20: string[20];
  TStr25: string[25];
  TStr30: string[30];
  TStr10: string[10];
  TStr80: string[80];
```

Given these declarations, you can write code that looks like this:

```
var
  S1: TStr20;
  S2: TStr30;
```

The syntax shown here can help you save memory without having to perform much extra work. In fact, the types shown here are so useful that I have added them to the STRBOX unit so that you can access them easily at any time. I have also added a few other string declarations that can prove useful when you are working with files in 16-bit Windows:

```
DirStr = string[67];
PathStr = string[79];
NameStr = string[8];
ExtStr = string[4];
```

The only problem with limiting the length of strings through the technique shown here is that it still requires you to know the length of a string at design time. Working with `AnsiStrings`, or working with `PChars` and the `GetMem` function, it is possible to set the length of a string at runtime, which means you can make strings that are exactly long enough to hold the characters stored in them. (You can learn more about pointers and the `GetMem` function in Chapter 4, "Pointers and PChars.") You also can declare a pointer to a standard short string, predeclared by Delphi as a `PString`, and then allocate just the amount of memory you need for it.

It might be easier to use the default behavior of `AnsiStrings` when you want to limit memory usage rather than going to the bother of declaring the special types of strings shown above. However, you should study the techniques shown here carefully—in case you ever need them. Remember also that strings declared as part of an object or procedure are local to that object or procedure, and will be in memory only as long as the object or procedure that owns them.

Working with Text Files

A text file provides a place for you to store strings. The PAS and DPR source files for your programs are text files. So are the DOF files that accompanies them, as well as the WIN.INI and SYSTEM.INI files that you use to configure Windows 3.1. Even the lowly AUTOEXEC.BAT and CONFIG.SYS files, which may have been the very first thing you ever learned about a computer, are nothing more than text files.

Delphi provides an extremely simple method for reading and writing these text files. To get started, you need only declare a variable of type `TextFile`:

```
var
  F: TextFile;
```

Variable `F` now represents a text file, and it can be used to specify where you want data to be read or written.

NOTE

Pascal has traditionally used the identifier `Text` rather than `TextFile` in situations like the one shown above. You can, in fact, still use the `Text` type. However, you will probably also need to qualify the identifier `Text` with the name of the unit where it is declared, which is the SYSTEM unit. This is necessary because the TForm object already has a variable with this name inside it, thereby causing a name conflict, since you can't use a variable as a type. To remedy the situation, you need to specify which instance of the identifier `Text` you want to reference. Specifically, you are saying that you want to reference the `Text` type that is declared in the SYSTEM unit: `SYSTEM.Text`. The same problem occurs with the identifiers `Assign` and `Close`.

Needless to say, the name conflict shown here never should have occurred, and its presence in the shipping version of Delphi is a testament to the fact that even the developers of Delphi are fallible.

After declaring the file variable, the next step is to associate it with a particular filename:

```
var
  F: TextFile;
begin
  AssignFile(F, 'MYFILE.TXT');
  ...
```

It is traditional to assign the extension TXT to a text file. Of course, many files don't follow this convention. For instance, INI files don't use the TXT extension, and neither do files labeled READ.ME. However, most text files do have a TXT extension, and this is the accepted and traditional way to treat them.

After the assignment statement, the next step is to open the file with the Reset, Rewrite, or Append routine. The Reset procedure opens an existing file:

```
var
  F: TextFile;
begin
  AssignFile(F, 'MYFILE.TXT');
  Reset(F);
  ...
end;
```

The ReWrite procedure creates a file or overwrites an existing file. The Append routine opens an existing file. It does not overwrite its current contents, but it enables you to append new strings to the end of a file:

```
var
  F: TextFile;
begin
  AssignFile(F, 'MYFILE.TXT');
  Append(F);
  ...
end;
```

NOTE

There is no simple way to open a text file and insert a string into it at a particular location. You can create a new file, overwrite an existing file, or append a string onto an existing file. You can't easily add a new string in the fourth line of a twenty-line text file. I say you can't do this easily, but there are ways to do this. They usually involve opening the file in either binary or text mode, reading its entire contents into an array or other complex data structure, inserting a string, and finally writing the file back out to disk.

Once you have opened a text file, you can write a string to it with the Write or WriteLn procedure:

```
var
  F: TextFile;
begin
  AssignFile(F, 'MYFILE.TXT');
  ReWrite(F);
  WriteLn(F, 'Call me Ishmael.');
  CloseFile(F);
end;
```

Notice that the WriteLn statement begins by referencing the file variable as its first parameter.

The method shown here ends with a CloseFile statement. If you want to use the more traditional Close statement, you probably need to qualify it by referencing SYSTEM.PAS. (I say *probably,* since you will not need to qualify it if you are in a stand-alone procedure that is not part of an object that contains a method called Close.)

Bugs can be introduced into your program if you forget to call CloseFile. More specifically, there is an internal buffer associated with each text file that will probably not be flushed if you fail to call CloseFile. If the buffer isn't flushed, a portion of the file will remain in memory rather than being written to disk. As a result, it appears that your program is not writing properly to the file, and programmers can spend a long time looking for a memory corruption problem when the source of the trouble is simply failing to call CloseFile. See the Flush procedure, found in the online help.

NOTE

The SYSTEM file is buried deep in the Delphi runtime library. Every Delphi program you create will automatically have the system file linked into it, even if you don't explicitly reference it in your uses clause. Most of the SYSTEM unit contains assembly language code for elemental routines such as WriteLn, Assign, ReWrite, Reset, and a few other functions that have survived since the earliest versions of the Turbo Pascal compiler. If you want to know more about this unit, you can look it up in the online help or look for the source code on disk. The availability of the source code depends on which version of Delphi you bought. That is, it comes with the client/server version, but not the desktop version. If it exists on your system, it would be stored somewhere beneath the source subdirectory. You can purchase the RTL separately from Borland.

If you want to read a string from a text file, you can use the Read or ReadLn statement:

```
var
  F: TextFile;
  S: String;
begin
  AssignFile(F, 'MYFILE.TXT');
  Reset(F);
```

```
  ReadLn(F, S);
  WriteLn(S);
  CloseFile(F);
end;
```

Notice that this code uses the `Reset` procedure to open an existing file and then uses `ReadLn` to retrieve the first string from this file.

You can also read and write numbers from a text file. For instance, the following code is entirely legal:

```
var
  F: System.Text;
  S: String;
  i: Integer;
begin
  System.Assign(F, 'MYFILE.TXT');
  ReWrite(F);
  S := 'The secret of the universe: ';
  i := 42;
  WriteLn(F, S, i);
  System.Close(F);
end;
```

This code, which uses the word `System` as a qualifier, writes the following line into a text file:

```
The secret of the universe: 42
```

If you had a text file with the following contents:

```
10 101 1001
20 202 2002
```

you could read the first line from this file with the following code:

```
var
  F: TextFile;
  i, j, k: Integer;
begin
  AssignFile(F, 'MYFILE.TXT');
  Reset(F);
  ReadLn(F, i, j, k);
  CloseFile(F);
end;
```

The code shown here would read the numbers 10, 101, and 1001 from the file. If you wanted to read both lines from the file, you could write

```
var
  F: TextFile;
  i, j, k, a, b, c: Integer;
begin
  AssignFile(F, 'MYFILE.TXT');
  Reset(F);
  ReadLn(F, i, j, k);
  ReadLn(F, a, b, c);
  CloseFile(F);
end;
```

You can use a function called EOF to determine if you are at the end of a text file. For instance, if you had a file that contained several hundred lines of numbers like those shown in the small file listed earlier, you could read the entire file in the following manner:

```
var
  F: TextFile;
  i, j, k, Sum: Integer;
begin
  AssignFile(F, 'MYFILE.TXT');
  Reset(F);
  while not EOF(F) do begin
    ReadLn(F, i, j, k);
    Sum := I + j + k;
    WriteLn(F, 'i + j + k := ', Sum);
  end;
  CloseFile(F);
end;
```

The EASYFILE program, shown in Listing 3.3, demonstrates how to use the TTEXTREC structure to determine a file's name and whether a file is open for input, open for output, or closed. Specifically, you can typecast a variable of type Text so that you can test its state, as shown here:

```
var
  F: TextFile;
begin
  if TTextRec(F).Mode := fmClosed then OpenTheFile;
end;
```

TTextRec is in the online help. The Mode constants are declared in SYSUTILS.PAS as follows:

```
fmClosed = $D7B0;
fmInput  = $D7B1;
fmOutput = $D7B2;
fmInOut  = $D7B3;
```

Listing 3.3. The EASYFILE program demonstrates some basic techniques for handling TextFiles.

```
unit Main;

{ Program copyright (c) 1995 by Charles Calvert }
{ Project Name: EASYFILE }

{
  This program shows how to work with strings and
  with text based files.

  Constants for using with the MODE field
  of TTextRec, declared in SYSUTILS.PAS :

  fmClosed = $D7B0;
  fmInput  = $D7B1;
  fmOutput = $D7B2;
  fmInOut  = $D7B3;
```

This program gives a general workout on
file IO issues. In particular, it shows
how to use the TTextRec structure to determine
if a file is open, closed, etc.

As declared in SYSUTILS:

```
PTextBuf = ^TTextBuf;
TTextBuf = array[0..127] of Char;
TTextRec = record
  Handle: Word;
  Mode: Word;
  BufSize: Word;
  Private: Word;
  BufPos: Word;
  BufEnd: Word;
  BufPtr: PTextBuf;
  OpenFunc: Pointer;
  InOutFunc: Pointer;
  FlushFunc: Pointer;
  CloseFunc: Pointer;
  UserData: array[1..16] of Byte;
  Name: array[0..79] of Char;
  Buffer: TTextBuf;
end;

}
interface

uses
  WinTypes, WinProcs, Classes,
  Graphics, Forms, Controls,
  StdCtrls, SysUtils, ExtCtrls,
  Dialogs;

type
  TForm1 = class(TForm)
    RunTest: TButton;
    OpenInput: TButton;
    OpenOutPut: TButton;
    CloseFile: TButton;
    Panel1: TPanel;
    Panel2: TPanel;
    Label1: TLabel;
    Label2: TLabel;
    procedure RunTestClick(Sender: TObject);
    procedure OpenInputClick(Sender: TObject);
    procedure OpenOutPutClick(Sender: TObject);
    procedure CloseFileClick(Sender: TObject);
  private
    F: TextFile;
  end;

var
  Form1: TForm1;

implementation
```

continues

Listing 3.3. continued

```pascal
uses
  StrBox;

{$R *.DFM}

function GetMode(var F: Text): string;
begin
  case TTextRec(F).Mode of
    fmClosed: Result := 'Closed';
    fmInput: Result := 'Open for Input';
    fmOutPut: Result := 'Open for Output';
    fmInOut: Result := 'Open for input and output';
  end;
end;

procedure TForm1.RunTestClick(Sender: TObject);
var
  i: Integer;
begin
  AssignFile(F, GetTodayName('EZ', 'txt'));
  Label1.Caption := TTextRec(F).Name;
  Label2.Caption := GetMode(F);
  for i := 0 to ComponentCount - 1 do
    if Components[i] is TButton then
      TButton(Components[i]).Enabled := True;
end;

{ Exception handling is explained in the
  chapter entitled "Exceptions". The
  exception will be raised if a file
  with the filename generated above
  does not exist.    }
procedure TForm1.OpenInputClick(Sender: TObject);
begin
  try
    Reset(F);
  except
    on EInOutError do
      MessageDlg('File must be created first', mtInformation, [mbOk], 0);
  end;
  Label2.Caption := GetMode(F);
end;

procedure TForm1.OpenOutPutClick(Sender: TObject);
begin
  ReWrite(F);
  Label2.Caption := GetMode(F);
end;

procedure TForm1.CloseFileClick(Sender: TObject);
begin
  if TTextRec(F).Mode <> fmClosed then
    System.Close(F);
  Label2.Caption := GetMode(F);
end;

end.
```

When using this program, it is important that you push the buttons on the main form in the order in which they appear. That is, push the top one first, the next button down, and so on. If you press the buttons out of order, the program could raise an exception. You could, of course, disable and enable buttons in order to force the user to proceed in a particular fashion, but I decided against that approach in order to keep the code as simple as possible.

Notice that the following method uses exceptions to handle the errors that would occur if the user pushed the buttons in the wrong order:

```
procedure TForm1.OpenInputClick(Sender: TObject);
begin
  try
    Reset(F);
  except
    on EInOutError do
      MessageDlg('File must be created first', mtInformation, [mbOk], 0);
  end;
  Label2.Caption := GetMode(F);
end;
```

The code first attempts to open the file with the Reset function. If this attempt fails, the user is notified that an error occurred, and the function immediately terminates.

In this section, you learned the basics about text files. One of the most important points to remember is that you can open a file one of three ways:

- ReWrite opens a new file or overwrites an existing file.
- Reset opens an existing file for reading.
- Append opens an existing file and enables you to append text to the end of it. If the file does not exist, an error condition results.

Summary

In this chapter, you explored strings and text files. You saw that strings are really just a special form of array, and that you can manipulate them in myriad ways by treating them as vectors filled with chars. You also saw that there are many functions used to manipulate strings. In particular, you were exposed to the Move, FillChar, Delete, Copy, and Pos routines. You also learned something about the differences between ShortStrings and AnsiStrings.

The last part of the chapter presented a basic introduction to TextFiles. You saw how to open and close these files, how to read and write to them, and how to detect if you are at the end of a text file. Look on the CD for programs showing how to parse text files.

Pointers and PChars

4

In the 16-bit world, manipulation of pointers was probably the single most powerful skill in the repertoire of experienced programmers. However, the need to understand pointers is not quite as pressing in the 32-bit world. In fact, you can write many very good programs without understanding pointers. Nevertheless, pointers still lie at the heart of most advanced programming techniques. If you really understand pointers, little in computer programming is likely to be beyond you.

I don't mean to imply that understanding pointers makes computer programming easy. That is not at all the case. Pointers tend to be a relatively difficult subject, even in their easiest and most comprehensible forms. Furthermore, the advent of 32-bit flat model, programming for PCs means that the need for pointers in your code has gone way down. You had to use pointers in the 16-bit world, but you don't have to in the 32-bit world. If you are in doubt about whether or not you need to use pointers, don't use them.

Pointers are worth the struggle, however, because they enable you to directly manipulate memory, or at least simulate the act of directly manipulating memory. When you are dealing with pointers, there are few barriers between you and the raw bytes of memory that exist in RAM, or in other portions of the computer's memory. With pointers, you are able to manipulate the raw material that forms the life blood of every computer.

> **NOTE**
>
> Actually, protected-mode programming under Win32 puts at least one layer of indirection between you and the memory you want to manipulate, but it also gives you the very realistic illusion that you are manipulating real memory.

This chapter covers the following:

- The theory behind manipulating memory with pointers
- Using New and Dispose to allocate memory
- Using GetMem and FreeMem to allocate memory
- The relationship between objects and pointers
- Working with PChars

In the first edition of this book, this was probably one of the four or five most important chapters. In this edition, the subject is not nearly as important. In fact, its attraction is mostly for people who want to explore advanced programming techniques. Even the section on PChars is not nearly as important as it was in the first edition. In Delphi 1.0, you usually had to use PChars if you wanted to call Windows API functions that took strings as parameters. However, in Delphi 2.0, you can just use AnsiStrings in these cases, doing nothing more than typecasting them before passing them in.

Once again, pointers are not nearly as important in Delphi 2.0 as they were in Delphi 16. I suggest that under most circumstances you shy away from using either pointers or PChars. Avoid them as much as possible because they can lead to bugs! It's easy to make a mistake using pointers. For the speed demons in the crowd who want to use pointers for performance reasons, please note that all Delphi objects, as well as AnsiStrings, are actually disguised pointers. That is, they are pointers masquerading as static values. The apparent absence of pointers in your program does not mean that your code is taking a speed hit.

Pointers and Win32

It might be helpful to start this chapter off by talking about what happened to pointers when the Intel-based world switched from 16-bit real-mode DOS to Windows 95 and Windows NT. What is the difference between pointers in a 16-bit world and pointers in a 32-bit world?

> **NOTE**
>
> Memory manipulation on Intel computers is a very complex subject, and in this section of the book I am going to make some assumptions that will help simplify the topic. In particular, I'm going to act as if the world jumped directly from real-mode DOS to protected-mode Win32. In reality, Windows 3.1 usually ran in protected mode, so some of the innovations that I attribute to Win32 were actually in place in Windows 3.1. However, for the sake of making the subject more comprehensible, I'm going to pretend that the Intel world jumped directly from DOS to Win32, even though there was a five-year transition in which Windows 3.0 and Windows 3.1 helped the PC world migrate from real mode to protected mode. (I am also aware that the entire world has not yet made the jump to 32-bits; however, it's a fairly safe assumption that most people reading this book have made the jump.)

In the 16-bit world, pointers were bound by the 64KB limitation imposed by the 8086 and 286 architectures. In that world, pointers consisted of two different pieces: the first referencing a particular 64KB segment in the first megabyte of memory and the second referencing an offset in that segment. 16-bit, protected-mode implementations did some hand waving that allowed programmers to access memory outside of the first megabyte, but the actual numbers out of which the pointers were made were still bound by extreme limitations. In particular, you could not reference more than 64 KB of memory at one time. That was the limit; a 16-bit number simply can't address more than 64 KB of memory. (The HUGE pointers in C made it appear that we were addressing more than 64 KB at a time, but this was never more than a rather tenuous mirage.)

In the 32-bit world, the limitation is no longer 64 KB, but 4 GB. That is, the maximum number of addressable bytes in a single pointer is 65,536 in the 16-bit world, and 4,294,967,296 in the 32-bit world. The maximum amount of addressable memory in real mode is 1,048,576 bytes, in 16-bit protected mode 16,777,216, and in 32-bit protected mode 4,294,967,296. The switch to 32 bits turns the computer world on its head. Before we had more memory than we could easily address. Now we have more address space than memory—much more address space.

To step from the 16-bit world to the 32-bit world is a bit similar to the northern Europeans starting to circumnavigate the globe with ships. Before that, the world was limited to just a few small countries, and then all at once the entire world was within reach. On a more modest scale, the same thing happened when planes and cars were developed. Before these technologies were available, most people lived entire lives within a 50-square-mile radius of their home. Afterward, nearly everyone began to travel across entire countries, and many now travel regularly between continents. The same thing will happen if we ever begin to seriously explore space. The limitations of our reach will switch from a single planet to an entire solar system, and perhaps some day to an entire galaxy.

When you are thinking in terms of pointers, the switch from the 16-bit to the 32-bit world is a vast reorientation in space and time. The world isn't just one or two times bigger, it's thousands of times bigger.

I mention all this because it has a rather strong impact on the memory theater. In the 16-bit world, you could imagine the dimensions of the Memory Theater. It was huge, holding at least 640,000 seats. That's bigger than any known existing theater, but it's still an imaginable number. The million man march, for instance, was probably approximately that big. Four gigabytes worth of seats, however, is just beyond the range of imagining. It's just plain flat-out incomprehensible, at least from my point of view.

So, the first thing to grasp about 32-bit pointers is that they reference spaces that are almost unimaginably large. You have to start thinking in terms of interplanetary, perhaps even interstellar, distances before you can find analogies for the size of the numbers addressed by a 32-bit operating system.

A second key point about 32-bit pointers is that they almost all address virtual memory. Under Windows 95, for instance, most programs are loaded into memory at the 4MB mark and can access memory up to the 2GB mark. Clearly, none of the machines currently running Windows 95 have anything like 2 GB of memory on them.

To have a program access memory at the 2GB mark clearly involves a certain amount of handwaving. In particular, there is a table in memory called a *descriptor table*. Each address used in Win32 is really a reference into this table, and not a reference into a real place in memory. To find the actual address of a variable residing in memory, you would have to first take the address you are working with, which is a virtual address, and then see what that address really points to by looking it up in the descriptor table. In other words, addresses aren't really addresses; they are just references to a look up in the descriptor table. The descriptor table contains the actual addresses of places in RAM. Under normal circumstances you never look at these real addresses, and there is rarely any practical reason to do so.

Well, even that last paragraph is a bit of a simplification. Windows actually has a paging scheme that complicates matters even further, but this is not the time to go into these details. If you want to find out the specifics, you should read Jeffrey Richter's *Advanced Windows,* by Microsoft Press, and *Extending DOS,* by Ray Duncan, et al, Addison Wesley Press. I will address some of the issues in Chapter 8, "Multitasking, Threads, and Memory: The Windows 95 Environment."

This is not the part of this book where I want to dig deeply into the nature of memory under Windows 95. Instead, I want to make clear that the memory theater analogy is strained by the appearance of Win32. However, underneath all the descriptors, and all the paging, all the virtual memory, Microsoft and Intel still want you to be able to think of memory as if it were something tangible. The operating system goes to enormous lengths to make memory seem simple, to make it appear to be as straightforward as it seems when I discuss the memory theater.

In the memory theater, the CPU addresses the audiences and asks them to participate in the play currently being enacted. It's an audience-participation theater. In particular, the CPU, from its position on the stage, might tell four bytes out in the audience that it is their job to remember an integer value. It takes four members of the audience to remember a single integer value because an integer is four bytes in size.

The purpose of this section, then, has been twofold:

- I want to make it clear that the memory theater analogy is less than perfect when you are working under Win32. Don't take it too literally.

- Windows goes to great lengths to make the virtual addresses you use in your program seem as if they reference actual places in RAM, and not just a series of tables and pages. You are running your program inside a virtual machine that emulates in software a real-mode, 4GB machine. Most of the time it is a good idea to buy into this illusion.

Maybe under Win32, the memory theater should be given a new name: the *virtual memory theater.* When you play Doom, Heretic, or Phantasmagoria, you don't think you are moving through a real world. Nevertheless, the illusions created by these games are clever enough to make users grasp the rules of the virtual world in which they play, and to see how it has parallels to the real world. In the same way, Windows makes programmers feel as though the addresses they get are real addresses. It's a virtual memory theater.

In real mode memory the CPU addressed the actual bytes sitting in the audience. It talked to "real" bytes of memory. In Win32, the CPU addresses a set of virtual bytes. The programs running in the theater think they are standing in front of an audience 4 GB in size, but they are actually sitting in front of an elaborate virtual display that simulates a theater four gigabytes in size.

Of course, there is real RAM in a computer, but your program never addresses it directly. Instead, it addresses virtual RAM, and the operating system then moves beyond the scenes to translate these simulated actions into actual events that effect RAM, your hard disk, video memory, or some other part of your computer. Your program, however, very rarely actually directly touches any of these things. It's working with a simulation of memory, not with real memory.

The memory theater under Win32 is based upon an illusion. There isn't a one-to-one analogy between the seats in a theater and the bytes of memory in RAM because programmers no longer address actual bytes of memory in RAM. Instead, programmers address descriptor tables, they address virtual pages of memory. However, it appears to the programmer that they are addressing actual bytes of memory, just as it appears that you walk through a real house when you play Phantasmagoria. To the imaginative it can appear that the virtual bytes of memory in Win32 are like seats in a vast theater. The whole thing is an illusion within an illusion, yet it can still help you understand how memory works—as long as you don't start taking it too literally!

If all this doesn't come home to you right away, don't worry. I'm going to talk a lot about memory in this book, and for most readers a clear conception of memory under Win32 will probably sink in only slowly, over a considerable period of time. In particular, I spend copious amounts of time discussing these subjects in Chapter 7, "Multitasking and Threads," and Chapter 8, "Win32 Memory Management."

If you've come out of your reading of the last few paragraphs with an understanding that there is an important difference between virtual memory and real memory, you probably have enough knowledge to go on from here. Later on, however, you will want to be sure that you have a clearer conception of the exact nature of virtual memory.

Pointers and the Memory Theater

It's time now to start talking about pointers. When you first start to think about pointers, you should try to keep in mind the memory theater—the virtual memory theater, that is!. Pointers simply refer to seats in the memory theater. In fact, pointers are blocks of four seats in the memory theater that remember the location of other seats.

> **NOTE**
>
> During this discussion you should stop trying to see through virtual memory and should instead allow yourself to be fooled by the illusion it presents. There is no danger in doing this because the illusion is very carefully constructed and follows a very clearly laid-out set of predefined rules. You should now believe that virtual memory is real memory, just as an air traffic controller comes to believe that the blips on a screen are actual airplanes.

Suppose you have a list of 100 sentences, each of which is between 100 and 150 characters in length. Furthermore, suppose this list of sentences is not part of the body of a text, but is the list of error messages displayed by your program. In other words, you don't necessarily want to show this entire list to the user at once, but you might want to grab the 12th string, or 23rd string, or some other particular string, and show it to the user.

Given this scenario, it might be helpful to keep a set of references to these strings, rather than wandering through the seats of the memory theater trying to find a particular string at a particular time. As it happens, there are a number of different ways you can keep these references, but one convenient way to do it would be by keeping pointers to these strings.

In the 32-bit Intel architecture, pointers occupy four bytes. That is, they take up four seats in the memory theater. These four bytes contain the address of a particular location in the memory theater. In other words, the four seats occupied by a pointer contain the reference number, or address, of other seats in the memory theater.

Suppose the first of the 100 strings you want to reference is located in seat 255A. One simple way to reference this number would be to create the following simple piece of syntax:

$255A

Though this syntax might not make much sense to a total stranger, it is easily understood by someone who recognizes it purpose. It's the hexadecimal number for a seat in the memory theater. You just start numbering the seats: The first one is $1, the second is $2, and so on.

> **NOTE**
>
> Before the emergence of Win32, all the seats in the memory theater were referenced by segment and offset. For instance, a typical 16-bit addresses might look like this: 25:5A. In the memory theater analogy, the number before the colon referred to a section number and the number after the colon referred to a seat number. In the real world, the first number referenced a 64KB segment of memory, and the second number referenced an offset in that 64KB block. This is no longer the system. Now the world is greatly simplified, and each of the 4GB worth of seats in the memory theater has its own unique number, with $FFFFFFFF being the largest possible number. (Ironically, the above number is -1, if you considered it to be a signed number.)

The addresses of the seats in the 32-bit memory theater are very simple. They are just hexadecimal numbers. Besides its simple syntax, another advantage of this construction is that it can easily be stored in a small area. For instance, it takes only four members of the audience to remember the entire number. In particular, each person is remembering an 8-bit value, which can be as high as 256, which is $FF. The result would be that the entire 32-bit number could be memorized by four members of the audience: $FF FF FF FF.

> **NOTE**
>
> To understand exactly what is going on here, you need to recall that while one member of the audience can remember a number between 0 and 255, two members of the audience working together can remember numbers between 0 and 65,364. Four members working together can remember a number between 0 and 4,294,967,296.

Using a system in which four members of the audience remember the seat number of another group of people in the audience, it is possible to have a relatively manageable block of 100 sets of pointers, where each pointer is really just four seats in the memory theater.

100×4 is equal to 400, which is a fairly large number of seats. However, if each of the strings being referenced averaged 125 characters in length, the approximate number of bytes in the group is 100×125, or 12,500 seats. 12,500 is a large number of seats to have to sort through, even for a computer. Obviously, it would be helpful to be able to refer to a smaller lookup table, consisting of 400 seats, that can be broken down into groups of 4 seats each. This is what pointers do for you. Because each pointer is the same size, you can jump to the tenth pointer by moving in 40 bytes. You could not, however, jump to the 10 string by moving in any particular number of bytes because you don't know the length of each string ahead of time.

Suppose you want to find the 20th string in the group of strings. One way to find it would be to start wandering through the section where the strings are stored, looking for the beginning and end of each string, and keep looking until you finally find the string you want. A second method would be to go to the 20th pointer to see which seat number is stored there. Then you could go directly from the pointer to the string itself. In effect, the people who sit in the four seats of the 20th pointer can stand up and point directly at the seat that represents the beginning of the string you want to find, as shown in Figure 4.1.

FIGURE 4.1.

Four members of the memory theater save the seat number where a string is stored.

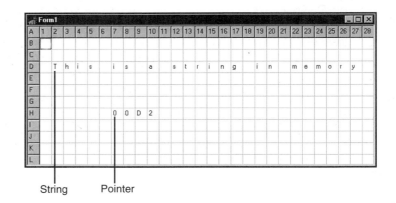

It doesn't take much imagination to see that pointers can help speed up operations inside a computer. By using pointers, you can avoid lengthy searches through hundreds of thousands of bytes, and instead be directed quickly and efficiently to the seat you want to find.

Furthermore, if you want to change the order of the strings you are referencing, you don't actually have to move a 150-character string from one place to another. Instead, you can simply change the addresses stored in the pointers. For instance, if one pointer references a string starting in seat $00001A2B and the next pointer references a string in seat $00005A6B, reversing the order of these strings is a simple matter of swapping two 4-byte pointers. This is obviously much faster than trying to move hundreds of bytes around.

Some readers might be inclined at this point to take this whole matter back one step further and ask what it is that points at the pointer. In other words, it is easy enough to imagine how the pointers described here can help you reference a particular place in memory, but how does one get to the pointer in the first place?

The short answer is that the locations of certain pointers are stored in your executable. In other words, when you write a program, code is generated that says, in effect, go to this spot, find a pointer, and then do something with the memory referenced by the pointer. The code usually points to a place in your address space or stack segment where the pointers you declare are stored. However, you also can have a pointer in your program's data that points to a pointer on your heap, which points to yet another pointer on the heap, and so on.

You can trace this answer back even further, to the moment when a computer is first switched on. At that moment, pointers are loaded into memory that reference instructions for booting up a computer and loading the operating system. These instructions and data in turn use pointers to reference other places inside the computer, and so on. What really ends up happening is that a computer follows an endless stream of pointers, each of which keeps referencing some other place in memory where data or instructions are stored.

NOTE

Pointers are sometimes referred to as addresses because that is really all that a pointer represents. For instance, you might hear someone say, "Pass the address of variable J to the FooBar function." What this means is that you should pass a pointer to the variable J to the FooBar function. Pointers are really nothing more than addresses. Furthermore, you can obtain the address of any variable by appending the @ symbol before it:

```
var
  A: Integer;
  P: Pointer;
begin
  Caption := Format('$%p <<=>> $%p', [@A, P]);
end;
```

The code shown here would write the address of the variable A to the caption at the top of a window. It would also write the pointer value P to the caption. The result might look something like this: $0065F8DC <<=>> $0065F938, where the <<=>> symbol is just a randomly chosen separator to help you keep the two address separate in your mind.

Remember that addresses are normally written in hex notation, so I prepend a $ to the above result. Another way to see a meaningful version of the address of the variable A is to type @A in the Watch Window. Be sure that the variable A is in scope when you view it in the integrated debugger.

Once again, I want to stress that you don't have to understand all this in order to write code. However, if you can begin to see what I am driving at, or if this material is already old hat to you, you are sitting in the catbird's seat, with all the vast realms of the computer spread out before you. Pointers are the keys to the kingdom, and with them you can unlock virtually any door.

Finally, I want to remind you once again that the addresses in memory are not real addresses, they are virtual addresses. The memory theater is not a perfect analogy, but it does create a virtual world that you can play within your mind. Because you never actually touch real memory in a protected-mode operating system, there is something appropriate about creating a virtual memory theater to help you imagine the inside of a computer. Programming is like a game. Everything about memory and computer languages is an illusion, just as games like Phantasmagoria or Doom are illusions. Computer-based illusions, however, can be both interesting and useful. In truth, I have always found programming more interesting in the long run than even the cleverest computer games and, conversely, what really interests me in computer games is how they are programmed.

My point is that virtual memory might not be real memory, but that doesn't make it any less powerful or valuable! At some level, it's hard to give up a slide rule and start using a calculator. It's difficult to move from a typewriter to a word processor. It's hard to give up eye-to-eye contact and instead rely on sonar or radar. But in the long run, all but the most starry-eyed ludite would agree that you are better off making all of these changes. In the same way, you are better off moving from real memory to virtual memory. It's all an illusion, but a very useful one.

Allocating Memory with *New* and *Dispose*

The simplest way to allocate memory is by using New or Dispose. These functions automatically allocate the amount of memory needed to hold a particular variable. In this section, you are going to learn about what it means to allocate and deallocate memory, and how these acts can be performed by using New and Dispose.

There is a parallel between the act of allocating memory in a computer and the act of reserving seats in the memory theater. When you allocate memory in a computer, all you are really doing is telling the operating system that you want to reserve a certain section of RAM until further notice. It is as if you go to the ticket office in the memory theater and say, "I want to reserve 256 seats so that I can put a string into them. Don't use those seats for anything else. They are reserved." If your needs are somewhat different, you might tell the ticket office, "I need room for an integer. Please reserve four seats for me." Once you make this request, the owners of the memory theater are honor-bound to reserve those seats until you tell them you want to dispose of them.

It is very important that whenever you allocate memory, you eventually come along and deallocate it. The problem is that there are only a certain number of seats in the memory theater. If you allocate memory and then forget to deallocate it, eventually you will go to the ticket office and ask for more seats, and you will be told that the house is all booked up, or more likely, you will find that the request is honored, but that the performance on your system becomes very slow. In particular, protected mode provides a kind of virtual memory that can be swapped to your hard disk. Therefore, it can keep swapping between RAM and your hard disk for a very long time before it actually runs out of potential memory. However, long before all the possible bytes are allocated, there will come a time when you machine's performance will become unacceptably slow, or when some particular resource on your system will be depleted. However, you will not actually run out of memory until you run out of hard disk space. If you have 2 GB of empty hard drive space on your system, you have at least 2 GB of memory available to your program.

NOTE

One of the key problems that has haunted the worlds of DOS and Windows has been that there is very little to keep an ill-behaved program from taking up more seats than it reserved. Some programs simply write over the seats reserved by another program. That is, they start acting as if they owned those seats, when the seats were clearly reserved for someone else. If Windows is able to detect that this is happening, it generates a General Protection Fault (Windows 3.1) or an Access Violation (Windows 95 or NT), which says that some program is trying to write to memory that it does not own, and that the operating system is going to try to protect those violated seats by shutting down the program that is out of line.

This is not the place to do much more than hint at this subject, but the move toward Windows NT, Windows 95, and OS/2 is fueled in large part by the desire to use protected-mode operating systems that are good at protecting the memory that belongs to a program. In particular, the goal is to give each program its own virtual memory theater with 4 GB worth of seats in it. The program doesn't really have its own memory theater, but it has the illusion that it has its own memory theater. The theater, of course, isn't really 4 GB in size, it's really probably only some 8-, 16-, or 32MB in size, plus whatever free space is available on the hard drive. The illusion is so complete, however, that the program thinks it has 4 GB worth of memory allocated to it, and that all of it is in RAM. Your program doesn't know or care that it might be reference memory that has been paged to disk. All the addresses that it can access belong to that one program and that one program alone. Therefore (at least in theory), it can't access memory that belongs to another program.

If you call New to allocate memory, the operating system literally sets up a table where it keeps track of your request, and it will not give the memory you have reserved to anyone else until you come back and say, "Okay, I'm through with this memory. You can deallocate it." (The table in question is called a *descriptor table,* and it can be thought of as an internal database or spreadsheet used to keep track of pointers.)

If a programmer comes to the operating system and requests memory that is not available, the request fails and the user usually sees a sign that says "Out of Memory," or more likely, "Out of Resources." In these cases, the operating system absolutely will not give up any reserved seats no matter how important the need. The issue, of course, is that information vital to the user or to the integrity of the operating system might be stored in any particular allocation. As a result, it is not possible to give it up until the module that allocated the memory gives the sign okaying the deallocation.

NOTE

Memory allocation and maintenance inside Windows can become quite complex. For instance, as mentioned previously, it is possible for Windows to swap memory to disk. In terms of the memory theater, this is a bit like telling a group of people in one set of seats that they will have to step out into the lobby for a time, so that other people can come in and participate for a bit. The issue is that there are 4 GB of potential seats, but the theater itself might hold only 8 MB or 16 MB, or however much RAM you have in your machine. When the first set of people is needed again, they can be swapped back into the memory theater, and the second set of people is sent out into the lobby—that is, they are swapped to disk. These kinds of trades can and do continue indefinitely until the seats in question are deallocated. Furthermore, it is possible for the programmer to specify that certain seats can't be swapped in and out of memory in this manner, although this capability is greatly limited in Win32 when compared to Windows 3.1.

However, this is not the time to get into all these esoteric issues. For now it is simplest to imagine the audience in the memory theater as being entirely static. There will be time enough later to get into all the tricks people have created to expand the capabilities of the memory theater. The facts of the matter, however, are very simple: There are *x* number of seats in the memory theater. You can reserve these seats by allocating memory. If you reserve many seats and do not ever deallocate them, you will run out of seats and produce an error condition.

Declaring Pointers: A Practical Example

It is time now to start getting down to examples. Consider the case discussed previously, where you want to declare pointers to strings. If you wanted to work with a pointer to a string, what you really need is a special type of pointer.

Listing 4.1 shows the simplest possible program that shows how to declare a pointer to string, allocate memory for it, and dispose of it.

Listing 4.1. The SimpMem program shows how to perform simple memory allocations and deallocations.

```
unit main;

interface

uses
  Windows, Messages, SysUtils,
  Classes, Graphics, Controls,
  Forms, Dialogs, StdCtrls;

type
  TForm1 = class(TForm)
    Button1: TButton;
    procedure Button1Click(Sender: TObject);
  private
    { Private declarations }
  public
    { Public declarations }
  end;

var
  Form1: TForm1;

implementation

{$R *.DFM}


procedure TForm1.Button1Click(Sender: TObject);
type
  PShortString = ^ShortString;
var
  MyString: PShortString;
begin
  New(MyString);        { Allocate 256 bytes for the string }
  MyString^ := 'Hello'; { Assign a value to string          }
  Canvas.TextOut(10, 10, MyString^); { Write to the screen  }
  Dispose(MyString);    { Deallocate the memory             }
end;

end.
```

When creating this program, I set the color of the form to white, turned off the button's Parent Font property, and set the font of the form to Arial, 24-point, bold-italic. The result is shown in Figure 4.2.

FIGURE 4.2.

The main form for the SimpMem project.

I spend several paragraphs discussing this program, so if it doesn't make complete sense to you yet, don't worry. I want to start by describing the program once at a fairly high speed, go through the whole program again very slowly, and finally come back and summarize what has been said.

The program starts by declaring a new type, which is a pointer to a ShortString:

```
type
  PShortString = ^ShortString;
```

Notice that I am not declaring a pointer to an AnsiString, since an AnsiString is really a pointer. You can work with pointers to pointers if you want to, but this isn't the place to start an examination of this topic. So I am working with pointers to a ShortString—that is, a pointer to an array. I am not working with pointers to AnsiString. Note also that there is an internal Object Pascal type called PString, which is a pointer to an AnsiString. The native Pascal PString type is declared in the System unit. I'm not referencing that type here, but only the type that is explicitly declared previously as a pointer to a ShortString.

The program declares a variable of the type PShortString:

```
var
  MyString: PShortString;
```

In the body of the code, memory is allocated for the variable, and then the variable is assigned a value and is written to the screen:

```
New(MyString);          { Allocate 256 bytes for the string }
MyString^ := 'Hello'; { Assign a value to string         }
Canvas.TextOut(10, 10, MyString^);   { Write the value to the screen    }
```

Finally, the memory that was allocated is disposed—that is, it is given back to the operating system:

```
Dispose(MyString);      { Deallocate the memory            }
```

In the preceding paragraph I gave you a quick overview of the program, but many readers probably need the action to be slowed down much further so that they can get a careful look at exactly what happened. As I said earlier, pointers are a complicated subject, so it is very appropriate that they be covered in the clearest possible terms. I therefore slow the camera way down and consider each frame of the film in detail.

In chapters found on the CD, you work with variables of type `Integer`, type `Word`, or type `string`. You can declare these types of variables with syntax that might look something like this:

```
var
  A: Word;
  B: Integer;
  C: ShortString;
```

If you wanted to change the third variable from a string to a pointer to a string, you would write

```
var
  C: ^ShortString;
```

In this code fragment, the caret symbol (^) identifies the variable as a pointer.

If you wanted to read the line aloud, you would say, "C is a pointer to a string," or, if you prefer, "C colon up-caret string." Of the two options, I much prefer the former. The syntax itself is merely a convention. In other words, the colon and the caret were symbols that were picked more or less at random by the developers of Object Pascal. They don't have any particular significance. What is significant is the actual meaning of the syntax, which is best expressed by the sentence "C is a pointer to a string." Here are a few more examples of bits of syntax, and a reasonable method for speaking them aloud:

```
A: ^Word;
"A is a pointer to a word."
B: ^Char;
"B is a pointer to a character."
```

Of course, if you would rather say "B colon up-caret Char," there is no harm in it. I simply happen to prefer a more literal translation of the syntax. Experienced programmers will readily comprehend either manner of speaking.

Now it is possible to go back and take a second look at the declarations at the top of the SimpMem program:

```
type
  PShortString = ^ShortString;

var
  MyString: PShortString;
```

The type declaration shown here states that a `PShortString` is a pointer to a string. The var statement then declares a variable called `MyString` that is of type `PShortString`.

The classic mistake made in cases such as this would be to write the following:

```
type
  PShortString = ^ShortString;

var
  MyString: PShortString;

begin
  MyString := 'Hello';
```

```
  Caption := MyString;
end;
```

The are two problems with this code. The first is that no allocation is made for the `MyString` variable, and the second is that the variable is not dereferenced when it is used.

Dereferencing a variable is a fancy way of talking about using the caret syntax. This is a dereferenced variable:

```
MyString^
```

This variable is not dereferenced:

```
MyString
```

Often, the compiler will catch you up if you forget to dereference a variable. You will get a compiler error telling you that you have a type mismatch or some other problem. The way to fix the problem is to deference the variable involved.

Consider this statement:

```
MyString := 'Hello';
```

Given the declarations shown here, you know that `MyString` is a pointer, and the string literal `Hello` is a string. You can't assign a string to a pointer. It is a type mismatch. You can, however, write the following:

```
MyString^ := 'Hello';
```

This statement says that the memory that `MyString` points to is going to be assigned a certain value. Because `MyString` points to a string, it's okay to assign a string to it.

> **NOTE**
>
> Many programmers like to append `Ptr` to pointer variables so that they can easily be recognized. For instance, these programmers might write
>
> ```
> MyStringPtr: PShortString;
> ```
>
> Other programmers prefer to prepend letters designating the type of variable being declared and the fact that it is a pointer:
>
> ```
> lpstrMyString: PShortString;
> ```
>
> This syntax states that `MyString` is a long pointer—that is, a 32-bit pointer—to a string. I usually don't use syntax of this type, primarily because I think it makes my code harder to read. However, there are very good arguments on the other side of this issue, and you should take the path that you find most comfortable. (You will, however, find that I sometimes distinguish one type of component from another type by using syntax closely akin to this Hungarian notation. Like certain politicians, I tend to waffle a bit on this issue!)

As I said previously, the compiler will usually warn you if you forget to dereference a variable. There are exceptions, such as when you are using the Move command, or when you are using the BlockRead or FillChar commands. These functions enable you to use a pointer without dereferencing it, which can lead you down the primrose path to some fairly serious crashes. The point here is not that BlockRead, FillChar, and Move are poorly designed functions, but merely that they are flexible enough to enable you to make some fairly serious mistakes. As a result you should always use these powerful functions with care.

Access Violations: Courting Trouble!

As stated earlier, the compiler will never murmur a peep if you write code like this:

```
type
  PShortString = ^ShortString;

var
  MyString: PShortString;

begin
  MyString^ := 'Hello';
  WriteLn(MyString^);
end.
```

In fact, there are even occasions when you will be able to run code like this without ever receiving an error message. However, the fact that the preceding code does not allocate any memory for MyString is a very serious bug, and it will eventually catch up with a programmer and cause real trouble, if it doesn't surface right away by causing the program to produce an access violation. Access violations, shown in Figure 4.3, are caused when you try to access memory that does not belong to your program or that you do not have rights to access.

FIGURE 4.3.

Access violations cause Delphi to act in a disgruntled and irritable manner.

I want to emphasize, however, that you can sometimes use a pointer for which you have not allocated memory without causing an Access Violation. This is called *blind luck*, and it would happen if the address of the variable you are referencing happens to point to valid memory. Note that before you allocate memory for a pointer, it will contain a random address, and it's possible that this address might point at valid memory. However, a mistake of this kind is very serious, and it will almost certainly catch up with you sooner or later. Furthermore, unless more powerful debugging tools appear in the future, there is no way to ensure that you never make this mistake. There currently are no tools that test to see if this is the case. The only way to check for these errors is to comb over your code carefully looking for slip-ups!

The short program shown in Listing 4.2 will help you get a feeling for what happens when you forget to allocate memory for a pointer.

Listing 4.2. The Buggy1 program seeks to intentionally create an access violation.

```
unit main;

{$R+,S+}

interface

{ This programs demonstrates the fact that you
  need to allocate memory for a pointer before
  you use it. If you don't allocate the memory,
  you risk generating an Access Violation (used
  to be called a GPF.) You are not okay if the Access
  Violation happens not to occur — you are just
  lucky.

  If it occurs, this error will automatically generate an
  EAccessViolation exception. }

uses
  Windows, Messages, SysUtils,
  Classes, Graphics, Controls,
  Forms, Dialogs, StdCtrls;

type
  PAnsiString = ^string;

  TForm1 = class(TForm)
    bMayRaiseException: TButton;
    bWillRaiseException: TButton;
    procedure bMayRaiseExceptionClick(Sender: TObject);
    procedure bWillRaiseExceptionClick(Sender: TObject);
  private
    NilString: PAnsiString;
  end;

var
  Form1: TForm1;

implementation

{$R *.DFM}

procedure TForm1.bMayRaiseExceptionClick(Sender: TObject);
type
  PString = ^ShortString;
var
  MyString: PString;
begin
  // MyString := nil;  // Uncomment to force exception
  MyString^ := 'Hello';
  Caption := MyString^;
end;
```

```
// The data in an object is set to nil, so this
// function will always raise an access violation.
procedure TForm1.bWillRaiseExceptionClick(Sender: TObject);
begin
  NilString^ := 'Sam';
  Caption := NilString^;
end;
end.
```

When you run this program, it will probably produce an access violation. However, you might be able to run it without error because MyString might accidentally reference valid memory. If this happens, you could try adding more units to the uses clause, or new variables in the var section. These might alter the program's image so that the MyString variable will point at invalid memory. Most of the time, however, this program will automatically generate an access violation. (Though it has similar results, this is not exactly the same thing as using the Access database program. Access violations, Access databases—related concepts, different implementations!)

> **NOTE**
>
> As mentioned earlier, one of the insidious things about pointer errors is that the line of code that causes them will often compile and run just fine. On occasion, a detectable problem will not surface until much later in your program. As a result, it appears that the error occurs in a portion of your code that is actually error-free. Tracking down pointer errors can be a task strewn with red herrings.
>
> In the 16-bit version, you could set HeapLimit equal to zero in the first line of your program, which would effectively turned off the suballocator. You would then have a better chance of finding the error in the location it occurred. However, this is not an option in the 32-bit version. In fact, there are no panaceas when it comes to pointer problems. Many of them are, by definition, insidious and hard to track down. One of the ways that good programmers earn their reputation is by finding pointer errors in record time.
>
> In the future, there might be a Code Guard or Bounds Checker for Delphi. If this type of product appears, this would be a big boon for programmers. However, in its absence, you can do little more than concentrate hard on writing good code, and use the Microsoft debug kernel if it's available.

Another thing you should notice about the Buggy1 program is that it includes the following compiler directives:

```
{$R+,S+}
```

This code turns on stack-checking and range-checking, both of which can help you detect pointer errors at the places they occur.

The key point about the BUGGY1 program is that it does not include any code to allocate memory for a pointer. It might seem as if I am spending an awfully long time on this point, but you will find that even the most experienced programmers frequently forget to allocate memory for pointers. It is a simple mistake to fix once you have found the error, but tracking down pointer errors is not always easy.

Here is a second version of the body of the BUGGY1 program:

```
begin
  New(MyString);
  MyString^ := 'Hello';
  WriteLn(MyString^);
end.
```

This version of the program will compile and run just fine. However, it also contains a very common, and very serious, error.

Many alert readers are probably aware that this code is missing a statement to deallocate the memory assigned to MyString. When you are thinking about this kind of thing, it is simple enough to see what is wrong. The problem, however, is that in a program containing tens of thousands of lines of code, it is easy to forget to deallocate memory in one place or another. Once you make this mistake, it can be very difficult to track it down and eradicate it. The issue being, of course, that it will not produce an immediate error condition in your program.

Here is how the body of BUGGY1 should look:

```
begin
  New(MyString);
  MyString^ := 'Hello';
  WriteLn(MyString^);
  Dispose(MyString);
end.
```

If you accidentally left off the last line and failed to deallocate memory, the program would still run fine. However, omitting the last line of this program is the type of error that can slowly drain the system of all its available memory.

NOTE

The very important Drain program, found only on the Unleashed CD, shows what happens when you allocate memory and don't free it. It includes working with the THeapStatus record from the Windows API:

```
THeapStatus = record
  TotalAddrSpace: Cardinal;s
  TotalUncommitted: Cardinal;
  TotalCommitted: Cardinal;
  TotalAllocated: Cardinal;
  TotalFree: Cardinal;
  FreeSmall: Cardinal;
  FreeBig: Cardinal;
  Unused: Cardinal;
  Overhead: Cardinal;
  HeapErrorCode: Cardinal;
end;
```

In particular, suppose I have written a small utility that runs constantly on my system. Suppose further that inside that utility there happens to be an error like the one shown earlier. The first time the utility runs, I lose about 256 bytes, which on most systems happens to be no major problem. However, if that keeps executing in a loop, after a few hours or days, my system will crash with an "Out of Memory" or "Out of Resources" error.

The error, of course, could occur while I am running some other program, which means that it would be very difficult to figure out where the error was coming from. Even if I did track the error back to its home program, it might still be difficult for me to sift through a few thousand lines of code looking for the one place where I forgot to call Dispose.

Once again, I am belaboring this point because I want to make it absolutely clear that you have to remember to call New and Dispose nearly every time you use a pointer. Furthermore, it is very natural for the soggy little computer residing between our ears to occasionally forget to call New or Dispose, even if it thoroughly understands the importance of the calls. As a result, there are times when you have to track this error down at great expense in terms of time and sanity.

NOTE

The GetMem and FreeMem routines are closely related to New and Dispose. In fact, in their implementation, New and Dispose call GetMem and FreeMem. The difference between the two sets of routines is that one set automatically calculates the size of the variables for which you want to allocate memory, whereas the other asks you to specifically state how much memory you need:

```
var
  S, S1: ^ShortString;
begin
  New(S);
  GetMem(S1, 256);
  Dispose(S);
  FreeMem(S1, 256);
end;
```

> In the code shown here, the calls to GetMem and the calls to New perform exactly the same function; that is, they each allocate 256 bytes on the heap.

In Chapter 7, "Multitasking and Threads," you will learn about ways to allocate memory by calling into the operating system. In particular, you will learn about calling VirtualAlloc and HeapAlloc, and about memory-mapped files.

I should also add that all programs running under Windows 3.1 and most 16-bit programs running under Windows 95 will end up sharing the same address space. This means that if one program is corrupting memory, it can affect all the other programs in its address space. Any corruption or any unallocated memory associated with that program will live on, even after the program closes. That is, it will live on until the Windows 3.1 session is shut down or until all the other 16-bit programs run under Windows 95 are shut down. 32-bit programs, on the other hand, do not operate in this fashion. After you close a 32-bit program under Windows 95 or Windows NT, all the memory associated with that program will be disposed by the operating system. This is not, however, a license to forget about deallocating memory. Any time you don't dispose a pointer, you are courting trouble. If you know what you are doing, you can get away with it in a 32-bit program, but it is a very bad habit to develop.

In this section you have learned some of the basic facts about pointers. The next section goes on to show you one very practical use for the new tool you have been studying.

Pointers and Objects

Like AnsiStrings, all Delphi objects are really pointers to objects. Delphi allows you to write

```
Edit1.Text := 'Sam';
```

However, it is vital to understand that Edit1 is really a pointer to an object. Under normal circumstances, you would have to write

```
Edit1^.Text := 'Sam';
```

You don't have to do this because the developers of Delphi have intentionally tried to conceal the fact that Edit1 is a pointer. They don't want to burden you with that difficulty, so they never force you to dereference an object. Furthermore, it is not possible to create an instance of an object that is not a pointer. All objects are pointers in Delphi.

I stressed earlier in this chapter that it is very important to allocate and deallocate memory for pointers. This is usually not a problem when you are dealing with objects because the system will allocate and deallocate the memory for you. In particular, memory gets allocated for an object when you pull it off the Component Palette and drop it on a form. When a program ends, its forms are automatically disposed. Furthermore, each form knows how to dispose the objects that are placed on it. This subject will be discussed in depth in the chapters on components and objects.

There are times, however, when you do need to explicitly create and destroy objects. For instance, if you are using a TStringList variable, you must allocate memory for it and deallocate that memory when you are done:

```
var
  L: TStringList;
begin
  L := TStringList.Create;
  // Do something with the string list.
  L.Free;
end;
```

In the code shown here, notice that there is a special syntax for allocating memory for objects. In particular, you don't call New or GetMem. It would normally be an error, or lead to an error, if you tried to call New or GetMem on an object. Instead, you call the Create method of the object. Furthermore, you don't dispose an object by calling Dispose or FreeMem. Instead, you call the object's Free method.

That's all I'm going to say about objects in this chapter. The subject is covered in depth in Part 5, "Objects."

Setting a Pointer to *nil*

Pointers can be set to a value called nil:

```
var
  P: ^ShortString;
  I: Pinteger;
begin
  P := nil;
  I := nil;
end;
```

This code in effect zeros out the pointer value itself. It sets the pointer to zero. This does not mean that it sets the memory associated with the pointer to zero, it means that the pointer itself is set to zero. It does not affect what the pointer is pointing at, since all nil pointers by definition are not pointing at anything.

By definition, nil pointers have no memory associated with them. That is, they have not been allocated. Further, you can test to see if a pointer is set to nil:

```
var
  P: Pointer;
begin
  ...
  if P = nil then
    GetMem(P, 1000)
  else
    Move(P^, MyVariable, 1000);
  ...
  if P <> nil then Dispose(P);
end;
```

This code illustrates the main reason for adding the value nil to the Object Pascal language. Specifically, it allows you to explicitly set a pointer to nil and then test to see if it has that value. If it is set to nil, it cannot have any memory associated with it. In other words, you can check to see if a pointer has been allocated by seeing whether it is equal to nil. If it is equal to nil, it has no memory associated with it. If it is not equal to nil, it might have a valid address in it or it might have garbage characters that just look like an address.

If you declare a pointer as a local variable in a function and do not explicitly set it to nil, it will probably contain a randomly chosen address. That is, it will not necessarily automatically be set to nil, and might appear to be a valid pointer. However, the address in the variable is probably random garbage unless you have explicitly declared memory for it. Pointer values that you declare inside an object declaration will automatically be zeroed out—that is, be set to nil.

The compiler will not stop you from setting a valid pointer to nil. This will not cause an error in your program, but it will strand the memory associated with the pointer. That is, you will not be able to access that memory, and it will not be possible to easily dispose it.

PChars and Arrays of Char

Both C and Object Pascal are very powerful languages that give you full access to all the features of a computer. However, there are certain places where one language branched in one direction and the second branched in a different direction. In particular, C used to have a radically different way of handling strings than Object Pascal.

Both C and Pascal are old languages that have been around since the late sixties or early seventies. During much of that time, it didn't matter that they had such radically different philosophies regarding the best way to treat strings. However, once C was chosen as a key building block for Windows, it became necessary to extend Object Pascal's syntax to include the methods C employs when working with strings. In the past, Delphi depended on PChars and arrays of Char to represent strings because that is the native way that Windows handles strings. You can still use these types if you want, but the new AnsiStrings used in Delphi 2.0 automatically give you compatibility with Windows API functions.

NOTE

You can pass AnsiStrings directly to Windows functions by typecasting them as a PChar. In fact, beneath the surface, AnsiStrings and PChars are nearly identical, except for the undocumented data kept at negative offsets in AnsiStrings. Therefore, you can simply typecast an AnsiString and pass it off as a PChar, that is, you can safely trick the system into believing that an AnsiString is a PChar. This makes it very easy to call Windows functions in Delphi. In fact, it's simpler to do so than it is to call them from C. This is because it's easier to work with AnsiStrings than with PChars (LPSTRs), or with C-style, null-terminated strings.

The developers of Delphi go out of their way to ensure that you can write complex, full-featured programs without ever having to use a PChar. That is, they intentionally make sure that you can use Delphi strings to access most of the basic functionality of a computer, including the Windows API functions. The reasoning behind this decision is simply that strings are much easier to use than PChars. However, whenever you decide to step outside the native Delphi calls and start accessing the Windows API directly, you might decide to use PChars, although this is no longer necessary.

> **NOTE**
>
> The PChar type is a special kind of pointer. You need to allocate memory for it, but you usually do not need to dereference it. This can cause some confusion at first, but the key thing to remember about PChars is that they are pointers, so you have to be sure that memory is allocated for them and that the memory associated with them is later freed.

There are two ways to create a PChar. The first is simply to declare a variable as a PChar:

```
var
  S: PChar;
```

The other method is to declare it as a zero-based array of Char:

```
var
  S: array[0..100] of Char;
```

The most fundamental difference between the two declarations shown here is that the second has memory allocated for it and the first does not. In other words, the character array shown here has 101 bytes allocated for it, whereas the PChar has no bytes allocated for it. Otherwise, the two declarations are nearly identical. This identity comes about because the compiler has a special set of rules for handling PChars and zero-based arrays of Char. In other words, the array of Char shown earlier has special properties associated with it, just as a standard Delphi string is really just an array of Char with special properties.

In Chapter 3, "Strings and Text Files," you were introduced to some of the basic facts about PChars. In that chapter, you learned that both strings and PChars are really just arrays of Char. ShortStrings, however, track their length in the first byte of their data structure, AnsiStrings track them at an undocumented negative offset, and PChars place a NULL character (#0) at their end to signal their length. Because Delphi ShortStrings use a length byte, they are limited by definition to only 255 characters. PChars, on the other hand, have no inherent limitations under the 32-bit version of Delphi. AnsiStrings also have no inherent limits, and they also have a null character (#0) at their end. They differ from PChars in that you usually don't have to explicitly allocate memory for them; and when you allocate memory for them, you do so with the SetLength function. Furthermore, AnsiStrings have undocumented data stored at negative offsets.

When working with strings, you can use the Length function to determine their size. With PChars, however, you must use the StrLen function, which is stored in the SysUtils unit:

```
uses
  SysUtils;

procedure TForm1.Button2Click(Sender: TObject);
var
  MyString: array[0..100] of Char;
begin
  StrCopy(MyString, 'Null terminated strings');
  Edit1.Text := IntToStr(StrLen(MyString));
end;
```

The code first calls StrCopy to assign a string to the PChar called MyString. It then calls StrLen to find out the length of the string. StrLen returns a Word, so that value must be translated into a string before it can be shown in an edit control.

Here is a list of the commonly used string functions found in the Strings unit:

StrAlloc	Allocates a buffer for a null-terminated string with a maximum length of Size −1
StrBufSize	Returns the maximum number of characters that may be stored in a string buffer allocated by StrAlloc
StrCat	Appends a copy of one string to the end of another and returns the concatenated string
StrComp	Compares two strings
StrCopy	Copies one string to another
StrDispose	Disposes a string on a heap
StrECopy	Copies one string to another and returns a pointer to the end of the resulting string
StrEnd	Returns a pointer to the end of a string
StrFmt	Formats a series of arguments
StrLFmt	Formats a series of arguments; the result contains a pointer to the destination buffer
StrLCat	Appends characters from one string to the end of another and returns the concatenated string
StrIComp	Compares two strings without case sensitivity
StrLComp	Compares two strings, up to a maximum length
StrLCopy	Copies characters from one string to another
StrLen	Returns the number of characters in Str
StrLIComp	Compares two strings, up to a maximum length, without case sensitivity

StrLower	Converts a string to lowercase
StrMove	Copies characters from one string to another
StrNew	Allocates a string on a heap
StrPas	Converts a null-terminated string to a Pascal-style string
StrPCopy	Copies a Pascal-style string to a null-terminated string
StrPLCopy	Copies a maximum of MaxLen characters from the Pascal-style string Source into the null-terminated string Dest
StrPos	Returns a pointer to the first occurrence of a string in another string
StrScan	Returns a pointer to the first occurrence of a character in a string
StrRScan	Returns a pointer to the last occurrence of a character in a string
StrUpper	Converts a string to uppercase

A list very similar to this can be found in the online help, and you should refer to it whenever you have questions about the best way to handle PChars. The next few paragraphs comment on the routines in the Strings unit and offer some simple examples on how to use them.

It is easy to confuse the functionality of StrCopy and StrCat. StrCopy copies one string to another, thereby obliterating the contents of the first string. StrCat, on the other hand, appends one string onto the end of another string. The classic error to make in this regard is to attempt to use StrCat on a string that is currently set to a random value:

```
var
  S1, S2: array[0..100] of Char;

begin
  StrCat(S1, 'Hello');
  StrCat(S2, ', gentle reader');
  StrCat(S1, S2);
end;
```

The code shown here might not perform as expected, because there may be random characters in S1. As a result, the word Hello will be appended onto the end of these random characters rather than being copied into the first six letters of string S1. The correct way to handle the situation shown earlier is this:

```
var
  S1, S2: array[0..100] of Char;

begin
  StrCopy(S1, 'Hello');
  StrCopy(S2, ', gentle reader');
  StrCat(S1, S2);
  Edit1.Text := S1;
end;
```

This code always ends up with the string Hello, gentle reader in string S1. The first example might end up with this string in S1, but it is not guaranteed.

The StrNew and StrDispose functions are very useful ways of allocating memory for a string:

```
var
  S1: PChar;
begin
  S1 := StrNew('Hello');
  Edit1.Text := S1 + ' Length: ' + IntToStr(StrLen(S1));
  StrDispose(S1);
end;
```

When using StrNew, you never have to specify exactly how many bytes you want to allocate for string S1. Instead, the compiler makes the calculation for you. This technique can be very useful when you want to make sure you are not wasting memory by preallocating arbitrarily large blocks of memory at design time. The StrDispose function provides a simple way to dispose of memory that was allocated with StrNew. In fact, you must use StrDispose whenever you use StrNew. Notice that you don't have to tell the compiler how many bytes to deallocate. You should also look at the StrAlloc function, which is clearly explained in the online help.

If you are working in Delphi 16, the code shown previously would need to use the StrPas function, which converts a null-terminated string into a Delphi string:

```
Edit1.Text := StrPas(S1) + ' Length: ' + IntToStr(StrLen(S1));
```

To use StrPas, simply pass it the PChar you want to convert, and the string equivalent will be returned by the function. Nothing could be simpler.

The opposite of the StrPas function is StrPCopy, which converts a Delphi string into a null-terminated string. In both Delphi 16 and Delphi 32, you must use StrPCopy when working with arrays of Char:

```
var
  S1: String;
  S2: array[0..100] of Char;
begin
  S1 := 'Confront the difficult while it is still easy';
  StrPCopy(S2, S1);
  Edit1.Text := S2;
end;
```

In Delphi 2.0, however, you can, with the aid of typecast, simply assign a PChar to a string, as long as Huge Strings is turned on in the Compiler Options page:

```
procedure TForm1.Button3Click(Sender: TObject);
var
  S1: string;
  S2: PChar;
begin
  S1 := 'Confront the difficult while it is still easy';
  S2 := PChar(S1);
  Edit1.Text := S2;
end;
```

Notice that the code shown here does not need to allocate memory for S2 because it is being assigned to the same pointer as S1. This chore is handled for you automatically by the compiler. Please understand, however, that some strange things are happening when you assign S1 to S2, that is, when you write S2 := PChar(S1). If you are an experienced assembly language programmer, you should use the standalone debugger to see if you can suss out exactly how the shipping version of Delphi handles these situations.

> **NOTE**
>
> There are subtle differences between the ways that the compiler handles PChars and arrays of Char. By definition, they should be identical as long as extended syntax is turned on {$X+}, which is the default setting. This is not always the case, however, as shown above.

All of the code you have seen in the last few pages can be found on the CD in a program called PCHAR1. I don't bother to reproduce that program here, because it is nothing more than a series of buttons, each one of which is associated with one of the examples shown previously. The form for the PCHAR1 program is shown in Figure 4.4.

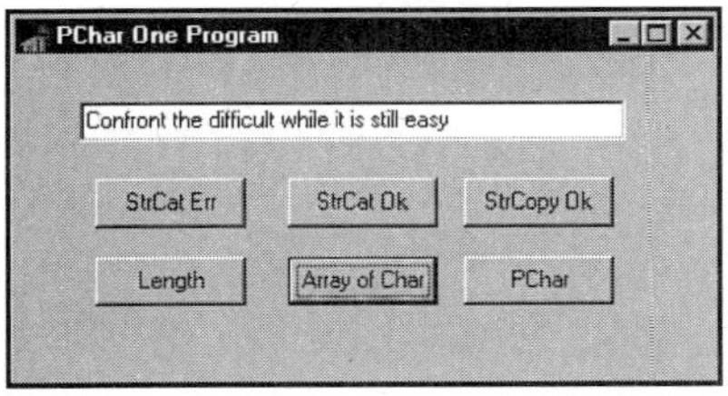

FIGURE 4.4.

The PCHAR1 program demonstrates some of the basic traits of null-terminated strings.

Before closing this chapter, there is one final point I want to make about PChars. If you create a procedure that returns a PChar, you should always make the routine that calls the procedure allocate the memory for the PChar. For instance, suppose you wanted to return a string from a procedure that supplies the current date. The following implementation would be incorrect:

```
procedure GetDate(Date: PChar);
begin
  GetMem(Date, 100);
  StrCopy(Date '11/01/94');
end;
```

The problem with this code fragment is that it allocates memory inside a function and then returns the string to a place that lies outside the scope of the current function. As a result, there is no guaranteed way to ensure clean up of the memory. The correct way to handle a situation like this is to insist that the calling routine allocate memory:

```
procedure GetDate(Date: PChar);
begin
  StrCopy(Date, '11/01/94');
end;
```

A simple way to call this routine would be to write a procedure that looks like this:

```
procedure CallDate;
var
  S: array[0..100] of char;
begin
  GetDate(S);
  Edit1.Text := S;
end;
```

or like this:

```
procedure CallDate;
var
  S: PChar;
begin
  S := StrAlloc(100);
  GetDate(S);
  Edit1.Text := S;
  StrDispose(S);
end;
```

In this case, the CallDate procedure handles memory allocation for the string that will hold a date. This is always the correct way to handle this type of situation. The golden rule is that a procedure that returns a modified PChar should never be responsible for allocating its memory. The calling procedure should always handle this task.

There is a program on the CD called PCHARFUN that illustrates the ideas discussed in the preceding paragraphs. The key point to remember is that any function that returns a PChar should have the calling function perform any necessary memory allocation. It is always a mistake for the called function to return a PChar that it has allocated. If you make this mistake, one of two things will happen:

- The returned value will no longer be valid because it was a pointer that was allocated on the function's stack.

- The returned value will probably never be properly deallocated because there is no one who owns it and who therefore has responsibility for its deallocation.

Summary

In this chapter you have learned the basics about pointers and PChars. Pointers are one of the most elemental types supported by a computer. Delphi enables you to write a good deal of code without ever forcing you to think about pointers.

This chapter also explored PChars. PChars can be very confusing to newcomers, in part because they are a special kind of pointer that rarely needs to be dereferenced. As a result, it is easy to make a mistake when using this type.

The next chapter takes a more in-depth look at pointers. In particular, you will get a look at linked lists and the way addresses look when you explore them with the debugger. You will also see how to perform arithmetic on pointers.

Pointers, Linked Lists, and Memory

5

In the last chapter you learned the basic facts about pointers. In this chapter you get a chance to explore the subject in more depth. In particular, you will look at

- Pointer arithmetic
- Linked lists
- Using the stand-alone debugger to explore pointers.

As in the last chapter, much of this material does not carry the burden of extreme importance that it had in the 16-bit version of Delphi. However, this is still significant material, and it is worthy of careful perusal by serious students of Delphi. In particular, it is now possible to be a reasonably respectable, intermediate level programmer without having a good understanding of pointers. It's not recommended, and it would be considered idiosyncratic by most professionals, but it is now possible to write useful professional level code that makes no explicit use of pointers. However, if you want to be an expert, you have to understand pointers on the deepest level of your consciousness. Nobody could lay claim to mastery of any field of Delphi programming without a thorough, and instinctive, understanding of pointers. In short, you can use Delphi without understanding pointers, but you will never be a really good Delphi programmer until you have the subject under your belt.

Pointer Arithmetic on PChars

The plus (+) and minus (-) operators, as well as the Inc and Dec procedures, can increment and decrement the offset part of a PChar. A sample program demonstrating this technique is shown in Listing 5.1.

Listing 5.1. The PMath program shows how you can do some simple pointer math using PChars.

```
unit Unit1;

interface

uses
  Windows, Messages, SysUtils,
  Classes, Graphics, Controls,
  Forms, Dialogs, StdCtrls;

type
  TForm1 = class(TForm)
    Button1: TButton;
    procedure Button1Click(Sender: TObject);
  end;
```

```
var
  Form1: TForm1;

implementation

{$R *.DFM}

procedure TForm1.Button1Click(Sender: TObject);
var
  A, B: PChar;
begin
  GetMem(A, 100);
  StrCopy(A, 'This-long-sentence');
  B := A;
  Inc(B, 2);
  Caption := B;
  FreeMem(A, 100);
end;

end.
```

This program lets you perform simple arithmetic on a PChar in order to iterate through its characters. After setting B equal to A with an assignment statement (B := A), the string B is pointing at a sentence that reads: "This-long-sentence". The next line:

```
Inc(B, 2);
```

moves the pointer value along two characters so that the sentence now reads: 'is-long-sentence'. You could have done the same thing by writing code like

```
B := B + 2;
```

It's important to understand that this is an unusual thing to do with pointers. It's a feature supported by C, so some folks tend to see it as a natural action; but it's quite peculiar and will work in Delphi only in particular circumstances, such as when you are working with PChars.

Some programmers tend to avoid this kind of syntax since it is a bit counter-intuitive and can lead to confusing and hard-to-read code. When you increment the value of a pointer, you are moving the place in memory that a pointer points to up by a certain value. For instance, the pointer might initially have pointed at seat 500 in the memory theater. If you increment it by two, it will point at seat 502. This is a simple concept, but the syntax that accomplishes these ends is not necessarily transparent to a reader of the code.

Linked Lists

It's time now to look at linked lists, which can be used to store lists of any type of item in a relatively small area of memory. Linked lists are known for their power and flexibility.

Conceptually, linked lists are fairly simple data structures. The basic idea behind them is that they are used for stringing a series of records together out on the heap. The main advantages of the system are twofold:

■ Linked lists are a very quick and convenient way to store many records in a single data structure.

■ Linked lists are very flexible data structures that enable you to allocate memory on the fly. If you don't know how many records of a particular type you need, linked lists can easily grow and shrink to meet your current demands.

NOTE

Delphi has a number of built-in objects such as TStrings, TStringList, and TList, all of which are really just object-oriented variations of linked lists. Obviously, it usually makes more sense to use these built-in structures than to create tools of your own.

Customized linked lists of various kinds, however, are so useful, and have played such a crucial role in computing over the years, that I can't really imagine finishing this book without covering them in at least some detail. If you are a good programmer, you can use linked lists to provide small, flexible solutions to a large number of problems.

Listing 5.2 shows the code for the LinkLst1 program. It demonstrates the core facts about linked lists. This is a console application. To make it run, go to the Project | Options | Linker menu option and check the Generate Console Application option. I have chosen to make this a console application not because this code couldn't be incorporated into a standard VCL project, but simply because I wanted it to be as simple as possible.

Listing 5.2. Basic details about allocating and deallocating memory for linked lists are shown in the LINKLST1 program.

```
program LinkLst1;

{ Program copyright (c) 1996 by Charles Calvert }
{ Project Name: LINKLST1 }

uses
  SysUtils; // Added to suppress IDE errors

type
  PMyRecord = ^TMyRecord;
  TMyRecord = Record
    Name: String;
    Next: PMyRecord;
  end;

var
```

```
    Total: Integer;


function Int2Str(L : LongInt) : string;
var
  S : string;
begin
  Str(L, S);
  Int2Str := S;
end; { Int2Str }

procedure CreateNew(var Item: PMyRecord);
begin
  New(Item);
  Item^.Next := nil;
  Item^.Name := '';
end;

procedure GetData(var Item: PMyRecord);
begin
  Item^.Name := 'Sam' + Int2Str(Total);
end;

procedure DoFirst(var First, Current: PMyRecord);
begin
  CreateNew(Current);
  GetData(Current);
  First := Current;
end;

procedure Add(var Current: PMyRecord);
var
  Prev: PMyRecord;
begin
  Prev := Current;
  CreateNew(Current);
  GetData(Current);
  Prev^.Next := Current;
end;

{ Here is an alternate version of the Add procedure }
procedure Add2(var Current: PMyRecord);
var
  Temp: PMyRecord;
begin
  CreateNew(Temp);
  GetData(Temp);
  Current^.Next := Temp;
  Current := Temp;
end;

procedure Show(Head: PMyRecord);
begin
  while Head^.Next <> nil do begin
    WriteLn(Head^.Name);
    Head := Head^.Next;
```

continues

Listing 5.2. continued

```
    end;
  WriteLn(Head^.Name);
end;

procedure FreeAll(var Head: PMyRecord);
var
  Temp: PMyRecord;
begin
  while Head^.Next <> nil do begin
    Temp := Head^.Next;
    Dispose(Head);
    Head := Temp;
  end;
  Dispose(Head);
end;

var
  First,
  Current: PMyRecord;
begin
  Total := 1;
  DoFirst(First, Current);
  repeat
    Inc(Total);
    Add(Current);
  until Total > 20;
  Show(First);
  FreeAll(First);
end.
```

LinkLst1 displays a simple list of strings that look something like this:

```
Sam1
Sam2
Sam3
Sam4
etc...
```

The list is comprised of strings that were parts of a very simple record:

```
  PMyRecord = ^TMyRecord;
  TMyRecord = Record
    Name: String;
    Next: PMyRecord;
  end;
```

This record has two fields. The first is a string, and the second is a pointer to a record of type TMyRecord. I explain this latter field in a moment.

In this program, the Name field of the records used in the program gets set to values such as Sam1, Sam2, Sam3, and so forth. The code that creates these strings is very simple and should be easy for most students of Object Pascal to read:

```
procedure GetData(var Item: PMyRecord);
begin
  Item^.Name := 'Sam' + Int2Str(Total);
end;
```

All that is happening here is that a variable called Total is being incremented inside a loop, and each time it is incremented, the function GetData is called. GetData sets the Name field of the record to the word Sam plus the value of the variable Total after it has been translated into a string.

The Name field of TMyRecord is easy enough to understand. The tricky part is the second field, the one called Next. The Next field is declared to be of type PMyRecord. In other words, it is a pointer to a record of the same type as the record to which it belongs.

If you are new to linked lists, you might mistakenly be tempted to think of them as a series of Chinese boxes, each of which contains another box of its same type, only slightly smaller. A better image for a linked list might be a series of helium-filled balloons each attached to the next by a string, with the very first member tied down to a stake fixed firmly in the ground.

Picture a metal stake with a ring on the top of it fixed into an area of ground where your executable resides in memory. This stake has a string tied to it, and on the end of the string is a balloon. At the very bottom of the balloon, right next to the place where the string is attached, there is a second string, which in turn leads off to a second balloon. Tied to the bottom of this balloon is a third string, which leads to a third balloon, which in turn leads to a fourth string, and so on, for ten, twenty, even a thousand or more balloons.

At the very bottom of each linked list is a pointer, which is fixed firmly in the solid earth of your program's EXE image. This pointer points off like a long string that leads to a record that is floating out on the heap. Inside this record another pointer exists, which in turn leads off like a long string to the next member in the list. This process continues until you have strung together all the records you want to work with at any one time. The only limits you have to wrestle with are those imposed by the operating system or the amount of available virtual memory. The key image I want you to grasp here is that the pointer field, which in this case is called Next, acts exactly like a string that leads you to the next record in the list of records that comprise what is called a linked list. The pointers link the list together the same way the strings link the balloons together.

Suppose you had 20 of these records linked together. If you wanted to find the tenth record, you could start at the pointer in your executable's data, feel your way along to the first record, find the pointer field in that record, feel your way along to the second record, and so on, until you had iterated through ten records. Then you would be standing smack dab in the middle of the record you wanted to find.

Furthermore, if you had a list of this type, you could count the total members in the list by starting at the first record and proceeding until you came to a point where there was no string to lead you to another record. The question is how can you tell that you are out of records? How do you know that the next pointer you look at is the end of the road and doesn't point at another record?

The answer to this question is fairly simple. Every pointer can be set to one of three states. It can contain a valid address, a nonsense address, or an address that is set to zero. It is very difficult to tell the difference between a valid address and a nonsense address, because they both simply contain a set of numbers. However, pointers that are set to zero are clearly defined as invalid pointers. Therefore, you can mark the end of a linked list by setting the Next field of the record to zero, which is called setting a pointer to nil. You can set a pointer to nil by writing the following:

```
MyRecord^.Next := nil;
```

> **CAUTION**
>
> I stated earlier that it is hard to tell from just looking at it whether a pointer contains a valid address or just some randomly chosen set of numbers that happened to be in a particular section of memory. The inability to make this distinction is a very serious problem.
>
> In particular, if a program is feeling its way along the length of a linked list and it suddenly stumbles across a Next pointer that points off at a random place in memory, the computer will try to feel its way along that string to the imaginary or nonsensical location. Because there is no valid memory at this new location, the computer becomes effectively lost the moment it arrives at the end of its string. Once a computer gets lost, it is very difficult for it ever to get back on track again. Jumping to an invalid address is an excellent way to crash a computer, or at least to cause a process running under a multitasking system to be frozen and ultimately terminated by the system.
>
> As a result of the problem outlined here, it is absolutely essential that you construct all linked lists entirely out of valid addresses, and that you mark the end of each linked list with the value nil. Assigning nil to the last Next field in a linked list clearly marks that node as being the end of the road.

Here is one way to create a node in a linked list:

```pascal
procedure CreateNew(var Item: PMyRecord);
begin
  New(Item);
  Item^.Next := nil;
  Item^.Name := '';
end;
```

This procedure starts by allocating memory for the node with the New procedure. The code then sets the Next pointer to nil and sets the Name field to an empty string. After this procedure is through, the node passed to it is fully initialized.

As stated earlier, the very first node in a linked list is attached to the data in your executable. As a result, it is an exception and needs to be treated differently than all the other nodes in a list. Here is one way to create the first node in a linked list:

```
procedure DoFirst(var First, Current: PMyRecord);
begin
  CreateNew(Current);
  GetData(Current);
  First := Current;
end;
```

DoFirst calls CreateNew, and then GetData, and sets the variable First equal to Current. You have already heard about both CreateNew and GetData, but it will still take a moment to explain the last line in the DoFirst procedure.

In addition to the Total variable, the LINKLST1 program lists the following global variables:

```
var
  First,
  Current: PMyRecord;
```

These two variables are used to keep track of the members of the linked list. The First variable always points to the member of the list that is staked into the data or stack segment. The Current variable always points to the currently selected member of the linked list, which in this particular program will always be the last member of the linked list. In more complex linked list programs, a variable like Current might address a node that is in the middle of the list.

The DoFirst procedure first creates a valid node, fills it with valid data, and finally sets First equal to this node. In other words, the following line of code

```
First := Current;
```

is equivalent to the act of driving the stake attached to the first balloon into the ground. After this, the linked list is attached to the data in your executable, by means of the variable called First.

After getting the list started, all other nodes are added onto the list by means of the Add procedure:

```
procedure Add(var Current: PMyRecord);
var
  Prev: PMyRecord;
begin
  Prev := Current;
  CreateNew(Current);
  GetData(Current);
  Prev^.Next := Current;
end;
```

Add gets passed a copy of the currently selected member of the linked list. Remember that in this linked list, Current could just as easily have been called Last.

> **NOTE**
>
> It's important to understand that in a different type of linked list, the Current item might not necessarily be the Last item. In fact, there are many different kinds of linked lists, and you need to be aware that some of the comments I make in this chapter refer to this particular implementation of a very simple form of linked list, and not necessarily to all linked lists.
>
> Other types of linked lists include circular linked lists and double linked lists. In circular linked lists the last item points back to the first item, rather than being marked as nil. In double linked lists, each item contains a pointer to both the next item in the list, and the previous item in the list. There is also an entire series of structures called binary trees that can be built out of the concepts used in constructing the simple linked list found in this chapter. However, thoroughly describing all these types of data structures would take up hundreds of pages of text, and there is no room for that kind of undertaking within the limits of the current book.
>
> Remember, the main point of this chapter is not so much to teach you about a specific type of linked list, as it is to make sure that you understand pointers. Of course, linked lists also happen to be a very important type of data structure, and most programmers use them in a wide variety of circumstances. In fact, no programmer could ever lay claim to being an expert without having a solid understanding of linked lists.

The Add procedure declares a second pointer to PMyRecord, called Prev. Prev is set equal to Current, and then CreateNew is called. In other words, Prev remembers what Current was pointing at, then Current is used to hold a newly created node, which is then immediately filled with data by the GetData procedure. Finally, the new Current variable is tied on to the end of the linked list with the following piece of code:

```
Prev^.Next := Current;
```

There are many, many ways to implement a linked list. The following routine represents a second take on the Add procedure:

```
procedure Add2(var Current: PMyRecord);
var
  Temp: PMyRecord;
begin
  CreateNew(Temp);
  GetData(Temp);
  Current^.Next := Temp;
  Current := Temp;
end;
```

In this example, a variable called Temp is used when a new node is created. The Next field of Current is set equal to Temp, and finally the Current variable is set equal to the newly created node. Both examples take the same amount of time to execute, and both accomplish the same goal. However, looking at a second version of the Add procedure will help you understand exactly how linked lists work and exactly what needs to be accomplished to add a new node to the end of a list.

The main body of the LINKLST1 program uses the following code to create 21 nodes:

```
repeat
Inc(Total);
Add(Current);
until Total > 20;
```

> **NOTE**
>
> The main body of a Delphi program is always encapsulated in a begin..end pair that is terminated with a period. Most Delphi programs use this main block simply to initialize one or more forms and then call Application.Run. The LINKLST1 program uses this main block far more extensively than VCL programs, but there is no difference in the way the compiler handles this section of the program. In other words, it simply executes the code between the begin..end pair, regardless of whether that code reads
>
> ```
> Application.Run,
> ```
>
> or whether it reads
>
> ```
> CreateNew(Current, First);
> ```

After the list has been created, the following procedure shows it to the user:

```
procedure Show(Head: PMyRecord);
begin
  while Head^.Next <> nil do begin
    WriteLn(Head^.Name);
    Head := Head^.Next;
  end;
  WriteLn(Head^.Name);
end;
```

This procedure is passed the variable called First:

```
Show(First);
```

First is passed to Show because the procedure simply displays each record in the list, starting with the first and traveling through to the end. As you will see in a moment, it is not possible to iterate backwards through this particular linked list. Instead, you must always iterate through the list by starting at the beginning and moving one link at a time.

Here is how to move from the currently selected item to the next item in the list:

```
Head := Head^.Next;
```

If you pass First to the Show procedure, calling this line once will move you from the first item in the list to the second item. Calling it a second time will move you from the second item to the third item, and so forth.

The trick in the Show procedure is to know when you are at the end of the list. This is accomplished with the while statement, which enables the line shown previously to be called until the moment when the current record has a Next field that is set equal to nil. The significance of the nil Next pointer was described earlier:

```
while Head^.Next <> nil do begin
```

There are two other important points about the Show procedure. The first is that after the while loop ends, one more item still must be displayed to the user, so the code does that in its last line. Furthermore, you should note that First is passed to the Show procedure, not as a var parameter:

```
procedure Show(var Head: PMyRecord);
```

but as a simple parameter:

```
procedure Show(Head: PMyRecord);
```

That is, it is passed by value, not by reference. This is done because you don't want to change the node addressed by First.

Because this is an important point, let's look at the same issue again from a second angle. You want to be able to pass Show the first member of the list:

```
Show(First);
```

If Show uses the following code:

```
Head := Head^.Next;
```

to iterate from the first member of the list to the second member, you don't want the variable called First to be affected. As a result, the correct thing to do is pass First by value, rather than by reference. This means a copy of the pointer will be passed to the function and not the First pointer itself.

One last function in the LinkLst1 program still needs to be explained:

```
procedure FreeAll(var Head: PMyRecord);
var
  Temp: PMyRecord;
begin
  while Head^.Next <> nil do begin
    Temp := Head^.Next;
    Dispose(Head);
    Head := Temp;
  end;
  Dispose(Head);
end;
```

The purpose of this procedure is to dispose of all the nodes in the linked list. In other words, it deallocates all the memory allocated by the CreateNew procedure.

Just like the Show procedure, FreeAll is passed First, and it iterates through the linked list in exactly the same manner as Show. However, as each node is reached, the FreeAll procedure disposes of it. In order to do this correctly, it must first keep a copy of the next member of the list, so that it has something to hang on to after it has deleted the current member. Then the current member, called Head in this procedure, is set equal to what was the second member of the list. In this way, the procedure iterates through the whole list, deleting the member behind it as it goes. Note that it is safe to pass First to free all as a var parameter.

The 16-bit version of the LINKLST1 program used Delphi's built-in MemAvail procedure to list the currently available memory both at the beginning and at the end of a run. This function is not used in the 32-bit version because there is no sensible way to keep track of the exact amount of available memory in a 32-bit system. One reason for this is that more memory can often be created by simply swapping RAM to disk. (In fact, there was no really sensible way to keep track of the amount of available memory under Windows 3.1 either, but the developers still tried to make it possible.)

If you took the LinkLst1 program and removed the uses clause, or changed the uses clause so that it referenced Crt instead of SysUtils, you could then run this program from the DOS prompt as an old style Turbo Pascal program. To do so, you would, of course, have to compile it with an old version of Turbo Pascal, if you have one available. You could then call MemAvail, and you would find that the LINKLST1.EXE program created by this code will report the same amount of memory available at startup as at the end.

NOTE

It's important to understand that neither the 16-bit nor the 32-bit versions of Delphi are meant to produce DOS code. Some clever programmers have been able to coax this kind of code out of Delphi 16 and there might be ways to get console applications to run under a 32-bit DOS DPMI extender, but this is not one of the goals set for the compiler by the developers. There is no definitive answer to the question of whether or not the developers will someday create a version of Turbo Pascal for DOS that supports all, or some major subset, of the Delphi syntax. Certainly it is possible that such a tool will be created, but you should not, by any means, count on it.

I mention all this in part because it is hard to tell whether a Win32 program is leaking memory. With a real mode program, however, you can use the MemAvail command to get an exact reading of program memory usage. Sometimes it's worthwhile taking a piece of code like a linked list back into real-mode DOS, and testing it to see that it is absolutely clean. Of course, there are tools that test this kind of thing in Windows 95 and Windows NT, but a quick real-mode compile can be one way to check your work. A real-mode compile can be particularly appealing if you are operating on a limited budget, or if your company is a bit slow approving funding requests!

A Second Linked List Example

The LINKLST1 program introduces you to linked lists and to the mechanisms that drive them. It is, however, such a stripped-down and simple example that you might not be able to see quite how useful linked lists can be. As a result, I have created a second linked list program, called LINKLST2, which has three new features:

- It is integrated into the Delphi VCL environment.
- It enables you to manually enter new records.
- It enables you to delete records.

The LINKLST2 program is also unusual in that it is broken into three parts. The main form for the program, shown in Figure 5.1, enables you to iterate through the records in the linked list, to search for them by name, and to delete them. The second form in the program, shown in Figure 5.2, is used when you want to add a new entry to the linked list. The third unit has no form attached to it and is used only to declare variables common to both units, as well as one short routine that creates some dummy records to be displayed in the linked list.

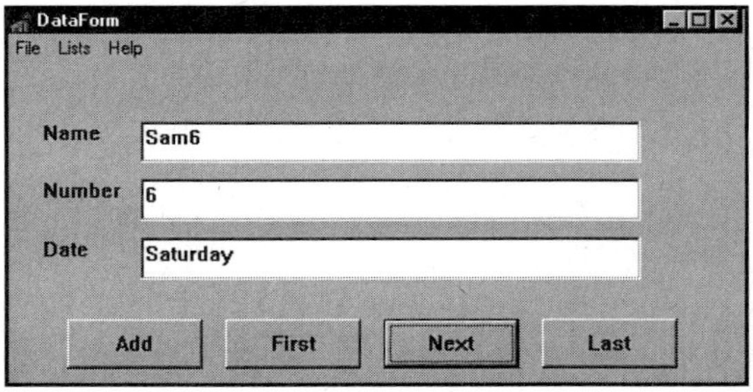

FIGURE 5.1.

The main form for the LINKLST2 program enables you to browse the list and delete records.

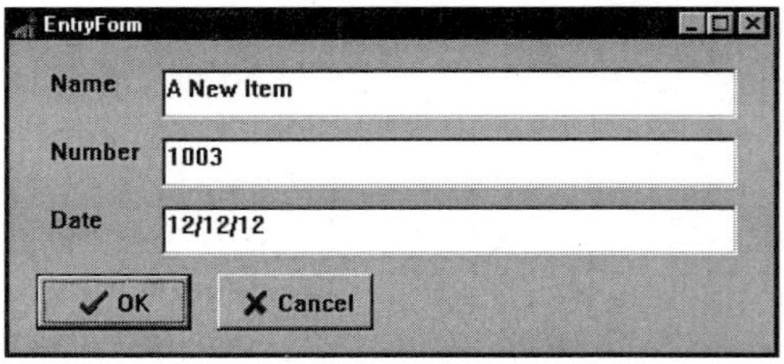

FIGURE 5.2.

The second form in the LINKLST2 program is used for entering new data into the list.

With the capability to add, delete, browse, and search for records, the LINKLST2 program gives you most of the functionality you want in a simple linked list. The one thing that is missing is the capability to move both backward and forward through the list. This capability is granted by a data structure called a *double-linked list.* An example of a double-linked list is available on the CD in the file DBLIST.PAS. DBLIST is stored in the UNITS subdirectory on the CD.

Listing 5.2. The LINKLST2 program gives you access to adding, deleting, and searching for records.

```
unit Main;

{ Program copyright (c) 1995 by Charles Calvert }
{ Project Name: LINKLST2 }

{ This a simple linked list program. It supports Adding,
  Deleting and Searching.

  The first time you run this program you should
  choose Create New List from the File menu. Thereafter
  you should always choose Read Data after starting the
  program. }

interface

uses
  WinTypes, WinProcs, Classes,
  Graphics, Forms, Controls,
  Menus, StdCtrls, SysUtils,
  Entry;

const
  FileName = 'LinkExp.dta';

type
  TDataForm = class(TForm)
    MainMenu1: TMainMenu;
    File1: TMenuItem;
    CreateList1: TMenuItem;
    Save1: TMenuItem;
    Lists1: TMenuItem;
    Add1: TMenuItem;
    Delete1: TMenuItem;
    ReadData1: TMenuItem;
    N1: TMenuItem;
    Exit1: TMenuItem;
    N2: TMenuItem;
    Edit1: TEdit;
    Edit2: TEdit;
    Edit3: TEdit;
    Label1: TLabel;
    Label2: TLabel;
    Label3: TLabel;
    First: TButton;
    Next: TButton;
    Count1: TMenuItem;
    bAdd: TButton;
    Last: TButton;
    Find1: TMenuItem;
    Help1: TMenuItem;
    procedure CreateList1Click(Sender: TObject);
    procedure ReadData1Click(Sender: TObject);
    procedure FirstClick(Sender: TObject);
```

continues

Listing 5.2. continued

```pascal
    procedure NextClick(Sender: TObject);
    procedure Save1Click(Sender: TObject);
    procedure Count1Click(Sender: TObject);
    procedure bAddClick(Sender: TObject);
    procedure LastClick(Sender: TObject);
    procedure Find1Click(Sender: TObject);
    procedure Delete1Click(Sender: TObject);
    procedure Help(Sender: TObject);
    procedure Exit1Click(Sender: TObject);
  private
    FirstNode,
    Current: PMyNode;
    procedure CreateNewBinaryFile;
    procedure ShowRecord;
    procedure NewNode(var Item: PMyNode);
    function ReadBinaryFile(var First, Current: PMyNode): Boolean;
    function ReadTextFile(var FirstNode, Current: PMyNode): Boolean;
    procedure Working;
    procedure GoLast;
    function Find(S: String): PMyNode;
    procedure DeleteNode(var Node: PMyNode);
    procedure FreeAll(var FirstNode: PMyNode);
    function ErrorCondition: Boolean;
  public
    { Public declarations }
  end;

var
  DataForm: TDataForm;

implementation

uses
  Dialogs;

{$R *.DFM}


procedure CreateTextFile;
const
  Max = 100;

  Days: array[0..6] of String = ('Sunday', 'Monday', 'Tuesday',
                                 'Wednesday','Thursday',
                                 'Friday', 'Saturday');
var
  F: Text;
  i: Integer;

begin
  Assign(F, 'data.txt');
  ReWrite(F);
  for i := 1 to Max do begin
    WriteLn(F, 'Sam' + IntToStr(i));
    WriteLn(F, i);
    WriteLn(F, Days[i Mod 7]);
  end;
```

```
  Close(F);
end;

procedure TDataForm.CreateNewBinaryFile;
var
  F: File of TMyNode;
  Head: PMyNode;
begin
  Head := FirstNode;
  System.Assign(F, FileName);
  ReWrite(F);
  while Head^.Next <> nil do begin
    Write(F, Head^);
    Head := Head^.Next;
  end;
  Write(F, Head^);
  System.Close(F);
end;

procedure TDataForm.FreeAll(var FirstNode: PMyNode);
var
  Temp: PMyNode;
begin
  if FirstNode = nil then Exit;
  while FirstNode^.Next <> nil do begin
    Temp := FirstNode^.Next;
    Dispose(FirstNode);
    FirstNode := Temp;
  end;
  Dispose(FirstNode);
end;

procedure TDataForm.NewNode(var Item: PMyNode);
begin
  New(Item);
  Item^.Next := nil;
  Item^.Name := '';
  Item^.Flight := 0;
  Item^.Day := '';
end;

function TDataForm.ReadBinaryFile(var First, Current: PMyNode): Boolean;
var
  F: File of TMyNode;
  Prev: PMyNode;
begin
  ReadBinaryFile := False;
  System.Assign(F, FileName);
  try
    Reset(F);
  except
    on E:EInOutError do Exit; // Don't report error
  end;
  NewNode(Current);
  Read(F, Current^);
  FirstNode := Current;
```

continues

Listing 5.2. continued

```pascal
  while not Eof(F) do begin
    Prev := Current;
    NewNode(Current);
    Read(F, Current^);
    Prev^.Next := Current;
  end;
  System.Close(F);
  ReadBinaryFile := True;
end;

{ Read a Text File }
function TDataForm.ReadTextFile(var FirstNode, Current: PMyNode): Boolean;
var
  F: System.Text;
  Prev: PMyNode;
  i: Integer;
begin
  Result := False;
  System.Assign (F, 'data.txt');
  try
    Reset(F);
  except
    on E:EInOutError do begin
      ShowMessage(E.Message + ': Data.Txt. Use Create New List.');
      Exit;
    end;
  end;
  NewNode(Current);
  ReadLn(F, Current^.Name);
  ReadLn(F, Current^.Flight);
  ReadLn(F, Current^.Day);
  FirstNode := Current;
  i := 0;
  while not Eof(F) do begin
    Prev := Current;
    NewNode(Current);
    ReadLn(F, Current^.Name);
    ReadLn(F, Current^.Flight);
    ReadLn(F, Current^.Day);
    Prev^.Next := Current;
    Inc(i);
  end;
  System.Close(F);
  CreateNewBinaryFile;
  Result := True;
end;

procedure TDataForm.ShowRecord;
begin
  Edit1.Text := Current^.Name;
  Edit2.Text := IntToStr(Current^.Flight);
  Edit3.Text := Current^.Day;
end;

procedure TDataForm.CreateList1Click(Sender: TObject);
begin
  Working;
```

```
    FreeAll(FirstNode);
    CreateTextFile;
    ReadTextFile(FirstNode, Current);
    Current := FirstNode;
    ShowRecord;
end;

procedure TDataForm.Working;
begin
    Edit1.Text := 'Please wait';
    Edit2.Text := 'Working';
    Edit3.Text := '';
    Application.ProcessMessages;
end;

procedure TDataForm.ReadData1Click(Sender: TObject);
begin
    Working;
    if not ReadBinaryFile(FirstNode, Current) then
        if not ReadTextFile(FirstNode, Current) then Exit;
    Current := FirstNode;
    ShowRecord;
end;

procedure TDataForm.FirstClick(Sender: TObject);
begin
    if ErrorCondition then Exit;
    Current := FirstNode;
    ShowRecord;
end;

procedure TDataForm.NextClick(Sender: TObject);
begin
    if ErrorCondition then Exit;
    if Current^.Next <> nil then
        Current := Current^.Next;
    ShowRecord;
end;

procedure TDataForm.Save1Click(Sender: TObject);
begin
    if ErrorCondition then Exit;
    CreateNewBinaryFile;
end;

procedure TDataForm.Count1Click(Sender: TObject);
var
    i: Integer;
    Head: PMyNode;
begin
    i := 1;
    Head := FirstNode;
    while Head^.Next <> nil do begin
        Head := Head^.Next;
        Inc(i);
    end;
    MessageDlg('Total = ' + IntToStr(i), mtInformation, [mbOk], 0);
```

continues

Listing 5.2. continued

```
end;

procedure TDataForm.GoLast;
begin
  while Current^.Next <> nil do
    Current := Current^.Next;
end;

function TDataForm.ErrorCondition: Boolean;
begin
  Result := True;
  if FirstNode = nil then begin
    ShowMessage('Create or read list first');
    Exit;
  end;
  Result := False;
end;

procedure TDataForm.bAddClick(Sender: TObject);
var
  Temp: PMyNode;
begin
  if ErrorCondition then Exit;
  NewNode(Temp);
  if EntryForm.Add(Temp) then begin
    GoLast;
    Current^.Next := Temp;
    Current := Temp;
  end;
  ShowRecord;
end;

procedure TDataForm.LastClick(Sender: TObject);
begin
  if ErrorCondition then Exit;
  GoLast;
  ShowRecord;
end;

function TDataForm.Find(S: String): PMyNode;
var
  Head,
  Temp: PMyNode;
begin
  Head := FirstNode;
  Temp := nil;
  while Head^.Next <> nil do begin
    if Head^.Name = S then begin
      Temp := Head;
      break;
    end;
    Head := Head^.Next;
  end;
  if Head^.Name = S then Temp := Head;
  Find := Temp;
end;

procedure TDataForm.Find1Click(Sender: TObject);
```

```
var
  S: String;
begin
  S := '';
  InputQuery('Search', 'Search for: ', S);
  Current := Find(S);
  ShowRecord;
end;

procedure TDataForm.DeleteNode(var Node: PMyNode);
var
  Temp: PMyNode;
begin
  Temp := FirstNode;
  if Temp = Node then begin          { First Node? }
    Temp := Temp^.Next;
    FirstNode := Temp;
  end else
    while Temp^.Next <> Node do
      Temp := Temp^.Next;
  Current := Temp;
  if Temp^.Next^.Next <> nil then    { A Middle Node? }
    Temp^.Next := Temp^.Next^.Next
  else
    Temp^.Next := nil;               { Last Node? }
  Dispose(Node);
end;

procedure TDataForm.Delete1Click(Sender: TObject);
var
  S: String;
  Temp: PMyNode;
begin
  if ErrorCondition then Exit;
  if MessageBox(Handle, 'Delete node?', 'Question', mb_YesNo) = idNo then Exit;
  S := Edit1.Text;
  Temp := Find(S);
  if Temp <> nil then
    DeleteNode(Temp);
  ShowRecord;
end;

procedure TDataForm.Help(Sender: TObject);
var
  S: string;
begin
  S := 'The first time you run the program ' +
       'choose Create New List from the File menu. ' +
       'Thereafter, you must always choose ' +
       'Read Data from the File menu when you start the program. ';
  ShowMessage(S);
end;

procedure TDataForm.Exit1Click(Sender: TObject);
begin
  FreeAll(FirstNode);
  Close;
end;

end.
```

Listing 5.3. The Entry module allows you to add records to the LNKLIST2 program.

```
unit Entry;

{ Program copyright (c) 1995 by Charles Calvert }
{ Project Name: LINKLST2 }

interface

uses
  WinTypes, WinProcs, Classes,
  Graphics, Forms, Controls,
  StdCtrls, Buttons, MakeData,
  SysUtils;

type
  TEntryForm = class(TForm)
    Edit1: TEdit;
    Edit2: TEdit;
    Edit3: TEdit;
    Label1: TLabel;
    Label2: TLabel;
    Label3: TLabel;
    BitBtn1: TBitBtn;
    BitBtn2: TBitBtn;
  private
    { Private declarations }
  public
    function Add(var Current: PMyNode): Boolean;
  end;

var
  EntryForm: TEntryForm;

implementation

{$R *.DFM}

function TEntryForm.Add(var Current: PMyNode): Boolean;
begin
  if ShowModal = mrOk then begin
    Current^.Name := Edit1.Text;
    Current^.Flight := StrToInt(Edit2.Text);
    Current^.Day := Edit3.Text;
    Result := True
  end else
    Result := False;
end;

end.
```

The LINKLST2 program reads and writes data from both a binary and a text file. The binary file is the main storage for the program. The text file exists as an option for you to manually enter data into a text file when you are starting the program. You can then automatically read the text file into the program's linked list. In other words, the text file is just part of a utility, and the binary file is the main data storage. The ReadData method will call the text file routines only if there is no binary file for it to read.

The LnkLst2 program can automatically create its own text file. The only reason I'm leaving open the possibility of needing to read in a text file is because it is a common operation that occasionally confuses some programmers. I therefore include an example of it here, on the grounds that it might be helpful to some people. However, there is no reason why this program could not have automatically generated a binary file, and skipped the text file altogether. In short, the text file is there only as an added service, and you shouldn't think of it as a necessary part of this type of program.

The File menu item in the LINKLST2 program has the following entries:

```
Read Data
Create New List
Save
Exit
```

The capability to create a new list is granted to the CreateData function in the MakeData unit:

```
procedure CreateData;
var
  F: Text;
  i: Integer;

begin
  Assign(F, 'data.txt');
  ReWrite(F);
  for i := 1 to Max do begin
    WriteLn(F, 'Sam' + Int2Str(i));
    WriteLn(F, i);
    WriteLn(F, Days[i Mod 7]);
  end;
  Close(F);
end;
```

This function creates a simple text file that looks like this:

```
Sam1
1
Monday
Sam2
2
Tuesday
Sam3
...
```

The file goes through as many iterations as you specify in the Integer constant called Max. The first time you run the program, you need to call this function.

The following rather plodding function reads the text file into a linked list:

```
function TDataForm.ReadTextFile(var FirstNode, Current: PMyNode): Boolean;
var
  F: System.Text;
  Prev: PMyNode;
  i: Integer;
begin
  Result := False;
  System.Assign (F, 'data.txt');
  try
    Reset(F);
  except
    on E:EInOutError do begin
      ShowMessage(E.Message + ': Data.Txt. Use Create New List.');
      Exit;
    end;
  end;
  NewNode(Current);
  ReadLn(F, Current^.Name);
  ReadLn(F, Current^.Flight);
  ReadLn(F, Current^.Day);
  FirstNode := Current;
  i := 0;
  while not Eof(F) do begin
    Prev := Current;
    NewNode(Current);
    ReadLn(F, Current^.Name);
    ReadLn(F, Current^.Flight);
    ReadLn(F, Current^.Day);
    Prev^.Next := Current;
    Inc(i);
  end;
  System.Close(F);
  CreateNewBinaryFile;
  Result := True;
end;
```

You should call one of the preceding functions via the menu each time you load the program—except the very first time, when it should be the second function you call, after the CreateData routine. After having read this list the first time from a text file, LINKLST2 stores its data in a binary file of the type first seen at the end of Chapter 13, "The Windows API and DLLs." The CreateNewFile procedure is used to actually write the binary data to disk:

```
procedure TDataForm.CreateNewFile;
var
  F: File of TMyNode;
  Head: PMyNode;
begin
  Head := FirstNode;
  Assign(F, FileName);
  ReWrite(F);
  while Head^.Next <> nil do begin
    Write(F, Head^);
    Head := Head^.Next;
  end;
  Write(F, Head^);
  System.Close(F);
end;
```

You can call this function from the Save menu item. This procedure iterates over all the nodes in the linked list and writes each one to disk. The entire file is rewritten from scratch each time the procedure is called. Like all the procedures in the LINKLST2 program, it would not matter if there were 5 or 5,000 records in the list. The procedures would work exactly the same under either condition. The only limit to the size of the list is the amount of available memory on your system.

The LINKLST2 program knows how to count all the nodes in the linked list:

```
procedure TDataForm.Count1Click(Sender: TObject);
var
  i: Integer;
  Head: PMyNode;
begin
  i := 1;
  Head := FirstNode;
  while Head^.Next <> nil do begin
    Head := Head^.Next;
    Inc(i);
  end;
  MessageDlg('Total = ' + IntToStr(i), mtInformation, [mbOk], 0);
end;
```

The procedure begins by moving to the first node in the list:

```
Head := FirstNode;
```

It then proceeds to iterate over all the nodes

```
while Head^.Next <> nil do begin
  Head := Head^.Next;
  Inc(i);
end;
```

while doing nothing more than incrementing the variable i after visiting each node. At the end, i will be equal to the total number of records in the list, and the MessageDlg procedure is then called on to display that number to the user.

The Find procedure searches through all the records in the list until it finds one that has a Name field equal to a string entered by the user:

```
function TDataForm.Find(S: String): PMyNode;
var
  Head,
  Temp: PMyNode;
begin
  Head := FirstNode;
  Temp := nil;
  while Head^.Next <> nil do begin
    if Head^.Name = S then begin
      Temp := Head;
      Break;
    end;
    Head := Head^.Next;
  end;
```

```
  if Head^.Name = S then Temp := Head;
  Find := Temp;
end;
```

Notice that when the sought-after record is found, the routine exits the `while` loop by calling `Break`. Delphi provides two commonly used ways for getting out of a loop:

- A call to the `Exit` procedure breaks you out of the loop and also out of the current procedure. If the current procedure is the main body of a program, a call to `Exit` ends the entire program.

- A call to `Break` causes the code to exit the current loop but not the entire procedure. For instance, in the preceding example, `Break` exits the `while` loop, but the following two lines are still executed:

```
  if Head^.Name = S then Temp := Head;
  Find := Temp;
```

Notice that the lines that exist outside the loop are necessary for special cases—for instance, when there is only one node.

Perhaps the most important, and most difficult, procedure from the LINKLST2 program is the `DeleteNode` procedure:

```
procedure TDataForm.DeleteNode(var Node: PMyNode);
var
  Temp: PMyNode;
begin
  Temp := FirstNode;

  if Temp = Node then begin          { First Node? }
    Temp := Temp^.Next;
    FirstNode := Temp;
  end else
    while Temp^.Next <> Node do
      Temp := Temp^.Next;

  Current := Temp;

  if Temp^.Next^.Next <> nil then    { A Middle Node? }
    Temp^.Next := Temp^.Next^.Next
  else
    Temp^.Next := nil;               { Last Node? }
  Dispose(Node);
end;
```

There are three different sections in this routine. The first section checks to see if the node to be deleted is the first node in the list. If so, the code iterates down to the second node of the list, sets `FirstNode` equal to it, and then deletes the node that was at the head of the list.

The second section in the `DeleteNode` procedure checks to see if the node to be deleted is somewhere in the middle of the list. If it is, the `Next` field in the node before the one to be deleted is set equal to the node after the one to be deleted. The node between these two locations is disposed of.

The third section of the `DeleteNode` method checks to see if the last node in the list is the one that needs to be deleted. If it is, the `Next` field in the next to last node is set to nil, and the final node is disposed of.

The logic in the `DeleteNode` procedure is interesting primarily because it shows how you can use `if` statements to track down special cases. If the first or last nodes in the list need to be deleted, each one needs to be handled as a special case; otherwise, a default method is used for deleting any of the nodes in the middle of the list.

I have also included a third program, called LINKLST3, that shows the LINKLST2 transformed into a console application. This third example is provided as an afterthought, and I do not mention it again, other than to say that it is available on disk. After you start the program, choose Create New List from the menu before trying to iterate through any of the records.

Examining Pointers in the Debugger

This is one of the sections of this book that will probably glaze the eyes of beginners, and of those who don't want to dig deeply into the Object Pascal language. If that happens to you, don't worry about it. Even after my first two years of steady programming, I'm not sure I could have made much sense of this material. Certainly it took a good five years of hard work before I felt ready to write about material like this with any confidence. In other words, this subject is by definition of interest primarily to advanced programmers who are serious about Delphi. If you are an intermediate programmer who wants to make the jump to the advanced level, this is one of the areas where you will want to concentrate. I should perhaps add, however, that understanding this material does not make you, ipso facto, a great programmer. That is a gift that can be given only by God (or, if you prefer, by Fate). However, if you do master this stuff, nobody is going to call you a neophyte. That part of your career is well behind you once you are comfortable with this discussion of pointers.

Consider the program shown in Listing 5.4.

Listing 5.4. The POINTER5 program explores the strange world of pointers and the Intel addressing scheme.

```
program Pointer5;

var
  A: Pointer;
  B: PChar;
begin
  A := Ptr(HInstance);    { A "fake" pointer to nothing,    }
  B := Ptr($000045FF);    { There is no memory allocation! }
  A := nil;               { Set pointer to nil              }
  B := nil;               { Set pointer to nil              }
  New(A);                 { Pointer will STILL equals nil! }
  Dispose(A);             { Does nothing                    }
```

continues

Listing 5.4. continued

```
GetMem(A, 100);          { Allocate a hundred bytes          }
GetMem(B, 100);          { Allocate a hundred bytes          }
StrCopy(B, 'Test data');{ Use the allocation                }
FreeMem(A, 100);         { Deallocate 100 bytes              }
A := nil;                { Set pointer to nil                }
FreeMem(B, 100);         { Deallocate 100 bytes              }
asm                      { Set pointer to nil (B := nil;)    }
  mov longint ptr B, 0;  { Zero out pointer                  }
end;                     { Close ASM block                   }
end.                     { Close program                     }
```

You can see that POINTER5 contains an unusually large number of comments. I have done this because I want to give you something concrete to hang on to while I discuss some pretty abstract concepts. There is, however, a second version (POINTER5A) of the program available on disk that does not have any comments. If you find the comments confusing, switch to the other version.

A quick look at this program reveals that it doesn't do anything useful. In fact, it does strange things such as create pointers that don't point at valid data. When it finally does allocate some memory, it never uses it in any conventional sense but quickly proceeds to dispose of it.

I wrote this program primarily to give you a chance to watch pointers in the stand-alone debugger. You will probably be able to follow the first part of this discussion if all you have is the integrated debugger, but the real meat of the discussion requires the stand-alone tool.

NOTE

When you compile for the stand-alone debugger, you must make sure that the "Include TDW Debug Info" switch is turned on. To set this switch, choose the Project | Options menu selection and turn to the Linker page. The switch is near the bottom of the window, and it is turned on when there is an X in front of it. Make sure also that the Debug Information and Compiler Symbols options are turned on in the Compile page. You must also be sure that Optimizations is turned off! The Optimizations option is also found on the Project | Options | Compiler page.

For safety's sake, it is probably a good idea to choose Build from the Run menu now. The debug symbols won't be embedded into the executable unless the program is rebuilt. Once the settings are correctly identified, and the entire project has been rebuilt, the next step is to pop up the stand-alone debugger by choosing the Tools | Turbo Debugger menu option, or else by starting the debugger from the command line and passing it the POINTER5.EXE program as a parameter.

Turbo Debugger may not ship with your version of Delphi 2.0. You can, however, purchase it from Borland as a stand-alone product. It usually comes bundled with

TASM, which is Borland's assembler. If you have Borland C++ 4.5 or later, you may already have a copy of a Delphi-compatible, stand-alone debugger, which is called TDW.EXE. The only way to know for sure whether your version of TDW or TD32 works with Delphi is to try it. Remember that it won't work properly unless you compile with debug symbol info. You must pass the executable you want to run as a parameter to TD32.EXE, or else you must load your program from the File menu.

The first time you step through the program, you should set the following watches in the Watch Window of either the integrated or the stand-alone debugger. Use the stand-alone debugger if possible, because it is designed from the bottom up for this kind of analysis of a program or code fragment.

```
A
B
@A
@B
A^
B^
```

The @ symbol tells the debugger to return the address of a variable. You can use the @ symbol inside the code of your own programs if you want to reference, not the contents of a variable, but its address.

After pressing F8 for the first time, the Watch Window at the bottom of the screen should look something like this:

```
B^              #158 : CHAR
A^              @:00000000 : UNTYPED
@B              :00406528 [Pointer5.B] : POINTER
@A              :00406524 [Pointer5.A] : POINTER
B               :00000000 : PCHAR
A               :00000000 : POINTER
```

Of course the actual addresses for the first, third and fourth entries you see in the Watch Window might not be identical to those you see here, but the general layout should be similar. (However, in Win32 it is at least probable that the numbers you see will be identical to the ones I see, particularly if we happened to be using the same shipping version of the compiler, which in this case is unlikely. The issue here is that programs are loaded at a prespecified virtual address, and the data is stored at offsets from that virtual address.)

NOTE

Some curious readers may wonder how I copied the information from the Watch Window in the debugger. Actually, it isn't difficult—you just need to know your way around. One way is to show the debugger as a child window on the desktop, and then choose Edit from the System menu. A second method involves the Log Window, which can be accessed from the View menu in the stand-alone debugger. Simply follow these steps:

1. After opening the Log Window, click it once with the right mouse button.
2. Choose "Open Log File" and click the OK button to accept the default name given to you by the debugger.
3. Select the window whose contents you want to save.
4. Pull down the Edit menu and choose "Dump Pane to Log."
5. Click the right mouse button again on the Log window and close the file.

When you return to DOS, you will find a file saved under the default name containing the contents of the window that was focused when you chose "Dump Pane to Log."

You probably won't have to do this kind of thing very often, but when the time finally comes around, the need is usually fairly urgent.

Two of the addresses in the Watch Window are important to use during this initial stage of the program analysis:

```
@B                        :00406528 [Pointer5.B] : POINTER
@A                        :00406524 [Pointer5.A] : POINTER
```

Notice that there is no segment and offset format for the display of these pointers. Instead, you have a single flat model address: $00406524. This is just a simple hexadecimal value which, when translated into base ten, is revealed to be slightly larger than 4 megabytes: 4,220,196.

The pointer here is that there is no longer any data segment in your program. Win32 has a non-segmented architecture. Your executable is loaded into memory at a particular place, usually 4 MB, and its data will usually appear at some virtual address slightly higher than that. You can specify the exact virtual address at which your program will be loaded by selecting the Project | Options | Linker page, and checking the Image Base entry.

In this particular case, variable A is stored $00406524. Four bytes further on you can find B, which resides at $00406528. Once again, this should not surprise anyone, because the variables were declared right next to each other in the code, and they are each four bytes in size. In other words, B is found 4 bytes further into the program's image than A because the intervening space is taken up by pointer A, which is four bytes in size.

NOTE

Two quick points might be helpful for some readers. First, if you ever forget how large a variable is, you can run the SizeOf function on it. Generally you don't have to recompile your code but can simply type SizeOf(A) in the Watch Window, and the debugger will tell you the size of the object, which in this case is 4.

Second, don't forget that Windows ships with a calculator that can help you translate hex numbers into decimal numbers. The calculator is kept in the Accessories group, and you can start it the way you would any other Windows program. Once it's running, choose the View | Scientific menu item. Type 170 into the calculator and click the button labeled Hex to see its hex value, which is AA. Conversely, you can first click the Hex button, then type AE, and the calculator will translate the number into its decimal value if you click the Dec button.

Once again, you don't need to know any of these things to program in Delphi. However, if you want to get really serious about programming, you ought to know this material, or at least aspire to know it one day.

The key point that has been established so far is that the pointers A and B both reside in the main executable image for the program. When you load a program, it is sucked into memory by the operating system via a mechanism called a memory-mapped file. In effect, the entire executable is mapped into a series of virtual addresses which I am referring to as the executable's image.

In the simplest case scenario, the program is literally read into one area of memory in one fell swoop, without any concern for creating the segmented areas that were common in 16-bit Windows. Of course, in some cases portions of an executable may reside on disk even after they have been mapped into virtual memory. The point of memory mapped files is that you can treat data on disk as if it were residing in RAM. That is, the file on disk has been mapped into virtual addresses, and can be accessed the same way you would access any area in memory, and with the same commands. That is, you can call functions like StrCat or Move on files that reside on disk. It is of no concern to you whether this memory is actually in RAM or actually swapped to disk. The operating system lets you treat the memory exactly the same, regardless of its real location.

There is a big difference between the address at which A and B reside and the items they point at. In fact, at this time, A and B aren't pointing at anything. Their value is currently nil.

NOTE

Delphi initializes all global variables to nil, or 0, on start up. If you are following along on a DOS version of Pascal which doesn't do this, you should add two lines of code to the program, which will initialize these values to nil.

Here comes the important part. A and B point at nil. That much is clear. But what exactly does this mean? What specifically does it mean to say that a pointer is equal to nil? To find out, you need to open the Dump Pane from the Watch Window. Click it once with the right mouse button and select the option that says Goto. (See Figure 5.3.) A dialog box will appear and you can type the letter A into it and press Enter. This takes you to a pictorial representation of the place in the executable image where A actually resides:

```
:00406524 00 00 00 00 00 00 00 00
:0040652C 00 00 00 00 00 00 00 00
:00406534 00 00 00 00 00 00 00 00
:0040653C 00 00 00 00 00 00 00 00
```

As you can see, the four bytes shown immediately after $00406524 are all zeros. This is what it means to say that A is equal to nil. Just so you're sure to understand what I mean, let me show you the line again, with the relevant four bytes in brackets:

```
$00406524 [00 00 00 00] 00 00 00 00
```

The last four bytes in the preceding line also happen to be set to zero, which once again should not come as a surprise, because they belong to B. As you saw earlier, B is also set to nil, so of course the four bytes in its portion of the data segment are set to zero.

FIGURE 5.3.

Searching for an address in the Dump Pane.

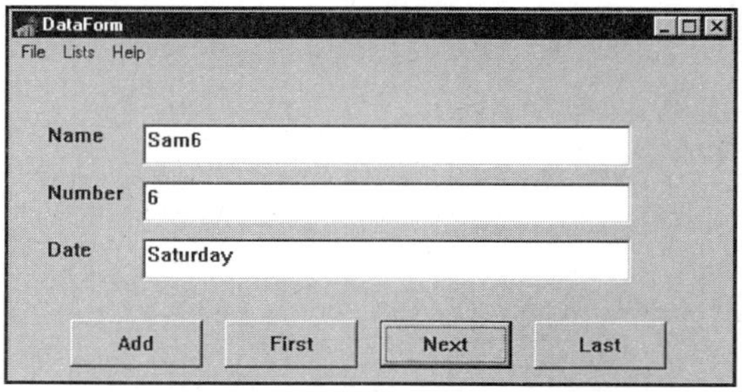

To verify the value of B, you can click once on the right mouse button, select Goto, and enter B. The Dump Pane you see will look something like this:

```
:00406528 00 00 00 00 00 00 00 00
:00406530 00 00 00 00 00 00 00 00
:00406538 00 00 00 00 00 00 00 00
:00406540 00 00 00 00 00 00 00 00
```

Once again, it is the first 4 bytes after $00406528 that are important. As you can see, they are set to zero, and that means that B has the value of nil.

After spending all this time getting set up, and after carefully examining the initial state of the program, it is at last time to step through the first real lines in the program:

```
A := Ptr(HInstance);    { A "fake" pointer to nothing,   }
B := Ptr($000045FF);    { There is no memory allocation! }
```

The Ptr function creates a pointer that addresses a particular place in memory. Specifically, the preceding code sets the first two bytes at the address $00406524 to the address of the place in memory where the program is loaded:

```
:00406524 00 00 40 00 FF 45 00 00    @ _E
:0040652C 00 00 00 00 00 00 00 00
:00406534 00 00 00 00 00 00 00 00
:0040653C 00 00 00 00 00 00 00 00
```

Here is the significant line again, with the relevant address offset in brackets:

```
:00406524 [00 00 40 00] FF 45 00 00    @ _E
```

HInstance is always set to the place in memory where your program is loaded. This is specified in the Project | Options | Linker page from the menu, and should normally be set to $00400000.

The most obvious facts about the preceding line are that the numbers in the address are reversed. Specifically, the high byte is where you would expect the low byte to be, and vice versa. If this strikes you as peculiar, you are a considerably calmer and more controlled person than myself. Even after years of working with the Intel architecture, I am still completely floored by the fact that such a topsy-turvy memory scheme managed to win out over more logical alternatives. The simple moral of this story is that it is not reason, but the free market, that dictates the major decisions made in the computer industry. All in all, the free market is probably a respectably admirable arbiter in matters like this, yet it does yield some surprising results at times. (Given the flap over the floating point Pentium errors, I should perhaps add that I think Intel is a fine company, although I don't understand why they had to leave us with such a topsy-turvy method for storing addresses in memory.)

> **NOTE**
>
> Connoisseurs of the DOS EXE format should use the Dump Pane to Goto the actual address in memory pointed to by both HInstance and A:
>
> ```
> 00400000 4D 5A 70 00 05 00 00 00 MZp .
> 00400008 20 00 00 00 FF FF 47 00     __G
> 00400010 00 02 00 00 5C 02 00 00 . \ .
> 00400018 40 00 00 00 01 00 FB 50 @ . _P
> ```
>
> Notice the familiar MZ signature! Memory-mapped files just suck the executable into virtual memory!

At any rate, the second line of code shown previously looks like this:

```
B := Ptr($000045FF);    { There is no memory allocation! }
```

After it is run, the place in the data segment where B resides looks like this:

```
00406528 FF 45 00 00 00 00 00 00 _E
00406530 00 00 00 00 00 00 00 00
00406538 00 00 00 00 00 00 00 00
00406540 00 00 00 00 00 00 00 00
```

Once again, here are the relevant portions marked with parentheses around the segment and brackets around the offset:

```
00406528 [FF 45 00 00] 00 00 00 00 _E
```

As you can see, the address is obviously set to $45FF, with the bytes reversed, as dictated by the whims of the good folks at Intel.

To sum up what has been said here, you can look down at the Watch Window, which now shows A and B equal to the following:

```
B                        :000045FF : PCHAR
A                        :00400000 : POINTER
```

This representation of the address is much more readable than what is seen in the Dump Pane. However, the view in the Dump Pane is perhaps more important, because it shows exactly what is happening in the memory that belongs to the program. Specifically, it shows that the values that had been set to nil are now pointing at particular addresses.

> **NOTE**
>
> The List Pane used to examine the validity of pointers will probably not be included in the shipping version of Delphi. As a result, I have cut that section of this chapter. However, it might be of use to some readers, so I placed it in the POINTER5 directory on disk, in a text file, and in a Word 7.0 (WordPad) file.

More on *nil* Pointers

The next couple lines of code in the program set A and B back to nil:

```
A := nil;            { Set pointer to nil            }
B := nil;            { Set pointer to nil            }
```

When you step through these lines, you should set up the Dump Pane so that it gives you a view of the place in the data segment where A and B reside. If you do this, you will see them both being set back to zero.

> **NOTE**
>
> Under normal circumstances you should never set the value of a valid pointer to nil without first deallocating the memory associated with it. However, this time it is okay to do this with variable A, because it was simply set equal to memory that had already been allocated by the system. In other words, A was not the owner of the memory it addressed, it was simply borrowing it for a time. As a result, there is no need to deallocate the memory that A addresses, and there is no harm in setting its value back to zero.

Review of Key Points Covered So Far

There is still considerably more to be said about the POINTER5 program, but it might be worthwhile to take a moment to consider what has been said so far:

- The pointers A and B are global data that reside in the executable image for the POINTER5 program.

- The addresses of pointers A and B do not necessarily have anything to do with the value at which they point. One way to find out about the values A and B point at is to bring up the Dump Pane and go to the appropriate address, as shown above when you go to address $00400000.

- When A and B are set to nil, the four bytes at $ 00406524 and $00406528 are set to zero. You can use the Ptr function to put an actual address in these bytes, and you can use the Dump Pane to watch these addresses change during the assignment.

- Merely placing an address in the bytes at $00406524 and $00406528 does not necessarily mean that these pointers are going to address valid data. For instance, you can use the Selector List Pane to examine the selector (or the entire address) of pointer B. Performing this exercise reveals that B almost certainly references completely invalid data.

- Finally, you learned that it is possible to use the Ptr function to create a pointer that addresses valid data. However, you must be very careful when you attempt to do something like this, and you must remember that the memory you are addressing probably does not belong to your pointer but to some other object in the system.

Before continuing on, let me remind you that this material is not for everybody. Peering deep into the bowels of the Intel architecture is not necessarily what programming is all about. However, if you can master this material you will find that it can save you hours or even days of work when you stumble across certain kinds of bugs that are usually related to pointers. Furthermore, pointers are the keys to the kingdom of programming. Master them, and everything else about computer programming lies open before you, yours for the taking.

Another Type of Invalid Pointer

Someone new to pointers might write code that looks like this:

```
var
  A: Pointer;
begin
  New(A);
  ...
```

This seems like a reasonable thing to do, because you know that the New function allocates memory for pointer values, and A is indubitably declared as a pointer.

The problem with this code is that the New function simply allocates enough memory to cover the area addressed by a particular pointer. Because an ordinary pointer variable by default does not address any memory, a call to New in this case will not result in a change to the status of A. That is, it will still equal nil. If you want to allocate memory for a variable of type Pointer, you need to call the GetMem function. Use new on pointers that point to data structures, such as a pointer to a ShortString, a pointer to an array, or a pointer to a record.

Before looking at the GetMem function, pop up the CPU window again and step through the assembler code that gets executed as a result of a New(A) statement:

```
Pointer5.17:  New(A); { Pointer will STILL equals nil! }
:00404EF2 33C0          xor    eax,eax
:00404EF4 E85FD3FFFF    call   @GetMem
:00404EF9 A324654000    mov    [Pointer5.A],eax
```

As you can see, the compiler generates code that zeros out EAX:

```
xor eax, eax
```

and then calls a function that allocates memory from the operating system. When this call returns, EAX holds the address of some allocated memory. However, the value in EAX is still zero, so A is still set to nil.

Compare the preceding example with the following code:

```
Pointer5.19:  GetMem(A, 100); { Allocate a hundred bytes }
:00404F0A B864000000    mov    eax,00000064
:00404F0F E844D3FFFF    call   @GetMem
:00404F14 A324654000    mov    [Pointer5.A],eax
```

If you remember that decimal 100 and hex 64 are equivalent, you can see that the following code first loads the value 100 into EAX, then calls the function that allocates memory. When it returns, EAX no longer contains zero, so this time A is not set to nil.

The address that is listed at $00406524 in the program's image now references real memory on the heap that belongs to variable A. To prove this to yourself, put the address shown in the Watch Window next to variable A into the List Pane. You will see that the debugger lists it as belonging to a valid selector that has nothing to do with your program's executable image. (See Figure 5.4.) This address is to be found somewhere out on the heap, but it is now a portion of the heap that temporarily belongs to your program.

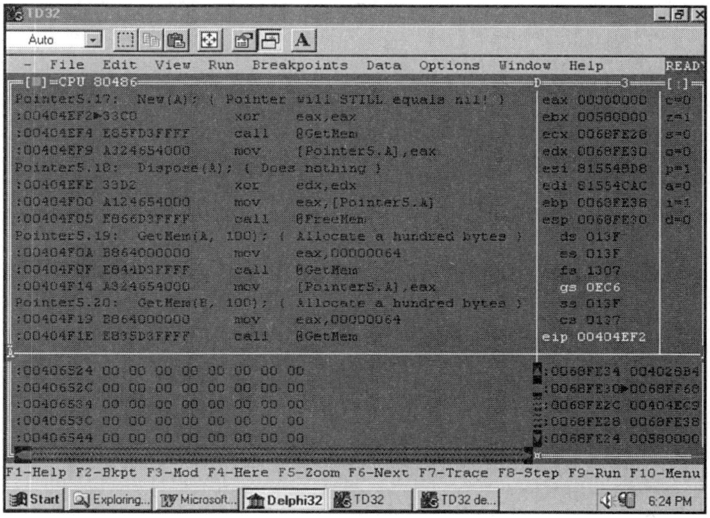

FIGURE 5.4.

Take the address ($XXXX) shown in the Watch Window and enter it in the List Pane to see if you have a valid selector.

One final portion of the POINTER5 program should be mentioned:

```
FreeMem(A, 100);        { Deallocate 100 bytes      }
A := nil;               { Set pointer to nil        }
FreeMem(B, 100);        { Deallocate 100 bytes      }
asm                     { Set pointer to nil (B := nil;) }
mov longint ptr B, 0; { Zero out pointer            }
end;                    { Close ASM block           }
```

The code shown here deallocates the memory associated with A and B. After these pointers are deallocated, you can put them in the List Pane to see that they are no longer considered valid pointers. Furthermore, this shows two different ways of setting a variable to nil. The first method simply makes an assignment:

```
A := nil;               { Set pointer to nil        }
```

The second method uses Delphi's built-in assembler to move zero into the bytes occupied by the variable B:

```
asm                     { Set pointer to nil (B := nil;) }
mov longint ptr B, 0; { Zero out the pointer        }
end;                    { Close ASM block           }
```

This discussion has been fairly involved, but it should help you begin to grasp exactly how pointers are constructed, and how you can use the stand-alone debugger to spy on their inner workings.

One of the main points I'm trying to stress in the second half of this chapter is that the stand-alone debugger is a good tool to use when you need to track down pointer bugs. In the last few sections of the chapter you have seen how valid pointers, nil pointers, and invalid pointers look in the debugger. Use this knowledge to help you track problems if something goes wrong with your program.

Summary

This chapter presented you with several full-length linked lists, and it showed you how you can manipulate these lists and how you can use them to store large amounts of data. In particular, you learned how to iterate through a linked list, how to count the nodes in a list, how to add and delete data from a list, and how to search for a record stored in a linked list. You also got a good look at some code that read a linked list from disk, and which enabled you to modify and then restore the list to its original location on disk.

Most of the time, built-in Delphi objects or tools such as TStringLists, TLists, and Paradox or dBASE tables will provide the simplest possible means for tracking long lists of data. However, linked lists can still be convenient if you need to create a custom list with particular properties, or if you want to write portable code that can be used both in Delphi and at the DOS prompt. The biggest advantage linked lists can bring you, however, is that they have almost no overhead. As a result, if memory usage has become a big problem in your program, you can use linked lists. However, under normal circumstances you will probably use a database table, TStringList, or TList. In particular, serious Delphi programmers should take the time to explore the TList object. On the CD, you will find the OBJECT4 program and the EXPLORER program, both of which use the TList object.

The text of this lengthy chapter also discussed the particulars of the Intel addressing scheme, and it showed you how you can use the debugger to learn about the pointers in your programs.

Exceptions

6

In this chapter, you will learn how to add error-handling to your programs. This is done almost entirely through a mechanism called *exceptions*.

In particular, the following subjects are covered:

- Exception-handling theory
- Basic exception classes
- `try..except` blocks
- `try..finally` blocks
- Raising exceptions
- Creating your own exception classes
- Saving error strings in resources and retrieving them with `LoadString`
- Internationalizing your program with string tables
- Overriding the default exception handler

To a large degree, Delphi and the VCL make it possible for you to write programs that almost entirely ignore the subject of error-checking. The reason for this is that exceptions are built into most classes and standalone routines so that they will be raised automatically whenever something goes wrong. However, professional programmers will want to go beyond even this level of safety and add additional error-checking to their code, or else change the default error handling performed by Delphi. Also, your programs might need to raise their own errors, so you will need to add and raise new exception classes.

The Theory Behind Exceptions

Exceptions enable you to designate specific areas of your code designed to handle the cases wherein something goes wrong. In particular, you can "guard" whole sections of code in such a way that if errors occur inside them, the problem will be handled in a different area by a set of routines designed explicitly for that purpose. This technique covers nested functions, too, so you can begin a guarded block, move in six or seven levels of procedure calls, and then, if something goes wrong, bounce directly back out to a single area in your code designed to handle error conditions.

> **NOTE**
>
> Right at the start, it's important to recognize the difference between Delphi exceptions, which cover language issues, and hardware exceptions, which involve hardware and hardware interrupts. You can (and Delphi often does) wrap a hardware exception inside a Delphi exception, and handle the event that way, but hardware exceptions are different than Delphi exceptions.

For instance, running out of paper in a printer causes a hardware exception. Object Pascal doesn't get an exception in this case, but a component might raise an exception if the situation is detected. Raising the exception does not cause the hardware error; it already exists outside the program.

Traditionally, error-handling has been a matter of setting flags and then responding to a flag that designates an error condition. For instance, if you tried to open a file that does not exist, an IOResult or DosError flag would be set and you could detect the condition by checking the flag. Under the new system, instead of a flag being set, an exception is raised.

The easiest way to start appreciating the advantages that exceptions bring to your code is to imagine a situation in which three different levels of code are called. Suppose, for instance, that you wanted to display data in a grid, where the data in question is stored in a text file. You might have the following set of calls, all nested inside each other:

```
function DisplayDataInGrid: Word;
  function RetrieveData: Word;
    function OpenFile: Word;
    function ReadFile: Word;
    function CloseFile: Word;
```

In this scenario, DisplayDataInGrid calls RetrieveData, and RetrieveData calls OpenFile, ReadFile, and CloseFile. After CloseFile was called, control would return to DisplayDataInGrid, and the actual data would be shown to the user.

If something went wrong during the time the file was being opened, OpenFile would have to pass that information back to RetrieveData. RetrieveData would have to include code ensuring that ReadFile and CloseFile didn't get called; then it would have to pass the error condition back to DisplayDataInGrid. In turn, DisplayDataInGrid would have to ensure that it did not try to display data which was never correctly retrieved. This whole process of passing information in a daisy chain forces you to write complicated, confusing, and error-prone code.

As a child, you might have played a game called "telephone." In particular, you might have had a teacher, camp counselor, or friend who arranged a large group of people in a circle and then whispered something to the person on his or her left. That person in turn whispered the message to someone on his left, and so on, until the message went all the way around the circle. When the message had made the whole trip, it almost always ended up changing radically from the time that it started, until the time when the trip was complete. The same thing can happen in a program if you use the daisy chain method of conveying error conditions. The worst case, of course, is when one link in the chain is broken altogether and the rest of the code continues merrily on its way, oblivious of the fact that something serious has gone wrong.

Exceptions don't use the daisy chain theory of error processing. Instead, if an exception is raised in the function OpenFile, the code automatically unwinds back to DisplayDataInGrid, where you can write code that handles the error. Exceptions automatically pop procedures and data off the stack, and they automatically ensure that no other routines behind or in front of it are called until the code is found that is intended to handle the exception.

> **NOTE**
>
> When code is being popped off the stack, Delphi checks for one particular block of code that needs to be executed, even if an exception has occurred. This special code is enclosed in `try..finally` blocks, as you will see in the next-to last section of this chapter.

If an exception occurs and you do not handle it explicitly, a default exception handler will process the exception. Most exceptions are not handled explicitly. When the VCL default exception handler is invoked, it displays a message dialog describing the exception to the user, and then your program resumes its normal processing of Windows messages. Your program does not return to the code that raised the exception. When an exception is raised, special code in your program (in the system unit) checks the most recently entered `try` block on the call stack for a suitable exception handler. If that `try` block has no exception handlers suitable for the current exception, the next outward `try` block is checked, and so on, until an exception handler is found or it reaches the default exception handler. Normal program execution resumes at the next statement following the code that handles the exception.

There is another default exception handler below the VCL default handler, called the RTL default exception handler. If an exception occurs in code that is not part of VCL's normal event or message handling (or in a Delphi program that doesn't use VCL) and that exception goes unhandled, it will be caught by the RTL default exception handler. The RTL default exception handler displays a rather technical error via a `MessageBox` and then terminates your program.

For some reason, all this always sounds considerably more complex in theory than it is in practice. If what I have said here does not quite make sense to you, just forage on anyway, and I think it will come clear in time. The previous few paragraphs lay out the theory behind a fairly simple set of syntactical routines. Play with the syntax for awhile, using the descriptions below as a guide, and then if you want, come back and read the theory a second time.

Exception Classes

Delphi comes with a rich set of built-in exception classes meant for handling a wide range of exceptions. You can easily create your own exception classes for handling the key events in your program that might be susceptible to error. Here is the base class for exception handling, as it is declared in SYSUTILS.PAS:

```
Exception = class(TObject)
```

```
private
  FMessage: string;
  FHelpContext: Integer;
public
  constructor Create(const Msg: string);
  constructor CreateFmt(const Msg: string; const Args: array of const);
  constructor CreateRes(Ident: Integer);
  constructor CreateResFmt(Ident: Integer; const Args: array of const);
  constructor CreateHelp(const Msg: string; AHelpContext: Integer);
  constructor CreateFmtHelp(const Msg: string; const Args: array of const;
    AHelpContext: Integer);
  constructor CreateResHelp(Ident: Integer; AHelpContext: Integer);
  constructor CreateResFmtHelp(Ident: Integer; const Args: array of const;
    AHelpContext: Integer);
  property HelpContext: Integer read FHelpContext write FHelpContext;
  property Message: string read FMessage write FMessage;
end;
```

The key point to grasp here is that all exceptions have a message that can be displayed to the user. You can pass in this message through a number of different constructors, and you can retrieve it through the Message function.

> **NOTE**
>
> Delphi classes sometimes have multiple constructors because you may have more than one way in which you want to create a class. Sometimes you might want to initialize a class by passing in one type of string, and another time you might want to pass in a second type of string or perhaps an integer. To give you the flexibility you need, Delphi enables you to declare multiple constructors. Needless to say, you still call only one constructor when creating a class; it's just that you have a choice of which constructor you want to choose.

Here are some additional built-in exceptions, all quoted directly from SYSUTILS.PAS:

```
EOutOfMemory = class(Exception)
public
  destructor Destroy; override;
  procedure FreeInstance; override;
end;

EInOutError = class(Exception)
public
  ErrorCode: Integer;
end;

EIntError = class(Exception);
EDivByZero = class(EIntError);
ERangeError = class(EIntError);
EIntOverflow = class(EIntError);

EMathError = class(Exception);
EInvalidOp = class(EMathError);
```

```
EZeroDivide = class(EMathError);
EOverflow = class(EMathError);
EUnderflow = class(EMathError);

EInvalidPointer = class(Exception);

EInvalidCast = class(Exception);

EConvertError = class(Exception);

EAccessViolation = class(Exception);
EPrivilege = class(Exception);
EStackOverflow = class(Exception);
EControlC = class(Exception);

EVariantError = class(Exception);

EPropReadOnly = class(Exception);
EPropWriteOnly = class(Exception);
```

You can see that there are error codes for divide by zero errors, file I/O errors, invalid type casts, and various other conditions both common and obscure.

The preceding list, however, is far from complete. Many other exceptions classes are declared in other modules of the VCL. To get a feeling for their complete scope, you should use the Browser and also the online help. Figure 6.1 shows the Browser as it looks when it is in the thick of the exception hierarchy.

FIGURE 6.1.

The Browser is a good tool to use when you want to see if Delphi has a class for handling a particular type of exception.

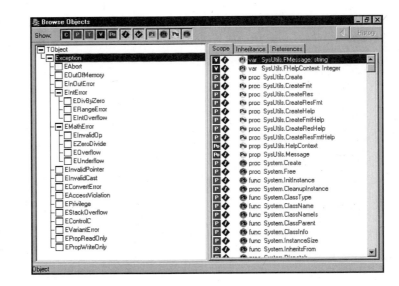

Basic Exception Syntax

When working with the code presented in this chapter, you will be raising a lot of exceptions. If you set Options | Environment | Preferences | Break on Exception to True, exceptions raised by your program will cause the debugger to take you as near as possible to the place in your code where the exception occurred. Only after you start running again will you see the error message as it will be reported to the user. As a result, you should probably keep Break on Exception set to False, except when you explicitly want to step through your code during an exception.

The SIMPEXEP program, referenced in Listing 6.1, gives four examples of how to raise and handle exceptions in Delphi. The first two examples shown are of the simplest possible kind, and are meant to get you started with the concepts involved in this process. The latter two examples in this program are a bit more complex, but are still relatively straightforward.

Remember to turn Optimizations off when running this program. You can find the Optimizations settings in the Project | Options | Compiler menu option.

Listing 6.1. The SIMPEXP program demonstrates basic techniques for handling exceptions.

```
unit Main;

{ Program copyright (c) 1996 by Charles Calvert }
{ Project Name: SIMPEXP }

{ This program shows how to raise exceptions. Compile
  with Optimizations turned off. }

interface

uses
  SysUtils, WinTypes, WinProcs,
  Messages, Classes, Graphics,
  Controls, Forms, Dialogs,
  StdCtrls, Buttons;

type
  TForm1 = class(TForm)
    DelExcept: TBitBtn;
    UserExcept: TBitBtn;
    Declare: TBitBtn;
    CalcAdd: TBitBtn;
    procedure DelExceptClick(Sender: TObject);
    procedure UserExceptClick(Sender: TObject);
    procedure DeclareClick(Sender: TObject);
    procedure CalcAddClick(Sender: TObject);
  private
    { Private declarations }
  public
    { Public declarations }
  end;

var
  Form1: TForm1;

implementation
```

continues

Listing 6.1. continued

```pascal
uses
  StrBox;

{$R *.DFM}

procedure TForm1.DelExceptClick(Sender: TObject);
var
  i, j, k: Integer;
begin
  j := 0;
  k := i div j;
end;

procedure TForm1.UserExceptClick(Sender: TObject);
var
  i, j, k: Integer;
begin
  j := 0;
  try
    k := i div j;
  except
    on EDivByZero do
      MessageDlg('Like wow! Don''t divide by zero, man!',
                 mtError, [mbOk], 0);
  end;
end;

procedure TForm1.DeclareClick(Sender: TObject);
var
  i, j, k: Integer;
begin
  j := 0;
  try
    k := i div j;
  except
    on E:EDivByZero do
      MessageDlg(Self.ClassName + ': ' + E.Message, mtError, [mbOk], 0);
  end;
end;

procedure TForm1.CalcAddClick(Sender: TObject);
const
  CR = #13#10;
var
  i, j, k: Integer;
begin
  j := 0;
  try
    k := i div j;
  except
    on E:EDivByZero do
      MessageDlg(E.Message + CR +
                 ' MyCalc: ' + Address2Str(ExceptAddr),
                 mtError, [mbOk], 0);
  end;
end;

end.
```

This program contains four TBitBtns that, when pressed, raise exceptions. In the first case, the code lets Delphi's built-in routines handle the exception; in the rest of the examples, a custom error handler is invoked.

Here is the simplest way to raise and handle an exception:

```
procedure TForm1.DelExceptClick(Sender: TObject);
var
  i, j, k: Integer;
begin
  j := 0;
  k := i div j;
end;
```

The code shown here causes a divide by zero error, and it will automatically pop up the dialog shown in Figure 6.2.

FIGURE 6.2.

The default mechanism for handling a divide by zero error.

The error message shown in Figure 6.2 is useful to programmers, since it provides an address you can use in the Search | Find Error menu choice. However, it is not a particularly friendly message to send to a user of your program.

The following code demonstrates how to set up a try..except block that gives you a place to handle an error:

```
procedure TForm1.UserExceptClick(Sender: TObject);
var
  i, j, k: Integer;
begin
  j := 0;
  try
    k := i div j;
  except
    on EDivByZero do
      MessageDlg('Division by zero error detected!',
                 mtError, [mbOk], 0);
  end;
end;
```

The code that you want to test appears right after the reserved word try. In this case, all that goes on in this section is that you force a divide by zero error. When the error occurs, the code after the word except is executed. In this section, you designate that you want to handle EDivByZero messages explicitly, and you do so by popping up an error message.

In the first part of the try block, you could make a procedure call. That procedure could in turn call another procedure, and so on, for six, ten, or however many levels of nested calls. If any of the routines in that block raised an EDivByZero error, the code would automatically jump to the MessageDlg shown in the preceding code.

Or, to state the same fact somewhat differently, if the code looked like this:

```
j := 0;
try
  k := i div j;
  DoSomething;
  DoSomethingElse;
   DoThis;
   DoThat;
except
  on EDivByZero do
    MessageDlg('Like wow! Don't divide by zero, man!',
              mtError, [mbOk], 0);
end;
```

then `DoSomething`, `DoSomethingElse`, `DoThis`, and `DoThat` would never be executed. Instead, the code would jump immediately from the division statement to the except section.

You can combine the convenience of having Delphi report an error with the luxury of being able to define your own error strings:

```
procedure TForm1.DeclareClick(Sender: TObject);
var
  i, j, k: Integer;

begin
  j := 0;
  try
    k := i div j;
  except
    on E:EDivByZero do
      MessageDlg(Self.ClassName + ': ' + E.Message,
                mtError, [mbOk], 0);
  end;
end;
```

In this code, Delphi is in effect allowing you to map an identifier onto the already existing exception object instance that was raised. This is not a variable declaration, since no new storage is being allocated. It's simply giving you a convenient way to access the exception object instance so that you can extract additional information carried by the object instance, such as the error message string:

```
E.Message
```

where `Message` returns the string that Delphi would associate with this error. To understand where `Message` comes from, refer to the declaration of `TException` shown previously.

After you have access to the `message` associated with an exception, you can add your own information to it. For instance, in this case I snag the name of the object whose method is raising the exception, thereby helping me know right away where the problem has occurred:

```
S := Self.ClassName + ': ' + E.Message,
```

The string created in this line of code is shown in Figure 6.3.

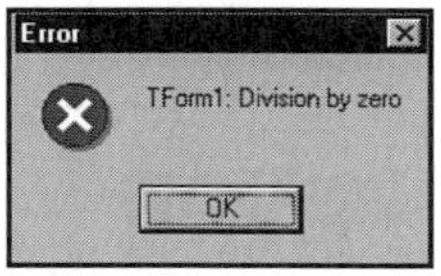

FIGURE 6.3.

An exception that shows a string created in part by Delphi and in part by the programmer.

You also might want to display the actual address at which an exception is raised. The built-in ExceptAddr function returns this address:

```
procedure TForm1.CalcAddClick(Sender: TObject);
const
  CR = #13#10;
var
  i, j, k: Integer;
begin
  j := 0;
  try
    k := i div j;
  except
    on E:EDivByZero do
      MessageDlg(E.Message + CR + ' MyCalc: ' +
                 Address2Str(ExceptAddr),
                 mtError, [mbOk], 0);
  end;
end;
```

This code displays the regular error message associated with an EDivByZero exception and then immediately converts the result of the ExceptAddr function into a string so that you can see that it returns the same address displayed by a Delphi exception. You can use this address in the Search | Find Error menu option, which will take you to the place in your code where the error occurred.

To convert a pointer into a string, you can use the following function from the StrBox unit:

```
function Address2Str(Addr : Pointer) : string;
begin
  Result := Format('%p', [Addr]);
end;
```

This function uses the Format function to perform a routine string operation that returns a string version of an address.

In this section, you learned how to handle simple exceptions. The actual logistics of handling these situations can be quite complex at times, but you are now armed with the basics needed to go into battle and wage war with the compiler. Note that I arranged the examples in this section in increasing order of complexity, where the first two are more typical of the code you will use in most programs, whereas the latter two are useful when you want to use advanced techniques.

Creating and Raising Your Own Exceptions

In this section, I will show how you can create your own exceptions and how to raise exceptions when errors occur. The code explored in this section is from the MYEXCEPT program shown in Listing 6.2. The form for the program has three buttons and an edit control.

Listing 6.2. The MYEXCEPT program shows how to create and raise custom exceptions.

```pascal
unit Main;

{ Program copyright (c) 1996 by Charles Calvert }
{ Project Name: MYEXCEPT }

{ This program shows how to create and raise your
  own exceptions. }

interface

uses
  SysUtils, WinTypes, WinProcs,
  Messages, Classes, Graphics,
  Controls, Forms, Dialogs,
  StdCtrls, Buttons;

type
  ESillySpellingError = class(Exception);

  TForm1 = class(TForm)
    ERead: TBitBtn;
    EReadAddr: TBitBtn;
    DelphiRaise: TBitBtn;
    Edit1: TEdit;
    Label1: TLabel;
    procedure RaiseEReadClick(Sender: TObject);
    procedure EReadAddrClick(Sender: TObject);
    procedure DelphiRaiseClick(Sender: TObject);
  private
    { Private declarations }
  public
    { Public declarations }
  end;

var
  Form1: TForm1;

implementation

uses
  StrBox;

{$R *.DFM}
```

```
procedure TForm1.RaiseEReadClick(Sender: TObject);
begin
  raise EReadError.Create('EReadError has occurred');
end;

function GetAddr: string;
var
  P: Pointer;
begin
  P := Form1.MethodAddress('EReadAddrClick');
  GetAddr := Address2Str(P);
end;

procedure TForm1.EReadAddrClick(Sender: TObject);
var
  S: string;
begin
  S := Edit1.Text;
  if UpperCase(S) = 'OCCURED' then begin
    S := 'A Silly Spelling Error has occured! ' +
         'The correct spelling is occuRRed, not occured: ';
    raise ESillySpellingError.Create(S + GetAddr);
  end;
end;

function StrToInt(S: string): LongInt;
var
  E: Integer;
begin
  Val(S, Result, E);
  if E <> 0 then raise EConvertError.Create('Can''t convert ' + S +
                                            ' into an integer');
end;

procedure TForm1.DelphiRaiseClick(Sender: TObject);
begin
  StrToInt('23a');
end;

end.
```

To use this program, just press any of the three buttons on the form. The third button won't raise an exception unless the edit control is set to the misspelled string occured.

Exceptions occur because they are explicitly raised. For instance, here is another version of the Str2Int routine:

```
procedure Str2Int(S: string);
var
  E: Integer;
begin
  Val(S, Result, E);
  if E <> 0 then
    raise EConvertError.Create('Can''t convert ' + S +
                               ' into an integer');
end;
```

This procedure uses the Delphi Val procedure to convert a string into an integer. If all is successful, Result is set equal to the transmuted string and E is set to 0. If there is a problem, E is non-zero. When an error condition exists, the Str2Int routine raises an EConvertError and passes in a string that explains what has gone wrong.

TIP

Val is one of many built-in routines for handling strings and numbers. If you are trying to find out whether Delphi contains a particular type of function, you can search on "Procedures and Functions (Categorical)" in the online help.

EConvertError is a built-in Delphi type meant to be used in situations where an error occurs in a conversion routine. If you look in SYSUTILS.PAS, you will find that Delphi uses this exception quite a bit, but tends to raise it via the good graces of the ConvertError routine.

There is nothing in Delphi that forces you to use a particular class of exceptions in a particular situation. For instance, in the following method I raise an EReadError, even though nothing has gone wrong in the program:

```
procedure TForm1.RaiseEReadClick(Sender: TObject);
begin
  raise EReadError.Create('Fake EReadError has occurred');
end;
```

Exceptions are triggered when you use the reserved word raise and then construct an instance of a particular type of exception. In and of themselves, exceptions have nothing to do with errors, and indeed you could use them for some entirely different purpose. In other words, exceptions are a good means of reporting errors, but they do not occur because an error occurs; they occur because you use the reserved word raise!

Many of the exception classes that are built into Delphi may be useful to you at times. For instance, you might need to convert some variable from one type to another; or there may be an occasion when you need to read some value. If errors occur during such tasks, it would make sense to raise an EConvertError or an EReadError. That way, the code that depends upon your conversion routines doesn't have to worry about what to do when the conversion routines fail. On failure, they will raise an exception and will never return bad data or error codes to the caller. That can go a long way toward simplifying your code.

Despite the usefulness of many of Delphi's built-in exception classes, there are many occasions when you are going to need to create exception classes of your own. To do so, you should first declare a new class:

```
type
  ESillySpellingError = class(Exception);
```

This code states that class ESillySpellingError is a descendant of type Exception.

```
   private
     { Private declarations }
   public
     { Public declarations }
   end;

var
  Form1: TForm1;

implementation

{$R *.DFM}
{$R RESMAIN.RES}
{$I RESMAIN.INC}

function GetError(ID: Integer): string;
const
  Max = 150;
var
  S: array[0..Max] of Char;
begin
  LoadString(HInstance, ID, S, Max);
  Result := S;
end;

procedure TForm1.TestLoadStrClick(Sender: TObject);
begin
  Edit1.Text := GetError(ErrorOne);
  Edit2.Text := GetError(ErrorTwo);
end;

procedure TForm1.RaiseErrorOneClick(Sender: TObject);
begin
  raise EErrorOne.Create(GetError(ErrorOne));
end;

procedure TForm1.RaiseErrorTwoClick(Sender: TObject);
begin
  raise EErrorTwo.Create(GetError(ErrorTwo));
end;

end.
```

Listing 6.4. The RESMAIN.INC file lists the errors used by the RESERROR program.

```
const
  ErrorOne = 1;
  ErrorTwo = 2;
```

Listing 6.5. The RESMAIN.RC file can be converted in a RES file by typing `BRCC32 -r RESMAIN.RC` at the DOS prompt.

```
#include "resmain.inc";

STRINGTABLE
{
  ErrorOne, "First error"
  ErrorTwo, "Second error"
}
```

The RESERROR program loads error strings from a resource and displays them to the user when an exception is raised. One button on the main form of the program is used to test to see that the strings found in the resource can be retrieved, and the other two buttons actually raise exceptions.

NOTE

String tables can help you during development and during maintenance by allowing you to change strings in one place and see the changes reflected throughout your program. Needless to say, this technique can be very useful when you are trying to create multiple versions of a program for internationalization purposes.

When foreign languages are involved, you might store your string resources in a DLL, so that you can change the strings without having to recompile your main program. In short, you can create DLLs that contain nothing but string resources. Each DLL will contain strings from a different language so that you have a version that is French, another that is German, and so on. You can then ship a different DLL with the products that you ship to different countries. When using these DLLs, call `LoadString`, but pass in the `HInstance` of the DLL where the string is stored.

Note also that the string resources in your EXE can be removed and replaced without recompiling the EXE. All you have to do is use BRCC32.EXE to tack the new resources onto the precompiled EXE.

To create a string resource, you could use the following syntax in an RC file:

```
STRINGTABLE
{
  1, "First error"
  2, "Second error"
}
```

where 1 and 2 are the IDs of the strings, and the strings themselves are shown in double quotes.

Notice, however, that RESERROR does not hard-code numbers into its string table:

```
#include "resmain.inc";

STRINGTABLE
{
  ErrorOne, "First error"
  ErrorTwo, "Second error"
}
```

Instead, it uses constants that are declared in RESMAIN.INC:

```
const
  ErrorOne = 1;
  ErrorTwo = 2;
```

You can compile a RC file into a RES file by typing this line at the DOS prompt:

```
brcc32 -r resmain.rc
```

BRCC32.EXE uses the C-like #include to reference the include file created. You reference the same include file in a Delphi program by writing this:

```
{$I 'resmain.inc'}
```

NOTE

Windows 95 can make life miserable for denizens of the command line. In particular, programs are sometimes installed in deeply nested paths that contain long filenames. For instance, my current version of Delphi is installed in the c:\program files\borland\delphi32 subdirectory. Given this rather bleak scenario, the correct command line for compiling the RES file would be:

```
c:\progra~1\borland\delphi32\bin\brcc32.exe -r resmain.rc
```

The issue here, of course, is that the directory 'program files' is referenced as shown above under DOS 7.0, though it may be referenced differently on your system. I have heard that 4DOS for Windows 95 supports long filenames. Without command line support for long file names, the best approach may be for you to create a batch file with the above line in it. (See GO.BAT on the CD-ROM.)

Once you have created a RES file and an include file, you can load the strings into your program with a relatively simple routine:

```
function GetError(ID: Integer): string;
const
  Max = 150;
var
  S: array[0..Max] of Char;
begin
  LoadString(HInstance, ID, S, Max);
  Result := S;
end;
```

LoadString is part of the Windows API, so it works with PChars. PChars will be automatically translated into strings for ease of use inside Delphi. Notice that once again, I avoid hard-coding numbers into the program but instead declare a constant called Max. Even if you reference a number only once, it's still a good habit to declare it as a constant. The reasoning, of course, is that you can change the number in one place and be sure that all references to that number will change. Yes, it is overkill in this one case, but still it is good programming practice.

It's worth noting that the VCL and Delphi use resources to store error strings. If you open up SYSUTILS.PAS, you will find that it makes heavy use of a more complex version of the logic shown in RESERROR.DPR. In general, string resources are one of the more valuable tools in the repertoire of any Windows programmer, and you should consider making use of them whenever you need to hard-code strings into your program.

The following excerpts from SYSUTILS.RC show a portion of a string table used by Delphi to aid in reporting errors:

```
#include "sysutils.inc"

STRINGTABLE
{
  SInvalidInteger, "'%s' is not a valid integer value"
  SInvalidFloat, "'%s' is not a valid floating point value"
  SInvalidDate, "'%s' is not a valid date"
  SInvalidTime, "'%s' is not a valid time"
  SInvalidDateTime, "'%s' is not a valid date and time"
  STimeEncodeError, "Invalid argument to time encode"
  SDateEncodeError, "Invalid argument to date encode"
  SOutOfMemory, "Out of memory"
  ...
}
```

Notice that this table obviously relies on Format and related functions to enable the program to insert data into a string before showing it to the user.

The following constants are excerpted from a Delphi source file called SYSUTILS.INC and are used as IDs that reference the errors in the string table shown previously:

```
const

  SInvalidInteger = 65408;
  SInvalidFloat = 65409;
  SInvalidDate = 65410;
  SInvalidTime = 65411;
  SInvalidDateTime = 65412;
  STimeEncodeError = 65413;
  SDateEncodeError = 65414;
  SOutOfMemory = 65415;
  ...
```

These string constants end up being linked into most of your programs, so you might want to open up SYSUTIL.RC and see if you can use any of them in your own code.

try..finally Blocks

Sometimes you need to ensure that a particular block of code is executed even if something goes wrong in the code that proceeds it. For instance, you may allocate memory, perform several actions, and finally intend to deallocate the memory. However, if an exception is raised between the time you allocate memory and the time you want to deallocate the memory, the code that deallocates the memory might never get executed. To ensure that this doesn't happen, you can use a try..finally block.

Here is a second way to think of try..finally blocks. As you know, a try..except block can cause the execution pointer for your program to jump from the place that an error occurs directly to the place where you handle that error. That is all well and good under most circumstances, but sometimes you want to make sure that some code between the error and the exception handler is executed regardless of circumstances. try..finally blocks represent solution to this problem.

The code shown in Listing 6.6 demonstrates how to use a try..finally block. The program is run in a simple form that contains a button and an edit control.

Listing 6.6. The FINAL program shows how to use a `try..finally` block.

```
unit Main;

{ Program copyright (c) 1996 by Charles Calvert }
{ Project Name: FINAL }

{ This program shows how to use a try..finally block.
  Turn optimizations off when running this program. }

interface

uses
   SysUtils, WinTypes, WinProcs,
   Messages, Classes, Graphics,
   Controls, Forms, Dialogs,
   StdCtrls, Buttons;

type
   TForm1 = class(TForm)
     BitBtn1: TBitBtn;
     Edit1: TEdit;
     Label1: TLabel;
     procedure BitBtn1Click(Sender: TObject);
   private
     GlobalString: string;
     procedure RunCalculation;
   end;

var
   Form1: TForm1;
```

continues

Listing 6.6. continued

```
implementation

{$R *.DFM}

procedure TForm1.RunCalculation;
var
  i,j,k: Integer;
begin
  j := 0;
  try
    k := i div j;
    Label1.Caption := 'Sam';
  finally
    GlobalString := 'RunCalculation called!';
  end;
  GlobalString := 'Toot';
end;

procedure TForm1.BitBtn1Click(Sender: TObject);
begin
  try
    GlobalString := '';
    Edit1.Text := GlobalString;
    RunCalculation
  except
    on EDivByZero do
      MessageDlg('You divided by zero again!', mtError, [mbOk], 0);
  end;
  Edit1.Text := GlobalString;
end;

end.
```

The key point to grasp about the FINAL program is that it nests a try..finally block inside a try..except block. Of course, in a Delphi program, all try..finally blocks are always nested inside a try..except block, because each Delphi program in fact occurs inside a try..except block. However, it helps to see a small example that shows exactly how try..execpt blocks and try..finally blocks are nested one inside the other. You might want to duplicate code like that shown in the Final program in many places in your own programs. Furthermore, sometimes try..except and try..finally blocks are nested in a single procedure. Remember to turn Optimizations off when running this program.

The FINAL program contains a private field of TForm1 called GlobalString. At the start of the BitBtn1Click method, this string is zeroed out and displayed in the edit control:

```
try
  GlobalString := '';
  Edit1.Text := GlobalString;
  RunCalculation
except
  on EDivByZero do
    MessageDlg('You divided by zero again!', mtError, [mbOk], 0);
```

```
  end;
  Edit1.Text := GlobalString;
```

The `RunCalculation` method called in `BitBtn1Click` looks like this:

```
procedure TForm1.RunCalculation;
var
  i,j,k: Integer;
begin
  j := 0;
  try
    k := i div j;
  finally
    GlobalString := 'RunCalculation called!';
  end;
end;
```

This function forces an exception to be raised, but it does so inside a `try..finally` block. Normally, the code pointer jumps from the place where the exception is raised straight to the place it is handled. The `try..finally` block, however, slows this process down long enough to ensure that the `GlobalString` variable will be set to a new value.

If there were code after the place where the exception is raised, that code would not be executed—and yet anything in the `finally` block would be executed. Consider this example:

```
  j := 0;
  try
    k := i div j;
    Label1.Caption := 'Foo';
  finally
    GlobalString := 'RunCalculation called!';
  end;
```

Here, the code that changes the caption would not get executed, but the code that changes the `GlobalString` would. If you changed the preceding code so that it first sets j to 1 instead of to 0, both the label and the `GlobalString` would be changed.

It's probably worthwhile for me to make a few brief comments on execution speed. As a rule, `try..finally` blocks are not particularly expensive in terms of clock cycles. As a result, you should feel free to scatter them through your code with a good degree of liberalism. On the other hand, `try..except` blocks can be fairly costly in terms of clock cycles, so you should show some caution when deciding how often you want to insert them into your programs.

NOTE

In my opinion, it is always better to play it safe than to try to optimize your code to the final and ultimate clock cycle. If you've been using a product like Visual Basic or PowerBuilder, then the move to Delphi is going to give you huge gains in speed. Let the developers put in all the optimizations; you should just concentrate on writing programs that work! Of course, many expert programmers can afford to ignore this advice, but I personally strive first to write reliable code, and I worry about optimizations only if I'm sure everything is already working correctly.

Replacing the Default Exception Handler

You might want to override the default exception handler either because you want to customize your program or because you want to be sure some things happen, regardless of how your program ends. Delphi provides an event called OnException in the Application class that can be used for this purpose. A sample program, called ONEXCEPT, demonstrates how to use this event. The code for the program is in Listing 6.7. The form for this program consists of two buttons, one called DivByZero and the other called ReadError.

Listing 6.7. The code for the ONEXCEPT program shows how to create a generic error handler for all exceptions raised in your program.

```
unit Main;

{ Program copyright (c) 1995 by Charles Calvert }
{ Project Name: ONEXCEPT }

interface

uses
  SysUtils, WinTypes, WinProcs,
  Messages, Classes, Graphics,
  Controls, Forms, Dialogs,
  StdCtrls;

type
  TForm1 = class(TForm)
    DivByZero: TButton;
    ReadError: TButton;
    procedure DivByZeroClick(Sender: TObject);
    procedure FormCreate(Sender: TObject);
    procedure ReadErrorClick(Sender: TObject);
  private
    procedure HandleExcepts(Sender: TObject; E: Exception);
  public
    { Public declarations }
  end;

var
  Form1: TForm1;

implementation

{$R *.DFM}

procedure TForm1.HandleExcepts(Sender: TObject; E: Exception);
begin
  if E is EDivByZero then
    MessageDlg('EDivByZero', mtError, [mbOk], 0)
  else
    MessageDlg('Other error', mtError, [mbOk], 0)
end;
```

```
procedure TForm1.DivByZeroClick(Sender: TObject);
begin
  raise EDivByZero.Create('Exception');
end;

procedure TForm1.FormCreate(Sender: TObject);
begin
  Application.OnException := HandleExcepts;
end;

procedure TForm1.ReadErrorClick(Sender: TObject);
begin
  raise EReadError.Create('Read Error');
end;

end.
```

The ONEXCEPT program will handle all exceptions in a single routine defined by the programmer. It is not meant as an example of how to write exceptions or how to construct a program. However, it does provide advanced programmers with an illustration of how to use the OnException event.

The OnException property for TApplication is declared like this:

```
property OnException: TExceptionEvent;
```

Here is the declaration for TExceptionEvent:

```
TExceptionEvent =
  procedure (Sender: TObject; E: Exception) of object;
```

Normally, the code for an OnXXX handler is created for you automatically when you click the Events page of the Object Inspector. In this case, however, TApplication never appears in the Object Inspector, so you must manually create the call as a method of TForm1:

```
TForm1 = class(TForm)
  ...
  procedure HandleExcepts(Sender: TObject; E: Exception);
end;
```

After declaring the procedure, you can assign it to the TApplication OnException property in the FormCreate method:

```
procedure TForm1.FormCreate(Sender: TObject);
begin
  Application.OnException := HandleExcepts;
end;
```

The HandleExcepts method will now be called when an exception occurs as long as you don't declare any intervening try..except blocks. In the example shown here, the HandleExcepts procedure explicitly handles EDivByZero errors but responds to all other errors through a generic handler:

```
procedure TForm1.HandleExcepts(Sender: TObject; E: Exception);
begin
  if E is EDivByZero then
    MessageDlg('EDivByZero', mtError, [mbOk], 0)
  else
    MessageDlg('Other error', mtError, [mbOk], 0)
end;
```

Needless to say, it is usually not a very good idea to create OnException handlers. You should use them only if you are absolutely sure you know what you are doing and why you want to do it.

Reraising Exceptions, Streams, Freeing Memory

The final example in this chapter catches a few key ideas that have not yet been sufficiently emphasized. In particular, the CreateExp program shows how to:

- Reraise an exception. This allows you to do some preliminary handling of an exception, and then pass the exception to Delphi's default handlers.

- Ensure that memory allocated for an object is properly deallocated, even if an error occurs.

Both concepts handled in this section of the chapter are very important. In many ways, the earlier parts of this chapter serve only to lead up to this section, which includes some very important, and very commonly used, programming techniques.

The CreateExp example has just two short methods in it, both of which are fairly easy to understand. Despite the brevity and simplicity of the code, the techniques shown here are still quite important. The program is shown in Listing 6.8.

Listing 6.8. The CreateExp program shows how to reraise an exception, and how to ensure that allocated memory is properly deallocated.

```
unit main;

interface

uses
  Windows, Messages, SysUtils,
  Classes, Graphics, Controls,
  Forms, Dialogs, StdCtrls;
```

```
type
  TForm1 = class(TForm)
    bAutoRaise: TButton;
    bMemRelease: TButton;
    procedure bAutoRaiseClick(Sender: TObject);
    procedure bMemReleaseClick(Sender: TObject);
  private
    { Private declarations }
  public
    { Public declarations }
  end;

var
  Form1: TForm1;

implementation

{$R *.DFM}

procedure TForm1.bAutoRaiseClick(Sender: TObject);
var
  i, j, k: Integer;
begin
  j := 0;
  try
    k := i div j;
  except
    k := -1;
    raise;
  end;
end;


procedure TForm1.bMemReleaseClick(Sender: TObject);
var
  F: TFileStream;
  S: PChar;
begin
  F := TFileStream.Create('c:\autoexec.bat', fmOpenRead);
  try
    GetMem(S, F.Size + 1);
    F.Read(S^, F.Size);
    S[F.Size] := #0;
    MessageBox(Handle, S, 'Info', mb_Ok);
  finally
    F.Free;
  end;
end;

end.
```

The main form for this program has two simple buttons on it. The first is called bMemRelease and the bAutoRaiseClick. If you press either of these buttons then code will execute which demonstrates some important feature of exceptions.

The `AutoRaiseClick` method shows how to reraise an exception:

```
procedure ¯Form1.bAutoRaiseClick(Sender: TObject);
var
  i, j, k: Integer;
begin
  j := 0;
  try
    k := i div j;
  except
    k := -1;
    raise;
  end;
end;
```

Reraising an exception involves nothing more than making a simple call to the raise function. The above example intentionally creates an `EDivByZero` error. (Be sure that Optimizations is turned off so that this code will execute properly.)

After the exception is raised, the program performs some error processing, which in this case involves nothing more than setting k to -1. Though setting k to 0 has no significant impact in this program, it might be helpful in other programs as a way of signaling that k contains not a valid result, but is instead in an error condition. In other words, setting k to -1 is a signal to the rest of the program that k should not be used, and that some kind of error has occurred.

After setting k to 0, you may still want to tell the user what kind of error has occurred. One way to do this would be to display a `MessageBox` containing your own string, or the string found in the `Message` field of the `EDivByZero` object. However, you may not want to handle things this way, particularly if you are not sure exactly which exception occurred. If this is the case, you can first set k to -1, and then reraise the exception by calling `raise`. When you reraise the exception, the default Delphi handlers kick in, and the error will be reported to the user automatically.

Reraising an exception allows you to get the best of both worlds. You get to perform some custom handling, and you also allow Delphi to automatically inform the user exactly what has gone wrong. One nice aspect of this kind of handling is that it frees you from trying to explicitly handle all possible exceptions. Instead, you can simply do some default handling that ensures your program knows about and handles a generic error condition. Once you have set everything up, you can then let the system specify the exact type of error that occurred.

One of the most common uses for exceptions is to ensure that memory that has been allocated will be deallocated:

```
procedure TForm1.bMemReleaseClick(Sender: TObject);
var
  F: TFileStream;
  S: PChar;
begin
  F := TFileStream.Create('c:\autoexec.bat', fmOpenRead);
  try
    GetMem(S, F.Size + 1);
```

```
    F.Read(S^, F.Size);
    S[F.Size] := #0;
    MessageBox(Handle, S, 'Info', mb_Ok);
  finally
    F.Free;
  end;
end;
```

In the example shown here, memory is allocated for the variable F. In a protected mode 32-bit development environment there isn't much chance that anything is going to go wrong while an object is being created. In other words, it's unlikely that you will run out of memory. If, however, something does go wrong, then there are internal Delphi exception handlers which will almost certainly catch the error, deal with it correctly, and then inform the user of what went wrong.

So it's fairly save to assume that the creation of the stream in the bMemReleaseClick method is going to succeed. If it did happen to fail, you can rest assured that Delphi has internal routines for handling and reporting the error. However, once the stream has been created, there is still a likely chance that an error will occur while the function is attempting to read from a file. If something did go wrong, Delphi would probably automatically catch the error. However, after the exception is raised, the program still needs to be sure that the memory for the stream is deallocated. The purpose of the try..finally block in the above routine is to ensure that the memory for the TFileStream object will be deallocated even if something goes wrong while reading from the file.

In particular, if something goes wrong during the execution of this block of code:

```
GetMem(S, F.Size + 1);
F.Read(S^, F.Size);
S[F.Size] := #0;
MessageBox(Handle, S, 'Info', mb_Ok);
```

You can still be sure that the stream will be deallocated:

```
F.Free;
```

The mechanism that ensure that the Free method gets called is nothing more than a simple try..finally block. This is a very common usage of the try..finally syntax, and it is one you should be sure you understand.

The above code also demonstrates how to open up a simple TFileStream object and read in some data. The newly collected data is then displayed to the user via the auspices of the MessageBox function. Once the stream is no longer needed, it is destroyed by a call to Free.

The Create method for a stream takes two parameters. The first is a string specifying the name of the file you want to read. The second is a constant that informs that system what kind of operation you want to perform. The following are the constants associated with Delphi streams, as found in the online help:

fmOpenRead	Open the file for reading only
fmOpenWrite	Open the file for writing only

fmOpenReadWrite	Open the file for reading or writing
fmShareExclusive	Open the file, disallowing other applications to open it for reading or writing.
fmShareDenyWrite	Open the file, disallowing other applications to open it for writing.
fmShareDenyRead	Open the file, disallowing other applications to open it for reading.
fmShareDenyNone	Open the file, disallowing other applications to open it for exclusive use.
fmCreate	Create a new file, replacing any existing file with the same name.

Streams have several methods associated with them, including generic Read and Write methods, and custom methods that allow you to easily read or write a component to a stream. These latter routines are called ReadComponent and WriteComponent. Streams also have a Size property that reports on the size of the file being read, and a Position property, which identifies your current position in the stream. For further information, see the online help entries for both TFileStream and TStream.

Summary

In this chapter you learned about exceptions. Exceptions are a vital part of all well-written programs. However, you should remember that Delphi declares a large number of exceptions for handling the errors that occur in your program. As a result, many errors will be handled gracefully without your intervention. For instance, the error popped up in the first EDivByZero example shown in this chapter is perfectly suitable for many programs. That exception was raised without you having to write special error-handling syntax.

Exceptions are one of the most important parts of Delphi's syntax, and you should dedicate considerable time to learning how they work. Overall, the mechanics, of exceptions are fairly simple. However, there is an art to learning exactly when and how to use exceptions. Gaining a skill in this art takes time, and will in most cases evolve over a period of months or years, rather than hours or days.

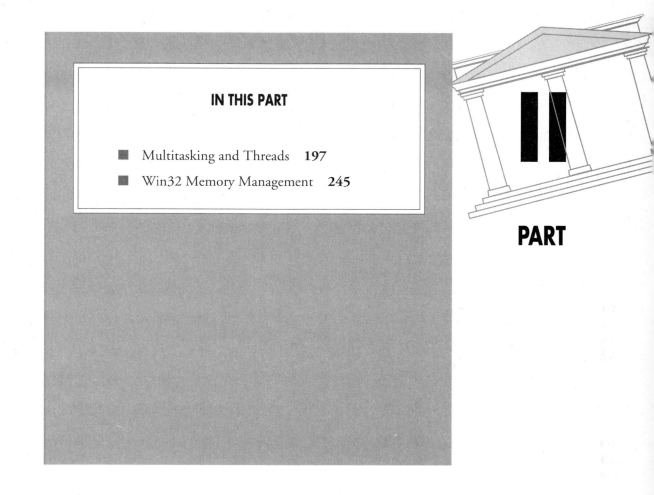

PART

II

Win32

Part II of this book covers Win32. These pages include a long look at multitasking, threading, and memory management. Specific information about mutexes, critical sections, virtual memory, heaps, memory-mapped files, and other Win32 programming issues are examined in both text and in sample programs.

Multitasking and Threads

7

This chapter is about advanced Windows 95 and Windows NT programming. It is a gateway to the upper echelons of Windows programming and introduces you to some of the most powerful capabilities of Win32.

In particular, this chapter covers the following:

- The basics of the Win32 architecture
- Processes
- Threads
- Critical sections
- Mutexes
- The VCL TThread object
- Setting thread priority

All of these are advanced subjects that are entirely Windows 95– and Windows NT–specific. The programs included in this chapter will not run under Windows 3.1 no matter how you dice or slice them.

My goal is to isolate some of the most important aspects of advanced Windows programming and introduce you to them in clear language so you can use them in your applications. I present five different programs in this chapter, each designed to show off a key feature related to threads and multitasking.

I have used the word "advanced" in this overview several times, but you will find that most of the code in this chapter is easy to use. I have sought to show you simple ways to get at some of the most powerful new features in Windows 95. I would need another five or six hundred pages to cover these subjects in depth, but the material you find here will get you started with these invaluable technologies. In fact, there is plenty of information in this lengthy chapter to enable you to incorporate threading into your own programs.

This chapter is meant as a companion piece to Chapter 8, "Win32 Memory Management." The chapters are closely related, and they should be read in order, with this chapter first. When you are done reading both chapters, you should have a good sense of what Win32 is all about and why it's important.

Processes and Memory

Process is the hip Win32 term for a program that is currently loaded. An executable file on disk is just a file. If it's been started, it's a process.

If you want to create a process, call `CreateProcess`. This function does what the `WinExec` function did in Windows 3.1. `WinExec` is now obsolete, and you should use `CreateProcess` in its stead.

Processes don't do anything. They just exist. The thing that does something inside a program is called a thread. Each program has at least one thread, and most programs that currently run on Windows have only one thread. All Windows 3.1 programs by definition have only one thread. The idea that each program can have its own thread, or that a program can have multiple threads, is specific to fancy operating systems like UNIX, OS/2, Windows NT, and Windows 95.

When Windows loads a process, it simply opens up a memory-mapped file and sucks the contents of an executable file or DLL into memory. Processes are inert. They don't do anything. Threads do things. Processes merely exist.

All processes have an `HInstance` associated with them. This parameter is declared globally inside all Delphi programs. You don't have to do anything to get hold of this variable. It's there automatically at program startup. Object Pascal programs have an advantage over C programs in that `WinMain` never has to be called, and the variables that are passed to it never have to be pushed on the stack. Startup is very fast in an Object Pascal program, yet `HInstance` is there for you as a global variable if you need it.

The `HInstance` of an application is the base memory address where it is loaded. In Windows 95, this value is typically 10×00400000, or 4,194,304. In other words, the program is usually loaded in at the 4 MB mark. It then ranges from that point up to the 2 GB mark. This means a Windows 95 program has 2 GB minus 4 MB worth of room in which to stretch out. Both the program's code and its data are loaded into this 2 GB address space. This means the operating system gives you virtually unlimited resources in which to run your program. (Your hardware might not, however, share the operating system's largesse.)

The specific value at which your program is loaded is under your control. If you select the Project | Options | Linker page from the menu, you will see that this value is accessible to you as the Image base.

NOTE

A *kilobyte* (KB) is approximately one thousand (1,000) bytes. A *megabyte* (MB) is approximately one million (1,000,000) bytes. A *gigabyte* (GB) is approximately one billion (1,000,000,000) bytes. Therefore, there are a thousand megabytes in one gigabyte. (Here are the precise figures: KB: 1024, MB: 1,048,576, GB: 1,073,741,824. If you are interested, here's 4 GB: 4,294,967,296.)

What does it mean to say that a program is loaded into a 4 GB address space? If you have only a few megabytes of memory on your machine, what sense does it make to talk about such huge amounts of memory?

The answer is that each program is assigned not an actual area in physical RAM, but only a virtual address space. That is, it's assigned a range of addresses. When you need to access that memory, physical addresses are assigned to it. The act of assigning physical addresses to virtual memory is called "mapping."

Windows is constantly mapping virtual memory into physical address spaces. That is, it's assigning physical addresses to virtual memory. Because of this system, people with only 8 MB of memory on their system can have variables, or even entire processes, that have addresses in the 3 to 4 GB range. Every program thinks it's running in its own private 4 GB address space, and that it can use 2 GB of this space as it pleases. What's really happening in some cases is that pages of that virtual 4 GB space are being mapped into the actual 8 MB of memory available on your system.

> **NOTE**
>
> Because each process runs in its own 4 GB address space, the global hPrevInstance variable from Windows 3.1 is meaningless in Win32. There can't be a previous instance of a program because each program is running in its own virtual world, and there is only one virtual world in all the universe. (Actually, there is more than one world inside a computer. But each process is convinced that it is alone, the only virtual world in existence. Its world is 4 GB in size, guaranteed, and the inhabitants of that world are prepared to prove it to you. And it's the only one there is. Any science fiction writers want to pick up this ball and run with it?)

A page of memory is typically 4 KB in size, which is 4,096 bytes. Windows 95 is always mapping pages of virtual memory into physical address spaces. When this happens, the address your program sees does not change. There is another table that Windows maintains that translates these virtual addresses into physical addresses. This is called indirection, or perhaps more accurately, double indirection. (The pointer itself is one level of indirection, the virtual address a second level.) The addresses that you see in your program are never direct references to real memory. Instead they are indirect references. You see one address in your program, and then Windows maintains a table that enables the virtual addresses you see to be mapped into physical memory that resides in RAM. RAM is physical memory; the addresses you see are virtual memory. Virtual memory is not real memory any more than virtual reality is reality.

Why does Windows maintain this elaborate fiction of having virtual addresses? The main reason is to protect one process from another. Each process is running in its own 4 GB address space. It thinks it owns the whole computer. It has no idea that there are other processes on the computer.

Because each process is totally separated from the other processes on the computer, there is much less chance that they will overwrite one another. This means it is unlikely that an invalid memory access by one program will overwrite another program, or overwrite some part of the operating system. Each process is boxed away in a safe virtual world where it can't get at any other programs. This makes interprocess communication very different than it was in Windows 3.1. However, it also makes it much less likely that your computer will crash.

Furthermore, when you close down a Win32 program, all the resources allocated to it are automatically closed out. By definition they can reside only inside that program's one virtual world. When the virtual world is closed out, all the resources associated with that process are also closed out. If you forget to deallocate memory, or if you forget to deallocate resources, all your mistakes are covered up the moment you close your program. (This is not, however, a theory on which to base program memory management! You should at least *try* to handle memory correctly. However, if you make a mistake, you are not permanently sullying the operating system's environment the way you did in Windows 3.1.)

> **NOTE**
>
> All 16-bit Windows programs that run on Windows 95 by default share the same address space. It's as if they are all running on their own miniature version of Windows 3.1. That means errors made by one 16-bit process can affect other 16-bit processes. However, when you close out all the 16-bit applications, their virtual world disappears, and all the resources dedicated to it are reclaimed. If one 16-bit program is giving you trouble, don't just close it. Close all the 16-bit programs in your Windows 95 session, then reopen the ones that you feel are running properly. That one program dirtied the water that all the other 16-bit programs used. The only thing to do in that case is to close all the 16-bit programs, then create a new, pristine virtual 16-bit world by reopening one of them. Remember, this is Windows 95 I'm talking about here, not Windows NT.

That's all I'm going to say about processes. The key point is that a process is a loaded program. It's not running; it's not executing. Processes don't run; they don't execute. They just exist in a vast 4 GB virtual address space. They have direct access to about 2 GB of that space, and the operating system owns the rest. Threads run. Threads execute. Threads are the doers.

Multitasking and Threads

Each process has one or more threads assigned to it. Threads are the part of a program that execute.

Windows 95 is a true multitasking operating system. At any one time, it has X number of threads running. It assigns a time slice to each of these threads. The technical name for a time slice is a quantum, but don't worry, I'm not going to call them that.

Each thread on the system has something called a context. A TContext record is a data structure that contains information about the state of a thread. More specifically, it contains information about the state of the registers in the CPU when that thread is running. If you want to see one of these structures, look for the TContext declaration in WINDOWS.PAS:

```
PContext = ^TContext;
TContext = record
  ContextFlags: DWORD;
  Dr0: DWORD;
  Dr1: DWORD;
  Dr2: DWORD;
  Dr3: DWORD;
  Dr6: DWORD;
  Dr7: DWORD;
  FloatSave: TFloatingSaveArea;
  SegGs: DWORD;
  SegFs: DWORD;
  SegEs: DWORD;
  SegDs: DWORD;
  Edi: DWORD;
  Esi: DWORD;
  Ebx: DWORD;
  Edx: DWORD;
  Ecx: DWORD;
  Eax: DWORD;
  Ebp: DWORD;
  Eip: DWORD;
  SegCs: DWORD;
  EFlags: DWORD;
  Esp: DWORD;
  SegSs: DWORD;
end;
```

The record quoted here is stripped of all its comments, which are by far the most enlightening part of the declaration. The comments are extensive, however, and of true interest to only a very small number of readers. The rest of us can get by with only a quick glance at the general lineaments of the structure.

For the moment, think of all the threads in a computer as if they were placed on a big wheel, like the wheels that spin around at a gambling casino. (Now, now! That analogy is not meant to be a commentary on the Windows 95 operating system!) As the wheel spins, there is a time when each of the threads is near the top of the wheel. Starting a few degrees before it reaches the top of the wheel, and extending a few degrees after, is the period of time when a thread is actually executing. The moment the thread comes into that range, its context is loaded. That is, the CPU register values that it stores in its TContext record are loaded into the physical CPU found on the computer. Then that thread begins executing at the point where its instruction pointer is currently located. It executes for a few cycles, until the wheel that owns it spins out of range. Just before it goes out of range, its TContext record is updated with the current state of the CPU.

This is one way to think of how multitasking works under Windows 95. The key point is that each thread is given a time slice. It executes during the duration of its time slice, and then another thread gets a chance. While it is running, the thread has its own unique set of register values. When its time slice is over, the values are stored in a `TContext` record, and the next thread's CPU values are loaded into memory.

No two threads are ever running at the same time (unless you have more than one processor on the machine). However, it seems to you as if they are all running at the same time. That's because computers are fast. Like most sleight-of-hand tricks, a computer's multitasking capability is based on speed and dexterity. Computers don't really do the impossible; they just seem to be doing the impossible.

> **NOTE**
>
> It's important to understand that threads can be assigned priorities. A thread with a high priority gets called more frequently than a thread with a low priority. This means you can (at least theoretically) start a thread that performs a task entirely in the background. It never takes up any of the system's time unless all the other threads are idle.

There's a lot of loose talk going on about Windows 95 right now. Some of it is valid. However, don't let anyone convince you that Windows 95 is not a real multitasking operating system. This book teaches you how to write 32-bit programs. 32-bit programs that run on Windows 95 are really multitasked. (The 16-bit programs in their single address space are not really multitasked, but you don't have to run them if you don't want to. Also, they can't steal the show entirely from 32-bit applications—only from each other. Therefore you are not so bad off if you run only one 16-bit process at a time.)

Preemptive and Nonpreemptive Multitasking

Windows 95 has what is called *preemptive multitasking*. Preemptive multitasking is the process that I described earlier. When a task's time slice is up, it is preempted. It's cut off, and it can't do any more damage until it gets another time slice. This means that no one program can hog the CPU.

Windows 3.1 had what is called *non-preemptive multitasking*. Non-preemptive multitasking enables a program to take over control of the CPU and return it only when it is good and ready. In truth, most good Windows 3.1 programmers tried hard not to hog the CPU. They used timers, `PeekMessage` loops, `PostMessage`, and other tools to ensure that the system could get the CPU back if it needed it. However, there were times when a program would not give the CPU back to the system. For instance, it might get stuck in an infinite loop. When the program started looping, it would not give you a chance to preempt it. Therefore, you could not even switch to another program long enough to save your data before the system crashed. You just sat there helplessly, while everything went to hell.

Preemptive multitasking puts an end to this nightmare. If a program is stuck in an infinite loop, or if it is just busy doing something that takes a long time, the user can usually switch away to another program. That new program keeps getting time slices, as regular as clockwork, right on schedule, despite what might be going on in the first program. This often enables you to save your work in one program, then press Ctrl+Alt+Del so you can shut down an ill-behaved program. If all goes well, you can just continue your Windows session. If the ill-behaved program won't give up the ghost, at least you had a chance to save your work before rebooting.

> **NOTE**
>
> For what it's worth, I don't know any operating system that is truly crash proof. Some UNIX systems have a reputation for being very solid, but somehow the ones I have been connected to do seem to crash from time to time. Windows NT is also a very stable operating system, but I have definitely managed to bring it weeping to its knees. Windows 3.11 was a much more stable operating system than many people gave it credit for, but still, one ill-behaved 16-bit application could knock the wind out of its sails with relative ease. Windows 95 seems to lie somewhere between Windows 3.11 and Windows NT. If you have a new computer with 16 or more MB of memory on it, Windows 95 is usually pretty stable, but it too will crash given the right set of circumstances. My point, once again, is that no operating system that runs on a PC is truly crash-proof.

This new system of preemptive multitasking is better from two different perspectives. First, it means that users have a better chance of recovering if something goes wrong. Second, programmers don't have to work so hard to make sure that their programs are polite and well-behaved.

That's enough theory for now. I discuss Win32 memory-related issues more carefully after you get some hands-on experience with threads. Remember, the stuff I'm talking about here regards advanced 32 programming issues. Intermediate programmers don't have to know about this stuff. However, you will be a better programmer if you do learn how processes, threads, multitasking, and memory work.

Threads: A Simple Example

There is something about the topic of threads that is innately intimidating. Somehow it sounds as if it must be part of the guru's bag of tricks.

As it turns out, simple thread programs are almost embarrassingly easy to write. In fact, all the issues surrounding threads that are discussed in this chapter are fairly easy to understand. In some cases, threads might become complicated in the sense that any programming problem can be complicated. You start out with a fairly simple idea, then add another fairly simple layer of complexity to it. Then you add another layer on top of that, and then another, and before you know it you have about twenty balls up in the air at the same time. The same is true of threads. Just starting a single thread is simple. Not quite as simple as a blank form Delphi RAD application, but still simple.

It's only when you get multiple threads running at the same time, and only when they are concurrently trying to access the same data, that things can get a bit more complex. Thread synchronization, thread local storage, and related topics do have their complex sides. However, I think you will be surprised at how easy it is to add threads to your programs. Even some of the more advanced thread synchronization-related topics such as critical sections and mutexes are both fairly simple, at least in principle.

As usual, it's hard to get specific without having an example program to examine. Listing 7.1 shows how to create a simple thread. Go ahead and run the program, then come back and read about how it works.

Remember: Don't worry about this one. Basic thread theory is simple.

Listing 7.1. The main module of the Thread1 program.

```
unit main;

interface

uses
  Windows, Messages, SysUtils,
  Classes, Graphics, Controls,
  Forms, Dialogs, StdCtrls;

type
  TForm1 = class(TForm)
    bUseThread: TButton;
    bNoThread: TButton;
    procedure bUseThreadClick(Sender: TObject);
    procedure bNoThreadClick(Sender: TObject);
  end;

var
  Form1: TForm1;

implementation

{$R *.DFM}

function ThreadFunc(P: Pointer): LongInt; stdcall;
var
  i: Integer;
  DC: HDC;
  S: string;
begin
  DC := GetDC(Form1.Handle);
  for i := 0 to 100000 do begin
    S := IntToStr(i);
```

continues

Listing 7.1. continued

```
    TextOut(DC, 10, 10, PChar(S), Length(S));
  end;
  ReleaseDC(Form1.Handle, DC);
end;

procedure TForm1.bUseThreadClick(Sender: TObject);
var
  hThread: THandle;
  ThreadID: DWord;
begin
  hthread := CreateThread(nil,          //Security attribute
                          0,            //Initial Stack
                          @ThreadFunc,  //Starting address of thread
                          nil,          // argument of thread
                          0,            // Create flags
                          ThreadID);    // thread ID

  if hthread = 0 then
    MessageBox(Handle, 'No Thread', nil, MB_OK);
end;

procedure TForm1.bNoThreadClick(Sender: TObject);
begin
  ThreadFunc(nil);
end;

end.
```

When this program begins, it displays the simple window shown in Figure 7.1. There are two buttons on the main window. If you select the one labeled Use Thread, the program counts from 1 to 100,000 using a thread. While this process is going on, you can use the mouse to move or resize the main window. If you press the second button, the program also counts from 1 to 100,000. However, this second counting process is not run in a separate thread, so you cannot move or resize the window until the loop that performs the counting is finished.

FIGURE 7.1.

The Thread1 program counts from 0 to 100,000 when the user selects either button on its main form.

The structure of the Thread1 program is very simple. There are two button response methods. The first runs a function called ThreadFunc as a separate thread, and the second runs the same function as part of the main thread of the program. If you press the first button, the program has two threads running simultaneously; if you press the second button, the program has only its main thread running.

When working with threads, you have two main tasks:

1. Create the thread.
2. Create a function that serves as the *thread entry point*.

As you learned earlier, each program has one thread by default. In a sense, this thread is started at the moment your program is launched. Just as a BEGIN..END pair at the bottom of a DPR file is the entry point for a program, so is the thread function you create the entry point for a thread. Unlike the code in the project source file, the thread function or functions you create can be located anywhere in your program.

The Windows API call to create a thread is known (naturally enough) as CreateThread. As you learned earlier, the thread function itself can have any name. However, it always takes one 32-bit pointer or variable as a parameter. It always returns a 32-bit value. The parameter of the function is of type Pointer. That is, it's just a generic pointer. As such you can pass in a pointer to almost any structure in this variable. You can also pass in a 32-bit integer value in this parameter. More on this later.

Here is the code that creates the thread:

```
hthread := CreateThread(nil,        //Security attribute
                        0,          //Initial Stack
                        @ThreadFunc, //Starting address of thread
                        nil,        // argument of thread
                        0,          // Create flags
                        ThreadID);  // thread ID

if hthread = 0 then
  MessageBox(Handle, 'No Thread', nil, MB_OK);
```

This code does nothing more than attempt to create a thread. If something goes wrong, it pops up a message box informing the user that there has been an error.

This is the CreateThread syntax:

```
function CreateThread(
  lpThreadAttributes: Pointer; // address of thread security attributes
  dwStackSize: DWORD;          // size of stack for thread
  lpStartAddress: TFNThreadStartRoutine; // address of thread function
  lpParameter: Pointer;        // argument for new thread
  dwCreationFlags: DWORD;      // creation flags
  var lpThreadId: DWORD):      // Returned thread identifier
  THandle; stdcall;            // Returns handle to thread
```

The first parameter takes a series of security attributes. If this parameter is nil, the default security attributes are used. On Windows 95, it is standard to set this parameter to nil. The only time you might want to vary from this pattern is if you want child processes to inherit the thread.

If the second parameter for the thread is 0, the stack size for the thread is the same as the stack size for the application. In other words, the primary thread and the thread you are starting both have stacks that are the same size. The stack automatically grows, if necessary. In short, you can usually set this parameter to 0.

The lpStartAddress parameter is the most important portion of the function call. It is where you specify the name of the thread function that is called when the thread begins execution. Just enter the name of the function in this field and put an at sign (@) in front of it.

WINDOWS.PAS declares a TFNThreadStartRoutine like this:

```
TFarProc = Pointer;
TFNThreadStartRoutine = TFarProc;
```

In short, you can pass in just about anything in this parameter. However, if you want your call to succeed, you should pass in the address of function like the ThreadFunc routine described earlier.

If you want to pass a parameter to your function, you specify it in lpParameter. Typically, you create a structure and pass in its address in this parameter. The variable you use does not have to be a structure—it could be a string or some other type of variable.

dwCreationFlags enables you to pass in certain flags that are associated with your thread. The Microsoft documentation I have seen so far specifies only one possible flag for this field. That flag is called CREATE_SUSPENDED. If you create a suspended thread, the thread itself is created, its stack is created, and its TContext structure is filled with CPU values, but the thread is never assigned any CPU time. It's all set to go, but it won't execute until you call ResumeThread. If you want, you can then suspend the thread again by calling SuspendThread. This whole subject of suspended threads is really an advanced topic relating to thread synchronization. For now, you should just pass in 0 in this parameter.

The final parameter, lpThreadID, holds a var parameter that is assigned a unique ID by the system. On Windows 95 this parameter can be 0, and indeed most of the time you won't use the thread ID, so you might have an inclination to set it to 0. On Windows NT, however, this parameter cannot be 0. If you are interested in portability between Windows 95 and Windows NT, you should not set this value to 0. In other words, if your application goes into general release, you should pass in 32-bit DWORD and should not set this value to 0. Remember, you are not passing anything to Windows in this parameter, rather you are passing in a variable that is assigned a value by Windows.

Here's an example:

```
var
  hThread: THandle;
  ThreadID: DWord;
begin
  CreateThread(nil, 0, ThreadFunc, nil, 0, ThreadID);
```

After you have created a non-suspended thread, the function you passed to it is automatically called. In other words, after you create a thread, the function representing the entry point for that thread is called almost immediately. Here is the thread for the Thread1 program:

```
function ThreadFunc(P: Pointer): LongInt; stdcall;
var
  i: Integer;
  DC: HDC;
  S: string;
begin
  DC := GetDC(Form1.Handle);
  for i := 0 to 100000 do begin
    S := IntToStr(i);
    TextOut(DC, 10, 10, PChar(S), Length(S));
  end;
  ReleaseDC(Form1.Handle, DC);
end;
```

It would not be safe to use the Canvas object for Form1 in this routine, because most of the visual objects in the VCL are not thread-safe. As you will see in the discussion of the TThread object, there is a way to safely use the VCL inside threads. However, as a general rule, you should consider using the Windows API exclusively when working with threads. This does not mean that your program cannot be VCL-based. In fact, there is no restriction on the number or kind of VCL objects you use in multithreaded programs. However, if the code in one of your threads wants to talk to a VCL object, it should use the Windows API, and in particular, it should use SendMessage or, occasionally, PostMessage.

> **NOTE**
>
> The six chapters of this book numbered Chapters 9 through 14 are dedicated to a discussion of the Windows API. In those chapters, and particularly in Chapter 14, you learn about using SendMessage and PostMessage to talk to Windows controls. This subject is also broached on several occasions in this chapter.
>
> I want to emphasize that the TThread object provides a way to call the VCL from inside threads. That object is explored later in this chapter. Furthermore, certain key commands, such as TQuery.Open, are safe to perform inside threads. Lastly, if you have a little knowledge of the Windows API, you can talk to your Delphi VCL objects using the SendMessage command. This enables you to build complex VCL-based applications, and to use threads inside them where necessary. One of the big goals of this book is to provide you with sufficient understanding of the VCL to use it with threads, and to use it in the countless other places in Windows development where that kind of knowledge can prove invaluable.
>
> One last comment needs to be made in this context. There are many parts of the VCL that you can use inside a thread function. It's mostly just TComponent descendants that you need to watch out for, and then only within certain parameters. This topic is addressed in more depth in the section on the TThread object.

The routine shown earlier first gets the device context from the system, then uses the device context to write 100,000 short strings to the surface of the form. When the loop is finished, the device context is returned to the system.

While this function is operating, there are two threads running simultaneously in the Thread1 program. If you resize the main window, or if you move it, then you are using the main thread for your program. The code that increments and paints numbers to the screen is part of the second thread. You can switch back and forth between the two threads just by moving the form or resizing it.

If you call the ThreadFunc routine directly, rather than as a thread, you cannot move or resize the main window until the loop is finished. That is because the program is entirely occupied with the loop and has no second thread available to handle other tasks. The point of this example program is to show how you can get one program to do two things at the same time. Part of the program is painting numbers to the screen, but the other part is free to handle resizing or any other task you might give it.

As you can see, there isn't anything very complicated about threads when you are looking at them from the most elemental level. What's complicated is when you have multiple threads trying to access the same data at the same time. When that happens, you need to find a way to get the threads to synchronize with one another, so that they are working together and not working at cross purposes.

One Program, Multiple Threads

Now that you know the basics about threads, the next step is to see how to run multiple threads from inside the same program. This is a bit like multitasking inside a single program, although of course the operating system doesn't necessarily treat two threads inside one program any differently than it would treat two threads from separate executables.

The example program in Listings 7.2 and 7.3 shows how a program can have four separate threads running at the same time. Three of the threads are painting graphics to the screen. The fourth thread, which does some simple math, is the main thread for the program. It continues functioning normally even when the other threads are active.

Listing 7.2. The main code for the Thread2 program.

```
unit main;

interface

uses
  Windows, Messages, SysUtils,
  Classes, Graphics, Controls,
  Forms, Dialogs, StdCtrls,
  Menus;
```

```
const
  Margin = 20;

type
  PData = ^TData;
  TData = record
    XPos: Integer;
    YPos: Integer;
  end;

  TForm1 = class(TForm)
    MainMenu1: TMainMenu;
    Start1: TMenuItem;
    Edit1: TEdit;
    bSquare: TButton;
    procedure FormPaint(Sender: TObject);
    procedure FormCreate(Sender: TObject);
    procedure Button1Click(Sender: TObject);
    procedure StartMenu(Sender: TObject);
    procedure FormResize(Sender: TObject);
    procedure bSquareClick(Sender: TObject);
  private
    EarthMap: HBitmap;
    procedure DrawBitmap(PaintDC: HDC; Bitmap: HBitMap;
                         XVal, YVal: Integer);
  end;

var
  Form1: TForm1;
  AWidth, AHeight: Integer;

implementation

uses
  MathBox;

{$R *.DFM}
{$R earth.res}

procedure TForm1.DrawBitmap(PaintDC: HDC; Bitmap: HBitMap;
                            XVal, YVal: Integer);
var
  MemDC: HDC;
  OldBitmap: HBitmap;
begin
  MemDC := CreateCompatibleDC(PaintDC);
  OldBitmap := SelectObject(MemDC, Bitmap);
  BitBlt(PaintDC, XVal, YVal, AWidth,
         AHeight, MemDC, 0, 0, SRCCOPY);
  SelectObject(MemDC, OldBitmap);
  DeleteObject(MemDC);
end;

procedure TForm1.FormPaint(Sender: TObject);
begin
  if EarthMap <> 0 then
    DrawBitmap(GetDC(Handle), Earthmap, Margin, 0);
end;
```

continues

Listing 7.2. continued

```
procedure TForm1.FormCreate(Sender: TObject);
var
  BStruct: Windows.TBitmap;
begin
  EarthMap := LoadBitmap(hInstance, 'Earth');
  GetObject(EarthMap, sizeof(Windows.TBitMap), @BStruct);
  AWidth := BStruct.bmWidth;
  AHeight := BStruct.bmHeight;
  PostMessage(Handle, wm_Size, 0, 0);
end;

function ThreadFunc(Ptr: Pointer): LongInt; stdcall;
var
  i, j: Integer;
  P: TColorRef;
  DC: HDC;
  Data: PData;
begin
  Data := PData(Ptr);
  DC := GetDC(Form1.Handle);
  for j := 0 to AHeight do
    for i := Margin to AWidth + Margin do begin
      P := GetPixel(DC, i, j);
      SetPixel(DC, i + Data^.Xpos, Data^.YPos + j, P);
    end;
  ReleaseDC(Form1.Handle, DC);
  Dispose(Data);
end;

procedure TForm1.StartMenu(Sender: TObject);
var
  hThread1, hThread2, hThread3: THandle;
  ThreadID: DWORD;
  Data: PData;
begin
  New(Data);
  Data^.xPos := AWidth;
  Data^.YPos := 0;
  hThread1 := CreateThread(nil, 0, @ThreadFunc,
                           Data, 0, ThreadID);

  New(Data);
  Data^.xPos := 0;
  Data^.YPos := AHeight;
  hThread2 := CreateThread(nil, 0, @ThreadFunc,
                           Data, 0, ThreadID);

  New(Data);
  Data^.xPos := AWidth;
  Data^.YPos := AHeight;
  hThread3 := CreateThread(nil, 0, @ThreadFunc,
                           Data, 0, ThreadID);

  if ((hTHread1 = 0) or (hThread2 = 0) or (hThread3 = 0)) then
    MessageBox(Handle, 'No Thread!', nil, mb_Ok);
end;
```

```
procedure TForm1.FormResize(Sender: TObject);
begin
  Edit1.Left := ClientWidth - (Edit1.Width + Margin);
  bSquare.Left := ClientWidth - (bSquare.Width + Margin);
end;

procedure TForm1.bSquareClick(Sender: TObject);
var
  r: Double;
begin
  r := Str2Real(Edit1.Text);
  Edit1.Text := Format('%f', [Sqrt(r)]);
end;

end.
```

Listing 7.3. The Resource file for the Thread2 program.

```
////////////////////////////////////////////////////
// EARTH.RC
// Copyright (c) 1996 Charlie Calvert.
////////////////////////////////////////////////////

Earth BITMAP "earth.bmp"
```

When you first run this program, a bitmap appears in the upper-left corner of the screen. If you select the program's sole menu item, three other copies of this bitmap are slowly painted in, as shown in Figure 7.2. There is also a button and edit control in the upper-right corner of the screen. You can enter data in this edit control and then press the button to find its square root.

FIGURE 7.2.

The Thread2 program after three copies of the original bitmap were made by three separate threads.

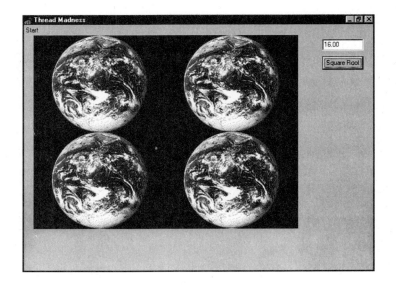

What's interesting about the program is that you can perform mathematical calculations at the same time that the program is very busy painting three bitmaps to the screen. The program appears to be doing four things at once, which would have been impossible under Windows 3.1. (You could have faked this same kind of capability in Windows 3.1 by using a series of PostMessage commands, but that kind of code is awkward to implement and difficult to maintain.)

Working with Bitmaps Using the Windows API

When the Thread2 program starts, it loads a bitmap from a secondary resource file via a call to LoadBitmap in the OnCreate handler. The RC file for this second bitmap looks like this:

```
Earth BITMAP "earth.bmp"
```

You can compile it by entering the following command on the DOS prompt:

```
brcc32 -r earth.rc
```

EARTH.RC is the name of the RC file. Note that the resource file that will be created is explicitly declared in the source:

```
{$R earth.res}
```

Don't try to combine EARTH.BMP with the default THREAD2.RES resource file. Let Delphi handle THREAD2.RES, and you can create your own resource.

> **NOTE**
>
> If do not have any experience with resource files, this subject is covered in some depth in Chapter 10, "Dialogs and Resources." The preceding resource file is so simple that you are unlikely to have trouble with it. However, if you can't get it to compile, just use the copy of the EARTH.RES file that ships with this book. If you can't find EARTH.RES, you could also try copying EARTH.RC and EARTH.BMP into the Delphi 2.0\bin subdirectory, and then running BRCC32.EXE from there. Once again, the whole subject of compiling from the command line is covered in Chapter 10.

Here is the code that loads the bitmap from the resource file:

```
EarthMap := LoadBitmap(hInstance, 'Earth');
GetObject(EarthMap, sizeof(Windows.TBitMap), @BStruct);
AWidth := BStruct.bmWidth;
AHeight := BStruct.bmHeight;
```

The LoadBitmap function is a Windows API routine that snags a bitmap from the resource that resides in the executable whose hInstance you pass in the first parameter. The name you gave the bitmap in the resource file is passed in the second parameter. For instance, here is the code for the resource:

```
Earth BITMAP "earth.bmp"
```

In this case you called the resource Earth, which is the first word in the preceding line. You therefore retrieve this resource by passing the word Earth in the second parameter to LoadBitmap.

The call to GetObject retrieves the following structure, declared in WINDOWS.PAS:

```
TBitmap = packed record
  bmType: Longint;        // Type of bitmap, always zero
  bmWidth: Longint;       // The width in pixels of the bitmap
  bmHeight: Longint;      // The height in pixels of the bitmap
  bmWidthBytes: Longint;  // Number of bytes in each scanline
  bmPlanes: Word;         // The number of color planes
  bmBitsPixel: Word;      // Number of bits per pixel
  bmBits: Pointer;        // A pointer to the actual bits
end;
```

In this case, the Thread2 program is concerned only with the width and height of the current bitmap, so it saves those values in global variables called AWidth and AHeight.

This original bitmap from the resource is shown in the upper-left corner of the screen. It is placed there by a call to DrawBitmap from the OnPaint handler:

```
procedure TForm1.DrawBitmap(PaintDC: HDC; Bitmap: HBitMap;
                            XVal, YVal: Integer);
var
  MemDC: HDC;
  OldBitmap: HBitmap;
begin
  MemDC := CreateCompatibleDC(PaintDC);
  OldBitmap := SelectObject(MemDC, Bitmap);
  BitBlt(PaintDC, XVal, YVal, AWidth,
         AHeight, MemDC, 0, 0, SRCCOPY);
  SelectObject(MemDC, OldBitmap);
  DeleteObject(MemDC);
end;
```

This is the traditional method of painting a bitmap, and it is relatively fast. There is, however, no reason not to use a Delphi TBitmap object if you find that approach easier. The preceding code starts by creating a device context compatible with the screen's device context:

```
MemDC := CreateCompatibleDC(PaintDC);
```

This means that it creates a device context that knows how to work with your video card and your monitor.

The next step is to select the bitmap into this newly created device context:

```
OldBitmap := SelectObject(MemDC, Bitmap);
```

Notice that the code saves the original bitmap stored in the new device context. This original bitmap is probably only a very small one pixel by one pixel image, but you need to conserve the resources associated with the bitmap.

The next step is to Blt the bitmap from the newly minted device context to the screen's device context:

```
BitBlt(PaintDC, XVal, YVal, AWidth,
       AHeight, MemDC, 0, 0, SRCCOPY);
```

BitBlt is declared like this in WINDOWS.PAS:

```
function BitBlt(
  DestDC: HDC;                 // Device context of screen.
  X, Y: Integer;               // Where on screen to blit.
  Width, Height: Integer;      // Width and height of bitmap.
  SrcDC: HDC;                  // Device context that contains the bitmap.
  XSrc: Integer;               // Location in the source
  YSrc: Integer;               // bitmap from which to blt.
  Rop: DWORD):                 // Logical operation to perform when blitting.
  BOOL; stdcall;               // Use GetLastError if it returns False.
```

After blitting the bitmap to the screen, you need to first restore the old bitmap into the newly created device context

```
SelectObject(MemDC, OldBitmap);
```

and then dispose of the new device context because it is no longer needed:

```
DeleteObject(MemDC);
```

Remember, you wouldn't ever want to dispose of the screen device context, because it is going to be needed throughout the life of the program.

The preceding call to DrawBitmap could be easily converted into a general purpose utility routine by changing the header so that it accepted the width and height of the bitmap:

```
procedure DrawBitmap(PaintDC: HDC; Bitmap: HBitMap;
                     XVal, Yval, AWidth, AHeight: Integer);
```

A copy of this procedure is found on disk in UTILBOX.PAS from the UNITS subdirectory.

Using Threads in the Thread2 Program

I could have made additional copies of the bitmap by blitting it to the screen multiple times in different locations. However, in this case I didn't want to do things the fast way. Instead, I wanted things to go slowly so you could watch a thread at work. In other words, I didn't want the thread to be over before it had seemingly begun, which is what would have happened if I had called BitBlt from inside each of the three secondary threads in the program.

So instead of BitBlt, I had each of the secondary threads read the original bitmap, one pixel at a time, and then copy it, again one pixel at a time, to another portion of the screen:

```
for j := 0 to AHeight do
  for i := Margin to AWidth + Margin do begin
    P := GetPixel(DC, i, j);
    SetPixel(DC, i + Data^.Xpos, Data^.YPos + j, P);
  end;
```

This time-consuming process has the side benefit of being fun to watch.

So now you understand the core of the Thread2 program. A bitmap is blitted to the screen. Three threads are started. Each of the threads laboriously copies the original bitmap to the screen, one pixel at a time.

You probably noticed that the Thread2 program also created a button and an edit control. If you enter a number in the edit control, you will find that pressing the program's button gives you its square root. In fact, the program starts out with an outrageously high number (4 GB) in the edit control. If you press the button several times, this number has its square root taken multiple times, until you start approaching the number 1.

What's interesting about the Thread2 program is not that it knows how to get a square root. (It's a given that a computer can do that for you.) What's amazing is that you can be asking it to calculate square roots at the same time that all three threads are busy copying the original bitmap.

The point here is that there is no apparent degradation in the way the button and edit control respond. The computer is obviously very busy copying pixels, yet it always lets you type in numbers and calculate square roots almost exactly as it would if you had the entire CPU to yourself. This is what preemptive multitasking is all about. When the time slices for the secondary threads are up, the processor is given over to the other threads on the system. No delay or degradation of performance is apparent to the user. The computer appears to be doing at least four things at the same time. In fact, for all practical purposes, it *is* doing four things at the same time!

The Thread2 program takes advantage of the lpParameter parameter of CreateThread, as shown by the Data parameter in the following code sample:

```
hThread1 := CreateThread(nil, 0, @ThreadFunc,
                         Data, 0, ThreadID);
```

The thread function is called ThreadFunc, and the parameter passed to it is of type PData:

```
PData = ^TData;
TData = record
  XPos: Integer;
  YPos: Integer;
end;
```

The x and y fields of this structure are used to designate the point at which each thread should start its copy of the picture.

Now here's the interesting part. Suppose you declared Data to be a global variable. Then suppose you assigned this global variable a starting x and y location for a picture, and passed it to a thread. Then suppose you assigned this same variable a new value and started a new thread. When you assigned the global variable a new value, it automatically changed the value passed to the first thread. This means that the first thread would now start painting at the place where the second picture should be, rather than in the place you originally asked it to paint. (One way around this type of problem is to use something called *thread local storage*, but that is beyond the scope of this book.)

As you saw in the last paragraph, simply declaring a global variable is not a solution to the problem presented by these three threads. A second possible idea would be to declare the Data variable as local to the StartMenu method, which is the method called when the Start menu item is selected. However, if you did this you would get into even deeper trouble. Specifically, you would assign the variable a value, then pass it to the thread. At that point the StartMenu method would go out of scope, and the value that the thread was trying to use would suddenly disappear from underneath it. So this alternative won't work either.

A third alternative, and the one used in this program, involves using pointers. First allocate memory for a variable, then pass it to the first thread. Next allocate memory for a second variable, and pass it to the second thread. Finally, you could allocate memory for a third variable, and pass it in to the third thread. Each thread is responsible for disposing the memory passed in to it. Each variable would of course contain a different set of coordinates:

```
procedure TForm1.StartMenu(Sender: TObject);
var
  hThread1, hThread2, hThread3: THandle;
  ThreadID: DWORD;
  Data: PData;
begin
  New(Data);
  Data^.xPos := AWidth;
  Data^.YPos := 0;
  hThread1 := CreateThread(nil, 0, @ThreadFunc,
                          Data, 0, ThreadID);

  New(Data);
  Data^.xPos := 0;
  Data^.YPos := AHeight;
  hThread2 := CreateThread(nil, 0, @ThreadFunc,
                          Data, 0, ThreadID);

  New(Data);
  Data^.xPos := AWidth;
  Data^.YPos := AHeight;
  hThread3 := CreateThread(nil, 0, @ThreadFunc,
                          Data, 0, ThreadID);

  if ((hTHread1 = 0) or (hThread2 = 0) or (hThread3 = 0)) then
    MessageBox(Handle, 'No Thread!', nil, mb_Ok);
end;
```

The preceding code calls New three times, once for each copy of the PData structure. The calls to New allocate memory for the PData structure. The code assigns values to the structure's fields and then passes them into the appropriate thread.

Given the scenario outlined earlier, each thread is then responsible for deallocating the structure passed in to it:

```
function ThreadFunc(Ptr: Pointer): LongInt; stdcall;
var
  i, j: Integer;
  P: TColorRef;
  DC: HDC;
  Data: PData;
begin
  Data := PData(Ptr);
  DC := GetDC(Form1.Handle);
  for j := 0 to AHeight do
    for i := Margin to AWidth + Margin do begin
      P := GetPixel(DC, i, j);
      SetPixel(DC, i + Data^.Xpos, Data^.YPos + j, P);
    end;
  ReleaseDC(Form1.Handle, DC);
  Dispose(Data);
end;
```

The relevant call in this case is the last one, where the Data variable is disposed of.

The process described here shows one way of handling data that is passed in to a thread. The issue here is that you have one thread but create three instances of it. This means you have to create three separate instances of the data you pass in to it.

As it turns out, the basic problem of how a thread handles data is one that has many implications. As a rule, the issues surrounding this subject are categorized under a topic called thread synchronization. The reason they are given this name becomes clear in just a moment.

Critical Sections: Getting Threads to Work Together

The classic problem encountered when using threads involves a piece of global data that is being accessed by more than one thread. Variations on this theme involve a series of threads, all of which have to access the same file, the same DLL, the same communications resource, or any of a number of different objects.

To take a classic database-related problem, imagine what would happen if two threads were accessing the same database. Suppose one of them opened a record and made some changes to the record's data. Then suppose a second program came along and made some changes to a different part of the same record and wrote them to the database. Now the first program writes its changes to the database, and in the process effectively undoes the changes made by the second program.

This scenario described in the last paragraph is a classic, and very familiar, problem as it would apply to thread synchronization. There are many different variations on this type of problem, and many different solutions to them. The programs you are about to see use critical sections and mutexes to resolve this problem.

Critical sections solve the problem described earlier by effectively blocking the second thread from accessing the sensitive data when it is being used by the first thread. In particular, it stops the second thread from executing by ensuring that it doesn't get any time slices. The parallel in the database world would be locking a record, but the analogy is not exact.

The mechanisms involved in this process are not hard to understand. Critical sections are a simple solution to what sounds like a fairly complex problem. Go ahead and get the CritSect program, shown in Listing 7.4, up and running. After you read the description of how it works, you'll see that this whole issue is easy to resolve.

Listing 7.4. The main module of the CritSect program.

```
unit main;

interface

uses
  Windows, Messages, SysUtils,
  Classes, Graphics, Controls,
  Forms, Dialogs, StdCtrls, Menus;

const
  TotalCount = 20;

type
  TForm1 = class(TForm)
    ListBox1: TListBox;
    ListBox2: TListBox;
    MainMenu1: TMainMenu;
    Options1: TMenuItem;
    RunThread1: TMenuItem;
    CritSects1: TMenuItem;
    procedure FormCreate(Sender: TObject);
    procedure FormDestroy(Sender: TObject);
    procedure RunThread1Click(Sender: TObject);
    procedure CritSects1Click(Sender: TObject);
  end;

var
  Form1: TForm1;

implementation

{$R *.DFM}

var
  CritSects: Boolean;
  Sect1: TRTLCriticalSection;
  GlobalData: Integer;

//////////////////////////////////////////////////////////
// The thread routine
//////////////////////////////////////////////////////////
function ThreadFunc1(P: Pointer): LongInt; stdcall;
var
```

```
  i, j: Integer;
  S: string;
begin
  Form1.ListBox1.Items.Clear;

  for j := 0 to TotalCount do begin
    if (CritSects) then EnterCriticalSection(Sect1);
    Sleep(3);
    Inc(GlobalData, 3);
    i := GlobalData - 3;
    S := Format('Information: %d', [i]);
    SendMessage(Form1.ListBox1.Handle, lb_AddString, 0, LongInt(S));
    Dec(GlobalData, 3);
    if (CritSects) then LeaveCriticalSection(Sect1);
  end;
  Result := 0;
end;

//////////////////////////////////////////////////////
// The thread routine
//////////////////////////////////////////////////////
function ThreadFunc2(P: Pointer): LongInt; stdcall;
var
  i, j: Integer;
  S: string;
begin
  Form1.ListBox2.Clear;

  for j := 0 to TotalCount do begin
    if (CritSects) then EnterCriticalSection(Sect1);
    Sleep(3);
    Dec(GlobalData, 3);
    i := GlobalData + 3;
    S := Format('Information: %d', [i]);
    SendMessage(Form1.ListBox2.Handle, lb_AddString, 0, LongInt(S));
    Inc(GlobalData, 3);
    if (CritSects) then LeaveCriticalSection(Sect1);
  end;

  Result := 0;
end;

procedure TForm1.FormCreate(Sender: TObject);
begin
  InitializeCriticalSection(Sect1);
  CritSects := False;
end;

procedure TForm1.FormDestroy(Sender: TObject);
begin
  DeleteCriticalSection(Sect1);
end;

procedure TForm1.RunThread1Click(Sender: TObject);
var
  ThreadID1: DWord;
  ThreadID2: DWord;
```

continues

Listing 7.4. continued

```
  ThreadHandles: array [0..1] of THandle;
begin
  GlobalData := 100;

  ThreadHandles[0] := CreateThread(nil, 0, @ThreadFunc1,
                      nil, 0, ThreadID1);

  ThreadHandles[1] := CreateThread(nil, 0, @ThreadFunc2,
                      nil, 0, ThreadID2);

  if (ThreadHandles[0] = 0) or (ThreadHandles[1] = 0) then
    MessageBox(Handle, 'No Thread', nil, MB_OK);
end;

procedure TForm1.CritSects1Click(Sender: TObject);
begin
  CritSects1.Checked := not CritSects1.Checked;
  CritSects := CritSects1.Checked;
end;

end.
```

The CritSect program has a single window with two list boxes and a menu. If you select the Run Thread menu item, the list boxes are filled with numbers, as shown in Figure 7.3.

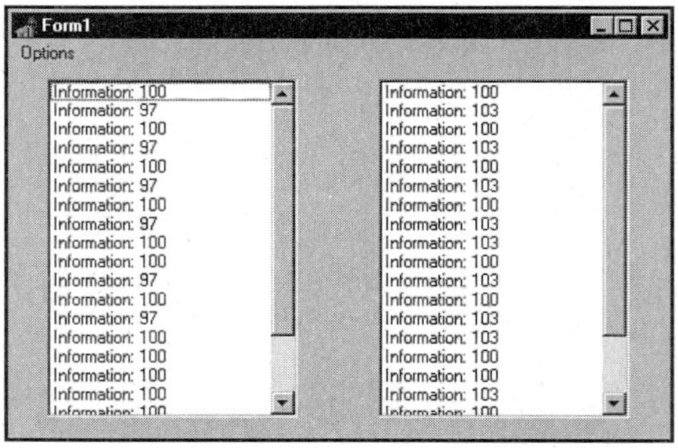

FIGURE 7.3.

The CritSect program as it appears when its threads are not synchronized.

As you can see, the two columns of numbers are not identical. For reasons that are explained in just a moment, this is the way the program appears when its threads are not synchronized. If you selected the Toggle CritSections menu and then choose Run Thread a second time, you see that the two columns are now identical in appearance, as shown in Figure 7.4. For reasons that are explained shortly, this is the way program looks when its threads are synchronized.

FIGURE 7.4.

The CritSect program as it appears when its threads are synchronized.

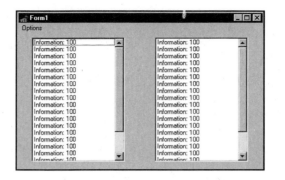

The CritSect program has a single global variable called GlobalData, which is of type Integer. Each thread in the program manipulates this global data and then restores it to its original value. For instance, the first thread adds 3 to this number, then sets a second variable called i to the new value GlobalData - 3, and then shows the number in the first list box:

```
Inc(GlobalData, 3);
    i := GlobalData - 3;
    S := Format('Information: %d', [i]);
    SendMessage(Form1.ListBox1.Handle, lb_AddString, 0, LongInt(S));
    Dec(GlobalData, 3);
```

If you add 3 to a number, and then subtract 3 from that same number, it should be restored to its original value. In fact, one would have to be living in a very non-Euclidean, non-linear world if adding 3 to a number and then subtracting it out did not take you back to the original number. 100 plus 3 equal 103, and 103 minus 3 equals 100. That's all there is to it, and there's no point in talking about the matter any further—except for the fact that when the CritSect program tries to do this, sometimes it gets 100, and sometimes it gets 97.

> **NOTE**
>
> In the example shown above, I can typecast S as a LongInt because it is a long string. You cannot use the exact same syntax with ShortStrings, the issue being that ShortStrings have a length byte at position zero. This length byte would confuse Windows.

The other thread in the program, the one that writes to the second list box, does the exact opposite thing. It subtracts 3 from 100, and then adds 3 back to the new number. Obviously this process would have to yield 100 as a result each and every time. That's the way the universe is put together, and that's the way things have to be. Only it doesn't turn out that way. Instead of getting the result you would expect, there are times when you do not get 100, but 103. Clearly there is something very wrong here.

What's going on is not some metaphysical curiosity, but only the kind of complication that ensues when two threads are accessing and manipulating the same data. Specifically, one thread adds 3 to the global data, thereby setting it equal to 103. Then the second thread accesses the data and subtracts 3 from it, thereby setting it equal to 100. When the second thread then adds back the 3 that it took away, the result is not 100, but 103. Or conversely, when the first thread subtracts 3 back out, it gets not 100, but 97. It's all a matter of timing.

As you can see, what's happening here is the same type of problem that I described when I talked about two threads simultaneously accessing the same record. The problem is one of synchronization. One thread needs to be able to tell the other that the global data is in a sensitive or critical state and that it shouldn't be touched!

Clearly, this is what critical sections are all about. They are a way of designating that a particular piece of data is currently off-limits and can't be touched.

The implementation of the solution to this problem is extremely literal minded. What you do is mark the blocks of code that manipulate the data as "critical sections." Before the code in these sections can be executed, the computer has to check a global record that records whether another thread is currently in the middle of a critical section. (Furthermore, it checks to see if this critical section is related to the first critical section. That is, you could have different sets of critical sections in the same program.)

Here's how it works. In the OnCreate handler, the CritSect program initializes a variable of type TRTLCriticalSection:

```
Sect1: TRTLCriticalSection;
InitializeCriticalSection(Sect1);
```

> **NOTE**
>
> It's not really important what TRTLCriticalSection looks like, but you can in fact find the structure defining its type in WINDOWS.PAS:
>
> ```
> TRTLCriticalSection = record
>   DebugInfo: PRTLCriticalSectionDebug;
>   //  The following three fields control entering
>   //  and exiting the critical
>   //  section for the resource
>   LockCount: Longint;
>   RecursionCount: Longint;
>   OwningThread: THandle;
>   LockSemaphore: THandle;
>   Reserved: DWORD;
> end;
> ```

Here is how you mark a section of code as a critical section:

```
EnterCriticalSection(Sect1);
...
// First swatch of Critical code appears here ...
```

```
...
LeaveCriticalSection(Sect1);
```

The moment `EnterCriticalSection` is passed `Sect1`, it sets one or more of its field to reflect the fact that a critical section is active. Now, if a second critical section is called by another thread, `EnterCriticalSection` can see that a critical section is active, so it puts the second thread to sleep:

```
EnterCriticalSection(Sect1);
...
// Second swatch of Critical code appears here ...
...
LeaveCriticalSection(Sect1);
```

While the second thread is asleep, it does not get any time slices. It's marked as inactive and the CPU wastes no time trying to call it. This is an extremely efficient system, and very few clock cycles are wasted by a process that has been put to sleep.

When the first critical section exits, `LeaveCriticalSection` is called. The variables in Sect1 are then changed, and the second thread is free to execute. The second thread immediately enters its own critical section, thereby preventing the first thread from executing the offending code. At this stage, the two critical sections in this program end up swapping back and forth, with each given a chance to execute while the other waits.

By using the process described earlier, you can mark the areas where a thread accesses the `GlobalData` variable as critical. Therefore, only one thread is able to access the data at a time. This effectively solves the problem. When the critical sections are active, the program always produces the results you would expect, as shown in Figure 7.4.

When you are through using a variable of type `CRITICAL_SECTION`, you should always delete it:

```
DeleteCriticalSection(Sect1);
```

This is an important step because it frees up system resources. However, you want to be sure that you do not call `EnterCriticalSection` or `LeaveCriticalSection` with an invalid variable. To do so causes an exception.

I have spent a fair amount of time on critical sections only because they are probably a new concept to most readers. They were new to me when I first saw them in Windows 95. As a result, I have tried to explain them in some depth, even though the concepts behind them are quite simple. As I said earlier, the whole issue of synchronization at least seems like a fairly complex problem. However, the solution to the problem is very simple. Critical sections are easy to use.

Working with Mutexes

Mutexes are very similar to critical sections, except they work not only in one process, but in multiple processes at the same time. In other words, they can help to synchronize not only two or more threads in a single application, but two or more threads that might reside in separate applications.

Mutexes get their name from the words "mutually exclusive." Only one thread can own a mutex at a time. If a thread owns that mutex, the mutex is said to be *signaled*. If no thread owns the mutex, the mutex is said to be *non-signaled*. (This is confusing terminology for a very simple concept. If you want, you can just think of the mutex as being owned or free.)

To create a mutex, you call `CreateMutex`. Here is the `CreateMutex` syntax:

```
function CreateMutex(
  lpMutexAttributes: PSecurityAttributes; // address of security attributes
  bInitialOwner: BOOL;                    // flag for initial ownership
  lpName: PChar):                         // address of mutex-object name
  THandle; stdcall;                       // If Result = 0, use GetLastError
```

The first parameter is a structure that defines the security attributes for the mutex. If you set this field to `nil`, the mutex is assigned a default set of security attributes. For more information on this field, see the online help.

The second parameter specifies whether the mutex is owned by the calling thread. An owned mutex is signaled, and an unowned mutex is non-signaled. You can use this parameter to specify whether the mutex should go immediately into the signaled state.

The final parameter is used to give the mutex a name. If one process creates a mutex and gives it a name, then a second process attempts to create or open a mutex of the same name, it gets the same mutex back in return. The two processes can then use the mutex to synchronize their actions. You can pass in `nil` in this parameter if you like. This produces an unnamed mutex.

Here's an example:

```
hMutex := CreateMutex(nil, FALSE, nil);
```

Listing 7.5 shows the Mutex program. It is nearly identical to the CritSect program. The only difference is that the Mutex program uses mutexes rather than critical sections.

Listing 7.5. The main module for the Mutex program.

```
unit main;

interface

uses
  Windows, Messages, SysUtils,
  Classes, Graphics, Controls,
  Forms, Dialogs, StdCtrls,
  Menus;

const
  TotalCount = 20;

type
```

```
  TForm1 = class(TForm)
    ListBox1: TListBox;
    ListBox2: TListBox;
    MainMenu1: TMainMenu;
    Options1: TMenuItem;
    RunThread1: TMenuItem;
    UseMutex1: TMenuItem;
    procedure FormCreate(Sender: TObject);
    procedure FormDestroy(Sender: TObject);
    procedure RunThread1Click(Sender: TObject);
    procedure UseMutex1Click(Sender: TObject);
  end;

var
  Form1: TForm1;

implementation

{$R *.DFM}

var
  UseMutex: Boolean;
  hMutex: THandle;
  GlobalData: Integer;

//////////////////////////////////////////////////////
// The thread routine
//////////////////////////////////////////////////////
function ThreadFunc1(P: Pointer): LongInt; stdcall;
var
  i, j: Integer;
  S: string;
begin
  Form1.ListBox1.Items.Clear;

  for j := 0 to TotalCount do begin
    if (UseMutex) then WaitForSingleObject(hMutex, INFINITE);
    Sleep(3);
    Inc(GlobalData, 3);
    i := GlobalData - 3;
    S := Format('Information: %d', [i]);
    SendMessage(Form1.ListBox1.Handle, lb_AddString, 0, LongInt(S));
    Dec(GlobalData, 3);
    if (UseMutex) then ReleaseMutex(hMutex);
  end;
  Result := 0;
end;

//////////////////////////////////////////////////////
// The thread routine
//////////////////////////////////////////////////////
function ThreadFunc2(P: Pointer): LongInt; stdcall;
var
  i, j: Integer;
  S: string;
begin
  Form1.ListBox2.Clear;
```

continues

Listing 7.5. continued

```
  for j := 0 to TotalCount do begin
    if (UseMutex) then WaitForSingleObject(hMutex, INFINITE);
    Sleep(3);
    Dec(GlobalData, 3);
    i := GlobalData + 3;
    S := Format('Information: %d', [i]);
    SendMessage(Form1.ListBox2.Handle, lb_AddString, 0, LongInt(S));
    Inc(GlobalData, 3);
    if (UseMutex) then ReleaseMutex(hMutex);
  end;

  Result := 0;
end;

procedure TForm1.FormCreate(Sender: TObject);
begin
  hMutex := CreateMutex(nil, False, nil);
  UseMutex := False;
end;

procedure TForm1.FormDestroy(Sender: TObject);
begin
  CloseHandle(hMutex);
end;

procedure TForm1.RunThread1Click(Sender: TObject);
var
  ThreadID1: DWord;
  ThreadID2: DWord;
  ThreadHandles: array [0..1] of THandle;
begin
  GlobalData := 100;

  ThreadHandles[0] := CreateThread(nil, 0, @ThreadFunc1,
                       nil, 0, ThreadID1);

  ThreadHandles[1] := CreateThread(nil, 0, @ThreadFunc2,
                       nil, 0, ThreadID2);

  if (ThreadHandles[0] = 0) or (ThreadHandles[1] = 0) then
    MessageBox(Handle, 'No Thread', nil, MB_OK);
end;

procedure TForm1.UseMutex1Click(Sender: TObject);
begin
  UseMutex1.Checked := not UseMutex1.Checked;
  UseMutex := UseMutex1.Checked;
end;

end.
```

As I stated earlier, the Mutex and CritSect programs are nearly identical. In fact, from the user's point of view, their behavior is indistinguishable.

Mutex calls `CreateMutex` in the part of the `OnCreate` handler where CritSect called `InitializeCriticalSection`. Instead of calling `EnterCriticalSection`, the Mutex program calls `WaitForSingleObject`. Instead of calling `LeaveCriticalSection`, the Mutex program calls `ReleaseMutex`:

```
if (UseMutex) then WaitForSingleObject(hMutex, INFINITE);
Sleep(3);
Inc(GlobalData, 3);
i := GlobalData - 3;
S := Format('Information: %d', [i]);
SendMessage(Form1.ListBox1.Handle, lb_AddString, 0, LongInt(S));
Dec(GlobalData, 3);
if (UseMutex) then ReleaseMutex(hMutex);
```

`WaitForSingleObject` takes two parameters. The first is the handle to a mutex, and the second is the number of milliseconds the function should wait before returning. `WaitForSingleObject` returns only if the mutex becomes signaled, or if the time specified has elapsed. That is, it returns when it owns the mutex or when the time interval specified in the second parameter elapses. If you pass in the `INFINITE` flag in this parameter, the routine returns only when the mutex is signaled. (There is a function called `WaitForMultipleObjects`. The name says it all, although you can look up the particulars in the online help.)

When a thread is finished with a mutex it should call `ReleaseMutex`, which takes a handle to a mutex as a parameter. After the call to `ReleaseMutex`, the mutex is free, and other code that has been waiting to own the handle can now execute. It's a bit like passing a baton between teams of runners. The ones that own the mutex run, and the others wait for it to be passed to them.

When you are completely done with a mutex and don't need it any more, you should close it:

```
CloseHandle(hMutex);
```

NOTE

Both the Mutex and the CritSect program call the `Sleep` function. `Sleep` suspends the execution of a thread for a specified number of milliseconds. A value of `INIFINITE` causes the thread to sleep for an indefinite period of time.

I call `Sleep` in the Mutex and CritSect program because I want to exaggerate the two threads' innate lack of synchronicity. In other words, I use this call to force the two threads out of sync so that it is almost certain that they will not both normally print out 100 each time. Because I use the function, the chance of coincidental synchronicity between the two threads is low. This means I have to use critical sections or mutexes to get them in line.

Threads and the VCL

With a few crucial exceptions, the VCL in Delphi 2.0 is not thread-safe. The reason for this is simply that making it thread-safe would make it both bigger and slower. In particular, critical sections or mutexes would have to be wrapped around certain portions of the VCL code. The sheer number of these sections would be so great that the VCL would end up being noticeably bigger and slower. To avoid this situation, a compromise of some kind had to be reached, and that compromise is called the TThread object.

> **NOTE**
>
> Code that is not thread-safe is code that will be corrupted if it gets called at random times. The CritSect program, when run without the CritSects optioned turned on, is not thread safe. The data it uses because corrupt, as you can see from the out put in the listboxes. When you turn CritSects on, the program becomes thread safe, and the data displayed in the listboxes is valid. This is, however, a relatively benign example of non-thread-safe code. If you try to call the visual elements of VCL from inside a thread, you will almost certainly end up crashing your program sooner or later. The crash will not, however, necessarily occur right away.

The TThread object gives you two big advantages:

- It provides a Synchronize function that enables you to make calls to the VCL from inside a thread.
- It provides an alternative to thread local storage that is literally about ten times faster to use.

Synchronize is a method of the TThread object. You wrap it around the call to a method that is going to call the VCL. For instance, if you access the VCL from inside a function called ShowData, you should call ShowData like this:

```
Synchronize(ShowData);
```

As a rule, the only way you can call the VCL inside a thread is to use the Synchronize method. In particular, Synchronize performs some hand waving that essentially makes your thread a temporary part of the main thread of the application. During this time, you can access the VCL. The moment you don't need the VCL anymore, you should break out of the synchronized section of your code. Your program will then once again have multiple threads.

The point is that most of the VCL is not thread-safe, so you can't access it while you are in a thread. Period. That's it. The solution, then, is to call Synchronize, which in effect puts a temporary end to you thread and makes it part of the main thread for the application. During this time, you can call the VCL. The moment your call to the VCL is finished, you should break out of the synchronized section of your code. The function gets its name because it synchronizes your thread with the main thread of the application.

In general, descendants of TComponent are not thread-safe. There are, however, some big parts of the VCL that do not descend from TComponent. For instance, there are no TComponent descendants anywhere in CLASSES.PAS.

> **NOTE**
>
> This is one of the early occasions in this book when I am going to remind you of the importance of having the source to the VCL. I return to this theme a number of times, but the key point to grasp is that really good Delphi programmers almost all have a copy of the VCL. The VCL ships with some versions of Delphi, and it is available as an up-sell directly from Borland or possibly from some third-party shops such as the Programmers Shop (1-800-421-8006) or Programmer's Paradise (1-908-389-9228). It is also possible that you have some files that have an INT extension on your system. Look for CLASSES.INT, for instance. This file would have the interface to CLASSES.PAS, but not the implementation.

Here are some of the objects declared in CLASSES.PAS:

```
TList
TStrings
TStringList
TStream
TFileStream
TMemoryStream
TFiler
TReader
TWriter
TBits
TParser
TComponent
```

It's safe to use these classes, as well as TObject or the exception classes, in a thread. You could even design your own thread-safe TComponent descendants if you were very careful and knew exactly what you are doing.

If you think about it for a moment, it becomes obvious that at least part of the VCL has to be thread-safe. For instance, the TThread object itself is part of the VCL, and obviously it is thread-safe. It's just a question of learning what you can and can't do.

The key to creating a thread-safe TComponent descendant would be judicious use of critical sections or mutexes. In other words, if you wrapped all the dangerous sections of your TComponent object in a critical section, you could access it in a thread. Clearly this is a big opportunity for some third parties to come along and make some hay while the sun shines. You need to work quickly, however, because the VCL might well be thread-safe in future versions.

Most of the rest of the VCL is out of bounds, with yet a few more key exceptions. One of the most important exceptions is calling the open methods of TQuery, TDatabase, and TTable objects. If you create a session in a thread using the TSession object, you could hook a TTable object to it and open that table in a thread. While you are opening the table, you should not have the TTable object attached to anything else, including a TDataSource. The moment the open procedure finishes, you could hook up the thread to a grid in a Synchronize method.

The point here is that you could compose a complex query, put it in the SQL property of a TQuery object that is part of a thread, and then call Open. While all those calculations are going on in the background, you could use the main thread of your program, or other threads of your program, to interact with the user. The moment the SQL statement was through executing, you could pop the results into a grid or other data-aware control and show them to the user.

The *TThread* Object

The following short example, found in Listings 7.6, 7.7, and 7.8, shows how to use the TThread object. It is based on the Thread1 example shown earlier. The program has two threads. One thread is designed correctly; the other is designed incorrectly. By studying the difference between the two threads you will see how to use the TThread object.

Listing 7.6. The Thread1a program shows how to use the VCL object called TThread.

```
unit main;

{ Copyright 1996 by Charlie Calvert

  Example program shows how to use TThread object
  that ships with Delphi.

  Using the TThread object makes the VCL thread
  safe. }

interface
```

```
uses
  Windows, Messages, SysUtils,
  Classes, Graphics, Controls,
  Forms, Dialogs, StdCtrls,
  MyThrd1, MyThrd2, Buttons, ExtCtrls;

const
  wm_ThreadDone = wm_User + 0;

type
  TForm1 = class(TForm)
    bGoodThread: TButton;
    bBadThread: TBitBtn;
    Memo1: TMemo;
    Panel1: TPanel;
    procedure bGoodThreadClick(Sender: TObject);
    procedure bBadThreadClick(Sender: TObject);
    procedure FormCreate(Sender: TObject);
    procedure GoodThreadDone(Sender: TObject);
    procedure BadThreadDone(Sender: TObject);
  private
    BadThread: TBadThread;
    T2: TMyThread2;
    procedure ButtonsOff(Setting: Boolean);
  end;

var
  Form1: TForm1;

implementation

{$R *.DFM}

procedure TForm1.ButtonsOff(Setting: Boolean);
var
  i: Integer;
begin
  for i := 0 to ComponentCount - 1 do
    if Components[i] is TButton then
      TButton(Components[i]).Enabled := not Setting;
end;

procedure TForm1.bBadThreadClick(Sender: TObject);
begin
  ButtonsOff(True);
  BadThread := TBadThread.Create(False);
  BadThread.OnTerminate := BadThreadDone;
end;

procedure TForm1.bGoodThreadClick(Sender: TObject);
begin
  ButtonsOff(True);
  T2 := TMyThread2.Create(False);
  T2.OnTerminate := GoodThreadDone;
end;

procedure TForm1.GoodThreadDone(Sender: TObject);
```

continues

Listing 7.6. continued

```
begin
  T2.Free;
  ButtonsOff(False);
  ShowMessage('On Terminate for Thread 2 received');
end;

procedure TForm1.BadThreadDone(Sender: TObject);
begin
  BadThread.Free;
  ShowMessage('On Terminate for Bad Thread received');
end;

procedure TForm1.FormCreate(Sender: TObject);
const
  S = 'Press the Good Thread button and you will find that you can move ' +
      'the window around, or resize it, while the thread is running. Press ' +
      'the Bad Thread button and you will find that the window is inert ' +
      ' while the thread is running.';
begin
  Memo1.Text := S;
end;

end.
```

Listing 7.7. How not to use the TThread object.

```
unit mythrd1;

{ An example of how NOT to use the TThread object. }

interface

uses
  Classes, Windows;

type
  TBadThread = class(TThread)
  private
    procedure RunUpdate;
  protected
    procedure Execute; override;
  end;

implementation

uses
  Main, SysUtils;

{ TBadThread }

procedure TBadThread.RunUpdate;
var
  i: Integer;
```

```
begin
  for i := 1 to 20000 do begin
    Form1.Panel1.Caption := IntToStr(i);
    Form1.Panel1.Update; // Wouldn't have to do this in good thread
  end;
end;

procedure TBadThread.Execute;
begin
  Windows.InvalidateRect(Form1.Handle, nil, True);
  Synchronize(RunUpdate);
  PostMessage(Form1.Handle, wm_ThreadDone, 1, 0);
end;

end.
```

Listing 7.8. The correct way to use the TThread object.

```
unit mythrd2;

{ Simple TThread object example. Thread is used properly. }

interface

uses
  Classes;

type
  TMyThread2 = class(TThread)
  private
    FCount: Integer;
    procedure RunUpdate;
  protected
    procedure Execute; override;
  end;

implementation

uses
  Main, SysUtils, Windows;

procedure TMyThread2.RunUpdate;
begin
  Form1.Panel1.Caption := IntToStr(FCount);
end;

procedure TMyThread2.Execute;
var
  i: Integer;
begin
  Windows.InvalidateRect(Form1.Handle, nil, True);
  for i := 1 to 20000 do
    if i mod 10 = 0 then begin
      FCount := i;
      Synchronize(RunUpdate);
```

continues

Listing 7.8. continued

```
    end;
  PostMessage(Form1.Handle, wm_ThreadDone, 2, 0);
end;

end.
```

This program has two buttons on it. If you press the button labeled Bad Thread, you will start a thread that is poorly designed. In particular, while it is running you will find that it takes up all the cycles allocated to the program. You can't do anything else in the program while this thread is running. The second button in the program, labeled Good Thread, enables you to move or resize the program while it is running. It is a well-behaved thread.

Here is the declaration for the TThread object in CLASSES.PAS:

```
TThread = class
  private
    ...
protected
    procedure DoTerminate; virtual;
    procedure Execute; virtual; abstract;
    procedure Synchronize(Method: TThreadMethod);
    property ReturnValue: Integer read FReturnValue write FReturnValue;
    property Terminated: Boolean read FTerminated;
  public
    constructor Create(CreateSuspended: Boolean);
    destructor Destroy; override;
    procedure Resume;
    procedure Suspend;
    procedure Terminate;
    function WaitFor: Integer;
    property FreeOnTerminate: Boolean read FFreeOnTerminate write FFreeOnTerminate;
    property Handle: THandle read FHandle;
    property Priority: TThreadPriority read GetPriority write SetPriority;
    property Suspended: Boolean read FSuspended write SetSuspended;
    property ThreadID: THandle read FThreadID;
    property OnTerminate: TNotifyEvent read FOnTerminate write FOnTerminate;
  end;
```

The key methods in this object are as follows:

```
Create
Execute
Synchronize
```

The Create method is meant to start and run the thread. It doesn't just allocate memory for the thread, it actually creates and calls the thread:

```
constructor TThread.Create(CreateSuspended: Boolean);
var
  Flags: Integer;
begin
  inherited Create;
```

```
    … // Additional code
    FHandle := CreateThread(nil, 0, @ThreadProc, Pointer(Self),
                            Flags, FThreadID);
end;
```

As you can see, the thread is actually running by the time the Create method has ended. Notice that the object passes itself as a parameter to the thread. The thread function (ThreadProc) does little more than call the Execute routine.

If you go back and look at the declaration for Execute, you can see that it is declared as abstract. This means that it is never implemented. It is up to you to implement the Execute method by overriding it. In essence, the Execute method becomes the thread function itself!

Whenever you use a TThread object, you first create a descendant of it:

```
TMyThread2 = class(TThread)
private
  FCount: Integer;
  procedure RunUpdate;
protected
  procedure Execute; override;
end;
```

Every time you create a descendant of a TThread object, you override the Execute method. That's a given. In the case shown here, I have also included an FCount variable and a procedure called RunUpdate.

Here is the implementation of TMyThread2, which is the "good" thread in the Thread1a example:

```
procedure TMyThread2.RunUpdate;
begin
  Form1.Panel1.Caption := IntToStr(FCount);
end;

procedure TMyThread2.Execute;
var
  i: Integer;
begin
  Windows.InvalidateRect(Form1.Handle, nil, True);
  for i := 1 to 20000 do
    if i mod 10 = 0 then begin
      FCount := i;
      Synchronize(RunUpdate);
    end;
  PostMessage(Form1.Handle, wm_ThreadDone, 2, 0);
end;
```

The purpose of this code is simply to count from 1 to 100,000 while regularly updating the user as to the status of the operation.

The thread begins by clearing the screen. It doesn't do this by calling the internal VCL function called Invalidate. Instead, it calls the Windows API function called InvalidateRect. The reason for this is simple: Invalidate is a method of TForm, and as such is out of bounds to call inside a thread. That's no big deal—you can just call InvalidateRect instead.

After clearing the screen, the code iterates through a loop 100,000 times. Each time it completes ten cycles of the loop it prints out the current iteration to the screen with a standard VCL routine:

```
Form1.Panel1.Caption:= IntToStr(FCount);
```

It does not, however, call the VCL directly. Instead it wraps the function inside a method call RunUpdate, and it wraps the call to that function inside a method call Synchronize:

```
Synchronize(RunUpdate);
```

While Synchronize is executing, your thread temporarily becomes part of the main thread for the executable. This means that the main thread for the program is temporarily halted. It is not running. Instead, your thread is running. As soon as the Synchronize method is finished, the thread resumes.

The point here is that when Synchronize is called, the main thread is not running, and therefore the VCL cannot be receiving any other messages. This means that it is safe for you to call the VCL during the time that Synchronize is executing.

The key point to remember is that you want to get out of the Synchronize procedure as quickly as possible. The moment you are through executing the VCL statement, you get out of the Synchronize method.

Here is how not to do it:

```
procedure TBadThread.RunUpdate;
var
  i: Integer;
begin
  for i := 1 to 20000 do begin
    Form1.Panel1.Caption := IntToStr(i);
    Form1.Panel1.Update; // Wouldn't have to do this in good thread
  end;
end;

procedure TBadThread.Execute;
begin
  Windows.InvalidateRect(Form1.Handle, nil, True);
  Synchronize(RunUpdate);
  PostMessage(Form1.Handle, wm_ThreadDone, 1, 0);
end;
```

In this case, the entire loop executes inside the call to Synchronize. This might seem like the right thing to do, because most of the time spent in the loop is dedicated to updating the main screen of the program. The flaw in this theory, however, is that the main thread of the application never gets a chance to execute while Synchronize is being called. As a result, the program doesn't really have two threads running, it has just one. The secondary thread has taken over the main thread, thereby rendering the whole enterprise worthless. It isn't really a bug, and it doesn't threaten the stability of the program, but it's a classic case of poor design. (Not that you should feel bad if you have done this. Needless to say, I wouldn't have the example here to present if I hadn't fallen in this trap once myself!)

There are a couple of other things I ought to say about the TThread object before closing this section. Notice, for instance, that the code specifies a method to be called when the thread is terminated:

```
T2.OnTerminate := GoodThreadDone;
```

Here is how to write the GoodThreadDone procedure:

```
procedure TForm1.GoodThreadDone(Sender: TObject);
begin
  T2.Free;
  ButtonsOff(False);
  ShowMessage('On Terminate for Thread 2 received');
end;
```

Notice that the signature for the procedure takes a single parameter of type TObject. This is the standard TNotifyEvent that is used in response to OnClick events, and in many other places in Delphi. You create this function yourself, typing out the entire declaration by hand, rather than having the IDE create it for you automatically. Inside the method you need do nothing more than free the thread itself, and handle any other cleanup chores that you might want to specify. In particular, the code shown above sets the buttons to valid values and uses a message box to let the user know that the thread has terminated.

A trap that you need to avoid involves the WaitFor method of TThread. This method enables the main program to wait until the thread finishes executing. It is a serious error to call WaitFor if the thread is going to call Synchronize. Then you end up with a deadlock where the thread waits for the main program and the main program waits for the thread. In the meantime, nothing happens, and you are forced to shut the program down through the IDE or through Ctrl+Alt+Del. In Delphi, a call to WaitFor under these circumstances should raise an exception.

In this section you have seen how to use the TThread object to run a thread. The two key points to remember about the TThread object are that it gives you a safe way to call the VCL while a thread is running and it gives you way to create local variables that are used only by the thread. These variables are the fields of your TThread descendant. Windows also provides a technique for doing this called Thread Local Storage. TLS is a powerful technique, but is, literally, about ten times slower than using a TThread object to obtain the same end.

Setting a Thread's Priority

Not all threads need to be created equal. You can set a thread's priority level so that it gets more or less CPU cycles than other threads. The call to set a thread's priority level is called SetThreadPriority. (There is a SetPriority method in the TThread object.)

The actual number of cycles a thread gets depends on its priority level and the priority class of its process. You can call GetPriorityClass to get the priority of your process, and SetPriorityClass to set the priority of your process. All of the functions mentioned in this paragraph are Windows API routines.

The program shown in Listing 7.9 was written by David Intersimone, a fellow Borland employee. The code has some historical significance, as it was written on the flight to the Windows 95 launch in Seattle. The fact that David was able to do some serious coding on a West Coast shuttle flight shows that almost anything is possible if you set your mind to it!

Listing 7.9. David Intersimone's Dreaded Sorts program. This program needs two other blank forms saved in units called SecForm and ThForm.

```
unit main;

{
  Dreaded Sorts
  copyright (c) 1996 by David Intersimone

  This example program shows how to set a thread's priority.
}

interface

uses
  SysUtils, WinTypes, WinProcs,
  Messages, Classes, Graphics,
  Controls, Forms, Dialogs,
  StdCtrls, ComCtrls, Buttons;

const
  aMax = 300;

type
  TForm1 = class(TForm)
    Edit1: TEdit;
    Label2: TLabel;
    Label1: TLabel;
    Label3: TLabel;
    Label4: TLabel;
    Label5: TLabel;
    BitBtn1: TBitBtn;
    BubbleTrackBar: TTrackBar;
    QuickTrackBar: TTrackBar;
    procedure Button1Click(Sender: TObject);
  private
    T1 : THandle;
    T2 : THandle;
  end;

var
  Form1: TForm1;
  a,b : array[0..aMax-1] of integer;
  numItems : integer;

implementation

uses
  secform, thform;

{$R *.DFM}
```

```
procedure BubbleSort(var ia:array of integer; items: integer);
var
  i,j,t : integer;
  DC: HDC;
begin
  DC := GetDC(Form2.Handle);
  for i := items downto 0 do
  begin
    for j := 0 to items-1 do
      if ia[j] < ia[j+1] then
      begin
        t := ia[j];
        SetPixel(DC, ia[j+1]+5, j+1+5, clBlue);
        SetPixel(DC, ia[j]+5, j+5, clBlue);
        ia[j] := ia[j+1];
        ia[j+1] := t;
        Setpixel(DC, ia[j+1]+5,j+1+5, clYellow);
        Setpixel(DC, ia[j]+5,j+5, clYellow);
      end;
  end;
  ReleaseDC(Form2.Handle, DC);
end;

procedure QuickSort(var ia:array of integer; iLo,iHi : integer);
var
  Lo,Hi,Mid,T : integer;
  DC: HDC;
begin
  Lo := iLo;
  Hi := iHi;
  mid := ia[(Lo+hi) div 2];
  repeat
    DC := GetDC(Form3.Handle);
    while ia[Lo] < mid do Inc(Lo);
    while ia[Hi] > mid do Dec(Hi);
    if Lo <= Hi then
    begin
      T := ia[Lo];
      SetPixel(DC, ia[Lo]+5,Lo+5, clBlue);
      SetPixel(DC, ia[Hi]+5,Hi+5, clBlue);
      ia[Lo] := ia[Hi];
      ia[Hi] := T;
      SetPixel(DC, ia[Lo]+5,Lo+5, clLime);
      SetPixel(DC, ia[Hi]+5,Hi+5, clLime);
      inc(Lo);
      dec(Hi);
    end;
  until Lo > Hi;
  if Hi > iLo then QuickSort(ia,iLo,Hi);
  if Lo < iHi then QuickSort(ia,Lo,iHi);
  ReleaseDC(Form3.Handle, DC);
end;

function BubbleThread(parms:pointer) : LongInt; far;
begin
  BubbleSort(a,numItems-1);
end;
```

continues

Listing 7.9. continued

```
function QuickThread(parms:pointer) : LongInt; far;
begin
  QuickSort(b,0,numItems-1);
end;

procedure TForm1.Button1Click(Sender: TObject);
var
  i : integer;
  ThreadID : dWord;
begin
  numItems := strToInt(Edit1.Text);
  if numItems <= aMax then
  begin
    form2.free;
    form2 := TForm2.Create(self);
    form2.top := 140;
    form2.left := 2;
    form2.clientheight := numItems+10;
    form2.clientwidth := numItems+10;
    form2.color := clBlue;
    form2.caption := 'Bubble Sort';
    form2.show;

    form3.free;
    form3 := TForm3.Create(self);
    form3.top := 140;
    form3.left := 320;
    form3.clientheight := numItems+10;
    form3.clientwidth := numItems+10;
    form3.color := clBlue;
    form3.caption := 'Quick Sort';
    form3.show;

    Randomize;
    for i := 0 to numItems-1 do
    begin
      a[i] := random(numItems);
      b[i] := a[i];
      form2.canvas.pixels[a[i]+5,i+5] := clYellow;
      form3.canvas.pixels[b[i]+5,i+5] := clLime;
    end;
    T1 := createThread(nil,0,@BubbleThread,nil,0,threadID);
    setThreadPriority(T1, BubbleTrackBar.Position);
    T2 := createThread(nil,0,@QuickThread,nil,0,threadID);
    setThreadPriority(T2, QuickTrackBar.Position);
  end
  else
    Form1.Caption := 'Too Large!';
end;

end.
```

The Dreaded Sorts program creates two threads. One thread runs a bubble sort and the second runs a quick sort. If you want, you can use trackbars to adjust the priority of the bubble sort upward, so that it gets lots of clock cycles, while simultaneously lowering the priority of the quick sort. The end result is that the bubble sort finishes in about the same time as the quick sort, even thought it is a much slower algorithm. The two extra blank forms used by the project visually depict the progress of the sorts, as shown in Figure 7.5.

FIGURE 7.5.

The bubble sort, shown on the left, is naturally slower than the quick sort, shown on the right.

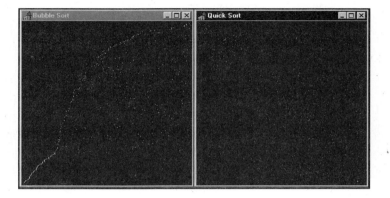

The key code in this program looks like this:

```
T1 := createThread(nil,0,@BubbleThread,nil,0,threadID);
SetThreadPriority(T1, BubbleTrackBar.Position);
T2 := createThread(nil,0,@QuickThread,nil,0,threadID);
SetThreadPriority(T2, QuickTrackBar.Position);
```

Here you can see both sorts being created. Each thread is assigned a priority by the SetThreadPriority function:

```
function SetThreadPriority(
  hThread: THandle;      // The handle of the thread.
  nPriority: Integer):   // The threads priority.
  BOOL; stdcall;         // Call GetLastError if the function fails
```

The following constants can be passed in the second parameter of SetThreadPriority:

```
THREAD_PRIORITY_LOWEST = THREAD_BASE_PRIORITY_MIN;
THREAD_PRIORITY_BELOW_NORMAL = THREAD_PRIORITY_LOWEST + 1;
THREAD_PRIORITY_NORMAL = 0;
THREAD_PRIORITY_HIGHEST = THREAD_BASE_PRIORITY_MAX;
THREAD_PRIORITY_ABOVE_NORMAL = THREAD_PRIORITY_HIGHEST - 1;
THREAD_PRIORITY_ERROR_RETURN = MAXLONG;
THREAD_PRIORITY_TIME_CRITICAL = THREAD_BASE_PRIORITY_LOWRT;
THREAD_PRIORITY_IDLE = THREAD_BASE_PRIORITY_IDLE;
```

Here are the constants you can use to help make sense of the values shown earlier:

```
THREAD_BASE_PRIORITY_LOWRT = 15;{ value that gets a thread to LowRealtime-1 }
THREAD_BASE_PRIORITY_MAX = 2;   { maximum thread base priority boost }
THREAD_BASE_PRIORITY_MIN = -2;  { minimum thread base priority boost }
THREAD_BASE_PRIORITY_IDLE = -15;{ value that gets a thread to idle }
```

Related functions that you should look up in the online help include SetPriorityClass and GetPriorityClass.

Delphi Threads Revisited

You have seen that even fairly sophisticated manipulation of threads is not difficult. Using the information presented in this book, you can add a great deal of powerful thread technology to your programs. However, I would be careful not to make your whole program nothing but a series of threads. If you get too carried away, you are likely to get into some very complicated design problems. Use threads when you need them, and when you can see how they fit into your program from beginning to end. Try to avoid creating programs that become a mangled tangle of threads. This could become a new form of spaghetti code called Mangled Tangled code! Avoid it.

Clearly, this is a revolutionary subject that is going to change the way you write code. In particular, on multiprocessor systems, different threads can end up in effect executing on different processors, which is an enormously powerful concept. Just imagine one Pentium Pro executing your graphics code, while the second parses a spreadsheet, and the third opens an SQL query! In the future you might have even have threads executing on separate machines, with one machine working on one part of your program, while a second machine works on another part!

The information presented here is complete in itself, and it can serve as a reliable basis for using threads in an application. However, it is not the whole story, and you should pursue the matter further if you are interested in the subject and its possibilities. In particular, the major subject I did not have time to cover here was thread local storage, though I did mention that the TThread object serves as a more than adequate substitute for this technology. You can find out more about Thread Local Storage in Jeffrey Richter's book, *Advanced Windows*, published by Microsoft Press.

Summary

When working with threads, you saw how to create single threads. You also saw how to allocate memory so that you can pass in data to a single thread that has multiple copies of itself running at one time. You also saw the reverse of this process: how to synchronize multiple threads so that they can all share access to a single block of data. In particular, you studied critical sections and mutexes.

You also got a good look at the TThread object that's part of the Delphi VCL. The TThread object enables you to use both the VCL and threads at the same time. This statement is somewhat misleading, in that there are no inherent conflicts between the VCL and threads, and indeed, the TThread object is very much a part of the VCL. However, most of the TComponent descendants are not compatible with threads. There are some exceptions, such as the TOpenDialog component, which works properly as long as it is created in code. The TQuery and TTable objects also work inside threads, as long as you handle them properly. However, most visual VCL objects won't work inside threads unless you use the TThread object.

Win32 Memory Management

8

In this chapter you get a look at memory-management issues under Windows 95 and Windows NT. In particular, you get a look at:

- The structure of memory in the four-gigabyte (4 GB) Win32 address space
- Creating, freeing, and using heaps
- Memory-mapped files
- Virtual memory and, particularly, the `VirtualAlloc` and `VirtualFree` functions

This chapter is a companion piece to the previous chapter, "Multitasking and Threads." The last chapter concentrated on multitasking and threads; this chapter concentrates on memory management. Put the two sides of the story together and you have a fairly clear picture of the most important features in Win32. These chapters show why Windows 95 and Windows NT are so important, and how they differ from Windows 3.1.

The end of this chapter provides a brief bit of Object Pascal code that shows how to manipulate a Delphi memory manager. This code is relatively straightforward when compared to the rest of the material in this chapter, but it helps to emphasize the power of Delphi, and the artfulness of its design. The subject fits in with the rest of the chapter because it involves memory management.

Win32 Memory Management at a Glance

This book teaches you how to program Windows. Once you understand how to write Windows applications, the next step is to learn the theory behind Windows so that you can improve the scope and design of your applications. The remainder of this chapter holds valuable information, but it is also a pointer toward those more-advanced realms that would be a natural next step in your exploration of Win32.

Win32 memory management is as different from Win16 memory management as a lion is from a house cat. They are two different beasts, and it is wrong to assume that knowledge of 16-bit, protected-mode memory applies to Windows 95 or Windows NT.

Let me say this again, just for the sake of clarity: the Win32 memory-management scheme is totally different from the memory-management scheme in 16-bit Windows. It uses different calls, has a different structure, uses different ranges of memory, and has several major new features that are different from anything you had in the old 16-bit world. For instance, in Win32:

- Each 32-bit process has a 4 GB, flat memory-model address space. That is, it has a nonsegmented architecture. Contrast this with Windows 3.1, where all processes share a single address space in a segmented architecture. Remember that you can think of a process as an executable or DLL loaded into memory, as explained in the beginning of this chapter.

■ Each program has only one type of heap, but it can have multiple copies of these heaps, and can create them on-the-fly. This enables you to isolate one set of objects from another. For instance, you can place a linked list in its own heap, where it can endanger only itself and no other parts of your program. Contrast this with Windows 3.1, where each program had two heaps: the local heap and the global heap.

■ Each Win32 heap belongs to one, and only one, process. There is no such thing as a global, shared heap in a 32-bit Windows 95 process. Contrast this with Windows 3.1, where each application has a local heap and then shares a single global heap with every other application on the system. The single Windows 3.1 global heap contained memory allocations not only from the current task, but from all the tasks on the system. It was a huge stew of different kinds of allocations from different kinds of programs, all mixed together in one potentially dangerous concoction. (Note also that the lack of Win32 local heaps means that DLLs no longer can be used to share memory between processes—at least, not by using the same techniques exploited in Windows 3.1.)

■ There is a powerful set of routines for manipulating virtual memory. Virtual memory is treated just like normal memory, but you can keep it either in RAM or in a "paging file" that is stored on disk. You can call the VirtualAlloc function to allocate memory in that paging file. You then can read and write to this memory. Reserving virtual memory and writing to it is called *committing physical storage*. Use VirtualAlloc to reserve or commit physical storage, and VirtualFree to decommit physical storage.

■ Win32 supports memory-mapped files, which can help you share memory between applications and also access files on disk. The system uses memory-mapped files to load executables and DLLs. As their name implies, memory-mapped files enable you to map a file on the disk into the address space of your program. It is then possible to manipulate the file using standard library routines, such as memcpy and even strcpy.

These points make it clear that Win32 has not one, but three different ways of handling memory. The first is through virtual memory, the second is through memory-mapped files, and the third is through heaps. Large arrays of data can usually be best stored in virtual memory. If you need to share memory between processes, or if you need to work with large streams of data (files), you can use memory-mapped files. If you want to create a linked list, or some similar structure that requires lots of small memory allocations, you probably should use the heap.

As you can see, there's more to Windows 95 memory management than just the bare presence of a 4GB address space. Furthermore, you can see that your program doesn't just get loaded into the bottom of this 4GB space. Nor does it then proceed to use the remaining 3.9 GB for its personal playground. Instead, in Windows 95, your program usually gets loaded in at the 4MB mark, and at least half of the rest of the address space is reserved for the system. In Windows NT, programs usually get loaded in at the 64KB mark, and can range up to within 64 KB of the 2GB mark. The two 64 KB blocks are used to trap errant pointers.

Windows 3.*x* had three possible modes of operation: real mode, standard mode, and enhanced mode. Windows 95 does not support either real mode or standard mode when running Windows applications. (It does support DOS real-mode programs running in a virtual DOS box.) Take this limitation as part and parcel of your vision of Windows 95 as a true 32-bit operating system. Real mode and standard mode are ways of handling 16-bit applications. By their definition they are tied to applications that have very limited address spaces. Windows 95 is about wide-open address spaces.

You'll be glad to hear that most of the key 16-bit Windows memory-management routines port over to Windows 95 applications. However, they are available just for compatibility, and are inefficient when compared to the new memory calls. In particular, the old `GlobalAlloc` call has been replaced with `HeapAlloc`, `VirtualAlloc`, and memory-mapped files. For compatibility reasons, `GlobalAlloc` still works. However, it is not as efficient as `HeapAlloc` or `VirtualAlloc`. Furthermore, there is no longer any distinction between `GlobalAlloc` and `LocalAlloc`. Both calls end up allocating memory from the process's primary heap. But I'm getting ahead of myself.

> **NOTE**
>
> People who argue that Windows 95 is just a thin veneer over a bunch of 16-bit DOS calls are ignoring some very important aspects of this new operating system. Yes, there still are portions of Windows 95 that are 16-bit. However, the memory model for Windows 95 is totally different from Windows 3.1. What computer programs do is manipulate memory. Every significant API or Delphi library call made on a computer ends up manipulating memory in one way or another. You can't even make the call without manipulating memory. If the memory model has changed radically, then everything has changed radically.
>
> It's interesting to study the similarities between Windows 95 and Windows 3.1, but it's a gross misstatement of the facts to claim that they are just two versions of the same operating system. I can be as cynical about Windows 95 as the next guy. But look again at the list of new Win32 memory features near the top of this section. Say what you will, Windows is in the big leagues now. Windows 95 is a real operating system, and a powerful one at that. The mere presence of some 16-bit code does not cancel out the extraordinary developments in multithreading and multitasking described in Chapter 7, "Multitasking and Threads," and in memory management shown earlier.

This section has given you a general overview of some of the key points about Win32 memory management. Further information is available in advanced books on Windows programming, or on the Microsoft Developer Network CD.

Why You Don't Need to Understand This Stuff

Memory management is an extremely important topic. However, Windows 95 has such a huge address space that it's often not important for intermediate-level Windows programmers to master the subject. In 16-bit Windows, everyone had to know at least something about memory management. If you didn't understand the DGROUP and 64KB segments, you were going to get in trouble.

Why is Windows 95 different? Part of the reason is that each process has its own 4GB address space. A gigabyte is one billion bytes, or a thousand megabytes. A megabyte is a million bytes. DOS programs used to run in one megabyte of memory. In other words, you can fit 4,000 DOS machines inside one 4GB address space. Back in the 1980s, you could have powered several hundred medium-sized companies with 4,000 DOS machines.

A program's data and code both are loaded into a 2GB virtual address space. This means that you're not going to run out of code and data space in your programs. The whole subject of code segments and data segments is essentially moot for intermediate-level Windows programmers. You just don't have to worry about it. (OK, you have to worry about whether the machines you are running on have enough physical RAM to give your programs reasonable performance. However, there usually is no practical reason to be concerned that you will exceed the limits of the operating system. It's possible, but not likely.)

Furthermore, each process, and each thread in that process, by default gets its own 1MB stack. (It's exactly 1 MB in Windows NT, and 1 MB plus 128 KB in Windows 95.) In the past, you always had to be thinking about the size of the stack in your application. Now, by default, you get a stack that is 1 MB. Most of the time a 1MB stack is going to give you all the memory you need, and then some. Managing stacks in Windows 3.1 often was a subtle and difficult process that nearly every programmer had to consider to some degree. Now most programmers can simply ignore the subject, and the system takes care of it automatically.

> **NOTE**
>
> The only reason there's a 1MB limit on the size of the stack is to catch runaway recursive processes before they get totally out of control.
>
> *Recursive* functions call themselves. Every time they call themselves, information is pushed on the stack. A recursive process should end automatically after it reaches some predefined goal. However, sometimes something goes wrong and the recursive process keeps calling itself over and over again, pushing more data on the stack with each call. Because the stack has a 1MB limit, the operating system has a chance to automatically stop this process before it consumes all the memory on the system.

250

The key point to understand is that most Windows 95 programmers don't have to worry a great deal about memory management under most circumstances. Advanced programmers need to understand this subject; indeed, an in-depth understanding of this subject is what defines advanced Windows programmers. If you want to be really good, you should know this stuff cold.

So yes, it's always good to know about memory. However, if you don't, you are not nearly as likely to get bit by Windows 95 or Windows NT as you were by Windows 3.1. When compared to Windows 3.1, Win32 gives you more power and more freedom, with less work and less anxiety.

A Closer Look at the 4GB Virtual Address Space

As I stated earlier, each program that you create has a virtual address space of 4 GB. The reason this number is chosen is that a 32-bit value can hold a number between 0 and 4 GB. In decimal notation, that's 0 to 4,294,967,296; in hex, that's $0 to $FFFFFFFF.

If you have trouble counting all those Fs in 4 GB, remember that there are eight of them, twice as many as in a 16-bit system. Here's 16 bits: $FFFF; here's 32 bits: $FFFF-FFFF, where I've put a dash in the middle of the 32-bit number to show that it is twice as large as the 16-bit number. Don't let that dash confuse you by making you think that Win32 is in any sense a segmented architecture. It is not. It's one single, flat address space of 4 GB. If the 16-bit world had been a flat address model, the most memory we could have had on our machines is 64 KB, which is 65,535 in decimal or $FFFF in hex. There's a fair amount of difference between 65,535 and 4,294,967,296.

Just because Win32 has a flat memory model does not mean that this memory is totally undifferentiated. For instance, both Windows 95 and Windows NT have different schemes for creating partitions in this memory. In Windows 95:

- The bottom 4 MB of memory are reserved for maintaining compatibility with MS-DOS and Windows 3.1. The bottom 4 KB of this region is totally *verbotten*. You can't write to it. The rest of this memory should be left alone by your 32-bit programs, but for technical reasons it is not guarded by Windows. This is one of the weaknesses in Windows 95. The memory should be totally off limits to 32-bit programs.

- The rest of the bottom 2 GB of memory is where your program resides.

- The third gigabyte of memory, $80000000 through $BFFFFFFF, is reserved for the system's DLLs, such as KERNEL32.DLL, USER32.DLL, and GDI32.DLL. This is also the place where memory-mapped files live. I discuss memory-mapped files later in this chapter.

■ The top 1 MB of memory, $C000000 through $FFFFFFF, is home to the operating system and, in particular, the virtual device drivers on which it is based. This memory is not protected by Windows 95, which is another reason that Windows 95 is not as stable as Windows NT.

The Windows NT memory scheme is much simpler. Basically, the bottom 2 GB belong to your program and the top 2 GB belong to Windows. Unlike Windows 95, you simply cannot access the memory in the top 2 GB. It belongs to Windows, which helps to make Windows NT a robust operating system. In fact, the bottom and top 64 KB of that 2 GB owned by your program are also off-limits. In particular, they are there to help catch you when you use nil or errant pointers.

The Theory Behind Allocating Virtual Memory

Gird your loins! This is the tough section of the chapter.

The most fundamental Win32 memory-management routine is `VirtualAlloc`. This is the primary call that allocates memory for use in a program. In more technical terms, Microsoft states that "it reserves or commits a region of pages in the virtual address space of the calling process." *Reserve* and *commit* are not synonyms. They are two different operations, as shown in this section.

As you saw in the last section, the virtual address space of the calling process is 4 GB, but you usually are working with only the bottom 2 GB of that area. Using the `VirtualAlloc` function, you can do two things with this memory: you can reserve it or you can commit it. Reserved regions in memory are just set aside for some part of your program and can't be used by any other allocations your program might make. Committed memory is actually being used by your program. It's physical storage, either in RAM or swapped to disk.

> **NOTE**
>
> You commit physical storage and reserve regions. All regions reserved by your program begin on 64KB boundaries. The size of the region must be a multiple of the page size on your computer. For the Intel architecture, the page size is 4 KB. Physical storage is allocated in pages, where the finest granularity is 4 KB.

Remember that virtual memory is virtual memory whether it's in RAM or swapped to disk. Memory management under Windows 95 or Windows NT is radically different from what it was under Windows 3.1. Win32 is even radically different from enhanced-mode Windows 3.1, which had a swap file.

You can think of physical storage in Win32 as a huge file that resides not so much in RAM as on disk. At times this huge paging file may have certain portions loaded into RAM, but it's just as much at home on your hard disk. In fact, it may be even more at home on your hard disk.

On the Intel architecture, paging files are divided up into pages of 4 KB each. If you ask for only 2000 bytes of memory using VirtualAlloc, the system still returns a full 4096 bytes. That's the size of a page of memory under Windows 95 or Windows NT on the Intel platform. In fact, all Win32 platforms except for the DEC Alpha work in 4KB chunks. The Alpha works in 8KB chunks.

> **NOTE**
>
> Your executable, or a DLL you create, does not reside in a paging file. Instead, it resides in a memory-mapped file.
>
> The allocations you make are from a paging file, but the actual code and data from your program resides in a memory-mapped file. This memory-mapped file is simply sucked into memory in one huge chunk when you first load the program. A region of memory is reserved for your executable, and the committed physical storage for that executable is simply the .EXE file residing on disk. This makes it easy for Windows to commit the memory for an executable!

Each page of memory in a paging file has a protection attribute associated with it. These attributes have names like PAGE_READONLY, PAGE_READWRITE, PAGE_EXECUTE, and so on. You pass in these attributes when you call VirtualAlloc.

Using *VirtualAlloc*

OK, you can take a deep breath now. The hard part is over. Actually, using VirtualAlloc is not nearly as hard talking about what it does.

> **NOTE**
>
> Remember, you don't have to do any of this stuff. If you want to allocate memory, you can use New and Dispose, or you can just declare a big array and work with that. The point of this chapter, and indeed of much of this book, is to let you look beneath the surface to see how Windows and Delphi work behind the scenes. The goal is not just to see how to do a particular job as quickly and easily as possible, but how to become a better programmer!

Here is a simple example of how to use `VirtualAlloc`:

```
P2 := VirtualAlloc(nil, Size, mem_Commit or mem_Reserve, Page_ReadWrite);
DoSomethingWithPointer(P2);
VirtualFree(P2, 0, mem_Release);
```

The code shown here assumes that P2 is declared as a pointer.

Here is the same code with some error checking:

```
P2 := VirtualAlloc(nil, Size, mem_Commit or mem_Reserve, Page_ReadWrite);
if P2 = nil then
  ShowMessage('No allocation');
DoSomethingWithPointer(P2);
if not VirtualFree(P2, 0, mem_Release) then
  ShowMessage('Error freeing memory');
```

The `VirtualAlloc` function takes four parameters:

```
function VirtualAlloc(
  lpvAddress: Pointer;      // Starting address for allocation
  dwSize: DWORD;            // Size of the allocation
  flAllocationType: DWORD;  // mem_Reserve or mem_Commit
  flProtect: DWORD          // page_ReadOnly, page_NoAccess, etc
  ): Pointer; stdcall;      // nil if the allocation fails
```

The first parameter is a suggested location where you might want to allocate memory. In most cases, just pass `nil` in this parameter, and let the system choose the location to allocate the memory.

The second parameter is the size of the allocation. If you are asking to reserve memory, this number is rounded up to 64 KB, even if you ask for less. If you are asking to commit memory, the figure is rounded up to the nearest 4KB boundary, even if you asked for less. (It's 8 KB on an Alpha machine.)

The third parameter specifies the allocation type. You can either reserve memory or commit memory. You cannot access memory that you have reserved. However, neither can any other part of your program. This way you can arrange to reserve a contiguous range of memory without necessarily having to commit it all. This might be useful if you need to allocate a 2MB array, but don't actually use more than a few thousands bytes of the array at one time.

NOTE

Suppose that you were mapping the battle of Gettysburg on a grid. Each cell in the grid might represent a certain area of the battlefield that is 100 yards square. Some of the areas are marked as containing Union troops and some as containing Confederate troops. Most of the squares, however, would be blank. This is an ideal time to explicitly use `VirtualAlloc`. Don't use `New` or `GetMem` in this case; it's time to turn to the Windows API. You can use `VirtualAlloc` to reserve memory for the entire grid, which might be several megabytes in size. Then you can commit memory only for those areas where there actually are troops. The result is that you can use the array syntax, but actually commit only a relatively small portion of the memory to physical storage.

The third parameter describes the type of access you want to have to the memory. As of this writing, Windows 95 supports only PAGE_NOACCESS, PAGE_READONLY, and PAGE_READWRITE.

If the operation succeeds, you get a pointer to some memory back. If it fails, the function returns nil.

You don't necessarily have to reserve memory first and then commit memory later. If you want, you can perform both actions at the same time:

```
P2 := VirtualAlloc(nil, Size, mem_Commit or mem_Reserve, Page_ReadWrite);
```

In this case, I use an or operation on the mem_Commit and mem_Reserve flags, which is the approach suggested by the Microsoft documentation. However, I appear to have the same results if I pass in only the mem_Commit flag.

The program in Listing 8.1, called VirtAll, performs some experiments with the VirtualAlloc function. In particular, it allocates some memory, and then displays some facts about that memory.

Listing 8.1. The VirtAll program explores virtual memory.

```
unit main;

interface

uses
  Windows, Messages, SysUtils,
  Classes, Graphics, Controls,
  Forms, Dialogs, StdCtrls,
  Grids, Buttons, ExtCtrls;

type
  TForm1 = class(TForm)
    SG: TStringGrid;
    Panel1: TPanel;
    bAllocate: TButton;
    bbHInstance: TBitBtn;
    bbMethod: TBitBtn;
    fForm: TBitBtn;
    bDLL: TBitBtn;
    procedure bAllocateClick(Sender: TObject);
    procedure FormCreate(Sender: TObject);
    procedure bbHInstanceClick(Sender: TObject);
    procedure bbMethodClick(Sender: TObject);
    procedure fFormClick(Sender: TObject);
    procedure bDLLClick(Sender: TObject);
  private
    procedure ShowPointer(P: Pointer; Col: Integer; S: string);
  end;

var
  Form1: TForm1;

implementation
```

```
var
  hLIb: THandle;
begin
  hLib := LoadLibrary('USER32.DLL');
  ShowPointer(Ptr(hLib), 7, 'USER32');
  FreeLibrary(hLib);
end;

end.
```

When you run this program, you see several buttons along the bottom of the form, as shown in Figure 8.1. You can press the first button to view information about three addresses, labeled P, P1, and P2. These three addresses are pointers allocated by the program. The HInstance button lets you view information on the HInstance for the program, which is the address at which the program is loaded into memory. The other three buttons enable you to view information on the form, on a function used in the program, and on the HInstance of USER32.DLL, as shown in Figure 8.2.

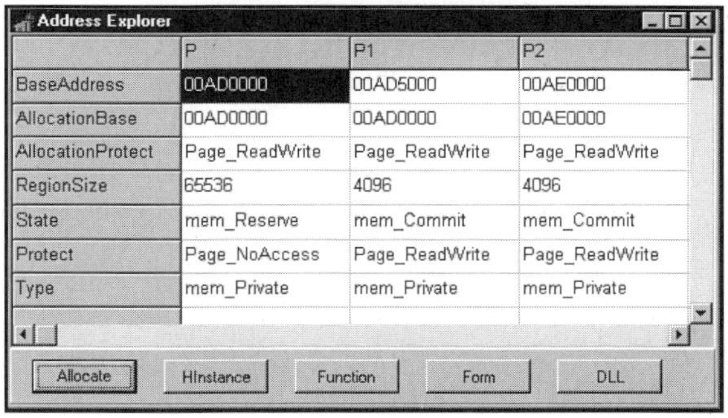

FIGURE 8.1.

The VirtAll program reports information about pointers allocated in a method of Form1.

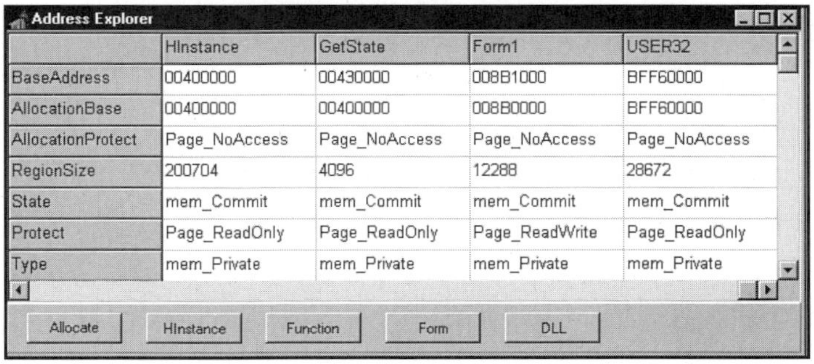

	P	P1	P2
BaseAddress	00AD0000	00AD5000	00AE0000
AllocationBase	00AD0000	00AD0000	00AE0000
AllocationProtect	Page_ReadWrite	Page_ReadWrite	Page_ReadWrite
RegionSize	65536	4096	4096
State	mem_Reserve	mem_Commit	mem_Commit
Protect	Page_NoAccess	Page_ReadWrite	Page_ReadWrite
Type	mem_Private	mem_Private	mem_Private

Allocate HInstance Function Form DLL

FIGURE 8.2.

The VirtAll program reports information about variables used by the system.

	HInstance	GetState	Form1	USER32
BaseAddress	00400000	00430000	008B1000	BFF60000
AllocationBase	00400000	00400000	008B0000	BFF60000
AllocationProtect	Page_NoAccess	Page_NoAccess	Page_NoAccess	Page_NoAccess
RegionSize	200704	4096	12288	28672
State	mem_Commit	mem_Commit	mem_Commit	mem_Commit
Protect	Page_ReadOnly	Page_ReadOnly	Page_ReadWrite	Page_ReadOnly
Type	mem_Private	mem_Private	mem_Private	mem_Private

Allocate HInstance Function Form DLL

Besides the calls to VirtualAlloc and VirtualFree, the VirtAll program also makes calls to VirtualQuery. This function retrieves information on pointers that are passed to it, and any contiguous memory beyond it that has the same attributes:

```
function VirtualQuery(
  lpAddress: Pointer;                      // Pointer you want to know about
  var lpBuffer: TMemoryBasicInformation;  // Record containing requested info
  dwLength: DWORD;                         // Size of TMemoryBasicInformation
  ): DWORD; stdcall;                       // Num Bytes returned in lpBuffer
```

The call to `VirtualQuery` is trivial. What is a bit more difficult is parsing the information retrieved in `lpBuffer`:

```
TMemoryBasicInformation = record
  BaseAddress : Pointer;
  AllocationBase : Pointer;
  AllocationProtect : DWORD;
  RegionSize : DWORD;
  State : DWORD;
  Protect : DWORD;
  Type_9 : DWORD;
end;
```

The `BaseAddress` is a rounded-off version of the address of the variable that you passed in to `VirtualQuery`.

The `AllocationBase` is the address of the reserved area to which the memory belongs. Suppose you first call `VirtualAlloc` with the `mem_Reserve` flag, and then call `VirtualAlloc` with the `mem_Commit` flag. In that case, the `BaseAddress` holds the address at which the variable you are asking about resides, and the `AllocationBase` shows the beginning of the reserved area to which the allocation belongs. I return to this subject in a moment, but you can see examples of this in the columns labeled P1 in Figure 8.1 and GetState in Figure 8.2.

The `AllocationProtect` field shows the protection given to the region when it was initially reserved. This is the reserved region, not the committed physical storage. In other words, when you call `VirtualAlloc` to reserve space for a region, you pass in certain protection flags. This field reports on which flags you passed in.

The `RegionSize` is the size of the allocation.

The `State` field is set to `mem_Reserve`, `mem_Commit`, `mem_Free`, or some combination of these three values.

The `Protect` field is the protection level of the actual memory in question. This is set to `PAGE_READONLY`, `PAGE_READWRITE`, `PAGE_NOACCESS`, and so on.

The `Type_9` field is set to either `mem_Private`, `mem_Image`, or `mem_Mapped`. In Windows 95, it is always `mem_Private`, but in Windows NT you have more scope.

If you press the Allocate button on the main form of the VirtAll program, the following code is the first to execute:

```
S := 'Sam';
  Size := Length(S) + 1;
  P := VirtualAlloc(nil, Size, mem_reserve, Page_ReadWrite);
  ShowPointer(P, 1, 'P');
```

This code is reserving memory, not committing it. Nothing physical happens on the system when you call this function. All it does is reserve a block of virtual memory for use by the pointer variable P.

As you can see by looking at Figure 8.1, the function happened to reserve memory at $00AD0000. The AllocationBase and the BaseAddress are the same in this case because the pointer occupies the same address as its reserved area. The code asks for four bytes of memory, but you can see in Figure 8.1 that VirtualAlloc actually set aside 64 KB. That's the finest resolution you can get when reserving memory. The state for the allocation is mem_Reserve, which makes good sense under the circumstances.

The memory was allocated with the PAGE_READWRITE flag, but you can see the system paid no attention to that request and gave the memory a PAGE_NOACCESS flag. This fact would be born out if you tried to access the memory:

```
Move(S, P^, Size);
```

would raise an exception. It is, therefore, probably better to reserve memory with the PAGE_NOACCESS flag:

```
P := VirtualAlloc(nil, Size, mem_reserve, Page_NoAccess);
```

If you now look at the second allocation made by the program, you see a quite different story:

```
P1 := VirtualAlloc(Ptr(Integer(P) + $5000), Size, mem_Commit, Page_ReadWrite);
ShowPointer(P1, 2, 'P1');
Move(S, P1^, Size);
```

This code allocates four bytes from a block of memory $5000 bytes into the 64KB block of memory reserved by the first call to VirtualAlloc. I first cast P as an integer so that I can perform integer math on the pointer. I then add $5000 to the pointer, which takes me $5000 bytes into the pointer. The next step is to convert this integer value back into a pointer that can be passed to VirtualAlloc. (This code is a stunning example of how cryptic Object Pascal can get under the worst possible circumstances, but at least it does let us do some pointer math.)

When you look at the pointer returned by this call to VirtualAlloc, shown in Figure 8.1, you see that its BaseAddress and AllocationAddress are different. In fact, they are separated by exactly $5000 bytes, which is what you would expect in this case. Both the AllocationProtect and the actual protect for the pointer are set to PAGE_READWRITE. Had I reserved the memory for its region with PAGE_NOACCESS rather than PAGE_READWRITE, the AllocationAddress for both this column and the P column would be set to PAGE_NOACCESS. However, the Protect field for P1 would still be correctly set to PAGE_READWRITE, if that was what I requested. To test this, modify the code on the *Unleashed* CD-ROM so that it passes PAGE_NOACCESS to the first call to VirtualAlloc. By all means, experiment with this code. That's why it's there!

The last of the three allocations does not explicitly reserve any memory, but instead commits four bytes of memory:

```
P2 := VirtualAlloc(nil, Size, mem_Commit or mem_Reserve, Page_ReadWrite);
```

In Figure 8.1 you can see that this appears to create a new allocation, only 4 KB in size. The code asks for PAGE_READWRITE protection, so you get it for both the page that was allocated and the reserved area to which it belongs.

The most interesting thing about this third call to VirtualAlloc is that occurs exactly 64 KB further down the pike from the first call. This shows that Windows is indeed reserving a 64KB block of memory for the pointer called P. VirtAll uses only four bytes of that memory, but still the entire block is reserved. Remember, though, that only four bytes of physical storage were ever committed from that 64KB block. This is virtual memory, and there's a big difference between virtual memory and the physical RAM on your system.

It's important to note that if I allocate another block of memory only four bytes in size immediately after the third allocation, its AllocationBase is set to 64 KB down from the last allocation:

```
P3 := VirtualAlloc(nil, Size, mem_Commit, Page_ReadWrite);
ShowPointer(P3, 4, 'P3');
```

The point is that P2 is really taking up (that is, reserving) 64 KB of virtual memory, although it appears to be taking up only 4 KB. Once again, that's 64 KB of virtual memory that is reserved, but only 4 KB of physical storage is committed. It's wasteful to expend reserved memory to no good effect; nearly as serious as wasting physical storage. You have to grasp the difference between reserving memory and committing memory!

Had I reserved a 64KB chunk of memory, and then committed two four-byte chunks inside of that, it would have taken up only 64 KB of virtual memory rather than 128 KB of virtual memory. In other words, the technique shown for committing the memory for P1 is the right choice to use in this case, and the method shown for the variable called P2 is the wrong choice! If you need to make only one allocation, it's OK to use the P2 technique. If you're going to make several small allocations in a row, reserve some memory first, then commit portions of it as needed!

The following code would place the second 4-byte memory allocation in the same 4KB page as the second allocation shown earlier:

```
P3 := VirtualAlloc(Ptr(Integer(P) + $5004), Size, mem_Commit, Page_ReadWrite);
ShowPointer(P3, 4, 'P3');
```

That means the code allocates only 4 KB of physical storage for two four-byte allocations.

The VirtAll program clearly provides a fascinating platform for exploring virtual memory. Notice that it also takes a look at the whole block of memory allocated for the code and data of your program. It does this by converting HInstance into a pointer, then passing it in to VirtualQuery. You also can obtain the HInstance for USER32.DLL, and then take a look at the memory allocated for that key system file.

When you are through with the memory used in the VirtAll program, you should free it. You can use the mem_Decommit flag to free the memory that you committed at an address inside the first reserved, 64KB region:

```
if not VirtualFree(P1, Size, mem_Decommit) then
  ShowMessage('Error decommitting memory');
```

Notice that you specify the exact amount of memory you want to free.

If you want to free the memory associated with the reserved pointer, you should not specify the amount of memory you want to release:

```
if not VirtualFree(P, 0, mem_Release) then
  ShowMessage('Error freeing memory');
```

Take a moment to compare these two examples. The first uses the mem_Decommit flag, and the second uses the mem_Release flag. One simply frees up some committed memory, while the other actually returns a block of memory to the system. If you are releasing memory that has been reserved, then you don't need to specify the size of the block. The system knows how big the block is and will perform the necessary calculations for you. If you are decommitting memory, you should say how large an area inside the reserved space you want to free.

You also should free the memory that was committed without first reserving a region for it. Do not specify the amount of memory to release:

```
if not VirtualFree(P2, 0, mem_Release) then
  ShowMessage('Error freeing memory');
```

It would, in fact, be an error to attempt to specify the amount of memory to release.

That's all I'm going to say about VirtualAlloc and VirtualFree. Once again, these are the primary means for allocating and deallocating memory in Win32. In Delphi programs, you would normally call New or Dispose, but there are times when you may need to go behind the scenes and use the raw API calls. In particular, VirtualAlloc is a great call to use if you want to reserve a huge amount of memory for an array, but you don't want to actually commit a lot of physical storage. That way you can use the array syntax without having to first physically allocate the whole block of memory that you want to access.

Allocating Memory and Creating Heaps

The next example program, called HeapMem, shows how to allocate memory from a program's default heap. It also shows how to create new heaps when you need them.

Here's a brief overview of the key points covered in this section: You can get the current Win32 heap by calling GetProcessHeap. You can create a new heap by calling CreateHeap, and destroy it by calling HeapDestroy. You can manipulate memory in a heap by calling HeapAlloc, HeapReAlloc, HeapSize, and HeapFree. (HeapFree deallocates a single memory allocation; HeapDestroy destroys the entire heap. Don't get them confused.)

As I explained earlier, heaps don't necessarily play the same role in Windows 95 as they did in Windows 3.1 or DOS. For one thing, you are not nearly as likely to run out of room in your program's address space for data or code. If there is plenty of RAM on your machine, there's plenty of room for even very large amounts of code and data in your program's address space.

Even if there is a shortage of RAM, Windows usually can swap memory to disk to make room for the core parts of your program. You code will run much slower in that case, but it still will run.

If you do need additional room, there's always the virtual memory in your paging file, or you could use memory-mapped files, as described in this section. However, if you want to make a series of relatively small allocations, your program's heap would be a good place to make them.

Your program can have more than one heap. As I've mentioned, you can create and destroy new heaps by calling CreateHeap and HeapDestroy. There are two primary reasons to create a heap:

- You might want to isolate a sensitive memory operation from the rest of the program so that it cannot corrupt the core routines in your code. For example, you could put a linked list in its own heap.

- You might want to optimize routines by placing allocations of similar size in their own unique heap. This helps prevent heap fragmentation, and increases the access time when you need to get at the memory.

Despite the seemingly esoteric nature of this subject, the actual calls to HeapAlloc, HeapFree, CreateHeap, and HeapDestroy are simple enough to master. Listing 8.2 contains a program that exercises each of these calls.

Listing 8.2. The main module for the HeapMem program shows how to work with Win32 heaps.

```
unit main;

interface

uses
  Windows, Messages, SysUtils,
  Classes, Graphics, Controls,
  Forms, Dialogs, StdCtrls,
  Buttons;

type
  TForm1 = class(TForm)
    bDoAlloc: TBitBtn;
    bNewHeap: TBitBtn;
    procedure bDoAllocClick(Sender: TObject);
    procedure bNewHeapClick(Sender: TObject);
  private
    { Private declarations }
  public
    { Public declarations }
  end;

var
  Form1: TForm1;
```

```
implementation

{$R *.DFM}

const
  HEAP_ZERO_MEMORY = $00000008; // Not in WINDOWS.PAS?
  MaxSize = 256;

procedure DoAlloc(hWindow: hwnd; AHeap: THandle; S: string);
var
  ASize: DWord;
  DC: HDC;
  MemStr: PChar;
  AllocStr: string;

begin
  MemStr := HeapAlloc(AHeap, HEAP_ZERO_MEMORY, MAXSIZE);

  StrCopy(MemStr, PChar(S));
  ASize := HeapSize(AHeap, 0, MemStr);
  AllocStr := Format('Alloc Size: %d', [ASize]);

  DC := GetDC(hWindow);
  SetBkColor(DC, GetSysColor(Color_BtnFace));
  TextOut(DC, 10, 10, MemStr, StrLen(MemStr));
  TextOut(DC, 10, 40, PChar(AllocStr), Length(AllocStr));
  ReleaseDC(hWindow, DC);

  if not HeapFree(AHeap, 0, MemStr) then
    ShowMessage('No Heapfree');
end;

procedure DoNewHeap(HWindow: hwnd);
var
  NewHeap: THandle;
begin
  NewHeap := HeapCreate(0, $4000, 0);

  DoAlloc(hWindow, NewHeap, 'Using the new heap  ');

  if not (HeapDestroy(NewHeap)) then
    ShowMessage('No HeapDestroy!');
end;

procedure TForm1.bDoAllocClick(Sender: TObject);
begin
  DoAlloc(Handle, GetProcessHeap, 'Using process heap  ');
end;

procedure TForm1.bNewHeapClick(Sender: TObject);
begin
  DoNewHeap(Handle);
end;

end.
```

This program enables you to print two simple strings to the screen, as shown in Figure 8.3. When you select one of the program's menu options, the memory for the strings is allocated from the default process heap. When you choose the other option, the memory for the strings is allocated from a new, custom heap.

FIGURE 8.3.

The HeapMem program shows how to allocate memory using native Win32 routines.

The following code shows how to allocate memory for a string, how to check the size of the allocation, and how to free the memory:

```
procedure DoAlloc(hWindow: hwnd; AHeap: THandle; S: string);
var
  ASize: DWord;
  DC: HDC;
  MemStr: PChar;
  AllocStr: string;

begin
  MemStr := HeapAlloc(AHeap, HEAP_ZERO_MEMORY, MAXSIZE);

  StrCopy(MemStr, PChar(S));
  ASize := HeapSize(AHeap, 0, MemStr);
  AllocStr := Format('Alloc Size: %d', [ASize]);

  DC := GetDC(hWindow);
  SetBkColor(DC, GetSysColor(Color_BtnFace));
  TextOut(DC, 10, 10, MemStr, StrLen(MemStr));
  TextOut(DC, 10, 40, PChar(AllocStr), Length(AllocStr));
  ReleaseDC(hWindow, DC);

  if not HeapFree(AHeap, 0, MemStr) then
    ShowMessage('No Heapfree');
end;
```

This routine calls `HeapAlloc` to allocate memory, `HeapSize` to check the size of the allocation, and `HeapFree` to free the memory. Here's the declaration for the `HeapAlloc` function:

```
function HeapAlloc(
  hHeap: THandle;     // The handle of the heap you want to use.
  dwFlags: DWORD;     // Flags such as HEAP_ZERO_MEMORY
  dwBytes: DWORD      // The amount of memory you need
  ): Pointer; stdcall; // On failure generates exception or returns nil
```

Use `HeapAlloc` to allocate memory, just as you use `New` or `GetMem`, or `GlobalAlloc` from Windows 3.1. (Well, it's not exactly the same, as you're suballocating the memory from the heap. But it's similar.) The memory allocated may be larger than the amount you request, in which case you can use the entire amount returned. Use the `HeapSize` function to find out how much memory was actually allocated. You do not have to lock down this memory as you did in Windows 3.1. However, this memory is nonmoveable.

The first parameter is the handle to the heap you want to use. To use the default heap for your program, just call GetProcessHeap. If you want to create a new heap, call HeapCreate, as shown later in this chapter.

There are three flags you can pass to this routine in its second parameter. One is HEAP_GENERATE_EXCEPTION, which means that on failure the operating system generates an error rather than returning nil. The HEAP_ZERO_MEMORY flag causes the system to fill the block of memory with zeros. You also can pass in HEAP_NO_SERIALIZE, but this option is beyond the scope of this book.

The last parameter is the size of the block of memory you want to create. In principle, this number can be as large as you want. However, if you want to request large chunks of memory, you should consider calling VirtualAlloc rather than HeapAlloc. Furthermore, requests for large chunks of memory usually are satisfied by the system calling VirtualAlloc automatically, even though you made the request with HeapAlloc. The only concrete limitation on this number occurs if you explicitly called CreateHeap, and you explicitly made the heap you created nongrowable. In that case, this number should not exceed $7FFF8, which is 524,280.

Here's an example:

```
MemStr := HeapAlloc(GetProcessHeap, HEAP_ZERO_MEMORY, 4096);
```

The HeapSize routine returns the size of the current heap allocation. In other words, if you allocate 500 bytes with HeapAlloc and then call HeapSize, the value returned is 500. Remember that Windows sometimes returns more memory than you requested, in which case HeapSize returns a value larger than the amount you requested. It's the value returned by HeapSize that is correct, not the value you requested.

Here is the declaration:

```
function HeapSize(
  hHeap: THandle; // handle to the heap
  dwFlags: DWORD; // heap size control flags
  lpMem: Pointer // The memory you want to query
): DWORD; stdcall;
```

This is a simple function to use. Just pass in a heap in the first parameter, zero in the second parameter, and the pointer you want to know about in the third parameter. (The second parameter can be set to HEAP_NO_SERIALIZE but, as I mentioned earlier, that's an advanced topic not covered in this book.)

Here's the declaration for the HeapFree function:

```
function HeapFree(
  hHeap: THandle; // Value returned by CreateHeap or GetProcessHeap
  dwFlags: DWORD; // usually zero, can be HEAP_NO_SERIALIZE
  lpMem: Pointer // pointer to the memory to free
): BOOL; stdcall; // returns False on failure
```

This function frees memory allocated with HeapAlloc. The first parameter is the handle to the heap. The second usually is set to zero. The third parameter is a pointer to the memory you want to free.

The function returns True when successful.

Here's an example:

```
HeapFree(AHeap, 0, MemStr);
```

The following code fragment shows how to create a new heap:

```
var
  NewHeap: THandle;
begin
  NewHeap := HeapCreate(0, $4000, 0);
  DoAlloc(hWindow, NewHeap, 'Using the new heap  ');
  if not (HeapDestroy(NewHeap)) then
    ShowMessage('No HeapDestroy!');
end;
```

The declaration for HeapCreate looks like this:

```
function HeapCreate(
  flOptions: DWORD;      // heap allocation flag
  dwInitialSize: DWORD;  // initial heap size
  dwMaximumSize: DWORD   // maximum heap size
): THandle; stdcall;     // returns 0 on failure
```

You can pass in zero in the first parameter, or one of the flags HEAP_GENERATE_EXCEPTIONS or HEAP_NO_SERIALIZE. Use HEAP_GENERATE_EXCEPTIONS if you want the operating system to report errors, rather than simply returning nil.

The second parameter is the amount of memory you want to allocate for the heap. If you pass in zero in the third parameter, the heap grows automatically if you request more than dwInitialSize bytes of memory through calls to HeapAlloc. If you do not pass in zero in dwMaximumSize, the heap does not grow, and requests for memory beyond the limits of the heap fail.

When you want to destroy a heap, call HeapDestroy and pass in the handle to the heap as the sole parameter:

```
HeapDestroy(AHeap);
```

This section of the chapter telegraphed to you the information you need to manipulate native Win32 heaps. You now know how to allocate memory, how to free it, and how to create and destroy your own heaps.

Remember that this is not the only way to manipulate memory. Windows 95 and Windows NT also provide memory-mapped files and VirtualAlloc. If you want to allocate very large chunks of memory, then see the description of the VirtualAlloc function in this section. If you want to create a series of small allocations, as in a linked list, use `HeapAlloc` and its related functions. To get started with memory-mapped files, see the next (and last) section of this chapter.

Mapping a File into Memory

Memory-mapped files are one of the more interesting, and powerful, features of the Win32 landscape. They enable you to map the memory on your hard disk into the address space of your program. This means that you can manipulate the bytes in a file as if they resided in memory. Instead of using one set of routines for manipulating files and another set of routines for manipulating memory, you now can use the same set of routines in both places. Furthermore, two processes can map the same file simultaneously, thus giving them a relatively simple way to share memory.

Use `CreateFile` to create or open a memory-mapped file. Use `CloseHandle` to close a memory-mapped file. Other important APIs include `MapViewOfFile`, `UnmapViewOfFile`, and `CreateFileMapping`.

Listing 8.3 shows an example of memory-mapped files. I have to confess that this example does not represent a complete examination of this subject. Instead, my goal is to introduce you to the topic so that you understand what memory-mapped files are all about. After all, seeing is believing—and in this case I think most programmers will be intrigued by what they see. If you're interested in exploring this subject in depth, you should get a book on advanced Windows programming, or else study the Delphi online Help.

Listing 8.3. The main unit for the MemFile program shows how to work with memory-mapped files.

```
unit main;

interface

uses
  Windows, Messages, SysUtils,
  Classes, Graphics, Controls,
  Forms, Dialogs, StdCtrls,
  Buttons;

type
  TForm1 = class(TForm)
    BitBtn1: TBitBtn;
    OpenDialog1: TOpenDialog;
    Memo1: TMemo;
    procedure BitBtn1Click(Sender: TObject);
  private
    hMapping: THandle;
    Data: Pointer;
```

continues

Listing 8.3. continued

```
    function OpenMappedFile(FileName: string;
                           var FileSize: DWORD): Boolean;
  end;

var
  Form1: TForm1;

implementation

{$R *.DFM}

//////////////////////////////////////////////////////////
// Open a map file and prepare to access it
//////////////////////////////////////////////////////////
function TForm1.OpenMappedFile(FileName: string; var FileSize: DWORD): Boolean;
var
  hFile: THandle;
  HighSize: DWORD;
begin
  Result := False;

  if Length(FileName) = 0 then Exit;

  hFile := CreateFile(PChar(FileName), GENERIC_READ,
            FILE_SHARE_READ, nil, OPEN_EXISTING,
            FILE_FLAG_SEQUENTIAL_SCAN, 0);

  if (hFile = 0) then Exit;

  FileSize := GetFileSize(hFile, @HighSize);

  hMapping := CreateFileMapping(hFile, nil, PAGE_READONLY,
                                0, 0, nil);

  if (hMapping = 0) then begin
    CloseHandle(hFile);
    Exit;
  end;

  CloseHandle(hFile);

  Data := MapViewOfFile(hMapping, FILE_MAP_READ, 0, 0, 0);

  if (Data <> nil) then Result := True;
end;

procedure TForm1.BitBtn1Click(Sender: TObject);
var
  Size: Integer;
  S: PChar;
begin
  if OpenDialog1.Execute then begin
    if not OpenMappedFile(OpenDialog1.FileName, Size) then Exit;
    GetMem(S, Size);
    Move(Data^, S^, Size);
    S[Size - 2] := #0;
```

```
    SetWindowText(Memo1.Handle, S);
    if not UnMapViewOfFile(Data) then
      ShowMessage('No unmapping');
    if not CloseHandle(hMapping) then
      ShowMessage('No closing');
    FreeMem(S, Size);
  end;
end;

end.
```

The MemFile program, shown in Figure 8.4, has a standard window, a TMemo object, and one button. If you select the menu item, the program opens a file in read-only mode, reads it into memory, uses move to copy its contents into a string variable, and then sends the file to a memo control with SetWindowText.

FIGURE 8.4.

The MemFile program maps a file from your hard drive into memory.

I should point out that one of the advantages of memory-mapped files is that you can use them to work with huge blocks of memory. In other words, you can open up a file that is several gigabytes in size, and manipulate it using the routines in the MemFile program.

> **NOTE**
>
> Memory-mapped files are powerful enough to work with huge files. However, the MemFile program displays the contents of the file you choose in an edit control, which means this particular program cannot work with huge files. If you want to use these routines with really big files, combine this program with the RichText control.

You should note, however, that it usually doesn't make any sense to map a really big file into memory all at once. Instead, you want to read in sections of the file and then work with these sections one at a time. (You'll find that the routines I show you in the HeapMem example have provisions for this kind of process, although I did not exploit those routines.) In particular, you can specify the offset at which you want to begin mapping a file. You can use this offset to map in chunks of a file at a time. Note, however, the provisions mentioned later in this chapter regarding the granularity of memory allocations.

There are two important routines in the MemFile program. The first prepares the memory-mapped file, and the second reads it into memory and manipulates it. The first routine is called OpenMappedFile. The second is just a button's OnClick handler.

Here is the routine that maps the file into memory:

```
function TForm1.OpenMappedFile(FileName: string; var FileSize: DWORD): Boolean;
var
  hFile: THandle;
  HighSize: DWORD;
begin
  Result := False;

  if Length(FileName) = 0 then Exit;

  hFile := CreateFile(PChar(FileName), GENERIC_READ,
            FILE_SHARE_READ, nil, OPEN_EXISTING,
            FILE_FLAG_SEQUENTIAL_SCAN, 0);

  if (hFile = 0) then Exit;

  FileSize := GetFileSize(hFile, @HighSize);

  hMapping := CreateFileMapping(hFile, nil, PAGE_READONLY,
                        0, 0, nil);

  if (hMapping = 0) then begin
    CloseHandle(hFile);
    Exit;
  end;

  CloseHandle(hFile);

  Data := MapViewOfFile(hMapping, FILE_MAP_READ, 0, 0, 0);

  if (Data <> nil) then Result := True;
end;
```

The routine shown here uses the CreateFile Windows API call to open the file. Because this program displays its output in an edit control, there's a limit on the size of the file you can read.

Here's the lowdown on `CreateFile`:

```
function CreateFile(
  lpFileName: PChar;                              // File Name
  dwDesiredAccess,                                // Read-write access
  dwShareMode: Integer;                           // Can other apps read it?
  lpSecurityAttributes: PSecurityAttributes;      // Security
  dwCreationDisposition,                          // overwrite, truncate, etc
  dwFlagsAndAttributes: DWORD;                     // hidden, system, etc
  hTemplateFile: THandle                          // file with attributes to copy
): THandle; stdcall;                              // INVALID_HANDLE_VALUE on error
```

This is the standard Windows routine for opening and closing files. You don't just use it to create a file: You also can use it to open an existing file. It can also be used with named pipes, communications tools, storage devices, and consoles.

This is one of the most complex calls in the whole Windows API. In saying this, I don't mean that the function is necessarily hard to use; rather, it has many, many flags that can be passed into it. If you want a full explanation of the routine, see the Delphi online Help. Here I'll only give you enough information so you can use the routine to open and close standard disk files.

The first parameter is simple, in that it takes a pointer to a filename. The second parameter can have the following values:

0	You can query the device without actually accessing the device.
GENERIC_READ	You can read the file and move the file pointer.
GENERIC_WRITE	You can write to the file and move the file pointer.

The `dwShareMode` parameter can have one of the following values:

0	The file cannot be shared.
FILE_SHARE_READ	Others can open the file for read access.
FILE_SHARE_WRITE	Others can open the file for write access.

Security issues generally are relevant only to Windows NT, so Windows 95 programmers can set the `lpSecurityAttributes` parameter to nil.

The `dwCreationDistribution` field can have the following values:

CREATE_NEW	The function fails if the specified file already exists.
CREATE_ALWAYS	The function overwrites the file if it exists.
OPEN_EXISTING	The function fails if the file does not exist.
OPEN_ALWAYS	If the file does not exist, the function creates it.
TRUNCATE_EXISTING	The function truncates the file to 0 bytes. (Use this with GENERIC_WRITE.)

The `dwFlagsAndAttributes` field can have the following values:

FILE_ATTRIBUTE_ARCHIVE	The function archives the file. (It's been changed.)
FILE_ATTRIBUTE_COMPRESSED	The file or directory is compressed.

FILE_ATTRIBUTE_NORMAL	No attributes. This is valid only if you use it alone.
FILE_ATTRIBUTE_HIDDEN	The file is hidden.
FILE_ATTRIBUTE_READONLY	The file is read-only.
FILE_ATTRIBUTE_SYSTEM	This field is used exclusively by the operating system.

It happens that there are many other possible attributes that you can use with CreateFile. However, the list shown here should be all you need for standard file operations.

Before moving on, I should point out that it usually is OK to use standard Pascal library routines instead of CreateFile. Delphi library file I/O calls generally map through to CreateFile or other acceptable routines, but the Pascal routines are much easier to use. I would, however, feel remiss if I wrote a long book on Windows programming without ever mentioning the standard routines used by the operating system. You ought to know what these routines are, and how to use them, even if they are not part of your day-to-day programming practice.

Here's an example:

```
HANDLE hFile := CreateFile('A CreateFile long name.txt',
                GENERIC_WRITE or GENERIC_READ,
                0, nil, CREATE_ALWAYS,
                FILE_ATTRIBUTE_NORMAL, nil);
```

The file handle returned by CreateFile is used to determine the file's size, and to create a file-mapping object.

Here is the CreateFileMapping function:

```
function CreateFileMapping(
  hFile: THandle;            // handle of file to map
  lpFileMappingAttributes: PSecurityAttributes; //optional security attributes
  flProtect,                 // protection for mapping object
  dwMaximumSizeHigh,         // high-order 32-bits of object size
  dwMaximumSizeLow: DWORD;   // low-order 32-bits of object size
  lpName: PAnsiChar          // name of file-mapping object
): THandle; stdcall;         // zero on failure, use GetLastError
```

The first parameter of this function contains the handle of the file you want to map. You get this handle by calling CreateFile.

You can pass in nil in the second parameter to use the default security attributes.

The flProtect parameter can have one of the following values, plus some additional values described in the online Help:

PAGE_READONLY	The committed part of the file has read-only access.
PAGE_READWRITE	CreateFile must use GENERIC_READ and GENERIC_WRITE.
Page_WriteCopy	CreateFile must use GENERIC_READ and GENERIC_WRITE.

If you set the dwMaximumSizeHigh and dwMaximumSizeLow parameters to zero, the system automatically fills them in with the size of the file associated with the handle passed to this function.

The last parameter contains the name of the file-mapping object. This parameter allows different processes to enter the same name when calling this function, thereby gaining access to the same file. This enables you to share memory between two applications. You can pass `nil` in this parameter if you don't need to specify a name.

Here's an example:

```
hMapping := CreateFileMapping(hFile, nil, PAGE_READONLY,
                             0, 0, nil);
```

After successfully calling and using `CreateFile` and `CreateFileMapping`, you should call `CloseHandle` to close out the files.

A call to `CreateFileMapping` does not actually allow you to use mapped files. It opens up a file-mapping object, but does not return a pointer to the "memory" in that file. To get at the actual contents of that file, call `MapViewOfFile` or `MapViewOfFileEx`.

Here is the declaration for a call to `MapViewOfFile`:

```
function MapViewOfFile(
  hFileMappingObject: THandle;  // Object returend by CreateFileMapping
  dwDesiredAccess: DWORD;       // Access mode (FILE_MAP_READ)
  dwFileOffsetHigh,             // high-order 32-bits of file offset
  dwFileOffsetLow,              // low-order 32-bits of file offset
  dwNumberOfBytesToMap: DWORD   // number of bytes to map
): Pointer; stdcall;           // returns nil on failure
```

The first parameter is the mapping object you want to work with. This value is obtained by calling `CreateFileMapping`. The next parameter specifies the kind of access you want. It can contain the following values:

FILE_MAP_WRITE	Read-write access.
FILE_MAP_READ	Read-only access.
FILE_MAP_ALL_ACCESS	Same as FILE_MAP_WRITE.
FILE_MAP_COPY	Copy on write access.

See the online Help for additional information.

The `dwFileOffsetHigh` and `dwFileOffsetLow` are the high and low DWORDS of the value specifying the offset into the file at which you want to read. The file has to be very large before you need to use the `dwFileOffsetHigh` parameter. The `dwFileOffsetLow` parameter must be a multiple of the system's memory allocation granularity. You obtain this number using a call to `GetSystemInfo`. If you want to start reading from the beginning of the file, set both `dwFileOffsetHigh` and `dwFileOffsetLow` to zero.

The final parameter is the number of bytes to map. If you want to read the whole file, just set this value to zero. Otherwise, set it to either the granularity value returned by `GetSystemInfo` or some amount smaller than the granularity.

Once you have the pointer to the data in a file, you can use it to access the contents of the file. To help illustrate this point, I use Move to copy the contents of the file into a string. I then set the last byte in the string to 0, and send it off to the edit control so you can look at it:

```
if not OpenMappedFile(OpenDialog1.FileName, Size) then Exit;
GetMem(S, Size);
Move(Data^, S^, Size);
S[Size - 2] := #0;
SetWindowText(Memo1.Handle, S);
if not UnMapViewOfFile(Data) then
  ShowMessage('No unmapping');
if not CloseHandle(hMapping) then
  ShowMessage('No closing');
FreeMem(S, Size);
```

The point here is that file-mapping enables you to treat the contents of a file as if it were memory. (You're calling Move on the contents of a file.) If the last bytes in two files both were 0, you could append them by using StrCopy or StrCat, or the simple string concatenation operator (+). You could even compare two files with StrComp! If you had a routine that reversed the bytes in a block of memory, or that scanned memory for data, you could use it with memory-mapped files. Furthermore, you can allow two programs to share memory by giving them both access to the same file.

When you're through using a file, you should close out the variables you have been using:

```
UnmapViewOfFile(Data);
CloseHandle(hMapping);
```

Once again, the purpose of this discussion of memory-mapped files is not to give you an encyclopedic overview of the entire, rather complex, subject. Instead, I just want to give you a feeling for what memory-mapped files can do for you. This is a taste of something powerful that's meant to inspire you to pursue the subject further.

Memory Manager Basics

I end this chapter by returning from the depths of the Windows API to talk about a simple VCL tool called a memory manager. The memory manager is implemented in SYSTEM.PAS, and provides a way for you to keep track of the number of times your program calls GetMem and FreeMem. If you find that your program is calling GetMem more than FreeMem, you have a problem. The memory manager does not track calls to New and Dispose, however, so you have to design your code a certain way to make this work.

The very short example shown in Listing 8.4, quite frankly, leans rather heavily on some sample code in the Delphi online Help. It's a just simple example, however, and I'm not going to make much of it. Simplicity aside, this code can help you write programs that make good and legal use of memory!

Listing 8.4. The MemMgr program shows how to track the number of calls you make to `GetMem` and `FreeMem`.

```
unit main;

interface

uses
  Windows, Messages, SysUtils,
  Classes, Graphics, Controls,
  Forms, Dialogs, StdCtrls;

type
  TForm1 = class(TForm)
    bAllocate: TButton;
    bCheckStatus: TButton;
    procedure FormCreate(Sender: TObject);
    procedure bAllocateClick(Sender: TObject);
    procedure bCheckStatusClick(Sender: TObject);
  end;

var
  Form1: TForm1;
  GetMemCount: Integer;
  FreeMemCount: Integer;
  ReallocMemCount: Integer;
  OldMemMgr: TMemoryManager;

implementation

{$R *.DFM}

function NewGetMem(Size: Integer): Pointer;
begin
  Inc(GetMemCount);
  Result := OldMemMgr.GetMem(Size);
end;

function NewFreeMem(P: Pointer): Integer;
begin
  Inc(FreeMemCount);
  Result := OldMemMgr.FreeMem(P);
end;

function NewReallocMem(P: Pointer; Size: Integer): Pointer;
begin
  Inc(ReallocMemCount);
  Result := OldMemMgr.ReallocMem(P, Size);
end;

const
  NewMemMgr: TMemoryManager = (
    GetMem: NewGetMem;
    FreeMem: NewFreeMem;
    ReallocMem: NewReallocMem);

procedure TForm1.FormCreate(Sender: TObject);
```

continues

Listing 8.4. continued

```
begin
  GetMemoryManager(OldMemMgr);
  SetMemoryManager(NewMemMgr);
end;

procedure TForm1.bAllocateClick(Sender: TObject);
var
  P: Pointer;
  i: Integer;
begin
  for i := 1 to 10 do
    GetMem(P, 500);
  FreeMem(P, 500);
end;

procedure TForm1.bCheckStatusClick(Sender: TObject);
var
  LostMem: Integer;
begin
  LostMem := GetMemCount - FreememCount;
  ShowMessage('LostMem: ' + IntToStr(LostMem));
end;

end.
```

The code in Listing 8.4 tracks the number of times you call GetMem and the number of times you call FreeMem. It then subtracts the one number from the other, thereby informing you that you may have called GetMem more times that you called FreeMem. In particular, this program has a button called Allocate, which allocates 500 bytes 10 times, while only calling FreeMem once. The result is that you find a skewed balance of calls to GetMem and FreeMem.

Inside SYSTEM.PAS there's a record called MemoryManager of type TMemoryManager:

```
PMemoryManager = ^TMemoryManager;
TMemoryManager = record
  GetMem: function(Size: Integer): Pointer;
  FreeMem: function(P: Pointer): Integer;
  ReallocMem: function(P: Pointer; Size: Integer): Pointer;
end;
```

The instance of this record in SYSTEM.PAS contains pointers to three functions that perform the basic memory-management routines for Delphi: GetMem, FreeMem, and ReAllocMem. In particular, you want to declare a record that looks like this:

```
NewMemMgr: TMemoryManager = (
  GetMem: NewGetMem;
  FreeMem: NewFreeMem;
  ReallocMem: NewReallocMem);
```

This record contains a set of pointers to new routines that replaces the old memory-manager routines.

By calling `GetMemoryManager`, you can get hold of the old `MemoryManger`; by calling `SetMemoryManager`, you can put a new memory manager in place. You should therefore pass your new memory manager record to `SetMemoryManager`, which makes the replacement official.

In this case, the new memory manager simply increments a number and then calls the routines in the old `MemoryManger`. As a result, it can track the number of times you call `GetMem` and `FreeMem`. This technique can help you be sure that you are not committing memory without also taking the time to free it. Because these calls to `GetMem` and `FreeMem` have a small overhead, you might want to remove this memory manager when you ship your code.

Summary

This chapter introduced you to some of the advanced features of Windows 95. In particular, you got a broad overview of Win32 memory-management issues, such as allocation, memory-mapped files, and heaps.

Besides providing specific coding examples, in the last two chapters I presented an overview of Windows 95 multitasking and memory management. These are complex subjects, introduced here in broad, general terms. However, this material should make you aware of some of the major theories behind Windows 95 and Windows NT. Hopefully, I've pointed you in the right direction so you can see where to concentrate your future studies.

At the end of this chapter I also presented a short example of how to use the Delphi memory manager. I tacked this on in part because it had no better home, and in part because it provided a rather light and easy way to end a difficult chapter. In particular, it emphasized the fact that Delphi programming often is much simpler than Windows API programming.

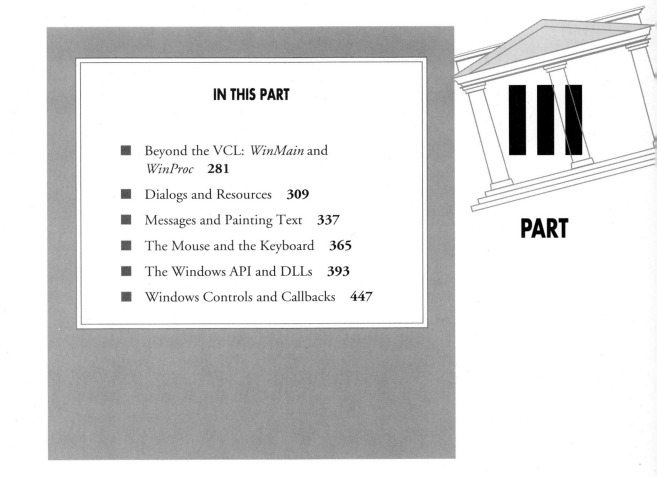

PART

The Windows API

The third part of this book delves into the Windows API. These chapters show how to go beyond the VCL and construct executables and DLLs out of nothing but Windows API calls. This part also shows how the Windows API is used in the VCL and how you can enhance VCL programs with the Windows API.

Beyond the VCL: WinMain and WinProc

9

In this chapter, you get a look at the core API code that makes Windows programming possible. My goal is to show you not only how to write a Windows program with only API calls, but also how to find the role this same code plays in the VCL.

The VCL has a magical quality to it. It seems to create your forms out of whole cloth and present them to you as complete entities fabricated by the Delphi environment or compiler. However, the VCL is really just a wrapper around the Windows API. It's a very sophisticated, very clever wrapper, but it's still just a wrapper. The goal of this chapter is to begin to show you how that wrapper works.

A second theme, however, runs in the background of this entire chapter. I am of the opinion that Object Pascal is an excellent language to use if you want full access to all the features of the Windows programming environment. Delphi allows low-level access to the most esoteric aspects of the operating system. In short, if you want to do sophisticated system programming, there is no need to switch to another tool. Delphi has everything you need.

If you are new to the material in this chapter, you may find it a bit overwhelming at first. One of the key points to remember is that the code that forms the core of each Windows program generally needs to be written only once. Each subsequent Windows application that you build can reuse this code with only minor changes. It's difficult to get the code right the first time, and it can be confusing to understand, or at least it was confusing to me the first time I saw it. Once I had the basics down, then I could reuse the code as often as I liked just by copying it from one application to the next with only minor changes.

All Delphi RAD programs have to include the Windows API calls shown in this chapter. However, the VCL intentionally goes to great lengths to hide this code from your sight. It's pushed down the hierarchy of VCL objects and out of the view of casual Delphi programmers. Still, this is the core code that lies at the bottom of all Delphi programs, and no programmer could ever claim to understand either Windows or the VCL without knowing this material both inside and out.

Straight—No Chaser

If you are new to the Windows API, you may find the pace of this chapter fairly arduous. Because I need to cover a lot of ground in a limited amount of space, I'm going to deal out the whole deck in one sitting. These are core programming issues under discussion in this chapter, and half the fun is wagering more than a little on each hand that's dealt.

> **NOTE**
>
> A number of books are available that discuss Windows API programming in depth. My personal favorite, needless to say, is *Teach Yourself Windows 95 Programming in 21 Days,* Second Edition by Charlie Calvert, published by Sams. A well-known book that covers this same material is *Programming Windows,* by Charles Petzold, published by Microsoft Press. If the material I'm about to discuss comes at you too fast for you to assimilate, you might turn to either of these books. They are both written about the C programming language, but when you are down to the Windows API level, it's hard to tell the difference between Pascal and C. They are virtually identical at this level.

The great advantage of exploring the Windows API in depth is that it helps you understand how Delphi and the operating system on which it is built really work. If you can see the core techniques used to create Windows programs, you can extrapolate from that information to see how Delphi really works and what it can and can't do.

Many people use Delphi because it allows you to build complex applications with relative ease and rapidity. This is an excellent use of the tool, and one that I myself take advantage of on many occasions. However, if you want to create really powerful programs, or if you want to create components, you need to know about more than just the high-level tools. You need to understand how Delphi works and why it works. This chapter, and the remaining chapters in this part of the book, show you the underlying theory behind Windows programming and the Delphi tools. Armed with that knowledge, you will find that there is no computer-based task you cannot conquer with the Object Pascal language.

A Windows API Program: The Simplest Possible Case

Listing 9.1 provides a simple Windows API program that does nothing more than pop up a window. After you have had a chance to compile and run it, most of the rest of the chapter discusses how it works. If you are new to this kind of code, take the time to study it in some depth, because it provides a foundation on which you can build an in-depth understanding of Delphi.

Listing 9.1. The source code for the Window1 program.

```
program Window1;

{ Standard Windows API application written in Object Pascal }

uses
  Windows;
```

continues

Listing 9.1. continued

```pascal
const
  AppName = 'Window1';

function WindowProc(Window: HWnd; AMessage, WParam,
                    LParam: Longint): Longint; stdcall; export;
begin
  WindowProc := 0;

  case AMessage of
    wm_Destroy: begin
      PostQuitMessage(0);
      Exit;
    end;
  end;

  WindowProc := DefWindowProc(Window, AMessage, WParam, LParam);
end;

{ Register the Window Class }
function WinRegister: Boolean;
var
  WindowClass: TWndClass;
begin
  WindowClass.Style := cs_hRedraw or cs_vRedraw;
  WindowClass.lpfnWndProc := @WindowProc;
  WindowClass.cbClsExtra := 0;
  WindowClass.cbWndExtra := 0;
  WindowClass.hInstance := HInstance;
  WindowClass.hIcon := LoadIcon(0, idi_Application);
  WindowClass.hCursor := LoadCursor(0, idc_Arrow);
  WindowClass.hbrBackground := HBrush(Color_Window);
  WindowClass.lpszMenuName := nil;
  WindowClass.lpszClassName := AppName;

  Result := RegisterClass(WindowClass) <> 0;
end;

{ Create the Window Class }
function WinCreate: HWnd;
var
  hWindow: HWnd;
begin
  hWindow := CreateWindow(AppName, 'Object Pascal Window',
             ws_OverlappedWindow, cw_UseDefault, cw_UseDefault,
             cw_UseDefault, cw_UseDefault, 0, 0, HInstance, nil);

  if hWindow <> 0 then begin
    ShowWindow(hWindow, CmdShow);
    UpdateWindow(hWindow);
  end;

  Result := hWindow;
end;
```

```
var
  AMessage: TMsg;
  hWindow: HWnd;
begin
  if not WinRegister then begin
    MessageBox(0, 'Register failed', nil, mb_Ok);
    Exit;
  end;
  hWindow := WinCreate;
  if hWindow = 0 then begin
    MessageBox(0, 'WinCreate failed', nil, mb_Ok);
    Exit;
  end;

  while GetMessage(AMessage, 0, 0, 0) do begin
    TranslateMessage(AMessage);
    DispatchMessage(AMessage);
  end;
  Halt(AMessage.wParam);
end.
```

You can compile this program simply by loading it into the IDE and pressing the green compilation arrow. Alternatively, you can compile it from the DOS prompt by issuing the following command:

```
DCC32 WINDOW1.DPR
```

Note that this application has no form during design time. It is, therefore, radically different from standard Delphi applications. Probably the best way to create this application is in a text editor such as Notepad. You can then save the file as WINDOW1.DPR and compile it from the command prompt.

If you want to create the file in the IDE, perform the following steps:

1. First, start a new project.
2. Remove unit one from the project using the Project Manager found in the View menu. (First select UNIT1 in the Project Manager, then delete it by pressing the button with a red minus symbol on it.)
3. Select View | Project Source from the menu and edit the main module so that it looks like the code in Listing 9.1.

When you are done, compile and run the program. The code pops up a simple window.

This program is roughly equivalent to the form you would see in the simplest possible standard RAD-based Delphi applications. That is, if you opened up Delphi, then compiled and ran the default "PROJECT1" application, the result would be very similar to what you see when you compile and run Window1.

NOTE

In this section of the book, I refer to "RAD" applications and "Windows API" applications. By the former, I mean applications that are written in the Delphi IDE using the Component Palette, Form Designer, and Object Inspector. By the latter, I mean applications like WINDOW1.DPR that do not use visual tools. This section of the book is about Windows API-based applications, but I constantly compare them to applications that are built using the RAD tools. Of necessity, this meant that I needed to come up with terms I could use to distinguish the two types of applications.

There is one very significant difference between a default Delphi RAD-based application and the Window1 application just shown. This difference will become obvious if you copy the executables from both projects into a single directory and run the DIR command.

```
Volume in drive C is HOST FOR C    Serial number is 1ADA:2A4F
 Directory of  c:\foo\*.exe

project1.exe   153088   10-11-95   20:46
window1.exe      9216   10-11-95   20:37
      162,304 bytes in 2 files and 0 dirs     172,032 bytes allocated
    33,030,144 bytes free
```

As you can see, PROJECT1.EXE is about 16 times larger than WINDOW1.EXE. In fact, WINDOW1.EXE is probably the smallest stand-alone Windows executable you have ever seen. Visual Basic produces small executables, but they depend on a large DLL nearly half a megabyte in size, so they are really some fifty times larger than a standard Delphi app. PowerBuilder typically needs several megabytes worth of support files before its applications can be run. C also produces small, tight executables, but even the smallest C-based Windows applications are usually considerably larger than the Window1 executable produced by Delphi.

Why is WINDOW1.EXE so much smaller than PROJECT1.EXE? The key issue here is that the Window1 source code makes no use of Delphi objects. In short, the VCL is not linked into WINDOW1.EXE, except perhaps in some very vestigial form.

The VCL takes up a lot of space. This should be no secret to people who read computer magazines. In fact, many magazine editors, in their infinite wisdom, complain about something they call "code bloat." They state that applications keep getting bigger and bigger, and many of them say that object-oriented libraries such as the VCL, OWL, or MFC represent one of the major reasons for this rapid increase in the size of executables.

When read from a particular perspective, these pundits of the computer press are right on target in their colorful fulminations against "ignorant programmers." After all, the code created for a standard Delphi application is much larger than the code produced by a typical non-object-oriented project.

I probably don't need to spend much time defending OOP for the typical reader of this book, however. Objects, and particularly component-based objects, save months of development time on most projects. RAD tools make it easier to quickly develop applications that are relatively free of bugs. Windows API programs, on the other hand, have a tendency to attract bugs just as flypaper attracts flies. All RAD-based Delphi programmers, as well as OWL and MFC programmers, trade performance and size for the benefits of objects. Tools like Delphi that add Rapid Application Development to the mix are even more appealing to developers who want to quickly create bug-free programs.

When you weigh the relative merits of these systems, compiled RAD tools like Delphi win hands down over both the straight Windows API applications and the applications based on non-RAD object libraries like MFC or OWL. After all, users will always choose a larger, slower, currently available application over a smaller, faster application that is promised to be delivered "real soon now."

So, you might now ask, why do I bother to show you this Windows API-based application? After all, it's not a RAD-based program. It's one of the smaller, faster applications championed by the pundits of the computer press. If the Windows API is so hard to work with, and if I personally prefer RAD tools, why should I bother to discuss Windows API programs in this book? Well, the reason is that everything done in the Delphi VCL is ultimately handled through the Windows API. Remember, the VCL is just a wrapper around the Windows API! The Windows API lies at the heart of Delphi and at the heart of every other Windows tool, utility, or service. If you understand the Windows API, you will be well on your way to understanding the VCL. In fact, all of Windows programming will start to open out in front of you. Understand Windows API-based applications, and you will know much more about how to get Delphi RAD applications to do anything you want!

In other words, I don't think most readers of this book really want to develop applications using the techniques shown in WINDOW1.DPR. The only people who should try to build production-quality applications using this technique are experienced programmers who have a very good reason to try to build the smallest, fastest application possible. Of course, programmers who are building VCL components may also have good reason to use this kind of code in their tools, but it probably will not appear in exactly this same form.

No, my point is not to promote development of Windows API-based applications. Instead, I want to show how Delphi really works. I want to take this subject down to the metal, so that you can see what is really going on. One of the benefits of that knowledge will be the ability to create really tiny executables if you need them. However, my main goal is not so much optimization as education. If you don't already understand them, learn about Windows API applications, and then apply that knowledge to the RAD tools given to you by Delphi. You should only build Windows API-based applications if you are sure you know what you are getting into, and you are sure you know why you want to do it. You should, however, find many times when this kind of code can help you construct VCL components. In those situations, you may want to use variations on this kind of code, but you will also want to protect consumers of your components from the complexity of your implementation.

Into the Code

Enough of the philosophical background—it's time now to get down to work. The entry point for the Window1 application appears at the bottom of the program's source code:

```
var
  AMessage: TMsg;
  hWindow: HWnd;
begin
  if not WinRegister then begin
    MessageBox(0, 'Register failed', nil, mb_Ok);
    Exit;
  end;
  hWindow := WinCreate;
  if hWindow = 0 then begin
    MessageBox(0, 'WinCreate failed', nil, mb_Ok);
    Exit;
  end;

  while GetMessage(AMessage, 0, 0, 0) do begin
    TranslateMessage(AMessage);
    DispatchMessage(AMessage);
  end;
  Halt(AMessage.wParam);
end.
```

C programmers know that their entry point for a Windows application looks roughly like this:

```
int WINAPI WinMain(HINSTANCE hInst, HINSTANCE hPrevInstance,
                   LPSTR lpszCmdParam, int nCmdShow)
```

In an Object Pascal application, you don't have to set up a function that takes all these parameters. Instead, the startup code for your app saves this information in global variables called hInstance, ParamStr, and CmdShow. A PrevInstance variable was available in 16-bit Delphi (and may still be available in 32-bit Delphi), but it serves no purpose in Win32 because there can be only one executable in each virtual address space. The C WinMain code already shown still references hPrevInstance in Win32, but this is only for portability reasons, and its value will always be set to zero.

The point here is that the WinMain function in a C program is analogous to the main block of code in a Delphi program. By the main block of code, I mean the body of code between the begin..end pair that appears at the bottom of the main module of your program. The beginning of this block of code is a begin statement, and the end is an end statement with a period after it.

There is no reason to assume that there is any inherent advantage in having your compiler pass parameters to WinMain, rather than saving them off earlier in global variables. In fact, it is probably actually slower to push these variables on the stack before executing a function call to WinMain, rather than just saving the variables in the data segment and then calling the initialization sections of your units, which is what happens in Object Pascal. In other words, my guess is that the Object Pascal technique for starting a Windows program is probably better optimized than the technique used in standard C programs. However, there is no significant difference between the two techniques, and either is completely acceptable. After all, every program takes several computer ages to be loaded into memory. The user is going to notice the load time, not the overhead of a single function call!

In general, I would discourage hard-core Delphi developers from trying to claim that Delphi is faster than C. The two languages perform more or less identically overall. There are areas in which one language is faster than the other, but overall, neither has a significant difference in terms of performance. (If you are the spirited type who is determined to champion Object Pascal over C, then the most significant feature to push is the size of the binary files it produces.)

NOTE

Remember that the `initialization` sections of your units will be called before the main body of your code. Consider what would happen if you added the following unit to the Window1 project:

```
unit Unit2;

interface

uses
  Windows;

implementation

initialization
  MessageBox(0, 'hi', nil, mb_Ok);
end.
```

Given the presence of this unit, and a reference to it in the `uses` clause for the main body of your program, then this `MessageBox` function would be called before the main body of your code in the primary unit. This means that in multiunit projects, the first line of executable code is likely to be the initialization section of some unit!

I am now going to take you through the code for the Window1 program in very general terms. This is the 25,000-foot overview. To begin, here are the first few lines from the main program block of the Window1 program:

```
if not WinRegister then begin
  MessageBox(0, 'Register failed', nil, mb_Ok);
  Exit;
end;
hWindow := WinCreate;
if hWindow = 0 then begin
  MessageBox(0, 'WinCreate failed', nil, mb_Ok);
  Exit;
end;
```

The `WinRegister` and `WinCreate` functions are two local routines that first register and then create the main window for the program. These two functions must complete successfully, or there is no point in trying to run your program! These two functions are a little bit like the act of starting a car and putting it in gear. If you can't complete these steps correctly, there is no point in talking about trying to take a drive to a particular location.

After the main window is created, the `ShowWindow` command is used to make it visible, and the `UpdateWindow` command is used to force it to paint itself. The code then enters a message loop that captures certain kinds of incoming messages, translates them, and sends them off to the `WindowProc`. This loop continues until the user closes the main window, at which time the application terminates and passes Windows the `wParam` value of the current message as an exit code:

```
Halt(AMessage.wParam);
```

`Halt` is a common Pascal call for terminating an application. You can look it up in the online help if you are interested, though it plays no important part in the current discussion. It's just a way to guarantee that your application exits with a certain exit code that you can define. If you omitted the call, your program would still end without mishap, but it would not be quite as kosher.

This section has given you the first of three overviews of the Window1 program that you will get in this chapter. This overview has been very brief, painting a general picture in the broadest possible outlines. The next three sections go over this material in more detail and from a slightly different perspective. After you have read once about the `WinRegister`, `WinCreate`, and `WindowProc` functions, I will review the whole process one more time. I'm using repetition here to help reinforce some fairly complex ideas that might not be well understood ahead of time by all readers of this book. It's essential that you come to terms with this material. If you understand how to register a window, create a window, and run its `WindowProc`, then you have laid a good foundation on which to build an in-depth understanding of Windows programming.

Registering a Window

The first thing the main program block does is call `WinRegister`:

```
function WinRegister: Boolean;
var
  WindowClass: TWndClass;
begin
  WindowClass.Style := cs_hRedraw or cs_vRedraw;
  WindowClass.lpfnWndProc := @WindowProc;
  WindowClass.cbClsExtra := 0;
  WindowClass.cbWndExtra := 0;
  WindowClass.hInstance := HInstance;
  WindowClass.hIcon := LoadIcon(0, idi_Application);
  WindowClass.hCursor := LoadCursor(0, idc_Arrow);
  WindowClass.hbrBackground := HBrush(Color_Window);
```

```
WindowClass.lpszMenuName := nil;
WindowClass.lpszClassName := AppName;

Result := RegisterClass(WindowClass) <> 0;
end;
```

The TWndClass structure contains a good deal of information about the type of window you want to register with the operating system. For instance, it specifies the icon associated with the window:

```
WindowClass.hIcon := LoadIcon(0, idi_Application);
```

It specifies the cursor associated with the window:

```
WindowClass.hCursor := LoadCursor(0, idc_Arrow);
```

It also specifies the window's background color, menu, and class name. Note that the following code gives the background of your main window the same color given to the background for a standard Delphi RAD-based form:

```
WindowClass.hbrBackground := HBrush(Color_Window);
```

In particular, Color_Window is a variable set in the Display applet from the Control Panel. It happens that you can typecast this constant as a brush in order to get this color for your main window. Delphi performs a similar trick for the main form in a standard RAD application.

Perhaps the single most important thing that happens in the WinRegister method is that you tell Windows where it should send the messages associated with a window. For instance, if the user clicks the mouse on the window, what function should be called in order to give your application a chance to respond to the mouse click? Well, in this case, all messages associated with the main window are passed to the function called WindowProc. The specific line of code that tells Windows to pass the message to looks like this:

```
WindowClass.lpfnWndProc := @WindowProc;
```

If you look at the source for the Window1 program, you will see the WindowProc procedure. In just a little while, I will discuss that procedure and explain how it works.

NOTE

This book is not meant to explain Windows API programming from the ground up. That's a major challenge, and the last time I took it on, the book I wrote turned out to be about 1300 pages in length. It's simply too much to attempt an explanation of both Windows API programming and Delphi OOP programming, all within the same volume. Nevertheless, I want some of the major concepts of Windows programming to come through to you in fairly clear and easy-to-understand terms. As a result, I will dedicate portions of this and the next two chapters to the subject of messages. I will frequently revisit the subject of the WindowProc and the role it plays in Windows API programming. In short, you need not worry if you don't yet fully grasp how Windows handles messages. That topic will be covered carefully in this book. If you need additional information, you can read *Teach Yourself Windows 95 Programming in 21 Days*, Second Edition or *Programming Windows*.

Once you have filled out all the fields of the `TWndProc` structure, you can pass it to the `RegisterClass` procedure:

```
Result := RegisterClass(WindowClass) <> 0;
```

This function is not the same as the VCL `RegisterClass` function used in component creation. Indeed, in a regular OOP-based Delphi application, you would have to qualify the call if you did not want to get a type mismatch:

```
Result := Windows.RegisterClass(WindowClass) <> 0;
```

The `RegisterClass` function registers your window with the operating system. It returns an atom that uniquely identifies the class that you plan to create. If the call fails, then the function returns 0, so you can assume that it succeeded if the call does not equal zero. In fact, the preceding code line sets `Result` to `True` as long as the function does not return `0`. (Note that this code is not compatible with Win16 applications because 16-bit Windows defined the `RegisterClass` as a Boolean function. I will touch briefly on a method for compiling Windows API code under 16-bit Windows in Chapter 10, "Dialogs and Resources.")

> **NOTE**
>
> What does it mean to say that Windows defines `RegisterClass`? Why do I word things this way?
>
> Well, the point is that `RegisterClass` is a Windows API function. It's defined by the operating system. You can call this same `RegisterClass` function from a C program if you like. There is no difference in calling this function from a Delphi program or a C program.
>
> It happens that Delphi also defines an internal routine called `RegisterClass` that is part of the VCL. This internal routine is not part of the operating system. One of the big chores that a Delphi programmer must face is discovering which routines are part of the operating system, which are part of the core Object Pascal language, and which are part of the VCL.
>
> Routines that are defined in SYSTEM.PAS and SYSUTILS.PAS are generally considered to be part of the core Object Pascal language. At the time of this writing, if you have the source code to Delphi, you will find these core Object Pascal files in the ..\DELPHI32\SOURCE\RTL\SYS subdirectory.

Routines that are defined in WINDOWS.PAS are part of the operating system. These are the core functions supplied by Windows to all programs that want to run under Windows 95 and Windows NT. Other files such as OLE2.PAS, WINSOCK.PAS, DDEML.PAS, COMMCRTL.PAS, COMMDLG.PAS, and so on are also calls that are resolved by the operating system. At the time of this writing, these files are found in the ..\DELPHI32\SOURCE\RTL\WIN subdirectory of the source code to Delphi.

In general, all the other files or routines found in the ..\DELPHI32\LIB subdirectory that are not part of the two categories previously mentioned are by default part of the VCL. The core units in the VCL are CLASSES.PAS, FORMS.PAS, COMCTRLS.PAS, GRAPHICS.PAS, STDCTRLS.PAS, and EXTCTRLS.PAS. There are many other units that make up the VCL, many of which are very important. At the time of this writing, these VCL files are found in the ..\DELPHI32\SOURCE\VCL and ..\DELPHI32\SOURCE\LIB subdirectory.

All of the files mentioned in this note come precompiled with every copy of Delphi. The compiled versions of these files are stored in the ..\DELPHI32\LIB subdirectory. At the time of this writing, the interfaces for these files are found in the ..\DELPHI32\DOCS subdirectory. In other words, if you don't have the source code to Delphi, you can find out quite a bit about the core source files by looking in the DOCS subdirectory for files that end with an INT extension. I strongly recommend getting the source code if you don't have it already.

The TWndClass structure (defined in WINDOWS.PAS) is fairly long and complex. Nevertheless, the actual act of filling it out and passing it to RegisterClass is fairly straightforward from a conceptual point of view. Specifically, you need to register your window class with the system. To do so, you first fill out a record that describes your window class, and then you pass that record to RegisterClass. It can be a bit confusing if it's the first time you've seen it, but the basic principles involved in registering a class are really fairly straightforward. Once again, here are the steps:

1. Fill out the TWndClass record.
2. Pass it to RegisterClass.

If the call succeeds, you can go on to create the window. If the call fails, you should abort your application immediately, as shown in the main block of code for the Window1 program.

A Delphi programmer, however, can be confused by all this talk of classes and class registration. It's crucial to understand that the RegisterClass method has nothing to do with the Delphi VCL, and in fact, a window class is not a Delphi object. In and of itself, Windows is not object-oriented, and it does not support polymorphism, inheritance, or encapsulation. The TWndClass structure and the Windows.RegisterClass method belong to the Windows API, not to the VCL. They are part of the operating system, and Windows is not an object-oriented operating system. The Windows classes referenced by TWndClass and RegisterClass are not real objects, but are only vaguely object-like. Delphi wraps these object-like entities inside real objects.

Creating a Window

After the Window1 class is registered with the system, the next step is to create it:

```
function WinCreate: HWnd;
var
  hWindow: HWnd;
begin
  hWindow := CreateWindow(AppName, 'Object Pascal Window',
              ws_OverlappedWindow, cw_UseDefault, cw_UseDefault,
              cw_UseDefault, cw_UseDefault, 0, 0, HInstance, nil);

  if hWindow <> 0 then begin
    ShowWindow(hWindow, CmdShow);
    UpdateWindow(hWindow);
  end;

  Result := hWindow;
end;
```

The core of this function is the call to CreateWindow. The other two functions, ShowWindow and UpdateWindow, are really just very simple routines that get the window up on the screen and make sure it is painted correctly. From the programmer's point of view, these latter calls are essential, but relatively trivial. The hard part is calling CreateWindow.

The first parameter passed to CreateWindow is the name of a registered class. In this case, the window you want to create is called Window1, and you just finished registering it in the call to WinRegister. There are, however, various preregistered classes such as edits, listboxes, richedits, listviews, and so on, and you can use the CreateWindow call to create these windows without having to explicitly call RegisterWindow. The distinction between windows you register yourself and those that are preregistered by Windows can be confusing at first. Take your time with this subject. It's not really that hard; there is just a lot of detail to master.

The second parameter you pass to CreateWindow is the title of your window, and the next four parameters are its dimensions. If you want the window to open in a default size and shape selected by Windows, then you can pass in cw_UseDefault rather than a specific number in the four dimension parameters.

The next three parameters are the Windows parent, its menu, and its hInstance. Because this is the main window of the application, it will have no parent. Menus also play no role in this simple application. The hInstance of the program is available as a global variable, per the explanation given earlier in this chapter.

The final parameter can be filled with user-defined data, or it can play a particular role in the creation of MDI windows. However, for the purposes of the current discussion, it can simply be set to nil and then ignored.

Here's how the call to `CreateWindow` is defined:

```
function
CreateWindow(ClassName: PChar;  { address of registered class name }
             WindowName: PChar;  { address of window name }
             Style: LongInt;     { window style }
             X: Integer;         { horizontal position of window }
             Y: Integer;         { vertical position of window }
             Width: Integer      { window width }
             Height: Integer;    { window height }
             WndParent: HWnd;    { handle of parent or owner window }
             Menu: HMenu;        { handle of menu }
             Instance: THandle;  { handle of application }
             Param: Pointer      { address of window-creation data }
             ): HWnd;
```

Remember, these functions are not defined in the main Delphi help, but in a separate help file accessible from the help menu. In the shipping version of Delphi, this file will probably be called WINAPI32.HLP.

If you want to know more about the `CreateWindow` function, you can read the online help, you can buy a book like *Teach Yourself Windows 95 Programming in 21 Days*, Second Editon, or you can browse the Microsoft Developer's CD. From my point of view, I find that it really doesn't matter much if the book or help file I am reading is meant for C programmers or Pascal programmers. `CreateWindow` looks the same in C or in Pascal, with a few minor differences. For instance, this is what the call looks like in C:

```
HWND CreateWindow(
    LPCTSTR  lpClassName,   // address of registered class name
    LPCTSTR  lpWindowName,  // address of window name
    DWORD  dwStyle,         // window style
    int  x,                 // horizontal position of window
    int  y,                 // vertical position of window
    int  nWidth,            // window width
    int  nHeight,           // window height
    HWND  hWndParent,       // handle of parent or owner window
    HMENU  hMenu,           // handle of menu or child-window identifier
    HANDLE  hInstance,      // handle of application instance
    LPVOID  lpParam         // address of window-creation data
    );
```

To me, there is no significant difference in making this call from a C application or a Delphi application. It's the same function either way—it's just that each language has slightly different type names.

> **NOTE**
>
> If I seem to be making a big point of the similarities between C and Pascal, that's just because I have found that many people don't seem to understand how similar the two languages are to each other, especially when you are down at the level being discussed in this chapter. Once again, my point is not that one is better than the other, but just that there are many parallels between the two languages.

If the call to CreateWindow fails, the return value will be zero:

```
if hWindow <> 0 then begin
  ShowWindow(hWindow, CmdShow);
  UpdateWindow(hWindow);
end;
```

There is no hope for an application if it does not have a main window, so you need to shut down your app if this call fails.

Before closing this section, I should point out that a call to CreateWindow causes Windows to send a wm_Create message to the WindowProc associated with the window in question. This wm_Create message gives you a chance to initialize data associated with the window. I will explain more about this process later in this chapter and in several other places in this book.

A First Look at the *Window* Procedure

Here is the Window procedure for the Window1 program:

```
function WindowProc(Window: HWnd; AMessage, WParam,
                    LParam: Longint): Longint; stdcall; export;
begin
  WindowProc := 0;

  case AMessage of
    wm_Destroy: begin
      PostQuitMessage(0);
      Exit;
    end;
  end;

  WindowProc := DefWindowProc(Window, AMessage, WParam, LParam);
end;
```

This procedure takes four parameters. This isn't a matter of choice. It has to take four parameters, and they have to be of the exact same type shown. The name you give to the procedure does not matter, and the names of the parameters you pass to it do not matter. However, the types of the parameters passed to this procedure are set in stone.

> **NOTE**
>
> Remember that this procedure was assigned to the `lpfnWndProc` field of the `TWndClass` structure. Your duty as a Windows programmer is to declare a procedure that takes the types defined in the call to `WindowProc`. To create a standard Windows program, you must declare a procedure of this type, and you must assign it to the `lpfnWndProc` field of the `TWndClass` structure passed to `RegisterClass`.
>
> There are other ways to write Windows programs, but 98 percent of all Windows programs, including all Delphi RAD programs, are built in just this way. In other words, Delphi RAD programs also have a `WndProc`, and it is identical in kind to the one shown here. Delphi goes to great length to hide this fact from you, but at bottom, there is no easy way to escape this architecture. Windows programs are built around `WndProc`s; that's all there is to it!
>
> Please note that I use the term `WndProc` when I am referring to the generic concept of a window procedure, but that I frequently name explicit instances of this procedure `WindowProc`. The spelling `WndProc` comes from Microsoft type declarations in various C header files, whereas the easier-to-read-and-use `WindowProc` is associated more with explicit instances of the function. Both words are correct, and for most practical purposes they are interchangeable. However, `WndProc` hints at a concept, whereas `WindowProc` usually refers to a specific procedure in my code.

The signature of a `WndProc` function is predefined by Windows. You can even look it up in the online help if you want. Just search in the help index for `WindowProc`, and you will find something like the following definition:

```
Function WindowProc(
  Window: HWnd;    /* handle of window    */
  AMsg: LongInt;   /* message    */
  wParam: LongInt; /* first message parameter    */
  lParam: LongInt; /* second message parameter    */
  ): LongInt;
```

The first parameter is the handle of your main window. The handle of your window is like the handle of a file: it's a number that uniquely identifies your window. Whenever you need to talk to Windows about the traits of a particular window, you can identify the window in question by passing the operating systems its handle, that is, its `HWnd`.

The second parameter of this function is the type of the message coming in. Each message in Windows has its own unique identifier. For instance, when you move the mouse, the `window` procedure gets a `wm_MouseMove` message. When you press a key, it gets a `wm_KeyDown` message. When the window is about to close, it gets a `wm_Destroy` message. There are thousands of these messages, and expert Windows programmers know many of them by heart. Macho dudes pump iron, macho Window programmers memorize Windows messages, but I survive by mastering the online help system! To each his own.

The last two parameters, wParam and lParam, hold data that will differ depending on the type of message being sent. For instance, if you move the mouse, the X and Y coordinates of the mouse's new position will be passed in these parameters. Don't worry about getting at that information quite yet. I will explain more about message handling in several other places in this book.

The body of a window procedure consists primarily of a case statement that handles all the messages sent to the window. Most of these messages can be passed on untouched to a default internal window procedure referenced by the DefWindowProc function. However, there are usually some messages that require explicit handling. In this case, the only one you need to worry about is the wm_Destroy message. This message is sent to tell you that the user or operating system is closing down this window. Because this is the only window in this application, the appropriate response to this request is to close down the whole application. You can do this by calling PostQuitMessage.

Once again: wm_Destroy messages are sent to your window when it is time for that window to close. When the main window of an application is closed, its duty is to shut down the whole application. You can close the application by calling PostQuitMessage. PostQuitMessage sets a flag that tells the application it's time to exit the message loop; that is, it causes Windows to send a wm_Quit message:

```
while GetMessage(AMessage, 0, 0, 0) do begin
  TranslateMessage(AMessage);
  DispatchMessage(AMessage);
end;
```

GetMessage returns false after PostQuitMessage has been called, that is, after it retrieves a wm_Quit message from the message queue. Once again: the message loop continues until it gets a wm_Quit message. A call to PostQuitMessage causes a wm_Quit message to be placed in the thread's message queue.

A message queue is just a place where messages can be stacked up while they are waiting to be processed. There is a function called SendMessage that sends messages directly to a WndProc. There is a second function called PostMessage that places messages in the message queue. Each thread in a Win32 application has its own message queue. Don't worry if some of this doesn't quite make sense yet. Messages are a little complex at first, but the experienced programmers who are reading this book could tell you that this subject is much simpler than it seems at first.

Before leaving this subject, I should point out that if there had been other memory allocations associated with your window, then you could deallocate that memory in response to a wm_Destroy message. In other words, the response to a wm_Destroy message can include code for disposing memory:

```
wm_Destroy: begin
  Dispose(MyRecord);
  FreeMem(MyPointer, MySize);
  PostQuitMessage(0);
  Exit;
end;
```

I will touch on this subject again in the next chapter, "Dialogs and Resources."

The call to DefWindowProc at the end of this window procedure is simply a way of letting Windows handle the default behavior for your window. For instance, all windows know by default how to handle certain aspects of being redrawn, and how to handle being resized. To make sure that all this behavior occurs automatically, you must pass all unhandled messages through to DefWindowProc. DefWindowProc passes your call on to an internal routine that can be thought of as something like a mirror image of your own window procedure. Of course, the body of the routine is different, but its structure and purpose are similar to your own window procedure. As explained previously, its job is to execute any default behavior associated with your window.

If you explicitly handle a message, then you have a choice of passing it on to DefWindowProc or not, depending on your circumstances, and depending on the nature of the particular window in question. Some classic bugs are introduced into programs because someone handles a particular message and then forgets to pass it on to DefWindowProc.

In this section, you have had a first look at window procedures. These little jewels are the heart and soul of most Windows programs. I will therefore go over this material several more times, in several different contexts, in various different parts of this book. It's okay if it doesn't make sense to you yet, but you will never really understand the Windows API until you understand what WndProcs do, and how they should be constructed.

Taking Another Perspective

By this point in the chapter, you have been through all the major aspects of the Windows1 program. You have had a chance to look at the whole thing from start to finish. However, this material is so important that it's worthwhile taking a moment to review some of the key points covered so far in this chapter. I'm reviewing this material in part because I know it can be very difficult to grasp when you first encounter it. Taking another shot at this material also gives me a chance to emphasize certain points.

The Window1 program has two major parts:

1. One is the main program block.
2. The other is the WndProc function.

The next few paragraphs take a brief look at each part.

The code inside or called from the main program block can be divided into three sections:

■ The first section is where the window is registered:

```
WindowClass.Style := cs_hRedraw or cs_vRedraw;
WindowClass.lpfnWndProc := @WindowProc;
WindowClass.cbClsExtra := 0;
WindowClass.cbWndExtra := 0;
WindowClass.hInstance := HInstance;
WindowClass.hIcon := LoadIcon(0, idi_Application);
WindowClass.hCursor := LoadCursor(0, idc_Arrow);
```

```
WindowClass.hbrBackground := HBrush(Color_Window);
WindowClass.lpszMenuName := nil;
WindowClass.lpszClassName := AppName;

Result := RegisterClass(WindowClass) <> 0;
```

The WinRegister procedure tells Windows about the characteristics of a window class. A window class is registered so that Windows will know about its existence and will know what traits you want to have associated with it. The key point is that this is the first thing that happens in a typical main block for an API program.

■ The next step is to create the window (lines 26-30):

```
hWindow := CreateWindow(AppName, 'Object Pascal Window',
            ws_OverlappedWindow, cw_UseDefault, cw_UseDefault,
            cw_UseDefault, cw_UseDefault, 0, 0, HInstance, nil);
if hWindow <> 0 then begin
  ShowWindow(hWindow, CmdShow);
  UpdateWindow(hWindow);
end;
```

The act of creating a window involves two steps. The first is the call to CreateWindow, and the second is the two calls to ShowWindow and UpdateWindow. As with the registration procedure, the act of creating a window is usually handled in its own separate procedure. This is done to isolate complexity and to create a well-structured, robust program.

■ The third portion of the WinMain procedure is called the message loop (lines 32-36):

```
while GetMessage(AMessage, 0, 0, 0) do begin
  TranslateMessage(AMessage);
  DispatchMessage(AMessage);
end;
```

The GetMessage procedure retrieves messages from the application's message queue. Windows sends certain types of messages to the message queue first, and then lets you pass them on to the WindowProc through TranslateMessage and DispatchMessage. The actual mechanisms involved here will be discussed more in the chapter on the Windows API and events, or you can look them up in the online help. The key point to grasp is that when the user moves the mouse or strikes a key, these events are sent to your program in the form of messages. These and other messages are usually handled by the message loop of your application.

The message loop is the *driver's seat* for a Windows program. This is command central, a loop that keeps repeating throughout much of the life of a program. However, you should be aware that many messages are sent directly to the WindowProc and never pass through the message loop. Posted messages, however, pass through the message loop.

The message queue in Win32 programs will grow automatically to accommodate the number of messages sent to it. There are, however, many tricks you can use to grab messages from the message queue in a particular order, or in a particular manner.

These are very advanced programming issues and will not be given much consideration in this book. If you want to futz around with the message queue, you should read books by Jeffrey Richter, Andrew Schulman, Kim Crouse, or Matt Pietrek.

Don't worry if all of this doesn't make sense to you yet—it's not supposed to. The point of this section of the chapter is simply to give you an overview of a typical Windows program.

Right now, you only need to think about the broadest issues, such as the three steps in the main block of the Window1 program:

1. Register the window.
2. Create the window.
3. Enter the message loop.

There it is, just as simple as one, two, three!

The other key part of the program is the WndProc procedure, which responds to messages a program receives:

```
function WindowProc(Window: HWnd; AMessage, WParam,
                    LParam: Longint): Longint; stdcall; export;
begin
  WindowProc := 0;

  case AMessage of
    wm_Destroy: begin
      PostQuitMessage(0);
      Exit;
    end;
  end;

  WindowProc := DefWindowProc(Window, AMessage, WParam, LParam);
end;
```

The Window1 program only responds explicitly to wm_Destroy messages. All other messages get passed on to DefWindowProc. The DefWindowProc procedure does nothing more than handle the default behavior associated with a window. In other words, when you maximize a window or minimize a window, the DefWindowProc procedure supplies the necessary know-how to execute these maneuvers.

DefWindowProc doesn't, however, handle wm_Destroy messages. That is your duty as a programmer. When the message comes down the pike, just call PostQuitMessage; this will cause a wm_Quit message to be placed in the queue. After PostQuitMessage has been called, you can exit WndProc with a return value of 0.

For now, that's all you need to know about the Window1 program. To summarize:

■ There are two main parts in a program. The first is the main block of the program; the second is the WndProc procedure.

- The main block of the program has three parts. The first part *registers* the Window, the second *creates* the window, and the third sends *messages* to the window through a loop.

- Any messages sent to a window pass through WndProc. This window procedure can explicitly handle the messages, or it can pass them on to DefWindowProc, which is the default message handler. In fact, some programs first handle the message, and then pass it on to DefWindowProc for further processing.

I hope the repetition in the preceding sections hasn't driven you totally insane. I've used it so heavily here because I want to do everything I can to drive home some complicated, but very important, issues. My hope is that even newcomers to this subject will finally throw up their hands and say: "Okay, Charlie, I get it! You don't have to say it again. It's clear to me now!" If that happens, then you can rest assured that you understand the overall flow of a typical Windows program. Just get the broad issues clear in your mind, and then the details will become clear in the future. Armed with this knowledge, there are many, many important Windows programming issues that you are now prepared to grasp.

What Does This Have to Do with Delphi?

It's time now for me to tie some of this stuff together in terms that will make sense to a Delphi programmer. In particular, it's time to explain exactly what WinMain, WinRegister, and WinCreate have to do with a RAD tool like Delphi.

To get right at the core of this subject, you need only take a quick look at the constructor for the TApplication object, as seen in the VCL source code:

```
constructor TApplication.Create(AOwner: TComponent);
const
  WindowClass: TWndClass = (
    style: 0;
    lpfnWndProc: @DefWindowProc;
    cbClsExtra: 0;
    cbWndExtra: 0;
    hInstance: 0;
    hIcon: 0;
    hCursor: 0;
    hbrBackground: 0;
    lpszMenuName: nil;
    lpszClassName: 'TApplication');
var
  P: PChar;
  TempClass: TWndClass;
  ModuleName: array[0..255] of Char;
begin
  inherited Create(AOwner);
  ... // code not germane to current example is omitted here
  if not IsLibrary then
  begin
    FObjectInstance := MakeObjectInstance(WndProc);
    if not GetClassInfo(HInstance, WindowClass.lpszClassName, TempClass) then
```

```
  begin
    WindowClass.hInstance := HInstance;
    if Windows.RegisterClass(WindowClass) = 0 then
      raise EOutOfResources.CreateRes(SWindowClass);
  end;
  FHandle := CreateWindow(WindowClass.lpszClassName, ModuleName,
    WS_POPUP + WS_VISIBLE + WS_CLIPSIBLINGS + WS_SYSMENU + WS_MINIMIZEBOX,
    GetSystemMetrics(SM_CXSCREEN) div 2,
    GetSystemMetrics(SM_CYSCREEN) div 2,
    0, 0, 0, 0, HInstance, nil);
  SetWindowLong(FHandle, GWL_WNDPROC, Longint(FObjectInstance));
  if NewStyleControls then
    SendMessage(FHandle, WM_SETICON, 1, GetIconHandle);
  end;
end;
```

Note in particular the TWndClass structure and the calls to RegisterClass:

```
if Windows.RegisterClass(WindowClass) = 0 then
      raise EOutOfResources.CreateRes(SWindowClass);
```

Or how about the call to CreateWindow:

```
FHandle := CreateWindow(WindowClass.lpszClassName, ModuleName,
    WS_POPUP + WS_VISIBLE + WS_CLIPSIBLINGS + WS_SYSMENU + WS_MINIMIZEBOX,
    GetSystemMetrics(SM_CXSCREEN) div 2,
    GetSystemMetrics(SM_CYSCREEN) div 2,
    0, 0, 0, 0, HInstance, nil);
```

The point here is that the Delphi VCL makes the same calls that are made in WINDOW1.DPR. In fact, it has to make these calls! There is no other way to create a standard window and show it to the user.

Let's move away from the Forms unit, and take a look at the TWinControl implementation in the Controls unit:

```
procedure TWinControl.CreateWindowHandle(const Params: TCreateParams);
begin
  with Params do
    FHandle := CreateWindowEx(ExStyle, WinClassName, Caption, Style,
      X, Y, Width, Height, WndParent, 0, HInstance, Param);
end;
```

CreateWindowEx is just like CreateWindow, except that it takes one extra parameter that shows up in the first position. The point here is that TForm, TEdit, TListBox, and many of the other major controls are all descended from TWinControl. The CreateWindowHandle procedure demonstrates that these core Delphi components all have their bases in the fundamental call to CreateWindow that is shown in the Window1 example.

Going on just one step further, let's look at the TCreateParams structure:

```
TCreateParams = record
  Caption: PChar;
  Style: Longint;
  ExStyle: Longint;
  X, Y: Integer;
  Width, Height: Integer;
```

```
    WndParent: HWnd;
    Param: Pointer;
    WindowClass: TWndClass;
    WinClassName: array[0..63] of Char;
end;
```

This vitally important structure holds most of the parameters that are passed to `CreateWindow`. As it happens, you have direct access to this structure through a call to a function called `CreateParam`. Every form calls `CreateParam` before it is shown. This is a virtual method, and you can override it if you want to change the default values passed in the `TCreateParams` structure. The Provider program, discussed later in this book, makes heavy use of this programming technique. Here is an excerpt from that program:

```
procedure TCompanyForm.CreateParams(var Params: TCreateParams);
begin
  inherited CreateParams(Params);
  Params.Style := Params.Style and not ws_Caption;
  Params.Style := Params.Style and not ws_ThickFrame;
  Params.Style := Params.Style or ws_Border;
end;
```

This code gives you the same control over the parameters passed to `RegisterClass` as you would get in a standard Windows API application. It's not as fast, nor quite as clean, as standard API code, but the control is there if you need it.

Overriding *TForm.WndProc*

Besides the `CreateParam` function, another `TForm` routine you might want to override is called `TForm.WndProc`. All the messages sent to your application pass through this routine, just as all the messages sent to the Window1 program pass through the `WindowProc` routine.

The NWndProc program, shown in Listing 9.2, demonstrates how to override the `TForm.Wnd` procedure.

The NWndProc program gives you some of the clues you need to start digging into the structure of the Delphi VCL from the perspective of a Windows API programmer. You should use this program as a starting point and beginner's guide to the types of riches found when you study the VCL. (See Listing 9.2.)

Listing 9.2. The NWndProc program shows how to override the window procedure of a form.

```
unit main;

interface

uses
  SysUtils, Windows, Messages,
  Classes, Graphics, Controls,
  Forms, Dialogs, StdCtrls;
```

```
type
  TForm1 = class(TForm)
    procedure FormClick(Sender: TObject);
  private
    ShowMessages: Boolean;
  protected
    procedure WndProc(var Msg: TMessage); override;
  end;

var
  Form1: TForm1;

implementation

uses
 MsgForm;

{$R *.DFM}

procedure ShowMsg(S: string);
begin
  if MessageForm <> nil then
    with MessageForm do begin
      Edit1.Text := S;
      ListBox1.Items.Add(S);
      if ListBox1.Items.Count > 10 then
        ListBox1.TopIndex := ListBox1.Items.Count - 5;
  end;
end;

procedure HandleMessages(var Msg: TMessage);
var
  S: string;
begin
  if Msg.Msg = wm_Paint then begin
    S := 'wm_Paint';
    ShowMsg(S);
  end else
  if Msg.Msg = wm_MouseMove then begin
    S := IntToStr(TWMMouse(Msg).XPos) + ' ' + IntToStr(TWMMouse(Msg).YPos);
    S := 'wm_MouseMove ' + S;
    ShowMsg(S);
  end else
  if Msg.Msg = wm_KeyDown then begin
    S := IntToStr(TWMKeyDown(Msg).CharCode) + ' ' +
         IntToStr(TWMKey(Msg).KeyData);
S := 'wm_KeyDown ' + S;
    ShowMsg(S);
  end else
  if Msg.Msg = wm_NCHITTEST then begin
    S := 'wm_NCHitTest';
    ShowMsg(S);
  end else begin
    S := Format('$%x', [Msg.Msg]);
    ShowMsg(S);
  end;
end;
```

continues

Listing 9.2. continued

```
procedure TForm1.WndProc(var Msg: TMessage);
begin
  if Msg.Msg = wm_Close then ShowMessages := False;
  if ShowMessages then
    HandleMessages(Msg);
  inherited WndProc(Msg);
end;

procedure TForm1.FormClick(Sender: TObject);
begin
  MessageForm.Show;
  ShowMessages := not ShowMessages;
end;

end.
```

When you first launch the NWndProc program, it appears as a normal form with some text on it. If you click it once, however, a second form pops up. This second form will process all the messages sent to the main form and display them in a list box. (In Windows 95, it will be possible to fill up the list box, so run the program for only a few minutes at a time.)

The overridden WndProc procedure itself is very simple:

```
procedure TForm1.WndProc(var Msg: TMessage);
begin
  if Msg.Msg = wm_Close then ShowMessages := False;
  if ShowMessages then
    HandleMessages(Msg);
  inherited WndProc(Msg);
end;
```

This code first checks to see if the message passed in is wm_Close. If so, it is simply passed to the inherited WndProc, which is roughly the equivalent of calling DefWindowProc. If the message is not wm_Close, then it is passed on to HandleMessages, which displays the message to the user. After it has been displayed, the message is then passed on to DefWindowProc through the inherited WndProc call.

Note that the TForm.WndProc procedure takes only one parameter. This is clearly not the original WndProc that handles four separate parameters. Instead, it is a secondary function called by internal VCL routines. Nevertheless, you will find that all the information stored in lParam and wParam has been encapsulated inside the TMessage structure and is there for your perusal if you need it. In fact, you will find that the TMessage structures have parsed this information and made it more readily available for your use. Here is the TMessage structure as it appears in MESSAGES.PAS:

```
TMessage = record
    Msg: Cardinal;
    case Integer of
      0: (
        WParam: Longint;
```

```
      LParam: Longint;
      Result: Longint);
   1: (
      WParamLo: Word;
      WParamHi: Word;
      LParamLo: Word;
      LParamHi: Word;
      ResultLo: Word;
      ResultHi: Word);
 end;
```

The HandleMessages routine explicitly handles certain very frequently delivered messages, and then gives you the Hex value of any other message. If you want to find out what these other messages are, you can look them up in MESSAGES.PAS, using the Hex value as a key to search on. Here is a simplified version of the routine that highlights its structure:

```
procedure HandleMessages(var Msg: TMessage);
var
  S: string;
begin
  if Msg.Msg = wm_Paint then …
  if Msg.Msg = wm_MouseMove then …
  if Msg.Msg = wm_KeyDown then …
  if Msg.Msg = wm_NCHITTEST then …
  end else begin
    S := Format('$%x', [Msg.Msg]);
    ShowMsg(S);
  end;
```

Note that this function acts like a simplified version of the WinSight utility that ships with Delphi. If you want, you can try to rewrite the Window1 program so that it acts in the same way as NWndProc. If you try this latter idea, you should use the Windows TextOut function to display text on the main screen of the application.

I'm not going to spend any more time describing the NWndProc program. It's not really that complex, and it is meant only to show you the type of things you can do with a solid understanding of standard Windows programs. If you want to be a really good Delphi programmer, then you should take the information you have seen in this chapter and plunge into the Delphi source code with a will. This knowledge forms the basis for the skillsets of all the best Windows programmers I've met.

If you already know this material from your experiences with C or Turbo Pascal, this chapter has shown you how to apply that knowledge to Delphi applications. The key point to grasp is that most Windows programs are the same underneath. Fortunately, Delphi offers you a transparent object wrapper that lets you dig down to these core routines when you need them.

Summary

In this chapter, you have learned some of the key points about the Windows API. In particular, you have seen how to write a Delphi program that uses straight Windows API code in lieu of VCL objects. You also saw how to apply your knowledge of Windows API code to VCL objects. One of the main themes of this chapter is that the VCL builds applications using the techniques shown in the Window1 program. If you understand Window1, then you understand some of the core functions in the VCL.

This chapter has also showered the Object Pascal language with rather lavish praise. I want to stress that my point is not to fight a language war, but only to point out that Pascal is an excellent language for writing low-level system code. In fact, Delphi itself is written in Object Pascal because there was no need to turn to another language for aid in accessing low-level routines.

Object Pascal is a very fast, very tight language with a clean syntax and a quick compilation time. C is also a very fine language, with a number of great strengths, some of which have no parallel in the Pascal language. However, you may find that you prefer working in Pascal, especially when you need to dig into the darkest, most obscure recesses of the Windows API. Pascal is a very well-constructed language, and Delphi's developers have found a way to polish it so that it gleams in the sun and glows in the moonlight.

Dialogs and Resources

10

This chapter contains several different topics, most of which are related to the Windows API, dialogs, or resources. In particular, you will see the following:

- How to create old style Windows dialogs in a straight API-based program.
- How to compile Delphi applications from the command line.
- How to write one set of Windows API code that compiles under both 16-bit Windows and Win32.

The obvious themes of this chapter are dialog boxes and messages. However, the main focus is still the Windows API, and I spend considerable time refining and explaining the way standard Windows API programs are designed and written. In particular, there is an introduction to handling messages in the WndProc function and a discussion about how this task can be optimized in a Windows application. This basic subject is carried over into the next two chapters, which serve to nail down the whole topic of the Windows messaging system.

This chapter spends a considerable amount of time discussing compiling from the command line and creating batch and makefiles that you can use from the command line. This material might appear to be not quite as earth-shattering in its importance as the rest of the code in this chapter nor as the code you saw in the previous chapter or will see in the next chapter. However, this material has to be covered, because it is essential programming information. Have a little patience with the command line material, but be sure not to miss the information on dialog boxes and resources. That's key information.

Use the Source, Luke!

One of the best reasons to learn the Windows API is that it enables you to begin a quest to understand Delphi from top to bottom. The core of Delphi is hidden in the details of the VCL, and the VCL is just a wrapper around the Windows API.

The best programmers live inside the source modules that make up the core of their language. For C programmers, that means gaining a thorough knowledge of the header files that ship in the INCLUDE directory. For Delphi programmers, the key source files are the VCL files that ship with the high-end versions of Delphi or that can be purchased separately via the RAD pack and other sources. To understand those files you must understand the Windows API. As the folks around Borland are fond of saying, "Use the *source*, Luke!"

Ten calls to Tech Support are unlikely to be as valuable as 10 minutes spent in intelligent study of the source to the VCL. The core of the language is the source code, and all I am doing is attempting to make it comprehensible to you. The core tool for all the best programmers is the source code found in the VCL and in WINDOWS.PAS. The best books serve only as a commentary on that source, and like the key Star Wars episodes, they continually remind the user, "Use the *source*, Luke!"

Old Style Windows Dialog Boxes

The dialog boxes that you create with the Delphi RAD tools are not made in the same manner as the dialog boxes you see in a typical Windows program. Specifically, when you are in Delphi you usually make a dialog box by changing the BorderStyle property of a TForm object to bsDialog. This gives your window the same look and feel as a dialog box, but it does not create exactly the same type of dialog box found in most Windows programs.

The Window2 program shown later demonstrates how to create a real Windows dialog box using Delphi. In other words, this is a classic Windows dialog box, not the kind made with the Delphi RAD tools. It's important to note that standard Delphi RAD programs can use standard dialog boxes, but you don't normally use this technique because the Delphi visual tools provide a better solution.

One of the original reasons for the existence of standard Windows dialog boxes is that they made it easy for vendors to provide a set of tools that help to simplify the creation of windows that contain controls such as buttons, list boxes, and scrollbars. In particular, the Resource Workshop that ships with Borland C++, the Delphi RAD Pack, and Borland Pascal can help you to design old style dialog boxes using visual tools.

In Delphi, there is no need to simplify the task of creating dialog boxes other than a desire to save memory and speed up your programs. Creating dialog boxes visually is part of the core functionality of the Delphi RAD tools, and it is one of the first things you notice when you use the environment. In short, Delphi represents a better solution to the problem of creating dialog boxes than the one represented by the technology behind standard Windows dialog boxes.

So, if Delphi has a better way to do this, why am I bothering to show you the old technique? What is to be gained?

There are two reasons to learn about old style dialog boxes:

1. The old style dialog boxes enable you to easily create windows and controls without using objects. If you want to create a very small DLL that pops up a dialog box, you can use the technique shown here to produce DLLs that are only a few thousand bytes in size. If you do things the Delphi RAD way, the task itself is easier, but you end up with a DLL that is at least 150,000 bytes in size. Sometimes nothing else matters more than speed and size. In those situations, you can use the classic, old style Windows dialog boxes described in this chapter.

2. Standard Windows dialog boxes represent one of the common features of the Windows API. The goal of the current section of the book is to show you how Windows works. You can use this knowledge to help you create better programs.

Before going on I should emphasize that the dialog boxes built with Delphi RAD tools are in no way inferior, or superior, to standard old style Windows dialog boxes. The VCL just provides another, easier, way to do the same thing. In one case, the message loop for the dialog box is handled by the operating system, whereas in the other it's handled by the VCL. But this is not a significant difference, and in fact you will find that both types of dialog boxes look, act, and feel exactly the same. The only difference is in the amount of memory they consume and the speed at which they execute.

> **NOTE**
>
> One final note of clarification is needed here. Adding a VCL dialog box to a Delphi program does not necessarily provide a 150KB hit to your program. If you put one dialog box in a DLL, you will get a 150KB hit. If you put two VCL dialog boxes in that DLL, the DLL remains essentially the same size. It's the first hit that is costly. In a standard Delphi program, all the code required to build a dialog box is also required to build the main form for the program. So adding one dialog box to an existing Delphi program is unlikely to make your code significantly larger. The first hit is costly, but once you have added that code into your project you can reuse it at relatively little cost to the size of your project. As a result, it's primarily when you start putting dialog boxes into DLLs that the technique shown here becomes valuable.

This chapter concentrates on creating dialog boxes and using resources. However, I offer several examples of putting dialog boxes in DLLs. This code appears in Chapter 13, "The Windows API and DLLs," and in Chapter 14, "Windows Controls and Callbacks."

Use the Source, Luke: Into the Windows API

Enough theory. It's time now to look at a program that uses the Windows API to create dialog boxes. The Window2 program, shown in Listings 10.1 through 10.3, features a standard Window, a menu, and a dialog box. The program itself is shown in Figure 10.1, and is found on disk in the WINDOW2 subdirectory, as opposed to the WINDOW2a subdirectory. The program in the WINDOW2a directory is very similar to this one but differs in some minor ways. It is discussed later in this chapter.

The source code shown here is much like the code you saw in the last chapter, but it has a few significant differences. In particular, you get a chance to see how to create a dialog box procedure and how to call `DialogBox`.

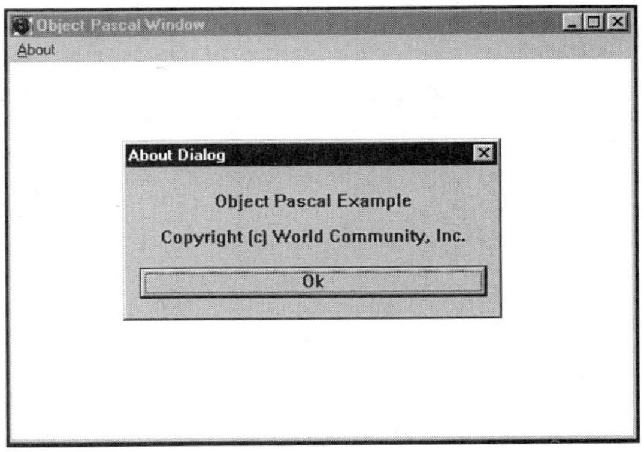

FIGURE 10.1.

The main window, menu, and dialog box for the Window2 program.

Listing 10.1. The source for the Window2 Program.

```
program Window2;

{ Standard Windows API application written in Object Pascal }

uses
  Windows, Messages;   // The wm_XXX constants moved from Windows to Messages

{$I WINDOW2.INC}
{$R WINDRES.RES}

const
  AppName = 'Window2';

function About(Dialog: HWnd; AMessage, WParam: UINT;
               LParam: LPARAM): Bool; stdcall; export;
begin
  About := True;
  case AMessage of
    wm_InitDialog: Exit;

    wm_Command:
      if (WParam = idOk) or (WParam = idCancel) then begin
        EndDialog(Dialog, 1);
        Exit;
      end;
  end;
  Result := False;
end;

function WindowProc(Window: HWnd; AMessage, WParam: UINT;
                    LParam: LPARAM): Longint; stdcall; export;
var
  AboutProc: TFarProc;
begin
  Result := 0;
```

continues

Listing 10.1. continued

```pascal
  case AMessage of
    wm_Command:
      if LoWord(WParam) = cm_About then begin
        DialogBox(HInstance, 'About', Window, @About);
        Exit;
      end;

    wm_Destroy:
      begin
        PostQuitMessage(0);
        Exit;
      end;
  end;

  Result := DefWindowProc(Window, AMessage, WParam, LParam);
end;

{ Register the Window Class }
function DoRegister: Boolean;
var
  WindowClass: TWndClass;
begin
  WindowClass.Style := cs_hRedraw or cs_vRedraw;
  WindowClass.lpfnWndProc := @WindowProc;
  WindowClass.cbClsExtra := 0;
  WindowClass.cbWndExtra := 0;
  WindowClass.hInstance := HInstance;
  WindowClass.hIcon := LoadIcon(HInstance, 'WindowIcon');
  WindowClass.hCursor := LoadCursor(0, idc_Arrow);
  WindowClass.hbrBackground := GetStockObject(white_Brush);
  WindowClass.lpszMenuName := 'WindowMenu';
  WindowClass.lpszClassName := AppName;

  Result := RegisterClass(WindowClass) <> 0;
end;

{ Create the Window Class }
function Create: HWnd;
begin
  Result := CreateWindow(AppName, 'Object Pascal Window',
            ws_OverlappedWindow, cw_UseDefault, cw_UseDefault,
            cw_UseDefault, cw_UseDefault, 0, 0, HInstance, nil);
end;


var
  AMessage: TMsg;
  HWindow: HWnd;

begin
  if not DoRegister then begin
    MessageBox(0, 'Register failed', nil, mb_Ok);
    Exit;
  end;
  HWindow := Create;
  if HWindow = 0 then begin
```

```
      MessageBox(0, 'Create failed', nil, mb_Ok);
      Exit;
    end;

  ShowWindow(hWindow, CmdShow);
  UpdateWindow(hWindow);

  while GetMessage(AMessage, 0, 0, 0) do begin
    TranslateMessage(AMessage);
    DispatchMessage(AMessage);
  end;

  Halt(AMessage.wParam);
end.
```

Listing 10.2. The Include file for the Window2 program.

```
{        Name : WINDOW2.INC
       Author : Copyright (c) 1995 by Charlie Calvert
  Description : Include file for WINDOW2.DPR }

const
  cm_About = 100;
```

Listing 10.3. The Resource file for the Window2 program.

```
//////////////////////////////////////////////////////
//          File: WINDRES.RC
//        Author: Copyright (c) 1995 by Charlie Calvert
//          From: Delphi Unleashed
// Description: The resource for the WINDOW2 program
//////////////////////////////////////////////////////

#include "window2.inc"

// The Icon
WindowIcon ICON "WINDOW2.ICO"

// The Menu
WindowMenu MENU
BEGIN
  MENUITEM "&About", cm_About
END

// The About Dialog
About DIALOG 18, 18, 141, 58
STYLE DS_MODALFRAME ¦ WS_POPUP ¦ WS_CAPTION ¦ WS_SYSMENU
CAPTION "About Dialog"
BEGIN
  PUSHBUTTON "Ok", IDOK, 5, 39, 132, 12,
             WS_CHILD ¦ WS_VISIBLE ¦ WS_TABSTOP
```

continues

Listing 10.3. continued

```
CTEXT "Object Pascal Example", -1, 1, 9, 140, 8,
          WS_CHILD | WS_VISIBLE | WS_GROUP
  CTEXT "Copyright (c) World Community, Inc.",
       -1, 1, 23, 140, 10,
          WS_CHILD | WS_VISIBLE | WS_GROUP
END
```

To compile this program you first need to compile its resource from the command prompt using the following command:

```
BRCC32 -r windres.rc
```

This produces a file called WINDRES.RES. Once this file exists, the Window2 program compiles smoothly inside the IDE.

> **NOTE**
>
> A more detailed discussion of resource files is included later in the chapter, along with a lengthy discussion of compiling from the command prompt. If you can't get this application to compile successfully right away, don't despair. There are plenty of clues as to what might be wrong scattered among the next few pages of this book.

When this program is first launched, it appears as a standard window with a simple menu at the top. If you select the sole item in the menu, a dialog box appears. The dialog box has a button and some text in it. If you press the button, the dialog box closes.

Using the Delphi RAD tools, it would be trivial to construct a program of this type. However, the task is considerably more complex when you are working with the straight Windows API. The primary benefit of the Window2 program, however, is that it's about one tenth the size of a standard Delphi VCL program of similar capability. To get started understanding how it works, you first need to understand something about resources.

The Resource File for the Window2 Program

Delphi treats RES files as binary entities, but traditionally they begin as text files with an RC extension. To convert an RC file to an RES file, use the BRCC32.EXE resource compiler. BRCC32 stands for Borland Resource CommandLine Compiler, 32-bit. Microsoft compilers typically come with a program called RC.EXE or RC32.EXE. This does the same thing that BRCC32 does, but Borland's tool has several extensions that speed up compilation and add niceties such as support for Pascal syntax. However, you can use the 32-bit Microsoft resource compiler to create resources for Delphi programs.

RC text files have code in them that follows a very simple syntax for defining which icons and bitmaps you want to build into your application, as well as any menus, dialog boxes, or custom resources you might want to add.

The Window2 program has one RES file called WINDRES.RES. The source for this file is shown in Listing 10.3. It contains an icon, a simple menu, and a simple dialog box.

Here is the code found in WINDRES.RC for including a simple icon:

```
// The Icon
WindowIcon ICON "WINDOW2.ICO"
```

The first line of the file shown here contains a C style comment, which is the traditional way to add comments to resource files. The second line of code tells BRCC32 to find a file called WINDOW2.ICO. Furthermore, it states that the content of WINDOW2.ICO is an ICON, and that it should be compiled into a resource and labeled WindowIcon:

- Filename: Window2.ico
- Resource Type: ICON
- Identifier labeling resource: WindowIcon

As a rule, a word such as ICON is not processed by BRCC32—it is simply stored for later use. In other words, resource files are just chunks of binary data sorted by name and type, where anyone can define a new type whenever they want. Resource files store names like ICON so that you can find out what kind of resource is available, not because they treat icons any differently than any other chunk of binary data you might pass to them.

The following code adds a menu to the resource:

```
// The Menu
WindowMenu MENU
BEGIN
  MENUITEM "&About", cm_About
END
```

The word WindowMenu is an identifier selected by the programmer to label the menu for later retrieval. Writing

```
WindowMenu MENU
```

is roughly equivalent to writing the following in the body of a Delphi program:

```
var
  WindowMenu: TMainMenu;
```

That is, the word WindowMenu is a variable declaration for a resource file, and the word MENU is a type declaration for a resource file. (Obviously, the syntax for RC files has nothing to do with Object Pascal.) The code tells the resource compiler that you want to define a menu, and that you want the menu to be called WindowMenu.

The BEGIN..END pair that follows the opening line of the menu declaration is used exactly as a BEGIN..END pair would be used in a Delphi application. In other words, it's a syntactical construct for designating the beginning and ending of a block of code. In RC files you can also use C style curly braces:

```
WindowMenu MENU
{
  MENUITEM "&About", cm_About
}
```

From a performance point of view, no advantage adheres to either syntactical construct. You can simply choose the technique that you feel is clearest and easiest to read.

The single line between the BEGIN..END pair defines the only visible part of this menu:

```
MENUITEM "&About", cm_About
```

This code tells BRCC32 that you want to create a menu item with the text "About" in it. A menu item is the visible, textual, part of a menu. In a typical pop-up File menu, menu items include Open, Save, and Close.

NOTE

If you want to work with a more complex menu, you can view the code shown here:

```
MENU_1 MENU
BEGIN
     POPUP "&File"
     BEGIN
          MENUITEM "&New", CM_NEW
          MENUITEM "&Open...", CM_OPEN
          MENUITEM "&Save", CM_SAVE
          MENUITEM "Save &as...", CM_SAVEAS,
          MENUITEM SEPARATOR
          POPUP "&Print..."
          BEGIN
               MENUITEM "Print To Disk", CM_PRNDISK
               MENUITEM "Print LPT1", CM_PRNLPT1
          END
          MENUITEM "Page se&tup...", CM_PAGESETUP
          MENUITEM "P&rinter setup...", CM_PRINTERSETUP
          MENUITEM SEPARATOR
          MENUITEM "E&xit", CM_EXIT
     END
     POPUP "&Cursors"
     BEGIN
          MENUITEM "&Round Cursor\tAlt+F1", CM_ROUNDCURSOR
          MENUITEM "&Diamond Cursor\tCtrl+F2", CM_DIAMONDCURSOR
          MENUITEM "&Draw Icon\tShift+F3", CM_ICONCURSOR
     END
     POPUP "BitCursors"
     BEGIN
          MENUITEM "Item", CM_BITMENU1
          MENUITEM "Item", CM_BITMENU2
          MENUITEM "Item", CM_BITMENU3
```

```
    END
        MENUITEM "&Help", CM_HELP
    END
```

This menu has a series of pop-up menus like the kind you would find in a standard Windows program such as Notepad or WordPad. You could define the following constants inside the RC file so that it would compile:

```
#define CM_NEW 101
#define CM_OPEN 102
#define CM_SAVE 103
#define CM_SAVEAS 104
#define CM_PRNDISK 151
#define CM_PRNLPT1 152
#define CM_PAGESETUP 105
#define CM_PRINTERSETUP 106
#define CM_EXIT 107

#define CM_ROUNDCURSOR 201
#define CM_DIAMONDCURSOR 202
#define CM_ICONCURSOR 203

#define CM_BITMENU1 301
#define CM_BITMENU2 302
#define CM_BITMENU3 303

#define CM_HELP     401
#define ID_HELPEDIT 402
```

If you want to experiment with this code, I have included it on the CD in a small file called README.TXT. You can just cut and paste between README.TXT and WNDRES.RC to begin your exploration of creating complex menus by hand.

The menu item with a label that reads &About declared earlier has an ID associated with it. This ID is represented by the constant CM_ABOUT. Whenever the user clicks this menu item, a message with the value CM_ABOUT associated with it is sent to your WndProc.

cm_About is a standard constant defined like this:

```
const
  cm_About  = 100;
```

You should not define this constant inside the main body of WINDOW2.DPR, nor inside the RC file. The issue is that the value needs to be seen by both WINDOW2.DPR and WINDRES.RC. The best solution in cases like this is to start a small separate file meant for storing global variables that will be used by two or more modules in your program.

In this case, the small global file is called WINDOW2.INC, and it looks like this:

```
const
  cm_About = 100;
```

This is the entire include file, complete with all the syntax necessary to make it compile properly. In other words, there is no interface section, no implementation, no anything. It's just a code fragment.

You can link an include file into any Object Pascal program with the following syntax:

```
{$I WINDOW2.INC}
```

This code tells the compiler to insert the file called WINDOW2.INC at this place in the file. In terms of the final binary executable produced by the compiler, there is absolutely no difference between placing code in an include file and placing code in a module at the exact location where the {$I ...} directive is located.

In the preceding example, the include directive looks like this:

```
uses
  Windows;

{$I WINDOW2.INC}

{$R WINDRES.RES}

const
  AppName = 'Window2';
```

If I removed the include directive and inserted the constant declaration for cm_About directly into the code, there would be no change in the binary imprint of the executable:

```
uses
  Windows;

const
  cm_About = 100;

{$R WINDRES.RES}

const
  AppName = 'Window2';
```

In other words, the two code fragments shown here are, for all intents and purposes, identical. One happens to use an include file and the other doesn't, but they both say the exact same thing, and the compiler interprets both code fragments as being identical.

If you want to link an include file into an RC file, you can use the following syntax:

```
#include "window2.inc"
```

This inserts the code from WINDOW2.INC into the RC file, just as the {$I WINDOW2.INC} syntax inserts the code into the DPR file.

> **NOTE**
>
> You can also insert references to PAS files into RC files that are to be compiled by BRCC32. (However, this won't work with Microsoft's resource compiler.)
>
> For instance, you could create the following file in lieu of WINDOW2.INC:
>
> ```
> unit Globals;
> ```

```
{       Name : GLOBALS.PAS
Author : Copyright (c) 1995 by Charlie Calvert
 Description :   Contains variables used in WINDOW2.DPR }

interface

const
  cm_About = 100;

implementation

end.
```

You could then link this file into WINDOW2.DPR as you would link in any other
PAS file, and you could link it into WINDRES.RC with the following syntax:

```
#include "globals.pas"
```

So that you can have examples of both types of syntax, I have implemented this
technique in a version of the Window2 program that is included on disk in the
subdirectory called Window2a.

The following code fragment shows how to define a dialog box in a resource file:

```
// The About Dialog
About DIALOG 18, 18, 141, 58
STYLE DS_MODALFRAME | WS_POPUP | WS_CAPTION | WS_SYSMENU
CAPTION "About Dialog"
BEGIN
  PUSHBUTTON "Ok", IDOK, 5, 39, 132, 12,
             WS_CHILD | WS_VISIBLE | WS_TABSTOP
  CTEXT "Object Pascal Example", -1, 1, 9, 140, 8,
             WS_CHILD | WS_VISIBLE | WS_GROUP
  CTEXT "Copyright (c) World Community, Inc.",
        -1, 1, 23, 140, 10,
        WS_CHILD | WS_VISIBLE | WS_GROUP
END
```

The opening line of this code gives the dialog box a name, declares its type so the resource
compiler knows what to do with it, and defines its dimensions:

```
About DIALOG 18, 18, 141, 58
```

The next line of code defines the styles associated with the dialog box. These are the same styles
you would pass in the third parameter of a call to CreateWindow.

The code that appears between the BEGIN..END pair defines the three controls that reside on the
dialog box's surface. One is a button, of essentially the same type as created by the TButton
object found on the Component Palette. The other two controls are like the TLabel controls
found on the Component Palette. However, unlike the button controls, these controls are not
identical to the Delphi TLabel controls. They look, feel, and act very much the same, but at
bottom they are quite different. In particular, the CTEXT items shown earlier use the static class
defined by Windows.

TLabel components are defined inside Delphi. In particular, they are Delphi objects that have no Window handle, and they are drawn on the surface of the object on which they lie. The main point, however, is that they are not part of the operating system. TLabel objects are not the same as static controls defined with the CTEXT directive.

The TButton, TEdit, TListBox, TComboBox, TRadioBox, and TCheckBox controls from the Component Palette are all real Windows controls. For instance, the push button control in the preceding dialog box is the same type of push button control used in Delphi RAD programs. The TLabel and TShape controls are fabrications made up of Delphi objects. The developers of Delphi chose to create the TLabel control because they could make something smaller, faster, and less expensive to use than the standard static control displayed in Window2's dialog box.

NOTE

You can compile many different resources into a single RES file. For instance, the following short RC file would compile six bitmaps, an icon, and a string resource into an RES file that could be linked into your executable:

```
Body    BITMAP "body.bmp"
Head    BITMAP "head.bmp"
Pattern BITMAP "pattern.bmp"
Grass   BITMAP "grass.bmp"
Road    BITMAP "road.bmp"
Road2   BITMAP "road2.bmp"
Icon    ICON   "file1.ico"

STRINGTABLE
BEGIN
    0, "Woodnotes (Part 1)"
    1, "by Ralph Waldo Emerson"
    2, ""
    3, "When the pine tosses its cones"
    4, "To the song of its waterfall tones,"
    5, "..."
    6, "Wealth to the cunning artist who can work"
    7, "This matchless strength. Where shall he find, O waves!"
    8, "A load your Atlas shoulders cannot lift?"
END
```

You could retrieve the bitmaps at runtime by calling LoadBitmap and the strings from the stringtable by calling LoadString.

That's all I'm going to say about RC files for now. If you have had trouble compiling this example, hold on just a moment longer, and I will discuss compiling from the command prompt.

Working with Resources in a Standard Delphi RAD Program

This section explores the RES file that is included in nearly all standard Delphi RAD programs. The discussion in this section is a bit of an aside to Window2 program, but I feel that it's important that you understand how Delphi normally treats RES files. Once you see their significance in a standard RAD program, the role the RES file plays in Window2 should come into sharper relief.

Almost all Delphi RAD-based programs use a simple resource file that contains an icon. You can find these files in the directory where you compile your programs. The name of the resource file defaults to the name of your application, with the letters RES as an extension.

In the DPR file for your program, you find the following syntax:

```
{$R *.RES}
```

This code tells Delphi to search for and load a resource file with the same name as the current source module, but with an RES extension.

> **NOTE**
>
> I call the RES file for the Window2 program WINRES.RES. This is because Delphi, by default, works with a resource file that has the same name as the executable. This resource file belongs to Delphi, the programming environment, and it's best not to have a RES file that you have created with the same name as the executable itself. Just consider the executable name as reserved when you are working with a resource file for a Delphi program.

The following very short RC file, called CLIENT1.RC, defines the standard RES file that accompanies a Delphi application:

```
/*   Client1 Icon        */
Icon ICON "client1.ico"
```

These standard Delphi resource files contain nothing more than an icon. Normally these files are automatically built for you by Delphi, but I am showing how to make one so that you will understand the technology involved. You can use the Resource Workshop to examine a standard VCL resource file. Ask it to convert the file into an RC file. If you do this, you will see that its code is identical to the code shown earlier.

BRCC32.EXE compiles the RC file if you enter the following command at the DOS prompt:

```
BRCC32 -r CLIENT1.RC.
```

This command produces a file called CLIENT1.RES that contains a single icon. You can examine this file in the Image Editor from the Tools menu. It can also be loaded into the Resource Workshop, if you have that tool available.

> **NOTE**
>
> Experienced Borland C++ and Borland Pascal programmers probably know about the Resource Workshop, which can be used to simplify the process of working with RES files. You can still use the Resource Workshop with Delphi exactly as you would have used it with BP7 or BC45. If you don't have a copy of this tool, you can almost certainly buy it from Borland as an up-sell. Note that there is a difference between the 16- and 32-bit versions of the Resource Workshop. BC45 ships with a 32-bit version of this tool.
>
> BRCC32.EXE can do everything that the Resource Workshop can do except enable you to browse through existing resources or executables. The advantage that Resource Workshop has over BRCC32 is that it's easier to use.
>
> The Image Editor that ships with Delphi has much of the functionality of the Resource Workshop built into it, but it does not handle version resources, dialog boxes, or string tables. The very first versions of the Image Editor that shipped with Delphi 16 were buggy. However, this product is much cleaner now, and I have found myself relying on it more often with reasonably good results.

Besides the standard icon, you can add additional resources to standard Delphi RAD programs. However, when you do this, you should not attempt to insert your resources into the default RES file used to hold the program's icon. For instance, if you had a program called CLIENT1, Delphi would automatically create a RES file for it called CLIENT1.RES. In content, it would be similar, or identical, to the resource file shown earlier. Do not attempt to add your own resources to this file. Instead, add a second resource file to this project, for the reasons explained earlier when I talked about resource naming conventions.

When adding additional resource files to a standard Delphi RAD project, I prefer to put them in the main form, right next to the reference to the DFM file:

```
implementation

{$R *.DFM}
{$R MYRES.RES}
```

The code shown here adds a second resource file to a Delphi RAD project. The resource file is called MYRES.RES, and it would typically be made with a copy of BRCC32.EXE and a text file called MYRES.RC. The assumption here is that the executable for the preceding program is named anything else besides MYRES.EXE, because you should not add a resource file to a Delphi project that has the same name as the DPR file.

Creating and Handling the Dialog Box

Here is the code that actually pops up the dialog box you created using BRCC32 or the Resource Workshop:

```
function WindowProc(Window: HWnd; AMessage, WParam: UINT;
                    LParam: LPARAM): Longint; stdcall; export;

var
  AboutProc: TFarProc;
begin
  WindowProc := 0;

  case AMessage of

    wm_Command:
      if LoWord(WParam) = cm_About then begin
        DialogBox(HInstance, 'About', Window, @About);
        Exit;
      end;
      ...

end;
```

wm_Command messages are sent to a WndProc whenever the user chooses an item from a menu, selects an accelerator key stroke, or performs certain other actions such as selecting a button. When you receive a wm_Command message, WParam is set to the constant associated with the control that sent it. In this case, that value is cm_About.

In Win32, the high-order Word of WParam is set to the value 1 if the message is from an accelerator, or to 0 if the message is from a menu. The high order word specifies a notification code if the message is from a control. Because this message is being sent by a menu, there is no need to use the LoWord function. However, this is still the cautious thing to do, and it helps you form the right habits. In Win16, there is no value specified in the high-order word of WParam, in part because this is only a 16-bit value in Win16, and therefore there is no high-order Word.

Once you have parsed WParam and know what message you are going to receive, the next step is to create the dialog box itself:

```
DialogBox(HInstance, 'About', Window, @About);
```

The relatively straightforward DialogBox command takes the following arguments:

- The HInstance for the application in the first parameter.
- The name of the resource in the second parameter. This is the name you specified in the RC file.
- The HWnd of the owner in the third parameter.
- The address of the dialog box procedure in the fourth parameter. The dialog box procedure plays the same role for a dialog box that WndProc plays for window.

In Win32, calling the `DialogBox` procedure is trivial. In Win16, it can be complicated by the need to call `MakeProcInstance` before the `DialogBox` call, and `FreeProcInstance` after the `DialogBox` call. It is not an error to call `MakeProcInstance` and `FreeProcInstance` in Win32; however, these calls do not do anything in Win32. I return to this subject later in the chapter, when you see the Win232 program, which compiles in both Win16 and Win32.

`DialogBox` creates a modal dialog box. If you want to create a modeless dialog box, you should use `CreateDialog` instead of `DialogBox`.

After creating the dialog box, the focus of the program moves to the `About` function, which is to the About dialog box what the `WindowProc` is to the main window:

```
function About(Dialog: HWnd; AMessage, WParam:UINT;
               LParam: LPARAM): Bool; stdcall; export;
begin
  Result := True;
case AMessage of
    wm_InitDialog: Exit;

    wm_Command:
      if (WParam = idOk) or (WParam = idCancel) then begin
        EndDialog(Dialog, 1);
        Exit;
      end;
  end;
  Result := False;
end;
```

If you compare the `About` function and the `WindowProc` function, you will see that they take the same parameters but return a different value. In general, the two routines are very similar, both in appearance and in function.

You can use the `wm_InitDialog` message to perform any initialization needed for the dialog box. The dialog box should be closed whenever the user presses the OK button or cancels out of the dialog box. To close a dialog box, call the `EndDialog` procedure, passing in the `HWnd` of the dialog box in the first parameter. The second parameter of `EndDialog` contains the value you want the `DialogBox` procedure to return.

This whole process is not really that complicated. However, if it seems a bit intimidating, remember that you can just cut and paste this code from one application to the next. All modal dialog boxes are created the same way, and all dialog box procedures have the same basic structure as the `About` procedure. So whenever you need to create one of these dialog boxes, just cut and paste the code from this program. Write once, use many. It's not really that hard.

Batch File Issues

The next two sections of this chapter discuss compiling Delphi applications from the command prompt. If you have a copy of the Resource Workshop, you don't have to do any work at the command line. If you don't have the Resource Workshop, you have to compile the RC files from the command prompt, but you can still compile the executables from inside the Delphi IDE.

I'm discussing the command line now only because it can be helpful to know how to work outside the IDE. It is not a necessity to work from the command prompt, and indeed I only do so under unusual circumstances. However, it can be a very fast way to compile and test applications. The command prompt also enables you to easily automate procedures with batch or makefiles, which can be a very convenient aid under certain circumstances of the type frequently encountered by serious programmers.

NOTE

If you want to compile from the command line, it's probably best not to have Delphi installed in a subdirectory that includes long filenames anywhere in its path. In particular, I would install it into C:\DELPHI32, if possible. If you decide to move Delphi from its current directory to a new location, remember that you have to change the entries in the registration database. Under most circumstances, this means that you should probably first uninstall Delphi using the Control Panel, and then reinstall to a new location where there are no long pathnames leading to the Delphi directory. If you have a CD, and you choose the automated Uninstall from the Control Panel, it really isn't that difficult to move Delphi's location.

You should note that the 4DOS command processors, version 5.51 and greater, do understand long filenames. These tools are made by JP software and are available as shareware on CompuServe and elsewhere. 4DOS makes life with long filenames bearable, but in general, I still think it is a good idea not to install Delphi into a subdirectory that uses long filenames.

Just to make my point clear, at the time of this writing I was not able to get Delphi applications to compile cleanly from the command prompt unless I could eliminate long filenames in the path leading to the Delphi directory. Perhaps this will be fixed in the shipping version of the product, but for now I would recommend installing Delphi in C:\DELPHI32, or in some other location that has a simple path leading to it. My other programs can be buried behind the c:\program files\ directory, but Delphi seems to work best if it has a simple path leading to it.

By now you know how to construct and compile a very simple RES file. The following code shows a simple DOS batch file. It would compile the resources used by the Window2 program, as well as the Window2 program itself:

```
BRCC32 -r windres.rc
dcc32 -b window2.dpr
```

This batch file enables you to compile Delphi programs from the command prompt, without ever opening DELPHI32.EXE. The -b parameter specifies that you want to perform a build rather than a simple compile. You must have the DELPHI32\BIN directory on your path for this to work correctly. Furthermore, you should define a DCC32.CFG file that points to the LIB directory:

```
-rC:\Delphi32\Lib
-uC:\Delphi32\Lib
```

The -r switch specifies the resource directory, and the -u switch designates the directory or directories where your units are stored. The code shown here should be placed in a separate file called DCC32.CFG and should be stored in the DELPHI32\BIN subdirectory. In the case shown here, I'm assuming Delphi was installed in the c:\delphi32 subdirectory. That enables me to avoid atrocities that look like this:

```
-uC:\Progra~1\Borland\Delphi~1.0\Lib
```

Note that the WINDRES.RC won't compile successfully unless you have an icon called WINDOW2.ICO in the same directory. There are icons that ship both with this book and with Delphi, or you can build an icon with the Resource Workshop or with the Image Editor from the Tools menu. If you don't want to build your own icon, you can safely rename an existing icon to WINDOW2.ICO, or copy an existing icon to a file of that name.

The WINDRES.RES file is automatically linked into your program because of the $R line found in WINDOW2.DPR:

```
{$R WINDRES.RES}
```

The Command Line Revisited

I want to take a few paragraphs to look a little more closely at what happens when you compile from the command line rather than from inside DELPHI32.EXE. I also want to lay some groundwork for rewriting the Window2 application so it compiles under both WIN16 and WIN32.

Here is the original simple batch file composed earlier:

```
BRCC32 -r windres.rc
dcc32 -b window2.dpr
```

This kind of batch file works fine for small projects. However, there are occasions when you need to compile large, multifile projects. In those cases, you need a more sophisticated tool, such as a makefile.

In one moment, I'll show an example makefile. However, it's at least arguable that a makefile's syntax is such that it should be used only as a last resort. For those who feel that way, the following is a useful batch file trick that can get you through even very complex projects.

The key point to consider when reading the following batch file is that the Borland compilers set the DOS ERRORLEVEL to 1 if something goes wrong:

```
@echo off

BRCC32 -r wind232.rc
if ErrorLevel 1 goto Error

DCC32 -b -AWINPROCS=WINDOWS -AWINTYPES=WINDOWS wind232.dpr
if ErrorLevel 1 goto Error
goto AllDone

:Error
echo Error occured!

:AllDone
```

The batch file tries to compile each of the files in your project. If something goes wrong, the batch file prints out "Error occurred!" and terminates. Even if you had hundreds of different compilations specified in your batch file, the run would always either terminate successfully or terminate with the last few lines showing the action that caused the error. It's this error detection mechanism that makes these batch files useful.

Notice the change to the command line where DCC32.EXE is called. This change sets up aliases for the WinProcs and WinTypes units. These aliases tell the 32-bit compiler to substitute the word WINDOWS whenever it sees the words WinTypes or WinProcs. (Inside the IDE, you can set up the same changes by selecting Tools | Options | Library | Aliases from the menu.) The switch for declaring an alias is -A. Needless to say, you need to put WinProcs and WinTypes in your uses clause for this option to make any sense.

Assuming that you don't want to use batch files, here is a makefile that can be used to compile the WINDOW2 project:

```
#------------------------------------------------------------------
# WINDOW2.MAK
# Copyright (c) 1996 by Charlie Calvert
# You must have MAKE.EXE on your path to run this file.
# Syntax: MAKE -f WINDOW2.MAK
#------------------------------------------------------------------

!if !$d(WIN16)
COMPILER = DCC32.EXE
RCCOMPILER = BRCC32.EXE
FLAGS = -B -AWINPROCS=WINDOWS -AWINTYPES=WINDOWS
!else
COMPILER = DCC.EXE
RCCOMPILER = BRC.EXE
FLAGS = -B
!endif

APPNAME = WINDOW2
```

```
# link EXES
$(APPNAME).exe: WINDRES.res
  $(COMPILER) $(FLAGS) $(APPNAME).DPR

# resource
.rc.res:
  $(RCCOMPILER) -r { $< }
```

Here is the syntax for using a makefile from the command line:

```
make -f window2.mak
```

This is not the time or place to get involved in a long discussion of makefiles. I'm including this one mostly to let hard-core C/C++ programmers see how they can use some of their favorite tools with Delphi. Note that this MAK file has a rule for building resources, and it provides a mechanism for creating 16-bit files as well as 32-bit. If you want to create a 16-bit executable, you should enter the following line at the command prompt:

```
make -DWIN16 -f window2.mak
```

The -D option shown here defines WIN16 so that it appears to be part of the environment. The makefile sets up the COMPILER and RCCOMPILER macros differently when WIN16 is defined. In the next section I describe how to change WINDOW2.DPR so it compiles under 16-bit and 32-bit.

You cannot create the 16-bit Delphi executable unless you have Delphi 16 installed on your system. Furthermore, you need to be able to switch your DOS path back and forth between the DELPHI\BIN and DELPHI32\BIN subdirectories before switching targets.

NOTE

Next you find a batch file that I use to switch my path dynamically without having to reboot my system or my Windows 95 DOS session. This file assumes you have a command processor running that passes parameters to batch files. 4DOS does this for you, as do all versions of DOS up to, but not including, version 7. Here is the batch file:

```
@echo off
if %1==1 goto delphi
if %1==2 goto BC45
if %1==3 goto Delphi32

echo 1): Delphi
echo 2): BC45
echo 3): Delphi32
goto end

:delphi
path=c:\delphi\bin
goto mostpaths

:bc45
```

```
path=c:\bc45\bin\

goto mostpaths

:delphi32
path=c:\delphi32\bin
goto mostpaths

:mostpaths
path=c:\iblocal\bin;c:\windows\command;c:\idapi;%path%;
set BCROOT=c:\bc45
goto end

:end
```

Note that the %path% syntax enables me to reference the current DOS path. Therefore, the path statement in MOSTPATHS prepends a few new subdirectories onto the path statement defined in one of the earlier sections of the batch file. For example, the early sections of the batch file might set the path to the following:

```
c:\delphi32\bin
```

The mostpaths section would then set it to

```
c:\iblocal\bin;c:\windows\command;c:\idapi;c:\delphi32\bin
```

On my system this batch file is called NEWP.BAT. If I type NEWP directly at the DOS prompt with no parameters, I get a list of the available paths. If I want to switch to the Delphi 16 path, I type NEWP 1. If I want to switch to the DELPHI32 path, I type NEWP 3. There is a call to NEWP 3 (CALL NEWP 3) in my AUTOEXEC.BAT file.

Achieving 16- and 32-Bit Windows API Compatibility

The references to 16-bit applications in the preceding makefile are academic, because the WINDOW2.DPR project does not compile as is for 16 bits. To remedy this problem, I have created a second project called WIN232.DPR, which exists in its own subdirectory on the CD. The sources for these files are not quoted in their entirety in this book, although I do quote the entire DPR file in Listing 10.4.

In the 16-bit version, the WindowProc function is no longer declared stdcall, and the AMessage and wParam parameters passed to it are of type Word. Similar changes are made in the dialog box procedure. Finally, the RegisterClass procedure is declared differently in Win16 and Win32, so some changes have to be made to it. In all cases, I use conditional compilation so as to have one source file that compiles under both Win16 and Win32. For instance, here is one way to ifdef the WndProc so that it compiles on both platforms:

```
...
{$ifdef WIN32}
function WindowProc(Window: HWnd; AMessage, WParam,
                LParam: Longint): Longint; stdcall; export;
```

```
{$else}
function WindowProc(Window: HWnd; AMessage, WParam: Word;
                    LParam: Longint): Longint; export;
{$endif}
var
  AboutProc: TFarProc;
begin
  WindowProc := 0;

  case AMessage of
    ...
```

This code assumes that Win32 is defined automatically when you run DCC32 or DELPHI32.

In my opinion, a better way to handle this problem would be to declare types that can be redefined in 16- and 32-bit Windows:

```
type
  UINT  = Cardinal;
  WPARAM = UINT;
  LPARAM = LongInt;

function WindowProc(Window: HWnd; AMessage, WParam: UINT;
  LParam: LPARAM): Longint; {$ifdef WIN32} stdcall; {$endif} export;
```

A UINT would then be declared as a 16-bit value in Win16 and a 32-bit value in Win32. The same code would then compile in both versions without a need to resort to perhaps overly obtrusive ifdefs. Some of these types might be predefined for you in the file WINDOWS.PAS that ships with your version of Delphi 2.0. However, they won't be defined in Delphi 16. The complete code for the program is shown below in Listing 10.4.

Listing 10.4. A version of the Window2 program that compiles under both Win32 and Win16.

```
program Wind232;

{ Standard Windows API application written in Object Pascal }

uses
  WinTypes, WinProcs, Messages;

{$I WIND232.INC}

{$R WINDRES.RES}

const
  AppName = 'Wind232';

type
  UINT = Cardinal;
  WPARAM = UINT;
  LPARAM = LongInt;

function About(Dialog: HWnd; AMessage, WParam: UINT;
  LParam: LPARAM): Bool; {$ifdef WIN32} stdcall; {$endif} export;
```

```
begin
  Result := True;
case AMessage of
    wm_InitDialog: Exit;

    wm_Command:
      if (WParam = idOk) or (WParam = idCancel) then begin
        EndDialog(Dialog, 1);
        Exit;
      end;
  end;
  Result := False;
end;

function WindowProc(Window: HWnd; AMessage, WParam: UINT;
  LParam: LPARAM): Longint; {$ifdef WIN32} stdcall; {$endif} export;
var
  AboutProc: TFarProc;
begin
  Result := 0;

  case AMessage of

    wm_Command:
      if WParam = cm_About then begin
        AboutProc := MakeProcInstance(@About, HInstance);
        DialogBox(HInstance, 'About', Window, AboutProc);
        FreeProcInstance(AboutProc);
        Exit;
      end;

    wm_Destroy:
      begin
        PostQuitMessage(0);
        Exit;
      end;
  end;

  Result := DefWindowProc(Window, AMessage, WParam, LParam);
end;

{ Register the Window Class }
function DoRegister: Boolean;
var
  WindowClass: TWndClass;
begin
  WindowClass.Style := cs_hRedraw or cs_vRedraw;
  WindowClass.lpfnWndProc := @WindowProc;
  WindowClass.cbClsExtra := 0;
  WindowClass.cbWndExtra := 0;
  WindowClass.hInstance := HInstance;
  WindowClass.hIcon := LoadIcon(HInstance, 'WindowIcon');
  WindowClass.hCursor := LoadCursor(0, idc_Arrow);
  WindowClass.hbrBackground := GetStockObject(white_Brush);
  WindowClass.lpszMenuName := 'WindowMenu';
  WindowClass.lpszClassName := AppName;

  {$ifdef WIN32}
```

continues

Listing 10.4. continued

```
Result := RegisterClass(WindowClass) <> 0;
{$else}
Result := RegisterClass(WindowClass);
{$endif}
end;

{ Create the Window Class }
function Create: HWnd;
begin
  Result := CreateWindow(AppName, 'Object Pascal Window',
              ws_OverlappedWindow, cw_UseDefault, cw_UseDefault,
              cw_UseDefault, cw_UseDefault, 0, 0, HInstance, nil);
end;

var
  AMessage: TMsg;
  Window: HWnd;

begin
  if not DoRegister then begin
    MessageBox(0, 'Register failed', nil, mb_Ok);
    Exit;
  end;
  Window := Create;
  if Window = 0 then begin
    MessageBox(0, 'Create failed', nil, mb_Ok);
    Exit;
  end;

  ShowWindow(Window, CmdShow);
  UpdateWindow(Window);

  while GetMessage(AMessage, 0, 0, 0) do begin
    TranslateMessage(AMessage);
    DispatchMessage(AMessage);
  end;

  Halt(AMessage.wParam);
end.
```

This program acts identically to the Window2 program. The only differences involve the places where Win32 is defined. For instance, note the DoRegister procedure:

```
{$ifdef WIN32}
Result := RegisterClass(WindowClass) <> 0;
{$else}
Result := RegisterClass(WindowClass);
{$endif}
```

Register class is defined to return an Atom in 32-bit code, and to return a BOOL in 16-bit.

The call to the `DialogBox` procedure also looks considerably different:

```
if WParam = cm_About then begin
  AboutProc := MakeProcInstance(@About, HInstance);
  DialogBox(HInstance, 'About', Window, AboutProc);
  FreeProcInstance(AboutProc);
  Exit;
end;
```

The code shown here compiles fine in both WIN16 and WIN32. The issue is that `MakeProcInstance` and `FreeProcInstance` don't do anything in WIN32:

```
function MakeProcInstance(Proc: FARPROC; Instance: THandle): FARPROC;
begin
  Result := Proc;
end;

procedure FreeProcInstance(Proc: FARPROC);
begin
end;
```

This is the kind of code sample that makes you think, "Hey, maybe I could have written Windows after all!" Of course, these routines are a little more complicated in their 16-bit versions.

All this dancing around when switching back and forth between 16 and 32 bits is necessary only because the code shown here is Windows API code and not VCL code. One of the significant functions of the VCL is that it makes it easy to move back and forth between 16 and 32 bits. The little exercises shown here should help to make it clear how much work is saved by using the VCL.

Summary

In this chapter you got a look at dialog boxes, resources, and messages. In addition, you got a good look at compiling applications from the DOS prompt, and at writing the appropriate batch files and makefiles to complete this task.

Remember that if you absolutely need to see this material in more depth, you can pick up a standard C reference on the Windows API such as Petzold's *Windows Programming*, published by the Microsoft Press, or *Teach Yourself Windows 95 Programming*, published by Sams. One of the goals of this chapter is to make it easy for you to use the reference books on Windows that are written in C. The key piece you need to grasp is how all that raw C API code relates to Delphi, and the answer to that query is supplied in these chapters.

Remember that the discussions about DLLs and messages begun in this chapter are picked up again in the next chapter. There is much more to be said about both topics, so you should tune in to the next chapter for additional information. One of the best ways to get used to all this Windows API code is simply through repetition. The first time you see a `WinProc`, it's a bit overwhelming. But once you have seen a dozen of them, they start to look awfully familiar.

They start by seeming alien, but they end up being old friends.

Messages and Painting Text

11

Two major subjects are covered in this chapter:

- The basic facts about messages
- The most fundamental I/O issue—how to display text

Many of the traits that give Windows its special flavor owe their character to the fact that Windows is an *event-oriented* (or message-based) system. If you don't understand messages, you won't understand Windows.

In this chapter, you get a chance to learn about event-oriented, message-based systems. You get an in-depth look at window procedures, messages, and message crackers. This is material that lies very much at the heart of Windows.

In particular, this chapter covers the following:

- Messages
- The MESSAGES.PAS file that ships with Delphi
- Message crackers
- Message handler functions
- Responses to WM_PAINT messages
- Device contexts
- Two ways to write text in a window

Much of the information in this chapter is of equal importance to RAD programmers and those who want to spelunk through the hard core of the Windows API. In other words, this information is of general interest, even though it is given in the context of a Windows API program. It's perhaps also worth pointing out that the Windows API program shown in this chapter produces an executable about one-tenth the size of its equivalent RAD program.

MESSAGES.PAS

This chapter uses a powerful message-cracking technique built into Delphi that helps you write clean, portable code. In particular, MESSAGES.PAS contains a series of special records that help you handle messages in a simple, easy-to-read manner, while at the same time creating code that is portable between Win16 and Win32.

Each message sent by the operating system is accompanied by two parameters of type LongInt called WParam and LParam. In Win16, WParam is declared as a 16-bit value, but in Win32, it is declared as 32-bit value. LParam is declared as a 32-bit value under both operating systems. These changes mean that the information accompanying some messages is encoded differently in Win32 than it was in 16-bit Windows. The message-cracking records in MESSAGES.PAS hide these implementation details from you. More specifically, Delphi 16 and Delphi 32 ship with two different versions of MESSAGES.PAS: one for 16-bit code and one for 32-bit code.

MESSAGES.PAS helps you avoid having to typecast most of your code that involves processing LParam and WParam. Normally Windows programming requires a huge number of typecasts, all of which circumvent the normal type-checking procedures that help you write safe code. MESSAGES.PAS lets you avoid typecasts and reasserts the primacy of type checking.

What Is a Message?

Chapter 9, "Beyond the VCL: WinMain and WinProc," presented a bird's-eye view of a standard Windows program. It gave you a flyby over all the major portions of a Windows program, including the WinMain, Register, Create, and WndProc functions, as well as the message loop. The next step is to narrow the focus so that you get a closer look at the window procedure and the messages that are sent to it.

By now you should have a feeling for the difference between a message-based (or event-driven) program and a standard procedural program. In the former case, the operating system tells a program that an event has occurred. In the latter case, the program queries the system to find out what has happened.

Here's a more in-depth look at the differences between the traditional DOS and Windows programming worlds:

- **Windows message-based model:** Once the program is launched, it simply waits for messages to be sent to it and then responds accordingly. Windows itself detects if a key has been pressed or if the mouse has been moved. When an event of this type occurs, Windows sends a predefined message to the program, telling it what has happened. The program usually has the option of either ignoring the message or responding to the message.

- **DOS procedural model:** DOS code usually executes linearly; that is, it starts at the beginning of a program and advances through to the end by stepping through code one line at a time or by branching or looping through various segments of code. The program discovers the user's commands by querying the system. That is, the program calls interrupt-based subroutines that are built into the operating system or the hardware. In return, these interrupts report whether a key has been pressed or the mouse has been moved. Special APIs such as Turbo Vision lived in a never-never-land halfway between DOS and Windows, but the standard DOS program followed the system outlined in the first part of this paragraph.

It should come as no surprise to hear that messages are really just constants defined in WINDOWS.PAS. Here, for instance, are the declarations for messages that handle keyboard and mouse movements:

```
// Keyboard Messages
WM_KEYDOWN        = $100; // Key was pressed
WM_KEYUP          = 257;  // Key was released
WM_CHAR           = 258;  // Processed keystroke
WM_DEADCHAR       = 259;  // Composite key
```

```
WM_SYSKEYDOWN      = 260;   // Alt key was pressed
WM_SYSKEYUP        = 261;   // Alt key was released
WM_SYSCHAR         = 262;   // Processed system keystroke
WM_SYSDEADCHAR     = 263;   // Composite system keystroke

// Mouse Messages
WM_MOUSEMOVE       = $200;  // Mouse was moved
WM_LBUTTONDOWN     = 513;   // Left button pressed
WM_LBUTTONUP       = 514;   // Left button released
WM_LBUTTONDBLCLK   = 515;   // Double click of left button
WM_RBUTTONDOWN     = 516;   // Right button down
WM_RBUTTONUP       = 517;   // Right button released
WM_RBUTTONDBLCLK   = 518;   // Double click of right button
WM_MBUTTONDOWN     = 519;   // Middle button down
WM_MBUTTONUP       = 520;   // Middle button up
WM_MBUTTONDBLCLK   = 521;   // Double click of middle button
```

Don't try to memorize these messages. Just look them over and become familiar with the way they look and the kinds of services they provide.

NOTE

C programmers might be a bit confused by capitalization issues here, so I will take a moment to review this issue. Object Pascal is not case sensitive, so it does not matter if you write WM_PAINT or wm_Paint. The compiler simply does not care, and these are not two separate identifiers as they would be in C/C++. My personal preference is wm_Paint, in part because I think it looks nicer on the page, but you might find me using the other technique in certain isolated instances. For instance, the previous examples are taken from the Delphi source files and, as you can see, they follow a somewhat different philosophy when it comes to these matters. On the other hand, here are some constants taken from the Delphi SYSTEM.PAS file:

```
varEmpty     = $0000;

varNull      = $0001;

varSmallint = $0002;
```

As you can see, this code follows a syntax similar to the one I have adopted. Perhaps the internal rule on the Delphi team is that Windows constants follow C conventions, and native Delphi declarations follow the style I prefer. At any rate, there are clearly some conflicting schools of thought at work here, and as a result, I don't place great weight on this issue (although I do tend to avoid declaring anything in all caps unless it is an acronym). However, you will undoubtedly find that I use both conventions in various places in this book. This is perhaps regrettable, but it is not a serious issue because the compiler simply does not care how I capitalize my code!

Clearly, nothing is very mysterious about the messages themselves. They are simply constants with useful names that inform a program about the current state of the system. When an event occurs, these messages are bundled with other useful bits of information and sent to one or more appropriate window procedures. Exactly what should then be done with those messages is the topic of this chapter.

You don't need to understand how Windows knows that the user moved the mouse or pressed a key. All you need to do is trap messages and then decode them. For instance, whenever a message with the number hexadecimal 200 comes down the pike, it's an indication that the user moved the mouse.

Accompanying the message are additional codes that tell something about the location and state of the mouse. This information lies encoded in parameters called wParam and lParam.

Your Second Full-Scale Windows Program

The next few pages of this chapter focus on a three-part process that outlines exactly how messages are treated in a WndProc:

- Step one is to get a working example program up and running.
- Step two is to discuss MESSAGES.PAS and message crackers. The discussion focuses primarily on two particular messages: wm_Destroy and wm_Create.
- Step three takes a brief look at how to treat a WndProc so as to make it easy to use.

Most of the code in the program I am about to show you is similar to the code you saw in Chapters 9 and 10. In fact, most Windows API programs are based on a common template that changes little from program to program. As a result, you might want to copy the files used in making WINDOW1.EXE into a new subdirectory called EASYTEXT. Go through the files, changing the words Window1 to EasyText and renaming the files from WINDOW1.* to EASYTEXT.*. To perform this latter duty, enter the following command at the DOS prompt:

```
ren WINDOW1.* EASYTEXT.*
```

The three steps previously outlined are very important. Almost every piece of Windows API code you write rests on the basic components created in Chapters 9 and 10. In other words, that code is very much reusable. In fact, you might want to keep it in a separate subdirectory where you can access it whenever you need to start a new program. As you probably know, the idea of reusing packets of code is very important in most modern programming endeavors.

> **NOTE**
>
> Don't try to copy old makefiles or DSK files from directory to directory without carefully reviewing them. DSK files generated by the Delphi IDE often contain the pathname of the files you add to a project. Don't make the mistake of moving your files to a new subdirectory and accidentally modifying WINDOW1.DPR (or some other member of the original program) simply because it is still listed in your project file.

It's now time to take a look at the code from the EASYTEXT program, found in Listing 11.1. Take the time to get this program up and running. It will help you understand the rest of this chapter.

Listing 11.1. The EASYTEXT.DPR main source file.

```
program EasyText;
//////////////////////////////////////
//   Program Name: EASYTEXT.DPR
//   Programmer: Charlie Calvert
//   Description: Demonstrate simple text I/O
//   Date: Dec 30, 1995
//////////////////////////////////////

uses
  Windows, Messages;

const
  AppName = 'EasyText';

var
  Directions: string;

//////////////////////////////////////
// The destructor handles WM_DESTROY
//////////////////////////////////////
procedure EasyText_OnCreate(hWindow: HWnd; var Msg: TWMCreate);
begin
  Directions := 'Try resizing this window.';
  Msg.Result := 0; // Continue. Return -1 on error
end;

//////////////////////////////////////
// The destructor handles WM_DESTROY
//////////////////////////////////////
procedure EasyText_OnDestroy(hWindow: HWnd; var Msg: TWMDestroy);
begin
  PostQuitMessage(0);
end;

//////////////////////////////////////
// Handle WM_PAINT messages
// Show how to use TextOut and DrawText.
//////////////////////////////////////
```

```
procedure EasyText_OnPaint(hWindow: HWnd; var Msg: TWMPaint);
var
  PaintStruct: TPaintStruct;
  Rect: TRect;
  PaintDC: HDC;
begin
  PaintDC := BeginPaint(hWindow, PaintStruct);

  SetBkMode(PaintDC, TRANSPARENT);

  TextOut(PaintDC, 10, 10, PChar(Directions), Length(Directions));

  GetClientRect(hWindow, Rect);

  DrawText(PaintDC, 'The middle of the road', -1, Rect,
           DT_SINGLELINE or DT_CENTER or DT_VCENTER);

  EndPaint(hWindow, PaintStruct);
end;

//////////////////////////////////////
// The Window Procedure
//////////////////////////////////////
function WindowProc(Window: HWnd; AMessage, WParam,
                    LParam: Longint): Longint; stdcall; export;
var
  AMsg: TMessage;
begin
  AMsg.Msg := AMessage;
  AMsg.WParam := WParam;
  AMsg.LParam := LParam;
  AMsg.Result := 0;

  case AMessage of
    wm_Create: EasyText_OnCreate(Window, TWMCreate(AMsg));
    wm_Destroy: EasyText_OnDestroy(Window, TWMDestroy(AMsg));
    wm_Paint: EasyText_OnPaint(Window, TWMPaint(AMsg));
  else
    WindowProc := DefWindowProc(Window, AMessage, WParam, LParam);
    Exit;
  end;

  Result := AMsg.Result
end;

//////////////////////////////////////
// Register the Window Class
//////////////////////////////////////
function DoRegister: Boolean;
var
  WindowClass: TWndClass;
begin
  WindowClass.Style := cs_hRedraw or cs_vRedraw;
  WindowClass.lpfnWndProc := @WindowProc;
  WindowClass.cbClsExtra := 0;
  WindowClass.cbWndExtra := 0;
  WindowClass.hInstance := HInstance;
  WindowClass.hIcon := LoadIcon(HInstance, 'WindowIcon');
```

continues

Listing 11.1. continued

```
  WindowClass.hCursor := LoadCursor(0, idc_Arrow);
  WindowClass.hbrBackground := hBrush(Color_Window);
  WindowClass.lpszMenuName := 'WindowMenu';
  WindowClass.lpszClassName := AppName;

  Result := RegisterClass(WindowClass) <> 0;
end;

////////////////////////////////////////
// Create the Window Class
////////////////////////////////////////
function Create: HWnd;
begin
  Result := CreateWindow(AppName, 'Object Pascal Window',
            ws_OverlappedWindow, cw_UseDefault, cw_UseDefault,
            cw_UseDefault, cw_UseDefault, 0, 0, HInstance, nil);
end;


var
  AMessage: TMsg;
  HWindow: HWnd;

begin
  if not DoRegister then begin
    MessageBox(0, 'Register failed', nil, mb_Ok);
    Exit;
  end;
  HWindow := Create;
  if HWindow = 0 then begin
    MessageBox(0, 'Create failed', nil, mb_Ok);
    Exit;
  end;

  ShowWindow(hWindow, CmdShow);
  UpdateWindow(hWindow);

  while GetMessage(AMessage, 0, 0, 0) do begin
    TranslateMessage(AMessage);
    DispatchMessage(AMessage);
  end;

  Halt(AMessage.wParam);
end.
```

The purpose of this program is to show you how to use message crackers and how to respond to wm_Paint messages. The code pops up a standard window, shown in Figure 11.1, and prints two pieces of text on it. Notice that one piece of text always stays in the middle of the window, even when you resize it.

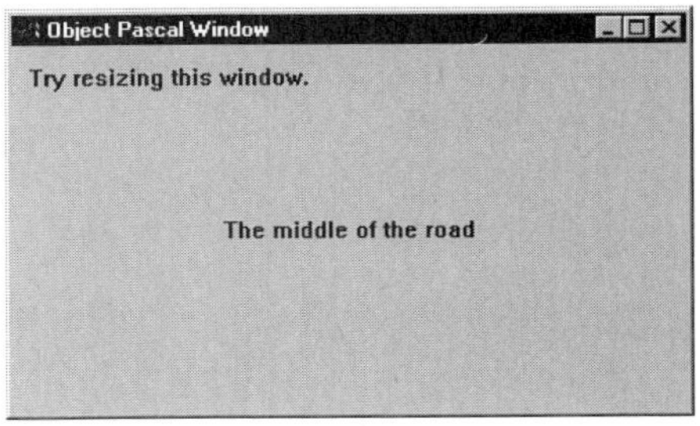

FIGURE 11.1.

EASYTEXT.EXE displays two pieces of text: one in the upper-left corner of the window, and one centered in the middle of the window.

Case Statements, MESSAGES.PAS, and Message Crackers

The most obvious new feature of this program is the presence of text in the client area of the window. Before taking a look at how that text is painted onscreen, it's important to first understand the mechanisms at play in the WndProc function:

```
function WindowProc(Window: HWnd; AMessage, WParam,
                    LParam: Longint): Longint; stdcall; export;
var
  AMsg: TMessage;
begin
  AMsg.Msg := AMessage;
  AMsg.WParam := WParam;
  AMsg.LParam := LParam;
  AMsg.Result := 0;

  case AMessage of
    wm_Create: EasyText_OnCreate(Window, TWMCreate(AMsg));
    wm_Destroy: EasyText_OnDestroy(Window, TWMDestroy(AMsg));
    wm_Paint: EasyText_OnPaint(Window, TWMPaint(AMsg));
  else
    WindowProc := DefWindowProc(Window, AMessage, WParam, LParam);
    Exit;
  end;

  Result := AMsg.Result
end;
```

> **NOTE**
>
> The code I am showing you here is very close to compiling in both Win16 and Win32. However, you would need to tweak the WindowProc header very slightly before the code would recompile in 16-bit land. I covered the changes you would need to make in the last chapter, in the Wind232 program. The basic structure of this program, however, is designed so that it can run on either platform. The EZText16 program, found on disk, compiles on both platforms. However, I wanted to avoid any ifdefs in the code I'm showing you in this book.

If the message crackers in MESSAGES.PAS did not exist, the window procedure could become an extremely formidable foe that Windows programmers would have to wrestle to the mat on a daily basis. The source of the trouble is the notorious case statement found in window procedures. Even moderately complex Windows API programs that don't use message crackers contain WndProcs that tend to stretch on for page after page of mind-boggling code.

Now that message crackers are here, the case statement still exists, but it has been tamed by a series of predeclared TWMXXX records that fairly effectively defang the serpent waiting within every window procedure. The message crackers do this by finding a simple way to move the body of your response to a message out of the WndProc and into functions that obey the basic rules of structured programming. Of course, using message crackers isn't an absolutely effortless process, but I believe you'll find them much easier to use than a lengthy case statement.

The EasyText program explicitly handles three messages:

```
wm_Create: EasyText_OnCreate(Window, TWMCreate(AMsg));
wm_Destroy: EasyText_OnDestroy(Window, TWMDestroy(AMsg));
wm_Paint: EasyText_OnPaint(Window, TWMPaint(AMsg));
```

As you can see, the messages are wm_Create, wm_Destroy, and wm_Paint. In the next few pages, you'll see how message crackers simplify the use of not only these messages, but all standard API messages.

When reading this discussion, remember that the TWMXXX messages help shield you from complexity. Unfortunately, I have to delve right into the heart of that complexity in order to explain how message crackers work. After you have a few basic ideas clear in your mind, you'll find that message crackers smooth the way for you over and over again.

> **NOTE**
>
> Message crackers help you use standard structured programming techniques throughout your WndProc. When I first learned structured programming, it seemed a bit complex. Over the years, however, it has saved me many, many frustrating days of painful debugging. The same is true of message crackers—for many of the same reasons.

All right. It's time to gird your loins and focus your mind. The next few paragraphs contain a good deal of important information.

To begin, you need to know that wm_Destroy messages are sent to a window whenever it's about to be closed. In the main window of an application, it's crucial that you remember to call PostQuitMessage in response to a wm_Destroy message. If you don't do this, you'll immediately become involved in an inexplicable mass of bugs from which you'll never extract yourself until you finally figure out the nature of your error. If you forget to call PostQuitMessage, your application is toast!

NOTE

PostQuitMessage sends a WM_QUIT message to Windows, which is the signal to break out of the message loop back in WinMain. In other words, the message loop would continue indefinitely were it not for the call to PostQuitMessage. Therefore, this call is absolutely essential for proper application termination.

In EasyText, the PostQuitMessage call is made in the EasyText_OnDestroy function:

```
procedure EasyText_OnDestroy(hWindow: HWnd; var Msg: TWMDestroy);
begin
  PostQuitMessage(0);
end;
```

If message crackers were not being used, this whole process would have been handled in the WndProc:

```
switch (Message)
{
  case WM_DESTROY:
    PostQuitMessage(0);
    break;

  case WM_PAINT:
  etc..
}
```

With the TWMXXX records, however, programmers have the option of easily handling wm_Destroy messages in a separate function. This helps promote good structured programming techniques.

In the source for MESSAGES.PAS, you can view the message cracker records. These nuggets of code "pick apart" the parameters to WndProc. The macros then pass on the important finds to your message handler function. The issue is that every message sent to a window can be accompanied by additional information—which usually comes in the form of the hwnd, wParam, and lParam parameters.

Three problems occur as the result of sending messages in the hwnd, wParam, and lParam parameters:

■ Not all messages use all three of these parameters. As a result, programmers always have to look in their reference books to see which of these parameters are utilized by a particular message.

■ Different pieces of information often are packed into a particular parameter. For instance, a programmer might have to look in the first word of lParam to get a piece of information, and look in the first and second words of wParam to get different pieces of information. After engaging in this trying process, the programmer often needs to typecast the information before it's usable.

■ The way information is packed into lParam and wParam sometimes differs depending on whether you are in 16-bit Windows or in Win32.

You have learned that message crackers are really just a series of records designed to pick apart the various parameters passed to WndProc. The first stage in understanding this technique is to take a look at the TMessage structure, used as the type for the AMsg local variable in the WndProc:

```
TMessage = record
  Msg: Cardinal;
  case Integer of
    0: (
      WParam: Longint;
      LParam: Longint;
      Result: Longint);
    1: (
      WParamLo: Word;
      WParamHi: Word;
      LParamLo: Word;
      LParamHi: Word;
      ResultLo: Word;
      ResultHi: Word);
end;
```

This is a typical variant record that can be interpreted in two different ways. In particular, you can see it as containing three 32-bit values, six 16-bit values, or some combination of the two. It's up to you to interpret the structure as you please.

Delphi has its own internal ways of filling out TMessage structures, but in this case the code simply makes some quick and dirty assignments:

```
AMsg.Msg := AMessage;
AMsg.WParam := WParam;
AMsg.LParam := LParam;
AMsg.Result := 0;
```

After these assignments are made, all the values sent to the WndProc are encapsulated in a single structure. A default return value for the WndProc is also designated, although you could, if you wanted, change this setting before passing it back to the operating system at the end of the WndProc:

```
  Result := AMsg.Result
end;
```

NOTE

Some programmers might get a little nervous when they see the assignment statements shown here. After all, thousands of messages can come into a WndProc during the life of a procedure, and the act of assigning values to the fields of TMessage seems a bit time-consuming. However, if you look at the actual assembler generated for that code you will see that it is not very lengthy:

```
mov    [ebp-10],eax  // AMsg.Msg := Amessage;
mov    [ebp-0C],edx  // AMsg.WParam := WParam;
mov    [ebp-08],ecx  // AMsg.LParam := LParam;
xor    ebx,ebx       // AMsg.Result := 0;
mov    [ebp-04],ebx
```

On a Pentium, these few instructions take place almost instantaneously. Certainly they aren't worth fretting about.

The TMessage record type is 16 bytes in size. So is the TWMNoParams record shown here:

```
TWMNoParams = record
  Msg: Cardinal;
  Unused: array[0..3] of Word;
  Result: Longint;
end;
```

What is the relationship between TWMNoParams and TMessage? Well, they are both the same size, so you can effectively map them into the same memory area or copy the value of one to the other through typecast:

```
var
  A: TMessage;
  B: TWMNoParams;
begin
  A.Msg := wm_Destroy;
  A.WParam := 3;
  A.LParam := 3;
  B := TWMNoParams(A);
end;
```

It's okay to typecast a TMessage variable as a TWMNoParams variable because they both take up the same number of bytes. There is no loss of information when you make the assignment.

What good is the TWMNoParams record? Why would you want to use it? In some cases, LParam and WParam contain no information. They are simply empty. For instance, the wm_Destroy message doesn't take advantage of either LParam or WParam. These values are simply along for the ride. As a result, MESSAGES.PAS associates wm_Destroy messages with TWMNoParams:

```
type
  TWMDestroy = TWMNoParams;
```

You can now safely typecast the TMessage structure associated with wm_Destroy messages so that it fills TWMDestroy records that can be passed to a function that handles wm_Destroy messages:

```
…
AMsg.Msg := AMessage;
AMsg.WParam := WParam;
AMsg.LParam := LParam;
AMsg.Result := 0;
…
wm_Destroy: EasyText_OnDestroy(Window, TWMDestroy(AMsg));
…
```

The EasyText_OnDestroy function will now receive a copy of a record that has automatically parsed LParam and WParam. In this case, the parsing does nothing more than designate that LParam and WParam are Unused:

```
TWMNoParams = record
  Msg: Cardinal;
```

```
    Unused: array[0..3] of Word;
    Result: Longint;
  end;
```

This might seem like a small accomplishment, but the point is that `LParam` and `WParam` have now been automatically parsed for you in a way that prevents you from making an error. The `TWMDestroy` record makes it impossible for you to accidentally try to use `LParam` and `WParam`. The record informs you that these values do not exist for this record. They are `Unused`!

It's now time to revisit this issue when looking at a second message called `wm_Create`:

```
  TWMCreate = record
    Msg: Cardinal;
    Unused: Integer;
    CreateStruct: PCreateStruct;
    Result: Longint;
  end;
```

In this case `WParam` is mapped into a variable called `Unused`, but `LParam` is mapped into a variable of type `PCreateStruct`:

```
  TCreateStruct = packed record
    lpCreateParams: Pointer;
    hInstance: HINST;
    hMenu: HMENU;
    hwndParent: HWND;
    cy: Integer;
    cx: Integer;
    y: Integer;
    x: Integer;
    style: Longint;
    lpszName: PAnsiChar;
    lpszClass: PAnsiChar;
    dwExStyle: DWORD;
  end;
```

Now when you try to parse the `WParam` and `LParam` variables associated with a `wm_Create` message, there is no guessing. Delphi automatically does the parsing for you and assigns the `PCreateParams` parameter to `lParam`:

```
  ...
  AMsg.Msg := AMessage;
  AMsg.WParam := WParam;
  AMsg.LParam := LParam;
  AMsg.Result := 0;

  case AMessage of
    wm_Create: EasyText_OnCreate(Window, TWMCreate(AMsg));
  ...
```

The key points of this system are the following:

■ It automatically parses `WParam` and `LParam` for you so that you don't make a careless error.

■ The records can be parsed differently in 16 and 32 bits, without you having to think about portability issues. In other words, Delphi can just define a different TWMCreate method for 16-bit Delphi if necessary.

One key point to remember is that this technique works just as effectively in a Delphi RAD program as it does in a Windows API program. For instance, in Chapter 25, "Handling Messages," you see the following object definition:

```
TEvents = class(TForm)
  … // Additional code
  procedure FormMouseDown(Sender: TObject; Button: TMouseButton;
    Shift: TShiftState; X, Y: Integer);
  … // Additional code
private
  procedure MyMouseMove(var M: TWMMouse); message wm_MouseMove;
public
  { Public declarations }
end;
```

This code shows two ways of handling wm_MouseMove messages in a standard Delphi RAD application. Notice that the second technique uses a TWMMouse message cracker parameter:

```
TWMMouse = record
  Msg: Cardinal;
  Keys: Longint;
  case Integer of
    0: (
      XPos: Smallint;
      YPos: Smallint);
    1: (
      Pos: TSmallPoint;
      Result: Longint);
end;
```

As you can see, the TWMMouse parameter does the same job of parsing out the parameters passed to it as the FormMouseDown event handler does. In fact, there is quite a bit in common between the MyMouseMove function and the EasyText_On*XXX* events shown earlier.

That's all I'm going to say about message crackers for now. However, this subject comes up again several times in the next few chapters. If it's not already obvious, over time it will begin to come clear to you how these message crackers work and what they can do for you.

Creating Message Handlers

Now that you understand how message crackers work, it's probably also worth spending a few moments talking about the EasyText_On*XXX* methods shown earlier. Here, for instance, is the OnCreate handler:

```
procedure EasyText_OnCreate(hWindow: HWnd; var Msg: TWMCreate);
begin
  Directions := 'Try resizing this window.';
  Msg.Result := 0; // Continue. Return -1 on error
end;
```

The name of this function is designed to make it look like a method. I append the word EasyText before the name, just as you would append Form1 before an event in a standard Delphi application. This gives you the artificial sense that your code is being categorized and organized as it would be in an object-oriented program.

The name of the event being handled is appended onto the name of the "object class":

```
ClassName_OnMessageName
EasyText_OnCreate
```

This gives you the sense that you are just responding to an event the way you would in a Delphi application. In general, the naming convention used here is designed to help you write the cleanest, clearest possible code.

All the message handling functions should take two parameters:

```
EasyText_OnCreate(hWindow: HWnd; var Msg: TWMCreate);
```

The first is the HWnd of the window you are working with, and the second is the message cracking record described earlier.

> **NOTE**
>
> There is actually an argument in favor of just declaring the HWnd as a global variable and not bothering to pass it in to each function you declare. You could, for instance, pick up the global HWnd in the Create method for the entire application in the place where you call CreateWindow. You could then use that global variable in all your message handlers. My tendency to expend a few extra clock cycles passing the parameter to functions is all part and parcel of my belief that it is always best to write the clearest possible code. This is a judgment call, however, and certainly I can see good arguments on both sides of the issue.

The body of the EasyText_OnCreate method is fairly straightforward. First the global string Directions is assigned a value, then the Msg parameter is given a result value:

```
begin
  Directions := 'Try resizing this window.';
  Msg.Result := 0; // Continue. Return -1 on error
end;
```

If this function returned -1, the whole application would shut down immediately. In particular, wm_Create messages get sent when you call CreateWindow. The call to CreateWindow fails if the wm_Create handler returns -1. In this case, there is no reason why the string assignment would ever be likely to fail, so the code returns 0 automatically. If you had more complicated allocations to make, you might write code that could set Msg.Result to -1 if one of the allocations failed.

You can use the Msg.CreateStruct parameter to access any of the values in the TCreateStruct structure passed to this procedure. If you look back a page or two, you will see that a

`TCreateStruct` record holds all the variables that were passed to `CreateWindow`. This mechanism provides an easy way for you to access these variables, and to change them if necessary.

If it weren't for the message cracker, you would have to handle the typecasting yourself, as follows:

```
CreateStruct = PCreateStruct(lParam);
```

This is a tedious and error-prone process that is particularly worrisome to beginners. The best thing to do is to follow the template shown earlier and let the typecast occur automatically when the `TMessage` value gets passed to an `EasyText_OnXXX` handler.

> **NOTE**
>
> It might be helpful for you to know that whenever I explicitly handle either `wm_Create` or `wm_Destroy` messages, I try to do it at the very beginning of a window procedure. That way, readers of my code can easily find the place where I handle the initialization (`wm_Create`) and the destruction (`wm_Destroy`) of my window. Exactly why these two processes are so important is probably obvious to you intuitively and will certainly become apparent to you over time. For now, you need to remember only that I like to handle these two chores first and then handle all other messages in alphabetical order.

The `wm_Command` message cracker works with `HWnd`, `wParam`, and `lParam`. As a result, you might want to look it up in MESSAGES.PAS to see what a really complex message cracker looks like.

MESSAGES.PAS and the Default Window Procedure

As you might recall from Chapter 9, throughout the life of an application, the `WndProc` function is usually being bombarded by a vast array of messages. Indeed, there are times when these messages pour down in the same way that raindrops pour down on your head during a storm. In many applications, most of these messages are being handled by the default window procedure. The purpose of this section is to show how to handle `DefWindowProc`.

Most of the time, if you handle a message explicitly, you don't want to also call `DefWindowProc`. However, there are occasions when you might want to both handle a message and also call `DefWindowProc`. In such cases, you have several different choices:

- You can explicitly call `DefWindowProc` from inside the function that wants to pass the message on.
- You can change the signature of the message handle, turn it into a function, and have it return False. This could change a variable called `AllDone` to False, which informs the `WndProc` that there is additional processing that needs to take place.

> **NOTE**
>
> If you choose the latter technique, there is one last detail that needs to be taken care of. On occasion, when you handle a message, you might change the values stored in LParam and WParam. This means that you need to pass these changed values on to the DefWindProc, which is the purpose of the following code:
>
> ```
>   if not AllDone then begin
>     WParam := AMsg.WParam;
>     LParam := AMsg.LParam;
>       Result := DefWindowProc(Window, AMessage, WParam, LParam);
> Exit;
>   end;
> ```

Most of the time, you will either want to handle the message yourself or pass it on directly to DefWindowProc. That kind of default processing is handled automatically by the WndProc provided earlier. However, there are occasions when you might want to pass your handled message on to DefWindProc. I discuss these latter occasions in this section. I'm aware that neither of the solutions provided in this section are particular elegant, but they would resolve the problem with only a minimum of fuss.

Summing Up Message Crackers

Before moving on to discuss the all-important wm_Paint message, it might be worth indulging in a short recap of the last few sections.

Message crackers help simplify Windows programs and eliminate careless errors. They do this by three means:

- They break up the endless case statements typically found in WndProcs and help make your code conform to good structured programming practices.
- They help pick apart or parse the hwnd, lParam, and wParam parameters by singling out the important ones and subjecting them to proper typecasting.
- They unify all the functions related to a window class under a single title, by virtue of the MyClass_OnXXX naming convention.

I hope that all this has sunk in; I don't cover it again in any detail. From here on out, message crackers are going to be taken for granted and treated as if they were the only sane non-OOP way to handle messages in a window procedure. Indeed, I believe that to be the case.

This kind of concision can help you organize and clean up your code quickly. Let other programmers continue to flounder in the void; the message crackers in MESSAGES.PAS provide you with a simple means to write clean code.

Painting Text

Every message sent to a window procedure is important. Yet somehow, the wm_Paint message strikes me as being the central message around which most applications revolve. Certainly, nobody could deny that wm_Paint messages perform a vital function in the life of nearly all Windows applications.

wm_Paint messages are sent to a window every time it needs to redraw the contents of its client area. When programmers speak of the client area of a window, they are usually referring to the area inside a window's borders and title bar (see Figure 11.2). The client area is the space that programmers usually draw in, whereas Windows tends to take care of the rest of the application.

FIGURE 11.2.

The client area is the portion of a window beneath the title bar and inside the frame or border.

If there is a part of the client area that you do not specifically take control of, Windows fills it in with the designated background color. That is, it does so if you don't prevent it from getting the required messages from the default window procedure. Specifically, trouble can occur if you don't pass some messages on to DefWndProc that need additional processing by the system. This is a subject to which I return in Chapter 12, "The Mouse and the Keyboard."

wm_Paint messages get sent to a window by the operating system whenever it needs to be drawn or redrawn. Think for a moment what this means. If a window has been hidden under another window and is suddenly uncovered, it receives a wm_Paint message. It gets the message because it needs to redraw the area covered by the other window. If a window has been maximized or minimized, it receives a wm_Paint message when restored to normal size. If a user switches back from a full-screen DOS window, all the visible windows on the desktop receive wm_Paint messages.

> **NOTE**
>
> Windows provides programmers with an enormous number of very valuable services to which DOS programmers have no access. For instance, Windows automatically takes care of the border, background, and title of a window. Furthermore, the operating system works in the background to reliably remind every window on the desktop to redraw itself when necessary. It's true that Windows demands quite a bit from its programmers, but it gives a great deal back in the form of default services.

BeginPaint, EndPaint, and Device Contexts

Take a close look at the wm_Paint message handler function for EasyText:

```
procedure EasyText_OnPaint(hWindow: HWnd; var Msg: TWMPaint);
var
  PaintStruct: TPaintStruct;
  Rect: TRect;
  PaintDC: HDC;
begin
  PaintDC := BeginPaint(hWindow, PaintStruct);

  SetBkMode(PaintDC, TRANSPARENT);

  TextOut(PaintDC, 10, 10, PChar(Directions), Length(Directions));

  GetClientRect(hWindow, Rect);

  DrawText(PaintDC, 'The middle of the road', -1, Rect,
           DT_SINGLELINE or DT_CENTER or DT_VCENTER);

  EndPaint(hWindow, PaintStruct);
end;
```

To help you understand exactly what's going on here, it might help if I strip the function of everything but its most fundamental parts:

```
procedure EasyText_OnPaint(hWindow: HWnd; var Msg: TWMPaint);
var
  PaintStruct: TPaintStruct;
  PaintDC: HDC;
begin
  PaintDC := BeginPaint(hWindow, PaintStruct);

  EndPaint(hWindow, PaintStruct);
end;
```

This example can serve as a template from which you can build all your paint routines. The basic elements are the calls to BeginPaint and EndPaint. Note also the variables called PaintDC and PaintStruct.

The key role of the BeginPaint function is to give you access to a *device context* (HDC) for a window. Device contexts might be a totally new concept for some people who come from DOS. As a result, you might want to pay special attention during this brief discussion to one of the key concepts in Windows programming.

NOTE

In a RAD program, you can get hold of the device context for a window by accessing Canvas.Handle. In particular, the following OnPaint handler method for a TForm object is roughly parallel to the short version of the EasyText_OnPaint method shown earlier:

```
procedure TForm1.FormPaint(Sender: TObject);
var
```

```
   PaintDC: HDC;
begin
   PaintDC := Canvas.Handle;
end;
```

This code retrieves `PaintDC` from the `Canvas` object in much the way the `EasyText_OnPaint` function retrieves it from the call to `BeginPaint`. For people with a slightly more technical bent, the following code more precisely mirrors inside a RAD program the code shown in the `EasyText_OnPaint` function:

```
type
   TForm1 = class(TForm)
     private
        procedure wmPaint(var Msg: TWMPaint); message wm_Paint;
     end;

implementation

procedure TForm1.wmPaint(var Msg: TWMPaint);
var
   PaintDC: HDC;
   PaintStruct: TPaintStruct;
begin
   inherited Paint;  // possibly not needed?
   PaintDC := BeginPaint(Handle, PaintStruct);
   TextOut(PaintDC, 5, 5, 'hi', 2);
   EndPaint(Handle, PaintStruct);
end;
```

Device contexts form a link between your program and certain external output devices that can be attached to a computer. In particular, most device contexts form the interface between your application and a printer or video card.

It's probably safe to say that if device contexts did not already exist, somebody would have to invent them. They form an essential part of any robust programming environment. Until Windows came along, all DOS programmers either consciously or unconsciously felt their lack.

Device contexts make it easy to deal with a wide variety of video cards and printers. For instance, there are VGA, EGA, CGA, Hercules, and who-knows-how-many different SuperVGA cards lying in wait for unwary programmers. Printers are even more numerous and varied.

In the past, every application needed its own drivers to run these different devices. WordPerfect, for instance, was famous for its wonderful printer drivers. Their existence gave the product a kind of flexibility that users loved. But of course, not every start-up company that came down the pike could afford to develop its own set of drivers; even if they could, all that redundant effort would not make a great deal of sense.

To resolve this problem, Windows made it possible for manufacturers of hardware output devices to write drivers that could be hooked into any Windows program. The key to this whole process is the development of device contexts, which form the link between your application, a device driver, and an actual hardware device. Their existence makes it possible for you to write one set of code that can, at least in theory, use multiple devices.

It is quite feasible under Windows to write one set of code that works equally well with a CGA, VGA, or EGA monitor. This can be done without ever having to write any device-specific code. Any DOS programmer who has done serious work in the graphics world is bound to recognize that this is a major accomplishment, even if it does come replete with a few caveats illustrated at various points in this book.

By now, you should start to understand why it is so important to begin every paint procedure with a call to BeginPaint. BeginPaint is the function that retrieves the device context for a particular window, and without the device context you aren't going to get very far when attempting to display graphics.

> **NOTE**
>
> There are several different ways to get device contexts from the system. One of the most convenient is called GetDC. To my mind, GetDC is so well named, and so easy to use, that there is a temptation to use it in place of BeginPaint. Don't ever do this—it causes all kinds of inexplicable and undefined behavior. BeginPaint is specifically designed to be used in conjunction with wm_Paint messages. If you try to work without it, your window is likely not to respond correctly when brought to the top from behind another window or when it needs to be repainted. Inside a RAD program, however, you can almost always get the device context by just referencing Canvas.Handle.

Just as BeginPaint is the proper way to start a paint function, EndPaint is the proper way to close it off. Be sure to encapsulate the heart of your response to every wm_Paint message within these two functions.

BeginPaint and EndPaint both take an HWnd and a PaintStruct as parameters. Here are the fields of a PaintStruct:

```
TPaintStruct = packed record
  hdc: HDC;
  fErase: BOOL;
  rcPaint: TRect;
  fRestore: BOOL;
  fIncUpdate: BOOL;
  rgbReserved: array[0..31] of Byte;
end;
```

Here's a description of the fields of a PaintStruct:

- hdc: A copy of the device context for the window.
- fErase: Whether the background of the window should be redrawn.
- rcPaint: The rectangle inside of which the drawing will occur. It is important to understand that this rectangle is not synonymous with the area of the client rectangle. The reason for this is that Windows is smart enough to tell a window exactly how much of itself needs to be redrawn. This can be important when a window in the

background is half-revealed by a movement of a window in the foreground. The rcPaint field says, in effect: "Don't bother to repaint your whole surface, just paint this little section that has been revealed to the user."

■ The remaining three fields of the PaintStruct are reserved by Windows and need not concern you in this context.

TextOut and *DrawText*

The BeginPaint and EndPaint functions form bookends around the core of the paint routine:

```
SetBkMode(PaintDC, TRANSPARENT);

TextOut(PaintDC, 10, 10, PChar(Directions), Length(Directions));

GetClientRect(hWindow, Rect);

DrawText(PaintDC, 'The middle of the road', -1, Rect,
         DT_SINGLELINE or DT_CENTER or DT_VCENTER);
```

This code starts by setting the background mode to TRANSPARENT. This is necessary because the background of the window can be any of a number of different colors as a result of this line from the Register procedure:

```
WindowClass.hbrBackground := hBrush(Color_Window);
```

This code uses a system-wide color choice as the background of the main window. If you right-click the desktop, you can access the Display Properties dialog box. Use the Item combo box in this display to select the option called "Window," and then set it to some color of your own choosing. Thereafter, all the properly designed windows on your desktop will have the new color that you selected. As a programmer, your job is to respect whatever choice the user makes in the Display Properties dialog box. To do this, you set the background of your windows to the COLOR_WINDOW constant and then set the background of the text you output to transparent:

```
SetBkMode(PaintDC, TRANSPARENT);
```

If you neglect to call SetBkMode, your text appears with a white background even if the surrounding window is blue, gray, or some other color. The end result is not good, and you might want to comment out the call to SetBkMode once in your code just to appreciate how bad this looks. Of course, you must first set the COLOR_WINDOW constant to something other than white if you want to see this effect. This issue also applies to Windows 3.1, but the use of non-white background colors in that platform was less prevalent.

In the EasyText program, you can examine the two most common ways of displaying text in a Windows program. The first is called TextOut, and the second is DrawText.

TextOut is the easiest to use of the two functions. All that is required is a device context, some starting coordinates, a string, and the length of the string. The most common means of determining the string length is to call the Length function. If you happen to be working with PChar rather than a long string, you can call on one of the Pascal language's built-in functions, such as StrLen, or Windows own lstrlen.

The higher level DrawText function takes a device context, a string, a string length, a RECT, and some flags as parameters. If you pass DrawText a NULL-terminated string, you can pass -1 in the third parameter, which lets Windows calculate the length of the string. Long strings are by default NULL-terminated.

The RECT parameter designates the area inside which the string will be painted. In this case, I have used the GetClientRect function to retrieve the area of the entire client window and then passed in three flags that instruct Windows to center the string in the RECT. Figure 11.3 illustrates how Windows continues to center the string, regardless of what shape the window happens to assume. Notice that the string output by TextOut remains resolutely in place, regardless of the shape or size of the window.

FIGURE 11.3.

The string output by DrawText always finds the center of the client area— no matter how often you drag or reshape its boundaries.

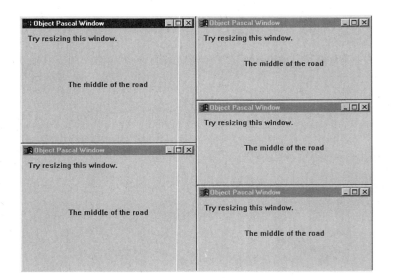

I should point out that the previous paragraphs are really only an introduction to the subject of outputting text in a Windows application.

Relating the Windows API to RAD Delphi

Before ending this chapter, I should perhaps take a moment to place some of this information within the context of Delphi RAD development. The purpose of this chapter has been to show how Windows handles messages. However, Delphi RAD programs can't get anything to the screen without using these same techniques. Sometimes the relationship between Delphi techniques and the WinAPI techniques shown in this chapter are obvious, and sometimes the relationship turns out to be surprisingly skewed. In the remainder of this chapter I provide a few quick examples illustrating what I mean.

The Delphi `Canvas.TextOut` function makes internal calls to the Windows `TextOut` function:

```
procedure TCanvas.TextOut(X, Y: Integer; const Text: String);
begin
  Changing;
  RequiredState([csHandleValid, csFontValid, csBrushValid]);
  Windows.TextOut(FHandle, X, Y, PChar(Text), Length(Text));
  MoveTo(X + TextWidth(Text), Y);
  Changed;
end;
```

The third line in this function is expected. Somewhere in the midst of this process the function has to call the Windows API function `TextOut`. However, it's not obvious that Delphi is also going to call functions called `Changing` and `Changed`, as well as `RequiredState`.

The calls to `Changing` and `Changed` are really fairly trivial functions that just ensure that any one method that hooks the `OnChanging` or `OnChange` event gets called. In essence, these are just courtesy functions to let anyone who happens to be interested in the fact that the HDC is about to change be notified that the change is going to occur.

The `RequiredState` function, however, ensures that the Handle, Font, and Brush associated with the device context are valid and are set to the proper values. For instance, if the user has changed the Font property associated with the Form, the proper font has to be created and selected into the device context.

Finally, the call to `MoveTo` sets off another call to `RequiredState`, this time one that again checks to be sure the device handle is valid. Once all is well, the Windows API `MoveToEx` function is called.

The point here is that there is a huge difference between calling `Windows.TextOut` and calling `Canvas.TextOut`. `Canvas.TextOut` provides many services for you that `Windows.TextOut` does not provide. On the other hand, it also must take many more clock cycles to execute. To really understand Delphi, you need to understand the difference between these functions, and you need to understand that you have a choice. You can call `Windows.TextOut`, or you can call `Canvas.TextOut`. However, the importance of your choice will not become clear to you until you start writing the kind of Windows API program demonstrated by the `EasyText` example shown earlier.

It's noteworthy that there is no Delphi equivalent of the `DrawText` function, although you can construct one if necessary:

```
procedure TForm1.FormPaint(Sender: TObject);
var
  Rect: TRect;
begin
  Windows.GetClientRect(Handle, Rect);
  DrawText(Canvas.Handle, 'The middle of the road', -1, Rect,
          DT_SINGLELINE or DT_CENTER or DT_VCENTER);
end;
```

After writing the code shown here, you would think you would be done. However, in my version of Delphi, this code does not act as you would expect. In particular, it is not updated each time the Window is resized.

To get this kind of code to act as you would expect, you need to give it a little push in a `FormResize` method:

```
procedure TForm1.FormResize(Sender: TObject);
begin
  InvalidateRect(Handle, nil, True);
end;
```

Once again, my point is that the Delphi VCL does not always act as you expect it to act. The Delphi VCL is not necessarily as thin a wrapper around the Windows API as you might expect. In fact, sometimes the VCL seems to take over altogether and to in effect rewrite Windows.

Using the `DrawText` example shown earlier, try playing with the font for the form. Notice that when you use `Canvas.Handle` as your device context, the output for your program reflects changes you make to the `Form1.Font` property. Now try the following code:

```
procedure TForm1.FormPaint(Sender: TObject);
var
  Rect: TRect;
  DC: HDC;
begin
  DC := GetDC(Handle);
  Windows.GetClientRect(Handle, Rect);
  DrawText(DC, 'The middle of the road', -1, Rect,
           DT_SINGLELINE or DT_CENTER or DT_VCENTER);
  ReleaseDC(Handle, DC);
end;
```

This code doesn't use the HDC kept by the `TCanvas` object. Instead, it gets the HDC directly from Windows:

```
DC := GetDC(Handle);
```

In this situation, changes that you make to the `Form1.Font` property are not reflected in the text that is output by the `DrawText` function. In particular, I'm setting things up so that Delphi never gets a chance to call `TCanvas.RequiredState`. These seemingly minor details have a huge impact on the way Delphi programs perform. It's one thing to look at Delphi as a simple RAD tool, and it's another to start digging in and seeing how Delphi is really put together under the hood.

Notice, for instance, that Delphi would make it very hard for you to use `TCanvas.TextOut` to write multiple fonts to a window at the same time. However, if you grab hold of the DC directly, you can select what fonts you want into it, even if you are using the Delphi `TFont` object to create the font. It's all a question of knowing how the tools work, finding their limits, and finding their special capabilities. Dig down to the Windows API level, and it all starts to make sense.

Summary

In this chapter, you have had a chance to get an overview of messages, message crackers, and the wm_Paint message handler function.

One of the most important passages in this chapter discusses the way MESSAGES.PAS uses records to parse the otherwise somewhat cryptic parameters passed to the WndProc. Message crackers also are important because they help to break WndProcs up into structured code that is relatively easy to debug and to understand.

You have also learned about the necessity of handling wm_Destroy messages, and you have gotten a glimpse of wm_Create messages and the crucial role they can play in your application.

The final sections of the chapter concentrate on device contexts and the BeginPaint and EndPaint functions. You have seen that text can be output to a window with either the TextOut or DrawText functions.

One final key point needs to be emphasized. If you create the Delphi RAD equivalent of the EasyText program, it will be about 150,000 bytes in size, assuming you have all the optimizations turned on. The EasyText program itself is about 15,000 bytes in size. That is, it's one-tenth the size of a standard Delphi application. Both applications are smaller than their equivalent C applications. That is, EASYTEXT.DPR produces a smaller application than a similar C application does, and the Delphi RAD equivalent produces a smaller application than a C++ OWL application. Despite the innate strength of the Delphi development environment, it's still interesting to see that you can have a tenfold improvement in size just by dropping to the API level.

The Mouse and the Keyboard

12

In this chapter, you learn how to use the Windows API to get control over the mouse and keyboard. In particular, you will see the following:

- How to detect when a key has been pressed
- How to detect which key has been pressed
- How to detect if the system (Alt) key has been pressed
- How to track the position of the mouse
- How to detect mouse button presses
- How to detect double-clicks

In addition, you'll learn a number of tips about painting text to the screen that complement the knowledge you picked up in Chapter 11, "Messages and Painting Text."

Once again, the reason for presenting this material is simply to introduce you to the Windows API. Delphi can call any Windows API function and can respond to any Windows message. Furthermore, it is possible to structure an Object Pascal program along the basic lines of a standard C Windows API program with WinMain and WndProc. The potential to tap into the full power of Windows is there, but you can't do it unless you understand how the code works. These chapters show how Windows works and how to tap into its resources using Delphi.

Most of the material in this chapter isn't particularly difficult, but it is important because it covers many fundamental I/O services. When you finish this chapter, you should have a good feeling for how to handle messages and how to structure a Windows API application.

Though they don't follow each other in direct sequence, you should read this chapter in coordination with Chapter 24, "Objects, Encapsulation, and Properties," which is an entirely VCL-based chapter that covers very similar material. If you understand both chapters, you can feel confident that you truly understand Windows-based event-oriented programming. This is one of the key aspects of both Delphi and Windows. Serious programmers will benefit on a daily basis from understanding it thoroughly on both the API and VCL levels.

A Program That Reports Mouse and Keyboard Events

Now that you have explored the window procedure and basic text output, you are ready for a brief introduction to more advanced topics, such as the keyboard and mouse. Through the good graces of the message system, Windows enables you to get immediate and relatively complete control over these two hardware devices.

To begin your exploration, type in and run the program shown in Listing 12.1.

Listing 12.1. The KeyMouse program shows how to trap keyboard and mouse input.

```
program KeyMouse;
//////////////////////////////////////
//   Program Name: KEYMOUSE.DPR
//   Programmer: Charlie Calvert
//   Description: Show how to trap keyboard and mouse input.
//   Date: Dec 30, 1995
//////////////////////////////////////

uses
  Windows, Messages, SysUtils;

// --------------------------------------------------------
// Interface
// --------------------------------------------------------

// Some variables
const
  XVal: Integer = 10;
  YVal: Integer = 30;
  AppName       = 'KeyMouse';

var
  hWindow: HWnd;

// TKeyMouse
procedure KeyMouse_OnDestroy(var Msg: TWMDestroy); forward;
procedure KeyMouse_OnChar(var Msg: TWMChar); forward;
procedure KeyMouse_OnKeyUp(var Msg: TWMKeyDown); forward;
procedure KeyMouse_OnKeyDown(var Msg: TWMKeyDown); forward;
procedure KeyMouse_OnLButtonDown(var Msg: TWMLButtonDown); forward;
procedure KeyMouse_OnLButtonDblClk(var Msg: TWMLButtonDblClk); forward;
procedure KeyMouse_OnLButtonUp(var Msg: TWMLButtonUp); forward;
procedure KeyMouse_OnMouseMove(var Msg: TWMMouseMove); forward;
procedure KeyMouse_OnPaint(var Msg: TWMPaint); forward;
procedure KeyMouse_OnSysKeyUp(var Msg: TWMSysKeyUp); forward;
procedure KeyMouse_OnSysKeyDown(var Msg: TWMSysKeyDown); forward;

// --------------------------------------------------------
// Initialization
// --------------------------------------------------------


//////////////////////////////////////
// Program entry point
//////////////////////////////////////

type
  TWMChar2 = record
    Msg: Cardinal;
    CharCode: Word;
    Unused: Word;
    cRepeat: Word;
    ScanCode: Byte;
    KeyData: Byte;
```

continues

Listing 12.1. continued

```pascal
    Result: Longint;
  end;

procedure KeyMouse_OnChar2(var Msg: TWMChar2);
var
  S: string;
  DC: HDC;
begin
  DC := GetDC(hWindow);

  S := Format('wm_Char ==> Ch = %S   cRepeat = %d Scan = %d          ',
              [Char(Msg.CharCode), Msg.cRepeat, Msg.ScanCode]);

  SetBkColor(DC, GetSysColor(Color_BtnFace));
  TextOut(DC, XVal, YVal + 20, PChar(S), Length(S));

  ReleaseDC(hWindow, DC);
end;

procedure KeyMouse_OnKeyDown2(var Msg: TWMKeyDown);
var
  S: string;
  DC: HDC;
begin
  DC := GetDC(hWindow);

  case Msg.CharCode of
    vk_Left:    S := 'Left arrow pressed.                    ';
    vk_Right:   S := 'Right arrow pressed.                   ';
    vk_F1:      S := 'F1 key pressed.                        ';
    vk_F12:     S := 'F12 key pressed.                       ';
    vk_Clear:   S := 'Numeric keypad 5, NumLock off';
    vk_NumPad5: S := 'Numeric keypad 5, NumLock on ';
  else
    S := 'Out to lunch, back in five!              ';
  end;

  SetBkColor(DC, GetSysColor(Color_BtnFace));
  TextOut(DC, XVal, YVal + 140, PChar(S), Length(S));

  ReleaseDC(hWindow, DC);
end;


/////////////////////////////////////
// The Window Procedure
/////////////////////////////////////
function WindowProc(Window: HWnd; AMessage, WParam,
                    LParam: Longint): Longint; stdcall; export;
var
  AMsg: TMessage;
begin
  AMsg.Msg := AMessage;
  AMsg.WParam := WParam;
  AMsg.LParam := LParam;
  AMsg.Result := 0;
```

```
  case AMessage of
    wm_Destroy: KeyMouse_OnDestroy(TWMDestroy(AMsg));
    wm_Char: KeyMouse_OnChar(TWMChar(AMsg));
    wm_KeyDown: KeyMouse_OnKeyDown(TWMKeyDown(AMsg));
    wm_KeyUp: KeyMouse_OnKeyUp(TWMKeyUp(AMsg));
    wm_MouseMove: KeyMouse_OnMouseMove(TWMMouseMove(AMsg));
    wm_LButtonDblClk: KeyMouse_OnLButtonDblClk(TWMLButtonDblClk(AMsg));
    wm_LButtonDown: KeyMouse_OnLButtonDown(TWMLButtonDown(AMsg));
    wm_LButtonUp: KeyMouse_OnLButtonUp(TWMLButtonUp(AMsg));
    wm_Paint: KeyMouse_OnPaint(TWMPaint(AMsg));
    wm_SysKeyup: KeyMouse_OnSysKeyUp(TWMSysKeyUp(AMsg));
    wm_SysKeyDown: KeyMouse_OnSysKeyDown(TWMSysKeyDown(AMsg));
  else
    Result := DefWindowProc(Window, AMessage, WParam, LParam);
    Exit;
  end;
  Result := AMsg.Result
end;

////////////////////////////////////
// Handle wm_DESTROY
////////////////////////////////////
procedure KeyMouse_OnDestroy(var Msg: TWMDestroy);
begin
  PostQuitMessage(0);
end;

////////////////////////////////////
// Handle regular keyboard hits
// Use if you want to trap the letter keys or number keys.
////////////////////////////////////
procedure KeyMouse_OnChar(var Msg: TWMChar);
var
  S: string;
  DC: HDC;
begin
  DC := GetDC(hWindow);

  S := Format('wm_Char ==> Ch = %S   cRepeat = %d         ',
              [Char(Msg.CharCode), LoWord(Msg.KeyData)]);

  SetBkColor(DC, GetSysColor(Color_BtnFace));
  TextOut(DC, XVal, YVal + 20, PChar(S), Length(S));

  ReleaseDC(hWindow, DC);
end;

////////////////////////////////////
// Any key is released
////////////////////////////////////
procedure KeyMouse_OnKeyUp(var Msg: TWMKeyUp);
var
  S: string;
  DC: HDC;
begin
  DC := GetDC(hWindow);
```

continues

Listing 12.1. continued

```
  S := Format('wm_KeyUp == > vk = %d   Repeat = %d          ',
                [Msg.CharCode, LoWord(Msg.KeyData)]);

  SetBkColor(DC, GetSysColor(Color_BtnFace));

  TextOut(DC, XVal, YVal + 40, PChar(S), Length(S));

  ReleaseDC(hWindow, DC);
end;

/////////////////////////////////////////
// Handle a key press
// Don't try to process letter or number keys here. Instead,
// use wm_CHAR messages.
/////////////////////////////////////////
procedure KeyMouse_OnKeyDown(var Msg: TWMKeyDown);
var
  S: string;
  DC: HDC;
begin
  DC := GetDC(hWindow);

  S := Format('wm_KeyDown == > vk = %d   cRepeat = %d ',
                [Msg.CharCode, LoWord(Msg.KeyData)]);

  SetBkColor(DC, GetSysColor(Color_BtnFace));

  TextOut(DC, XVal, YVal + 40, PChar(S), Length(S));

  ReleaseDC(hWindow, DC);
end;


/////////////////////////////////////////
// Click on left mouse button
/////////////////////////////////////////
procedure KeyMouse_OnLButtonDown(var Msg: TWMLButtonDown);
var
  S: string;
  DC: HDC;
begin
  DC := GetDC(hWindow);

  S := Format('wm_LButtonDown ==> Db = %d x = %d y = %d Flags = %d  ',
      [Msg.Keys, Msg.XPos, Msg.YPos, Msg.Keys]);

  SetBkColor(DC, GetSysColor(Color_BtnFace));
  TextOut(DC, XVal, YVal + 100, PChar(S), Length(S));

  ReleaseDC(HWindow, DC);
end;

/////////////////////////////////////////
// This function is called when the user double-clicks the mouse
/////////////////////////////////////////
procedure KeyMouse_OnLButtonDblClk(var Msg: TWMLButtonDblClk);
```

```
var
  S: string;
  DC: HDC;
begin
  DC := GetDC(hWindow);

  S := Format('wm_LButtonDblClk ==> Db = %d x = %d y = %d Flags = %d  ',
      [Msg.Keys, Msg.XPos, Msg.YPos, Msg.Keys]);

  SetBkColor(DC, GetSysColor(Color_BtnFace));
  TextOut(DC, XVal, YVal + 100, PChar(S), Length(S));

  ReleaseDC(HWindow, DC);
end;

//////////////////////////////////////
// This function is called when the mouse button is released
//////////////////////////////////////
procedure KeyMouse_OnLButtonUp(var Msg: TWMLButtonUp);
var
  S: string;
  DC: HDC;
begin
  DC := GetDC(hWindow);

  S := Format('wm_LButtonUp ==> x = %d y = %d F = %d   ',
              [Msg.XPos, Msg.YPos, Msg.Keys]);

  SetBkColor(DC, GetSysColor(Color_BtnFace));
  TextOut(DC, XVal, YVal + 120, PChar(S), Length(S));

  ReleaseDC(hWindow, DC);
end;

//////////////////////////////////////
// This function is called whenever the mouse moves
//////////////////////////////////////
procedure KeyMouse_OnMouseMove(var Msg: TWMMouseMove);
var
  S: string;
  DC: HDC;
begin
  DC := GetDC(hWindow);
  S := Format('wm_MouseMove ==> x = %d y = %d keyFlags = %d    ',
              [Msg.XPos, Msg.YPos, Msg.Keys]);
  if ((Msg.Keys and MK_CONTROL) = MK_CONTROL) then
    SetTextColor(DC, RGB(0, 0, 255));
  if ((Msg.Keys and MK_LBUTTON) = MK_LBUTTON) then
    SetTextColor(DC, RGB(0, 255, 0));
  if ((Msg.Keys and MK_RBUTTON) = MK_RBUTTON) then
    SetTextColor(DC, RGB(255, 0, 0));
  if ((Msg.Keys and MK_SHIFT) = MK_SHIFT) then
    SetTextColor(DC, RGB(255, 0, 255));

  SetBkColor(DC, GetSysColor(Color_BtnFace));
  TextOut(DC, XVal, YVal + 80, PChar(S), Length(S));
```

continues

Listing 12.1. continued

```
  ReleaseDC(hWindow, DC);
end;

//////////////////////////////////////
// Handle wm_PAINT messages.
//////////////////////////////////////
procedure KeyMouse_OnPaint(var Msg: TWMPaint);
const
  Message : array[0..5] of string =
  (
  'wm_Char',
  'wm_Key',
  'wm_SysKey',
  'wm_MouseMove',
  'wm_MousdDown',
  'wm_MouseUp');

var
  PaintStruct: TPaintStruct;
  Rect: TRect;
  PaintDC: HDC;
  OldFont: HFont;
  i: Integer;
begin
  PaintDC := BeginPaint(hWindow, PaintStruct);

  SetBkColor(PaintDC, GetSysColor(Color_BtnFace));

  OldFont := SelectObject(PaintDC, GetStockObject(OEM_FIXED_FONT));

  GetClientRect(hWindow, Rect);
  Rect.top := 5;
  DrawText(PaintDC, 'MOUSE AND KEYBOARD DEMONSTRATION', -1, Rect, DT_CENTER);
  Rect.top := 25;
  Rect.bottom := 45;
  DrawText(PaintDC,
           '(Try experimenting with the mouse and keyboard)',
           -1, Rect, dt_Center);

  SelectObject(PaintDC, OldFont);

  for i := 0 to 5 do
    TextOut(PaintDC, XVal, YVal + (20 * (i + 1)),
            PChar(Message[i]), Length(Message[i]));

  EndPaint(hWindow, PaintStruct);
end;

//////////////////////////////////////
// This function is called whenever the ALT key is lifted.
//////////////////////////////////////
procedure KeyMouse_OnSysKeyUp(var Msg: TWMSysKeyUp);

var
  S: string;
  DC: HDC;
```

```
begin
  DC := GetDC(hWindow);
  SetBkColor(DC, GetSysColor(Color_BtnFace));

  S := Format('wm_SysKeyUp == > ' +
              ' vk = %d   cRepeat = %d          ',
              [Msg.CharCode, LoWord(Msg.KeyData)]);

  TextOut(DC, XVal, YVal + 60, PChar(S), Length(S));

  ReleaseDC(hWindow, DC);
end;

///////////////////////////////////////
// This function is called whenever the ALT key is pressed.
///////////////////////////////////////
procedure KeyMouse_OnSysKeyDown(var Msg: TWMSysKeyDown);
var
  S: string;
  DC: HDC;
begin
  DC := GetDC(hWindow);
  SetBkColor(DC, GetSysColor(Color_BtnFace));

  S := Format('wm_SysKeyDown == > vk = %d   cRepeat = %d         ',
              [Msg.CharCode, LoWord(Msg.KeyData)]);

  TextOut(DC, XVal, YVal + 60, PChar(S), Length(S));

  ReleaseDC(hWindow, DC);
end;

///////////////////////////////////////
// Register the Window Class
///////////////////////////////////////
function DoRegister: Boolean;
var
  WindowClass: TWndClass;
begin
  WindowClass.Style := cs_hRedraw or cs_vRedraw or cs_dblClks;
  WindowClass.lpfnWndProc := @WindowProc;
  WindowClass.cbClsExtra := 0;
  WindowClass.cbWndExtra := 0;
  WindowClass.hInstance := HInstance;
  WindowClass.hIcon := LoadIcon(0, idi_Application);
  WindowClass.hCursor := LoadCursor(0, idc_Arrow);
  WindowClass.hbrBackground := hBrush(Color_Window);
  WindowClass.lpszMenuName := nil;
  WindowClass.lpszClassName := AppName;

  Result := RegisterClass(WindowClass) <> 0;
end;

///////////////////////////////////////
// Create the Window Class
///////////////////////////////////////
function Create: HWnd;
```

continues

Listing 12.1. continued

```
begin
  Result := CreateWindow(AppName, 'Object Pascal Window',
            ws_OverlappedWindow, cw_UseDefault, cw_UseDefault,
            cw_UseDefault, cw_UseDefault, 0, 0, HInstance, nil);
end;


var
  AMessage: TMsg;

begin
  if not DoRegister then begin
    MessageBox(0, 'Register failed', nil, mb_Ok);
    Exit;
  end;
  hWindow := Create;
  if hWindow = 0 then begin
    MessageBox(0, 'Create failed', nil, mb_Ok);
    Exit;
  end;

  ShowWindow(hWindow, CmdShow);
  UpdateWindow(hWindow);

  while GetMessage(AMessage, 0, 0, 0) do begin
    TranslateMessage(AMessage);
    DispatchMessage(AMessage);
  end;

  Halt(AMessage.wParam);
end.

Color_BtnFaceColor_BtnFaceColor_BtnFaceColor_BtnFaceColor_BtnFaceColor
➥_BtnFaceColor_BtnFaceColor_BtnFaceColor_BtnFaceColor_BtnFace
```

When KEYMOUSE.DPR is run, it produces the output shown in Figure 12.1.

FIGURE 12.1.

KEYMOUSE.DPR shows the information conveyed by the most important mouse and keyboard messages.

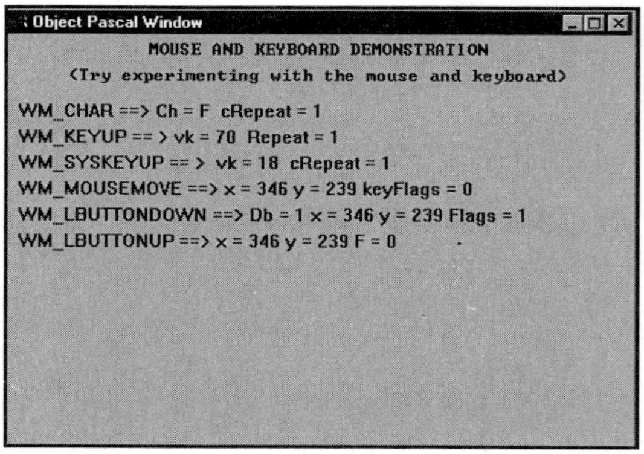

```
Object Pascal Window                                    _ □ ×
            MOUSE AND KEYBOARD DEMONSTRATION
         <Try experimenting with the mouse and keyboard>

WM_CHAR ==> Ch = F  cRepeat = 1
WM_KEYUP == > vk = 70  Repeat = 1
WM_SYSKEYUP == > vk = 18  cRepeat = 1
WM_MOUSEMOVE ==> x = 346 y = 239 keyFlags = 0
WM_LBUTTONDOWN ==> Db = 1 x = 346 y = 239 Flags = 1
WM_LBUTTONUP ==> x = 346 y = 239 F = 0
```

The KeyMouse program provides two major services:

- It shows how to detect when a key has been pressed. In particular, it shows the value of the pressed key and a few pieces of related information.

- It shows how to detect when the mouse has been moved and if a mouse button has been pressed. In particular, it prints output to the screen showing the current location and status of the mouse.

Take a few moments to play with this program. Note the way it reacts when you move the mouse or press a key. Remember that whenever you press the Alt key, the system menu on the upper-left corner of the title bar is activated. Regular keyboard response won't resume until you press the Alt key again or take some other action that changes the focus. Detecting Alt key presses is discussed in the section on WM_SYSKEY messages.

> **NOTE**
>
> The concept of *focus* is extremely important in Windows programming. Focused windows respond to keyboard and mouse input, whereas nonfocused windows don't respond. For instance, if the Windows Explorer has the focus, it responds to a press of the Alt+F key by opening its File menu. However, if you bring the KeyMouse program to the foreground of the desktop, the Windows Explorer no longer responds to the press of a keystroke. This occurs because the KeyMouse program now has the focus. You often can tell if a particular program has the focus by checking to see if its title bar is highlighted.
>
> It's important to understand that only one window has the focus at a time. For instance, if you open the File menu, that newly opened menu has the focus, and the main window of the program is inactive. The same thing happens when you open the Options dialog box from the View menu of the My Computer window. When the Options dialog box has the focus, the rest of My Computer is inactive.

From a technical point of view, I have opted to go with a global copy of hWindow and therefore to pass each of my message handlers only the TMessage variant that they need to process. I discussed this approach in the last chapter, and I implement it here so that you can compare the two techniques. Notice that the global hWindow is declared at the top of the program that all the message handler routines utilize. Other than this brief note, I'm not going to spend much more time discussing how the message handlers are dispersed from the WndProc. If you want to review that kind of material, see the previous chapter, "Messages and Painting Text." Most of this chapter focuses on the implementation of these message handlers, rather than how they were set up or why they were created.

forward Declarations

One minor technical point you might want to consider when looking at the KeyMouse program is that all the `MessageHandler` routines are predeclared with `forward` declarations:

```
// TKeyMouse
procedure KeyMouse_OnDestroy(var Msg: TWMDestroy); forward;
procedure KeyMouse_OnChar(var Msg: TWMChar); forward;
procedure KeyMouse_OnKeyUp(var Msg: TWMKeyDown); forward;
procedure KeyMouse_OnKeyDown(var Msg: TWMKeyDown); forward;
procedure KeyMouse_OnLButtonDown(var Msg: TWMLButtonDown); forward;
procedure KeyMouse_OnLButtonDblClk(var Msg: TWMLButtonDblClk); forward;
procedure KeyMouse_OnLButtonUp(var Msg: TWMLButtonUp); forward;
procedure KeyMouse_OnMouseMove(var Msg: TWMMouseMove); forward;
procedure KeyMouse_OnPaint(var Msg: TWMPaint); forward;
procedure KeyMouse_OnSysKeyUp(var Msg: TWMSysKeyUp); forward;
procedure KeyMouse_OnSysKeyDown(var Msg: TWMSysKeyDown); forward;
```

Needless to say, predeclaring all these functions is not necessary. I do it only because it provides a place in your code that serves the same purpose as an object declaration. In other words, it lets you get an overview of all the functions in the KeyMouse family, just as the `TForm` object at the head of the Delphi RAD module gives you an overview of the code in a PAS file.

Some readers might find this technique useful, primarily because it's always a good idea to consider carefully any technique that helps you write clean, easy-to-read, self-documenting code. You can just glance at the preceding declarations and learn a lot about this program. If you are new to the KeyMouse program, you can get a quick overview of the program by just glancing at these `forward` declarations. C programmers are also going to find this technique familiar because it is strongly encouraged in that language.

All that you are doing with the `forward` directive is stating that you might call some of the functions before you have defined them. That is, you might call them at a point one-third down the page of the source file, and yet you implement them down near the very bottom, as is done in the KeyMouse program. By writing out the header and following it with the word `forward`, you can legally do this without confusing the compiler. Once again, this is not a necessity in this particular case, it's just a technique that might have appeal to careful programmers who want to make their code as easy to maintain as possible. (To make sure I'm not confusing anyone, let me state the matter again slightly differently: There may be occasional times when it is necessary to use the forward directive, but this is not one of them.)

Windows Keyboard and Mouse Messages

KeyMouse is designed to show off nine Windows messages associated with the keyboard and mouse. These are shown in Table 12.1.

Table 12.1. Windows messages associated with the keyboard and mouse.

Message	Result
WM_CHAR	A number or letter key was pressed.
WM_KEYDOWN	A key was pressed.
WM_KEYUP	A key was released.
WM_LBUTTONDOWN	The left mouse button was pressed.
WM_LBUTTONUP	The left mouse button was released.
WM_LBUTTONDBLCLK	The left mouse button was double-clicked.
WM_MOUSEMOVE	The mouse was moved.
WM_SYSKEYDOWN	The Alt key was pressed.
WM_SYSKEYUP	The Alt key was released.

The majority of the rest of this chapter is dedicated to discussing these messages in one form or another. There are a few side trips to discuss matters such as painting the screen, but the main focus is on these very important messages.

Handling *wm_Char* Messages

wm_Char messages get sent whenever the user presses an alphanumeric key. That is, if you press one of the letters A–Z, or one of the numbers at the top of the keyboard, you get a wm_Char message. wm_KeyDown messages are sent whenever any key is pressed, regardless of whether it's alphanumeric. For instance, pressing the Delete key produces a wm_KeyDown message but not a wm_Char message.

Here is the wm_Char handler for the KeyMouse program:

```
procedure KeyMouse_OnChar(var Msg: TWMChar);
var
  S: string;
  DC: HDC;
begin
  DC := GetDC(hWindow);

  S := Format('WM_CHAR ==> Ch = %S   cRepeat = %d        ',
              [Char(Msg.CharCode), LoWord(Msg.KeyData)]);

  SetBkColor(DC, GetSysColor(Color_BtnFace));
  TextOut(DC, XVal, YVal + 20, PChar(S), Length(S));

  ReleaseDC(hWindow, DC);
end;
```

In just a moment, I talk about the actual purpose of the KeyMouse_OnChar function and about how it handles wm_Char messages. Before I get to that subject, however, I want to make sure you understand the crucial difference between the way the KeyMouse_OnChar and the KeyMouse_OnPaint functions handle the device context. This is a point you have to get clear in your head or you'll never get your programs to act correctly.

The first thing the KeyMouse_OnChar function does is get a device context. It does this not by calling BeginPaint and EndPaint but by snagging the device context with calls to GetDC and ReleaseDC. The TextOut method uses this device context to output information to the screen, just as the EasyText program did in Chapter 11.

To understand the difference between calling GetDC and calling BeginPaint, you only need to drag another program over the KeyMouse window. If, for instance, you were to temporarily obscure the left half of the KeyMouse window, the scene visible in Figure 12.2 would greet your eyes when the KeyMouse window is again brought to the fore.

FIGURE 12.2.

The KeyMouse program with some of its information blotted out after it was temporarily obscured by another program.

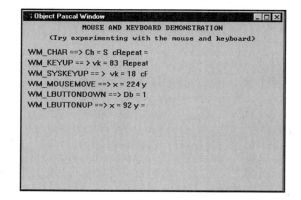

If you understand what has happened here, you are definitely getting a feel for the mechanisms employed by the Windows messaging system. A wm_Paint message is sent to a window every time a portion obscured by another window is uncovered. Therefore, the title and the words on the left portion of the KeyMouse program are visible whenever the window is visible. However, any text painted in, say, the KeyMouse_OnChar function, won't be repainted. The reason for this, of course, is that only wm_Char messages are sent to the KeyMouse_OnChar method. It doesn't know, or care, if a wm_Paint message is sent!

> **NOTE**
>
> In DOS programs, the contents of windows are frequently saved wholesale in a buffer and then restored whenever a window is brought back on top. This isn't the way Windows usually works. Instead, the contents of a window are restored by sending a wm_Paint message to the window that needs to be repainted. When a window gets a

wm_Paint message, it explicitly performs the acts necessary to repaint itself. The point here is that KeyMouse gets wm_Paint messages when it needs repainting, but it doesn't get wm_Char messages when it needs repainting. Therefore, any painting done in the wm_Char handler won't be updated automatically if it gets obscured by another window.

Nothing about the mechanism I'm describing is terribly complicated. Here are the two sides to the story:

- When responding to wm_Paint messages, you should use BeginPaint and EndPaint.
- At all other times, you should use GetDC and ReleaseDC.

Now that you have a feeling for the difference between BeginPaint and GetDC, the next step is to tackle the wm_Char message. wm_Char messages are sent to a program whenever a user presses one of the standard alphanumeric keys. That is, if a user presses the A key or B key, a wm_Char message is sent. Notice that wm_Char messages are not sent when the user presses one of the function keys or the arrow keys on the numeric keyboard.

Here is the TWMChar structure that is passed to the KeyMouse_OnChar routine:

```
TWMKey = record
  Msg: Cardinal;
  CharCode: Word;
  Unused: Word;
  KeyData: Longint;
  Result: Longint;
end;

TWMChar = TWMKey;
```

In particular, notice that TWMChar messages are handled by the TWMKey record. If this isn't clear to you, open up a copy of MESSAGES.PAS or MESSAGES.INT, if you have them available, and study the way they are put together. Remember, time spent studying the source code is never wasted! It's one of the most valuable ways you can expend your time. If you get paid by the hour, you should ask your boss or contractor to pay you twice as much for the time you spend studying the Delphi source code! (I'm pulling your leg just a bit here, but still, nothing is more valuable than the time you spend studying the source code!)

The value associated with a keypress is sent to the KeyMouse_OnChar function in the Msg.CharCode variable, which is declared to be a word. In other words, if the user presses the A key, Msg.CharCode is set to ASCII value 97, which is the letter a. If the user holds down the Shift key while pressing A, the ASCII value 65 is sent in the Msg.CharCode variable. ASCII 65, of course, represents the letter A.

If a key is pressed repeatedly between calls to wm_Char, the number of key presses that occurred is sent in the low word of the Msg.KeyData variable. Although this information is usually not very important, Windows still passes it on to you in case you have some use for it.

NOTE

It's worth noting here that it would not be hard to break up the TWMKey record into additional fields for use with TWMChar messages:

```
type
  TWMChar2 = record
    Msg: Cardinal;
    CharCode: Word;
    Unused: Word;
    cRepeat: Word;
    ScanCode: Byte;
    KeyData: Byte;
    Result: Longint;
  end;

procedure KeyMouse_OnChar2(var Msg: TWMChar2);
var
  S: string;
  DC: HDC;
begin
  DC := GetDC(hWindow);

  S := Format('WM_CHAR ==> Ch = %S  cRepeat = %d Scan = %d       ',
              [Char(Msg.CharCode), Msg.cRepeat, Msg.ScanCode]);

  SetBkColor(DC, GetSysColor(Color_BtnFace));
  TextOut(DC, XVal, YVal + 20, PChar(S), Length(S));

  ReleaseDC(hWindow, DC);
end;
```

The code shown here breaks the KeyData field of TWMKey into three separate fields called cRepeat, ScanCode, and KeyData. I know to do this by referring to the online help for wm_Char, found in WIN32.HLP. There I learn that bits 0–15 of LParam contain the repeat count, bits 16–23 hold the OEM scancode, and the top eight bits contain various pieces of miscellaneous data, as shown here:

24	Specifies whether the key is an extended key, such as the right-hand Alt and Ctrl keys that appear on an enhanced 101- or 102-key keyboard. The value is 1 if it is an extended key; otherwise, it is 0.
25-28	Reserved; do not use.
29	Specifies the context code. The value is 1 if the Alt key is held down while the key is pressed; otherwise, the value is 0.
30	Specifies the previous key state. The value is 1 if the key is down before the message is sent; it is 0 if the key is up.
31	Specifies the transition state. The value is 1 if the key is being released; it is 0 if the key is being pressed.

As you can see, I choose to ignore the feast of information in the high byte of LParam, and instead concentrate on the lower 24 bits. The code shown in this note is available in the copy of KeyMouse that appears on disk. You can call KeyMouse_OnChar2 just by changing one letter in the wm_Char response in the WndProc:

```
WM_CHAR: KeyMouse_OnChar2(TWMChar(AMsg));
```

Note that there is nothing to prevent you from creating as many custom TWMXXX messages as you might need. In fact, you can define your own messages and create your own TWMXXX records to go with them. What I am showing you in this chapter is in part a code resource found in MESSAGES.PAS and in part a coding technique that you can exploit for your own purposes.

The KeyMouse_OnChar function serves as a set piece for the virtues of MESSAGES.PAS. If KeyMouse didn't take advantage of message crackers, it would have to parse the wParam and lParam variables sent to the program's WndProc to determine the correct value of the keypress and the repeat count. To help get hold of this issue you might want to look up wm_KeyDown and wm_Char in the online help, as shown in Figure 12.3.

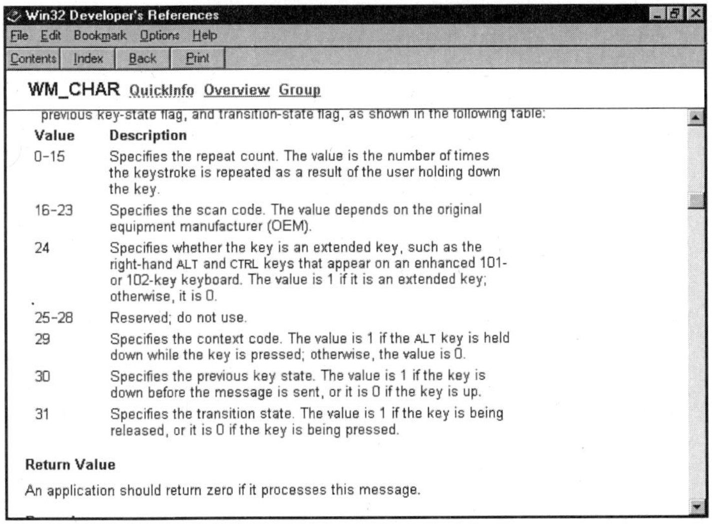

FIGURE 12.3.

A Borland help screen shows how information about keypresses is packed into lParam and wParam. Thanks to MESSAGES. PAS, detailed understanding of this information is no longer needed.

Before message crackers came along, programmers ferreted out all this information on their own by reading the fine print in the reference manuals, and by studying the actual bits in wParam and lParam.

Before closing this section it might be worth taking a moment to review some key points. You should use wm_Char messages for reading the alphanumeric keys. These key presses are correctly translated by Windows before the wm_Char message is sent. Therefore, wm_Char messages are an ideal way to tell if a number or letter is selected by the user.

Don't try to use wm_Char to detect whether function keys and letter keys have not yet been properly translated (via the TranslateMessage function in the message loop) when wm_KeyDown messages are sent. Hence, you can easily misinterpret the value of the keystroke associated with a wm_KeyDown message. More information about wm_KeyDown messages is presented in the next section.

Detecting Key Presses with *wm_KeyDown*

As you saw earlier, the wm_Char message is, from the point of view of a DOS programmer, one of the most essential messages sent to the window procedure. The CharCode field, which is passed to the KeyMouse_OnChar message handler function, contains the value of the key pressed (as long as that key is a letter or number). The other parameters provide other information, such as keeping track of how many times that key was pressed since the last time a wm_Char message was sent.

To handle other keypresses, such as a left-arrow, right-arrow, or function key, you should process the wm_KeyDown message:

```
procedure KeyMouse_OnKeyDown(var Msg: TWMKeyDown);
var
  S: string;
  DC: HDC;
begin
  DC := GetDC(hWindow);

  S := Format('WM_KEYDOWN == > vk = %d  cRepeat = %d ',
              [Msg.CharCode, LoWord(Msg.KeyData)]);

  SetBkColor(DC, GetSysColor(Color_BtnFace));

  TextOut(DC, XVal, YVal + 40, PChar(S), Length(S));

  ReleaseDC(hWindow, DC);
end;
```

#### Chapter 12

Windows makes it very easy for programmers to discover when a right-arrow key, left-arrow key, or function key has been pressed. This information is packed into the message handler's TWMKey record in the CharCode field. (Once again, TWMKeyDown is set equal to TWMKey in MESSAGES.PAS.)

The CharCode parameter plays the same role in the KeyMouse_OnKey function that it played in the KeyMouse_OnChar function. In other words, if the user presses the A key, that value is passed to the KeyMouse_OnChar function in the CharCode field. However, if the user presses the left-arrow key, the VK_LEFT constant is passed to the KeyMouse_OnKey method via the CharCode parameter. By default, this information is passed along as a raw number, and it's up to you to know which numbers are associated with which keystrokes.

The VK_LEFT constant is one of several predefined constants declared in the WINDOWS.PAS. Here is an excerpt from that list:

```
VK_END       = 35;
VK_HOME      = 36;
VK_LEFT      = 37;
VK_UP        = 38;
VK_RIGHT     = 39;
VK_DOWN      = 40;
VK_SELECT    = 41;
VK_PRINT     = 42;
VK_EXECUTE   = 43;
VK_SNAPSHOT  = 44;
VK_INSERT    = 45;
VK_DELETE    = 46;
VK_HELP      = 47;
{ VK_0 thru VK_9 are the same as ASCII '0' thru '9' ($30 - $39) }
{ VK_A thru VK_Z are the same as ASCII 'A' thru 'Z' ($41 - $5A) }
VK_LWIN      = 91;
VK_RWIN      = 92;
VK_APPS      = 93;
VK_NUMPAD0   = 96;
VK_NUMPAD1   = 97;
VK_NUMPAD2   = 98;
```

You can also find this information in various reference books or in your online help files.

The following modified version of the KeyMouse_OnKey function shows how to explicitly detect a few of these keystrokes:

```
procedure KeyMouse_OnKeyDown2(var Msg: TWMKeyDown);
var
  S: string;
  DC: HDC;
begin
  DC := GetDC(hWindow);

  case Msg.CharCode of
    vk_Left:   S := 'Left arrow pressed.      ';
    vk_Right:  S := 'Right arrow pressed.     ';
    vk_F1:     S := 'F1 key pressed.          ';
    vk_F12:    S := 'F12 key pressed.         ';
```

```
   vk_Clear:   S := 'Numeric keypad 5, NumLock off';
   vk_NumPad5: S := 'Numeric keypad 5, NumLock on ';
 else
   S := 'Out to lunch, back in five!                    ';
 end;

 SetBkColor(DC, GetSysColor(Color_BtnFace));
 TextOut(DC, XVal, YVal + 140, PChar(S), Length(S));

 ReleaseDC(hWindow, DC);
end;
```

```
Color_BtnFace
```

When examining this procedure, you might note the VK_CLEAR and VK_F12 constants. Capturing both of these keystrokes could be a bit complicated for DOS programmers working with certain compilers, but in Windows this kind of information is readily available.

For now, that's all I'm going to say about the wm_KeyDown message. I won't comment directly on the wm_KeyUp message because it is simply the converse of wm_KeyDown. This subject is really very straightforward. If you want to know more about the wm_KeyUp message, review the KeyMouse_OnKeyUp routine, or spend some time with the wm_KeyUp entry in the WIN32.HLP file that ships with Delphi.

> **NOTE**
>
> There is some chance that you did not install the Windows API help file when you ran the Delphi setup program. The file is about 10 MB in size, so some people opt to leave it on the CD-ROM. If you want, you can load it from the CD-ROM or you can copy it over to your hard drive now.

The System Key

In Windows, the system key is the Alt key. In other words, when you hold down the Alt key, you are holding down the system key. As a rule, choosing the system key forces a program to select the menu or the system menu, which in effect puts the program in a different mode.

Windows often gives more information than a user is ever likely to need. The KeyMouse program, for instance, traps wm_SysKeyDown and wm_SysKeyUp messages, which usually should be passed on directly to DefWndProc without any need for processing on your part. In Windows 3.1, these messages had to be passed on to DefWndProc because the system keys handle a lot of default Windows keyboard behavior, such as the famous Alt+Tab keystroke that switches between applications. Passing this message on is apparently not necessary in Windows 95.

In general, it's important to remember that erratic, inexplicable behavior in an application can sometimes be attributed to missing calls to the default window procedure. If one day you find yourself stuck in the midst of some lengthy, hair-pulling, patience-trying debugging session, you might want to consider the possibility that you have simply forgotten to pass a message on to the default window procedure for further processing. This seems to be less of an issue in Windows 95 than it was in Windows 3.1, but you should still keep the thought in mind.

The code for handling wm_SysKeyDown messages is shown here:

```
procedure KeyMouse_OnSysKeyDown(var Msg: TWMSysKeyDown);
var
  S: string;
  DC: HDC;
begin
  DC := GetDC(hWindow);
  SetBkColor(DC, GetSysColor(Color_BtnFace));

  S := Format('WM_SYSKEYDOWN == > vk = %d   cRepeat = %d        ',
              [Msg.CharCode, LoWord(Msg.KeyData)]);

  TextOut(DC, XVal, YVal + 60, PChar(S), Length(S));
  ReleaseDC(hWindow, DC);
end;
```

TWMSysKeyDown is again just another way of referencing TWMKey. As a result, the code shown here is very similar to the code in the wm_KeyDown handler, so it needs no further comment. You should, however, view the wm_SysKeyDown entries in the online help. I don't repeat them here because there is little point in my writing a book that does nothing more than rehash the online help.

The *wm_MouseMove* Message

There is something truly remarkable about the Windows messaging system. Even the simple act of moving a mouse across a window has a kind of fascination to it, especially when the co-ordinates being sent to the window are made visible, as they are in KeyMouse.

Stop for a moment and take a look at the wm_MouseMove message response function:

```
procedure KeyMouse_OnMouseMove(var Msg: TWMMouseMove);
var
  S: string;
  DC: HDC;
begin
  DC := GetDC(hWindow);
  S := Format('WM_MOUSEMOVE ==> x = %d y = %d keyFlags = %d     ',
              [Msg.XPos, Msg.YPos, Msg.Keys]);
  if ((Msg.Keys and MK_CONTROL) = MK_CONTROL) then
    SetTextColor(DC, RGB(0, 0, 255));
  if ((Msg.Keys and MK_LBUTTON) = MK_LBUTTON) then
    SetTextColor(DC, RGB(0, 255, 0));
  if ((Msg.Keys and MK_RBUTTON) = MK_RBUTTON) then
    SetTextColor(DC, RGB(255, 0, 0));
  if ((Msg.Keys and MK_SHIFT) = MK_SHIFT) then
    SetTextColor(DC, RGB(255, 0, 255));
```

```
SetBkColor(DC, GetSysColor(Color_BtnFace));
TextOut(DC, XVal, YVal + 80, PChar(S), Length(S));

ReleaseDC(hWindow, DC);
end;
```

The first thing to notice is what a good job the message cracker does of passing on relevant information to the KeyMouse_OnMouseMove function. In particular, note that the TWMMouseMove record ends up resolving to a more primary structure, which in this case is called TWMMouse:

```
TWMMouse = record
  Msg: Cardinal;
  Keys: Longint;
  case Integer of
    0: (
      XPos: Smallint;
      YPos: Smallint);
    1: (
      Pos: TSmallPoint;
      Result: Longint);
end;
```

If you look in a reference book, you see that when a window procedure gets a wm_MouseMove message, information is packed into the hwnd, wParam, and lParam parameters. The latter of these parameters carries information about the column the mouse is on in its low-order word, and it carries information about the row it's on in its high-order word. Thanks to the message crackers, this obscure information is translated into the *x* and *y* coordinates visible in the record passed to the KeyMouse_OnMouseMove function.

The KeyMouse_OnMouseMove function makes the x, y, and Keys parameters visible onscreen by first translating them into a string and then displaying them through the TextOut function. This is the same system you saw previously when studying the response to a keypress.

Sometimes it seems to me that the WndProc function is weathering a storm of messages that come in at a rate that boggles the mind. You can get a feeling for how many wm_MouseMove messages are sent to the program by studying the KeyMouse_OnMouseMove function in action. Remember that every time a new set of mouse coordinates is shown onscreen, another message has been processed by the WndProc. It's as if the window procedure is walking through a blizzard of messages that descends on it in great flurries of activity.

Besides the *x* and *y* coordinates of the mouse, the other piece of information sent with every wm_MouseMove message is contained in the Msg.Keys argument. This parameter can have one of the following values:

Constant	Significance
MK_CONTROL	The Ctrl key is down.
MK_LBUTTON	The left mouse button is down.
MK_RBUTTON	The right mouse button is down.

| MK_MBUTTON | The middle mouse button is down. |
| MK_SHIFT | The Shift key is down. |

These constants are bit flags, which means that you have to use bitwise operators to test whether they are set. Doing this is really very simple. For instance, if you want to test to see if the Ctrl key is pressed while the mouse is moving, all you need to do is AND keyFlags with MK_CONTROL and then test the result:

```
if ((Msg.Keys and MK_CONTROL) = MK_CONTROL) then
    SetTextColor(DC, RGB(0, 0, 255));
```

This code changes the color of the line output to the screen, depending on whether the Ctrl key is pressed.

If you review the KeyMouse_OnMouseMove function, you will see that it changes colors depending on which mouse button is pressed or depending on whether the Ctrl or Shift key is pressed. It does this just by testing the bits in the Msg.Keys field.

KeyMouse_OnMouseMove shows off the powers inherent in the Windows messaging system. The line associated with the wm_MouseMove message smoothly changes colors as the mouse buttons and Ctrl and Shift keys are pressed. Watching it in action helps you get a feeling for the agility and flexibility of a message-based operating system. In practice, it turns out to be a much more powerful and flexible system than it first appeared to me when I read descriptions of how it worked.

NOTE

The SetTextColor and RGB API calls are used over and over again in Windows programs. As a result, if you don't already understand them, you might want to take a few moments to get a feeling for how they work.

The RGB macro returns a 4-byte value that designates a color. The color to be returned is defined by the three parameters passed to the macro, each of which can have a value of from 0 to 255.

If the third parameter is set to 255 and the others are set to 0, the resulting color is dark blue. If the first parameter is set to 255, and the others to 0, the resulting color is red. The middle parameter controls the amount of green in the color returned by the RGB macro.

In the fourth example of the previous function, both the blue and the red are turned on all the way, resulting in a deep purple. If you wanted to produce a gray color, you could set all three values to 127. Setting them all to 0 produces a deep black, and setting them all to 255 produces white. If you turn on green and red simultaneously, you produce a bright yellow. With just a few minutes of experimentation, you should begin to get a feeling for all the interesting combinations you can produce with this powerful macro.

The SetTextColor function is easier to understand than the RGB macro because it does nothing more than its name implies. That is, it sets the text color output with the device context passed to it. In other words, it copies the result of the RGB function into the device context.

Processing Button Selections and Double-Clicks

The KeyMouse program uses the KeyMouse_OnLButtonDown, KeyMouse_OnLButtonDblClk, and KeyMouse_OnLButtonUp functions to record button presses. These functions work very much like the other routines presented in this chapter, so you shouldn't have much trouble with them.

It's as easy to understand what happens when a button is released as it is to understand what happens when a button is pressed. Therefore, there is no reason not to start with the KeyMouse_OnLButtonUp function:

```
procedure KeyMouse_OnLButtonUp(var Msg: TWMLButtonUp);
var
  S: string;
  DC: HDC;
begin
  DC := GetDC(hWindow);

  S := Format('WM_LBUTTONUP ==> x = %d y = %d F = %d    ',
              [Msg.XPos, Msg.YPos, Msg.Keys]);

  SetBkColor(DC, GetSysColor(Color_BtnFace));
  TextOut(DC, XVal, YVal + 120, PChar(S), Length(S));

  ReleaseDC(hWindow, DC);
end;
```

All in all, nothing could be much simpler than this little fellow. Its purpose, of course, is simply to let the user know where the mouse was when the user released the left mouse button. This is accomplished through the tried-and-true method of snagging hold of the device context and using it to print information to the screen.

Handling button presses has one gray area, however, because it is necessary to distinguish between ordinary button presses and button presses that are really double-clicks. Fortunately, Windows has a system that makes it relatively easy to distinguish between these two conditions, as long as you know how to get started.

Here comes a gotcha that can trip up many unsuspecting Windows programmers. If you want to process double-clicks on the left or right mouse button, you must begin by setting the window class style to CS_DBLCLKS. This is done in the Register method:

```
WindowClass.Style := cs_hRedraw or cs_vRedraw or cs_dblClks;
```

In this case, you can see that the style associated with the window class now contains three flags. I covered the first two earlier in this book, and they are also covered in the online help. The cs_dblClks style informs Windows that this class needs to know when the user double-clicks the mouse in its client area. If you forget to do this, and if you don't figure out what's wrong, you will begin pulling your hair out in about five minutes flat. I guarantee it.

Assuming you have the flags set up correctly, the message sent when the user double-clicks the left mouse button is wm_LButtonDblClk:

```
procedure KeyMouse_OnLButtonDblClk(var Msg: TWMLButtonDblClk);
var
  S: string;
  DC: HDC;
begin
  DC := GetDC(hWindow);

  S := Format('WM_LBUTTONDBLCLK ==> Db = %d x = %d y = %d Flags = %d  ',
      [Msg.Keys, Msg.XPos, Msg.YPos, Msg.Keys]);

  SetBkColor(DC, GetSysColor(Color_BtnFace));
  TextOut(DC, XVal, YVal + 100, PChar(S), Length(S));

  ReleaseDC(HWindow, DC);
end;
```

Take the time to study exactly how the KeyMouse_OnLButtonDblClk function works. When it is called, the function prints out a string stating that a wm_LButtonDblClk message has been sent; the function also informs the user about the current coordinates and other settings.

As I suggested earlier, Windows programs respond to changes in their environment just as a well-driven car responds to highway signs, or to curves in the road. In other words, Windows makes sure that a program is sent plenty of information about its environment. The job of the programmer is to teach a program how to respond to these messages. You have seen that a Windows program can respond to a blizzard of keyboard and mouse messages yet still stay on the road.

Handling *wm_Paint*

It's probably worth taking just a moment to discuss handling wm_Paint messages in the KeyMouse program:

```
procedure KeyMouse_OnPaint(var Msg: TWMPaint);
const
  Message : array[0..5] of string =
  (
  'WM_CHAR',
  'WM_KEY',
  'WM_SYSKEY',
  'WM_MOUSEMOVE',
  'WM_MOUSEDOWN',
  'WM_MOUSEUP');
```

```
var
  PaintStruct: TPaintStruct;
  Rect: TRect;
  PaintDC: HDC;
  OldFont: HFont;
  i: Integer;
begin
  PaintDC := BeginPaint(hWindow, PaintStruct);

  SetBkColor(PaintDC, GetSysColor(Color_BtnFace));

  OldFont := SelectObject(PaintDC, GetStockObject(OEM_FIXED_FONT));

  GetClientRect(hWindow, Rect);
  Rect.top := 5;
  DrawText(PaintDC, 'MOUSE AND KEYBOARD DEMONSTRATION', -1, Rect, DT_CENTER);
  Rect.top := 25;
  Rect.bottom := 45;
  DrawText(PaintDC,
           '(Try experimenting with the mouse and keyboard)',
           -1, Rect, DT_CENTER);

  SelectObject(PaintDC, OldFont);

  for i := 0 to 5 do
    TextOut(PaintDC, XVal, YVal + (20 * (i + 1)),
            PChar(Message[i]), Length(Message[i]));

  EndPaint(hWindow, PaintStruct);
end;
```

Unlike the code shown in the various other message handlers, anything printed by this routine stays onscreen even if the program is temporarily pushed into the background and covered by other applications. This helps to illustrate the significance of wm_Paint messages. If you wanted this program to always keep all its information current, you would have to output all its data in response to wm_Paint messages.

This function starts by using DrawText to print some general instructions to the user at the top of the screen. Notice that these calls to DrawText use the Rect function to constrain the output inside two small rectangular areas at the top of the screen. At the same time, the function uses the DT_CENTER flag to say that the text should be centered within these rectangles.

The code also changes the font that is used to output the top two instructional lines. To do this, it first selects a system font into the current device context:

```
OldFont := SelectObject(PaintDC, GetStockObject(OEM_FIXED_FONT));
```

When you select a font into a device context, the font that was previously selected is spit out the back end of the SelectObject function. It's as if the device context has room for only one font, and indeed, it probably does contain a record that has only one field for tracking fonts.

The key point here is that you don't want to waste system resources by just throwing the old font away. Instead, you need to preserve it in a temporary variable, which in this case is called `OldFont`. When you are finished using the new font, you need to restore the old font:

```
SelectObject(PaintDC, OldFont);
```

In some cases you would also need to destroy the font that you originally selected into the device context. In this case, however, that is not necessary because you selected one of the system fonts, which are created and maintained by Windows. In particular, you selected the `OEM_FIXED_FONT`, which is just a standard font that Windows keeps around for anyone or anything that needs it.

The little loop at the bottom of the program is used to write the system messages down the left side of the program. If you play with the KeyMouse program, you will notice that these labels, which read `wm_Char`, `wm_Key`, and so forth, never disappear as long as the program is onscreen. They are painted in response to a `wm_Paint` message, so they are permanently fixed to the main screen of the program. In a sense, this whole program is designed to emphasize the fact that `wm_Paint` messages are sent by the system whenever the screen needs to be updated, whereas `wm_Char`, `wm_Key`, and all the other messages shown in this program are sent only when the user explicitly triggers them.

In this program I use `SetBkColor` rather than `SetBkMode`, which I used in the last chapter. It's important to understand why I made this change. `SetBkColor` causes `TextOut` to overwrite the text that underlies it, whereas `SetBkMode` leaves the old text exposed, unless it is directly overwritten by the characters themselves. In other words, `SetBkColor` causes a letter to wipe out a rectangular area, whereas `SetBkMode` just wipes out the area directly beneath the black part of a letter. Clearly this has something to do with the bit modes Windows uses when blitting the text to the screen.

Because the output from this program writes multiple lines of text at the same coordinates, it is necessary to ensure that the text that is being overwritten is entirely blanked out. `SetBkColor` does the job. I also tend to append a few blank spaces onto the end of the output strings in case the new text is a little shorter than the old text. The blank spaces wipe out the occasional letters that might stick out farther in the old text than in the new. You should notice that built-in Delphi controls such as `TLabel` or `TEdit` take care of this kind of thing for you automatically. Once again, you can better understand how and when to use Delphi VCL controls if you understand exactly what they do for you and exactly when they need to expend extra clock cycles performing a task that may or may not be necessary for you.

Summary

In this chapter, you have dug beneath the surface of a Windows program to see how keyboard and mouse messages are handled.

In particular, you have taken a look at GetDC, ReleaseDC, RGB, and the SetTextColor functions. You have also been introduced to a slew of Windows constants, such as VK_CLEAR, wm_LButtonDblClk, and MK_CONTROL. Obviously, most people are never going to be able to memorize all these identifiers, so you must learn how to use the reference books and online help services available to you. Don't try to memorize the constants; instead, memorize the places where you can find them.

Of course, some messages are so important that you should always have them in mind. Messages that fit in this category include wm_Paint, wm_KeyDown, wm_Char, wm_MouseMove, and wm_1ButtonDown. These easy-to-comprehend messages prove their usefulness again and again when you are programming Windows applications.

To help you understand the main messages shown in this program, you should also read Chapter 24, "Objects, Encapsulation, and Properties," which is the VCL counterpart to this chapter. Perhaps I should have placed these two chapters back to back, but I instead opted to put chapters directly involving the Windows API in one place, and chapters directly involving the Windows VCL in a second place. It would not be inappropriate, however, for you to go directly from this chapter to Chapter 24 to see how to write a VCL program that does essentially the same thing as KeyMouse.

A key point to remember is that wm_KeyDown messages occur whenever a key is pressed. However, when this message is sent to a window procedure, Windows has not yet translated the keystroke. As a result, it's easy to become confused about exactly which key has been pressed. wm_Char messages, however, are an ideal place to find out about which alphanumeric key the user has pressed.

The BeginPaint and EndPaint functions are used only when responding to wm_Paint messages. Because wm_Paint messages are sent to a window whenever it needs to be updated, anything painted to the screen (with a DC retrieved by BeginPaint) is always visible when the window is visible. The GetDC function, however, can be called at virtually any time during the life of an application. As a result, it gives you considerably more flexibility than the BeginPaint function does. However, if you call GetDC, the screen won't be updated automatically after it was covered up by some other object (such as a window or dialog box). You can use BeginPaint only in response to wm_Paint messages, and you should not use GetDC in response to a wm_Paint message.

It doesn't take a genius to see that the Windows message system works. It gives programmers the kind of control over the computer's hardware that DOS programmers often longed in vain to achieve. So, take the time to linger over the riches revealed in this chapter.

The Windows API and DLLs

13

This chapter concentrates on events and DLLs. In particular, you will learn how to:

- Load and unload a DLL at runtime.
- Create Delphi DLLs that contain Delphi dialogs. You can call these DLLs from standard Delphi programs, from Delphi Windows API programs, and from other environments such as Borland C++ or Paradox.
- Use the Windows API to create old-style dialogs in tiny DLLs that can be called from Delphi programs, C programs, or any tool that supports DLLs.
- Share long strings between executables and DLLs with the ShareMem unit.

Like the last chapter, this one has lots of information in it, much of it presented on a large but tightly woven tapestry. Windows is a complicated operating system, and many of its key features will be laid bare. The chapter starts with a basic overview of DLLs, and quickly moves on to more advanced material. Concentrate on the main threads of the discussion, and you'll end up with a considerable amount of useful information by the end of this chapter.

DLL Basics

DLL stands for *dynamic link library*. DLLs are simple binary files containing sets of routines that can be called by any application or even by another DLL. They are called *dynamic* link libraries because they are linked into a program at runtime as they are needed.

DLLs are valuable because they enable you to write a single set of routines that can be called by a number of different programs. You can create smaller executables by avoiding the wasteful habit of linking the exact same code into multiple programs. Furthermore, DLLs can be loaded or unloaded from memory at runtime, allowing you to build applications that are many megabytes in size but which may never occupy more than a few hundred kilobytes of memory at any one time. The trick, of course, is to design DLLs that contain modules specific to a particular part of your program. That way you can load one DLL in memory when the user is working with one set of tools, then unload it and load another when the user wants to move to another part of your program.

You also can produce multiple DLLs that have the same interface, but that work slightly differently. For example, if you create a DLL that contains functions for displaying text to the user, you could build multiple copies of this DLL, each copy containing language-specific information. The first DLL might contain Spanish phrases, the second French phrases, the third Chinese, and so on. You could ship different versions of this DLL with different versions of your product. That way the core of your program could make the same calls to what appears to be the same DLL, but will in fact be a language-specific DLL. The calls will have the same names in each DLL, and the DLL itself will always have the same name, but the results of a call will depend on which particular DLL is shipped with that version of the product.

DLLs are one of the most important constructs inside Windows. In fact, Windows itself is in large part nothing but a collection of DLLs. If you look inside the WINDOWS\SYSTEM directory, you find files such as GDI32.DLL, KRNEL32.DLL, and USER32.EXE. The logic that runs Windows is stored in these and other files, all of which are DLLs.

> **NOTE**
>
> Most DLLs have the letters DLL as an extension. You can, however, give a DLL file any extension you want by using the DOS Rename command. For example, files with a DRV extension are also almost always DLLs. These are driver files that run things like your printer or your video display.
>
> In Windows 3.1, the core of the Windows API was stored in files called GDI.EXE, KERN386.EXE, and USER.EXE. These were DLLs, and in fact you will still find copies of these binary files shipping with Windows 95. They are provided to supply the strong 16-bit compatibility available in Windows 95.

To get a feeling for what role DLLs play in your environment, open up WINDOWS.PAS and look at the declarations it contains. WINDOWS.PAS, of course, is the unit that serves as an interface between Delphi and the Windows API. Here is a small excerpt:

```
function MessageBeep; external user32 name 'MessageBeep';
function MessageBoxA; external user32 name 'MessageBoxA';
function MessageBoxW; external user32 name 'MessageBoxW';
function MessageBox; external user32 name 'MessageBoxA';
function ModifyMenuA; external user32 name 'ModifyMenuA';
function ModifyMenuW; external user32 name 'ModifyMenuW';
function ModifyMenu; external user32 name 'ModifyMenuA';
function MoveWindow; external user32 name 'MoveWindow';
```

This business of calling MessageBoxA and MessageBoxW is simply a way to handle the Unicode versions of these functions. MessageBoxA is the standard ASCII version that you call on most occasions, and MessageBoxW is the Wide, or Unicode, version of the call.

The code excerpt from WINDOWS.PAS states that the MessageBox function is stored in USER32.DLL, and that it can be looked up in the module by searching for the name or string 'MessageBoxA'. If you scan through the rest of WINDOWS.PAS, you can see that there are more than a thousand functions, most of which are in the major DLLs such as GDI32.DLL, USER32.DLL, and KRNEL32.DLL.

NOTE

Under Windows 3.1, KRNL386 and KRNL286 are both referred to as 'KERNEL' inside of the old WINPROCS unit:

```
function FindResource; external 'KERNEL' index 60;
function LoadResource; external 'KERNEL' index 61;
function LockResource; external 'KERNEL' index 62;
function FreeResource; external 'KERNEL' index 63;
```

Needless to say, Windows decides that 'KERNEL' refers to one or the other of these DLLs, depending on the particulars of your current system and setup. In Windows 95 and Windows NT, there is no support for 286 computers, so there was no need to have two versions of KERNEL32.DLL.

Another DLL that Delphi uses all the time is CMPLIB32.DCL. Once again, don't let the extension fool you. CMPLIB32.DCL is a DLL with its extension renamed. To see the source for this DLL, go to the Options | Tools | Library menu option and choose *Save Library Source Code*. Then recompile CMPLIB32.DCL, as explained in Chapter 1. When you are done, you will be able to find the source for your copy of CMPLIB32.DCL. Here, for instance, are the opening lines of my DPR file for CMPLIB32:

```
library cmplib32;

uses
  ShareMem,
  ...
```

As you already know, CMPLIB32.DCL is the file that you recompile when you add components, OCXs, or other tools to the Delphi environment. In other words, Delphi itself is in part just a series of DLLs. Your ability to extend Delphi's IDE is a simple result of the fact that you can recompile a key DLL that is in fact part of Delphi itself. In particular, you can rebuild CMPLIB32.DCL. (Another seemingly mysterious and complex concept that ends up being quite simple!)

One last thing you should know about DLLs is that they can be explored using the TDUMP.EXE utility that ships with Delphi 1.0, C++, BP7, and other Borland products. To use this file, go to the DOS prompt and type:

```
tdump filename
```

For instance, you might write:

```
tdump krnl386.exe > kernel.txt
```

where > kernel.TXT pipes the output into a text file. When you are done, KERNEL.TXT will list all the functions available in KERNEL, even if they are not documented elsewhere:

```
Name: TOOLHELPHOOK              Entry:   341
    Name: ISTASK                   Entry:   320
    Name: FATALEXITHOOK            Entry:   318
    Name: MEMORYFREED             Entry:   126
    Name: A20PROC                  Entry:   165
    Name: MAKEPROCINSTANCE         Entry:    51
    Name: SETERRORMODE             Entry:   107
    Name: REGISTERWINOLDAPHOOK     Entry:   343
    Name: SWAPRECORDING            Entry:   204
    Name: ISWINOLDAPTASK           Entry:   158
    Name: _LLSEEK                  Entry:    84
    Name: LOCKCURRENTTASK          Entry:    33
    Name: FLUSHCACHEDFILEHANDLE    Entry:   319
    Name: GETFREEMEMINFO           Entry:   316
    Name: GETCODEHANDLE            Entry:    93
    Name: FREEPROCINSTANCE         Entry:    52
    Name: GETNUMTASKS              Entry:   152
```

If you are interested in this information, I have included the output from USER.EXE and KRNL386.EXE in the files USER.TXT and KERNEL.TXT on the disk accompanying this book. If you are *very* interested in this topic and want to explore it in depth, you should refer to Andrew Schulman's *Undocumented Windows* and *Unauthorized Windows 95*.

A Simple DLL

Also on the CD is a simple DLL example stored in a directory called SimpDLL. If you've never created a DLL before, you can use this example to examine the most basic facts about DLLs. Because it's so simple, I'll discuss it only briefly here and then move on to the meat of this chapter, which involves several much more complex examples.

The SimpDLL directory contains one DLL called DLLTEST.DLL and one very simple executable called RUNDYNLK.DPR, which stands for "Run Dynamic Link Library." The code for the DLL and the executable appear below in Listings 13.1 and 13.2. If you get an error message about the uses clause for the DllTest library, you can safely ignore it.

Listing 13.1. The DllTest module is a "simplest possible case" DLL that shows the basics of putting together a dynamic link library.

```
library Dlltest;

{ Program copyright (c) 1995 by Charles Calvert }
{ Project Name: SIMPDLL }

{ You can ignore the error about the uses
  clause that you will get when you open
  this program in Delphi. }

function TestTen: Integer; export;
begin
```

continues

Listing 13.1. continued

```
  Result := 10;
end;

exports
  TestTen name 'TestTen';

begin
end.
```

Listing 13.2. The main module for the executable that calls the DllTest library.

```
unit Testcall;

{ Program copyright (c) 1995 by Charles Calvert }
{ Project Name: SIMPDLL }

interface

uses
  SysUtils, WinTypes, WinProcs,
  Messages, Classes, Graphics,
  Controls, Forms, Dialogs,
  StdCtrls;

type
  TForm1 = class(TForm)
    Button1: TButton;
    Edit1: TEdit;
    procedure Button1Click(Sender: TObject);
  end;

var
  Form1: TForm1;

implementation

{$R *.DFM}

function TestTen: Integer; external 'DLLTEST' name 'TestTen';

procedure TForm1.Button1Click(Sender: TObject);
begin
  Edit1.Text := IntToStr(TestTen);
end;

end.
```

Before running this program, make sure that the DLLTEST.DPR module is compiled. Compiling that module will produce a DLL called DLLTEST.DLL, which must exist or this example will not run.

When you run the main program a simple dialog containing a button and an edit control appears, as shown in Figure 13.1. If you press the button, the number 10 appears in the edit control. This number is retrieved from the DLL's sole function, which does nothing more than return the number 10.

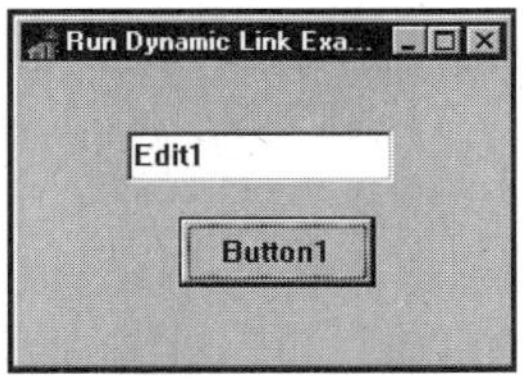

FIGURE 13.1.

The simple interface for RUNDYNLK.EXE.

The business end of the code in TESTDLL.DPR is simple:

```
function TestTen: Integer; export;
begin
  Result := 10;
end;

exports
  TestTen name 'TestTen';
```

Notice that the first line of the function called TestTen contains the word "export." This word indicates that the function will be exported from this DLL. In other words, this function can be called not only by routines residing inside the DLL, but it can also be called from outside the DLL.

Besides the export directive, also notice the mandatory exports clause. This clause lists all the functions that will be exported from the DLL, along with the name under which each will be exported. While you may have several exported functions listed in various units attached to your DLL, the exports clause should appear only in the DPR file, to list all the exported functions in one place. The purpose of the exports directive is to provide the name or index under which the function will be exported.

NOTE

Don't confuse the exports directive used to list all the functions exported from a DLL with the export directive used to designate one particular function as being marked for export.

This DLL exports its sole function by name. That is, it uses the name directive, and follows that directive with the name of the function that needs to be exported. In Windows 3.1, it was faster to look up functions in DLLs by index, but in Win32 you can use the name directive. Delphi imports all its functions by name.

Here is how the exports clause would look if you exported functions by name rather than by index:

```
exports
  TestTen index 1;
```

You can export by both name and index if you wish:

```
exports
  TestTen index 1 name 'TestTen';
```

You now know the basics of creating any DLL. And it is easy to create an Object Pascal DLL.

You import the TestTen function into the executable with the following line of code:

```
function TestTen: Integer; external 'DLLTEST' name 'TestTen';
```

This declaration states the header for the function; that is, it gives it a signature or type. The external directive states that the function is implemented outside of the current module, and, in particular, it is implemented in a DLL called DLLTEST.DLL. The declaration also states that the function is exported from the DLL under the name 'TestTen'.

After importing the function as shown above, you call it as you would any other Object Pascal or Windows API function:

```
procedure TForm1.Button1Click(Sender: TObject);
begin
  Edit1.Text := IntToStr(TestTen);
end;
```

Here the TestTen function is called, and its result is translated into a string and shown in Edit1.Text. You could also call the function this way:

```
X := TestTen;
```

where x is declared as an integer.

This brief introduction to DLLs is meant to get people who have not seen DLLs before up and running. I've included most of the information you need to use DLLs, although I will talk more about importing functions from DLLs later in this chapter.

Technical Details about DLLs

A DLL does not have its own stack, so it uses the stack of the program that calls it. Likewise, if you allocate memory in a DLL, it is stored in the address space of the calling program.

Unlike the situation in Windows 3.1, you cannot automatically use a DLL to share memory between multiple programs. Each program usually has a separate copy of any variables stored in a DLL and of any allocations made in a DLL. As a rule, use memory-mapped files, or OLE automation, to share memory or variables between applications.

The main program that calls a DLL can use the handles opened by a DLL function, and vice versa. You can, therefore, pass the handle of your main window to a DLL if you want to make the windows in that DLL child windows of the main window, or if you want them to exist as modal windows whose parents reside in the main executable. We'll look at examples of both these cases later in this chapter.

The whole C/C++ business about `LibMain`, `DllEntryPoint`, and WEPs does not apply to Object Pascal DLLs. Instead, you can use the `initialization` section of a DLL unit as the entry point, and you can use the `finalization` section as the exit point:

```
unit fileio;

interface

implementation

var
  F: Text;

initialization
  AssignFile(F, 'c:\Sam.txt');
  ReWrite(F);
  WriteLn(F, 'Init');
  Flush(F);
finalization
  WriteLn(F, 'Close');
  CloseFile(F);
end.
```

In the example shown here, the `initialization` code is executed as the DLL is loaded into memory, and the `finalization` section is executed as the DLL is unloaded. A similar example is supplied on the accompanying disk.

You cannot include the `initialization` and `finalization` sections in the DPR file for a library, but you can include them in a unit listed in the DPR file's uses clause. This has the same effect, as the unit's initialization clause is executed before any code in the DPR file.

The `begin..end` clause at the bottom of the DPR file for a library is executed at load time, but after the initialization section for any units included with the code. You can therefore initialize variables in the `begin..end` clause, but it is not a great place to allocate memory, since there is no good way to guarantee that the memory will be disposed.

If you use load-time dynamic linking (that is, if you don't call `LoadLibrary`), the links to the functions in a DLL are mapped at load time, but the code for each of the functions may or may not stay in memory. The code will, of course, be loaded into memory when you actually call the functions in question; the rest of the time, however, the code may be swapped to disk. In WIN32 it doesn't matter if you use the PRELOAD or LOADONCALL directives; they have no effect.

Calling Delphi Dialogs from an API Application

Working from the raw API level is very helpful if you want to build small, fast applications. It is not much help, however, if you want to build applications quickly.

Fortunately, when working in Delphi, it is not absolutely necessary for you to choose one option over the other. Moreover, you can create Delphi DLL's that you call from straight Windows API applications, and vise versa.

To show how this works, it's perhaps easiest to start with a straight Windows API application, then add a Delphi VCL DLL to it. Later in this chapter, I demonstrate the reverse scenario.

Suppose a programmer has constructed a very small, very fast Windows API application. In the middle of the project, the programmer realizes that she needs to retrieve a date from the user. She could just pop up a dialog containing an edit control, and ask the user to enter a date in the edit control. The programmer could not, however, just assume that the date was entered in the proper format. She would have to verify the entry for accuracy through considerable checking and cross-checking.

Just thinking about writing this code, the beleaguered programmer might begin to long for the tools available from the Delphi Component Palette. If only she could access a few Delphi components to create the form shown in Figure 13.2. Then she could present the user with a nice graphical tool for entering the date, and be assured that the input contained no formatting errors. Without Delphi's visual tools, the task of creating the dialog would be, to say the least, an enormous effort.

FIGURE 13.2.

A dialog built in Delphi for retrieving a date from the user.

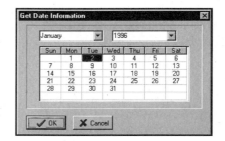

The point, of course, is that deciding to write a straight Windows API application does not force you to give up all the advantages of the Delphi RAD tools. In particular, you can create a DLL using the visual tools, and then call that DLL from inside your API-based application. This technique keeps the size of your application down, while simultaneously allowing you to use certain RAD development tools. Your application's memory usage will suffer somewhat for a short period of time while the DLL is being accessed, but you will be free of the DLL's weight once it is no longer needed. Most of the time you will have a small, fast executable in memory, and only temporarily will you also have the DLL in memory.

To make this work correctly, you need to call `LoadLibrary` and `FreeLibrary`. These two calls allow you to launch your application without having to simultaneously load your application's DLLs into memory. If you need to access a DLL, you can call `LoadLibrary` to read the DLL into memory and give you a handle to its functions, but the DLL must be in memory only during the times that you need it.

Two sample API programs appear below. The first, called SMALL1.DPR, shows how to call a DLL without using `LoadLibrary`. The second shows how to access a DLL through the good graces of the `LoadLibrary` function. Before creating either of these programs, however, it's necessary to first take a moment to put together a Delphi VCL-based DLL.

The form of the DLL is illustrated previously in Figure 13.2. The project source file appears below, in Listings 13.3 and 13.4.

Listing 13.3. The project source file for the DATEINFO DLL.

```
library dateinfo;

uses
  ShareMem,
  main in 'main.pas' {DateInformation};

exports
  GetDate index 1 name 'GetDate';

begin
end.
```

Listing 13.4. The main module for the DATEINFO library.

```
unit main;

interface

uses
  SysUtils, Windows, Messages,
  Classes, Graphics, Controls,
```

continues

Listing 13.4. continued

```
  Forms, Dialogs, StdCtrls,
  Buttons, Grids, Calendar,
  ExtCtrls;

const
  { From SYSUTILS.INC }
  SShortMonthNames = 65472;
  SLongMonthNames = 65488;
  SShortDayNames = 65504;
  SLongDayNames = 65511;

type
  TDateInformation = class(TForm)
    Cal: TCalendar;
    bbOk: TBitBtn;
    bbCancel: TBitBtn;
    Bevel1: TBevel;
    cbMonth: TComboBox;
    cbYear: TComboBox;
    procedure FormCreate(Sender: TObject);
    procedure cbMonthChange(Sender: TObject);
    procedure cbYearChange(Sender: TObject);
  public
    function GetDate: string;
  end;

var
  DateInformation: TDateInformation;

procedure GetDate(Handle: THandle; var S: string);

implementation

{$R *.DFM}

function TDateInformation.GetDate: string;
begin
  Result := IntToStr(Cal.Month) + '/' + IntToStr(Cal.Day) + '/' +
IntToStr(Cal.Year);
end;

procedure TDateInformation.FormCreate(Sender: TObject);
var
  i: Integer;
begin
  for i := 0 to 11 do
    cbMonth.Items.Add(LoadStr(SLongMonthNames + i));
  cbMonth.ItemIndex := Cal.Month - 1;
  for i := 1990 to 2100 do
    cbYear.Items.Add(IntToStr(i));
  cbYear.ItemIndex := cbYear.Items.IndexOf(IntToStr(Cal.Year));
end;

procedure TDateInformation.cbMonthChange(Sender: TObject);
begin
```

```
  Cal.Month := cbMonth.ItemIndex + 1;
end;

procedure TDateInformation.cbYearChange(Sender: TObject);
begin
  Cal.Year := StrToInt(cbYear.Items.Strings[cbYear.ItemIndex]);
end;

procedure GetDate(Handle: THandle; var S: string); export;
begin
  Application.Handle := Handle;
  DateInformation := TDateInformation.Create(Application);
  if DateInformation.ShowModal <> mrCancel then
    S := DateInformation.GetDate
  else
    S := 'Unknown';
  DateInformation.Free;
end;

end.
```

This DLL enables the user to select a date from a calendar. There are two combo boxes on the main form, one containing the 12 months of the year, and one holding a list of the years between 1900 and 2100 AD. The user can select a year and a month from the combo boxes, and can select a date from the calendar component in the middle of the form.

Notice the reference to ShareMem in the first position of the uses clause of both the DLL and the executable that calls it. This is necessary because the memory allocated for the long strings used in both modules must be shared. In other words, you are going to allocate memory for a string in the DLL, and then use the string in the executable. This will not work properly unless you add ShareMem to your uses clause. This unit loads DELPHIMM.DLL into memory. (DELPHIMM.DLL ships with Delphi in the DELPHI32\BIN directory, and contains the memory manager.)

Ensuring that DELPHIMM.DLL is loaded in memory before your application runs can be trying. As a result, you might prefer to use ShortStrings or PChars rather than long strings. If so, you can remove the reference to ShareMem from your uses clause. The version of DATEINFO.DLL that ships with this book uses the latter approach, and eschews ShareMem. This is probably the wisest course to take when shipping any application that you produce with Delphi. Here is how GetDate looks if you use ShortStrings:

```
procedure GetDate(Handle: THandle; var S: ShortString); export;
begin
  Application.Handle := Handle;
  DateInformation := TDateInformation.Create(Application);
  if DateInformation.ShowModal <> mrCancel then
    S := DateInformation.GetDate
  else
    S := 'Unknown';
  DateInformation.Free;
end;
```

Notice that the variable s is declared as a ShortString, and not as a string. I will discuss this procedure in a moment. The only point I'm making at this stage is that you have a choice between using ShareMem and not using it. The choice involves a decision whether or not to use long strings, and the function above shows the particular method that needs to be changed if you don't use ShareMem. This method needs to be changed because it is the one that will be exported from the library.

The project source code uses the reserved word Library to tell the compiler that this is a DLL and not an executable. This word will be inserted automatically if you choose File | New | DLL from the menu. Alternatively, you can create a normal project, save it, and then change the word project to library:

```
project DateInfo; => library DateInfo;
```

The reserved word exports is used to list the names of the functions exported by the DLL. The DLL's sole function can be exported by name alone, or by name and index. Win32 handles exporting functions equally well by either method. Here is the way the main module would look if you did not use ShareMem and exported GetDate by name only:

```
library dateinfo;

uses
  main in 'main.pas' {DateInformation};

exports
  GetDate name 'GetDate';

begin
end.
```

Understanding the Code in the DateInfo DLL

The most important method in the DLL is called when the form is created:

```
procedure TDateInformation.FormCreate(Sender: TObject);
var
  i: Integer;
begin
  for i := 0 to 11 do
    cbMonth.Items.Add(LoadStr(SLongMonthNames + i));
  cbMonth.ItemIndex := Cal.Month - 1;
  for i := 1990 to 2100 do
    cbYear.Items.Add(IntToStr(i));
  cbYear.ItemIndex := cbYear.Items.IndexOf(IntToStr(Cal.Year));
end;
```

The first lines in this method fill a combo box with a list of the names of the months of the year:

```
for i := 0 to 11 do
  cbMonth.Items.Add(LoadStr(SLongMonthNames + i));
```

SLongMonthNames is a constant declared in SYSUTILS.INC, which ships with the compiler. I've copied this constant out of the include file and placed it at the top of the main module. These numbers reference some strings held in SYSUTILS.RC:

```
SLongMonthNames + 1,  "February"
  SLongMonthNames + 2,  "March"
  SLongMonthNames + 3,  "April"
  SLongMonthNames + 4,  "May"
  SLongMonthNames + 5,  "June"
  SLongMonthNames + 6,  "July"
  SLongMonthNames + 7,  "August"
  SLongMonthNames + 8,  "September"
  SLongMonthNames + 9,  "October"
  SLongMonthNames + 10, "November"
  SLongMonthNames + 11, "December"
```

You can access these strings by calling the LoadStr function, found in the SYSUTILS unit. It's worth your effort to spend some time examining SYSUTILS.PAS, SYSUTILS.RC, and SYSUTILS.INC so that you become familiar with the various routines, constants, and resources available in these files. If you are having trouble understanding the way RC and include files work, turn back to Chapter 10, "Dialogs and Resources."

The Calendar object has a property called UseCurrentDate that defaults to TRUE. When turned on, this property sets the calendar automatically to the current date. To make the month combo box reflect this date you can enter the following line of code:

```
cbMonth.ItemIndex := Cal.Month - 1;
```

The items in the combo box are numbered 0 through 11. The numbers used to represent the months of the year in the TCalendar object are based on the number 1. That is, they are labeled 1 through 12, where 1 is January and 12 is December. To synchronize these two sets of numbers, I subtract one from the currently selected month of the calendar object. For instance, if the current month is October, then Cal.Month will be equal to 10. Subtract one from that number, and you get 9, which is the offset of the word October in the list held by the combo box. To set a combo box to a particular string in its string list, just find out the number of that string in the string list, and assign that number to the ItemIndex property of the combo box, as shown above.

After filling the second combo box with the years from 1900 to 2100, you must initialize the box to the current year:

```
cbYear.ItemIndex := cbYear.Items.IndexOf(IntToStr(Cal.Year));
```

This code fragment shows several of the traits of the TStringList object associated with a combo box. As in the example above, the code selects a particular string in the combo box by finding the string's index in the Items list, and then setting the ItemIndex property to that number. To retrieve the index of the string, the code translates the Year property of the TCalendar object into a string, then calls the TStringList IndexOf function, which returns the index of that string. This index is then assigned to the ItemIndex property. This approach is not the only way to solve this problem, but it's reasonably efficient.

Once you have filled out the combo boxes at the top of the DateInformation form, there are only a few additional steps you need to take to make this form behave properly. In particular, you need to keep track of when a new month is selected in the combo box:

```
procedure TDateInformation.cbMonthChange(Sender: TObject);
begin
  Cal.Month := cbMonth.ItemIndex + 1;
end;
```

This code performs the opposite action from the code shown in the FormCreate method. It is called whenever the user changes the selection in the list box. In response to this action, the code tells the calendar to switch to the newly selected month chosen in the combo box. In this case, of course, you need to add 1 to the currently selected combo box index in order to properly synchronize it with the months of the year tracked by the TCalendar object.

Another important method in this unit is the one which returns the currently selected date:

```
function TDateInformation.GetDate: string;
begin
  Result := IntToStr(Cal.Month) + '/' + IntToStr(Cal.Day) + '/' +
            IntToStr(Cal.Year);
end;
```

This code is trivial in the extreme, and is noteworthy only in that it shows a little something about string concatenation in Delphi.

The object in this DLL will not be initialized automatically in the project source. In particular, there is no code like this in the DPR file:

```
begin
  Application.CreateForm(TForm1, Form1);
  Application.Run;
end.
```

As a result, I have created my own function for this purpose, and exported the function so it can be called from outside the DLL. Note that this is the same function referenced in the export statement shown previously, and the same one I quoted when discussing the ShareMem versus ShortStrings issue:

```
procedure GetDate(Handle: THandle; var S: string); export;
begin
  Application.Handle := Handle;
  DateInformation := TDateInformation.Create(Application);
```

```
  if DateInformation.ShowModal <> mrCancel then
    S := DateInformation.GetDate
  else
    S := 'Unknown';
  DateInformation.Free;
end;
```

Note that this version of the code assumes that you are using `ShareMem`.

This code first creates an instance of the `TDateInformation` object. This is the moment when memory is allocated, and is roughly equivalent to calling the Object Pascal functions `GetMem` or `New`, or the WinAPI functions `HeapAlloc` or `VirtualAlloc`. In fact, ultimately this call resolves into a call to `VirtualAlloc`. The next step is to show the form to the user. When the user has selected a date and pressed OK, you can free up the form's memory and return the selected date.

Remember! You won't be able to share the string between the two units unless you add `ShareMem` to the `uses` clause of both the DLL and the executable, or unless you use `ShortStrings`. The reference to `ShareMem` should be the first entry in the `uses` clause for the main module of both files. This crucial fact is not documented clearly, so it is also unclear whether it will change in future versions of the product!

Overall this is not a particularly complicated DLL. I've explained it in some depth, however, because it provides an interesting example of how to use Delphi components. Make sure you compile a version of this DLL, and place it in the same directory as the program that will use its services.

Making Calls to the DLL

Now that the DLL exists, the only thing left to do is to call it from an executable. I'm going to show two versions of this executable. The first version will load the DLL at the same time the executable is launched. This means that the DLL and the executable will always be in memory together. The second executable launches normally, but does not load the DLL into memory until it needs it. The executable then discards the DLL as soon as it is finished using it. The mechanism employed in the second version involves calls to `LoadLibrary` and `FreeLibrary`. (There is also a third executable, Test1, on the accompanying disk. You can use this program to call the DLL from a standard Delphi application. I've included it so you can check out the DLL easily, without having to worry about composing the Windows API application.)

Listing 13.5 shows the version of the executable that calls the DLL without using `LoadLibrary`. This file is found on the CD-ROM in the directory called DELDLL. Notice that the program lists `ShareMem` as the first item in its `uses` clause. This reference makes it possible to share strings back and forth between the DLL and the executable.

Listing 13.5. The Small1 program allows the user to use code stored in a DLL.

```pascal
program Small1;

{ Copyright (c) 1996 by Charles Calvert

  Shows how to launch a DLL from a Windows API program. }

uses
  ShareMem, Windows;

const
  AppName = 'SmallOne';

var
  DateStr: string;

procedure GetDates(Handle: THandle; var S: string);
  external 'DATEINFO' name 'GetDate';

function WindowProc(Window: HWnd; AMessage, WParam,
                    LParam: Longint): Longint; stdcall; export;
var
  PaintDC: HDC;
  PaintStruct: TPaintStruct;

begin
 Result := 0;

  case AMessage of
    wm_Destroy: begin
      PostQuitMessage(0);
      Exit;
    end;

    wm_LButtonDown: begin
      GetDates(Window, DateStr);
      InvalidateRect(Window, nil, True);
      Exit;
    end;

    wm_Paint: begin
      PaintDC := BeginPaint(Window, PaintStruct);
      SetBkMode(PaintDC, TransParent);
      TextOut(PaintDC, 10, 10, PChar(DateStr), Length(DateStr));
      EndPaint(Window, PaintStruct);
    end;

  end;

Result := DefWindowProc(Window, AMessage, WParam, LParam);
end;

{ Register the Window Class }
function WinRegister: Boolean;
var
  WindowClass: TWndClass;
```

```
begin
  WindowClass.Style := cs_hRedraw or cs_vRedraw;
  WindowClass.lpfnWndProc := @WindowProc;
  WindowClass.cbClsExtra := 0;
  WindowClass.cbWndExtra := 0;
  WindowClass.hInstance := HInstance;
  WindowClass.hIcon := LoadIcon(0, idi_Application);
  WindowClass.hCursor := LoadCursor(0, idc_Arrow);
  WindowClass.hbrBackground := GetStockObject(LtGray_Brush);
  WindowClass.lpszMenuName := nil;
  WindowClass.lpszClassName := AppName;

  Result := RegisterClass(WindowClass) <> 0;
end;

{ Create the Window Class }
function WinCreate: HWnd;
begin
  Result := CreateWindow(AppName, 'Object Pascal Date Window',
              ws_OverlappedWindow, cw_UseDefault, cw_UseDefault,
              cw_UseDefault, cw_UseDefault, 0, 0, HInstance, nil);
end;

var
  AMessage: TMsg;
  Window: HWnd;

begin
  DateStr := 'Click here to start';
  if not WinRegister then Exit;
  Window := WinCreate;
  if Window = 0 then Exit;

  ShowWindow(Window, CmdShow);
  UpdateWindow(Window);

  while GetMessage(AMessage, 0, 0, 0) do begin
    TranslateMessage(AMessage);
    DispatchMessage(AMessage);
  end;

  Halt(AMessage.wParam);
end.
```

This code pops up a regular window. If you click the window, the date dialog from the DLL appears, and you can select a date. If you click the OK button in the dialog, the string is returned to the executable and displayed in its main window.

The executable imports one routine from the DLL, called GetDates:

```
procedure GetDates(Handle: THandle; var S: string);
  external 'DATEINFO' name 'GetDate';
```

If you look in the DLL itself, you will find that there is no routine in the DLL called GetDates. The name of the exported function is GetDate. This works because the code above states that the routine to search for is called `GetDate`. The point is that the "name" under which the function is exported is `GetDate`, and what it's called inside the executable is irrelevant. Of course, most of the time you should try to call the function by the same name in the DLL and in the executable, but you don't have to do this. Be careful, however, to make sure you give the function the same signature in the DLL and in the executable. That is, the parameters passed to the function should be identical in both cases.

The `external` directive in the above code specifies the DLL in which the function resides. In this case, the name of the DLL is `DATEINFO`, and so I explicitly name that string. It is, of course, necessary to specify this name exactly.

Once you have included this declaration in your code, you are free to call the `GetDates` method. The above declaration automatically loads DATEINFO.DLL into memory and assures that you can call the `GetDate` method when needed:

```
wm_LButtonDown: begin
  GetDates(Window, DateStr);
  InvalidateRect(Window, nil, True);
  Exit;
end;
```

If you need to export many functions from a DLL, you should put them all in a single unit and list the unit in your `uses` clause. To do this, you should declare the function normally in the interface, and specify the relevant DLL and name in the implementation:

```
unit DLLUnit;

interface

uses
  Windows;

procedure GetDates(Handle: THandle; var S: string);

implementation

procedure GetDates; external 'DATEINFO' name 'GetDate';

end.
```

The above code represents a complete unit that will compile correctly and can be added to an application. Clearly this is overkill for importing a single function. However, if you have a complex set of routines that you need to work with, this is the preferred method for handling them. See WINDOWS.PAS or WINSOCK.PAS for classic examples of this type of unit.

The *WndProc* Revisited

Now that you have imported the routine from the DLL, the next step is to use it in your application. Basically all you need to do is call the routine as you would any other function or procedure:

```
var
  Window: Hwnd;
  DateStr: string;
  ...
begin
  GetDates(Window, DateStr);
  ...
end;
```

This is simple enough in principle, but it turns out there are a few more concepts to grasp before you have a good understanding of the role of this function in the program.

Take a moment to study the WindowProc routine:

```
function WindowProc(Window: HWnd; AMessage, WParam,
                    LParam: Longint): Longint; stdcall; export;
var
  PaintDC: HDC;
  PaintStruct: TPaintStruct;

begin
 Result := 0;

  case AMessage of
    wm_Destroy: begin
      PostQuitMessage(0);
      Exit;
    end;

    wm_LButtonDown: begin
      GetDates(Window, DateStr);
      InvalidateRect(Window, nil, True);
      Exit;
    end;

    wm_Paint: begin
      PaintDC := BeginPaint(Window, PaintStruct);
      SetBkMode(PaintDC, TransParent);
      TextOut(PaintDC, 10, 10, PChar(DateStr), Length(DateStr));
      EndPaint(Window, PaintStruct);
      Exit;
    end;

  end;

  Result := DefWindowProc(Window, AMessage, WParam, LParam);
end;
```

Each message that comes into this routine passes through the filter of a single, potentially very large, case statement. In this particular example, the three messages handled are wm_Destroy, wm_LButtonDown, and wm_Paint. (As you can see, I am not using message crackers in this particular program. I will in the next version of the code, but I thought it would be interesting to omit them on this occasion just to remind you of how a program looks that doesn't use them.)

> **NOTE**
>
> Remember that wm_Destroy messages are sent to all windows after they are removed from the screen. It's your chance to do any cleanup of variables allocated by your window. A window may have a series of child windows or other allocations. For instance, a window might be associated with various data structures for which memory is allocated. This is the chance to deallocate the memory associated with those structures. If the window receiving a wm_Destroy message is the main window for an application, it should call PostQuitMessage. PostQuitMessage terminates an application, using its sole parameter as the application's exit code. In particular, PostQuitMessage tells the program to break out of the message loop.

When you actually break it down, a typical API program like Small1 isn't really that complex, but it appears complex, and it takes a long time to code. It's worth contemplating, however, because Delphi RAD programs go way out of their way to hide this kind of code from the user.

One of the major goals of tools like Delphi is to make the basic mechanisms that lie at the heart of Windows intuitively obvious to the developer. If you click the Events page in the Object Inspector and start handling OnMouseDown messages, you don't have to think much about the process involved. It comes naturally. However, if you want to create components that handle wm_LButtonDown messages, you have to put the old nose to the grindstone! In short, Delphi's ability to protect you from the innards of Windows is a benefit up to a point, but it can become a liability because it can prevent you from ever understanding what is really going on.

Once you think about it, it's obvious the OnMouseDown events in the Object Inspector are just Delphi's way of handling wm_LButtonDown and wm_RButtonDown messages. Furthermore, OnKeyPress events correspond to wm_Char messages, OnKeyDown events correspond to wm_KeyDown messages, OnPaint to wm_Paint messages, and so on.

Sometimes this analogy breaks down, at least in part. For instance, OnDestroy events are not exactly analogous to wm_Destroy messages. They are similar, but there are some slight differences in the way they behave. For instance, a Windows HWnd is still valid when you get a wm_Destroy message, but it is not valid when you handle an OnDestroy event in Delphi.

The beauty of Delphi, of course, is that if you need to handle wm_Destroy messages instead of OnDestroy messages, the system is flexible enough to allow you to do so. (See Chapter 22, "Handling Messages," for more information on this type of maneuver.) However, if you want to decide whether you need to handle OnDestroy, or wm_Destroy messages, you first need to understand the Windows API. That's one of the primary reasons I'm taking the trouble to write this chapter and the ones related to it. If you want to be really good at using Delphi, you have to understand not only how to use Delphi, but also how Delphi actually works. Furthermore, to create first class components you need to understand this stuff at some fairly deep-seated level.

wm_Paint and InvalidateRect

When the user clicks the window, the wm_LButtonDown part of the case statement is called:

```
wm_LButtonDown: begin
  GetDates(Window, DateStr);
  InvalidateRect(Window, nil, True);
  Exit;
end;
```

The call to GetDates is the key line that causes the date dialog in the DLL to be shown to the user. In fact, if you compile both the DLL and the executable with TDW information, then load the executable into the stand-alone debugger, you can step into the GetDates routine, and into the code in DATEINFO.DLL. Alternatively, you can load the executable into the stand-alone debugger, then right-click the main pane of the debugger. Now select the Modules option, and use its dialog to load the DLL into the debugger.

> **NOTE**
>
> Remember that you need to select the Project | Options | Linker | Include TDW Debug menu option before you can use the stand-alone debugger. The stand-alone debugger does not ship with all versions of Delphi, but it can be bought as an "up sell" from Borland or through third-party retail stores. Programmer's Paradise (800-445-7899) is one mail-order store that carries these kinds of tools.

After the call to GetDates, the next line of code forces a wm_Paint message to be sent to the WndProc:

```
InvalidateRect(Window, nil, True);
```

InvalidateRect takes three parameters. The first is the Window that contains the WndProc to which the wm_Paint message should be sent. The second is a Trect variable designating the area in that window that needs to be repainted. If you pass nil in this parameter, the entire window will be repainted. The final parameter specifies whether or not to erase the window before re-painting it.

After InvalidateRect is called, the window is repainted as soon as the wm_Paint message hits the WndProc. wm_Paint messages are sent whenever there are no other messages in the queue for that window. In other words, wm_Paint messages are low priority, and they don't get through until other messages have already been processed. Another message with a low priority is wm_Timer.

Loading DLLs Dynamically at Runtime

The Small2 program, shown below in Listing 13.6, uses the same DATEINFO.DLL employed by the Small1 program seen earlier in this chapter. The big difference, of course, is in the way the DLL is loaded and unloaded from memory.

Listing 13.6. The Small2 program calls `LoadLibrary` and `FreeLibrary`.

```
program small2;

{ Copyright (c) 1996 by Charles Calvert

  Shows how to use a DLL without having the DLL loaded at program
  launch. That is, shows how to use LoadLibrary and FreeLibary. }

uses
  ShareMem, Windows, Messages, SysUtils;

const
  AppName = 'SmallTwo';

type
  TGlobalVars = record
    XSpot: Integer;
    YSpot: Integer;
    DateStr: string[200];
  end;

var
  GlobalVars: TGlobalVars;

{ -- Miscelaneous Routines -- }

procedure GetDate(Window: HWnd);
type
  TDateProc = procedure(Handle: THandle; var S: string);
var
  hLib: THandle;
  DateProc: TDateProc;
  S: ShortString;
begin
  hLib := LoadLibrary('DATEINFO.DLL');
  if hLib < 32 then begin
    MessageBox(Window, 'No DLL', nil, mb_Ok);
    Exit;
  end;
  DateProc := TDateProc(GetProcAddress(hLib, 'GetDate'));
  DateProc(Window, S);
  GlobalVars.DateStr := S;
  FreeLibrary(hLib);
end;

{ -- Message Functions -- }
```

```
procedure wmDestroy(Window: HWnd; var Msg: TWMDestroy);
begin
  PostQuitMessage(0);
end;

procedure wmLButtonDown(Window: HWnd; var Msg: TWMLButtonDown);
begin
  with GlobalVars do begin
    GetDate(Window);
    XSpot := Msg.XPos;
    YSpot := Msg.YPos;
  end;
  InvalidateRect(Window, nil, True);
end;

procedure wmPaint(Window: HWnd; var Msg: TWMPaint);
var
  PaintDC: HDC;
  PaintStruct: TPaintStruct;
  S: array[0..100] of Char;
begin
  PaintDC := BeginPaint(Window, PaintStruct);
  SetBkMode(PaintDC, TransParent);
  with GlobalVars do
    TextOut(PaintDC, XSpot, YSpot, StrPCopy(S, DateStr), Length(DateStr));
  EndPaint(Window, PaintStruct);
end;

{ -- Core Windows Routines -- }

function WindowProc(Window: HWnd; AMessage, WParam,
                    LParam: Longint): Longint; stdcall; export;
var
  AMsg: TMessage;
begin
  AMsg.Msg := AMessage;
  AMsg.WParam := WParam;
  AMsg.LParam := LParam;
  AMsg.Result := 0;

  case AMessage of
    wm_Destroy: wmDestroy(Window, TWMDestroy(AMsg));
    wm_LButtonDown: wmLButtonDown(Window, TWMLButtonDown(AMsg));
    wm_Paint: wmPaint(Window, TWMPaint(AMsg));
  else
    Result := DefWindowProc(Window, AMessage, WParam, LParam);
Exit;
  end;

  Result := AMsg.Result
end;

{ Register the Window Class }
function WinRegister: Boolean;
var
  WindowClass: TWndClass;
```

continues

Listing 13.6. continued

```
begin
  WindowClass.Style := cs_hRedraw or cs_vRedraw;
  WindowClass.lpfnWndProc := @WindowProc;
  WindowClass.cbClsExtra := 0;
  WindowClass.cbWndExtra := 0;
  WindowClass.hInstance := HInstance;
  WindowClass.hIcon := LoadIcon(0, idi_Application);
  WindowClass.hCursor := LoadCursor(0, idc_Arrow);
  WindowClass.hbrBackground := GetStockObject(LtGray_Brush);
  WindowClass.lpszMenuName := nil;
  WindowClass.lpszClassName := AppName;

  Result := RegisterClass(WindowClass) <> 0;
end;

{ Create the Window Class }
function WinCreate: HWnd;
begin
  Result := CreateWindow(AppName, 'Object Pascal Date Window',
            ws_OverlappedWindow, cw_UseDefault, cw_UseDefault,
            cw_UseDefault, cw_UseDefault, 0, 0, HInstance, nil);
end;

var
  AMessage: TMsg;
  Window: HWnd;

begin
  GlobalVars.DateStr := 'UnKnown';

  if not WinRegister then Exit;
  Window := WinCreate;
  if Window = 0 then Exit;

  ShowWindow(Window, CmdShow);
  UpdateWindow(Window);

  while GetMessage(AMessage, 0, 0, 0) do begin
    TranslateMessage(AMessage);
    DispatchMessage(AMessage);
  end;

  Halt(AMessage.wParam);
end.
```

This program looks and acts almost exactly the same as the Small1 program seen earlier in this chapter. The main difference, from the user's point of view, is that the string recording the date is always printed out at the location where the user clicked the window, rather than in the upper left-hand corner of the window. This refinement occurs because of the way the program responds to wm_LButtonDown events.

> **NOTE**
>
> Remember that the version of this program on the CD-ROM passes Shortstrings back and forth rather than using the ShareMem unit. If you are unclear about which technique you want to use, then use the technique found on the CD-ROM.
>
> I might also add that if there is a discrepancy between the book's version of the code and version on disk, you should always trust the code on the CD-ROM. That code will be tested against the latest version of Delphi, and it has the highest certainty of being correct.

Despite the obvious similarities between the Small1 and Small2 programs, they contain a number of fairly significant differences. Most of these differences are due to Small2 using message crackers and message handling routines.

The key function in the program is the GetDate routine:

```
procedure GetDate(Window: HWnd);
type
  TDateProc = procedure(Handle: THandle; var S: string);
var
  hLib: THandle;
  DateProc: TDateProc;
  S: string;
begin
  hLib := LoadLibrary('DATEINFO.DLL');
  if hLib < 32 then begin
    MessageBox(Window, 'No DLL', nil, mb_Ok);
    Exit;
  end;
  DateProc := TDateProc(GetProcAddress(hLib, 'GetDate'));
  DateProc(Window, S);
  GlobalVars.DateStr := S;
  FreeLibrary(hLib);
end;
```

This function begins by loading the DateInfo DLL into memory:

```
hLib := LoadLibrary('DATEINFO.DLL');
```

This code has a rough parallel to the external directive used when importing a routine from a DLL using the technique shown earlier in this chapter:

```
procedure GetDates(Handle: THandle; var S: string);
  external 'DATEINFO' name 'GetDate';
```

The difference, of course, is that the external directive loads the DLL when the executable is launched, while the LoadLibrary loads the DLL only when your program calls for it.

> **NOTE**
>
> Some DLLs will already be loaded into memory when your program starts. For instance, GDI32.DLL or USER32.DLL are core Windows modules that are almost surely loaded in memory at any given moment. The only reason you would ever call LoadLibrary on DLLs of this type would be because you explicitly needed a handle that referenced them.
>
> In particular, what LoadLibrary really does is map a DLL into your program's address space. Its primary purpose is to give you access to a DLL, not to load it into memory. If, however, you create a DLL for use with only your program, and you load it by using LoadLibrary, it is unlikely that the DLL would be in memory before you explicitly referenced it. It is not a certainty, however, that a call to FreeLibrary will force your DLL to be unloaded from memory.
>
> You can call LoadLibrary on an executable. The most likely reason for doing this is that you want access to resources in another executable.
>
> Note also that all the Windows API function calls that you make are calls into the standard DLLs such as USER32.DLL. Every API call that you make is a call into a DLL. This means that you call DLLs all the time; what's new in this chapter is that you are also building the DLL into which you are making the call.

To find out whether LoadLibrary succeeded, check if its return value is larger than 32:

```
if hLib < 32 then begin
  MessageBox(Window, 'No DLL', nil, mb_Ok);
  Exit;
end;
```

If the result were less than 32, it would be set equal to an error value. That is, hlib would contain not a handle to a DLL, but an error number. To get information on the error, call GetLastError.

Assuming that the call to the function succeeded, you have the handle to a DLL in your hands. This handle is very much like the hInstance value given you at startup, or like the hWnd to a window in your application. In particular, you can use this handle to call GetProcAddress:

```
DateProc := TDateProc(GetProcAddress(hLib, 'GetDate'));
```

GetProcAddress returns the address of an exported routine in a DLL. GetProcAddress takes two parameters. The first is a handle to a DLL module, and the second is a reference to an exported routine. The reference can be either a string or a numeric value, although in Win32 string values are almost always used. If you want to reference the function by number, rather than by name, place the index value in the low-order word, and set the high-order word to zero.

GetProcAddress returns a TFarProc, which resolves to a Pointer. In this case, the specific signature of the requested function is known, so the result of the function is typecast as a TDateProc:

```
type
  TDateProc = procedure(Handle: THandle; var S: string);
```

Procedural types always look a bit strange to programmers who haven't worked with them before. In particular, I often want to see the name of a function in a declaration of this type. "Procedure *what?*" one wants to ask! Of course, there is no particular function associated with this type, any more than there is a particular integer associated with the (hidden) declaration of the integer type in Object Pascal. It's just an abstract type, and it just happens, in this particular case, to match directly with the declaration of a function in the DateInfo DLL. There is more information on procedural types, function pointers, method pointers, and related matters in Chapter 23, "Objects and Inheritance."

Once you've retrieved the address of the specified function from the DLL, you are free to call the function in a normal fashion:

```
DateProc(Window, S);
GlobalVars.DateStr := S;
FreeLibrary(hLib);
```

This call to DateProc looks just the same as a similar call in the Small1 program. In particular, you pass a window handle in the first parameter. This window handle assures that the modal dialog which you are going to create knows its parent. In particular, the date dialog in the DLL is going to be shown in a modal state, so it's best if it has a specific parent. That parent is passed in the first parameter. The second parameter is a pointer to the string you want to retrieve. It's a var parameter, and var parameters are always passed by address. That is, they are passed as pointers, even though you don't have to treat them explicitly as such.

The retrieved string is stored in a global variable, and the library is freed, which means that Windows can now move it out of memory if need be. As I said earlier, you should not assume that the DLL will always be discarded the moment you call FreeLibrary. In some circumstances, Windows simply notes the fact that you are no longer using the DLL. It might not, however, unload the DLL, because it is easiest to leave it where it is for the time being. Once again, LoadLibrary and FreeLibrary are intended as means for accessing a DLL. It's just coincidence that they can also help you manage memory.

Before closing this section I want to mention once again that Windows is built on top of a series of DLLs. Nearly all the calls in the WINDOWS.PAS unit are stored in the DLLs named KERNEL32.DLL, USER32.DLL, and GDI32.DLL. These DLLs are handled by Delphi programs using the techniques shown in Small1. There is no need to load and unload these DLLs, since they are kept in memory continuously almost by definition. Windows itself resides in these DLLs, and nothing can happen without first calling them. If they are not in memory, however, the declarations referencing them in WINDOWS.PAS ensure that they will be loaded when needed.

In general, don't be afraid to break your code up into DLLs. They are the core technique holding the Windows technology together. Take a look in the Delphi32\Bin directory and you will find many more DLLs. Within reason, feel free to build as many DLLs as you want. They present a fast, efficient way to handle memory. DLLs are the operating system's bread and butter, and you should use them to help you construct robust, well-organized, programs.

Understanding the MESSAGES.PAS

The Small2 program is included in this book not only because of the way it handles DLLs, but also for the way it handles messages. The WndProc for this program follows the pattern established in the last two chapters. In particular, notice that it encapsulates the messages sent to the WndProc in a message cracking record, then passes this record on to a series of functions:

```
function WindowProc(Window: HWnd; AMessage, WParam,
                    LParam: Longint): Longint; stdcall; export;
var
  AMsg: TMessage;
begin
  AMsg.Msg := AMessage;
  AMsg.WParam := WParam;
  AMsg.LParam := LParam;
  AMsg.Result := 0;

  case AMessage of
    wm_Destroy: wmDestroy(Window, TWMDestroy(AMsg));
    wm_LButtonDown: wmLButtonDown(Window, TWMLButtonDown(AMsg));
    wm_Paint: wmPaint(Window, TWMPaint(AMsg));
  else
    WindowProc := DefWindowProc(Window, AMessage, WParam, LParam);
    Exit;
  end;

  Result := AMsg.Result
end;
```

The goal of this code is break up the case statement in the WndProc so that it is easier for you to handle messages.

In a standard Delphi program, you don't have to handle messages in a case statement. Instead, each message is delivered to you in a custom message handler, or handled internally by the VCL. The WndProc shown above delivers similar functionality. In particular, notice that there are separate functions for handling wmPaint, wmLButtonDown, and wm_Destroy messages.

One of the themes of the last few chapters has been to point out how the VCL processes many messages passed to your program without your knowledge. For instance, every wm_Paint message or wm_Size message that your RAD program receives is parsed automatically by the TForm object. The interesting thing about the programs shown in these chapters on the API is that you are explicitly handling many of the messages yourself. Of course there are many other messages that are being passed on to DefWindowProc and being handled by the operating system. There is a good deal of difference, however, between having the message handled by Windows, and having it handled by the VCL.

DLLs Written Entirely with Windows API Calls

The next program is a RAD Delphi program that calls one DLL written entirely using the Windows API, and a second DLL that makes heavy use of the Windows API.

The main showpiece here is the straight Windows API DLL. It contains two normal windows and one dialog, but weighs in at a little over 15KB. This is about one-tenth the size the same DLL would be if it were built using the RAD tools.

This program features a second DLL that contains three standard Delphi forms. The first form (shown in Figure 13.3) shows some pictures of Saturn, the second form (see Figure 13.4) has some fun with geometric shapes, and the third form (see Figure 13.5) draws a fractal fern. The presence of a number of Windows API calls in the third of these three Windows won the DLL its inclusion in a chapter that focuses primarily on the Windows API. On the CD-ROM, however, you will find a second version of the Squares form that also uses a number of Windows API functions.

FIGURE 13.3.

The Saturn form from FRACTDLL.DLL.

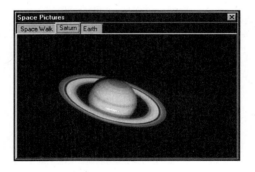

FIGURE 13.4.

The Squares form from FRACTDLL.DLL.

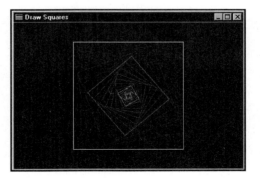

FIGURE 13.5.
*The Ferns form from
FRACTDLL.DLL.*

The source code for the program is shown in Listings 13.7 through 13.14. Listing 13.8 is the most important of these listings, as it contains the code for the straight Windows API DLL. The main form and all of the straight Windows API DLL forms are shown in Figure 13.6. In particular, the code for the windows with captions that read "Child without VCL," "Popup without VCL," and "About" all reside in a DLL. That is, they are not Delphi RAD windows and dialogs, but straight API windows and dialogs.

FIGURE 13.6.
*The child, pop-up, and
dialog windows are all
created by straight
Windows API code that
resides in a 15KB DLL.*

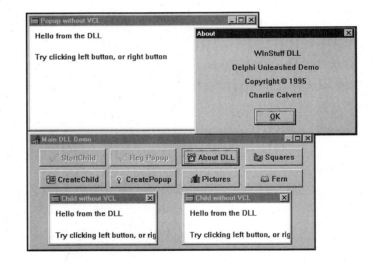

Listing 13.7. The Windows API DLL exports seven functions.

```
library Apidll;

{ Program copyright (c) 1996 by Charles Calvert }
{ Project Name: RUNDLL }

uses
  Winstuff in 'Winstuff.pas';

exports
```

```
   About index 1,
   HandleButton index 2,
   ShowAbout index 3,
   RegisterWinPopup index 4,
   CreateWinPopup index 5,
   RegisterChild index 6,
   CreateChild index 7;

begin
end.
```

Listing 13.8. The Windows API DLL features two windows and one dialog.

```
unit Winstuff;

{ Program copyright (c) 1996 by Charles Calvert }
{ Project Name: WINSTUFF }

{
  This unit shows four types of routines exported from a DLL:

    HandleButton: Simple MessageBox routine

    About
    ShowAbout: Launch and run a modal dialog

    RegisterWinPopup
    CreateWinPopup: Create and show a popup window

    RegisterChild
    CreateChild: Register, Create, and Show a child window
}

interface

uses
  Windows, Messages;

procedure HandleButton(Window: HWnd); export;
function About(Dialog: HWnd; AMessage, WParam,
               LParam: Longint): Bool; stdcall export;
procedure ShowAbout(Window: Hwnd); export;
function RegisterChild(ParentWindow: HWnd): HWnd; export;
function CreateChild(ParentWindow: HWnd): Hwnd; export;
function RegisterWinPopup: Boolean; export;
function CreateWinPopup: Boolean; export;

implementation

{$R WINSTUFF.RES}

{ A trivial routine showing that it is easy to pass
  a window handle into a DLL }
procedure HandleButton(Window: HWnd);
```

continues

Listing 13.8. continued

```pascal
begin
  MessageBox(Window, 'Hello', 'Sam', MB_OK);
end;

{-- The About Dialog --}

const
  idm_About = 100;

{ This is the main routine for the About Dialog. It
  handles all messages sent to the dialog, and is responsible
  for telling it to close itself when the user clicks on the
  Ok or Cancel button. }
function About(Dialog: HWnd; AMessage, WParam: LParam;
  LParam: Longint): Bool; stdcall export;
begin
  Result := True;
  case AMessage of
    wm_InitDialog:
      Exit;
    wm_Command:
      if (WParam = idOk) or (WParam = idCancel) then begin
        EndDialog(Dialog, 1);
        Exit;
      end;
  end;
  Result := False;
end;

{ Create, show, and destroy a modal dialog }
procedure ShowAbout(Window: Hwnd);
begin
  DialogBox(HInstance, 'AboutBox', Window, @About);
end;

{ -- Popup Window -- }

const
  PopupName = 'PopStuff';

{ The WindProc for the Popup Window. }
function PopupWinProc(Window: HWnd; AMessage, WParam: UINT;
                      LParam: LPARAM): Longint; stdcall export;
const
  S = 'Hello from the DLL';
  S1 = 'Try clicking left button, or right button';
var
  PS: TPaintStruct;
  PaintDC: HDC;

begin
  Result := 0;
  case AMessage of
    wm_LButtonDown: begin
      HandleButton(Window);
      Exit;
    end;
```

```
    wm_RButtonDown: begin
      ShowAbout(Window);
      Exit;
    end;

    wm_Paint: begin
      PaintDC := BeginPaint(Window, PS);
      TextOut(PaintDC, 10, 10, PChar(S), Length(S));
      TextOut(PaintDC, 10, 50, PChar(S1), Length(S1));
      EndPaint(Window, PS);
    end;
  end;
  Result := DefWindowProc(Window, AMessage, WParam, LParam);
end;

{ The Create routine for the Popup Window. Basically, its
  just a wrapper around the complex CreateWindow call. The
  call to ShowWindow makes the window visible, with sw_ShowNormal
  specifying that it is shown in a normal state, and not
  minimized or maximized. }

function CreateWinPopup: Boolean;
var
  Window: Hwnd;
begin
  Window := CreateWindow(
    PopupName, 'Popup without VCL', ws_OverLappedWindow,
    cw_UseDefault, cw_UseDefault, cw_UseDefault, cw_UseDefault,
    0, 0, HInstance, nil);

  CmdShow := Sw_ShowNormal;

  if Window = 0 then begin
    Result := False;
    Exit;
  end;

  ShowWindow(Window, CmdShow);
  UpdateWindow(Window);
  Result := True;
end;

{ The Register routine for the Popup Window. The main chore
  is to fill out the complex TWndClass structure, and pass it
  to RegisterWindow. After the window has been registered,
  the call to the local CreateWinPopup routine actually creates
  it and shows it on screen. Only call RegisterWindow once
  for each window in your application.}

function RegisterWinPopup: Boolean;
var
  WndClass: TWndClass;
begin
  if HPrevInst = 0 then begin
    WndClass.Style := 0;
    WndClass.lpfnWndProc := @PopupWinProc;
    WndClass.cbClsExtra := 0;
```

continues

Listing 13.8. continued

```pascal
    WndClass.cbWndExtra := 0;
    WndClass.hInstance := HInstance;
    WndClass.hIcon := LoadIcon(0, idi_Application);
    WndClass.hCursor := LoadCursor(0, idc_Arrow);
    WndClass.hbrBackground := GetStockObject(white_Brush);
    WndClass.lpszMenuName := PopupName;
    WndClass.lpszClassName := PopupName;

    if RegisterClass(WndClass) = 0 then begin
      Result := False;
      Exit;
    end;
  end;

  Result := CreateWinPopUp;
end;

{ -- Child Window -- }

const
  ChildName = 'ChildWindow';

{ This is the WindProc for the child Window.
  It paints text to the window, and handles right and
  left button clicks. }
function ChildProc(Window: HWnd; AMessage, WParam: UINT;
  LParam: LPARAM): Longint; stdcall export;
const
  S = 'Hello from the DLL';
  S1 = 'Try clicking left button, or right button';
var
  AboutProc: TFarProc;
  PS: TPaintStruct;
  PaintDC: HDC;

begin
  ChildProc := 0;

  case AMessage of
    wm_LButtonDown: begin
      HandleButton(Window);
      Exit;
    end;

    wm_RButtonDown: begin
      AboutProc := MakeProcInstance(@About, HInstance);
      DialogBox(HInstance, 'AboutBox', Window, AboutProc);
      FreeProcInstance(AboutProc);
      Exit;
    end;

    wm_Paint: begin
      PaintDC := BeginPaint(Window, PS);
        TextOut(PaintDC, 10, 10, PChar(S), Length(S));
        TextOut(PaintDC, 10, 50, PChar(S1), Length(S1));
      EndPaint(Window, PS);
      Exit;
    end;
```

```
   end;

   ChildProc := DefWindowProc(Window, AMessage, WParam, LParam);
end;

{ The Create routine for the Child Window. Basically, its
  just a wrapper around the complex CreateWindow call. The
  call to ShowWindow makes the window visible, with sw_ShowNormal
  specifying that it is shown in a normal state, and not
  minimized or maximized. }
function CreateChild(ParentWindow: Hwnd): Hwnd;
var
  ASimpleWindow: HWnd;
begin
  ASimpleWindow := CreateWindow(
    ChildName, 'Child without VCL',
    ws_ChildWindow or ws_Caption or ws_ClipSiblings or
    ws_visible or ws_ThickFrame or ws_SysMenu,
    1, 75, 200, 100, ParentWindow, 0, HInstance, nil);

  if ASimpleWindow <> 0 then
    ShowWindow(ASimpleWindow, sw_ShowNormal);

  Result := ASimpleWindow;
end;

{ The Register routine for the Child Window. The main chore
  is to fill out the complex TWndClass structure, and pass it
  to RegisterWindow. After the window has been registered,
  the call to the local CreateChild routine actually creates
  it and shows it on screen. Only call RegisterWindow once
  for each window in your application.}
function RegisterChild(ParentWindow: HWnd): HWnd;
var
  WndClass: TWndClass;
begin
  if HPrevInst = 0 then begin
    WndClass.Style := cs_HRedraw or cs_VRedraw;
    WndClass.lpfnWndProc := @ChildProc;
    WndClass.cbClsExtra := 0;
    WndClass.cbWndExtra := 0;
    WndClass.hInstance := HInstance;
    WndClass.hIcon := LoadIcon(0, idi_Application);
    WndClass.hCursor := LoadCursor(0, idc_Arrow);
    WndClass.hbrBackground := GetStockObject(White_Brush);
    WndClass.lpszMenuName := ChildName;
    WndClass.lpszClassName := ChildName;

    if RegisterClass(WndClass) = 0 then begin
      Result := 0;
      Exit;
    end;
  end;

  Result := CreateChild(ParentWindow);
end;

end.
```

Listing 13.9. The project source for the second DLL exports three functions, one for each of its forms.

```
library Fractdll;

{ Program copyright (c) 1996 by Charles Calvert }
{ Project Name: RUNDLL }

uses
  Pics in 'PICS.PAS' {SpacePict1},
  Squares in 'SQUARES.PAS' {DrawSqr},
  Fern in 'FERN.PAS' {Ferns};

exports
  ShowPictures index 1,
  ShowSquares index 2,
  ShowFerns index 3;

begin
end.
```

Listing 13.10. The `Pics` form is written entirely using the VCL. Its sole function pops up a window containing some `TImage` and `TTabbedNotebook` controls.

```
unit Pics;

{ Program copyright (c) 1996 by Charles Calvert }
{ Project Name: RUNDLL }

interface

uses
  SysUtils, WinTypes, WinProcs,
  Messages, Classes, Graphics,
  Controls, Forms, Dialogs,
  ExtCtrls, TabNotBk, ComCtrls;

type
  TSpacePict1 = class(TForm)
    TabbedNotebook1: TTabbedNotebook;
    Image1: TImage;
    Image2: TImage;
    Image3: TImage;
  end;

var
  SpacePict1: TSpacePict1;

procedure ShowPictures(Handle: THandle); export;

implementation

{$R *.DFM}

procedure ShowPictures(Handle: THandle);
```

```
begin
  Application.Handle := Handle;
  SpacePict1 := TSpacePict1.Create(Application);
  try
    SpacePict1.ShowModal;
  finally
    SpacePict1.Free;
  end;
end;

end.
```

Listing 13.11. The Squares form shows off the TCanvas object.

```
unit Squares;

{ Program copyright (c) 1995 by Charles Calvert }
{ Thanks to Danny Thorpe for cleaning this one up and showing how
  to make good use of the TCanvas object. }
{ Project Name: RUNDLL }

interface

uses
  SysUtils, WinTypes, WinProcs,
  Messages, Classes, Graphics,
  Controls, Forms, Dialogs,
  StdCtrls, ExtCtrls;

const
  BoxCount = 25;
type
  TDrawSqr = class(TForm)
    Timer1: TTimer;
    procedure Timer1Timer(Sender: TObject);
    procedure FormCreate(Sender: TObject);
  private
    { Private declarations }
    Colors: array [1..BoxCount] of TColor;
    procedure DrawSquare(Scale: Double; Theta: Integer);
  public
    { Public declarations }
  end;
var
  DrawSqr: TDrawSqr;

procedure ShowSquares(Handle: THandle); export;

implementation

{$R *.DFM}

type
  TSquarePoints = array [0..4] of TPoint;
```

continues

Listing 13.11. continued

```
const
  Square : TSquarePoints =
    ((x: -100; y: -100),(x: 100; y: -100),(x: 100; y: 100),
     (x: -100; y: 100),(x: -100; y: -100));

procedure ShowSquares(Handle: THandle);
begin
  Application.Handle := Handle;
  DrawSqr := TDrawSqr.Create(Application);
  try
    DrawSqr.ShowModal;
  finally
    DrawSqr.Free;
  end;
end;

procedure TDrawSqr.DrawSquare(Scale: Double; Theta: Integer);
var
  i: Integer;
  CosTheta, SinTheta: Double;
  Path: TSquarePoints;
begin
  { precalculate rotation and scaling }
  CosTheta := Scale * cos(Theta * PI / 180);
  SinTheta := Scale * sin(Theta * PI / 180);
  for i := 0 to 4 do
  begin
    Path[i].X := Round(Square[i].X * CosTheta +  Square[i].Y * SinTheta);
    Path[i].Y := Round(Square[i].Y * CosTheta -  Square[i].X * SinTheta);
  end;
  Canvas.Polyline(Path);
end;

procedure TDrawSqr.Timer1Timer(Sender: TObject);
var
  i: Integer;
  Scale: Double;
  Theta: Integer;
begin
  Scale := 1.0;
  Theta := 0;
  SetViewPortOrgEx(Canvas.Handle, ClientWidth div 2, ClientHeight div 2, nil);
  Canvas.Pen.Color := clWhite;
  for i := 1 to BoxCount do
  begin
    DrawSquare(Scale, Theta);
    Theta := Theta + 10;
    Scale := Scale * 0.85;
    Canvas.Pen.Color := Colors[i];
  end;
  { Shift all colors down one for special spinning effects }
  Move(Colors[1], Colors[2], sizeof(Colors) - Sizeof(TColor));
  Colors[1] := Colors[1] + RGB(Random(64), Random(64), Random(64));
end;
```

```
procedure TDrawSqr.FormCreate(Sender: TObject);
var
  X: Integer;
begin
  Randomize;
  Colors[1] := RGB(Random(255), Random(255), Random(255));
  for X':= 2 to BoxCount do
    Colors[X] := Colors[X-1] + RGB(Random(64), Random(64), Random(64));
end;

end.
```

Listing 13.12. The Fern unit shows how to draw a fractal shape in a VCL window.

```
unit Fern;

{ Program copyright (c) 1995 by Charles Calvert }
{ Project Name: RUNDLL }

interface

uses
  SysUtils, WinTypes, WinProcs,
  Messages, Classes, Graphics,
  Controls, Forms, Dialogs,
  StdCtrls, ExtCtrls;

type
  TDAry = array[0..3] of Double;

  TFerns = class(TForm)
    Timer1: TTimer;
    procedure FormResize(Sender: TObject);
    procedure Timer1Timer(Sender: TObject);
    procedure FormCreate(Sender: TObject);
  private
    MaxX, MaxY: Integer;
    MaxIterations, Count: INteger;
    x, y: Double;
  public
    procedure DoPaint;
  end;

const
  a: TDAry = (0, 0.85, 0.2, -0.15);
  b: TDAry = (0, 0.04, -0.26, 0.28);
  c: TDAry = (0, -0.04, 0.23, 0.26);
d: TDAry = (0.16, 0.85, 0.22, 0.24);
  e: TDAry = (0, 0, 0, 0);
  f: TDAry = (0, 1.6, 1.6, 0.44);

var
```

continues

Listing 13.12. continued

```
  Ferns: TFerns;

procedure ShowFerns(Handle: THandle); export;

implementation

{$R *.DFM}

procedure ShowFerns(Handle: THandle);
begin
  Application.Handle := Handle;
  Ferns := TFerns.Create(Application);
  try
    Ferns.ShowModal;
  finally
    Ferns.Free;
  end;
end;

procedure TFerns.DoPaint;
var
  k: Integer;
  TempX, TempY: Double;
begin
  k := Random(100);
  if ((k > 0) and (k <= 85)) then  k := 1;
  if ((k > 85) and (k <= 92)) then k := 2;
  if (k > 92) then k := 3;
  TempX := a[k] * x + b[k] * y + e[k];
  TempY := c[k] * x + d[k] * y + f[k];
  x := TempX;
  y := TempY;
  if ((Count >= MaxIterations) or (Count <> 0)) then
    Canvas.Pixels[Round(x * MaxY / 11 + MaxX / 2),
                  Round(y * - MaxY / 11 + MaxY)] :=  clGreen;
  Count := Count + 1;
end;

procedure TFerns.FormResize(Sender: TObject);
begin
  MaxX := Width;
  MaxY := Height;
  MaxIterations := MaxY * 50;
end;

procedure TFerns.Timer1Timer(Sender: TObject);
var
  i: Integer;
begin
  if Count > MaxIterations then begin
    Invalidate;
    Count := 0;
  end;

  for i := 0 to 200 do
    DoPaint;
end;
```

```
procedure TFerns.FormCreate(Sender: TObject);
begin
  Count := 0;
  x := 0;
  y := 0;
end;

end.
```

Listing 13.13. The main unit for the program that calls the DLLs listed above.

```
unit Testem;

{ Program copyright (c) 1995 by Charles Calvert }
{ Project Name: RUNDLL }

{ RunDLL is an excerpt from Delphi Programming Unleashed, a SAMS book. }

{ This is an example program showing how to create and call DLLs in Delphi.

  This program will test FRACTDLL and APIDLL. FRACTDLL has Delphi forms
  stored in it, APIDLL, creates windows by directly calling
  the Windows API.

  You must compile and link FRACTDLL and APIDLL before
  running this program. }

interface

uses
  SysUtils, WinTypes, WinProcs,
  Messages, Classes, Graphics,
  Controls, Forms, Dialogs,
  StdCtrls, Buttons, DLLUnit;

type
  TBigNumber = class(TForm)
    CreateChild: TBitBtn;
    AboutDLL: TBitBtn;
    Pictures: TBitBtn;
    Fern: TBitBtn;
    Squares: TBitBtn;
    Start: TBitBtn;
    RegPopup: TBitBtn;
    CreatePopup: TBitBtn;
    procedure StartClick(Sender: TObject);
    procedure PicturesClick(Sender: TObject);
    procedure AboutDLLClick(Sender: TObject);
    procedure CreateChildClick(Sender: TObject);
    procedure RegPopupClick(Sender: TObject);
    procedure CreatePopupClick(Sender: TObject);
  private
    DLLWnd: HWnd;
  end;
```

continues

Listing 13.13. continued

```
var
  BigNumber: TBigNumber;

implementation

{$R *.DFM}

{ Call Delphi forms stored in a DLL }
procedure TBigNumber.PicturesClick(Sender: TObject);
begin
  case (Sender as TBitBtn).Tag of
    100: ShowPictures(Application.Handle);
    101: ShowSquares(Application.Handle);
    102: ShowFerns(Application.Handle);
  end;
end;

{ Show the About Box from the APIDLL }
procedure TBigNumber.AboutDLLClick(Sender: TObject);
begin
  ShowAbout(Handle);
end;

{ This routine registers and shows a child window. It
  can only be called once during the run of the program.
  It calls routines from APIDLL.}
procedure TBigNumber.StartClick(Sender: TObject);
begin
  if RegisterChild(Handle) = 0 then
    ShowMessage('No Child');
  Start.Enabled := False;
end;

{ This routine creates and runs a child window
  It calls routines from APIDLL}
procedure TBigNumber.CreateChildClick(Sender: TObject);
begin
  DLLUnit.CreateChild(Handle);
end;

{ This routine registers and shows a Popup window. It
  can only be called once during the run of the program.
  It calls routines from APIDLL. }
procedure TBigNumber.RegPopupClick(Sender: TObject);
begin
  RegisterWinPopup;
  RegPopup.Enabled := False;
end;

{ Create a popup window. Calls APIDLL }
procedure TBigNumber.CreatePopupClick(Sender: TObject);
begin
  CreateWinPopup;
end;

end.
```

Listing 13.14. The DLL containing the import statements for the calls in the DLLs.

```
unit Dllunit;

{ Program copyright (c) 1995 by Charles Calvert }
{ Project Name: RUNDLL }

interface

uses
  Windows;


procedure ShowPictures(Handle: THandle);
procedure ShowSquares(Handle: THandle);
procedure ShowFerns(Handle: THandle);
function About(Dialog: HWnd; Message, WParam: Word; LParam: Longint): Bool;
procedure HandleButton(Window: HWnd);
procedure ShowAbout(Window: Hwnd);
function RegisterWinPopup: Boolean;
function CreateWinPopup: Boolean;
function RegisterChild(ParentWindow: HWnd): HWnd;
function CreateChild(ParentWindow: HWnd): Hwnd;

implementation

procedure ShowPictures; external 'FRACTDLL' index 1;
procedure ShowSquares; external 'FRACTDLL' index 2;
procedure ShowFerns; external 'FRACTDLL' index 3;

function About; external 'APIDLL' index 1;
procedure HandleButton; external 'APIDLL' index 2;
procedure ShowAbout; external 'APIDLL' index 3;
function RegisterWinPopup; external 'APIDLL' index 4;
function CreateWinPopup; external 'APIDLL' index 5;
function RegisterChild; external 'APIDLL' index 6;
function CreateChild; external 'APIDLL' index 7;

end.
```

Before launching this program, make sure that both the APIDLL.DLL and the FRACTDLL.DLL are compiled. When you launch the main program, a simple form containing eight buttons appears. Each button, as shown in Figure 13.7, calls one or more of the functions that reside in the DLLs listed above.

FIGURE 13.7.

The main form for the MainDemo program has eight buttons on it.

The StartChild button on the main form will call into the DLL and create a child window that appears only within the scope of its parent, which in this case is the main form of the executable. This is an interesting example of how the handles for a window work across the boundary of a DLL. The "Child Without VCL" window created inside the DLL acts as if it is very much a part of the main executable. Most users would never guess that it resides inside a DLL.

If you want to create multiple instances of this "Child Without VCL" window, you can press the CreateChild button on the main form for the application. This function calls a `CreateWindow` procedure in the DLL. The difference between pressing the StartChild button and the CreateChild button is that the former calls both `RegisterClass` and `CreateWindow`, while the latter calls only `CreateWindow`. Notice that the StartChild button becomes disabled after you press it. This is because you only need to register a window once. After that you can create multiple instances of the child window by calling `CreateWindow` multiple times. I create the child window in the exact same place each time, so you'll need to move the first instance of the window if you want to see the secondary instances.

The RegPopup button registers and creates a pop-up window inside the DLL. The CreatePopup button calls `CreateWindow` on the pop-up window, in case you want to see more than one instance of the window. There is no practical limit on the number of pop-up windows you can create. A pop-up window appears as a separate, free-floating window that is not attached to the main form. Notice that child windows stay within their owner window, while pop-up windows float free.

I discuss the difference between pop-up and child windows in more depth a bit later, but the key point is that you use the `ws_ChildWindow` flag when calling `CreateWindow` on a child window:

```
ASimpleWindow := CreateWindow(
    ChildName, 'Child without VCL',
    ws_ChildWindow or ws_Caption or ws_ClipSiblings or
    ws_visible or ws_ThickFrame or ws_SysMenu,
    1, 75, 200, 100, ParentWindow, 0, HInstance, nil);
```

You use a different style to call `CreateWindow` on a pop-up window:

```
Window := CreateWindow(
    PopupName, 'Popup without VCL', ws_OverLappedWindow,
    cw_UseDefault, cw_UseDefault, cw_UseDefault, cw_UseDefault,
    0, 0, HInstance, nil);
```

Notice that the child window has a parent window handle specified in the fourth to last parameter, while the pop-up window has 0 in this spot. The child needs a parent, while the pop-up does not.

NOTE

Unfortunately, this book is not long enough to cover all the styles you can pass to a window. The subject is covered in many other C reference books, however. By this time, you should be able to read any C reference book on the Windows API with little trouble. The code in such books is almost identical to the Windows API programs you have seen here. Be sure to look for a straight Windows API book like *Teach Yourself Windows 95 Programming in 21 Days*, published by Sams. Don't get a book that concentrates on OWL or MFC.

At any rate, the ws_OverLappedWindow style is actually a compound style defined like this in WINDOWS.PAS:

```
WS_OVERLAPPEDWINDOW = (WS_OVERLAPPED or WS_CAPTION or WS_SYSMENU or
  WS_THICKFRAME or WS_MINIMIZEBOX or WS_MAXIMIZEBOX);
```

Here are three other styles of WINDOWS.PAS that might come in handy in the context of this discussion:

```
WS_TILEDWINDOW = WS_OVERLAPPEDWINDOW;
WS_POPUPWINDOW = (WS_POPUP or WS_BORDER or WS_SYSMENU);
WS_CHILDWINDOW = (WS_CHILD);
```

The AboutDLL button on the main form of the MainDemo application will pop up a stand-alone dialog. I will comment on this dialog in more depth down below, but the basic code for creating it is the same as that shown in the Window2 program discussed in Chapter 10, "Dialogs and Resources." Note that you can pop up this same dialog by clicking the child and pop-up windows mentioned above.

The last three buttons on the MainDemo window call standard VCL forms that make only limited use of the Windows API. I won't discuss them in any great depth in this book, in large part because this chapter has already become a bit long.

Probably the most interesting of these three forms is the Fern form, which calls some nice fractal code originally given to me by Borland employee and expert programmer Lar Mader. In general, both the Squares form and the Fern form are interesting because they contain a good deal of math. If you have mathematical code that depends on fast execution, Object Pascal is a good language to work in, because it is both very fast and very tight.

Below I take a somewhat closer look at WINSTUFF.PAS, which is the module that contains the core Windows API code of interest to readers of this chapter. Most of the code in WINSTUFF.PAS may not make sense to you unless you have read the previous four chapters of this book.

The *APIDLL*

This APIDLL contains seven routines that are grouped here into four basic types:

```
// Simple MessageBox routine
HandleButton

// Launch and run a modal dialog
About
ShowAbout

// Register, Create, and Show a child window
RegisterChild
CreateChild

// Register, Create and show a popup window
RegisterWinPopup
CreateWinPopup
```

The simplest code in the DLL belongs to the HandleButton routine, which enables you to pass in a window handle to be used by the MessageBox function:

```
procedure HandleButton(Window: HWnd);
begin
  MessageBox(Window, 'Hello', 'Sam', MB_OK);
end;
```

This routine is not meant to be particularly useful because you can pass in 0 as the first parameter to MessageBox if you don't have a handle, and because you can call MessageBox directly from a program just as easily as you can wrap it in a DLL. However, I provide the routine because it serves to remind you that you often need to pass in a handle to a parent window when you are creating child windows in a DLL. It's easy to do this, and the Window handle will serve as a link between your application and the DLL. This becomes a crucial point when you want to show a modal dialog.

The ShowAbout function allocates memory for a dialog, shows it modally, and then destroys it:

```
procedure ShowAbout(Window: Hwnd);
begin
  DialogBox(HInstance, 'AboutBox', Window, @About);
end;
```

If you wanted this same code to compile under both Windows 3.1 and Win32, you would have to write this:

```
procedure ShowAbout(Window: Hwnd);
var
  AboutProc: TFarProc;
begin
  AboutProc := MakeProcInstance(@About, HInstance);
  DialogBox(HInstance, 'AboutBox', Window, AboutProc);
  FreeProcInstance(AboutProc);
end;
```

I won't discuss the actual Windows API calls shown here, but you'll remember that they were discussed in depth in Chapter 10. Notice that this code calls `MakeProcInstance` and `FreeProcInstance`, which provide compatibility with 16-bit code.

There are two other pairs of calls in the `WINSTUFF` unit. The first pair launches a pop-up window that has no parent and that roves freely across the Windows desktop:

```
RegisterWinPopup
CreateWinPopup
```

The second pair of calls launches a child window that lives inside its parent and cannot escape its confines:

```
RegisterChild
CreateChild
```

Child windows never get the focus. Although it's not the case in this particular example, they are usually shown without a caption or a thick-framed border. As a result, they usually appear in one place in a larger window, just like a button or an edit control. In particular, they usually don't have a caption. I don't treat them that way in this example, since I want you to be able to move them around on their parent. (The Music program, presented in the chapters on databases, shows how to turn a standard Delphi form into a child window.)

I have two pairs of routines for each window because it is necessary to first register the window before you create and launch it. The `RegisterWinPopup` and `RegisterChild` routines are both used to register windows. These routines should be called only once for each window. The `CreateChild` and `CreateWinPopup` routines create and launch windows, and they can be called multiple times during a session.

The register routines fill out a `TWndClass` structure and then call `RegisterWindow`:

```
function RegisterWinPopup: Boolean;
var
  WndClass: TWndClass;
begin
  if HPrevInst = 0 then begin
    WndClass.Style := 0;
    WndClass.lpfnWndProc := @PopupWinProc;
    WndClass.cbClsExtra := 0;
    WndClass.cbWndExtra := 0;
    WndClass.hInstance := HInstance;
    WndClass.hIcon := LoadIcon(0, idi_Application);
    WndClass.hCursor := LoadCursor(0, idc_Arrow);
    WndClass.hbrBackground := GetStockObject(white_Brush);
    WndClass.lpszMenuName := PopupName;
    WndClass.lpszClassName := PopupName;

    if RegisterClass(WndClass) = 0 then begin
      Result := False;
      Exit;
    end;
  end;

  Result := CreateWinPopUp;
end;
```

Notice that the call to `RegisterClass` is checked to see if it returns zero. `RegisterClass` returns an atom that uniquely identifies the class on success, or zero on failure.

The pop-up window in WINSTUFF.PAS uses the `PopupWinProc` routine as its window procedure, whereas the child window uses `ChildProc`. You don't have to do anything special to call `CreateWindow` or `RegisterClass` in a DLL. The principles are the same as in a normal executable such as the Window1 program you saw earlier.

In the `CreateChild` and `CreateWinPopup` methods, you find calls to the complex `CreateWindow` function, which, as you know, takes a fairly baffling array of parameters:

```
function CreateChild(ParentWindow: Hwnd): Hwnd;
var
  ASimpleWindow: HWnd;
begin
  ASimpleWindow := CreateWindow(
    ChildName, 'Child without VCL',
    ws_ChildWindow or ws_Caption or ws_ClipSiblings or
    ws_visible or ws_ThickFrame or ws_SysMenu,
    1, 75, 200, 100, ParentWindow, 0, HInstance, nil);

  if ASimpleWindow <> 0 then
    ShowWindow(ASimpleWindow, sw_ShowNormal);

  Result := ASimpleWindow;
end;
```

Not to beat a dead horse, but please notice the fourth-to-last parameter in the `CreateWindow` call from the `CreateChild` routine. It's the handle of the parent window. Notice that this same parameter is zeroed out in the `CreateWinPopup` method. The parent window parameter is an important part of what distinguishes a child window from a pop-up window. Another key factor is the presence of the `ws_ChildWindow` style. You should almost always use the `ws_ClipSiblings` style to avoid problems when painting the child windows.

> **NOTE**
>
> The previous paragraph is perhaps a bit misleading in that you can specify the parent of a pop-up window. However, it is not absolutely necessary.

The `CreateChild` routine calls `ShowWindow` only if the call to `CreateWindow` succeeds. If `CreateWindow` fails, the function automatically returns zero, thereby signifying a failure.

Once again, this section of the book strives to illustrate how to use the Windows API, and how to create very small binary files that do the same thing as standard Delphi RAD programs. The Windows API lies at the heart of the operating system most of us use day in and day out. It is also the foundation on which Delphi is built. Understand the API, and everything else is possible. If you don't understand the Windows API, you will keep running into brick walls.

An Alternative Squares Unit

Below you will find an alternative to the Squares unit included in the FRACTDLL. This unit is not quite as fancy as the code shown above, but it does show some interesting features of the Windows API. In particular, note the use of pens and the GDI calls such as LineTo and MoveToEx.

```
type
  TDrawSqr = class(TForm)
    Timer1: TTimer;
    procedure Timer1Timer(Sender: TObject);
  private
    { Private declarations }
  public
    { Public declarations }
  end;

var
  DrawSqr: TDrawSqr;

procedure ShowSquares; export;

implementation

{$R *.DFM}

procedure ShowSquares;
begin
  DrawSqr := TDrawSqr.Create(Application);
  DrawSqr.ShowModal;
  DrawSqr.Free;
end;

procedure DrawSquare(PaintDC: HDC; Scale: Double; Theta: Integer);
type
  TCDS = array[0..5] of TPoint;
var
  X1, Y1: Integer;
  XT, YT: Integer;
  i, j: Integer;
  Pens: array[0..4] of HPen;
  OldPen: HPen;
  CDS: TCDS;
begin
  j := Random(25);
  Pens[0] := CreatePen(PS_SOLID, 1, RGB(255, 255, 255));
  Pens[1] := CreatePen(PS_SOLID, 1, RGB(Random(255), 0, 0));
  Pens[2] := CreatePen(PS_SOLID, 1, RGB(0, Random(255), 0));
  Pens[3] := CreatePen(PS_SOLID, 1, RGB(0, 0, Random(255)));
  Pens[4] := CreatePen(PS_SOLID, 1, RGB(Random(255), 0, Random(255)));

  CDS[0].X := -100;
  CDS[0].Y := -100;
  CDS[1].X := 100;
  CDS[1].Y := -100;
  CDS[2].X := 100;
  CDS[2].Y := 100;
```

```
  CDS[3].X := -100;
  CDS[3].Y := 100;
  CDS[4].X := -100;
  CDS[4].Y := -100;

  for i := 0 to 4 do begin
    x1 := CDS[i].X;
    y1 := CDS[i].Y;
    xt := Round(Scale * (x1 * cos(Theta * PI / 180) + y1 * sin(Theta * PI/180)));
    yt := Round(Scale * (y1 * cos(Theta * PI / 180) - x1 * sin(Theta * PI/180)));
    if (i = 0) then
      MoveToEx(PaintDC, xt, yt, nil)
    else begin
      if Scale = 1.0 then
        OldPen := SelectObject(PaintDC, Pens[0])
      else
        OldPen := SelectObject(PaintDC, Pens[i]);
      LineTo(PaintDC, xt, yt);
      SelectObject(PaintDC, OldPen);
    end;
  end;
  for I := 0 to 4 do
    DeleteObject(Pens[i]);
end;

procedure TDrawSqr.Timer1Timer(Sender: TObject);
var
  i: Integer;
  Scale: Double;
  Theta: Integer;
  PaintDC: HDC;
  R: TRect;
begin
  Scale := 1.0;
  Theta := 0;
  PaintDC := GetDC(Handle);
  R := GetClientRect;
  SetViewPortOrg(PaintDC, R.Right div 2, R.Bottom div 2);
  for i := 1 to 25 do begin
    DrawSquare(PaintDC, Scale, Theta);
    Theta := Theta + 10;
    Scale := Scale * 0.85;
  end;
  ReleaseDC(Handle, PaintDC);
end;

end.
```

The following call creates a pen:

```
Pens[0] := CreatePen(PS_SOLID, 1, RGB(255, 255, 255));
```

`CreatePen` takes a constant in the first parameter that specifies the kind of pen you want to create. The following excerpt from the online help shows the kinds of pens you can create:

PS_SOLID	Pen is solid.
PS_DASH	Pen is dashed. This style is valid only when the pen width is 1 or less in device units.
PS_DOT	Pen is dotted. This style is valid only when the pen width is 1 or less in device units.
PS_DASHDOT	Pen has alternating dashes and dots. This style is valid only when the pen width is 1 or less in device units.
PS_DASHDOTDOT	Pen has alternating dashes and double dots. This style is valid only when the pen width is 1 or less in device units.
PS_NULL	Pen is invisible.
PS_INSIDEFRAME	Pen is solid. When this pen is used in any graphics device interface (GDI) drawing function that takes a bounding rectangle, the dimensions of the figure are shrunk so that it fits entirely in the bounding rectangle, taking into account the width of the pen. This applies only to geometric pens.

You use pens to draw lines and curves. For instance, the outside line in a rectangle or ellipse is painted in the current pen.

The second parameter passed to `CreatePen` designates the width, in pixels, of the pen you want to create. The third parameter designates the color of the pen you want to create. You can use the RGB function to return the 32-bit value designated in this parameter. The RGB function is discussed in several other places in this book, but remember that the first number passed to the function designates how much red will be in the color, the second parameter designates the amount of green, and the third the amount of blue. The numbers range from 0 to 255.

Once you have a pen, you can select it into the current device context:

```
OldPen := SelectObject(PaintDC, Pens[0])
```

Notice that the old pen that resided in the device context needs to be saved in a temporary variable. When you are finished with the pen, reselect the original pen into the device context:

```
SelectObject(PaintDC, OldPen);
```

The other important method to notice in this example is the `MoveToEx` function. It replaces the `MoveTo` function commonly used in Windows 3.1. `MoveToEx` is portable between Windows 3.1 and Win32, but `MoveTo` works only in Windows 3.1. After calling `MoveToEx`, you can call the `LineTo` function to draw a line from the point specified in `MoveToEx` to the point specified in `LineTo`. `MoveToEx` will move from one point to another without drawing a line, while `LineTo` moves the point from one place to another and draws a line in the process. Both `MoveToEx` and

LineTo are GDI functions that require a device context. The line drawn by these functions will have the color and size of the current pen. In other words, if you want to change the size, type, or color of the line drawn with LineTo, you should create a new pen and select it into the device context.

Summary

In this chapter you have looked at some DLLs and seen how they can be handled by a Delphi program. Most of these DLLs make heavy use of Windows API functions. In fact, you have seen DLLs that are made entirely out of Windows API calls, as well as DLLs that are standard Delphi RAD productions but that make heavy use of the Windows API.

The key points from this chapter are the techniques used for creating DLLs, and the techniques for calling functions in a DLL. In particular, you saw two techniques for importing functions from a DLL. The first technique loaded the DLL at the launch of the program, which is called *load time dynamic linking*. The second technique allowed you to control more explicitly the moment the DLL was loaded into memory by calling LoadLibrary, GetProcAddress, and FreeLibrary.

If you call LoadLibrary and FreeLibrary, you are performing what is known as runtime dynamic linking. If you call into a DLL without using these calls, you are using load time dynamic linking.

When you call into the Windows API functions, you are always using load time dynamic linking. In particular, when you import a function using external and then use the name or index directive, you are always using load time dynamic linking, which means the DLL will be loaded at the same time as your executable and won't be freed until your executable is closed down. This is the technique used most often in all Object Pascal programs, and indeed it is the standard in most Windows programs regardless of the language used to create them.

To use runtime dynamic linking, you have to explicitly call LoadLibrary, GetProcAddress, and FreeLibrary. It's more work to do things this way, but you can reap advantages in terms of speed and memory usage.

Windows Controls and Callbacks

This chapter presents a relatively complex program written entirely in the Windows API. The program is called the FontsExp program because it experiments with fonts. FontsExp makes heavy use of standard Windows controls to display all the fonts on the current system. One of the main points of the program is that it shows how to use Windows controls without using the VCL.

The examination of FontsExp is divided into two sections. The first section focuses on the various Window controls introduced in the FontsExp program. In particular, it includes an examination of the following controls:

- Static controls, used primarily to display text that the user can't edit.
- List boxes, used to display lists of one-line strings that can be scrolled by the user.
- Edit controls, which enable the user to edit a string.
- Check boxes, which are like the tiny boxes on a ballot or school quiz—if an X is in the box, the item is selected. Otherwise, it's either gray or blank.

The second half of this chapter presents an explanation of how to communicate with controls and how to use a callback function to retrieve the fonts available on the system. In particular, those sections show:

- How to use SendMessage and PostMessage
- How to communicate with list boxes and check boxes
- How to create user-defined messages
- How to use the EnumFontFamilies callback

Controls form a key part of the Windows operating environment; as a result, this chapter explores them in considerable depth. However, I obviously don't want you to interpret this chapter as advocating the use of Windows API code rather than Delphi RAD tools. The reasons for including this chapter are:

- The Delphi TListBox, TComboBox, TButton, TRadioButton, and other controls are, of course, constructed out of calls to the Windows API. After reading this chapter, you will have the basic knowledge you need to create your own TButton, TRadioButton, and similar controls, or to modify or extend the existing controls.
- Sometimes you may want to optimize your code by making direct Windows API calls. You also might want to get at functionality that is not available in the standard Delphi controls.
- When you construct your own components, you usually need to understand the Windows API. This chapter reveals a lot of key details about the inner workings of Windows. You can use that knowledge when you create your own custom controls.

■ You can communicate with Delphi controls using the techniques shown here. You don't have to use properties to talk to Delphi components. The components that are wrappers around standard Windows controls such as TEdit, TButton, and the like will respond to direct calls from the Windows API.

Of course, an in-depth knowledge of Windows pays off in more ways than just those listed here. However, these points should help to put the code you are about to see into context.

Understanding Controls and Messages

This chapter digs deeply into the subject of controls. As a result, it might be worth taking a moment to think about what controls do for programmers and users.

Controls are interface elements (or interface tools) that help present information to the user in a clear and easily comprehensible manner.

It's possible to imagine a parallel between a window (or a series of windows) and the control panel for a stereo, tape recorder, or radio. When seen this way, visual tools, such as buttons, radio buttons, and check boxes, are like knobs or buttons on a stereo. Just as a button turns a stereo on and off and a knob adjusts its volume, controls manage the flow of events inside a computer.

Interface elements, such as controls, become very important when you are wrestling with large quantities of information. For instance, some graphic design shops have an incredibly large number of fonts on their machines. A simple written list of these fonts gets to be as overwhelming as the list of fields in a big Windows structure. What people need is some sort of visual interface that can present these fonts to them in a readily comprehensible fashion. Controls help provide the interface needed to properly present lists of fonts to the user.

Readers, writers, and users—all of us—need a way to grasp the vast amount of information that comes streaming at us in this confusing and fascinating information age. Windows controls are about presenting information to people. They're about interface design. Overall, they're one of the most important elements of the inspired vision that drives GUI environments such as Windows.

The Font Display Program: Phase One

You can get started working with controls on the raw API level by taking a look at an actual example that shows how to manipulate the elements of a Windows interface. The window that the FontsExp program creates is shown in Figure 14.1.

FIGURE 14.1.

The FontsExp program enables you to iterate through all the fonts on the system.

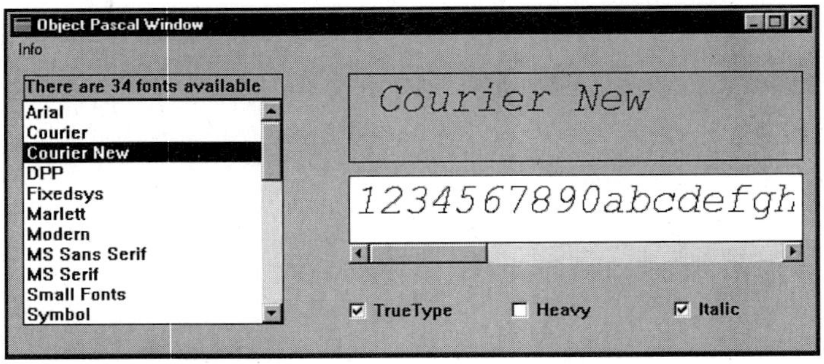

The visual front end of the FontsExp program bears a slight resemblance to the view you see when you pop up a Fonts common dialog (TFontDialog). From a programmer's perspective, however, FontsExp is a very different type of program. It takes you inside the world of Windows fonts, letting you control how, where, and with what degree of detail fonts are presented to the user.

You can build on the knowledge presented in the next few pages to expand the FontsExp program into a world-class tool that many Windows users would love to have at their disposal. As always in the world of programming, there are plenty of opportunities. Start with a look at the code shown in Listings 14.1 through 14.4.

Listing 14.1. The FontsExp program demonstrates techniques for using fonts and controls.

```
program FontsExp;

//////////////////////////////////////
//   Program Name: FONTSEXP.DPR
//   Copyright (c) 1996 by Charlie Calvert
//   Description: FontsExp Windows program
//////////////////////////////////////

uses
  Windows,
  Messages,
  FontStr in 'FontStr.pas',
  SysUtils;

{$I FONTSEXP.INC}
{$R FONTEXP.RES}

const
  AppName = 'FontsExp';
  WM_STARTFONTS = (WM_USER + 0);
  WM_NEWFONT = (WM_USER + 1);

type
  PEnumStruct = ^TEnumStruct;
  TEnumStruct = record
```

```
    Count: Integer;
    hWindow: HWnd;
  end;

var
  TextMetrics: TTextMetric;
  TextFace: string;
  hFontList, hNumFonts: HWnd;
  hFontName, hAlphaEdit: HWnd;
  ButtonWindows: array[0..2] of HWnd;
  TheFont: HFont;

////////////////////////////////////
// FontCallback
////////////////////////////////////
function FontCallBack(lpnlf: PEnumLogFont;
                      lpntm: PNewTextMetric;
                      FontType: Integer;
                      Data: PEnumStruct): Integer; stdcall;
var
  S: string;
begin
  S := (lpnlf.elfLogFont.lfFaceName);
  SendMessage(Data.hWindow, LB_ADDSTRING, 0, LongInt(S));
  Inc(Data.Count, 1);
  Result := 1;
end;

////////////////////////////////////
// DescribeFontCallback
////////////////////////////////////
function DescribeFontCallBack(lpnlf: PEnumLogFont;
                             lpntm: PNewTextMetric;
                             FontType: Integer;
                             Data: PEnumStruct): Integer; stdcall;

begin
  SendMessage(Data.hWindow, WM_NEWFONT, 0, LPARAM(@lpnlf.elfLogFont));
  Result := 1;
end;


////////////////////////////////////
// HandleMetrics
////////////////////////////////////
procedure HandleMetrics(TextMetrics: TTextMetric);
begin
  if ((TextMetrics.tmPitchAndFamily and TMPF_TRUETYPE) = TMPF_TRUETYPE) then
    SendMessage(ButtonWindows[0], BM_SETCHECK, 1, 0)
  else
    SendMessage(ButtonWindows[0], BM_SETCHECK, 0, 0);

  if TextMetrics.tmWeight > 600 then
    SendMessage(ButtonWindows[1], BM_SETCHECK, 1, 0)
  else
    SendMessage(ButtonWindows[1], BM_SETCHECK, 0, 0);
```

continues

Listing 14.1. continued

```
  if TextMetrics.tmItalic <> 0 then
    SendMessage(ButtonWindows[2], BM_SETCHECK, 1, 0)
  else
    SendMessage(ButtonWindows[2], BM_SETCHECK, 0, 0);
end;

//////////////////////////////////////
// Handle WM_CREATE
//////////////////////////////////////
procedure FontsExp_OnCreate(Window: HWnd; var Msg: TWMCreate);
const
  Titles: array[0..2] of string = ( 'TrueType' , 'Heavy', 'Italic') ;
var
  i: Integer;
begin
  SetLength(TextFace, 250);

  hFontList := CreateWindow('listbox', nil,
                    WS_CHILD or WS_VISIBLE or LBS_STANDARD,
                    9, 30, 201, 180, Window, HMENU(ID_LISTBOX),
                    hInstance, nil);

  hNumFonts := CreateWindow('static', nil,
                    WS_CHILD or WS_VISIBLE or WS_BORDER,
                    10, 10, 200, 20, Window, -1,
                    hInstance, nil);

  hFontName := CreateWindow('edit', nil, WS_CHILD or ES_LEFT or
                    WS_VISIBLE or WS_BORDER or ES_READONLY,
                    260, 10, 350, 70, Window, HMENU(-1),
                    hInstance, nil);

  hAlphaEdit := CreateWindow('edit', nil, WS_CHILD or
                    WS_VISIBLE or WS_BORDER or WS_HSCROLL or
                    ES_LEFT or ES_AUTOHSCROLL or ES_MULTILINE,
                    260, 90, 350, 70, Window, HMENU(-1),
                    hInstance, nil);

  for i := 0 to 2 do
    ButtonWindows[i] := CreateWindow('button', PChar(Titles[i]),
                    WS_CHILD or WS_VISIBLE or BS_CHECKBOX,
                    260  + (i * 125), 180, 100, 35, Window,
                    HMENU(-1), hInstance, nil);

  TheFont := 0;

  PostMessage(Window, WM_STARTFONTS, 0, 0);

end;

//////////////////////////////////////
// Handle WM_DESTROY
//////////////////////////////////////
procedure wmDestroy(Window: HWnd; var Msg: TWMDestroy);
begin
  if (TheFont <> 0) then
```

```
      DeleteObject(TheFont);
    PostQuitMessage(0);
end;

/////////////////////////////////////
// ShowTheFont
/////////////////////////////////////
procedure ShowTheFont(hWindow: HWnd);
var
  Buffer: string;
  EnumStruct: TEnumStruct;
  Index: LResult;
  DC: HDC;
  Alpha: string;
  SaveIt: hFont;
begin
  SaveIt := 0;
  SetLength(Buffer, 250);
  Alpha := '1234567890abcdefghijklmnopqrstuvwxyz' +
           'ABCDEFGHIJKLMNOPQRSTUVWXYZ';

  DC := GetDC(hWindow);

  Index := SendMessage(hFontList, LB_GETCURSEL, 0, 0);
  SendMessage(hFontList, LB_GETTEXT, WPARAM(Index), LPARAM(Buffer));
  EnumStruct.Count := 0;
  EnumStruct.hWindow := hWindow;
  if not EnumFontFamilies(DC, PChar(Buffer), @DescribeFontCallback,
                          LongInt(@EnumStruct)) then Exit;

  if TheFont <> 0 then
    SaveIt := SelectObject(DC, TheFont);
  GetTextMetrics(DC, TextMetrics);
  HandleMetrics(TextMetrics);
  GetTextFace(DC, 150, PChar(TextFace));
  if TheFont <> 0 then
    SelectObject(DC, SaveIt);

  ReleaseDC(hWindow, DC);

  SendMessage(hFontName, WM_SETTEXT, 0, LPARAM(Buffer));
  SendMessage(hFontName, WM_SETFONT, WPARAM(TheFont), 0);

  SendMessage(hAlphaEdit, WM_SETTEXT, 0, LPARAM(Alpha));
  SendMessage(hAlphaEdit, WM_SETFONT, WPARAM(TheFont), 0);
end;

procedure ShowFontString(hWindow: HWnd);
var
  S: string;
begin
  S := GetFontString(S, TextMetrics, TextFace);
  MessageBox(hWindow, PChar(S), 'Info', MB_OK);
end;

/////////////////////////////////////
// Handle WM_COMMAND
/////////////////////////////////////
```

continues

Listing 14.1. continued

```pascal
procedure FontsExp_OnCommand(hWindow: HWnd; var Msg: TWMCommand);
begin
  case Msg.ItemID of
    ID_LISTBOX:
      case Msg.NotifyCode of
        LBN_SELCHANGE: ShowTheFont(hWindow);
        LBN_DBLCLK: ShowFontString(hWindow);
      end;

    CM_INFO: ShowFontString(hWindow);
  end;
end;

procedure NewFont(lParam: LongInt);
var
  LogFont: PLogFont;
begin
  if TheFont <> 0 then
    DeleteObject(TheFont);
  LogFont := PLogFont(lParam);
  TheFont := CreateFontIndirect(LogFont^);
end;

procedure StartFont(hWindow: HWnd);
var
  DC: HDC;
  EnumStruct: TEnumStruct;
  S: string;
begin
  DC := GetDC(hWindow);
  EnumStruct.Count := 0;
  EnumStruct.hWindow := hFontList;
  if not EnumFontFamilies(DC, nil, @FontCallBack, LongInt(@EnumStruct)) then
    Exit;
  ReleaseDC(hWindow, DC);

  S := Format('There are %d fonts available', [EnumStruct.Count]);
  SetWindowText(hNumFonts, PChar(S));

  SetFocus(hFontList);
  SendMessage(hFontList, LB_SETCURSEL, 0, 0);
  ShowTheFont(hWindow);
end;

function WindowProc(hWindow: HWnd; AMessage, WParam,
                    LParam: Longint): Longint; stdcall; export;
var
  AMsg: TMessage;
begin
  AMsg.Msg := AMessage;
  AMsg.WParam := WParam;
  AMsg.LParam := LParam;
  AMsg.Result := 0;

  case AMessage of
    wm_Create: FontsExp_OnCreate(hWindow, TWMCreate(AMsg));
```

```
      wm_Destroy: wmDestroy(hWindow, TWMDestroy(AMsg));
      wm_Command: FontsExp_OnCommand(hWindow, TWMCommand(AMsg));
      wm_NewFont: NewFont(lParam);
      wm_StartFonts: StartFont(hWindow);
    else
      WindowProc := DefWindowProc(hWindow, AMessage, WParam, LParam);
      Exit;
    end;

  Result := AMsg.Result
end;

{ Register the Window Class }
function WinRegister: Boolean;
var
  WindowClass: TWndClass;
begin
  WindowClass.Style := cs_hRedraw or cs_vRedraw;
  WindowClass.lpfnWndProc := @WindowProc;
  WindowClass.cbClsExtra := 0;
  WindowClass.cbWndExtra := 0;
  WindowClass.hInstance := HInstance;
  WindowClass.hIcon := LoadIcon(0, idi_Application);
  WindowClass.hCursor := LoadCursor(0, idc_Arrow);
  WindowClass.hbrBackground := HBrush(Color_Window);
  WindowClass.lpszMenuName := 'FontMenu';
  WindowClass.lpszClassName := AppName;

  Result := RegisterClass(WindowClass) <> 0;
end;

{ Create the Window Class }
function WinCreate: HWnd;
var
  hWindow: HWnd;
begin
  hWindow := CreateWindow(AppName, 'Object Pascal Window',
             ws_OverlappedWindow, cw_UseDefault, cw_UseDefault,
             625, 275, 0, 0, HInstance, nil);

  if hWindow <> 0 then begin
    ShowWindow(hWindow, CmdShow);
    UpdateWindow(hWindow);
  end;

  Result := hWindow;
end;


var
  AMessage: TMsg;
  hWindow: HWnd;
begin
  if not WinRegister then begin
    MessageBox(0, 'Register failed', nil, mb_Ok);
    Exit;
  end;
  hWindow := WinCreate;
```

continues

Listing 14.1. continued

```
if hWindow = 0 then begin
  MessageBox(0, 'WinCreate failed', nil, mb_Ok);
  Exit;
end;

while GetMessage(AMessage, 0, 0, 0) do begin
  TranslateMessage(AMessage);
  DispatchMessage(AMessage);
end;
Halt(AMessage.wParam);
end.
```

Listing 14.2. The FontStr Module provides code for examining the features of a font.

```
unit FontStr;

///////////////////////////////////////
//  Program Name: FONTSTR.DPR
//  Copyright (c) 1996 by Charlie Calvert
//  Description: Create description of a font
///////////////////////////////////////

interface

uses
  Windows, SysUtils;

var
  TextMetrics: TTextmetric;
  TheFaceName: string;


function GetFontString(var S: string; TextMetric: TTextMetric;
                       FaceName: string): string;
implementation

function GetType(var S: string): string;
begin
  S := 'Font Type: ';

  if ((TextMetrics.tmPitchAndFamily and TMPF_FIXED_PITCH) =
      TMPF_FIXED_PITCH) then
    S := S + 'Fixed <> ';
  if ((TextMetrics.tmPitchAndFamily and TMPF_VECTOR) = TMPF_VECTOR) then
    S := s + 'Vector <> ';
  if ((TextMetrics.tmPitchAndFamily and TMPF_TRUETYPE) = TMPF_TRUETYPE) then
    S := s + 'TrueType <> ';
  if ((TextMetrics.tmPitchAndFamily and TMPF_DEVICE) = TMPF_DEVICE) then
    s := S + 'Device <> ';

  if Length(S) > 11 then
    SetLength(S, Length(S) - 3);
```

```
    Result := S;
end;

function GetFamily(var S: string): string;
var
  R: Integer;
begin
  R := TextMetrics.tmPitchAndFamily and $F0;
  S := 'Family: ';
  case R of
    FF_DONTCARE: S := S + 'Don''t Care or don''t know';
    FF_ROMAN: S := S + 'Roman';
    FF_SWISS: S := S + 'Swiss';
    FF_MODERN: S := S + 'Modern';
    FF_SCRIPT: S := S + 'Script';
    FF_DECORATIVE: S := S + 'Decorative';
  end;
  Result := S;
end;

function GetCharSet(var S: string): string;
begin
  S := 'Char Set: ';
  case TextMetrics.tmCharSet of
    ANSI_CHARSET: S := S + 'Ansi';
    DEFAULT_CHARSET: S := S + 'Default';
    SYMBOL_CHARSET: S := S + 'Symbol';
    OEM_CHARSET: S := S + 'OEM';
  end;
  Result := S;
end;

function GetFontString(var S: string; TextMetric: TTextMetric;
                       FaceName: string): string;
var
  szType: string;
  szFamily: string;
  szCharSet: string;
  Len: Integer;
begin
  TextMetrics := TextMetric;
  TheFaceName := FaceName;          // Facename had its length set to 250
  Len := StrLen(PChar(FaceName));   // We have to shorten the string
  SetLength(TheFaceName, Len);      // To use it with Format!!!

  GetType(szType);
  GetFamily(szFamily);
  GetCharSet(szCharSet);

  S := Format('Font: %s ' + #13 +
              'Height: %d ' + #13 +
              'Ascent: %d ' + #13 +
              'Descent: %d ' + #13 +
              'AveCharW: %d ' + #13 + 'MaxCharW: %d ' + #13 +
              'Weight: %d ' + #13 + 'Italic: %d ' + #13 +
              'Underlined: %d ' + #13 + '%s ' + #13 +
              '%s ' + #13 + '%s ',
              [TheFaceName,
```

continues

Listing 14.2. continued

```
                TextMetrics.tmHeight,
                TextMetrics.tmAscent,
                TextMetrics.tmDescent,
                TextMetrics.tmAveCharWidth,
                TextMetrics.tmMaxCharWidth,
                TextMetrics.tmWeight,
                TextMetrics.tmItalic,
                TextMetrics.tmUnderlined,
                szType, szFamily, szCharSet]);

  Result := S;
end;

end.
```

I adopt a bunch of Richs suggestions in new versin I adopt a bunch of Richs suggestions in new versin I adopt a bunch of Richs suggestions in new version I adopt a bunch of Richs suggestions in new versin I adopt a bunch of Richs suggestions in new versin I adopt a bunch of Richs suggestions in new versin

Listing 14.3. The include file for the FontsExp program.

```
//////////////////////////////////////
//   Program Name: FONTSEXP.INC
//   Programmer: Charlie Calvert
//   Description: FontsExp include file
//////////////////////////////////////

const
  id_ListBox = $FF;
  cm_Info = id_ListBox + 1;
```

Listing 14.4. The resource file for the FontsExp program.

```
{    Program Name: FONTSEXP.INC
     Programmer: Charlie Calvert
     Description: FontsExp include file  }

const
  id_ListBox = $FF;
  cm_Info = id_ListBox + 1;
```

The FontsExp program creates a window and populates it with static controls, edit controls, check boxes, and list boxes. These controls enable the user to display a series of fonts. As shown in Figure 14.2, the FontInfo menu choice lets the user view information about the current font.

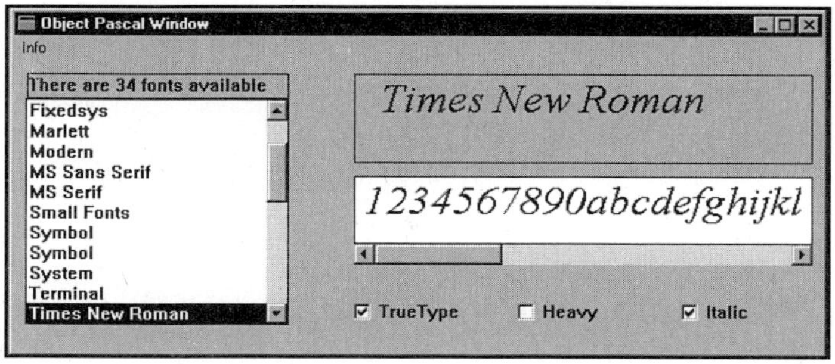

FIGURE 14.2.

*The FontsExp program,
displaying the system font
in its list box and the Times
Roman font in an edit and
static control.*

Now that you've seen the code, it's time to rev up your engines and pay special attention to the rest of this chapter. Most Windows programmers work with controls on a daily basis. Understand them thoroughly, and you'll be well on your way to creating powerful, robust programs that users love.

Static Controls

Users never interact with static controls, like the TLabel control. Such controls are meant only to display text. Static controls are the easiest controls to utilize. Here are the minimum steps involved:

- Call CreateWindow.
- Fill in the first field of CreateWindow, called lpszClassname, with the string *static*.
- Fill in the third field, called dwStyle, with the WS_CHILD and WS_VISIBLE styles and any others you might need to add, such as SS_LEFT or SS_SIMPLE.
- Specify the control's dimensions.
- Fill in the program's hwndParent field with the HWnd from the main window.
- Give the control a unique ID by filling in the hMenu field with a predefined constant. (Or, on occasion, you might calculate the number in a loop or some other code fragment. The point is that you should be able to predict what the ID will be, so that you can reference it from other parts of your code.)
- Either specify the caption at creation, or else use SetWindowText to fill the control with a string.

As you'll see, there are a few other factors to keep in mind, but these steps form the core procedures used when creating static controls. In fact, you can use these steps as a template for creating all window controls. In other words, all controls are brought kicking and screaming into the world by calls to CreateWindow. Figure 14.3 shows the FontsExp program.

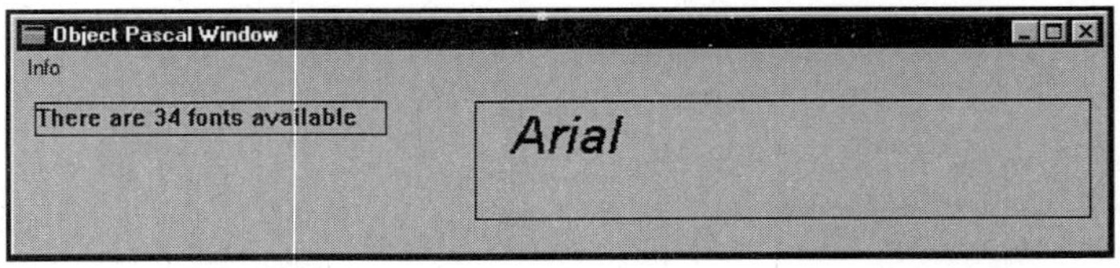

FIGURE 14.3.

A static control displays the number of fonts and a read-only edit control displays the font name.

Following is the call that creates the static control in the FontsExp program:

```
hNumFonts := CreateWindow('static', nil,
                    WS_CHILD or WS_VISIBLE or WS_BORDER,
                    10, 10, 200, 20, Window, HMENU(-1),
                    hInstance, nil);
```

As you can see, this code looks like the routines used to create a main window, except that there's no need to first register a class. The reason for this omission is simply that the `static` class has been preregistered for you. That's what controls are all about. They are preregistered classes.

> **NOTE**
>
> The fact that a static control is just a preregistered window is such an important point that I want to take a moment to emphasize it.
>
> In this book, you have learned how to create a number of different windows that behave in a particular way. You did this by filling out their `TWndClass` structure with values of your own choosing, and then writing message response functions called from a window procedure. In the process, you created several classes of potentially reusable windows that behave in various, predefined ways.
>
> This is exactly what has already been done for you with the `static`, `listbox`, `combobox`, `button`, and `scrollbar` classes. Microsoft has already registered these classes and defined how they will respond to certain messages. The same is true of the Windows 95 and Windows NT specific classes such as toolbars, rich edits, progress bars, property sheets, and up/down controls.

You have been calling `CreateWindow` regularly in the last few chapters. When creating child window controls, however, you need to take special note of a few key points. The next few paragraphs outline those points for you while showing you how to create a static control.

The `dwStyle` field of `CreateWindow` ORs together `WS_CHILD`, `WS_VISIBLE`, and `WS_BORDER`. The first and last styles simply tell Windows that this is a child window with a border. The `WS_VISIBLE` style is a nifty little flag that requests Windows to call the `ShowWindow` function. In past chapters, most calls to `CreateWindow` have been followed by calls to `ShowWindow` and `UpdateWindow`:

```
ShowWindow(hwnd, nCmdShow);
UpdateWindow(hwnd);
```

If you use the WS_VISIBLE style, this isn't necessary, because Windows does the dirty work for you.

The next set of fields you need to be concerned with are those that define the size of the border surrounding the static control. When CreateWindow is being called for a main window, these fields are usually filled with CW_USEDEFAULT constants. With static controls, however, you should explicitly fill in these fields with the actual dimensions you want associated with your control.

The next step is to fill out the hwndParent parameter to CreateWindow. Controls are child windows, and children need parents. In this case, of course, the parent is the main window.

Another field you need to be aware of is the ninth, called hMenu. In this field, you normally designate the number to be associated with a window. Because objects such as static controls and child windows don't have menus, this field can be available as a place to specify an ID for a window.

The ID number you choose can prove important later when you set up a line of communication between a control and its parent window. As a result, if you decide to specify a value in this field, you should pick a unique ID number for each control. This is especially true for controls that are embedded in dialogs. In those cases, the ID number is the only link between a dialog and a control.

Because programmers develop a lot of these ID constants in their programs, they've fallen into the habit of using constants to act as mnemonics:

```
const
  id_ListBox = $FF;
  cm_Info = id_ListBox + 1;
```

It is not strictly necessary to typecast these constants before passing them on to Windows, but doing so is a nicety that helps specify exactly what your code means.

NOTE

The FontsExp program usually communicates with a control through its HWnd, which is carefully saved after every call to CreateWindow. This technique is easy to use when working with controls embedded in Windows. Within dialogs, however, it's simpler to use an ID and the GetDlgItem Windows API function.

To make static controls useful objects, all you need to do is place a bit of text in them with the SetWindowText call:

```
SetWindowText(hNumFonts, PChar(S));
```

hNumFonts is the handle to a static or edit control, and S is the string that appears in the control's window.

Static controls are the simplest controls you're likely to use in a Windows program. Of course, nothing in the Windows API is ever totally devoid of syntactical verbosity. For instance, there are a number of changes you can run on static texts. You can change their border and color or use them to seat icons or bitmaps.

Following are some of the valid styles that can be ORed into the dwStyle field of a static control:

SS_BLACKRECT	SS_BLACKFRAME
SS_GRAYRECT	SS_GRAYFRAME
SS_WHITERECT	SS_WHITEFRAME
SS_LEFT	SS_RIGHT
SS_CENTER	SS_ICON

Feel free to experiment with these styles. Take special note, however, of the simple examples I've included in the FontsExp program. They can remain as an image of what lies at the heart of every control: an ordinary window with something painted inside it.

> **NOTE**
>
> In this sample program, a great deal goes on in the WM_CREATE message function handler. It's the place in which all the controls used in the program are created. This, of course, only makes sense. In fact, the idea of creating controls in response to a WM_CREATE message really defines what the message is all about. A WM_CREATE message is sent to a window specifically to say: "Hey, wake up there! It's time for you to create all your child windows and to do any other initialization you think necessary!"

List Boxes

Of particular interest in the context of the current chapter is the code for creating list box controls:

```
hFontList := CreateWindow('listbox', nil,
                WS_CHILD or WS_VISIBLE or LBS_STANDARD,
                9, 30, 201, 180, Window, HMENU(ID_LISTBOX),
                hInstance, nil);
```

List boxes, of course, are rectangular windows that present the user with an array of items to select. A list box and a static control are shown in Figure 14.4.

In the list box, the most important field is the third, in which you can define the style of the class:

WS_CHILD or WS_VISIBLE or LBS_STANDARD

By this time, I'm sure it won't come as a surprise to you to learn that the LBS_STANDARD flag is part of another lengthy array of options. This is the Windows way of doing things. Good

Windows programmers eventually develop something of a love/hate relationship with these tables full of options and possibilities. After all, each list may be a bit confusing, but it also contains numerous tidbits that can be used to spice up your program.

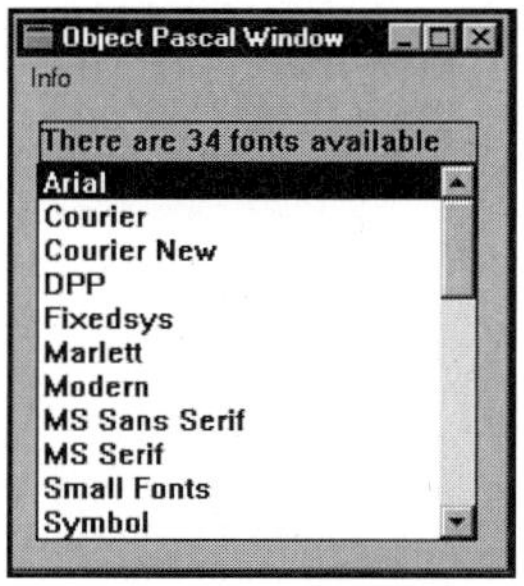

FIGURE 14.4.

A static control with a string in it. Immediately beneath it is a list box filled with font names.

The online help has already provided you with several copies of this list, so I'll show you only the ones programmers are likely to use on a regular basis:

LBS_MULTIPLESEL	User can select more than one item at a time.
LBS_EXTENDEDSEL	Enables the user to select multiple items by using the Shift key and the mouse or special key combinations.
LBS_NOTIFY	When this flag is turned off, the parent window doesn't know whether the user has clicked or double-clicked a string.
LBS_STANDARD	The standard list box with a border and with LBS_NOTIFY turned on.
LBS_OWNERDRAW	The style you need if you want to display bitmaps or other nonstandard items in a list box.
LBS_USETABSTOPS	Used for simulating multiple columns in a single list box.
LBS_WANTKEYBOARDINPUT	Enables the programmer to pick up on keyboard input when the list box has the focus.

Of these items, the two most important are LBS_STANDARD and LBS_MULTIPLESEL. Multiple selection list boxes work like the windows in the File Manager: they let you select multiple items at one time. Of course, they don't have all the capabilities of the windows in the File Manager, but they do enable multiple selections.

Even without the Delphi RAD tools, creating a list box is a trivial task that you can accomplish in just a few moments. Simply cut and paste the call from another program, or copy the CreateWindow call from your main window. There's really nothing to it. This is true whether you are inside a RAD program, or inside straight Windows API code. Once you've got one sample to work from, it's easy to create all the other list boxes you ever need to create.

The subject of communicating with a list box can become fairly involved. For now, a few simple examples should suffice. If you want to add a string to a list box, you can do so by sending it an LB_ADDSTRING message:

```
MyString = 'Sambo';
SendMessage(hListBox, LB_ADDSTRING, 0, LPARAM(MyString));
```

The code shown here typecasts the last parameter to SendMessage as an LPARAM. LPARAM is a type declared in WINDOWS.PAS that resolves into a LongInt:

```
type
  WPARAM = UINT;
  LPARAM = Longint;
  LRESULT = Longint;
```

The reason I use LPARAM rather than LongInt is twofold:

■ If you ever need to port the code to a different operating system, you could just redefine LPARAM, whereas you might not be able to redefine LongInt because it is a built-in Object Pascal type.

■ Windows was originally written in C, and in C it is traditional to use a type called LPARAM in this parameter. LPARAM is defined in C very much as it is defined in WINDOWS.PAS, and for the same reasons described in the preceding paragraph. At any rate, much of the documentation on the Windows API is written using C as the example language, so it helps to write Windows API code that mirrors the C language as much as possible. However, one should be careful not to enter into the confusing syntactical excesses of that venerable language and its more egregious sibling C++. (Pascal is a great language because of its clarity; C is great because of its flexibility. I think it is wrong to obscure Pascal's virtues in an attempt to emulate C's virtues. C is meant to be concise; Object Pascal is meant to be easy to read. Let each language stick to its innate virtues.)

You can retrieve a string from a list box by first getting the index of the currently selected item with an LB_GETCURSEL message:

```
var
  Index: Integer;
begin
  Index = SendMessage(hFontList, LB_GETCURSEL, 0, 0);
```

Use the index to retrieve the string by using an LB_GETTEXT message:

```
SendMessage(hFontList, LB_GETTEXT, WPARAM(Index), LPARAM(Buffer));
```

This material is being presented here mostly as a reference tool and brief introduction to list boxes. To really get a deep insight into this material, you should turn to the Windows API documentation, which you now have enough knowledge to read, whether the examples in those docs are written using Pascal or C.

You should also be getting a sense that there is nothing you can't do in Object Pascal. It's all there—all the techniques for accessing the Windows API are at your fingertips whenever you need them.

Check Boxes

Following are the calls that create all three of the check boxes used in this program:

```
const
  Titles: array[0..2] of string = ( 'TrueType' , 'Heavy', 'Italic') ;
var
  i: Integer;
begin
  ...
  for i := 0 to 2 do
    ButtonWindows[i] := CreateWindow('button', PChar(Titles[i]),
                        WS_CHILD or WS_VISIBLE or BS_CHECKBOX,
                        260  + (i * 125), 180, 100, 35, Window,
                        HMENU(-1), hInstance, nil);
  ...
end;
```

To create a check box, you should specify the "button" class name and use the BS_CHECKBOX style. The preceding example also shows how to use constant arrays and FOR loops to create a series of three controls. This is a technique you'll probably use on many occasions if you work regularly with the Windows API.

> **NOTE**
>
> *Check boxes* are little square bordered windows with a name attached to them, as shown in Figure 14.4. If the bordered window has an X in it, that item is selected; otherwise, it's not selected. In most cases, users click a check box with a mouse to select or deselect an option. FontsExp, however, sends messages to select or deselect a check box, and the user never interacts with the box directly.

Figure 14.5 shows check boxes and the list box of the FontsExp program. If you use the arrow keys to move the highlight bar up and down the list, the check boxes blink on and off like Christmas lights. Well, okay, like black-and-white Christmas lights.

I'm sure you've already guessed that the BS_CHECKBOX style is only one of many different possible styles that can be associated with a button control. This versatile class is one that Windows programmers rely on time and time again. Take a careful look at the following button styles:

BS_CHECKBOX	Creates a check box.
BS_DEFPUSHBUTTON	Has a heavy black border and is chosen by default when the user presses the Enter key in a dialog.

BS_GROUPBOX	Brings a group of controls together into a group.
BS_3STATE	Can be grayed as well as checked and unchecked.
BS_AUTO3STATE	Responds automatically to being selected.
BS_AUTOCHECKBOX	Responds when the user selects it.
BS_AUTORADIOBUTTON	Responds when the user selects it.
BS_LEFTTEXT	Text on the left (not the right) side of a check box or radio button.
BS_OWNERDRAW	Enables the programmer to define the appearance of a button.
BS_PUSHBUTTON	Standard button.
BS_RADIOBUTTON	A small round button that can appear to be either selected or not selected. When these buttons are placed in a group, the user usually only can select one of these at a time.

FIGURE 14.5.

A selected check box has a check mark in it, whereas unselected check boxes are blank.

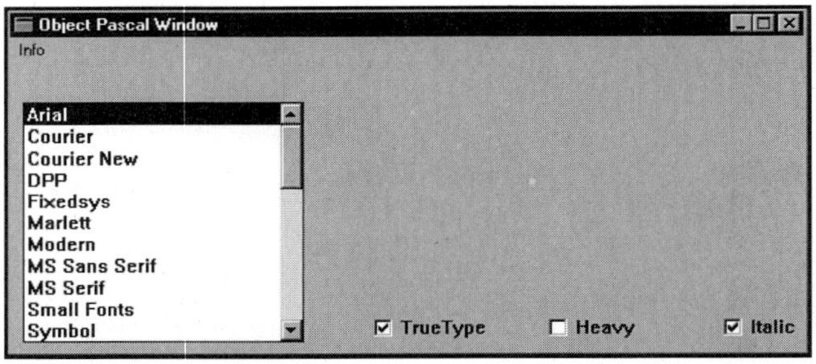

This list shows that buttons are very versatile tools. At first, you might not even make the connections among standard OK buttons, check boxes, and radio buttons. However, all these tools belong to the same class, and you should learn to think of them as being closely related.

Communicating with check boxes can be a fairly delicate matter. For now, I'll just say that you can use the BM_SETCHECK messages to perform the most important aspects of the job. The key point to remember is that passing 1 in the WPARAM field of SendMessage sets the check, whereas passing 0 clears the check mark:

```
SendMessage(ButtonWindows[0], BM_SETCHECK, 1, 0);
```

If you want to query a check box as to the state of its button, use BM_GETCHECK:

```
var
  IsCheck: Integer;
begin
  IsCheck := SendMessage(ButtonWindows[0], BM_GETCHECK, 0, 0);
  ...
```

Buttons with the BS_3STATE or BS_AUTO3STATE have a third grayed state selected by sending the value 2 to them.

An in-depth discussion of this topic is presented later in the chapter. There you'll see how FontsExp uses messages to control and query check boxes.

Edit Controls

The FontsExp program also makes use of two edit controls, one of which is shown in Figure 14.6 and the other in Figure 14.3. Edit controls are used for getting input from a user through the keyboard, as in a text editor. In fact, edit controls can be used to create small text editors that can handle a few pages of text at a time.

You can also create read-only edit controls by giving them the ES_READONLY style. The ES_READONLY style makes an edit control behave as if it were a souped-up static control. Compared to static controls, you have better control over fonts and highlighting in an edit control even if it has the ES_READONLY style.

The following code creates a read-only edit control:

```
hFontName := CreateWindow('edit', nil, WS_CHILD or ES_LEFT or
              WS_VISIBLE or WS_BORDER or ES_READONLY,
              260, 10, 350, 70, Window, HMENU(-1),
              hInstance, nil);
```

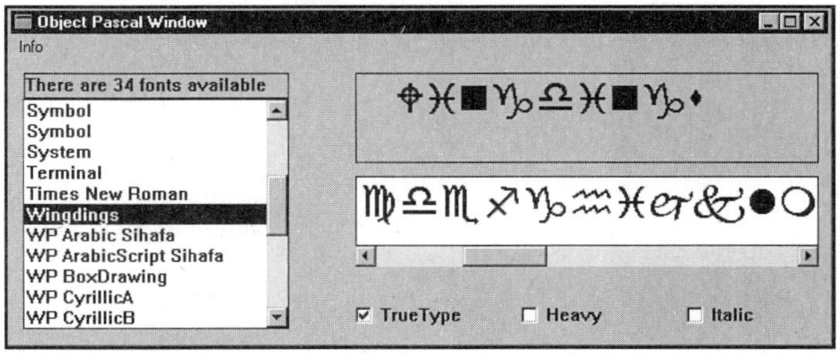

FIGURE 14.6.

An edit control, with its scrollbar, displays the ever-useful Wingdings font.

In this particular program, you might never type in either edit control; you might prefer to simply scroll the text back and forth. However, it's easy to see how a user might want to look at a particular combination of letters, so I've designed the program to respond to that contingency. Notice, however, that this is the only part of the program that requires any typing skills.

The call to initialize the second edit control uses six different styles ord together to form the third parameter:

```
hAlphaEdit := CreateWindow('edit', nil, WS_CHILD or
              WS_VISIBLE or WS_BORDER or WS_HSCROLL or
              ES_LEFT or ES_AUTOHSCROLL or ES_MULTILINE,
              260, 90, 350, 70, Window, HMENU(-1),
              hInstance, nil);
```

> **NOTE**
>
> You can add the WS_BORDER style if you want the control to be outlined in black. Scrollbars are handled automatically by Windows. You can add this feature to your edit controls simply by using the WS_HSCROLL style.
>
> Don't confuse this style with either the ES_AUTOHSCROLL or ES_AUTOVSCROLL styles. These two styles let the user scroll text into view if it is hidden behind the right or bottom edge of a control. They seem to imply that this latter process involves using scrollbars, but that is not actually the case.

I'm sure the astute reader has already prepared him or herself for another long list of identifiers. So, without further delay, here are the edit control styles:

ES_AUTOHSCROLL	Automatically scrolls horizontally.
ES_AUTOVSCROLL	Automatically scrolls vertically.
ES_CENTER	Centers the text.
ES_LEFT	Aligns text on the left margin.
ES_LOWERCASE	Converts text to lowercase.
ES_MULTILINE	Uses multiple lines.
ES_NOHIDESEL	Forces Windows to keep the text highlighted, even if you set the focus to another control. (If you highlight a text fragment, Windows normally will not preserve the selection after the control loses focus.)
ES_OEMCONVERT	Helps preserve characters outside the range of normal letters and numbers.
ES_PASSWORD	Helps prevent other users from seeing what is being typed into an edit control.
ES_READONLY	Uses the edit control only for viewing text.
ES_RIGHT	Aligns text on the right margin.
ES_UPPERCASE	Sets all input to uppercase.
ES_WANTRETURN	Treats carriage returns normally, rather than sending them on to the default button.

This list is invaluable. Countless Windows programmers have spent hours trapping WM_KEYDOWN messages to handle carriage returns or to create edit controls appropriate for handling passwords. Don't become one of these poor, overworked programmers. Instead, take a careful look at these styles, so you don't have to reinvent the proverbial wheel.

Check the online help for additional styles. You should get used to popping up the Win32 help on a moment's notice to see what's available.

> **NOTE**
>
> Don't bother memorizing all the styles shown in this chapter. Instead, just absorb the fact that every control has a set of styles that can be used to fine-tune, or even radically change, its appearance and behavior. Another helpful point is that the styles associated with each of the controls begin with a particular set of letters. For instance, edit-control styles all begin with ES. To help you understand how this works, here is a list of letters associated with each of the major control types:
>
> | | |
> |---|---|
> | Button | BS |
> | Combo box | CBS |
> | Edit | ES |
> | List box | LBS |
> | Static | SS |

Communicating with edit controls is a fairly simple process. To insert text into an edit control, call SetWindowText, just as you do with a static control:

```
SetWindowText(hAlphaEdit, PChar(S));
```

To retrieve text from an edit control, call GetWindowText:

```
SetLength(S, 250);
GetWindowText(hAlphaEdit, PChar(S), Length(S));
```

With GetWindowText, the first parameter is the HWnd of the edit control; the second is a buffer to hold the string displayed in the control; the third is the maximum number of bytes the string can hold. Because you are passing in a string, you need to allocate memory for it, as Windows won't know how to do this. At the time of this writing, Length returns the amount of memory allocated for a string, not its length. You can use the following code to return the true length of a long string:

```
Len := StrLen(PChar(S));
```

In the later sections of this chapter, you'll see that the SendMessage function provides an alternative to this technique. For instance, the following call passes the string Alpha to an edit control:

```
SendMessage(hAlphaEdit, WM_SETTEXT, 0, LPARAM(Alpha));
```

Besides WM_SETTEXT, edit controls also respond to a series of messages that enable you to directly manipulate their text. Most of these messages involve relatively advanced Windows programming issues, but you should at least be aware of their existence. Here is a small sample:

EM_CANUNDO	Checks whether an operation can be undone.
EM_GETMODIFY	Checks whether contents have changed.

EM_GETRECT	Gets a control's coordinates.
EM_GETSEL	Gets the position of the current selection.
EM_LIMITTEXT	Limits text in an edit control.
EM_REPLACESEL	Replaces current selection.
EM_SETPASSWORDCHAR	Sets password character.
EM_SETREADONLY	Sets the read-only state.
EM_SETSEL	Selects text.
EM_UNDO	Undoes the preceding operation.

It's very important for you to remember that all of these calls also work with Delphi controls. Just because an edit control is wrapped in a TEdit component doesn't meant that it isn't still really an edit control, underneath the wrapper. You can send all these messages to standard TEdit controls, and they will respond appropriately. You can get the handle of the control by addressing the handle field of the TEdit:

```
var
  Alpha: string;
  MyEdit: TEdit;

begin
  ...
  SendMessage(MyEdit.Handle, WM_SETTEXT, 0, LPARAM(Alpha));
  ...
end;
```

An Examination of FontsExp: Phase Two

This is a long chapter, and for people who are new to the Windows API, it is probably one of the most difficult in the book. You might want to take a little break at this point, in order to catch your breath.

The second half of this chapter has four main themes, most of which involve communication between controls and the main body of a program. In particular, the rest of the chapter seeks to do these things:

- Use the FontsExp program to continue the exploration of controls. In particular, you will hear more about talking to list boxes, radio buttons, check boxes, and push buttons.

- Show how to use callbacks to access the fonts on your system. In particular, you'll see the EnumFontFamilies function and the EnumFontFamilies callback.

- Demonstrate the use of the debugger to see how Windows communicates with list boxes, edit controls, static controls, and buttons.

- Explain the SendMessage and PostMessage functions. SendMessage passes messages directly to the window procedure, while PostMessage places messages in the message queue.

When you are reading this chapter, try to pay particular attention to the material on the debugger. It's almost impossible for most people to do any serious programming without having an in-depth knowledge of the debugger.

> **NOTE**
>
> This book is aimed at intermediate and advanced programmers. I consider basic debugging skills to be an introductory topic, so I don't cover them in this book. The material on the debugger shown below is not difficult, nor particularly advanced, but it does assume a basic knowledge of the integrated debugger. You can find this kind of basic information in the user's guide that ships with Delphi. Some relatively advanced tips on using the stand alone debugger are included in Chapter 5, "Pointers, Linked Lists, and Memory". For those who want even more information, some years ago Tom Swan wrote a good DOS-based book on the stand-alone Turbo Debugger, called *Mastering Turbo Debugger*, published by Hayden books. This book covers both C and Pascal debugging techniques. I should add, however, that purchasing a separate book on debugging would be overkill for most readers of this book.
>
> Let me emphasize, however, that it is completely impossible for most people to do serious programming without a complete, thorough, and instinctive knowledge of how to set breakpoints, examine variables in a watch window, and step through code. You shouldn't have to think about how to do these things; they should be an automatic part of your skills. You should be able to set a breakpoint as easily as you save a file.

From a purely conceptual point of view, the second half of this chapter covers fairly complex material. The theme for the day is communication—specifically the way Windows communicates with messages and callbacks. In an attempt to make this material as comprehensible as possible, I have arranged it around the life history of a single event. In particular, the agenda is as follows:

- Learn about a user-defined message called WM_STARTFONTS.
- Trace WM_STARTFONTS from the moment of its conception until it sets off two calls to EnumFontFamilies, thereby causing messages to be sent that fill up the list box and other visual elements of the FontsExp program.

Each step on the agenda is explained methodically, starting from point one and working to the end. The narrative flow is provided by the life history of WM_STARTFONTS. In other words, the narrative starts by describing the declaration of WM_STARTFONTS, then follows through by describing how the message is sent and processed. My theory is that if you watch a message from the moment it's defined, until it's finally delivered and processed, you'll get a complete overview of the subject—without any major gaps or omissions.

Delivering the Mail

WM_STARTFONTS is a user-defined message. It is not defined in WINDOWS.PAS; it is defined by the FontsExp program.

To begin the discussion of WM_STARTFONTS, it might be helpful to recall what was said earlier about the WM_CREATE method response function for the FontsExp program. As you recall, that code created edit controls, static controls, list boxes, and check boxes in the FontsExp_OnCreate procedure.

The earlier discussion didn't mention one command in FontsExp_OnCreate—the call to PostMessage:

```
PostMessage(hwnd, WM_STARTFONTS, 0, 0);
```

To understand how PostMessage works, it's best to start out by defining messages from a new, and hopefully elucidating, perspective. WM_STARTFONTS is a user-defined message sent to tell the main window that it's time to fill up the list box and other controls with the names and descriptions of all the fonts on the system. There are two differences between user-defined messages and other messages:

- User-defined messages are declared by the programmer, whereas normal Windows messages are declared in WINDOWS.PAS, or in other units that come with the system such as WINSOCK.PAS.

- User-defined messages normally have only local scope. This means that they can be defined for one class only.

More specifically, user-defined messages are calculated in terms of a constant called WM_USER, which is defined in WINDOWS.PAS:

```
{ NOTE: All Message Numbers below $0400 are RESERVED.
  Private Window Messages Start Here: }

  WM_USER = $400;
```

As you can see, the comment in WINDOWS.H specifies that messages below 1024 (0X400) are reserved for internal use by Windows.

The WM_STARTFONTS message is defined in FONTSEXP.DPR:

```
  WM_STARTFONTS = (WM_USER + 0);
```

The preceding line of code simply states that WM_STARTFONTS should be assigned a number that will enable Windows to recognize it as a message of local import. By definition, it is intended specifically for the FontsExp class. To define additional messages, simply add 1 to the value of WM_STARTFONTS, and so on:

```
  WM_STARTFONTS = (WM_USER + 0);
  WM_NEWFONT = (WM_USER + 1);
```

It is sometimes possible to have two messages that have the same value. This is not necessarily a problem. All messages are designed to be sent to a particular window. The window in question is designated by the HWnd in the first parameter to PostMessage or SendMessage:

```
var
  MainWindow, hCheckBox;  // Handles to windows
  IsCheck: Integer;
...
// Code to initialize hMainWindow and hCheckbox.
...
PostMessage(hMainWindow, WM_STARTFONTS, 0, 0);
IsCheck := SendMessage(hCheckBox, BM_GETCHECK, 0, 0);
...
```

Suppose (just hypothetically) that in this example, WM_STARTFONTS and BM_GETCHECK had the same value. This call states explicitly that WM_STARTFONTS is being sent to the program's main window. If WM_STARTFONTS were accidentally sent to a check box, Windows would cheerfully ignore all the fonts on your system and return the state of the check box. The point here is that all will be on the up and up as long as you send the message to the correct window! The name of a message, however, is meaningless. What's important is its underlying integer-based value.

There are times when you need to create a message that is sent across the desktop to more than one application. To do so, call RegisterWindowMessage. This call returns a unique message, defined at runtime, to be used by your applications.

NOTE

Use WM_USER as an offset for messages that are going to be sent to only one class.

Don't try to send these messages between applications. Use the RegisterWindowMessage function to assign numbers to messages that will be sent between applications. The numbers returned from RegisterWindowMessage are in the following range: $C000 through $FFFF. Refer to the online help for more information on this process.

I should add, however, that in Delphi 2.0 using OLE Automation is probably the best way to set up interprocess communication. At any rate, it should be considered carefully whenever you are contemplating methods for getting two applications to communicate. For the record, mutexes and memory mapped files can also be used when two processes need to share memory or communicate with one another.

SendMessage and PostMessage

Now that you know how WM_STARTFONTS is declared, you're ready to take a look at PostMessage and SendMessage. These are two of the more interesting API calls. They perform functions that appear to be similar but are actually quite different. As a result, they should occupy separate, but adjacent, living quarters in your imagination.

The basic purpose of both SendMessage and PostMessage is to tell a particular window to perform a task. The SendMessage function does this by explicitly calling the window procedure associated with the HWnd in its parameter list. SendMessage doesn't return from that window procedure until the window has processed the message in question.

The PostMessage function, however, doesn't explicitly call a window procedure. Instead, it posts a message to the application's message queue and immediately returns.

The old 16-bit Windows applications had a message queue that would, by default, handle up to eight messages at a time. WIN32 applications can automatically resize the queue; that is, it will grow or shrink as needed.

Messages are retrieved from the queue by the GetMessage function. If you glance at FontsExp's WinMain function, you can see that after GetMessage is called, a message is passed on to the window procedure with the DispatchMessage function.

What it all boils down to is that SendMessage delivers a message directly to a window procedure, whereas PostMessage just plops a message into a queue. In other words, SendMessage is the express route, and PostMessage is the slower, more laid-back way to deliver the mail. (See Figure 14.7.) SendMessage lets you deliver a message immediately, while PostMessage lets you immediately continue processing the code in the current routine.

FIGURE 14.7

SendMessage *delivers a message directly to a window procedure, whereas* PostMessage *takes a more roundabout route.*

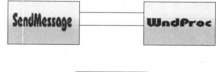
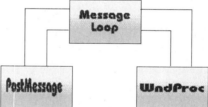

> **NOTE**
>
> Use SendMessage when time is of the essence; that is, when you want to be sure a message is processed before the SendMessage call ends. Don't use SendMessage if you can possibly put off processing the message. Remember that SendMessage won't return until its message has been processed. Don't forget that PostMessage returns immediately, enabling your program to continue on the next line of code, usually well before the message is processed.

In this particular case, FontsExp uses `PostMessage` for two reasons. The first reason is that there is no immediate need to process the message; the second reason is that the creation of the window should end before the WM_STARTFONTS message is processed.

How can FontsExp be sure that the creation of the window will be completed before the message is processed? To understand the reasoning, simply trace through the steps involved in starting a Windows application.

Start the debugger and place a breakpoint at the first call to `CreateWindow`. Next, start stepping through the program from the beginning, after `WinMain` is called. The first step is the call to `RegisterWindow`. Then, there are the calls to `CreateWindow`, `ShowWindow`, `UpdateWindow`, and `GetMessage`.

The WM_STARTFONTS message is posted at the end of a WM_CREATE message handler function. WM_CREATE messages are sent during the call to `CreateWindow`. This means that a window will finish creation, be shown, and be updated before `GetMessage` ever has a chance to pull the WM_STARTFONTS message out of the application queue.

> **NOTE**
>
> Because this book assumes a certain amount of knowledge on the programmer's part, I'm not going to take the time to describe exactly how to use your debugger. If you are not yet familiar with your debugger, you should take the time to learn about it by reading Delphi's documentation.
>
> For most programmers, there is nothing more important than a thorough knowledge of their debugger. You should take the time to get to know that tool, which in Delphi's case is particularly easy because the debugger is built right into the IDE. Specifically, be sure you know how to set breakpoints, how to watch a variable, and how to step through your code one line at a time. Believe me, it will be well worth it. If everything goes wrong, it will take about 30 minutes to learn all these things. On a good day, you can learn them in five minutes. Use the docs!

Here's a step-by-step view of the process that occurs when you first start the FontsExp program:

1. Register the window.
2. Call `CreateWindow`. This is the stage at which a window handles WM_CREATE messages. This is also the stage when the WM_STARTFONTS message is posted.
3. Show and update the window.
4. Start the message loop. It's during this stage that the WM_STARTFONTS message is actually passed on to `WndProc`. The message loop has to be running before any messages can be pulled out of the queue!

That's the end of my introduction to Windows messages. I've discussed this topic in-depth because the whole idea of sending and posting messages is a crucial part of the life of a Windows application. Furthermore, you won't really understand what's being said in the rest of this chapter unless you first understand, at least in general terms, how SendMessage and PostMessage works.

Callbacks: Enumerating the System Fonts

This section of the chapter deals with callbacks, which have the reputation of being rather nasty. I think you will find this reputation is not deserved. What's complicated about Windows is the sheer accumulation of detail. No one particular feature is hard to implement. The developers of Windows always tried to find the simplest possible way to do everything. The problem, of course, is that there are so many different things to do, not that any one of them is particularly difficult.

In the last section, you saw the mail being delivered. You saw the posting of the WM_STARTFONTS message and then saw it through to its address in the WndProc procedure. After the post office has done its job, the next step is to process the message in the body of the WndProc. To follow this with your debugger, place a breakpoint on the beginning of the StartFont handler. Now run the FontsExp program again from the beginning, and continue until you reach the breakpoint in the WM_STARTFONTS handler.

```
procedure StartFont(hWindow: HWnd);
var
  DC: HDC;
  EnumStruct: TEnumStruct;
  S: string;
begin
  DC := GetDC(hWindow);
  EnumStruct.Count := 0;
  EnumStruct.hWindow := hFontList;
  if not EnumFontFamilies(DC, nil, @FontCallBack,
                          LongInt(@EnumStruct)) then
    Exit;
  ReleaseDC(hWindow, DC);

  S := Format('There are %d fonts available', [EnumStruct.Count]);
  SetWindowText(hNumFonts, PChar(S));

  SetFocus(hFontList);
  SendMessage(hFontList, LB_SETCURSEL, 0, 0);
  ShowTheFont(hWindow);
end;
```

The goal of this code is to enumerate through the system fonts. It asks the system: "What fonts do you have available?" The system answers back, "Arial, Times New Roman, Courier" (and so on). This process becomes somewhat complex, primarily because it is Windows (not the FontsExp program) that knows which fonts are available. Therefore, the FontsExp program has to find a way to ask Windows which fonts are available on the system.

The solution is to set up an address for Windows to mail the information to and then to simply wait at that address while Windows iterates through all the available fonts. Each time a font is found, Windows sends a letter to the proper address in FontsExp. It's just like ordering something from the Land's End catalog. You send something in the mail and wait for the goodies to arrive. Anybody can do it. (See Figure 14.8.)

FIGURE 14.8.

FontsExp asks Windows what fonts are available, and Windows sends information back.

The first step is to set up the mailing address, which in this case happens to be a function called FontCallBack. Right now, don't worry about how this function works; just concentrate on the fact that it exists. It's a little post office box with its own address.

To set up the post office, you call EnumFontFamilies and pass it the address of FontCallBack:

```
if not EnumFontFamilies(DC, nil, @FontCallBack,
                        LongInt(@EnumStruct)) then
```

What you are doing here is talking to Windows, telling it that you want to set up a post office called FontCallBack. You say: "Here, Windows, is the address of the place where I want you to send the mail. It's in the third parameter."

> **NOTE**
>
> Calling EnumFontFamilies involves a similar process to the one you went through when you were learning how to set up a DialogBox procedure. All the issues are the same. In particular, the FontCallBack function is part of FontsExp, but it's going to be called by Windows. In the dialog procedure, DialogBox is like EnumFontFamilies, and the dialog procedure is like the FontCallBack function.
>
> Don't forget that in 16-bit Windows, you would have to call MakeProcInstance before calling EnumFontFamilies, just as you had to call it before calling DialogBox.

If, by chance, the last few sentences don't make a great deal of sense to you, you should turn back to the discussion of the DialogBox procedure, and reread that section of the book. The point is that Windows and your program need to agree on the mailing address to which the list of fonts will be delivered, just as Windows and your program had to agree on where the address of the About dialog was located. (Dialogs were discussed in Chapter 10, "Dialogs and Resources.")

Now that you understand the general concept involved, I want to go back over the call to EnumFontFamilies in more detail. The key lines look like this:

```
DC := GetDC(hWindow);
EnumStruct.Count := 0;
EnumStruct.hWindow := hFontList;
if not EnumFontFamilies(DC, nil, @FontCallBack, LongInt(@EnumStruct)) then
  Exit;
ReleaseDC(hWindow, DC);
```

The center of focus is the EnumFontFamilies call, which takes a device context as its first parameter. The HDC is needed because fonts are part of the GDI. The second parameter is the name of a font family, which in this case is set to nil. The third parameter is the address of the callback function, which is the post office box to which information will be sent. The final parameter is the address of some data that you can pass to the FontCallBack function. In many cases, you can set this last parameter to 0. However, I have filled it in here, primarily so you can see how to use it.

> **NOTE**
>
> FontsExp performs a typecast so it can treat a TEnumStruct as a LongInt. It's saying: "As far as you are concerned, we're just delivering a car, but I know that this particular car is a Mustang, and I have to explicitly declare it that way." It's as if the guy who does the trucking just thinks: "Okay, I'm delivering a load of cars. I don't know what make they are and I don't care." However, the dealer who loads his truck knows exactly what kinds of cars are being shipped. He tells his workers: "Go down to the shipping bay and put a Mustang on that truck that's coming in."
>
> In the analogy presented here, the Mustang is a TEnumStruct, and the truck is EnumFontFamiles. EnumFontFamilies doesn't care exactly what kind of 32-bit value you pass in the last parameter; it just wants a 32-bit integer, any 32-bit integer. But the guys who load EnumFontFamilies have to know exactly what kind of 32-bit value is involved. So they load in a TEnumStruct, and then just tell the driver that it's a plain old regular 32-bit value, "just like I'm always loading on your truck."
>
> Remember, the address of a record is a 32-bit value, and it can be treated as if it were an integer, even if it's really an address! Don't just think on the surface level—this book is about what things look like beneath the surface!

```
  if TextMetrics.tmItalic <> 0 then
    SendMessage(ButtonWindows[2], BM_SETCHECK, 1, 0)
  else
    SendMessage(ButtonWindows[2], BM_SETCHECK, 0, 0);
end;
```

Notice that the BM_SETCHECK message always takes 0 as its last parameter. You should set WPARAM to 1 to set the check, and 0 to erase the check. Once again, no one expects you to remember how to use the BM_SETCHECK message. All that's important is that you know it exists and that you know how to look up the information. If remembering all these bits of information comes to you easily, that's fine. But don't waste time struggling to remember all these details. Just know how to look them up when you need them.

The last few calls in ShowTheFont send the information to the two edit controls with the WM_SETTEXT message, which wants a string buffer sent in the last parameter. After sending the text to the control, set the font with the WM_SETFONT message. You'll probably want to take a close look at those two SendMessage calls, because they perform an important task that you might want to utilize in your own programs. Anyway, the FontsExp program wouldn't be nearly as useful, or as much fun, if the text on-screen weren't written in the current font.

Hit Me with the Highlights!

Take a moment to review the steps of the ShowTheFont function (and if possible, follow along with your debugger):

- Query the list box to find the currently selected font name.
- Send the font name to Windows via a call to EnumFontFamilies.
- Wait for Windows to send a TLogFont structure to the DescribeFontCallBack function.
- Use the TLogFont supplied by Windows to create a global font.
- Use the font's TEXTMETRIC to retrieve a few bits of detailed information for the user's perusal.

None of these steps are particularly difficult to perform. You just need to remember what has to be done, and then go about doing it in a logical, straightforward manner.

NOTE

Focus for a moment on just one segment of this process:

- FontsExp calls EnumFontFamilies.
- EnumFontFamilies calls Windows.
- Windows sends information to the callback procedure.

■ The callback function sends a message to the main window.

■ The main window creates a copy of the font.

As you've seen by using the debugger, the logic outlined here is radically different from the sequential programming that goes on in most DOS programs. Messages are flying all over the place, and the instruction pointer is flying from one part of your program to the next.

This is a classic example of what event-oriented programming is all about. Grasp these concepts, cup them in the palms of your hands, and examine them one by one. See how they all fit together and admire their complexity.

Don't waste time trying to decide whether this system is better or worse than the one that is familiar from command-line environments. That's an interesting topic in and of itself, but it's not the theme of this book. For now, concentrate on how Windows does things. It's a fascinating process, and it's not over yet, as you'll see in the next section.

The Return of *ShowTheFont*

Before I close this chapter, I want to turn your attention to the WM_COMMAND message function handler, which receives a message every time the user selects another item from the list box. To follow along with the debugger, set a breakpoint on the ShowTheFont function of FontExp_OnCommand:

```
procedure FontsExp_OnCommand(hWindow: HWnd; var Msg: TWMCommand);
var
  S: string;
begin
  case Msg.ItemID of
    ID_LISTBOX:
      if Msg.NotifyCode = LBN_SELCHANGE then
        ShowTheFont(hWindow);

    CM_INFO: begin
      S := GetFontString(S, TextMetrics, TextFace);
      MessageBox(hWindow, PChar(S), 'Info', MB_OK);
    end;
  end;
end;
```

This code uses the TWMCommand structure from MESSAGES.PAS:

```
TWMCommand = record
  Msg: Cardinal;
  ItemID: Word;
  NotifyCode: Word;
  Ctl: HWND;
  Result: Longint;
end;
```

The code checks to see whether the `ItemID` field is set to `ID_LISTBOX` and whether the message being sent signifies that the selection in the list box has changed. If both statements are true, `ShowTheFont` is called. As mentioned, `ShowTheFont` knows how to set the controls in the window to exhibit an example and a description of the current font.

It's quite typical of Windows to make it so very easy to find out whether a selection has changed in a list box. Information about things the user has done almost always comes to you free of charge, courtesy of the people at Microsoft. However, it's also typical of Windows to make it fairly difficult for you to send information back to the user. Windows is such an ornate and powerful tool that creating an effective interface can sometimes be a little bit tricky, which is where the RAD tools come in.

Finally, you should notice that this program calls the `GetFontString` function in FONTSTR.PAS. This function displays additional information about the current font.

GetTextMetrics and the *FontStr* Module

When you create a font, you usually fill out a TLogFont (or its equivalent fields) in a `CreateFontIndirect` call. You need to perform this operation in reverse when getting this information back from the system.

To reverse the process, call `GetObject`, and pass the handle to a font in the first parameter, the size of a logfont structure in the second parameter, and a logfont structure in the third parameter. This will enable you to retrieve a logfont structure when all you have to start with is the handle to the font.

Windows also provides detailed information about the current font through the `GetTextMetrics` call, and the `TTextMetric` structure that it retrieves. The `TTextMetric` structure tells you how big the font is, whether it's underlined or italicized, what pitch and family it has, and so on.

Not to be outdone by the `TLogFont` structure, the `TTextMetric` structure includes no less than 20 fields! This proliferation of minutiae enables you to learn more than you most likely ever wanted to know about the current font:

```
TTextMetricA = packed record
  tmHeight: Longint;
  tmAscent: Longint;
  tmDescent: Longint;
  tmInternalLeading: Longint;
  tmExternalLeading: Longint;
  tmAveCharWidth: Longint;
  tmMaxCharWidth: Longint;
  tmWeight: Longint;
  tmOverhang: Longint;
  tmDigitizedAspectX: Longint;
  tmDigitizedAspectY: Longint;
  tmFirstChar: AnsiChar;
  tmLastChar: AnsiChar;
  tmDefaultChar: AnsiChar;
```

```
    tmBreakChar: AnsiChar;
    tmItalic: Byte;
    tmUnderlined: Byte;
    tmStruckOut: Byte;
    tmPitchAndFamily: Byte;
    tmCharSet: Byte;
  end;
  TTextMetric = TTextMetricA;
```

SimpFont wrestles with the TTextMetric structure in an isolated module called FontStr. FontStr returns most of the TTextMetric fields in a single string. This module is designed so it can be easily linked to another program, in case you have use for it. (Always strive for reuse. Reuse is arguably even better than optimization.)

The core of FontStr is the GetFontString function. It contains the following straightforward, but lengthy, call to Format:

```
TheFaceName := FaceName;              // Facename had its length set to 250
Len := StrLen(PChar(FaceName));       // We have to shorten the string
SetLength(TheFaceName, Len);          // To use it with Format!!!

GetType(szType);
GetFamily(szFamily);
GetCharSet(szCharSet);

S := Format('Font: %s ' + #13 +
            'Height: %d ' + #13 +
            'Ascent: %d ' + #13 +
            'Descent: %d ' + #13 +
            'AveCharW: %d ' + #13 + 'MaxCharW: %d ' + #13 +
            'Weight: %d ' + #13 + 'Italic: %d ' + #13 +
            'Underlined: %d ' + #13 + '%s ' + #13 +
            '%s ' + #13 + '%s ',
            [TheFaceName,
             TextMetrics.tmHeight,
             TextMetrics.tmAscent,
             TextMetrics.tmDescent,
             TextMetrics.tmAveCharWidth,
             TextMetrics.tmMaxCharWidth,
             TextMetrics.tmWeight,
             TextMetrics.tmItalic,
             TextMetrics.tmUnderlined,
             szType, szFamily, szCharSet]);

Result := S;
```

As you can see from Figure 14.11, most of the information from the TEXTMETRIC structure is transferred into a single string. This string is returned to the WM_COMMAND handler function in the program's main module and displayed through a call to the MessageBox function:

```
S := GetFontString(S, TextMetrics, TextFace);
MessageBox(hWindow, PChar(S), 'Info', MB_OK);
```

GetFontString is the only function in the FontStr module that is made global so it can be accessed from other modules.

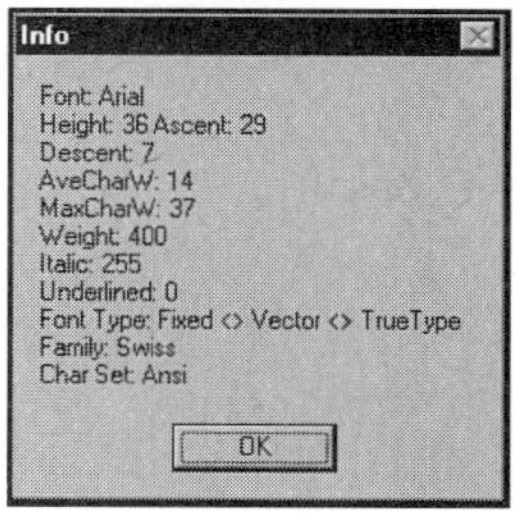

FIGURE 14.11.

The SimpFont program pops up a message box relating important information about the currently selected font.

The parts of the FontStr module described so far are fairly straightforward. The tricky sections involve deciphering the contents of the tmPitchAndFamily and the tmCharSet fields:

- The four low-order bits of tmPitchAndFamily describe the type of font, which can be one of the following values:

TMPF_FIXED_PITCH	A fixed-pitch font
TMPF_VECTOR	A vector font
TMPF_TRUETYPE	A TrueType font
TMPF_DEVICE	A device font

  Many times, a font combines one or more of these values.

- The four high-order bits can be ANDed together with the hexadecimal value $F0 and then used to determine the current font family. Common font families include Roman, Swiss, Script, and Modern.

- The tmCharSet field is set to one of the following values:

ANSI_CHARSET	0
DEFAULT_CHARSET	1
SYMBOL_CHARSET	2
SHIFTJIS_CHARSET	128
OEM_CHARSET	255

Extracting this information from a TEXTMETRIC structure is the job of the following functions, all found in the FontStr module:

```
function GetType(var S: string): string;
function GetFamily(var S: string): string;
function GeTCharSet(var S: string): string;
```

The GetType function uses BitWise operations to find the current font type. The GetFamily function uses the hex value F0 to determine the font family, and the GetCharSet functions retrieves the current CharSet. If you want to understand these functions in-depth, you should crank up the debugger and start stepping through them one line at a time.

> **NOTE**
>
> Although SimpFont doesn't use it, I should probably also mention the `GetDeviceCaps` routine. It enables you to ask Windows what capabilities are associated with a particular device, such as a video screen or printer. You can use this function to discover whether the device can, for instance, print very large fonts, clip fonts, or stroked fonts.
>
> You should keep both the `GetDeviceCaps` and `GetTextMetrics` functions in mind, because no serious work with fonts can be conducted without them.

Summary

In this chapter, you've had a chance to become acquainted with Windows controls. You have seen that these tools can be used to form an interactive interface between your program and a user.

This chapter covers the creation of four controls:

- Static controls
- List boxes
- Check boxes
- Edit controls

This is an incomplete, but representative, selection of Windows controls. The information presented here should be enough to allow you to start working with any type of control, even the new Windows 95 controls.

When creating window controls, the most important step is to fill in the first field of `CreateWindow`, called `lpszClassName`, with the class name of a control. For instance, if you want to create an edit control, copy the word *edit* into `lpszClassName`. Other controls are created by copying in one of the following words: *static, scrollbar, list box,* or *button.*

This chapter also presents an in-depth discussion of the various styles used to define the behavior of a control. For instance, you have seen that the `ES_CENTER` style centers text in an edit control and the `BS_CHECKBOX` style converts an ordinary button into a check box.

All in all, this chapter covers a lot of ground. You've learned about communicating with static controls, list boxes, check boxes, and edit controls. You've had another look at fonts and learned how to put them at your absolute beck and call with the `EnumFontFamilies` and `GetTextMetrics` calls.

By now you should be getting the sense that you have the ability to completely control your presentation of textual materials. You know all about TLogFonts, TTextMetrics, and the `EnumFontFamilies` callbacks. This knowledge should help you begin to understand how Windows is put together.

Once again, the point of this chapter is not to suggest an alternative to the RAD tools that ship with Delphi. This information is meant to help you understand the RAD tools, to help you extend them so they do exactly what you want, and to help you create new components of your own. However, there is one virtue to the code in this chapter that does not cling to the VCL. The FontsExp program is 33 KB in size. Its much smaller than a similar program built in the VCL.

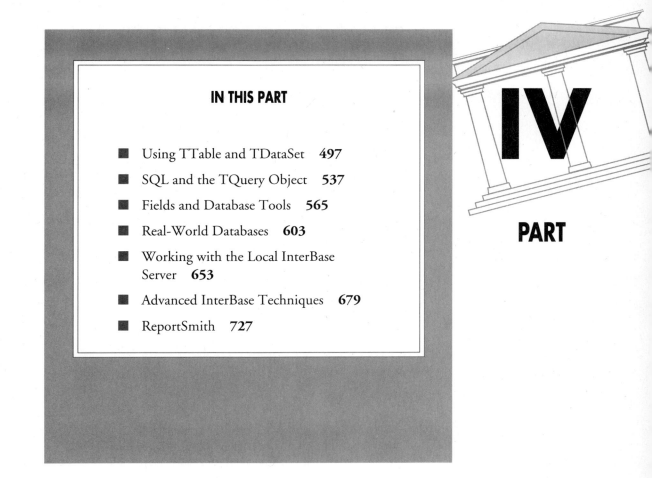

PART

IV

Databases

The fourth part of this book is about databases. After the theoretical issues explored in Parts II and III, these chapters help to ground the book in more concrete examples of how to perform specific tasks. This is similar to a how-to section of the book. It explores new features of Delphi, such as data modules, data dictionaries, lookups, filters, cached updates, and the new grids and multi-record objects. On a more theoretical note, the database material also explores what it means to create a relational database and how Delphi's tools can be used to design and construct relational databases. The last chapter in this section, written by Andy Fears, takes a highly professional, in-depth look at ReportSmith.

Using TTable and TDataSet

15

In this chapter, you learn some of the basics about accessing database tables. In the examples given here, you will be explicitly working with local Paradox tables, but nearly everything explained here applies equally to dBase files or to files located on a server.

If you are already familiar with the Delphi 1.0 database tools, you still might want to read this chapter in order to learn about the TDataModule, the Object Repository, the Database Explorer, and a new method for filtering on non-keyed fields. There is also a new and much easier technique for accessing fields by name.

Looking a little more deeply at the content of this chapter, you can expect to find information on the following:

- The TTable object, which provides the fastest and simplest access to tables.
- The TQuery object, which is the gateway to the flexible and powerful world of SQL.
- The TDataSet object, an ancestor of TTable and TQuery, which provides the core functionality for accessing tables and the records that lie within them.
- The TField object, which gives you access to the fields in a table or dataset. This object has powerful descendants such as TStringField and TIntegerField, all of which can be created automatically by a visual tool called the Fields Editor.
- The TDataSource object, which serves as an intermediary between data-aware controls and the TTable and TQuery objects.
- The TDBGrid object, which provides a simple and easy way to display the contents of tables to the user. TDBGrid objects support editing, deletion, and insertion. They also have support for dropdown lists in lookup fields and the ability to assign colors to a column.
- The TDBEdit component, which enables you to display a single field from a single record and to edit or insert the contents of that field.

Here is a second way to categorize the objects listed:

- Nonvisual: TTable, TQuery, TDataSet, TField
- Visual: TDBGrid, TDBEdit
- Link (also nonvisual): TDataSource

This latter view of the major database components breaks them down into two major categories. The nonvisual components enable you to open, close, edit, and otherwise manipulate tables, records, and fields. The visual components display the tables to the user and enable the user to edit them. The powerful TDataSource object forms a link between the visual and nonvisual database controls.

This chapter also discusses the TDataModule object, which enables you to place nonvisual components, and particularly nonvisual database components, on a special window designed for this purpose. This window can be stored in an object repository and can be used to specify business rules that can be reused by a wide range of projects and programmers.

The overriding purpose of this chapter is to give you a good overview of the basic facts about using a Delphi database component called TDataSet. TDataSet is the driving force behind both the TTable and TQuery objects.

Specific information about other database issues will be presented in subsequent chapters. For instance, the TQuery object will be treated in depth in the next chapter, and a more detailed explanation of TDBGrid, TField, TStringField, and TIntegerField is found in Chapter 17, "Fields and Database Tools."

Database Basics

To create a simple database application, start by placing a TTable, a TDataSource, and a TDBGrid component on a form, as shown in Figure 15.1.

FIGURE 15.1.

TTable, TDataSource, and TDBGrid arranged on a form.

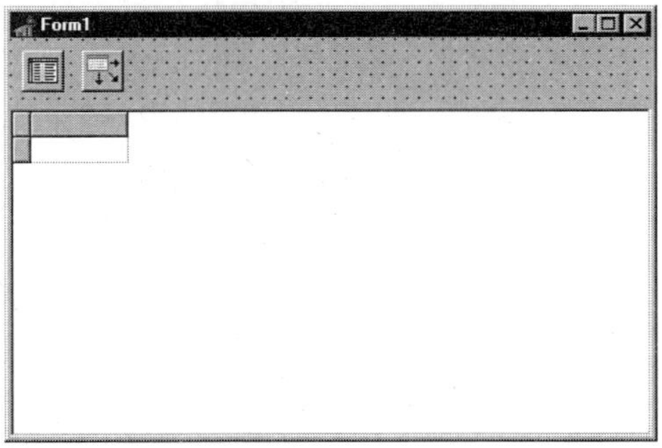

Wire these three controls together by completing the following simple steps:

1. Connect the DataSource property of the TDBGrid to DataSource1.
2. Connect the DataSet property of the TDataSource control to Table1.

After completion of these steps, the three components are hooked together and can communicate with one another.

Connecting the TTable object to a table that resides on disk is a three-step process:

1. Set the DatabaseName property either to a valid alias or to the subdirectory where your data resides. In this case, you can set the DatabaseName property to the DBDEMOS alias, which is created by default during Delphi's installation. Alternatively, you could type c:\delphi32\demos\data into the DatabaseName Property Editor, where you might need to change some aspects of this path to fit the needs of your system.
2. Set the TableName property to the name of the table you want to view; for instance, you might choose the CUSTOMER.DB table. The Property Editor drops down a list of available tables, so there is no need for you to type anything.

3. Set the Active property, found at the very top of the Object Inspector, to True. (See Figure 15.2 for the Object Inspector.)

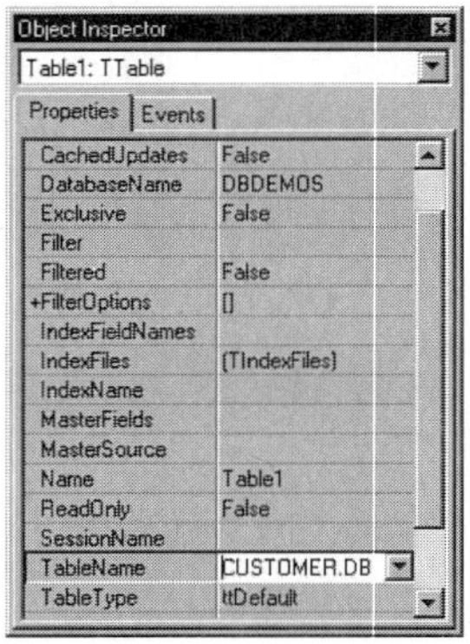

FIGURE 15.2.

The Object Inspector after connecting to a table called Customer, using an alias called DBDEMOS.

If you have completed all these steps properly, you should now be looking at the data from the table you chose, as shown in Figure 15.3. To take this process one step further, you can compile and run the program, and then begin browsing and editing your data.

FIGURE 15.3.

Simple form displaying the contents of CUSTOMER.DB.

If you want to simplify the task of browsing through the data in your application, you can go back into design mode and add the TDBNavigator control to the program described earlier. To hook this control into the loop, all you need to do is set its DataSource property to DataSource1. Now you can run the program and begin iterating through the records with the navigator, as shown in Figure 15.4. In Figure 15.4, most of the functionality of the dbNavigator has been turned off by manipulating the VisibleButtons property. For instance, a navigator can automatically enable you to edit, insert, delete, post, cancel, and refresh. All of those capabilities have been disabled and hidden in the form shown here.

FIGURE 15.4.

*A simple database program
with a TDBNavigator
control.*

CustNo	Company	Addr1
1221	Kauai Dive Shoppe	4-976 Sugarloaf Hwy
1231	Unisco	PO Box Z-547
1351	Sight Diver	1 Neptune Lane
1354	Cayman Divers World Unlimited	PO Box 541
1356	Tom Sawyer Diving Centre	632-1 Third Frydenhoj
1380	Blue Jack Aqua Center	23-738 Paddington Lane
1384	VIP Divers Club	32 Main St.
1510	Ocean Paradise	PO Box 8745
1513	Fantastique Aquatica	Z32 999 #12A-77 A.A.
1551	Marmot Divers Club	872 Queen St.

The DataModule

In the previous example, you placed a TTable and TDataSource component on the same form
with your visual components. When you ran the program, the icons representing these
components disappeared. However, they are visible at design time and have a tendency to clutter
up the form. In order to eliminate this clutter, the 32-bit version of Delphi has a new component
called a TDataModule, which can be used to store nonvisual controls such as TTable and
TDataSource.

To get started working with TDataModules, first start a new application. Now choose File |
New and select the DataModule component from the New page of the New Items dialog, as
shown in Figure 15.5.

FIGURE 15.5.

*Selecting the TDataModule
component from the New
Items dialog.*

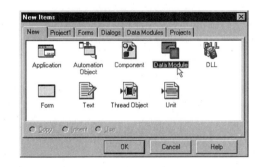

NOTE

I'm calling the TDataModule a component because it is a direct descendant of
TComponent. When you first see a TDataModule object, there is a tendency to view it
as merely a special kind of form, which is, to some degree, true. However, the
hierarchy for a TForm component looks like this:

```
-TComponent
-TControl
-TWinControl
-TScrollingWinControl
-TForm
```

The hierarchy for a TDataModule, on the other hand, looks like this:

```
-TComponent
-TDataModule
```

Clearly, TForms and TDataModules are two very different beasts, despite some apparent similarities between them.

If you have the source to the VCL, the TDataModule object is found in FORMS.PAS.

After adding a TDataModule object to your application, click Form1, open the File menu, and choose the Use Unit menu option. In the Use Unit dialog, select Unit2 and press OK. This is a simple way of automatically inserting a line into the uses clause of Unit1. In particular, the following changes are made to your code:

```
implementation

uses Unit2;  // This is the new line added by Use Unit dialog.

{$R *.DFM}

end.
```

Arrange Form1 and DataModule2 on the screen so you can view them both at the same time. Drop a TTable and TDataSource component on the datamodule, as shown in Figure 15.6.

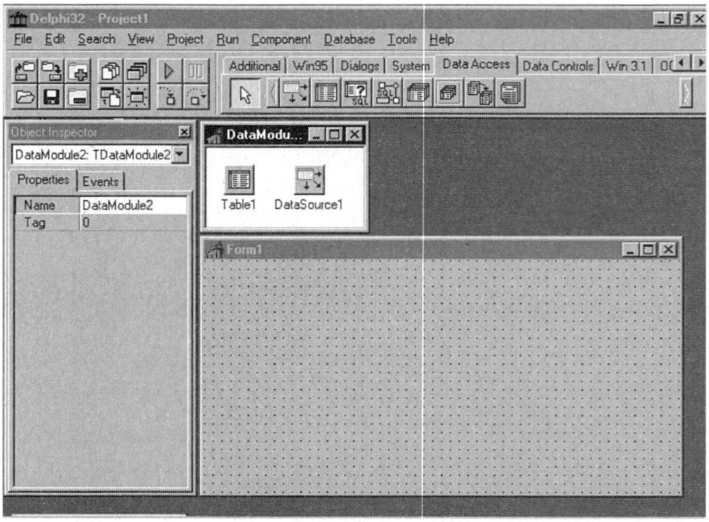

FIGURE 15.6.

Form1 and DataModule2 arranged on the screen so that you can easily view them both at the same time.

Wire the TDataSource to the TTable object, and set the `DatabaseName` of the TTable object to DBDEMOS and the TableName to BioLife. Set the `Active` property of the TTable object to `True`.

Right-click the TTable object and bring up the Fields Editor. Right-click the Fields Editor, and bring up the AddFields dialog. Make sure all the fields in the dialog are selected, which is the default behavior for the tool. Click the OK button.

The Fields Editor now contains a list of all the fields in the BioLife table. To add these files to your form, simply click one or more fields, hold the left mouse button down, and drag them onto the form. For instance, select the Graphic field, making sure that it is the only one highlighted. Now drag it onto the form. When you release the left mouse button, this graphics field will automatically display itself in a TDBImage component. Drag over several other fields, and create a form that looks something like the image in Figure 15.7.

FIGURE 15.7.

Some of the fields of the BioLife table arranged in visual controls on a TForm object.

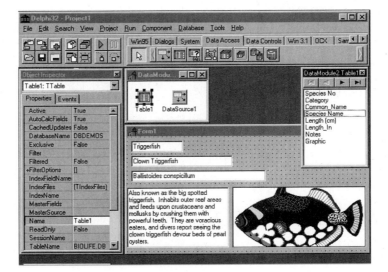

The Object Repository

The simplest way to introduce you to the Object Repository is to just lead you step by step through the process of using it. After you have seen how it works, then I will take a moment to explain its significance.

Save the program you created in the last section. Save Unit1 as Main, Unit2 as DataInfo, and the project file as Test1. Select the datamodule, and use the Object Inspector to rename it from DataModule2 to DataInfo. Right-click the datamodule and select Add To Repository. Fill in the Add To Repository dialog by setting the Title, Description, and Author fields as you see fit. In the Page dropdown combo, select DataModules. Use the Browse button to select an icon from the ..Delphi32\images\icon subdirectory, or from any place else where you might have some icons stored.

Start a new project. Choose File | New. This time, instead of choosing the DataModule component from the New page, select the DataModules page and choose the DataInfo component that you just finished creating. When it appears on the screen, you will see that it contains a TTable and TDataSource component. The components are wired together, and the TTable object is set to the BioLife table with its `Active` property set to `True`.

To access this table from Form1, you must first employ the Use Unit menu option from the File menu to add Unit2 to the uses clause in Unit1. Go to the DataControls page of the Component Palette, and drop down a TDBGrid object on Form1. In the Object Inspector, dropdown the `DataSource` property of the TDBGrid object, and you will see the TDataSource object from the DataInfo module listed. Select this item, and the grid will automatically fill up with data.

If you drop down a TDBEdit control instead of a TDBGrid control, then you proceed the same way, except that you will need to fill in not only the `DataSource` property in the Object Inspector, but also the `DataField` property. There is no need to type information into the `DataField` property because it will automatically contain a list of the available fields in the BioLife table.

> **NOTE**
>
> The whole point of adding Unit2 to the uses clause of Unit1 is so that you can access the components in Unit2 from Form1. For instance, if you did not have Unit2 listed in Unit1's uses clause, then you would find the `DataSource` property of the TDBGrid object empty when you dropped it down to search for a TDataSource component.
>
> Of course, you don't have to do things manually. Instead, you can use the Fields Editor to drag and drop objects from the datamodule onto Form1, as described earlier. What I've done here is show you two different techniques for hooking up Form1 and the datamodule. In practice, you will probably sometimes use the drag-and-drop technique and sometimes manually hook the visual tools to the datasource.

The true significance of the object repository is only hinted at by this example. The importance of this tool is made more obvious if you have six or seven tables dropped onto a datamodule. You might then define several relationships between the tables and add other related code. For instance, you might have some one-to-many relationships established, possibly a many-to-many relationship established, and you might have several filters, lookups, and several calculated fields defined.

Altogether, a datamodule of this type might encapsulate several sets of business rules defining exactly how tables should be accessed and how they relate to each other. The ability to save all this work in the Repository, and to then automatically reuse it in multiple projects, is extremely valuable. I am, however, getting ahead of myself. Discussions of filters, lookups, calculated fields, and other database issues will occur in various places over the next few chapters.

The Database Explorer

In addition to the datamodule, another key tool to use when working with databases is the Database Explorer. You can access the Database Explorer by choosing the Database | Explore menu item. The Explorer is a stand-alone executable, so you can also access it from the Windows Start button on the TaskBar. You can use the Explorer even if Delphi is not running.

Once you have loaded the Explorer, make sure you have selected the Databases page and not the Dictionary page. Click the DBDEMOS node to expose the Tables node. Now click the little plus sign before the Tables node. A list of all the tables in the database will appear. Select the BioLife table and choose the Data page to view the contents of the table, as shown in Figure 15.8.

FIGURE 15.8.

Exploring the BioLife table in the Database Explorer.

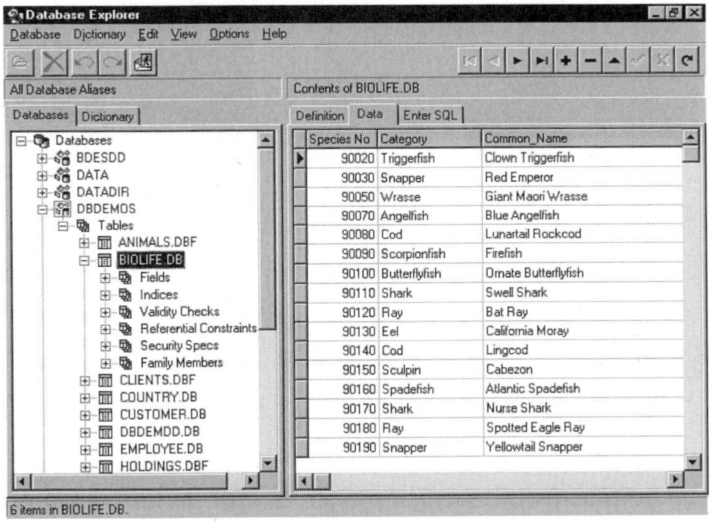

Click the little plus symbol in front of the BIOLIFE.DB node, and you will see a list of properties for the BioLife table. The properties listed are Fields, Indices, Validity Checks, Referential Constraints, Security Specs, and Family Members. You can expand each of these nodes to view their properties. For instance, if you select the Fields node, you will see a list of all the fields in the table. As you select each individual field, you will see a description of its primary characteristics.

The Database Explorer is a fairly complex tool with a number of powerful traits, many of which will undoubtedly be expanded in future versions of the product. In particular, you should note that it contains a DataDictionary, and that it enables you to define a new alias or to modify existing aliases. Chapter 17, "Fields and Database Tools," examines the Explorer in more depth.

At this stage, I want to show you only one key trait of the Database Explorer. Arrange your screen so you can view both the Explorer and Form1 at the same time. Select the BioLife table in the Explorer with the mouse, and then drag and drop it onto Form1. If you want, you can experiment further by expanding the BioLife node in the Explorer and dragging and dropping individual fields of the table onto Form1, just as you did when using the Fields Editor.

If you start a new application, and then drag and drop the BioLife table onto Form1 from the Explorer, you will find that the TTable and TDataSource objects are placed on Form1. If you want to move them off the form, you can add a TDataModule object to the project, and then select both the TTable and TDataSource objects and choose Edit | Cut from the menu. Now select the TDataModule object and choose Edit | Paste. Make sure the uses clause for Form1 contains a reference to the unit that contains the TDataModule, and then hook up the grid to the TDataSource object in the TDataModule. This sounds like a fairly complicated process when written out, but you can perform this task in just a few seconds using Delphi's visual tools.

> **NOTE**
>
> Dragging a table from the Explorer onto a form is one of the fastest ways to get access to a table. When I need to get data quickly and easily, this is the technique I prefer to use. The viability of this method, will, of course, depend a little on the power of the machine you are currently using. If it takes a long time for the Database Explorer to launch itself into memory, then this technique will be less appealing.
>
> You can also drag a table from the Explorer directly onto a TDataModule. You may get a message that its not being legal to add controls to a TDataModule, but the operation should still succeed.

Once again, the last few paragraphs have done nothing more than introduce you to the Database Explorer. This is a complex tool that will prove useful to you in many different ways, some of which might not even have been apparent to its creator. For now, the key point to grasp about it is that it gives you an overview of all the data in a database and enables you to drag and drop fields and tables onto your forms.

Understanding the TDataSet Class

Now that you have had an introduction to using the Database Explorer, and TDataModule, it is time to start digging into some of the technical details of the TTable object. Learning something about these details will go a long way towards helping you understand the structure of the database tools supplied by Delphi.

TTable and TQuery inherit most of their functionality from TDataSet. As a result, the TDataSet class is one of the most important database objects. To get started working with it, you need to concentrate on the following hierarchy:

```
TDataSet
    |
   TDBDataSet
    |
   / \
TTable  TQuery
```

TDataSet contains the abstractions needed to directly manipulate a table. TDBDataSet knows how to handle passwords and other tasks directly associated with linking to a specific table. TTable knows how to handle indices and the specific chores associated with linking two tables in a one-to-many relationship. As you will see in the next chapter, TQuery has specific knowledge of how to process SQL statements.

The methods of the TDataSet object enable you to open and navigate through a table. Of course, you will never directly instantiate an object of type TDataSet. Instead, you will usually be working with TTable, TQuery, or some other descendant of TDataSet. The exact way this system works, and the precise significance of TDataSet, will become clear as you read through this chapter.

On the most fundamental level, a dataset is nothing more than a set of records, as depicted in Figure 15.9.

FIGURE 15.9.

A dataset consists of series of records, each containing X number of fields and a pointer to the current record.

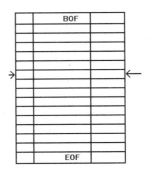

On many occasions, a dataset has a direct, one-to-one correspondence with a physical table that exists on disk. However, at other times, you may perform a query or other action that returns a dataset that contains either a subset of one table, or else a join between multiple tables. The text that follows, however, sometimes uses the terms dataset and table interchangeably if it helps to simplify the explanation of a particular concept.

You will normally instantiate an object of type TTable or TQuery in order to access the functionality of TDataSet. Because of this relationship, the code in the next few sections will always assume the existence of an instance of class TTable called Table1. Remember, however, that the functions under discussion are part of TDataSet, unless the text specifically states otherwise.

It's now time for you to begin a direct exploration of TDataSet. As you become familiar with its capabilities, you will begin to understand exactly how Delphi accesses the raw data saved to disk as a database. The key point to remember is that nearly every time a Delphi programmer opens a table, he or she will be using a class such as TTable or TQuery, which are merely thin wrappers around TDataSet.

Opening and Closing Datasets

The simplest thing you can do with a TDataSet is open or close it. This is therefore an appropriate starting point for an exploration of datasets. In the sections that follow, you will drill down deeper and learn more about the thorough access to databases provided by Delphi.

If you are writing code rather than working through the Object Inspector, there are two different ways to open or close a dataset. You can write the following line of code:

```
Table1.Open;
```

Or, if you prefer, you can set the Active property equal to True:

```
Table1.Active := True;
```

There is no difference between the effects produced by these two statements. Open, however, ends up setting Active to True, so it may be ever so slightly more efficient to use the Active property directly.

Just as there are two ways to open a table, there are two ways to close a table. The simplest way is to call Close:

```
Table1.Close;
```

Or, if you want, you can write:

```
Table1.Active := False;
```

Once again, there is no substantial difference between these two calls. You should note, however, that Close and Open are procedures, but Active is a property.

You should also know about the TDatabase object, which exists primarily to give you a means of staying connected to a database even if you are continually opening and closing a series of tables. If you use TDatabase, you can be connected to Oracle, InterBase, or other servers without ever opening any tables. You can then begin opening and closing tables over and over without having to incur the overhead of connecting to the database each time you call Open.

The TDatabase object also enables you to start server-based applications without specifying a password, and it gives you access to transactions. For further information on TDataBase, see the TRANSACTS program, which is discussed at the end of Chapter 19, "Working with the Local InterBase Server."

In this section, you have learned about two methods:

```
procedure Open;
```

```
procedure Close;
```

You also learned about one property:

```
property Active;
```

You also learned about the TDatabase object, which can be used to optimize code that is continually connecting and disconnecting from tables that belong to one database.

Navigational Routines

After opening a dataset, the next step is to learn how to move about inside it. The following rich set of methods and properties from TDataSet provides all the tools you need to access any particular record inside a dataset:

```
procedure First;
procedure Last;
procedure Next;
procedure Prior;
property BOF: Boolean read FBOF;
property EOF: Boolean read FEOF;
procedure MoveBy(Distance: Integer);
```

Experienced programmers will find these procedures very easy to use. Here is a quick overview of their functionality:

- Calling `Table1.First` moves you to the first record in a table.
- `Table1.Last` moves you to the last record.
- `Table1.Next` moves you one record forward, unless you are at the end of a table.
- `Table1.Prior` moves you one record back, unless you are at the beginning of the table.
- You can check the `BOF` or `EOF` properties in order to see if you are at the beginning or the end of a table.
- The `MoveBy` procedure moves x number of records forward or backward in a table. There is no functional difference between calling `Table1.Next` and calling `Table1.MoveBy(1)`. Furthermore, calling `Table1.Prior` has the same effect as calling `Table1.MoveBy(-1)`. In fact, `Next` and `Prior` are one-line procedures that call `MoveBy`, exactly as shown here.

Most of these properties and methods are demonstrated in the example program found on the CD accompanying this book as NAVY.DPR. You can open this example directly, or construct it piece-by-piece by following the description that follows.

To get started using these navigational routines, you should:

1. Place a TTable, TDataSource, and TDBGrid on a form.

2. Hook the grid to the datasource and the datasource to the table.

3. Set the `DatabaseName` property of the table to the `DBDEMOS` alias, or type in the path to the demos subdirectory (`..\delphi 2.0\demos\data`).

4. Set the `TableName` property to the CUSTOMER table.

If you are having trouble completing these steps refer to NAVY.DPR, which comes on the CD that accompanies this book.

If you run a program that contains a TDBGrid control, you will find that you can iterate through the records in a dataset by manipulating the scrollbars on the edges of the grid. You can gain the same functionality by using the TDBNavigator component. However, there are times when you want to move through a table programmatically, without the use of the built-in visual tools. The next few paragraphs explain how this process works.

Place two buttons on a form and label them Next and Prior, as shown in Figure 15.10.

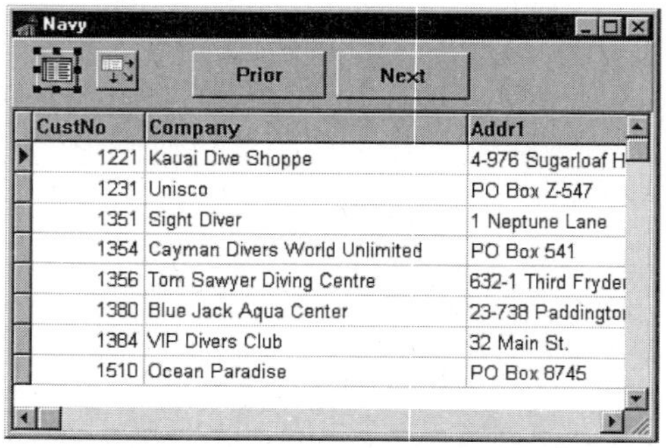

FIGURE 15.10.

The Prior and Next buttons in NAVY.DPR enable you to maneuver through a database.

Double-click once on the Next button to create an `OnClick` method, and fill it in like this:

```
procedure TForm1.bNextClick(Sender: TObject);
begin
  Table1.Next;
end;
```

Perform the same action with the Prior button, so that the function associated with it looks like this:

```
procedure TForm1.bPriorClick(Sender: TObject);
begin
  Table1.Prior;
end;
```

Now run the program and click the two buttons. You will find that they easily let you iterate through the records in a dataset.

Now drop down two more buttons and label them First and Last, as shown in Figure 15.11.

FIGURE 15.11.

The Navy program with all four buttons inserted.

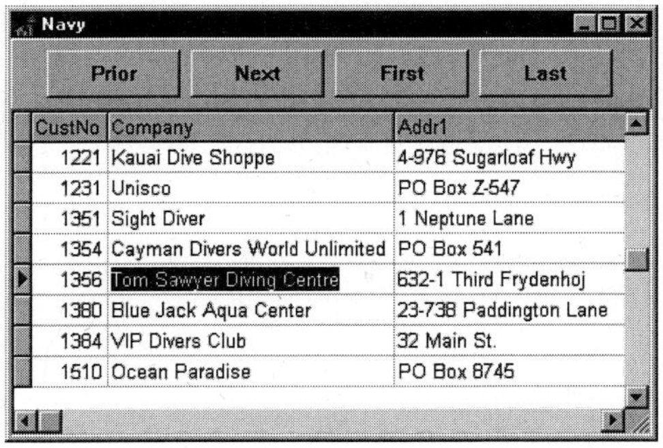

Proceed to do the same thing for the calls to Table1.First and Table1.Last as you did with Next and Prior:

```
procedure TForm1.bFirstClick(Sender: TObject);
begin
  Table1.First;
end;

procedure TForm1.bLastClick(Sender: TObject);
begin
  Table1.Last;
end;
```

Nothing could be more straightforward than these navigational functions. First takes you to the beginning of a dataset, Last takes you to the end, and the Next and Prior functions move you one record forward or backward.

Checking for the End or Beginning of a DataSet

TDataSet.BOF is a read-only Boolean property used to check whether you are at the beginning of a dataset. The BOF property returns True on three occasions:

- After you first open a file
- After you call TDataSet.First
- After a call to Prior fails

The first two items listed should be obvious. Specifically, when you open a dataset, Delphi places you on the first record, and when you call First, Delphi again moves you to the beginning of the dataset. The third item, however, requires a little more explanation: after you have called Prior enough times to get to the beginning of a file, and have then tried one more time and found that the call failed, BOF will return True.

The following code shows a very common method for using `Prior` to get to the beginning of a file:

```
while not Table1.BOF do begin
  DoSomething;
  Table1.Prior;.
end;
```

In the code shown here, the hypothetical function `DoSomething` is called on the current record and then on every other record between the current location and the beginning of the dataset. The loop continues until a call to `Table1.Prior` fails to move you back any further in the table. At that point `BOF` returns `True`, and the program breaks out of the loop.

To optimize the code, set `DataSource1.Enabled` to `False` before beginning the loop, and then reset it to `True` after the loop is finished. These two lines of code allow you to iterate through the table without having to update the visual tools at the same time.

Everything said previously about `BOF` also applies to `EOF`. In other words, the code that follows provides a simple means of iterating over all the records in a dataset:

```
Table1.First;
while not Table1.EOF do begin
  DoSomething;
  Table1.Next;
end;
```

The classic error in cases like this is to enter into a `while` or `repeat` loop but to forget to call `Table1.Next`:

```
Table1.First;
repeat
  DoSomething;
until Table1.EOF;
```

If you accidentally wrote code like this, your machine would appear to lock up. You could break out of the loop only by hitting Ctrl+Alt+Del and asking Windows to kill the current process. Also, this code could cause problems if you opened an empty table. Because the code uses a `repeat` loop, `DoSomething` would still be called once, even though there was nothing to process. As a result, it's better to use `while` loops rather than `repeat` loops in situations like this.

`EOF` returns `True` in the following three cases:

- If you open an empty dataset
- If you call `Table1.Last`
- If a call to `Table1.Next` fails

The last navigational routine that I want to cover is called `MoveBy`. `MoveBy` enables you to move *X* number of records forward or backward in a dataset. If you want to move two records forward, you would write:

```
MoveBy(2);
```

And if you wanted to move two records backward, you would write:

```
MoveBy(-2)
```

When using this function, you should always remember that when you are working on a network, datasets are fluid entities, and the record that was five records back a moment ago may now be back four records, or six records, or who knows how many records. In other words, when you are on a network, someone on another machine may delete or add records to your database at any time. If that happens, `MoveBy` might not work exactly as you expect. One solution to this "fluidity" problem is to use the Bookmark functions mentioned later in this chapter.

> **NOTE**
>
> `Prior` and `Next` are simple one-line functions that call `MoveBy`. If you have the source, look up TDataSet.Next in DB.PAS. The TDataSet object is a beautifully written wrapper around the core functionality in the BDE.

After reading the last two sections, you should have a good feeling for how to move around in a dataset. The navigational commands you have been learning about are very easy to use, but it is essential that you understand them because they are likely to be part of your day-to-day Delphi programming experience.

Fields

On most occasions when you want to programmatically access the individual fields of a record, you can use one of the following properties or methods, all of which belong to TDataSet:

```
property Fields[Index: Integer];
function FieldByName(const FieldName: string): TField;
property FieldCount;
Table1['MyField'];
```

The Fields object also has a number of useful descendant classes with names such as TStringField and TIntegerField. These child objects are discussed in Chapter 17, "Fields and Database Tools."

The `FieldCount` property returns an integer that specifies the number of fields in the current record structure. If you wanted a programmatic way to read the names of these fields, you could use the `Fields` property:

```
var
  S: String;
begin
  S := Table1.Fields[0].FieldName;
end;
```

If you were working with a record with a first field called CustNo, the code shown would put the string "CustNo" in the variable S. If you wanted to access the name of the second field in the example, you could write:

```
S := Table1.Fields[1].FieldName;
```

In short, the index passed to Fields is zero-based, and it specifies the number of the field you want to access, where the first field is number zero, the second is referenced by the number one, and so on.

If you want to find out the current contents of a particular field from a particular record, you can use the Fields or FieldByName property, or you could access the entire table as an array of fields. To find the value of the first field of a record, index into the first element of the Fields array:

```
S := Table1.Fields[0].AsString;
```

Assuming that the first field in a record contains a customer number, the code shown would return a string such as '1021', '1031', or '2058'. If you wanted to access this variable as an integer value, you could use AsInteger in place of AsString. Similar properties of Fields include AsBoolean, AsFloat, and AsDate.

If you want, you can use the FieldByName function instead of the Fields property:

```
S := Table1.FieldByName('CustNo').AsString;
```

As used in the examples shown, both FieldByName and Fields return the same data. The two different syntaxes are used solely to provide programmers with a flexible and convenient set of tools for programmatically accessing the contents of a dataset. When in doubt, use FieldByName because it won't be affected if you change the order of the fields in your table.

You can also treat TTable as a variant array, which will let you access the fields of a table with the following syntax:

```
S := Table1['CustNo'];
```

This is obviously a considerable improvement over the FieldByName method. However, it is not supported in 16-bit Delphi. If you need to run your program under both Windows 95 and Windows 3.1, then you should use the FieldByName technique. However, if you are only targeting WIN32 platforms, then you should definitely use the variant array.

The FIELDER program that ships with this book demonstrates some simple ways to use the Fields property of TDataSet. If you want to construct the program dynamically, place a TTable, two buttons, and two list boxes on a form, as shown in Figure 15.12. Hook up the TTable object to the CUSTOMER table that ships with Delphi.

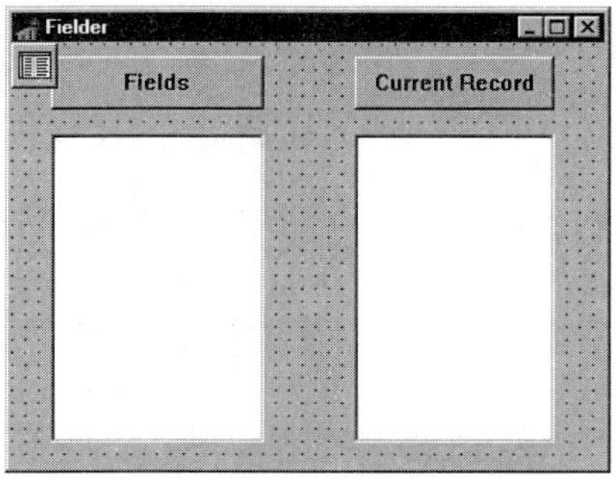

FIGURE 15.12.

The Fielder program shows how to use the Fields property.

Double-click the Fields button and create a method that looks like this:

```
procedure TForm1.bFieldsClick(Sender: TObject);
var
  i: Integer;
begin
  ListBox1.Clear;
  for i := 0 to Table1.FieldCount - 1 do
    ListBox1.Items.Add(Table1.Fields[i].FieldName);
end;
```

This method starts by clearing the current contents of the first list box, and then it iterates through each of the fields, adding their names one by one to the list box. Notice that the for loop shown here counts from 0 to FieldCount - 1. If you don't remember to subtract one from FieldCount, you will get a "List Index Out of Bounds" error, because you will be attempting to read the name of a field that does not exist.

If you enter the code correctly, you will fill the list box with the names of all the fields in the current record structure. Delphi provides other means to get at the same information, but this is a simple, programmatic way for you to access these names at runtime.

In the FIELDER example, you can associate the following code with the second button you placed on the program's form:

```
procedure TForm1.bCurRecordClick(Sender: TObject);
var
  i: Integer;
begin
ListBox2.Clear;
  for i := 0 to Table1.FieldCount - 1 do
    ListBox2.Items.Add(Table1.Fields[i].AsString);
end;
```

This code adds the contents of each of the fields to the second list box. Notice that once again, it is necessary to iterate from zero to FieldCount - 1. The key point here is that the indices to Fields are zero-based.

> **NOTE**
>
> Much of the functionality of TField can be achieved with visual tools. In particular, you can manipulate fields with the Fields Editor, which you can access by clicking once with the right mouse button on the top of a TTable or TQuery object. This subject is explored in more depth in Chapter 17, "Fields and Database Tools." However, good programmers know how to use both the methods of TDataSet and the Fields Editor. Furthermore, the Fields Editor can be used to best advantage if you understand how to enhance its functionality with some of the code you are learning about in this chapter.

In this section you have learned how to access the fields of a record. In the next section you will see how to use this knowledge when you want to append, insert, or edit records in a dataset.

Changing Data

The following methods enable you to change the data associated with a table:

```
procedure Append;
procedure Insert;
procedure Cancel;
procedure Delete;
procedure Edit;
procedure Post;
```

All these routines are part of TDataSet, and they are inherited and used frequently by TTable and TQuery.

Whenever you want to change the data associated with a record, you must first put the dataset you are using into edit mode. As you will see, most of the visual controls do this automatically. However, if you want to change a table programmatically, then you need to use the functions listed above.

Here is a typical sequence you might use to change a field of a given record:

```
Table1.Edit;
Table1['CustNo'] := '1234';
Table1.Post;
```

The first line shown places the database in edit mode. The next line assigns the string '1234' to the field labeled 'CustNo'. Finally, the data is written to disk when you call Post.

The very act of moving on to the next record automatically posts your data to disk. For instance, the following code has the same effect as the code shown previously, plus it moves you on to the next record:

```
Table1.Edit;
Table1['CustNo'] := '1234';
Table1.Next;
```

Calls to First, Next, Prior, and Last all perform Posts, as long as you are in edit mode. If you are working with server data and transactions, the rules explained here do not apply. However, transactions are a separate matter with their own special rules, as explained in the next section.

Even if you are not working with transactions, you can still undo your work at any time, as long as you have not yet either directly or indirectly called Post. For instance, if you have put a table into edit mode, and have changed the data in one or more fields, you can always change the record back to its original state by calling Cancel. For instance, you can edit every field of a record, and then call the following line to return to the state you were in before you began editing:

```
Table1.Cancel;
```

There is also a Cancel button on the TDBNavigator control. You can use this button to cancel an operation without having to write any code.

There are two methods, called Append and Insert, which you can use whenever you want to add another record to a dataset. It obviously makes more sense to use Append on datasets that are not indexed, but Delphi won't throw an exception if you use it on an indexed dataset. In fact, it is always safe to use either Append or Insert whenever you are working with a valid dataset.

On your disc you will find a simple program called INSERTS, which shows how to use the Insert and Delete commands. To create the program by hand, first use a TTable, TDataSource, and TDBGrid to open up the COUNTRY table from the demos subdirectory. Then place two buttons on the program's form and call them Insert and Delete. When you are done, you should have a program like the one shown in Figure 15.13.

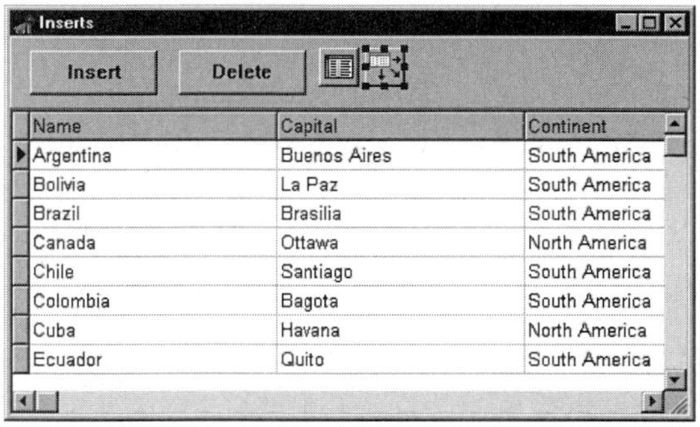

FIGURE 15.13.

The INSERTS program knows how to insert and delete a record from the COUNTRY table.

NOTE

To spice up the Inserts program, you can drop a panel on the top of the form and then add the buttons to the panel. Set the panel's Align property to alTop, and set the TDBGrid's Align property to alClient. If you run the program, you can then maximize and resize the form without damaging the relationship between the various visual components.

The next step is to associate code with the Insert button:

```
procedure TForm1.InsertClick(Sender: TObject);
begin
  Table1.Insert;
  Table1['Name'] := 'Erehwon';
  Table1['Capital'] := 'None';
  Table1['Continent'] := 'Imagination';
  Table1['Area'] := 0;
  Table1['Population'] := 1;
  Table1.Post;
end;
```

The procedure shown here first puts the table into insert mode, which means that a new record filled with blank fields is automatically inserted into the current position of the dataset.

After inserting the record, the next job is to assign strings to one or more of its fields. There are, of course, several different ways to enter this data. Using the current program, you could simply type the information into the current record in the grid. Or, if you wanted, you could place standard edit controls on the form and then set each field equal to the value the user has typed into the edit control:

```
Table1['Name'] := Edit1.Text;
```

If you place a table in edit mode, or if its TDataSource object has AutoEdit set to True, you can use data-aware controls to insert information directly into a record.

The intent of this chapter, however, is to show you how to enter data programmatically. Therefore you are presented with an example in which information is hardwired into the code segment of the program:

```
Table1['Name'] := 'Erehwon';
```

> **NOTE**
>
> One of the interesting (or perhaps "frustrating" would be a more appropriate word) byproducts of this technique is that pressing the Insert button twice in a row automatically triggers a "Key Violation" exception. To remedy this situation, you must either delete the current record or manually change the Name and Capital fields of the newly created record.
>
> Note also that you can pass either a string or a number into a field using this technique. The array of Fields property is of type Variant, and so you can, to a considerable degree, ignore type issues in this situation.

Looking at the code shown previously, you will see that the mere act of inserting a record and of filling out its fields is not enough to change the physical data that resides on disk. If you want the information to be written to disk, then you must call Post.

After calling `Insert`, if you change your mind and decide to abandon the current record, you should call `Cancel`. As long as you do this before you call `Post`, everything you have entered is discarded, and the dataset is restored to the condition it was in before you called `Insert`.

One last related property that you should keep in mind is called `CanModify`. A table might be set to `ReadOnly`, in which case `CanModify` would return `False`. Otherwise `CanModify` returns `True` and you can enter edit or insert mode at will. `CanModify` is itself a read-only property. If you want to set a dataset to read-only, you should use the `ReadOnly` property, not `CanModify`.

In this section, you have learned how to use the `Insert`, `Delete`, `Edit`, `Post`, `Cancel` and `Append` commands. Most of the actions associated with these commands are fairly intuitive, though it can take a little thought to see how they interact with the `Fields` property.

Using *SetKey* or *FindKey* to Search Through a File

If you want to search for a value in a dataset, you can call on five Delphi procedures, called `FindKey`, `FindNearest`, `SetKey`, `GotoNearest`, and `GotoKey`. These procedures assume that the field you are searching on is indexed. This book ships with a demonstration program called SEARCH that shows how to use these calls.

To create the SEARCH program, place TTable, TDataSource, TDBGrid, TButton, TLabel, and TEdit controls on a form, and arrange them so the result looks like the image shown in Figure 15.14. Be sure to name the button Search, and then to wire the database controls so you can view the Customer table in the grid control.

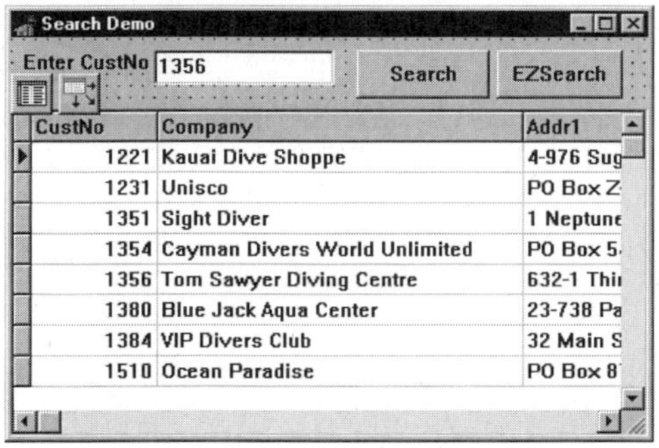

FIGURE 15.14.

The SEARCH program enables you to enter a customer number and then search for it by pressing a button.

The functionality for the SEARCH program is encapsulated in a single method that is attached to the Search button. This function retrieves the string entered in the edit control, searches the CustNo column until it finds the value, and finally switches the focus to the record it found. In its simplest form, here's how the code attached to the Search button looks:

```
procedure TSearchDemo.SearchClick(Sender: TObject);
begin
  Table1.SetKey;
  Table1.Fields[0].AsString := Edit1.Text;
  Table1.GotoKey;
end;
```

The first call in this procedure sets `Table1` into search mode. Delphi needs to be told to switch into search mode simply because you use the `Fields` property in a special way when Delphi is in search mode. Specifically, you can index into the `Fields` property, and assign it to the value you want to find.

In the example shown, the CustNo field is the first column in the database, so you set the `Fields` index to zero. To actually carry out the search, simply call `Table1.GotoKey`. `GotoKey` is a Boolean function, so you could write code that looks like this:

```
If not Table1.GotoKey then DatabaseError('');
```

The DatabaseError routine raises an EDatabase exception.

If you are not sure of the value you are looking for, call `Table1.GotoNearest`. `GotoNearest` will take you to the numerical or string value closest to the one you specify.

If you are not searching on the primary index of a file, you must use a secondary index and specify the name of the index you are using in the `IndexName` property for the current table. For instance, the `Customer` table has a secondary index called `ByCompany` on the field labeled `Company`. You would have to set the `IndexName` property to the name of that index if you wanted to search on that field. You could then use the following code when you searched on the Company field:

```
Table1.IndexName := 'ByCompany';
Table1.Active := True;
Table1.SetKey;
Table1.FieldByName('Company').AsString := Edit1.Text;
Table1.GotoKey;
```

In this case, you set the `Fields` index to 3, since `City` is the fourth field in the `Customer` database. Remember: this search will fail unless you first assign the correct value to the `IndexName` property. Furthermore, you should note that `IndexName` is a property of TTable and would therefore not automatically be included in any direct descendant of TDataSet or TDBDataSet that you might create yourself.

When you are searching for a value in a database, there is always a strong possibility that the search might fail. You can raise an exception in such a case and handle the error by writing the code like this. Delphi will not automatically throw an exception in such a case, so if you want to handle the error, you might write code that looks like this:

```
procedure TSearchDemo.SearchClick(Sender: TObject);
begin
  Table1.SetKey;
  try
```

```
    Table1.Fields[0].AsString := Edit1.Text;
    If not Table.GoToKey then raise DatabaseError.create(');
    Table1.GotoKey;
  except
    on EDataBaseError do
      MessageDlg('Value not found', mtError, [mbOk], 0);
  end;
end;
```

In the code shown, either an illegal assignment to the Fields property or a failure to find the value on which you are searching would automatically force the code to pop up an error message stating "Value not found." For more information on exceptions, see Chapter 6, "Exceptions."

The FindKey and FindNearest routines perform the same function GotoKey or GotoNearest, but they are much easier to use. Here, for instance, is the technique for using FindKey:

```
Table1.FindKey([Edit1.Text]);
```

Here's how FindNearest looks:

```
Table1.FindNearest([Edit1.Text]);
```

There is no need to first call SetKey or to use the FieldByName property.

FindKey and FindNearest take a comma-delimited array of values in their sole parameter. You would pass multiple parameters to FindKey or FindNearest if you have a table that was indexed on multiple fields. You may need to set the IndexName property before calling FindKey and FindNearest, just as you needed to do this when using GotoKey or GotoNearest. (Needless to say, internally FindKey and FindNearest end up calling GotoKey and GotoNearest.)

A neat trick you can use with the FindNearest method involves performing an incremental search across a table. Start a new project and drag the Country table off the Database Explorer and onto Form1. You will end up with a TTable, TDataSource, and TDBGrid on the form, with the TTable hooked up to the Country table. Put a panel on the top of the form and set its Align property to alTop. Set the Align property of the TDBGrid for the Country table to alClient.

Place a TEdit component on the panel and create an OnChange event with the following code attached to it:

```
procedure TForm1.Edit1Change(Sender: TObject);
begin
  Table1.FindNearest([Edit1.Text]);
end;
```

Run the program. When you type into the edit control, you will automatically begin incrementally searching through the table. For instance, if you type in **c**, you will go to the record for Canada, if you type in **Cu**, you will go to the record for Cuba.

The incremental search example is available on disc as the IncSrch program. It's perhaps worth pointing out that this program is interesting in part because it shows how you can use the built-in features of Delphi to easily implement additional features that were never planned by the developers. For instance, there is no Incremental Search component in Delphi. However, if you need to build one, the tools come readily to hand.

Filtering the Records in a DataSet with *ApplyRange*

The `ApplyRange` procedure lets you set a filter that limits the range of the records you view. For instance, in the Customers database, the CustNo field ranges from just over 1,000 to a little under 10,000. If you wanted to see only those records that had a customer number between 2000 and 3000, you would use the `ApplyRange` procedure and two related routines. When using this procedure, you must work with a field that is indexed. (As explained in the next chapter, you can perform this same type of operation on a non-indexed field by using a TQuery object rather than TTable object.)

Here are the four procedures that make up the suite of routines you will use when setting up filters:

```
procedure ApplyRange;
procedure SetRangeEnd;
procedure SetRangeStart;
procedure CancelRange
```

To use these procedures:

1. Call `SetRangeStart` and then use the `Fields` property to designate the start of the range.

2. Call `SetRangeEnd` and use the `Fields` property a second time to designate the end of the range you are specifying.

3. The first two actions prepare the filter; now all you need to do is call `ApplyRange`, and the new filter you have specified will take effect.

4. If you want to undo the effects of a call to `ApplyRange` or `SetRange` then you can call the `CancelRange` procedure.

The RANGER program, which is located on the CD that came with this book, shows you explicitly how to use these procedures. To create the program, drop a TTable, TDataSource, and TDBGrid onto a form. Wire them up so that you can view the CUSTOMERS table from the demos subdirectory. You need to set `Table.Active` to `True`. Next drop two labels on the form and set their captions to Start Range and End Range. Place two edit controls next to the labels. Finally, add a single button with the caption ApplyRange. When you are done, you should have a form like the one shown in Figure 15.15.

FIGURE 15.15.

The RANGER program shows how to limit the number of records from a table that are visible at any one time.

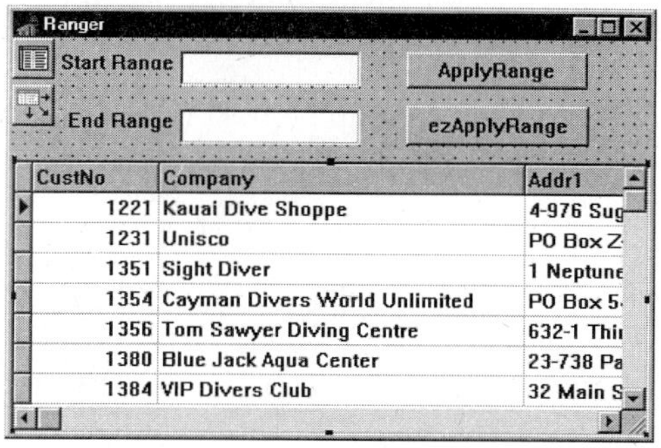

The `SetRangeStart` and `SetRangeEnd` procedures enable you to declare the first and last members in the range of records you want to see. To get started using the procedures, first double-click the ApplyRange button, and then create a procedure that looks like this:

```
procedure TForm1.bApplyRangeClick(Sender: TObject);
begin
  Table1.SetRangeStart;
  Table1.Fields[0].AsString := Edit1.Text;
  Table1.SetRangeEnd;
  Table1.Fields[0].AsString := Edit2.Text;
  Table1.ApplyRange;
end;
```

The `bApplyRangeClick` procedure first calls `SetRangeStart`, which puts the table into range mode and blanks out the records seen in the TDBGrid control. Once in range mode, the program next expects you to specify the beginning range, which in this case you grab from the first edit control. Setting the end range for the program involves following a very similar pattern. First you call `SetRangeEnd`, and then you snag an appropriate value from the second `Edit` control.

Note that you can use the `Fields` property to specify the actual range you want to use:

```
Table1.Fields[0].AsString := Edit2.Text;
```

This use of the `Fields` property is obviously a special case, since the syntax shown here is usually used to set the value of a field, not to define a range. This special case comes into effect only after you have put `Table1` into range mode by calling `SetRangeStart`.

The final step in the procedure just shown is the call `ApplyRange`. This is the routine that actually puts your request into effect. When the call to `ApplyRange` ends, the table is no longer in range mode, and the `Fields` property returns to its normal functionality.

If you want to undo the results of a call to `ApplyRange`, then you can call the `CancelRange` function:

```
procedure TForm1.UndoClick(Sender: TObject);
begin
  Table1.CancelRange;
end;
```

A typical run of the program might involve the user typing in the number 4000 in the first edit control and the number 5000 in the next edit control. After entering the data, a click on the ApplyRange button would then put the request into effect.

In this section, you have learned how to filter the functions from a table or dataset so that you view only a particular range of records. The steps involved are threefold:

1. Call SetRangeStart and specify the beginning value in the range of records you want to see.
2. Call SetRangeEnd and specify the ending value in the range of records you want to see.
3. Call ApplyRange in order to view the results of your request.

Delphi also provides a shorthand method calling the SetRangeStart, SetRangeEnd, and ApplyRange methods:

```
procedure TForm1.ezApplyRangeClick(Sender: TObject);
begin
  Table1.SetRange([Edit1.Text], [Edit2.Text]);
end;
```

This method performs exactly the same chore as the bApplyRangeClick method shown above.

Filtering with the OnFilterRecord Event

The OnFilterRecord event enables you to set up filters on fields at are not keyed. You can use this event in two different ways.

The first technique involves setting the TTable Filtered property to True. When you do this, then you will see only the records that are designated by the formula defined in the OnFilterRecord event. For instance, if you had a State field in your dataset, and the OnFilterRecord event said to accept only records from New Hampshire, then you would see only the records from New Hampshire when Filtered was set to True.

The second technique enables you to search for records even when Filtered is set to False. For instance, if you set up an OnFilterRecord event that accepted only records from New Hampshire, then you could call Table1.FindFirst to find the first of these records, and Table1.FindNext to find the next one, and so on. There are also FindPrior and FindLast properties that you can use with the OnFilterRecord event.

An example of the OnFilterRecord event is shown in the Filter program found on this book's CD-ROM. The rest of this section describes how to create that program from scratch.

To see the OnFilterRecord event in a live program, start by dragging the Country table off the Database Explorer onto a blank form from a new project. (It sometimes helps to close the Database Explorer after the drop operation, rather than trying to switch between the two tools by changing their focus.) Drop down a panel and set up the Align property for the panel and for the TDBGrid as explained in the previous examples from this chapter.

Place a TCheckBox object on the panel and set its Caption to Filtered. Associate the following method with the OnClick event for the checkbox:

```
procedure TForm1.CheckBox1Click(Sender: TObject);
begin
  Table1.Filtered := CheckBox1.Checked;
end;
```

This code ensures that the table will be filtered whenever the checkbox is checked.

Use the Fields Editor for the Table1 object to create field objects for all the fields in the database. Drag the Continent field of the Fields Editor onto the form, as shown in Figure 15.16.

FIGURE 15.16.

The main form for the Filter program includes a grid, a panel, a checkbox, a TDBEdit control, and a button.

Turn to the Events page for the TTable object, and associate the following code with the OnFilterRecord event:

```
procedure TForm1.Table1FilterRecord(DataSet: TDataSet;
  var Accept: Boolean);
begin
  Accept := Table1['Continent'] = dbEdit1.Text;
end;
```

This code states that the OnFilterRecord event will accept all records where the Continent field of the Country table equals the value in the dbEdit control. The continent field will have either the value North America or South America in it. If you run the program, then view a record that lists a country in South America, then the dbEdit control will say South America. If you then click the checkbox to turn the filter on, you will see only the records from South America. In short, the filter will automatically accept only those records whose Continent field matches the value of the current record.

It's important to note that the Accept field of the OnFilterRecord event is a Boolean value. This means that you can set up any kind of a Boolean statement in order to set the value of this field. For instance, in addition to the = operator, you could also use the following operators: <>, > or <.

The FindNext, FindFirst, FindPrior, and FindLast functions are extremely easy to use. For instance, if you wanted to find the next record in the database that satisfied the requirements specified in the OnFilterRecord event, then you could write the following code to be fired in response to a click on a button:

```
procedure TForm1.bFindNextClick(Sender: TObject);
begin
  Table1.FindNext;
end;
```

The other functions work exactly the same way. This is a Boolean function that will return False if the search fails. Remember that these methods work even if the Filtered property of the TTable object is set to False.

Using the *Refresh* Function

As you already know, any table that you open is always subject to change. In short, you should regard a table as a fluid, rather than as a static, entity. Even if you are the only person using a particular table, and even if you are not working in a networked environment, there is always the possibility that the program you are running may have two different ways of changing a piece of data. As a result, you should always be aware of the need to update, or refresh, your current view of a table.

The Refresh function is related to the Open function, in that it retrieves the data, or some portion of the data, associated with a given table. For instance, when you open a table, Delphi retrieves data directly from a database file. Similarly, when you refresh a table, Delphi goes out and retrieves data directly from a table. You can therefore use this function to update a table if you think it might have changed. It is faster, and much more efficient, to call Refresh than to call Close and then Open.

> **NOTE**
>
> In a networked environment, refreshing a table can sometimes lead to unexpected results. For instance, if a user is viewing a record that has been deleted, it will seem to disappear out from under the user the moment the program calls Refresh. Similarly, if another user has edited data, then a call to Refresh can result in data dynamically changing while a user is viewing it. Of course, it is unlikely that one user will change or delete a record while another is viewing it, but it is possible. As a result, you should use calls to Refresh with caution.

Bookmarks

It is often useful to mark a particular location in a table so that you can quickly return to it when desired. Delphi provides this functionality through three methods that use the metaphor of a bookmark. When you use these functions, it is as if you have left a bookmark in the dataset, and you can therefore turn back to it quickly whenever you want:

```
procedure FreeBookmark(Bookmark: TBookmark);
function GetBookmark: TBookmark;
procedure GotoBookmark(Bookmark: TBookmark);
```

As you can see, the GetBookmark call returns a variable of type TBookmark. A TBookmark contains enough information to enable Delphi to find the location to which it refers. Therefore, you can simply pass this bookmark to the GotoBookmark function, and you will immediately be returned to the location with which the bookmark is associated.

It's important to note that a call to GetBookmark allocates memory for the bookmark, and so you must remember to call FreeBookmark before you exit your program, and before every attempt to reuse a bookmark. For instance, here is a typical set of calls for freeing, setting, and moving to a bookmark:

```
procedure TForm1.MarkClick(Sender: TObject);
begin
  if Bookmark = nil then
    Bookmark := Table1.GetBookmark;
end;


procedure TForm1.bReturnClick(Sender: TObject);
begin
  if Bookmark <> nil then begin
    Table1.GotoBookmark(Bookmark);
    Table1.FreeBookmark(Bookmark);
    Bookmark := nil;
  end;
end;
```

The code shown here is excerpted from a program called BOOKMARK.DPR, which comes with this book. In the declaration for TForm1, a variable called BookMark is declared in the private section. Every time the MarkClick procedure is called, the first step is to be sure the BookMark is freed. It is never a mistake to call FreeBookmark, as the procedure checks to make sure BookMark is not set to nil. After de-allocating any existing copies of the Bookmark, a new one is allocated. You can then call GotoBookmark and repeat the cycle.

Bookmarks are powerful features that can be of great benefit under certain circumstances. The developers of Delphi, for instance, used bookmarks frequently in order to develop the database components. They often have several different bookmarks open at the same time.

TTable

TTable adds several frequently used properties to TDataSet:

```
property DetailFields
property Exclusive
property MasterFields
property MasterSource
property ReadOnly
property TableName
```

Of the properties shown here, the most common ones are probably TableName and ReadOnly. You can use the TableName property to specify the table you want to open, and you can set the ReadOnly property to True or False depending on whether you want to allow the user to change the data in a dataset. Neither of these properties can be used when a table is active.

The Exclusive property lets you open up a table in a mode that guarantees that no other user will be able to access it at the same time. You will not be able to set Exclusive to True if another user is currently accessing the table.

The MasterSource property is used to specify a TDataSource from which the current table needs to obtain information. For instance, if you linked two tables in a master/detail relationship, the detail table can track the events occurring in the first table by specifying the first table's datasource in this property. This technique is demonstrated in the following section on linked cursors.

Creating Linked Cursors

Linked cursors enable programmers to easily define a one-to-many relationship. For instance, it is sometimes useful to link the CUSTOMER and ORDERS tables so that each time the user views a particular customer's name, he or she can also see a list of the orders related to that customer. In short, the user can view one customer's record, and then see only the orders related to that customer.

To understand linked cursors, you first need to see that the CUSTOMER table and the ORDERS table are related to one another through the CustNo field. This relationship exists specifically because there needs to be a way to find out which orders are associated with which customer.

The LINKS program on your disc demonstrates how to create a program that uses linked cursors. To create the program on your own, place two tables, two datasources, and two grids on a form. Wire the first set of controls to the CUSTOMER table and the second set to the ORDERS table. If you run the program at this stage, you should be able to scroll through all the records in either table, as shown in Figure 15.17.

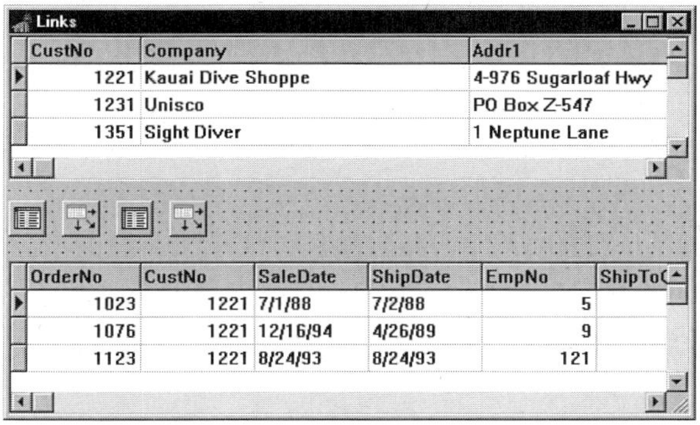

FIGURE 15.17.

The LINKS program shows how to define a relationship between two tables.

The next step is to link the ORDERS table to the CUSTOMER table so that you view only those orders associated with the current customer record. To do this, you must take three steps, each of which requires some explanation:

1. Set the `MasterSource` property of `Table2` to `DataSource1`.
2. Set the `MasterField` property in `Table2` to `CustNo`
3. Set the `IndexName` property of `Table2` to `ByCustNo`.

If you now run the program, you will see that both tables are linked together, and that every time you move to a new record in the CUSTOMER table, you can see only those records in the ORDERS table that belong to that particular customer.

The `MasterSource` property in `Table2` specifies the `DataSource` from which `Table2` can draw information. Specifically, it allows the ORDERS table to know which record currently has the focus in the CUSTOMERS table.

The question then becomes this: what other information does `Table2` need in order to properly filter the contents of the ORDERS table? The answer to this question is twofold:

1. It needs the name of the field that links the two tables.
2. It needs the index of the field in the ORDERS table that is going to be linked to the CUSTOMER table.

In order to correctly supply the information described here, you must first ensure that both the CUSTOMER table and the ORDERS table have the correct indices. Specifically, you must ensure that there are indices on both the CustNo field and the CustNo field in the ORDERS table. If the index in question is a primary index, there is no need to specifically name that index, and therefore you can leave the IndexName field blank in both tables. However, if either of the tables is linked to the other through a secondary index, you must explicitly designate that index in the IndexName field of the table that has a secondary index.

In the example shown here, the CUSTOMER table has a primary index on the CustNo field, so there is no need to specify the index name. However, the ORDERS table does not have a primary index on the CustNo field, and so you must explicitly declare it in the IndexName property by typing in or selecting the word CustNo.

> **NOTE**
>
> To simplify the process described above, the developers put in a dialog that appears when you click the `MasterFields` property. This dialog simplifies the process described here and helps to automate the task of setting up a link between two tables.
>
> In particular, to use the MasterFields dialog, start a new project and drag the Customer and Orders tables off the Explorer onto the main form. Arrange the grids with the Customer grid on top and the Orders grid beneath it. Set the `DataSource` property of the Orders TTable object to the TDataSource object associated with the Customer table.
>
> Pop up the MasterFields dialog and make sure the Available Indexes is set to Primary Index. Click the CustNo field in both Detail Fields and MasterFields list boxes. Click Add. The two fields will appear in the Joined Fields list box. At this stage, you are all done, and so you can click the OK button.

Some indices can contain multiple fields, so you must explicitly state the name of the field you want to use to link the two tables. In this case, you should enter the name `CustNo` in the `MasterFields` property of `Table2`. If you wanted to link two tables on more than one field, you should list all the fields, placing a pipe symbol between each one:

```
Table1.MasterFields := 'CustNo | SaleData | ShipDate';
```

In this particular case, however, the statement shown here makes no sense, since the SaleData and ShipDate fields are neither indexed nor duplicated in the CUSTOMER table. Therefore, you should only enter the field called CustNo in the `MasterFields` property. You can specify this syntax directly in a property editor, or else write code that performs the same chore.

It's important to note that this section covered only one of several ways you can create linked cursors using Delphi. Chapter 16, "SQL and the TQuery Object," describes a second method that will appeal to people who are familiar with SQL. The Database Expert provides a third means of achieving this end. As you have seen, the Database Expert is an easy-to-use visual tool. The Query Builder is yet a fourth way of creating a one-to-many relationship between two tables. Like the Database Expert, the Query Builder is a visual tool that can save you much time. However, it's best not to rely entirely on the visual tools, since there are times when you might feel limited by their functionality.

TDataSource Basics

Class TDataSource is used as a conduit between TTable or TQuery and the data-aware controls such as TDBGrid, TDBEdit, and TDBComboBox. Under most circumstances, the only thing you will do with a TDataSource object is to set its `DataSet` property to an appropriate TTable or TQuery object. Then, on the other end, you will also want to set a data-aware control's `DataSource` property to the TDataSource object you are currently using.

> **NOTE**
>
> Visual tools such as TDBEdit or TDBGrid all have a `DataSource` property that connects to a TDataSource object. When reading this chapter, you need to distinguish between a visual control's `DataSource` property and the TDataSource object to which it is attached. In other words, the word DataSource can refer to either a property or a class, depending on the context. I tend to refer to the class as a TDataSource and the property as a `DataSource`, but you should watch the context in which these words are used.

A TDataSource also has an `Enabled` property, and this can be useful whenever you want to temporarily disconnect a table or query from its visual controls. This functionality might be desirable if you need to programmatically iterate through all the records in a table. For instance, if a TTable is connected to a data-aware control, each time you call `TTable.Next`, the visual control needs to be updated. If you are quickly going through two or three thousand records, then it can take a considerable time to perform the updates to the visual controls. In cases like this, the best thing to do is set the TDataSource object's Enabled field to `False`, which will allow you to iterate through the records without having to worry about screen updates. This single change can improve the speed of some routines by several thousand percent.

The `AutoEdit` property of `TDataSource` enables you to decide whether or not the data-aware controls attached to it will automatically enter edit mode when you start typing inside them. Many users prefer to keep `AutoEdit` set to `True`, but if you want to give a user more precise control over when the database can be edited, this is the property you need. In short, if you set `AutoEdit` to `False`, you have essentially made the table read-only.

Using TDataSource to Check the State of a Database

TDataSource has three key events associated with it:

```
OnDataChange
OnStateChange
OnUpdateData
```

OnDataChange occurs whenever you move on to a new record. In other words, if you call Next, Previous, Insert, or any other call that is likely to lead to a change in the data associated with the current record, an OnDataChange event will get fired. If someone begins editing the data in a data-aware control, an OnResync event occurs.

A TDataSource OnStateChange event occurs whenever the current state of the dataset changes. A dataset always knows what state it's in. If you call Edit, Append, or Insert, the table knows that it is now in edit mode. Similarly, after you Post a record, the database knows that it is no longer editing data, and it switches back into browse mode. If you want more control, the next section in this chapter explains that a dataset also sends out messages just before and just after you change states.

The dataset has five different possible states, each of which are captured in the following enumerated type:

```
TDataSetState = (dsInactive, dsBrowse, dsEdit,
                 dsInsert, dsSetKey, dsCalcFields);
```

During the course of a normal session, the database will frequently move back and forth between browse, edit, insert, or the other modes. If you want to track these changes, you can respond to them by writing code that looks like this:

```
procedure TForm1.DataSource1StateChange(Sender: TObject);
var
  S: String;
begin
  case Table1.State of
    dsInactive: S := 'Inactive';
    dsBrowse: S := 'Browse';
    dsEdit: S := 'Edit';
    dsInsert: S := 'Insert';
    dsSetKey: S := 'SetKey';
    dsCalcFields: S := 'CalcFields';
  end;
  StatusBar1.Panels[0].Text := S;
end;
```

An OnUpdateData event occurs whenever the data in the current record is about to be updated. For instance, an OnUpdateEvent will occur between the time Post is called and the time information is actually posted.

> **NOTE**
>
> The above code assumes that you have dropped one of the Windows 95 TStatusBar objects on the form. To create one or more Panels in the StatusBar, use the `Panels` property of the TStatusBar object. In the Statusbar Panels Editor dialog, click New to create a new panel.

The events belonging to `TDataSource` can be extremely useful. To help illustrate them, you will find a program on your disc called DSEVENTS that responds to all three `TDataSource` events. This program shows an easy way to set up a "poor man's" data-aware edit control that automatically shows and posts data to and from a database at the appropriate time.

This example works with the COUNTRY database, and it has a TTable, TDataSource, five edits, six labels, eight buttons, and a panel on it. The actual layout for the program is shown in Figure 15.18. Note that the sixth label appears on the panel located at the bottom of the main form.

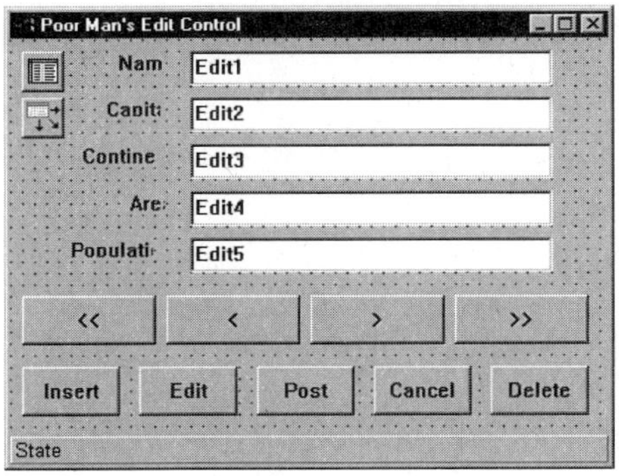

FIGURE 15.18.

The DSEVENTS program shows how to track the current state of a table.

DSEVENTS has one small conceit that you need to understand if you want to learn how the program works. Because there are five separate edit controls on the main form, you need to have some way to refer to them quickly and easily. One simple method is to declare an array of edit controls:

```
Edits: array[1..5] of TEdit;
```

To fill out the array, you can respond to the forms `OnCreate` event:

```
procedure TForm1.FormCreate(Sender: TObject);
var
  i: Integer;
begin
  for i := 1 to 5 do
    Edits[i] := TEdit(FindComponent('Edit' + IntToStr(i)));
end;
```

The code shown here assumes that the first edit control you want to use is called Edit1, and the second is called Edit2, and so on.

Given the existence of this array of controls, it is very simple to use the OnDataChange event to keep them in sync with the contents of the current record in a dataset:

```
procedure TForm1.DataSource1DataChange(Sender: TObject;
                                       Field: TField);
var
  i: Integer;
begin
  for i := 1 to 5 do
    Edits[i].Text := Table1.Fields[i - 1].AsString;
end;
```

This code iterates through each of the fields of the current record and puts its contents in the appropriate edit control. Whenever Table1.Next is called, or whenever any of the other navigational methods are called, the procedure shown previously is called. This assures that the edit controls always contain the data from the current record.

Whenever Post gets called, you will want to perform the opposite action. That is, you will want to get the information from the edit controls and place it inside the current record. To perform that action, simply respond to TDataSource.OnUpdateData events, which are generated automatically whenever Post is called:

```
procedure TForm1.DataSource1UpdateData(Sender: TObject);
var
  i: Integer;
begin
  for i := 1 to 5 do
    Table1.Fields[i - 1].AsString := Edits[i].Text;
end;
```

The DSEVENTS program automatically switches into edit mode whenever you type anything in one of the edit controls. It does this by responding to OnKeyDown events:

```
procedure TForm1.Edit1KeyDown(Sender: TObject;
                              var Key: Word;
                              Shift: TShiftState);

begin
  if DataSource1.State <> dsEdit then
    Table1.Edit;
end;
```

This code shows how you can use the State variable of a TDataSource object to find out the current mode of the dataset.

Tracking the State of a DataSet

In the last section, you learned how to use TDataSource to keep tabs on the current state of a TDataSet and to respond just before certain events are about to take place.

Using a TDataSource object is the simplest way to perform all these functions. However, if you would like to track these events without using TDataSource, you can respond to the following events from TDataSet, all of which are naturally inherited by TTable or TQuery:

```
property OnOpen
property OnClose
property BeforeInsert
property AfterInsert
property BeforeEdit
property AfterEdit
property BeforePost
property AfterPost
property OnCancel
property OnDelete
property OnNewRecord
```

Most of these properties are self-explanatory. The `BeforePost` event, for instance, is functionally similar to the `TDataSource.OnUpdateData` event that is explained and demonstrated previously. In other words, the DSEVENTS program would work the same if you responded to `DataSource1.OnUpdateData` or to `Table1.BeforePost`. Of course, in one case you would not need to have a `TDataSource` on the form, while the other requires it.

Summary

In this chapter, you have learned how to use the TDataSet, TField, TDBDataSet, TTable, and TDataSource classes. Through the simple techniques of exposition, example, and repetition, all the major ideas associated with objects of these types should now be clear to you.

The key points to remember are as follows:

- TDataSet encapsulates the basic functions you will perform on a table.
- TField is a property of TDataSet that allows you to access the contents or name of each field in a record.
- TDBDataSet gives you the ability to associate a dataset with a given table.
- TTable encapsulates all the functionality of a dataset, but it also gives you access to table-specific chores such as setting indices or creating linked cursors.
- TDataSource forms a link between TTable or TQuery and any of the data-aware components such as TDBEdit or TDBGrid. TDataSource also contains three useful events that keep you informed about the current state of the database.

In the next chapter, you will learn about the TQuery object and SQL. SQL is especially useful when you want to access the advanced capabilities associated with servers and server data.

SQL and the TQuery Object

This chapter is about queries. It's a subject that lies at the heart of client/server programming, so this is one of the most important chapters in the book.

The material will be broken down into the following main sections:

- Using the TQuery object
- Using SQL with local and remote servers to select, update, delete, and insert records
- Using SQL statements to create joins, linked cursors, and programs that search for individual records

The acronym SQL stands for Structured Query Language and is usually pronounced as "Sequel" or by saying each letter ("Ess Que El"). Whatever way you choose to pronounce it, SQL is a powerful database language that is easily accessible from within Delphi but is distinct from Delphi's native language. Delphi can use SQL statements to view tables, to perform joins between tables, to create one-to-many relationships, or to perform almost any action that your underlying database tools can perform.

Delphi ships with two local SQL engines, one built into the BDE and the other built into InterBase. As a result, you can perform SQL queries even if you're working on a stand-alone machine and don't have access to a server.

Delphi provides support for pass-through SQL, which means that you can compose SQL statements and then have them sent directly (with one or two exceptions) to an Oracle, Sybase, InterBase, or other server. Pass-through SQL is a powerful feature for two different reasons:

1. Most servers can process SQL statements very quickly, which means that you can use SQL on remote data to get an extremely fast response to your requests.
2. You can compose SQL statements that ask a server to perform specialized tasks unavailable through Delphi's native language.

In the last chapter, you learned a lot about how Delphi works internally and about how to utilize its native capabilities. Now it's time to see how Delphi interacts with the database tools that exist either on your current machine or on a network.

TQuery Basics

You can create a Delphi SQL statement by using a TQuery component in the following manner:

1. Drop down a TQuery, TDataSource, and TdbGrid object on a form and wire them together.
2. Assign an alias to the DatabaseName property of the TQuery object. For instance, use the DBDEMOS alias.
3. Use the SQL property to enter a SQL statement such as Select * from Country.

4. Set the `Active` property to `True`. If you completed each step correctly, and if the BDE is set up correctly, the grid should now contain the records from the Country table.

If you're working with local data, you can substitute a fully qualified subdirectory path for an alias. When using the latter method, it's best if you don't include the actual name of a table, but only the subdirectory in which one or more tables exist. In my opinion, however, it is almost always better to work with an alias rather than specify the path directly in the `DatabaseName` property.

There are two general points that you need to understand before you proceed further:

- This chapter isn't intended to be a SQL primer, but rather a description of the TQuery object and the basic tasks you can perform with it. Even if you don't know anything about SQL, this chapter will still be helpful to you, and you'll end up learning a number of basic facts about how to compose a SQL statement. However, for a detailed analysis of the language, you should turn to one of the many books and public documents available on this subject. You also can refer to the handy reference in the online help for the WISQL utility. Additional information is available in the form of a LOCALSQL.HLP file that ships with Delphi. (Open help, press Alt+F+O, and then choose LOCALSQL.HLP. You need to be in a help file for this work, not in the Index or Content section. Also, you may have to browse to the ..\delphi 2.0\help subdirectory to find this file.)

- Because Delphi uses pass-through SQL, you'll find that you can access the unique features of the servers to which you connect. For instance, the Borland Database Engine, which ships with Delphi, provides a special, if somewhat limited, local SQL engine. To learn about the specific capabilities of that engine, you should read not only this chapter, but also the LOCALSQL.HLP file that is included with Delphi.

Overall, you'll find that the TQuery object is one of the most useful and flexible features available inside the Delphi environment. With it, you can tap into the power inherent in some of today's premier servers such as Interbase, Oracle, or Sybase.

The *SQL* Property

The `SQL` property is probably the single most important part of TQuery. You can access this property from the Object Inspector during design time or programmatically at runtime. You've already seen how to access the `SQL` property at design time, so the next few sections concentrate on ways to manipulate it programmatically.

Most people want to access the `SQL` property at runtime in order to dynamically change the statement associated with a query. For instance, if you want to issue three SQL statements while your program is running, there's no need for you to place three TQuery components on your form. Instead, you can just place one on the form and simply change its `SQL` property three times. The most efficient, most powerful, and simplest means of doing this is through parameterized queries, which are explained in the next section. However, this chapter first examines the basic features of the SQL property and then covers more advanced topics, such as parameterized queries.

The SQL property is of type TStrings, which means that it is a series of strings kept in a list. The list acts very much as if it were an array, but it's actually a special class with its own unique capabilities. If you want to find out everything you can about the SQL property, you should study the class TStrings or TStringList. However, the next few paragraphs review its most commonly used features.

When using TQuery programmatically, you should first close the current query and clear out any strings that might already be residing in the SQL property:

```
Query1.Close;
Query1.SQL.Clear;
```

It's always safe to call Close. If the query is already closed, the call will not cause an error.

The next step is to add the new strings that you want to execute:

```
Query1.SQL.Add('Select * from Country');
Query1.SQL.Add('where Name = ''Argentina''');
```

You can use the Add property to append from one to *x* number of strings to an SQL query, where *x* is limited only by the amount of memory on your machine.

> **NOTE**
>
> For those not familiar with Object Pascal strings, I should point out that this code specifies that there should be single quotes around the word Argentina. Argentina is a string within a string, so it is necessary to add double single quotes each time you want to enter single quotes inside a string.
>
> You can, if you want, set the Argentina off with double quotes:
>
> ```
> Query1.SQL.Add('where Name = "Argentina"');
> ```
>
> This is probably the preferred method, but you should also be aware of how to handle single quotes in an Object Pascal string.

To ask Delphi to process the statement and return a cursor containing the results of your query, you can issue the following statement:

```
Query1.Open;
```

Whenever you want to change the SQL statement, you can simply alter the strings you pass to the Add property:

```
Query1.Close;
Query1.SQL.Clear;
Query1.SQL.Add('Select * from Country');
Query1.Open;
```

The sample program called EASYSQL demonstrates this process. EASYSQL is shown in Figure 16.1.

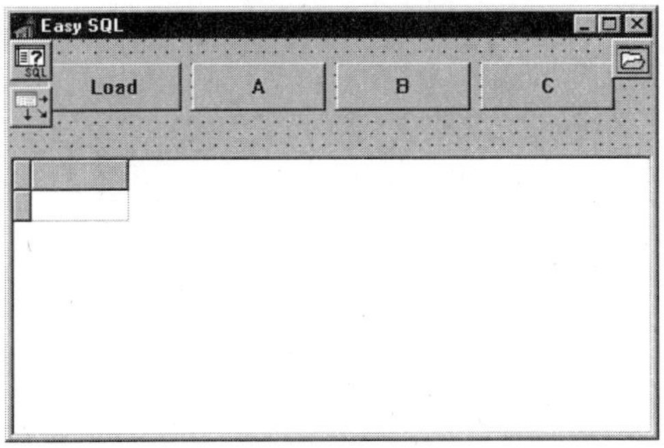

FIGURE 16.1.

The EASYSQL program shows how to issue multiple queries from a single TQuery object.

The EASYSQL program uses a feature of local SQL that lets you use case-insensitive wild cards. For instance, the following SQL statement returns a dataset containing all the records in which the Name field begins with the letter C:

```
Select * from Country where Name like 'C%'
```

The following syntax enables you to see all the countries that have the letter C embedded somewhere in their name:

```
Select * from Country where Name like '%C%';
```

Here's a statement that finds all the countries whose name ends in the letters ia:

```
Select * from Country where Name like '%ia';
```

If you want to compose a series of statements like the preceding one, you can expedite matters by using either parameterized queries or the Format function. Both of these techniques will be explained in this chapter.

One of the most powerful features of the SQL property is its capability to read files directly from disk. This feature is also demonstrated in the EASYSQL program.

Here's how it works. In the EASYSQL subdirectory, there are several files with the extension SQL. These files contain SQL statements such as the ones shown previously. The EASYSQL program has a Load button that enables you to select one of these text files and then run the SQL statement stored in that file. Be sure that your DatabaseName property for your TQuery object is assigned an alias before you try this code. In particular, I am working with the DBDEMOS alias in all these examples.

The Load button has the following response method for its `OnClick` event:

```
procedure Form1.LoadClick(Sender: TObject);
begin
  if OpenDialog1.Execute then begin
    Query1.Close;
    Query1.SQL.LoadFromFile(OpenDialog1.FileName);
    Query1.Open;
  end;
end;
```

The `LoadClick` method first loads the `OpenDialog` component and enables the user to select a file with an SQL extension. The code checks to see whether the user has selected a file. If a file has been selected, the current query is closed, and the selected file is loaded from disk and displayed to the user.

`OpenDialog1` has its `Filter` property set to the following value:

```
OpenDialog1.Filter := 'SQL(*.SQL)¦*.SQL'
```

As a result, it lists only files that have an SQL extension, as shown in Figure 16.2.

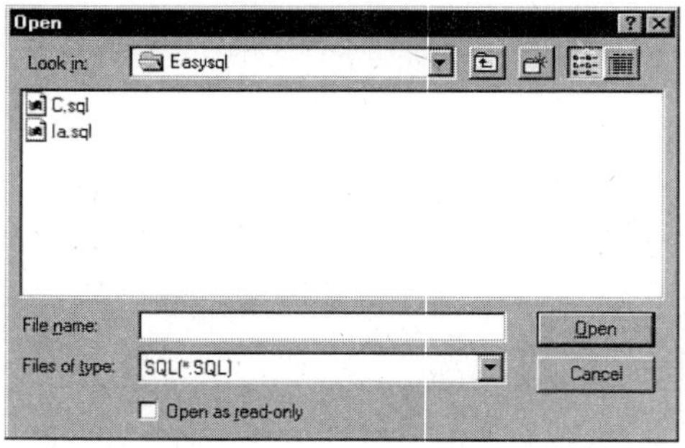

FIGURE 16.2.

The Open dialog from the EASYSQL program enables you to select a prepared SQL statement from an ASCII file stored on disk.

The `LoadFromFile` procedure enables you to load an entire text file at runtime by issuing a single command. The trick, then, is to store SQL statements in text files and load them at runtime. Because the `SQL` property can contain an essentially unlimited number of strings, there is no practical limit to the size of the SQL statement that you could load in this fashion. You can use this technique to quickly execute a series of very complex SQL statements.

In this section, you have seen two methods of changing the `SQL` property at runtime. The first technique enables you to add strings to the `SQL` property, run a query, change the strings, and run the query again. The second technique enables you to load one or more statements from a file. The `LoadFromFile` technique is obviously quite elegant. The first technique can be very powerful at times, but it can be a bit awkward if all you want to do is change one word in a SQL statement. In the next section, you'll learn about how you can eliminate this awkwardness by using parameterized queries.

TQuery and Parameters

Delphi enables you to compose a flexible form of query statement called a *parameterized query*. A parameterized query enables you to substitute variables for single words in the where or insert clause of a SQL statement. These variables can then be changed at any time throughout the life of the query. (If you're using local SQL, you'll be able to make substitutions on almost any word in a SQL statement, but this same capability is not included on most servers.)

To get started using parameterized queries, consider again one of the simple SQL statements listed earlier:

```
Select * from Country where Name like 'C%'
```

To turn this statement into a parameterized query, just replace the right side of the like clause with a variable called NameStr:

```
select * from County where Name like :NameStr
```

In this SQL statement, NameStr is no longer a predefined constant, but instead can change at either design time or runtime. The SQL parser knows that it is dealing with a parameter instead of a constant because a colon is prepended to the word NameStr. That colon tells Delphi that it should substitute the NameStr variable with a value that will be supplied at some future point.

It's important to note that the word NameStr was chosen entirely at random. You can use any valid variable name in this case, just as you can choose a wide range of identifiers when you declare a string variable in one of your programs.

There are two ways to supply variables to a parameterized SQL statement. One method is to use the Params property to supply the value at runtime. The second is to use the DataSource property to supply information from another dataset at either runtime or design time. Here are the key properties used to accomplish these goals:

```
property Params[Index: Word];
function ParamByName(const Value: string);

procedure Prepare
```

When you substitute bind variables in a parameterized query by using the Params property, you usually take four steps:

1. Make sure the table is closed.
2. Ready the Query object by issuing the Prepare command (optional, but highly recommended).
3. Assign the correct values to the Params property.
4. Open the query.

Here's a sample code fragment showing how this might be done in practice:

```
Query1.Close;
Query1.Prepare;
Query1.Params[0].AsString := 'Argentina';
Query1.Open;
```

If you're not familiar with parameterized queries, the preceding code might appear a bit mysterious. To understand it thoroughly, you'll need to do a careful line-by-line analysis. The simplest way to begin is with the third line because it is the `Params` property that lies at the heart of this process.

`Params` is an indexed property that uses a syntax similar to the `Fields` property from `TDataSet`. For instance, you can access the first bind variable in a SQL statement by referring to element 0 in the `Params` array:

```
Params[0].AsString := 'Argentina';
```

If you combine a simple parameterized SQL statement such as

```
select * from Country where Name like :NameStr
```

with the `Params` statements shown previously, the end result is the following SQL statement:

```
select * from Country where Name like 'Argentina'
```

What's happened here is that the variable `:NameStr` has been assigned the value `Argentina` by the `Params` property, thereby enabling you to complete a simple SQL statement.

If you have more than one parameter in a statement, you can access them by changing the index of the `Params` property:

```
Params[1].AsString :=  'SomeValue';
```

So far, you've seen that a parameterized query uses bind variables, which always begin with a colon, to designate the places where parameters will be passed. With this concept in mind, you can move on to the other lines in the previous code fragment.

Before you use the `Params` variable, you should first call `Prepare`. A call to `Prepare` causes Delphi to parse your SQL statement and ready the `Params` property so that it's prepared to accept the appropriate number of variables. If you try to assign a value to the `Params` variable without first calling `Prepare`, your code will still work, but the routine may not be as highly optimized. There is also an `UnPrepare` statement that you should use if you are very concerned about taking up database resources.

After you've called `Prepare` and assigned the correct values to the `Params` variable, you should call `Open` to complete the binding of the variables and produce the dataset that you hope to find. In this particular case, given the input shown previously, the dataset includes the contents of the record where the name field is set to `Argentina`.

In the examples subdirectory, you'll find a program called EASYSQL2 that demonstrates how to use parameterized queries. The EASYSQL2 program performs a function very similar to the one shown earlier in the first EASYSQL program. However, this new version shows how parameterized queries can be used to increase the flexibility of a SQL statement.

To create the program, place TQuery, TDataSource, TdbGrid, and TTabSet components on a form. Hook up the data controls and set the query's DatabaseName property to the demos subdirectory in which the COUNTRY table is found. Fill in the tabset so that it lists the alphabet from *A* to *Z*, as shown in Figure 16.3.

FIGURE 16.3.

The EASYSQL2 program shows how to use parameterized queries.

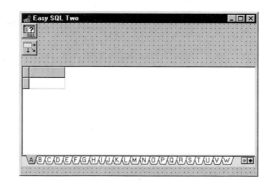

Enter the following string in the SQL property for the query component:

```
select * from Country where Name like :NameStr
```

Now all that's left to create is a response method for the OnChange property of the tabset:

```
procedure TForm1.TabSet1Change(Sender: TObject;
                               NewTab: Integer;
                               var AllowChange: Boolean);
var
  S: String;
begin
  S := TabSet1.Tabs.Strings[NewTab] + '%';
  Query1.Close;
  Query1.Prepare;
  Query1.Params[0].AsString := S;
  Query1.Open;
end;
```

The code shown here follows the four simple steps outlined previously. This is what the code does:

1. Closes the query.
2. Prepares the Params property.
3. Assigns a string to the Params property.
4. Executes the resultant SQL statement by calling Query1.Open.

The actual string assigned to the `Params` property consists of one of the letters of the alphabet plus the % symbol. A typical query produced by this method might look like this:

```
Select * from Country where Name like 'C%'
```

The end result, then, is that the EASYSQL2 program lets you view the contents of the table in alphabetical sequence. Press the tab labeled A, and you see only those records in the database for which the first letter of the Name field begins with an A. Press the B tab, and you see only those items with a first letter of B.

The important point, of course, is that you were able to produce the previous program by writing only five lines of code:

```
S := TabSet1.Tabs.Strings[NewTab] + '%';
Query1.Close;
Query1.Prepare;
Query1.Params[0].AsString := S;
Query1.Open;
```

You also wrote one line of SQL:

```
Select * from Country where Name like :NameStr
```

This combination of SQL and Delphi's native language provides maximum power and flexibility when you want to produce your own applications.

NOTE

In the last chapter, I showed you how to write this same type of program using the TTable object rather than the TQuery object. The question then becomes, which one is better?

Well, there is no definitive answer to this question. If you come from the client/server world and have been writing SQL statements for years, you will almost certainly prefer the TQuery object. If you come from the Turbo Pascal or C++ world, you will probably prefer the TTable component because you are likely to find SQL awkward to write, at least at first.

Ultimately, I can only call them as I see them. I have to confess that after considerable experience trying both methods, I tend to use the TTable object unless I'm forced into a corner and have to use the TQuery object. In some cases, I use a combination of the TTable and TStoredProc object and add in a TQuery object only when absolutely necessary.

Just so I don't mislead anyone, I should emphasize that a stated preference for the TTable object over the TQuery object is likely to be greeted with boos and hisses from an experienced client/server-oriented crowd. I honestly don't know whether this preference is just machismo, or perhaps a failure to appreciate the true power of the TTable object, or whether it is grounded in the bitter fruit of experience. Certainly it

> would be a mistake to read this note as a ringing endorsement of the TTable object over the TQuery object. I am merely mentioning the two opposing viewpoints on this issue and expressing a very tentative personal opinion on this matter.
>
> Finally, I should add that no one can hope to do any serious contemporary database development without understanding something about SQL. SQL is a vital part of the client/server world, and if you don't understand how to use the TQuery object, your viability as a professional client/server programmer would be seriously, perhaps hopelessly, impaired.

Further examples of parameterized queries are found on the CD that accompanies this book as PARAMS2 and PARAMS3. The PARAMS2 program is particularly interesting because it shows how to work with two parameterized variables at once.

To create the PARAMS2 program, drop a query, datasource, and dbgrid on a form, and place two list boxes and TdbImage above the grid, as shown in Figure 16.4. Use TLabel objects to put the word Size above the first list box, and the word Weight above the second list box. Set the DataSource property of the TdbImage control to DataSource1, and type the word BMP in the editor for its DataField property.

FIGURE 16.4.

The form for the PARAMS2 program, as it appears at design time.

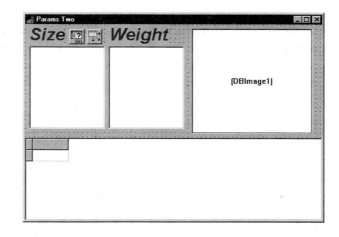

The SQL statement used in the PARAMS2 program looks like this:

```
select * from Animals
  where
    Animals."Size" > :Size and
    Animals."Weight" > :Weight
```

To satisfy the two parameters specified in this SQL statement, you should create the following method:

```
procedure TForm1.ListBox1Click(Sender: TObject);
begin
  Query1.Close;
  Query1.Prepare;
  Query1.Params[0].AsInteger :=
    strtoInt(ListBox1.Items.Strings[ListBox1.ItemIndex]);
  Query1.Params[1].AsInteger :=
    strtoInt(ListBox2.Items.Strings[ListBox2.ItemIndex]);
  Query1.Open;
end;
```

The OnClick events for both list boxes should be set to the previous routine.

When you run the PARAMS2 program, both list boxes are automatically filled with numbers that range from 0 to 42. By selecting a value from the first list box, you specify the size of the animal you want to find. By selecting one from the second list box, you select its weight. Using both values together, you are able to resolve both parameterized variables, thereby effectively selecting a range of animals to view. For instance, select 4 in the Size list box, and then iterate through the choices 2, 4, 6, 8, and 10 in the Weight list box.

As a final touch, the PARAMS2 program displays a picture of the animals in question in the TdbImage control. The blob field of the table that contains the picture is called BMP. The TdbImage control asks only that you set its DataSource property to a valid TDataSource object and its DataField property to the name of the blob field you want to display. In this case, the DataSource is DataSource1, and the blob field is called BMP. (See Listing 16.1.)

Listing 16.1. The PARAMS2 program shows how to work with a parameterized query that has two fields.

```
unit Main;

{ Program copyright (c) 1996 by Charlie Calvert }
{ Project Name: PARAMS2 }

interface

uses
  WinTypes, WinProcs, Classes,
  Graphics, Forms, Controls,
  DB, StdCtrls, dbTables,
  DBGrids, DBCtrls, Grids;

type
  TForm1 = class(TForm)
    Query1: TQuery;
    DataSource1: TDataSource;
    ListBox1: TListBox;
    DBGrid1: TDBGrid;
    ListBox2: TListBox;
    Label1: TLabel;
```

```
    Label2: TLabel;
    DBImage1: TDBImage;
    procedure ListBox1Click(Sender: TObject);
    procedure FormCreate(Sender: TObject);
  private
    { Private declarations }
  public
    { Public declarations }
  end;

var
  Form1: TForm1;

implementation

uses
  SysUtils;

{$R *.DFM}

procedure TForm1.ListBox1Click(Sender: TObject);
begin
  Query1.Close;
  Query1.Prepare;
  Query1.Params[0].AsInteger :=
    StrToInt(ListBox1.Items.Strings[ListBox1.ItemIndex]);
  Query1.Params[1].AsInteger :=
    StrToInt(ListBox2.Items.Strings[ListBox2.ItemIndex]);
  Query1.Open;
end;

procedure TForm1.FormCreate(Sender: TObject);
var
  i: Integer;
  S: string;
begin
  for i := 0 to 21 do begin
    S := IntToStr(i * 2);
    ListBox1.Items.Add(S);
    ListBox2.Items.Add(S);
  end;
  ListBox1.ItemIndex := 0;
  ListBox2.ItemIndex := 0;
end;

end.
```

The *SQL* Property and the *Format* Function

I stated earlier that normally you can only use parameterized variables in cases in which there is a where clause or an insert clause. There are times, however, when these guidelines can be a bit limiting. If you find that you need more flexibility, you can use Delphi's Format function to create your own special version of parameterized variables.

Consider the following SQL statement:

```
Select * from Country
```

There are definitely times when you might want to parameterize the last word in this statement so that it could vary over the life of a program:

```
Select * from :ACountry
```

Unfortunately, most SQL servers won't support this syntax, so you're forced to find another solution.

At times like these, the Format function can come to the rescue. The Format function works a lot like the printf function found in the C language. A detailed explanation of this function is available in Chapter 2, "Delphi Types Under Win32;" for now, all you really need to know about it is that it enables you to substitute variables of almost any type for certain words in a string. More specifically, you can compose a string that looks like this:

```
S := 'Select * from %s';
```

In this string, the syntax %s performs the same role that the :FileName syntax does in a parameterized query. The one difference, of course, is that you should only use %s when you're working with a string. If you're working with an integer, use %d. Once again, you should refer to Chapter 3 or the online documentation if you want more details on how this function works.

The second parameter passed to Format is an array of values separated by commas. To start an array, use an open bracket. Then include a series of values and mark the end of the array with a closed bracket:

```
Format(S, [value1, value2]);
```

When you've declared a string like this:

```
S := 'Select * from %s';
```

you can plug it into a Format statement:

```
Format(S, [Args]);
```

Given the preceding code, if Args were a string set to the value Country, after the Format function was executed you would end up with the following string in the variable S:

```
'Select * from Country'
```

Needless to say, this was exactly what you hoped to achieve, and the Format function enables you to reach your goal without any of the restrictions placed on parameterized variables.

Of course, this example was fairly simplistic, but if you wanted, you could create a string that looks like this:

```
S = 'Select * from %s where %s = %d';
```

This string contains three variables that can be changed at runtime, and it should give you some hints as to the kind of flexibility you can achieve using this system. For instance, you could write code that looks like this:

```
function GetQuery(S1, S2: string; Value: Integer): string;
begin
  Result := Format('Select * from %s where %s = %d', [S1, S2, Value]);
end;

procedure TForm1.Button1Click(Sender: TObject);
begin
  Caption := GetQuery('Customer', 'CustNo', 42);
end;
```

After substitutions are made, this sets the Caption of Form1 to the following string:

```
select * from Customer where CustNo = 42.
```

To see this entire process in action, refer to the PARAMS1 program in the CHAP16 subdirectory on the CD-ROM that comes with this book. This program, shown in Listing 16.2, lets you pick from a list of tables and display the contents of each table in a data grid.

Listing 16.2. The PARAMS1 program shows how to use the `Format` function with an SQL query.

```
unit Main;

{ Program copyright (c) 1995, 1996 by Charles Calvert }
{ Project Name: PARAMS1 }

interface

uses
  WinTypes, WinProcs, Classes,
  Graphics, Forms, Controls,
  DB, DBGrids, StdCtrls,
  DBTables, Grids;

const
  BaseStr = 'Select * from %s';

type
  TForm1 = class(TForm)
    Query1: TQuery;
    DataSource1: TDataSource;
    DBGrid1: TDBGrid;
    ListBox1: TListBox;
    procedure ListBox1Click(Sender: TObject);
    procedure FormCreate(Sender: TObject);
  private
    { Private declarations }
  public
    { Public declarations }
  end;
```

continues

Listing 16.2. continued

```
var
  Form1: TForm1;

implementation

uses
  StrBox,
  SysUtils;

{$R *.DFM}

procedure TForm1.ListBox1Click(Sender: TObject);
var
  S: String;
begin
  S := ListBox1.Items.Strings[ListBox1.ItemIndex];
  S := StripLastToken(S, '.');
  Query1.Close;
  Query1.SQL.Clear;
  S := Format(BaseStr, [S]);
  Query1.SQL.Add(S);
  Query1.Open;
end;

procedure TForm1.FormCreate(Sender: TObject);
begin
  Session.GetTableNames(Query1.DatabaseName, '', False, False, ListBox1.Items);
end;

end.
```

To create the PARAMS1 program, place a query on the form, and set its DatabaseName property to DBDEMOS. To create the list of tables, place a TListBox object on the form and create the following FormCreate method:

```
procedure TForm1.FormCreate(Sender: TObject);
begin
  Session.GetTableNames(Query1.DatabaseName, '',
                        False, False, ListBox1.Items);
end;
```

The call to Delphi's built-in GetTableNames routine returns a complete list of valid table names from the database specified in the first parameter. The second parameter is a string that can contain a file mask, if you so desire. For instance, you can enter c*.* to get a list of all tables beginning with the letter C. The fourth parameter is a Boolean value that specifies whether you want to work with system tables, and the final parameter is a value of type TStrings that holds the output from the function.

To enable the user to view the contents of the tables listed in the FormCreate method, you should add a TDataSource and TdbGrid to the form, and then wire them up.

At the very top of the unit that holds your main form, you should declare a string constant:

```
const
  BaseStr = 'Select * from %s';
```

Next, create a response method for the `ListBox1.OnClick` event:

```
procedure TForm1.ListBox1Click(Sender: TObject);
var
  S: String;
begin
  S := ListBox1.Items.Strings[ListBox1.ItemIndex];
  Query1.Close;
  Query1.SQL.Clear;
  Query1.SQL.Add(Format(BaseStr, [S]));
  Query1.Open;
end;
```

The first line of the code shown here assigns a string the value from the currently selected item from a list box.

The next line of code checks to make sure that the query is closed:

```
Query1.Close
```

The next line then clears out any strings currently sitting in the `SQL` property:

```
Query1.SQL.Clear;
```

The next line in the program adds a new SQL statement to the query. To do this, it calls on the `Format` function, the `BaseStr` constant, and the string selected from the list box. The result is a new SQL statement that requests a dataset containing the contents of a table. For example, the string might look like this:

```
select * from Orders
```

The PARAMS1 program, shown in Listing 16.2, demonstrates how to use the `Format` function in lieu of parameterized queries. The `Format` function is useful because it is more flexible than parameterized queries.

Later in this chapter, you'll revisit this program again to see how you can automatically list all the tables in a particular database or subdirectory.

Passing Parameters Through TDataSource

In the last chapter, you learned about a technique for creating a one-to-many relationship between two tables. Now, you'll learn about a second technique for performing the same action, this time using a TQuery object.

The TQuery object has a `DataSource` property that can be used to create a link between itself and another dataset. It doesn't matter whether the other dataset is a TTable object, TQuery object, or some other descendant of TDataSet that you or another programmer might create.

All you have to do is ensure that the dataset is connected to a datasource, and then you're free to make the link.

In the following explanation, assume that you want to create a link between the ORDERS table and the CUSTOMERS table, so that whenever you view a particular customer record, only the orders associated with that customer will be visible.

Consider the following parameterized query:

```
Select * from Orders where CustNo = :CustNo
```

In this statement, :CustNo is a bind variable that needs to be supplied a value from some source. Delphi enables you to use the TQuery.DataSource field to point at another dataset, which can supply that information to you automatically. In other words, instead of being forced to use the Params property to manually supply a variable, the appropriate variable can simply be plucked from another table. Furthermore, Delphi always first tries to satisfy a parameterized query by using the DataSource property. Only if that fails does it expect to get the variable from the Params property.

Take a moment to consider exactly what happens in these situations. As you saw in the last chapter, the CustNo field forms a link between the ORDERS table and the CUSTOMER table. Therefore, if both tables are visible on a form, the appropriate CustNo value is always available in the current record of the Customer table. All you need to do is point the query object in the appropriate direction.

To obtain the bind value, just set the DataSource for the Query object to the TDataSource object that's associated with the CUSTOMER table. That's all there is to it! Just enter a short SQL statement, then link up the DataSource property, and Bingo! You've established a one-to-many relationship like the linked cursors example from the last chapter!

On the CD that accompanies this book, you'll find an example called QLINKS that demonstrates how this technique works. To create the QLINKS program, place two TQuery, two TDataSource, and two TdbGrids on a form, as shown in Figure 16.5.

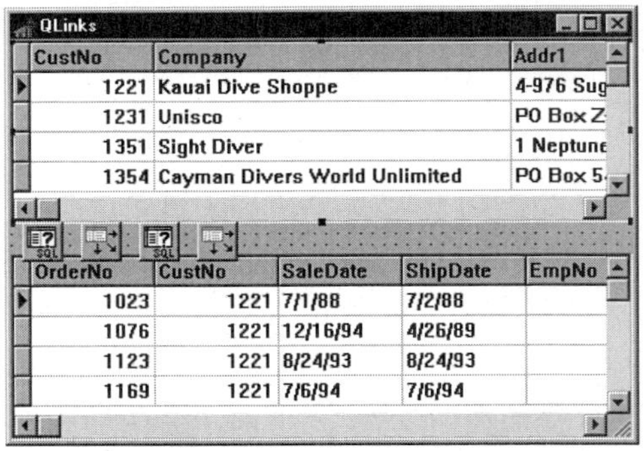

FIGURE 16.5.

The QLINKS program shows how to create a one-to-many relationship using the TQuery object.

In the SQL property for the first TQuery component, enter the following:

```
select * from Customer
```

In the second TQuery component, enter the following:

```
select * from Orders where CustNo = :CustNo
```

To complete the program, all you have to do is wire up the controls by attaching dbGrid1 to DataSource1 and DataSource1 to Query1. Perform the same action for the second set of controls, and then set the Query2.DataSource property to DataSource1. This last step is the main action that forms the link between the two tables. If you now run the program, you'll see that the two tables work together in the desired manner.

If you want to create a link between two tables using multiple fields, you can simply specify the relevant fields in your query:

```
select * from Orders
    where CustNo = :CustNo and
    CustCountry = :CustCountry
```

The important point to understand is that this one-to-many example works simply because Delphi supports parameterized variables. There is no other hand-waving going on in the background. All that's happening is that you're using a basic SQL statement to view the members of the ORDERS table that happen to have a particular customer number. The customer number in question was passed to you through the DataSource property and the bind variable you created.

The examples you've seen so far in this chapter should give you some feeling for the extreme power and flexibility inherent in the TQuery object. If you're looking for a lever powerful enough to move the roadblocks in your client/server programming world, TQuery is likely to be the tool you require.

NOTE

The RequestLive field of the TQuery object can play a very important role in SQL programming. By default, any query you make with the TQuery object will return a read-only dataset. However, you can attempt to get a live query by setting the TQuery RequestLive property to True. At the time of this writing, it is not clear exactly when you will be able to get live datasets back from a query. As a rule, if your query involves only one table, then you can set RequestLive to True. If your query involves multiple tables, then setting RequestLive to True might not produce the desired result. You can check the CanModify property to see if your request has succeeded.

In general, I use the TTable object rather than the TQuery object when I want to edit the results of a join between one or more tables. The SQL language is designed to prevent indiscriminate updating of a table. In particular, if you want to update a table with a SQL query, then you should use the SQL `Update` command. That's the way SQL is supposed to work. It's a very conservative language. If you want to let the user edit tables at will, then you should use the TTable object.

Whatever limitations the `RequestLive` property may have are not unique to Delphi. If you want to edit tables quickly, with a high-performance system, then use the TTable object. Of course, you can try to use the TQuery object first, and see how these requests are handled with your particular server.

In the next section, you'll learn more about the TQuery object when you see how to join two tables together so that you can view them both in a single dataset.

Performing Joins Between Multiple Tables

You've seen that the CUSTOMERS and ORDERS tables are related in a one-to-many relationship based on the `CustNo` field. The ORDERS table and ITEMS tables are also bound in a one-to-many relationship, only this time the field that connects them is called `OrderNo`.

More specifically, each order that exists in the ORDERS table will have one or more records from the ITEMS table associated with it. The records from the ITEMS table specify characteristics, such as price and part number, of the items associated with a particular sale.

Consider what happens when you go to a restaurant and order steamed shrimp, a steamed artichoke, Caesar salad, and a mineral water. The result of this pleasurable exercise is that you've made one order that has four different line items associated with it:

```
Suzie Customer (Oct 1, 1994):
   ITEMS1: Shrimp          $12.95
   ITEMS2: Artichoke       $6.25
   ITEMS3: Caesar salad    $3.25
   ITEMS4: Mineral water   $2.50
```

In a situation like this, it's sometimes simplest to join the data from the ORDERS table and the ITEMS table, so that the resulting dataset contains information from both tables:

```
Suzie      Oct 1, 1994    Shrimp         $12.95
Suzie      Oct 1, 1994    Artichoke      $6.25
etc...
```

The act of merging these two tables is called a join, and it is one of the fundamental operations you can perform on a set of two or more tables.

Given the ORDERS and ITEMS tables from the demos subdirectory, you can join them in such a way that the CustNo, OrderNo, and SaleDate fields from the ORDERS table are merged with the StockNo, Price, and Qty fields from the ITEMS table to form a new dataset containing all six fields. A grid containing the resulting dataset is shown in Figure 16.6.

FIGURE 16.6.

The QJOIN program joins the ORDERS and ITEMS table producing a dataset with fields from each table.

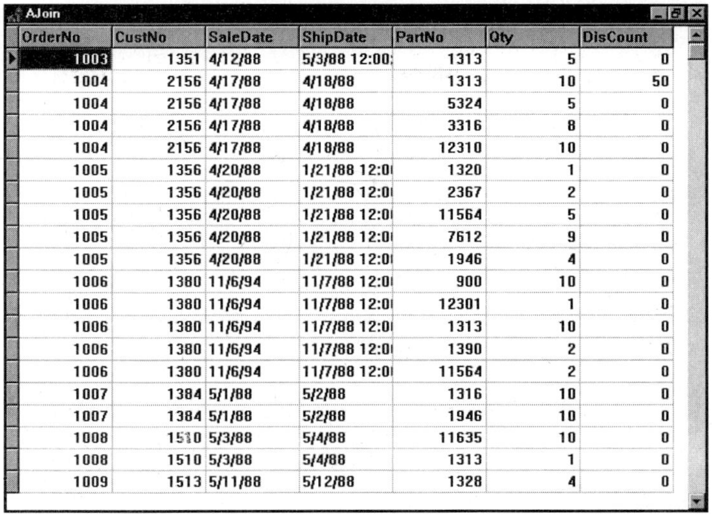

OrderNo	CustNo	SaleDate	ShipDate	PartNo	Qty	DisCount
1003	1351	4/12/88	5/3/88 12:00:	1313	5	0
1004	2156	4/17/88	4/18/88	1313	10	50
1004	2156	4/17/88	4/18/88	5324	5	0
1004	2156	4/17/88	4/18/88	3316	8	0
1004	2156	4/17/88	4/18/88	12310	10	0
1005	1356	4/20/88	1/21/88 12:0(	1320	1	0
1005	1356	4/20/88	1/21/88 12:0(	2367	2	0
1005	1356	4/20/88	1/21/88 12:0(	11564	5	0
1005	1356	4/20/88	1/21/88 12:0(	7612	9	0
1005	1356	4/20/88	1/21/88 12:0(	1946	4	0
1006	1380	11/6/94	11/7/88 12:0(	900	10	0
1006	1380	11/6/94	11/7/88 12:0(	12301	1	0
1006	1380	11/6/94	11/7/88 12:0(	1313	10	0
1006	1380	11/6/94	11/7/88 12:0(	1390	2	0
1006	1380	11/6/94	11/7/88 12:0(	11564	2	0
1007	1384	5/1/88	5/2/88	1316	10	0
1007	1384	5/1/88	5/2/88	1946	10	0
1008	1510	5/3/88	5/4/88	11635	10	0
1008	1510	5/3/88	5/4/88	1313	1	0
1009	1513	5/11/88	5/12/88	1328	4	0

There's a substantial difference between linking cursors and joining tables. However, they both have two things in common:

■ They both involve two or more tables.

■ Each table is linked to the other by one or more shared fields.

The act of joining the ORDERS and ITEMS tables can be accomplished by a single SQL statement that looks like this:

```
select
  O."OrderNo", O."CustNo",
  O."SaleDate", O."ShipDate",
  I."PartNo ", I."Qty",  I."Discount "
from
  Orders O, Items I
where
  O.OrderNo = I.OrderNo
```

This statement consists of four different parts:

■ The select statement specifies that you expect a cursor to be returned containing some form of dataset.

■ Next, there is a list of the fields that you want included in the dataset you are requesting. This list includes the OrderNo, CustNo, SaleDate, ShipDate, PartNo, Qty, and Discount fields. The first four fields originate in the ORDERS table, and the next three fields originate in the ITEMS table.

■ The from clause states that you're working with two tables, one called ORDERS and the other called ITEMS. For the sake of brevity, the statement uses an optional SQL feature that lets you specify the ORDERS table with the letter O, and the ITEMS table with the letter I.

■ The where clause is vitally important, because it specifies which field will link the two tables. Some servers are capable of returning valid datasets even if you don't include a where clause in your join, but the resulting set of records will almost surely not be what you want. To get the results you're looking for, be sure to include a where clause.

When you've created the SQL statement that you want to use, there is nothing at all difficult about performing a join. The QJOIN example that ships with Delphi demonstrates exactly how to proceed. All you need do is drop a TQuery, TDataSource, and TdbGrid onto a form and then wire them up in the standard way. When you're hooked up, you can paste the query statement in the SQL property of the query, fill in the DatabaseName property, and then set Active to True. Now, compile and run the program and take a moment to scroll through the new dataset you've created from the raw materials in the ORDERS and ITEMS tables.

> **NOTE**
>
> When you are composing SQL statements in the SQL field of the TQuery object, you may find that the space you are working in is a little cramped. To open up your horizons, click on the Code Editor button in the String List Editor dialog box. Your code will then be transferred from the String List Editor to Delphi's main editor. The main editor gives you more room to work, and provides syntax highlighting for your SQL statements.

There is not much point to showing you the actual source code for the QJOIN program because all the magic occurs in the SQL statement quoted previously.

Parameterized Queries and *join* Statements

You can mix parameterized queries and join statements. This is useful if you want to show the CUSTOMER table at the top of a form, and then beneath it, show another dataset that contains records with information from both the ORDERS and ITEMS table. The end result is a program that enables you to iterate through a list of customers in the top half of a form, while the bottom half of the form shows only the purchases associated with any particular customer, including a list of the line items that were bought. This is the type of form you'd produce if you wanted to create an electronic invoice.

The QJOIN2 program on your system shows how a program of this type looks in practice. The main form for the QJOIN2 program is shown in Figure 16.7.

FIGURE 16.7.

The QJOIN2 program shows three tables linked together in a logical and coherent fashion.

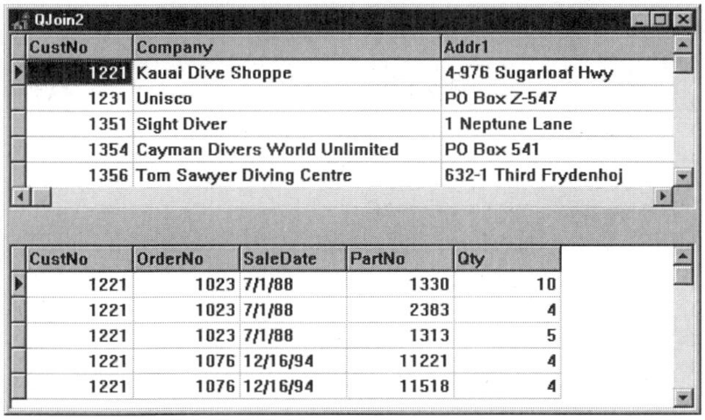

To create this program, drop down a TTable, a TQuery, two datasources, and two data grids. Hook up the TTable, the first datasource, and the first grid to the CUSTOMER table. Wire up the remaining controls, and specify `DataSource1` in the `Query1.DataSource` property. Now add the following SQL statement in the `Query1.SQL` property:

```
select
  O.CustNo, O.OrderNo, O.SaleDate,
  L.PartNo, L.Discount, L.Qty
from
  Orders O, Items L
where
  O.CustNo = :CustNo and
  O.OrderNo = L.OrderNo
```

The statement pictured here is very much like the one you saw in the last section, except that the `where` clause has been expanded to include a bind variable:

```
where
  O.CustNo = :CustNo and
  O.OrderNo = L.OrderNo
```

This clause now specifies two different relationships: one between the CUSTOMER table and the ORDERS table, and the second between the ORDERS table and the ITEMS table. More specifically, the value for the `CustNo` variable will be supplied by the current record of the CUSTOMER table through the link on the `Query1.DataSource` property. The link between the ORDERS table and ITEMS table will be the OrderNo field.

Conceptually, the QJOIN2 program forces you to wrestle with some fairly complex ideas. This complexity is inherent in the task being performed. Delphi, however, enables you to encapsulate these complex ideas in a few very simple mechanical steps. In short, once you understand the goal you want to achieve, Delphi enables you to perform even complex data operations with just a few minutes of work.

Open Versus ExecSQL

After you've composed an SQL statement, there are two different ways to process it. If you need to get a cursor back from the Query, you should always call Open. If you don't need to return a cursor, you should call ExecSQL. For instance, if you're inserting, deleting, or updating data, you should call ExecSQL. To state the same matter in slightly different terms, you should use Open whenever you compose a select statement, and you should use ExecSQL whenever you write any other kind of statement.

Here's a typical SQL statement that you might use to delete a record from a table:

```
delete from Country where Name = 'Argentina';
```

This statement deletes any record from the COUNTRY database that has Argentina in the Name field.

It doesn't take long to see that this is a case in which you might want to use a parameterized query. For instance, it would be nice to be able to vary the name of the country you want to delete:

```
delete from Country where Name = :CountryName
```

In this case, CountryName is a variable that can be changed at runtime by writing code that looks like this:

```
Query2.Prepare;
Query2.Params[0].AsString := 'Argentina';
Query2.ExecSQL;
Query1.Refresh;
```

The code shown here first calls Prepare to inform Delphi that it should parse the SQL statement you gave it and ready the Params property. The next step is to insert a value into the Params property, and then to execute the newly prepared SQL statement. Note that you execute the statement not by calling Open but by calling ExecSQL. Call ExecSQL when you don't need to return a dataset! Finally, you display the results of your actions to the user by asking the first query to refresh itself.

The Insert2 program from the examples subdirectory demonstrates this technique. That program uses three different TQuery objects. The first TQuery object works with a TDataSource and TdbGrid object to display the COUNTRY database on screen. In Figure 16.8, you can see that the program has two buttons: one for deleting records, and the other for inserting records.

The second TQuery object in the INSERT2 program is used to insert a record into the COUNTRY table, as explained next. The third TQuery object is used for deleting records. It has the following statement in its SQL property:

```
delete from Country where Name = :Name;
```

FIGURE 16.8.

The INSERT2 program uses three TQuery components and one TDataSource component.

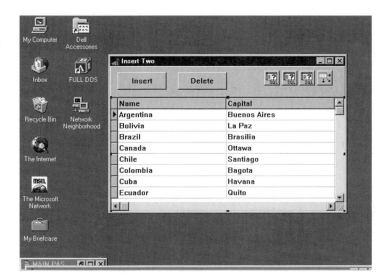

The code associated with the Delete button looks like this:

```
Query3.Prepare;
Query3.Params[0].AsString := Query1.Fields[0].AsString;
Query3.ExecSQL;
Query1.Refresh;
```

Query3 snags the name of the record to delete from the currently selected record in the first query. This enables the user to scroll through the list of records using the TdbGrid tool, and then delete whatever record is current. After the deletion, Query1.Refresh is called. A call to Refresh forces the Query to obtain the most recent data from the disk, thereby allowing the program to reflect the deletion at almost the same moment it is made. (Note that a real-world program meant to be used with a typical set of users would query the user before performing a deletion of this sort.)

Here is a typical SQL statement for inserting data into a table:

```
insert into
  Country
  (Name, Capital, Continent, Area, Population)
values
  ('Argentina', 'Buenos Ares',
   'South America', 2777815, 32300003)
```

This is a convenient system, but it has the disadvantage of forcing you to hard-code values into the statement. To avoid this problem, the Query2 object has the following code in its SQL property:

```
insert
  into Country (Name, Capital, Continent, Area,  Population)
  values (:Name, :Capital, :Continent, :Area, :Population)
```

Note that in this code, all the actual values intended for insertion are specified by bind variables. These bind variables are convenient because they enable you to write code that looks like this:

```
procedure TForm1.InsertClick(Sender: TObject);
begin
  Query2.Prepare;
  Query2.Params[0].AsString := 'Erewhen';
  Query2.Params[1].AsString := 'None';
  Query2.Params[2].AsString := 'Imagination';
  Query2.Params[3].AsFloat : =  0.0;
  Query2.Params[4].AsFloat : =  1.0;
  Query2.ExecSQL;
  Query1.Refresh;
end;
```

In the code shown here, you can use edit controls to dynamically specify the values that you want to insert at runtime. Notice that once again, the program calls ExecSQL rather than Open. This is because there's no need to return a cursor from an SQL insert statement. The procedure ends with a call to Refresh, which assures that Query1 goes out to the disk and gets the most recent data.

> **NOTE**
>
> You might want to compare this version of the Insert program with the Insert1 application that uses the TTable object. There are advantages to both techniques, but you should remember that keeping code as simple as possible is one way to construct applications that are robust and easy to maintain.

In this section, you've learned about the differences between ExecSQL and Open. The major point to remember is that select statements return a cursor and therefore require a call to Open. delete, insert, and update don't return a cursor, and should therefore be accompanied by calls to ExecSQL. All of this is demonstrated on the CD in the INSERT2 program. The call to Refresh ensures that the data displayed to the user reflects the changes made by the delete statement.

Specialized TQuery Properties

By this time, you should have a good feeling for how to use Delphi to create and execute SQL statements. There are, however, a few properties belonging to TQuery that have not yet been mentioned:

```
property UniDirectional: Boolean;
property Handle: HDBICur;
property StmtHandle: HDBIStmt;
property DBHandle: HDBIDB;
```

The UniDirectional property is used to optimize your access to a table. If you set UniDirectional to True, you can iterate through a table more quickly, but you'll only be able to move in a forward direction.

The StmtHandle property is related to the Handle property from TDataSet; it's included solely so you can make your own calls directly to the Borland Database Engine. Under normal circumstances, there would be no need for you to use this property, because Delphi's components can handle the needs of most programmers. However, if you're familiar with the Borland Database Engine, and if you know that it has some particular capability that isn't encapsulated in the VCL, you can use TQuery.StmtHandle or TQuery.Handle to make calls directly to the engine.

The following short code fragment shows two calls being made directly to the BDE:

```
var
  Name: array[0..100] of Char;
  Records: Integer;
begin
  dbiGetNetUserName(Name);
  dbiGetRecordCount(Query1.Handle, Records);
end;
```

The DBIPROCS unit contains a list of all the possible calls made to the Borland Database Engine. This file may appear on your system as either DBIPROCS.PAS or DBIPROCS.INT.

Summary

In this chapter, you have learned the main features of the TQuery component. You have seen that you can use this component to create SQL statements that enable you to manipulate tables in a wide variety of useful ways.

One of the keys to understanding TQuery's SQL property is the ability to manipulate it at runtime. In this chapter, you saw three different methods of manipulating this property. The first, and conceptually simplest, is to merely use the Query1.SQL.Add function whenever you need to change a query at runtime. Parameterized queries are less wasteful than using the Add property, but there are some limits on what you can do with parameterized queries. To get beyond these limits, you can use the Format function, which enables you to create almost any kind of SQL statement you could want at runtime.

Regardless of how you treat the SQL property, there is no doubt that it is one of the power centers in the Delphi environment. Programmers who want to write powerful SQL applications need to know almost everything they can about the SQL property.

In the next chapter, you will learn how to use the Fields Editor, the Database Explorer, the DataDictionary, QBE, and the Query Builder to automate some of the database tasks you have been performing in the last two chapters.

I should perhaps add that almost all the code in this chapter will compile without change in either the 16- or 32-bit version of Delphi. This ability to write one source file that compiles fine under 16- or 32-bit Windows is one of Delphi's great strengths.

Fields and Database Tools

17

IN THIS CHAPTER

This chapter covers a set of visual tools you can use to simplify database development. The major areas of concentration are as follows:

- Relational databases
- The Fields Editor
- TField descendant objects
- Calculated fields
- The TdbGrid Component
- Lookup fields
- The Database Explorer
- The Database Desktop
- Query by example (QBE)
- MultiRecord objects—TdbCtrlGrid

The general theme that ties these subjects together is how you can use Delphi's visual and programmatic tools to create relational databases. Delphi has become a very sophisticated database tool, and it takes time to get a feeling for the breadth of the tools available to client/server developers. One of the goals of this chapter is to give you some sense of the key components used when designing database applications.

One of the most frequently mentioned tools in this chapter is the Fields Editor. By using the Fields Editor, you can create objects that you can use to influence the manner and types of data that appear in visual controls such as `TdbEdit` and `TdbGrid`. For instance, you can use the objects made in the Field Editor to format data so that it appears as currency or as a floating-point number with a defined precision. These same changes can be accomplished through the Data Dictionary in the Database Explorer, or through the Database Desktop. These latter tools, however, have a global impact on the field's potential values, whereas the changes made in the Object Inspector affect only the current application.

The new `Columns` property of the TdbGrid control can be used to change the appearance of a grid so that its columns are arranged in a new order or are hidden. You can also use the `Columns` property to change the color of columns in a grid, or to insert dropdown combo boxes into a grid.

The lessons you learn in this chapter will demonstrate a key part of the techniques used by most programmers when they present database tables to their users. Much of the material involves manipulating visual tools, but the basic subject matter is fairly technical and assumes a basic understanding of the Delphi environment and language.

If you are an experienced database programmer, don't be fooled by the relatively basic overview of relational databases found in the first few pages of this chapter. There is a lot of important subject matter to be found here, and much of it is unique to Delphi in general and to Delphi 2.0 in particular.

Relational Databases

In order to make sure everyone is following the discussion in the next few chapters, I'm going to spend a few pages giving a quick-and-dirty introduction to relational databases. This discussion will also include a brief overview of the Database Explorer and the Database Desktop.

There are many different kinds of possible databases, but in today's world, on the PC, there are only two kinds that have any significant market share:

1. Flat-file databases
2. Relational databases

Flat-file databases consist of a single file. The classic example would be an address book that contains a single table with six fields in it: Name, Address, City, State, Zip, and Phone. If that is your entire database, then what you have is a flat-file database. In a flat-file database, the words table and database are synonymous.

In general, relational databases consist of a series of tables related to each other by one or more fields in each table. In Chapter 15, "Using TTable and TDataSet," and Chapter 16, "SQL and the TQuery Object," you saw how to use the TTable and TQuery objects to relate the Customer and Orders table together in a one-to-many relationship. As you recall, the two tables were joined on the CustNo field. The relationship established between these two tables on the CustNo field is very much at the heart of all relational databases.

What are the differences between the address book example and the Customer and Orders example? Well, here are three key differences:

1. The address book database consists of one single table. That's the whole database. There is nothing more to say about it.
2. The Customer and Orders example consists of two tables. Relational databases always contain multiple tables. As you will see, there are in fact more than just these two tables in the DBDEMOS database, but for now just concentrate on the Customer and Orders tables.
3. The Customer and Orders tables are related to one another by the CustNo field.

The key differences, then, are that relational databases consist of multiple tables, at least some of which are related together by one or more fields. Flat-file databases, on the other hand, consist of only one single table, which is not related to any other table.

What advantages do relational databases have over flat-file databases? Here are two key advantages:

- Relational databases save disk space. The Customer table holds information about customers, including their address, phone, and contact information. The Orders table holds information about orders, including their date, cost, and payment method. If you were forced to keep all this information in a single table, then each order would also have to list the customer information, which would mean that some customers' addresses would be repeated dozens of times in the database. That's wasteful of space. It's better to use a relational database because each customer's address would be entered only once. You could also have two flat-file databases, one holding the customer information and the other holding the orders information. The problem with this second scenario is that flat-file databases provide no means of relating the two tables so that you can easily see which orders belong to which customer.

■ Relational databases provide flexibility. If you combined the Customer and Orders table into one single table, that might be good on some occasions, but it would mean that you would have no immediately intuitive way to view the orders information separately from the customer information, or the customer information separately from the orders information. (You could make certain fields invisible, but how could you intuitively know which fields belonged to which group?) A relational database offers these possibilities:

1. You can view the Customer table alone if you want and view the Orders table alone, if you want.

2. You can place the two tables in a one-to-many relationship, so that you can see them side by side, but only see the Orders relating to the currently highlighted customer.

3. Yet another alternative would be to perform a join between the two tables, so that you see them as one combined table, much like the combined table you would be forced to use if you wanted to "join" the customer and orders table in a single flat-file database. However, you can decide which fields from both tables will be part of the join, leaving out any you don't want to view.

The one disadvantage that relational databases have when compared to flat-file databases is that they are more complicated to use. This is not just a minor sticking point. Neophytes are literally completely baffled by relational databases. They don't have a clue as to what to do with them. Even if you have a relative degree of expertise, anyone can still become overwhelmed by a relational database consisting of three dozen tables related to one another in some hundred different ways.

NOTE

One common feature of relational databases is that most records will have a unique number associated with them, and these numbers will be used as the indexes that relate one table to another. For instance, if you have a list of Customers, there will be a unique CustNo field in each record. Furthermore, if you have a list of Orders, then there will be a unique OrderNo associated with the orders table. The Orders table will also have a CustNo field that will relate it to the Customer table. These CustNo, OrderNo, AuthorNo, BookNo, and similar fields might also be used in flat-file databases, but they play a key and unique role in relational databases because they are the indexes used to relate different tables.

One-to-Many Relationships: The Data and the Index

One good way to start to understand relational databases is by working with the Customer, Orders, Items, and Parts tables. All four of these tables are related in one-to-many relationships, each to each. That is, the Customer table is related to the Orders table, the Orders table to the Items table, and the Items table to the Parts table.

Master	Detail	Connector
Customer	Orders	CustNo
Orders	Items	OrderNo
Items	Parts	PartNo

The preceding list shows that the Customer and Orders tables are related in a one-to-many relationship, with Customer being the Master table and Orders being the detail table. The connector between them is the CustNo field. The relationship between these tables can be reversed. For instance, the Parts table could become the master table and the Items table the detail table, and so on, back down the line.

All of these tables have various indexes. An index enables you to sort tables on a particular field, or to otherwise group related bits of information. For now, I'll draw a distinction between only two different kinds of indexes:

1. Primary Index or Key: This is the default sort order for the table. With Paradox tables, each entry in the Primary Index must be unique. You can, however, have multiple fields in the Primary Index of a Paradox table. These fields must be sequential, starting with the first field in the table.

2. Secondary Index: These are secondary methods of sorting on a particular table. You can create composite, secondary keys.

NOTE

If you are new to databases, you will undoubtedly be frustrated to discover that different databases have varying rules for setting up indexes, keys, and so on. In this book, I tend to use Paradox tables as the default, but I also spend considerable time describing InterBase tables. If you use some other database, such as dBASE, Oracle, or Sybase, then you should be sure to read up on the basic rules for using those tools.

If you are not sure what database to use, then I would tentatively suggest using Paradox to get started. It has a robust set of rules for enforcing data integrity, a rich set of types, and some nice features such as autoincrement fields. It works fine on a network, as long as everyone can attach their PCs to one centralized server and you aren't expecting a large number of simultaneous users.

If you are expecting 20 or more simultaneous users, then I would bite the bullet financially and switch to InterBase or to another standard SQL server such as Oracle, Sybase, or MS SQL Server. These tools will:

- Let you talk to the server over TCP/IP, or some other network protocol
- Put much of the computational burden on the server rather than the client machine
- Prove to be much more robust
- Allow you to use stored procedures, triggers, views, and other advanced server-side technologies

Remember that when I make suggestions about databases or about anything else, I am usually not so much trying to establish a definitive standard as I am trying to give reasonable advice to those readers who are not sure which way to turn.

Here is a list of the keys and indexes on the Customers, Orders, Items, and Parts tables:

Table Name	Primary Index	Secondary Indexes
Customer	CustNo	Company
Orders	OrderNo	CustNo
Items	OrderNo	CustNo
Parts	PartNo	VendorNo, Description

If you do not have a premade list like this one, you could find this information in at least three ways:

- The Object Inspector
- The Database Explorer
- The Database Desktop

I will explain all three methods and then discuss some possible alternative techniques.

If you drag the Customer table off the Explorer and onto a form, you will be able to view its indexes in the Object Inspector. If you drop down the IndexName property editor, you will see that there is one index listed there. This is the secondary index, called ByCompany. If you select this index, the table will sort on the Company field. If you set the IndexName property back to blank, then the table will sort automatically on the Primary Index, which is the CustNo field. You can also drop down the IndexFieldNames property, which gives you a list of the fields that are indexed, in this case the CustNo and Company fields.

The IndexName and IndexFieldNames properties give you a handy way of tracking indexes at design time. They don't, however, give you all the information you need, such as exactly what fields make up which parts of the Primary and Secondary Indexes. In this case, you could probably guess, but it would still be nice to get a more definitive answer.

If you open up the Database Explorer, expand the DBDEMOS node, the Tables node, the Customer node, and finally the Indexes node, you get (naturally enough) a list of the indexes on the Customer table! This is a great feature, and you should use it whenever possible. Figure 17.1 shows the expanded nodes of the Indexes for the Customer table.

FIGURE 17.1.

The Indexes of the Customer table viewed in the Database Explorer.

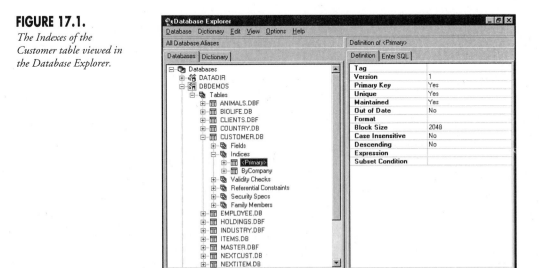

While you have the Explorer open, you should also expand the Fields node, as shown in Figure 17.2. This gives a quick list of all the fields and their types. Notice that you can drag and drop individual fields onto a form.

A third way to get a look at the structure of a table is through the Database Desktop (DBD). You can open this program from the Tools menu in Delphi. Use the File menu in the DBD to set the Working Directory to the DBDEMOS Alias. Open up the Customer table and choose the Table | Info Structure menu choice. Drop down the Table Properties combo box and look up the Secondary Indexes, as shown in Figure 17.3. The Primary Index is designated by the asterisks after the keyed fields in the Key Roster. In this case, only the CustNo field is starred, since it is the sole keyed field.

> **NOTE**
>
> Over time, the Database Desktop will probably be replaced entirely by the Explorer. However, there are still some things that the DBD does better than the Explorer, so both products are shipped with Delphi.

FIGURE 17.2.

The Fields view of the Customer table from the Database Explorer.

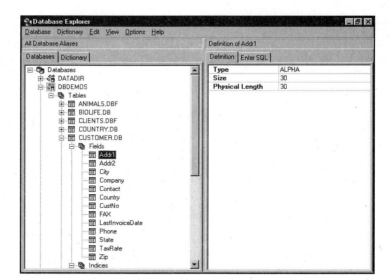

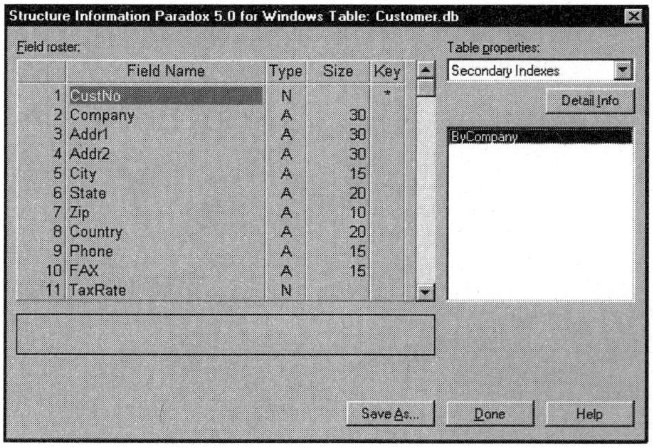

FIGURE 17.3.

The Database Desktop struts its venerable features by displaying the indexes on the Customer table.

Notice the Save As button on the Info Structure dialog. You can use this to save a table that contains the structure of the Customer table. You can then print this out on a printer using Report Smith or TQuickReports. Be sure to use a fixed-size font, not a proportional font:

```
Field Name      Type    Size Key

CustNo          N              *
Company         A       30
Addr1           A       30
Addr2           A       30
City            A       15
State           A       20
Zip             A       10
Country         A       20
```

> **NOTE**
>
> In this particular example, you might notice that the Parts table is always arranged in a one-to-one relationship with the Items table. However, if you reverse the order of these table and make the Parts table the Master, then the arrangement will look more like a proper one-to-many relationship. However, it is not wrong to make either table the master. The point is simply to arrange the tables so that you get the information from that you want to obtain.

This discussion of the Relate program has given you a look at some of the important features in the Database Explorer and Database Desktop. It has also given you a quick run-down on some of the key ideas behind the construction of relational databases. The point here is that Delphi has lots of built-in tools that help you construct relational databases. There is more that I want to say about these topics, however, even in this rather sketchy overview of a complicated subject. In particular, I have not yet talked about joins.

Relational Databases and Joins

In the last section, you saw how to relate the Customers, Orders, Items, and Parts table in a one-to-many relationship that is sometimes called a master-detail relationship. In this section, you will again relate all four tables, but in a different kind of relationship called a join.

You had a look at joins in the last chapter, "SQL and the TQuery Object." This time the query that you need to build is a bit longer:

```
SELECT DISTINCT d.Company, d1.AmountPaid, d2.Qty,
                d3.Description, d3.Cost, d3.ListPrice
FROM "Customer.db" d, "Orders.db" d1,
     "Items.db" d2, "Parts.db" d3
WHERE (d1.CustNo = d.CustNo)
      AND (d2.OrderNo = d1.OrderNo)
      AND (d3.PartNo = d2.PartNo)
ORDER BY d.Company, d1.AmountPaid, d2.Qty,
         d3.Description, d3.Cost, d3.ListPrice
```

Though not horrendously complicated, the syntax shown here is still ugly enough to give some people pause.

The basic principles involved in this kind of statement are simple enough to describe. All that's happening is that the Customer, Orders, Items, and Parts tables are being joined together into one large table of the type you would have to create if you were trying to track all this information in a single flat-file database. The one proviso, of course, is that not all the fields from the four tables are being used, in fact, the only ones mentioned are:

```
d.Company, d1.AmountPaid, d2.Qty,
d3.Description, d3.Cost, d3.ListPrice
```

Here the d, d1, d2, and d3 are described in the following From clause:

```
"Customer.db" d, "Orders.db" d1,
"Items.db" d2, "Parts.db" d3
```

The Order By clause, of course, simply defines the sort order to be used on the table created by this join.

You can create a program that performs this join by dropping a TQuery, TDataSource, and TdbGrid on a form. Wire the objects together, wire the TQuery to the DBDEMOS database, and set its SQL property to the query shown above. An example program called RelJoin demonstrates this process. The output from the program is shown in Figure 17.6.

FIGURE 17.6.

The RelJoin program demonstrates a join between four tables.

Company	AmountPaid	Qty	Description	Cost	ListPrice
Action Club	$134.85	3	Krypton Flashlight	$20.68	$44.95
Action Club	$1,004.80	1	95.1 cu ft Tank	$130.00	$325.00
Action Club	$1,004.80	4	Flashlight (Rechargeable)	$50.98	$169.95
Action Club	$10,152.00	54	Depth/Pressure Gauge Console	$73.32	$188.00
Action Club	$20,108.00	8	Safety Knife	$13.12	$41.00
Action Club	$20,108.00	46	Regulator System	$154.80	$430.00
Action Diver Supply	$536.80	1	Second Stage Regulator	$95.79	$309.00
Action Diver Supply	$536.80	4	Medium Titanium Knife	$26.77	$56.95
Adventure Undersea	$0.00	1	Navigation Compass	$9.18	$19.95
Adventure Undersea	$0.00	2	Depth/Pressure Gauge	$48.30	$105.00
Adventure Undersea	$0.00	3	Electronic Console	$120.90	$390.00
Adventure Undersea	$0.00	3	Flashlight (Rechargeable)	$50.98	$169.95
Adventure Undersea	$0.00	3	Underwater Diver Vehicle	$504.00	$1,680.00
Adventure Undersea	$0.00	3	Welded Seam Stabilizing Vest	$109.20	$280.00
Adventure Undersea	$0.00	4	Depth/Pressure Gauge	$48.30	$105.00
Adventure Undersea	$0.00	5	Compass Console Mount	$10.15	$29.00
Adventure Undersea	$0.00	15	Flashlight	$29.25	$65.00
Adventure Undersea	$0.00	45	Depth/Pressure Gauge Console	$73.32	$188.00
Adventure Undersea	$2,195.00	5	Sonar System	$215.11	$439.00
Adventure Undersea	$3,117.00	3	60.6 cu ft Tank	$57.28	$179.00
Adventure Undersea	$3,117.00	6	Stabilizing Vest	$146.20	$430.00
Adventure Undersea	$3,304.85	1	Medium Titanium Knife	$26.77	$56.95
Adventure Undersea	$3,304.85	1	Wrist Band Thermometer (C)	$6.48	$18.00
Adventure Undersea	$3,304.85	2	Halogen Flashlight	$19.18	$59.95

If you are not familiar with this kind of join, you might want to bring up the Relate and RelJoin tables side by side and compare them. Look, for instance, at the Action Club entries in the RelJoin program and trace them through so that you see how they correspond to the entries in the Relate program. Both programs describe an identical set of relationships—they just show the outcome in a different manner.

Notice that the AmountPaid column in the RelJoin program has the same number repeated twice in the Action Club section, as shown in Figure 17.6. In particular, the numbers $1,004.80 and $20,108 both appear twice. This is because there are two different Items associated with these orders, as you can tell from glancing at the Parts table in the Relate program.

NOTE

Unless you are already familiar with this material, be sure to run the RelJoin and Relate programs and switch back and forth between them until you understand why RelJoin program works as it does. I find it easy to understand the Relate program at a glance, but the RelJoin program is a bit more subtle.

Joins and QBE

The RelJoin program is a good advertisement for the power of SQL. Once you had the SQL statement composed, it was simple to put the program together. All the work is embodied in just a few lines of code, and everything else was trivial to construct. SQL can help concentrate the intelligence of a program in one small area—or at least it does in this one example.

The sticking point, of course, is that not everyone is a whiz at composing SQL statements. Even if you understand SQL thoroughly, it can still be confusing to try to string together all those interrelated Select, Order By, From, and Where clauses. What is needed here is a way to automate this process.

Most of the versions of Delphi ship with a very useful tool that makes it easy to compose even relatively complex SQL statements. In particular, I'm talking about the QBE tool in the Database Desktop. If you want, you can use the Query Builder instead, or some other third-party tool that you might favor. However, in this section of the book, I will concentrate on the QBE tool, since it will be available to nearly all readers of this book.

Start the DBD and set the Working Directory to the DBDEMOS alias. Choose File | New | QBE Query from the menu. A dialog will appear listing the tables in the DBDEMOS database. Select the Customer table. Reopen the Select File dialog by clicking on the Add Table icon in the Toolbar. You can find the Add Table icon by holding the mouse over each icon until the fly-by help comes up or until you see the hint on the status bar. You can also simply look for the icon with the plus sign on it. Continue until you have added the Customer, Orders, Items, and Parts tables to the query. You can resize the query window until all four tables are visible, as shown in Figure 17.7.

To join these tables together, select the Join Tables icon, located just to the right of the lightning bolt. Click once on the Join Tables icon, and then click the CustNo fields for the Customer and Orders table. The symbol "join1" will appear in each field. Click the Join Tables icon again, and link the Orders and Items table on the OrderNo field. Join the Parts and Items table on the PartNo field.

After joining the tables, select the fields you want to show by clicking once in the check box associated with the fields you want to view. When you are done, the result should look like Figure 17.8.

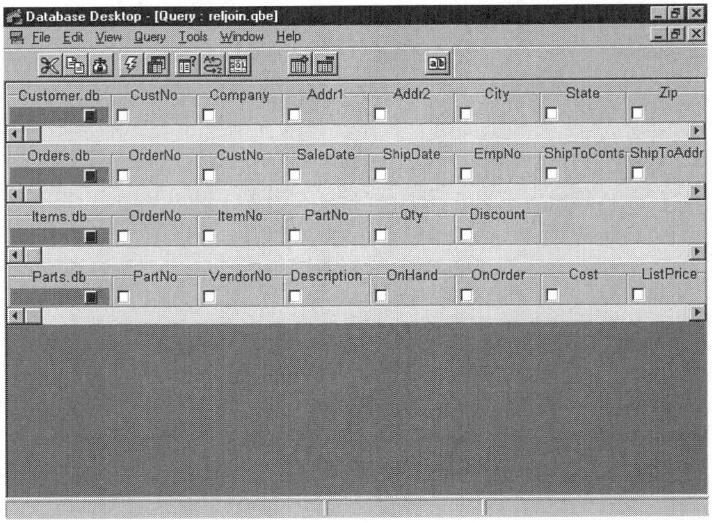

FIGURE 17.7.

Four tables used in a single QBE example.

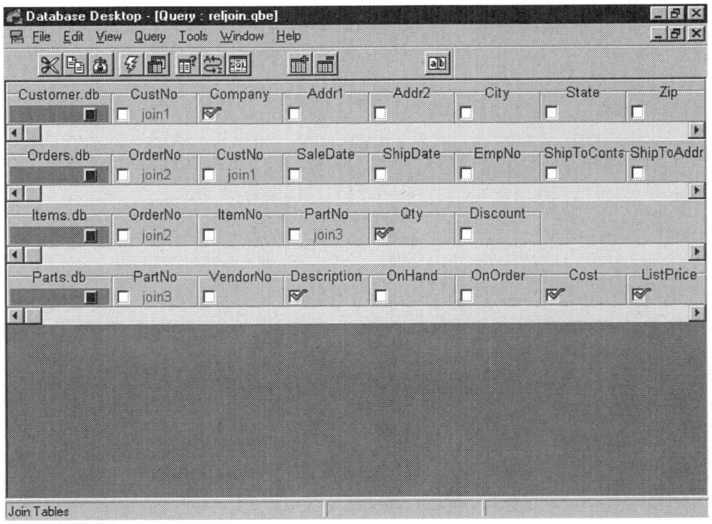

FIGURE 17.8.

The complete QBE query for joining the Customer, Orders, Items, and Parts tables.

To test your work, click the lightning bolt icon once. You should get a table that looks just like the one in the RelJoin program.

To translate the QBE statement into SQL, first close the result table so you can view the query shown in Figure 17.8. Click once on the SQL icon to perform the translation. You can save this SQL to disk, or just block-copy it and deposit it in the SQL property of a TQuery object.

On paper, this process takes a few minutes to explain. However, once you understand the QBE tool, you can use it to relate multiple tables in just a very few seconds. For most people, QBE is probably the simplest and fastest way to compose all your SQL Select statements. Don't neglect learning to use this tool. It's a simple, easy-to-use tool that can save you hours of time.

> **NOTE**
>
> The only peculiarity of the QBE tool is that by default it saves its output in a text-based language called QBE, rather than in SQL. However, once you press the SQL button, it converts the QBE code to SQL, thereby rendering the exact same results produced by standard SQL query builders. Once again, the great advantage of the QBE tool over other SQL tools is that it ships with the DBD product that accompanies nearly all versions of Delphi. If you have access to a more powerful SQL builder, then you might want to use it instead of the QBE tool. However, QBE works fine in most circumstances, even when running against SQL data in an InterBase table.

That's it for the discussion of the basic principles of relational databases. You've seen how to build master detail relationships, and how to construct joins. More importantly, you've seen how Delphi encapsulates these key aspects of relational database design. The rest of this chapter digs in further and discusses other tools Delphi uses to help you create client/server or standard database applications.

The Fields Editor

The Fields Editor enables you to associate custom objects with some or all of the fields from a table. By associating a custom object with a field, you can control the way a field displays, formats, validates, and inputs data. The Fields Editor also enables you to add new fields to a table at runtime and to then calculate the values that will be shown in the new fields. This latter procedure is referred to as *calculated fields*.

In this section and the next, you will be building a program called MASS, which illustrates both the Fields Editor and calculated fields. This is an important program, so you should try to use your copy of Delphi to follow the steps described.

You can access the Fields Editor from either a TTable or TQuery object. To get started, drop a TQuery object on a form, set up the DBDEMOS alias, enter the SQL statement select * from animals, and make the table active.

Drop down the Object Selector at the top of the Object Inspector. Notice that you currently have two components in use: TForm and TQuery.

Right-click the TQuery object and select the Fields Editor menu choice to bring up the Fields Editor. Right-click the Fields Editor and select Add Fields from the menu to pop up the Add Fields dialog, as shown in Figure 17.9.

FIGURE 17.9.

The Add Fields dialog box from the Fields Editor.

By default, all of the fields in the dialog box are selected. Click the OK button to select all five fields, and then close the Fields Editor.

Open the Object Selector a second time; notice that there are now five new objects on your form, as shown in Figure 17.10.

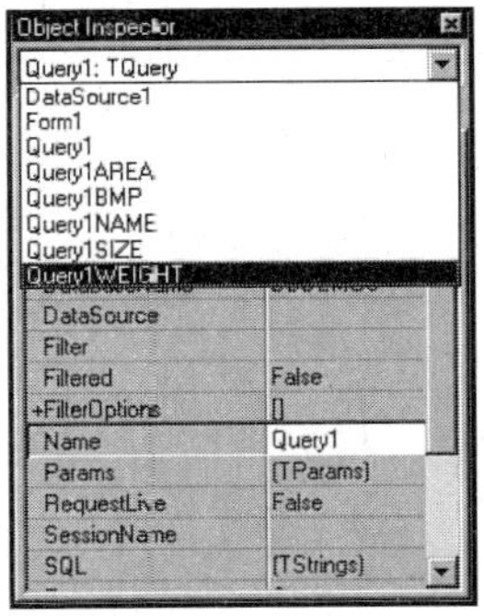

FIGURE 17.10.

The Object Selector lists the objects created in the Fields Editor. You also can find this list in the TForm1 class definition.

These objects help you control your presentation of the Animals table to the user.

Here's a complete list of the objects you just created:

```
Query1NAME: TStringField;
Query1SIZE: TSmallintField;
Query1WEIGHT: TSmallintField;
Query1AREA: TStringField;
Query1BMP: TBlobField;
```

I cut and pasted this list from the TForm1 class definition found in the Editor Window. The origins of the names shown here should be fairly obvious. The Query1 part comes from the default name for the TQuery object, and the second half of the name comes from the fields in the Animals Table. If I had renamed the Query1 object to Animal, I would have produced names that looked like this:

```
AnimalNAME
AnimalSIZE
AnimalWEIGHT
```

This kind of convention can be very useful if you are working with several tables and want to know at a glance which table and field are being referenced by a particular variable.

> **NOTE**
>
> The names of the fields in the example shown here are capitalized only because the table in question is a dBASE table. dBASE tables automatically capitalize all letters in field names. If I had chosen to work with some other type of table, the capitalization of the letters in the field name would have followed the rules defined by the current database software.

Each of the objects created in the Fields Editor is a descendant of TField. The exact type of descendant depends on the type of data in a particular field. For instance, the Query1WEIGHT field is of type `TSmallIntField`, whereas the Query1NAME field is of type `TStringField`. These are the two field types you will see most often. Other common types include `TDateField` and `TCurrencyField`, neither of which are used in this particular table. Remember that these types were selected to correspond with the field types in the table itself.

`TStringField`, `TSmallIntField`, and the other objects shown here are all descendants of `TField` and share its traits. If you want, you can treat these objects exactly as you did the `TField` objects that you learned about in Chapter 20, "Using TTable and TDataSet." For instance, you can write this:

```
S := TIntegerField.AsString;
```

and this:

```
S := TIntegerField.Name.
```

However, these descendants of TField are very smart objects and have several traits that go beyond the functionality of their common ancestor.

To start getting a feel for what you can do with TField descendants, you should open up the Browser, turn off the option to view Private and Protected fields, and then scroll through the Public and Published properties and methods.

The most important property you will see is called `Value`. You can access it like this:

```
procedure TForm1.Button1Click(Sender: TObject);
var
  i: Integer;
  S: string;
begin
  i := Query1SIZE.Value;
  S := Query1NAME.Value;
  Inc(i);
  S := 'Foo';
  Query1SIZE.Value := i;
```

```
   Query1NAME.Value := S;
end;
```

The code shown here first assigns values to the variables i and S. The next two lines change these values, and the last two lines reassign the new values to the objects. It usually wouldn't make much sense to write code exactly like this in a program, but it serves to illustrate the syntax used by TField descendants.

The Value property always conforms to the type of the field you have instantiated. For instance, TStringFields are strings, whereas TCurrencyFields always return floating-point double values. However, if you show a TCurrencyField in a data-aware control, it will return a string that looks like this: "$5.00". The dollar sign and the rounding to decimal places are simply part and parcel of what a TCurrencyField is all about.

The preceding example might make you think that these variables are declared as Variants. The point here is that TCurrencyField.Value is declared as a Double. If you tried to assign a string to it, you would get a type mismatch. Likewise, TIntegerField.Value is declared as an LongInt, and so on. TSmallIntField and TWordField are both descendants of TIntegerField and inherit the Value declaration as a LongInt. However, they have other internal code that affects the Value field, just as TCurrencyField rings some changes on its Value field to make it look like a monetary value. If you have the source, look up DBTABLES.PAS and DB.PAS to find the details of these constructions. At any rate, the point here is that the preceding code is an example of polymorphism; it is not an example of relaxed type-checking. The Value field has a specific type—it's just that it undergoes polymorphic changes.

If you want the names of each field in the current dataset, you should reference the FieldName property through one of the following two methods:

```
S := Query1.Fields[0].FieldName;
S := Query1NAME.FieldName;
```

If you want the name of an object associated with a field, you should use the Name property:

```
S := Query1.Fields[0].Name;
S := Query1NAME.Name;
```

When using the ANIMALS table, the first two examples shown above yield the string "Name", while the second two lines yield "Query1NAME".

Special properties are associated with most of the major field types. For instance, TIntegerFields have DisplayFormat and DisplayEdit properties, as well as MinValue and MaxValue properties. TStringFields, on the other hand, have none of these properties, but they do have an EditMask property, which works just like the TEditMask component found on the Additional Page of the Component Palette. All these properties are used to control the way data is displayed to the user, or the way that input from the user should be handled.

> **NOTE**
>
> I don't want to get ahead of myself, but properties such as MinValue and MaxValue are also used in the Data Dictionary, as will be explained later in this chapter. Changes made in the Data Dictionary will affect these values as seen in the Object Inspector, but changes in the Object Inspector will not affect the Data Dictionary. Don't worry if this doesn't make the slightest bit of sense yet, as I will get to the Data Dictionary in just a little while.

You should be aware of one more thing about the Fields Editor. You can use this tool not only to build objects that encapsulate existing fields, but also to build objects that represent new fields. For instance, suppose you wanted to create a sixth field, MASS, which contains the product of the SIZE and WEIGHT fields, in the Animals table.

To create the MASS field, open the Field Editor again, right-click it, and select the New Field menu choice. In the top part of the New Field dialog, enter the word MASS. Now set its type to Integer, and leave its field type as calculated, as shown in Figure 17.11.

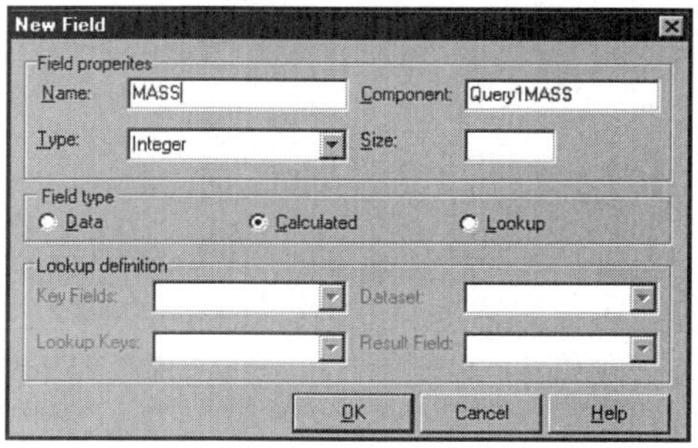

FIGURE 17.11.

Creating the MASS field in the Field Editor.

If you close the Field Editor and add a TDataSource and TdbGrid to your project, you will see that the Animals table now appears to have six fields, the last of which is called MASS.

Of course, it's one thing to create a field, and another to fill it in at runtime with an appropriate value. The act of placing a value in the new field you have created involves calculated fields, which are addressed in the next section.

Calculated Fields

Calculated fields are one of the most valuable fruits of the Fields Editor. You can use these fields for several different purposes, but two stand out:

■ If you need to perform calculations on two or more of the fields in a dataset and want to show the results of the calculations in a third field, you can use calculated fields. A scenario describing this type of situation was set up in the last section and will be explained further in this section.

- If you are viewing one dataset and want to perform calculations or display data that involve lookups in at least one additional dataset, you can use the Field Editor and Calculate Fields to show the results of these calculations in a new field of the first dataset. There is also a second, much better method for doing lookups. I will talk about that method later in this chapter. As a rule, you should do calculations in calculated fields, and lookups in lookup fields, though calculated fields are powerful enough to fill a number of different roles in your programs.

The MASS program illustrates one example of the first of the two uses for calculated fields described previously. You got this program started in the last section when you created the field called MASS and displayed it in a grid.

To continue working with the MASS program, highlight the Query1 object and set the Object Inspector to the events page. Now create an `OnCalcFields` event that looks like this:

```
procedure TForm1.Query1CalcFields(DataSet: TDataset);
begin
  Query1MASS.Value := Query1SIZE.Value * Query1WEIGHT.Value;
end;
```

The code shown here assigns the value of the Query1MASS object to the product of the Query1SIZE and Query1WEIGHT fields. This kind of multiplication is legal to do because all of the fields are of the same type.

`OnCalcField` methods get called each time a record is first displayed to the user. As a result, all of the MASS fields displayed in the grid are properly filled in, as shown in Figure 17.12.

FIGURE 17.12.

The MASS field contains the product of the WEIGHT and SIZE fields. A TdbImage control contains a bitmap from the BMP field of the table.

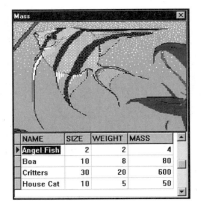

To get the image shown in Figure 17.12, I opened the `Column` property in the TdbGrid object and selected Add All Fields. I then deleted the Area and BMP fields and closed the `Column` property editor. I will talk more about the grid object later in this chapter.

If you choose to never instantiate a particular field in the field editor, the current dataset you are working with no longer contains that field. It can't be accessed programmatically or visually at runtime. Usually, this is exactly the effect you want to achieve, and so this trait will generally be perceived as a strong benefit. However, there are times when it might not serve your purposes, and in those cases you should either create an object for all the fields in a table or stay away from the Field Editor altogether.

TdbGrid at Runtime

dbGrids can be completely reconfigured at runtime. You can hide and show columns, change the order of columns, the color of columns, and change the width of columns.

The MOVEGRID (see Figure 17.13) program shows how to take a TdbGrid through its paces at runtime. The program is fairly straightforward except for two brief passages. The first passage involves creating check box controls on the fly, whereas the second shows how to change the order of items in a list box on the fly.

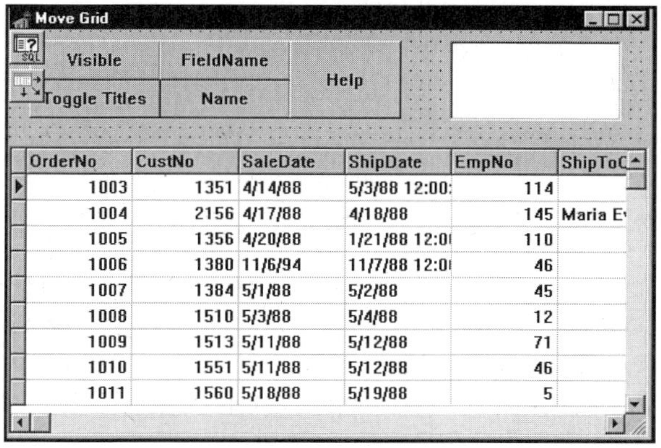

FIGURE 17.13.

The main MOVEGRID program enables you to change the appearance of a grid at runtime.

When the user wants to decide which fields are visible, MOVEGRID pops up a second form and displays the names of all the fields from the ORDERS table in a series of check boxes. The user can then select the fields that he or she wants to make visible. The selected check boxes designate fields that are visible, whereas the nonselected ones represent invisible fields. The program also enables you to set the order and width of fields, as well as to hide and show the titles at the top of the grid. (See Listings 17.1 and 17.2.)

Listing 17.1. The code for the MOVEGRID program is in the CHAP17 directory on this book's CD-ROM.

```pascal
unit Main;

{ Program copyright (c) 1995 by Charlie Calvert }
{ Project Name: MOVEGRID }

interface

uses
  SysUtils, WinTypes, WinProcs,
  Messages, Classes, Graphics,
  Controls, Forms, Dialogs,
  Grids, DBGrids, DB,
  DBTables, StdCtrls, Buttons;

type
  TForm1 = class(TForm)
    Query1: TQuery;
    DataSource1: TDataSource;
    DBGrid1: TDBGrid;
    Name: TButton;
    ListBox1: TListBox;
    Button3: TButton;
    Visible: TButton;
    FieldName: TButton;
    Help: TButton;
    Query1OrderNo: TFloatField;
    Query1CustNo: TFloatField;
    Query1SaleDate: TDateTimeField;
    Query1ShipDate: TDateTimeField;
    Query1EmpNo: TIntegerField;
    Query1ShipToContact: TStringField;
    Query1ShipToAddr1: TStringField;
    Query1ShipToAddr2: TStringField;
    Query1ShipToCity: TStringField;
    Query1ShipToState: TStringField;
    Query1ShipToZip: TStringField;
    Query1ShipToCountry: TStringField;
    Query1ShipToPhone: TStringField;
    Query1ShipVIA: TStringField;
    Query1PO: TStringField;
    Query1Terms: TStringField;
    Query1PaymentMethod: TStringField;
    Query1ItemsTotal: TCurrencyField;
    Query1TaxRate: TFloatField;
    Query1Freight: TCurrencyField;
    Query1AmountPaid: TCurrencyField;
    procedure NameClick(Sender: TObject);
    procedure Button3Click(Sender: TObject);
    procedure FormCreate(Sender: TObject);
    procedure CustNoIndexClick(Sender: TObject);
    procedure FieldNameClick(Sender: TObject);
    procedure VisibleClick(Sender: TObject);
    procedure ListBox1DblClick(Sender: TObject);
    procedure BitBtn1Click(Sender: TObject);
    procedure DBGrid1DblClick(Sender: TObject);
  private
```

```
      ShowTitles: Boolean;
    public
      { Public declarations }
    end;

var
  Form1: TForm1;

implementation
uses
  VisForm;
{$R *.DFM}

procedure TForm1.NameClick(Sender: TObject);
var
  i: Integer;
begin
  ListBox1.Clear;
  for i := 0 to Query1.FieldCount - 1 do
    ListBox1.Items.Add(Query1.Fields[i].Name);
end;

procedure TForm1.Button3Click(Sender: TObject);
begin
  if ShowTitles then
    DBGrid1.Options := DBGrid1.Options + [dgTitles, dgIndicator]
  else
    DBGrid1.Options := DBGrid1.Options - [dgTitles, dgIndicator];
  ShowTitles := not ShowTitles;
end;

procedure TForm1.FormCreate(Sender: TObject);
var
  i: Integer;
begin
  ListBox1.Clear;
  for i := 0 to Query1.FieldCount - 1 do
    ListBox1.Items.Add(Query1.Fields[i].Name);
end;

procedure TForm1.CustNoIndexClick(Sender: TObject);
var
  S: String;
begin
  S := '';
  InputQuery('Get Index of CustNo', 'Enter a number between 0 and 10: ', S);
  Query1CustNo.Index := StrToInt(S);
  DBGrid1.SelectedField := Query1CustNo;
end;

procedure TForm1.FieldNameClick(Sender: TObject);
var
  i: Integer;
begin
  ListBox1.Clear;
  for i := 0 to Query1.FieldCount - 1 do
    ListBox1.Items.Add(Query1.Fields[i].FieldName);
end;
```

continues

Listing 17.1. continued

```
procedure TForm1.VisibleClick(Sender: TObject);
begin
  VisiForm.ShowMe(Query1);
end;

procedure TForm1.ListBox1DblClick(Sender: TObject);
var
  Input, Temp, CurPos: string;
  StartPos: Integer;
begin
  Input := '';
  Temp := ListBox1.Items.Strings[ListBox1.ItemIndex];
  StartPos := ListBox1.ItemIndex;
  CurPos := 'Current Position: ' + IntToStr(StartPos);
  InputQuery(CurPos, 'New Position', Input);
  ListBox1.Items.Delete(ListBox1.ItemIndex);
  ListBox1.Items.Insert(StrToInt(Input), Temp);
  Query1.Fields[StartPos].Index := StrToInt(Input);
end;

procedure TForm1.BitBtn1Click(Sender: TObject);
const
  CR = #13#10;
  S :PChar = 'Grid: Double click a column to change its width.' + CR +
        'ListBox: Double-click to change order of Fields. ' + CR +
        'Visible Btn: Hide Fields. '+ CR +
        'FieldName Btn: Show names of fields.' + CR +
        'Name Btn: Show names of field objects.' + CR +
        'ToggleTitles Btn: Hide/Show titles & indicators.';
  S1:PChar = 'Example program for changing a Grid at runtime.';
begin
  MessageBox(Handle, S, S1, mb_Ok or mb_IconInformation);
end;

procedure TForm1.DBGrid1DblClick(Sender: TObject);
var
  S, Name: string;
begin
  S := '';
  Name := DBGrid1.SelectedField.Name;
  if not InputQuery(Name, 'Enter New Length', S) then Exit;
  DBGrid1.SelectedField.DisplayWidth := StrToInt(S);
end;

end.
```

Listing 17.2. The VisiForm unit, displays a set of check boxes, where the user designates which fields are to be made visible.

```
unit Visform;

{ Program copyright (c) 1995 by Charlie Calvert }
{ Project Name: MOVEGRID }
```

```
interface

uses
  SysUtils, WinTypes, WinProcs,
  Messages, Classes, Graphics,
  Controls, Forms, Dialogs,
  DBTables, StdCtrls;

const
  RadSize = 25;

type
  TVisiForm = class(TForm)
  private
    R: array[0..25] of TCheckBox;
    procedure CreateRad(Index: Integer; Name: String; Visible: Boolean);
  public
    { Public declarations }
    procedure ShowMe(Query1: TQuery);
  end;

var
  VisiForm: TVisiForm;

implementation

{$R *.DFM}

procedure TVisiForm.CreateRad(Index: Integer; Name: String; Visible: Boolean);
begin
  R[Index] := TCheckBox.Create(Self);
  R[Index].Parent := VisiForm;
  R[Index].Caption := Name;
  R[Index].Left := 10;
  R[Index].Top := Index * RadSize;
  R[Index].Width := 200;
  R[Index].Checked := Visible;
end;

procedure TVisiForm.ShowMe(Query1: TQuery);
var
  i: Integer;
begin
  for i := 0 to Query1.FieldCount - 1 do
    CreateRad(i, Query1.Fields[i].Name, Query1.Fields[i].Visible);
  Height := i * (RadSize + 5);
  ShowModal;
  for i := 0 to Query1.FieldCount - 1 do
    Query1.Fields[i].Visible := R[i].Checked;
end;

end.
```

In the next few paragraphs, you will find descriptions of the key parts of the MOVEGRID program. Understanding its constituent parts will help you to take control over the grids you display in your programs.

Most of the code in the MOVEGRID program is fairly simple. However, the program performs a number of separate tasks. To grasp the program, it's necessary to divide and conquer, that is, take the tasks performed by the program one at a time. Find out how each one works, and then move on to the next one. If you proceed in this fashion, you will find the program easy to understand.

You can use the Options field of a TdbGrid to change its appearance. The Options property has the following possible values:

dgEditing	Set to True by default, it enables the user to edit a grid. You can also set the grid's ReadOnly property to True or False.
dgTitles	Designates whether titles can be seen.
dgIndicator	Determines whether to show the small icons on the left of the grid.
dgColumnResize	Designates whether or not the user can resize columns.
dgColLines	Determines whether or not to show the lines between columns.
dgRowLines	Designates whether or not to show the lines between rows.
dgTabs	Enables the user to tab and shift+tab between columns.

Here is the declaration for the enumerated type where these values are declared:

```
TDBGridOption = (dgEditing, dgAlwaysShowEditor, dgTitles,
                 dgIndicator, dgColumnResize, dgColLines,
                 dgRowLines, dgTabs);
```

For instance, you can set the options at runtime by writing code that looks like this:

```
DBGrid1.Options := [dgTitles, dgIndicator];
```

If you want to toggle an option on and off, you can do so with a logical operator. For instance, the following code will add a set of titles to DBGrid1:

```
DBGrid1.Options := DBGrid1.Options + [dgTitles];
```

Given the presence of a Boolean variable called ShowTitles, the following code enables you to toggle an option back and forth at the press of a single button:

```
procedure TForm1.Button3Click(Sender: TObject);
begin
  if ShowTitles then
    DBGrid1.Options := DBGrid1.Options + [dgTitles]
  else
    DBGrid1.Options := DBGrid1.Options - [dgTitles];
  ShowTitles := not ShowTitles;
end;
```

To move the location of a column at runtime, you can simply change its index, which is a zero-based number:

```
Query1.FieldByName('CustNo').Index := 1;
Query1CustNo.Index := 2;
```

By default, the CustNo field in the Customer table is at the top of the record, in the zero (first) position. The code in the first example above moves it to the second position, whereas the code that reads `Query1CustNo.Index := 2;` moves it to the third position. Remember, the Index field is zero-based, so moving a field to Index 1 moves it to the second field in a record. The first field is at Index 0.

When you change the index of a field, you do not need to worry about the indexes of the other fields in a record. They will be changed automatically at runtime.

The MOVEGRID program contains a list box that displays the current order of the fields in a dataset. The code shown following responds to a double-click in a list box by querying the user if he or she wants to change the position of the currently selected item in the list box. The user can then enter the number to which he wants to move the currently selected field. For instance, if the user clicked the CustNo string in the list box and entered the number 2, CustNo would move from the first to the third position in the list box. The code shown here also moves the index of the real field from 0 to 2, thereby changing the actual position of the field in the grid. These changes are being made only to the visual representation of a dataset. The actual data on a disk is not changed by this procedure.

The following code is activated whenever the user double-clicks the list box:

```
procedure TForm1.ListBox1DblClick(Sender: TObject);
var
  Input, Temp, CurPos: string;
  StartPos: Integer;
begin
  Input := '';
  Temp := ListBox1.Items.Strings[ListBox1.ItemIndex];
  StartPos := ListBox1.ItemIndex;
  CurPos := 'Current Position: ' + IntToStr(StartPos);
  InputQuery(CurPos, 'New Position', Input);
  ListBox1.Items.Delete(ListBox1.ItemIndex);
  ListBox1.Items.Insert(StrToInt(Input), Temp);
  Query1.Fields[StartPos].Index := StrToInt(Input);
end;
```

The last line in the preceding example is what actually changes the index of the column the user wants to move. The two lines directly before it delete the currently selected string in the list box and then insert it into a new position.

If you want to change the width of a column at runtime, just change the `DisplayWidth` property of the appropriate TField object:

```
Query1.FieldByName('CustNo').DisplayWidth := 12;
Query1CustNo.DisplayWidth := 12;
```

The value 12 refers to the number of characters that can be displayed in the control.

If you want to hide a field at runtime, you can set its Visible property to False:

```
Query1.FieldByName('CustNo').Visible := False;
Query1CustNo.Visible := False;
```

Both lines of code perform identical tasks. To show the fields again, simply set Visible to True:

```
Query1.FieldByName('CustNo').Visible := True;
Query1CustNo.Visible := True;
```

In order to allow the user to decide which fields are visible, MOVEGRID pops up a second form with a series of check boxes on it. (See VISFORM.PAS.) The program actually creates each of these check boxes at runtime. In other words, it doesn't just pop up a form with the correct number of check boxes on it, but instead iterates through the Query1 object, finds out how many check boxes are needed, and then creates them dynamically at runtime.

To perform these tasks, MOVEGRID passes a copy of the Query1 object through to the form that displays the check boxes:

```
procedure TForm1.VisibleClick(Sender: TObject);
begin
  VisiForm.ShowMe(Query1);
end;
```

The ShowMe method of the VisiForm first calls a routine called CreateRad, which creates the check boxes, displays the form, and finally sets the state of the check boxes:

```
procedure TVisiForm.ShowMe(Query1: TQuery);
var
  i: Integer;
begin
  for i := 0 to Query1.FieldCount - 1 do
    CreateRad(i, Query1.Fields[i].Name, Query1.Fields[i].Visible);
  Height := i * (RadSize + 5);
  ShowModal;
  for i := 0 to Query1.FieldCount - 1 do
    Query1.Fields[i].Visible := R[i].Checked;
end;
```

The ShowMe method iterates through the Query1 object and assigns one check box to each field. It also asks TQuery for the names of the fields, and whether each field is currently hidden or visible. Here is the code that creates a check box on the fly:

```
procedure TVisiForm.CreateRad(Index: Integer;
                              Name: String;
                              Visible: Boolean);
begin
  R[Index] := TCheckBox.Create(Self);
  R[Index].Parent := VisiForm;
  R[Index].Caption := Name;
  R[Index].Left := 10;
  R[Index].Top := Index * RadSize;
  R[Index].Width := 200;
  R[Index].Checked := Visible;
end;
```

Most of the code in this example is performing relatively mundane tasks, such as assigning names and locations to the check boxes. These are the two key lines:

```
R[Index] := TCheckBox.Create(Self);
R[Index].Parent := VisiForm;
```

The first line actually creates the check box and gives it an owner. The second line assigns a parent to the check box.

> **NOTE**
>
> The difference between a parent and an owner can be confusing at times. A form is always the owner of the components that reside inside it. As such, it is responsible for allocating and deallocating memory for these components. A form might also be the parent of a particular component, which means that the component will be displayed directly on the form. However, one component might also find that another component is its parent, even though both components are owned by the form. For instance, if you place a TPanel on a form and then two TButtons on the TPanel, all three components will be owned by the form; however, the buttons will have the panel as a parent, whereas the TPanel will have the form as a parent. Ownership has to do with memory allocation. Parenthood usually describes what surface a component will be displayed on. If you get confused about this while in the midst of a lengthy programming session, you can look it up in the online help by searching on the topic, Parent.

The grids supplied with the first version of Delphi are reasonably flexible objects that perform most of the tasks required of them. If you feel you need some additional functionality, check with third-party tool makers such as TurboPower software. A number of third-party grids with extended capabilities are available on the market, and some of them are well worth the purchase price.

New features of the TdbGrid object not found in Delphi 1.0 include the ability to add combo boxes to the grid, and to color the columns of your grids. Both of these processes are discussed elsewhere in this chapter, particular in the next section on Lookups.

Lookup Fields

You can use Lookup fields to look up a value in one table that you want to use in a second table. For instance, suppose you had two tables, one of which contained a list of books, and the other contained a list of authors. It would be nice if you could automatically view a list of the existing authors whenever you needed to add a new book to the Book table. That way you could enter the book's name, then just look up the author in a dropdown list, and presto, you would be done. The Book table would then automatically contain a reference to the appropriate author in the Author table. That is, the author number from the Author table would automatically be inserted in the Book table.

Needless to say, Delphi gives good support for using Lookup fields. You can now perform automatic lookups inside grids, list boxes and combo boxes. The Lookup program on disk shows how to proceed. The listings for this application are shown in Listings 17.3 through 17.4. Two views of the program are shown in Figures 17.14 and 17.15.

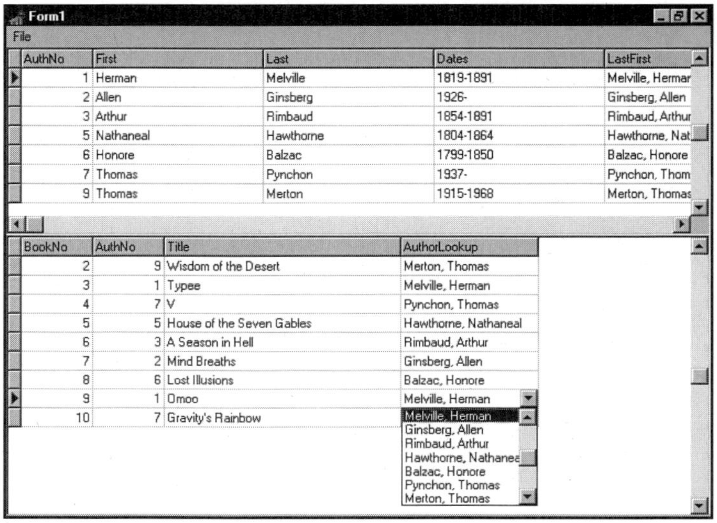

FIGURE 17.14.

The AuthorLookup field in the grid for the Books table is a lookup into the Authors table.

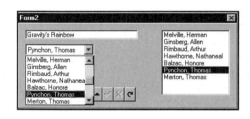

FIGURE 17.15.

This form features a list box and combo box that let you performs lookups from the Book table into the Author table.

NOTE

Delphi 1.0 had a dbLookupCombo control and a dbLookupList control that had certain limited capabilities. Both of these controls are still present in Delphi 2.0, but they have been moved off the Data Controls page onto the Win 3.1 page. They are being kept around solely for compatibility with 16-bit programs. The dbLookupComboBox control and the dbLookupListBox control now replace the old 16-bit controls, and they outperform them on several fronts. In particular, the dbLookupComboBox and dbLookupListBox will automatically be filled up with the data from the lookup table. Don't confuse the old control with the new ones! This is an area where Delphi has become much more powerful in version 2.0 than it was version 1.0.

Listing 17.3. The main work for the program is done in the Object Inspector for the TData object.

```
unit DMod;

interface

uses
  Windows, Messages, SysUtils,
  Classes, Graphics, Controls,
  Forms, Dialogs, DB,
  DBTables, Menus;

type
  TData = class(TDataModule)
    tblAuthor: TTable;
    tblAuthorAuthNo: TIntegerField;
    tblAuthorFirst: TStringField;
    tblAuthorLast: TStringField;
    tblAuthorDates: TStringField;
    tblAuthorLastFirst: TStringField;
    dsAuthor: TDataSource;
    dsBook: TDataSource;
    tblBookBookNo: TIntegerField;
    tblBookAuthNo: TIntegerField;
    tblBookTitle: TStringField;
    tblBookAuthorLook: TStringField;
    tblAuthorBirthPlace: TStringField;
    tblBook: TTable;
    procedure tblAuthorCalcFields(DataSet: TDataSet);
  private
    { Private declarations }
  public
    { Public declarations }
  end;

var
  Data: TData;

implementation

{$R *.DFM}

procedure TData.tblAuthorCalcFields(DataSet: TDataSet);
begin
  tblAuthorLastFirst.Value := tblAuthorLast.Value + ', ' +
                              tblAuthorFirst.Value;
end;

end.
```

Listing 17.4. Form1 gives you a look at both the Author table and the Book table. A dropdown in dbGrid2 lets you view the lookup field.

```
unit main;

interface

uses
  Windows, Messages, SysUtils,
  Classes, Graphics, Controls,
  Forms, Dialogs, DB,
  Grids, DBGrids, DBTables,
  DBCtrls, Menus;

type
  TForm1 = class(TForm)
    DBGrid1: TDBGrid;
    DBGrid2: TDBGrid;
    MainMenu1: TMainMenu;
    File1: TMenuItem;
    ViewEntryForm1: TMenuItem;
    OneToMany1: TMenuItem;
    Exit1: TMenuItem;
    procedure Form21Click(Sender: TObject);
    procedure Exit1Click(Sender: TObject);
  private
    { Private declarations }
  public
    { Public declarations }
  end;

var
  Form1: TForm1;

implementation

uses
  DMod, fieldvew;

{$R *.DFM}

procedure TForm1.Form21Click(Sender: TObject);
begin
  Form2.Show;
end;

procedure TForm1.Exit1Click(Sender: TObject);
begin
  Close;
end;

end.
```

Listing 17.5. Form2 shows how to use dbLookupListBoxes and dbLookupComboBoxes.

```
unit FieldVew;

interface

uses
  Windows, Messages, SysUtils,
  Classes, Graphics, Controls,
  Forms, Dialogs, ExtCtrls,
  DBCtrls, StdCtrls, Mask;

type
  TForm2 = class(TForm)
    Panel1: TPanel;
    DBEdit3: TDBEdit;
    DBLookupComboBox1: TDBLookupComboBox;
    DBLookupListBox1: TDBLookupListBox;
    DBNavigator1: TDBNavigator;
  private
    { Private declarations }
  public
    { Public declarations }
  end;

var
  Form2: TForm2;

implementation

uses dmod;

{$R *.DFM}

end.
```

The Lookup program enables you to easily fill in the key fields of the Book table by looking them up in the Author table. To understand why this capability is important, notice that the only way to tell which author is associated with which book is by placing the appropriate author number in the AuthNo field of the Book table. This is convenient from the point of view of the programmer who wants to construct a well-made relational database. In particular, it allows for saving space through the construction of one-to-many relationships. However, the user isn't going to want to have to remember that Herman Melville is associated with the number 2, Jack Kerouac with the number x, and so on. The point of a lookup field is that it lets you look up a list of authors in the author table, then automatically assigns the chosen author number to the AuthNo field in the book table.

This program uses two tables called, not surprisingly, AUTHOR.DB and BOOK.DB. Both of these tables are found on the CD that accompanies this book. Tables 17.1 and 17.2 show the schema for the tables.

Table 17.1. AUTHOR.DB table structure.

Name	Type	Keyed
AuthNo	AutoInc	Key
First	Character(25)	
Last	Character(25)	
Dates	Character(25)	
BirthPlace	Character(25)	

Table 17.2. BOOK.DB table structure.

Name	Type	Keyed
BookNo	AutoInc	Key
AuthNo	LongInt	
Title	Character (35)	

NOTE

Notice the use of the AutoIncrement fields in the table definitions shown in Tables 17.1 and 17.2. These fields will automatically be filled in when the user adds a new record at runtime. For instance, when you add the first record to the Books table, it will automatically be given a BookNo of 1. The second record will automatically be given a BookNo of 2, and so on. AutoIncrement fields are read-only, and frequently there is no need to show them to the user at runtime.

There is little actual work required to construct this program. In particular, look over the source code shown earlier, and you will see that the only significant line of code in the whole program is the one for the OnCalcFields event. Other than that, it's just a matter of manipulating the visual tools.

To get started, create a new application and add a data module to it. Drag both the Authors and Books tables out of the Explorer and onto a form. Cut and paste them from there onto the data module. Bring up the Fields Editor for both tables and create objects for all of their fields. Give the tables and their datasources appropriate names, as shown in Figure 17.16.

FIGURE 17.16.

The datamodule for the Lookup program.

Inside the Author table, create a Calculated Field called LastFirst. To create the calculated field, first right-click the TTable object, then right-click the Field's editor and select New from the menu. After creating the calculated field, assign the following method to the OnCalcFields event:

```
procedure TData.tblAuthorCalcFields(DataSet: TDataSet);
begin
  tblAuthorLastFirst.Value := tblAuthorLast.Value + ', ' +
                              tblAuthorFirst.Value;
end;
```

This field will be the one that is looked up in the second table. The issue here is that just looking up the last name of an author is not sufficient—you need to look up both first and last names in order to be sure you are finding a unique author. It would be wasteful of disk space to permanently add a field to the table that combined the first and last names, but you can create a temporary copy of that field with a calculated field.

Bring up the Fields Editor for the Book table. Right-click it and create a new field called AuthorLookup. Set its Type to string and its Field Type to Lookup. The KeyField should be set to AuthNo, the Dataset to tblAuthor, the Lookup Key to AuthNo, and the Result field to LastFirst. Figure 17.17 shows how the New Field dialog should look when you are done. Notice that you can also fill in this same information in the Object Inspector if you first select the tblBookAuthorLookup object. (In other words, you could create a new object and then close the Fields Editor without specifying any of its properties. Later, you could select the object and designate its type, its lookup fields, and so on.)

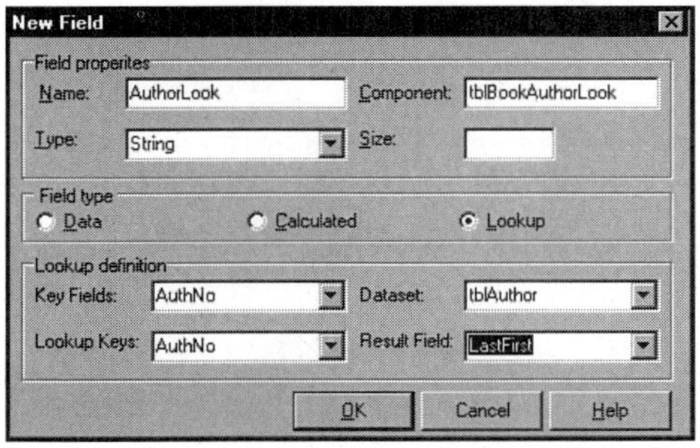

FIGURE 17.17.

Filling in the New Field dialog.

Go back to Form1 and make sure the two dbGrids are arranged one above the other and are hooked up properly to the tables on the datamodule. Run the application.

The AuthorLookup field in the dbGrid object associated with the Book table is now a dropdown combo box. If you click it once, then dropdown its list, you can then perform a lookup into the LastFirst field of the Author table. This lookup will automatically fill in the AuthNo field of the book table. You can use this lookup to insert a new author into a new record, or to change the author of an existing record.

NOTE

The capability to have a dropdown list in a grid object comes for free in Delphi 2.0. Go back in design mode, and open up the Columns property of a grid object. Add all the fields to the Columns list box. You can now select one of the fields, such as Title, and choose the PickList button in order to create a set of default values available for the field. The user can access these values at runtime by clicking the field and dropping down the combo box, per the lookup example discussed above.

Besides the dbGrid object, there are two other controls in Delphi that understand lookup fields. Both of these controls are shown on Form2. The first is a TdbLookupComboBox, which is the default control you will get if you drag and drop the AuthorLookup field from the Fields Editor onto a form. If you perform the drag-and-drop operation, then the control will be hooked up automatically. If you want to hook it up manually, just connect its DataSource to the dsBook object and its DataField to the AuthorLookup field. There is also a TdbLookupListBox, which works exactly the same way as the TdbLookupComboBox.

NOTE

Both the dbLookupListBox and dbLookupComboBox have fields that correspond to the ones you filled in with the New Fields dialog shown in Figure 17.17. However, there is no need to fill these fields in a second time. Just hook up the DataSource and DataFields properties, and you are ready to go.

When you are working with the Lookup program, you should note that Form1 is a bit artificial. It's meant to help you scan through all the available data so you can grok the significance of the lookup process. Form2 is somewhat closer to the type of display you would want to present to the user in a real program.

When working with Form2, notice how easy it is to simply type in a new book name, then click an author in the list box, and click the Post button on the TdbNavigator. The process is very simple from the user's point of view. In particular, a new BookNo is being assigned automatically by the AutoIncrement field, and the new AuthNo is being filled in automatically by the lookup process.

If you want to change the author associated with a particular record, then you just click a new item in the list box. The author number will be changed automatically for you by the lookup. It's all very simple and intuitive when viewed from the user's perspective.

MultiRecord Objects

Another object that deserves mention is the dbCtrlGrid, shown in Figure 17.8. You can use this object to view multiple records from a single table at one time without using the TdbGrid component. In other words, you can dropdown TdbEdit controls onto a TdbCtrlGrid, and these edit controls will automatically be duplicated in a series of rows, where the first set of controls shows the first record, the second set the second record, and so on. You only have to dropdown one set of controls—the extra sets are duplicated for you automatically by the dbCtrlGrid, as shown in Figure 17.18.

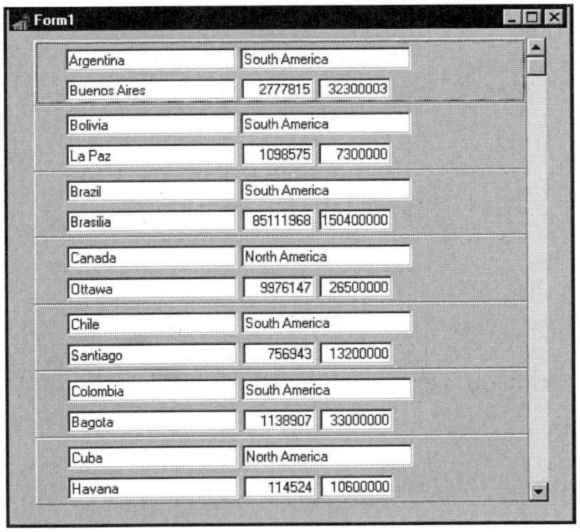

FIGURE 17.18.

The TdbCtrlGrid object on the form the CtrlGrid application.

To get started with this object, drag and drop the Country table off the Explorer. Delete the dbGrid object, and add the TdbCtrlGrid object off the Data Controls page of the Component Palette. Use the Fields Editor to drag and drop all the fields from Country table onto the top section of the dbCtrlGrid. Arrange them as shown in Figure 17.18. Notice that dbCtrlGrids have RowCount and ColCount properties that enable you to define the number of rows and columns in the object. In this case, I have set the RowCount to 7.

The dbCtrlGrid component doesn't bring any new functionality to Delphi. It's useful, however, as it eliminates the need to have the user slide the scrollbar back and forth on a TdbGrid object. In other words, the TdbGrid object sometimes forces you to use the scrollbar in order to view all the fields of a record. That can be inconvenient, but the ability to view multiple records at once is so valuable that users are willing to put up with the minor annoyance of the scrollbar. The point of the dbCtrlGrid object is that it lets you view multiple records at one time, while eliminating the need to scroll back and forth when viewing the data. It's hardly earth-shattering in its importance, but it can be very useful under some circumstances. It's a way to make the presentation of your data potentially more viable to the user.

Summary

In this chapter you learned some fairly sophisticated methods for displaying the data from multiple tables. In particular, you saw how Delphi handles the key features of a relational database.

The tools discussed in this chapter include

- The Fields Editor
- The Database Explorer
- The Database Desktop
- The Query by Example tool in the DBD

The components discussed in this chapter include

- TField descendant objects
- The TdbCtrlGrid, TdbLookupComboBox, TdbLookupListBox objects
- The TdbGrid component

The properties discussed in this chapter include

- Calculated fields
- Lookup fields

Good database programmers will find that there is a considerable amount of hidden power in the TField object and in the Fields Editor, as well as the other tools and components mentioned in this chapter. These database tools represent a very strong aspect of Delphi, which is further expanded on by the work of third-party developers such as TurboPower software, Woll2Woll, and Shoreline.

Real-World Databases

In this chapter, you will get a look at a simple address book program called ADDRESS2. This program is designed to represent the simplest possible database program that is still usable in a real-world situation.

In particular, you will look at the following:

- Sorting data
- Filtering data
- Searching for data
- Printing data
- Dynamically moving a table in and out of a read-only state
- Forcing the user to select a field's value from a list of valid responses
- Allowing the user to choose the colors of a form at runtime
- Saving information to an .INI file

After finishing this chapter, you will have learned something about the kinds of problems experienced when writing even a very basic database program. The final product, though not quite up to professional standards, provides solutions to many of the major problems faced by programmers who want to create tools that can be used by the typical user.

You will find that the final program is relatively long when compared to most of the programs you have seen so far in this book. The reason is that this program is meant not just to show you how to perform a particular action, but to show you how to accomplish some of the basic effects expected in real-world settings and provide a minimum degree of robustness.

Supporting 16- and 32-Bit Platforms

I go to Delphi user group meetings all across the country; people constantly ask about compatibility between the 16- and 32-bit versions of Delphi. It's a big issue. As a result, I have chosen to make sure that the program shown in this chapter will compile in both 16- and 32-bit mode. It's proof that you can write at least a reasonably complex program that will compile in both 16 and 32 Delphi.

There is a reason I have chosen to keep this particular program compatible between 16 and 32 bits. I use the program shown in this chapter in my day-to-day work. In fact, I use it a lot, and so do a few other people. I have found that I have to keep both a 16- and 32-bit version of this program available, because the code runs on boxes that support Windows 3.11, Windows 95, and Windows NT. Most versions of Delphi 2.0 ship with both the 16- and the 32-bit compiler, so obviously the developers of Delphi knew that this was a real-world issue that had to be addressed. In keeping with this theme, I have made sure that the code shown in this chapter will compile on both platforms. As I stated, this is not a whim, but a real-world necessity for me. At the risk of making too gross an understatement, let me add that I am sure many other programmers will find themselves in the same boat. The 16-bit world will apparently not die too quickly.

Defining the Data

When considering an address program, it's easy to come up with a preliminary list of needed fields:

```
First Name
Last Name
Address
City
State
Zip
Phone
```

After making this list and contemplating it for a moment, you might ask the following questions:

- What about complex addresses that can't be written on one line?
- Is one phone number enough? What about times when you need a home phone and a work phone?
- Speaking of work, what about specifying the name of the company that employs someone on the list?
- What about faxes?
- This is the 1990s, so what about an e-mail address?
- What about generic information that doesn't fit into any of these categories?

This list of questions emerges only after a period of gestation. In a real-world situation, you might come up with a list of questions like this only after you talk with potential users of your program, after viewing similar programs that are on the market, and after experimenting with a prototype of the proposed program. Whichever way you come up with questions, the key point is that you spend the time to really think about the kind of data you need.

> **NOTE**
>
> Many books will tell you to complete your plan before you begin programming. The only thing wrong with that theory is that I have never seen it work out as expected in practice.
>
> Nearly all the real-world programs that I have seen, both my own and others, whether produced by individuals or huge companies, always seem to go through initial phases that are later abandoned in favor of more sophisticated designs. This is part of what Delphi and RAD programs in general are all about. They make it possible for you to create a draft of your program and then rewrite it.

Think hard about what you want to do, then get a prototype up in fairly short order, critique it, then rethink your design. It's rarely necessary to totally abandon the first draft, but you are almost certainly going to have to rewrite. This is why it's not a good idea to concentrate on details at first. Get things up and running, then if they look okay, go back and optimize.

The point is that it's an iterative process. You keep rewriting, over and over, the same way authors keep rewriting the chapters in their books. RAD programming tools help make this kind of cycle possible.

If you have to write everything in code from scratch, then you have to try to get it right the first time. That's almost impossible to do, which is why so many programming projects have failed. The issue was that people were using the wrong tools. The interesting thing about Delphi is that the same tool that lets you prototype quickly is also the tool that lets you optimize down to the last clock cycle.

After considering the preceding questions, you might come up with a revised list of fields for your program:

```
First Name
Last Name
Company
Address1
Address2
City
State
Zip
Home Phone
Work Phone
Fax
EMail1
EMail2
Comment
```

This list might actually stand up to the needs of a real-world user. Certainly it doesn't cover all possible situations, but it does represent a reasonable compromise between the desire to make the program easy to use and the desire to handle every possible variety of potential user demand.

At this stage, you might start thinking about some of the basic functionality you want to associate with the program. For instance, you might decide that a user of the program should be able to search, sort, filter, and print the data. After stating these needs, you'll find that there is going to be a need to break the data up into various categories so that it can be filtered. The question, of course, is how these categories can be defined.

After considering the matter for some time, you might decide that two more fields should be added to the list. The first field can be called Category, and it holds a name that describes the type of record currently being viewed. For instance, some entries in an address book might consist of family members, whereas other entries might reference friends, associates from work, companies where you shop, or other types of data. A second field will be called Marked, and it designates whether a particular field is marked for some special processing.

Here is the revised list, with one additional field called Category, which is used to help the user filter the data he or she might be viewing:

```
First Name
Last Name
Company
Address1
Address2
City
State
Zip
Home Phone
Work Phone
Fax
EMail1
EMail2
Comment
Category
Marked
```

After carefully considering the fields that might be used in the ADDRESS2 program, the next step is to decide how large and what type the fields should be. Table 18.1 shows proposed types and sizes.

Table 18.1. The length, type, and size of fields used by the ADDRESS2 program.

Name	Type	Size
FName	Character	40
LName	Character	40
Company	Character	40
Address1	Character	40
Address2	Character	40
City	Character	40
State	Character	5
Zip	Character	15
HPhone	Character	15

continues

Table 18.1. continued

Name	Type	Size
WPhone	Character	15
Fax	Character	15
EMail1	Character	45
EMail2	Character	45
Comment	Memo	20
Category	Character	15
Marked	Logical	

As you can see, I prefer to give myself plenty of room in all the fields I declare. In particular, notice that I have opted for wide EMail fields to hold long Internet addresses, and I have decided to make the Comment field a memo field so that it can contain long entries, if necessary. The names of some of the fields have also been altered so that they don't contain any spaces. This might prove useful if the data is ever ported to another database.

Now that you have decided upon the basic structure of the table, the next thing is to work out some of the major design issues. In particular, the following considerations are important:

- ■ The program should run off local tables, because this is the kind of tool likely to be used on individual PCs rather than on a network. It's a toss-up as to whether to use Paradox or dBASE tables, but I'll opt to use Paradox tables because they provide a bit more flexibility.

- ■ The user should be able to sort the table on the FName, LName, and Company fields.

- ■ It should be possible to search on the FName, LName, and Company fields.

- ■ The user should be able to set up filters based on the Category field.

- ■ It should be absolutely clear whether or not the table is editable, and the user should be able to move in and out of read-only mode easily.

- ■ It should be possible to print the contents of the table based on the filters set up by the Category field.

- ■ It's very difficult to choose a set of colors that will satisfy all tastes, so the user should be able to set the colors of the main features in the program.

A brief consideration of the design decisions makes it clear that the table should have a primary index on the first three fields and secondary indexes on the FName, LName, Company, and Category fields. The primary index can be used in place of a secondary index on the FName field, but the intent of the program's code will be clearer if a secondary index is used for this purpose. In other words, the code will be easier to read if it explicitly sets the IndexName to something called FNameIndex rather than simply defaulting to the primary index. Table 18.2

shows the final structure of the table. The three stars in the fourth column of the table show the fields that are part of the primary index.

Table 18.2. The fields used by the ADDRESS2 program.

Name	Type	Size	PIdx	Index
FName	Character	40	*	FNameIndex
LName	Character	40	*	LNameIndex
Company	Character	40	*	CompanyIndex
Address1	Character	40		
Address2	Character	40		
City	Character	40		
State	Character	5		
Zip	Character	15		
HPhone	Character	15		
WPhone	Character	15		
Fax	Character	15		
EMail1	Character	45		
EMail2	Character	45		
Comment	Memo	20		
Category	Character	15		CategoryIndex
Marked	Logical			

Now that there is a clear picture of the type of table that needs to be created, you can open up the Database Desktop and create the table, its primary index, and its four secondary indexes. When you are done, the structure of the table should look like that in Figure 18.1. You can save the table under the name ADDRESS.DB.

Here is another way of looking at the indexes for this table:

```
Primary Index
FName
LName
Company

Category Index
Category
Company Index
Company
FName
LName
```

```
LName Index
LName
FNameCompany
{the sort order should be Company, LName then FName.  The last name is more
significant than the first name.}
```

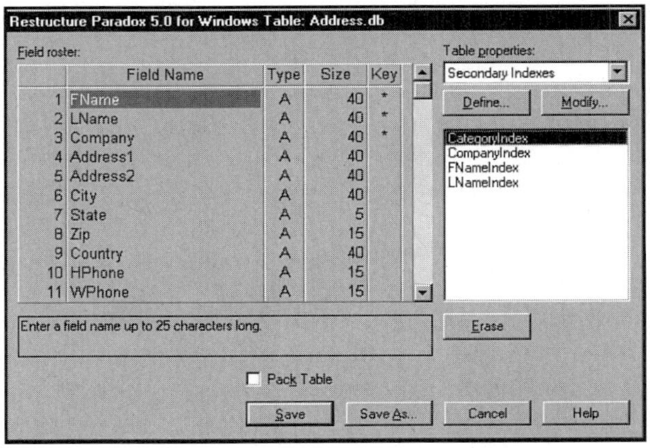

FIGURE 18.1.

Designing the main table for the ADDRESS2 program.

Defining the Program's Appearance

Before beginning the real programming chores, you need to create a main form and at least one of the several utility forms that will be used by the program. You can let the Database Expert perform at least part of this task for you, but I prefer to do the chore myself in order to give my program some individuality.

The main form of the ADDRESS2 program, shown in Figure 18.2, contains two panels. On the top panel are all the labels and data-aware controls necessary to handle basic input and output chores. All of the main fields in the program can be encapsulated in TdbEdit controls, except for the Comment field, which needs a TdbMemo, and the Category field, which needs a TdbComboBox. The names of the data-aware controls should match the field with which they are associated, so the first TdbEdit control is called eFName, the second eLName, and so on. The TdbComboBox would therefore be called cbCategory, and the memo field mComment.

The bottom panel should contain four buttons for navigating through the table's records, as well as Edit, Insert, and Cancel buttons. The bottom half of the second panel contains one or more labels for optionally reporting on the current status of the program. You might want to divide the two portions of the second panel into separate areas by running a TBevel control horizontally across the center of the control.

FIGURE 18.2.

The main form for the ADDRESS2 program.

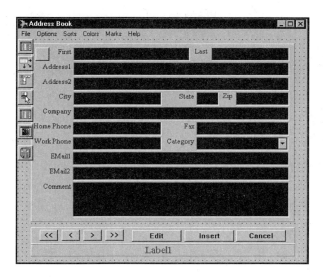

The top of the program contains a menu with the following format:

```
Caption = 'File'
  Caption = 'Print'
  Caption = '-'
  Caption = 'Exit'
Caption = 'Options'
  Caption = 'Delete'
  Caption = 'Search'
  Caption = 'Filter'
  Caption = 'Set Category'
Caption = 'Sorts'
  Caption = 'First Name'
  Caption = 'Last Name'
  Caption = 'Company'
Caption = 'Colors'
  Caption = 'Form'
  Caption = 'Edits'
  Caption = 'Edit Text'
  Caption = 'Labels'
  Caption = 'Panels'
Caption = 'Marked'
  Caption = 'Mark All'
  Caption = 'Clear All Marks'
  Caption = 'Print Marked to File'
Caption = 'Help'
  Caption = 'About'
```

Each line represents the caption for one entry in the program's main menu. The indented portions are the contents of the dropdown menus that appear when you select one of the menu items visible in Figure 18.2.

After creating the program's interface, dropdown a TTable and TDataSource, wire them up to ADDRESS.DB, and hook up the fields to the appropriate data-aware control. To make this work correctly, you should create an alias, called Address, that points at the location of ADDRESS.DB.

The only tricky part of this process involves the Category field, which is connected to the TdbComboBox. You make the basic connection to the TdbComboBox by setting its DataSource field to DataSource1 and its DataField to Category.

If you run the program, you will find that the TdbComboBox for the Category field does not contain any entries. The purpose of this control is to enable the user to select categories from a prepared list, rather than forcing the user to make up categories on the fly. The list is needed to prevent users from accidentally creating a whole series of different names for the same general purpose. For instance, if you want to be able to set a filter for the program, which presents you with a list of friends, you should create a category called Friend and assign it to all the members of the list that fit that description. If you always choose this category from a dropdown list, it will presumably always be spelled the same. However, if you rely on users to type this word, you might get a series of related entries that look like this:

```
Friend
Friends
Frends
Acquaintances
Buddies
Buds
Homies
HomeBoys
Amigos
Chums
Cronies
Companions
```

This mishmash of spellings and synonyms won't do you any good when you want to search for the group of records that fits into the category called Friend.

The simplest way to make the TdbComboBox perform its required function is to simply pop open the Property Editor for the Items property and type in a list of categories such as the following:

```
Home
Work
Family
Local Business
Friend
```

Now when you run the program and drop down the Category combo box, you will find that it contains the preceding list.

The only problem with typing names directly into the Items property for the TdbComboBox is that it is impossible to change this list at runtime. To do away with this difficulty, the program stores the list in a separate table, called CATS.DB. This table has a single character field that is 20 characters wide. After creating the table in the Database Desktop, you can enter the following five strings into five separate records:

> Home
> Work
> Family
> Local Business
> Friend

The program loads these records into the TdbComboBox during the OnCreate method for the main form:

```
Table2.Open;
Table2.First;
while not Table2.EOF do begin
  cbCategory.Items.Add(Table2.Fields[0].AsString);
  Table2.Next;
end;
Table2.Close;
```

This code makes use of a second TTable object dropped onto the form. This object has its DatabaseName set to the address alias and its TableName property set to the CATS table.

NOTE

In the last chapter, you saw the TdbLookupComboBox, which is smart enough to load itself with values automatically. I'm not using that here because I still use the AD-DRESS2 program on some 16-bit machines. That means I need to be careful not to include features that work only in Delphi 2.0.

To enable the user to change the contents of the CATS table, you can create a form like that shown in Figure 18.3. This form needs only minimal functionality because it's best to discourage the user from changing the list except when absolutely necessary. Note that you need to add the CATS unit to the uses clause in order for this code to run.

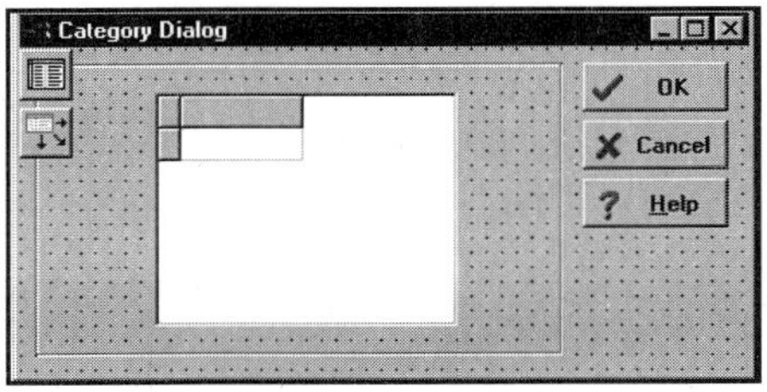

FIGURE 18.3.

The Category form enables the user to alter the contents of CATS.DB.

There is no need for the Category dialog, and the memory associated with it, to be created and allocated at program startup. As a result, you should open the Options | Project menu, select the Forms page, and move the Category dialog into the Available Forms column. In response to a selection of the Set Category menu item from the main form of the ADDRESS2 program, you can write the following code:

```
procedure TfrAddress.Category1Click(Sender: TObject);
begin
  CatsDlg := TCatsDlg.Create(Self);
  CatsDlg.ShowModal;
  CatsDlg.Free;
end;
```

This code creates the Category dialog, shows it to the user, and finally deallocates its memory after the user is done. This approach is taken because it assures that the Category dialog and CATS.DB are only in memory when absolutely necessary.

The skeletal structure of the ADDRESS2 program is starting to come together. However, there is one remaining task that must be completed before the core of the program is complete. A number of basic commands are issued by the program, and these can be defined in a single enumerated type:

```
TCommandType = (btClose, btInsert, btPrior,
                btEdit, btNext, btCancel,
                btPrint, btFirst, btLast);
```

This type enables you to associate each of the program's commands with the Tag field of the appropriate button or menu item, and then to associate all of these buttons or menu items with a single method that looks like this:

```
procedure TfrAddress.CommandClick(Sender: TObject);
begin
  case TCommandType((Sender as TComponent).Tag) of
    btClose: Close;
    btInsert: tblAddress.Insert;
    btPrior: tblAddress.Prior;
    btEdit: HandleEditMode;
    btNext: tblAddress.Next;
    btCancel: tblAddress.Cancel;
    btPrint: PrintData;
    btFirst: tblAddress.First;
    btLast: tblAddress.Last;
  end;
end;
```

All of the code in this program will compile at this stage except for the references to `HandleEditMode` and `PrintData`. For now, you can simply create dummy `HandleEditMode` and `PrintData` private methods and leave their contents blank.

There is no reason why you can't have a different method associated with each of the buttons and menu items in the program. However, it's neater and simpler to handle things this way, and the code you create is much easier to read. The key point here is to be sure that the Tag property of the appropriate control gets the correct value and that all of the controls listed here have the OnClick method manually set to the CommandClick method.

Table 18.3 gives a brief summary of the commands passed to the CommandClick method:

Table 18.3. Commands passed to CommandClick.

Command	Type	Name	Tag
Exit	TMenuItem	btClose	0
Insert	TButton	btInsert	1
Prior	TButton	btPrior	2
Edit	TButton	btEdit	3
Next	TButton	btNext	4
Cancel	TButton	btCancel	5
Print	TMenuItem	btPrint	6
First	TButton	btFirst	7
Last	TButton	btLast	8

At this stage, you are ready to run the ADDRESS2 program. You can now insert new data, iterate through the records you create, cancel accidental changes, and shut down the program from the menu. This is the bare functionality needed to run the program.

NOTE

The program as it exists now is what I mean by creating a "rough draft" of a program. It gets the raw functionality of the program up and running with minimum fuss, and it lets you take a look at it to see if it passes muster.

If you were working for a third-party client, or for a demanding boss, this would be the time to call the person or persons in question and have them critique your work.

"Is this what you are looking for?", you might ask. "Are there any fields you think need to be there that aren't yet visible? Do you feel that the project is headed in the right direction?"

Nine times out of ten, they will come back to you with a slew of suggestions, most of which have never occurred to you. If there are irreconcilable differences of opinion about the project, this is the time to find out. If there are some good ideas you never considered, now is the time to add them.

This is also your chance to let everyone know that after this point, it may become impossible to make major design changes. Let them know that you are about to start doing the kind of detail work that is very hard to undo. If people need a day or two to think about your proposed design, give it to them. It's better to make changes now, at the start, than after you have everything polished and spit-shined. By presenting them with a prototype, you give them a sense of participating in the project, which at least potentially puts them on your side when you turn in the finished project.

Creating a Finished Program

The remaining portions of this chapter will tackle the issues that improve this program to the point that it might be useful in a real-world situation. All but the most obvious or irrelevant portions of the code for the ADDRESS2 program are explained in detail in the remainder of this chapter.

Listing 18.1 shows the code for the finished program. I discuss most of this code in one place or another in this chapter. Once again, the goal of this program is to show you something that is reasonably close to being useful in a real-world situation. It's that gap between the sketchy outline of a program, as discussed earlier, and a product that is actually usable that forms the heart of the discussion that follows. In fact, most of the discussion of databases that you have heard in the last few chapters has concentrated on the bare outlines of a real database program. You have to know those raw tools in order to write any kind of database program. However, they are not enough, and there comes a time when you have to start putting something together that might be useful. That's the burden of the rest of this chapter.

Listing 18.1. The source code for the ADDRESS2 program has several different modules.

```
unit Main;

{ Program copyright (c) 1995, 1996 by Charles Calvert }
{ Project Name: ADDRESS2 }

interface

uses
  WinTypes, WinProcs, Classes,
  Graphics, Controls, Printers,
  Forms, ExtCtrls, StdCtrls,
  DB, DBTables, DBCtrls,
  Mask, Menus, Dialogs,
  DBLookup, Report, Search, Buttons;

const
  mfClearMarks = 100;
```

```
    mfMarkAll    = 101;
    ReadOnlyStr  = ' [Read Only Mode]';
    EditModeStr  = ' [Edit Mode]';

type
  TColorType   = (ccForm, ccEdit, ccEditText, ccLabel, ccPanel);
  TChangeType  = (tcColor, tcFontColor);
  TCommandType = (btClose, btInsert, btPrior,
                  btEdit, btNext, btCancel,
                  btPrint, btFirst, btLast);

  TfrAddress = class(TForm)
    tblAddress: TTable;
    Panel1: TPanel;
    ELName: TDBEdit;
    EFName: TDBEdit;
    Panel2: TPanel;
    BNext: TButton;
    BPrevious: TButton;
    EAddress1: TDBEdit;
    EAddress2: TDBEdit;
    ECity: TDBEdit;
    EState: TDBEdit;
    EZip: TDBEdit;
    ECompany: TDBEdit;
    Insert: TButton;
    EEdit: TButton;   {Shouldn't this just be called 'Edit'}
    DataSource1: TDataSource;
    MainMenu1: TMainMenu;
    File1: TMenuItem;
    Print1: TMenuItem;
    N1: TMenuItem;
    Exit1: TMenuItem;
    Options1: TMenuItem;
    Search1: TMenuItem;
    Help1: TMenuItem;
    About1: TMenuItem;
    First: TButton;
    Last: TButton;
    Sorts1: TMenuItem;
    FirstName1: TMenuItem;
    LastName1: TMenuItem;
    Company1: TMenuItem;
    EHomePhone: TDBEdit;
    EWorkPhone: TDBEdit;
    EFax: TDBEdit;
    EEMail1: TDBEdit;
    Delete1: TMenuItem;
    Label3: TLabel;
    Address1: TLabel;
    Address2: TLabel;
    City: TLabel;
    State: TLabel;
    Zip: TLabel;
    Company: TLabel;
    HPhone: TLabel;
    WPhone: TLabel;
    Fax: TLabel;
```

continues

Listing 18.1. continued

```
    Comment: TLabel;
    EMail1: TLabel;
    Category: TLabel;
    EMail2: TLabel;
    EEMail2: TDBEdit;
    Table2: TTable;
    cbCategory: TDBComboBox;
    Filter1: TMenuItem;
    Colors1: TMenuItem;
    FormColor1: TMenuItem;
    EditColor1: TMenuItem;
    EditText1: TMenuItem;
    Labels1: TMenuItem;
    ColorDialog1: TColorDialog;
    Panels1: TMenuItem;
    Report1: TReport;
    Cancel: TButton;
    Category1: TMenuItem;
    Marks1: TMenuItem;
    MarkAll1: TMenuItem;
    ClearAllMarks1: TMenuItem;
    SpeedButton1: TSpeedButton;
    PrintMarkedtoFile1: TMenuItem;
    DBMemo1: TDBMemo;
    Edit1: TMenuItem;
    Copy1: TMenuItem;
    Cut1: TMenuItem;
    Paste1: TMenuItem;
    procedure About1Click(Sender: TObject);
    procedure Category1Click(Sender: TObject);
    procedure ColorClick(Sender: TObject);
    procedure CommandClick(Sender: TObject);
    procedure Delete1Click(Sender: TObject);
    procedure Filter1Click(Sender: TObject);
    procedure FormCreate(Sender: TObject);
    procedure SortMenu(Sender: TObject);
    procedure Search1Click(Sender: TObject);
    procedure Marks1Click(Sender: TObject);
    procedure DataSource1DataChange(Sender: TObject; Field: TField);
    procedure SpeedButton1Click(Sender: TObject);
    procedure PrintMarkedtoFile1Click(Sender: TObject);
    procedure Copy1Click(Sender: TObject);
    procedure Paste1Click(Sender: TObject);
    procedure Cut1Click(Sender: TObject);
  private
    FCaptionStr: string;
    FSortType: TSortType;
    FEditing: Boolean;
    BookOpen: HBitMap;
    BookShut: HBitmap;
    procedure CheckForIni;
    procedure DoSearch(S: string);
    procedure DoSort;
    function GetIni(CType: TColorType): TColor;
    function GetPath: string;
    procedure HandleEditMode;
```

```
      procedure PrintData;
      procedure SetCategoryList;
      procedure SetEdits(TypeChange: TChangeType; NewValue: TColor);
      procedure SetIni(CType: TColorType; C: TColor);
      procedure SetLabels(C: TColor);
      procedure SetPanels(C: TColor);
      procedure SetReadOnly(NewState: Boolean);
      procedure WriteRecord(var F: System.Text);
    end;

var
  frAddress: TfrAddress;

implementation

uses
  About, Cats, Filter,
  IniFiles, StrBox, SysUtils,
  UtilBox, ClipBrd;

{$R *.DFM}
{$R BITS.RES}

{========= Private Methods ==========}
procedure TfrAddress.About1Click(Sender: TObject);
begin
  AboutBox.Color := GetIni(ccForm);
  AboutBox.ShowModal;
end;

procedure TfrAddress.CommandClick(Sender: TObject);
begin
  case TCommandType((Sender as TComponent).Tag) of
    btClose: Close;
    btInsert: tblAddress.Insert;
    btPrior: tblAddress.Prior;
    btEdit: HandleEditMode;
    btNext: tblAddress.Next;
    btCancel: tblAddress.Cancel;
    btPrint: PrintData;
    btFirst: tblAddress.First;
    btLast: tblAddress.Last;
  end;
end;

procedure TfrAddress.Category1Click(Sender: TObject);
begin
  CatsDlg := TCatsDlg.Create(Self);
  CatsDlg.ShowModal;
  CatsDlg.Free;
end;

procedure TfrAddress.ColorClick(Sender: TObject);
begin
  if not ColorDialog1.Execute then Exit;
  case TColorType((Sender as TMenuItem).Tag) of
    ccForm: frAddress.Color := ColorDialog1.Color;
    ccEdit: SetEdits(tcColor, ColorDialog1.Color);
```

continues

Listing 18.1. continued

```
    ccEditText: SetEdits(tcFontColor, ColorDialog1.Color);
    ccLabel: SetLabels(ColorDialog1.Color);
    ccPanel: SetPanels(ColorDialog1.Color);
  end;
  SetIni(TColorType((Sender as TMenuItem).Tag), ColorDialog1.Color);
end;

procedure TfrAddress.Delete1Click(Sender: TObject);
begin
  if MessageDlg('Are you sure you want to delete?',
            mtInformation, [mbOk,mbCancel], 0) = idOk then
    tblAddress.Delete;
end;

procedure TfrAddress.Filter1Click(Sender: TObject);
var
  S: string;
begin
  if Filter1.Caption = 'Filter' then begin
    S := FilterDlg.GetFilter(cbCategory.Items);
    if S = '' then Exit;
    Filter1.Caption := 'Cancel Filter';
    tblAddress.IndexName := 'CategoryIndex';
    tblAddress.SetRangeStart;
    tblAddress.FieldByName('Category').AsString := S;
    tblAddress.SetRangeEnd;
    tblAddress.FieldByName('Category').AsString := S;
    tblAddress.ApplyRange;
  end else begin
    Filter1.Caption := 'Filter';
    tblAddress.CancelRange;
  end;
end;

procedure TfrAddress.FormCreate(Sender: TObject);
var
  i: Integer;
begin
  FSortType := stLast;
  FCaptionStr := Caption;
  Caption := FCaptionStr + ReadOnlyStr;

  CheckForIni;
  for i := 0 to 4 do
    case TColorType(i) of
      ccForm: Color := GetIni(TColorType(i));
      ccEdit: SetEdits(tcColor, GetIni(TColorType(i)));
      ccEditText: SetEdits(tcFontColor, GetIni(TColorType(i)));
      ccLabel: SetLabels(GetIni(TColorType(i)));
      ccPanel: SetPanels(GetIni(TColorType(i)));
    end;

  tblAddress.Open;
  DataSource1.AutoEdit := False;
  SetCategoryList;
end;
```

```
procedure TfrAddress.SortMenu(Sender: TObject);
begin
  FSortType := TSortType((Sender as TComponent).Tag);
  DoSort;
  DoSearch('A');
end;

procedure TfrAddress.Search1Click(Sender: TObject);
var
  S: string;
begin
  if not SearchDlg.GetSearchStr(FSortType, S) then Exit;
  DoSort;
  DoSearch(S);
end;

{========= Private Methods ==========}

procedure TfrAddress.CheckForIni;
var
  F: System.Text;
  Path: string;
begin
  Path := GetPath + 'address.ini';
  if not FileExists(Path) then begin
    System.Assign(F, Path);
    System.ReWrite(F);
    System.WriteLn(F, '[Colors]');
    System.WriteLn(F, 'Form=7045184');
    System.WriteLn(F, 'Edits=8421376');
    System.WriteLn(F, 'EditText=0');
    System.WriteLn(F, 'Labels=0');
    System.WriteLn(F, 'Panels=12639424');
    System.Close(F);
  end;
end;

procedure TfrAddress.DoSearch(S: string);
begin
  tblAddress.SetKey;
  case FSortType of
    stFirst: tblAddress.FieldByName('FName').AsString := S;
    stLast:tblAddress.FieldByName('LName').AsString := S;
    stCompany:tblAddress.FieldByName('Company').AsString := S;
  end;
  tblAddress.GotoNearest;
end;

procedure TFrAddress.DoSort;
begin
  case FSortType of
    stFirst: tblAddress.IndexName := 'FNameIndex';
    stLast: tblAddress.IndexName := 'LNameIndex';
    stCompany: tblAddress.IndexName := 'CompanyIndex';
  end;
end;
```

continues

Listing 18.1. continued

```
function TfrAddress.GetIni(CType: TColorType): TColor;
var
  Ini: TIniFile;
  Path, S: string;
begin
  Ini := TIniFile.Create(GetPath + 'address.Ini');
  case CType of
    ccForm: S := 'Form';
    ccEdit: S := 'Edits';
    ccEditText: S := 'EditText';
    ccLabel: S := 'Labels';
    ccPanel: S := 'Panels';
  end;
  Result := Ini.ReadInteger('Colors', S, clBlue);
  Ini.Free;
end;

function TfrAddress.GetPath: string;
begin
  Result := ExtractFilePath(ParamStr(0));
end;

procedure TfrAddress.HandleEditMode;
begin
  Insert.Enabled := not DataSource1.AutoEdit;
  Cancel.Enabled := not DataSource1.AutoEdit;
  Delete1.Enabled := not DataSource1.AutoEdit;
  if not DataSource1.AutoEdit then begin
    SetReadOnly(True);
    EEdit.Caption := 'ReadOnly';
    Caption := FCaptionStr + EditModeStr;
  end else begin
    if tblAddress.State <> dsBrowse then tblAddress.Post;
    SetReadOnly(False);
    EEdit.Caption := 'Edit';
    Caption := FCaptionStr + ReadOnlyStr;
  end;
end;

procedure TfrAddress.PrintData;
begin
  Cursor := crHourGlass;
  Report1.ReportDir := GetPath;
  Report1.Run;
  Cursor := crDefault;
end;

procedure TfrAddress.SetCategoryList;
begin
  Table2.Open;
  while not Table2.EOF do begin
    cbCategory.Items.Add(Table2.Fields[0].AsString);
    Table2.Next;
  end;
  Table2.Close;
end;
```

```
procedure TfrAddress.SetEdits(TypeChange: TChangeType; NewValue: TColor);
var
  i: Integer;
begin
  for i := 0 to ComponentCount - 1 do
    if (Components[i] is TdbEdit) or (Components[i] is TdbComboBox) or
         (Components[i] is TdbMemo) then
    case TypeChange of
      tcColor: TdbEdit(Components[i]).Color := NewValue;
      tcFontColor: TdbEdit(Components[i]).Font.Color := NewValue;
    end;
end;

procedure TfrAddress.SetIni(CType: TColorType; C: TColor);
var
  Ini: TIniFile;
  Path, S: string;
begin
  Ini := TIniFile.Create(GetPath + 'address.ini');
  case CType of
    ccForm: S := 'Form';
    ccEdit: S := 'Edits';
    ccEditText: S := 'EditText';
    ccLabel: S := 'Labels';
    ccPanel: S := 'Panels';
  end;
  Ini.WriteInteger('Colors', S, C);
  Ini.Free;
end;

procedure TfrAddress.SetLabels(C: TColor);
var
  i: Integer;
begin
  for i := 0 to ComponentCount - 1 do
    if (Components[i] is TLabel) then
      TLabel(Components[i]).Font.Color := C;
end;

procedure TfrAddress.SetPanels(C: TColor);
var
  i: Integer;
begin
  for i := 0 to ComponentCount - 1 do
    if (Components[i] is TPanel) then
      TPanel(Components[i]).Color := C;
end;

procedure TfrAddress.SetReadOnly(NewState: Boolean);
begin
  DataSource1.AutoEdit := NewState;
end;

procedure TfrAddress.Marks1Click(Sender: TObject);
var
  B: TBookmark;
  Value: string;
```

continues

Listing 18.1. continued

```
begin
  case (Sender as TMenuItem).Tag of
    mfMarkAll: Value := 'T';
    mfClearMarks: Value := 'F';
  end;
  DataSource1.Enabled := False;
  B := tblAddress.GetBookmark;
  tblAddress.First;
  while not tblAddress.EOF do begin
    tblAddress.Edit;
    tblAddress.FieldByName('Marked').AsString := Value;
    tblAddress.Next;
  end;
  tblAddress.GotoBookmark(B);
  tblAddress.FreeBookmark(B);
  DataSource1.Enabled := True;
end;

{ Delphi disposes of TBitMaps when the
  handle is assigned to a new value, so we have
  to keep reloading it. At least it's part of the
  executable this way, and not a separate file. }
procedure TfrAddress.DataSource1DataChange(Sender: TObject; Field: TField);
begin
  if tblAddress.FieldByName('Marked').AsBoolean then begin
    BookOpen := LoadBitmap(HInstance, 'BookOpen');
    SpeedButton1.Glyph.Handle := BookOpen
  end else begin
    BookShut := LoadBitmap(HInstance, 'BookShut');
    SpeedButton1.Glyph.Handle := BookShut;
  end;
end;

{ -----------------------------------------
  Toggle the Boolean value of the marked field
  ---------------------------------------}
procedure TfrAddress.SpeedButton1Click(Sender: TObject);
begin
  tblAddress.Edit;
  tblAddress.FieldByName('Marked').AsBoolean :=
    not tblAddress.FieldByName('Marked').AsBoolean;
  tblAddress.Post;
end;

procedure TfrAddress.WriteRecord(var F: System.Text);
begin
  with tblAddress do begin
    Write(F, FieldByName('FName').AsString, ' ');
    WriteLn(F, FieldByName('LName').AsString);
    if FieldByName('Company').AsString <> '' then
      WriteLn(F, FieldByName('Company').AsString);
    WriteLn(F, FieldByName('Address1').AsString);
    if FieldByName('Address2').AsString <> '' then
      WriteLn(F, FieldByName('Address2').AsString);
    Write(F, FieldByName('City').AsString, ', ');
    Write(F, FieldByName('State').AsString, ' ');
```

```
      WriteLn(F, FieldByName('Zip').AsString);
      WriteLn(F);
      WriteLn(F, '*************');
  end;
end;

procedure TfrAddress.PrintMarkedtoFile1Click(Sender: TObject);
const
  Caption = 'File Name Dialog';
  Hint = 'Enter File Name';
var
  S: string;
  F: System.Text;
  S1, S2: array[0..100] of Char;
begin
  S := '';
  if not InputQuery(Caption, Hint, S) then Exit;
  System.Assign(F, S);
  System.ReWrite(F);
  while not tblAddress.EOF do begin
    if tblAddress.FieldByName('Marked').AsBoolean then
      WriteRecord(F);
    tblAddress.Next;
  end;
  System.Close(F);
  StrCopy(S1, 'notepad.exe ');
  StrPCopy(S2, S);
  StrCat(S1, S2);
  WinExec(S1, sw_ShowNormal);
end;

procedure TfrAddress.Copy1Click(Sender: TObject);
begin
  if ActiveControl is TDBEdit then
    TDBEdit(ActiveControl).CopyToClipBoard
  else if ActiveControl is TDBMemo then
    TDBMemo(ActiveControl).CopyToClipBoard
  else if ActiveControl is TDBComboBox then
    ClipBoard.AsText := cbCategory.Text;
end;

procedure TfrAddress.Paste1Click(Sender: TObject);
begin
  if not DataSource1.AutoEdit then begin
    ShowMessage('Must be in edit mode');
    Exit;
  end;
  if ActiveControl is TDBEdit then
    TDBEdit(ActiveControl).PasteFromClipBoard
  else if ActiveControl is TDBMemo then
    TDBMemo(ActiveControl).PasteFromClipBoard
  else if ActiveControl is TDBComboBox then
    cbCategory.Text := ClipBoard.AsText;
end;

procedure TfrAddress.Cut1Click(Sender: TObject);
begin
  if not DataSource1.AutoEdit then begin
```

continues

Listing 18.1. continued

```
    ShowMessage('Must be in edit mode');
    Exit;
  end;
  if ActiveControl is TDBEdit then
    TDBEdit(ActiveControl).CutToClipBoard
  else if ActiveControl is TDBMemo then
    TDBMemo(ActiveControl).CutToClipBoard
  else if ActiveControl is TDBComboBox then begin
    cbCategory.Text := ClipBoard.AsText;
    cbCategory.Text := '';
  end;
end;

end.
```

Listing 18.2. The About dialog contains only visual elements.

```
unit About;

{ Program copyright (c) 1995 by Charles Calvert }
{ Project Name: ADDRESS2 }

interface

uses
  WinTypes, WinProcs, Classes,
  Graphics, Forms, Controls,
  StdCtrls, Buttons, ExtCtrls;

type
  TAboutBox = class(TForm)
    Panel1: TPanel;
    OKButton: TBitBtn;
    ProgramIcon: TImage;
    ProductName: TLabel;
    Version: TLabel;
    Copyright: TLabel;
    Comments: TLabel;
  private
    { Private declarations }
  public
    { Public declarations }
  end;

var
  AboutBox: TAboutBox;

implementation

{$R *.DFM}

end.
```

Listing 18.3. The Cats dialog enables the user to work with the category table.

```
unit Cats;

{ Program copyright (c) 1996 by Charles Calvert }
{ Project Name: ADDRESS2 }

interface

uses
  WinTypes, WinProcs, Classes,
  Graphics, Forms, Controls,
  Buttons, StdCtrls, Grids,
  DBGrids, DB, DBTables,
  ExtCtrls;

type
  TCatsDlg = class(TForm)
    OKBtn: TBitBtn;
    CancelBtn: TBitBtn;
    HelpBtn: TBitBtn;
    Bevel1: TBevel;
    tblCats: TTable;
    DataSource1: TDataSource;
    DBGrid1: TDBGrid;
    procedure FormCreate(Sender: TObject);
    procedure FormDestroy(Sender: TObject);
  end;

var
  CatsDlg: TCatsDlg;

implementation

{$R *.DFM}

procedure TCatsDlg.FormCreate(Sender: TObject);
begin
  tblCats.Open;
end;

procedure TCatsDlg.FormDestroy(Sender: TObject);
begin
  tblCats.Close;
end;

end.
```

Listing 18.4. The Filter dialog enables the user to set a range on the visible records.

```
unit Filter;

{ Program copyright (c) 1995 by Charles Calvert }
{ Project Name: ADDRESS2 }

interface

uses
  SysUtils, WinTypes, WinProcs,
  Messages, Classes, Graphics,
  Controls, Forms, Dialogs,
  StdCtrls, Buttons;

type
  TFilterDlg = class(TForm)
    ListBox1: TListBox;
    BitBtn1: TBitBtn;
    BitBtn2: TBitBtn;
  private
    { Private declarations }
  public
    { Public declarations }
    function GetFilter(SList: TStrings): string;
  end;

var
  FilterDlg: TFilterDlg;

implementation

{$R *.DFM}

function TFilterDlg.GetFilter(SList: TStrings): string;
begin
  ListBox1.Items := SList;
  if ShowModal = mrCancel then
    Result := ''
  else
    Result := ListBox1.Items.Strings[ListBox1.ItemIndex];
end;

end.
```

Listing 18.5. The Search dialog lets the user decide which fields to search on.

```
unit Search;

{ Program copyright (c) 1995 by Charles Calvert }
{ Project Name: ADDRESS2 }

interface
```

```
uses
  WinTypes, WinProcs, Classes,
  Graphics, Forms, Controls,
  Buttons, StdCtrls, ExtCtrls;

type
  TSortType = (stFirst, stLast, stCompany);

  TSearchDlg = class(TForm)
    OKBtn: TBitBtn;
    CancelBtn: TBitBtn;
    HelpBtn: TBitBtn;
    Bevel1: TBevel;
    Edit1: TEdit;
    GroupBox1: TGroupBox;
    FirstName: TRadioButton;
    LastName: TRadioButton;
    Company: TRadioButton;
    Label1: TLabel;
    procedure FormActivate(Sender: TObject);
  private
    { Private declarations }
  public
    { Public declarations }
    function GetSearchStr(var ST: TSortType; var S: string): Boolean;
  end;

var
  SearchDlg: TSearchDlg;

implementation

{$R *.DFM}

function TSearchDlg.GetSearchStr(var ST: TSortType; var S: string): Boolean;
begin
  Result := False;

  if ShowModal = mrCancel then Exit;

  S := Edit1.Text;

  if FirstName.Checked then
    ST := stFirst
  else if LastName.Checked then
    ST := stLast
  else
    ST := stCompany;

  Result := True;
end;

procedure TSearchDlg.FormActivate(Sender: TObject);
begin
  Edit1.Text := '';
  Edit1.SetFocus;
end;

end.
```

It's important to note that a lot of the code ends up being considerably less formidable than it might appear at first glance. For instance, the code for the About dialog or the Category dialog is primarily created visually with very little effort on your part. Even the Search dialog, which is perhaps the most complicated of the utility dialogs, really consists of nothing more than a dozen fairly straightforward lines of code. The code for the main form is a bit more meaty, but most of it will become fairly transparent if you study the logic one step at a time.

Moving In and Out of Read-Only Mode

Perhaps the most important single function of the ADDRESS2 program is its capability to move in and out of read-only mode. This is valuable because it enables the user to open the program and browse through data without ever having to worry about accidentally altering a record. In fact, when the user first opens the program, it is impossible to type into any of the data-aware controls, which ensures that there is no possible way to accidentally alter a record. The only way for the program to get into edit mode is for the user to press the Edit button, which then automatically makes the data live.

When the program is in read-only mode, the Insert and Cancel buttons are grayed out, and the Delete menu item is also dimmed. When the user switches into edit mode, all of these controls become live and the text in the Edit button switches to read-only. All these visual clues help make the current mode of the program obvious to the user.

The functionality described is quite simple to implement. The key methods to trace are the HandleEditMode and SetReadOnly methods.

The HandleEditMode routine is called from the CommandClick method described in the last section:

```
procedure TfrAddress.HandleEditMode;
begin
  Insert.Enabled := not DataSource1.AutoEdit;
  Cancel.Enabled := not DataSource1.AutoEdit;
  Delete1.Enabled := not DataSource1.AutoEdit;
  if not DataSource1.AutoEdit then begin
    SetReadOnly(True);
    EEdit.Caption := 'ReadOnly';
    Caption := FCaptionStr + EditModeStr;
  end else begin
    if tblAddress.State <> dsBrowse then tblAddress.Post;
    SetReadOnly(False);
    EEdit.Caption := 'Edit';
    Caption := FCaptionStr + ReadOnlyStr;
  end;
end;
```

The primary purpose of this code is to ensure that the proper components are enabled or disabled, depending on the current state of the program. After altering the appearance of the program, the code calls SetReadOnly:

```
procedure TfrAddress.SetReadOnly(NewState: Boolean);
begin
  DataSource1.AutoEdit := NewState;
end;
```

The center around which both of these routines revolve is the `DataSource1.AutoEdit` property. When this property is set to False, all the data-aware controls on the form are disabled and the user won't be able to type in them, as shown in Figure 18.4. When the property is set to True, the data becomes live and the user can edit or insert records, as shown in Figure 18.5.

FIGURE 18.4.

ADDRESS2 as it appears in read-only mode.

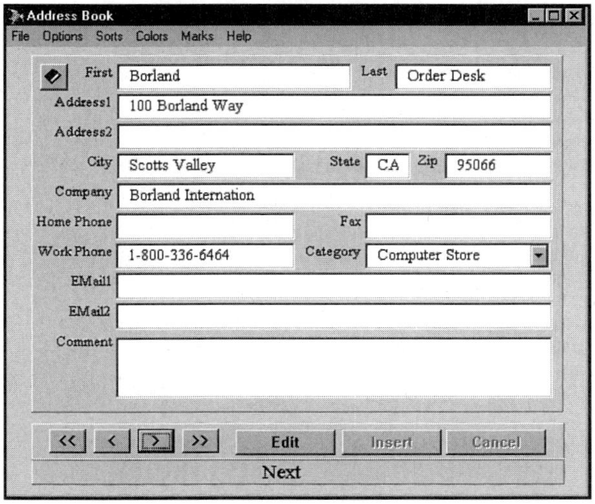

The purpose of the `AutoEdit` property is to determine whether or not a keystroke from the user can put a table directly into edit mode. When `AutoEdit` is set to False, the user can't type information into a data-aware control. When `AutoEdit` is set to True, the user can switch the table into edit mode simply by typing a letter in a control. It's important to note that even when `AutoEdit` is set to False, you can set a table into edit mode by calling `tblAddress.Edit` or `tblAddress.Insert`. As a result, the technique shown here won't work unless you gray out the controls that give the user the power to set the table into edit mode. (See Figure 18.5.)

The code in the `HandleEditMode` method is concerned entirely with interface issues. It enables or disables the Insert, Cancel, and Delete controls, depending on whether the table is about to go in or out of read-only mode. The code also ensures that the caption for the Edit button provides the user with a clue about the button's current function. In other words, the button doesn't report on the state of the program, but on the functionality associated with the button.

The `HandleEditMode` method is written so that the program is always moved into the opposite of its current state. At startup time the table should be set to read-only mode (`AutoEdit = False`), and the appropriate controls should be disabled. Some of the code in the `FormCreate` method ensures that this is, in fact, the state of affairs at startup. Thereafter, every time you press the

Edit button, the program will switch from its current state to the opposite state, from read-only mode to edit mode, and then back again.

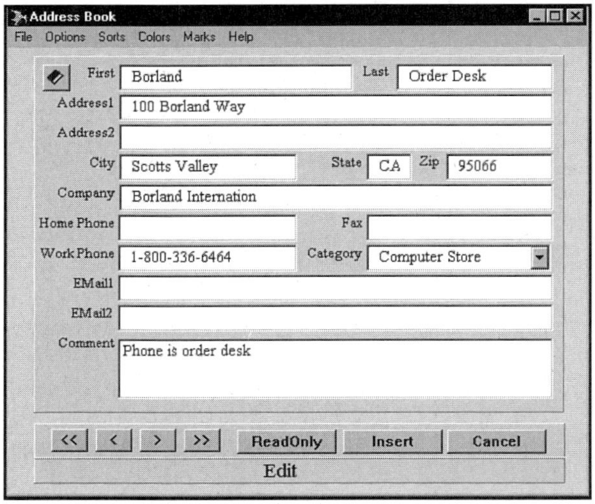

FIGURE 18.5.

The ADDRESS2 program as it appears in edit mode.

In addition to the TDataSource AutoEdit property, there is a second way to take a table in and out of read-only mode. This second method is really more powerful than the first, because it makes the table itself completely resistant to change. However, this second method is a bit more costly in terms of time and system resources. The trick, naturally enough, is to change the ReadOnly property of a TTable component. Here is how the SetReadOnly procedure would look if you employed this second technique:

```
procedure TfrAddress.SetReadOnly(NewState: Boolean);
var
  Bookmark: TBookmark;
begin
  Bookmark := tblAddress.GetBookMark;
  tblAddress.Close;
  tblAddress.ReadOnly := NewState;
  tblAddress.Open;
  tblAddress.GotoBookMark(Bookmark);
  tblAddress.FreeBookmark(Bookmark);
end;
```

It turns out that you cannot set a table in or out of read-only mode while it is open. Therefore, you have to close the table every time you change the ReadOnly property. Unfortunately, every time you close and open a table, you are moved back to the first record. As a result, it is necessary to set a bookmark identifying your current location in the table, close the table, and then move the table in or out of read-only mode. When you are done, you can open the table and jet back to the bookmark. This sounds like quite a bit of activity, but in fact it can usually be accomplished without the user being aware that anything untoward has occurred. The entire functionality described in this paragraph is encapsulated in the second version of the SetReadOnly method, shown previously.

If you choose this second method, you would have to set the tblAddress.ReadOnly property to True at program startup and rewrite the HandleEditMode method so that it looks like this:

```
procedure TfrAddress.HandleEditMode;
begin
  Insert.Enabled := tblAddress.ReadOnly;
  Cancel.Enabled := tblAddress.ReadOnly;
  Delete1.Enabled := tblAddress.ReadOnly;
  if tblAddress.ReadOnly then begin
    SetReadOnly(False);
    EEdit.Caption := 'ReadOnly'
  end else begin
    if tblAddress.State <> dsBrowse then tblAddress.Post;
    SetReadOnly(True);
    EEdit.Caption := 'Edit';
  end;
end;
```

With the ADDRESS2 program, it is clear that the first technique for moving a program in and out of read-only mode is best. In other words, it's much faster and much easier to switch DataSource1 in and out of AutoEdit mode than it is to switch tblAddress in and out of read-only mode. However, I have shown you the second technique because there may be a time when you have to quickly open and close a table, and it is useful to have a routine to use in such cases.

On the whole, the act of moving ADDRESS2 in and out of read-only mode is fairly trivial. The key point to grasp is the power of the TDataSource AutoEdit method. If you understand how it works, you can provide this same functionality in all your programs.

Sorting Data

At various times, you might want the records stored in the program to be sorted by first name, last name, or company. These three possible options are encapsulated in the program's menu, as depicted in Figure 18.6, and also in an enumerated type declared in SEARCH.PAS:

```
TSortType = (stFirst, stLast, stCompany);
```

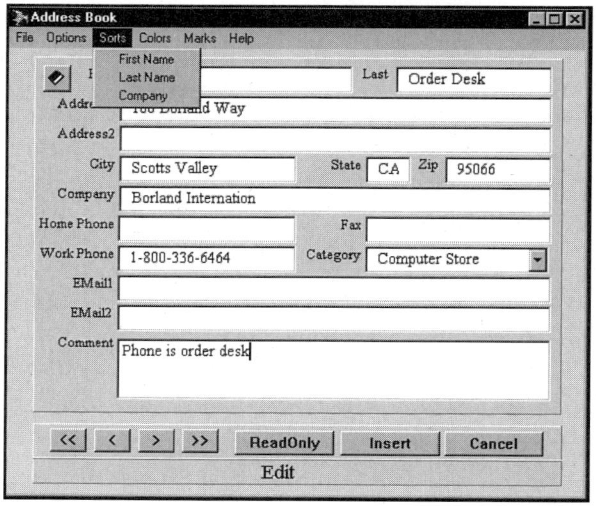

FIGURE 18.6.

The Sorts menu has three different options.

Once again, it is the Tag field from the Sorts dropdown menu that makes it possible to detect which option the user wants to select:

```
procedure TfrAddress.SortMenu(Sender: TObject);
begin
  FSortType := TSortType((Sender as TComponent).Tag);
  DoSort;
  DoSearch('A');
end;
```

FSortType is a field of TfrAddress that is declared to be of TSortType.

The key point is to be sure to associate a different value between 0 and 2 for the Tag property of each menu item, and to then associate the SortMenu method with the OnClick event for each menu item. If the Tag property for a menu item is zero, it gets translated into stFirst, and so on.

After finding out whether the user wants to sort by first name, last name, or company, you must perform the actual sort, which is done by simply changing indexes:

```
procedure TFrAddress.DoSort;
begin
  case FSortType of
    stFirst: tblAddress.IndexName := 'FNameIndex';
    stLast: tblAddress.IndexName := 'LNameIndex';
    stCompany: tblAddress.IndexName := 'CompanyIndex';
  end;
end;
```

This is about as straightforward a method as you'll encounter. Changing an index involves nothing more than changing the IndexName property, and I have isolated this trivial chore in its own method so it can be called from multiple and unrelated locations in the source.

After sorting, there may be a group of blank records at the beginning of the table. For instance, if you choose to sort by the Company field, it is likely that many of the records in the AD-DRESS table will not have anything in the company field. As a result, there could be several hundred, or even several thousand, records at the beginning of the table that are of no interest to someone who wants to view only companies. The solution, of course, is to search for the first record that has a non-blank value in the company field. You can do this by searching for the record that has a company field that is nearest to matching the string "A". The actual details of searching for a record are covered in the next section.

That's all there is to sorting the records in the ADDRESS2 program. Clearly, this is not a difficult subject. The key points to grasp are that you must create secondary indexes for all the fields you want to sort on, and then performing the sort becomes as simple as swapping indexes.

Searching for Data

Searching for data in a table seems like an extremely simple subject, and indeed it is quite straightforward, except for one minor catch. The problem, of course, is that when working with local tables in the 16-bit version of Delphi, you can only use the GotoKey, FindKey, FindNearest or GotoNearest methods on fields that are currently keyed. In other words, if you want to search on the Company field, it's not enough to simply declare a secondary index called CompanyIndex. To perform an actual search, you must make the CompanyIndex the active index and then perform the search. As a result, before you can make a search, you must do three things:

1. Ask the user for the string he or she wants to find.
2. Ask the user for the field where the string resides.
3. Set the index to the proper field.

Only after jumping through each of these hoops are you free to perform the actual search.

> **NOTE**
>
> It's important to note that some databases don't force you to search only on actively keyed fields. Some SQL servers, for instance, don't have this limitation. But local Paradox and dBASE tables in the 16-bit version of the BDE are restricted in this manner, so you must use the techniques described here when searching for fields in these databases. Remember that these limitations do not apply to the 32-bit version of Delphi, where you can search with the OnFilterRecord process.

To find out what string and field interests the user, the ADDRESS2 program pops up the dialog shown in Figure 18.7. This dialog contains three radio buttons and an edit control, along with a few buttons.

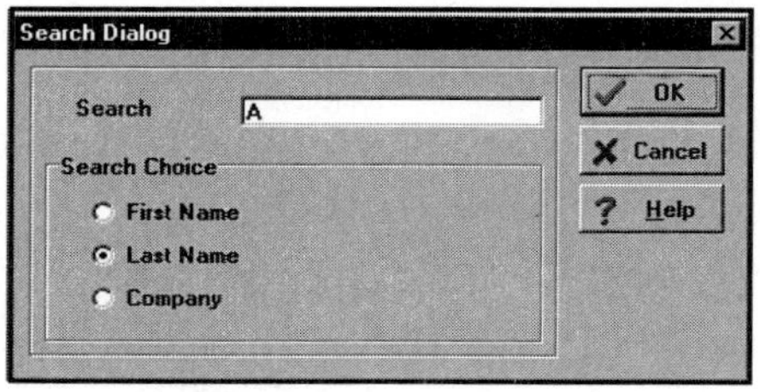

FIGURE 18.7.

The Search Dialog from the ADDRESS2 program.

The code to call the Search Dialog is simple enough:

```
procedure TfrAddress.Search1Click(Sender: TObject);
var
  S: string;
begin
  if not SearchDlg.GetSearchStr(FSortType, S) then Exit;
  DoSort;
  DoSearch(S);
end;
```

This code retrieves the relevant string and search field, calls the DoSort method, and finally calls a method that performs the actual search. Here is the code for the GetSearchStr method:

```
function TSearchDlg.GetSearchStr(var ST: TSortType; var S: string):
  Boolean;
begin
  Result := False;

  if ShowModal = mrCancel then Exit;

  S := Edit1.Text;

  if FirstName.Checked then
    ST := stFirst
  else if LastName.Checked then
    ST := stLast
  else
    ST := stCompany;

  Result := True;
end;
```

This code first pops up the Search dialog in modal mode. If the user selects the OK button, the selected string is retrieved and the selected radio button is translated into a variable of type TSortType. In other words, the user must select a string to search on and also choose a radio button in order to indicate the field he or she believes contains the string.

If the GetSearchStr method returns True, the Search1Click method calls DoSort, which sets the current index to the field that interests the user. Because the program now knows the string that needs to be found and because the index has been set to the appropriate field, it is now safe to perform a search:

```
procedure TfrAddress.DoSearch(S: string);
begin
  tblAddress.SetKey;
  case FSortType of
    stFirst: tblAddress.FieldByName('FName').AsString := S;
    stLast:tblAddress.FieldByName('LName').AsString := S;
    stCompany:tblAddress.FieldByName('Company').AsString := S;
end;
  tblAddress.GotoNearest;
end;
```

The DoSearch method sets the table into SetKey mode and then tells the table to look for a particular string in the field that is currently indexed. Finally, tblAddress.GotoNearest is called, and the table is brought as close to the sought-after record as possible.

This sounds a bit complex, but it has some hidden virtues. Because the table has already been indexed on the appropriate field, you will find that you can perform partial searches that take you close to the record you seek, even if you can't remember its exact spelling. For instance, if you know someone's name begins with Gab, but can't recall if the rest is Gabfest, Gabfald, or Gabheld, you can search on the string Gab and iterate forward from that point in search of the record in question. This is the technique used by the SortMenu method when it calls DoSearch with "" as its parameter.

Once again, it turns out that the actual code for searching for data in a Paradox table is fairly straightforward. A curve is thrown at you here in that you are forced to set the table to a particular index before you can search for a value, but even this seeming inconvenience can turn out to have some fairly important hidden benefits. However, you should remember that many SQL servers enable you to search on fields that are not currently part of the active index.

Filtering Data

It turns out that setting up a filter and performing a search are very similar tasks. The first step is to find out the string the user wants to use as a filter. To do this, you can call the Filter dialog, passing it the contents of the cbCategory combo box as a parameter:

```
function TFilterDlg.GetFilter(SList: TStrings): string;
begin
  ListBox1.Items := SList;
```

```
  if ShowModal = mrCancel then
    Result := ''
  else
    Result := ListBox1.Items.Strings[ListBox1.ItemIndex];
end;
```

This code accepts the list from the combo box as a parameter, displays it inside a list box, and shows the Filter form as a modal dialog. If the user presses OK, the `GetFilter` function returns the selected string. If Cancel is pressed, an empty string is returned.

After retrieving the string, the ADDRESS2 program sets up the CategoryIndex and then performs a normal filter operation:

```
procedure TfrAddress.Filter1Click(Sender: TObject);
var
  S: string;
begin
  if Filter1.Caption = 'Filter' then begin
    S := FilterDlg.GetFilter(cbCategory.Items);
    if S = '' then Exit;
    Filter1.Caption := 'Cancel Filter';
    tblAddress.IndexName := 'CategoryIndex';
    tblAddress.SetRangeStart;
    tblAddress.FieldByName('Category').AsString := S;
    tblAddress.SetRangeEnd;
    tblAddress.FieldByName('Category').AsString := S;
    tblAddress.ApplyRange;
  end else begin
    Filter1.Caption := 'Filter';
    tblAddress.CancelRange;
  end;
end;
```

This is a simple process that lets you narrow the number of records displayed at any one time. The key point to remember is that this whole process works only because the user enters data in the Category field by selecting strings from a dropdown combo box. Without the TdbComboBox, the number of options in the Category field would likely become unmanageable.

Note that the code also lets you cancel the filter operation after it has been implemented. In doing so, the program toggles the Caption for Filter1 between Filter and Cancel Filter. This way, the currently available menu item is always appropriate.

Printing Records

Chapter 21, "ReportSmith," is set aside in this book to discuss ReportSmith. However, I will touch on this subject briefly, just to give you a few clues about how to proceed.

To start creating a report, bring up ReportSmith using Tools | ReportSmith and select the type of report you want to make, which is probably a label-based report. Go to the Tables page in the Report Query dialog, choose Add Table, and select ADDRESS.DB.

Next, go to the Report Variables page and create a new variable called Filter. Set its type to String, its Title to Filter List, and the prompt to "What filter do you want?". Set the Entry to Type-in, as shown in Figure 18.8. When you are done, choose Add.

NOTE

You do not have to choose Type-in as the Entry method. In fact, the ADDRESS2 program is ideally suited for using the "Choose from a Table" method. After you select this method, a workspace will appear in the bottom-right corner of the Report Variables page that enables you to choose a table and field that contain a list of available entries. In this case, you can choose the CATS.DB table and the Category field. Now when the user wants to run the report, he or she will be prompted with a list of valid categories and can choose the appropriate one, without the likelihood of an error being introduced.

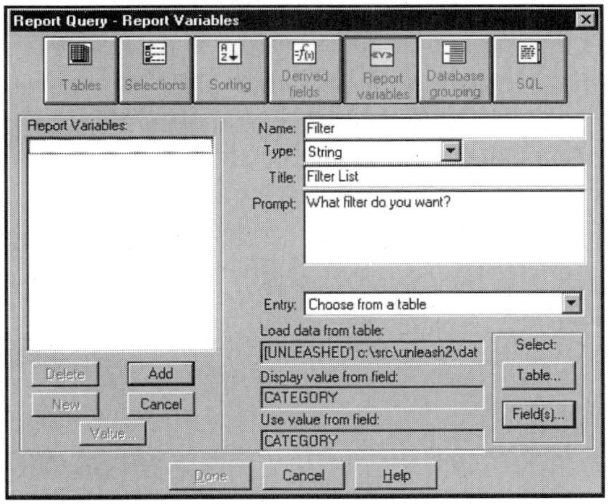

FIGURE 18.8.

Creating report variables in ReportSmith.

Turn to the Selections page, click on the yellow number "1" in the center of the page, and choose "Select SQL selection criteria" from the dropdown list. Select the Category field from the DataFields list box on the left, and choose "x=y" from the Comparison Operators in the middle list box. Go back to the left-hand list box, and change the combo box at the top so it reads "Report Variables" rather than "Data Fields". Choose Filter, and then set this variable in quotes:

```
'ADDRESSxDB'.'CATEGORY' = '<<Filter>>'
```

When you are done, the dialog should look like that in Figure 18.9. Now click the OK button at the bottom of the dialog.

FIGURE 18.9.

Creating SQL selection criteria in ReportSmith.

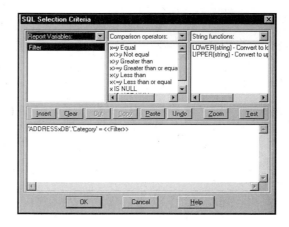

The final step in this process is to create derived fields in the Derived Fields page of the Report Query dialog. The first derived field should combine the FName and LName fields, so you might want to call this field FirstLast. After typing in the name, select Add, and the Edit Derived Fields dialog box will appear. Select FName from the left column:

```
'ADDRESSxDB'.'FName'
```

Choose Addition from the middle column:

```
'ADDRESSxDB'.'FName' +
```

Add a space by writing the string ' ':

```
'ADDRESSxDB'.'FName' + ' '
```

Choose Addition again from the middle column:

```
'ADDRESSxDB'.'FName' + ' ' +
```

End by adding the LName field. The string you create should look like this:

```
'ADDRESSxDB'.'FName' + ' ' + 'ADDRESSxDB'.'LName'
```

This statement combines the FName and LName fields so that they produce a single string out of a first and last name:

```
Kurt Weill
```

You should then create a second derived field called CityStateZip, which combines the City, State, and Zip fields:

```
'ADDRESSxDB'.'CITY' + ', ' + 'ADDRESSxDB'.'STATE' + ' ' +
  'ADDRESSxDB'.'ZIP'
```

You have now created the logic behind a report, and so you should choose Done from the bottom of the Report Query dialog. ReportSmith will then pop up a dialog to fill in the report variable you created. In other words, it's time for you to fill in the Filter portion of the following statement:

```
'ADDRESSxDB'.'CATEGORY' = '<<Filter>>'
```

You can type the word Family, Work, or whatever value you feel will return a reasonably sized dataset.

The Insert Field dialog now appears, and you can enter the fields and derived fields that you have created. The combo box at the top of the dialog enables you to switch back and forth between data fields and derived fields; you should do so when you think it's appropriate. For instance, the first field you select will probably be the derived field called FirstLast, whereas the second will probably be the data field called Address1. When you are done, the report you create should look something like the image shown in Figure 18.10.

FIGURE 18.10.

A "live data" label report produced by ReportSmith.

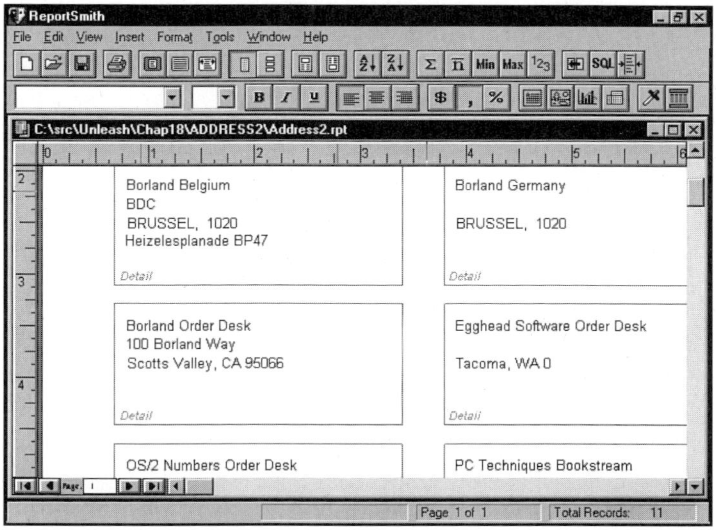

Even the report shown here is probably not totally complete; you might want to rearrange the location of the fields inside each label and change the size and location of each individual label. You will find that you can move individual fields around by simply dragging them with the mouse. The actual decisions you make will be based on your personal tastes and on the type of labels you have in your office or home. When you are performing these tasks, you will probably find it easiest to do so by choosing the File | Page Setup menu option from the ReportSmith main menu.

If you want to change the fonts used in your report, select one of the fields in a label, then right-click on the page, and choose Character from the popup menu. Other options, such as adjusting borders and field height, and inserting pictures, are available when you right-click a report.

When you are completely finished preparing a report, choose File | Save to save the report you have created under the name Address, in the same directory where the ADDRESS2 program resides.

As I stated previously, this brief tutorial on ReportSmith is not meant to be anything more than a very loosely structured primer. ReportSmith is very easy to use, and most of the actions you will perform are intuitive variations on the simple steps already outlined. However, you will probably also want to study the ReportSmith manuals, the online help, and perhaps a third-party book dedicated to this subject.

NOTE

> ReportSmith has a fairly sophisticated query builder in the Selections page of the Report Query Dialog. On several occasions, I have actually abandoned Delphi's query builder and opened up ReportSmith to construct a SQL statement. When I'm done, I just block-copy the SQL code from ReportSmith into the SQL property of my current Delphi TQuery object. This is a major kludge, but under some circumstances you might want to consider it as an option.

As easy as it is to use ReportSmith, it is even easier to link this tool into a standard Delphi program.

Drop a TReport object on a form and set the ReportName to the name of the report you want to use. You can resolve the path to the report at runtime, by calling the GetPath method, which will be described later in this chapter.

The actual code for printing the report is encapsulated in the PrintData method. As you recall, you blocked out the code from this routine when you were setting up the CommandClick method. Here is the code for PrintData:

```
procedure TfrAddress.PrintData;
begin
  Cursor := crHourGlass;
  Report1.ReportDir := GetPath;
  Report1.Run;
  Cursor := crDefault;
end;
```

This routine finds the path in which ADDRESS.RPT resides, and then it loads ReportSmith by calling `Report1.Run`. As long as you have the RS_RUN subdirectory on your path, the ReportSmith runtime will load automatically after a call to `Run`, and you can then enter the name of the category you want to set up as a filter. Because ReportSmith can take a few moments to load, you should probably set the program's cursor to `crHourGlass` before calling `Run`.

It's important to understand that there are two versions of ReportSmith. The main version of the program resides in the RPTSMITH subdirectory. This is the version you should use when you are designing reports. The runtime version of ReportSmith resides in the RS_RUN subdirectory; it is the one you can distribute with your programs. Specifically, it is RS_RUN.EXE that gets loaded when you are running a Delphi program.

After RS_RUN is loaded, you have two options. If you have set the `AutoUnload` property to True, ReportSmith will be taken out of memory automatically after the print job finishes. However, because it takes a while for RS_RUN to load, you might want to leave it running while you complete several print jobs. To do this, just set `AutoUnload` to False. You can then perform your print jobs and close RS_RUN by calling `CloseApplication` and passing it a Boolean parameter specifying whether the program should prompt the user to save reports, and so on. Because `CloseApplication` uses DDE commands, it is possible that the routine might fail. As a result, you should test to see if `CloseApplication` succeeds, and repeat the command if it fails:

```
function CloseReportSmith: Boolean;
begin
  Result := Report1.CloseApplication(False);
end;
```

It is possible to set up macros inside ReportSmith. The `RunMacro` method of TReport can be used to execute a ReportSmith macro. `RunMacro` takes a single parameter, which is the name of the report you want to run.

You can pass parameters to ReportSmith by using the InitialValues field. The InitialValues fields lets you automatically pass a string to ReportSmith, rather than having the user type in a value in a dialog. In short, you can pass the category you want to filter through the InitialValues field, and then the user will not need to enter the value. This can be particularly useful if you want to set up error-free input methods.

> **NOTE**
>
> As mentioned, ReportSmith can associate a table with a report variable, thereby letting the user select a value from the table, rather than typing it in. In my experience, this technique works fine and may be preferable to using the InitialValues field.

You should also note that it is possible to change a report variable at runtime by using the `SetVariable` and `SetVariableLines` methods. After using these methods, you should call `ReCalcReport` to make sure that ReportSmith assimilates the changes you have made. `SetVariable` and `SetVariableLines` use DDE, so you should test to make sure the calls succeed.

Another property of TReport that you might want to use is the Preview property, which lets a user determine whether the correct report has been generated. You can use the MaxRecords and StartPage properties to control the number of records that ReportSmith prints.

ReportSmith is a good tool that has the enormous advantage of being easy to use. In fact, ReportSmith is so easy to use that it turns the task of generating reports into something very similar to play. As a result, you can quickly generate elegant-looking reports and then get back to the more interesting task of writing code.

Setting Colors

The Colors menu, shown in Figure 18.11, lets you set the colors for most of the major objects in the program. The goal is not to give the user complete control over every last detail in the program, but to let him or her customize the most important features.

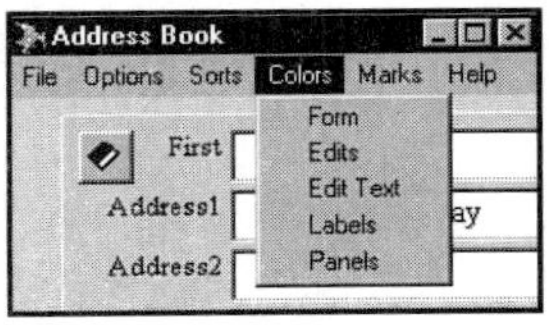

FIGURE 18.11.

The options under the Colors menu enable you to change the appearance of the ADDRESS2 program.

The ColorClick method uses the time-honored method of declaring an enumerated type and then sets up the Tag property from a menu item to specify the selection of a particular option. Here is the enumerated type in question:

```
TColorType = (ccForm, ccEdit, ccEditText, ccLabel, ccPanel);
```

The routine begins by enabling the user to select a color from the Colors dialog and then assigns that color to the appropriate controls:

```
procedure TfrAddress.ColorClick(Sender: TObject);
begin
  if not ColorDialog1.Execute then Exit;
  case TColorType((Sender as TMenuItem).Tag) of
    ccForm: frAddress.Color := ColorDialog1.Color;
    ccEdit: SetEdits(tcColor, ColorDialog1.Color);
    ccEditText: SetEdits(tcFontColor, ColorDialog1.Color);
    ccLabel: SetLabels(ColorDialog1.Color);
    ccPanel: SetPanels(ColorDialog1.Color);
  end;
  SetIni(TColorType((Sender as TMenuItem).Tag), ColorDialog1.Color);
end;
```

If the user wants to change the form's color, the code to do so is simple enough:

```
ccForm: frAddress.Color := ColorDialog1.Color;
```

However, it is a more complicated process to change the color of all the data-aware controls. To accomplish this goal, the ColorClick method calls the SetEdits routine:

```
procedure TfrAddress.SetEdits(TypeChange: TChangeType;
                              NewValue: TColor);
var
  i: Integer;
begin
  for i := 0 to ComponentCount - 1 do
    if (Components[i] is TdbEdit) or
       (Components[i] is TdbComboBox) or
       (Components[i] is TdbMemo) then
      case TypeChange of
        tcColor: TdbEdit(Components[i]).Color := NewValue;
        tcFontColor: TdbEdit(Components[i]).Font.Color := NewValue;
      end;
end;
```

This code iterates though all the components belonging to the main form of the program and checks to see if any of them are TdbEdits, TdbComboBoxes, or TdbMemos. When it finds a hit, the code casts the control as a TdbEdit and sets its color to the new value selected by the user:

```
tcColor: TdbEdit(Components[i]).Color := NewValue;
```

This code will very quickly change all the data-aware controls on the form to a new color.

The SetEdits routine works for both setting the color of the data-aware controls themselves, and for setting the fonts displayed in these controls. To tell which property the user wants to change at any particular moment, the SetEdits routine uses the following enumerated type:

```
TChangeType  = (tcColor, tcFontColor);
```

The code for setting labels and panels works exactly the same way as the code for the data-aware controls. The only difference is that you don't need to worry about looking for multiple types of components:

```
procedure TfrAddress.SetLabels(C: TColor);
var
  i: Integer;
begin
  for i := 0 to ComponentCount - 1 do
    if (Components[i] is TLabel) then
      TLabel(Components[i]).Font.Color := C;
end;

procedure TfrAddress.SetPanels(C: TColor);
var
  i: Integer;
begin
  for i := 0 to ComponentCount - 1 do
    if (Components[i] is TPanel) then
      TPanel(Components[i]).Color := C;
end;
```

When working with the colors of the program, the final step is to make sure that the program "remembers" the user's selections. To do this, ADDRESS2 makes use of an INI file that looks something like this:

```
[Colors]
Form=8421440
Edits=8421376
EditText=0
Labels=0
Panels=12639424
```

This INI file has only one section, which contains five different items, one for each of the colors specified by the user. The colors themselves are stored as integers, each representing one of the possible values captured in the TColor enumerated type.

> **NOTE**
>
> In this chapter, I assume that all readers are familiar with INI files. The most common INI files are WIN.INI and SYSTEM.INI. However, most major programs have their own INI files, such as the DELPHI.INI file that is stored in the WINDOWS subdirectory. These files are used to store settings for a program; you can read more about them in any good book on Windows basics. In Windows 95, INI files are still supported, but the Registry provides an appealing alternative. This program, however, provides support for both 16- and 32-bit programs, so it does not use the Registry. Many powerful new programs, such as Delphi 2.0 itself, use a combination of the Registry and an INI file. (See the DELPHI32.INI file in the Windows subdirectory.)

The following code writes new values to the INI file:

```
procedure TfrAddress.SetIni(CType: TColorType; C: TColor);
var
  Ini: TIniFile;
  Path, S: string;
begin
  Ini := TIniFile.Create(GetPath + 'address.ini');
  case CType of
    ccForm: S := 'Form';
    ccEdit: S := 'Edits';
    ccEditText: S := 'EditText';
    ccLabel: S := 'Labels';
    ccPanel: S := 'Panels';
  end;
  Ini.WriteInteger('Colors', S, C);
  Ini.Free;
end;
```

This method takes advantage of the TIniFile type, which is found in a source file, called INIFILES.PAS, that ships with Delphi.

You create a TIniFile object by passing in the name of the INI file you want to work with to the object's Create method:

```
Ini := TIniFile.Create(GetPath + 'address.ini');
```

The `GetPath` method performs some hand-waving to return the subdirectory from which the ADDRESS2 program was launched. In particular, it uses Delphi's built in ExtractFilePath method:

```
function TfrAddress.GetPath: string;
begin
  Result := ExtractFilePath(ParamStr(0));
```

Before discussing the key methods of TIniFile, I should mention that after you are through with the object, you must deallocate the memory you created for it:

```
Ini.Free;
```

There are a number of methods you might want to call between the time you create a TIniFile object and the time you free it. However, you cannot call these methods successfully without first allocating memory for the object, and you must free that memory when you are through with the object.

Windows supplies a set of functions called `GetPrivateProfileString`, `WritePrivateProfileString`, `GetPrivateProfileInt`, and `WritePrivateProfileInt` that let you talk with INI files. These routines work well enough, and they are fairly easy to use, but they expect you to pass in PChars in their numerous parameters. TIniFile simplifies this process by enabling you to pass in Pascal strings rather than PChars. For instance, the `WriteInteger` method replaces `WritePrivateProfileInt`:

```
procedure WriteInteger(const Section, Ident: string;
                       Value: LongInt);
```

This function expects the name of a section in the first parameter, the name of an item in the second parameter, and the value you want to write in the third parameter. For instance, the INI file has an entry in it labeled Form. if you wanted to change the Form entry to black, you would enter the following code:

```
WriteInteger('Colors', 'Form', 0);
```

This will change the Form entry in the INI file to zero:

```
[Colors]
Form=0
```

With this knowledge in hand, it's easy enough to go back to the `SetIni` function and see exactly how it works. The key, of course, is simply that the second parameter passed to `WriteInteger` is designated by using an enumerated type in a `case` statement:

```
case CType of
  ccForm: S := 'Form';
  ccEdit: S := 'Edits';
  ccEditText: S := 'EditText';
  ccLabel: S := 'Labels';
  ccPanel: S := 'Panels';
end;
Ini.WriteInteger('Colors', S, C);
```

It's not enough, however, simply to write the values to an INI file. You must also read these values whenever the program starts. Here's how you can read an integer value from an INI file:

```
function TfrAddress.GetIni(CType: TColorType): TColor;
var
  Ini: TIniFile;
  Path, S: string;
begin
  Ini := TIniFile.Create(GetPath + 'address.Ini');
  case CType of
    ccForm: S := 'Form';
    ccEdit: S := 'Edits';
    ccEditText: S := 'EditText';
    ccLabel: S := 'Labels';
    ccPanel: S := 'Panels';
  end;
  Result := Ini.ReadInteger('Colors', S, clBlue);
  Ini.Free;
end;
```

This code is almost the exact reverse of the `SetIni` method, except that `ReadInteger` takes a default value in its last parameter. This default value will be returned if the program is unable to locate the INI file, or if it can't find the item requested in the INI file.

The code in the `FormCreate` method that calls the `GetIni` method looks like this:

```
for i := 0 to 4 do
  case TColorType(i) of
    ccForm: Color := GetIni(TColorType(i));
    ccEdit: SetEdits(tcColor, GetIni(TColorType(i)));
    ccEditText: SetEdits(tcFontColor, GetIni(TColorType(i)));
    ccLabel: SetLabels(GetIni(TColorType(i)));
    ccPanel: SetPanels(GetIni(TColorType(i)));
  end;
```

Though somewhat complex, this code should be fairly easy to understand at this stage because you have already seen all the various routines called in this loop. It's just a question of bringing them all together so the program can read the INI file and set the appropriate controls to the appropriate colors.

There is always the possibility that the INI file in question does not exist or cannot be found. In such a case, the ADDRESS2 program is smart enough to create a new INI file containing default values:

```
procedure TfrAddress.CheckForIni;
var
  F: System.Text;
  Path: string;
begin
  Path := GetPath + 'address.ini';
  if not FileExists(Path) then begin
    System.Assign(F, Path);
    System.ReWrite(F);
    System.WriteLn(F, '[Colors]');
    System.WriteLn(F, 'Form=7045184');
    System.WriteLn(F, 'Edits=8421376');
    System.WriteLn(F, 'EditText=0');
```

```
      System.WriteLn(F, 'Labels=0');
      System.WriteLn(F, 'Panels=12639424');
      System.Close(F);
   end;
end;
```

The `CheckForIni` routine is called from the `FormCreate` method. It begins by using the built-in `FileExists` method to check for the existence of the INI file. If the file can't be found, a new one is created, using standard text file operations.

In this section, you have learned how to change the colors of components at runtime and how to save the value of these colors in an INI file. The key fact you learned is that you can use the `Components` array to iterate through the components owned by a form, and you can check to see the type of each component you iterate past. When you find a component of a particular type, you can then perform a typecast and change its color.

Marking Files

I have also added the ability to mark files to the ADDRESS2 application. In the current version, the only thing you can do with a marked file is write it to disk in a text file. Still, it's useful to see how to work with a logical field in a table, and to see an interesting technique for displaying these marked fields to the user.

The Marked field in this table is declared to be of type Boolean. (Remember that one of the fields of ADDRESS.DB is actually called Marked, so in the last sentence I'm not referring to an attribute of a field, but to its name.) Here is a method for showing the user whether the Boolean Marked field is set to True or False:

```
procedure TfrAddress.DataSource1DataChange(Sender: TObject; Field: TField);
begin
  if tblAddress.FieldByName('Marked').AsBoolean then begin
    BookOpen := LoadBitmap(HInstance, 'BookOpen');
    SpeedButton1.Glyph.Handle := BookOpen
end else begin
    BookShut := LoadBitmap(HInstance, 'BookShut');
    SpeedButton1.Glyph.Handle := BookShut;
  end;
end;
```

If the field is marked, then a bitmap called BookOpen is loaded from one of the program's two resource files. This bitmap is then assigned to the Glyph field of a speedbutton. If the Marked field is set to False, then a second bitmap is loaded, and shown in the speedbutton. The bitmaps give a visual signal to the user as to whether or not the record is marked.

As hinted in the last paragraph, the ADDRESS2 program has two resource files. The first is the standard resource file, which holds the program's icon. The second is a custom resource build from the following RC file:

```
bookopen BITMAP "BOOKOPEN.BMP"
bookshut BITMAP "BOOKSHUT.BMP"
```

This file is called BITS.RC, and it compiles to BITS.RES, and is linked into the executable by the last of these lines quoted from MAIN.PAS:

```
uses
  About, Cats, Filter,
  IniFiles, StrBox, SysUtils,
  UtilBox;

{$R *.DFM}
{$R BITS.RES}
```

Whenever the user toggles the SpeedButton where the Bookshut and BookOpen bitmaps are displayed, then the logical Marked field in the database is toggled:

```
procedure TfrAddress.SpeedButton1Click(Sender: TObject);
begin
  tblAddress.Edit;
  tblAddress.FieldByName('Marked').AsBoolean :=
not tblAddress.FieldByName('Marked').AsBoolean;
  tblAddress.Post;
end;
```

Note that this code never checks the value of the Marked field—it just sets it to the opposite of its current state.

There are several other routines in the ADDRESS2 program that relate to this logical field. However, none of them are very complicated to understand once you understand the logic from the SpeedButton1Click and the DataSource1DataChange methods.

The Clipboard: Cut, Copy, and Paste

Delphi makes it very easy to cut information from a database to the Clipboard. The key point to understand is that the currently selected control will always be accessible from the ActiveControl property of the main form:

```
procedure TfrAddress.Copy1Click(Sender: TObject);
begin
  if ActiveControl is TDBEdit then
    TDBEdit(ActiveControl).CopyToClipboard
  else if ActiveControl is TDBMemo then
    TDBMemo(ActiveControl).CopyToClipboard
  else if ActiveControl is TDBComboBox then
    Clipboard.AsText := cbCategory.Text;
end;
```

This method is called when the user chooses Copy from the Edit menu. The code first checks to see if the currently selected control is one of those that contains data from the Address table; that is, it checks to see if it is a TDBEdit, TDBMemo, or TDBComboBox. If it is, the control is typecast so that its properties and methods can be accessed.

The TDBEdit and TDBComboBox controls have CopyToClipBoard, PasteFromClipBoard, and CutToClipBoard commands. Each of these commands simply copies, cuts, or pastes data from the live database control to or from the Clipboard. The TDBComboBox does not have quite so rich a set of built-in functions, so it is handled as a special case. In particular, note that I have to use the built-in ClipBoard object, which can easily be a part of every Delphi project. To access a fully allocated instance of this object, simply include the `ClipBrd` unit in your `Uses` clause.

You can see that working with the clipboard is a trivial operation in Delphi. The `Paste1Click` and `Cut1Click` methods from the ADDRESS2 program demonstrate a specific technique you can use when pasting and cutting from or to the clipboard.

Summary

You have had a chance to look at all the major portions of the ADDRESS2 program. The only items not mentioned in this chapter were the construction of the About dialog and the use of the Object Repository to expedite the creation of some of the forms. These techniques have been examined in previous chapters, so you shouldn't find them challenging.

I went into such detail about the ADDRESS2 program because it contains many of the features that need to be included in real-world programs. As stated earlier, the ADDRESS2 program isn't quite up to the standards expected from a professional program, but it does answer some questions about how you can take the raw database tools described in the last few chapters and use them to create a useful program.

Working with the Local InterBase Server

19

Delphi ships with the Local InterBase Server, which is sometimes simply called LIBS. This tool provides all the capabilities of the full InterBase server, but it runs on a local machine. In other words, you do not need to be connected to a network in order to run the Local InterBase Server.

The goal of this chapter is to provide a useful introduction to LIBS and also a brief overview of transactions. In particular, you will see how to do the following:

- Connect to local InterBase tables
- Connect without having to specify a password
- Create databases
- Work with TDatabase objects
- Create tables
- Commit and roll back transactions in both local and InterBase tables
- Maintain the data you have created
- Work with cached updates
- Work with many-to-many relationships

Almost everything that is said about the local InterBase in this chapter applies equally to the full server version of InterBase, so this chapter will also be of interest to people who use InterBase on a network.

Most readers of this book will probably find this an interesting chapter, including those who have access to the full-blown version of InterBase. In particular, this chapter shows how you can use a local system to create a database that is fully compatible with the network version of InterBase.

Some readers come from the world of "big iron," where the only kinds of databases that exist are servers such as Oracle, Sybase, InterBase, or DB2. Other readers come from the world of PCs, where tools such as dBASE, Paradox, Access, or FoxPro are considered to be the standard database tools. It is almost impossible to overemphasize the huge gap that exists between these two worlds.

Readers who are familiar with "big iron" and large network-based servers are likely to find the Local InterBase Server very familiar. Readers who come from the world of PCs are likely to find InterBase very strange indeed, especially at first.

InterBase is meant to handle huge numbers of records, which are stored on servers. It does not come equipped with many of the amenities of a tool such as dBASE or Paradox. In fact, InterBase supplies users with only the most minimal interface and instead expects you to create programs with another front end such as Delphi.

Setting Up the Local InterBase

LIBS is installed for you automatically when you install Delphi 2.0. In most cases, InterBase will run smoothly without any need for you to worry about setup. However, there are several key steps you should take to ensure that all is as it should be.

First, find out if LIBS is running. By default, it will load into memory every time you boot up the system. If you are running Windows 95, you should see it as a little splash of green on the system tray to the right of the toolbar. On Windows NT, it's just an icon at the bottom of your screen. Click on this green object, and you will see a report on the Local InterBase Server configuration.

You need to know where your copy of LIBS is installed. Most likely, it is in the ..\BORLAND\INTRBASE subdirectory on the drive where you installed Delphi. For instance, my copy of the local InterBase is in C:\BORLAND\INTRBASE. To find out for sure, open up the InterBase Configuration applet that ships with Delphi. It will report on the InterBase root subdirectory and enable you to change that directory if need be.

To find this same information in the Registry, run REGEDIT.EXE, and open HKEY_LOCAL_MACHINE/SOFTWARE/BORLAND/INTERBASE. There are several nodes reporting on the location of your server and other related information.

In the INTRBASE subdirectory, you find a copy of a file called INTERBAS.MSG. You should also be able to locate a copy of GDS32.DLL somewhere on your system, most likely in the ..\WINDOWS\SYSTEM subdirectory, but possibly in either your BDE or INTRBASE subdirectory.

A common problem occurs when InterBase users end up with more than one copy of GDS32.DLL. If you work with the networked version of InterBase, you probably already have a copy of the InterBase Client on your system. If this is the case, you should make sure that you don't have two sets of the file GDS32.DLL on your path. On my system, I use the copy of GDS32.DLL that comes with the local InterBase. These tools communicate with both LIBS and the full networked version of InterBase. This setup works fine for me.

To find out which version you are currently using, run the Interbase Communications Diagnostics Tool that ships with Delphi. Use the Browse button to find the EMPLOYEE.GDB file, which is probably located in the ..\BORLAND\INTRBASE\EXAMPLES subdirectory. Enter SYSDBA as the User Name and masterkey as the password, all lowercase. You should get the following read-out, or something like it:

```
Path Name    = C:\WINDOWS\SYSTEM\gds32.dll
Size         = 348672 Bytes
File Time    = 04:10:00
File Date    = 12/18/1995
Version      = 4.1.0.6
This module has passed the version check.
```

```
Attempting to attach to C:\Borland\Intrbase\EXAMPLES\Employee.gdb
        Attaching       ...Passed!
        Detaching       ...Passed!


InterBase versions for this connection:
InterBase/Windows NT (access method), version "WI-B4.1.0"
on disk structure version 8.0

InterBase Communication Test Passed!
```

The key piece of information you are getting here is the location of GDS32.DLL.

> **NOTE**
>
> Readers who want to connect to the full server version of InterBase will find that the procedure I have just outlined works fine, except that you must have a network protocol such as TCP/IP loaded first. This book does not include a description of the wizardry needed to successfully set up a network protocol, though the task is usually handled automatically by either Windows 95 or Windows NT. I assume that you will turn to another source in order to learn how to ping your server and how to test the connection with a few simple FTP sessions. When you have gotten that far, you can open this book and follow the directions that I give here.
>
> Almost everything I have said about databases in this book applies equally to local databases and servers. The key point is that you have to set up the network connection first, then turn to this book to learn how Delphi talks to databases. Of course, I am fully aware of how difficult and frustrating it can be to set up a network connection, and how little clear and easy-to-understand prose there is on the subject. Nevertheless, it is simply too large a topic for me to tackle in this book. My goal here is to write about Delphi, and you will have to turn elsewhere to learn about setting up network connections. I should add, however, that setting up an InterBase connection is usually a fairly straightforward process when compared to setting up other servers.

Setting Up an InterBase Alias

When you have the local InterBase set up, you should take a few minutes to make sure the connection is working correctly. In particular, you should make sure there is an alias that points to one of the sample tables that ship with LIBS. For instance, there should be an alias called IBLOCAL that points to the EMPLOYEE.GDB file installed by Delphi.

The next few paragraphs describe how to set up an alias identical to the IBLOCAL alias in all but name. To begin, open the Database Explorer and turn to the Databases page. Select the first node in the tree, the one that's called Databases. Select the Database | New menu option and select IntrBase as the Database Driver Name in the New Database Alias page dialog. Click OK.

Name the new alias TESTGDB, or give it whatever name you prefer. The ServerName property for this alias should be set to:

```
c:\program files\borland\intrbase\examples\employee.gdb
```

You can adjust the drive letter and path for the way you have set up the files on your machine.

The user name should be set to SYSDBA, and the Password you will use is masterkey. All the other settings can have their default values, as shown in Figure 19.1. When you have everything set up correctly, choose Database | Apply from the menu.

FIGURE 19.1.

A sample InterBase alias, as it appears in the Database Explorer.

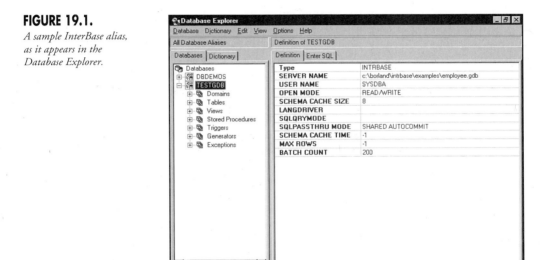

After you have set up and saved your alias, you can connect to the TESTGDB alias exactly as you would with any other set of data. From inside the Explorer, just click on the plus symbol before the TESTGDB node. A dialog will pop up prompting you for a password. Make sure the USER NAME is set to SYSDBA, and then enter masterkey as the password. Everything else will then be the same as when working with a Paradox table, except that you will find many new features such as stored procedures and triggers. Most of these new features will be described in this chapter and the next.

To connect to the database from inside Delphi proper, first drop a table onto a form, and set its DatabaseName property to TESTGDB. When you try to drop down the list of TableNames, you will be prompted for a password. You should enter masterkey at this point, all in lower-case. After taking these steps, you can set the Active property for Table1 to True. If this call succeeds, everything is set up correctly, and you can begin using the local InterBase to create Delphi database programs. If you can't set Active to True, you should go over the steps outlined previously and see whether you can correct the problem.

> **NOTE**
>
> I usually use SYSDBA and masterkey as the user name and password combination for the InterBase databases in this book. However, I sometimes work with USER1 and USER1 instead, simply because it is easier to type in USER1 than it is to type in masterkey.

In the last two sections, you have learned the basic facts about using LIBS. The next step is to learn how to create your own databases and tables.

Creating Databases

Unlike local Paradox or dBASE files, InterBase tables are not stored in separate files located within a directory. Instead, InterBase tables are stored in one large file called a database. This means that you need to first go out and create a database, and then you can create a series of tables inside this larger database.

The simplest way to create a database is with the WISQL program that ships with the Local InterBase Server. WISQL stands for Windows Interactive Standard Query Language, or simply the Interactive SQL tool. WISQL is fundamentally a tool for entering SQL statements, with a few other simple features thrown in for good measure.

> **NOTE**
>
> In addition to WISQL, the other important tool that ships with InterBase is the InterBase Server Manager, IBMGR32.EXE. It enables you to test connections to servers and perform simple maintenance tasks such as backing up and restoring databases and setting passwords. You can use IBMGR32 to back up your data so that you can recover if disaster strikes. What little information you need for this easy-to-use tool is available in the InterBase documentation. The IBMGR32 will not be mentioned further in this book, but you should take the few minutes required to browse through its online help and take it through its paces.

After starting up WISQL, choose Create Database from the File menu. A dialog like the one shown in Figure 19.2 appears. Set the Location Info to Local Engine. Because you are working with local InterBase, in fact, there is no need for an active network protocol.

FIGURE 19.2.

The dialog used for creating databases inside WISQL.

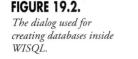

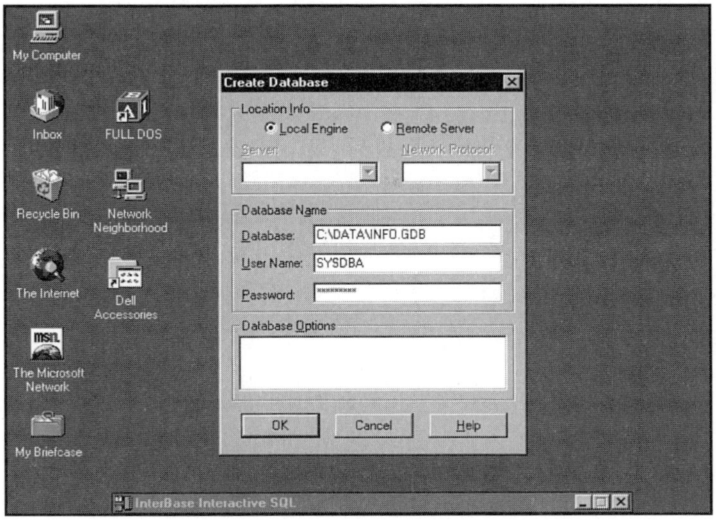

In the Database field, enter the name of the table you want to create. If the table is to be located inside a directory, include that directory in the database name. For practice, you should create a database called INFO.GDB that is located in a subdirectory called DATA. If it does not already exist on your system, you should first go to DOS and create the DATA subdirectory. When you are all set up, enter the following in the Database field:

```
E:\DATA\INFO.GDB
```

You can replace E: with the letter for the appropriate drive on your system. The extension .GDB is traditional, though not mandatory. However, I suggest always using this extension so that you can recognize your databases instantly when you see them. It can be a tragedy if you accidentally delete a database.

The user name can be set to anything you want, although the traditional entry is SYSDBA, and the traditional password is masterkey. When you first start out with InterBase, it is probably best to stick with this user name and password combination. Even if you assign new passwords to your database, the SYSDBA/masterkey combination will still work unless you explicitly remove it using the IBMGR.

After you have entered a user name and password, you can create the database by clicking the OK button. If all goes well, you are then placed back inside WISQL proper. At this stage, you can either quit WISQL or add a table to your database. If something went wrong, an error message will appear. Click the Details button to try to track down the problem.

Assuming all went well, the following SQL statement can be run inside WISQL if you want to create a very simple table with two fields:

```
CREATE TABLE TEST1 (FIRST VARCHAR(20), LAST INTEGER);
```

Enter this line in the SQL Statement field at the top of WISQL, and then press the Run button. If all goes smoothly, your statement will be echoed in the ISQL output window without being accompanied by an error dialog. The lack of an error dialog signals that the table has been created successfully. The preceding code creates a table with two fields. The first is a character field containing 20 characters, and the second is an integer field.

> **NOTE**
>
> The table-creation code shown here is used to describe or create a table in terms that WISQL understands. Indeed, throughout most of this chapter and the next, I work with WISQL rather than with the DBD. In describing how to perform these actions in WISQL, I do not mean to imply that you can't use the Database Desktop to create or alter InterBase tables. In fact, the 32-bit version of DBD provides pretty good support for InterBase tables. Still, I have found WISQL to be considerably more powerful than I suspected when I first started using it.

After creating a database and table, you should select Commit Work from the File menu. This command causes WISQL to actually carry out the commands you have issued. At this stage you should choose File | Disconnect from Database.

In this section, you have learned the basic steps required to use InterBase to create a database and table. The steps involved are not particularly complicated, although they can take a bit of getting used to if you are new to the world of server tools.

Exploring a Database with WISQL

WISQL provides a number of tools that can help you explore a database and its contents. In the last section, you created a database with a single table. In this section, you will learn how to connect to the table from inside WISQL, and how to examine the main features of that table.

To connect to INFO.GDB, select File | Connect to Database, which brings up the dialog shown in Figure 19.3. Enter the drive and the database as e:\data\info.gdb, where e: represents the appropriate drive on your machine. Enter the user as SYSDBA, and the password as masterkey. If all goes well, you should be able to connect to the database by clicking on the OK button. Once again, success is signaled by the lack of an error message.

FIGURE 19.3.

Connecting to the INFO.GDB database using the WISQL tool.

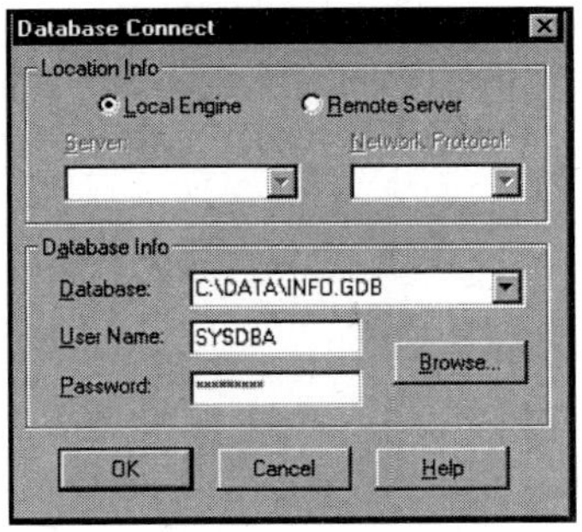

Go to View | Metadata Information, and set "View Information On" to Database, as shown in Figure 19.4. After you choose the OK button, the information displayed in the ISQL output window should look something like this:

```
SHOW DB
Database: c:\data\info.gdb
        Owner: SYSDBA
PAGE_SIZE 1024
Number of DB pages allocated = 210
Sweep interval = 20000
```

FIGURE 19.4.

Preparing to view information on the INFO.GDB database.

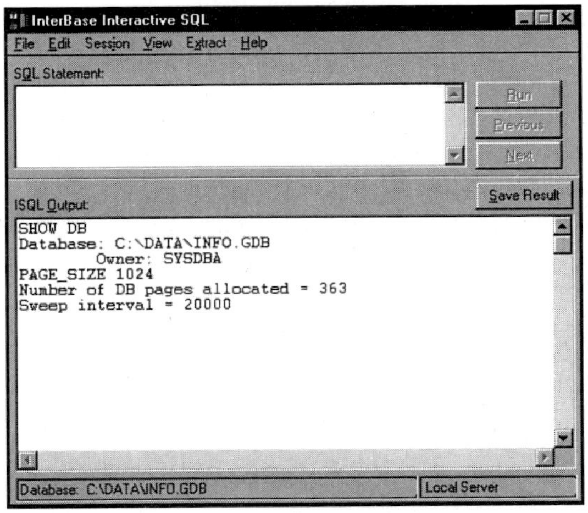

To see the tables available in a database, select View | Metadata Information from the menu, and set "View Information On" to Table. Select the Run button, and view the information in the ISQL output window, which should look like this:

```
SHOW TABLES
     TEST1
```

Browsing through the Metadata Information menu choices, you can see that InterBase supports triggers, stored procedures, views, and a host of other advanced server features.

The Extract menu choice enables you to find out more detailed information about the database and its tables. For instance, if you choose Extract | SQL Metadata for Database, you get output similar to the following:

```
/* Extract Database e:\data\info.gdb */
CREATE DATABASE "e:\data\info.gdb" PAGE_SIZE 1024
;


/* Table: TEST1, Owner: SYSDBA */
CREATE TABLE TEST1 (FIRST VARCHAR(20),
      LAST INTEGER);



/* Grant permissions for this database */
```

If you choose Extract | SQL Metadata for Table, you get the following output:

```
/* Extract Table TEST1 */

/* Table: TEST1, Owner: SYSDBA */
CREATE TABLE TEST1 (FIRST VARCHAR(20),
      LAST INTEGER);
```

You should note that WISQL often asks whether you want to save the output from a command to a text file, and the File menu gives you some further options for saving information to files. You can take advantage of these options when necessary, but 90 percent of the time, I pass them by with barely a nod.

> **NOTE**
>
> The WISQL program accepts most SQL statements. For instance, you can perform Insert, Select, Update, and Delete statements from inside WISQL. Just enter the statement you want to perform in the SQL Statement area, and then select the Run button.
>
> You should also be aware that WISQL bypasses the BDE altogether, so you can use it to test your connections to InterBase even if you are not sure that you have the BDE set up correctly. For instance, if you are having trouble connecting to InterBase and you're not sure where the problem lies, start by trying to connect with WISQL. If that works but you can't connect from inside Delphi, it might be that the problem lies not with your InterBase setup, but with the way you have deployed the BDE.
>
> WISQL also comes equipped with a handy online reference to SQL. If you have questions about how to format an Alter, Drop, Insert, Create Index, or other SQL statement, you can look it up in the help for WISQL.

After reading the last three sections, you should have a fair understanding of how WISQL works and how you can use it to manage a database. The information provided in this chapter is nothing more than an introduction to a complex and very sophisticated topic. However, you now know enough to begin using the local InterBase. This is no insignificant accomplishment. Tools such as InterBase, Oracle, and Sybase lie at the heart of the client/server activity that is currently so volatile and lucrative. If you become proficient at talking to servers such as InterBase, you might find yourself at an important turning point in your career.

Transactions

The TRANSACT program, found on the *Unleashed* CD that accompanies this book, gives a brief introduction to Transactions. To use Transactions, you must have a TDatabase component on your Form, and you must use a real server such as Sybase, Informix, InterBase, or the local InterBase. It won't work with Paradox or dBASE files. (In just a moment I'll show you a second technique, called Cached Updates, that works with local tables and InterBase tables.)

To begin, drop down a TDatabase component. Set the AliasName property of the TDataBase object to a valid alias such as IBLOCAL. Create your own string, such as IBNAME, to fill in the DatabaseName property of the TDatabase object. In other words, when you are using a TDatabase component, you make up the DatabaseName, rather than picking it from a list of available aliases.

Drop down a TQuery object and hook it up to the EMPLOYEE.GDB file that ships with Delphi. In particular, set the DatabaseName property of the TQuery object to IBNAME, not to IBLOCAL. In other words, set the DatabaseName property to the string you made up when filling in the DatabaseName property of the TDatabase component. You will find that DBNAME, or whatever string you chose, has been added to the list of aliases you find when you use the Query1.DatabaseName Property Editor.

Finally, set the Query1.SQL property to the following string:

```
select * from employee
```

Then set the Active property to True and set RequestLive to True.

Once you've connected to the database, you can add a TDataSource and a Tdbgrid so you can view the data. Also add four buttons, and give them the following captions:

> Begin Transaction
> Rollback
> Commit
> Refresh

The code associated with these buttons should look like this:

```
procedure TForm1.BeginTransactionClick(Sender: TObject);
begin
```

```
  Database1.StartTransaction;
end;

procedure TForm1.RollbackClick(Sender: TObject);
begin
  Database1.Rollback;
end;

procedure TForm1.CommitClick(Sender: TObject);
begin
  Database1.Commit;
end;

procedure TForm1.RefreshClick(Sender: TObject);
begin  Query1.Close;
  Query1.Open;
end;
```

Run the program, click Begin Transaction, and edit three or four records. If you click RollBack and then Refresh, you will find that all of your work is undone, as if none of the editing occurred. If you edit three or four records and then click Commit, you will find that your work is preserved. To learn more about this subject, you should read the very important online help entry called "Transaction Isolation Levels."

NOTE

I don't call `Refresh` directly because the table I am using is not uniquely indexed. In lieu of this call, I close the table and then reopen it. You could use bookmarks to preserve your location in the table during this operation.

Note that when you run the TRANSACT program included on the disk, you don't have to specify a password. This occurs because the `LoginPrompt` property of the `TDatabase` object is set to False, and the `Params` property contains the following string:

```
password=masterkey
```

Cached Updates

One of the fanciest new features in the BDE is cached updates. Cached updates are like the transactions just described, only considerably fancier. Like transactions, cached updates enable you to edit a series of records without committing any of your work, and indeed, without causing any network activity at all. When you are ready to commit your work, cached updates enable you to do so on a record-by-record basis, where any records that violate system integrity can be repaired or rolled back on a case-by-case basis.

NOTE

One of the interesting things about cached updates is that they work with both local and server data. To illustrate this point, the example in this section will work with the local DBDEMOS alias. You could, however, do the same things with an InterBase table.

Some users have reported remarkable increases in performance on some operations when they use cached updates.

Cached updates are relatively complex mechanisms that enable you to keep track of the status of each record on a field-by-field basis. In particular, when cached updates are turned on, you can query your records one at a time and ask them if they have been updated. Furthermore, if they have been updated, you can ask the current value of each field in the updated record, and you can also retrieve the old, or original, value of the field.

You can do three things with the records in a dataset once the CachedUpdates property for the dataset has been set to True:

1. You can call ApplyUpdates on the dataset, which means that you will try to commit all the other records updated since CachedUpdates was set to True, or since the last attempt to update the records. This is analogous to committing a transaction.

2. You can call CancelUpdates, which means that all the updates made so far will be canceled. This is analogous to rolling back a transaction.

3. You can call RevertRecord, which will roll back the current record, but not any of the other records in the dataset.

There is an excellent example program in the Delphi DEMOS subdirectory that shows how to use cached updates. In this particular case, the example program is so good that it's hard to imagine improving on it. So, instead of trying to go it one better, I will create a sample program that takes the basic elements of cached updates and presents them in the simplest possible terms.

The CacheUp program, shown in Figure 19.5, has one form. On the form is a copy of the Orders table. The Orders table, as you recall, is related to both the Customer table and the Items table. As a result, it is difficult to change either the OrderNo or CustNo fields without violating system integrity in one way or another. When working with this program, you should change these fields to values like 1 or 2, which will almost surely be invalid values. You can then watch what happens when you try to commit the records you have changed.

The code for the CacheUp program is shown in Listing 19.1. Go ahead and get this program up and running, and then come back for a discussion of how it works. When implementing the code shown here, the key point to remember is that none of it will work unless the CachedUpdates property of Table1 is set to True.

Listing 19.1. The form for the CacheUp program.

```
unit main;

interface

uses
  Windows, Messages, SysUtils,
  Classes, Graphics, Controls,
  Forms, Dialogs, DB,
  Grids, DBGrids, DBTables,
  StdCtrls, Buttons, TypInfo, ExtCtrls;

type
  TForm1 = class(TForm)
    Table1: TTable;
    DBGrid1: TDBGrid;
    DataSource1: TDataSource;
    bApply: TBitBtn;
    bRevert: TBitBtn;
    BitBtn1: TBitBtn;
    Panel1: TPanel;
    Edit1: TEdit;
    Edit2: TEdit;
    Label1: TLabel;
    Label2: TLabel;
    ListBox1: TListBox;
    BitBtn2: TBitBtn;
    Label3: TLabel;
    procedure bApplyClick(Sender: TObject);
    procedure bRevertClick(Sender: TObject);
    procedure Table1UpdateError(DataSet: TDataSet; E: EDatabaseError;
      UpdateKind: TUpdateKind; var UpdateAction: TUpdateAction);
    procedure BitBtn1Click(Sender: TObject);
    procedure DataSource1DataChange(Sender: TObject; Field: TField);
    procedure BitBtn2Click(Sender: TObject);
  private
    { Private declarations }
  public
    { Public declarations }
  end;

var
  Form1: TForm1;

implementation

{$R *.DFM}

procedure TForm1.bApplyClick(Sender: TObject);
begin
  Table1.ApplyUpdates;
end;

procedure TForm1.bRevertClick(Sender: TObject);
begin
  Table1.RevertRecord;
end;
```

```
procedure TForm1.Table1UpdateError(DataSet: TDataSet; E: EDatabaseError;
  UpdateKind: TUpdateKind; var UpdateAction: TUpdateAction);
var
  S: string;
begin
  S := GetEnumName(TypeInfo(TUpdateKind), Ord(UpdateKind)) + ': ' + E.Message;
  ListBox1.Items.Add(DataSet.Fields[0].OldValue + ': ' + S);
  UpdateAction := uaSkip;
end;

procedure TForm1.BitBtn1Click(Sender: TObject);
begin
  Table1.CancelUpdates;
end;

procedure TForm1.DataSource1DataChange(Sender: TObject; Field: TField);
begin
  Panel1.Caption := GetEnumName(TypeInfo(TUpdateStatus),
                              Ord(Table1.UpdateStatus));
  if Table1.UpDateStatus = usModified then begin
    Edit1.Text := Table1.Fields[0].OldValue;
    Edit2.Text := Table1.Fields[0].NewValue;
  end else begin
    Edit1.Text := 'Unmodified';
    Edit2.Text := 'Unmodified';
  end;
end;

procedure TForm1.BitBtn2Click(Sender: TObject);
begin
  Close;
end;

end.
```

The first thing to notice about the CacheUp program is that it tracks which records have been modified. For instance, change the OrderNo field of the first two records to the values 1 and 2. If you now select one of these records, you will see that the small panel in the upper right-hand corner of the screen gets set to usModified. This means that the update status for this field has been set to modified.

Here is the TUpdateStatus type:

```
TUpdateStatus = (usUnmodified, usModified, usInserted, usDeleted);
```

Any particular record in a database is going to be set to one of these values.

Here is the code that sets the value in the TPanel object:

```
procedure TForm1.DataSource1DataChange(Sender: TObject; Field: TField);
begin
  Panel1.Caption := GetEnumName(TypeInfo(TUpdateStatus),
                              Ord(Table1.UpdateStatus));
  if Table1.UpDateStatus = usModified then begin
```

```
    Edit1.Text := Table1.Fields[0].OldValue;
    Edit2.Text := Table1.Fields[0].NewValue;
  end else begin
    Edit1.Text := 'Unmodified';
    Edit2.Text := 'Unmodified';
  end;
end;
```

The relevant line in this case is the first one. In particular, notice that it reports on the value of Table1.UpdateStatus. This value will change to reflect the update status of the currently selected record. In order to show this value to the user, the code calls a routine in the TypInfo unit that gets the name of an enumerated value. To use this routine, pass in the type that you want to examine, as well as the ordinal value of the element in that type whose name you want to see. For instance, in this case you are working with a variable of type TUpdateStatus, so you should pass that type in the first parameter. You should then pass the ordinal value of your current record in the second parameter. The routine will return the value of the type in string form.

At the same time that the CacheUp program reports that a record has been modified, it also reports on the old and new value of the OrderNo field for that record. In particular, if you changed the first record's OrderNo field to 1, it will report that the old value for the field was 1003, and the new value is 1. (This assumes that you have the original data as it shipped with Delphi. Remember that if you end up ruining one of these tables performing these kinds of experiments, you can always copy the table over again from the CD!)

In the code that reports on the old and new value of the OrderNo field, you should examine these lines in particular:

```
  Edit1.Text := Table1.Fields[0].OldValue;
  Edit2.Text := Table1.Fields[0].NewValue;
```

As you can see, this information is easy enough to come by—you just have to know where to look.

If you have entered the values 1 and 2 into the OrderNo fields for the first two records, you are going to encounter errors when you try to commit the data. In particular, if you try to apply the data, the built-in referential integrity will complain that there are detail records associated with the OrderNo fields numbered 1003 and 1004. As a result, it is not possible to commit the records. The code then rolls back the erroneous records to their original state.

> **NOTE**
>
> Referential integrity is a means of enforcing the rules in a database. This subject is discussed in some detail in Chapter 20, "Advanced InterBase Techniques." For now, you should not be concerned with the details of how referential integrity works. The key point is simply that there are rules that some tables have to obey, and the BDE will not let users enter invalid data that violates these rules.

Here is the code that reports on the errors in the OrderNo field and rolls the data back to its original state:

```
procedure TForm1.Table1UpdateError(DataSet: TDataSet; E: EDatabaseError;
  UpdateKind: TUpdateKind; var UpdateAction: TUpdateAction);
var
  S: string;
begin
  S := GetEnumName(TypeInfo(TUpdateKind), Ord(UpdateKind)) + ': ' + E.Message;
  ListBox1.Items.Add(DataSet.Fields[0].OldValue + ': ' + S);
  UpdateAction := uaSkip;
end;
```

This particular routine is an event handler for the OnUpdateError event for the Table1 object. To create the routine, click once on the Table1 object, select its Events page in the Object Inspector, and then double-click on the OnUpdateError entry.

The Table1UpdateError method will get called only if an error occurs in attempting to update records. It will get called at the time the error is detected, and before Delphi tries to commit the next record.

Table1UpdateError gets passed four parameters. The most important is the last, which is a var parameter. You can set this parameter to one of the following values:

```
TUpdateAction = (uaAbort, uaSkip, uaRetry, uaApplied);
```

If you set the UpdateAction variable to uaAbort, then the entire attempt to commit the updated data will be aborted. None of your changes will have taken place, and you will return to edit mode as if you had never attempted to commit the data. The changes you have made so far will not be undone, but neither will they be committed. You are aborting the attempt to commit the data, but you are not rolling it back to its previous state.

If you choose uaSkip, then the data will be committed, but the record that is currently in error will be rolled back to its previous value. This will not affect any of the other records in the dataset—it's just the current record that is being reverted.

If you set UpdateAction to uaRetry, that means you have attempted to update the information in the current record, and that you want to retry committing it. The record you should update is the current record in the dataset passed as the first parameter to Table1UpdateError.

In the Table1UpdateError method, I always choose uaSkip as the value to assign to UpdateAction. Of course, you could pop up a dialog and show the user the old value and the new value of the current record. The user would then have a chance to retry committing the data. Once again, you retrieve the data containing the current "problem child" record from the dataset passed in the first parameter of Table1UpdateError. I show an example of accessing this data when I retrieve the old value of the OrderNo field for the record:

```
ListBox1.Items.Add(DataSet.Fields[0].OldValue + ': ' + S);
```

Needless to say, the OldValue field is declared as a Variant in the source code to DB.PAS, which is where TDataSet's declaration is located.

Two other values are passed to the `TableUpdateError` method. The first is an exception reporting on the current error, and the second is a variable of type `TUpdateKind`:

```
TUpdateKind = (ukModify, ukInsert, ukDelete);
```

The variable of type `TUpdateKind` just tells you how the current record was changed. Was it updated, inserted, or deleted? The exception information is passed to you primarily so that you can get at the message associated with the current error:

```
E.Message;
```

If you handle the procedure by setting UpdateAction to a particular value, say uaSkip, then Delphi will not pop up a dialog reporting the error to the user. Instead, it assumes that you are handling the error explicitly, and it leaves it up to you to report the error or not, as you see fit. In this case, I just dump the error into the program's list box, along with some other information.

That is all I'm going to say about cached updates. At this point, you should go back and run the dbCache program that ships with Delphi. It covers all the same ground covered in the last few pages, but it does so in a slightly different form. In particular, it shows how to pop up a dialog so that you can handle each `OnUpdateError` event in an intelligent and sensible manner.

In general, cached updates give you a great deal of power you can tap into when updating the data in a dataset. If necessary, go back and play with the CacheUp program until it starts to make sense to you. This subject isn't prohibitively difficult, but it does take a few moments thought to absorb the basic principles involved.

Many-To-Many Relationships

Many-to-many relationships are necessities in most relational database projects. Suppose, for instance, that you have a set of software routines that you want to store in a database. Some of the routines you can use in DOS, some in Windows 3.1, some in Windows NT, and some in Windows 95. Some routines, however, apply to two or more of the operating systems.

To track this information, you might try adding an OS field to your Routines table, where OS stands for Operating System. It all sounds simple enough. However, there is one problem. The issue, of course, is that some routines will work with more than one OS. For instance, you may have a routine that works in Windows NT and Windows 95, but not in Windows 3.1 or DOS. This means that the fairly simple one-to-many relationship you tried to establish with the OS fields really needs to be converted into a many-to-many relationship.

This section describes how to create many-to-many relationships. This is an annoyingly complex subject, but one that you can master if you take a little time to think things through. My basic goal is to break this process down into a series of steps that you can follow whenever you have to create one of these many-to-many relationships. It might be going too far to say that these steps make the process simple. They do make it manageable, however.

In Listing 19.2, you will find the database definition for a simple set of InterBase tables. You can run this definition through WISQL, using the File | Run ISQL Script menu option. Alternatively, you can create a new database and pass the key statements shown here through one at a time.

Beneath the data definition for the database, you will find the code to a program called Man2Man. This code is found in Listings 19.3 and 19.4, and it shows how to handle a many-to-many relationship in a Delphi program.

Listing 19.2. The schema for a simple database that can capture a many-to-many relationship.

```
/* Extract Database c:\src\unleash2\data\man2man.gdb */
CREATE DATABASE "c:\src\unleash2\data\man2man.gdb" PAGE_SIZE 1024;


/* Table: ATTRIBS, Owner: SYSDBA */
CREATE TABLE ATTRIBS (ATTRIBNO INTEGER NOT NULL,
        ATTRIB VARCHAR(34),
PRIMARY KEY (ATTRIBNO));

/* Table: CUSTOMERS, Owner: SYSDBA */
CREATE TABLE CUSTOMERS (CUSTNO INTEGER NOT NULL,
        NAME VARCHAR(35),
PRIMARY KEY (CUSTNO));

/* Table: MIDDLE, Owner: SYSDBA */
CREATE TABLE MIDDLE (CUSTNO INTEGER,
        ATTRIBNO INTEGER);

/* Grant permissions for this database */
```

Listing 19.3. The main form for the Man2Man program.

```
unit Main;

interface

uses
  Windows, Messages, SysUtils,
  Classes, Graphics, Controls,
  Forms, Dialogs, Grids,
  DBGrids, DB, DBTables,
  StdCtrls, Buttons;

type
  TForm1 = class(TForm)
    Table1: TTable;
    DataSource1: TDataSource;
    DBGrid1: TDBGrid;
    bAttribs: TBitBtn;
```

continues

Listing 19.3. continued

```
    Database1: TDatabase;
    procedure bAttribsClick(Sender: TObject);
  private
    { Private declarations }
  public
    { Public declarations }
  end;

var
  Form1: TForm1;

implementation

uses relate;

{$R *.DFM}

procedure TForm1.bAttribsClick(Sender: TObject);
begin
  Relater := TRelater.Create(Self);
  Relater.RunDialogModal(Table1['CustNo']);
  Relater.Free;
end;

end.
```

Listing 19.4. The Relater form from the Man2Man program.

```
unit Relate;

interface

uses
  Windows, Messages, SysUtils,
  Classes, Graphics, Controls,
  Forms, Dialogs, StdCtrls,
  Buttons, Grids, DBGrids,
  DB, DBTables;

type
  TRelater = class(TForm)
    tblAttrib: TTable;
    dsAttrib: TDataSource;
    DBGrid1: TDBGrid;
    bbInsert: TBitBtn;
    bbDelete: TBitBtn;
    BitBtn3: TBitBtn;
    qInsert: TQuery;
    DBGrid2: TDBGrid;
    qViewAttrib: TQuery;
    dsViewAttrib: TDataSource;
    qDelete: TQuery;
    procedure bbInsertClick(Sender: TObject);
    procedure FormShow(Sender: TObject);
```

```
    procedure bbDeleteClick(Sender: TObject);
    procedure FormCreate(Sender: TObject);
  private
    FCustNo: Integer;
    procedure ViewAttribs;
  public
    procedure RunDialogModal(CustNo: Integer);
  end;

var
  Relater: TRelater;

implementation

{$R *.DFM}

procedure TRelater.RunDialogModal(CustNo: Integer);
begin
  FCustNo := CustNo;
  ShowModal;
end;

procedure TRelater.bbInsertClick(Sender: TObject);
begin
  qInsert.Params[0].AsInteger := FCustNo;
  qInsert.Params[1].AsInteger := tblAttrib['AttribNo'];
  qInsert.ExecSQL;
  ViewAttribs;
end;

procedure TRelater.ViewAttribs;
begin
  qViewAttrib.Close;
  qViewAttrib.Params[0].AsInteger := FCustNo;
  qViewAttrib.Open;
end;

procedure TRelater.FormShow(Sender: TObject);
begin
  ViewAttribs;
end;

procedure TRelater.bbDeleteClick(Sender: TObject);
begin
  qDelete.Params[0].AsInteger := FCustNo;
  qDelete.Params[1].AsInteger := qViewAttrib['AttribNo'];
  qDelete.ExecSQL;
  ViewAttribs;
end;

procedure TRelater.FormCreate(Sender: TObject);
begin
  tblAttrib.Open;
end;

end.
```

The Man2Man program enables you to pop up a dialog that contains two lists of attributes. The left-hand list shows all the possible attributes that can be associated with a record in the main table for this program. The second list shows the currently selected attributes for the current record in the main table. Buttons are supplied so that you can add items from the left-hand column to the column on the right. The dialog in question is shown in Figure 19.5.

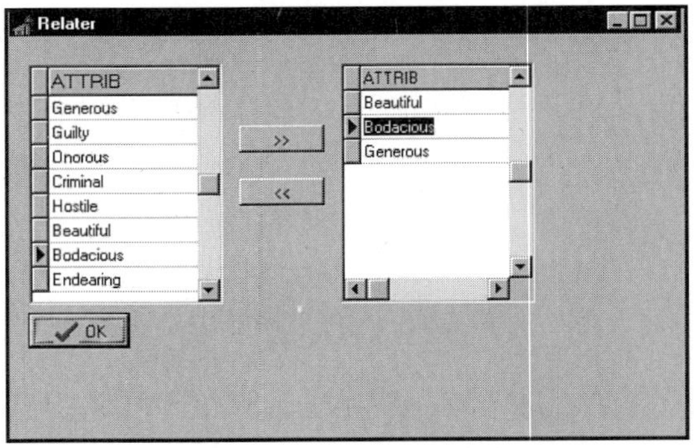

FIGURE 19.5.

The Relater dialog relates the Customer table to the Attributes table.

The basic idea behind a many-to-many relationship is that you need to have an intermediate table between the main table and the list of attributes that you assign to it. For instance, if you have the Routines and the OS tables described, you need a middle table that relates the Routine ID from the Routines table to the OS ID from the OS table.

In the database just shown, the Middle table serves as the intermediary between the Customers table and the Attribs table. Here's how it works.

The Customer table has a series of records in it like this:

```
select * from Customers

     CUSTNO NAME
=========== ====================================

          1 SAM
          2 MIKE
          3 FREDDY FREELOADER
          4 SUNNY SUZY
          5 LOU
          6 TYPHOID MARY
          7 SANDRA
          8 MICHELLE
          9 NICK
         10 NANCY
```

The Attribs table also has a set of attributes that can be assigned to these Customers:

```
select * from Attribs

    ATTRIBNO ATTRIB
=========== ====================================
```

```
 1 Nice
 2 Naughty
 3 Generous
 4 Guilty
 5 Onerous
 6 Criminal
 7 Hostile
 8 Beautiful
 9 Bodacious
10 Endearing
```

Suppose that Sunny Suzy was both Nice and Bodacious. To connect her to these two attributes, you could add two fields to the Middle table:

```
CustNo AttribNo
4      1
4      9
```

Now when you open up the Middle table, you will find two entries in it. The first entry has a CustNo of 4, which stands for Sunny Suzy, and an AttribNo of 1, which stands for Nice. Likewise, the second line translates into Sunny Suzy, Bodacious.

Now that you understand the principle behind creating a many-to-many relationship, the next step is to create a dialog that can capture this relationship in terms that the user can understand. The Man2Man program has a main form that contains a grid showing the fields of the Customer table. There is a button on the main form called Attribute. If you click this button, a dialog like the one shown in Figure 19.5 appears.

On the left-hand side of the Relater dialog is a list of possible attributes that can be assigned to a Customer. On the right-hand side of the dialog is a list of the attributes that have in fact been assigned to the current customer. In between the two lists are two buttons. If you push the button with the arrows pointing to the right, then the word selected on the left will be added to the list on the right. That is, the attribute will be assigned to the currently selected customer. (The Customer list, remember, is back on the main form.) The button with the arrows pointing left will delete the current selected attribute in the right-hand list. This, in effect, removes that attribute from the current Customer's list of traits.

At this stage, you are ready to prepare a list of things that you must do in order to complete the many-to-many relationship:

1. Create a way to insert a new item into the Middle table.
2. Assuming you know the CustNo of the current selected record, you need a way to view the attributes associated with the current customer.
3. Find a way to delete an item from the Middle table.

There are other tasks associated with creating the Relater dialog. For instance, you must put up the table showing the list of possible attributes, and you must add buttons and grids to the dialog. However, I am assuming that all these tasks are too trivial to be worth describing. The key tasks are the ones just listed. Keep your mind focused on them, and the rest will be easy.

To begin, drop down a table, datasource, and grid, and set up the list of possible attributes as shown in the left-hand side grid in Figure 19.5. Name the TTable object containing this dataset tblAttrib.

Now drop down a button that will move things from the left-hand grid to the right-hand grid. Put two arrows on it as shown in Figure 19.5. Drop down a TQuery object, call it qInsert, and place the following line of code in its SQL property:

```
insert into middle (CustNo, AttribNo)
 values (:CustNo, :AttribNo);
```

Here is the code you can create in order to fill in the two bind variables called :CustNo and :AttribNo. This code should be associated with the button that points to the right:

```
procedure TRelater.bbInsertClick(Sender: TObject);begin
  qInsert.Params[0].AsInteger := FCustNo;
  qInsert.Params[1].AsInteger := tblAttrib['AttribNo'];
  qInsert.ExecSQL;
  ViewAttribs;
end;
```

The FCustNo variable is assigned a value when the dialog is launched. It's the CustNo of the currently selected Customer, and it is passed in when the dialog is first called by the main form. The AttribNo value is retrieved from the currently selected record in the grid on the left. In order to actually insert the data into the database, you call ExecSQL.

The ViewAttribs routine shows the attributes associated with the current Customer. That is, it is the one responsible for filling in the grid on the right-hand side of the Relater dialog. The ViewAttribs routine is very simple:

```
procedure TRelater.ViewAttribs;
begin
  qViewAttrib.Close;
  qViewAttrib.Params[0].AsInteger := FCustNo;
  qViewAttrib.Open;
end;
```

This code does nothing more than resolve a single bind variable and then open the qViewAttrib query object. The SQL property of the qViewAttrib query object should look like this:

```
SELECT DISTINCT A.ATTRIB, A.ATTRIBNO
FROM MIDDLE M, ATTRIBS A
WHERE
  (M.CUSTNO = :CustNo)
  AND (A.ATTRIBNO = M.ATTRIBNO)
ORDER BY A.ATTRIB
```

This code selects the Attribute and AttribNo from the Attribs table in all the cases where the AttribNo in the Attribs table is also found in a record from the Middle table that has the CustNo of the currently selected Customer. (Phew!) The resulting set of data is shown in the grid on the right-hand side of the dialog shown in Figure 19.5.

To help make this process intelligible, consider the case I outlined, where Sunny Suzy was both Nice and Bodacious:

```
CustNo AttribNo
4      1
4      9
```

This SQL code searches through the Middle table and finds all the cases where Sunny Suzy is mentioned in it. In other words, it finds the two records shown. The code then performs a lookup in the Attribs table, finding the words that are associated with the two AttribNos shown in the preceding code. Whenever it finds a match, it displays it in the right-hand grid. When there are only two records in the Middle table, this does not seem like much of a trick, but the SQL shown here seems a bit smarter if there are thousands of records in the Middle table, only two of which relate to Sunny Suzy.

At this stage, you are two-thirds of the way through completing the many-to-many relationship. You have found out how to insert records and how to show the list of currently selected items associated with a particular customer. The only step left is to come up with a technique for deleting records.

The SQL to perform a delete from the Middle table looks like this:

```
delete from Middle where
  CustNo = :CustNo and
  AttribNo = :AttribNo;
```

Here is the code, associated with the leftward-pointing button, that fills in the bind variables in the SQL delete code shown in the preceding paragraph:

```
procedure TRelater.bbDeleteClick(Sender: TObject);begin
  qDelete.Params[0].AsInteger := FCustNo;
  qDelete.Params[1].AsInteger := qViewAttrib['AttribNo'];
  qDelete.ExecSQL;
  ViewAttribs;
end;
```

The CustNo bind variable is resolved easily enough because you had the appropriate CustNo passed in from the main form when the dialog was first created. The qViewAttrib query holds a list of the currently selected attributes and their AttribNo. Therefore, you can simply ask the qViewAttrib TQuery object for the AttribNo of the currently selected record in order to find out what item the user wants to delete. Now both bind variables are satisfied, and you can perform the deletion by calling ExecSQL!

All in all, a many-to-many relationship is not so bad as long as you are methodical about the process. Remember that there are three key steps involved:

- First you have to add to the Middle table.
- Then you have to show the records associated with the current Customer.
- And finally, you have to delete from the middle table.

Tackle these tasks one at a time, and the process will not prove to be terribly difficult.

Summary

This chapter gave you a basic introduction to the local InterBase and to several related subjects.

I should stress that InterBase is a very complex and powerful product, and what you have seen in this chapter should serve as little more than a brief introduction that will whet your appetite. In the next chapter, you will look at stored procedures, triggers, InterBase calls, and a few other tricks that should help you grasp the extent of the power in both the local and server-based versions of InterBase.

Delphi protects you from the details of how a server handles basic database chores. However, Delphi also enables you to tap into the power associated with a particular server. This was one of the most delicate balances that the developers had to consider when they created Delphi: How can you make a database tool as generic as possible, without cutting off a programmer's access to the special capabilities of a particular server? The same type of question drove the developers' successful quest to make Delphi's language as simple and elegant as possible without cutting off access to the full power of the Windows API.

Advanced InterBase Techniques

20

In this chapter you get a look at the Music program, which shows a good deal about working with relational databases in general, and about working with InterBase in particular. This chapter is also meant to sum up much of what has been said so far about databases.

This chapter features overviews of

- Relational database design
- Referential integrity
- Stored procedures and the TStoredProc components
- Triggers
- Generators
- Domains
- Table alteration

By the time you finish this chapter, you should have a pretty good feel for how to tap into the power of InterBase. This chapter is not meant to appeal only to InterBase developers, however. It also contains many general comments about working with relational databases.

Everything in this chapter also applies to working with Paradox tables. While Paradox might not support stored procedures, it provides parallel means of providing all the same features which the Music program accesses through stored procedures.

The Music program uses many of the new features of Delphi32. For instance, there are examples of lookups, filters, and searching a database with FindFirst. Many other standard database techniques are also used in this program, such as searching a database with FindNearest and working with ranges. There is also an example of how to search records in the detail table of a master-detail relationship.

In general, this chapter sums up and places in perspective everything said in Chapters 15 through 19. It describes the basic techniques for creating a professional-quality Delphi database.

The Music Program

The MUSIC.DPR program enables you to keep track of CDs, records, tapes, and books. The main goal of the program is to enable you to enter the name of an artist (a musician or a writer) and add one or more titles associated with that artist.

> **NOTE**
>
> Already there are potential problems emerging. *Artist* is a good word for the creator of a song or a work of fiction, but perhaps not a good word for the author of a book on computers! I could choose a more abstract word, such as *Creator*, but it's a bit awkward to refer to Vivaldi or Miles Davis as Creators. So I stay with the word Artist, despite its imperfections. Databases provide a great deal of power, but they have a rather rigid structure that is not always as flexible as one might wish.
>
> The danger with this kind of analysis is that you may consider the word Creator as a good choice for this field, or perhaps you have another choice that you think is more appealing. My emphasis, however, is not so much on the particulars of this situation, but on the necessity of thinking about the names you give to the fields in a table. You should make these decisions only after serious thought, and you should consider discussing the matter with others so you can get a wide range of opinions.

The program has two main tables, related in a one-to-many relationship. The master table is called Artist, and the detail table is called Album. The Album table holds either albums or books, so perhaps it is poorly named. However, the only other words that work are abstract terms like Creations, or Items, both of which perhaps have their own problems.

Besides the two main tables, there are several lookup tables used to store the various lists of possible categories to which the albums and books can belong. For instance, a record can be of type Jazz, Rock, Folk, Blues, and so on, and a book can be of type Fiction, Computer, Mystery, Science Fiction, Reference, and so on. These words are stored in the lookup tables.

There is no need to create a complex database, so I will stop with the short list presented above. Even with this simple structure, however, there are still enough tables to provide some food for thought. In particular, how will these tables be related, and how can you put constraints on them so that it's difficult for the user to accidentally break a dependency? For instance, if there are six albums associated with an artist, a user should not be able to delete the artist without first deleting or reassigning the albums. And how about generating the IDs for each artist and each album? This is not Paradox, so there is no auto-increment field. This means that generators have to be created, and some means of accessing the generators needs to be employed. (If you are new to the concept of generators, don't worry, as you will hear more about them later in this chapter.)

Clearly there are enough questions to keep someone busy for an hour or two. To resolve these issues, a specific database schema needs to be generated.

Creating the Database Schema

In cases like this, it's probably best to start at the top with the Artist table:

```
CREATE TABLE ARTIST (CODE CODE_DOM NOT NULL,
        LAST VARCHAR(30),
        FIRST VARCHAR(30),
        TYPE VARCHAR(15),
        BORN DATE,
        DIED DATE,
        BIRTHPLACE VARCHAR(35),
        COMMENT BLOB SUB_TYPE TEXT SEGMENT SIZE 80,
        PRIMARY KEY (CODE));
```

The definition for this table assumes the presence of a domain called CODE_DOM. You can create a domain in WISQL with the following code:

```
CREATE DOMAIN CODE_DOM AS INTEGER;
```

This code states that CODE_DOM is a domain of type Integer.

A *domain* is an alias for a type that will be used more than once in the program. For instance, the Code field used in the Album table will be referenced in the Album table in the GroupCode field:

```
CREATE TABLE ALBUM (CODE CODE_DOM NOT NULL,
        ALBUM VARCHAR(25) NOT NULL,
        TYPES SMALLINT,
        LOUDNESS SMALLINT,
        MEDIUM SMALLINT,
        RATING SMALLINT,
        GROUPCODE CODE_DOM NOT NULL,
        PRIMARY KEY (CODE));
```

Make sure you understand what is happening here. The GroupCode field in the Album table references the Group, or Artist, associated with this particular album. For instance, if Bob Dylan's code was 57, and the name of the current album was *Blonde on Blonde*, the GroupCode field in the album table would be set to 57. This would tie the album Blonde on Blonde to the artist Bob Dylan.

Creating a domain called CODE_DOM allows you to easily assign the same type to the Code field in the Artist table and the GroupCode field in the Album table. It's not earth-shattering in importance, but it can be helpful.

> **NOTE**
>
> Notice that the Code field is declared as Not Null. This means that the user cannot leave this field blank. This rule is implemented by the server and will be enforced regardless of which front end you use to access the data.

Deciding which fields should be given the value Not Null is one of the more difficult chores in creating a database. This is one of those situations where I almost never call it right every time in design-mode. Instead, I am forced to go back and massage my data after having created a first draft of the data definition.

To change a table using WISQL, you have to call an SQL command called ALTER TABLE:

```
ALTER TABLE MYTABLE
ADD NAME VARCHAR(25),
DROP NAMES;
```

This code adds a field called NAME to a table and drops a field called NAMES. You don't have to add and drop fields at the same time; for instance, you can write:

```
ALTER TABLE MYTABLE
ADD NAME VARCHAR(25)
```

or:

```
ALTER TABLE MYTABLE
  DROP NAMES
```

Because you often have to go back and alter the structure of an existing table, make sure you run many tests on your program before entrusting a large amount of data to your tables.

After the Code field, the next five fields in the Artist table are pretty straightforward:

```
LAST VARCHAR(30),
FIRST VARCHAR(30),
TYPE VARCHAR(15),
BORN DATE,
DIED DATE,
BIRTHPLACE VARCHAR(35),
COMMENT BLOB SUB_TYPE TEXT SEGMENT SIZE 80,
```

The code for creating a BLOB field is a bit tricky-looking, but basically you can just repeat this code any time you need to create a text blob in InterBase.

The final line in the definition for the Artist table defines the primary key:

```
PRIMARY KEY (CODE));
```

This states that the primary key is the Code field. It's important that Code be a keyed field, since it will be referenced by a foreign key in the Album table.

Here, once again, in slightly different form, is the definition for the Album table:

```
CREATE TABLE ALBUM (CODE CODE_DOM NOT NULL,
       ALBUM VARCHAR(25) NOT NULL,
       TYPES SMALLINT,
       LOUDNESS SMALLINT,
       MEDIUM SMALLINT,
       RATING SMALLINT,
```

```
GROUPCODE CODE_DOM NOT NULL,
PRIMARY KEY (CODE),
FOREIGN KEY (TYPES) REFERENCES TYPES(CODE),
FOREIGN KEY (LOUDNESS) REFERENCES LOUDNESS(CODE),
FOREIGN KEY (MEDIUM) REFERENCES MEDIUM(CODE),
FOREIGN KEY (GROUPCODE) REFERENCES ARTIST(CODE)
);
```

Once again, the Code field is the primary key. This field contains a unique number for each new Album record that is entered by the user. There is a CHAR field designating the name of the album or book, and also the GroupCode field that relates each record to the Artist table.

Notice that the GroupCode field is a foreign key referencing the Code field of the Artist table. A foreign key provides *referential integrity.* The foreign key asserts that:

- Every GroupCode entry must have a corresponding Code field in the Artist table.
- You can't delete an Artist record if there is a corresponding record in the Album table with a GroupCode the same as the Code field of the record you are trying to delete.

These two rules go a long way toward describing what foreign keys are all about. They also help to explain some key aspects of what referential integrity is all about. In particular, note that these rules are enforced by the server, and they will be implemented regardless of which front end attempts to alter the table.

> **NOTE**
>
> Referential integrity is not unique to InterBase. In fact, Paradox supplies good tools for supporting referential integrity. It's built right into the Database Desktop, and every Paradox table that you create can have referential integrity if you want it. In most cases, you do indeed want it!

To see referential integrity in action, run the Music program that comes with this book and try to delete one of the Artist records that has an Album associated with it. For instance, try to delete Bob Dylan, Miles Davis, or Philip Glass. Your efforts will be stymied because there are albums associated with all of these artists.

Go into the Database Desktop, enter a new album, and try to give it a GroupCode that does not have a corresponding entry in the Code field of the Artist table. The Database Desktop won't let you do it. (Note that there are other fields that have foreign keys in this table, so you have to give valid values all the way round, or you won't be able to enter a record. You can, however, leave the other fields blank if you wish.)

The key point here is that referential integrity is being enforced automatically in Delphi, and automatically in the Database Desktop. In fact, the rules are being enforced on the server side, and so no matter how you try to get at the data, you have to obey the rules. It's not just some client-side code in Delphi; the rule is built into the database itself, which is what you want.

This concept is so important that I will repeat it once more: These rules are enforced automatically no matter what front end the user attempts to use on the table!

The `Types`, `Loudness`, `Medium`, and `Rating` fields are all integers. `Types`, `Loudness`, and `Medium` are all foreign keys that reference one of three small tables called, logically enough, TYPES, LOUDNESS, and MEDIUM:

```
/* Table: LOUDNESS, Owner: SYSDBA */
CREATE TABLE LOUDNESS (LOUDNESS VARCHAR(15) NOT NULL,
        CODE INTEGER NOT NULL,
        PRIMARY KEY (CODE));

/* Table: MEDIUM, Owner: SYSDBA */
CREATE TABLE MEDIUM (MEDIUM VARCHAR(15) NOT NULL,
        CODE INTEGER NOT NULL,
        PRIMARY KEY (CODE));

/* Table: TYPES, Owner: SYSDBA */
CREATE TABLE TYPES (TYPES VARCHAR(15) NOT NULL,
        CODE INTEGER NOT NULL,
        PRIMARY KEY (CODE));
```

The structure of these tables ought to be intuitively obvious. The `Types` table, for instance, is designed to hold the following records:

```
select * from types

TYPES               CODE
=============== ===========

JAZZ                   1
ROCK                   2
CLASSICAL              3
NEW AGE                4
FOLK                   5
BLUES                  6
COMPUTER            1000
FICTION             1001
SCIFI               1002
MYSTERY             1003
REFERENCE           1004
```

What you have here are six types for albums and five types for books. I separate the two "types of types" by a large range, so that you can add a virtually unlimited number of additional types of either kind. (If you want to work with more than 999 different types of music, you have a problem! I could, of course, have made the split at 10,000 or 100,000 instead of at 1,000, but it's unlikely you would want to have more than 999 distinct types of music in this database.)

The key point to grasp here is that you cannot add a number to the `Types` field of the `Album` table unless it has a corresponding entry in the `Types` table. The foreign key on the TYPES field is placed there explicitly to enforce this rule. Furthermore, you can't delete an entry from the `Types` table if it has a corresponding element in the TYPES field of the `Album` table. You could, however, change the content of one of the strings in the `Types` table, and thereby either enhance, or totally trash, your data.

Astute readers probably noticed that I designed the relationship between the TYPES field of the Album table and the Types table itself so that it is easy to perform lookups on the Types table when necessary. You will hear more about this topic later in the chapter, or you can refer to the discussion of lookup fields in Chapter 17, "Fields and Database Tools."

A Few More Indices

By now, you have seen most of the data definition for MUSIC.GDB. However, there are a few more details to discuss before moving on to take a look at the interface for the program.

Besides foreign keys, the following indices are also defined:

```
CREATE INDEX ALBUM_IDX ON ALBUM(ALBUM, CODE);
CREATE INDEX ARTIST_LASTFIRST_NDX ON ARTIST(LAST, FIRST);
CREATE INDEX ARTIST_TYPE_NDX ON ARTIST(TYPE, LAST, FIRST);
CREATE UNIQUE INDEX LOUDNESS_IDX ON LOUDNESS(LOUDNESS);
CREATE UNIQUE INDEX MEDIUM_IDX ON MEDIUM(MEDIUM);
CREATE UNIQUE INDEX TYPE_IDX ON TYPES(TYPES);
```

If you want to create a new index in WISQL, you can do so with the SQL CREATE INDEX command, as shown in the preceding code excerpt. The command takes the name of the index, the name of the table on which the index will be enforced, and finally, in parentheses, the names of the fields in the index. For more information on this and other commands, see the *InterBase Workgroup Server Language Reference.*

The first two indices listed above allow you to perform sorts on the Album table or the Artist table so that the data is easy to read. For instance, it's only natural that you would want to sort the Artist table on the artist's first and last names.

The ARTIST_TYPE_NDX is provided so you can filter out either the books or the albums, depending on your current needs. This index is not strictly needed anymore because of the new OnFilterRecord event, but force of habit makes me feel that filtering on an indexed field is faster than filtering on a non-indexed field. Also, I will have another use for the OnFilterRecord event for the Artist table.

The last three indices are provided in case you ever need them. These are such small tables that the indices probably won't be of much use, but there isn't any harm in creating them.

Generators, Triggers, and Stored Procedures

Two generators provide unique numbers to use in the CODE fields of the Artist and Album tables. Generators provide almost the same functionality in InterBase tables that autoincrement fields provide in Paradox tables. That is, they provide numbers to use in the keyed fields that relate tables together.

Autoincrement fields are filled in automatically at runtime. Generators, however, merely generate random numbers in sequence, where the first number generated might be one, the second two, and so on. You can tell a generator to start generating numbers at a particular starting value, where the first number might be X, the next X + 1, and so on.

Here is how to create a generator in WISQL and set it to a particular value:

```
CREATE GENERATOR MUSIC_GEN;
SET GENERATOR MUSIC_GEN TO 300;
```

As a result of this code, the first generated number would be 300, the next, 301, and so on.

Here is how to write a trigger that will automatically put this value into the CODE field of the Artist table whenever an Insert occurs:

```
CREATE TRIGGER SETMUSICGEN FOR ARTIST
BEFORE INSERT AS
BEGIN
  NEW.CODE = GEN_ID(MUSIC_GEN, 1);
END
```

This code appears on the server side. It's not Delphi code. You enter it exactly as in WISQL and the procedure runs on the server end; it is not processed by Delphi. There is never any need to call this procedure explicitly. The whole point of triggers is that they run automatically when certain events occur. This one is designed to run right before an Insert occurs. In other words, the way to call this procedure is to perform an Insert!

This code states that you want to create a trigger called SetMusicGen to be run on the Artist table. The generator is called before an insert operation:

```
BEFORE INSERT AS
```

The actual body of the code is simple:

```
NEW.CODE = GEN_ID(MUSIC_GEN, 1);
```

The NEW statement says that you are going to define the new value for a particular field that is about to be inserted into a table. In this case you are referencing the new value for the CODE field of the Artist table.

GEN_ID is a function built into InterBase that produces an integer value. It takes a generator as its first parameter and a step value as its second parameter. The step value will increase or decrease the value produced by the generator. For instance, the preceding code increments the value by 1.

You can get a generator to fill in a field automatically with the trigger shown above. Unfortunately, Delphi does not provide particularly good support for triggers, in part because each server generates a different kind of trigger. The developers of Delphi didn't want to run around finding out how to handle triggers for 30 different kinds of servers, and neither did the developers of the BDE. There are some third-party solutions to this problem, however, including a good one that works with InterBase.

In the example under discussion, Delphi's poor support for triggers is irrelevant because the table is not sorted on the CODE field. If it were, this trigger might cause Delphi to lose track of the current record after the insert operation. Delphi would not know that the Code value was inserted, because it would not know that the trigger fired. As a result, the current record might be lost because it had been sorted on a value of which Delphi was not aware. In other words, the index would cause the record to be moved to a particular place in the dataset, but Delphi would not know how to follow it. As far as Delphi is concerned, the CODE field would still be blank! (There would not, however, be a referential integrity exception raised, since the InterBase server would be aware that the field was inserted!)

You can now see that in this case there is no problem using a trigger because the table is sorted on the LAST and FIRST fields, not on the CODE field.

NOTE

Here is another example of how to create a trigger using WISQL:

```
CREATE TRIGGER SET_COMPANY_UPPER FOR COMPANY
ACTIVE BEFORE INSERT POSITION 1
AS
BEGIN
  NEW.COMPANY_UPPER = UPPER(NEW.COMPANY);
END
```

This code is called just before an insert operation on a table called Company. This table contains a string field also called Company, and a second field called Company_Upper. The second field is meant to mirror the Company field, but with all its characters in upper case. Having this second field takes up a lot of space, but you can conduct searches on the Company field without having to take character case into account. The goal of the trigger shown above, then, is to take the new value for the Company field and convert it into an uppercase version of the string for use in the COMPANY_UPPER field. The Upper macro shown here is built into InterBase.

Notice the line that states when this trigger will be fired:

```
ACTIVE BEFORE INSERT POSITION 1
```

For a detailed understanding of how to create triggers, turn to the *Language Reference* for the InterBase server.

I show you this trigger because it works fine when used with Delphi. Delphi does not need to know that the Set_Company_Upper trigger occurred. The trigger can take place in the background, without impacting Delphi's inner workings. However, if you use a trigger that affects a field that Delphi sorts on, you can have trouble. Delphi will not know that the new value for the field has been inserted, and thus will not know to search on that value to find the newly inserted record. Suppose, for instance, that you are sorting records on a field called CustNo, which can have values between 0 and 64 KB. If you insert a new record, and you use a trigger to assign a new CustNo value, Delphi will never know the number assigned by Interbase. The server will then automatically sort the records on the new number, but Delphi will be left in the lurch, not knowing that the record you were editing has been moved to a different part of the table based on the value of its CustNo field. As far as Delphi is concerned, the record you were editing just disappeared when you posted it. It won't know where to look for it!

If you find yourself in a situation where you can't use a trigger, there is no great need for alarm. The absence of trigger support is not a big concern under most circumstances. Instead of using a trigger, you can use a stored procedure to retrieve the next number from a generator.

A *stored procedure* is simply a routine that is stored on the server side rather than being listed in your Object Pascal source code. Like the language for writing triggers, there is a unique language for writing stored procedures that has nothing to do with Object Pascal or SQL. In fact, you need to keep in mind that there is no particular relationship between Delphi and InterBase. They are made by two different teams, using two different languages, with two different goals in mind. The stored procedure language was made up long before anyone ever thought of creating Delphi, and in general, the two languages have absolutely nothing to do with one another.

Stored procedures are not difficult to create. Here, for instance, is a stored procedure that returns the next number generated by the Music_Gen generator:

```
CREATE PROCEDURE GETMUSICGEN
RETURNS (NUM INTEGER)
AS
BEGIN
  NUM = GEN_ID(MUSIC_GEN, 1);
END
```

The first line tells WISQL that you are going to create a procedure called GetMusicGen. The next line states that it is going to return a value called Num, which is an integer. The AS statement tells InterBase that you are now ready to define the body of the procedure. The procedure itself appears between a BEGIN..END pair, and consists of a call to the GEN_ID function, which returns the next number from the MUSIC_GEN generator. When it retrieves the number, it asks InterBase to increment its value by one.

> **NOTE**
>
> Stored procedures are handled on the Delphi end with either a TStoredProc component, or by returning an answer set by way of a SQL statement. In general, if the stored procedure returns several rows of data, you access it by way of a SQL statement in a TQuery component. If the stored procedure returns only a single item of data, you can call it with a TStoredProc component. Examples of calling stored procedures from Delphi appear in the next section.

There are, as I said earlier, two generators, one trigger, and one stored procedure in the data definition for the MUSIC database. The stored procedure generates a unique number for the Code field in the Album table. As with the Artist table, I could have used a trigger instead of a stored procedure. However, I wanted to provide an example of using a stored procedure in this type of situation.

Stored Procedures from Delphi's End

The Album and Book pages of the Music program have stored procedures on them. Since both procedures are identical, I will describe only the one on the Album page.

To get started using a TStoredProc, drop it onto the Album page. Set the StoreProcName alias to the GetAlbumGen stored procedure. The procedure looks like this:

```
CREATE PROCEDURE GETALBUMGEN RETURNS (NUM INTEGER)
AS
BEGIN
  NUM = GEN_ID(ALBUM_GEN, 1);
END
```

As you can see, this is a simple stored procedure that does nothing more than return a single value.

> **NOTE**
>
> If GetAlbumGen returned several rows of data rather than a single value, you would call it by using a TQuery object rather than a TStoredProc object. The SQL statement to use in such a case would be Select * from GetAlbumGen.

After selecting the procedure to use with the TStoredProc, you can pop up the Params field to see the parameters passed to or returned by the function. In this case there is only one parameter, which is returned as the result of the function.

Whenever the user wants to insert a record into the Album table, the following procedure is called:

```
procedure TMusicAlbum.sbInsertClick(Sender: TObject);
var
  S: string;
begin
  S := '';
  if not InputQuery('Insert New Album Dialog', 'Enter album name', S) then Exit;
  Form1.tblAlbum.Insert;
  GetAlbum.ExecProc;
  Form1.tblAlbum.FieldByName('Code').AsInteger := GetAlbum.Params[0].AsInteger;
  Form1.tblAlbum.FieldByName('Album').AsString := S;
  Form1.tblAlbum.FieldByName('Types').AsString := '';
```

```
    Form1.tblAlbum.FieldByName('Loudness').AsString := '';
    Form1.tblAlbum.FieldByName('Medium').AsString := '';
    Form1.tblAlbum.Post;
    lcbType.SetFocus;
end;
```

The key lines of this procedure are the ones involving the stored procedure:

```
GetAlbum.ExecProc;
Form1.tblAlbum.FieldByName('Code').AsInteger := GetAlbum.Params[0].AsInteger;
```

This code first executes the stored procedure, then snags its return value from the Params field of the TStoredProc. The Params field for stored procedures works the same way as the Params field for TQuery objects.

NOTE

Here is an example of a stored procedure that uses SQL:

```
CREATE PROCEDURE CONTACTBYPRODUCT (PRODNAME VARCHAR(20))
RETURNS (SFIRST VARCHAR(30),
         SLAST VARCHAR(30),
         STITLE VARCHAR(30))
AS
BEGIN
  SELECT DISTINCT C.LAST, C.FIRST, C.TITLE
  FROM CONTACTS C, CONT2PROD C1, BORPRODS B
  WHERE
    (C1.CONTACTNO = C.CONTACTNO)
     AND (B.BORPRODID = C1.BORPRODID)
     AND (B.PRODUCT = :ProdName)
  ORDER BY C.LAST, C.FIRST, C.TITLE
  INTO : SLAST, SFIRST, STITLE;
  SUSPEND;
END
```

This code is part of the expression of a many-to-many relationship. The BorProds table contains a list of products that might be associated with the people listed in the Contacts table. This situation calls for a many-to-many relationship because there can be more than one product associated with each of the records listed in the contact table, and there can be more than one contact associated with each of the records in the BorProds table. As a result, there is an intermediate table that lists a series of IDs from the Contacts and BorProds tables.

The query shown above fulfills the request: Show me a list of contacts associated with one particular product. You pass in a product name, and you get back all the Contacts associated with that product. The product name passed in is bound to the query as a parameter:

```
AND (B.PRODUCT = :ProdName)
```

Notice that you are going to get back a dataset, not just three variables, when you call this function. In other words, you will get back a series of records, each containing the

SLAST, SFIRST, and STITLE fields. The results of the query are placed in the dataset via the syntax that reads:

```
INTO : SLAST, SFIRST, STITLE;
```

The SUSPEND statement temporarily delays the execution of the procedure while a Fetch statement is carried out. Imagine the moment after the first row has been calculated, and while it is being returned via the calling procedure. The loop is temporarily put on hold while this is going on; that is, it is SUSPENDed. After the fetch is complete, the next row is calculated, and so on. You would use SUSPEND statements in procedures that return rows of values, not in a simple procedure that returns only one value.

The point here is that you can store a particular query in a stored procedure, then call it from a TQuery or TStoredProc component. This approach can eliminate considerable complexity in programs that need to perform complex operations such as creating many-to-many relationships. This process allows you to keep a SQL statement on the server side rather than in the SQL property of a TQuery component.

As you can see, Delphi makes it easy for you to use stored procedures in your programs. In this particular case, you could have used a stored procedure rather than a trigger. However, it is not a great crisis if you have to use a stored procedure rather than a trigger. The one advantage triggers have over stored procedures is that they are called automatically, thereby helping you to ensure data integrity.

The Complete Data Definition for MUSIC.GDB

Here is the complete data definition for MUSIC.GDB:

```
/* Extract Database C:\SRC\UNLEASH2\DATA\MUSIC.GDB */
CREATE DATABASE "C:\SRC\UNLEASH2\DATA\MUSIC.GDB" PAGE_SIZE 1024
;

/* Domain definitions */
CREATE DOMAIN CODE_DOM AS INTEGER;

/* Table: ALBUM, Owner: SYSDBA */
CREATE TABLE ALBUM (CODE CODE_DOM NOT NULL,
        ALBUM VARCHAR(25) NOT NULL,
        TYPES SMALLINT,
        LOUDNESS SMALLINT,
        MEDIUM SMALLINT,
        RATING SMALLINT,
        GROUPCODE CODE_DOM NOT NULL,
PRIMARY KEY (CODE));

/* Table: ARTIST, Owner: SYSDBA */
```

```
CREATE TABLE ARTIST (CODE CODE_DOM NOT NULL,
        LAST VARCHAR(30),
        FIRST VARCHAR(30),
        TYPE VARCHAR(15),
        BORN DATE,
        DIED DATE,
        BIRTHPLACE VARCHAR(35),
        COMMENT BLOB SUB_TYPE TEXT SEGMENT SIZE 80,
PRIMARY KEY (CODE));

/* Table: LOUDNESS, Owner: SYSDBA */
CREATE TABLE LOUDNESS (LOUDNESS VARCHAR(15) NOT NULL,
        CODE INTEGER NOT NULL,
PRIMARY KEY (CODE));

/* Table: MEDIUM, Owner: SYSDBA */
CREATE TABLE MEDIUM (MEDIUM VARCHAR(15) NOT NULL,
        CODE INTEGER NOT NULL,
PRIMARY KEY (CODE));

/* Table: TYPES, Owner: SYSDBA */
CREATE TABLE TYPES (TYPES VARCHAR(15) NOT NULL,
        CODE INTEGER NOT NULL,
PRIMARY KEY (CODE));

/*  Index definitions for all user tables */
CREATE INDEX ALBUM_IDX ON ALBUM(ALBUM, CODE);
CREATE INDEX ARTIST_LASTFIRST_NDX ON ARTIST(LAST, FIRST);
CREATE INDEX ARTIST_TYPE_NDX ON ARTIST(TYPE, LAST, FIRST);
CREATE UNIQUE INDEX LOUDNESS_IDX ON LOUDNESS(LOUDNESS);
CREATE UNIQUE INDEX MEDIUM_IDX ON MEDIUM(MEDIUM);
CREATE UNIQUE INDEX TYPE_IDX ON TYPES(TYPES);
ALTER TABLE ALBUM ADD FOREIGN KEY (TYPES) REFERENCES TYPES(CODE);
ALTER TABLE ALBUM ADD FOREIGN KEY (LOUDNESS) REFERENCES LOUDNESS(CODE);
ALTER TABLE ALBUM ADD FOREIGN KEY (MEDIUM) REFERENCES MEDIUM(CODE);
ALTER TABLE ALBUM ADD FOREIGN KEY (GROUPCODE) REFERENCES ARTIST(CODE);

CREATE GENERATOR MUSIC_GEN;
CREATE GENERATOR ALBUM_GEN;

COMMIT WORK;
SET AUTODDL OFF;
SET TERM ^ ;

/* Stored procedures */
CREATE PROCEDURE GETALBUMGEN AS BEGIN EXIT; END ^

ALTER PROCEDURE GETALBUMGEN RETURNS (NUM INTEGER)
AS

BEGIN
  NUM = GEN_ID(ALBUM_GEN, 1);
END
  ^
SET TERM ; ^
COMMIT WORK ;
SET AUTODDL ON;
SET TERM ^ ;
```

```
/* Triggers only will work for SQL triggers */
CREATE TRIGGER SETMUSICGEN FOR ARTIST
ACTIVE BEFORE INSERT POSITION 0
AS
BEGIN
  NEW.CODE = GEN_ID(MUSIC_GEN, 1);
END
^
COMMIT WORK ^
SET TERM ; ^

/* Grant permissions for this database */
```

If you want to create this database from scratch, you can run this entire statement through WISQL from the File menu. Otherwise, you could create the database and pass the statements through one at a time. A third use for the code is simply to give you one place to look when you need a reference for MUSIC.GDB. To create the output shown above, select Extract ¦ SQL Data From Database from the WISQL menu.

Server Side Rules Versus Client Side Rules

A few more words about database design: In many people's minds, the Holy Grail of contemporary client/server development is to place as many rules as possible on the server side of the equation. This means that no matter how the user accesses the data, and no matter how many front ends are written to access the data, the basic rules of the database will be enforced.

To me, this means that you must create referential integrity on the server side using foreign keys, or whatever tools are at your disposal. Furthermore, you should use triggers whenever possible to enforce additional rules. For instance, some people would view it as an error to insert the Code field of the Album table using a stored procedure rather than a trigger.

Even using triggers and referential integrity is not enough for many hard-core adherents of the server side philosophy. This book, however, is being written about a client-side tool, and so I will generally promote just placing the referential integrity on the server side, and then maybe adding a few more triggers or stored procedures where necessary.

If you can use QBE, or some other SQL builder, to create powerful SQL statements that you will use in your programs, you should probably place those SQL statements in stored procedures, as shown above in the note that discusses the ContactByProduct procedure.

I find, however, that most other database chores are easier to perform on the Delphi side. Delphi is a powerful language, with powerful debuggers to back it up. Most servers have neither a powerful language nor a powerful debugger. That means that, for now, this particular writer still feels it's often wisest to keep certain kinds of database logic on your client side.

Besides these tentative opinions, the only thing I can say for certain is that there is a great deal of heated debate regarding this topic. Furthermore, the emergence of Distributed OLE and other tools that support Remote Procedure Calls (RPC), are likely to have a powerful impact on the future of this issue. If PC-based developers can use Distributed OLE to place rules easily on remote servers, the whole way databases are constructed is likely to change. In other words, if I could use Delphi to enforce a bunch of rules, then encapsulate those rules in an object that resides on the same machine as the InterBase server, I would do it. I would put all my database logic out there, and just provide a few entry points for my front-end program to call. This is not yet a reality, however, and so I would suggest not getting too heavily involved in placing complex logic out on a server where you can't debug it or maintain it easily. One man's opinion!

An Overview of the Interface for the Music Program

The interface for MUSIC.DPR presents the user with a main screen with four pages imbedded inside it. One page (shown in Figure 20.1) is meant only for performing searches. It gives you a view of both the Artist and Album tables. You can't insert new records in this screen, but you can edit the data that you see.

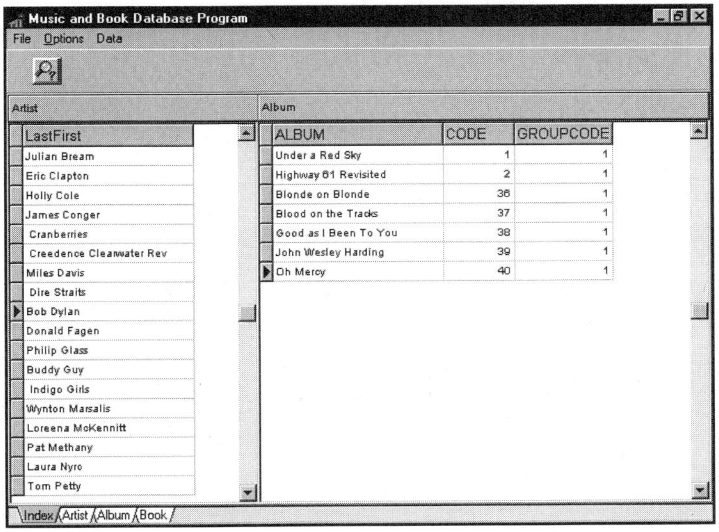

FIGURE 20.1.

The Index *page from MUSIC.DPR enables you to view artists and their related productions.*

NOTE

I use the following code to prevent the user from using the Insert key to insert a record into either of the grids on the Index page:

```
procedure TIndexForm.DBArtistGridKeyDown(Sender: TObject; var Key: Word;
  Shift: TShiftState);
```

```
begin
  if (Key = vk_Insert) or (Key = vk_Delete) then
    Key := 0;
end;
```

This code takes Insert keystrokes and Delete keystrokes and disarms them. Users never know the method is being called, but find that they can't use the Insert or Delete keys. The code is called in response to OnKeyDown events.

The second page in the Music program allows you to see one record from the Artist table, as shown in Figure 20.2. The general theory is that users can browse or search through the data using the Index page shown in Figure 20.1. If they want to look at a particular record, they can switch to the Artist, Album, or Book pages. Figures 20.3 and 20.4 show the latter two of these three pages.

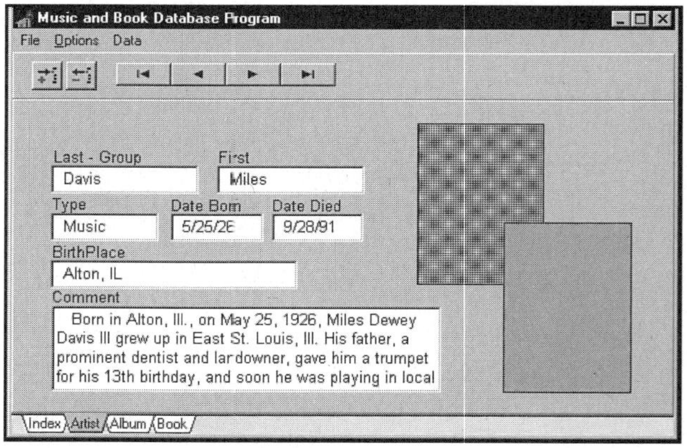

FIGURE 20.2.

The Artist page from the Music program.

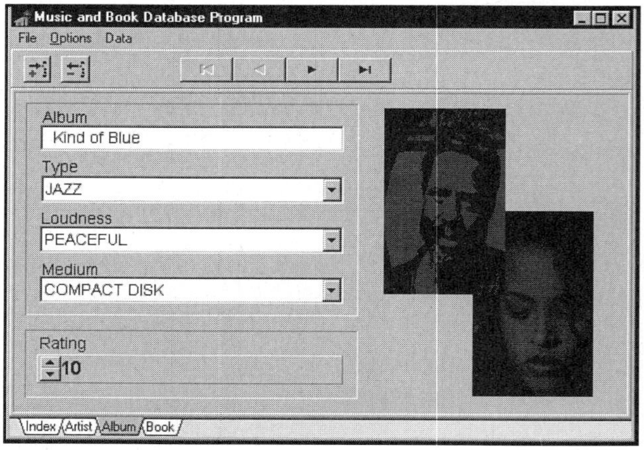

FIGURE 20.3.

The Album page from the Music program.

FIGURE 20.4.

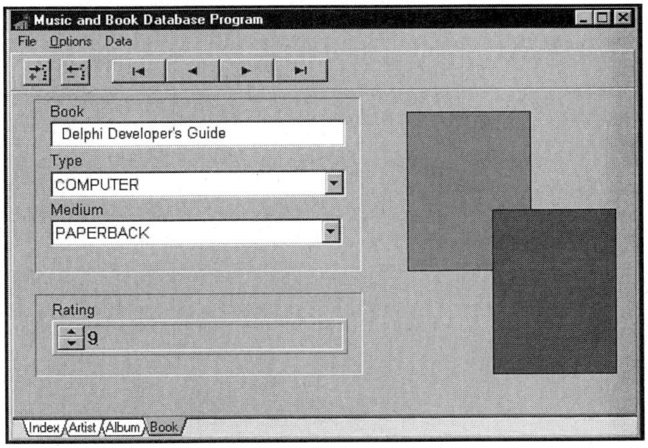

The Book *page from the Music program.*

Traditionally, relational databases have been shown to users all on one screen. The typical technique used is like that demonstrated in the Relate program in Chapter 17, "Fields and Database Tools." In general, the idea is to put the master table at the top of a screen, and to put the detail tables beneath it, finding room for all the fields as best one can.

I prefer to use pages, where each page represents a different table, because it cuts down on the use of cluttered, hard-to-comprehend screens. However, paged relational databases can be confusing to users who don't understand the structure of the database. There are plenty of examples of database programs that throw several tables onto one cluttered screen and let the user have at it. In this chapter you will get a look at an alternative structure for presenting relational databases to users.

Working with Paged Forms

Delphi provides a number of paged dialogs or notebooks that can be used to present data to the user. In this particular program, I use the TTabSet tool, but don't have any problem with using TNotebook, TTabbedNotebook, TPageControl, or TTabControl. My primary concern is allowing the programmer to place each major object in a separate unit, rather than forcing the combination of various different sets of functionality into one paged notebook. In other words, the Album page is a separate object, not a part of the TNotebook object. I, therefore, have found a method that enables you to give the object its own unit.

The Music program really has five major forms in it, the first representing the frame for the entire program, and the rest representing the Index, Artist, Album, and Book pages. The next few paragraphs describe how to make a form become a child of a second form, which is what is really going on inside the Music program.

The key point to grasp is that you need to convert the standard Delphi pop-up form to a child form that has Form1 as its parent. Here is how to proceed:

```
unit Ritchey1;

interface

uses
  Windows, Messages, SysUtils,
  Classes, Graphics, Controls,
  Forms, Dialogs;

type
  TRitchey = class(TForm)
  private
    { Private declarations }
  public
    procedure Loaded; override;
    procedure CreateParams(var Params: TCreateParams); override;
  end;

var
  Ritchey: TRitchey;

implementation

{$R *.DFM}

procedure TRitchey.Loaded;
begin
  inherited Loaded;
  Visible := false;
  Position := poDefault;
  BorderIcons := [];
  BorderStyle := bsNone;
  HandleNeeded;
  SetBounds(0,0,Width,Height);
end;

procedure TRitchey.CreateParams(var Params: TCreateParams);
begin
  inherited CreateParams(Params);
  Params.WndParent := (Owner as TForm).Handle;
  Params.Style := WS_CHILD or WS_CLIPSIBLINGS;
  Params.X := 0;
  Params.Y := 0;
end;

end.
```

This is the work of Pat Ritchey, a long-time Object Pascal developer who clearly understands how Windows, as well as Delphi, is put together.

When using this technique, you want the parent form to explicitly create the child forms. To do this, do not auto-create the forms, but choose Options | Project | Forms, and move the forms from the Auto-Create list box into the Available Forms list box. Then you can create the forms as needed inside Form1, with code that looks like this:

```
MusicAlbum := TMusicAlbum.Create(Self);
```

I will describe this process in more depth below, in the section that examines the FormCreate event for the main module.

To make sure the form adheres to the dimensions of its parent, you can respond to OnResize events:

```
procedure TForm1.FormResize(Sender: TObject);
var
  i: Integer;
begin
  for i := 0 to MaxForms do
    MoveWindow(ChildForms[i].Handle, 0, 0, Panel1.ClientWidth,
      Panel1.ClientHeight, True);
end;
```

The Code for the Music Program

Now that you understand the basic structure of the Music program, the next step is to take a look at the code, and analyze any sections that need explanation. The code appears in Listings 20.1 through 20.8.

Listing 20.1. The main form for the Music program.

```
unit Main;

interface

uses
  SysUtils, WinTypes, WinProcs,
  Messages, Classes, Graphics,
  Controls, Forms, Dialogs,
  DB, DBTables, Grids,
  DBGrids, ExtCtrls, Tabs,
  Menus;

const
  MaxForms = 3;

type
  TChildType = (cfIndex, cfArtist, cfAlbum, cfBook);

  TForm1 = class(TForm)
    TabSet1: TTabSet;
    Panel1: TPanel;
    MainMenu1: TMainMenu;
    File1: TMenuItem;
    Exit1: TMenuItem;
    Options1: TMenuItem;
    Search1: TMenuItem;
    N1: TMenuItem;
    Index1: TMenuItem;
```

continues

Listing 20.1. continued

```
    Album1: TMenuItem;
    Data1: TMenuItem;
    Delete1: TMenuItem;
    Insert2: TMenuItem;
    N2: TMenuItem;
    ShowOnlyMusic1: TMenuItem;
    ShowOnlyBooks1: TMenuItem;
    ShowAll1: TMenuItem;
    tblArtist: TTable;
    tblArtistCODE: TIntegerField;
    tblArtistLAST: TStringField;
    tblArtistFIRST: TStringField;
    tblArtistTYPE: TStringField;
    tblArtistLastFirst: TStringField;
    dsArtist: TDataSource;
    Database1: TDatabase;
    tblAlbum: TTable;
    tblAlbumALBUM: TStringField;
    tblAlbumCODE: TIntegerField;
    tblAlbumTYPES: TSmallintField;
    tblAlbumRATING: TSmallintField;
    tblAlbumLOUDNESS: TSmallintField;
    tblAlbumMEDIUM: TSmallintField;
    tblAlbumGROUPCODE: TIntegerField;
    tblAlbumluType: TStringField;
    tblAlbumluLoudness: TStringField;
    tblAlbumluMedium: TStringField;
    tblLoudness: TTable;
    tblTypes: TTable;
    tblMedium: TTable;
    dsAlbum: TDataSource;
    tblArtistBORN: TDateTimeField;
    tblArtistDIED: TDateTimeField;
    tblArtistBIRTHPLACE: TStringField;
    tblArtistCOMMENT: TMemoField;
    SearchAlbums1: TMenuItem;
    procedure FormCreate(Sender: TObject);
    procedure FormResize(Sender: TObject);
    procedure TabSet1Change(Sender: TObject; NewTab: Integer;
      var AllowChange: Boolean);
    procedure FormShow(Sender: TObject);
    procedure Index1Click(Sender: TObject);
    procedure Album1Click(Sender: TObject);
    procedure Search1Click(Sender: TObject);
    procedure Insert2Click(Sender: TObject);
    procedure Delete1Click(Sender: TObject);
    procedure ShowOnlyMusic1Click(Sender: TObject);
    procedure tblArtistCalcFields(DataSet: TDataSet);
    procedure tblTypesFilterRecord(DataSet: TDataSet;
      var Accept: Boolean);
    procedure tblMediumFilterRecord(DataSet: TDataSet;
      var Accept: Boolean);
    procedure SearchAlbums1Click(Sender: TObject);
    procedure tblArtistFilterRecord(DataSet: TDataSet;
      var Accept: Boolean);
  private
```

```
    FArtistCode: Integer;
    FChildType: TChildType;
    ChildForms: array[0..MaxForms] of TForm;
    { Private declarations }
  public
    { Public declarations }
  end;

var
  Form1: TForm1;

implementation

uses
  Index1, Mus2Alb, Artist1,
  Bookfrm1, Globals, Search1;

{$R *.DFM}

procedure TForm1.FormCreate(Sender: TObject);
var
  i: Integer;
begin
  tblArtist.Open;
  tblAlbum.Open;
  tblTypes.Open;
  tblLoudness.Open;
  tblMedium.Open;
  IndexForm := TIndexForm.Create(Self);
  MusicAlbum := TMusicAlbum.Create(Self);
  ArtistForm := TArtistForm.Create(Self);
  BookForm := TBookForm.Create(Self);
  ChildForms[0] := IndexForm;
  ChildForms[1] := ArtistForm;
  ChildForms[2] := MusicAlbum;
  ChildForms[3] := BookForm;
  for i := 0 to MaxForms do
    ChildForms[i].Show;
end;

procedure TForm1.FormResize(Sender: TObject);
var
  i: Integer;
begin
  for i := 0 to MaxForms do
    MoveWindow(ChildForms[i].Handle, 0, 0, Panel1.ClientWidth, Panel1.ClientHeight,
True);
end;

procedure TForm1.TabSet1Change(Sender: TObject; NewTab: Integer;
  var AllowChange: Boolean);
begin
  tblTypes.Filtered := False;
  tblMedium.Filtered := False;
  FChildType := TChildType(NewTab);
  if (FChildType = cfBook) or (FChildType = cfAlbum) then begin
    tblTypes.Filtered := True;
    tblMedium.Filtered := True;
```

continues

Listing 20.1. continued

```
  end;

  ChildForms[NewTab].BringToFront;
end;

procedure TForm1.FormShow(Sender: TObject);
begin
  ChildForms[0].BringToFront;
end;

procedure TForm1.Index1Click(Sender: TObject);
begin
  TabSet1.TabIndex := Ord(cfIndex);
  IndexForm.dbArtistGrid.SetFocus;
end;

procedure TForm1.Album1Click(Sender: TObject);
begin
  TabSet1.TabIndex := Ord(cfAlbum);
  MusicAlbum.dbAlbum.SetFocus;
end;

procedure TForm1.Search1Click(Sender: TObject);
begin
  Index1Click(nil);
  IndexForm.sbSearchClick(nil);
end;

procedure TForm1.Insert2Click(Sender: TObject);
begin
  case TChildType(TabSet1.TabIndex) of
    cfArtist: begin
      TabSet1.TabIndex := Ord(cfIndex);
      ArtistForm.sbInsertClick(nil);
    end;
    cfAlbum: begin
      TabSet1.TabIndex := Ord(cfAlbum);
      MusicAlbum.sbInsertClick(nil);
    end;
  else
    ShowMessage('Choose Artist or Album Page First');
  end;
end;

procedure TForm1.Delete1Click(Sender: TObject);
begin
  case TChildType(TabSet1.TabIndex) of
    cfArtist: begin
      TabSet1.TabIndex := Ord(cfIndex);
      ArtistForm.sbDeleteClick(nil);
    end;
    cfAlbum: begin
      TabSet1.TabIndex := Ord(cfAlbum);
      MusicAlbum.sbDeleteClick(nil);
    end;
    else
```

```
      ShowMessage('Choose Artist or Album Page First');
   end;
end;

procedure TForm1.ShowOnlyMusic1Click(Sender: TObject);
begin
   IndexMode := TIndexMode((Sender as TMenuItem).Tag);
   case IndexMode of
     imPrimary: tblArtist.IndexName := 'ARTIST_LASTFIRST_NDX';
     imMusic: begin
      tblArtist.IndexName := 'ARTIST_TYPE_NDX';
       tblArtist.SetRange(['Music'], ['Music']);
      end;
      imBook: begin
        tblArtist.IndexName := 'ARTIST_TYPE_NDX';
        tblArtist.SetRange(['Book'], ['Book']);
      end;
   end;
end;

procedure TForm1.tblArtistCalcFields(DataSet: TDataSet);
begin
   tblArtistLastFirst.Value := tblArtistFirst.Value + ' ' + tblArtistLast.Value;
end;

procedure TForm1.tblTypesFilterRecord(DataSet: TDataSet;
   var Accept: Boolean);
begin
   if FChildType = cfBook then
     Accept := tblTypes['Code'] > 999
   else if FChildType = cfAlbum then
     Accept := tblTypes['Code'] < 1000;
end;

procedure TForm1.tblMediumFilterRecord(DataSet: TDataSet;
   var Accept: Boolean);
begin
   if FChildType = cfBook then
     Accept := tblMedium['Code'] > 999
   else if FChildType = cfAlbum then
     Accept := tblMedium['Code'] < 1000;
end;

procedure TForm1.SearchAlbums1Click(Sender: TObject);
var
   OutCome: Integer;
begin
   AlbumSearch := TAlbumSearch.Create(Self);
   OutCome := AlbumSearch.AlbumSearchModal;
   AlbumSearch.Free;
   if OutCome = -1 then
     Exit
   else begin
     FArtistCode := OutCome;
     tblArtist.FindFirst;
   end;
end;
```

continues

Listing 20.1. continued

```
procedure TForm1.tblArtistFilterRecord(DataSet: TDataSet;
  var Accept: Boolean);
begin
  Accept := tblArtist['Code'] = FArtistCode;
end;

end.
```

Listing 20.2. The `Index` form for the Music program.

```
unit Index1;

interface

uses
  SysUtils, WinTypes, WinProcs,
  Messages, Classes, Graphics,
  Controls, Forms, Dialogs,
  Grids, DBGrids, DB,
  ExtCtrls, Buttons, DBTables;

type
  TIndexForm = class(TForm)
    Panel1: TPanel;
    Panel2: TPanel;
    Header1: THeader;
    DBArtistGrid: TDBGrid;
    DBGrid2: TDBGrid;
    sbSearch: TSpeedButton;
    Query1: TQuery;
    procedure sbSearchClick(Sender: TObject);
    procedure FormCreate(Sender: TObject);
    procedure Header1Sizing(Sender: TObject; ASection, AWidth: Integer);
    procedure DBArtistGridKeyDown(Sender: TObject; var Key: Word;
      Shift: TShiftState);
    procedure DBGrid2KeyDown(Sender: TObject; var Key: Word;
      Shift: TShiftState);
  private
    procedure Loaded; override;
    procedure CreateParams(var Params: TCreateParams); override;
  end;

var
  IndexForm: TIndexForm;

implementation

uses
  Main, NewArt, Globals;

{$R *.DFM}

procedure TIndexForm.Loaded;
```

```
begin
   inherited Loaded;
   Visible := false;
   Position := poDefault;
   BorderIcons := [];
   BorderStyle := bsNone;
   HandleNeeded;
   SetBounds(0,0,Width,Height);
end;

procedure TIndexForm.CreateParams(var Params: TCreateParams);
begin
   inherited CreateParams(Params);
   Params.WndParent := (Owner as TForm).Handle;
   Params.Style := WS_CHILD or WS_CLIPSIBLINGS;
   Params.X := 0;
   Params.Y := 0;
end;

procedure TIndexForm.sbSearchClick(Sender: TObject);
var
   S: string;
begin
   S := '';
   InputQuery('Search Dialog', 'Enter search string', S);
   case IndexMode of
     imPrimary: Form1.tblArtist.FindNearest([S]);
     imMusic: Form1.tblArtist.FindNearest([MusicStr, S]);
     imBook: Form1.tblArtist.FindNearest([BookStr, S]);
   end;
end;

procedure TIndexForm.FormCreate(Sender: TObject);
begin
   Header1.SectionWidth[0] := DBArtistGrid.Width;
end;

procedure TIndexForm.Header1Sizing(Sender: TObject; ASection,
   AWidth: Integer);
begin
   DBArtistGrid.Width := Header1.SectionWidth[0];
end;

procedure TIndexForm.DBArtistGridKeyDown(Sender: TObject; var Key: Word;
   Shift: TShiftState);
begin
   if (key = vk_Insert) or (key = vk_Delete) then
     Key := 0;
end;


end.
```

Listing 20.3. The `Artist` form for the Music program.

```
unit Artist1;

interface

uses
  SysUtils, WinProcs, Messages,
  Classes, Graphics, Controls,
  Forms, Dialogs, WinTypes,
  Grids, DBGrids, StdCtrls,
  Mask, DBCtrls, DB,
  ExtCtrls, Buttons;

type
  TArtistForm = class(TForm)
    Panel1: TPanel;
    Panel2: TPanel;
    dbeLast: TDBEdit;
    dbeFirst: TDBEdit;
    sbInsert: TSpeedButton;
    Label1: TLabel;
    Label2: TLabel;
    dbeType: TDBEdit;
    DBEdit2: TDBEdit;
    dbeDied: TDBEdit;
    dbeBirthPlace: TDBEdit;
    dbeComment: TDBMemo;
    Label3: TLabel;
    Label4: TLabel;
    Label5: TLabel;
    Label6: TLabel;
    Label7: TLabel;
    sbDelete: TSpeedButton;
    Shape3: TShape;
    Shape4: TShape;
    DBNavigator1: TDBNavigator;
    procedure sbInsertClick(Sender: TObject);
    procedure sbDeleteClick(Sender: TObject);
  private
    procedure Loaded; override;
    procedure CreateParams(var Params: TCreateParams); override;
  public
    { Public declarations }
  end;

var
  ArtistForm: TArtistForm;

implementation

uses
  Main, NewArt, Index1,
  Globals;

{$R *.DFM}

procedure TArtistForm.Loaded;
```

```
begin
   inherited Loaded;
   Visible := false;
   Position := poDefault;
   BorderIcons := [];
   BorderStyle := bsNone;
   HandleNeeded;
   SetBounds(0,0,Width,Height);
end;

procedure TArtistForm.CreateParams(var Params: TCreateParams);
begin
  inherited CreateParams(Params);
  Params.WndParent := (Owner as TForm).Handle;
  Params.Style := WS_CHILD or WS_CLIPSIBLINGS;
  Params.X := 0;
  Params.Y := 0;
end;

procedure TArtistForm.sbInsertClick(Sender: TObject);
begin
  Form1.tblArtist.Insert;
  case IndexMode of
    imBook: Form1.tblArtist.FieldByName('Type').AsString := 'Book';
    imMusic: Form1.tblArtist.FieldByName('Type').AsString := 'Music';
  else
     Form1.tblArtist.FieldByName('Type').AsString := 'Music';
  end;
  NewArtist.ShowModal;
end;

procedure TArtistForm.sbDeleteClick(Sender: TObject);
var
  S: string;
begin
  with Form1.tblArtist do
    S := FieldByName('Last').AsString + ', ' + FieldByName('First').AsString;
  if MessageDlg('Delete Record ' + S , mtConfirmation, [mbYes, mbNo], 0) = idYes
then
     Form1.tblArtist.Delete;
end;

end.
```

Listing 20.4. The Album form from the Music program.

```
unit Mus2alb;

interface

uses
  SysUtils, WinProcs, Messages,
  Classes, Graphics, Controls,
  Forms, Dialogs, WinTypes,
  Grids, DBGrids, DB,
```

continue.

Listing 20.4. continued

```
  DBTables, Spin, StdCtrls,
  DBCtrls, Mask, ExtCtrls, Buttons;

type
  TMusicAlbum = class(TForm)
    DataSource2: TDataSource;
    Panel1: TPanel;
    Label1: TLabel;
    Label2: TLabel;
    Label4: TLabel;
    dbAlbum: TDBEdit;
    Label5: TLabel;
    Panel2: TPanel;
    DBText1: TDBText;
    Panel3: TPanel;
    DBNavigator1: TDBNavigator;
    sbDelete: TSpeedButton;
    Image1: TImage;
    OpenDialog1: TOpenDialog;
    Bevel1: TBevel;
    Label3: TLabel;
    Spin1: TSpinButton;
    Bevel2: TBevel;
    Image2: TImage;
    lcbType: TDBLookupComboBox;
    lcbLoud: TDBLookupComboBox;
    lcbMedium: TDBLookupComboBox;
    GetAlbum: TStoredProc;
    sbInsert: TSpeedButton;
    procedure Spin1DownClick(Sender: TObject);
    procedure Spin1UpClick(Sender: TObject);
    procedure ComboChange(Sender: TObject);
    procedure sbInsertClick(Sender: TObject);
    procedure sbDeleteClick(Sender: TObject);
    procedure DataSource2StateChange(Sender: TObject);
    procedure FormKeyDown(Sender: TObject; var Key: Word;
      Shift: TShiftState);
  private
    procedure Loaded; override;
    procedure CreateParams(var Params: TCreateParams); override;
    procedure LoadCombos(T: TTable; C: TComboBox);
    procedure SetCombo(T: TTable; C: TComboBox);
    procedure SetField(T: TTable; C: TComboBox);
    procedure SetLabelColor(Color: TColor);
  public
    { Public declarations }
  end;

var
  MusicAlbum: TMusicAlbum;

implementation

uses
  Main, StrBox, Globals;

{$R *.DFM}
```

```
procedure TMusicAlbum.Loaded;
begin
   inherited Loaded;
   Visible := false;
   Position := poDefault;
   BorderIcons := [];
   BorderStyle := bsNone;
   HandleNeeded;
   SetBounds(0,0,Width,Height);
end;

procedure TMusicAlbum.CreateParams(var Params: TCreateParams);
begin
   inherited CreateParams(Params);
   Params.WndParent := (Owner as TForm).Handle;
   Params.Style := WS_CHILD or WS_CLIPSIBLINGS;
   Params.X := 0;
   Params.Y := 0;
end;

procedure TMusicAlbum.LoadCombos(T: TTable; C: TComboBox);
var
   S: string;
begin
   T.Open;
   while not T.EOF do begin
     S := T.Fields[0].AsString;
     C.Items.Add(S);
     T.Next;
   end;
   T.Close;
end;

procedure TMusicAlbum.Spin1DownClick(Sender: TObject);
var
   i: Integer;
begin
   i := Form1.tblAlbum.FieldByName('Rating').AsInteger;
   if i < 1 then i := 1;
   if i < 10 then Inc(i);
   Form1.tblAlbum.Edit;
   Form1.tblAlbum.FieldByName('Rating').AsInteger := i;
   Form1.tblAlbum.Post;
end;

procedure TMusicAlbum.Spin1UpClick(Sender: TObject);
var
   i: Integer;
begin
   i := Form1.tblAlbum.FieldByName('Rating').AsInteger;
   if i < 1 then i := 1;
   if i > 1 then Dec(i);
   Form1.tblAlbum.Edit;
   Form1.tblAlbum.FieldByName('Rating').AsInteger := i;
   Form1.tblAlbum.Post;
end;
```

continues

Listing 20.4. continued

```pascal
procedure TMusicAlbum.SetCombo(T: TTable; C: TComboBox);
var
  i: Integer;
  S: string;
begin
  T.Open;
  i := Form1.tblAlbum.FieldByName(Shorten(T.Name, 3)).AsInteger;
  T.IndexName := T.TableName + '_CODE_NDX';
  if T.FindKey([i]) then begin
    S := T.Fields[0].AsString;
    C.ItemIndex := C.Items.IndexOf(S);
  end else
    C.ItemIndex := -1;
  T.IndexName := '';
end;

procedure TMusicAlbum.SetField(T: TTable; C: TComboBox);
begin
  T.Open;
  T.FindKey([C.Items.Strings[C.ItemIndex]]);
  Form1.tblAlbum.Edit;
  Form1.tblAlbum.FieldByName(Shorten(T.Name, 3)).AsInteger :=
  ➥T.FieldByName('Code').AsInteger;
  Form1.tblAlbum.Post;
end;

procedure TMusicAlbum.ComboChange(Sender: TObject);
var
  S: string;
  T: TTable;
begin
  S := GetName((Sender as TComboBox).Name);
  T := TTable(FindComponent('tbl' +_ S));
  SetField(T, Sender as TComboBox);
end;

procedure TMusicAlbum.SetLabelColor(Color: TCclor);
var
  i: Integer;
begin
  for i := 0 to ComponentCount - 1 do
    if Components[i] is TLabel then
      TLabel(Components[i]).Font.Color := Color;
end;

procedure TMusicAlbum.sbInsertClick(Sender: TObject);
var
  S: string;
begin
  S := '';
  if not InputQuery('Insert New Album Dialog', 'Enter album name', S) then Exit;
  Form1.tblAlbum.Insert;
  GetAlbum.ExecProc;
  Form1.tblAlbum.FieldByName('Code').AsInteger := GetAlbum.Params[0].AsInteger;
  Form1.tblAlbum.FieldByName('Album').AsString := S;
  Form1.tblAlbum.FieldByName('Types').AsString := '';
  Form1.tblAlbum.FieldByName('Loudness').AsString := '';
```

```
      Form1.tblAlbum.FieldByName('Medium').AsString := '';
      Form1.tblAlbum.Post;
      lcbType.SetFocus;
end;

procedure TMusicAlbum.sbDeleteClick(Sender: TObject);
var
  S: string;
begin
  S := Form1.tblAlbum.FieldByName('Album').AsString;
  if MessageDlg('Delete ' + S + ' from Album Table?', mtConfirmation, [mbYes,
mbNo], 0) = idYes then
     Form1.tblAlbum.Delete;
end;

procedure TMusicAlbum.DataSource2StateChange(Sender: TObject);
begin
  case Form1.tblArtist.State of
   dsBrowse: SetLabelColor(clBlack);
   dsEdit: SetLabelColor(clRed);
   dsInsert: SetLabelColor(clRed);
  end;
end;

procedure TMusicAlbum.FormKeyDown(Sender: TObject; var Key: Word;
  Shift: TShiftState);
begin
  if ssAlt in Shift then
    ShowMessage('MusicAlbum');
end;

end.
```

Listing 20.5. The Book form from the Music program.

```
unit bookfrm1;

interface

uses
  SysUtils, WinProcs, WinTypes,
  Messages, Classes, Graphics,
  Controls, Forms, Dialogs,
  DB, StdCtrls, Mask,
  DBCtrls, DBTables, ExtCtrls,
  Buttons, Spin;

type
  TBookForm = class(TForm)
    Panel1: TPanel;
    Panel2: TPanel;
    DBEdit1: TDBEdit;
    DBNavigator1: TDBNavigator;
    sbInsert: TSpeedButton;
    sbDelete: TSpeedButton;
```

continues

Listing 20.5. continued

```
    Book: TLabel;
    Label2: TLabel;
    Label3: TLabel;
    Bevel1: TBevel;
    Label1: TLabel;
    Panel3: TPanel;
    DBText1: TDBText;
    Spin1: TSpinButton;
    Shape1: TShape;
    Shape2: TShape;
    Bevel2: TBevel;
    lcbTypes: TDBLookupComboBox;
    DBLookupComboBox2: TDBLookupComboBox;
    GetAlbum: TStoredProc;
    procedure ComboChange(Sender: TObject);
    procedure sbInsertClick(Sender: TObject);
    procedure sbDeleteClick(Sender: TObject);
    procedure Spin1DownClick(Sender: TObject);
    procedure Spin1UpClick(Sender: TObject);
    procedure Spin1Enter(Sender: TObject);
    procedure Spin1Exit(Sender: TObject);
  private
    procedure Loaded; override;
    procedure CreateParams(var Params: TCreateParams); override;
    procedure LoadCombos(T: TTable; C: TComboBox);
    procedure SetCombo(T: TTable; C: TComboBox);
    procedure SetField(T: TTable; C: TComboBox);
  public
    { Public declarations }
  end;

var
  BookForm: TBookForm;

implementation

uses
  StrBox, Main, Globals;

{$R *.DFM}

procedure TBookForm.Loaded;
begin
  inherited Loaded;
  Visible := false;
  Position := poDefault;
  BorderIcons := [];
  BorderStyle := bsNone;
  HandleNeeded;
  SetBounds(0,0,Width,Height);
end;

procedure TBookForm.CreateParams(var Params: TCreateParams);
begin
  inherited CreateParams(Params);
  Params.WndParent := (Owner as TForm).Handle;
  Params.Style := WS_CHILD or WS_CLIPSIBLINGS;
  Params.X := 0;
```

```
    Params.Y := 0;
  end;

procedure TBookForm.LoadCombos(T: TTable; C: TComboBox);
var
  S: string;
begin
  T.Open;
  while not T.EOF do begin
    S := T.Fields[0].AsString;
    C.Items.Add(S);
    T.Next;
  end;
  T.Close;
end;

procedure TBookForm.SetCombo(T: TTable; C: TComboBox);
var
  i: Integer;
  S: string;
begin
  T.Open;
  i := Form1.tblAlbum.FieldByName(Shorten(T.Name, 3)).AsInteger;
  T.IndexName := T.TableName + '_CODE_NDX';
  if T.FindKey([i]) then begin
    S := T.Fields[0].AsString;
    C.ItemIndex := C.Items.IndexOf(S);
  end else
    C.ItemIndex := -1;
  T.IndexName := '';
end;


procedure TBookForm.SetField(T: TTable; C: TComboBox);
begin
  T.Open;
  if not T.FindKey([C.Items.Strings[C.ItemIndex]]) then Exit;
  Form1.tblAlbum.Edit;
  Form1.tblAlbum.FieldByName(Shorten(T.Name, 3)).AsInteger :=
  ➥T.FieldByName('Code').AsInteger;
  Form1.tblAlbum.Post;
end;


procedure TBookForm.ComboChange(Sender: TObject);
var
  S: string;
  T: TTable;
begin
  S := GetName((Sender as TComboBox).Name);
  T := TTable(FindComponent(S + 'Tbl'));
  SetField(T, Sender as TComboBox);
end;

procedure TBookForm.sbInsertClick(Sender: TObject);
var
  S: string;
begin
```

continues

Listing 20.5. continued

```
  S := '';
  if not InputQuery('Insert New Album Dialog', 'Enter album name', S) then Exit;
  Form1.tblAlbum.Insert;
  GetAlbum.ExecProc;
  Form1.tblAlbum.FieldByName('Code').AsInteger := GetAlbum.Params[0].AsInteger;
  Form1.tblAlbum.FieldByName('Album').AsString := S;
  Form1.tblAlbum.FieldByName('Types').AsString := '';
  Form1.tblAlbum.FieldByName('Medium').AsString := '';
  Form1.tblAlbum.Post;
  lcbTypes.SetFocus;
end;

procedure TBookForm.sbDeleteClick(Sender: TObject);
var
  S: string;
begin
  S := Form1.tblAlbum.FieldByName('Album').AsString;
  if MessageDlg('Delete ' + S + ' from Album Table?', mtConfirmation, [mbYes,
  ➡mbNo], 0) = idYes then
    Form1.tblAlbum.Delete;
end;

procedure TBookForm.Spin1DownClick(Sender: TObject);
var
  i: Integer;
begin
  i := Form1.tblAlbum.FieldByName('Rating').AsInteger;
  if i < 1 then i := 1;
  if i < 10 then Inc(i);
  Form1.tblAlbum.Edit;
  Form1.tblAlbum.FieldByName('Rating').AsInteger := i;
  Form1.tblAlbum.Post;
end;

procedure TBookForm.Spin1UpClick(Sender: TObject);
var
  i: Integer;
begin
  i := Form1.tblAlbum.FieldByName('Rating').AsInteger;
  if i < 1 then i := 1;
  if i > 1 then Dec(i);
  Form1.tblAlbum.Edit;
  Form1.tblAlbum.FieldByName('Rating').AsInteger := i;
  Form1.tblAlbum.Post;
end;

procedure TBookForm.Spin1Enter(Sender: TObject);
begin
  Label1.Color := clBlue;
end;

procedure TBookForm.Spin1Exit(Sender: TObject);
begin
  Label1.Color := clBlack;
end;

end.
```

Listing 20.6. The `New Artist` form from the Music program.

```
unit Newart;

interface

uses
  SysUtils, WinTypes, WinProcs,
  Messages, Classes, Graphics,
  Controls, Forms, Dialogs,
  StdCtrls, Mask, DBCtrls,
  DB, Buttons, DBTables;

type
  TNewArtist = class(TForm)
    dbLast: TDBEdit;
    dbFirst: TDBEdit;
    Label1: TLabel;
    Label2: TLabel;
    bbCancel: TBitBtn;
    bbOk: TBitBtn;
    DataSource1: TDataSource;
    Label3: TLabel;
    DBComboBox1: TDBComboBox;
    MusicGen: TStoredProc;
    procedure bbOkClick(Sender: TObject);
    procedure bbCancelClick(Sender: TObject);
    procedure FormShow(Sender: TObject);
  end;

var
  NewArtist: TNewArtist;

implementation

uses
  Main;

{$R *.DFM}

procedure TNewArtist.bbOkClick(Sender: TObject);
begin
  MusicGen.ExecProc;
  Form1.tblArtist['Code'] := MusicGen.Params[0].AsInteger;
  Form1.tblArtist.Post;
end;

procedure TNewArtist.bbCancelClick(Sender: TObject);
begin
  Form1.tblArtist.Cancel;
end;

procedure TNewArtist.FormShow(Sender: TObject);
begin
  dbLast.SetFocus;
end;

end.
```

Listing 20.7. The `Globals` form tracks some global variables and contains some general-purpose utilities.

```
unit globals;

interface

const
  BookStr = 'book';
  MusicStr = 'music';

type
  TIndexMode = (imPrimary, imMusic, imBook);

var
  IndexMode: TIndexMode;

function GetName(S: string): string;
implementation

uses
  StrBox;

function GetName(S: string): string;
var
  Temp: string;
begin
  Temp := ReverseStr(S);
  Temp := Shorten(Temp, 2);
  Result := ReverseStr(Temp);
end;

end.
```

Listing 20.8. The `Search` unit lets you search on the `Album` table.

```
unit Search1;

interface

uses
  Windows, Messages, SysUtils,
  Classes, Graphics, Controls,
  Forms, Dialogs, StdCtrls,
  Buttons, ExtCtrls, Grids,
  DBGrids, DB, DBTables;

type
  TAlbumSearch = class(TForm)
    Table1: TTable;
    DataSource1: TDataSource;
    DBGrid1: TDBGrid;
    Panel1: TPanel;
    Edit1: TEdit;
    bbOk: TBitBtn;
```

```
    bbCancel: TBitBtn;
    procedure Edit1Change(Sender: TObject);
  public
    function AlbumSearchModal: Integer;
  end;

var
  AlbumSearch: TAlbumSearch;

implementation

{$R *.DFM}

function TAlbumSearch.AlbumSearchModal: Integer;
begin
  if ShowModal = mrCancel then
    Result := -1
  else
    Result := Table1['GroupCode'];
end;

procedure TAlbumSearch.Edit1Change(Sender: TObject);
begin
  Table1.FindNearest([Edit1.Text]);
end;

end.
```

You have already had several different explanations of how the Music program is structured and how it works, so I won't spend any time discussing the program itself. I would recommend, however, that you spend some time working with it so that you understand how to interact with it; practice inserting records, deleting records, and searching for records.

While working with this program you should remember that it is an example from a book, and not a polished professional program. You will probably be able to find some ways to improve this program, and it should not be difficult to crash it if you set your mind to it. As always, I have had to make a choice between keeping the program easy to understand, and loading it up with code that does nothing more than check for user errors.

What the Music program does well is show you how to work with a relational database in a Delphi program. There are five different interrelated tables in this program, all working together to produce a particular result. The thing to come away with when studying this program is how you can make the tables in a relational database work together seamlessly toward a particular end. This chapter is about how to construct a powerful relational database, and the Music program is the main exhibit.

Because this program uses InterBase, you could use it in a rigorous multiuser environment without fear that it would collapse under the load. For instance, there is no reason why this program, as is, could not handle two or three hundred simultaneous users.

NOTE

Most of the DataAccess controls for the Music program are placed on the main form. I could also have placed them on a datamodule, but on a paged program of this sort no visual tools are ever placed directly on the main form, so its surface is free. Given the circumstances, why bother with a datamodule?

Suppressing the Password: The *TDatabase* Object

The TDatabase object on the main form has its AliasName property set to the Music alias. This alias was defined in the Database Explorer, and it points to the tables that make up the music database. The alias is shown in Figure 20.5.

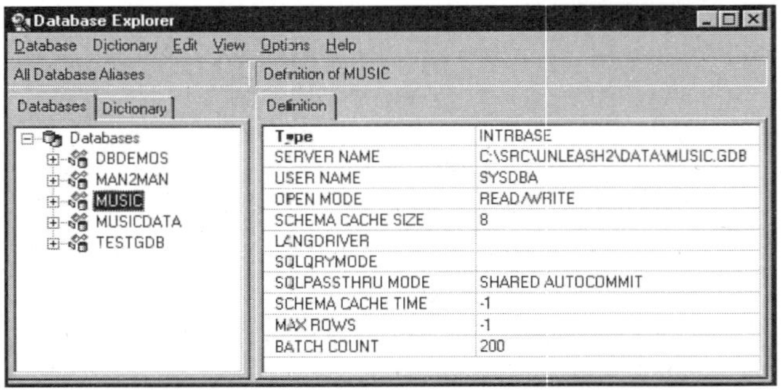

FIGURE 20.5.

The alias for MUSIC.GDB as it appears in the Database Explorer.

The DatabaseName property of the TDatabase object is set to the string MusicData, which is the alias attached to by all the other TTable, TStoredProc, and TQuery objects in the program. Remember: Only the TDatabase object attaches directly to the Music alias. This enables you to point the entire program at a second database by changing only one variable: the AliasName property. This feature can be handy if you need to experiment with the program, but don't want to be working with your primary data while you are doing the testing.

The Params property for the TDatabase object contains the following information:

```
USER NAME=SYSDBA
PASSWORD=masterkey
```

The LoginPrompt property is then set to False, which makes it possible to launch the program without having to enter a password. This is pretty much a necessity during development, and it's a useful trait in a program like this that will probably have little fear of hostile attacks on its data.

The *FormCreate* Event

It's up to the FormCreate event for the main form to create the child windows that hold all the main controls used in the program:

```
procedure TForm1.FormCreate(Sender: TObject);
var
  i: Integer;
begin
  IndexForm := TIndexForm.Create(Self);
  MusicAlbum := TMusicAlbum.Create(Self);
  ArtistForm := TArtistForm.Create(Self);
  BookForm := TBookForm.Create(Self);
  ChildForms[0] := IndexForm;
  ChildForms[1] := ArtistForm;
  ChildForms[2] := MusicAlbum;
  ChildForms[3] := BookForm;
  for i := 0 to MaxForms do
    ChildForms[i].Show;
end;
```

The first four lines of the routine create the forms. The next four lines assign them to an array of TForm objects. You can then use this array to iterate through all the main forms for the program, as shown in the last two lines of the routine, and in the OnResize response method shown above.

The following type is used to track the child forms:

```
TChildType = (cfIndex, cfArtist, cfAlbum, cfBook);
```

As you can see, cfIndex, with an ordinal value of 0, would give you immediate access to the Index form if you wrote code that looks like this:

```
ChildForms[cfIndex].Width := X;
```

The cfArtist, cfAlbum, and cfBook elements can also be used to access their appropriate related forms in the ChildForms array.

The importance of referencing the ChildForms array by number increases when you see that the TTabSet control has four tabs on it, with element zero equal to Index, element one to Artist, and so on. This means that the tabs clicked by the user also map into the enumerated type. To see this principle in action, see the FormResize method referenced above, and the TabSet1Change method discussed at the beginning of the next section.

Filters and Lookups

Whenever the user clicks one of the tabs in order to bring it to the front, the following routine is called:

```
procedure TForm1.TabSet1Change(Sender: TObject; NewTab: Integer;
  var AllowChange: Boolean);
```

```
begin
  tblTypes.Filtered := False;
  tblMedium.Filtered := False;
  FChildType := TChildType(NewTab);
  if (FChildType = cfBook) or (FChildType = cfAlbum) then begin
    tblTypes.Filtered := True;
    tblMedium.Filtered := True;
  end;

  ChildForms[NewTab].BringToFront;
end;
```

The key line here is the last, which is the one that brings the appropriate form to the top of the stack of visible forms.

The first seven lines of code in the TabSet1Change method are used to set up the Album and Books forms so that their dropdown combo boxes provide the right list of choices to the user. In particular, when you flip to the Album page, and drop down the Types combo box, you see a list of choices associated with albums, such as Jazz, Folk, and so on. If you then flip to the Book page, you see a list of options associated with books.

You saw earlier that the Types table is divided into two sections. Entries with an ID less than 1,000 are associated with music, and those with an ID of 1,000 or greater are associated with books. The OnFilterRecord event is used to filter this list so that the user sees the appropriate half of the list when viewing the appropriate page.

TabSet1Change starts filtering data only if the user chooses the Album or Book pages:

```
if (FChildType = cfBook) or (FChildType = cfAlbum) then begin
  tblTypes.Filtered := True;
  tblMedium.Filtered := True;
end;
```

The actual OnFilterRecord events look like this:

```
procedure TForm1.tblTypesFilterRecord(DataSet: TDataSet;
  var Accept: Boolean);
begin
  if FChildType = cfBook then
    Accept := tblTypes['Code'] > 999
  else if FChildType = cfAlbum then
    Accept := tblTypes['Code'] < 1000;
end;

procedure TForm1.tblMediumFilterRecord(DataSet: TDataSet;
  var Accept: Boolean);
begin
  if FChildType = cfBook then
    Accept := tblMedium['Code'] > 999
  else if FChildType = cfAlbum then
    Accept := tblMedium['Code'] < 1000;
end;
```

A quick glance shows that this code filters the records in the Types table so that the user can see only those that are appropriate to the currently selected page.

To actually show the types to the user, I employ a `TdbLookupComboBox`. In particular, note that the `Types` field can be assigned values by simply doing a lookup in the `Types` table. I define a lookup field for this purpose in the `Album` table, calling the field `luTypes`. There are also `luMedium` and `luLoudness` lookup fields. These are standard lookups of the kind described in Chapter 17, "Fields and Database Tools." As I mentioned earlier, the `Types`, `Loudness`, and `Medium` tables were designed to make it easy to do lookups in them from the `Album` table. The fruits of this forethought are the easy-to-use `TdbLookupComboBoxes` on the `Album` and `Book` pages. If you want to assign a type to an album, you just drop down the combo box and pick a `Type`: Jazz, Rock, Classical, and so on.

If you want to add more types, simply put more entries in the `Types` table. Make sure that musical entries have an ID under 1,000 and that book entries have an ID of 1,000 or greater.

Searching on the *Album* Table

You usually see the `Album` table as a detail table. For instance, you might be looking at the entries for Vivaldi or Neil Young, and in the detail table you could see the albums associated with these artists. But what if you want to search for a particular album and you don't know the artist associated with it? How do you go backwards from the detail table to the master table?

To begin, I created a search dialog like the one shown in Figure 20.6. This dialog allows the user to type into the edit control at the bottom of the screen in order to perform an incremental search on the albums listed in the grid at the top of the screen. The grid is just a view into the `Album` table, with the `Columns` property of the grid being used to filter out all but the `Album` field.

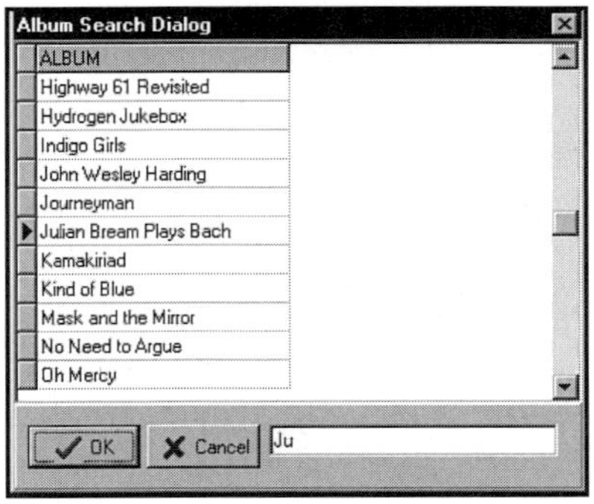

FIGURE 20.6.

The Search *dialog lets you search on the* Album *table.*

Here is the code, attached to the `OnChange` event of the edit control, that lets the user search through the `Album` table:

```
procedure TAlbumSearch.Edit1Change(Sender: TObject);
begin
  Table1.FindNearest([Edit1.Text]);
end;
```

Notice that this is a standard edit control, and not a TdbEdit control.

The dialog has one other method, used to report the results of the search back to the calling routine:

```
function TAlbumSearch.AlbumSearchModal: Integer;
begin
  if ShowModal = mrCancel then
    Result := -1
  else
    Result := Table1['GroupCode'];
end;
```

If the user clicks the Cancel button, the routine returns -1, which means that no further processing is necessary. If the user clicks the OK button, the GroupCode associated with the current record is returned. The GroupCode, of course, contains the Code from the record in the Artist table that you now want to locate.

Here is the routine on the main form that calls the SearchAlbum dialog:

```
procedure TForm1.SearchAlbums1Click(Sender: TObject);
var
  OutCome: Integer;
begin
  AlbumSearch := TAlbumSearch.Create(Self);
  OutCome := AlbumSearch.AlbumSearchModal;
  AlbumSearch.Free;
  if OutCome = -1 then
    Exit
  else begin
    FArtistCode := OutCome;
    tblArtist.FindFirst;
  end;
end;
```

The first three lines of the routine allocate memory for the dialog, call the AlbumSearchModal method, and free the memory associated with the dialog. Note that you should choose Project | Options | Forms and remove the SearchAlbum dialog from the Auto-Create list box in order to make this process work correctly.

After the dialog has been shown to the user, the integer OutCome variable holds either a -1 or the Code of the record that you want to find in the Artist table. If the value is -1, the user chooses Cancel, and the function immediately exits. If there is a valid code in the OutCome variable, it is assigned to a global variable called FArtistCode, and a FindFirst operation takes place on the Artist table.

FindFirst operations on database tables cause the OnFilterRecord event associated with the table to be called until a particular record is found. Here is the OnFilterRecord event for the Artist table:

```
procedure TForm1.tblArtistFilterRecord(DataSet: TDataSet;
  var Accept: Boolean);
begin
  Accept := tblArtist['Code'] = FArtistCode;
end;
```

Clearly this is a simple process. You should note, however, that code of this kind is highly optimized and will allow you to perform very fast searches.

> **NOTE**
>
> It's important to understand why this search is carried out in this manner rather than using a call to FindNearest or FindKey. These latter two calls are dependent on particular indices being in place. In this case, you don't want to switch indices, but want instead to perform a search in the background without doing anything that might change the way the data looks to the user. The FindFirst or FindNext procedures fit the bill in this case and allow you to perform the search in a rapid, unobtrusive manner.

Viewing a Range of Data

The Music program stores lists of books and albums. Naturally there are times when you will want to filter out either the books or albums and concentrate on just the type of record you are currently using. The Types field of the Artist table allows you to do this. In particular, this field contains either the word "Books," or the word "Music," depending on the type of the currently selected artist.

> **NOTE**
>
> This is another situation where the relentless inflexibility of databases can be a bit frustrating. For instance, what can you do about musicians, such as Arnold Schoenberg, Bob Dylan, and Jimmy Buffet, who also write books? The simplest solution, and the one I have opted for, is to simply ignore this situation. Another possible option would be to create a Type called BothAuthorAndMusician, but that has its own problems since Jimmy Buffet would suddenly not be listed in a filter set to catch musicians. A more thorough solution would be to turn the Types field into part of a many-to-many relationship. But then you are faced with difficulties whenever you want to perform a Range operation on this field, as well as the innate complexity of executing the many-to-many relationship. In general, I find that ignoring the exceptions to a rule really is the best way of handling certain annoying situations!

Because the Types field is expected to contain a certain kind of data, you must rigorously control the way data is put into this field. I am not going to discuss the input routines used in this program for inserting records, but you might want to glance at them and notice that I never leave it up to the user to just type characters into this field. Instead, I force the user to make a choice between the word "Book" or the word "Music." In situations like this, you should consider having the Types field declared as Not Null.

If the user chooses the menu choice that filters the Artist table so that only records of albums or books are shown, the following procedure is called:

```
procedure TForm1.ShowOnlyMusic1Click(Sender: TObject);
begin
  IndexMode := TIndexMode((Sender as TMenuItem).Tag);
  case IndexMode of
    imPrimary: tblArtist.IndexName := 'ARTIST_LASTFIRST_NDX';
    imMusic: begin
      tblArtist.IndexName := 'ARTIST_TYPE_NDX';
      tblArtist.SetRange(['Music'], ['Music']);
    end;
    imBook: begin
      tblArtist.IndexName := 'ARTIST_TYPE_NDX';
      tblArtist.SetRange(['Book'], ['Book']);
    end;
  end;
end;
```

The IndexMode is calculated by the Tag field of the menu item selected to call the routine. The possible menu choices are:

```
Show All
Show Only Music
Show Only Books
```

Here are the possible IndexModes as found in the Globals units:

```
TIndexMode = (imPrimary, imMusic, imBook);
```

If the user selects Show All, the default sort method for the table is selected:

```
imPrimary: tblArtist.IndexName := 'ARTIST_LASTFIRST_NDX';
```

If the user elects to see only albums, the following code is executed:

```
imMusic: begin
  tblArtist.IndexName := 'ARTIST_TYPE_NDX';
  tblArtist.SetRange(['Music'], ['Music']);
end;
```

This code selects an index that sorts on the Types, Last, and First fields. The range is then set so that only those records with a Type field of Music will be shown. Notice that in this situation, it's OK to re-sort the data in the middle of the operation, since the user expects the data to change in appearance after choosing this menu option. The user would not, however, expect the data to be resorted in the middle of a search operation.

Summary

That's all I'm going to say about the Music program. There are a few lines of code in the program that were never mentioned, but most of the program has been reviewed in this chapter.

Once again, this program contains a lot of the basic code that anyone uses when constructing a relational database with Delphi. The particular example shown is not robust enough to use in a professional setting, but it gives you a good feeling for how to proceed if you want to construct such an application.

In particular, you got a good look at the techniques used to create a robust database with referential integrity. You also saw how to use generators, triggers, and stored procedures, and how to perform filters and lookups on relational data. In general, this chapter is the one that sums up the core information necessary to produce a professional database program. If you understand all this material, you are not yet necessarily an expert, but you are ready to start building relational databases in a professional setting.

ReportSmith

21

by Andy Fears

IN THIS CHAPTER

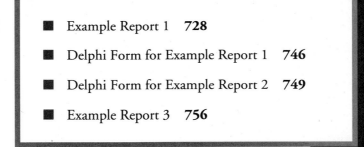

Now that you have finished the front end, it's time to write the reports. Which report writing tool do you use? The obvious choice for Delphi programmers is ReportSmith because it is bundled with Delphi. This chapter details the interface between Delphi and ReportSmith. Unfortunately, in only one chapter I cannot go into too much detail on the ReportSmith side, but I can provide firm foundation for further ReportSmith development.

You are going to build two reports, both with the exact same layout and functionality. "Why build the same report twice," I hear you ask, "are you crazy?" There is reason behind this madness. The first report is built in the traditional sense, using ReportSmith. It generates its own SQL statement and uses report variables to interface with Delphi. The second report takes advantage of the new Delphi32 features and interfaces with Delphi using the TQuery component.

The last section examines a third example of a Delphi form. This form is used to dynamically create a ReportSmith report using Delphi.

Example Report 1

This chapter demonstrates how to build two reports that are linked to a front-end Delphi application. In the examples that follow, assume that you are working on a project for a video rental store. You will use the demo tables that come with ReportSmith. These are dBASE databases that reside in the rptsmith\demos directory. The first report you will build is a Customer Invoice report that lists each customer and its corresponding invoices. The manager of the video rental store has asked for four specific criteria for the report she wants you to build:

- It must report either all customers or one specific customer.
- It must show the total amount owed by each customer.
- It must calculate a discounted total for each invoice according to a specified discount percentage.
- It must be able to highlight invoices that are over a certain dollar amount.

Building Reports

Having heard the requests from the rental manager, you can now begin. Start up ReportSmith and select Columnar Report as the report type. You are now presented with the Report Query dialog box, with the Tables page showing. (See Figure 21.1.)

The Report Query dialog box has several pages, including Tables, Selections, and Sorting. This dialog box is used to build the SQL statement for the report. (For example, adding a table adds a table to the SQL; adding a sort order adds an `Order By` statement to the SQL; adding Database Grouping adds a `Group By` statement.) Understanding how each page of the Report Query dialog box manipulates the SQL statement will greatly help your report building and will further your understanding of the SQL language, which is key to building reports.

FIGURE 21.1.

Adding the CUSTOMER and INVOICES tables to the report.

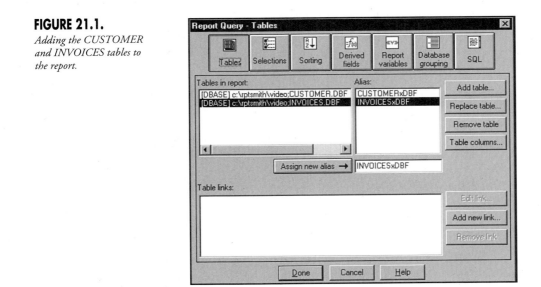

Select Add Table and choose the CUSTOMER.DBF table. Next choose Add Table and select the INVOICES.DBF table. Using the Table Columns button, select the following columns to be included in the report from each table:

CUSTOMER TABLE COLUMNS

CSTMR_ID
CSTMR_NAME

INVOICES TABLE COLUMNS

INVOICE_ID
CSTMR_ID
DATE
SUBTOTAL
FREIGHT
TOTAL

Choose the Done button. What happens? ReportSmith displays a warning, shown in Figure 21.2. This warning means that you have not linked the two tables within the report. If you proceed, each record from the Customer table will be linked to each record in the Invoices table. To avoid this you must show SQL how the two tables relate to each other. You link the two tables by adding a where clause. From the warning, choose Yes to return to the Report Query dialog box. Next choose Add New Link to display the Create New Table Link dialog box.

FIGURE 21.2.

ReportSmith displays a warning if the SQL query contains tables that are not joined.

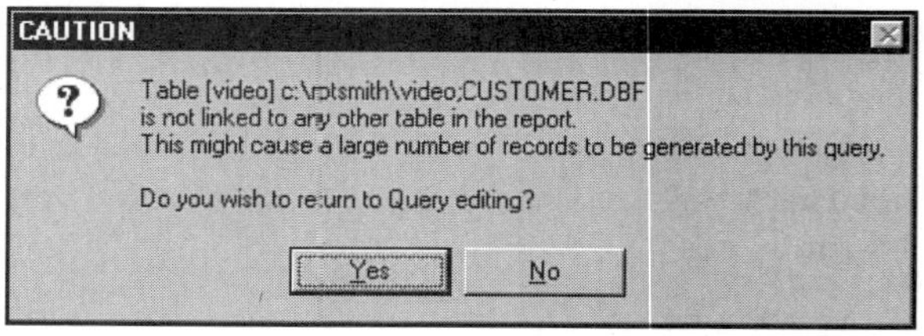

The Create New Table Link dialog box, shown in Figure 21.3, is used to link two tables together. The top section shows the tables included in the report, and the bottom half of the dialog box shows which columns are available within these tables.

Select the CSTMR_ID column from the Customer table and the CSTMR_ID column from the Invoices table. Link these columns using the relational operator (=).

NOTE

ReportSmith tries to guess the join for you by selecting columns that have the same name from each table. It is common practice among database designers to name columns that are used to join tables with the same name.

You will notice that on each side of the Create New Table Link dialog box is an Include Unmatched Records checkbox. When checked, it enables records from the table to be returned even if such records do not satisfy the join condition.

FIGURE 21.3.

Linking tables using the Create New Table Link dialog box.

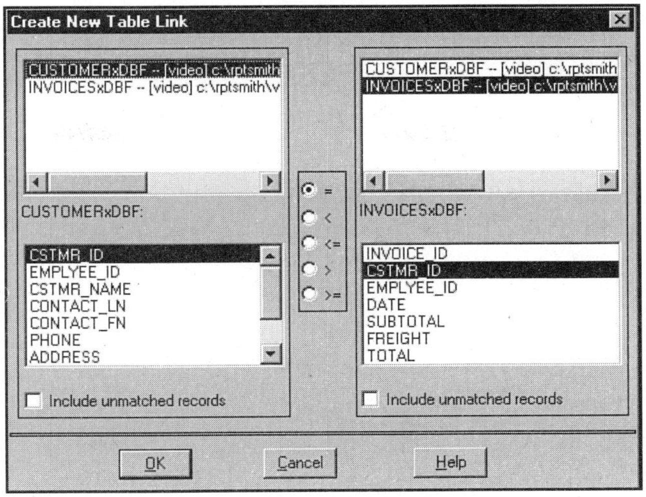

For example, customer "Fred Jones and Company" exists in the Customer table but does not have any invoices in the Invoices table. Because Fred has no matching invoice records, the preceding query skips Fred, and he does not appear in the report.

If you want to see cases like Fred (customers without invoices), check the Include Unmatched Records checkbox. Now customers with no invoices are also returned. The invoice information for these customers is automatically set to null by the SQL query. This option is known as an outer join and is specific for each server. Each server has its own level of support for outer joins; therefore, the checkbox is dynamic and appears only if an outer join is available.

NOTE

Use outer joins only where necessary, because a query with an outer join is not as efficient as a query with a straight join.

Now that you have completed the initial SQL statement for the report, choose the Done button. ReportSmith runs the SQL query and returns the data to the report. One of the first things you will notice is that you are presented with live data, not just a representation of the data. Within the ReportSmith design environment you always work with live data so that it is easy to see what the final report will look like to the user.

Initially all data is presented on one line (you will change this later). First, select the first column in the report, then hold down the Shift key and select the last column. All columns are now selected. Choose the Best Fit button from the toolbar. This compresses the column width for each column, so that now all columns fit on one page, as shown in Figure 21.4.

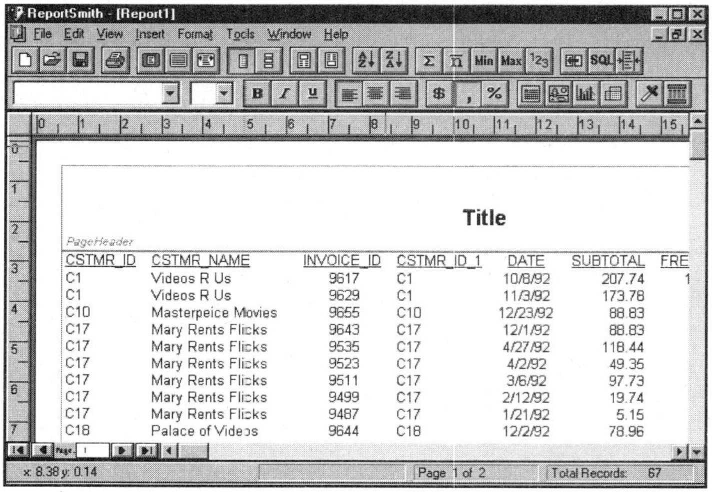

FIGURE 21.4.

The initial layout for the Customer Invoices report.

Now you are ready to lay out the report. Select the two CSTMR_ID columns by holding down the Ctrl key and clicking each column, then remove them by pressing the Del key. These columns are used internally to join the two tables, but they are not needed in the report layout.

NOTE

Deleting columns from the report layout does not remove them from the SQL query. If a column is deleted by mistake it can be added to the layout by using the Insert | Field menu item to display the Insert Field dialog box, shown in Figure 21.5.

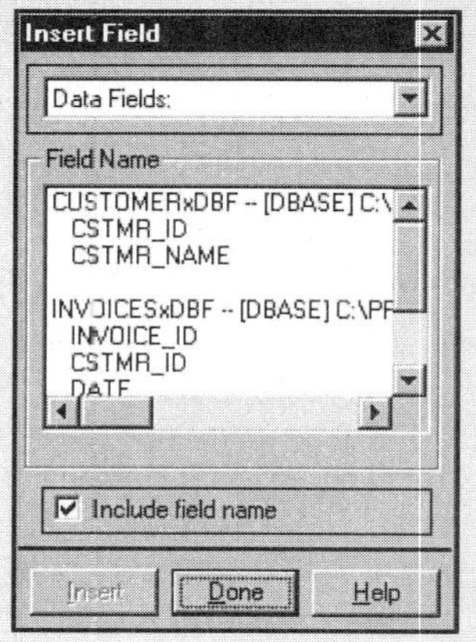

FIGURE 21.5.

The Insert Field dialog box can be used to add fields to the report layout.

As you can now see from the initial layout, the customer information is being repeated because some customers have more than one invoice. You need to tell ReportSmith to group information from the same customer together. In other words, you want to see each customer once, followed by that customer's invoices. To do this you must create a Report Group.

Report Groups are created as a logical way to group the data in your report. To create a Report Group, choose the Tools | Report Groupings menu item. This displays the Define Groups dialog box shown in Figure 21.6.

FIGURE 21.6.

Create Report Grouping using the Define Groups dialog box.

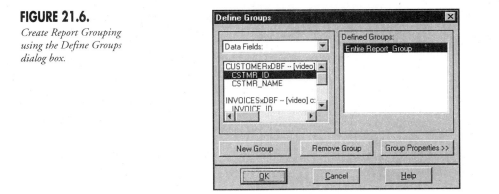

The Define Groups dialog box shows what groups are currently created. In this report the only group present is the Entire_Report_Group. The Entire_Report_Group encapsulates all the data within the report and cannot be deleted. Select the CSTMR_NAME field and the choose New Group. A new group is created and named CSTMR_NAME_Group.

Choose Group Properties, which displays the Group Properties dialog box. The Group Properties dialog box enables you to specify which fields to suppress and how the grouping is performed.

Use the Group By combo box to control how the grouping is performed. There are two options:

- SameValue: This keeps values that are the same together. In this example, you want invoices for the same customer to be kept together, so select this option.

- Every: This enables a hard-coded number of records to be grouped together. For example, you can create a group that groups every 10 records together, regardless of their values.

Select the CSTMR_NAME field and choose Suppress. An asterisk appears next to CSTMR_NAME; this means that the customer's name is no longer repeated for each invoice but appears only for each new customer, as shown in Figure 21.7.

FIGURE 21.7.

Adding properties to the CSTMR_NAME_Group.

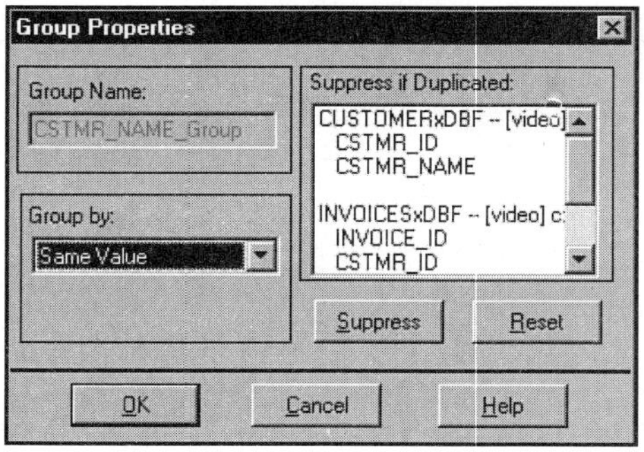

Choose the OK button to close both of these dialog boxes and return to the layout editor. The report layout is changed in accordance with the newly created CSTMR_NAME_Group. ReportSmith has separated the detail section into separate sections, each one belonging to an individual customer. One important point to remember is that Report Groups and the report order go hand in hand. Report grouping is performed by ReportSmith on the client machine. It expects the rows to be returned in the order specified by the Report Groups. To ensure that this is the case, you need to add an Order By statement to the SQL. Choose Tools | Sorting to display the Sorting page of the Report Query dialog box, shown in Figure 21.8. Select the CSTMR_NAME field and drag and drop this into the Sort list. Select Done to return to the report layout. You are now assured that CSTMR_NAME_Group will be correct, because you are also ordering on the CSTMR_NAME column.

FIGURE 21.8.

Sorting by CSTMR_NAME.

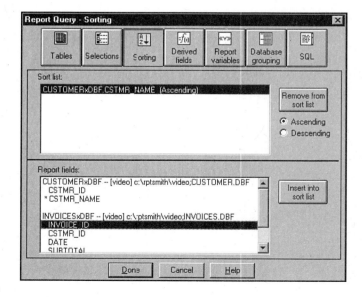

Report Groups can be nested. If the preceding report included customers, invoices, and then invoice items, it would be possible to create a second Report Group to group invoices by invoice ID. This group would be nested under the main customer name group. Again, the report order must match. In this example, it would be nested first on CSTMR_NAME and then on INVOICE_ID. You can try this by adding the table DETAIL to the report.

Report grouping can also be created by selecting the required column and using one of the toolbar buttons shown in Figure 21.9. When Report Groups are created in this way, the following actions are performed by ReportSmith:

1. The Report Group is created and named accordingly.
2. The Suppress attribute is automatically added to the group properties for the selected column.
3. The selected column is automatically included in the report's sort order.
4. A header or footer is created for the Report Group.

FIGURE 21.9.

Report Groupings can be created quickly using the toolbar buttons.

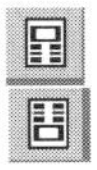

> **NOTE**
>
> Report grouping is a local operation performed by ReportSmith. This must not be confused with Database grouping, which uses the SQL `Group By` statement to group the data at the server level.

Returning to the report layout, you now have the Report Group as shown Figure 21.10. It would be nice to have each customer name appear above the list of invoices. To do this you need to create a new report section. In this case you will create a group header for the CSTMR_NAME_Group. Select the Insert | Header/Footer menu item. From the Header/Footer dialog box, choose CSTMR_Group and check the header checkbox to create a group header. The section CSTMR_NAME_Header now appears within the report above each detail section for the customer.

> **NOTE**
>
> Boundaries such as page headers, footers, and detail sections are always displayed at specific locations in a report. Feel free to resize, move horizontally, and manipulate boundaries with the Borders and Format Section dialog boxes, but do not move them

from their specific vertical location using the mouse. Problems occur when boundaries are moved out of the normal expected sequence. For example, do not move a group header to be displayed after its detail section!

FIGURE 21.10.

Creating the CSTMR_NAME_Group has split the detail section into sections, one for each Customer.

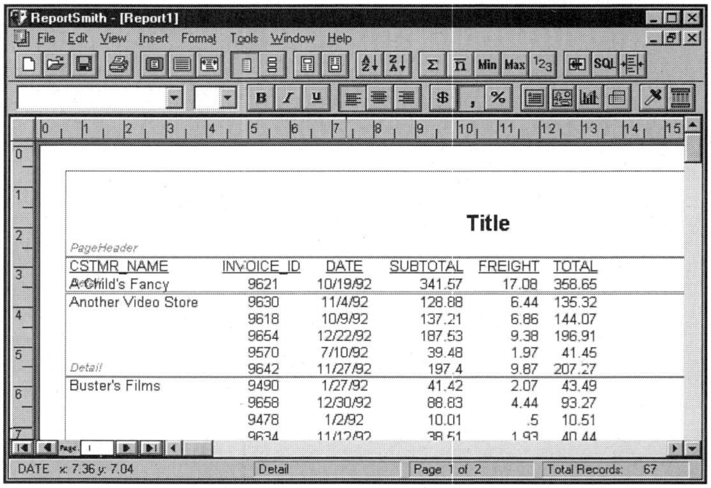

You can now drag and drop the CSTMR_NAME field from the detail section into the CSTMR_NAME_Header section. To do this, ensure that you are in Form Mode and not Column Mode. This is indicated by the buttons cn the toolbar (see Figure 21.11).

FIGURE 21.11.

Use the toolbar to toggle between Form Mode and Column Mode.

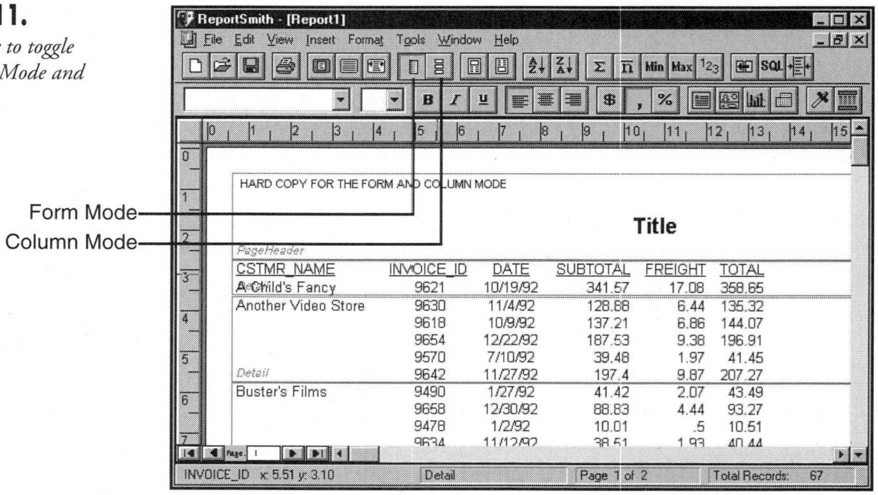

Form Mode
Column Mode

Use Column Mode when you are working on the detail section of a columnar report. It lets you move columns horizontally across the page. Column labels move along with the column. In Column Mode, ReportSmith automatically left-justifies columns with their headings, keeping them evenly aligned so you don't have to adjust alignment. When you move a column, ReportSmith displays a heavy line indicating where the column would drop if you released the mouse.

Form Mode enables you to move selected objects freely around the report page, horizontally and vertically. This is useful when you're positioning fields and labels on form reports or placing values into headers and footers. Form Mode does not reorder column positions. If you delete a column in Form Mode, columns do not reposition to fill in the blank space.

After the CSTMR_NAME field has been moved, return to Column Mode and delete the CSTMR_NAME column by deleting the column heading.

The section CSTMR_NAME_Group can have properties set using the Format | Sections menu item. This displays the Format Section dialog box, shown in Figure 21.12. Select the Keep Section Together checkbox for the detail section to prevent this section (the invoices for a customer) from being split over a page break.

FIGURE 21.12.

The Format Section dialog box can be used to control how sections are displayed.

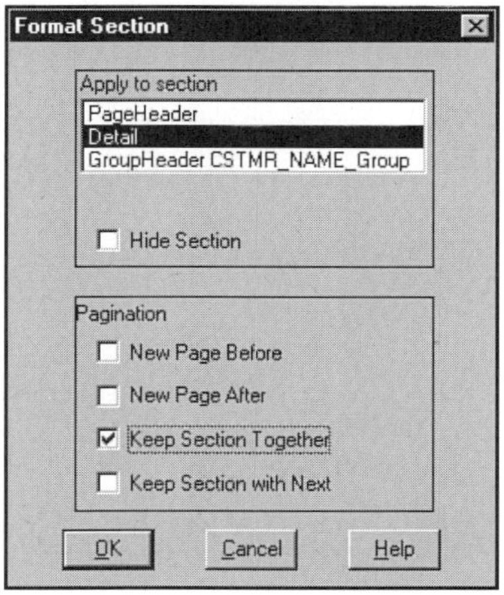

Now that the basic report layout is complete, it is time to add the rental manager's requests to this report.

Request 1: It Must Report Either All Customers or One Specific Customer

First a report variable must be created so that the user can interact with the report. Choose the Tools | Report Variables menu item to display the Report Variables page of the Report Query dialog box as shown in Figure 21.13. Create a new variable, name it Customer_name, set its type to String, its title to Customer, and the prompt to "Please enter the Customer (Use % for All Customers." After you have done this, choose Add to create the report variable.

Report variables are key to allowing your created report to interface with the user of the report. By using report variables, your report can become dynamic, responding specifically to a user's needs. When a report variable is created, ReportSmith automatically creates an individual dialog box that is used specifically to assign a value for that report variable. The dialog box is presented to the user of the report each time a report variable value is needed. You can use the various options from the Report Variables page of the Report Query dialog box to change the way the variable is entered. In this example, choosing the value from a table would be more appropriate. You are going to use a Delphi screen to set the values of the report variables you create, so there is no need to worry about the presentation of the Report Variable dialog box, because the user never needs to see this.

FIGURE 21.13.

A report variable is created to allow a specific customer to be entered.

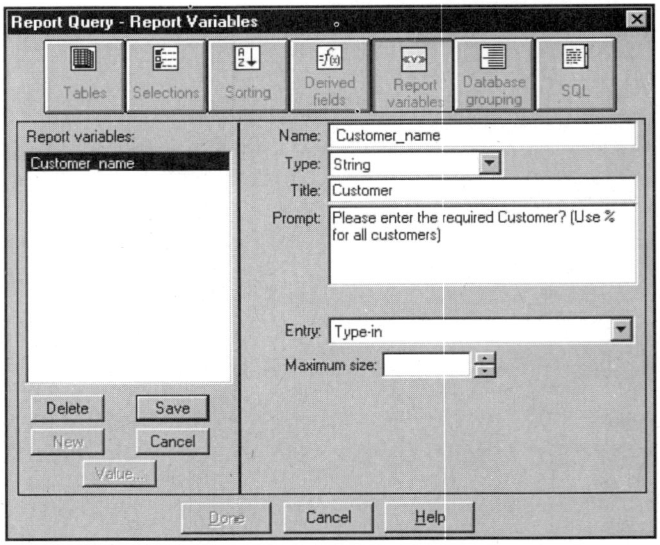

Choose Done and enter a valid customer for the value of the report variable, for example, Another Video Store. What happened? Nothing. You have created a report variable but have not yet used it. Select the Tools | Selections menu item to display the Selections page of the Report Query dialog box.

The Selections page of the Report Query dialog box is used to manipulate the where clause of the report's SQL statement. Selection criteria can be added in two ways:

- English-like manner. Using this option enables you to add selection criteria in English. You do not need to have knowledge of SQL to use this. Using this method you are assured that ReportSmith will generate correct SQL.

■ Using SQL language. This option displays the SQL Selection Criteria dialog box (see Figure 21.14). From here you can build the SQL where clause either by typing or by dragging and dropping fields, report variables, and operators from the list boxes. If you decide to use this method, you have taken on the responsibility of writing SQL that is syntactically correct. Within this dialog box you can enter anything for the selection criteria. This gives you great flexibility, allowing any SQL statement that the SQL server supports to be written. For example, a subquery could be written. Remember that ReportSmith returns a database error if SQL criteria is entered incorrectly.

FIGURE 21.14.

The SQL Section Criteria dialog box can be used to build an SQL where condition.

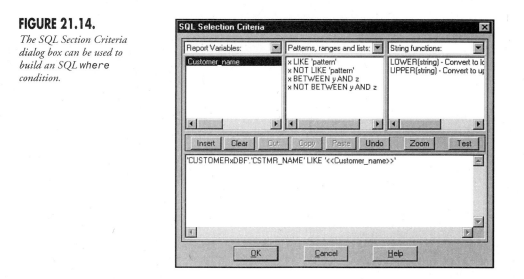

The SQL Selection Criteria dialog box is dynamic according to the server. This means that only the specific SQL functions that your server supports are shown to you. To advance your report writing prowess, you should become familiar with the specific functions that your server offers.

For this example, add selection criteria in an English-like manner. Choose Tools | Selections, choose the 1 button, then select Add selection criteria (see Figure 21.15). A default selection string is produced. Modify this by clicking each underlined item to be equal to this:

```
data field CUSTOMERxDBF.CSTMR_NAME is patterned like report variable customer_name.
```

When you examine the SQL statement, you will notice that the SQL now has an extra line (see Figure 21.16). This is the where clause that you added via the Selections page of the Report Query dialog box.

FIGURE 21.15.

Adding selection criteria.

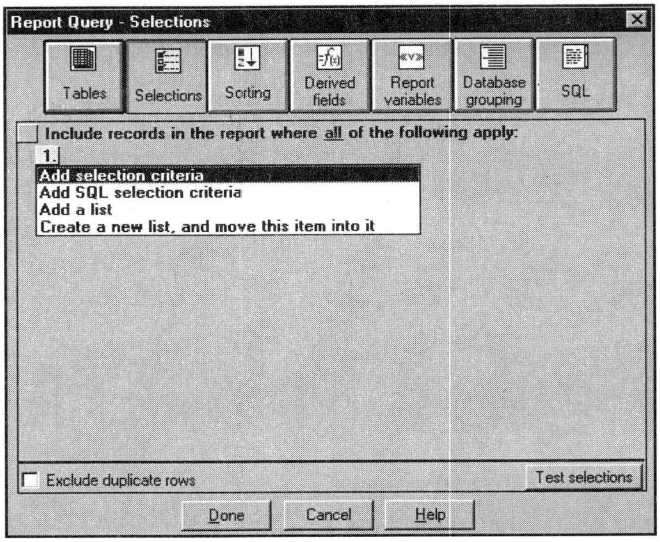

FIGURE 21.16.

Adding selection criteria simply adds a WHERE *clause to the SQL statement.*

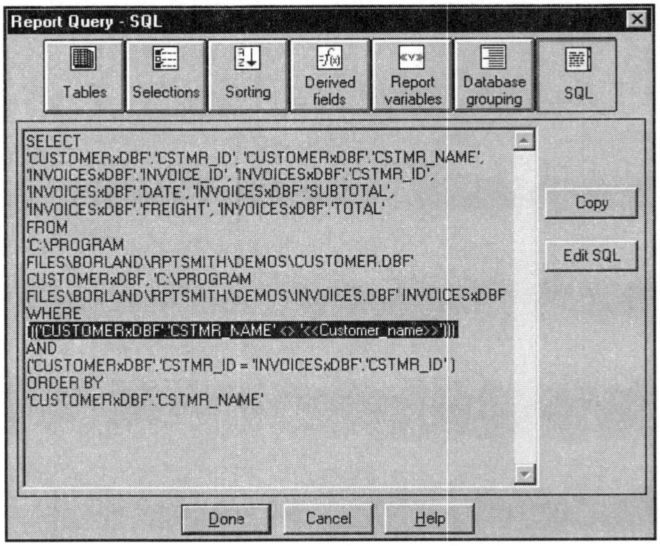

You have now completed Request 1. This report reports on only the specified customer. If % is entered for the Customer_name report variable, the report returns all customers.

Request 2: It Must Show the Total Amount Owed By Each Customer

This request is simple. Report summaries are needed for the CSTMR_NAME_Group. First use the Insert | Header/Footer menu item to create a group footer for the CSTMR_NAME_Group. Next select the three fields FREIGHT, SUBTOTAL, and TOTAL (hold down the Ctrl key and click each field) and use the Dollar button to format these columns as dollar amounts. Keeping the three fields selected, use the Sum Selected column button to create three summaries in the CSTMR_NAME_Group footer (see Figure 21.17). Remove the titles for these summaries and align them horizontally using the alignment palette available from the Tools | Alignment menu item. Request 2 is now complete.

FIGURE 21.17.

Toolbar buttons are a quick way to create summaries.

NOTE

Using the toolbar buttons is a quick way to create summaries. Such summaries are automatically created for each group in the report and are inserted into the group footer. You can also create summaries by using the Tools | Summary Fields dialog box.

Remember that summaries are a local operation calculated by ReportSmith. It is possible to hide the detail section and create a report that shows only summary information by using the Format Section dialog box (refer back to Figure 21.13). If all that is required is summary information, it is more efficient to use the Database Grouping features of ReportSmith to add a Group By statement to the SQL. By doing this, summaries can be calculated on the server, which is always more efficient.

Request 3: It Must Calculate a Discounted Total for Each Invoice According to a Specified Discount Percentage

This request requires interaction from the user. In this case, the manager wants to enter a variable percentage amount for the discount. Create a report variable named discount and set the type to Number. This is performed the same way as the report variable Customer_name, which was created earlier. This request requires an extra field for each invoice that shows the discounted total owed. This must be calculated and cannot be retrieved directly from the database. ReportSmith calls such fields derived fields. Choose Tools | Derived fields to display the Derived Fields page of the Report Query dialog box, enter the name of the derived field as discount_amt, and select the Add button (see Figure 21.18).

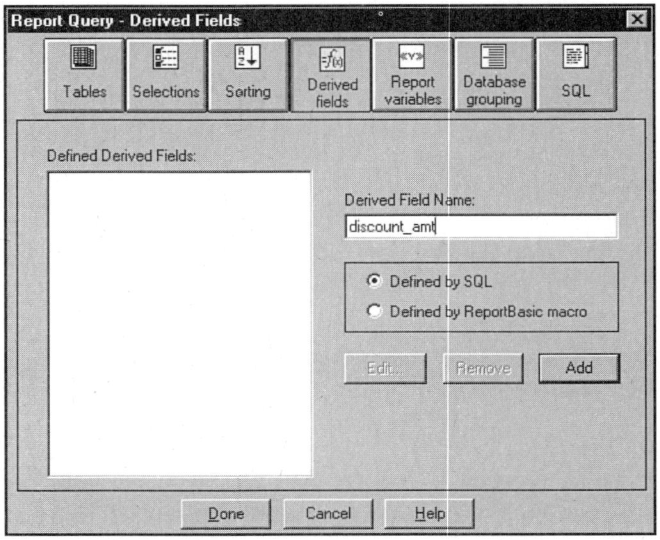

FIGURE 21.18.

Creating a derived field.

The Edit Derived Fields dialog box is now displayed. This dialog box is exactly the same as the SQL Selection Criteria dialog box in Figure 21.14. In this case you need to calculate the discount for the data field total. With the help of the three list boxes, enter the following calculation for the derived field:

```
'INVOICESxDBF'.'TOTAL'   -   (   (  'INVOICESxDBF'.'TOTAL'     /    100  )   *
➥<<discount>>   )
```

When calculation for the derived field has been entered, choose OK and Done. The derived field is added in the report layout as the rightmost column of the detail section for each invoice. A derived field created in this way simply adds to the SELECT section of the SQL statement (see Figure 21.19). Such a derived field can be manipulated in the same way as a normal data field. Create a summary for this derived field and align this summary with the other summaries in the CSTMR_GROUP_footer.

FIGURE 21.19.

*A derived field defined via
SQL simply adds to the
SQL SELECT statement.*

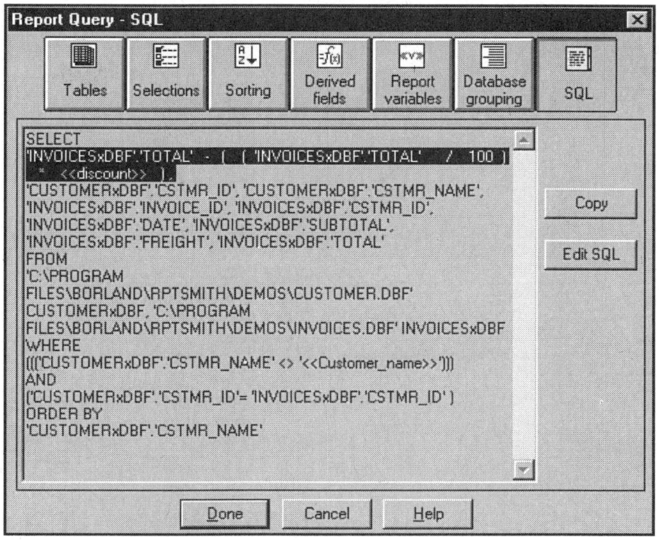

NOTE

As shown in Figure 21.19, a derived field can be defined via SQL as in this case, or
defined via a ReportBasic macro. A derived field defined via a ReportBasic macro has
its value calculated using a ReportBasic script. ReportBasic is a macro scripting
language that uses the same syntax as Basic. Whenever possible, always use derived
fields defined by SQL. It is always more efficient because the value for the derived field
is calculated by the server. A ReportBasic macro is not run by ReportSmith until the
answer set is returned by the server. ReportBasic can be used to perform complex
operations that SQL cannot do, such as `if..then..else` logic. ReportBasic is another
subject in itself, and there is no time here to examine this subject in detail; however,
please refer to the ReportSmith manuals for more information.

Request 4: It Must Be Able to Highlight Invoices that Are Over a Certain Dollar Amount

The rental manager has requested that she would like to identify invoices over a certain dollar
amount. If an invoice is over or equal to this amount, the invoice total should be highlighted
in red. If the invoice falls below this amount, it should be highlighted in green.

How do you do this? By using ReportBasic. Before you do this, however, you must create an-
other report variable and name it `Highlight`, then choose Tools | Macro to display the Macro
Commands dialog box (see Figure 21.20).

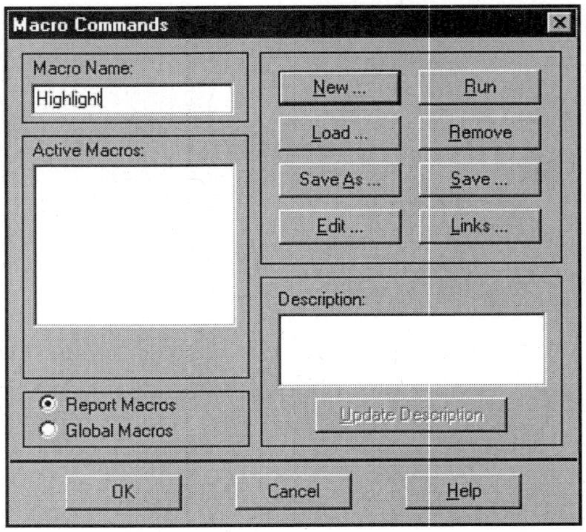

FIGURE 21.20.

The Macro Commands dialog box is used to maintain ReportBasic macros.

Enter Highlight as the macro name and choose New. The Edit Macro dialog box is displayed and now you can create the ReportBasic code for the macro. The code for this is shown in Listing 21.1. You should enter this code directly or choose Load to insert the example named highlite.mac from the CD.

Listing 21.1. Macro code to dynamically highlight a field.

```
Sub highlight()

'
'Uses the RGB function in order to set the variables Red and
'Green equal to the required values for these colors.
'

  Red = RGB( 255,0,0 )
  Blue = RGB( 0,0,255 )
  Green = RGB( 0,128,0)
  Purple = RGB(128,0,255)


' Get the value of the total field and store this in the local variable invtotal
'

  invtotal = val(Field( "TOTAL"))


' Get the value of the report variable  and store this in the local variable
' ➥breakpoint
'

breakpoint = val(getrepvar ("highlight"))



' Set the local variable color to Red if the Total for the invoice is over the
' ➥breakpoint
```

```
   if invtotal >= breakpoint then
     Color = Red
   else
     Color = Green
   end if

'
' Apply the color to the field.
' This will be applied to whichever field is linked to the macro
'

   FieldFont "",0,-1,Color,-1

End Sub
```

This macro first uses the RGB function to set the variables Red and Green equal to the required values for these colors. The function Field is called to return the value of the field total into the variable invtotal. The function GetRepVar is used to return the value of the report variable highlight into the variable breakpoint.

The two variables invtotal and breakpoint are then compared. If the variable invtotal is greater than or equal to the variable breakpoint, the variable color is set equal to the variable Red. Otherwise, color is set equal to the variable Green. The FieldFont function is called to set the field's color to the color as stored in the variable color. Although on the surface this macro might look complex to write in terms of syntax, the Edit Macro dialog box enables functions to be dragged and dropped into the code. For example, if a report variable is dropped into the macro from the first list box, the code GetRepVar("highlight") is automatically written.

Notice that the FieldFont function does not have the field explicitly stated. Choose Done to return to ReportSmith. What happens? Nothing! ReportSmith is unsure when to run the new macro. You must link this to a ReportSmith event. Choose the Tools | Macro menu item to again display the Macro Commands dialog box. Select the highlight macro and choose Links. Change the Object combo box to read DataField and the Event combo box to read display. Now select the field total and choose Link. The macro highlight is now linked to the display event of the data field total. The Macro Links dialog box should look like Figure 21.21 when you are finished.

Choose OK. The macro now runs, and the total field color changes. This is why no field was specified when the FieldFont function in the macro was called. This function acts on whichever field the macro is linked to. This means that this macro could be linked to many fields. Try linking this to the CSTMR_NAME field and see what happens.

Now that the report is complete, save it and close ReportSmith. You can go to Delphi and build a front-end screen to control this report. Why do this? You could give the report to the users as is, and the users could use the RunTime viewer that comes with ReportSmith to open the report. The report would then prompt them for the three report variables: Customer_name, discount, and highlight. Each of these would prompt the user for a value in a separate dialog box over which you have little control. Using Delphi to create a front-end screen for the report means that you have far more control over validating what the user enters, as well as a much improved interface.

FIGURE 21.21.

Linking the highlight *macro to the* display *event of the data field total.*

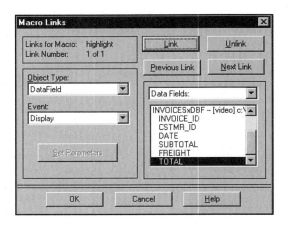

Delphi Form for Example Report 1

Before continuing, it is important to understand that there are two versions of ReportSmith. The main version resides inside the RPTSMITH subdirectory. This is the ReportSmith designer you just used. A RunTime version resides in the RS_RUN subdirectory. This is the one that can be freely distributed and can be used by users of your reports to view and print them. Specifically, RS_RUN.EXE gets loaded when you are running a Delphi program. For the following section, please ensure that the RS_RUN subdirectory is on your path.

Integrating ReportSmith reports and Delphi is done using the TReport component, which lives alongside its other data access friends in the Component Palette.

TReport

The TReport component encapsulates all the operations needed to control ReportSmith from Delphi. Start up Delphi and drop down a TReport component. First, step through the properties you need to set to control the previously built report:

- AutoUnload. Leave this set to False. AutoUnload automatically unloads ReportSmith RunTime once the report has finished. This is usually used when a report requires printing only. ReportSmith is loaded while the report is printed; when the report is finished, ReportSmith RunTime is closed.

- Start Page and End Page. These control which pages are printed. Leave these as default.

- **InitialValues.** InitialValues is used to populate the values for report variables the report uses when it first opens. You use this property to set the value for each report variable: Customer_name, discount, and Highlight. Once set, when the report opens the normal report variable dialog boxes do not appear because the report variables already have values. InitialValues is a TString, just like the Items property of a TListBox. This property is set by the code for the Start button (see Figure 21.22).

- **MaxRecords.** MaxRecords can be used to control how many records the report should return. For those who are familiar with ReportSmith, this is the same as running a report in draft mode. This can be useful during development to limit the number of records a report returns in order to speed the development process along.

- **Preview.** Preview is a Boolean property. Set this to True. This decides whether the report should be shown in the RunTime viewer or printed immediately. Setting Preview to False automatically prints the report.

- **ReportDir and ReportName.** These properties control which report the TReport component relates to. Set this to the Directory and ReportName of the report created in Example 1.

Now that you have set some initial properties of TReport, you can build the rest of the form. I am assuming that through reading this book you are already quite adept at building simple forms. Drop down three edit boxes, three labels (one for each report variable), and two buttons. Set the caption for the first button to Start and the caption for the second to Recalc. When you have completed this, the form should look like Figure 21.22.

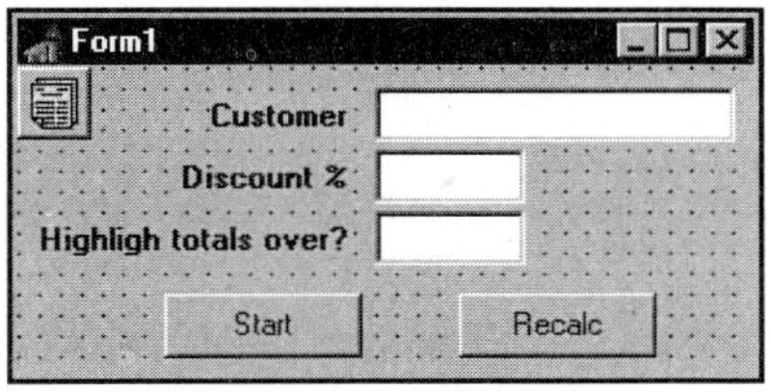

FIGURE 21.22.

Form to control the Example 1 report.

The three edit boxes are used to get the value for each report variable. The code is shown in Listing 21.2. The Start button needs to set the value of the report variables and then open the report.

Listing 21.2. Code for the Start button.

```
procedure TForm1.Button1Click(Sender: TObject);
begin
with report1 do
    begin
    initialvalues.clear;
    initialvalues.add('@customer_name = <' + edit1.text + '>');
    initialvalues.add('@discount = <'     + edit2.text + '>');
```

continues

Listing 21.2. continued

```
        initialvalues.add('@highlight = <'        + edit3.text + '>');
        run;
        end;
end;
```

This code first sets the `initialvalues` property for each report variable and then opens the report using the `run` method. This sets the value for each report variable when the report is opened. By setting `initialvalues` you are preventing the report from prompting for the values of the report variables. The `initialvalues` property can set the values of many variables, one on each line. The following syntax must be used for initial values:

```
@Reportvariablename = <reportvariablevalue>
```

The Recalc button is used to reset the report variables and recalculate the report using the new report variable values while the report is still open. The code is shown in Listing 21.3.

Listing 21.3. Code for the Recalc button.

```
procedure TForm1.Button2Click(Sender: TObject);
begin
with report1 do
      begin
      setvariable('customer_name',edit1.text);
      setvariable('discount',edit2.text);
      setvariable('highlight',edit3.text);
      recalcreport;
      end;
end;
```

The Recalc button sets the value of each report variable, but this cannot be done using the `initialvalues` property because the report is already open. Instead it uses the `setvariable` method to place a new value into each report variable. The `recalcreport` method is then used. This causes the SQL statement for the report to be rerun so that the new report variable values are used.

The form is now complete. Run the form, enter three values for each report variable, and choose Start. The report opens and the three values you entered are used within the report. Enter three more values and choose Recalc. The report reruns the SQL and uses the three new values you have entered. You have now completed the first report.

Before moving on, let's examine some other methods of `TReport` that are useful when building a report interface:

■ `CloseReport`. This method can be used to close down a report. This closes the current report that is open but does not close down ReportSmith RunTime.

- `CloseApplication`. This method closes down ReportSmith RunTime.
- `Connect`. This method can be used to connect ReportSmith RunTime to a required server. This is useful to prevent users from being prompted by ReportSmith to log on to the server.
- `Print`. This prints the report.
- `RunMacro`. This is a useful method that can be used to run a ReportBasic macro. The syntax for the method differs from that in the Delphi help and is shown here:

```
Report1.RunMacro ('"RunMacro","c:\mymacro.mac"," "').
```

`RunMacro` is not limited to running a ReportBasic macro—it can be used to call other specific ReportBasic commands. The following example uses the `RunMacro` method to call the ReportBasic procedure `msgbox` to display a ReportSmith message box:

```
report1.RunMacro('msgbox "Hello from ReportBasic:"');
```

The first report is now complete and has a working front-end Delphi interface.

Delphi Form for Example Report 2

For the second report you build the same report as in Example 1 except you use a Delphi `TQuery` as the datasource for the report. This is a new feature introduced in Delphi 2 and ReportSmith 3.0. You can now control the SQL for the report from within Delphi. For this report, create an alias named `rsdemo` and point it to access the ReportSmith demo tables located in RptSmith\demo.

First you must build the query to be used by the report. Start a new form and drop down a `TQuery`. Set the database name to `rsdemo` and set the SQL to the following:

(You can either cut and paste the SQL from the Sample 1 report or use the query builder.)

```
SELECT
    CUSTOMER."CSTMR_ID" ,
    CUSTOMER."CSTMR_NAME" ,
    INVOICES."INVOICE_ID" ,
    INVOICES."DATE" ,
    INVOICES."SUBTOTAL" ,
    INVOICES."FREIGHT",
    INVOICES."TOTAL"
FROM
    "CUSTOMER.DBF" CUSTOMER ,
    "INVOICES.DBF" INVOICES
WHERE
    ( CUSTOMER.CSTMR_ID = INVOICES.CSTMR_ID )
ORDER BY
    CUSTOMER.CSTMR_NAME
```

The initial query the report will use is complete. You must now modify the query to incorporate the rental manager's requests.

Request 1: It Must Report Either All Customers or One Specific Customer

To performthis you must change the query to take a bind parameter. Edit the SQL for the query to add the following `where` condition:

```
AND (CUSTOMER.CSTMR_NAME LIKE :CUSTOMER_NAME)
```

This creates a bind parameter for the query. The bind parameter is used to control which customers are returned by the query. Edit the `params` property of the query, set the parameter type to `String`, and enter a value of `%`. Now that the `Customer_name` parameter has been created, you must give the user control over it. To ensure that the SQL is correct, open and close the query by toggling the active property in the Object Inspector.

Drop down a `TComboBox` and set the text to `All Customers`. This combo box enables the user to select the required customer. Drop down a `TLabel` for the combo box and set the caption to Customer. Drop down a `TTable` and set the database name to rsdemo, the table name to CUSTOMER.DBF, and the index name to the CSTMR_NAME field. Setting this index ensures that the customers are ordered by name. This table is used to populate the dropdown list for the combo box. Enter the code shown in Listing 21.4 for the `FormCreate` event of the form.

Listing 21.4. Code to populate the `Items` property of the combo box.

```
procedure TForm1.FormCreate(Sender: TObject);
begin
table1.open;
table1.first;
ComboBox1.items.clear;
ComboBox1.items.Add('All Customers');
while not Table1.eof do
    begin
    ComboBox1.items.add(Table1.FieldbyName('CSTMR_NAME').asstring);
    Table1.next;
    end;
end;
```

When the form runs, this code populates the combo box with a list of all customers plus the first option, which is to choose All Customers.

Next you need to link the combo box into the query. To do this, add the code shown in Listing 21.5 to the `OnChange` event of the combo box. Now, when the user selects a customer from the dropdown list, the `OnChange` event fires and the query returns only the records for the selected customer.

Listing 21.5. Code to change the bind parameter of the query.

```
procedure TForm1.ComboBox1Change(Sender: TObject);
begin
with Query1 do
     begin
     close;
     if ComboBox1.text = 'All Customers' then
         ParamByName('Customer_name').asstring := '%'
     else
         ParamByName('Customer_name').asstring := Combobox1.text;
     open;
     end;
end;
```

You have now completed Request 1. When the user selects a customer from the combo box, the query reflects that selection. Skipping Request 2 for now, let's move on to Request 3.

Request 3: It Must Calculate a Discounted Total for Each Invoice According to a Specified Discount Percentage

First drop down a further TComboBox and a TLabel so that the user can enter the required discount percentage. Set the Label caption to Discount, set the items for the combo box to go from 10 to 100 in increments of 10, and the text to 10. You must now amend the SQL of the query to calculate the discounted total. This is performed using the same formula as the derived field in the Sample 1 report. Edit the SQL to include the following line (remember to add a comma after the previous line):

```
SELECT
     CUSTOMER."CSTMR_ID" ,
     CUSTOMER."CSTMR_NAME" ,
     INVOICES."INVOICE_ID" ,
     INVOICES."DATE" ,
     INVOICES."SUBTOTAL" ,
     INVOICES."FREIGHT",
     INVOICES."TOTAL",
     (INVOICES."TOTAL" - (INVOICES."TOTAL" / 100 * 10)) DISCOUNT
FROM
     "CUSTOMER.DBF" CUSTOMER ,
     "INVOICES.DBF" INVOICES
WHERE
     ( CUSTOMER.CSTMR_ID = INVOICES.CSTMR_ID )
ORDER BY
         CUSTOMER.CSTMR_NAME
```

This line calculates the discounted total using a default discount amount of 10 percent. Notice that you are using a column alias Discount, which means the column will be named Discount. Next add the code shown in Listing 21.6 to the OnChange event of the combo box.

> **NOTE**
>
> Using a column alias has two advantages. First, the column has a meaningful name. Second, you can change the calculation in the SQL without having any impact on the column name, because the column will be called Discount regardless of the calculation.

Listing 21.6. Code to amend the query according to the selected discount.

```
procedure TForm1.ComboBox2Change(Sender: TObject);
begin
with Query1 do
    begin
    sql.delete(8);
    sql.insert(8,(' INVOICES."TOTAL" - ( ( INVOICES."TOTAL" / 100  ) * ' +
    ➥ComboBox2.text + ') DISCOUNT,'));
    end;
end;
```

This code assumes that the SQL select line that calculates the discount is the ninth line in your SQL statement (remember that Delphi is zero-based, hence in code you reference this as line 8). Of course, in a real-world example you would not hard-code the line number, but I hope you will allow me a little leeway here. When the user selects a discount amount from the combo box, the OnChange event fires and the discount selected is reflected in the SQL for the query. Request 3 is now complete.

Request 4: It Must Be Able to Highlight Invoices that are Over a Certain Dollar Amount

Again, the actual highlighting of the field is performed by a ReportBasic macro. This time, however, instead of passing the highlight value using a report variable, you pass the highlight value as a field within the SQL. This is done by selecting the field as a constant within the SQL. Edit the SQL for the query and add the line shown here. Add this line as the last line of the select portion of the SQL statement. Remember to add a comma after the previous line. 100 is now selected as the default highlight amount.

```
SELECT
    CUSTOMER."CSTMR_ID" ,
    CUSTOMER."CSTMR_NAME" ,
    INVOICES."INVOICE_ID" ,
    INVOICES."DATE" ,
    INVOICES."SUBTOTAL" ,
    INVOICES."FREIGHT",
    INVOICES."TOTAL",
    (INVOICES."TOTAL" -  (INVOICES."TOTAL" / 100 * 10)) DISCOUNT,
    ➥100 HIGHLIGHT
FROM
```

```
    "CUSTOMER.DBF" CUSTOMER ,
    "INVOICES.DBF" INVOICES
WHERE
    ( CUSTOMER.CSTMR_ID = INVOICES.CSTMR_ID )
AND (CUSTOMER.CSTMR_NAME LIKE :CUSTOMER_NAME)
ORDER BY
        CUSTOMER.CSTMR_NAME
```

Again you must add the code and components to enable the user to manipulate this line of SQL. Drop down a further TCombobox and TLabel. Set the caption to HIGHLIGHT and the items for the combo box to go from 50 to 300 in increments of 50. Set the text to 100. Add the code shown in Listing 21.7 to the OnChange event of the combo box.

Listing 21.7. Code to amend the query according to the selected highlight amount.

```
procedure TForm1.ComboBox3Change(Sender: TObject);
begin
with Query1 do
    begin
    sql.delete(9);
    sql.insert(9,(ComboBox3.text +' HIGHLIGHT'));
    end;
end;
```

Now when the user selects a value from the Highlight combo box the OnChange event fires and the SQL is changed to include the selected highlight amount. Notice that here again you are using a column alias Highlight, which automatically names the field. The Delphi portion of Request 4 is now complete.

Request 2: It Must Show the Total Amount Owed by Each Customer

Before going back to ReportSmith, drop a TReport onto the form and set Preview to True. Start up ReportSmith, but do not close Delphi. Choose Create New Report, and select Type Columnar to display the Tables page of the Report Query dialog box. Choose Add Table, and the video tables are displayed. In this example you are not going to use these tables directly. Change the Type combo box to Delphi and choose Server Connect. The TQuery and TTable that are present in the Delphi application are displayed as shown by Figure 21.23. Select Query1 and choose Done. The report is now using the Delphi TQuery information to retrieve its data. You will notice that you are no longer allowed to manipulate the SQL from ReportSmith for this report. The options that normally change the SQL are no longer available. (These are Sorting, SQL Editing, Derived fields, Defined via SQL, Database Groupings, Selections, and report variables.) This is because all the SQL is now controlled by Delphi. This second report is available only from within the Delphi application, because Delphi must be available for the report to obtain its data.

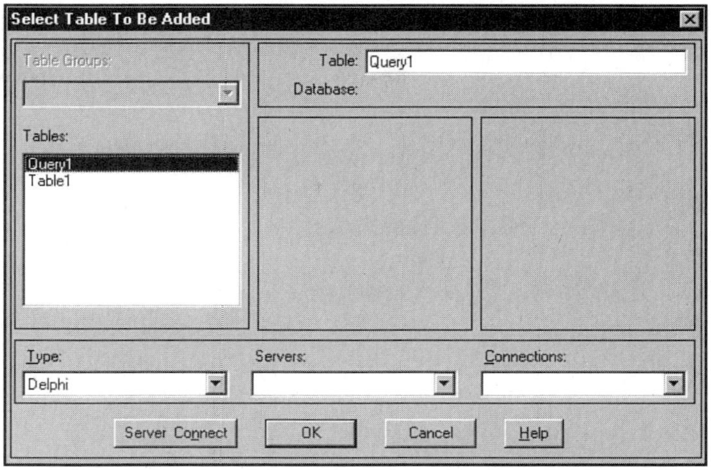

FIGURE 21.23.

ReportSmith 3.0 can use Delphi TTable *and* TQuery *to build a report.*

> **NOTE**
>
> For the server connect to work correctly, the Delphi application must have the TReport component present. Without this, the server connection will fail.

Follow the same steps as with the Sample 1 report to change the layout. Create the Report Group CSTMR_NAME_Group using the Define Groupings dialog box. Add a header and footer to this group using the Header/Footer dialog box. Move the CSTMR_NAME field into the CSTMR_NAME_Group header. Create summaries for the TOTAL, SUBTOTAL, FREIGHT, and DISCOUNT fields. Add these summaries to the CSTMR_NAME_Group footer. Select the Highlight field and click Del to remove it. This field is used by the macro highlight, but you do not need to display it in the report layout.

> **NOTE**
>
> You will notice that if you try to use the toolbar buttons to create the Report Groups, a warning is displayed stating that this operation is not allowed for the connection type. This is because the toolbar button is trying to amend the sort order for the SQL. You must create the report grouping by choosing the menu item Tools | Report Groups.

Now that the report layout is complete, you can finish the ReportSmith section of Request 4.

Request 4 Continued: It Must be Able to Highlight Invoices that are Over a Certain Dollar Amount

The process for this request is basically the same as the Sample 1 report, with the exception that you no longer pass the report variable `highlight` to the report. You pass the `highlight` value as a field. This means a change to the macro. Choose the Tools | Macro menu item to display the Macro Commands dialog box. Enter `highlight` as the macro name and choose New. The Edit Macro dialog box is displayed. From here you create the ReportBasic code for the macro. Enter this code directly or choose Load from the Macro Commands dialog box to insert the example named highlite.mac from the CD. Once this code is entered, change the following line:

```
breakpoint = val(getrepvar ("highlight"))
```

to read

```
breakpoint = val(field ("HIGHLIGHT"))
```

See Figure 21.24 for the Example Report 2 Form.

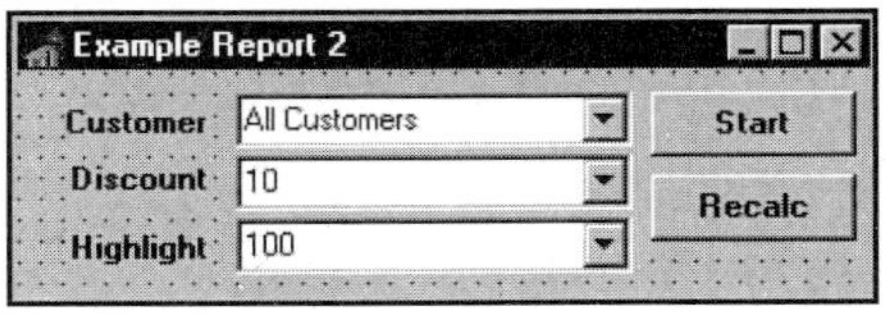

FIGURE 21.24.

Completed Delphi Form for the Example 2 report.

> **NOTE**
>
> You will notice that you also changed the case when returning the field highlight. ReportBasic is case-sensitive when it is returning values from fields and report variables. When you created the report variable, it was named `highlight` in lowercase; therefore, you referenced it as such in the function `GetRepVar`. When you created the field `HIGHLIGHT`, you named it using an alias in uppercase; therefore, it must be referenced as such using the `Field` function.

As with Example 1, link this macro to the display event for the data field TOTAL. The invoice total now changes color according to the field HIGHLIGHT. Request 4 is now complete.

Save the report and close down ReportSmith. Return to Delphi and set the `ReportDir` and `ReportName` to the report you created. Drop down two buttons and set their captions to Start and Recalc, respectively. The Start button is again used to start up ReportSmith RunTime and open the first report. Add the following code to the `OnClick` event of the Start button:

```
procedure TForm1.Button1Click(Sender: TObject);
begin
report1.run;
end;
```

Remember that the Start button does not need to set the initial values because you are controlling the report from the Delphi query. It is also not necessary to open the query. ReportSmith opens the query itself. Next, add the code for the `OnClick` event of the Recalc button:

```
procedure TForm1.Button2Click(Sender: TObject);
begin
report1.recalcreport;
end;
```

Again, you do not need to use any methods other than the `recalcreport`. All control is performed through the query, which you are changing according to the user's selections.

The form is now complete. Run the form. Choose a customer, a discount amount, and a highlight breakpoint. Choose Run. ReportSmith RunTime starts and opens the report. The report is using the SQL from the Delphi query that was set according to the options you selected. Next choose different values and select the Recalc button. The report reruns the SQL, which now uses the new values you selected.

Example Report 3

Sample Report 3 actually creates a ReportSmith report dynamically using Delphi. This example automatically creates a report that is based on the Customer table. Two named connections must be set up within ReportSmith for this example to work. To add these, start up ReportSmith and choose the File | Connections menu item to display the Connection dialog box. In this dialog box, choose New, enter Delphi as the name, select Delphi for the type, and choose Save. You have now created a named connection that you will use to connect to Delphi from ReportSmith. Create a second connection, name it Video, choose DBASE (IDAPI) as the type, and enter RptSmith\video as the path. This named connection is used to connect to the dBASE tables in the RptSmith\video directory.

> **NOTE**
>
> If you are having problems creating these named connections, copy the named connection file rptsmith.con from the CD to your Windows directory.

To look at this example, an additional component must first be installed. This new component is called a `TReportSmith`. Install this component by starting up Delphi and choosing the Component | Install menu item to display the Install Components dialog box. From this dialog box, choose Add and select the ReportSmith.dcu file from the CD, then choose OK to rebuild the library. `TReportSmith` should now appear on the Samples page of the component palette.

This new component is a `TReportSmith`, which is essentially the same as a `TReport` except that it has an additional property called `RunTime`, as shown in Figure 21.25.

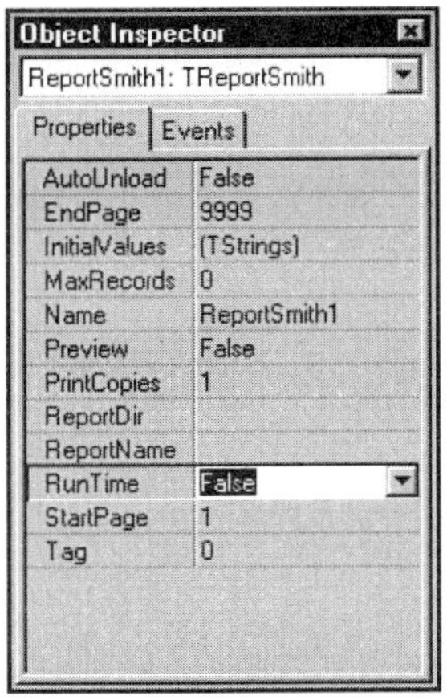

FIGURE 21.25.

The TReportSmith *component has an additional property called* RunTime.

Open up the project dynamicreport from the CD. This project uses a TReportSmith. Examine the TReportSmith component using the Object Inspector. This shows the additional property RunTime. This is a Boolean property. Setting this to True forces TReportSmith to always load ReportSmith RunTime; setting this to False forces TReportSmith to load the full-blown ReportSmith designer. In this project, RunTime is set to False. This is because this project dynamically creates reports and therefore you must access some of the functionality of ReportSmith that is not available in ReportSmith RunTime.

As shown in Figure 21.26, this project has two options: Standalone and Delphi Dependent. These two options enable two types of report to be created. When created, the Standalone report has its own SQL statement and therefore can be opened later independently of Delphi. (This is the same type of report as the Sample 1 report). The Delphi Dependent report does not have its own SQL query but uses a Delphi TQuery as its datasource. (This is the same as the Example 2 report.) The code that generates the reports is behind SpeedButton1 (see Listing 21.8). This is split into two blocks. The first is used to generate the Standalone report and the second the Delphi Dependent report.

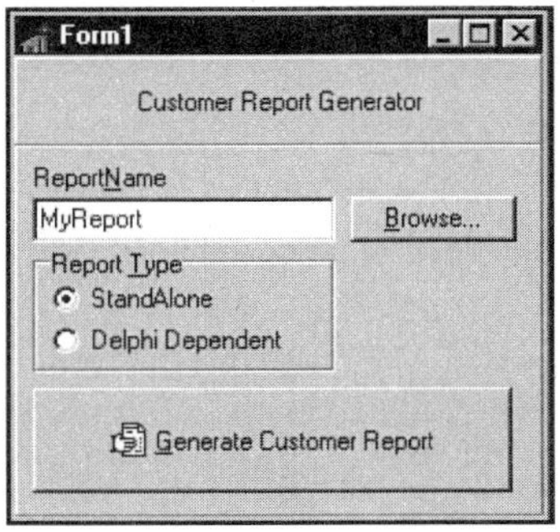

FIGURE 21.26.

The dynamicreport project creates a customer report on-the-fly.

Listing 21.8. Code that generates the ReportSmith reports.

```
procedure TForm1.SpeedButton1Click(Sender: TObject);
{
 Generate the report by passing ReportBasic commands via DDE
 to ReportSmith using the RunMacro method.
 If the user selects a standalone report then set the sql for the report
 else add Query1 as a table to the report
 }
begin
with ReportSmith1 do
     begin
     if RadioGroup1.itemindex = 0 then
        begin
        RunMacro('dim ds as dataset¦¦'+
        'ds.connect 0,"video"," "," "," "¦¦'+
        'ds.setusersql "select * from '+ chr(39)+'C:\PROGRAM
FILES\BORLAND\RPTSMITH\DEMOS\CUSTOMER.DBF'+chr(39)+' CUSTOMERxDBF"¦¦'+
        'ds.CreateReport¦¦'+
        'savereport "'+edit1.text+'"');
        end
     else
        begin
        RunMacro('dim ds as dataset¦¦'+
        'ds.connect 0,"delphi"," "," "," "¦¦'+
        'ds.AddTable "Query1"," "¦¦'+
        'ds.CreateReport¦¦'+
        'savereport "'+edit1.text+'"');
        end;
     end;
end;
```

Let's examine the first block of code, shown in Listing 21.9. This code generates the Standalone report.

Listing 21.9. Code block to generate the Standalone report.

```
begin
RunMacro('dim ds as dataset¦¦'+
'ds.connect 0,"video"," "," "," "¦¦'+
'ds.setusersql "select * from '+ chr(39)+'C:\PROGRAM
FILES\BORLAND\RPTSMITH\DEMOS\CUSTOMER.DBF'+chr(39)+' CUSTOMERxDBF"¦¦'+
'ds.CreateReport¦¦'+
'savereport "'+edit1.text+'"');
end
```

This code uses the `TReportSmith` method `RunMacro` to pass a series of ReportBasic commands to ReportSmith via DDE. Multiple ReportBasic commands can be passed by separating each one using ¦¦. The first ReportBasic command sent is

```
dim ds as dataset
```

This declares ds to be of type dataset. A dataset is what ReportSmith calls a control object. A dataset has various properties and methods that can be manipulated to define a new report or modify an existing one. The next line establishes a connection between the dataset and the datasource. This line therefore connects the dataset to the named connection video:

```
ds.connect 0,"video"," "," "," "
```

Once the connection is established, the method setusersql is called. This adds the SQL statement to the dataset:

```
ds.setusersql "select * from '+ chr(39)+'C:\PROGRAM
FILES\BORLAND\RPTSMITH\DEMOS\CUSTOMER.DBF'+chr(39)+' CUSTOMERxDBF"
```

Now that you have established a connection and set the SQL for the dataset, a new report can be created by calling the CreateReport method for the dataset:

```
ds.CreateReport
```

This line creates a new ReportSmith report using the dataset as its definition. Once created, the new report is saved to the filename specified in edit1.text using the ReportBasic command savereport.

The second block of code, used for the Delphi Dependent report, uses the same techniques. See Listing 21.10.

Listing 21.10. Code block to generate the Delphi Dependent report.

```
begin
RunMacro('dim ds as dataset¦¦'+
'ds.connect 0,"delphi"," "," "," "¦¦'+
'ds.AddTable "Query1"," "¦¦'+
'ds.CreateReport¦¦'+
'savereport "'+edit1.text+'"');
end;
```

Again a dataset is used to create the report, but the connect method is different. In this example you need to connect the dataset to Delphi and not to the dBASE tables directly. Therefore, you connect to the named connection called delphi, not the named connection video:

```
ds.connect 0,"delphi"," "," "," "
```

The other change needed is setting the SQL for the dataset. Instead of calling the setusersql method, you call another dataset method, AddTable. This adds the Delphi TQuery, Query1, to the dataset:

```
ds.AddTable "Query1"," "
```

Again the report can then be created and saved using the CreateReport and SaveReport methods.

NOTE

The more observant reader will notice there is a TReport component present on the form. This component was added solely to enable the join from ReportSmith to Delphi to work correctly for the Delphi Dependent report. The TReportSmith component does not perform this functionality.

This has been a simple example. The TReportSmith component was introduced only to enable the ReportSmith designer to be loaded instead of the RunTime. This example always creates a report that uses the Customer table, but in showing this I was hoping to pass on further insight into ReportBasic and also show some of the power that lies within ReportSmith.

Summary

I hope that through these examples I have demonstrated how easy it is to control ReportSmith reports from within Delphi. You are now able to control Standalone reports using report variables and also build reports that use Delphi as their query source. Using these two techniques, you should be able to easily integrate your reports within your Delphi application. Through the last example I hope you now understand some ReportBasic techniques and have a further appreciation for some of the power of ReportSmith.

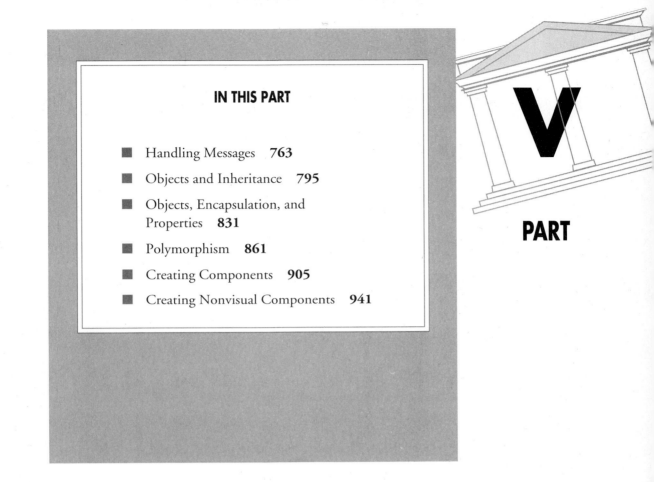

PART

V

Objects

The fifth section of the book plunges into the heart of object-oriented programming. There are chapters on inheritance, encapsulation, and polymorphism, as well as a description of how to create both visual and non-visual components. These pages include some of the most important material in the book, all of which should be well understood by any serious Delphi programmer.

Handling Messages

22

Event-oriented code is one of the central tenets of Windows programming. Some rapid-application development environments attempt to hide users from this feature altogether, as if it were something so complicated that most programmers couldn't understand it. The truth is that event-oriented programming is not, in itself, particularly complex. However, some features of the way it is implemented in Windows can be confusing under certain circumstances.

Delphi gives you full access to the event-oriented substructure that provides Windows with a high degree of power and flexibility. At the same time, it simplifies and clarifies the way a programmer handles those events. The end result is a system that gives you complete access to the power of Windows, while simultaneously protecting you from unnecessary complexity.

This chapter covers the following topics:

- Event-oriented programming basics
- Responding to mouse events or key events
- Accessing the information passed in events
- The basics of sets, which are used frequently in Delphi event handlers
- Circumventing Delphi's message handling tools and directly capturing messages
- Creating wm_Command handlers and finding the IDs of the components used in a program

Some of the ideas in this chapter were introduced in chapters 9–14, which are on the Windows API. However, this chapter looks at these ideas from the perspective of a Delphi RAD programmer, rather than the perspective of a Windows API programmer. To be really good at programming Windows, you need to be able to look at these subjects from both perspectives. That is, you need to know the VCL inside out, and you need to know the Windows API inside out. This chapter concentrates on the VCL side of that equation. Put both perspectives together and you can go on to create your own VCL components, or you can design elegant, well-structured Windows programs.

Before starting, let me reiterate that Delphi hides much of the complexity of Windows programming. However, the developers did not want to prevent programmers from accessing any portion of the Windows API. By the time you finish reading this chapter, you should be able to see that Delphi gives you access to the full range of power provided by an event-oriented system.

Delphi Events

Delphi makes it easy to handle keyboard and mouse events. Suppose, for instance, that you wanted to capture left mouse clicks in the main form of your program. Here's how to get started. Create a new project and name it EVENTS1.DPR. Go to the area in the code just underneath the word `implementation` and write the following uses statement, shown here with some surrounding text so you can see where to write it:

```
implementation

uses
 Dialogs;

{$R *.DFM}
```

In the Object Inspector for the main form, choose the Events Page and double-click the area to the right of the `OnClick` property. Create the following procedure:

```
procedure TForm1.FormClick(Sender: TObject);
begin
  MessageDlg('Hello', mtInformation, [mbOk], 0);
end;
```

This code tells Windows that a dialog box should appear every time the user clicks the left mouse button in the form. The dialog box is shown in Figure 22.1.

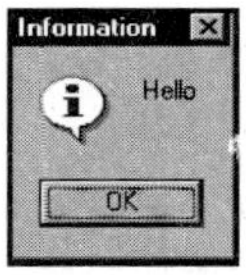

FIGURE 22.1.

The dialog box displayed by the EVENTS1 program when you click the left mouse button inside the main form.

The previous code presents one of the simplest possible cases of responding to an event in a Delphi program. It is so simple, in fact, that many programmers write this kind of code without ever understanding that they are writing event-oriented code. In this case, Delphi programmers get the event secondhand, because VCL massages the event before passing it on to the main form. Nonetheless, this is real event-oriented programming, albeit in a very simplified manifestation.

As you saw back in the section on the Windows API, the operating environment notifies you not only of the event, but of several related bits of information. For instance, when a mouse down event is generated, a program is informed about where the event occurred and which button generated the event. If you want to get access to this kind of relatively detailed information, you should turn to the Events Page for the form and create an `OnMouseDown` handler:

```
procedure TForm1.FormMouseDown(Sender: TObject;
                               Button: TMouseButton;
                               Shift: TShiftState;
                               X, Y: Integer);
begin
  if ssRight in Shift then
    Canvas.TextOut(X, Y, '* Button');
end;
```

This method writes text to the form every time the user clicks the right mouse button. To test this method, run the program and click the right mouse button in the form in several different locations. You'll see that each spot you click is marked, as shown in Figure 22.2.

FIGURE 22.2.

When you click the mouse button in the form of the EVENTS1 program, the location of the event is recorded.

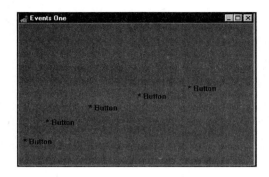

The `Canvas.TextOut` procedure prints text to the screen at the location specified by the variables X and Y. Both of these variables are supplied to you by Delphi, which received them in turn from the operating system. The X variable tells you the column in which the mouse was clicked, and the Y variable tells you the row.

As you can see, Delphi makes it very simple for you to respond to events. Furthermore, not only mouse events are easy to respond to. You can respond to key presses in a similar manner. For instance, if you create a method for the `OnKeyDown` property on the Events Page for the form, you can show the user which key was pressed on the keyboard whenever the EVENTS1 program has the focus:

```
procedure TForm1.FormKeyDown(Sender: TObject;
                            var Key: Word;
                            Shift: TShiftState);
begin
  MessageDlg(Chr(Key), mtInformation, [mbOk], 0);
end;
```

In the preceding code, the `Chr` function is used to translate a numerical value into an ASCII value. In other words, Delphi and the operating system both pass you not an actual letter like A, B, or C, but the number associated with the key you pressed. On PCs, the letter A is associated with the number 65. The `Chr` function translates the number 65 into the letter A. It wouldn't be appropriate for Delphi to perform this translation for you automatically because some keys, such as the F1 or Enter key, have no letter associated with them. Later in this chapter, you learn how to use `OnKeyDown` events to respond sensibly to keypresses on special keys such as F1, Shift, or Caps Lock.

Besides `OnKeyDown` events, Delphi also lets you respond to keyboard activity via the `OnKeyPress` event:

```
procedure TForm1.FormKeyPress(Sender: TObject; var Key: Char);
```

```
begin
  MessageDlg(Key, mtInformation, [mbOk], 0);
end;
```

You can see that this event is very similar to an OnKeyDown event. The difference is that the Key variable passed to OnKeyPress events is already translated into a Char. However, OnKeyPress events work only for the alphanumeric keys and are not called when special keys are pressed. In short, the OnKeyPress event is the same as a wm_Char event.

The code for the EVENTS1 program is shown in Listing 22.1. Get the program up and running and take whatever time is necessary to be sure it all makes sense to you. There is no point in trying to be a Windows programmer if you don't understand events.

Listing 22.1. The main form for the EVENTS1 program.

```
unit Main;

{ Program copyright (c) 1996 by Charles Calvert }
{ Project Name: EVENTS1 }

interface

uses
  WinTypes, WinProcs, Classes,
  Graphics, Forms, Controls;

type
  TEventsOne = class(TForm)
    procedure FormClick(Sender: TObject);
    procedure FormMouseDown(Sender: TObject; Button: TMouseButton;
      Shift: TShiftState; X, Y: Integer);
    procedure FormKeyDown(Sender: TObject; var Key: Word;
      Shift: TShiftState);
  private
    { Private declarations }
  public
    { Public declarations }
  end;

var
  EventsOne: TEventsOne;

implementation

uses
  Dialogs;

{$R *.DFM}

procedure TEventsOne.FormClick(Sender: TObject);
begin
  MessageDlg('Hello', mtInformation, [mbOk], 0);
end;

procedure TEventsOne.FormMouseDown(Sender: TObject;
```

continues

Listing 22.1. continued

```
                              Button: TMouseButton;
                              Shift: TShiftState;
                              X, Y: Integer);
begin
  if ssRight in Shift then
    Canvas.TextOut(X, Y, '* Button');
end;

procedure TEventsOne.FormKeyDown(Sender: TObject;
                          var Key: Word;
                Shift: TShiftState);
begin
  MessageDlg(Chr(Key), mtInformation, [mbOk], 0);
end;

end.
```

After this introduction to event-oriented programming, it's time to step back and see some of the theory behind the code. After explaining something of how the system works, this chapter goes on to give examples of how to take full advantage of Windows event-oriented code base.

> **NOTE**
>
> Some astute readers may notice that the code in this program, and in other programs in this book, still includes WINTYPES.PAS and WINPROCS.PAS in the Uses clause. These units are part of the 16-bit version of Delphi but not the 32-bit version. However, code that references them still compiles in the 32-bit version due to the Unit Alias option, which you can reach by choosing Project | Options | Directories/Conditionals. The default line automatically entered by Delphi into the Unit Alias directive reads as follows:
>
> WinTypes=Windows;WinProcs=Windows
>
> The directive means that the compiler should internally change the identifiers WinTypes or WinProcs into the identifier Windows during compilation.
>
> Going through all the programs in this book to make sure that all the references to WinTypes and WinProcs were changed to Windows obviously would not have been much work for me. I decided against doing so on the grounds that you may one day have some reason for wanting to compile this code under 16-bit Windows. Why deliberately make the code incompatible with 16-bit Windows doing so presents no advantage? Making this change would be especially strange in a time when the vast majority of professional programmers are forced to straddle a murky line between 16- and 32-bit Windows.
>
> Only one or two programs in this book were deliberately designed to run in both 16-bit Windows and 32-bit Windows. Many of the programs were designed to take

explicit advantage of 32-bit features and therefore will not compile under 16-bit Windows. However, the developers of Delphi went to great lengths to ensure that a tremendous amount of compatibility exists between the 16-bit and 32-bit versions of their compiler. This compatibility is one of the strengths of Delphi, and I saw no reason to obscure that compatibility deliberately to make this book appear artificially fancy or up to date. For instance, you will find very little difference between the way Delphi handles messages in the 16- and 32-bit versions. Therefore, all or most of the code in this chapter will compile under both versions of Delphi. This is a strength, not a weakness, and it is completely in accord with the carefully crafted plans of the Delphi developers.

If you are curious, the reason the units changed names in this version is that 32-bit Windows no longer enforces 64KB limitations on the internal tables that Delphi builds when it compiles a unit. Sans a 64KB limitation, the developers of Delphi could combine the WinTypes and WinProcs units into one large unit called WINDOWS.PAS.

Understanding Events

Event-oriented programming isn't unique to Windows, nor is it a chore that can be handled only by an operating system. For instance, any DOS program could be based around a simple loop that keeps running the entire time the program is in memory. Here is a hypothetical example of how such code might look:

```
repeat
  CheckForMouseEvent(Events);
  CheckForKeyPress(Events)
  HandleEvents(Events);
until Events.Done := True;
```

This code represents a typical event-oriented loop. A simple repeat..until statement checks for keyboard and mouse events and then calls HandleEvents to give the program a chance to respond to the events that are generated by the user or the operating system.

The variable called Events might be a record with a fairly simple structure:

```
TEvent = record
  X, Y: Integer;
  MouseButton: TButton;
  Key: Word;
  Done: Boolean;
end;
```

X and Y give the current location of the cursor, and Key contains the value of the top event in the key buffer. The TButton type might have a declaration that looks like this:

```
TButton = (lButton, rButton);
```

These structures permit you to track where the mouse is, what states its buttons are in, and what keys the user has pressed. Admittedly, this is a very simple type of event structure, but the principles involved mirror what is going on inside Windows, or inside other event-oriented systems such as Turbo Vision. If the program being written was an editor, the HandleEvent for the program might look like this:

```
procedure HandleEvent(Events: TEvent);
begin
  case Events.Key of
   'A..z': Write(Events.X, Events.Y, Events.Key);
    EnterKey: Write(CarriageReturn);
    EscapeKey: Events.Done := True;
  end;
end;
```

Given the preceding code, the program would go to location X,Y and write the letter most recently pressed by the user. If the Enter key was pressed, a carriage return would be written to the screen. A press on the Esc key would cause the program to terminate. All other key presses would be ignored.

Code like this can be very powerful, particularly if you're writing a program that requires animation. For instance, if you need to move a series of bitmaps across the screen, you want to move the bitmap a few pixels and then check to see whether the user has pressed a button or hit a keystroke. If an event has occurred, you want to handle it. If nothing occurred, you want to continue moving the bitmap.

I hope the short code samples shown here give you some feeling for the way event-oriented systems work. The only piece that's missing is an understanding of why Windows is event-oriented.

Microsoft made Windows event-oriented in part because multiple programs run under the environment at the same time. In multitasking systems, the operating system needs to know whether the user has clicked in a program, or whether the click was in the desktop window. If the mouse click occurred in a window that was partially hidden behind another window, it is up to the operating system to recognize the event and bring that window to the foreground. Clearly, it wouldn't be appropriate for the window itself to have to be in charge of that task. To ask that much would place an impossible burden on the programmer who created the window. As a result, it's best for the operating system to handle all the keystrokes and mouse clicks, and to then pass them on to the various programs in the form of events. Any other system would force every programmer to handle all the events that occurred when his or her program had the focus, and to manipulate the entire operating system in response to certain mouse events or keystrokes, such as Alt+Tab.

In short, Windows programmers almost never directly monitor the hardware or hardware interrupts. Instead, the operating system handles that task. It passes all external events on to individual programs in the form of messages. In a typical event-oriented system, the operating system continually polls the hardware in a loop and then sends each event off to its programs in the form of some kind of event structure or event variables. This is the same kind of activity you saw in the brief code snippets shown earlier.

You have seen that Windows handles mouse and keyboard events and passes them on to the appropriate window. The message that is generated in these cases gets sent to the default window procedure, which, as you know, is called `DefWindowProc`. `DefWindowProc` is analogous to the `HandleEvent` procedure shown earlier.

The important point to understand is that Windows messages contain the information that drives the entire operating environment. Almost everything that happens inside Windows is a message, and if you really want to tap into the power of Delphi, you need to understand how these messages work.

One of the tricky parts of Windows event-oriented programming is extracting information from the `wParam` and `lParam` variables passed to the window procedure. In most cases, Delphi frees you from the necessity of performing this task. For instance, if you create an event for the `OnMouseDown` property, Delphi directly tells you the `X` value and `Y` value where the event occurred. As a programmer, you don't have to struggle to get the event and its associated values. As you will see in the next section, everything about the event is shown to you in a simple and straightforward manner.

Using Sets to Track Messages

Rather than ask you to parse the `lParam` and `wParam` parameters, Delphi performs this chore for you and then passes the information on in the form of parameters:

```
procedure TForm1.FormMouseDown(Sender: TObject;
                               Button: TMouseButton;
                               Shift: TShiftState;
                               X, Y: Integer);
```

This is by far the most convenient way for you to handle events. Delphi can also give direct access to the values sent to you by the operating system. That is, you can handle `wParams` and `lParams` directly, if you want. After you have studied the EVENTS2 program and learned more about sets, I'll show you exactly how to get at that raw data.

Take a moment to consider the `Shift` parameter shown in the `FormMouseDown` header. `Shift` is declared to be of type `TShiftState`:

```
TShiftState = set of (ssShift, ssAlt, ssCtrl,
                      ssRight, ssLeft, ssMiddle,
                      ssDouble);
```

`TShiftState` is a set, and so far I have not spent much time on Delphi sets. As a result, that topic is covered in some detail throughout the rest of this section of the chapter.

To find out whether a particular element is a member of the set passed to you by Delphi, you can perform simple tests using the in operator:

```
if ssRight in Shift then Label1.Caption := 'ssShift';
```

This code asks whether the element ssRight is in the set passed to you via the Shift variable. If it is, the code assigns the word ssShift to the Caption of a label.

Here is how you can declare a set at runtime:

```
Shift := [ssright, ssShift, ssAlt, ssCtrl];
```

Given this set, the in operator from the if statement shown previously returns True. The following set causes the operator to return False:

```
Shift := [ssAlt, ssCtrl];
```

Besides in, there are three other operators you can use with sets:

```
+     Union
-     Difference
*     Intersection
```

All three of these operators return a set, whereas the in operator returns a Boolean value. The SETSEXP program, shown in Listing 22.2, shows how to work with all four operators.

Listing 22.2. The SETSEXP program shows how to use operators to track the members of sets such as TShiftState.

```
unit Main;

{ Program copyright (c) 1996 by Charles Calvert }
{ Project Name: SETSEXP }

interface

uses
  SysUtils, WinTypes, WinProcs,
  Messages, Classes, Graphics,
  Controls, Forms, Dialogs,
  StdCtrls, ExtCtrls, Buttons;

type
  TOptType = (otUnion, otIntersection, otDifference);

  TUnion = class(TForm)
    Panel1: TPanel;
    ControlKey: TCheckBox;
    ShiftKey: TCheckBox;
    LeftButton: TCheckBox;
    RightButton: TCheckBox;
    Union: TBitBtn;
    Intersection: TBitBtn;
    Difference: TBitBtn;
    Label1: TLabel;
```

```
    Label2: TLabel;
    Label3: TLabel;
    Panel2: TPanel;
    Label4: TLabel;
    procedure PanelMouseDown(Sender: TObject; Button: TMouseButton;
      Shift: TShiftState; X, Y: Integer);
    procedure SetBtnClick(Sender: TObject);
  private
    { Private declarations }
    procedure CheckState(Shift: TShiftState);
  public
    { Public declarations }
  end;

var
  Union: TUnion;

implementation

{$R *.DFM}

procedure TUnion.CheckState(Shift: TShiftState);
begin
  ShiftKey.Checked := ssShift in Shift;
  ControlKey.Checked := ssCtrl in Shift;
  LeftButton.Checked := ssLeft in Shift;
  RightButton.Checked := ssRight in Shift;
end;

procedure TUnion.PanelMouseDown(Sender: TObject;
                               Button: TMouseButton;
                               Shift: TShiftState;
                               X, Y: Integer);
begin
  CheckState(Shift);
end;

procedure TUnion.SetBtnClick(Sender: TObject);
const
  Operators: array[0..2] of string = ('+', '*', '-');
var
  FinalSet: TShiftState;
  LeftShift: TShiftState;
  LeftCtrl: TShiftState;
begin
  LeftShift := [ssLeft, ssShift];
  LeftCtrl := [ssLeft, ssCtrl];
  case TOptType((Sender as TBitBtn).Tag) of
    otUnion: FinalSet := LeftShift + LeftCtrl;
    otIntersection: FinalSet := LeftShift * LeftCtrl;
    otDifference: FinalSet := LeftShift - LeftCtrl;
  end;
  CheckState(FinalSet);
  Label2.Caption := Operators[(Sender as TBitBtn).Tag];
end;

end.
```

The SETSEXP program shows how you can read and manipulate sets. In particular, you work with sets of type TShiftState. When you are finished studying the program, you will have all the knowledge you need to work with Delphi sets.

The main form for the SETSEXP program consists of four checkboxes, two panels, four labels, and three bitbtns, as shown in Figure 22.3. The four checkboxes are placed on top of the first panel, and the fourth label is placed on the top of the second panel.

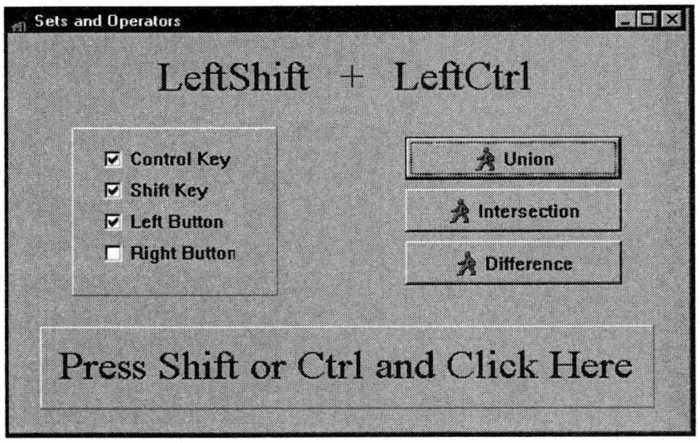

FIGURE 22.3.

The SETSEXP program's main form enables you to manipulate variables of type TShiftState.

SETSEXP tells you whether the Shift or Ctrl keys are pressed when the mouse is clicked, and it tells you whether the user pressed the right or left mouse button. The code also shows how to use the Intersection, Union, and Difference operators.

The key method in the SETSEXP program looks at a variable of type TShiftState and displays its contents to the user via the program's radio buttons:

```
procedure TUnion.CheckState(Shift: TShiftState);
begin
  ShiftKey.Checked := ssShift in Shift;
  ControlKey.Checked := ssCtrl in Shift;
  LeftButton.Checked := ssLeft in Shift;
  RightButton.Checked := ssRight in Shift;
end;
```

This code takes advantage of the fact that the in operator returns a Boolean variable, and the Checked property of a radio button is also declared to be of type Boolean. As a result, you can test to see whether a particular element is part of the Shift set. If it is, you can easily set the Checked state of a radio button to record the result. For example, in the preceding code, if ssShift is part of the current set, the ShiftKey radio button is checked.

Two different routines pass variables of type TShiftState to the CheckState method. The first routine is called whenever the user clicks in the panel at the bottom of the program or the label that rests on the panel:

```
procedure TUnion.PanelMouseDown(Sender: TObject;
                        Button: TMouseButton;
```

```
                            Shift: TShiftState;
                            X, Y: Integer);
begin
  CheckState(Shift);
end;
```

This code passes the Shift variable on to CheckState, which displays the contents of the variable to the user. For instance, if the Shift key is being held down and the right mouse button is pressed, PanelMouseDown is called. PanelMouseDown then passes the Shift variable to CheckState, and CheckState causes the ShiftKey and RightButton controls to be checked. The other two radio buttons are left unchecked.

There are three bitbtns on the right side of the main form. They are labeled Union, Intersection, and Difference. Clicking any of these buttons demonstrates one of the non-Boolean set operators. All three buttons have their OnClick event set to the following procedure:

```
procedure TUnion.SetBtnClick(Sender: TObject);
const
  Operators: array[0..2] of string = ('+', '*', '-');
var
  FinalSet: TShiftState;
  LeftShift: TShiftState;
  LeftCtrl: TShiftState;
begin
  LeftShift := [ssLeft, ssShift];
  LeftCtrl := [ssLeft, ssCtrl];
  case TOptType((Sender as TBitBtn).Tag) of
    otUnion: FinalSet := LeftShift + LeftCtrl;
    otIntersection: FinalSet := LeftShift * LeftCtrl;
    otDifference: FinalSet := LeftShift - LeftCtrl;
  end;
  CheckState(FinalSet);
  Label2.Caption := Operators[(Sender as TBitBtn).Tag];
end;
```

The SetBtnClick method declares three variables of type TShiftState. Two of these variables are used to declare sets that are used by the rest of the SetBtnClick method:

```
LeftShift := [ssLeft, ssShift];
LeftCtrl := [ssLeft, ssCtrl];
```

The first line assigns the LeftShift variable to a set that contains the values ssLeft and ssShift. The next line assigns the LeftCtrl variable to a set that contains ssLeft and ssCtrl. The rest of this method enables the user to see the union, intersection, and difference of these two sets.

The case statement in the middle of the SetBtnClick method detects which of the three bitbtns the user clicked. This is the old time-honored technique featuring the use of an enumerated type and the assignment of zero-based ordinal values to the Tag field of each button.

If the user clicks the Union button, the FinalSet variable is set to the union of the LeftShift and LeftCtrl variables:

```
FinalSet := LeftShift + LeftCtrl;
```

A click on the Intersection button executes the following code:

```
FinalSet := LeftShift * LeftCtrl;
```

The difference of the sets is calculated if the user clicks the Difference button:

```
FinalSet := LeftShift - LeftCtrl;
```

After the case statement ensures the selection of the proper operator, the FinalSet value is passed to CheckState and its contents are displayed to the user. For instance, if the user clicks the Union button, the LeftButton, ShiftKey, and ControlKey radio buttons are all checked. The Intersection button causes the LeftKey to be checked, and the Difference button causes the ShiftKey to be checked. Here is another way of looking at the work accomplished by these operators:

```
[ssLeft, ssShift] + [ssLeft, ssCtrl] = [ssLeft, ssShift, ssCtrl];
[ssLeft, ssShift] * [ssLeft, ssCtrl] = [ssLeft]
[ssLeft, ssShift] - [ssLeft, ssCtrl] = [ssShift]
```

To help the user understand exactly what is happening, the current set operation is displayed at the top of the form. For instance, if the user clicks the Union button, the following expression is shown to the user:

```
LeftShift + LeftCtrl
```

Throughout a run of the program, the words LeftShift and LeftCtrl are displayed to the user in a pair of TLabels. A third label displays +, -, or *, depending on the current state of the program:

```
Label2.Caption := Operators[(Sender as TBitBtn).Tag];
```

In this code, Operators is an array of three strings that contain the operators that return a set:

```
const
  Operators: array[0..2] of string = ('+', '*', '-');
```

The SETSEXP program gives you enough information that you should be able to work with the sets that are passed to Delphi event handlers. The code shown here defines the way sets are usually handled in all Delphi programs. However, you can actually directly manipulate the raw data that represents a Delphi set. Techniques for performing these manipulations are shown in the GetShift method, which is part of the program examined in the next section of this chapter.

Tracking the Mouse and Keyboard

You now know enough to be able begin an in-depth study of the main event handlers used by Delphi forms and controls. The EVENTS2 program, shown in Listing 22.3, enables you to trace the occurrence of all the keyboard or mouse interrupts generated during the run of a program.

Listing 22.3. The EVENTS2 program provides a detailed look at how to track events.

```
unit Main;

{ Program copyright (c) 1996 by Charles Calvert }
{ Project Name: EVENTS2 }

{ Events Two }

interface

uses
  WinTypes, WinProcs, Classes,
  Graphics, Forms, Controls,
  StdCtrls, vKeys, Messages,
  SysUtils, ExtCtrls;

const
  Space = 20;

type
  TEvents = class(TForm)
    Panel1: TPanel;
    Label1: TLabel;
    LMouseMove: TLabel;
    Label3: TLabel;
    LMouseDown: TLabel;
    Label5: TLabel;
    LKeyDown: TLabel;
    Label7: TLabel;
    LKeyUp: TLabel;
    Label9: TLabel;
    LMouseUp: TLabel;
    Label11: TLabel;
    LWidth: TLabel;
    Label13: TLabel;
    LHeight: TLabel;
    LSpecialMouse: TLabel;
    Label16: TLabel;
    procedure FormMouseDown(Sender: TObject; Button: TMouseButton;
      Shift: TShiftState; X, Y: Integer);
    procedure FormMouseMove(Sender: TObject; Shift: TShiftState; X,
      Y: Integer);
    procedure FormKeyDown(Sender: TObject; var Key: Word;
      Shift: TShiftState);
    procedure FormKeyUp(Sender: TObject; var Key: Word;
      Shift: TShiftState);
    procedure FormMouseUp(Sender: TObject; Button: TMouseButton;
      Shift: TShiftState; X, Y: Integer);
    procedure FormResize(Sender: TObject);
    procedure FormPaint(Sender: TObject);
  private
    procedure MyMouseMove(var M: TWMMouse); message wm_MouseMove;
  public
    { Public declarations }
  end;
```

continues

Listing 22.3. continued

```
var
  Events: TEvents;

implementation

{$R *.DFM}

procedure TEvents.FormMouseDown(Sender: TObject; Button: TMouseButton;
  Shift: TShiftState; X, Y: Integer);
begin
  LMouseDown.Caption := Buttons[Ord(Button)] + ' ' + GetShift(Shift);
end;

procedure TEvents.FormMouseMove(Sender: TObject;
                                Shift: TShiftState;
                                X, Y: Integer);
begin
  LMouseMove.Caption := 'X: ' + IntToStr(X) + ' Y: ' +
                        IntToStr(Y) + ' ' + GetShift(Shift);

end;

procedure TEvents.FormKeyDown(Sender: TObject; var Key: Word;
  Shift: TShiftState);
begin
  LKeyDown.Caption := GetKey(Key) + ' ' + GetShift(Shift);
end;

procedure TEvents.FormKeyUp(Sender: TObject; var Key: Word;
  Shift: TShiftState);
begin
  LKeyUp.Caption := GetKey(Key) + ' ' + GetShift(Shift);
end;

procedure TEvents.FormMouseUp(Sender: TObject;
                              Button: TMouseButton;
                              Shift: TShiftState;
                              X, Y: Integer);
begin
  LMouseUp.Caption := 'X: ' + IntToStr(X) + ' Y: ' +
                      IntToStr(Y) + ' ' + GetShift(Shift);
end;

procedure TEvents.FormResize(Sender: TObject);
begin
  LHeight.Caption := IntToStr(Width);
  LWidth.Caption := IntToStr(Height);
end;

procedure TEvents.MyMouseMove(var M: TWMMouse);
begin
  Inherited;
  LSpecialMouse.Caption := 'X: ' + IntToStr(M.XPos) +
                           ' Y: ' + IntToStr(M.YPos);
end;
```

```
procedure TEvents.FormPaint(Sender: TObject);
begin
  Canvas.Font.Name := 'New Times Roman';
  Canvas.Font.Size := 48;
  Canvas.TextOut(1, Panel1.Height, 'Mouse Zone');
end;

end.
```

Listing 22.4 shows the VKeys unit used by the EVENTS2 program.

Listing 22.4. The VKeys unit is used by the EVENTS2 program.

```
unit Vkeys;

{ Program copyright (c) 1996 by Charles Calvert }
{ Project Name: UNITS }

interface

uses
  Classes;

type
  T3StrAry = array[0..2] of String;
  T5StrAry = array[0..4] of String;
  T8StrAry = array[0..7] of String;

const
  AMessage: T5StrAry = ('WM_CHAR', 'WM_KEY', 'WM_MOUSEMOVE',
                        'WM_MOUSEDOWN', 'WM_MOUSEUP');
  Buttons: T3StrAry = ('mbLeft', 'mbRight', 'mbCenter');
  Shifty: T8StrAry = ('ssShift', 'ssAlt', 'ssCtrl', 'ssLeft',
                      'ssRight', 'ssMiddle', 'ssDouble', ssUnknown);

function GetShift(State: TShiftState): String;
function GetKey(K: Word): String;
implementation
uses
  WinTypes;

function GetShift(State: TShiftState): String;
var
  B, i: Byte;
begin
  Result := '';
  for i := 0 to 7 do begin
    B := Byte(1) shl i;
    if (B and Byte(State)) > 0 then Result := Result + ' ' +  Shifty[i];
  end;
end;

function GetKey(K: Word): String;
begin
  case K of
```

continues

Listing 22.4. continued

```
vk_LButton: Result := 'vk_LButton';
vk_RButton  : Result := 'vk_RButton';
vk_Cancel   : Result := 'vk_Cancel';
vk_MButton  : Result := 'vk_MButton';
vk_Back     : Result := 'vk_Back';
vk_Tab      : Result := 'vk_Tab';
vk_Clear    : Result := 'vk_Clear';
vk_Return   : Result := 'vk_Return';
vk_Shift    : Result := 'vk_Shift';
vk_Control  : Result := 'vk_Control';
vk_Menu     : Result := 'vk_Menu';
vk_Pause    : Result := 'vk_Pause';
vk_Capital  : Result := 'vk_Capital';
vk_Escape   : Result := 'vk_Escape';
vk_Space    : Result := 'vk_Space';
vk_Prior    : Result := 'vk_Prior';
vk_Next     : Result := 'vk_Next';
vk_End      : Result := 'vk_End';
vk_Home     : Result := 'vk_Home';
vk_Left     : Result := 'vk_Left';
vk_Up       : Result := 'vk_Up';
vk_Right    : Result := 'vk_Right';
vk_Down     : Result := 'vk_Down';
vk_Select   : Result := 'vk_Select';
vk_Print    : Result := 'vk_Print';
vk_Execute  : Result := 'vk_Execute';
vk_SnapShot : Result := 'vk_SnapShot';
vk_Insert   : Result := 'vk_Insert';
vk_Delete   : Result := 'vk_Delete';
vk_Help     : Result := 'vk_Help';
vk_NumPad0  : Result := 'vk_NumPad0';
vk_NumPad1  : Result := 'vk_NumPad1';
vk_NumPad2  : Result := 'vk_NumPad2';
vk_NumPad3  : Result := 'vk_NumPad3';
vk_NumPad4  : Result := 'vk_NumPad4';
vk_NumPad5  : Result := 'vk_NumPad5';
vk_NumPad6  : Result := 'vk_NumPad6';
vk_NumPad7  : Result := 'vk_NumPad7';
vk_NumPad8  : Result := 'vk_NumPad8';
vk_NumPad9  : Result := 'vk_NumPad9';
vk_Multiply : Result := 'vk_Multiply';
vk_Add      : Result := 'vk_vkAdd';
vk_Separator : Result := 'vk_Separator';
vk_Subtract : Result := 'vk_Subtract';
vk_Decimal  : Result := 'vk_Decimal';
vk_Divide   : Result := 'vk_Divide';
vk_F1       : Result := 'vk_F1';
vk_F2       : Result := 'vk_F2';
vk_F3       : Result := 'vk_F3';
vk_F4       : Result := 'vk_F4';
vk_F5       : Result := 'vk_F5';
vk_F6       : Result := 'vk_F6';
vk_F7       : Result := 'vk_F7';
vk_F8       : Result := 'vk_F8';
vk_F9       : Result := 'vk_F9';
vk_F10      : Result := 'vk_F10';
```

```
   vk_F11        : Result := 'vk_F11';
   vk_F12        : Result := 'vk_F12';
   vk_F13        : Result := 'vk_F13';
   vk_F14        : Result := 'vk_F14';
   vk_F15        : Result := 'vk_F15';
   vk_F16        : Result := 'vk_F16';
   vk_F17        : Result := 'vk_F17';
   vk_F18        : Result := 'vk_F18';
   vk_F19        : Result := 'vk_F19';
   vk_F20        : Result := 'vk_F20';
   vk_F21        : Result := 'vk_F21';
   vk_F22        : Result := 'vk_F22';
   vk_F23        : Result := 'vk_F23';
   vk_F24        : Result := 'vk_F24';
   vk_NumLock    : Result := 'vk_NumLock';
   vk_Scroll     : Result := 'vk_Scroll';
 else
   Result := Chr(K);
 end;
end;
end.
```

EVENTS2 shows how to extract the full content of a message sent to you by Delphi. The main form for the program (shown in Figure 22.4) provides information on a wide range of mouse and keyboard generated events.

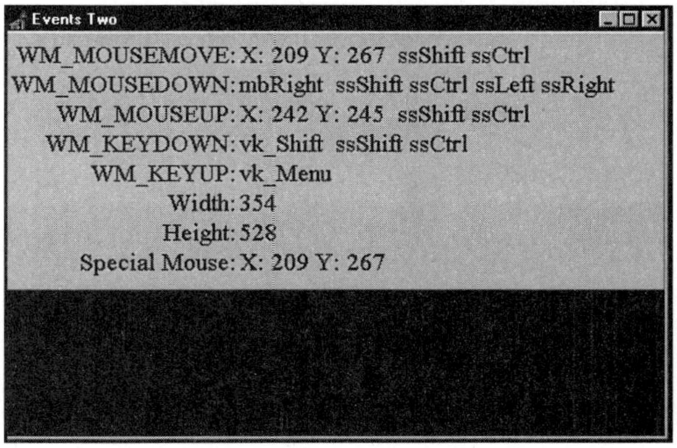

FIGURE 22.4.

The EVENTS2 program tracks key Windows events as they occur.

```
Events Two                                           _ □ ✕
WM_MOUSEMOVE: X: 209 Y: 267  ssShift ssCtrl
WM_MOUSEDOWN: mbRight  ssShift ssCtrl ssLeft ssRight
     WM_MOUSEUP: X: 242 Y: 245  ssShift ssCtrl
     WM_KEYDOWN: vk_Shift  ssShift ssCtrl
         WM_KEYUP: vk_Menu
               Width: 354
               Height: 528
         Special Mouse: X: 209 Y: 267
```

To use the program, simply compile and run. Click the mouse in random locations and strike any of the keys on the keyboard. Just rattle away; you won't do any harm unless you press Ctrl+Alt+Del. Every time you move the mouse, click the mouse, or strike a key, the exact nature of the event that occurred is shown in the main form of the program. For instance, if you move the mouse, its current location is shown on the form. If you strike the F1 key while the Ctrl key is pressed, those keys' values are displayed on the form.

The FormMouseMove event handler in the EVENTS2 window tracks the current location of the mouse and the state of its buttons. It does this by responding to OnMouseMove events:

```
procedure TEvents.FormMouseMove(Sender: TObject;
                                Shift: TShiftState;
                                X, Y: Integer);
begin
  LMouseMove.Caption := 'X: ' + IntToStr(X) + ' Y: ' +
                        IntToStr(Y) + ' ' + GetShift(Shift);

end;
```

The method for tracking the X and Y values is fairly intuitive. X stands for the current column, and Y stands for the current row, with columns and rows measured in pixels. Before these values can be shown to the user, they need to be translated into strings by the IntToStr function. Nothing could be simpler than the techniques used to record the current location of the mouse.

The technique for recording the current shift state, however, is a bit more complex. As you saw earlier, TShiftState is a predeclared structure that looks like this:

```
TShiftState = set of (ssShift, ssAlt, ssCtrl,
                      ssRight, ssLeft, ssMiddle,
                      ssDouble);
```

The elements of this set track all the possible states of the Shift, Alt, and Ctrl keys, as well as the mouse buttons.

Delphi records the state of a set in the individual bits of a variable, in which bit 0 corresponds to the first element in the set, bit 1 corresponds to the second element in the set, bit 2 corresponds to the third element in the set, and so on. This fact enables you to use bitwise operators to track the state of the shift button:

```
function GetShift(State: TShiftState): String;
var
  B, i: Byte;
begin
  Result := '';
  for i := 0 to 7 do begin
    B := Byte(1) shl i;
    if (B and Byte(State)) > 0 then Result :=
      Result + ' ' + Shifty[i];
  end;
end;
```

The preceding code takes advantage of the following constant array:

```
Shifty: T7StrAry = ('ssShift', 'ssAlt', 'ssCtrl', 'ssLeft',
                    'ssRight', 'ssMiddle', 'ssDouble');
```

as well as this type declaration:

```
T7StrAry = array[0..6] of String;
```

More specifically, the code checks to see whether the 0 bit is set, and if it is, 'ssShift' is added to the string returned by the function. If the first bit in the Shift variable is set to 1, the string 'ssAlt' is added to the string returned by the function, and so on. As you move through the bits in the State variable, you get a picture of the current state of the mouse and keyboard. For instance, if the Shift and Ctrl keys are pressed, as well as the right mouse button, the string returned by the function looks like this:

```
ssShift ssCtrl ssRight
```

Bitwise operators can be tricky at times, but anyone can call the GetShift function. (See the BINARY.PAS unit, included on the CD in the UNITS subdirectory, for additional routines that help simplify the process of working on the bit level.)

Trapping Virtual Keys

When keys are pressed in a Windows program, two different messages can be sent to your program. One message is called wm_KeyDown, and it is sent whenever any key on the keyboard is pressed. The second message is called wm_Char, and it is sent when one of the alphanumeric keys is pressed. In other words, if you press the A key, you get both a wm_KeyDown and a wm_Char message. If you press the F1 key, only the wm_KeyDown message is sent.

OnKeyPress event handlers correspond to wm_Char messages, and OnKeyDown events correspond to wm_KeyDown events. That's why OnKeyPress handlers are passed a Key variable that is of type Char, and OnKeyDown handlers are passed a Key variable that is of type word.

When you get a wm_KeyDown message, you need to have some way of translating that message into a meaningful value. To help with this chore, Windows declares a set of virtual key constants that all start with vk. For example, if you press the F1 key, the Key variable passed to an OnKeyDown event is set to vk_F1, in which the letters vk stand for virtual key. The virtual key codes are found in the WINDOWS unit and also in the online help if you search under "Virtual Key Codes."

You can test to see which virtual key has been pressed by writing code that looks like this:

```
if Key = vk_Cancel then DoSomething;
```

This code simply tests to see whether a particular key has been pressed. If it has, the code calls the DoSomething procedure.

To help you understand virtual keys, the GetKey method from the VKEYS unit returns a string stating exactly what key has been pressed:

```
function GetKey(K: Word): String;
begin
  case K of
    vk_LButton: Result := 'vk_LButton';
    vk_RButton  : Result := 'vk_RButton';
    vk_Cancel   : Result := 'vk_Cancel';
    vk_MButton  : Result := 'vk_MButton';
    vk_Back     : Result := 'vk_Back';
    vk_Tab      : Result := 'vk_Tab';
    vk_Clear    : Result := 'vk_Clear';
```

```
vk_Return    : Result := 'vk_Return';
vk_Shift     : Result := 'vk_Shift';
vk_Control   : Result := 'vk_Control';
vk_Menu      : Result := 'vk_Menu';
vk_Pause     : Result := 'vk_Pause';
vk_Capital   : Result := 'vk_Capital';
vk_Escape    : Result := 'vk_Escape';
vk_Space     : Result := 'vk_Space';
vk_Prior     : Result := 'vk_Prior';
vk_Next      : Result := 'vk_Next';
vk_End       : Result := 'vk_End';
vk_Home      : Result := 'vk_Home';
vk_Left      : Result := 'vk_Left';
vk_Up        : Result := 'vk_Up';
vk_Right     : Result := 'vk_Right';
vk_Down      : Result := 'vk_Down';
vk_Select    : Result := 'vk_Select';
vk_Print     : Result := 'vk_Print';
vk_Execute   : Result := 'vk_Execute';
vk_SnapShot  : Result := 'vk_SnapShot';
vk_Insert    : Result := 'vk_Insert';
vk_Delete    : Result := 'vk_Delete';
vk_Help      : Result := 'vk_Help';
vk_NumPad0   : Result := 'vk_NumPad0';
vk_NumPad1   : Result := 'vk_NumPad1';
vk_NumPad2   : Result := 'vk_NumPad2';
vk_NumPad3   : Result := 'vk_NumPad3';
vk_NumPad4   : Result := 'vk_NumPad4';
vk_NumPad5   : Result := 'vk_NumPad5';
vk_NumPad6   : Result := 'vk_NumPad6';
vk_NumPad7   : Result := 'vk_NumPad7';
vk_NumPad8   : Result := 'vk_NumPad8';
vk_NumPad9   : Result := 'vk_NumPad9';
vk_Multiply  : Result := 'vk_Multiply';
vk_Add       : Result := 'vk_vkAdd';
vk_Separator : Result := 'vk_Separator';
vk_Subtract  : Result := 'vk_Subtract';
vk_Decimal   : Result := 'vk_Decimal';
vk_Divide    : Result := 'vk_Divide';
vk_F1        : Result := 'vk_F1';
vk_F2        : Result := 'vk_F2';
vk_F3        : Result := 'vk_F3';
vk_F4        : Result := 'vk_F4';
vk_F5        : Result := 'vk_F5';
vk_F6        : Result := 'vk_F6';
vk_F7        : Result := 'vk_F7';
vk_F8        : Result := 'vk_F8';
vk_F9        : Result := 'vk_F9';
vk_F10       : Result := 'vk_F10';
vk_F11       : Result := 'vk_F11';
vk_F12       : Result := 'vk_F12';
vk_F13       : Result := 'vk_F13';
vk_F14       : Result := 'vk_F14';
vk_F15       : Result := 'vk_F15';
vk_F16       : Result := 'vk_F16';
vk_F17       : Result := 'vk_F17';
vk_F18       : Result := 'vk_F18';
vk_F19       : Result := 'vk_F19';
vk_F20       : Result := 'vk_F20';
```

```
      vk_F21        : Result := 'vk_F21';
      vk_F22        : Result := 'vk_F22';
      vk_F23        : Result := 'vk_F23';
      vk_F24        : Result := 'vk_F24';
      vk_NumLock    : Result := 'vk_NumLock';
      vk_Scroll     : Result := 'vk_Scroll';
    else
      Result := Chr(K);
    end;
  end;
end;
end.
```

This procedure is really just a giant `case` statement that checks to see whether the `Key` variable is equal to any of the virtual keys. If it is not, the code assumes that it must be one of the standard keys between A and Z. (See the `else` clause in the code to see how these standard keys are handled.)

As explained in the last paragraph, the virtual key codes do not cover normal letters such as A, B, and C. In other words, there is no value `vk_A` or `vk_B`. To test for these letters, just use the standard ASCII values. In other words, test whether `Key` is equal to 65, or whether `Chr(Key)` is equal to A. The point here is that these letters already have key codes. That is, the key codes for these letters are the literal values A, B, C, and so on. Because these are perfectly serviceable values, there is no need to create virtual key codes for the standard letters of the alphabet, or for numbers.

You probably won't have much use for the `GetKey` routine in a standard Delphi program. However, it is useful when you are trying to understand virtual keys and the `OnKeyDown` event. As a result, I have included it in this program.

Handling Events Directly

If you look at the bottom of the EVENTS2 form, you see that there is a special event that tracks the position of the mouse. The EVENTS2 program tracks the mouse movements in two different ways because I wanted to show you that you can get information about the mouse either by responding to `OnMouseMove` events or by directly tracking `wm_MouseMove` messages.

Here is how you declare a procedure that is going to directly capture a message:

```
procedure MyMouseMove(var M: TWMMouse);
  message wm_MouseMove;
```

The declaration shown here tells Delphi that you want to respond directly when the operating system informs your program that the mouse has moved. In other words, you don't want the Delphi VCL to trap the message first and then pass it on to you in an `OnMouseMove` event. Instead, you just want the message sent straight to you by the operating system, as if you were working with one of the Windows API programs shown earlier in the book. In short, you're telling the VCL: "Yes, I know you can make this task very simple and can automate nearly the entire process by using visual tools. That's nice of you, but right now I want to get the real event itself. I have some reason of my own for wanting to get very close to the metal. As a result, I'm going to grab the message before you ever get a chance to look at it!"

If you want to intercept messages directly, you should use the message keyword, as shown earlier in the MyMouseMove declaration. The proper way to use this syntax is to first write the word message and then follow it by the constant representing the message you want to trap. When you use the message directive, you are declaring a form of dynamic method, which means Delphi uses the dynamic method table to dispatch your message. In particular, Delphi maintains a list of dynamic methods used in your application, and it locates a particular method's address by using the offset implied in the wm_MouseMove constant.

Here's the code for the MyMouseMove procedure:

```
procedure TEvents.MyMouseMove(var M: TWMMouse);
begin
  Inherited;
  LSpecialMouse.Caption := 'X: ' + IntToStr(M.XPos) +
                           ' Y: ' + IntToStr(M.YPos);
end;
```

You can see that the code begins by calling the inherited wm_MouseMove handler. If you didn't make this call, the program would still run, but the OnMouseMove event would never be sent to the FormMouseMove procedure. It isn't an error if you don't pass the message back to Delphi. You can either keep the message for yourself or pass it on, as you prefer.

Normally, when you call an inherited method, you need to specify which function you mean to call. For instance, if you are in a Paint method, you write the following:

```
procedure Form1.Paint;
begin
  Inherited Paint;
  Canvas1.TextOut(1, 1, 'hi');
end;
```

When you are inside message handlers, however, there is no need to specify the inherited method you want to call, and you can therefore just write Inherited.

If you omit the call to Inherited from the MySpecialMouse procedure, the FormMouseMove method in the EVENTS2 program is no longer called. In other words, you are directly trapping wm_MouseMove messages and not passing them on to the VCL. As a result, the VCL does not know that the event occurred, and FormMouseMove is not called.

The explanation in the last paragraph might not be easy to grasp unless you actually experiment with the EVENTS2 program. You should run the program once with the default version of the MyMouseMove method, and once with the call to Inherited commented out:

```
procedure TEvents.MyMouseMove(var M: TWMMouse);
begin
  { Inherited; }
  LSpecialMouse.Caption := 'X: ' + IntToStr(M.XPos) +
                           ' Y: ' + IntToStr(M.YPos);
end;
```

Notice that when you run the program this way, the OnMouseMove message at the top of the form is left blank.

If you look at the header for the MyMouseMove function, you can see that it is passed a parameter of type TWMMouse. As you recall, the TWMMouse record, found in MESSAGES.PAS, looks like this:

```
TWMMouse = record
    Msg: Cardinal;
    Keys: Longint;
    case Integer of
      0: (
        XPos: Smallint;
        YPos: Smallint);
      1: (
        Pos: TSmallPoint;
        Result: Longint);
  end;
```

If you break out both of the options shown in this variant record, you can further simplify this record by writing

```
TWMMouse = record
  Msg: Cardinal;
  Keys: LongInt;
  XPos: SmallInt;
  YPos: SmallInt;
end;
```

or

```
TWMMouse = record
  Msg: Cardinal;
  Keys: LongInt;
  Pos: TSmallPoint;
  Result: Longint;
end;
```

For most users, one of these two views will be the most useful way to picture the record.

The same information is present in a TWMMouse record that you would find if you responded to an OnMouseMove or OnMouseDown event. If appropriate, you can find out the row and column where the mouse is located, what key is pressed, and what state the Shift, Alt, and Ctrl keys are in. To pursue this matter further, you should look up wm_MouseMove and wm_MouseDown messages in the online help, or refer to the earlier chapters on the Windows API, such as Chapter 12, "The Mouse and the Keyboard."

TWMMouse plays the same role in a Delphi program that message crackers from WINDOWSX.H play in a C++ program. In other words, they automatically break out the values passed in lParam or wParam. However, if you want, you can pass a variable of type TMessage as the parameter sent to the wm_MouseMove message handler:

```
procedure MyMouseMove(var M: TMessage);
  message wm_MouseMove;
```

Because TMessage and TWMMouse are both the same size, Delphi doesn't care which one you use when trapping wm_MouseMove events. It's up to you to decide how you want to crack the wParam and lParam parameters.

> **NOTE**
>
> Delphi is such a flexible tool that it lets you write Windows API code that can be totally specific to either the 16- or 32-bit versions of Windows. In other words, there is nothing in Delphi to prevent you from writing 32-bit code that takes advantage of threads. However, you cannot take that code to the 16-bit version of Windows and expect it to work. The rule to follow is very simple: If you write VCL code, it compiles under either the 16- or 32-bit compiler. However, if you start calling the Windows API directly, you take the chance that the call you make will change or not be supported under WIN32. Of course, most of the Windows API works in either 16- or 32-bit mode, but some calls can cause trouble, and you need to be aware of them if you are going to try to write portable code.

In this section, you have learned something about directly handling Windows messages. When you write code that captures messages directly, you are in a sense reverting back to the more complicated model of programming found in Borland Pascal 7.0. However, there are times when it is very helpful to get close to the machine, and Delphi lets you get there if that is what you need to do.

Handling *wm_Command*

In standard Windows programming as it was conducted before the appearance of visual tools, one of the most important messages was wm_Command. This message was sent to a program every time the user selected a menu item, a button, or clicked almost any other control that is part of the current program. Furthermore, each of the buttons, menu items, and other controls in a program had a special ID, which was assigned by the programmer. This ID was passed to wm_Command handlers in the wParam variable.

Delphi handles wm_Command messages in such a way that you almost never have to think about them. For instance, you can get clicks on a button or menu by using the delegation model. Standard Delphi controls still have IDs, but Delphi assigns these numbers automatically, and there is no obvious way for you to learn the value of these IDs.

Despite Delphi's capability to simplify this aspect of Windows programming, there are still times when you want to get down to the bare bones and start handling wm_Command messages yourself. In particular, you will want to find a way to discover the ID associated with a particular command, and you will want to trap that ID inside a wm_Command handler.

The MENUDEF program gives a general overview of this topic. The program enables you to discover the ID used by a series of menu items and then enables you to trap these IDs when they are sent to a wm_Command handler in the form of a TMessage.wParam variable.

Figure 22.5 shows the form for the MENUDEF program. Here are the menu items that you can't see in Figure 22.5:

```
Caption = 'File'
  Caption = 'Open'
  Caption = 'Close'
  Caption = 'Exit'
Caption = 'Edit'
  Caption = 'Cut'
  Caption = 'Copy'
  Caption = 'Paste'
```

FIGURE 22.5.

The MENUDEF program uses a TMemo, a TButton, and a TMainMenu control.

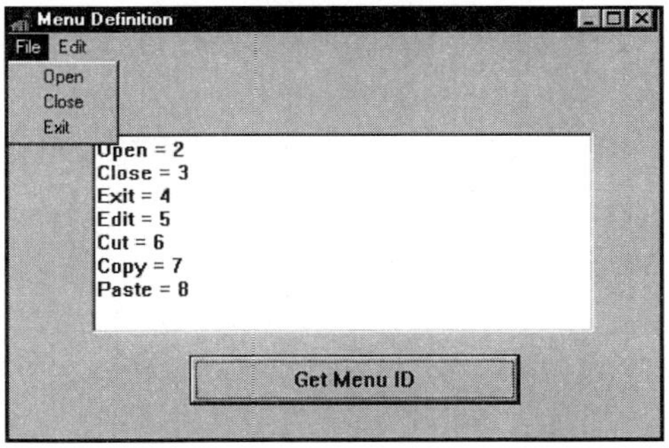

The code for the MENUDEF program is in Listing 22.5. You can see that it features two standard Delphi event handlers, as well as a wm_Command handler.

Listing 22.5. The MENUDEF program shows how to retrieve the ID of a Delphi menu item.

```
unit Main;

{ Program copyright  1996 by Charles Calvert }
{ Project Name: MENUDEF }

interface

uses
  SysUtils, WinTypes, WinProcs,
  Messages, Classes, Graphics,
  Controls, Forms, Dialogs,
  Menus, StdCtrls;

type
  TForm1 = class(TForm)
    MainMenu1: TMainMenu;
    File1: TMenuItem;
```

continues

Listing 22.5. continued

```
      Open1: TMenuItem;
      CLose1: TMenuItem;
      Exit1: TMenuItem;
      Exit2: TMenuItem;
      Cut1: TMenuItem;
      Copy1: TMenuItem;
      Paste1: TMenuItem;
      Memo1: TMemo;
      MenuID: TButton;
      procedure FormCreate(Sender: TObject);
      procedure MenuIDClick(Sender: TObject);
    private
      { Private declarations }
      TotalMenuItems: Word;
      MenuItemAry: array [0..100] of Word;
    public
      procedure WMCommand(var Message:TMessage); message wm_Command;
      { Public declarations }
    end;

var
  Form1: TForm1;

implementation

{$R *.DFM}

procedure TForm1.WMCommand(var Message: TMessage);
var
  i: Integer;
  S1, S2: string;
begin
  inherited;
  S2 := 'ID = ';
  for i := 1 to TotalMenuItems do
    if Message.WParam = MenuItemAry[i] then
      MessageBox(Handle, 'Not implemented',
                 PChar(S2 + IntToStr(Message.wParam)), mb_Ok);
end;

procedure TForm1.FormCreate(Sender: TObject);
var
  i: Integer;
begin
  for i := 0 to ComponentCount - 1 do
    if Components[i] is TMenuItem then begin
      MenuItemAry[TotalMenuItems] := TMenuItem(Components[i]).Command;
      Inc(TotalMenuItems);
    end;
end;

procedure TForm1.MenuIDClick(Sender: TObject);
var
  Command, i: Integer;
  Name: string;
begin
```

```
      Memo1.Lines.Clear;
      for i := 0 to ComponentCount - 1 do
        if Components[i] is TMenuItem then begin
          Command := TMenuItem(Components[i]).Command;
          Name := TMenuItem(Components[i]).Caption;
          Memo1.Lines.Add(Name + ' = ' + IntToStr(Command));
        end;
end;

end.
```

The MENUDEF program has two features:

- If you click the button at the bottom of the main form, the program's memo control displays a list of all the items in the menu, along with their IDs.

- If you click any of the menu items, a message box appears stating that the item is not yet implemented. This is the kind of message you want to show the user while you are still developing a program. You are stating, in effect, that the control has been placed on the form, but it doesn't do anything yet. Besides displaying the "Under development" message in the body of the message box, the caption shows the menu item's ID.

Here is the code that grabs the ID of all the menu items and displays the ID along with the menu item's caption in a TMemo:

```
procedure TForm1.MenuIDClick(Sender: TObject);
var
  Command, i: Integer;
  Name: string;
begin
  Memo1.Lines.Clear;
  for i := 0 to ComponentCount - 1 do
    if Components[i] is TMenuItem then begin
      Command := TMenuItem(Components[i]).Command;
      Name := TMenuItem(Components[i]).Caption;
      Memo1.Lines.Add(Name + ' = ' + IntToStr(Command));
    end;
end;
```

The code begins by clearing the current contents of the memo control. Then it iterates through all the components on the form and finds any of them that are of type TMenuItem. The next step is to get the ID and the caption of the menu items. To get the ID, you need only reference the Command property of the TMenuItem component. The caption can be retrieved the same way, and then you can add this information to the list box.

The use of the is operator in the previous code demonstrates Delphi's capability to work with Run Time Type Information (RTTI). RTTI enables you to test the type of a particular variable and respond accordingly. For instance, in this case, the program simply asks whether a particular component is of type TMenuItem; if this Boolean question returns True, the program examines the component in more depth. The capability to use the is and as operators to detect the type of an object at runtime is one of the sexier features of Delphi's language.

The remaining code in the program captures the IDs of the menu items in an array and then responds to wm_Command messages generated by clicks in one of the program's menu items. As explained earlier, the code displays a message box stating that the menus are not yet functional. In the caption of the menu box, you can read the ID of the control that was clicked.

The code that captures the menu items in an array occurs in a FormCreate method:

```
procedure TForm1.FormCreate(Sender: TObject);
var
  i: Integer;
begin
  for i := 0 to ComponentCount - 1 do
    if Components[i] is TMenuItem then begin
      MenuItemAry[TotalMenuItems] :=
        TMenuItem(Components[i]).Command;
      Inc(TotalMenuItems);
    end;
end;
```

This code is almost identical to the MenuIDClick method, except that the IDs of the TMenuItems are stored in an array, rather than being shown in a TMemo. The declaration for the array looks like this:

```
MenuItemAry: array [0..100] of Word;
```

The declaration for the wm_Command handler should be familiar to you by this time:

```
procedure WMCommand(var Message:TMessage);
  message wm_Command;
```

Here, the message directive tells the compiler that this is a dynamic method and the offset in the dynamic method table is established by the wm_Command constant.

The WMCommand method compares the values sent in Message.wParam to the values in the MenuItemAry. If it finds a match, it displays the message box previously described.

```
procedure TForm1.WMCommand(var Message: TMessage);
var
  i: Integer;
  S1, S2: string;
begin
  inherited;
  S2 := 'ID = ';
  for i := 1 to TotalMenuItems do
    if Message.WParam = MenuItemAry[i] then
      MessageBox(Handle, 'Not implemented',
                  PChar(S2 + IntToStr(Message.wParam)), mb_Ok);
end;
```

This code calls the Windows API MessageBox function rather than MessageDlg.

One final point about working with the IDs of a control: If you build the interface of your program and then don't change its menus or any other aspect of its interface, the IDs Delphi associates with each control will (at least theoretically) remain the same throughout the development of your application. This might give some people the idea of using the MenuIDClick method shown earlier as a temporary response to a click on one of your controls and to then store the output to a file. Thereafter, you would hope to know the ID associated with each of your controls and could handle them in a wm_Command routine. This technique is theoretically possible, but I wouldn't recommend it as part of the framework for any serious application. In short, if you have to know the ID of a particular control, I would determine it in the FormCreate method, thereby ensuring that the ID is correct for that build of your program.

Summary

In this section, you learned how to handle events using the standard Delphi delegation model. However, you saw that you can also circumvent this system and handle events directly by employing the message keyword. This is an important subject, and you shouldn't really move on until you have a good idea of what's going on in the EVENTS2 program.

This chapter also explained that you can start handling wParam and lParam variables directly. Furthermore, Delphi gives you a way to parse the information passed with events, so that you can place a custom record as the parameter to a message handler. For instance, if Windows conceals a set of X and Y coordinates inside the high and low words of wParam, Delphi enables you to define a custom record that automatically breaks up wParam into two separate variables called X and Y. This is the same functionality that is found in the message crackers provided in the WINDOWSX.H module that ships with Borland C++. The TWMMouse record discussed earlier is one of these records; TMessage is another. If you want, you can create your own records that parse the information associated with standard Delphi events or with events that you create yourself.

Objects and Inheritance

23

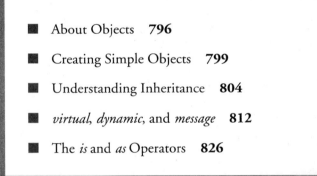

This chapter focuses on object-oriented programming (OOP). Specifically, it takes a close look at inheritance, which is one of the big three topics in object-oriented code. The other two key topics are encapsulation and polymorphism, which you learn about in the next few chapters.

In particular, this chapter covers the following topics:

- OOP theory and basics
- Inheritance
- Virtual and dynamic methods
- Method pointers and procedural variables
- Virtual and dynamic method tables
- The `is` and `as` operators, which provide valuable Run Time Type Information (RTTI)

This chapter focuses on several programs designed to show how objects are constructed and why object-oriented programming works. One of the programs is developed in several stages, so that you can see how an object hierarchy is developed. The program is not completed until halfway through the next chapter, but when you are finished you will know how to construct a useful object hierarchy.

After you read this chapter and Chapter 24, the next big step is to learn how to build components. In fact, the real justification for learning this material is that it gives you the ability to start creating your own components. Building your own components is one of the most important tasks you can tackle in Delphi, and I'm going to spend the next few chapters making sure that I properly lay the groundwork for this subject.

About Objects

It might seem a little strange to start focusing on objects this late in the book. After all, almost every program I have shown so far uses object-oriented code. So how could I wait this long to begin talking seriously about objects? To answer this question I need to discuss two different issues:

- How does Delphi treat objects?
- Why do people write object-oriented code?

The developers wanted Delphi to be very easy to use. By its very nature, OOP is not always a simple topic. As a result, Delphi goes to considerable lengths to hide some of the difficulties of object-oriented programming from the user. The biggest steps in this direction include the automatic construction of `Form1` as an object and the fact that the framework for most methods is produced automatically by the IDE.

Here are the same ideas looked at again from a slightly more in-depth perspective:

- **Visual Tools:** You can easily design a form using visual tools. To create a useful form, you want to be able to arrange and rearrange the elements of the visual design quickly and easily. Delphi excels at this.

- **Components:** You want to be able to manipulate objects not only as code, but as seemingly physical entities that you can handle with the mouse. Components provide an ideal solution to this problem. The plastic Lego sets you played with as a child were fascinating because they enabled you to build complex structures out of simple, easy-to-manipulate pieces. In other words, Legos let you concentrate on the design of structures, making the actual construction of a robust and easy-to-maintain building relatively trivial. Components give the same kind of flexibility.

- **OOP:** Objects, and particularly the ability to view object hierarchies in the Browser, make it easy to see the overall design of a program. It's possible to see how a program is constructed not only by looking at the code, but also by looking at an object hierarchy made up of reusable classes. These kinds of abstract, visual representations of a code base aid in the process of designing and maintaining a program. The key word here is reuse. You can write an object once and then reuse it over and over again. Reusability is what OOP is all about.

OOP, then, is part of a theory of design that is moving increasingly in the direction of reusable, visual components that can be manipulated with the mouse. Undoubtedly, this means some types of programs that are difficult to construct today will become trivial to build in the future. Delphi has already performed this magic with databases. A 10-year-old child could use Delphi to construct a simple database application. However, creating complex programs will probably always be difficult, simply because it is so hard to design a good program that performs anything more than trivial tasks. First printing presses, then typewriters, and finally word processors have made writing much easier than it used to be, but they have not succeeded in making us all into Shakespeare.

Delphi's object-oriented, component-based architecture makes programming easier than it used to be. That doesn't mean that now everyone will be able to program. It just means that now the best programmers can make better applications. The key terms are reuse, visual design tools, components, and objects.

Creating Simple Objects

If you start a new project, compile it, and then open the Browser, you see something like the image shown in Figure 23.1. There is a forest of objects depicted here and little question that the view can be intimidating to someone trying to get their hands around OOP.

FIGURE 23.1.

The Object Browser after compiling a minimal form-based application.

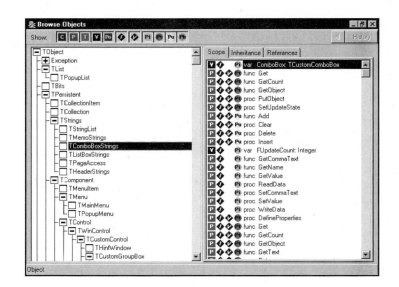

Start a new project. Bring up the Project Manager from the View menu and remove Form1. Go to the View menu again and choose Project Source. Go to Project | Options | Linker and chose Generate Console Application, as shown in Figure 23.2.

FIGURE 23.2.

Creating a console application in Delphi.

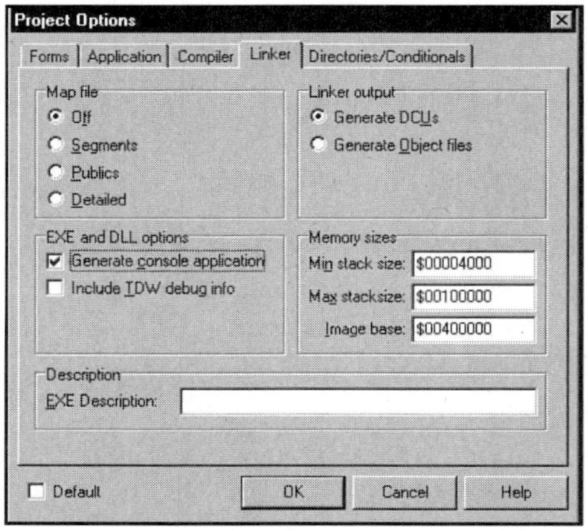

Edit the main source file for the project so it looks like this:

```
program Project1;

uses
  SysUtils;

begin
  WriteLn('Delphi');
end.
```

Save this file as OBJECT1.DPR. It is now a complete application that circumvents the VCL.

Go to the Tools | Options | Browser page, and in the Object Tree | Collapse Nodes section, type `exception`. This command tells the Browser not to expand the hierarchy for class `Exception`. If you now open the Browser, you find the scene depicted in Figure 23.3. This is the most simplified object hierarchy you can create with a normal Delphi application. All of the VCL has been eliminated, except for the class `TObject`, as well as `Exception` and its descendants. The latter objects cannot be eliminated because they are built into the heart and soul of the Delphi compiler.

FIGURE 23.3.

The Browser for an Object application, with the Exception *hierarchy collapsed.*

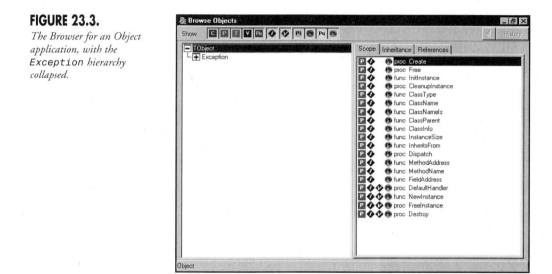

NOTE

The fact that Delphi has some built-in objects in all applications shows how deeply the OOP paradigm has been integrated into the compiler. The issue here is that Delphi has "carnal knowledge" of `TObject`; that is, its logic is built into the very heart and soul of the whole system. It's not something layered on top of the compiler; it's part of the very warp and weave of the whole system. To a somewhat lesser degree, the same can be said of exceptions, but they are not quite so deeply integrated.

The reference to the `SysUtils` unit is not absolutely necessary, but Delphi's visual environment seems to be less moody if you have a `uses` clause in the main project file.

It might seem strange to you that I have gone out of my way to eliminate so much of the object hierarchy in a chapter that is about objects. My goal, however, is to clear the boards so that you can view objects in a simplified state, thereby clearly delineating their most salient points.

The program that unfolds through the next few pages is called OBJECT1. This is a very simple object-oriented program that you will build on the console application framework established earlier. I'm not going to start by showing you the code for the whole program, because I want you to build it one step at a time, so that its structure emerges little by little. Before going any further, I ought to point out that this is not an extremely exciting application from a functional point of view. What's interesting is the technical aspect of the program.

To begin, you should create a small object at the top of the program:

```
program Object1;

uses
  SysUtils;

type
  TMyObject = class
  end;

begin
end.
```

All I have done here is added a `type` section with a simple class definition and removed the `WriteLn` statement.

If you now compile the application and open the Browser, you see that your new object has been added to the class hierarchy, as shown in Figure 23.4. Notice that this class is a descendant of `TObject`, even though you have done nothing to designate it as such. One of the fundamental rules of Delphi programming is that it is impossible to build a VCL object that is not a descendant of `TObject` or one of `TObject`'s children. The reason for this is that `TObject` contains some intelligence that is needed by all Delphi objects.

FIGURE 23.4.

The class hierarchy after `TMyObject` *has been added to it.*

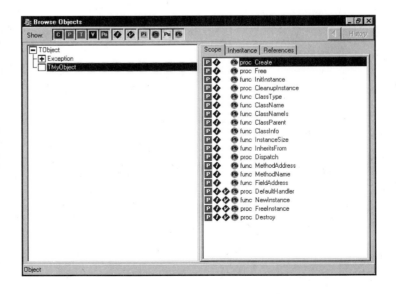

NOTE

You will find that I use the words *class* and *object* almost completely interchangeably. This is technically correct, although there is some merit in using the word class to describe the written declarations that appear in a text file and object to refer to a compiled class that is part of a binary file. In other words, programs are made up objects, whereas source files show class definitions.

To help clarify the hierarchy in this application, you should probably change TMyObject's definition so that it reads as follows:

```
program Object1;

uses
  SysUtils;

type
  TMyObject = class(TObject)
  end;

begin
end.
```

Logically, there is no difference between this declaration and the one you created earlier; however, now it is clear that TMyObject is a descendant of TObject.

The next step is to declare a variable of type TMyObject, then instantiate it and dispose of it:

```
program Object1;

uses
  SysUtils;

type
  TMyObject = class
  end;

var
  MyObject: TMyObject;

begin
  MyObject := TMyObject.Create;
  MyObject.Free;
end.
```

The code shown here doesn't do anything functional. Its only purpose is to teach you how objects work. Specifically, it declares a variable of type TMyObject:

```
var
  MyObject: TMyObject;
```

Next it allocates the memory for the object:

```
MyObject := TMyObject.Create;
```

Remember that this statement actually creates a pointer variable of type TMyObject. This means that you have to take this step if you want to use MyObject, and furthermore, you must dispose of this memory when you are finished with it. Here is the code that frees the memory allocated in the previous line:

```
MyObject.Free;
```

When you free an object, what you are really doing is calling the object's Destroy method. Here is code that shows approximately what takes place in the Free method of TObject:

```
procedure TObject.Free;
begin
  if Self <> nil then
    Destroy;
end;
```

The variable Self always points to the current object. In other words, if you are inside one of the methods of an object, you can refer to that object by using Self. (Self is passed as an implicit parameter to all Delphi methods. It is usually kept in EAX, if you need to access it on the assembler level.)

NOTE

Programmers use the words descendant, child object, derived class, and subclass as synonyms. I prefer to use either descendant or child object, because subclass is also used in another context and derived class seems unnecessarily obscure. My feeling is that it's best to stick to one metaphor: parent, child, ancestor, descendant, where child and descendant are synonymous, and parent and ancestor are synonymous.

Now that you know how to declare, allocate, and deallocate a simple object, it's time to narrow the focus and tackle the subject of inheritance. The next two sections are dedicated to this chore, and specifically to explaining the relationship between a parent and child object.

Understanding Inheritance

In general, a child object can use any of its parent's methods. A descendant of an object gets the benefit of its parent's capabilities, plus any new capabilities it might bring to the table. I say that this is true in general, because the private directive can limit the capability of a child to call some of its parent's routines. The private directive is explained in depth later in this chapter.

If you open the Browser again, you see that there are a number of methods associated with TObject. If you highlight TMyObject in the Browser and click the *I* icon at the top of the Browser, you see that all the methods associated with TMyObject are inherited from TObject. The *I* icon at the top of the Browser toggles on and off the ability to see inherited methods of an object. If you highlight TMyObject in the left Browser pane and then toggle inherited methods off, the right side of the Browser becomes blank. This is because all of TMyObject's methods and fields are inherited.

So, what are all these methods that are associated with TObject? Well, you can see their definitions, as well as their implementations, if you open up the SYSTEM.PAS file from the \DELPHI 2.0\SOURCE\RTL\SYS subdirectory:

```
TObject = class
  constructor Create;
  procedure Free;
  class function InitInstance(Instance: Pointer): TObject;
  procedure CleanupInstance;
  function ClassType: TClass;
  class function ClassName: ShortString;
  class function ClassNameIs(const Name: string): Boolean;
  class function ClassParent: TClass;
  class function ClassInfo: Pointer;
  class function InstanceSize: Longint;
  class function InheritsFrom(AClass: TClass): Boolean;
  procedure Dispatch(var Message);
  class function MethodAddress(const Name: ShortString): Pointer;
  class function MethodName(Address: Pointer): ShortString;
  function FieldAddress(const Name: ShortString): Pointer;
  procedure DefaultHandler(var Message); virtual;
  class function NewInstance: TObject; virtual;
  procedure FreeInstance; virtual;
  destructor Destroy; virtual;
end;
```

In the first version of Delphi, the implementation of TObject was hidden inside the compiler and there was no place in the RTL where you could see their source. This is not the case in the second version of Delphi; you can find the entire implementation of TObject in the System unit!

NOTE

Although I have mentioned this subject before, it's probably once again time to stress the importance of obtaining the source code to the VCL. Your version of Delphi may or may not ship with the source, but if you don't have it and can possibly afford to buy it, you should. If you are absolutely stuck and can't afford to get it, you should peruse the Delphi 2.0 subdirectories looking for files that have an INT extension. These files, usually found in the DOCS subdirectory, provide the interface for key Delphi units. They are not as good as having the source, but they are very valuable.

You can see that TObject has a few basic functions declared right at the top:

```
constructor Create;
destructor Destroy; virtual;
procedure Free;
```

The point to grasp here is that TMyObject has Create and Free methods because it inherits them from TObject.

To help illustrate this point, you can add a line of code to the nascent OBJECT1 program:

```
begin
  MyObject := TMyObject.Create;
  WriteLn(MyObject.ClassName);
  MyObject.Free;
end.
```

This code enables the object to write its name to the screen. The output from this program is a single string:

```
TMyObject
```

When you run the program, this string might flash by too quickly for leisurely perusal. To remedy the situation, add a ReadLn at the very end of the code, right before the end statement:

```
begin
  MyObject := TMyObject.Create;
  WriteLn(MyObject.ClassName);
  MyObject.Free;
  ReadLn;
end.
```

To end this program, press Enter. (That's the way it used to be done back in the DOS world. In fact, if you hang around a little longer, I will soon have you converted all the way back to CPM!)

If you want, you can even get this object to say its parent's name:

```
begin
  Write;
  MyObject := TMyObject.Create;
  WriteLn('Parent: ', MyObject.ClassParent.Classname);
  WriteLn('Self: ', MyObject.ClassName);
  MyObject.Free;
end.
```

The output from this code is the following:

```
Parent: TObject
Self: TMyObject
```

The point, of course, is that TMyObject inherits quite a bit of functionality from its parent, and as a result it has numerous capabilities that might not be obvious from merely viewing its declaration.

The ability to trace an object's ancestry is relatively appealing, so it might be nice to add it to TMyObject as a method:

```
program Object1;

uses
  SysUtils;
```

```
type
  TMyObject = class
    procedure ShowHierarchy;
  end;

procedure TMyObject.ShowHierarchy;
var
  AClass: TClass;
begin
  WriteLn(ClassName);
  AClass := ClassParent;
  while AClass <> nil do begin
    WriteLn(AClass.ClassName);
    AClass := AClass.ClassParent;
  end;
end;

var
  MyObject: TMyObject;

begin
  Write;
  MyObject := TMyObject.Create;
  MyObject.ShowHierarchy;
  MyObject.Free;
end.
```

This version of the OBJECT1 program includes a single method, which is listed in the TMyObject class declaration:

```
TMyObject = class
  procedure ShowHierarchy;
end;
```

The implementation of the method looks like this:

```
procedure TMyObject.ShowHierarchy;
var
  AClass: TClass;
begin
  WriteLn(ClassName);
  AClass := ClassParent;
  while AClass <> nil do begin
    WriteLn(AClass.ClassName);
    AClass := AClass.ClassParent;
  end;
end;
```

The type TClass is an Object Reference and is declared in SYSTEM.PAS as follows:

```
TClass = class of TObject;
```

Because ClassParent returns a variable of type TClass, it is obviously what needs to be used here.

NOTE

An Object Reference is a pointer that can be assigned to an object. Here is a unit that shows some legal things you can do with an Object Reference:

```
unit ClsRef;

interface

uses
  Forms;

type
  TObjectRef = class of Tobject;

  TDescendant = class(TObject)
  end;


procedure ShowClassReferences;
implementation

procedure ShowClassReferences;
var
  ObjectRef: TObjectRef;
begin
  WriteLn ('**start object references**');
  ObjectRef := Tobject;
  WriteLn(ObjectRef.ClassName);
  ObjectRef := Tdescendant;
  WriteLn(ObjectRef.ClassName);
  ObjectRef := Tform;
  WriteLn(ObjectRef.ClassName);
WriteLn ('*** end object references**');
end;

end.
```

Notice that you do not have to create an object before you can use it with an Object Reference.

You cannot use an Object Reference to refer to a field that belongs only to the child of the Object Reference type. For instance, this code does not compile because Caption is not a property of TObject:

```
ObjectRef.Caption := 'Sam';
WriteLn(ObjectRef.Caption);
```

You will find a version of the CLSREF unit in the same subdirectory as OBJECT1. You can use the Project Manager to add this file to the project, and you can then call it in the second line of the body of the OBJECT1 program. However, you should not leave this unit as part of the project because it will muddy the view of the object hierarchy that you get in the Browser.

When you get past the Object Reference, the remaining portions of the ShowHierarchy method are fairly straightforward:

```
begin
  WriteLn(ClassName);
  AClass := ClassParent;
  while AClass <> nil do begin
    WriteLn(AClass.ClassName);
    AClass := AClass.ClassParent;
  end;
end;
```

This code first writes the ClassName of the current object, which is TMyObject. Then it gets the ClassParent, which is TObject, and writes its name to the screen. The code then tries to get TObject's parent and fails, because TObject has no parent. At this point, AClass is set to nil, and the code exits the while loop.

> **NOTE**
>
> You should take a moment to open the Browser, highlight TMyObject in the left pane, and then toggle the view of inherited methods on and off as described earlier. The last time you did this, TMyObject had no methods, so the right pane was blank when the option to show inherited methods was toggled off. Now, the right pane has one method, called ShowHierarchy. It has a P in front of it because it is a Procedure, and a Pb in front of it because it is declared in the Published section by default.

In this section, you have learned about the Create, Destroy, Free, ClassParent, and ClassName methods of TObject. The declaration of TObject shows that several other methods are available to Delphi programmers. However, I do not discuss these methods in depth on the grounds that they are either self-explanatory (InheritsFrom), or beyond the scope of this book. I should mention, however, that some of these routines are used by the compiler itself when dispatching routines or performing other complex tasks. These are advanced programming issues that impact only a very small percentage of Delphi programmers.

Before going any farther, I want to make sure you understand inheritance, and specifically the functionality of the ClassParent and ClassName routines. As a result, I am going to take a brief foray into a second program that shows how inheritance looks in a standard form-based Delphi application.

Showing the Hierarchy of a VCL Program

To really appreciate the ShowHierarchy method, you need to add it to a regular Delphi application. For instance, if you make it a method of a standard Form1 class, here is the output you get:

```
TForm1
TForm
```

```
TScrollingWinControl
TWinControl
TControl
TComponent
TPersistent
TObject
```

This shows the whole hierarchy of class TForm1, starting with Self, moving to TForm, then back to TScrollingWinControl, and so on, all the way back to TObject. To make this object work, I had to modify the ShowHierarchy method slightly:

```
procedure TForm1.ShowHierarchy;
var
  AClass: TClass;
begin
  Memo1.Clear;
  Memo1.Lines.Add(ClassName);
  AClass := ClassParent;
  while AClass <> nil do begin
    Memo1.Lines.Add(AClass.ClassName);
    AClass := AClass.ClassParent;
  end;
end;
```

This code obviously depends on the presence of a TMemo object on the form, which is used in place of output to a console window. If you want to see this object in action, you can run the HIERARCHY.DPR program found on the CD. The form for the HIERARCHY program is shown in Figure 23.5, and the code is shown in Listing 23.1.

NOTE

The misspelling of the word Hierarchy is intentional due to the 8-3 format of DOS names. Delphi supports longer filenames, but the various compression and backup programs that I use don't support long filenames. I find it's fascinating to discover these little glitches that force me to keep using older technologies. This one will almost surely melt away over the next few months, yet it still has me rather firmly in its grip at the time of this writing.

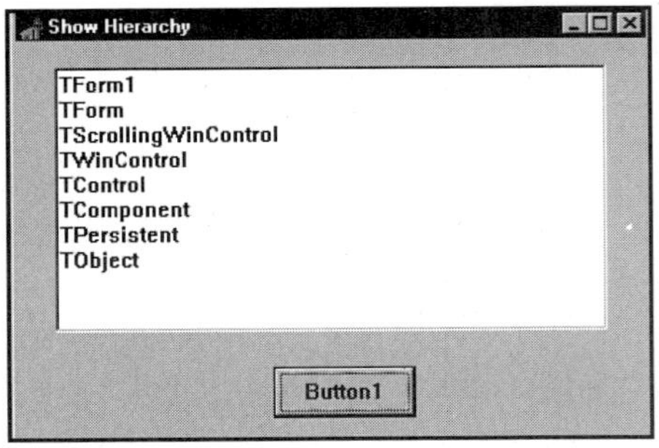

FIGURE 23.5.

The HIERARCHY form sports a TButton and a TMemo component.

Listing 23.1. The code for the HIERARCHY program.

```
unit Main;

{ Program copyright (c) 1995, 1996 by Charles Calvert }
{ Project Name: HIEARCHY }

interface

uses
  SysUtils, WinTypes, WinProcs,
  Messages, Classes, Graphics,
  Controls, Forms, Dialogs,
  StdCtrls;

type
  TForm1 = class(TForm)
    Button1: TButton;
    Memo1: TMemo;
    procedure Button1Click(Sender: TObject);
  private
    { Private declarations }
  public
    { Public declarations }
    procedure ShowHierarchy;
  end;

var
  Form1: TForm1;

implementation

{$R *.DFM}

procedure TForm1.ShowHierarchy;
var
  AClass: TClass;
begin
  Memo1.Clear;
  Memo1.Lines.Add(ClassName);
  AClass := ClassParent;
  while AClass <> nil do begin
    Memo1.Lines.Add(AClass.ClassName);
    AClass := AClass.ClassParent;
  end;
end;

procedure TForm1.Button1Click(Sender: TObject);
begin
  ShowHierarchy;
end;

end.
```

By this time, you should have a fairly good grasp of inheritance and hierarchies. The key point to understand is that, in general, a child object inherits the capability to use any of its parent's methods. In other words, it comes into an inheritance, where the inheritance is the methods, fields, and properties of its parent. Except for T0bject itself, all Delphi objects have parents that can trace their roots back to T0bject.

virtual, dynamic, and message

Inheritance, in itself, is an interesting feature, but it would not take on much significance were it not for the presence of virtual methods. Virtual methods can be overridden in a descendant class. As such, they provide the key to polymorphism, which is a trait of OOP programs that enables you to give the same command to two different objects but have them respond in different ways.

Delphi has three types of virtual methods, which use three different directives:

- virtual: This is the most commonly used of the three directives. It tells the compiler to store the address of the function in a virtual method table.

- dynamic: This tells the compiler to store the address of a function in a dynamic method table and generate a constant that can be used to identify the address during the lookup process.

- message: This tells the compiler to store the address of a function in a dynamic method table, but here the user supplies a particular constant to use during the lookup process.

This chapter covers the difference between virtual and dynamic method tables, but for now, all you need to know is that they exist. More specifically, I'm going to work with them for a while, then once you have seen them action, and you have become conscious of their presence, I'm going to come back and explain how they work.

Most of the time, you use the dynamic and virtual directives. However, the message directive also plays a key role in most programming projects, so it's worthwhile to spend some time explaining why it is needed. The actual syntax for using the message directive is explained in depth in Chapter 24, "Objects, Encapsulation, and Properties."

The OBJECT2 program (shown in Listing 23.2) has one virtual method and one dynamic method. The virtual method is overridden in a child object. When you are creating the OBJECT2 program, you should start with the source code for the OBJECT1 program. Modify the code by declaring ShowHierarchy as virtual, and by creating a descendant of TMyObject called THierarchy.

> **NOTE**
>
> If you want to copy the code from OBJECT1 into a separate directory called OB-JECT2, you should delete the DSK file. Otherwise, you might find yourself addressing files that are still stored in the OBJECT1 directory. If you rename OBJECT1.DPR to OBJECT2.DPR at the DOS prompt or in the File Manager, you should also change the project's title as it is declared in the first line of the DPR file. That is, change `program Object1` to `program Object2`. If you don't do this, you will get a `Module header is missing or incorrect` error message.
>
> Also, don't forget to check to be sure the program is set to work as a console application. If you don't have this option checked, you can get an `EInOutError` exception. After changing the setting, you should also rebuild your project so the new option takes effect.

Listing 23.2. The source code for the main unit in the OBJECT2 program.

```
program Object2;

{ Program copyright (c) 1995 by Charles Calvert }
{ Project Name: OBJECT2 }

uses
  SysUtils;

type
  THMethod = (hmScreen, hmDisk);

  TMyObject = class(TObject)
    procedure ShowHierarchy; virtual;
  end;

  THierarchy = class(TMyObject)
    HMethod: THMethod;
    procedure ShowHierarchy; override;
    procedure SetHierarchyMethod(Method: THMethod); dynamic;
  end;

procedure TMyObject.ShowHierarchy;
var
  AClass: TClass;
begin
  WriteLn(ClassName);
  AClass := ClassParent;
  while AClass <> nil do begin
    WriteLn(AClass.ClassName);
    AClass := AClass.ClassParent;
  end;
end;

procedure THierarchy.ShowHierarchy;
```

continues

Listing 23.2. continued

```
var
  F: Text;
  AClass: TClass;
begin
  if HMethod = hmscreen then
    inherited ShowHierarchy
  else begin
    Assign(F, 'inherit.txt');
    ReWrite(F);
    WriteLn(F, ClassName);
    AClass := ClassParent;
    while AClass <> nil do begin
      WriteLn(F, AClass.ClassName);
      AClass := AClass.ClassParent;
    end;
    Close(F);
  end;
end;


procedure THierarchy.SetHierarchyMethod(Method: THMethod);
begin
  HMethod := Method;
end;

var
  MyObject: THierarchy;
begin
  Write;
  MyObject := THierarchy.Create;
  MyObject.SetHierarchyMethod(hmScreen);
  MyObject.ShowHierarchy;
  MyObject.SetHierarchyMethod(hmDisk);
  MyObject.ShowHierarchy;
  MyObject.Free;
  ReadLn;
end.
```

In OBJECT1, the ShowHierarchy method wrote its output to the screen. Suppose you found this object somewhere and liked the way it worked but wanted to change its behavior so that it could also write its output to a file. The OBJECT2 program shows how you would proceed.

In the old world of structured programming, the most likely step would be to rewrite the original ShowHierarchy method. However, rewriting an existing method can be a problem for two different reasons:

- ■ You might not have the source code to the routine, so you can't rewrite it. However, you do have the binary file where the routine is kept, so you can still call it.

- ■ You might have the source code, but you know that this particular method is already being called by several different programmers. You might be afraid to rewrite it on the grounds that you might break the routine itself or you might break the other programmers' code.

A combination of design and maintenance issues might deter the impulse to rewrite the original method. Many projects have been delayed or mothballed because changes in their design have broken existing code and thrown the entire project into chaos.

OOP has a simple solution to this whole problem. Instead of declaring TMyObject as

```
TMyObject = class(TObject)
  procedure ShowHierarchy;
end;
```

thoughtful programmers declare it like this:

```
TMyObject = class(TObject)
  procedure ShowHierarchy; virtual;
end;
```

The difference is that in the second example the ShowHierarchy method is declared as virtual.

If ShowHierarchy is declared as virtual, you can override it, thereby changing the way the function works without ever changing the original version of the function. This means that all the other code that relies on the first version of the program continues to work, and yet you can rewrite the function for your own purposes. Here's how it looks:

```
THierarchy = class(TMyObject)
  procedure ShowHierarchy; override;
end;
```

This declaration states that class THierarchy is a descendant of class TMyObject, and that it overrides the ShowHierarchy method.

NOTE

BP7 programmers beware! The old object model performed the same chore by using the virtual directive in both the initial declaration and the overridden method. That's not the way VCL works. This is a major change between the new Delphi code and the old BP7 techniques.

The new version of the ShowHierarchy method looks like this:

```
procedure THierarchy.ShowHierarchy;
var
  F: Text;
  AClass: TClass;
begin
  if HMethod = hmscreen then
    inherited ShowHierarchy
  else begin
    Assign(F, 'inherit.txt');
    ReWrite(F);
    WriteLn(F, ClassName);
    AClass := ClassParent;
    while AClass <> nil do begin
      WriteLn(F, AClass.ClassName);
      AClass := AClass.ClassParent;
```

```
    end;
    Close(F);
  end;
end;
```

This code depends on a variable called HMethod, which is assigned a value through a mechanism I explain shortly. The HMethod variable is of type THMethod:

```
THMethod = (hmScreen, hmDisk);
```

If HMethod is set to hmScreen, the old ShowHierarchy routine is called. If it is set to hmDisk, the new technique is used. The new technique simply opens a text file and writes the data to it, rather than writing it to the screen. Notice that there is no need to qualify any of the file handling routines with the word System. This omission is possible because the parts of the VCL that cause a conflict are not included in this stripped-down program.

The final piece in this puzzle involves setting the HMethod variable. To do this, the declaration of THierarchy needs to be expanded:

```
type

  ...

  THMethod = (hmScreen, hmDisk);

  THierarchy = class(TMyObject)
    HMethod: THMethod;
    procedure ShowHierarchy; override;
    procedure SetHierarchyMethod(Method: THMethod); dynamic;
  end;
```

You can see that a field has been added to this object: THierarchy now contains not only procedures, but also data. One of the key aspects of class declarations is that they can contain both methods and data, so that you can bring all the code related to the THierarchy object together in one place. This is part of a concept called encapsulation, explained in the next chapter.

The SetHierarchyMethod method is declared as dynamic. From a high-level vantage point, there is no difference between declaring a method dynamic or virtual. The syntax for using the two terms is identical.

If you want to override a dynamic method, you do so with the override directive, just as you would if the method was declared as virtual. This technique is demonstrated in the OBJ23.DPR program, which is found on your disk. The relevant declaration from that program looks like this:

```
TFoo = class(THierarchy)
  procedure SetHierarchyMethod(Method: THMethod); override;
end;
```

Here, you can see that SetHierarchyMethod is overridden using the same technique used to override a virtual method.

The last issue involving the implementation of the OBJECT2 program is the SetHierarchyMethod method itself, which looks like this:

```
procedure THierarchy.SetHierarchyMethod(Method: THMethod);
begin
  HMethod := Method;
end;
```

This code is simple enough to understand, but a bit awkward to use. The clumsiness is eliminated in a later version of this program, after I explain how to create properties.

When you run the OBJECT2 program, the following code is executed in its main body:

```
var
  MyObject: THierarchy;
begin
  Write;
  MyObject := THierarchy.Create;
  MyObject.SetHierarchyMethod(hmScreen);
  MyObject.ShowHierarchy;
  MyObject.SetHierarchyMethod(hmDisk);
  MyObject.ShowHierarchy;
  MyObject.Free;
end.
```

This code creates an object of type THierarchy and then shows how you use the new functionality of the ShowHierarchy method.

> **NOTE**
>
> Two design issues should be discussed before abandoning the OBJECT2 program.
>
> OBJECT2 uses an enumerated type called THMethod. Programmers should be aware that enumerated types are not object-oriented and cannot be overridden. THMethod has two possible values: hmDisk and hmScreen. Suppose that another programmer comes along and wants to use both methods simultaneously. In other words, what this new programmer really wants is an hmBoth option. However, there is no way to supply this option without either breaking a lot of code or redeclaring THMethod. Because this new programmer might not have access to the source code, it might not be an option for him or her to rewrite the THMethod declaration. The point I'm making is that enumerated types are a bit dicey to use in object-oriented code, and you should consider using constants instead. You can always add one more constant to an object hierarchy, but you can't always change an enumerated type.
>
> The other design issue involves the fact that it's more expensive to call virtual or dynamic methods than it is to call a static method. As a result, you need to weigh the whole issue of whether you want to declare a method to be virtual. The SetHierarchy method, for instance, might not need to be declared dynamic. Such matters have to be considered in depth if you want to produce a well-written program.
>
> These two points are hardly earth-shattering in importance. However, I have said that OOP and design issues are intimately related concepts, so it's appropriate to discuss both issues in this chapter.

In this section, you have learned about the virtual, dynamic, and override directives. What you have learned here is very important, but its true significance won't be clear until you read about polymorphism. However, before you tackle that subject, it would be best to learn about virtual method tables (VMTs) and dynamic method tables (DMTs), and also about encapsulation.

Method Tables and Procedural Types

Dynamic and virtual method tables are some of the more esoteric features of object-oriented programming. Delphi has two different ways of dispatching virtual methods. Those declared with the virtual directive are relatively fast but take up a lot of space in memory. Dynamic methods, on the other hand, are a bit slower but conserve space.

To understand virtual and dynamic method tables, you need to understand that every function used in a program has an address. When it's time to call a particular function, the computer looks up the address of the function in memory, jumps to that address, and starts executing the code found at that address.

If you are new to the concept of procedures and functions having addresses, it would probably be helpful to see some concrete examples of procedural pointers. The FuncPtr program, shown in Listing 23.3, shows you how to get started.

Listing 23.3. The FuncPtr program shows how to work with the address of a function.

```
unit Main;

{ Program copyright (c) 1996 by Charles Calvert }
{ Project Name: FUNCPTR }

interface

uses
  SysUtils, WinTypes, WinProcs,
  Messages, Classes, Graphics,
  Controls, Forms, Dialogs,
  StdCtrls;

type
  TIntegerFunc = function(i: Integer): string;

  TForm1 = class(TForm)
    SimpleCall: TButton;
    Edit1: TEdit;
    PassNCall: TButton;
    procedure SimpleCallClick(Sender: TObject);
    procedure PassNCallClick(Sender: TObject);
  private
    { Private declarations }
  public
```

```
    { Public declarations }
  end;

var
  Form1: TForm1;

implementation

{$R *.DFM}

function IntegerFunc(i: Integer): string; far;
begin
  IntegerFunc := IntToStr(i);
end;

procedure TForm1.SimpleCallClick(Sender: TObject);
var
  Func: TIntegerFunc;
begin
  Func := IntegerFunc;
  Edit1.Text := Func(23);
end;

procedure CallFunc(Func: TIntegerFunc);
begin
  Form1.Edit1.Text := Func(2);
end;

procedure TForm1.PassNCallClick(Sender: TObject);
var
  Func: TIntegerFunc;
begin
  Func := IntegerFunc;
  CallFunc(Func);
end;

end.
```

The key line in this program is the type declaration in the `Button1Click` method:

```
TIntegerFunc = function(i: Integer): string;
```

This statement declares that `TIntegerFunc` is a pointer to a function that takes an integer as a parameter and returns an integer as a result.

The `IntegerFunc` procedure listed in this program is declared to be of this type:

```
function IntegerFunc(i: Integer): string;
begin
  IntegerFunc := IntToStr(i);
end;
```

NOTE

In the old days, the `IntegerFunc` routine would have been declared with the `far` directive. This is no longer necessary in the brave new 32-bit world. The issue, of course, is that all addresses are now 32 bits in size, so there is no need to explicitly declare a particular address as being 32 bits rather than 16 bits. The whole issue is moot. It is not, however, an error to use `far` in Win32. The directive is simply ignored.

Given a procedural variable of the correct type, it becomes trivial to declare and use a pointer to a function:

```
var
  Func: TIntegerFunc;
begin
  Func := IntegerFunc;
  Edit1.Text := Func(23);
end;
```

This code declares the variable `Func` to be of type `TIntegerFunc`. It then assigns the `IntegerFunc` function to the variable `Func` and calls it:

```
Func(23)
```

On most occasions when people need to use a pointer to a function, they want to pass the pointer to another location:

```
procedure TForm1.PassNCallClick(Sender: TObject);
var
  Func: TIntegerFunc;
begin
  Func := IntegerFunc;
  CallFunc(Func);
end;
```

In the `PassNCallClick` method, a procedural variable of type `TIntegerFunc` is declared, assigned, and passed to the `CallFunc` method:

```
procedure CallFunc(Func: TIntegerFunc);
begin
  Form1.Edit1.Text := Func(2);
end;
```

`CallFunc` then calls the `Func` method and displays its result in `Form1`'s `TEdit` control. I didn't make `CallFunc` a part of `TForm` simply because on most occasions when you use this technique, you are passing the function off to a DLL or some other remote part of the program that is not part of the current object.

The key point of the `CallFunc` program is that it shows how to use a pointer to a function. As I explained earlier, virtual method tables and dynamic method tables are simply lists of function addresses. In other words, they are tables that hold lists of addresses in which each address is a pointer to a method. When the program needs to call a particular method, it looks up the method's address in one of these tables, jumps to that location in memory, and starts executing code.

For instance, here is a simplified, conceptual, virtual method table:

```
StartOfTable
  … // Entries from ancestors not shown
  Func1: TIntegerFunc;
  Func2: TIntegerFunc;
  Func3: TIntegerFunc;
EndOfTable
```

Here is the object that would create such a table:

```
TMyObject = class(TSomething);
  function Func1(i: Integer): string; virtual;
  function Func2(i: Integer): string; virtual;
  function Func3(i: Integer): string; virtual;
end;
```

This is not an exact example, and as the earlier Note says, I am leaving out the part of this VMT that might be inherited from an ancestor. Still, this should help you get started visualizing what a VMT looks like in memory.

Virtual method tables have all the fields and functions available to an object in one table. Dynamic method tables are arranged hierarchically, so that each table corresponds to an object and contains addresses only of new dynamic methods or overridden dynamic methods. Each dynamic method table mirrors the declarations in a particular class, whereas a virtual method table looks more like the objects shown in the Browser.

Because of their structure, dynamic method tables take up less room than virtual method tables. However, if you want to call a dynamic method that is not introduced or overridden in the current object, the program must search through the DMTs of the object's ancestors until it finds the method in question by locating the numerical value associated with it. In short, it scans through a list of functions, looking for one that has a particular number assigned to it. This can involve iterating back through several method tables and therefore often takes longer than the quick one-stop lookup for virtual methods.

I said earlier that dynamic methods and methods that use the message directive are closely related. In fact, all dynamic methods are assigned a constant just the way message handlers are, except for the fact that you don't have to explicitly assign the constant because the compiler automatically picks a unique constant for you. A dynamic method still follows this format:

```
procedure MyDynoProc;
  dynamic MyConst;
```

This is the same format followed in message handlers:

```
procedure WMCommand(var Message: TMessage);
  message wm_Command;
```

However, there is no need for you to actually declare `MyConst`, because the compiler declares it for you and makes sure the constant is unique:

```
procedure MyDynoProc; dynamic;
```

The point here is that the constant you or the compiler declares in dynamic methods is the key the program looks for when it is scanning the dynamic method tables. It just starts iterating through the tables until it finds the constant in question, then it calls the address associated with that constant. Virtual method tables, on the other hand, work by offsets. Such and such a method is at such and such an offset in the table. It is quick and easy for a computer to jump to a particular offset, but setting up tables where methods appear at particular offsets can sometimes be costly in terms of the space used.

By now you should begin to have a general feeling for the way virtual and dynamic method tables work. I haven't given you enough information to write your own compiler, but I have told you what you need to know to start doing serious work with Delphi objects. In the next section, I briefly cover method pointers; encapsulation is covered in the next chapter.

Method Pointers

You have seen how to declare a procedural variable. However, these pointers work only with functions and procedures, not with methods. The METHPTR program, which follows, describes how to work with method pointers of the same kind that are stored in VMTs and DMTs.

Programmers frequently need to declare pointers to methods. A classic example of this need is when you have a unit or DLL that performs a series of complex activities and yet has no form associated with it. At times this unit needs to query the user, but its lack of a form makes this process needlessly complicated. One simple way to remedy this problem is to pass in the address of methods that have access to a form. That way, the DLL can call these methods when it needs to talk to the user.

The main form for the METHPTR program contains an edit control and a button. The code for the program is divided into two simple units, shown in Listings 23.4 and 23.5.

Listing 23.4. `CallMethodPtrClick` **passes a pointer to the** `ShowMethod` **routine into a second unit.**

```
unit Main;

{ Program copyright (c) 1995 by Charles Calvert }
{ Project Name: METHPTR }

interface

uses
  SysUtils, WinTypes, WinProcs,
  Messages, Classes, Graphics,
```

```
  Controls, Forms, Dialogs,
  StdCtrls;

type
  TForm1 = class(TForm)
    CallMethPtr: TButton;
    Edit1: TEdit;
    procedure CallMethPtrClick(Sender: TObject);
  private
    { Private declarations }
    procedure ShowMethod(S: string);
  public
    { Public declarations }
  end;

var
  Form1: TForm1;

implementation

uses
  Caller;
          {$R *.DFM}

procedure TForm1.ShowMethod(S: string);
begin
  Edit1.Text := S;
end;

procedure TForm1.CallMethPtrClick(Sender: TObject);
var
  AProc: TMyProc;
begin
  AProc := ShowMethod;
  CallProc(AProc);
end;

end.
```

Listing 23.5. METHPTR passes a method pointer to this small unit and then calls the method associated with the pointer from the `CallProc` procedure.

```
unit Caller;

{ Program copyright (c) 1995 by Charles Calvert }
{ Project Name: METHPTR }

interface

type
  TMyProc = procedure(S: string) of object;

procedure CallProc(MyProc: TMyProc);
implementation
```

continues

Listing 23.5. continued

```
procedure CallProc(MyProc: TMyProc);
begin
  MyProc('Sam');
end;

end.
```

Method pointer declarations look just like procedural variables except that they use the phrase of object:

```
type
  TMyProc = procedure(S: string) of object;
```

TMyProc is a pointer to a procedure that takes a single string as a parameter. It is declared in the CALLER unit because it needs to be used both there and in the program's main form.

Declaring and assigning a variable of this type inside the main form is exactly like calling a procedural variable:

```
procedure TForm1.CallMethPtrClick(Sender: TObject);
var
  AProc: TMyProc;
begin
  AProc := ShowMethod;
  CallProc(AProc);
end;
```

Because AProc is declared to be a pointer to a procedure that takes a string as a parameter, it can be assigned to the ShowMethod procedure:

```
procedure TForm1.ShowMethod(S: string);
begin
  Edit1.Text := S;
end;
```

ShowMethod is a simple routine that displays a string. This is exactly the kind of routine that a DLL or non-form-based unit might need if it wants to communicate with the user.

Finally, the CALLER unit declares and implements a short routine that calls the method pointer:

```
procedure CallProc(MyProc: TMyProc);
begin
  MyProc('Sam');
end;
```

This code calls ShowMethod and asks it to display the string Sam. To help you see how this logic works, you should step through the program with the debugger. Set the initial breakpoint at the beginning of the CallMethPtrClick routine and then press F7 until you get to ShowMethod.

> **NOTE**
>
> If you are having trouble understanding what I am saying here, just take a moment to step through the code with the debugger. This is not a complex program, but the ideas in it can be a bit confusing when you are first introduced to them.

After the FUNCPTR program, this code should be fairly transparent. The only difference between method pointers and procedural variables is that the of object syntax is added to the declaration of the procedural variable.

An Overview of Objects and Method Pointers

The subject matter in the latter half of this chapter is a bit abstract, so I want to take a moment to discuss it before moving on to look at RTTI. The key point to understand is that most objects have both methods and data in them:

```
THierarchy = class(TMyObject)
  HMethod: THMethod;
  procedure ShowHierarchy; override;
  procedure SetHierarchyMethod(Method: THMethod); dynamic;
end;
```

The ShowHierarchy and SetHierarchyMethod routines are both stored in memory as pointers. Furthermore, the data and methods in an object can be thought of as belonging to one large record that encapsulates them all. Records and objects have a lot in common. It's not entirely misleading to picture objects as physical records sitting in memory that contain data as well as pointers to methods. Of course, the structures that hold objects are referred to as tables, not as records.

Objects have data in them, and they have methods. It's easy to picture the data sitting in memory. An integer is a four-byte variable sitting somewhere in memory. A method pointer is also a four-byte variable sitting somewhere in memory. The actual types of pointers used in method pointers were shown to you explicitly in the METHPTR program. They are no longer abstractions to you—they are real entities, things you can pick up, pass around, and manipulate as you see fit. It's not inherently any harder to understand a method pointer than it is to understand an integer. They are just four bytes in memory. One contains data and the other contains the address of a routine, but otherwise they are the same.

You can think of objects as big records, or tables, that contain both data and method pointers. Complicating the matter slightly is the fact that most objects are represented by two types of tables. One type of table is for virtual methods and the other is for dynamic methods. However, this is just a slight variation on a theme. The point is that the object itself can still be pictured as a table full of method and variable addresses.

You need not despair at the idea of ever understanding how objects actually look in memory. Just picture those VMTs and DMTs sitting out there containing the essence of each object. They are just tables full of method addresses. You look up one kind of address by jumping to an offset in a VMT. You look up the other kind of address by scanning through a table looking for methods that are assigned a particular constant. Sure it would be complicated to implement, but you don't have to implement the object code itself. You can just use it!

If you jump to a particular offset in the TMyObject VMT, you will find the address of one version of the ShowHierarchy method. If you jump to the same offset in the THierarchy object, you will find a second pointer to the ShowHierarchy method. This latter pointer points to the second version of the method you created. That's what the override directive does. It says "replace the address of the original version of this method with the address of the new version." If you didn't use override, you would almost surely be telling the compiler to create a new entry in the table. Because you use override, you are saying not to create a new entry, but instead to change the address at a particular entry point in the table.

The *is* and *as* Operators

Run Time Type Information (RTTI) is implemented through the is and as operators. You can use the is operator to determine whether an object is of a particular type. The as operator uses exceptions to ensure that typecasts are made safely.

There are many different ways you can use RTTI in your programs. However, one of the most useful techniques involves checking the type of the object that generates an event. There are several examples of this technique in the RTTIOPS program, which is discussed next. The source for the program is shown in Listing 23.6.

Listing 23.6. Run Time Type Information is examined in the RTTIOPS program.

```
unit Main;

{ Program copyright (c) 1995 by Charles Calvert }
{ Project Name: RTTIOPS }

{ The Sender Parameter always points
  to the control that caused the event
  to occur, the one that delegated the
  action to the form. So if you click
  on a button, as in the ButtonTest
  method below, and you test to see if the
  sender is a button, then the is operator
  tells you that it is indeed a button that
  sent the message. However, if you click
  on a button and ask the is operator
  if it was an edit control that sent the
  message, you get a negative answer. Since
  a button is a descendant of a TComponent,
  you get a positive answer if you click on
  a button and ask if the Sender is a TComponent.
```

```
   When you are working with the as operator,
   in the examples shown below,
   you can turn off Break on Exception from
   the Options | Environment menu. That way
   you can see how to avoid popping up
   a dialog when you make an invalid
   type cast.

}

interface

uses
  SysUtils, WinTypes, WinProcs, Messages, Classes, Graphics, Controls,
  Forms, Dialogs, StdCtrls;

type
  TForm1 = class(TForm)
    IsTests: TGroupBox;
    ButtonTest: TButton;
    EditTest: TButton;
    Descendant: TButton;
    AsTests: TGroupBox;
    SafeCast: TButton;
    TryCast: TButton;
    Edit1: TEdit;
    Edit2: TEdit;
    procedure ButtonTestClick(Sender: TObject);
    procedure EditTestClick(Sender: TObject);
    procedure DescendantClick(Sender: TObject);
    procedure SafeCastClick(Sender: TObject);
    procedure TryCastClick(Sender: TObject);
  private
    { Private declarations }
  public
    { Public declarations }
  end;

var
  Form1: TForm1;

implementation

{$R *.DFM}

{ This method is attached to a button and an edit }
procedure TForm1.ButtonTestClick(Sender: TObject);
begin
  if Sender is TButton then
    Edit1.Text := 'ButtonTestClick: Ok'
  else
    Edit1.Text := 'ButtonTestClick: Error';
end;

{ This method is attached to the EditTest button }
procedure TForm1.EditTestClick(Sender: TObject);
begin
```

continues

Listing 23.6. continued

```
    if Sender is TEdit then
      Edit1.Text := 'EditTestClick: Ok'
    else
      Edit1.Text := 'EditTestClick: Error';
end;

{ This method is attached to the Descendant button }
procedure TForm1.DescendantClick(Sender: TObject);
begin
    if Sender is TComponent then
      Edit1.Text := 'Component'
    else
      Edit1.Text := 'Error';
end;

{ Attached to both the SafeCast button and the Form itself. }
procedure TForm1.SafeCastClick(Sender: TObject);
begin
    Edit2.Text := (Sender as TButton).Name;
end;

{ This procedure attempts to cast Sender as a
  TButton, if the cast fails, it then casts it
  as a TComponent, which will always succeed.
  The method is attached to a button and an edit.
}
procedure TForm1.TryCastClick(Sender: TObject);
begin
    try
      Edit2.Text := 'Good Cast: ' + (Sender as TEdit).Name;
    except
      Edit2.Text := 'Invalid cast: ' + (Sender as TComponent).Name;
    end;
end;

end.
```

The following method from the RTTIOPS program is attached to an OnClick event for a button and an edit control:

```
procedure TForm1.ButtonTestClick(Sender: TObject);
begin
    if Sender is TButton then
      Edit1.Text := 'ButtonTestClick: Ok'
    else
      Edit1.Text := 'ButtonTestClick: Error';
end;
```

The code first checks to see if the Sender is of type TButton. If it is, the program writes the words ButtonTestClick: Ok to the screen; if it is not, the words ButtonTestClick: Error appear on the screen. This is a fairly trivial example, but it shows the way RTTI works.

Remember that in OnClick events, the Sender parameter always points to the control that caused the event to occur; that is, the one that delegated the action to the form. So if you click a button, as in the ButtonTest method, and you test to see if Sender is a button, the is operator tells you that it is indeed a button that sent the message. However, if you click a button and ask the is operator if it was an edit control that sent the message, you get a negative answer.

You always get a positive answer if you ask whether a Delphi component is a TComponent. For instance, because a button is a descendant of a TComponent, you get a positive answer if you click a button and ask if the Sender is a TComponent. The DescendantClick method in the RTTIOPS programs demonstrates this technique.

> **NOTE**
>
> Before using the as operator (as discussed in the following section), you should turn off Break on Exception from the Options | Environment menu. If you turn the option off, you will see the exception only once, but if you leave it on, you will see the exception twice.

You can use the as operator to perform safe typecasts. Specifically, the as operator automatically checks a method's type and then performs a typecast. Here is one way to perform a safe typecast:

```
if Sender is TEdit then
  TEdit(Sender).Name := 'Data';
```

Here is a second way to perform a safe typecast:

```
(Sender as TEdit).Name := 'Data';
```

The second method raises an exception if Sender is not a TEdit.

The SafeTypeCast method from the RTTIOPS program typecasts Sender as a TButton by using the as operator. As long as the component attached to the code is indeed a TButton, the cast will succeed. If any other component is attached to the call, the typecast raises an exception:

```
procedure TForm1.SafeCastClick(Sender: TObject);
begin
  Edit2.Text := (Sender as TButton).Name;
end;
```

SafeCastClick is attached both to a button and to the program's main form. Therefore, clicks in the main form cause this method to raise an exception. The TryCastClick method, shown next, demonstrates how to use this same type of code without raising an exception.

The following method is attached to both a TButton and a TEdit:

```
procedure TForm1.TryCastClick(Sender: TObject);
begin
```

```
try
  Edit2.Text := 'Good Cast: ' + (Sender as TEdit).Name;
except
  Edit2.Text := 'Invalid cast: ' + (Sender as TComponent).Name;
end;
end;
```

If the user clicks TEdit, the function writes the words Goodcast: TEdit to the screen. If the user clicks the button control, the typecast in the try block fails and the code in the except block is executed. The code in the except block typecasts Sender as a TComponent, which is always safe. In other words, this code shows how to handle invalid typecasts without causing an exception.

Summary

In this chapter, you have had a good chance to start working with object-oriented programming. However, there are still several big topics to tackle, including encapsulation and polymorphism. Rather than trying to cover such big topics inside this already lengthy chapter, I have decided to break things up and give them their own chapter where they can have plenty of room to unfold naturally.

Declaring pointers to methods, functions, and procedures is one of the important techniques commonly used by advanced programmers. When you start treating a procedure as nothing more than a location in memory, you are finally moving past the syntax of a language and starting to manipulate the raw tools built into every computer. One of the ironies of modern computing is that programmers must simultaneously embrace both the leveraged abstractions inherent in objects and the raw power that comes from directly addressing locations in memory.

In the last part of the chapter, you got a look at RTTI. Run Time Type Information is one of the tools you need to write robust code in a visual environment. The objects in Delphi programs are constantly interacting. When you work in such a dynamic environment, you need a way to test the type of any one object. The solution to this problem is RTTI.

Objects, Encapsulation, and Properties

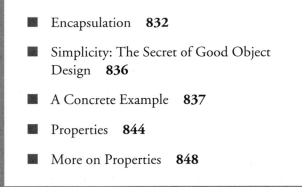

24

In this chapter, you continue the overview of object-oriented programming begun in the last chapter. In particular, the focus is on encapsulation and properties. The next chapter focuses on polymorphism.

This chapter covers the following topics:

- An overview of encapsulation, including the need to hide data and certain parts of the implementation
- An in-depth look at the `private`, `protected`, `public`, and `published` scoping directives
- Property creation
- The five basic types of properties
- Read-only properties
- Default value declarations for properties

This chapter features some of the syntactical jewels in the Delphi treasure chest. In particular, Delphi offers a complete array of scoping directives. These tools enable you to fine-tune access to your objects in a way that helps promote their reuse. Properties are also cutting-edge tools, and their implementation in Delphi yields some surprising fruits, such as arrays that are indexed on strings.

Encapsulation

The word *encapsulation* and the word *object* are closely linked in my mind. Encapsulation is one of the primary and most fundamental aspects of OOP. It is useful because it helps to enlist related methods and data under a single aegis, and to hide the implementation details that don't need to be exposed or that might change in future versions of an object.

The ability to encapsulate methods and data inside an object is important because it helps you design clean, well-written programs. To use a classic example, suppose that you were to create an object called `TAirplane`, which would represent (naturally enough) an airplane. This object might have fields such as `Altitude`, `Speed`, and `NumPassengers`; it might have methods such as `TakeOff`, `Land`, `Climb`, and `Descend`. From a design point of view, everything is simpler if you can encapsulate all these fields and methods in a single object, rather than leaving them spread out as individual variables and routines:

```
TAirplane = class(TObject)
  Altitude: Integer;
  Speed: Integer;
  NumPassengers: Integer;
  procedure TakeOff;
  procedure Land;
  procedure Climb;
  procedure Descend;
end;
```

There is a sleek elegance in this simple object declaration. Its purpose and the means for implementing its functionality are readily apparent.

Consider the class declaration from the current version of the OBJECT2 program:

```
THierarchy = class(TMyObject)
  HMethod: THMethod;
  procedure ShowHierarchy; override;
  procedure SetHierarchyMethod(Method: THMethod); dynamic;
end;
```

THierarchy encapsulates the ShowHierarchy method. If you want to call ShowHierarchy, you need to first instantiate an object of type THierarchy, then use that object as a qualifier when you call ShowHierarchy:

```
var
  H: THierarchy;

begin
  H := THierarchy.Create;
  H.ShowHierarchy;
  H.Free;
end.
```

This kind of encapsulation is useful primarily because it makes you treat everything about the THierarchy object as a single unit. There are some limitations to this technique, however. In particular, when you have declared an object of type THierarchy, you have full access to all its methods and fields. It's true that you have to jump through one hoop before you can access THierarchy's innards, but there is still a sense that a program's data is not very well protected.

To eliminate this problem, Delphi defines four directives meant to aid in the process of encapsulation:

private: Use this directive to declare a section in a class that can only be accessed from inside the current unit. For instance, if the HMethod variable is declared in a private section, it can't be accessed directly by code that is outside its unit. Private code and data can, however, be accessed by any object, method, procedure, or function that resides within the same unit.

protected: Code declared in a protected section can only be accessed by descendant objects. In other words, if HMethod is declared in a protected section, variables of type THierarchy do not have access to it. You have to declare a descendant of THierarchy before you can access this variable directly. Once again, this rule applies only when you are outside the unit in which the object was declared. The point here is that protected fields and methods are available only to other component developers, not to standard consumers of the object.

public: Code declared in a public section of an object is available to anyone who uses an object of that particular type. It's the standard interface of the object.

published: Properties that are declared in the published section are public variables that appear in the Object Inspector. Furthermore, you can discover the type of published properties at runtime; simple published properties can be streamed to disk automatically. (See the ENUMINFO program in the PROGRAMS directory for additional information on determining types or type of information at runtime.) Because published properties are for use in the Object Inspector, Delphi does not allow you to declare a property as published unless the object descends from TComponent or one of TComponent's children. TComponent is the base object from which all objects that appear on the Component Palette must descend. Without inheriting TComponent's functionality, no object would normally be able to show its properties in the Object Inspector.

NOTE

A directive called Automated is also used with the TAutomation object. Because the subject is separate, I cover it in Chapter 29, "OLE Automation Basics."

Given these scoping directives, the following might be a sensible way to declare THierarchy:

```
THierarchy = class(TMyObject)
private
  FHierarchyMethod: THMethod;
public
  procedure ShowHierarchy; override;
  procedure SetHierarchyMethod(Method: THMethod); dynamic;
end;
```

And here is a way to define TMyObject:

```
TMyObject = class(TObject)
public
  procedure ShowHierarchy; virtual;
end;
```

Notice that I have renamed HMethod to FHierarchyMethod. It is a standard Delphi convention to append an F before private fields, and to only use abbreviations like HMethod when it is absolutely clear what the H means. The F in these examples stands for Field.

All the data in your programs should be declared private and should be accessed through methods or properties. As a rule, it is a serious design error to ever give anyone access to the data of an object. Giving other objects or non-OOP routines direct access to data is a sure way to get into deep trouble when it comes time to maintain or redesign part of a program.

The whole idea that some parts of an object should remain forever concealed from other programmers is one of the hardest ideas for new OOP programmers to grasp. In fact, in early versions of Turbo Pascal with Objects, this aspect of encapsulation was given short shrift. Experience, however, has shown that many well-constructed objects consist of two parts:

■ Data and implementation sections hidden from the programmers who use the object.

■ A set of interface routines that enable programmers to talk to the concealed methods and data that form the heart of an object.

Data and implementation sections are hidden so that the developer of the object can feel free to change those sections at a later date. If you expose a piece of data or a method to the world and find a bug that forces you to change the type of that data, or the declaration for that method, you are breaking the code of people who rely on that data or that method. Therefore, it's best to keep all your key methods and data hidden from consumers of your object. Give them access to those methods and procedures only through properties and public methods. Keep the guts of your object private, so that you can rewrite it, debug it, or rearrange it at any time.

One way to approach the subject of hiding data and methods is to think of objects as essentially modest beings. An object doesn't want to show the world how it performs some task, and especially doesn't directly show the world the data or data structures it uses to store information. The actual data used in an object is a private matter that should never be exposed in public. The methods that manipulate that data should also be hidden from view because they are the personal business of that object. Of course, an object does not want to be completely hidden from view, so it supplies a set of interface routines that talk to the world, but these interface routines jealously guard the secret of how an object's functionality is actually implemented.

A well-made object is like a beautiful woman who conceals her charms from a prying world. Conversely, a poorly made object should also hide, much like an elderly man who doesn't want the world to see how his youth and virility has faded. These analogies are intentionally a bit whimsical, but they help to illustrate the extremely powerful taboo associated with directly exposing data and certain parts of the implementation.

Of course, the point of hiding data and implementations is not to conceal how an object works, but to make it possible to completely rewrite the core of an object without changing the way it interacts with the world. In short, the previous analogies collapse when it comes to a functional analysis of data hiding, but they serve well to express the spirit of the enterprise.

> **NOTE**
>
> If you have the source code to the VCL, you will find that at least half of most key objects in the Delphi code base are declared as `private`. A few complex objects contain several hundred lines of private declarations, and only 20 or 30 methods and properties that serve as an interface for that object. Objects near the top of a hierarchy don't always follow this model because they usually consist primarily of interface routines. It's the core objects that form the heart of a hierarchy that are currently under discussion.
>
> The internal methods of Delphi objects tend to reference their data through properties, rather than directly addressing the internal data storage. Not only consumers, but the objects themselves, should have the discipline to enforce data-hiding in their

implementation. Strictly speaking, this is the correct and wisest approach, but you will find that I sometimes allow methods of an object to directly reference the data declared in that same object. I am moving away from this practice gradually, however, because it has cost me during the maintenance phase of a project.

Whatever weaknesses I allow myself, however, I believe firmly that it is always wrong to declare a variable outside of a private section. Hiding data and methods is one of the most important aspects of OOP, and programmers who ignore this practice are simply asking to deliver products that are buggy and late.

Simplicity: The Secret of Good Object Design

Before moving on, I want to talk about the importance of creating easy-to-use interfaces. Notice, for instance, how easy it is to use the TTable, TDataSource, and TDBGrid objects. These examples are well-constructed objects with easy-to-use interfaces. If you take these objects away, however, and access the functions in the DBIPPROCS.PAS (or DBIPROCS.INT) unit directly, you see that TTable, TDBGrid, and TDataSource conceal a great deal of complexity. In other words, if you have to call the raw BDE functions directly to open and view a table, you will find that the process is both tedious and error prone. Using TTable, however, is very easy. You might need to have someone tell you how it works the first time you see it, but after that, the process of getting hooked up to a table and displaying data to the user is trivial. All good programmers should strive to make their objects this easy to use.

In the next few chapters, I discuss component creation. Components are very useful because they help guide you in the process of creating a simple, easy-to-use object. If you can drop an object onto a form and hook it up with just a few clicks in the Object Inspector, then you know that you have at least begun to create a good design. If you drop an object onto a form and then need to mess around with it for 15 or 20 minutes before you can use it, then you know something is probably wrong. Objects should be easy to use, whether they are placed on the Component Palette or not.

I do not mean to say that the act of creating an object is simple or easy. I have seen great programmers wrestle for months with the overwhelming minutiae of creating a complex object that is easy to use. A good programmer doesn't think the job is done just because the code works. Good code should not only work, but it should also be easy to use! Conversely, I often suspect that an object is poorly designed if it is difficult to use. In most cases, my suspicions turn out to be true, and a complex interface ends up being a wrapper around a buggy and ineptly coded object.

No hard-and-fast rules exist in the area of object design. However, the presence of an easy-to-use interface is a good sign. If you are working with a component, you should be able to drop it onto a form and hook it up in just a few seconds. If you are working with an object that is not encapsulated in a component, you should be able to initialize and use it by writing just a few lines of code. If hooking up takes more than a few minutes, you often have a reason to be suspicious of the entire enterprise.

The private methods of your objects should also be cleanly and logically designed. However, it is not a disaster if your private methods are difficult to understand as long as your public methods are easy to use. The bottom line is that the private methods should be designed to accomplish a task, and the public methods should be designed to be easy to use. When you look at the design this way, you can see a vast difference between the public and private methods in an object.

As you read through the next few chapters, you might consider thinking about the importance of creating a simple interface to your objects. Having a simple interface is particularly important for the top-level objects in your hierarchy.

A Concrete Example

Neither TMyObject nor THierarchy give us much scope for exploring encapsulation. As a result, it's time to introduce a new class called TWidget, which is a descendant of THierarchy. In the chapter on polymorphism, TWidget will become the ancestor of a series of different kinds of widgets that can be stored in a warehouse. In other words, in a computer factory TWidget might be the ancestor of several classes of objects such as TSiliconChip, TAddOnBoard, and TPowerSupply. Descendants of these objects might be called T486Chip, T386Chip, TVideoBoard, and so on. Object hierarchies always move from the general to the specific:

```
TWidget
TSiliconChip
TPentiumChip
```

The rule enforced here is simple enough:

1. A TWidget could be almost any object that is bought and sold.
2. A TSiliconChip is some kind of silicon-based entity.
3. A TPentiumChip is a specific kind of computer chip that has a real-world counterpart.

The movement is from the abstract toward the specific. It is almost always a mistake to embody specific traits of an object in a base class for a hierarchy. Instead, these early building blocks should be so broad in scope that they can serve as parents to a wide variety of related objects or tools.

The OBJECT3 program includes a declaration for class TWidget (see Listings 24.1 and 24.2). The declaration makes use of three of the four directives used for hiding and exposing data.

(I don't use the published directive since it is only allowed in TComponent descendants.) Notice also that the class declarations have been broken off into their own unit. This is done for two reasons:

- The program needs to be able to enforce the declaration of private data, which can only be accomplished if the classes involved are declared in their own unit.

- Class THierarchy is nearing the point of usefulness, so it's time for it to be broken off into a separate module that can be used by multiple programs and can exist as a single definable entity.

Listing 24.1. The main unit for the OBJECT3 program.

```
program Object3;

{ Program copyright (c) 1996 by Charles Calvert }
{ Project Name: OBJECT3 }

uses
  Classdef in 'CLASSDEF.PAS';

var
  W: TWidget;
begin
  W := TWidget.Create;
  W.HierarchyMethod := hmScreen;
  W.ShowHierarchy;
  WriteLn(W.Quantity);
  W.Stock;
  WriteLn(W.Quantity);
  W.Sell(2);
  WriteLn(W.Quantity);
  W.Col := 20;
  W.Row := 12;
  W.Paint;
  W.Free;
  ReadLn;
end.
```

Listing 24.2. The core of the OBJECT3 program is in the CLASSDEF unit.

```
unit Classdef;

{ Program copyright (c) 1995 by Charles Calvert }
{ Project Name: OBJECT3 }


interface

uses
  SysUtils, Windows;

type
  THMethod = (hmScreen, hmDisk);
```

```
  TMyObject = class(TObject)
  public
    procedure ShowHierarchy; virtual;
  end;

  THierarchy = class(TMyObject)
  private
    FHierarchyMethod: THMethod;
  public
    procedure ShowHierarchy; override;
    property HierarchyMethod: THMethod
      read FHierarchyMethod write FHierarchyMethod;
  end;

  TWidget = class(THierarchy)
  private
    FCol: Integer;
    FRow: Integer;
    FQuantity: LongInt;
    FBoxSize: LongInt;
    FMaxQuantity: LongInt;
    FDescription: string;
    function GetQuantity: string;
    procedure SetQuantity(S: string);
  protected
    function GetName: string; virtual;
  public
    constructor Create; virtual;
    procedure Sell(Amount: LongInt); virtual;
    procedure Stock; virtual;
    procedure Paint; virtual;
    property Quantity: string read GetQuantity write SetQuantity;
    property Col: Integer read FCol write FCol;
    property Row: Integer read FRow write FRow;
  end;

var
  HOut: THandle;

implementation

uses
  StrBox;

{ -- TMyObject -- }

procedure TMyObject.ShowHierarchy;
var
  AClass: TClass;
begin
  WriteLn(ClassName);
  AClass := ClassParent;
  while AClass <> nil do begin
    WriteLn(AClass.ClassName);
    AClass := AClass.ClassParent;
  end;
end;
```

continues

Listing 24.2. continued

```pascal
{ -- THierarchy -- }

procedure THierarchy.ShowHierarchy;
var
  F: Text;
  AClass: TClass;
begin
  if FHierarchyMethod = hmScreen then
    inherited ShowHierarchy
  else begin
    Assign(F, 'inherit.txt');
    ReWrite(F);
    WriteLn(F, ClassName);
    AClass := ClassParent;
    while AClass <> nil do begin
      WriteLn(F, AClass.ClassName);
      AClass := AClass.ClassParent;
    end;
    Close(F);
  end;
end;

{ -- TWidget -- }

constructor TWidget.Create;
begin
  inherited Create;
  FBoxSize := 5;
end;

function TWidget.GetQuantity: string;
begin
  Result := 'Quantity: ' + IntToStr(FQuantity);
end;

procedure TWidget.SetQuantity(S: string);
begin
  FQuantity := StrToInt(S);
end;

function TWidget.GetName: string;
begin
  Result := StripFromFront(ClassName, 1);
end;

procedure TWidget.Sell(Amount: LongInt);
begin
  if Amount = 0 then
    FQuantity := FQuantity - FBoxSize
  else
    FQuantity := FQuantity - Amount
end;

procedure TWidget.Stock;
begin
  FQuantity := FQuantity + FBoxSize;
```

```
end;

procedure GotoXY(X, Y: SmallInt);
var
  C: TCoord;
begin
  C.X := X;
  C.Y := Y;
  SetConsoleCursorPosition(HOut, C);
end;

procedure TWidget.Paint;
begin
  GotoXY(FCol, FRow);
  Write('* ' + GetName);
end;

begin
  HOut := GetStdHandle(STD_OUTPUT_HANDLE);
end.
```

The functionality associated with this program is still severely limited. An object of type TWidget is created, and its hierarchy is shown. The program next simulates the act of stocking up on a predefined number of these widgets. Finally, a bare representation of a widget is displayed on the screen:

```
W := TWidget.Create;
W.HierarchyMethod := hmScreen;
W.ShowHierarchy;
WriteLn(W.Quantity);
W.Stock;
WriteLn(W.Quantity);
W.Col := 20;
W.Row := 12;
W.Paint;
W.Free;
```

The output from this program is shown in Figure 24.1.

FIGURE 24.1.

The simple text output from the OBJECT3 program.

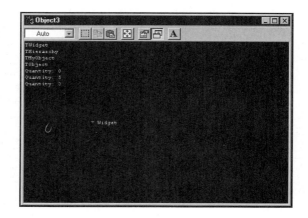

From a user's point of view, this is pretty tame stuff. However, the declaration for class TWidget shows programmers a good deal about how Delphi implements encapsulation:

```
TWidget = class(THierarchy)
private
  FCol: Integer;
  FRow: Integer;
  FQuantity: LongInt;
  FBoxSize: LongInt;
  FMaxQuantity: LongInt;
  FDescription: string;
  function GetQuantity: string;
  procedure SetQuantity(S: string);
protected
  function GetName: string; virtual;
public
  constructor Create; virtual;
  procedure Sell(Amount: LongInt); virtual;
  procedure Stock; virtual;
  procedure Paint; virtual;
  property Quantity: string read GetQuantity write SetQuantity;
  property Col: Integer read FCol write FCol;
  property Row: Integer read FRow write FRow;
end;
```

The private section of TWidget contains several fields of data and two methods:

```
private
  FCol: Integer;
  FRow: Integer;
  FQuantity: LongInt;
  FBoxSize: LongInt;
  FMaxQuantity: LongInt;
  FDescription: string;
  function GetQuantity: string;
  procedure SetQuantity(S: string);
```

All of the private data in the program have variable names that begin with the letter F. As stated before, this is a convention and not a syntactical necessity. These variables are called *internal storage*.

Internal storage should always be declared private, and as such cannot be accessed from outside of this unit. To reiterate, all of the data in any object should *always* be declared private. Other objects should never access any of this data directly, but should manipulate it through a predefined interface that appears in the protected, published, or public sections. If you want, you can think of the F in these names as standing for "Forbidden," as in "it is forbidden to directly access this data!"

> **NOTE**
>
> As I mentioned before, some of the programs in this book may place data in a public section. You won't see that happen often, but it may show up once or twice in small, simple, example programs. While it's one thing to write an example program that has

some public data, it's another thing to have public data in a production executable on which your own or a company's fortunes might depend. That's just not done.

Don't drive down an urban highway at eighty-five miles an hour. Don't drink and drive. Don't think that you are somehow miraculously going to be immune to crack's addictive qualities. Don't step between a mother grizzly bear and her cubs. Don't ask who's buried in Grant's tomb during the middle of a job interview. Don't swim with the sharks if you are bleeding. Don't declare public data in a production quality program!

The GetQuantity and SetQuantity functions are also declared private, and you will see that they are accessed through a property. Most objects have many more private methods, but TWidget is relatively bare in this department. The lack of private methods occurs because TWidget is such a simple object that there isn't much need to perform complex manipulations of its data.

The protected section is simple, and contains a single virtual method. This portion of the object can be accessed by descendants of TWidget, but not by an instance of the class. For example, if you make the declaration

```
var
  W: TWidget;
```

class W could not call GetName:

```
begin
  W := TWidget.Create;
  W.GetName;              { This line won't compile }
  W.Free;
end;
```

This functionality is available only from outside the unit in which the object is declared. That is, the rule enforcing the inaccessibility of GetName is valid only if you are outside the unit in which the object is declared. From inside the unit, the code shown above will compile.

The methods in the public section of the object make it possible to manipulate the widgets that you declare:

```
public
  constructor Create; virtual;
  procedure Sell(Amount: LongInt); virtual;
  procedure Stock; virtual;
  procedure Paint; virtual;
```

Here you can see a method for selling widgets, a method for stocking up on new widgets, and a method for painting pictures of widgets to the screen. All of these are common activities and need to be declared public.

The create method for the object sets the value of FBoxSize:

```
constructor TWidget.Create;
begin
```

```
  inherited Create;
  FBoxSize := 5;
end;
```

FBoxSize is meant to represent the number of items found in a box of widgets. Some items aren't sold individually, but only in boxes; this item describes how many widgets fit in one box.

Both Sell and Stock are simple methods:

```
procedure TWidget.Sell(Amount: LongInt);
begin
  if Amount := 0 then
    FQuantity := FQuantity - FBoxSize
  else
    FQuantity := FQuantity - Amount
end;

procedure TWidget.Stock;
begin
  FQuantity := FQuantity + FBoxSize;
end;
```

Because the calculations that occur here are trivial, there is no need to hide their implementations in private methods. However, if this were a more sophisticated program, and either Sell or Stock needed to call methods with names such as CalculateBoxSize or CalculateQuantity, those methods would be hidden behind a property because they might change in the future, and the user does not need to know of their existence.

You have now had an overview of all the code in the OBJECT3 program, except for its properties, which will be discussed in the next section. The discussion so far has concentrated on the Delphi object scoping directives. You have learned about the private, protected, public, and published sections of a program, and have seen why each is necessary.

Properties

Properties provide several advantages:

- Properties enable you to hide data.
- If you write a component and place it in the Component Palette, its published properties appear in the Object Inspector.
- Some properties can be made available at design time, while variables are only available at runtime.
- Properties can have side effects such as not only setting the value of the FWidth variable, but also physically changing the width of the object that appears on the screen.
- Property access methods can be declared virtual, which gives them more flexibility than simple variables.

The OBJECT3 program contains three properties:

```
public
  property Quantity: string read GetQuantity write SetQuantity;
  property Col: Integer read FCol write FCol;
  property Row: Integer read FRow write FRow;
```

If the TWidget object were a descendant of TComponent, all or some of these properties could be put in the published section and, therefore, could be seen from inside the Object Inspector if the object were compiled into Delphi's library.

There is no rule that says which properties should be declared in the published or public sections. In fact, properties often appear in public sections, although there is little reason for them to be in private or protected sections. In this case, all the properties appear in the public section because TWidget is not a descendant of TComponent.

The two properties shown here are simple tools that do nothing more than hide data and lay the groundwork for their use inside the Object Inspector:

```
property Col: Integer read FCol write FCol;
```

The declaration starts with the keyword property, which performs the same type of syntactical chore as procedure or function. Every property must be declared as having a certain type, which in this case is Integer.

Most properties can be both read and written. The read directive for the Col property states that the value to be displayed is FCol and the value to write is FCol. In short, writing

```
var
  i: Integer;
begin
  MyWidget.Col := 2;
  i := MyWidget.Col;
end;
```

sets FCol to the value 2, and sets i to the value of FCol (again, 2).

The reasons for doing this are two-fold:

- To hide data so that it is protected.
- To create a syntax that allows properties to be shown in the Object Inspector. Of course, you won't see these values in the Object Inspector until you metamorphose the object into a component, which is a subject that will be covered in Chapter 27, "Creating Nonvisual Components."

The Col and Row properties provide what is called *direct access*; they map directly to the internal storage field. The runtime performance of accessing data through a direct-access property is exactly the same as accessing the private field directly.

NOTE

The FCol and FRow properties are used to designate a location on the screen. To move to a location on a text-mode screen, Pascal programmers have traditionally called the GotoXY procedure. This procedure is not, however, automatically implemented in Delphi. Instead, I am forced to make up my own version of this routine:

```
procedure GotoXY(X, Y: SmallInt);
var
  C: TCoord;
begin
  C.X := X;
  C.Y := Y;
  SetConsoleCursorPosition(HOut, C);
end;
```

SetConsoleCursorPosition is a routine provided by Windows for those cases when you need to move the cursor in a console application. It is declared in WINDOWS.PAS. The TCoord type is also declared in WINDOWS.PAS:

```
PCoord = ^TCoord;
TCoord = packed record
  X: SHORT;
  Y: SHORT;
end;
```

A SHORT is declared as a SmallInt in WINDOWS.PAS. Remember that when you see a Delphi variable declared in all capital letters, it is likely that it is being included to provide compatibility with the variables declared in the official copy of WINDOWS.H (and its related files) provided by Microsoft.

The HOut variable of type THandle used in the first parameter of SetConsoleCursorPosition is a handle to standard out. You can retrieve it with the following code, which appears at the bottom of the ClassDef unit:

```
HOut := GetStdHandle(STD_OUTPUT_HANDLE);
```

GetStdHandle is provided by Windows and is declared in WINDOWS.PAS. The constant STD_OUTPUT_HANDLE is declared in WINDOWS.PAS, along with STD_INPUT_HANDLE:

```
STD_INPUT_HANDLE = DWORD(-10);
STD_OUTPUT_HANDLE = DWORD(-11);
STD_ERROR_HANDLE = DWORD(-12);
```

A large number of console functions are declared in one place in WINDOWS.PAS. Search on PeekConsoleInput to find the beginning of the function list.

The Col and Row examples represent the simplest possible case for a property declaration. The Quantity property presents a few variations on these themes:

```
property Quantity: string read GetQuantity write SetQuantity;
```

Rather than reading a variable directly, Quantity returns the result of a private function:

```
function TWidget.GetQuantity: string;
begin
  Result := 'Quantity: ' + IntToStr(FQuantity);
end;
```

SetQuantity, on the other hand, enables you to change the value of the FQuantity variable:

```
procedure TWidget.SetQuantity(S: string);
begin
  FQuantity := StrToInt(S);
end;
```

GetQuantity and SetQuantity are examples of access methods. Just as the internal storage for direct access variables begins by convention with the letter F, access methods usually begin with either "Set" or "Get."

Take a moment to consider what is happening here. To use the Quantity property, you need to use the following syntax:

```
 var
   S: string;
 begin
   S := W.Quantity;
   W.Quantity := '25';
 end;
```

In the preceding code, S is set to a string that might look like 'Quantity: 10' or 'Quantity: 25'. Note that when you are writing to the FQuantity variable, you *don't* write:

```
W.Quantity('25');
```

Instead, you use the simple, explicit syntax of a direct assignment. Delphi automatically translates the assignment into a function call that takes a parameter. C++ buffs will recognize this as a limited form of operator overloading.

If there were no properties, the previous code would look like this:

```
var
  S: string;
begin
  S := W.GetQuantity;
  W.SetQuantity('25');
end;
```

Instead of remembering one property name, this second technique requires you to remember two, and instead of the simple assignment syntax, you must remember to pass a parameter. Although it is not the main purpose of properties, it should now be obvious that one of their benefits is that they provide a clean, easy-to-use syntax.

In the last few pages, you had a good look at the OBJECT3 program. There are several additional traits of properties that should be explored, however, before moving on to the colorful warehouse simulation found in the next chapter.

More on Properties

Delphi provides support for five different types of properties:

- Simple properties are declared to be integers, characters, or strings.
- Enumerated properties are declared to be of some enumerated type. When shown in the Object Inspector, you can view them with a drop-down list.
- Set properties are declared to be of type Set. BorderIcons from TForm is an example of this type of property. You can only choose one enumerated value at a time, but you can combine several values in a property of type Set.
- Object properties are declared to be of some object type, such as the Items property from the TListBox component, which is declared to be of type TStrings.
- Array properties are like standard arrays, but you can index on any type, even a string. The classic example of this kind of property is the Strings property in a TStringList.

The PROPTEST program (referenced in Listings 24.3 and 24.4) gives an example of each of the five types of properties. It also gives the TStringList object a fairly decent workout. The program itself is only minimally useful outside the range of a purely academic setting such as this book.

Listing 24.3. The main unit for the PROPTEST program.

```
unit Main;

{ Program copyright (c) 1996 by Charles Calvert }
{ Project Name: PROPTEST }

interface

uses
  SysUtils, WinTypes, WinProcs,
  Messages, Classes, Graphics,
  Controls, Forms, Dialogs,
  StdCtrls;

type
  TForm1 = class(TForm)
    Button1: TButton;
```

```
    ListBox1: TListBox;
    ListBox2: TListBox;
    procedure Button1Click(Sender: TObject);
  private
    { Private declarations }
  public
    { Public declarations }

  end;

var
  Form1: TForm1;

implementation

uses
  MyObj1;

{$R *.DFM}

procedure TForm1.Button1Click(Sender: TObject);
var
  M: TMyProps;
  Ch: Char;
  i: Integer;
begin
  M := TMyProps.Create(Self);
  M.Parent := Self;
  M.SimpleProp := 25;
  M.EnumProp := teEnum;
  M.SetProp := [teEnum, TeSet];
  M.StrArrayProp['Jones'] := 'Sam, Mary';
  M.StrArrayProp['Doe'] := 'John, Johanna';
  ListBox1.Items.Add(M.StrArrayProp['Doe']);
  ListBox1.Items.Add(M.StrArrayProp['Jones']);
  for i := 0 to M.ObjectProp.Count - 1 do
    ListBox2.Items.Add(M.ArrayProp[i]);
  Ch := M.Default1;
end;

end.
```

Listing 24.4. The main unit for the PROPTEST program.

```
unit Myobj1;

{ Program copyright (c) 1996 by Charles Calvert }
{ Project Name: PROPTEST }

interface

uses
  Classes, Forms, Controls,
  StdCtrls, Graphics, SysUtils;
```

continues

Listing 24.4. continued

```
type
  TEnumType = (teSimple, teEnum, teSet, teObject, teArray);
  TSetProp = set of TEnumType;

  TCouple = class(TObject)
    Husband: string;
    Wife: string;
  end;

  TMyProps = class(TCustomControl)
  private
    FSimple: Integer;
    FEnumType: TEnumType;
    FSetProp: TSetProp;
    FObjectProp: TStringList;
    FDefault1: Char;
    function GetArray(Index: integer): string;
    function GetStrArray(S: string): string;
    procedure SetStrArray(Index: string; S: string);
  protected
    procedure Paint; override;
  public
    constructor Create(AOwner: TComponent); override;
    destructor Destroy; override;
    property ArrayProp[i: integer]: string read GetArray;
    property StrArrayProp[i: string]: string read GetStrArray write SetStrArray;
  published
    property SimpleProp: Integer read FSimple write FSimple;
    property EnumProp: TEnumType read FEnumType write FEnumType;
    property SetProp: TSetProp read FSetProp write FSetProp;
    property ObjectProp: TStringList read FObjectProp write FObjectProp;
    property Default1: Char read FDefault1 write FDefault1 default '1';
  end;

implementation

uses
  StrBox;
constructor TMyProps.Create(AOwner: TComponent);
begin
  inherited Create(AOwner);
  Width := 100;
  Height := 100;
  Left := (TForm(AOwner).ClientWidth div 2) - (Width div 2);
  Top := (TForm(AOwner).ClientHeight div 2) - (Height div 2);
  FObjectProp := TStringList.Create;
  Default1 := '1';
end;

destructor TMyProps.Destroy;
var
  i: Integer;
begin
  for i := 0 to FObjectProp.Count - 1 do
    FObjectProp.Objects[i].Free;
```

```
    FObjectProp.Free;
    inherited Destroy;
end;

procedure TMyProps.Paint;
begin
    Canvas.Brush.Color := clBlue;
    inherited Paint;
    Canvas.Rectangle(0, 0, Width, Height);
    Canvas.TextOut(1, 1, 'FSimple: ' + IntToStr(FSimple));
    Canvas.TextOut(1, Canvas.TextHeight('Blaise'), GetArray(0));
    Canvas.TextOut(1, Canvas.TextHeight('Blaise') * 2, FObjectProp.Strings[1]);
end;

function TMyProps.GetArray(Index: integer): string;
begin
    Result := FObjectProp.Strings[Index]
end;

function TMyProps.GetStrArray(S: string): string;
var
    Couple: TCouple;
begin
    Couple := TCouple(FObjectProp.Objects[FObjectProp.IndexOf(S)]);
    Result := Couple.Husband + ', ' + Couple.Wife;
end;

function GetHusband(S: string): string;
begin
    Result := StripLastToken(S, ',');
end;

function GetWife(S: string): string;
begin
    Result := StripFirstToken(S, ',');
end;

procedure TMyProps.SetStrArray(Index: string; S: string);
var
    Couple: TCouple;
begin
    Couple := TCouple.Create;
    Couple.Husband := GetHusband(S);
    Couple.Wife := GetWife(S);
    FObjectProp.AddObject(Index, Couple);
end;

end.
```

The structure of the PROPTEST program is simple. There is a main form with a button on it. If you click the button, you instantiate an object of type TMyObject. TMyObject has five properties, one for each of the major types of properties. These properties have self-explanatory names:

```
property SimpleProp;
property EnumProp;
property SetProp;
```

```
property ObjectProp;
property ArrayProp;
```

Before exploring these properties, I should mention that TMyObject is descended from the native Delphi object called TCustomControl. TCustomControl is intelligent enough to both display itself on the screen and store itself on the Component Palette. It has several key methods and properties already associated with it, including a Paint method and Width and Height fields. (This instance of TMyObject has nothing to do with the TMyObject from which THierarchy is descended. It's just a coincidence that the two objects have the same name.)

Because TCustomControl is so intelligent, it is easy to use its Paint method to write values to the screen:

```
procedure TMyProps.Paint;
begin
  Canvas.Brush.Color := clBlue;
  inherited Paint;
  Canvas.Rectangle(0, 0, Width, Height);
  Canvas.TextOut(1, 1, 'FSimple: ' + IntToStr(FSimple));
  Canvas.TextOut(1, Canvas.TextHeight('Blaise'), GetArray(0));
  Canvas.TextOut(1, Canvas.TextHeight('Blaise') * 2,
                 FObjectProp.Strings[1]);
end;
```

Note that you do not need to explicitly call the Paint method. Windows calls it for you whenever the object needs to paint or repaint itself. This means that you can hide the window behind others, and it will repaint itself automatically when it is brought to the fore. Inheriting functionality that you need from other objects is a big part of what OOP is all about. You will get a chance to look more closely at TCustomControl and similar objects in Chapter 26, "Creating Components."

The first three properties of TMyObject are extremely easy to understand:

```
property SimpleProp: Integer read FSimple write FSimple;
property EnumProp: TEnumType read FEnumType write FEnumType;
property SetProp: TSetProp read FSetProp write FSetProp;
```

These are direct access properties that simply read to and write from a variable. You can use them with the following syntax:

```
M.SimpleProp := 25;
M.EnumProp := teEnum;
M.SetProp := [teEnum, TeSet];
```

NOTE

I once asked one of the developers whether properties such as these didn't waste computer clock cycles. Looking somewhat miffed, he said, "Obviously, we map those calls directly to the variables!"

Chastened, and somewhat the wiser, I nodded sagely as if this were the answer I expected. Then, I ventured, "So they don't cost us any clock cycles?"

"Not at runtime, they don't!" he said, and concentrated once again on his debugger, which hovered over some obscure line in CLASSES.PAS.

The syntax for using the `ObjectProp` property is similar to the examples shown previously, but it is a bit harder to fully comprehend the relationship between an object and a property:

```
property ObjectProp: TStringList
      read FObjectProp write FObjectProp;
```

`ObjectProp` is of type `TStringList`, which is a descendant of the `TStrings` type used in the `TListBox.Items` property or the `TMemo.Lines` property. I use `TStringList` instead of `TStrings` because `TStrings` is essentially an abstract type meant for use only in limited circumstances. For general purposes, you should always use a `TStringList` instead of a `TStrings` object. (In fact, neither `TListBox` nor `TMemo` actually uses variables of type `TStrings`. They actually use descendants of `TStrings`, just as I do here.)

NOTE

A `TStringList` has two possible functions. You can use it to store a simple list of strings, and you can also associate an object with each of those strings. To perform the latter task, call `AddObject`, passing a string in the first parameter and a `TObject` descendant in the second parameter. You can then retrieve the object by passing in the string you used in the call to `AddObject`.

`TStringLists` do not destroy the objects that you store in them. It is up to you to deallocate the memory of any object you store on a `TStringList`.

If you want a simple list object that doesn't have all this specialized functionality, use a linked list or the versatile `TList` object that ships with Delphi.

After making the declaration for `ObjectProp` shown earlier, you can now use it as if it were a simple `TStringList` variable. This can sometimes be a bit inconvenient, however. For instance, the following syntax retrieves an object that is associated with a string:

```
S := 'StringConstant';
MyObject := FObjectProp.Objects[FObjectProp.IndexOf(S)]
```

Furthermore, you must be sure to allocate memory for the `FObjectProp` at the beginning of `TMyProps`'s existence, and you must dispose of that memory in the `TMyProps` destructor:

```
constructor TMyProps.Create(AOwner: TComponent);
begin
  inherited Create(AOwner);
  FObjectProp := TStringList.Create;
```

```
  ...
end;

destructor TMyProps.Destroy;
begin
  for i := 0 to FObjectProp.Count - 1 do
    FObjectProp.Objects[i].Free;
  FObjectProp.Free;
  inherited Destroy;
end;
```

This is the classic cycle so well known to BP7 programmers, but less frequently encountered in standard Delphi programming. The key point is that `TMyProps.Destroy` is called automatically whenever the form is freed.

Finally, you must also allocate memory for each object you place in a `TStringList`. That is, you must create not only a `TStringList`, but you must also create each object you pass to the `TStringList.AddObject` routine. When you are done with those objects, you must destroy them:

```
for i := 0 to FObjectProp.Count - 1 do
    FObjectProp.Objects[i].Free;
```

There is nothing you can do about the necessity of allocating and deallocating memory for an object of type `TStringList`. You can, however, use array properties to simplify the act of accessing it, and to simplify the act of allocating memory for each object you store in it. TESTPROP shows how this can be done. Specifically, it entertains the concept that you are creating a list for a party to which only married couples are being invited. Each couple's last name is stored as a string in a `TStringList`, and their first names are stored in an object that is stored in the `TStringList` in association with the last name. In other words, TESTPROP calls `AddObject` with the last name in the first parameter and an object containing their first names in the second parameter. This sounds complicated at first, but array properties can make the task trivial from the user's point of view.

In the TESTPROP program, I store a simple object with two fields inside the `TStringList`:

```
TCouple = class(TObject)
  Husband: string;
  Wife: string;
end;
```

Note that this object looks a lot like a simple record. In fact, I would have used a record here, except that `TStringLists` expect `TObject` descendants, not simple records. (Actually, you can sometimes get away with storing nonobjects in `TStringLists`, but I'm not going to cover that topic in this book.)

As described earlier, it would be inconvenient to ask consumers of `TMyObject` to allocate memory for a `TCouple` object each time they needed to be used. Instead, TESTPROP asks the user to pass in first and last names in this simple string format:

```
'HusbandName, WifeName'
```

TESTPROP also asks them to pass in the last name as a separate variable. To simplify this process, I use a string array property:

```
property StrArrayProp[i: string]: string read GetStrArray write SetStrArray;
```

Notice that this array uses a string as an index, rather than a number!

Given the StrArrayProp declaration, the user can write the following code:

```
M.StrArrayProp['Jones'] := 'Sam, Mary';
```

This is a simple, intuitive line of code, even if it is a bit unconventional. The question, of course, is how can Delphi parse this information?

If you look at the declaration for StrArrayProp, you can see that it has two access methods called GetStrArray and SetStrArray. SetStrArray and its associated functions look like this:

```
function GetHusband(S: string): string;
begin
  Result := StripLastToken(S, ',');
end;

function GetWife(S: string): string;
begin
  Result := StripFirstToken(S, ',');
end;

procedure TMyProps.SetStrArray(Index: string; S: string);
var
  Couple: TCouple;
begin
  Couple := TCouple.Create;
  Couple.Husband := GetHusband(S);
  Couple.Wife := GetWife(S);
  FObjectProp.AddObject(Index, Couple);
end;
```

Note the declaration for SetStrArray. It takes two parameters. The first one is an index of type string, and the second is the value to be stored in the array. So, 'Jones' is passed in as an index, and 'Sam, Mary' is the value to be added to the array.

SetStrArray begins by allocating memory for an object of type TCouple. It then parses the husband's and wife's names from the string by calling two token-based functions from the StrBox unit that ships with this book. Finally, a call to AddObject is executed. When the program is finished, you must be sure to deallocate the memory for the TCouple objects in the Destroy method:

```
destructor TMyProps.Destroy;
var
  i: Integer;
begin
  for i := 0 to FObjectProp.Count - 1 do
    FObjectProp.Objects[i].Free;
  FObjectProp.Free;
  inherited Destroy;
end;
```

The twin of SetStrArray is GetStrArray. This function retrieves a couple's name from the TStringList whenever the user passes in a last name. The syntax for retrieving information from the StrArray property looks like this:

```
S := M.StrArrayProp['Jones'];
```

In this case, S is assigned the value 'Sam, Mary'. Once again, note the remarkable fact that Delphi enables us to use a string as an index in a property array.

The implementation for GetStrArray is fairly simple:

```
function TMyProps.GetStrArray(S: string): string;
var
  Couple: TCouple;
begin
  Couple := TCouple(FObjectProp.Objects[FObjectProp.IndexOf(S)]);
  Result := Couple.Husband + ', ' + Couple.Wife;
end;
```

The code first retrieves the object from the TStringList, then performs some simple hand waving to re-create the original string passed in by the user. Obviously, it would be easy to add additional methods that retrieved only a wife's name, or only a husband's name.

I'm showing you this syntax not because I'm convinced that you need to use TStringLists and property arrays in exactly the manner showed here, but because I want to demonstrate how properties can be used to conceal an implementation and hide data from the user. The last two properties declared in this program show how to use important property types, and they also demonstrate how properties can be used to reduce relatively complex operations to a simple syntax that looks like this:

```
M.StrArrayProp['Doe'] := 'John, Johanna';
S := M.StrArrayProp['Doe'];
```

Consumers of this object don't need to know that I am storing the information in a TStringList, and they won't need to know if I change the method of storing this information at some later date. As long as the interface for TMyObject remains the same — that is, as long as I don't change the declaration for StrArrayProp — I am free to change the implementation at any time.

There is one other array property used in this program that should be mentioned briefly:

```
property ArrayProp[i: integer]: string read GetArray;
```

ArrayProp uses the traditional integer as an index. However, note that this array still has a special trait not associated with normal arrays: It is Read Only! Because no write method is declared for this property, it cannot be written to; it can be used only to query the TStringList that it ends up addressing:

```
function TMyProps.GetArray(Index: integer): string;
begin
  Result := FObjectProp.Strings[Index]
end;
```

You can call `ArrayProp` with this syntax:

```
S := M.ArrayProp[0];
```

This is an obvious improvement over writing the following:

```
S := M.FObjectProp.Strings[0];
```

Creating a simple interface for an object may not seem important at first, but in day-to-day programming a simple, clean syntax is invaluable. For instance, the TESTPROP program calls `ArrayProp` in the following manner:

```
for i := 0 to M.ObjectProp.Count - 1 do
  ListBox2.Items.Add(M.ArrayProp[i]);
```

In this case, it's very helpful that the call to `GetArray` is so simple. It would not be fun if you had to complicate matters further by writing this line:

```
ListBox2.Items.Add(M.FObjectProp.Strings[0]);
```

NOTE

Astute readers might be noticing that Delphi is flexible enough to enable you to improve even its own syntax. For instance, if you wanted to, you could create a list box descendant that enables you to write this syntax:

```
ListBox2.AddStr(S);
```

instead of

```
ListBox2.Items.Add(S);
```

In the chapter on creating components you will see that you can even replace the `TListBox` object on the Component Palette with one of your own making! The techniques you are learning in these chapters on the VCL will prove to be the key to enhancing Delphi so that it becomes a custom-made tool that fits your specific needs.

If you bury yourself in the Delphi source code, eventually you might notice the `default` directive, which can be used with properties:

```
property Default1: Char read FDefault1 write FDefault1 default '1';
```

Looking at this syntax, one would tend to think that this code automatically sets `FDefault1` to the value `'1'`. However, this is not its purpose. Rather, it tells Delphi whether this value needs to be streamed when a form file is being written to disk. If you make `TMyProp` into a component, drop it onto a form, and save that form to disk, Delphi explicitly saves that value if it is not equal to 1, but skips it if it is equal to 1.

An obvious benefit of the `default` directive is that it saves room in DFM files. Many objects have as many as 25, or even 50, properties associated with them. Writing them all to disk would be an expensive task. As it happens, most properties used in a form have default values that are never changed. The default directive merely specifies that default value, and Delphi thus knows whether to write the value to disk. If the property in the Object Inspector is equal to the default, Delphi just passes over the property when it's time to write to disk. When reading the values back in, if the property is not explicitly mentioned in the DFM file, the property retains the value you assigned to it in the component's constructor.

> **NOTE**
>
> The property is never assigned the default value by Delphi. You *must* ensure that you assign the default values to the properties as you indicated in the class declaration. This must be done in the constructor. A mismatch between the declared default and the actual initial value established by the constructor will result in lost data when streaming the component in and out.
>
> Similarly, if you change the initial value of an inherited published property in your constructor, you should also reassert/redeclare (partial declaration) that property in your descendant class declaration to change the declared default value to match the actual initial value.
>
> The default directive does nothing more than give Delphi a way of determining whether it needs to write a value to disk. It never assigns a value to any property. You have to do that yourself in your constructor.

Of course, there are times when you want to assign a property a default value at the moment that the object it belongs to is created. These are the times when you wish the default directive did what its name implies. However, it does not now, and never will, perform this action. To gain this functionality you must use the constructor, as shown in the TESTPROP application:

```
constructor TMyProps.Create(AOwner: TComponent);
begin
  inherited Create(AOwner);
  Width := 100;
  Height := 100;
  FDefault1 := 1;
  ...
```

Here, the Width and Height properties are set by default to 100. (As explained in the second paragraph of the preceding note, you need to be careful that you check to see whether a published property is declared as default.)

The TESTPROP program is obviously not meant to perform any useful function, but instead explores the world of properties from a syntactical point of view. Even the example of storing a couple's names in a TStringList is implemented primarily for the sake of exploring the syntax involved. It was just a fortuitous coincidence that it ended up yielding a fairly efficient, if idiosyncratic, solution to a real-life problem.

After reading this section, it should be clear that array properties represent one of the most powerful and flexible aspects of Delphi programming. I don't think it's stretching things to say that array properties provide the same kind of breakthrough flexibility that some people feel operator overloading brings to C++. However, operator overloading can be confusing because one never knows just what an operator in C++ does. Because it can be overloaded, a '+', '-', '/', or other operator in a C++ program might mean different things in different circumstances. Delphi array properties, on the other hand, always provide a clean, easy-to-read syntax that hides object data and implementations, without misleading users of the code.

Summary

That wraps up this introduction to properties and encapsulation. The key points you have explored are the `private`, `protected`, `public`, and `published` directives, as well as the art of creating useful properties. I have also attempted to browbeat you with the importance of hiding data and methods. Remember that robust, easily maintainable objects never directly expose their data! Instead, they present the user with a simple, custom-designed interface that should usually be easy to use.

In the next chapter, you will learn about polymorphism, which is the crown jewel of object-oriented theory.

Polymorphism

In this chapter you will learn about *polymorphism*. This feature is simultaneously one of the more esoteric and one of the most important concepts in object-oriented programming. Many people who write object-oriented code never use polymorphism. They may reap a number of the important benefits of OOP theory, but they miss out on a key tool that yields robust, flexible architectures.

A program called OBJECT4 forms the core of this chapter. OBJECT4 uses simple graphic objects to depict a warehouse in which several different kinds of widgets are stored. There are seven panels in this warehouse, each containing from 4 to 12 palettes full of widgets. You are able to stock each palette with new widgets and de-populate the palettes by selling off stock. It's also possible to reach a special view that shows the state of the widgets on an individual palette, and another view that uses graphs to show the state of the total stock.

The point of this chapter is to build up the object hierarchy begun in OBJECT1 to the point where it can be used for the relatively practical task just described. One of the main themes of the chapter is that OOP, which seems highly theoretical and intangible at first glance, actually turns out to be a natural tool for tracking and depicting the status of real objects, such as the inventory in a warehouse.

You don't need to understand polymorphism or much about objects to program in Delphi. However, if you want to be an expert Delphi programmer and want to create components, this is material you should master.

Polymorphism from 20,000 Feet

Polymorphism can be confusing even to experienced OOP programmers. My approach starts with a high-level overview of the subject, shows some real-world examples, and finally comes back to a second take on the high-level overview. Don't panic if you don't understand the information in the next few paragraphs right away. I cover this material several times in several different ways, and by the time you finish this chapter, you'll understand.

Let me start with a quick definition that may or may not make sense on first reading. If it doesn't sink in right away, don't worry.

Polymorphism is a technique that allows you to set a parent object equal to one or more of its child objects:

```
Parent := Child;
```

The interesting thing about this technique is that, after the change, the parent then acts in different ways, depending on the traits of the child that is currently assigned to it. One object, the parent, therefore acts in many different ways.

> **NOTE**
>
> The words "assign" and "equal" are ones that I find extremely tricky. If I am speaking off the cuff and use the word "assign" in three consecutive sentences, I will trip over myself for sure! Because this seemingly simple subject is so tricky, I'm going to take a moment to lay out some rules that you can reference while you're reading this chapter.
>
> Consider the following code fragment:
>
> ```
> Parent := Child;
> ```
>
> In this simple statement, the child is assigned to its parent. The parent is not assigned to its child. You could easily argue that this definition could be reversed, but I do not take that approach in this chapter.
>
> When referencing the preceding code fragment, I also say that the parent is set equal to its child. The child is not set equal to its parent. Once again, you can argue that this definition could be reversed, or that the action is reflexive. Throughout this chapter, however, I consistently state that the preceding code sets a parent equal to its child, and not a child equal to its parent.
>
> Because these seemingly simple English phrases are so confusing, at least to me, I try to illustrate exactly what I mean as often as possible. That is, I may write
>
> ```
> "You can set a parent equal to its child:
> Parent := Child;"
> ```
>
> Here I say the statement in English, insert a colon, and then follow the English phrase with code that provides an example of the meaning of my statement. I find the English phrases ambiguous and confusing, but the code is starkly clear. Don't waste too much time parsing the English; concentrate on the code!

The classic example of polymorphism is a series of objects all of which do the following:

1. Descend from one base class.
2. Respond to a virtual command called Draw.
3. Respond to the command in different ways.

For instance, you might have four objects called TRectangle, TEllipse, TCircle, and TSquare. Suppose that each of these objects is a descendant of a base class called TShape, and that TShape has a virtual method called Draw. (This is a hypothetical TShape object and is not necessarily the one that appears on Delphi's Component Palette.) All TShape's children also have Draw methods, but one draws a circle, one a square, the next a rectangle, and the last an ellipse. You could then assign any of these objects to a variable of type TShape, and that TShape variable would act differently after each assignment. That is, the object of type TShape would draw a square if set equal to a TSquare object:

```
Shape := Square
Shape.Draw;   // Draws a square.
```

an ellipse if set equal to a TEllipse object:

```
Shape := Ellipse;
Shape.Draw;  // Draws an ellipse;
```

and so on.

One object, called Shape, therefore acts in many different ways. That's polymorphism.

From a conceptual point of view, this description does much to explain what polymorphism is all about. However, there is one key aspect that still needs to be explained.

According to the rules of OOP, you can pass all these objects to a single function that takes an object of type TShape as a parameter. That single function can call the Draw method of each of these objects, and each one will behave differently:

```
procedure DrawIt(Shape: TShape);
begin
  Shape.Draw; // TShape draws different shapes depending on "assignment"
end;

var
  Rectangle: TRectangle;
  Square: TSquare;
  Ellipse: TEllipse;
begin
  … // Initialize variables;
  DrawIt(Rectangle);          // Draws a rectangle
  DrawIt(Square);             // Draws a square
  DrawIt(Ellipse);            // Draws an ellipse
  … // Free Variables
end.
```

When you pass an object of type TRectangle to a function that takes a TShape as a parameter, you are accessing the TRectangle object through an object of type TShape. Or, if you look at the act of passing a parameter from a slightly different angle, you are actually assigning a variable of type TRectangle to a variable of type TShape:

```
var
  Shape: TShape;
  Rectangle: TRectangle;
begin
  …
  Shape := Rectangle;
  …
end;
```

This assignment is the actual hub around which polymorphism revolves. Because this assignment is legal, you can use an object of a single type, yet have it behave in many different ways: Once again, that's polymorphism.

To fully understand the last few paragraphs, you have to grasp that children of an object are assignment-compatible with their parents. In other words, given the declarations you saw in the OBJECT1 program, the following is legal:

```
var
  Parent: TObject;
  Child: TMyObject;
begin
  Parent := Child;
end;
```

But this syntax is flagged as a type mismatch:

```
var
  Parent: TObject;
  Child: TMyObject;
begin
  Child := Parent;
end;
```

You can't set a child equal to a parent because the child is larger than its parent—that is, it has more methods or fields—and therefore all its fields and methods will not be filled out. All other things being equal, you can build a two-story building out of the pieces meant for a three-story building; but you can't build a three-story building out of the pieces meant for a two-story building!

Consider the following hierarchy:

```
type
  TParent = class(TObject)
    procedure Draw; virtual;
  end;

  TChild = class(TParent)
    procedure Draw; override;
    procedure ShowHierarchy; virtual;
  end;
```

The issue here is that setting child equal to a parent is not safe:

```
Child := Parent; // Don't do this!
```

If it were allowed, it would be legal to write the following:

```
Child.ShowHierarchy;
```

In this hypothetical world, the call might compile, but it would fail at runtime because Parent has no ShowHierarchy method; therefore, it could not provide a valid address for the function at the time of the assignment operation. I will return to this subject in the next section of this chapter.

If you set a parent equal to child, all the features of the parent will be filled out properly:

```
Parent := Child;
```

That is, all the functions of TParent are part of TChild, so you can assign one to the other without fear of something going wrong. The methods that are not part of TParent are ignored.

> **NOTE**
>
> When you are thinking about this stuff, you need to be sure you are reading statements about assigning parents to children correctly. Even if I manage to straighten my grammar out, there is still nothing in the English language that makes it totally clear which item in an assignment statement is on the left and which is on the right. I could use the terms lvalue and rvalue in this case, except that they don't quite fit the case either. However, if you take this as an analogy, you can consider a child to be an rvalue and a parent to be an lvalue. You can set a parent equal to a child:
>
> ```
> Parent := Child;
> ```
>
> but you can't set a child equal to a parent:
>
> ```
> Child  := Parent;
> ```
>
> You literally can't do this. It's a type mismatch. The compiler replies "Incompatible types." In this sense, Child becomes like an rvalue in this one case. Even though it's ultimately possible to assign values to Child, you can't assign a Parent to it. In this one case, it might as well be an rvalue!

Another View of Polymorphism

Here's another way of looking at polymorphism. A base class defines a certain number of functions that are inherited by all its descendants. If you assign a variable of the child type to one of its parents, all the parent's methods are guaranteed to be filled out with valid addresses. The issue here is that the child, by the very fact of its being a descendant object, must have valid addresses for all the methods used in its parent's Virtual Method Tables and Dynamic Method Tables. As a result, you can call one of these methods and watch as the child's functions get called. However, you cannot call one of the child's methods that does not also belong to the parent. The parent doesn't know about those methods, so the compiler won't let you call them. In other words, the parent may be able to call some of the child's functions, but it is still a variable of the parent type.

To help you understand this, picture the VMT for TParent. It has a pointer to a Draw method in it, but no pointer to a ShowHierarchy method. Therefore an attempt to call its ShowHierarchy method would fail, as would an attempt to fill out a TChild's ShowHierarchy through an assignment with a TParent object.

Consider this schema:

```
Simplified VMT for Parent        Simplified VMT for Child

StartTable                       StartTable
  Draw --------------------------- Draw
EndTable                           ShowHierarchy
                                 EndTable
```

This shows a parent being set equal to a child. As you can see, the address of the Draw method for the parent is assigned to the address for the Draw method for the child. There is no ShowHierarchy method in the parent, so it is ignored.

Here's what happens if you try to set the child equal to the parent:

```
Simplified VMT for Child         Simplified VMT for Parent

StartTable                       StartTable
  Draw --------------------------- Draw
  ShowHierarchy ------------------ ????
EndTable                         EndTable
```

As you can clearly see, there is no method pointer in the parent table that can be assigned to the ShowHierarchy method of the child table. Therefore it is left blank, which means a call to the ShowHierarchy method of the child almost certainly fails. Therefore it is illegal to assign a parent to a child. You can, however, assign a child to a parent, and it's this assignment that lies at the heart of polymorphism! For the sake of clarity, let me spell it out. Here is the legal assignment:

```
Parent := Child;
```

Virtual Methods and Polymorphism

If some of the methods in a base class are defined as virtual, each of the descendants can redefine the implementation of these methods. The key elements that define a typical case of polymorphism are a base class and the descendants that inherit a base class's methods. In particular, the fanciest type of polymorphism involves virtual methods that are inherited from a base class.

A classic example of polymorphism is evident if you examine the Delphi VCL. All these objects are descendants of a single base class called TObject; therefore, they all know how to obey a single virtual command called Destroy, which is originally defined in TObject's declaration. As a result, you can pass all the many hundreds of Delphi classes to a routine that takes a parameter of the same type as their base class:

```
procedure FreeAllClasses(O: TObject);
begin
  O.Free;
end;
```

You can pass any Delphi object to the FreeAllClasses method:

```
procedure TForm1.Button1Click(Sender: TObject);
var
  Child: TChild;
  Parent: TParent;
  Form1: TForm;
begin
  ...
  FreeAllClasses(Child);
  FreeAllClasses(Parent);
  FreeAllClasses(Form1);
end;
```

The issue here is that passing a parameter to FreeAllClasses is analogous to an assignment statement. You are writing, in effect:

```
O := Parent;
O := Child;
O := Form1;
```

You could not, however, do this:

```
procedure FreeAllClasses(O: TChild);
begin
  O.Free;
end;
procedure TForm1.Button1Click(Sender: TObject);
var
  Child: TChild;
  Parent: TParent;
begin
  ...
  FreeAllClasses(Child);
  FreeAllClasses(Parent);
end;
```

The issue, of course, is that by passing Parent to FreeAllClasses, you are, in effect, asking Delphi to make the following assignment:

```
Child := Parent;
```

Delphi is kind enough to tell you not to do this. It's bad practice.

Every object in the VCL can use polymorphism to some degree, because they all inherit methods from TObject. In particular, they all inherit a virtual Destroy method, as shown in this excerpt from SYSTEM.PAS:

```
TObject = class
  constructor Create;
  procedure Free;
  ...
  destructor Destroy; virtual;
end;
```

The VCL frequently iterates through a series of objects, calling Destroy on each in turn. Some use the Destroy method inherited from TObject; others override TObject.Destroy, and thereby implement the "highest form" of polymorphic behavior.

> **NOTE**
>
> Notice that the Free method for TObject is not declared as virtual. That's because there is never any need to override this method. Free just checks to see if Self is equal to nil, and if it's not, Free calls Self.Destroy. You can't improve on the method, and you shouldn't try. So it's not virtual. You may, however, need to destroy some of the objects which you create inside one of your own objects. You will need, therefore, to override Destroy, and so it is declared as virtual.

To help illustrate this point, you can use this simple example to step through in the debugger. In particular, you could create an example in which you implement the Draw method of a TChild and TParent object differently:

```
procedure TParent.Draw;
begin
  ShowMessage('Parent Draw');
end;

procedure TChild.Draw;
begin
  ShowMessage('Child Draw');
end;
```

You could then instantiate objects of both types and pass their parameters to a CallDraw method:

```
procedure CallDraw(O: TParent);
begin
  O.Draw;
end;

procedure TForm1.bPolymorphClick(Sender: TObject);
var
  Child: TChild;
  Parent: TParent;
begin
  Child := TChild.Create;
  Parent := TParent.Create;
  CallDraw(Parent);
  CallDraw(Child);
  Child.Free;
  Parent.Free;
end;
```

The CallDraw method works with a variable of type TParent. It has only one kind of object in it. It works only with variables of type TParent. And yet if you pass both a parent object and a child object into it, one instance will call the TChild's Draw method and the other will call the TParent's Draw method. This is polymorphism in action. The concept here is so important that I have placed this example on disk, and show it below in Listing 25.1.

Listing 25.1. The ChildPar program demonstrates a simple case of polymorphism.

```
unit main;

interface

uses
  Windows, Messages, SysUtils,
  Classes, Graphics, Controls,
  Forms, Dialogs, StdCtrls;

type
  TForm1 = class(TForm)
    bPolymorph: TButton;
    procedure bPolymorphClick(Sender: TObject);
  end;

var
  Form1: TForm1;

implementation

{$R *.DFM}

type
  TParent = class(TObject)
    procedure Draw; virtual;
  end;

  TChild = class(TParent)
    procedure Draw; override;
    procedure ShowHierarchy; virtual;
  end;

procedure TParent.Draw;
begin
  ShowMessage('Parent Draw');
end;

procedure TChild.Draw;
begin
  ShowMessage('Child Draw');
end;

procedure TChild.ShowHierarchy;
begin
  ShowMessage('Child Show Hierarchy');
end;

procedure CallDraw(O: TParent);
begin
  O.Draw;
end;

procedure TForm1.bPolymorphClick(Sender: TObject);
var
  Child: TChild;
```

```
    Parent: TParent;
begin
  Child := TChild.Create;
  Parent := TParent.Create;
  CallDraw(Parent);
  CallDraw(Child);
  Child.Free;
  Parent.Free;
end;
```

If you have any questions about what's going on in this code, run this program. Step through it with the debugger, if necessary, until it starts to make sense to you. The key point is that one variable, called O, which is of type TParent, behaves in two different ways. It's polymorphic. One variable acting in two different ways!

Polymorphism in the VCL

One place where Delphi uses polymorphism heavily is with the TField objects assigned to the Fields array in a TTable object. The objects in the Fields array are of type TField, but they behave as if they are of type TStringField, TIntegerField, TFloatField, and so on. The issue, of course, is that variables of type TStringField and TIntegerField can all be assigned to the Fields array because you can assign a child object to a variable of its parent type:

```
Parent := Child;
```

Here is the declaration of the Fields property:

```
property Fields[Index: Integer]: TField;
```

Clearly this is an array of objects of type TField. Suppose, however, that you execute the following method in a simple program containing a TTable object that's pointed at the Biolife table:

```
procedure TForm1.bViewFieldTypesClick(Sender: TObject);
var
  i : Integer;
begin
  for i := 0 to Table1.FieldCount - 1 do
    ListBox1.Items.Add(Table1.Fields[i].ClassName);
end;
```

According to the declaration of the Fields object, the type of each of the members of the Fields array should be TField. However, here is what actually gets printed in the program's list box:

```
TFloatField
TStringField
TStringField
TStringField
TStringField
TFloatField
TFloatField
```

```
TMemoField
TGraphicField
```

Clearly this isn't really an array of TField objects at all. So what's going on, anyway?

Well, by now the answer should be clear. Somewhere internally, Delphi is assigning TStringField, TFloatField, TMemoField, and TGraphicField objects to the members of the TField array. Why is this legal? Because it's always legal to set a parent object equal to a child object! In essence, this is what happens:

```
var
  Field: TField;
  StringField: TStringField;
begin
   Field := StringField;  // This is legal!
end;
```

Here is the hierarchy of some of the key TField descendants:

```
-TField
  -TStringField
  -TNumericField
    -TSmallIntField
    -TWordField
    -TAutoIncField
  -TFloatField
    -TCurrencyField
  -TBlobField
    -TMemoField
    -TGraphicField
```

Given this hierarchy, it's always legal to assign a TStringField or TFloatField object to a variable of type TField:

```
var
  Fields: array [1..3] of TField;
  StringField: TStringField;
  FloatField: TFloatField;
  GraphicField: TGraphicField;
begin
  Fields[1] := StringField;    // legal!
  Fields[2] := FloatField;     // legal!
  Fields[3] := GraphicField;   // legal!
end;
```

This is such an important point that I'm going to include the source code for a program, called POLYFLDS.DPR, which demonstrates the issue discussed in this section. Listing 25.2 contains the source for this program.

Listing 25.2. The PolyFlds program shows how Delphi makes practical use of polymorphism.

```
unit Main;

interface
```

```
uses
  Windows, Messages, SysUtils,
  Classes, Graphics, Controls,
  Forms, Dialogs, StdCtrls,
  DB, Grids, DBGrids,
  DBTables;

type
  TForm1 = class(TForm)
    Table1: TTable;
    DBGrid1: TDBGrid;
    DataSource1: TDataSource;
    bViewFieldTypes: TButton;
    ListBox1: TListBox;
    procedure bViewFieldTypesClick(Sender: TObject);
  end;

var
  Form1: TForm1;

implementation

{$R *.DFM}

procedure TForm1.bViewFieldTypesClick(Sender: TObject);
var
  i : Integer;
begin
  for i := 0 to Table1.FieldCount - 1 do
    ListBox1.Items.Add(Table1.Fields[i].ClassName);
end;

end.
```

This example program makes it clear how important polymorphism is to Delphi. The Fields array of TTable is one of the most commonly used elements in all of Delphi. And what lies at the heart of the whole thing? Polymorphism!

Another important point to grasp here is that there is very little about Delphi that is mysterious. If you work with Visual Basic or PowerBuilder, there are lots of elements of the code or environment where the only explanation for why they work a particular way is "because." How come? "Because!" With Delphi, it's never like that. There is an explanation for everything in Delphi, and there is no part of the VCL or the environment that you cannot build yourself using Delphi.

Delphi is built in Delphi. There are no mysteries here. If you know the language well enough, even the most esoteric parts of the VCL will make sense to you. How can the Fields array be so powerful? How does it do those things? Well, now you know the answer: It's polymorphic!

Polymorphism Encapsulated (Review of Main Points)

That's the end of the first high-level overview of polymorphism and virtual methods. The key points to remember are these:

- You can set a parent equal to a child object, but you can't set a child equal to a parent object:

```
Parent := Child; { Little set equal to big: OK}
Child := Parent; { Big set equal to little: Doesn't work}
```

    The ability to set a parent equal to a child object is what makes polymorphism tick.

- The defining elements in polymorphism are the methods of the parent object, particularly those methods that are declared virtual. Even if you assign a child to a parent object:

```
Parent := Child;
```

    the parent can't call methods of the child that are not also visible in the parent's class declaration. In short, a variable of type TParent can never call the ShowHierarchy method even if the TParent object has been assigned to a variable of type TChild.

The point is that you can take a whole slew of hierarchically arranged objects, assign each of them to their parent, call a virtual method belonging to the parent, and watch them all behave in different ways. Whee! Polymorphism!

For some readers, I'm sure this is old hat. Other readers might be new to the subject, but have grasped it completely from the descriptions given already. However, most readers probably still have some questions lingering in the back of their minds.

If you want, just reread the sections above as often as necessary. I know from personal experience that as many as three out of four object-oriented programmers don't really understand polymorphism. The subject, however, is not that complicated. Concentrate on these two sentences:

Polymorphism allows you to set one variable of type TParent equal to a series of child objects. When you call certain virtual methods of that parent it will behave in different ways, depending on the traits of the currently selected child.

It's a mouthful, but it's not impossible to comprehend.

I will now move on to some concrete examples that should shed more light on the issue. In particular, I am going to develop the OBJECT4 program, which builds on the code presented in the last two chapters, but finally brings it to some sort of useful fulfillment. The OBJECT4 program is quite long, so I will present it in its own section.

OBJECT4

As described at the beginning of this chapter, OBJECT4 is a warehouse simulation that features a series of panels arranged in a large room. Each panel has from 4 to 12 palettes on it, and each palette contains a certain number of widgets. Users can stock additional widgets on the palettes, or they can sell widgets. If a large number of widgets are sold, the program is smart enough to iterate through the palettes and empty them one by one.

> **NOTE**
>
> The OBJECT4 program shows the outlines of a clean approach to a real-world problem. However, it is not a complete business application. It shows how objects can be used to embody actual objects or entities that we find in day-to-day life, but it's a theoretical example, and not a real-world program.
>
> To bring this program up to the point where it might be used in an office would be a considerable chore, which would involve adding both features and error checking. However, in the construction of any large project, one key step is the development of a methodology that can support a large application. The foundation for a useful program is found in OBJECT4. It shows a lot about the way any good OOP tool should be constructed.
>
> For examples of real-world OOP programs, study the VCL. The TField object and its descendants show exactly how to construct polymorphic objects in a manner that can be used in the real world. However, that code is so complex that you need to step back and first see a simple example, like the one shown here. Then you can go back and study more complex examples, like the ones found in the VCL.

The OBJECT4 program is stocked with hypothetical widgets named after colors: TYellow, TBlue, TGreen, and TViolet. A real-world application might have TChairs, TTables, TBureaus, and so on, instead of colors. Or, a bit more to the point, a real-world program might have TStringField, TFloatField, and TGraphicField. The issue is not the names or traits of the individual widgets, but the fact that a series of different TWidget descendants needs to be created.

You will find that TYellow, TBlue, and the other colors share many traits. This is a somewhat artificial aspect of this program; in a real-world program, each of these objects would be more varied. For instance, a TChair would have an FLegs data store, a TBed would have an FFrame data store, and so on.

NOTE

When studying OBJECT4, you will find that the TWidget object has changed slightly from its appearance in OBJECT3. These types of minor structural changes should be expected in OOP. Developers don't start with a base class and build up a hierarchy without ever deciding that changes need to be made to the structures they are creating. Frameworks and hierarchies evolve over time; they do not burst into the world fully formed.

If you are building a certain kind of tool, after the first release, it is very dangerous to go back and start changing the way base classes work. Nevertheless, during development, changes need to be made to the base classes in your hierarchy. This is one of the major "gotchas" of object-oriented programming, and I would be remiss if I didn't lay it out in clear terms. Right now, there are no good remedies for this problem, but the lesson it teaches is clear: *Don't release objects to unsuspecting programmers until you are sure you have the proper design!* If you are looking for some relief, my experience has shown that most major companies don't think beta testers fit the definition of "unsuspecting."

This is probably also an interesting time to consider the object model used in COM. The Component Object Model does not directly support inheritance. Instead, they say you should rewrite the interface to an object entirely if you want to create a descendant; that is, if you want to add features to it.

The OBJECT4 program features five forms. The first depicts the floor of the warehouse. (See Figure 25.1.) The second depicts a report on the state of the widgets found on a particular palette. (See Figure 25.2.) The third enables you to specify how many objects of each type you want to sell. (See Figure 25.3.) The fourth depicts the status of the entire warehouse, using graphs to display the number and type of each object found in the warehouse. (See Figure 25.4.) The last form shows the hierarchy of a TWidget. (See Figure 25.5.)

FIGURE 25.1.

The Menagerie form shows the floor of the warehouse.

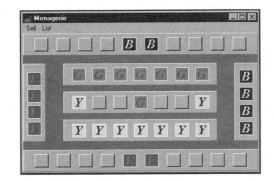

FIGURE 25.2.

The Report View form shows the status of the objects on an individual palette.

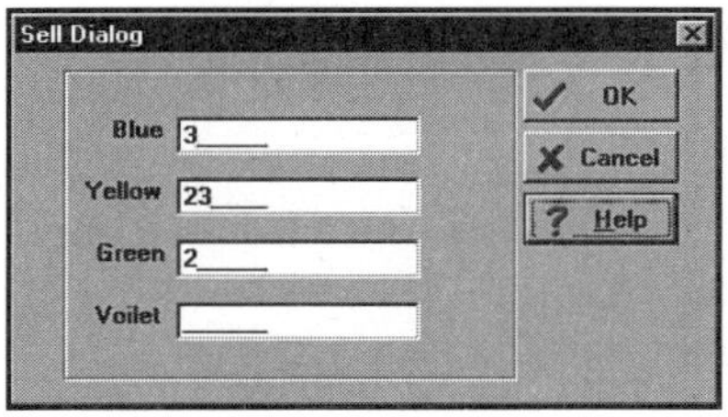

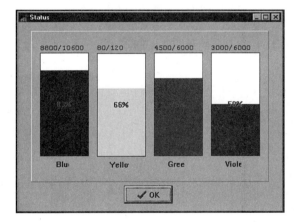

FIGURE 25.3.

The Sell dialog enables the user to specify how many widgets of each type are being sold during a transaction.

FIGURE 25.4.

The Status form shows how many of each type of widget are currently available in the warehouse.

The OBJECT4 program (shown in Listings 25.3 through 25.9) is fairly long on code, but once again you will find that many of the forms are relatively trivial, and that the core of the program can be found in a few, relatively simple lines of code.

FIGURE 25.5.

The Hierarchy dialog displays the hierarchy of a
`TWidget`.

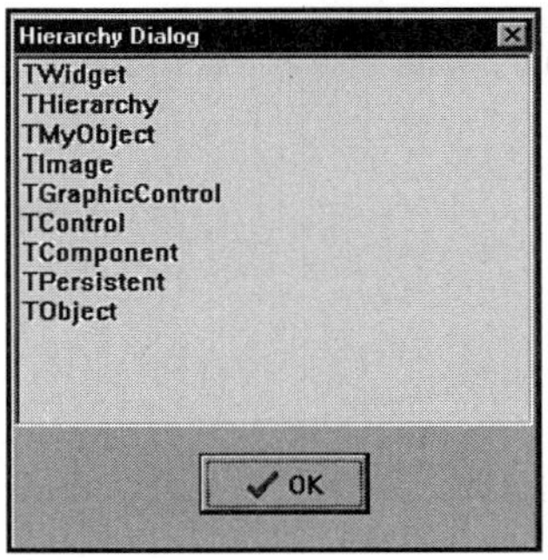

Listing 25.3. The project file for the OBJECT4 program is listed here; the rest of the program is found on the CD.

```
program Object4;

uses
  Forms,
  Main in 'MAIN.PAS' {Menagerie},
  Classdef in 'CLASSDEF.PAS',
  Reports in 'REPORTS.PAS' {Report},
  Status in 'STATUS.PAS' {StatusForm},
  Selldlgs in 'SELLDLGS.PAS' {SellDlg};

{$R *.RES}

begin
  Application.CreateForm(TMenagerie, Menagerie);
  Application.CreateForm(TReport, Report);
  Application.CreateForm(TStatusForm, StatusForm);
  Application.CreateForm(TSellDlg, SellDlg);
  Application.Run;
end.
```

Listing 25.4. The main form for the OBJECT4 program.

```
unit Main;

{ Program copyright (c) 1996 by Charles Calvert }
{ Project Name: OBJECT4 }

{ This program is a simplified warehouse simulation.

  When you open the program there are a number of
  empty palettes sitting in a large room. If you
  click on one of the palettes, you can "stock" it
  with either yellow, blue, green or violet widgets.

  If you click on a palette that has widgets, you
  can see the number and type of widgets on that
  palette.
```

```
begin
  FCurSp := TSpeedButton(Sender);
  P := Point(FCurSp.Left, FCurSp.Top);
  WinProcs.ClientToScreen(FCurSp.Parent.Handle, P);
  PopUpMenu1.Popup(P.X, P.Y);
end;

procedure TMenagerie.WidgetClick(Sender: TObject);
var
  WidgetType: Integer;
  Widget: TWidget;
begin
  WidgetType := (Sender as TMenuItem).Tag;
  case WidgetType of
    idBlue:  Widget := TBlue.Create(Self);
    idYellow:  Widget := TYellow.Create(Self);
    idGreen: Widget := TGreen.Create(Self);
    idViolet: Widget := TViolet.Create(Self);
  end;
  FCurSp.Enabled := False;
  FCurSp.Visible := False;
  Widget.Parent := FCurSp.Parent;
  Widget.Left := FCurSp.Left;
  Widget.Top := FCurSp.Top;
  Widget.Twin := FCurSp;
  Widget.Show;
end;

procedure TMenagerie.Timer1Timer;
var
  i: Integer;
  A: TWidget;
begin
  for i := 0 to ComponentCount - 1 do
    if Components[i] is TWidget then begin
      A := TWidget(Components[i]);
      if A.Quantity <= 0 then begin
        A.Twin.Enabled := True;
        A.Twin.Visible := True;
        A.Free;
        Exit;
      end;
    end;
end;

procedure TMenagerie.SellProduct(var Widget: TWidget; var DataRec: TDataRec);
var
  NewTotal: LongInt;
begin
  if Widget is TBlue then
    NewTotal := DataRec.BlueTotal
  else if Widget is TYellow then
    NewTotal := DataRec.YellowTotal
  else if Widget is TGreen then
    NewTotal := DataRec.GreenTotal
  else
    NewTotal := DataRec.VioletTotal;
```

continues

Listing 25.4. continued

```
  if NewTotal <= Widget.Quantity then begin
    Widget.Quantity := Widget.Quantity - NewTotal;
    NewTotal := 0;
  end else begin
    NewTotal := NewTotal - Widget.Quantity;
    Widget.Quantity := 0;
  end;

  if Widget is TBlue then
    DataRec.BlueTotal := NewTotal
  else if Widget is TYellow then
    DataRec.YellowTotal := NewTotal
  else if Widget is TGreen then
    DataRec.GreenTotal := NewTotal
  else
    DataRec.VioletTotal := NewTotal;
end;

procedure TMenagerie.Sell1Click(Sender: TObject);
var
  DataRec: TDataRec;
  i: Integer;
  Widget: TWidget;
begin
  if not SellDlg.GetData(DataRec) then exit;
  for i := 0 to ComponentCount - 1 do begin
    Widget := TWidget(Components[i]);
    if Components[i] is TWidget then
      SellProduct(Widget, DataRec);
  end;
end;

procedure TMenagerie.ListClick(Sender: TObject);
var
  i: Integer;
  List: TList;
begin
  List := TList.Create;
  for i := 0 to ComponentCount - 1 do
    if Components[i] is TWidget then
      List.Add(Components[i]);
  StatusForm.RunAll(List);
  List.Free;
end;

end.
```

Listing 25.5. The CLASSDEF unit, which is possibly the most important module in the OBJECT4 program.

```
unit Classdef;

{ Program copyright (c) 1996 by Charles Calvert }
{ Project Name: OBJECT4 }
```

```
interface

uses
  Classes, Controls, Graphics,
  Dialogs, ExtCtrls, Buttons;

const
  idBlue = 100;
  idYellow = 101;
  idGreen = 102;
  idViolet = 103;

type
  THMethod = (hmScreen, hmDisk);

  TMyObject = class(TImage)
  public
    procedure ShowHierarchy; virtual;
  end;

  THierarchy = class(TMyObject)
  private
    FHierarchyMethod: THMethod;
    procedure SetHierarchy(H: THMethod);
  public
    procedure ShowHierarchy; override;
  published
    property HierarchyMethod: THMethod read FHierarchyMethod write SetHierarchy;
  end;

  TWidget = class(THierarchy)
  private
    FQuantity: LongInt;
    FBoxSize: LongInt;
    FMaxQuantity: LongInt;
    FDescription: string;
    FTwin: TSpeedButton;
  protected
    procedure MouseDown(Sender: TObject; Button: TMouseButton;
                        Shift: TShiftState; X, Y: Integer);
  public
    constructor Create(AOwner: TComponent); override;
    procedure Sell(Amount: LongInt); virtual;
    procedure Stock; virtual;
    function GetName: string; virtual;
  published
    property Description: string read FDescription;
    property Quantity: LongInt read FQuantity write FQuantity;
    property Twin: TSpeedButton read FTwin write FTwin;
    property BoxSize: LongInt read FBoxSize write FBoxSize;
    property OnMouseDown;
  end;

  TBlue = class(TWidget)
    public
    constructor Create(AOwner: TComponent); override;
    procedure ShowHierarchy; override;
  end;
```

continues

Listing 25.5. continued

```
TYellow = class(TWidget)
  public
    constructor Create(AOwner: TComponent); override;
    procedure ShowHierarchy; override;
  end;

TGreen = class(TWidget)
  public
    constructor Create(AOwner: TComponent); override;
    procedure ShowHierarchy; override;
  end;

TViolet = class(TWidget)
  public
    constructor Create(AOwner: TComponent); override;
    procedure ShowHierarchy; override;
  end;

implementation

uses
  HierDlg,
  Reports,
  StrBox;

var
  FActive: Boolean;

{ -- TMyObject -- }

procedure TMyObject.ShowHierarchy;
const
  CR = #13#10;
var
  AClass: TClass;
  S: string;
begin
  S := ClassName;
  AClass := ClassParent;
  while AClass <> nil do begin
    S := S + CR + AClass.ClassName;
    AClass := AClass.ClassParent;
  end;
  MessageDlg(S, mtInformation, [mbOk], 0);
end;

{ -- THierarchy -- }

procedure THierarchy.ShowHierarchy;
var
  F: System.Text;
  AClass: TClass;
begin
  if FHierarchyMethod = hmscreen then
    inherited ShowHierarchy
```

```
    else begin
      System.Assign(F, 'inherit.txt');
      ReWrite(F);
      WriteLn(F, ClassName);
      AClass := ClassParent;
      while AClass <> nil do begin
        WriteLn(F, AClass.ClassName);
        AClass := AClass.ClassParent;
      end;
      Close(F);
    end;
end;


procedure THierarchy.SetHierarchy(H: THMethod);
begin
  FHierarchyMethod := H;
end;

{ -- TWidget -- }

constructor TWidget.Create(AOwner: TComponent);
begin
  inherited Create(AOwner);
  FBoxSize := 5;
  OnMouseDown := MouseDown;
  FDescription := 'I don''t talk!';
  ClientWidth := 25;
  ClientHeight := 25;
  FActive := True;
end;

function TWidget.GetName: string;
begin
  Result := StripFromFront(ClassName, 1);
end;

procedure TWidget.Stock;
begin
  FQuantity := FQuantity + FBoxSize;
end;

procedure TWidget.Sell(Amount: LongInt);
begin
  if FActive then
    FQuantity := FQuantity - FBoxSize;
end;

procedure TWidget.MouseDown(Sender: TObject; Button: TMouseButton;
                            Shift: TShiftState; X, Y: Integer);
begin
  FActive := False;
  Report.Run(Self);
  FActive := True;
end;

{ -- TBlue -- }
```

continues

Listing 25.5. continued

```pascal
constructor TBlue.Create(AOwner: TComponent);
begin
  inherited Create(AOwner);
  Picture.LoadFromFile('blue.bmp');
  FDescription := 'A blue widget!';
  FQuantity := 800;
  FBoxSize := 50;
  FMaxQuantity := 1000;
end;

procedure TBlue.ShowHierarchy;
begin
  if FHierarchyMethod = hmDisk then
    inherited ShowHierarchy
  else
    HierarchyDlg.Run(Self, clBlue);
end;

{ -- TYellow -- }

constructor TYellow.Create(AOwner: TComponent);
begin
  inherited Create(AOwner);
  Picture.LoadFromFile('yellow.bmp');
  FDescription := 'A yellow widget!';
  FQuantity := 10;
  FBoxSize := 1;
  FMaxQuantity := 15;
end;

procedure TYellow.ShowHierarchy;
begin
  if FHierarchyMethod = hmDisk then
    inherited ShowHierarchy
  else
    HierarchyDlg.Run(Self, clYellow);
end;

{ -- TGreen -- }

constructor TGreen.Create(AOwner: TComponent);
begin
  inherited Create(AOwner);
  Picture.LoadFromFile('green.bmp');
  FDescription := 'A green widget!';
  FQuantity := 500;
  FBoxSize := 50;
  FMaxQuantity := 650;
end;

procedure TGreen.ShowHierarchy;
begin
  if FHierarchyMethod = hmDisk then
    inherited ShowHierarchy
  else
    HierarchyDlg.Run(Self, clGreen);
end;
```

```
{ -- TViolet -- }

constructor TViolet.Create(AOwner: TComponent);
begin
  inherited Create(AOwner);
  Picture.LoadFromFile('violet.bmp');
  FDescription := 'Violet widget palette';
  FQuantity := 600;
  FBoxSize := 70;
  FMaxQuantity := 740;
end;

procedure TViolet.ShowHierarchy;
begin
  if FHierarchyMethod = hmDisk then
    inherited ShowHierarchy
  else
    HierarchyDlg.Run(Self, clPurple);
end;

end.
```

Listing 25.6. The REPORTS unit, which describes the state of an individual widget.

```
unit Reports;

{ Program copyright (c) 1996 by Charles Calvert }
{ Project Name: OBJECT4 }

interface

uses
  SysUtils, WinTypes, WinProcs,
  Messages, Classes, Graphics,
  Controls, Forms, Dialogs,
  StdCtrls, ExtCtrls, ClassDef, Buttons;

type
  TReport = class(TForm)
    Panel1: TPanel;
    LName: TLabel;
    Panel2: TPanel;
    LPanel: TLabel;
    LPalette: TLabel;
    Label2: TLabel;
    Label3: TLabel;
    Label4: TLabel;
    LDescription: TLabel;
    Label5: TLabel;
    LQuantity: TLabel;
    BitBtn1: TBitBtn;
    StockItems: TBitBtn;
    BitBtn2: TBitBtn;
    procedure BitBtn1Click(Sender: TObject);
```

continues

Listing 25.6. continued

```
    procedure StockItemsClick(Sender: TObject);
    procedure BitBtn2Click(Sender: TObject);
  private
    FWidget: TWidget;
    procedure ShowData;
  public
    procedure Run(Widget: TWidget);
  end;

var
  Report: TReport;

implementation

{$R *.DFM}

procedure TReport.ShowData;
begin
  LName.Caption := FWidget.GetName;
  LPalette.Caption := IntToStr(FWidget.Twin.Tag);
  LPanel.Caption := TPanel(FWidget.Parent).Name;
  LDescription.Caption := FWidget.Description;
  LQuantity.Caption := IntToStr(FWidget.Quantity);
end;

procedure TReport.Run(Widget: TWidget);
begin
  FWidget := Widget;
  ShowData;
  ShowModal;
end;

procedure TReport.BitBtn1Click(Sender: TObject);
begin
  Close;
end;

procedure TReport.StockItemsClick(Sender: TObject);
begin
  FWidget.Stock;
  ShowData;
end;

procedure TReport.BitBtn2Click(Sender: TObject);
begin
  FWidget.ShowHierarchy;
  ModalResult := mrNone;
end;

end.
```

Listing 25.7. The SELLDLGS unit, which enables the user to report the amount of a particular sale.

```
unit Selldlgs;

{ Program copyright (c) 1996 by Charles Calvert }
{ Project Name: OBJECT4 }

interface

uses
  WinTypes, WinProcs, Classes,
  Graphics, Forms, Controls,
  Buttons, StdCtrls, ExtCtrls,
  Mask, SysUtils;

type
  TDataRec = record
    BlueTotal: LongInt;
    YellowTotal: LongInt;
    GreenTotal: LongInt;
    VioletTotal: LongInt;
  end;

  TSellDlg = class(TForm)
    OKBtn: TBitBtn;
    CancelBtn: TBitBtn;
    HelpBtn: TBitBtn;
    Bevel1: TBevel;
    Label1: TLabel;
    Label2: TLabel;
    Label3: TLabel;
    Label4: TLabel;
    MaskEdit1: TMaskEdit;
    MaskEdit2: TMaskEdit;
    MaskEdit3: TMaskEdit;
    MaskEdit4: TMaskEdit;
    procedure FormActivate(Sender: TObject);
  public
    function GetData(var DataRec: TDataRec): Boolean;
  end;

var
  SellDlg: TSellDlg;

implementation

uses
  StrBox;

{$R *.DFM}

function CheckString(S: string): string;
begin
  S := CleanString(S);
  if S = '' then S := '0';
  Result := S;
end;
```

continues

Listing 25.7. continued

```
function TSellDlg.GetData(var DataRec: TDataRec): Boolean;
var
  i: Integer;
begin
  GetData := True;
  for i := 0 to ComponentCount - 1 do
    if Components[i] is TMaskEdit then
      TMaskEdit(Components[i]).Text := '';
  if ShowModal = mrOk then begin
    DataRec.BlueTotal := StrToInt(CheckString(MaskEdit1.Text));
    DataRec.YellowTotal := StrToInt(CheckString(MaskEdit2.Text));
    DataRec.GreenTotal := StrToInt(CheckString(MaskEdit3.Text));
    DataRec.VioletTotal := StrToInt(CheckString(MaskEdit4.Text));
  end else
    GetData := False;
end;

procedure TSellDlg.FormActivate(Sender: TObject);
begin
  MaskEdit1.SetFocus;
end;

end.
```

Listing 25.8. The STATUS dialog, which displays graphs depicting the current supplies of each widget.

```
unit Status;

{ Program copyright (c) 1996 by Charles Calvert }
{ Project Name: OBJECT4 }

interface

uses
  SysUtils, WinTypes, WinProcs,
  Messages, Classes, Graphics,
  Controls, Forms, Dialogs,
  StdCtrls, Gauges, ExtCtrls,
  Buttons, ClassDef;

const
  MaxBlue = 10600;
  MaxYellow = 120;
  MaxGreen = 6000;
  MaxViolet = 6000;

type
  TStatusForm = class(TForm)
    Panel1: TPanel;
    gBlue: TGauge;
    gYellow: TGauge;
    gGreen: TGauge;
```

```
    gViolet: TGauge;
    Label1: TLabel;
    Label2: TLabel;
    Label3: TLabel;
    Label4: TLabel;
    BitBtn1: TBitBtn;
    LBlue: TLabel;
    LYellow: TLabel;
    LGreen: TLabel;
    LViolet: TLabel;
    procedure FormCreate(Sender: TObject);
  private
    { Private declarations }
    FBlueTotal: LongInt;
    FYellowTotal: LongInt;
    FGreenTotal: LongInt;
    FVioletTotal: LongInt;
    procedure ZeroTotals;
    procedure TotalWidgets(Widget: TWidget);
  public
    { Public declarations }
    procedure RunAll(Components: TList);
    procedure CalcTotals(Components: TList);
  end;

var
  StatusForm: TStatusForm;

implementation

{$R *.DFM}

procedure TStatusForm.ZeroTotals;
begin
  FYellowTotal := 0;
  FBlueTotal := 0;
  FGreenTotal := 0;
  FVioletTotal := 0;
end;

procedure TStatusForm.TotalWidgets(Widget: TWidget);
begin
  if Widget is TYellow then
    FYellowTotal := FYellowTotal + Widget.Quantity;
  if Widget is TBlue then
    FBlueTotal := FBlueTotal + Widget.Quantity;
  if Widget is TGreen then
    FGreenTotal := FGreenTotal + Widget.Quantity;
  if Widget is TViolet then
    FVioletTotal := FVioletTotal + Widget.Quantity;
end;

procedure TStatusForm.CalcTotals(Components: TList);
var
  Widget: TWidget;
  i: Integer;
```

continues

Listing 25.8. continued

```
begin
  ZeroTotals;
  for i := 0 to Components.Count - 1 do begin
    Widget := TWidget(Components[i]);
    TotalWidgets(Widget);
  end;
end;

procedure TStatusForm.RunAll(Components: TList);
begin
  CalcTotals(Components);
  LBlue.Caption := IntToStr(FBlueTotal) + '/' + IntToStr(GBlue.MaxValue);
  LYellow.Caption := IntToStr(FYellowTotal) + '/' + IntToStr(GYellow.MaxValue);
  LGreen.Caption := IntToStr(FGreenTotal) + '/' + IntToStr(GGreen.MaxValue);;
  LViolet.Caption := IntToStr(FVioletTotal)+ '/' + IntToStr(GViolet.MaxValue);;
  GBlue.Progress := FBlueTotal;
  GYellow.Progress := FYellowTotal;
  GGreen.Progress := FGreenTotal;
  GViolet.Progress := FVioletTotal;
  ShowModal;
end;

procedure TStatusForm.FormCreate(Sender: TObject);
begin
  gBlue.MaxValue := MaxBlue;
  gYellow.MaxValue := MaxYellow;
  gGreen.MaxValue := MaxGreen;
  gViolet.MaxValue := MaxViolet;
end;

end.
```

Listing 25.9. The `Hierarchy` dialog, which shows the hierarchy of `TWidget`.

```
unit Hierdlg;

{ Program copyright (c) 1996 by Charles Calvert }
{ Project Name: OBJECT4 }

interface

uses
  SysUtils, WinTypes, WinProcs,
  Messages, Classes, Graphics,
  Controls, Forms, Dialogs,
  StdCtrls, Buttons, ClassDef;

type
  THierarchyDlg = class(TForm)
    ListBox1: TListBox;
    BitBtn1: TBitBtn;
  private
    { Private declarations }
  public
    { Public declarations }
```

```
    procedure Run(Widget: TWidget; AColor: TColor);
  end;

var
  HierarchyDlg: THierarchyDlg;

implementation

{$R *.DFM}

procedure THierarchyDlg.Run(Widget: TWidget; AColor: TColor);
var
  AClass: TClass;
  S: string;
begin
  ListBox1.Clear;
  ListBox1.Color := AColor;
  S := ClassName;
  AClass := Widget.ClassParent;
  while AClass <> nil do begin
    ListBox1.Items.Add(AClass.ClassName);
    AClass := AClass.ClassParent;
  end;
  ShowModal;
end;

end.
```

After starting the program, you can click any of the palettes shown in the warehouse. A menu appears asking you to specify the type of widget you want to place on the palette. You can choose to display a palette of Yellow, Blue, Green, or Violet widgets. After placing a few sets of widgets in the warehouse, you can click the List menu item to see the status of the entire warehouse. You can also click any individual palette that contains widgets to see a report on the type and number of widgets stored there. From inside the TReport form, you can add additional boxes of widgets to a palette. The final option in the program is the Sell menu item, which brings up a form called Sell Dialog that allows you to sell widgets. If you sell more than a full palette of widgets, a palette is emptied out and automatically deleted. If you sell less than a palette of widgets, the correct number of widgets is subtracted from one of the palettes. The program does no error checking in case you sell more widgets than there are in stock. Adding this feature, as the academicians would say, is left as an exercise for the reader!

> **NOTE**
>
> A key design issue in this program involves the ability to add new types at runtime. That is, the program supports TGreen, TBlue, TViolet, and TYellow widgets. Why can't you add a TRed widget at runtime? It might seem as if OBJECT4 is limited because you cannot dynamically add TPurple or TRed widgets at runtime, but must instead go back to the source to add this feature. Such a complaint stems from taking the program too literally.

For instance, you would not expect to be able to create new types of TField descendants dynamically at runtime. You could create many instances of a TStringField object, but you would not expect to be able to create a new type of TField descendant such as TAviField.

In a real-world program, you might have a TColoredWidget object and would dynamically add or delete colors at runtime by changing the widget's Color property. Here, I'm using colors as a metaphor for any kind of widget, where each widget is meant to contain a unique set of traits representative of a larger class. For instance, a programmer might have objects such as TChair, TBed, TTable, and so on. The program could then enable the user, at runtime, to add or delete various types of chairs such as Chippendale chairs, art deco chairs, and so on.

Major classes such as beds and chairs need to be differentiated as distinct objects, because beds will have FFrame and FMattress fields, while chairs will not have these fields, but FLegs, FSeat, and FBack fields instead. In short, this type of program does not allow the creation of a new class of objects at runtime, but it will enable you to add new types of a particular class. Deciding which types of objects need to be created at runtime is a major design issue worthy of serious consideration.

Before I begin talking about the code in this program, I should point out that I am not going to go through it in a line-by-line analysis. The program is too long for that kind of approach. At times, you may have to step through the code before you understand exactly how certain features are implemented, but that kind of activity can have unexpected benefits. In general, I'll assume that you know how to use the debugger to figure out the code in this program, so I will concentrate on discussing polymorphism.

Major Features of OBJECT4

The program begins by popping up a standard TForm descendant called TMenagerie. This form has a series of palettes on it, and you can place TWidget descendants on those palettes.

You can paint a direct descendant of TObject on the form of a Delphi program if you want, but in the long run it is probably better to display components on forms. In particular, I wanted to associate a bitmap with each TWidget descendant that I placed on a form. As a result, I decided to descend TMyObject from TImage, rather than directly from TObject. That way, I could inherit the capability to display a bitmap on a form, rather than having to create the functionality myself:

```
TMyObject = class(TImage)
public
  procedure ShowHierarchy; virtual;
end;
```

The most important single fragment of code in the OBJECT4 program contains the declarations for TYellow, TBlue, and the other widgets:

```
TBlue = class(TWidget)
public
  constructor Create(AOwner: TComponent); override;
  procedure ShowHierarchy; override;
end;

TYellow = class(TWidget)
public
  constructor Create(AOwner: TComponent); override;
  procedure ShowHierarchy; override;
end;

TGreen = class(TWidget)
public
  constructor Create(AOwner: TComponent); override;
  procedure ShowHierarchy; override;
end;

TViolet = class(TWidget)
public
  constructor Create(AOwner: TComponent); override;
  procedure ShowHierarchy; override;
end;
```

Notice that these declarations are fairly simple. You are merely redefining some fundamental traits of each object.

NOTE

If you have the Delphi source code, you might want to compare these declarations to the declarations for TStringField, TFloatField, and so on. These declarations are found in DBTABLES.PAS. Here, for instance, is the declaration for TWordField:

```
TWordField = class(TIntegerField)
public
  constructor Create(AOwner: TComponent); override;
end;
```

The Create methods for each of these objects are simple:

```
constructor TBlue.Create(AOwner: TComponent);
begin
  inherited Create(AOwner);
  Picture.LoadFromFile('blue.bmp');
  FDescription := 'A blue widget!';
  FQuantity := 800;
  FBoxSize := 50;
  FMaxQuantity := 1000;
end;
```

If you compare several of these Create methods, you see that certain fields of each object are assigned values that distinguish it from its peers.

The ShowHierarchy method is also straightforward.

```
procedure TBlue.ShowHierarchy;
begin
  if FHierarchyMethod = hmDisk then
    inherited ShowHierarchy
  else
    HierarchyDlg.Run(Self, clBlue);
end;
```

The Hierarchy dialog (shown in Figure 25.5) is a simple form containing a list box and a button. The list box displays the members of the hierarchy being shown. The key point here, however, is that each object differs slightly from the last, because the type of variable represented by the word Self passes a different color to HierarchyDlg.Run.

If you look at the form for TMenagerie, you see that the palettes laid out on the panels are really instances of TSpeedButton. If the user clicks on one of these palettes and asks to stock it with blue widgets, the following code is executed:

```
procedure TMenagerie.WidgetClick(Sender: TObject);
var
  WidgetType: Integer;
  Widget: TWidget;
begin
  WidgetType := (Sender as TMenuItem).Tag;
  case WidgetType of
    idBlue:  Widget := TBlue.Create(Self);
    idYellow:  Widget := TYellow.Create(Self);
    idGreen: Widget := TGreen.Create(Self);
    idViolet: Widget := TViolet.Create(Self);
  end;
  FCurSp.Enabled := False;
  FCurSp.Visible := False;
  Widget.Parent := FCurSp.Parent;
  Widget.Left := FCurSp.Left;
  Widget.Top := FCurSp.Top;
  Widget.Twin := FCurSp;
  Widget.Show;
end;
```

FCurSp is a pointer to the instance of TSpeedButton that the user selected. The assignment of the correct speedbutton to FCurSp occurs in a method called sp41Click:

```
procedure TMenagerie.sp41Click(Sender: TObject);
var
  P: TPoint;
begin
  FCurSp := TSpeedButton(Sender);
  P := Point(FCurSp.Left, FCurSp.Top);
  WinProcs.ClientToScreen(FCurSp.Parent.Handle, P);
  PopUpMenu1.Popup(P.X, P.Y);
end;
```

`WidgetClick` uses polymorphism. Specifically, it sets a parent class equal to a child class:

```
Widget := TBlue.Create(Self);
```

It then disables and hides the speedbutton:

```
FCurSp.Enabled := False;
FCurSp.Visible := False;
```

And, it completes the instantiation of the instance of type `TBlue`:

```
Widget.Parent := FCurSp.Parent;
Widget.Left := FCurSp.Left;
Widget.Top := FCurSp.Top;
Widget.Twin := FCurSp;
Widget.Show;
```

The point is that the parent object, `TWidget`, has `Parent`, `Top`, `Left`, `Twin`, and `Show` fields; so you can safely make these assignments regardless of whether the actual widget in question is of type `TYellow`, `TBlue`, `TGreen`, or `TViolet`. This is polymorphism in action.

> **NOTE**
>
> The `Twin` field of `TWidget` is a pointer to a `TSpeedButton`. While a `TWidget` descendant is visible on the screen, the speedbutton associated with it remains hidden and inactive. If the widgets on that palette are sold, the speedbutton is reactivated, and the instance of `TWidget` is destroyed. The `Twin` field is a mechanism that OBJECT4 employs in order to remember which speedbutton is associated with which `TWidget` descendant.

After reading the last few paragraphs, the core functionality of the OBJECT4 program should be clear to you. If it's not, try stepping through the program with the debugger. From now on, I will concentrate solely on explaining how the program implements various forms of polymorphism.

Classic Cases of Polymorphism

There are many examples of polymorphism in this program. Perhaps the most pure is found in REPORTS.PAS. Whenever the user clicks one of the `TWidget` descendants, the following mouse-down routine is called:

```
procedure TWidget.MouseDown(Sender: TObject; Button: TMouseButton;
                            Shift: TShiftState; X, Y: Integer);
begin
  FActive := False;
  Report.Run(Self);
  FActive := True;
end;
```

This is a method of TWidget, so all the TWidget descendants inherit it. As you can see, it calls Report.Run and passes itself as the parameter. Of course, each instance that is passed in is actually a reference to a variable of type TBlue, TYellow, TGreen, or TViolet. Once again, it is polymorphism that makes it possible to pass in objects of different types and assign them to a single variable of their ancestor's type:

```
procedure TReport.Run(Widget: TWidget);
begin
  FWidget := Widget;
  ShowData;
  ShowModal;
end;
```

Here, the variable called Widget is set equal to one of TWidget's descendants. The assignment occurs when a variable is passed as a parameter to the Run method. This is not what is traditionally thought of as an assignment, but in the end a variable of type TWidget is set equal to an object of type TBlue, TYellow, TGreen, or TViolet.

The ShowData method makes it clear that this technique is working:

```
procedure TReport.ShowData;
begin
  LName.Caption := FWidget.GetName;
  LPalette.Caption := IntToStr(FWidget.Twin.Tag);
  LPanel.Caption := TPanel(FWidget.Parent).Name;
  LDescription.Caption := FWidget.Description;
  LQuantity.Caption := IntToStr(FWidget.Quantity);
end;
```

In this example, calling FWidget.GetName resolves one way for a class of type TViolet, and another way for a class of type TBlue. In the first case, it retrieves the string 'Violet', and in the second case, it retrieves the string 'Blue'. The same principle applies to calls to FWidget.Description, except that this time a property is called rather than a method. Each of these calls is an example of polymorphism in action.

I said earlier that the highest form of polymorphism occurs when there are virtual methods involved. If you click the Hierarchy button in the Report dialog, a call to FWidget.ShowHierarchy is executed:

```
procedure TReport.BitBtn2Click(Sender: TObject);
begin
  FWidget.ShowHierarchy;
  ModalResult := mrNone;
end;
```

ShowHierarchy is a virtual method. As a result, if FWidget is set equal to an instance of TViolet, a different ShowHierarchy is called than if FWidget is set equal to a variable of type TGreen.

The kicker here, however, is that both methods display the object hierarchy not of TViolet, nor of TGreen, but of TWidget. Assigning a child to a parent object does not metamorphasize the parent object into its child; it only maps the child's functions to functions of the same type that exists in the parent.

If you are having trouble understanding all this, you should fire up Delphi and step through the code with the debugger. You can't just read about this kind of stuff; you have to make it happen yourself.

> **NOTE**
>
> This is definitely an excellent time to try to create your own objects and see whether you can get some polymorphism working. Create virtual methods that are resolved differently for different objects in your program. Get this subject down straight, and you can call yourself an expert in object-oriented programming!

As I said earlier, there are many examples of polymorphism in the OBJECT4 program. If you choose to explore it further, you will find examples scattered throughout every unit, and usually signaled by the declaration of a variable of type TWidget. These variables will, of course, be set equal to a child object. Every time this assignment occurs, polymorphism is taking place. But, as I said earlier, the purest — or at least the most interesting — forms of polymorphism occur when virtual methods are also added into the mix.

MaskEdits and Other Issues

The native Delphi TMaskEdit control used in the Sell dialog deserves at least a few sentences of comment. This component is a descendant of TEdit that enables you to control the kinds of characters that are entered into the control.

The key to the TMaskEdit component is the EditMask property, which enables you to enter a string that uses several special characters to define what the user can legally enter into the edit area. There is a property editor associated with the EditMask property. In this editor, you can find a number of default masks, as shown in Figure 25.6. However, on many occasions, none of these masks will suit your purpose.

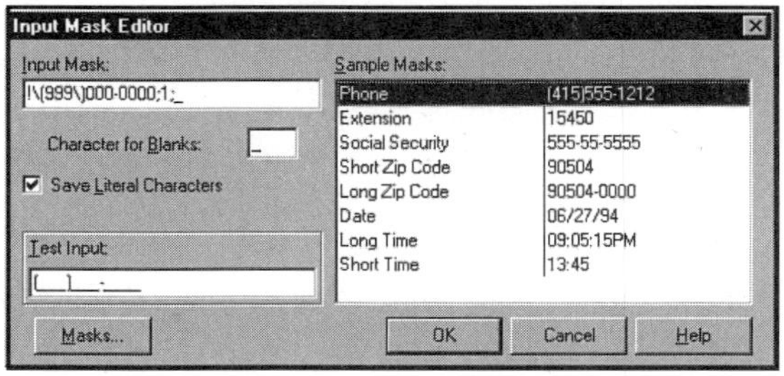

FIGURE 25.6.

The property editor for the
EditMask property.

In this program, I enter the following string as an EditMask:

```
######;0;_
```

The purpose of this string is to ensure that the user can enter only numeric values. In particular, these numeric values represent the number of widgets that the user wants to sell.

To understand the `EditMask` property, you need to study the entry associated with it in the online help. Here, you see all the characters that can be used to define a mask, along with a description of the effects associated with each character. Because this list is so readily available to you, I will not waste time or resources by reprinting it here. Instead, I will show how to use the information in the online help to achieve a specific purpose.

In the online help for the `EditMask` property, you will find that a pound sign (#) enables you to enter only numbers, spaces, and plus and minus characters. Notice, however, that there is also a 0 character, which requires that you enter a number in each location marked with that character. The question, then, is which special character should you use: # or 0?

In this particular case, the 0 character is *not* what you want, because it forces the user to enter a six-digit number, one for each of the 0s you place in the mask:

```
000000;0;_
```

The preceding mask would enable you to enter the number 123456, but it would reject 123. Because you want to give the user the freedom to enter a number of any size up to 999,999, you should use the # character rather than the 0 character. One way to sum this matter up is as follows: The 0 character means that the user has to fill in that place with a number, while the # character allows the user to fill in that space with either a number or a blank space.

The zero that appears after the semicolon in the previous string specifies that the mask entered is not saved as part of the data. If I had placed a 1 here, the mask would have been saved. In this particular case, there are no mask characters to either save or discard, so it doesn't matter what I placed in this location. The phone mask (shown in Figure 25.6) contains two parentheses that would be affected by this value.

Finally, the very end of the previous mask includes an underscore. This value is used to specify what will be used to designate the space character.

Notice that each field of the mask is separated from the last by a semicolon. Each mask consists of three fields, which were described earlier.

I am not completely enamored of this system, nor of the `TEditMask` component itself. Perhaps as I get better at using it, I will find that it has hidden strengths not yet evident to me. Only time will tell. But for now, I would say that this portion of your program is one you might want to entrust to a third party such as TurboPower Software. Or, perhaps you would like to create your own `TMaskEdit` component and place it on the market.

Method Addresses and Polymorphism

Polymorphism was not totally transparent to me until I began to think of it in terms of the actual method addresses involved in the assignment of a child to a variable of type parent:

```
Parent := Child;
```

If you really want to feel at home with this baby, look at the method addresses of an object of type TChild, assign it to an object of type TParent:

```
Parent := Child;
```

and look at the method addresses of the TParent object.

The HEXADDRESS program that follows demonstrates one way of looking at these addresses. This program uses the MethodAddress routine from TObject to get the address of a method of a child object. If you then assign a child object to a parent object:

```
Parent := Child;
```

you see that it has the same address for the Foo method as the child object did. That is why the parent starts to act as if it were a child object! When stated so boldly, the whole idea of polymorphism suddenly becomes transparent. Of course it works this way! How else could it work?

The form for the HEXADDRESS program, shown in Figure 25.7, contains three edit controls, one list box, two labels, and one button. The edit controls are used only for displaying data, and the user never needs to enter anything in them. I use them instead of labels just because I like the way they set the information off on the screen.

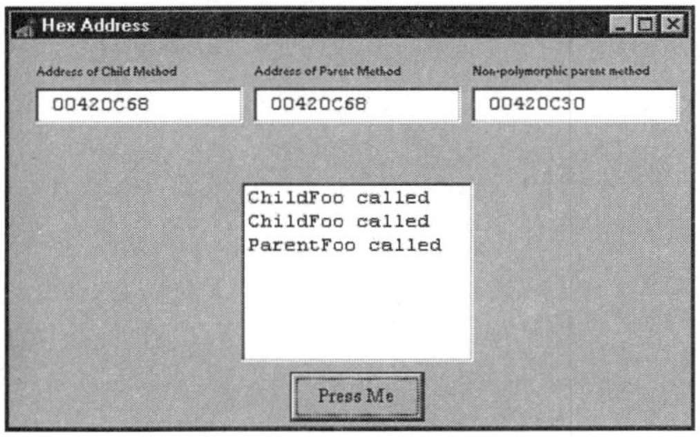

FIGURE 25.7.

The HEXADDRESS program shows that if you set a parent object equal to a child object, the two objects' methods will have the same addresses.

The complete code for the HEXADDRESS program is shown in Listing 25.10.

Listing 25.10. The HEXADDRESS program shows the address of polymorphic methods.

```
unit Main;

{ Program copyright (c) 1996 by Charles Calvert }
{ Project Name: HEXADDS }

{ This program shows what happens to method addresses
  in programs that implement polymorphism. }

interface

uses
  SysUtils, WinTypes, WinProcs,
  Messages, Classes, Graphics,
  Controls, Forms, Dialogs,
  StdCtrls;

type
  TForm1 = class(TForm)
    PressMe: TButton;
    Edit1: TEdit;
    Edit2: TEdit;
    ListBox1: TListBox;
    Edit3: TEdit;
    Label1: TLabel;
    Label2: TLabel;
    Label3: TLabel;
    Label4: TLabel;
    Label5: TLabel;
    procedure PressMeClick(Sender: TObject);
  end;

  TParent = class(TEdit)
  published
    procedure Foo; virtual;
  end;

  TChild = class(TParent)
  published
    procedure Foo; override;
  end;

var
  Form1: TForm1;

implementation

uses
  StrBox;

{$R *.DFM}

procedure TParent.Foo;
begin
  Form1.ListBox1.Items.Add('ParentFoo called');
end;
```

```
procedure TChild.Foo;
begin
  Form1.ListBox1.Items.Add('ChildFoo called');
end;

procedure TForm1.PressMeClick(Sender: TObject);
var
  P: TParent;
  C: TChild;
  Ptr: Pointer;
begin
  C := TChild.Create(Self);
  Ptr := C.MethodAddress('Foo');
  Edit1.Text := Address2Str(Ptr);
  C.Foo;
  P := C;
  Edit2.Text := Address2Str(P.MethodAddress('Foo'));
  P.Foo;
  C.Free;
  P := TParent.Create(Self);
  P.Foo;
  Edit3.Text := Address2Str(P.MethodAddress('Foo'));
  P.Free;
end;

end.
```

The HEXADDRESS program calls a routine found in the STRBOX unit that ships with this book. The Address2Str method converts a pointer address into a string:

```
function Address2Str(Addr: Pointer): string;
begin
  Result := Format('%p', [Addr]);
end;
```

The HEXADDRESS program reduces polymorphism to a principle so obvious that one feels foolish repeating it. Specifically, if you assign one object to another, of course their methods are going to have the same addresses! This is true even if one object is the parent of the other. The only tricky or unexpected part is the fact that Delphi enables you to set a parent equal to one of its children:

```
Parent := Child;
```

Given that, the rest is simple.

Summary

This chapter has tackled the complex subject of polymorphism. You saw that polymorphism is built on the fact that OOP languages enable you to assign a variable of type child to a variable declared to be of type parent. When you then call a method of the parent type, it will go to the address of the child object's methods. As a result, an object of type TParent, when assigned to four different objects of type TChild, might react in four different ways. One object, many different faces: polymorphism.

Creating Components

26

This chapter and the next cover building components. Components are one of the most important developments in contemporary programming, and there is not an environment on the market that makes them easier to use or to create than Delphi.

You build three types of components in this chapter:

- Descendants that change default settings in existing components.
- Descendants that add features to existing components.
- Tools built on top of abstract component base classes such as `TWinControl`, `TCustomControl`, `TComponent`, and `TGraphicControl`. These are the classes you descend from if you want to build your own components from the bottom up.

This chapter presents material on building visual components, and the next chapter explores building nonvisual components. Nonvisual components descend directly from `TComponent` and appear on the form only at design-time.

More specifically, the components built in this chapter fall into two categories:

- The first group is a set of `TEdit`, `TLabel`, and `TPanel` descendants that show how to change default colors, captions, and fonts. This section of the chapter also covers building components that consist of several different child components; that is, it shows how to group components together to form new components. The specific example included with this book shows a panel that comes with two radio buttons.
- The second tool is a clock component that can be dropped on a form, and stopped and started at will.

In the next chapter, you will see a nonvisual control that knows how to iterate through subdirectories. You can use it to build programs that search for files, delete all files with a certain extension, and so on.

Besides components, this chapter also briefly covers two related topics:

Property editors are used to edit the properties of components. The classic examples are the common dialogs that pop up when you edit the `Color` or `Font` properties that belong to most visible components. The drop-down lists and string editing capabilities found in the Object Inspector are also property editors.

Component editors are associated not with a single property, but with an entire component. An example is the Fields Editor used with `TTable` and `TQuery` components.

The property editors and component editors are related to a broader topic called the Tools API. The Tools API consists of a series of interfaces to the Delphi IDE that allow you to build experts, interfaces to version control systems, and similar utilities. The API for property editors, component editors, and the Tools API are defined in files with names that end in INTF, which stands for Interface. For instance, the TPropertyEditor class is found in DSGNINTF.PAS. The Tools API will be covered in a later chapter.

Components, component editors, and property editors are perhaps the most important topics in Delphi programming. In many ways, this chapter and the next are the keystones around which this entire book has been designed. Most of what I have said before was calculated to make these two chapters readily comprehensible.

Component Theory

Delphi components have three outstanding strengths:

- They are native components, built in Delphi's language. This means that you can write, debug, and test your components from inside standard Delphi programs. In short, it's about ten times easier to write a Delphi component as it is to write an OCX or VBX.
- They are fully object-oriented, which means you can easily change or enhance existing components by creating descendant objects.
- They are small, fast, and light, and can be linked directly into your executables.

Few people would claim that VBXs weren't groundbreaking, that OCX's aren't going to be very important, or that OLE2 is not an enormously promising architecture. However, Delphi components are relatively easy to create and come in a light, easy-to-use package. You can create Delphi components that do nearly anything, from serial communications, to database links, to multimedia. This gives Delphi a big advantage over other visual tools that force you to move to C++, or some other tool, if you want to build components.

NOTE

Most publicly available components cost in the range of $50 to $150. Many of these tools encapsulate functionality that might cost tens of thousands of dollars to produce in-house. For instance, a good communication library might take a year to build. However, if a company can sell it in volume, they can afford to charge $100 or $200 for the same product. That's a real bargain. And most of these tools are easy to use. Building components is a great way for relatively small third-party companies to make money, and buying components is a great way to save time on big projects. These are ground breaking tools that are changing everything about the way programs are constructed.

Delphi components are flexible tools easily built by anyone who knows OOP and the Delphi language. In this package you have explanations detailing all the prerequisite knowledge component builders need, from a description of Delphi itself, through a description of its language, and on to an overview of its implementation of OOP. From this foundation, it will be easy for you to begin building your own components.

Creating Descendants of an Existing Component

In this section, you will see how to create a series of custom TEdit, TPanel, and TLabel controls. The changes made to the standard TEdit and TLabel components involve tweaking their colors, as well as their fonts' colors, names, sizes, and styles. The goal is to show how to create a suite of custom controls that you can place on the component palette and use for special effects, or to define the look and feel of a certain set of applications belonging to a particular department or company.

With projects like this, it's best to start with one simple example and then move on to one with a larger number of objects. In Listing 29.1, you find the code for a first version of a unit that will hold the descendants of TEdit and TLabel controls. Scan through it, check out its basic structure, and then I will briefly discuss how to use the component editor to put it together.

Listing 26.1. The code for a simple component descending from TEdit.

```
unit Unleash1;

interface

uses
  SysUtils, WinTypes, WinProcs,
  Messages, Classes, Graphics,
  Controls, Forms, Dialogs,
  StdCtrls;

type
  TSmallEdit = class(TEdit)
  private
    { Private declarations }
  protected
    { Protected declarations }
  public
    { Public declarations }
    constructor Create(AOwner: TComponent); override;
  published
    { Published declarations }
  end;

procedure Register;

implementation

constructor TSmallEdit.Create(AOwner: TComponent);
begin
```

```
  inherited Create(AOwner);
  Color := clBlue;
  Font.Color := clYellow;
  Font.Name := 'Times New Roman';
  Font.Size := 12;
  Font.Style := [fsBold];
end;

procedure Register;
begin
  RegisterComponents('Edits', [TSmallEdit]);
end;

end.
```

Listing 26.2. The main form for the TestEds1 program serves as a test bed for the UNLEASH1 unit.

```
unit Main;

{ Program copyright (c) 1996 by Charles Calvert }
{ Project Name: TESTEDS1 }

interface

uses
  SysUtils, WinTypes, WinProcs,
  Messages, Classes, Graphics,
  Controls, Forms, Dialogs,
  StdCtrls;

type
  TForm1 = class(TForm)
    Button1: TButton;
    procedure Button1Click(Sender: TObject);
  private
    { Private declarations }
  public
    { Public declarations }
  end;

var
  Form1: TForm1;

implementation

uses
  UnLeash1;

{$R *.DFM}

procedure TForm1.Button1Click(Sender: TObject);
var
  MyEdit: TSmallEdit;
begin
```

continues

Listing 26.2. continued

```
  MyEdit := TSmallEdit.Create(Self);
  MyEdit.Parent := Self;
  MyEdit.Show;
end;

end.
```

It's simple to create this unit, test it, and compile it as a component that's merged in with the rest of the tools on the Component Palette. To get started, choose File | New and select Component from the first page of the Object Repository. The dialog shown in Figure 26.1 appears.

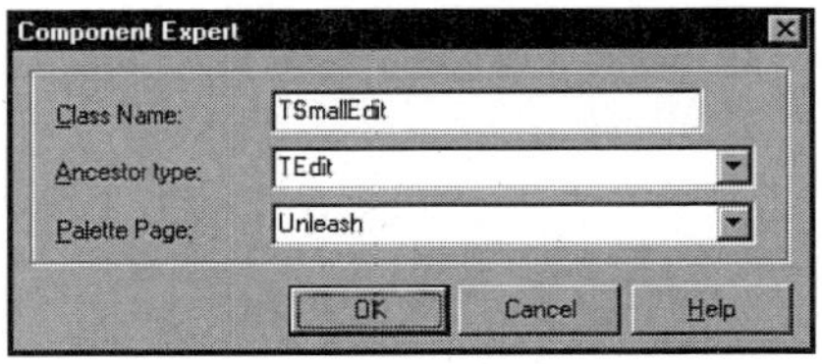

FIGURE 26.1.

The Component Expert dialog.

The Component Expert is a simple code generator of the type that any reader of this book who has made it this far should be able to write in an hour or two. All it does is ask you for the name of the component you want to create, and to then select its parent from a drop-down list. After you have defined the type of tool you want to create, you can select the page in the Component Palette where you want it to reside. You should fill in the blanks with the following information:

```
Class Name: TSmallEdit
Ancestor: TEdit
Palette Page: Unleash
```

For your efforts, the Component Expert churns out the code in Listing 26.3, in which everything is boilerplate except for the first line of the class declaration, the global var declaration, and the parameters passed to the RegisterComponents method.

Listing 26.3. The standard boilerplate output of the Component Expert.

```
unit Unit2;

interface

uses
  SysUtils, WinTypes, WinProcs,
  Messages, Classes, Graphics,
  Controls, Forms, Dialogs,
  StdCtrls;

type
  TSmallEdit = class(TEdit)
```

```
    private
      { Private declarations }
    protected
      { Protected declarations }
    public
      { Public declarations }
    published
      { Published declarations }
    end;

procedure Register;

implementation

procedure Register;
begin
  RegisterComponents('Unleash', [TSmallEdit]);
end;

end.
```

The Component Expert starts by giving you a uses clause designed to cover most of the bases you are likely to touch in a standard component:

```
uses
  SysUtils, WinTypes, WinProcs,
  Messages, Classes, Graphics,
  Controls, Forms, Dialogs,
  StdCtrls;
```

The next step is to give you a basic class declaration, in which the name and parent are filled in with the choices you specified in the Component Expert dialog. All this business about the scoping directives is just for your convenience, and you can delete any portion of it that you don't think you'll need.

```
type
  TSmallEdit = class(TEdit)
  private
    { Private declarations }
  protected
    { Protected declarations }
  public
    { Public declarations }
  published
    { Published declarations }
  end;
```

Before you can place a component on the Component Palette, you must first register it with the system:

```
procedure Register;
begin
  RegisterComponents('Unleash', [TSmallEdit]);
end;
```

Registering a class makes it known to the Delphi Component Palette when the unit is compiled into the Delphi component library. The `Register` procedure has no impact on programs compiled with this unit. Unless your program calls the `Register` procedure (which it should *never* do), the code for the `Register` procedure will never even appear in your executable.

After using the Component Expert, you should save the project. Proceed as you normally would by creating a directory for the project and saving MAIN.PAS and TESTEDS1.DPR inside it. The new unit that you created, however, should not be saved into the same directory, but should be placed in the directory where you store files such as STRBOX or MATHBOX. This code is now going to come into play as part of your system, and as such you want a single path that leads to all related files of this type. If you have all of your components in different subdirectories you will end up with a source path that is long and unwieldy. Furthermore, it's best not to open up the Project Manager and make this class a part of your project. Instead, merely add it to the uses clause of unit MAIN. If you add the class to your project, the path to it becomes hard-coded into your DPR file, which may cause problems later on.

The goal of this project is to give a component of type `TEdit` a new set of default behaviors, so that it starts out with certain colors and certain fonts. To do this, you need to override the `Create` method and change the fonts inside of it. To declare the method, write the following in your class declaration:

```
TSmallEdit = class(TEdit)
public
  constructor Create(AOwner: TComponent); override;
end;
```

Notice that in the declaration above I have removed the `private`, `published`, and `protected` directives created by the Component Expert. This is neither here nor there, and I do it just to keep the amount of code you need to look at as small as possible.

The `Create` method for `TSmallEdit` is declared as `public`. If you think about the process of creating a component dynamically, you will see in a moment that the `Create` method has to be `public`. This is one method that must be exposed.

`Create` is passed a single parameter of type `TComponent`, which is a base class that encapsulates the minimum functionality needed to be an owner of another component. In particular, whatever form you place a component on usually will be the owner of that component. Finally, use the `override` directive to specify that this is a virtual method that you want to redefine.

The implementation of the `Create` method is simple:

```
constructor TSmallEdit.Create(AOwner: TComponent);
begin
  inherited Create(AOwner);
  Color := clBlue;
  Font.Color := clYellow;
  Font.Name := 'Times New Roman';
  Font.Size := 12;
  Font.Style := [fsBold];
end;
```

The code first calls Create, passing in the variable AOwner. As stated above, the owner of a component will often, though not always, be the form on which the component is to be displayed. In other words, the user will drop the component onto a form, and that form will become the owner of the component. In such a case, AOwner is a variable that points at the form. The VCL uses it to initialize the Owner property, which is one of the fields of all components.

The next step is to define the color and font that you want to use, with Font.Style defined as follows:

```
TFontStyle = (fsBold, fsItalic, fsUnderline, fsStrikeOut);
TFontStyles = set of TFontStyle;
```

If you want to add the underline and bold style to the text in the edit control, write the following:

```
Font.Style := [fsBold, fsUnderline];
```

If you want to then add the italic style at runtime, write:

```
Font.Style := Font.Style + [fsItalic];
```

in which the plus symbol (+) is used as a set operator for unions, as explained in Chapter 22, "Handling Messages."

At this stage, the code is ready to go on the Component Palette. However, most of the time when you write components, you should test them first to see whether they work. The issue here is that, even on a fast machine, it takes 20 or 30 seconds to recompile CMPLIB32.DCL and add your component to the Component Palette. (Most of that time is taken up by Windows unloading the old CMPLIB32.DCL and then loading the new CMPLIB32.DCL into memory.) Perhaps I'm a bit impatient, but that's a little too long a wait for me if all I need to tweak is a few aspects of my code. As a result, I test things out first in a small program, and then add the component to the IDE.

To test the new class, drop a button on the program's main form, and create an OnClick handler:

```
procedure TForm1.Button1Click(Sender: TObject);
var
  MyEdit: TSmallEdit;
begin
  MyEdit := TSmallEdit.Create(Self);
  MyEdit.Parent := Self;
  MyEdit.Show;
end;
```

This code creates the component and shows it on the main form. Self, of course, is the way that TForm1 refers to itself from inside one of its own methods. The owner of the new component is Form1, which will be responsible for disposing of the component when finished with it. This happens automatically. You never need to worry about disposing of a visible component shown on a form.

The parent of the component is also Form1. The Parent variable is used by Windows when it is trying to decide how to display the form on the screen. If you place a panel on a form and drop a button on the panel, the owner of that button is the form, but the parent is the panel. Ownership determines when and how the component is deallocated, and parental relationships determine where and how the component is displayed. Ownership is fundamentally a Delphi issue, whereas parental relationships are primarily a concern of Windows.

> **NOTE**
>
> The next paragraph in the book explains how to recompile CMPLIB32.DCL. Remember that you should always keep a backup copy of CMPLIB32.DCL on your hard drive. CMPLIB32.DCL is stored in the ..\DELPHI 2.0\BIN directory. Beneath this directory I have created another directory called BAK where I keep a backup copy of CMPLIB32.DCL. If worse comes to worse, you can always copy the version of CMPLIB32.DCL on your install CD back into the BIN subdirectory. There is also a backup copy of CMPLIB32.DCL made when you try to recompile it. You can sometimes just rename this file, which is called CMPLIB32.~DC, to CMPLIB32.DCL.
>
> My personal experience is that everyone, sooner or later, makes a tasty Mulligan's Stew out of their copy of CMPLIB32.DCL. The worst case scenario is that you are on the road when this happens, and that you don't have access to your install disk. Don't let this happen to you! Keep a backup copy of CMPLIB32.DCL on your hard drive at all times!

After running the program and testing the component, the next step is to put it up on the Component Palette. To do this, select Components ¦ Install, and choose the Add button. Browse through the directories until you find the UNLEASH1 unit, select OK, and then close the Install Components dialog by selecting OK. At this point, a project called CMPLIB32.DPR is compiled. This project creates a huge DLL called CMPLIB32.DCL, which contains all the components in the Component Palette, all the component and property editors associated with those components, the form designer part of the IDE, the experts, and other support modules.

After CMPLIB32.DCL finishes recompiling, you can start a new project, turn to the newly created Unleash page, and drop your new component onto a form. It will have a blue background, default to Times New Roman, and have its font style set to bold and its font color to yellow. Notice that all the properties of TEdit have been inherited by TSmallEdit. That's OOP in action.

The CMPLIB32.DPR file used during compilation of CMPLIB32.DCL can be saved to disk if you choose Tools | Project | Library | Options | Save Library Source Code. After choosing this option and recompiling CMPLIB32.DCL, you can go to the \DELPHI\BIN directory and view your copy of CMPLIB32.DPR.

Extending the *UNLEASH* Unit

In the second version of the UNLEASH unit, a new edit control is added, along with two labels and two panels. The additional edits and labels show how quickly you can build on an idea or object when you understand where you're headed. One of the panels shows how you can get rid of the annoying label that always shows up in the middle of a panel, and the other shows how you can create a single component that contains other components. Specifically, it shows how to create a panel that already comes equipped with two radio buttons.

The code for the new version of the Unleash unit is shown in Listing 26.4, and its test bed appears in Listing 26.5. If you have two units on your system, both of which contain instances of TSmallEdit, it's probably best to uninstall the first instance before trying to install the new instance. In this case, you may have two files on your system, one called UNLEASH1.PAS and the second called UNLEASH.PAS. Both contain an instance of TSmallEdit. Under such circumstances it's best to use the Component | Install | Remove menu option to remove the first version of TSmallEdit before replacing it with a second version. If you have only one version of TSmallEdit, and you just want to update it, there is no need to remove the first instance before installing the updated instance.

Listing 26.4. The second version of the UNLEASH unit contains a panel that comes equipped with two radio buttons.

```
unit Unleash;

interface

uses
  SysUtils, WinTypes, WinProcs,
  Messages, Classes, Graphics,
  Controls, Forms, Dialogs,
  StdCtrls, ExtCtrls;

type
  TSmallEdit = class(TEdit)
  public
    constructor Create(AOwner: TComponent); override;
  end;

  TBigEdit = class(TSmallEdit)
  public
    constructor Create(AOwner: TComponent); override;
  end;

  TSmallLabel = class(TLabel)
  public
    constructor Create(AOwner: TComponent); override;
  end;

  TBigLabel = class(TSmallLabel)
  public
```

continues

Listing 26.4. continued

```pascal
    constructor Create(AOwner: TComponent); override;
  end;

  TEmptyPanel = class(TPanel)
  public
    constructor Create(AOwner: TComponent); override;
  end;

  TRadio2Panel = class(TEmptyPanel)
  private
    FRadio1: TRadiobutton;
    FRadio2: TRadioButton;
  public
    constructor Create(AOwner: TComponent); override;
    property Radio1: TRadioButton read FRadio1;
    property Radio2: TRadioButton read FRadio2;
  end;

procedure Register;

implementation

constructor TSmallEdit.Create(AOwner: TComponent);
begin
  inherited Create(AOwner);
  Color := clBlue;
  Font.Color := clYellow;
  Font.Name := 'Times New Roman';
  Font.Size := 12;
  Font.Style := [fsBold];
end;

constructor TBigEdit.Create(AOwner: TComponent);
begin
  inherited Create(AOwner);
  Font.Size := 24;
end;

constructor TSmallLabel.Create(AOwner: TComponent);
begin
  inherited Create(AOwner);
  Color := clBlue;
  Font.Color := clYellow;
  Font.Name := 'Times New Roman';
  Font.Size := 12;
  Font.Style := [fsBold];
end;

constructor TBigLabel.Create(AOwner: TComponent);
begin
  inherited Create(AOwner);
  Font.Size := 24;
end;

constructor TEmptyPanel.Create(AOwner: TComponent);
begin
```

```
  inherited Create(AOwner);
  Caption := ' ';
end;

constructor TRadio2Panel.Create(AOwner: TComponent);
begin
  inherited Create(AOwner);
  Width := 175;
  Height := 60;

  FRadio1 := TRadioButton.Create(Self);
  FRadio1.Parent := Self;
  FRadio1.Caption := 'Radio1';
  FRadio1.Left := 20;
  FRadio1.Top := 10;
  FRadio1.Show;

  FRadio2 := TRadioButton.Create(Self);
  FRadio2.Parent := Self;
  FRadio2.Caption := 'Radio2';
  FRadio2.Left := 20;
  FRadio2.Top := 32;
  FRadio2.Show;
end;

procedure Register;
begin
  RegisterComponents('Unleash', [TSmallEdit, TBigEdit,
                     TSmallLabel, TBigLabel,
                     TEmptyPanel, TRadio2Panel]);
end;

initialization
  RegisterClasses([TRadioButton]);
end.
```

Listing 26.5. The test bed for the UNLEASH unit.

```
unit Main;

{ Program copyright (c) 1996 by Charles Calvert }
{ Project Name: TESTEDS2 }

interface

uses
  SysUtils, WinTypes, WinProcs,
  Messages, Classes, Graphics,
  Controls, Forms, Dialogs,
  StdCtrls;

type
  TForm1 = class(TForm)
    Button1: TButton;
    procedure Button1Click(Sender: TObject);
```

continues

Listing 26.5. continued

```
private
  { Private declarations }
public
  { Public declarations }
end;

var
  Form1: TForm1;

implementation

uses
  UnLeash;

{$R *.DFM}

procedure TForm1.Button1Click(Sender: TObject);
var
  MyEdit: TBigEdit;
  R: TRadio2Panel;
begin
  MyEdit := TBigEdit.Create(Self);
  MyEdit.Parent := Self;
  MyEdit.Text := 'Inheritance!';
  MyEdit.Width := 200;
  MyEdit.Show;
  R := TRadio2Panel.Create(Self);
  R.Parent := Self;
  R.Left := 50;
  R.Top := 100;
  R.Radio1.Caption := 'Delphi';
  R.Radio2.Caption := 'Unleashed';
  R.Radio1.Checked := True;
  R.Show;
end;

end.
```

When you've created a component that does something you like, it's easy to create children of it. Class TBigEdit descends from TSmallEdit:

```
TBigEdit = class(TSmallEdit)
```

It inherits its font nearly unchanged from TSmallEdit, except that it sets Font.Size to 24, a nice hefty figure that helps the control live up to its name:

```
constructor TBigEdit.Create(AOwner: TComponent);
begin
  inherited Create(AOwner);
  Font.Size := 24;
end;
```

This elegant syntax is a good example of how OOP can save you time and trouble while still allowing you to write clear code.

The label controls shown in this code work in exactly the same way the edit controls do, except that they descend from TLabel rather than from TEdit. The TEmptyPanel component rectifies one of the petty issues that sometimes annoys me: Every time you put down a panel, it gets a caption. Most of the time, the first thing you do is delete the caption so you can place other controls on it without creating a mess!

Once again, you can change TPanel by overriding its constructor. This time, all you need to do is set the Caption property to an empty string:

```
constructor TEmptyPanel.Create(AOwner: TComponent);
begin
  inherited Create(AOwner);
  Caption := ' ';
end;
```

The last new component in this version of the UNLEASH unit enables you to drop down a panel that comes equipped with two radio buttons. This makes a single control out of a set of components that are often combined. You could create other controls that contained three, four, or more radio buttons. Or, you could even create a panel that would populate itself with a specific number of radio buttons.

The declaration for this new radio button is fairly simple:

```
TRadio2Panel = class(TEmptyPanel)
private
  FRadio1: TRadiobutton;
  FRadio2: TRadioButton;
public
  constructor Create(AOwner: TComponent); override;
  property Radio1: TRadioButton read FRadio1;
  property Radio2: TRadioButton read FRadio2;
end;
```

The actual radio buttons themselves are declared as private data, and access to them is given by the Radio1 and Radio2 properties.

You don't need write access to these radio button properties. Modifying a property of these radio buttons doesn't require write access to the radio button property. The following statement

```
RP.Radio1.Caption := 'hello'
```

performs one read of RP.Radio1 and one write to the Caption property of that radio button. You don't want write access to the properties, either, because that would allow the user to assign them garbage (or nil). The Create method for the Radio2Panel begins by setting the width and height of the panel:

```
constructor TRadio2Panel.Create(AOwner: TComponent);
begin
  inherited Create(AOwner);
  Width := 175;
  Height := 60;
```

```
    FRadio1 := TRadioButton.Create(Self);
    FRadio1.Parent := Self;
    FRadio1.Caption := 'Radio1';
    FRadio1.Left := 20;
    FRadio1.Top := 10;
    FRadio1.Show;

    FRadio2 := TRadioButton.Create(Self);
    FRadio2.Parent := Self;
    FRadio2.Caption := 'Radio2';
    FRadio2.Left := 20;
    FRadio2.Top := 32;
    FRadio2.Show;
end;
```

The next step is to create the first radio button. Notice that the code passes Self as the owner, and sets the parent to the panel itself. The rest of the code in the Create method is too trivial to merit comment.

At the very end of the unit, the TRadioButton class is registered:

```
RegisterClasses([TRadioButton]);
```

This event would normally occur when you drop a component on a form. However, in this case a TRadioButton is not necessarily ever dropped explicitly on a form. As a result, the safe thing to do is register the component.

When it comes time to test out the TRadio2Panel object, you can write the following code in the test-bed program to take it through its paces:

```
R := TRadio2Panel.Create(Self);
R.Parent := Self;
R.Left := 50;
R.Top := 100;
R.Radio1.Caption := 'Delphi';
R.Radio2.Caption := 'Unleashed';
R.Radio1.Checked := True;
R.Show;
```

Here, R is declared to be of type TRadio2Panel. Note that each of the radio buttons that belong to the panel act exactly as you would expect a normal radio button to act, only you have to qualify them differently before you access them.

NOTE

If you want, you can surface Radio1 and Radio2 as published properties of TRadio2Panel. However, when you first do so, they will have no property editors available because Delphi has no built-in property editors for TRadioButtons. To build your own, you can refer to the DSGNINTF.PAS unit that ships with Delphi, as well as the upcoming discussion of the Clock component and the Tools API.

Before closing this section I'd like to add some additional notes about how Delphi handles streaming chores. I owe most of my severely limited understanding of this advanced material to Danny Thorpe. Any holes or errors in this brief discussion of streaming are entirely mine, not Danny's.

The good news is that most of the time, you do not have to concern yourself with streaming at all. Delphi handles most streaming chores automatically. In particular, it will automatically stream published properties that are simple types. There are only limited circumstances under which you must explicitly stream the fields of your object.

If a property type is a TComponent or descendant, the streaming system assumes it must create an instance of that type when reading it in. If a property type is TPersistent but not TComponent, the streaming system assumes it is supposed to use the existing instance available through the property and read values into that instance's properties.

The Object Inspector knows to expand the properties of TPersistent but not TComponent descendants. This is not done for TComponent descendants because TComponents are likely to have a lot more properties, which would make navigating the Object Inspector difficult.

You will learn more about streaming objects in Chapter 30, "COM Object Basics."

Building Components from Scratch

In the previous examples, you were creating descendants of existing components. Now it's time to see how to create entirely new components. The main idea to grasp here is that there are three abstract objects from which you can descend a new component. The term "abstract" can have a specific technical meaning, but here I am using it to refer to any object that exists only so that you can create descendants of it. In short, the following three objects have built-in functionality that all components need to access, but you would never want to instantiate an instance of any of them:

- TWinControl and TCustomControl are base classes that can be used to produce a Windows control that can receive input focus and that has a standard Windows handle that can be passed to API calls. TWinControl descendants exist inside their own window. TEdit, TListBox, TTabbedNoteBook, TNoteBook, and TPanel are all examples of this type of control. Most components of this type actually descend from TCustomControl, which is in turn a descendant of TWinControl. The distinction between the two classes is that TCustomControl has a Paint method, and TWinControl does not. If you want to draw the display of your new component, you should inherit from TCustomControl. If the object already knows how to draw itself, inherit from TWinControl.

- TGraphicControl is for components that don't need to receive input focus, don't need to contain other components, and don't need a handle. These controls draw themselves directly on their parent's surface, thereby saving Windows resources. Not having a window handle eliminates a lot of Windows management overhead, and that translates into faster display updates. In short, TGraphicControls exist inside their parent's window. They use their parent's handle and their parent's device context. They still have Handle and Canvas fields that you can access, but they actually belong to their parent. TLabel and TShape objects are examples of this type of component.

■ TComponent enables you to create nonvisual components. If you want to make a tool such as the TTable, TQuery, TOpenDialog, or TTimer devices, this is the place to start. These are components you can place on the Component Palette, but they perform some internal function that you access through code, rather than appearing to the user at runtime. A tool such as TOpenDialog can pop up a dialog, but the component itself remains invisible.

Create a TWinControl or TCustomControl descendant whenever the user needs to directly interact with a visible control. If the user doesn't need to interact with a visible component, create a TGraphicControl descendant.

To get a handle on the issues involved here, you should place a TShape or TLabel control on a form and run the program. Clicking or attempting to type on these controls produces no noticeable result. These components don't ever receive the focus. Now place a TEdit control on the form. It responds to mouse clicks, gets the focus, and you can type in it. TEdit controls are descendants of TWinControl, and TShape is a descendant of TGraphicControl.

NOTE

I should add one caveat to the rules about TGraphicControl explained previously. In one limited sense, the user can interact with TGraphicControls. For instance, they do receive mouse messages, and you can set the mouse cursor when the mouse flies over them. They just can't receive keyboard input focus. If an object can't receive focus, it usually seems inert to the user.

If you are having trouble deciding whether you want to descend from TWinControl or TCustomControl, you should always go with TCustomControl. It has a real Paint method, and some other functionality that is useful when creating a component of your own. If you want to wrap an existing Windows control inside a VCL object, you should start with TWinControl. Most Delphi components that follow this path begin by creating intermediate custom objects, so that TEdit's hierarchy looks like this:

```
TWinControl
TCustomEdit
TEdit
```

TListBox's hierarchy looks like this:

```
TWinControl
TCustomListBox
TListBox
```

Of course, Delphi wraps all the major Windows controls for you, so you won't need to perform this operation unless you are working with a specialized third-party control of some sort.

Following are the declarations for TGraphicControl and TCustomControl, as they appear in CONTROLS.PAS or CONTROLS.INT:

```
TGraphicControl = class(TControl)
  private
    FCanvas: TCanvas;
    procedure WMPaint(var Message: TWMPaint); message WM_PAINT;
  protected
    procedure Paint; virtual;
    property Canvas: TCanvas read FCanvas;
  public
    constructor Create(AOwner: TComponent); override;
    destructor Destroy; override;
  end;

  TCustomControl = class(TWinControl)
  private
    FCanvas: TCanvas;
    procedure WMPaint(var Message: TWMPaint); message WM_PAINT;
  protected
    procedure Paint; virtual;
    procedure PaintWindow(DC: HDC); override;
    property Canvas: TCanvas read FCanvas;
  public
    constructor Create(AOwner: TComponent); override;
    destructor Destroy; override;
  end;
```

You can see that these are fairly simple objects. If you went back one step further in the hierarchy to TControl or TWinControl, you would see huge objects. For instance, the declaration for class TWinControl is nearly 200 lines long (not the implementation, mind you, just the type declaration).

I'm showing you this source code because component builders should work directly with the source, rather than using the on-line help or the DOCs. For simple jobs, it's easy to create your own components without the source. However, if you have a big project, you have to get the source code if it did not already ship with your product. The INT files that ship with all versions of Delphi are very helpful, but there is no replacement for the actual source. The source is available with the client/server version of Delphi, and also as an up-sell from Borland.

The *Clock* Component

It's now time to build a component from the ground up. The CLOCK unit (shown in Figure 26.2) is a simple little clock that you can pop onto a form, and activate and deactivate at will. You can start the clock running, and then tell it to stop by changing the value of a Boolean property called Running.

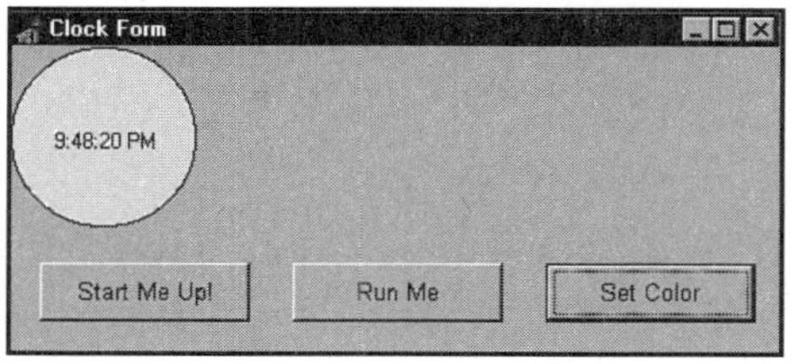

FIGURE 26.2.

The CLOCK unit as it appears on its own test bed, before being placed on the Component Palette.

When constructing class TClock, the first thing that needs to be decided is whether the clock is going to descend from TWinControl or TGraphicControl. If you've built a clock in Windows before, you know that one of the best ways to drive it is with a Windows timer. Timers require the presence of a Handle in order to be stopped and started; furthermore, they send their wm_Timer messages to the window that owns them. Because a TGraphicControl descendant isn't a real window, it will not automatically get the messages. As a result, TGraphicControl is not an ideal choice for this type of object.

Of course, the objections to using TGraphicControl raised in the last paragraph aren't insurmountable. If you really want to, you can still make it work. However, there is no point in expending effort that isn't strictly necessary, so I have opted for the simplest design possible and descended the class from TCustomControl. I chose TCustomControl rather than TWinControl because I needed a Paint method in which I could draw the clock.

> **NOTE**
>
> The decision to use Windows API calls to create a timer, rather than using a TTimer object, was driven by experience, not by a desire to save memory. I found that I had some buggy behavior when I placed four or five of these clocks on a single form. If I got rid of the TTimer object and made the calls directly, all went smoothly. Once again, when I ran into trouble, I didn't fight upstream, but instead followed the course of least resistance. I'll admit the exact issues involved here aren't clear to me, but I leave this note as a signpost to others who might pass this way. Hopefully you will have better luck (or skill) if you try the same ground where I trod.

You will see that the code, shown in Listing 26.6, also contains a special property editor, as well as a simple component editor. As you will see, neither of these tools are inherently difficult to build.

Listing 26.6. The code for the Clock component should be kept in the UNITS subdirectory where you store StrBox and other utility units.

```
unit Clock;

{ Program copyright (c) 1995 by Charles Calvert }
```

```
{ Project Name: CLOCK3 }

interface

uses
  SysUtils, WinTypes, WinProcs,
  Messages, Classes, Graphics,
  Controls, Forms, StdCtrls,
  DsgnIntf, Dialogs;

type
  TClock = class(TCustomControl)
  private
    FTimer: Integer;
    FRunning: Boolean;
    procedure SetRunning(Run: Boolean);
  protected
    procedure Paint; override;
    procedure WMTimer(var Message: TMessage); message WM_Timer;
    procedure WMDestroy(var Message: TMessage); message wm_Destroy;
  public
    constructor Create(AOwner: TComponent); override;
  published
    property Running: Boolean read FRunning write SetRunning;
  end;

  TClockEditor = class(TComponentEditor)
    procedure Edit; override;
  end;

  TColorClock = class(TClock)
  private
    FColor: TColor;
    procedure SetColor(Color: TColor);
  protected
    procedure Paint; override;
  public
    constructor Create(AOwner: TComponent); override;
  published
    property Color: TColor read FColor write SetColor;
  end;

  TColorNameProperty = class(TColorProperty)
  public
    function GetAttributes: TPropertyAttributes; override;
    procedure Edit; override;
  end;


procedure Register;

implementation

uses
  StrBox;

procedure Register;
begin
```

continues

Listing 26.6. continued

```pascal
  RegisterComponents('Unleash', [TClock, TColorClock]);
  RegisterComponentEditor(TClock, TClockEditor);
  RegisterPropertyEditor(TypeInfo(TColor),
                 TClock, 'Color',
                 TColorNameProperty);
end;

{ -- TClock -- }

constructor TClock.Create(AOwner: TComponent);
begin
  inherited Create(AOwner);
  Width := 100;
  height := 100;
  FTimer := 1;
end;

procedure TClock.wmDestroy(var Message: TMessage);
begin
  KillTimer(Handle, FTimer);
  FTimer := 0;
  inherited;
end;

procedure TClock.Paint;
begin
  Canvas.Ellipse(0, 0, 100, 100);
end;

procedure TClock.SetRunning(Run: Boolean);
begin
  if Run then begin
    SetTimer(Handle, FTimer, 50, nil);
    FRunning := True;
  end else begin
    KillTimer(Handle, FTimer);
    FRunning := False;
  end;
end;

procedure TClock.WMTimer(var Message: TMessage);
begin
  Canvas.TextOut(10, 40, GetTimeString);
end;

{ -- TColorClock -- }

constructor TColorClock.Create(AOwner: TComponent);
begin
  inherited Create(AOwner);
  FColor := clGreen;
end;


procedure TColorClock.Paint;
begin
```

```
  Canvas.Brush.Color := FColor;
  inherited Paint;
end;

procedure TColorClock.SetColor(Color: TColor);
begin
  FColor := Color;
  InvalidateRect(Handle, nil, True);
end;

{ --- TClockEditor --- }

procedure TClockEditor.Edit;
begin
  MessageDlg('Clock copyright (c) 1995 Charlie Calvert',
             mtInformation, [mbOK],0);
end;

{ --- TColorNameProperty --- }

function TColorNameProperty.GetAttributes;
begin
  Result := [paMultiSelect, paValueList, paDialog];
end;

procedure TColorNameProperty.Edit;
var
  S: String;
begin
  S := '';
  InputQuery('New Color', 'Enter Color', S);
  SetValue(S);
end;

end.
```

Listing 26.7. The test bed for the `Clock` component is stored in the CLOCK3 subdirectory.

```
unit Main;

{ Program copyright (c) 1995 by Charles Calvert }
{ Project Name: CLOCK3 }

{ CLOCK.PAS is stored in the UNITS subdirectory.
  That's the same place where STRBOX and other
  utility units are kept }

interface

uses
  SysUtils, WinTypes, WinProcs,
  Messages, Classes, Graphics,
  Controls, Forms, Dialogs,
```

continues

Listing 26.7. continued

```
Clock, StdCtrls;

type
  TForm1 = class(TForm)
    Button1: TButton;
    Button2: TButton;
    Button3: TButton;
    ColorDialog1: TColorDialog;
    procedure Button1Click(Sender: TObject);
    procedure Button2Click(Sender: TObject);
    procedure Button3Click(Sender: TObject);
  private
    { Private declarations }
  public
    { Public declarations }
  end;

var
  Form1: TForm1;
  MyClock: TColorClock;

implementation

{$R *.DFM}

procedure TForm1.Button1Click(Sender: TObject);
begin
  MyClock := TColorClock.Create(Self);
  MyClock.Parent := Form1;
end;

procedure TForm1.Button2Click(Sender: TObject);
begin
  MyClock.Running := True;
end;

procedure TForm1.Button3Click(Sender: TObject);
begin
  if ColorDialog1.Execute then
    MyClock.Color := ColorDialog1.Color;
end;

end.
```

To run this program, press the button that creates the clock and makes it visible on the form. The next logical step is to start the clock running; then, if you'd like, you can also change its color. You get an Access Violation if you click on the latter two buttons before pushing the first. The problem is that it is an error to call a method or property of the TClock object before the object itself has been created. To prevent this from happening, you could enable and disable the second two buttons.

The code for the clock components uses inheritance, virtual methods, and properties. TClock has two pieces of private data:

```
FTimer: Integer;
FRunning: Boolean;
```

One is an identifier for the timer, and the other is a Boolean value that specifies whether the clock is running.

Windows timers are managed by two Windows API calls. When you want to start a timer, use SetTimer; when you want to stop a timer, use KillTimer. SetTimer takes four parameters:

1. Handle is the HWND of your current window.

2. IDEvent is an integer identifier that uniquely identifies the timer inside of the window that created it. You can make this value up off the top of your head, although I generally set the IDTimer for the first timer in a window to 1, the second timer to 2, and so on. Because there is only going to be one timer in each instance of a TClock window, you can set its IDEvent to 1.

3. Elapse is the length of time between calls to the timer, measured in milliseconds.

4. TimerFunc is a callback function that is not used in this program. One of the developers' big goals was to create a Windows product that didn't need to use callbacks, and I see no reason to open that can of worms now if it can be avoided. (If you want to create a callback in Delphi, you will be able to do so, but it's usually not necessary.)

A typical call to SetTimer looks like this:

```
SetTimer(Handle, FTimer, 1000, nil);
```

1000 specifies that the timer is called once every 1000 milliseconds, or once a second. SetTimer returns zero if the call fails. This is a real possibility, so programs that include error checking should inspect this value and put up a MessageBox if the call fails.

KillTimer takes two parameters, the first being the handle of your window, and the second being the unique identifier associated with that timer:

```
KillTimer(Handle, FTimer);
```

When you are not using the callback function, timer events are sent to your window by way of messages:

```
procedure WMTimer(var Message: TMessage);
  message wm_Timer;
```

This is a classic dynamic method, of the kind covered in Chapter 22, "Handling Messages." The response to this event is a simple procedure that calls TextOut, and gets the time from a function in the StrBox unit called GetTimeString:

```
procedure TClock.WMTimer(var Message: TMessage);
begin
  Canvas.TextOut(10, 40, GetTimeString);
end;
```

The calls to SetTimer and KillTimer are managed primarily through a property called Running:

```
property Running: Boolean read FRunning write SetRunning;
```

The write mechanism, a procedure called SetRunning, is a fairly straightforward tool:

```
procedure TClock.SetRunning(Run: Boolean);
begin
  if Run then begin
    SetTimer(Handle, FTimer, 50, nil);
    FRunning := True;
  end else begin
    KillTimer(Handle, FTimer);
    FRunning := False;
  end;
end;
```

If the user sets the Running property to True, this procedure is executed and a call is made to the SetTimer function. If the user sets Running to False, KillTimer is called, and the clock immediately stops functioning.

The final issue involving the timer concerns the case in which the user closes a form while the clock is still running. In such a case, you must be sure to call KillTimer before the application exits. If you don't make the call, the timer keeps running even after the application closes. This wastes system resources, and also uses up one of the dozen or so timers that are available to the system at any one time.

The logical place to call KillTimer is the Destroy method for the TClock object. Unfortunately, the window associated with the clock has already been destroyed by the time this call is made, so there is no valid handle to use when you call KillTimer. As a result, you need to respond to wm_Destroy messages in order to be sure the timer is killed before the TClock window is closed:

```
procedure TClock.wmDestroy(var Message: TMessage);
begin
  KillTimer(Handle, FTimer);
  FTimer := 0;
  inherited;
end;
```

Before leaving this description of the TClock object, I should briefly mention the Paint method:

```
procedure TClock.Paint;
begin
  Canvas.Ellipse(0, 0, 100, 100);
end;
```

This procedure is called whenever the circle defining the circumference of the clock needs to be repainted. You never have to check for this circumstance, and you never have to call Paint directly. Windows keeps an eye on the TClock window, and if it needs to be painted, it sends you a wm_Paint message. Logic buried deep in the VCL converts the wm_Paint message into a call to Paint, the same way TClock translates wm_Timer messages into calls to TCanvas.TextOut.

NOTE

When writing components, sometimes it's easiest if you can get right down to the Windows API level, or as near to it as you would like to get. The following code reviews the techniques used to hook directly into the Window procedure:

```
procedure TMyObject.WndProc(var M: Tmessage);
begin
  case M.Msg of
    wm_Timer: DoSomething;
    wm_Paint: PaintSomething;
  else
    M.Result := DefWindowProc(Handle, M.Msg, M.wParam, M.lParam);
end;
```

WndProc is typically declared in the private section as:

```
procedure WndProc(var Msg: Tmessage);
```

See the Delphi VCL source for the TTimer object for another example of how to use the WndProc function.

The TColorClock component is a descendant of TClock that adds color to the control. I made TColorClock a separate object, rather than just adding color to TClock, for two different reasons (both of which are related to design):

1. You might want to create a descendant of TClock that doesn't have color, or that implements color differently than TColorClock does. By creating two objects, one called TClock and the other called TColorClock, I enable programmers to have the greatest amount of freedom when creating descendants. This principle has only minimal weight in a simple object such as TClock, but it can become extremely important when you are developing large and complex hierarchies. In short, be careful of building too much functionality into one object!

2. TClock and TColorClock also provide another example of inheritance, and vividly demonstrate how this technology can be utilized to your advantage.

TColorClock declares a private data store called FColor that is of type TColor. Users can set the FColor variable by manipulating the Color property:

```
property Color: TColor read FColor write SetColor;
```

SetColor is a simple procedure that sets the value of FColor, and calls the Windows API call InvalidateRect:

```
procedure TColorClock.SetColor(Color: TColor);
begin
  FColor := Color;
  InvalidateRect(Handle, nil, True);
end;
```

Just to be sure this makes sense, it's worth taking a paragraph or two to provide a refresher course on InvalidateRect. Here is the declaration for the routine:

```
procedure InvalidateRect(Wnd: HWnd; Rect: PRect; Erase: Bool);
```

InvalidateRect forces the window specified in the first parameter to completely redraw itself if the third parameter is set to True. If the third parameter is set to False, only the portions of the window that you specifically repaint are changed. The middle parameter is a pointer to the TRect structure that can be used to define the area that you want to redraw. Compare this function with the native Delphi function called Invalidate.

Calls to InvalidateRect naturally force calls to the TColorClick.Paint method:

```
procedure TColorClock.Paint;
begin
  Canvas.Brush.Color := FColor;
  inherited Paint;
end;
```

Paint sets the brush associated with the window's device context to the color specified by the user; then, it calls the Paint method defined in TClock.

To add this object to the Component Palette, you must first register it:

```
procedure Register;
begin
  RegisterComponents('Unleash', [TClock, TColorClock]);
  ...
end;
```

Here, I specify that the TClock and TColorClock objects should be placed in a group called Unleash.

> **NOTE**
>
> The second parameter to RegisterComponents takes an array of type TComponentClass:
>
> ```
> procedure RegisterComponents(const Page: string;
>   ComponentClasses: array of TComponentClass);
> ```
>
> Delphi supports open-arrays, which means that you do not have to declare how many members are going to be included in an array. Instead, you only need to declare the type of members that will go in the array, as shown earlier. Furthermore, when creating these arrays, you can build them on the fly rather than having to declare an array variable. To do this, write an open bracket and then enter the members of the array separated by commas. To close the array, write a closing bracket. For more information, look up Open-Array Construction in the online help.

That's all I'm going to say about TClock and TColorClock. Overall, these are fairly simple components, interesting primarily because they show you how to go about constructing your own controls from scratch. This kind of exercise lies very much at the heart of Delphi's architecture, and I expect many readers will be spending most of their time engaged almost exclusively in the business of building components.

Creating Icons for Components

The icon associated with a component and placed in the Component Palette is defined in a file with a .DCR extension. If you do not provide this file, Delphi uses the icon associated with the object's parent. If there is no icon anywhere in the component's ancestry, a default icon is used.

> **NOTE**
>
> A DCR file is a Windows resource file with the extension changed from RES to DCR. The resource file contains a bitmap resource with the same name as your component. For instance, the bitmap resource in a DCR file for a TCOLOR component would have a resource ID of TColor. This resource should be a 56×28 pixel (or smaller) bitmap that can be edited in the Image Editor. All you need to do is place this DCR file in the same directory as your component, and the images defined therein will show up on the Component Palette. Use the Image Editor to explore the DCR files that ship with Delphi. They are stored in the \DELPHI\LIB directory.

Here is a description of how to associate your own bitmaps with a particular component.

1. Open the Image Editor and choose New.
2. In the New Project dialog, choose Component Resource (DCR) and click OK.
3. A dialog called UNTITLED.DCR appears. Choose the New button.
4. A dialog called New Resource appears. Choose Bitmap and click OK.
5. A dialog called New Bitmap Attributes appears. Set Colors to 16 colors, because this technology is available on nearly all Windows systems. Set Size in Pixels to 56×28, with width being the larger number.
6. Draw a black line down the center of the bitmap, and paint the button-up bitmap on the right side of the line and the button-down bitmap on the left side of the line. To understand the difference between button-down and button-up bitmaps, just go to the Component Palette and press a component. You see that it has one image for depicting the unselected stage, and another for the selected stage.
7. Save the file as CLOCK.DCR. Rename the bitmap you have created to TCLOCK.

If you don't like the Image Editor, you can create a 56×28 bitmap in PBRUSH.EXE or some other bitmap editor, and then create an RC file that looks like this:

```
TCLOCK BITMAP clock.bmp
```

Save the file as CLOCK.RC. Run the Borland Resource Compiler from the command line:

```
brc -r clock.rc
```

The resulting file will be called CLOCK.RES. Rename that file CLOCK.DCR. An example of the latter method is used for the TColorClock component, and stored in the UNITS directory along with STRBOX.PAS and the other utility files.

Creating Help Files for Components

Delphi enables you to define help files that can ship with your components. These help files can be merged into the help that ships with Delphi, so users of your product will feel as though it is a native part of Delphi. Here are the two types of files involved.

- The HLP file is a standard Windows help file that contains information about the properties, methods, and events implemented by your component. I strongly recommend that you obtain a third-party tool to aid in the construction of these help files. For intance, you might buy a copy of FOREHELP from Borland, or you could turn to Blue Sky software, or some other third party that provides tools to help you create these files. As a last resort, you can use Word or WordPerfect to create RTF files, and then compile these RTF files into HLP files with the HCW.EXE help compiler that ships with Delphi. The EXPLORER program that ships with this book provides an example of using Word for Windows-based RTF files. (The copy of Forehelp sold by Borland has not been upgraded for Windows 95, but it is still many times better than having no help tool at all. Forehelp requires that you have a copy of HC.EXE or HCP.EXE on your system. These files ship with many compilers, and are available royalty free on Compuserve and the Internet.)

- The KWF file, generated by the Delphi KWGEN utility and later merged into Delphi's main help system with HELPINST.EXE, enables users to obtain context-sensitive help when working with your component.

All of the tools mentioned here play a peripheral role in the creation of components. They don't require a knowledge of the fascinating syntax used in component creation, but they help to make your tools attractive and easy to use.

The Five Main Tools APIs

There are five main Tools APIs, each accessible through a separate set of routines that ship with Delphi. These APIs enable you to write code that can be linked directly into the Delphi IDE. Specifically, you can link your tools into CMPLIB32.DCL the same way you link in components. Here is a list of the Tools APIs and the native Delphi source files that define them.

Experts:

- Enables you to write your own Experts
- EXPINTF.PAS
- VIRTINTF.PAS
- TOOLINTF.PAS (for enumerating the component pages and components installed, adding modules to the project, and so on)

Version Control:

- Enables you to write your own Version Control system, or to link in a third-party system
- VCSINTF.PAS
- VIRTINTF.PAS
- TOOLINTF.PAS (for opening and closing files in the editor)

Component Editors:

- Create dialogs associated with a control at design time (for instance, the DataSet Designer is a component editor)
- DSGNINTF.PAS

Property Editors:

- Create editors for use in the Object Inspector
- DSGNINTF.PAS

Editor Interfaces:

- EDITINTF.PAS
- FILEINTF.PAS

The letters INTF are an abbreviation for the word *interface*. This term was chosen because the Tools API is an interface between your own code and the Delphi developers' code.

Needless to say, most people will never use the Tools API. However, it will be important to a small minority of developers, and its existence means that everyone will be able to buy or download tools that extend the functionality of the IDE.

Property Editors

The Tools API for creating property editors is perhaps the most commonly used interface into the heart of the IDE. When you first use Delphi and start becoming familiar with the Object Inspector, you are bound to think that it is a static element that never changes. However, it should come as no surprise that you can change the functionality of the Object Inspector by adding new property editors to it.

As mentioned earlier, property editors control what takes place on the right side of the `Proper-ties` page of the Object Inspector. In particular, when you click on the `Color` property of a `TEdit`, you can select a new color from a dropdown list, from a common dialog, or by typing in a new value. In all three cases, you are using a property editor.

If you want to create a new property editor, you should create a descendant of `TPropertyEditor`, a class declared in DSGNINTF.PAS. Here is the declaration for the property editor associated with the `TColorClock` component:

```
TColorNameProperty = class(TColorProperty)
public
  function GetAttributes: TPropertyAttributes; override;
  procedure Edit; override;
end;
```

The DSGNINTF unit is unusual in that it is very carefully documented by the developer who created it. For instance, here are excerpts from that unit describing the two methods I call in my descendant of `TPropertyEditor`:

```
Edit
      Called when the '...' button is pressed or the
      property is double-clicked. This can, for example,
      bring up a dialog to allow the editing of the component
      in some more meaningful fashion than by text
      (e.g. the Font property).

GetAttributes
      Returns the information for use in the Object
      Inspector to be able to show the appropriate tools.
      GetAttributes return a set of type TPropertyAttributes.
```

I won't quote further, for fear of sounding like I'm plagiarizing. The point, however, is that these entries were written by the developers, and they extensively document this important interface to the core code inside the heart of the IDE. Here are declarations for `Edit` and `GetAttributes`, as well as the other key functions in `TPropertyEditor`:

```
TPropertyEditor = class
  public
    destructor Destroy; override;
    function AllEqual: Boolean; virtual;
    procedure Edit; virtual;
    function GetAttributes: TPropertyAttributes; virtual;
    function GetComponent(Index: Integer): TComponent;
    function GetEditLimit: Integer; virtual;
    function GetName: string; virtual;
    procedure GetProperties(Proc: TGetPropEditProc); virtual;
    function GetPropType: PTypeInfo;
    function GetValue: string; virtual;
    procedure GetValues(Proc: TGetStrProc); virtual;
    procedure Initialize; virtual;
    procedure SetValue(const Value: string); virtual;
    property Designer: TFormDesigner read FDesigner;
    property PrivateDirectory: string read GetPrivateDirectory;
```

```
    property PropCount: Integer read FPropCount;
    property Value: string read GetValue write SetValue;
  end;
```

Once again, all these methods are carefully documented inside DSGNINTF.PAS. You should study that file carefully if you want to learn more about creating complex property editors.

The Edit method of TPropertyEditor is the one you want to override to change the way a property editor actually edits data:

```
procedure TColorNameProperty.Edit;
var
  S: String;
begin
  S := '';
  InputQuery('New Color', 'Enter Color', S);
  SetValue(S);
end;
```

In this case, I am creating a substitute for the TColorDialog that pops up when you click on the ellipsis icon in Object Inspector. I am, of course, replacing the fancy Windows common dialog with a simpler one that asks the user to enter a string such as "clBlue" or "clGreen". The point, however, is that you are learning how to create your own property editors. In a more complex example, you might open a form that allowed the user to make extensive changes to a property. SetValue, called at the end of this procedure, is another method of TPropertyEditor.

The GetAttributes method is a way of defining what types of property editors you want to have associated with TColorDialog:

```
function TColorNameProperty.GetAttributes;
begin
  Result := [paMultiSelect, paValueList, paDialog];
end;
```

A property editor that has the paMultiSelect flag remains active even if the user has selected more than one component of that type. For instance, you can select 10 edit controls and change all their Fonts in one step. Delphi enables you to do that because TEdits have their paMultiSelect flag set.

The paValueList flag dictates that the property editor drops down a list of values from an enumerated or set type when the user presses the arrow button at the far right of the editor. This functionality is built into Delphi, and you need only set the flag to have it be supported by your property editor.

Finally, paDialog states that the property editor pops up a dialog. Because the Edit function shown earlier uses an InputQuery, I have decided that this flag should be set. Ultimately, the paDialog flag does little more than assure that the ellipsis button appears at the right of the property editor.

> **NOTE**
>
> When you choose both paDialog and paValuelist in a single component, the property editor button always winds up being a combo dropdown list button. In other words, the dialog button is obscured, even though the functionality is still present. See, for instance, the Color property of a TForm or TEdit.

You must register property editors with the system before compiling them into CMPLIB32.DCL:

```
procedure Register;
begin
  ...
  RegisterPropertyEditor(TypeInfo(TColor),
            TClock, 'Color',
            TColorNameProperty);
end;
```

The declaration for RegisterPropertyEditor looks like this:

```
procedure RegisterPropertyEditor(PropertyType: PTypeInfo;
                ComponentClass: TClass;
                const PropertyName: string;
                EditorClass: TPropertyEditorClass);
```

Here is what the various parameters mean:

- ■ PropertyType. The first parameter passed to this function states the type of data handled by the editor. In this case, it is TColor. Delphi uses this information as the first in a series of checklists that determine which properties should be associated with this editor.

- ■ ComponentClass. The second parameter further qualifies which components will use this editor. In this case, I have narrowed the range down to TClock and its descendants. If I had written TComponent instead of TClock, or if I had set this parameter to nil, all properties of type TColor would start using that editor. What this means is that you could build a new editor for Fonts or Colors, install it on a customer's system, and it would work with all properties of that type. In other words, you don't have to have created a component in order to write an editor for it.

- ■ PropertyName. The third parameter limits the scope to properties with the name passed in this string. If the string is empty, the editor is used for all properties that get passed the first two parameters.

- ■ EditorClass. This parameter defines the class of editor associated with the properties defined in the first three parameters.

If you want to find out more about this function, refer to the comments in DSGNINTF.

When you have seen how to build property editors, it is easy to understand component editors. These tools are descendants of TComponentEditor, just as property editors are descendants of TPropertyEditor:

```
TClockEditor = class(TComponentEditor)
  procedure Edit; override;
end;
```

The TColorDialog has a simple editor that pops up a dialog specifying a copyright:

```
procedure TClockEditor.Edit;
begin
  MessageDlg('Clock copyright (c) 1995 Charlie Calvert',
             mtInformation, [mbOK],0);
end;
```

This, of course, is the simplest possible component editor, but it gets you started working with these useful tools.

The Register method for TClockEditor looks like this:

```
procedure Register;
begin
  ...
  RegisterComponentEditor(TClock, TClockEditor);
  ...
end;
```

The declaration for this procedure looks like this:

```
procedure RegisterComponentEditor(ComponentClass: TComponentClass;
  ComponentEditor: TComponentEditorClass);
```

Clearly, the first parameter specifies the class with which the editor is associated, and the second parameter specifies the class of the editor.

In this section, you have had an introduction to property editors and component editors. These examples are important primarily because they help focus your attention on DSGNINTF.PAS, which is one of several files that ship with Delphi that define the Tools API. If you want to extend the Delphi IDE, you should get to know all the files that end in INTF.

Summary

In this chapter, you have learned about building components. Specifically, you learned how to create components that:

■ Change an ancestor's default settings. For instance, you created TEdit descendants with new default colors and fonts.

■ Add functionality not available in an ancestor object. For instance, the TColorClock object does things that TClock does not.

- Are built up from scratch so that they can add new functionality to the IDE. For instance, the TClock component brings something entirely new to Delphi programming that does not exist in any other component that ships with the product.

You also learned about tools and files associated with components, such as the DCR and KWF files. Finally, you learned something about the Tools API and specifically about the art of making property editors and component editors.

Creating Nonvisual Components

27

In this chapter, you will learn how to build a nonvisual component. In particular, the following topics will be emphasized:

- Creating your own event handlers and your own object references; creating your own OnXXX handlers.
- Descending directly from TComponent.
- Using and designing nonvisual components.
- Using FindFirst and FindNext to iterate through the files in directories.
- Creating your own stacks.
- Pushing and popping items off a stack.

Much of the material in this chapter follows naturally from the subject matter in the last chapter. However, the code shown here is more advanced, and the text looks a little more deeply into the theories involved in creating powerful, reusable components.

In particular, you will look at one reusable nonvisual component called TFileIterator, which is used in two different programs. The first program allows you to scan your directory looking for files, and then view them in an editor. The second program allows you to scan through files in your directory to see if there are certain types of files that you want to delete.

Both of these programs use the TFileIterator component. As a result, they graphically demonstrate the concept of component reuse. Write the TFileIterator component once, and you can reuse it in multiple programs. The big bonus here is that TFileIterator is a visual component, and thereby makes a relatively complex task simple enough that you can perform it by just dropping an object on a form and plugging it into your program.

The FindAllW Program

Below you will find the FindAllW program, which can be used to iterate through the subdirectories on a hard drive looking for files with a particular name or file mask. For instance, you could look for *.pas, or m*.pas, or ole2.pas. It will put all the files that match the mask you pass to it in a list box, and you can then double-click any item in the list box and it will be loaded into the Write or WordPad program. From there you can scan through the file, looking for particular entries, or whatever you want.

The FindAllW program depends on the TFileIterator component, which ships with this book. In order to use this component, you must first load it onto the Component Palette, using the techniques described in the last chapter. In general, all you have to do is choose Component ¦ Install from the menu, then press the Add button. Browse the Units subdirectory that ships with this book. There you will find the FileIter unit. Add it to CMPLIB32.DCL, and you are ready to build the FindAllW program, shown below in Listings 27.1 through 27.3.

The point here is that TFileIterator, like TTable and TQuery, is a nonvisual component. In particular, TFileIterator is a descendant of another custom object called TRunDirs. TRunDirs is a descendant of TComponent.

The TFileIterator and TRunDirs components complete your introduction to the basic component types by showing you how to build nonvisual components. You already know how to build visual components. Once you understand how to build nonvisual components, most of the power of Delphi will be open to you. The TRunDirs component is also important because it shows you how to create custom event handlers.

Listing 27.1. The FILEITER component enables you to iterate through directories, and have the name of each file found passed to ProcessNameFile.

```
unit Fileiter;

{ FILEITER.PAS copyright (c) 1996 by Charles Calvert }

interface

{$H+}

uses
  SysUtils, WinTypes, WinProcs,
  Messages, Classes, Graphics,
  Controls, Forms, AllDirs;

type
  TFileIterator = class(TRunDirs)
  private
    FFileList: TStringList;
    FDirList: TStringList;
    FUseFileList: Boolean;
    FUseDirList: Boolean;
    procedure SetFileList(UseList: Boolean);
    procedure SetDirList(UseList: Boolean);
  protected
    procedure ProcessName(FName: String; SR: TSearchRec); override;
    procedure ProcessDir(Start: String); override;
  public
    destructor Destroy; override;
    property FileList: TStringList read FFileList;
    property DirList: TStringList read FDirList;
  published
    property UseFileList: Boolean read FUseFileList write SetFileList;
    property UseDirList: Boolean read FUseDirList write SetDirList;
    property OnFoundFile;
    property OnProcessDir;
  end;

procedure Register;

implementation

procedure Register;
```

continues

Listing 27.1. continued

```
begin
  RegisterComponents('Unleash', [TFileIterator]);
end;

destructor TFileIterator.Destroy;
begin
  FFileList.Free;
  FDirList.Free;
  inherited Destroy;
end;

procedure TFileIterator.SetFileList(UseList: Boolean);
begin
  FUseFileList := UseList;
  if FUseFileList then
    FFileList := TStringList.Create
  else
    FFileList.Free;
end;

procedure TFileIterator.SetDirList(UseList: Boolean);
begin
  FUseDirList := UseList;
  if FUseDirList then
    FDirList := TStringList.Create
  else
    FDirList.Free;
end;

procedure TFileIterator.ProcessName(FName: String; SR: TSearchRec);
begin
  inherited ProcessName(FName, SR);
  if FUseFileList then FFileList.Add(FName);
end;

procedure TFileIterator.ProcessDir(Start: string);
begin
  inherited ProcessDir(Start);
  if FUseDirList then FDirList.Add(CurDir);
end;

end.
```

Listing 27.2. The ALLDIRS unit contains the brains for the FILEITER unit.

```
unit AllDirs;
{ Define Debug }

{ ALLDIRS.PAS copyright (c) 1996 by Charles Calvert }

interface

{$H+}
```

```
uses
  Classes,
  Controls,
  StrBox,
  SysUtils;

type
  TStack = class;
  TShortStack = class;

  TStackAry = array[1..1000] of PString;
  TStacksAry = array[1..1000] of TShortStack;

  TStack = class(TObject)
    First,
    Last: Word;
    constructor Create;
    procedure InitCount;
    function IsEmpty: Boolean;
    function Count: Integer;
  end;

  TBigStack = class(TStack)
    Stacks: TStacksAry;
    destructor Destroy; virtual;
    procedure Push(P: TShortStack);
    function Pop: TShortStack;
    function PopValue(var Num: Integer): String;
  end;

  TShortStack = class(TStack)
    StackAry: TStackAry;
    destructor Destroy; virtual;
    procedure Push(S: String);
    function Pop: String;
    function GetMoreDirs(Start: String): Integer;
    procedure Show;
  end;

  TFoundFileEvent = procedure(FileName: string;
                             SR: SysUtils.TSearchRec) of Object;
  TFoundDirEvent = procedure(DirName: string) of Object;

  TRunDirs = class(TComponent)
  private
    FOnFoundFile: TFoundFileEvent;
    FOnProcessDir: TFoundDirEvent;
    FFileMask: Str12;
    FCurDir: DirStr;
    FBigStack: TBigStack;
    FShortStack: TShortStack;
  protected
    procedure PushStack;
    procedure ProcessName(FName: String; SR: TSearchRec); virtual;
    procedure ProcessDir(Start: String); virtual;
  public
    constructor Create(Owner: TComponent); override;
    destructor Destroy; virtual;
```

continues

Listing 27.2. continued

```
    function Run(Start: PathStr; StartingDirectory: String): String;
  published
    property OnFoundFile: TFoundFileEvent
      read FOnFoundFile write FOnFoundFile;
    property OnProcessDir: TFoundDirEvent
      read FOnProcessDir write FOnProcessDir;
    property CurDir: DirStr read FCurDir;
  end;

implementation
{$IfDef Debug}
var
  F: Text;
{$EndIf Debug}

constructor TStack.Create;
begin
  inherited Create;
  InitCount;
end;

procedure TStack.InitCount;
begin
  First := 1;
  Last := 0;
end;

function TStack.IsEmpty: Boolean;
var
  OutCome: Boolean;
begin
  OutCome := First > Last;
  IsEmpty := OutCome
end;

function TStack.Count: Integer;
begin
  Count := Last - First;
end;

{=================================================}

destructor TBigStack.Destroy;
var
  i: Integer;
begin
  for i := First to Last do
    Stacks[i].Destroy;
  inherited Destroy;
end;

procedure TBigStack.Push(P: TShortStack);
begin
  Inc(Last);
  Stacks[Last] := P;
end;
```

```pascal
function TBigStack.Pop: TShortStack;
begin
end;

function TBigStack.PopValue(var Num: Integer): String;
begin
  Num := 0;
  if IsEmpty then begin
    PopValue := '-1';
    Num := -1;
    Exit;
  end;
  while Stacks[Last].IsEmpty do begin
    Inc(Num);
    Stacks[Last].Destroy;
    Dec(Last);
    if IsEmpty then begin
      PopValue := '-1';
      Num := -1;
      Exit;
    end;
  end;
  if Last = 0 then begin
    PopValue := '-1';
    Exit;
  end;
  PopValue := Stacks[Last].Pop;
end;


{===================================================}

destructor TShortStack.Destroy;
var
  i: Integer;
begin
  if not IsEmpty then
    for i := First to Last  do
      DisposeStr(StackAry[i]);
  inherited Destroy;
end;

procedure TShortStack.Show;
var
  i: Integer;
begin
  for i := First to Last do begin
    {$IfDef Debug}
    WriteLn(F, StackAry[i]^);
    {$EndIf}
    WriteLn(StackAry[i]^);
  end;
  {$IfDef Debug}
  WriteLn(F, '===============');
  {$EndIf}
end;

procedure TShortStack.Push(S: String);
```

continues

Listing 27.2. continued

```pascal
begin
  if (S <> '.') and (S <> '..') then begin
    Inc(Last);
    StackAry[Last] := NewStr(S);
  end;
end;

function TShortStack.Pop: String;
var
  S: PString;
  Temp: ShortString;
begin
  S := StackAry[First];
  if S <> nil then begin
    Temp := S^;
    DisposeStr(StackAry[First]);
    Inc(First);
    Pop := Temp;
  end
  else begin
    WriteLn('Error TShortStack.Pop');
    Halt;
  end;
end;

function TShortStack.GetMoreDirs(Start: String): Integer;
var
  SR: SysUtils.TSearchRec;
  Total: Integer;
begin
  Total := 0;
  if FindFirst(Start, faDirectory + faReadOnly, SR) = 0 then
    repeat
      if (SR.Attr = faDirectory) or
         (SR.Attr = faDirectory + faReadOnly) then begin
        Push(SR.Name);
        Inc(Total);
      end;
    until FindNext(SR) <> 0;
  FindClose(SR);
  GetMoreDirs := Total;
end;

{=======================================}

constructor TRunDirs.Create(Owner: TComponent);
begin
  inherited Create(Owner);
  {$IfDef Debug}
  Assign(F, 'DirLists.dat');
  ReWrite(F);
  {$EndIf}
  FShortStack := TShortStack.Create;
  FBigStack := TBigStack.Create;
end;
```

```
destructor TRunDirs.Destroy;
begin
  FShortStack.Free;
  FBigStack.Free;
  {$IfDef Debug}
  Close(F);
  {$EndIf}
  inherited Destroy;
end;

procedure TRunDirs.PushStack;
begin
  FBigStack.Push(FShortStack);
  FShortStack := TShortStack.Create;
end;

function RemoveDir(Start: String; NumDirs: Integer): String;
var
  i, j: Integer;
  CurDir: DirStr;
  FileMask: Str12;
begin
  SplitDirName(Start, CurDir, FileMask);
  i := Length(CurDir);
  for j := 1 to NumDirs + 1 do begin
    if CurDir[i] = '\' then  begin
      Dec(CurDir[0]);
      Dec(i);
    end;
    while CurDir[i] <> '\' do begin
      Dec(CurDir[0]);
      Dec(i);
    end;
{   Dec(CurDir[0]);
    Dec(i); }
  end;
  RemoveDir := CurDir;
end;

procedure TRunDirs.ProcessName(FName: String; SR: SysUtils.TSearchRec);
begin
  if Assigned(FOnFoundFile) then FOnFoundFile(FName, SR);
end;

procedure TRunDirs.ProcessDir(Start: String);
var
  SR: SysUtils.TSearchRec;
begin
  if Assigned(FOnProcessDir) then FOnProcessDir(FCurDir);
  if FindFirst(Start, faArchive, SR) = 0 then
    repeat
      ProcessName(UpperCase(FCurDir) + SR.Name, SR);
    until FindNext(SR) <> 0;
  FindClose(SR);
end;

function TRunDirs.Run(Start: PathStr; StartingDirectory: string): string;
var
```

continues

Listing 27.2. continued

```
  SR: TSearchRec;
  Finished: Boolean;
  NewDir, StartedAt: string;
  DirMask: ShortString;
  NumDirs: Integer;
  OutCome: Integer;
  SaveDir: string;
begin
  GetDir(0, SaveDir);
  ChDir(StartingDirectory);
  Start := ExpandFileName(Start);
  FCurDir := ''; FFileMask := '';
  DirMask := '*.*';
  OutCome := 3;
  Finished := False;
  StartedAt := Start;
  SplitDirName(Start, FCurDir, FFileMask);
  Start := FCurDir + DirMask;
  while not Finished do begin
    FCurDir := ExtractFilePath(Start);
    ProcessDir(FCurDir + FFileMask);
    OutCome := FShortStack.GetMoreDirs(Start);
    if OutCome > 2 then begin
      {ShortStack^.Show;}
      PushStack;
      Start := FCurDir + FBigStack.PopValue(NumDirs) + '\' + DirMask
    end else begin
      NewDir := FBigStack.  PopValue(NumDirs);
      FCurDir := RemoveDir(Start, NumDirs);
      Start := FCurDir + NewDir + '\' + DirMask;
      if (Start = StartedAt) or (NewDir = '-1') then Finished := True;
    end;
  end;
  ChDir(SaveDir);
end;
end.
```

Listing 27.3. The short code listing for the FindAllW program.

```
unit Main;

{ Program copyright (c) 1995 by Charles Calvert }
{ Project Name: FINDALLW }

{ Use this program to iterate through the directories
  on your hard drive and search for files. Enter
  the path where you want to start searching, with
  no backslash at the end, and then enter the mask
  that you want to search with, for instance '*.pas'.
}

interface
```

```
uses
  WinTypes, WinProcs, Classes,
  Graphics, Forms, Controls,
  AllDirs, StdCtrls, Fileiter,
  FileCtrl, Dialogs, SysUtils;

type
  TForm1 = class(TForm)
    BStartSearch: TButton;
    ListBox1: TListBox;
    Edit1: TEdit;
    Label1: TLabel;
    Label2: TLabel;
    FileIterator1: TFileIterator;
    DirectoryListBox1: TDirectoryListBox;
    DriveComboBox1: TDriveComboBox;
    procedure BStartSearchClick(Sender: TObject);
    procedure ListBox1DblClick(Sender: TObject);
    procedure FileIterator1FoundFile(FileName: string; SR: TSearchRec);
  end;

var
  Form1: TForm1;

implementation


{$R *.DFM}


{ Make sure the FILEITERATOR's UseFileList property
  is set to true! }
procedure TForm1.BStartSearchClick(Sender: TObject);
var
  RunDir, Start: String;
begin
  Start := Edit1.Text;
  FileIterator1.FileList.Clear;
  RunDir := DirectoryListBox1.Directory;
  ListBox1.Clear;
  FileIterator1.Run(Start, RunDir);
  ListBox1.Items := FileIterator1.FileList;
end;

procedure TForm1.ListBox1DblClick(Sender: TObject);
var
  S: string;
begin
  S := 'Write ' + ListBox1.Items.Strings[ListBox1.ItemIndex];
  WinExec(PChar(S), sw_ShowNormal);
end;

end.
```

To use the program, first point it at a subdirectory on your hard disk. Then type in a file mask in the edit control at the bottom of the form. For instance, you might type *.pas. When you click the button at the bottom of the program, the code iterates through all the directories beneath the one you pointed at, and finds all the files that have a *.pas extension. It then places these files in a list box, as shown in Figure 27.1. If you double-click one of the files in the list box, it will be loaded into the WordPad program that ships with Windows 95, or into the Write program that ships with Windows NT.

FIGURE 27.1.

The FindAllW program allows you to search through multiple directories looking for files with a particular extension.

Looking at the code listings shown above is in one sense deceptive. As a programmer, all you have to write is the code in the last of these three listings, which consists of three short methods. All the code in the FileIter and AllDirs units is wrapped up in a component that you just drop down on a form. The key point here is that the FindAllW program is incredibly easy to write, especially when you consider the functionality inherent in it.

Iterating Through Directories with TFileIterator

The FindAllW program uses the TFileIterator component to iterate through directories. The TFileIterator component sends events to your program whenever a new directory or a new file is found. The events include the name of the new directory or file, as well as information about the size and date of the files it finds. You can respond to these events in any way you want. The FindAllW program does not respond to the event that's triggered when a directory is found. However, it will respond to the events associated with finding files.

Here, for instance, is how the FindAllW program responds when a file with the proper extension is found:

```
procedure TForm1.FileIterator1FoundFile(FileName: string; SR: TSearchRec);
begin
  Edit1.Text := FileName;
  Edit1.Update;
end;
```

As you can see, the code does nothing more than show the filename to the user. In particular, the call to Update forces the editor to display the file before giving the processor any more clock cycles.

Part of the built-in functionality of the TFileIterator unit is to maintain lists of the files it finds. To get this functionality, you must set the UseFileList property to True. When you finish searching all the directories, the list is ready for you to do with as you wish. This list is kept in a TStringList object, so you can just assign it to the Items property in a list box, as shown in this excerpt from the BStartSearchClick method:

```
FileIterator1.Run(Start, RunDir);
ListBox1.Items := FileIterator1.FileList;
```

The first line shown above passes in the file mask that you want to search on. For instance, you might typically pass in *.pas in the Start parameter. The second parameter, RunDir, designates the directory where you want your search to start. By calling Run, you start the process. As each file that meets the requirements is found, it is passed to the FileIterator1FoundFile event handler, and displayed. When the run is finished, you can access the list of files as shown above.

Here is a more literal example of calling FileIterator1.Run:

```
FileIterator1.Run('*.pas', 'c:\Source');
```

In this example, you will find all files that have a .pas extension and that reside in the C:\SOURCE directory or one of its child directories.

Notice that the FileIterator1FoundFile method is an event handler. You create this handler by clicking once on the OnFoundFile event in the Object Inspector Events page for the TFileIterator. Notice that the TFileIterator has events for both finding files and for finding directories. The same is true of the lists it maintains. One is for finding files, the other for finding directories. The FindAllW program just works with the files that are found, it does not keep lists of directories that are found. It will, however, iterate over all the directories beneath the one you pass in via the second parameter of the Run method.

After the TFileIterator component has completed a run, you can view the files that were found in a list box. If you double-click one of these files, it is loaded into the Windows Write or WordPad program:

```
procedure TForm1.ListBox1DblClick(Sender: TObject);
var
  S: string;
begin
  S := 'Write ' + ListBox1.Items.Strings[ListBox1.ItemIndex];
  WinExec(PChar, sw_ShowNormal);
end;
```

The WinExec procedure launches an executable, then returns control to your program. It takes the name of the file, and any parameters you want to pass to it, in the first parameter. The second parameter tells WinExec how you want the program to start. For instance, sw_ShowMinimized would start the program in a minimized state.

> **NOTE**
>
> WinExec is a Windows API routine that is considered obsolete. It is, however, still part of this incarnation of Win32, and I personally am going to use it until it is no longer available, since the official Microsoft function for this purpose, called CreateProcess, is a bear to use. (The CreateProcess function is similar to the CreateFile function discussed in Chapter 8, "Win32 Memory Management.")
>
> If you can stand a rather abrupt change of topic, I might add that under the default installation of Windows 95, if you go to the Run menu on the taskbar, type the word Write, and press Enter, you will launch WordPad, not Write. The same results occur if you type Write from the command line, or if you pass it as a parameter to WinExec. I believe that the mechanism employed here involves a small stub program, called WRITE.EXE, that ends up launching WORDPAD.EXE. At any rate, my point is that I pass in Write to WinExec not because I am primarily a Windows NT user, but because the program name works in both Windows NT and Windows 95.

When Should Nonvisual Objects Become Components?

It is not always clear whether you should turn a particular object into a component. For instance, the TStringList object has no related component, and cannot be manipulated through visual tools. The question then becomes "Why have I taken the TFileIterator object and placed it on the Component Palette?"

As it turns out, the advantages of placing TFileIterator on the Component Palette are two-fold:

- There are several options that might need to be tweaked before you use this object. In particular, you need to decide whether you want to have the lists of directories and files that you find saved to memory in a TStringList. Letting the programmer decide these matters by clicking a property can go a long way toward presenting a clean, easy-to-use interface for an object.

- Secondly, the TFileIterator object has two features that can be accessed through the Events page. Specifically, custom event handlers can be notified every time a new file or directory has been found. However, it can be confusing to construct an event handler manually, particularly if you don't know what parameters will be passed to the functions involved. If you place a component on the Component Palette, there is no need for the programmer to guess about how to handle an event. All it takes is a quick click on the Events page and the event handler is created for you automatically!

Creating a component also has the enormous advantage of forcing, or at least enticing, programmers to design a simple interface for an object. Once I have placed an object on the Component Palette, I always want to ensure that the user can hook it into his or her program in only a few short seconds. I am therefore strongly inclined to create a simple, easy to use interface. If I don't place the component on the Component Palette, then I find it easier to attempt to slip by with a complex interface that takes many lines of code for myself and others to utilize. To my mind, good components are not only bug free, but also very easy to use.

The *AllDirs* and *FileIter* Units

The program shown in this chapter uses two units called AllDirs and FileIter. The AllDirs unit has built-in stacks and an object called TRunDirs that knows how to iterate through subdirectories. Notice that TRunDirs is a descendant of TComponent. Nonvisual components often descend directly from TComponent.

FileIter features a simple descendant of TRunDirs called TFileIterator that adds list management capabilities. In other words, TRunDirs knows how to iterate through subdirectories and how to call the OnFoundFile and OnFoundDir events. You may, however, want to add list-keeping to the set of skills found in TRunDirs. I have therefore added the TFileIterator component as a second layer of additional functionality.

This idea of layering your components so that you can create different objects, descending from different parents, under different circumstances, is key to object-oriented design. You don't want to push too much functionality up too high in the object hierarchy, or you will be forced to rewrite the object in order to get access to a subset of its functionality. For instance, if the Delphi developers had not created a TDataSet component, but had instead created one component called TTable, they would have had to duplicate that same functionality in the TQuery component. This is wasteful. The smart thing to do is to build a component called TDataSet, and end its functionality at the point at which the specific attributes of TQuery and TTable need to be defined. That way TQuery and TTable can both reuse the functionality of TDataSet, rather than having to rewrite that same functionality for both objects.

Before closing this section, let me reiterate some key points. The AllDirs unit is the brains of this particular operation. It knows how to iterate through directories, how to find all the files in each directory, and how to notify the user when new directories or files are found. The FileIter unit adds the capability to store lists of files and directories in TStringList objects. You can, of course, write these lists to disk by using the SaveToFile command.

Iterating Through Directories

The task of iterating through directories has a simple recursive solution. However, recursion is a slow and time-consuming technique that is also wasteful of stack space. As a result, AllDirs creates its own stacks and pushes the directories it finds onto them.

> **NOTE**
>
> Delphi has some built-in tools for creating stacks and lists. For instance, there are the TList and TStringList objects. I avoid these tools here because they either did not exist or I was not aware of their presence when I first created this program. However, the code I provide here does have the advantage of working in either DOS or Windows. That is, the core units will compile under either Delphi or Turbo Pascal.

Here are the objects in the ALLDIRS unit:

- The TStack object is an abstract class that provides some basic functionality for handling all classes of stacks. You'll never have a reason to instantiate an object of this type.

- The TShortStack object handles an array of up to 1000 long strings. It contains all the logic needed for storing and deleting these items. It holds them in an array that takes up only 4000 bytes of memory. That's 4 bytes per long string, times 1000 possible long strings, which equals 4000 bytes. This is a huge amount of overkill for this type of program, as it is very unlikely that you will encounter a case where there are 4000 nested directories.

- The TBigStack object creates stacks of TShortStack objects. One directory's worth of subdirectories can be stored in a TShortStack; but, if a directory has multiple subdirectories that have multiple subdirectories, you need TBigStack.

- The TRunDirs object is built around a series of FindFirst and FindNext calls. It uses these Delphi functions to find the files in a directory. It then pushes the directories it finds onto the TShortStack and TBigStack objects.

To dust off the classic analogy used in these situations, the FIFO (first in, first out) and LIFO (last in, first out) stacks implemented here are like piles of plates in a kitchen cabinet. You can put one plate down and then add another one to it. When you need one of the plates, you take the first one off either the top or the bottom depending on whether it's a FIFO or a LIFO stack. Putting a new plate on the top of a stack is called *pushing* the object onto the stack, and removing a plate is called *popping* the object off of the stack. For more information on stacks, refer to any book on basic programming theory.

Using *FindFirst, FindNext,* and *FindClose*

This section continues the examination of the stacks created in the AllDirs units. The core of these stacks are the calls to FindFirst, FindNext, and FindClose that search through directories looking for particular files.

Using FindFirst, FindNext, and FindClose is like typing DIR in a directory at the DOS prompt. FindFirst finds the first file in the directory, and FindNext finds the remaining files. You should call FindClose when you are finished with the process.

FindFirst is found in both the SysUtils unit and in the 16-bit WinDos unit, but you should use the version in the SysUtils unit because it uses Pascal strings, and because WinDos is not obsolete. The one in the WinDos unit used PChars. (WINDOS.PAS did not and will not make it across to the 32-bit version of Delphi.)

These calls enable you to specify a directory and file mask, as if you were issuing a command of the following type at the DOS prompt:

```
dir c:\aut*.bat
```

This command would, of course, show all files beginning with aut, and ending in .bat. This particular command would typically find AUTOEXEC.BAT and perhaps one or two other files.

When you call FindFirst, you pass in three parameters:

```
function FindFirst(const Path: string;
                   Attr: Word;
                   var F: TSearchRec): Integer;
```

The first parameter contains the path and file mask that specify the files you want to find. For instance, you might pass in 'c:\delphi32\source\vcl*.pas' or 'c:\program files\borland\delphi 2.0' in this parameter. The second parameter lists the type of files you want to see:

faReadOnly	$01	Read-only files
faHidden	$02	Hidden files
faSysFile	$04	System files
faVolumeID	$08	Volume ID files
faDirectory	$10	Directory files
faArchive	$20	Archive files
faAnyFile	$3F	Any file

Most of the time, you should pass in faArchive in this parameter. However, if you want to see directories, pass in faDirectory. The Attribute parameter is not a filter. No matter what flags you use, you will always get all normal files in the directory. Passing faDirectory causes directories to be included in the list of normal files; it does not limit the list to directories. You can

OR together several different faXXX constants, if you wish. The final parameter is a variable of type TSearchRec, which is declared as follows:

```
TSearchRec = record
  Fill: array[1..21] of Byte;
  Attr: Byte;
  Time: Longint;
  Size: Longint;
  Name: string[12];
end;
```

The most important value in TSearchRec is the Name field, which on success specifies the name of the file found. FindFirst returns zero if it found a file, and nonzero if the call fails.

FindNext works exactly like FindFirst, except that you only have to pass in a variable of type TSearchRec, because it is assumed that the mask and file attribute are the same. Once again, FindNext returns zero if all goes well, and a nonzero value if it can't find a file. You should call FindClose after completing a FindFirst/FindNext sequence.

Given this information, here is a simple way to call FindFirst, FindNext, and FindClose:

```
var
  SR: TSearchRec;
begin
  if FindFirst(Start, faArchive, SR) = 0 then
    repeat
      DoSomething(SR.Name);
    until FindNext(SR) <> 0;
  FindClose(SR);
```

That's all I'm going to say about the basic structure of the TRunDirs object. As I said earlier, you can learn more about stacks by studying a book on basic programming data structures. This book, however, is about Delphi, and so I'm going to move on to a discussion of creating event handlers.

Creating Your Own Event Handlers

Whenever TRunDirs is ready to process a new directory, it passes its name to a method called ProcessDir:

```
procedure TRunDirs.ProcessDir(Start: String);
var
  SR: SysUtils.TSearchRec;
begin
  if Assigned(FOnProcessDir) then FOnProcessDir(FCurDir);
  if FindFirst(Start, faArchive, SR) = 0 then
    repeat
      ProcessName(UpperCase(FCurDir) + SR.Name, SR);
    until FindNext(SR) <> 0;
  FindClose(SR);
end;
```

ProcessDir iterates through all the files in a directory and passes each file it finds to the ProcessName method:

```
procedure TRunDirs.ProcessName(FName: String;
                               SR: SysUtils.TSearchRec);
begin
  if Assigned(FOnFoundFile) then FOnFoundFile(FName, SR);
end;
```

Both ProcessDir and ProcessName are virtual methods. Therefore, you can create a descendant of TRunDirs, override either of these methods, and respond to them in any way you like.

Creating a descendant of TRunDirs is a simple enough operation, but it's even simpler to respond to event handlers through the delegation model. In other words, you could create a descendant of TRunDirs (or TFileIterator) and then override the ProcessName method. This would give you easy access to each name as it is processed. However, there is a simpler way to achieve the same end. Specifically, you could create an event handler, and have that event called each time a file is found.

To create an OnXXX event handler, you must first declare a pointer to a method. The method pointer you are creating will point at the method that will be called if the event takes place. Each particular type of method handler will have a signature. For instance, OnClick events always get passed a parameter called Sender, which is of type TObject. See the BStartSearchClick method in the source code for an example.

The Sender/TObject-type of routine is a called a TNotifyEvent, and is declared like this:

```
TNotifyEvent = procedure(Sender: TObject) of object;
```

If this code confuses you, remember that method pointers were discussed in Chapter 23, "Objects and Inheritance."

It's easy to see how you get from TNotifyEvent method pointer declaration to an event like this:

```
procedure Button1Click(Sender: TObject);
```

A Button1Click method is just an instance of a method of type TNotifyEvent. All an OnClick event does is provide an instance of a method that matches the OnClick method pointer stored inside an object.

Here is the way to declare the method pointer for the OnFoundDir event:

```
TFoundDirEvent = procedure(DirName: string) of Object;
```

This pointer references a procedure that takes a single string as a parameter. Methods of this type will be created when you click the OnFoundDir event in the Events page. It's exactly the same process that occurs when you click an OnClick event for a button, only the signature of the method types is different, and more particular, this time the signature is defined in the AllDirs unit, not in some unit that ships with Delphi.

> **NOTE**
>
> Here is what an OnFoundFile signature looks like:
>
> ```
> TFoundFileEvent = procedure(FileName: string;
>                             SR: SysUtils.TSearchRec) of Object;
> ```
>
> The OnFoundFile event is the one that is actually used in the FindAllW program, but I am concentrating on the OnFoundDir event because it takes only one parameter, and is therefore a bit easier to understand.

Here is how to declare a variable that can point at an object of this type:

```
FOnProcessDir: TFoundDirEvent;
```

Now the TRunDirs object has the tools it needs to use the delegation model. Specifically, it contains an internal variable that can be set equal to a method of the correct type. Whenever a particular event occurs, the TRunDirs object can use this variable to call the method delegated to handle the event:

```
if Assigned(FOnProcessDir) then FOnProcessDir(FCurDir);
```

This code is from the body of the ProcessDir method. It first checks to see whether FOnProcessDir is set to nil. If it is not nil, that means you have assigned a method to handle this event, and the event is called.

Event handlers are merely properties that consist of pointers to functions, rather than to some other kind of data. Here is the declaration for the OnProcessDir event:

```
property OnProcessDir: TFoundDirEvent
    read FOnProcessDir write FOnProcessDir;
```

You can see that this property is declared to be of type TFoundDirEvent, rather than being of some other, more common type such as a string, integer, or set. This property serves as an interface for the FOnProcessDir variable, mentioned above. FOnProcessDir is hidden from other objects in the private section:

```
 private
   FOnProcessDir: TFoundDirEvent;
```

As you can see, FOnProcessDir is just a method pointer. It's just another four-byte pointer to some variable, only this variable happens to be a method pointer, or more specifically, an event handler.

Event handlers are attractive because they can be accessed readily from the Object Inspector. Double-click the property editor for an event handler, and the method associated with that event is immediately inserted into your code. In short, event handlers are a modest form of code generator, in which the code that is generated is a declaration for any sort of method you might wish to define.

You now know how to create your own event handlers. This is important information that can set you free to start really taking advantage of the power of the programming environment in which you work!

The DelAllDb Program

The second program shown in this chapter is called DelAllDb. By using it you can iterate through subdirectories while deleting files that have particular extensions. The classic use for the program is to delete all files on one drive that have BAK for an extension. During a single run, DelAllDb can delete files with more than one specific extension. As a result, I often use the program for deleting the stray files created during the development process. For instance, I don't need to clutter my hard drive with hundreds of files that have extensions such as DCU, ~PA, DSM, or BAK. These are almost always effluvia that I can cast off when I am through building an EXE. DELALLWDB handles the chore for me.

The program also tracks the sizes of directories as it iterates through them. When you are done, there is a Paradox file listing all the directories you looked over, along with their current sizes. There are several commands you can give to this file so that it will sort itself, or calculate the combined size of all the directories it visited. You can therefore point this program at your entire hard drive, telling it to, for instance, delete all the files with a BAK extension. When you are done, you will have a list of the current directories on your hard drive sorted either by name or by size. There are many times when I have run this program, sorted the directories, and found that there was some backwater directory containing 20 megabytes of files that I'd meant to delete a month ago, but had forgotten about. All in all, I've found it a pretty useful program.

The program creates text files listing all the files that have been deleted. That way you can check right after the run of the program to see if you've accidentally deleted something you didn't mean to trash. This gives you time to boot up an old copy of DOS and give the Undelete command.

DelAllDb uses the TFileIterator component (found on the CD-ROM that ships with this book) to simplify the task of deleting certain files from a disk. However, as you have seen, you can use this component for many other useful tasks. For instance, you can create the file-finding utility shown above with it, or you can create a GREP program that searches through each file in a set of directories looking for a particular string. Another program provided on disk is used as a substitute for the Touch utility that shipped with Borland Pascal. The WTouch program iterates through directories, setting all the files found there to a certain time and date. The main point of all these programs, or proposed programs, is to show that you can easily create a nonvisual component that broadly expands Delphi's capabilities. Once you have the component, you can reuse it over and over again.

The code for the DelAllDb main unit, the FileIter unit, and the AllDirs unit are on this book's CD-ROM. The main program is with the other listings for Chapter 27, but the AllDirs and

`FileIter` unit are in the UNITS subdirectory. The main source code for DelAllDb is printed below in Listing 27.4. The `AllDirs` and `FileIter` units are shown above in Listings 27.2 and 27.3. The form for the DelAllDb program is shown in Figure 27.2.

FIGURE 27.2.

The main form for the DelAllDb program lists the extensions of the files that will be deleted.

Listing 27.4. The main unit for the DelAllDb program depends on `FILEITER` and `ALLDIRS`.

```
unit Main;

{ Contents copyright (c) 1996 by Charles Calvert }
{ Project Name: DELALLDB

{ This program allows you to selectively delete
  files from your hard drive. It deletes files
  by extension, so you can delete all the files
  with a BAK extension, etc. It cannot be used
  to delete files that have no extension.

  It will also count the size of directories
  on your system, and add up the total sizes.

  It saves the DirSizeList in a DB file which you
  can sort and perform calculations on. Other
  information is stored in text files that you
  can reach through the File menu for the program.

  A special file saves the list of extensions of
  the types of files you want to delete. This list
  can be edited at run time, and it is displayed
  in a list box.

  There are special cases for files that end with
  an EXE or ~?? extensions. To delete EXE files, '*.EXE'
  must be in the EXTLIST.TXT file, and also the
  Delete EXEs checkbox must be marked. To delete files
  whose extension begins with a tilde, just check
  the appropriate box. There is no need to put this
  extension in the EXTLIST file. }

interface
```

```
uses
   SysUtils, WinTypes, WinProcs,
   Messages, Classes, Graphics,
   Controls, Forms, Dialogs,
   StdCtrls, AllDirs, Fileiter,
   Menus, Buttons, ExtCtrls,
   FileCtrl, DB, DBTables;

type
   TForm1 = class(TForm)
      FileIterator1: TFileIterator;
      MainMenu1: TMainMenu;
      File1: TMenuItem;
      Open1: TMenuItem;
      N1: TMenuItem;
      Exit1: TMenuItem;
      DeleteBtn: TBitBtn;
      Panel1: TPanel;
      ExtBox: TListBox;
      BitBtn2: TBitBtn;
      DirectoryListBox1: TDirectoryListBox;
      DriveComboBox1: TDriveComboBox;
      OpenDelFile1: TMenuItem;
      Panel2: TPanel;
      DelExe: TCheckBox;
      DelTilda: TCheckBox;
      OpenDirSizeFile1: TMenuItem;
      Table1: TTable;
      Table1Directory: TStringField;
      Table1Size: TFloatField;
      pDirShow: TPanel;
      procedure FormDestroy(Sender: TObject);
      procedure FormCreate(Sender: TObject);
      procedure Exit1Click(Sender: TObject);
      procedure Open1Click(Sender: TObject);
      procedure BitBtn2Click(Sender: TObject);
      procedure DeleteBtnClick(Sender: TObject);
      procedure FileIterator1FoundFile(FileName: String; SR: TSearchRec);
      procedure FileIterator1ProcessDir(DirName: String);
   private
      FDelTilda: Boolean;
      FDelExes: Boolean;
      FDirSize: LongInt;
      FDeleteList: TStringList;
      FDirSizeList: TStringList;
      FStartPath: string;
      FDirName: string;
      FDirSizeName: string;
      FDelListName: string;
      FExtBoxName: string;
      procedure SaveDirList;
      procedure SetUpLists;
      function LoadExtBox: Boolean;
   end;

var
   Form1: TForm1;
```

continues

Listing 27.4. continued

```pascal
implementation

uses
  Grider,
  StrBox,
  UtilBox, textedit;

{$R *.DFM}


procedure TForm1.SaveDirList;
var
  ListStr: string;
  S1, S2: string;
  i: Integer;
begin
  Cursor := crHourGlass;
  try
    Table1.Close;
    Table1.EmptyTable;
    Table1.Open;
    for i := 0 to FDirSizeList.Count - 1 do begin
      Table1.Insert;
      ListStr := FDirSizeList.Strings[i];
      S1 := GetFirstToken(ListStr, '=');
      S2 := GetLastToken(ListStr, '=');
      Table1.FieldByName('Directory').AsString := S1;
      Table1.FieldByName('Size').AsString := S2;
      Table1.Post;
    end;
  finally
    Cursor := crDefault;
  end;
end;

function TForm1.LoadExtBox: Boolean;
begin
  ExtBox.Items.LoadFromFile(FExtBoxName);
end;

procedure TForm1.FormDestroy(Sender: TObject);
begin
  ExtBox.Items.SaveToFile(FExtBoxName);
  FDeleteList.Free;
  FDirSizeList.Free;
end;

procedure TForm1.SetUpLists;
begin
  FDeleteList.Free;
  FDirSizeList.Free;
  FDeleteList := TStringList.Create;
  FDirSizeList := TStringList.Create;
  FDirName := '';
  FDirSize := 0;
end;
```

```
procedure TForm1.FormCreate(Sender: TObject);
begin
  FStartPath := StripLastToken(ParamStr(0), '\');
  FDirSizeName := FStartPath + '\dirsize.txt';
  FDelListName := FStartPath + '\dellist.txt';
  FExtBoxName := FStartPath + '\extbox.txt';
  SetUpLists;
  LoadExtBox;
end;

procedure TForm1.Exit1Click(Sender: TObject);
begin
  Close;
end;

procedure TForm1.Open1Click(Sender: TObject);
var
  SPtr: array[0..150] of char;
  S: string;
begin
  case TMenuItem(Sender).Tag of
    100: S := FExtBoxName;
    101: S := FDelListName;
    102: begin
      GridView.DataSource1.DataSet := Table1;
      Table1.Open;
      GridView.ShowModal;
      Table1.Close;
      Exit;
    end;
  end;
  StrPCopy(SPtr, 'notepad.exe ' + S);
  TextEd.LoadModal(S);
  LoadExtBox;
end;

procedure TForm1.BitBtn2Click(Sender: TObject);
begin
  Close;
end;

{ Note that if you want to change the cursor for
  an entire application, then change Screen.Cursor. }
procedure TForm1.DeleteBtnClick(Sender: TObject);
var
  i: Integer;
  S: string;
begin
  FDelTilda := DelTilda.Checked;
  FDelExes := DelExe.Checked;
  s := DirectoryListBox1.Directory;
  if S[Length(S)] <> '\' then S := S + '\';
  if MessageDlg('Delete from: ' + S, mtConfirmation,
                [mbYes, mbNo], 0) = idNo then Exit;
  try
    Screen.Cursor := crHourGlass;
    SetUpLists;
```

continues

Listing 27.4. continued

```
    FileIterator1.Run('*.*', DirectoryListBox1.Directory);
    FDeleteList.SaveToFile(FDelListName);
    FDirSizeList.Add(FDirName + ' = ' + IntToStr(FDirSize));
    SysUtils.DeleteFile(FDirSizeName);
    SaveDirList;
    FDirSizeList.SaveToFile(FDirSizeName);
    for i := 0 to FDeleteList.Count - 1 do
      SysUtils.DeleteFile(FDeleteList.Strings[i]);
  finally
    Screen.Cursor := crDefault;
    pDirShow.Caption := '';
  end;
end;

{ This is the place where the list of files to delete is
  created. Get the extension, see if it is in the delete
  list, if it is, add it to the delete list.

  There are special cases for handling EXEs. Specifically, you
  want to add the files to the TotalDirSize always but only
  delete them if they are listed in the EXELIST.TXT file and
  Delete EXEs is checked. Also a special case for the files
  whose extension begin with a tilde. Finally, a special case
  for the possibility that the user put a carraige return
  at the end of the EXELIST thereby accidentally requesting
  that all files with NO extension get deleted. Because there
  is no way to check for this kind of user error, I've
  decided this program cannot be used to delete files
  that have NO extension. }

procedure TForm1.FileIterator1FoundFile(FileName: String; SR: TSearchRec);
var
  S: string;
  i: Integer;
  AddToDirSize: Boolean;
begin
  AddToDirSize := False;
  S := UpperCase(ExtractFileExt(FileName));
  for i := 0 to ExtBox.Items.Count - 1 do begin
    if (S = '.EXE') and (not FDelExes) then begin
      AddToDirSize := True;
      Continue;
    end;
    if (S = UpperCase(ExtBox.Items.Strings[i])) anc (StripBlanks(S) <> '') then
begin
      FDeleteList.Add(FileName);
      Exit;
    end;
    if not FDelTilda then
      AddToDirSize := True
    else if S[2] = '~' then begin
      FDeleteList.Add(FileName);
      Exit;
    end;
    AddToDirSize := True;
  end;
```

```
  if AddToDirSize then FDirSize := FDirSize + SR.Size;
end;

procedure TForm1.FileIterator1ProcessDir(DirName: String);
begin
  pDirShow.Caption := DirName;
  Application.ProcessMessages;
  if FDirName <> '' then
    FDirSizeList.Add(FDirName + ' = ' + IntToStr(FDirSize));
  FDirName := DirName;
  FDirSize := 0;
end;

end.
```

The DELALLWDB program depends on a text file called EXTBOX.TXT. This file contains the list of extensions used to determine which files should be deleted. For instance, here is the list I use when I want to go after the spare files generated when developing Delphi applications:

```
.bak
.dcu
.dsm
```

These extensions are displayed at runtime in a list box. You can open up the File menu in the DelAllDb program and select an option that enables you to edit this list. There is no real limit to the number of extensions you can store in this file, but most people would probably want to store only a few. The DelAllDb program could be improved by allowing the user to maintain different lists of extensions easily.

There are two radio buttons on the main form for the DELALLW program. These buttons let you decide whether you want to delete files with an EXE extension, or whether you want to delete files that have a tilde as the first character in their extension.

Delphi marks its backup files by placing a tilde in front of their extension. For example, a backup copy of MAIN.PAS is called MAIN.~PA, and a backup copy of DelAllDb.DPR is DelAllDb.~DP. Because Delphi produces a slew of files that have this tilde before their extension, it's simpler to delete all of the files of this type, rather than searching for each individual variety.

NOTE

To delete files with an EXE extension you must list .EXE in the EXTBOX.TXT file, and also have the Delete EXEs radio button set. If you select only one of these options, no EXE files will be deleted. The reason for this precaution is that EXE files can be rather valuable, and I want to be sure I don't delete them accidentally. This program could be improved by providing the same mechanism for DLL files.

In the DELALLW program, the code generated for the `OnProcessDir` event looks like this:

```
TForm1.FileIterator1ProcessDir(DirName: String);
begin
  FDirSizeList.Add(FDirName + ': ' + IntToStr(FDirSize));
  FDirName := DirName;
  FDirSize := 0;
end;
```

The body of any event handler is, of course, supplied by a programmer. In this case, it looks like this:

```
FDirSizeList.Add(FDirName + ': ' + IntToStr(FDirSize));
FDirName := DirName;
FDirSize := 0;
```

Here, the name and size of the last directory processed are added to a list, the new directory name is saved in a variable called `FDirName`, and the directory size is set to zero.

The actual size of each directory is calculated in the `OnFoundFile` event handler:

```
procedure TForm1.FileIterator1FoundFile(FileName: String; SR: TSearchRec);
var
  S: string;
  i: Integer;
  AddToDirSize: Boolean;
begin
  AddToDirSize := False;
  S := UpperCase(ExtractFileExt(FileName));
  for i := 0 to ExtBox.Items.Count - 1 do begin
    if (S = '.EXE') and (not FDelExes) then begin
      AddToDirSize := True;
      Continue;
    end;
    if (S = UpperCase(ExtBox.Items.Strings[i])) and
       (StripBlanks(S) <> '') then begin
      FDeleteList.Add(FileName);
      Exit;
    end;
    if not FDelTilda then
      AddToDirSize := True
    else if S[2] = '~' then begin
      FDeleteList.Add(FileName);
      Exit;
    end;
    AddToDirSize := True;
  end;
  if AddToDirSize then FDirSize := FDirSize + SR.Size;
end;
```

This one routine has several different pieces of logic in it. The most important logic determines whether the name passed in contains one of the extensions that the user wants to delete. If it does, the file's name is added to a list of files that will be deleted after visiting all the user-specified directories. Special cases are implemented for executables and backup files marked with a tilde. If it is determined that one of the files in the directory will not be deleted, its size is added to the current value of the `FDirSize` variable. `FDirSize` just keeps getting larger and larger until the entire directory is processed. At that point, DelAllDb stores the directory name and its size in a list, and the whole process begins again.

There are special cases for handling EXEs. Specifically, you always want to add the files to the TotalDirSize, but delete them only if they are listed in the EXELIST.TXT file and Delete EXEs is checked. Also, there is a special case for the files whose extension begins with a tilde. Finally, there is a special case for the possibility that the user put a carriage return at the end of the EXELIST, thereby accidentally requesting that all files with no extension get deleted. Because there is no practical way to check for this kind of user error, I've decided this program cannot be used to delete files that have no extension. A blank entry in the list is therefore ignored.

Summary

The FindAllW and DelAllDb programs, along with the TFileIterator component, point the way toward an understanding of Delphi's greatest strengths. TFileIterator and TRunDirs are not particularly difficult pieces of code, but they are sufficiently complex to highlight the fact that you can place almost any kind of logic inside a Delphi object. If you want to write multimedia code, talk on a network, or simulate the behavior of a submarine, you can write a Delphi component that will encapsulate the logic needed to reach your goal. More importantly, this component can then be placed on the Component Palette and dropped onto a form where it can easily be manipulated through the Object Inspector. Objects help you hide complexity, and help you reuse code.

The Object Inspector, and its related property editors and component editors, provide an elegant, easy-to-use interface to any object. Component architectures represent one of the most important tools in programming today, and it's quite possible that Delphi has by far the best implementation of a component architecture currently available in any market.

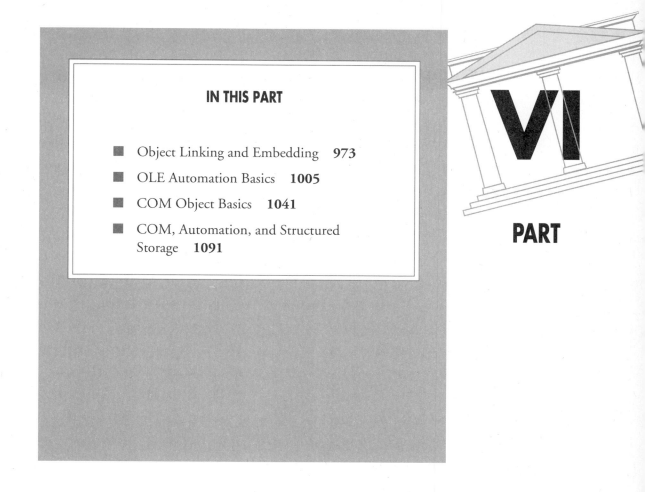

PART

VI

OLE and COM

The sixth section of this book explores OLE and the COM object model. As well as chapters on DDE, object linking and embedding, OLE automation, and the method for implementing the Component Object Model in Delphi, there is also some general discussion of OLE and DDE, though these topics are not explored in depth.

Object Linking and Embedding

28

This chapter explains a few basic facts about using OLE and DDE in a Delphi program. Inherently, the subject matter is extremely technical, but Delphi simplifies these interfaces, making them easy to use in most programming projects.

Of particular interest to most programmers is the greatly improved Delphi 2.0 `TOleContainer` component. This object now stands head and shoulders over the `TOleContainer` object that appeared in the first version of Delphi. With the appearance of this upgraded component, Delphi's support for object linking and embedding is now fast, flexible, and reliable.

Here are a few of the specific topics covered in this chapter:

- Creating OLE clients
- Inserting or pasting OLE objects at runtime
- OLE in-place activation
- Reading and writing OLE objects from files
- Working with OLE dialogs
- Accessing OLE verbs from your application
- DDE clients
- DDE servers
- Compiling from the command line with DCC32.EXE
- Configuring the command-line compiler with DCC32.CFG
- Modifying resource (RES) files
- Creating resource files with BRCC32.EXE

In the opening sections of this chapter, I assume that some readers know very little about either OLE or DDE. In particular, I include a few pages to introduce these topics to readers who are new to this material. My goal is to bring you from a standstill to the point where you can take these concepts for a mild walk around the track.

You should note, however, that this chapter serves as a warm-up exercise for the fairly interesting examination of OLE that stretches out over the next few chapters. The material found in this chapter on the `TOLEContainer` is quite important, but it is really only a prelude to the upcoming discussion of OLE automation, COM objects, and the Games SDK, all of which are covered in the next few chapters.

The Basics

OLE got its now anachronistic name from the acronym for object linking and embedding. However, current OLE technology extends far beyond the bounds of object linking and embedding, and Microsoft has officially stated that the letters of the word "OLE" no longer stand for anything. OLE is called OLE for historical reasons, but the party line is that OLE is now just a catchy word associated at least as closely with bullfights as it is with the specific technology that gave it birth.

In other words, OLE is so large a technology that it no longer refers explicitly to object linking and embedding. Instead, it refers to a host of technologies that include object linking and embedding, OCXs, structured storage, automation, and drag-and-drop technology. All these technologies are based on a software technology called the *Component Object Model,* or COM. It is the common thread that runs through all OLE technology, and to me it is also the defining element in that technology.

What is OLE technology? It is the set of objects built on top of the COM object model that allows for inter-process communication. All OLE technology is built on top of COM, and most of it has something to do with getting multiple applications, processes, binary files, machines, or operating systems to talk to one another. Whether it is a DLL talking to an executable, one executable talking to another executable, one object talking to another object, or one machine talking to another machine, OLE technology usually involves communication across some form of boundary. All this communication—indeed, nearly every line of OLE code—is built on top of COM. I discuss COM in some depth over the next few chapters, and you will find that it is the major theme of the OLE material found in this book.

Both OLE and DDE enable you to break out of the bounds of your current program and interact with other applications or other parts of the system. That is, they enable you to communicate across the boundaries that exist between executables. OLE, however, is a much more advanced technology, and it is of interest to a broader audience than its little brother DDE. In fact, DDE is historically just a precursor to the more grown-up technology found in OLE. DDE came first, but Microsoft all but abandoned it in favor of OLE.

> **NOTE**
>
> Most people access DDE features through a library called DDEML. DDEML stands for the Dynamic Data Exchange Management Library. It is built on top of the complex message-based interface called Dynamic Data Exchange, or DDE. Microsoft built DDEML to add increased power and flexibility to the original DDE message-based system. If you want to work with raw DDE code, you should use DDEML rather than the lowest levels of the DDE API.

Certain programs, such as Install utilities, still make heavy use of DDE. In fact, there are many DDE-aware applications on the market at this time. As a result, an understanding of this technology can still be very useful and will remain useful for the foreseeable future. One of the great lessons of the last 10 years has been the extraordinary persistence of legacy systems.

Dynamic Data Exchange gets its name because it lets two applications exchange data dynamically at runtime. That is, a link can be created between two programs so that changes to one application are reflected in the second application. For instance, if you change a number in a spreadsheet, a second application can be updated automatically so that it reflects the change.

OLE also enables you to implement this same feature, but with much more control and reliability. That is, a link can be established between your program and a spreadsheet so that your program is informed if changes are made to the data in the spreadsheet.

What then, are the differences between OLE and DDE? Basically, OLE takes the concepts inherent in DDE and makes much more of them. OLE is to DDE as a chicken is to an egg—it's more powerful, more sophisticated, more reliable, and has more diverse capabilities. It is also more difficult to understand and more demanding of system resources. However, you should always use OLE rather than DDE if you have choice. If resources are an issue, consider using OLE automation rather than object linking and embedding.

> **NOTE**
>
> OLE's demands on system resources are so high that it was originally tempting to think that it would never prove useful to a large number of users. However, more or less the same thing was said about GUIs, and now we are all using them—in fact, they are actually quite snappy if you have a Pentium. As the years have gone by, the demands of OLE have begun to seem less and less strenuous, and now a large number of systems run OLE-based programs with little apparent effort.
>
> As I explain later, one way to make OLE useful on slower systems is not to use huge applications as servers. For instance, it might be counter-productive to use Word or Excel as an OLE server. On at least some machines, OLE servers should be small modules that provide one particular type of functionality; they should not be massive applications that combine hundreds of features into one executable.

OLE Technologies: Embedding, In-Place Activation, and OCXs

You can not only link two applications with OLE, but actually embed the data from one application inside another application or document. This means that if you embed a spreadsheet document in a word processor document, the relationship between the two applications continues even if you remove the document from one computer and place it on a second computer. The embedded OLE object travels with the document and works as long as the necessary applications are also running on the second system.

OLE supports something called *in-place activation,* which enables an embedded object to temporarily take over a second application. For instance, if you embed a portion of a spreadsheet in a word processor document and then click in the spreadsheet document, the menus of your word processor disappear and the menus of the spreadsheet take their place. As you will see in later chapters, OLE automation lets you control another application from inside a first application. This means that one application can request services from a second application, without the user having to be concerned about the details.

OCX technology enables links between your application and free-floating objects that exist on your system. Or, to put the matter somewhat more generally, it's a technique for creating components that look and feel like Delphi components, but which can be used across multiple languages, applications, and perhaps, someday, even across platforms.

If you have an OCX toolbar object on your system, it can be embedded in your application in such a way that it appears to be a native part of your code. You could also do the same thing using Delphi objects. The difference between the two technologies is that Delphi objects can usually be used only in Delphi applications, whereas OCXs can be used in a wide range of tools.

OLE technology in general, and OCXs in particular, may point the way toward a new technique for building applications. For example, you can create several different toolbar OCXs, all of which have the same interface. Because they have a common interface, you could swap these different toolbars in and out of an application at will. As a result, this aspect of OLE might be utilized in the future to enable users to construct an application out of a series of interchangeable parts.

OCXs are easy to use. You can just plop them down on a form exactly as you would a VCL object. A page of OCXs ships with most versions of Delphi, and you can easily learn about them by experimentation and reference to their online help.

Building OCXs, on the other hand, is almost as difficult as using them is easy. You might, however, check the CD to see if there are any tools mentioned there that might help you convert VCL objects into OCXs. In particular, at the time of this writing, a company called Apiary based in Little Rock, Arkansas, was in the process of constructing such a tool. Technology of this kind is almost certain to be built into future versions of Delphi.

With the advent of Windows 95 and with the surge of Windows NT systems, it's finally time for object linking and embedding to start playing a role in the day-to-day life of at least some computer users. The introduction of cleaner 32-bit code is one possible cause of the improvement in the performance of this technology. However, the primary reason the technology now seems more feasible is likely to be simply the result of many people using bigger, more powerful machines. What seemed unbearably slow on a 4MB 386 now suddenly seems plausible on a 16MB Pentium. This turn of events probably does not come as a surprise to the original developers of this technology.

I hope this brief introduction to OLE and DDE brings you to the point that you can understand why this subject is of interest. Over the next few pages, you get a brief look at the TOleContainer object, which is well designed, easy to use, surprisingly fast, and plenty of fun. Using this object will get you used to working with well-constructed Delphi OLE objects and will hopefully prepare you for the more technical OLE-based chapters that lie ahead.

An OLE Example

To run an OLE example, you need to have a reliable OLE server on your system. A number of simple OLE 2-aware applications ship with Windows 95. Examples include Paintbrush and WordPad. You can use these two applications when testing the TOleContainer object. These OLE 2 applications even support in-place activation.

Some of my favorite servers are the applets that ship with Microsoft Word, Excel, and Powerpoint, or similar programs such as Visio. You can also use programs such as Paintbrush to good effect. These applications are small enough to load within a reasonable period of time, and they can reside in memory without claiming so many resources as to bring your system to a halt. If you have one of the Microsoft applets or another OLE server on your system, I suggest using them as servers rather than a big application such as Word, Paradox, or Excel. You can, however, effectively use big applications such as Word as an OLE client.

The code for the OleContainer example program is shown in Listing 28.1. This program shows how to insert OLE objects into a program at runtime, how to access their features, and how to save them to disk so that they can be loaded again at a later time. It also demonstrates in-place activation, returning from in-place activation to the original Delphi application, viewing OLE dialogs, and using OLE verbs.

Listing 28.1. The OleObj1 program shows the basic features of the TOleContainer object.

```
unit main;

{ Copyright (c) 1996 by Charlie Calvert

  TOleContainer example shows how to Insert OLE objects, link to OLE
  objects, save OLE objects, use in place activation, view OLE
  dialogs, query and use OLE verbs. }

interface

uses
  Windows, Messages, SysUtils,
  Classes, Graphics, Controls,
  Forms, Dialogs, StdCtrls,
  OleCtnrs, Menus, ExtCtrls;

type
  TForm1 = class(TForm)
    OpenDialog1: TOpenDialog;
    SaveDialog1: TSaveDialog;
    MainMenu1: TMainMenu;
    File1: TMenuItem;
    Open1: TMenuItem;
    Save1: TMenuItem;
    N1: TMenuItem;
    Exit1: TMenuItem;
```

```
      Dialogs1: TMenuItem;
      Property1: TMenuItem;
      Icon1: TMenuItem;
      Options1: TMenuItem;
      PasteSpecial1: TMenuItem;
      InsertObject1: TMenuItem;
      N2: TMenuItem;
      SourceDoc1: TMenuItem;
      OleClassName1: TMenuItem;
      LinkToFile1: TMenuItem;
      Panel1: TPanel;
      ListBox1: TListBox;
      Panel2: TPanel;
      OleContainer1: TOleContainer;
      ReturnMode: TMenuItem;
      procedure bOpenClick(Sender: TObject);
      procedure bSaveClick(Sender: TObject);
      procedure bGetPropertyDialogClick(Sender: TObject);
      procedure bIconDialogClick(Sender: TObject);
      procedure FormCreate(Sender: TObject);
      procedure Exit1Click(Sender: TObject);
      procedure MenuClick(Sender: TObject);
      procedure PasteSpecial1Click(Sender: TObject);
      procedure InsertObject1Click(Sender: TObject);
      procedure SourceDoc1Click(Sender: TObject);
      procedure OleClassName1Click(Sender: TObject);
      procedure LinkToFile1Click(Sender: TObject);
      procedure ReturnModeClick(Sender: TObject);
    private
      procedure FillMenu;
    end;

var
  Form1: TForm1;

implementation

{$R *.DFM}

procedure TForm1.FormCreate(Sender: TObject);
begin
  OpenDialog1.InitialDir := ExtractFilePath(ParamStr(0));
  SaveDialog1.InitialDir := ExtractFilePath(ParamStr(0));
end;

procedure TForm1.bOpenClick(Sender: TObject);
begin
  OpenDialog1.Filter := 'OleObject¦*.ole';
  if OpenDialog1.Execute then begin
    OleContainer1.LoadFromFile(OpenDialog1.FileName);
    ListBox1.Items := OleContainer1.ObjectVerbs;
    ListBox1.Items.Insert(0, 'Items added to Options Menu');
    ListBox1.Items.Insert(1, '------');
    FillMenu;
  end;
end;
```

continues

Listing 28.1. continued

```
///////////////////////////////////////
// Name: FillMenu
//    While loop: Delete Existing items under Options Menu
//    For loop: Add new items from list of OLE verbs to Options menu.
///////////////////////////////////////
procedure TForm1.FillMenu;
const
  Stub: string = 'MyItem';
var
  Temp: TMenuItem;
  i: Integer;
begin
  while MainMenu1.Items[2].Count > 0 do begin
    Temp := MainMenu1.Items[2].Items[0];
    MainMenu1.Items[2].Delete(0);
    Temp.Free;
  end;

  for i := 0 to OleContainer1.ObjectVerbs.Count - 1 do begin
    Temp := NewItem(OleContainer1.ObjectVerbs[i], 0, False, True,
                    MenuClick, 0, Stub + IntToStr(i));
    Temp.Tag := i;
    MainMenu1.Items[2].Insert(MainMenu1.Items[2].Count, Temp);
  end;
end;

// Called by temp items added to options menu
procedure TForm1.MenuClick(Sender: TObject);
begin
  OleContainer1.DoVerb(TMenuItem(Sender).Tag);
end;

procedure TForm1.bSaveClick(Sender: TObject);
begin
  if SaveDialog1.Execute then
    OleContainer1.SaveToFile(SaveDialog1.Filename);
end;

procedure TForm1.bGetPropertyDialogClick(Sender: TObject);
begin
  OleContainer1.ObjectPropertiesDialog
end;

procedure TForm1.bIconDialogClick(Sender: TObject);
begin
  OleContainer1.ChangeIconDialog;
end;

procedure TForm1.PasteSpecial1Click(Sender: TObject);
begin
  OleContainer1.PasteSpecialDialog;
  FillMenu;
end;

procedure TForm1.InsertObject1Click(Sender: TObject);
begin
```

```
    OleContainer1.InsertObjectDialog;
    FillMenu;
end;

procedure TForm1.LinkToFile1Click(Sender: TObject);
begin
    OpenDialog1.Filter := 'Common OLE File Types (*.avi, *.bmp, *.doc, *.wav '+
                          ' |*.avi;*.doc;*.wav;*.bmp';
    if OpenDialog1.Execute then begin
        OleContainer1.CreateLinkToFile(OpenDialog1.FileName, False);
        FillMenu;
    end;
end;

procedure TForm1.SourceDoc1Click(Sender: TObject);
begin
    ShowMessage(OleContainer1.SourceDoc);
end;

procedure TForm1.OleClassName1Click(Sender: TObject);
begin
    ShowMessage(OleContainer1.OleClassName);
end;

procedure TForm1.ReturnModeClick(Sender: TObject);
begin
    OleContainer1.Close;
end;

procedure TForm1.Exit1Click(Sender: TObject);
begin
    Close;
end;

end.
```

To create the preceding program, begin by dropping a TOleContainer component onto a form. You can wait until runtime to access the properties of the component, or you can right-click on it to bring up the InsertObject or PasteSpecial OLE dialogs. Both of these dialogs are part of the operating system, and Delphi merely accesses them to give you, or your users, access to their features. The InsertObject dialog is shown in Figure 28.1, and the PasteSpecial Dialog is shown in Figure 28.2.

If you choose the InsertObject dialog, you can select an application from the list supplied to you. If this dialog box is blank, no servers are available on your system. Otherwise, you can select an object, click OK, and bingo, you have written an OLE application. Now all you need to do is run the application and double-click the object whenever you want to activate it. Notice that the InsertObject dialog also enables you to browse for a file. You can use this option with WordPad files, BMP files, WAV files, or other file types supported by an OLE server.

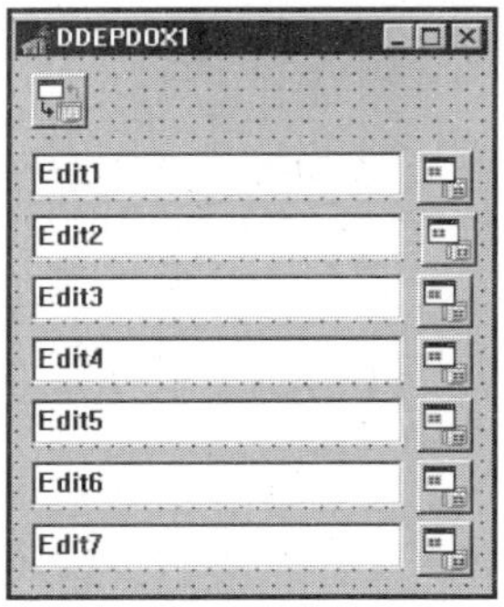

FIGURE 28.1.

The InsertObject dialog in action.

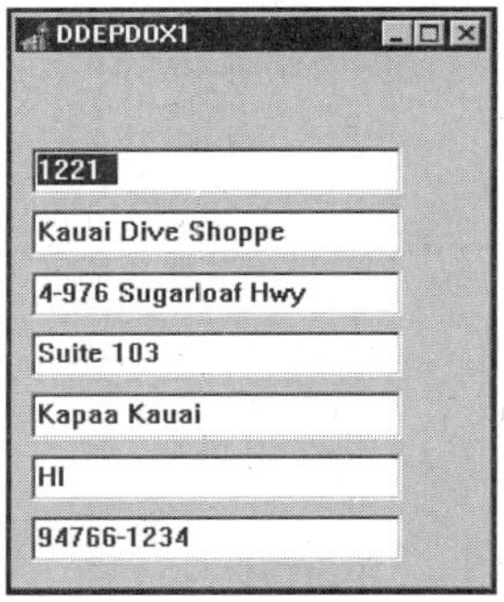

FIGURE 28.2.

The PasteSpecial dialog in action.

To use the PasteSpecial dialog, you should first run an OLE-aware application such as Write or WordPad. Enter some text in the application, copy it to the Clipboard, and return to Delphi. Now select the PasteSpecial dialog using the right mouse button. The type of the item stored in the Clipboard appears in the dialog, and you can first select it and then access it by clicking the OK button.

All the functionality of the InsertObject and PasteSpecial dialogs is available to you at runtime. However, I want to cover a few more general topics before discussing how to use the properties and methods of a TOleContainer.

After you right-click the TOleContainer object and select a server, the application you choose automatically starts up. If you select Paintbrush, for instance, you can draw a picture inside that application, select Return to form1 from Paintbrush's menu, and return to your Delphi application, which now contains a copy of your drawing. If you run the Delphi application, you find that you can begin modifying the painting at runtime just by double-clicking it.

Some servers, such as Paradox, Excel, and Word, are capable of providing in-place activation. To take advantage of that feature, simply place a menu component onto your form, fill in one or two items, drop down an OLEContainer, set the AllowInPlace property to True, and attach to one of these applications using the InsertObject or PasteSpecial dialogs. Run the application and double-click the OLEContainer. The menu in your application then takes on the appearance of the application to which you are linked. Two examples of the OleObj1 program using in-place activation are shown in Figures 28.3 and 28.4.

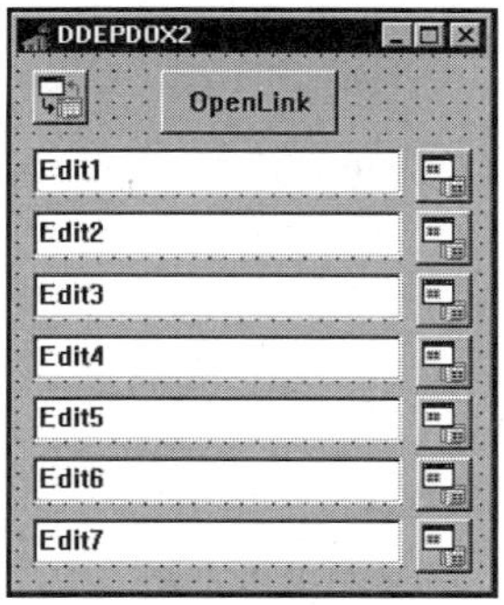

FIGURE 28.3.

The OleObj1 program uses in-place activation to perform a mind-meld with the Paint program.

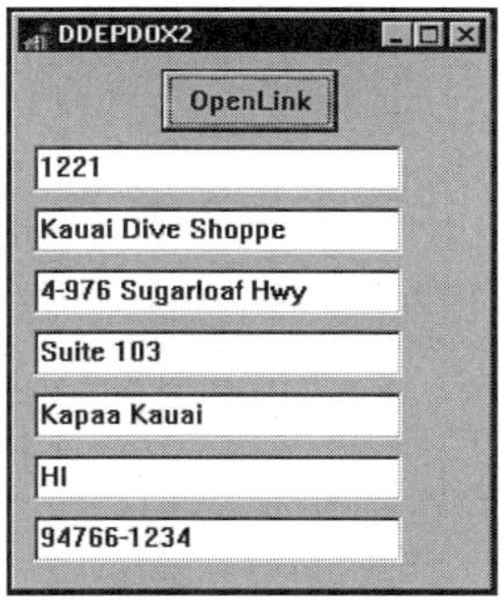

FIGURE 28.4.

The OleObj1 program and Word for Windows achieve digitalized holistic bliss through in-place activation.

In Windows 95, several available servers are small enough to use in-place activation to good purpose even on computers that have the minimal Win32 allotment of 16 MB of RAM. For instance, you can have a good deal of fun embedding Paintbrush into a Delphi application. (Remember the days when 256 KB of RAM seemed like a lot?)

Using *TOleContainer* at Runtime

You can use a TOleContainer object at runtime in three different ways. You can pop up a PasteSpecial dialog, you can pop up an InsertObject dialog, or you can link directly to an existing file. Each of these techniques is shown in the following simple methods:

```
procedure TForm1.PasteSpecial1Click(Sender: TObject);
begin
  OleContainer1.PasteSpecialDialog;
  FillMenu;
end;
```

```
procedure TForm1.InsertObject1Click(Sender: TObject);
begin
  OleContainer1.InsertObjectDialog;
  FillMenu;
end;

procedure TForm1.LinkToFile1Click(Sender: TObject);
begin
  OpenDialog1.Filter := 'Common OLE File Types (*.avi, *.bmp, *.doc, *.wav '+
                        ' ¦*.avi;*.doc;*.wav;*.bmp';
  if OpenDialog1.Execute then begin
    OleContainer1.CreateLinkToFile(OpenDialog1.FileName, False);
    FillMenu;
  end;
end;
```

Just a glance at these techniques tells you that there is nothing tricky about using either the `PasteSpecialDialog` or `InsertObjectDialog` functions. A simple call to either of these routines is all it takes to start using an OLE object at runtime. You can also open up an existing OLE file type and insert it into the `TOleContainer`. To do so, just pop up a `TOpenDialog`, select a file, and then pass it to the `CreateLinkToFile` method of `TOleContainer`. `CreateLinkToFile` takes two parameters; the first specifies the filename you want to use, and the second specifies whether you want the object to appear as an icon.

> **NOTE**
>
> You cannot just insert any file type into a `TOleContainer`. Instead, you must specify a file that is associated by the system with an OLE server. To find out what applications on your system are OLE servers, all you need do is open the InsertObject dialog. All the registered servers on your system appear in that dialog. Most of these servers have file types associated with them. For instance, BMP files are associated with Paint, DOC files are associated with WordPad or Word, AVI files are associated with MPLAYER.EXE, and so on. To find out more about file types and their associated applications, open the Windows Explorer, choose View | Options, and turn to the File Types page.

The `FillMenu` command shown in the preceding routines is local to the OleObj1 program. It takes the verbs supported by the current OLE object and displays them in the Options menu for the program. The code that displays the menu will not work correctly unless you have at least three top-level menuitems.

> **NOTE**
>
> The verbs associated with an OLE object describe the actions that you can ask the object to perform. The two most common and easiest-to-understand verbs are `Play` and `Edit`. If you work with the MPlayer application, for instance, you might ask it to

Play a file. Conversely, if you are working with Paint, you might ask it to Edit a file.

The verbs associated with an OLE server are registered with the system and can be viewed using the REGEDIT.EXE program. Go to the Run menu on the Taskbar and launch RegEdit. Open up HKEY_CLASSES_ROOT and search for the mplayer entry. Open up this entry as follows:

```
HKEY_CLASSES_ROOT/mplayer/protocol/StdFileEditing/verb
```

The verbs listed at this location are Edit, Play and Open. You can ask MPlayer to perform these actions when it is embedded or linked in your Delphi application.

After you have inserted an object into your TOleContainer, you can right-click it to see a list of the verbs supported by that object. As a rule, most objects support verbs such as Open, Play, or Edit. If you want to get a list of these verbs so that you can display them to the user, access the TOleContainer.ObjectVerbs array property.

The OleObj1 program does two different things with the verbs from the TOleContainer object:

- It inserts them into a listbox at the bottom of the program.
- It inserts them into the Options pop-up menu of the TMainMenu for the program.

Here is the code that inserts the verbs into a listbox:

```
ListBox1.Items := OleContainer1.ObjectVerbs;
```

Once again, this code is extremely simple to use. It takes advantage of the fact that ObjectVerbs and TListBox.Items are both instances of the TStrings object. Because of their mutual heritage, you can simply copy the string collection back and forth between the two objects.

The process of inserting these strings into the menu and then accessing them from an event handler is a little trickier:

```
procedure TForm1.FillMenu;
const
  Stub: string = 'MyItem';
var
  Temp: TMenuItem;
  i: Integer;
begin
  while MainMenu1.Items[2].Count > 0 do begin
    Temp := MainMenu1.Items[2].Items[0];
    MainMenu1.Items[2].Delete(0);
    Temp.Free;
  end;

  for i := 0 to OleContainer1.ObjectVerbs.Count - 1 do begin
    Temp := NewItem(OleContainer1.ObjectVerbs[i], 0, False, True,
                MenuClick, 0, Stub + IntToStr(i));
```

```
    Temp.Tag := i;
    MainMenu1.Items[2].Insert(MainMenu1.Items[2].Count, Temp);
  end;
end;

// Called by temp items added to options menu
procedure TForm1.MenuClick(Sender: TObject);
begin
  OleContainer1.DoVerb(TMenuItem(Sender).Tag);
end;
```

The preceding code first deletes any submenuitems that might be associated with the Options menu. It then iterates through all the verbs associated with the currently selected OLE server and uses the NewItem function from MENUS.PAS to create a menuitem for each one of them. Each menuitem has its Tag field set to the ordinal number associated with a particular verb. The code also associates each menuitem's OnClick event with the MenuClick method of TForm1.

Here is the declaration for NewItem:

```
function NewItem(
  const ACaption: string;   // Caption for menuitem
  AShortCut: TShortCut;     // Shortcut keys
  AChecked: Boolean;        // Is it checked?
  AEnabled: Boolean;        // Is it enabled?
  AOnClick: TNotifyEvent;   // What event is called if users selects it.
hCtx: Word;                 // The help context
  const AName: string       // The name of the new objects
): TMenuItem;               // Returns a newly created TMenuItem.
```

Most of this declaration is straightforward, with the possible exception of the AOnClick parameter. This parameter is a pointer to the method that will be called if the user clicks on the menuitem. It is the same method that is automatically associated with a menuitem if you double-click on it in design mode.

The MenuClick method passed in the AOnClick field of NewItem calls the DoVerb method of TOleContainer. DoVerb takes a single integer as a parameter. Each verb used by an OLE server has an ordinal number associated with it, where the first number is zero, and each successive verb has the next consecutive ordinal number. For instance, a typical OLE server might have the following numbers associated with it:

```
Play = 0
Edit = 1
Open = 2
```

Given these verbs, you could call DoVerb(0) to have the currently selected OLE server play the currently selected file. The key point to remember in the preceding code is that the Tag field of each newly created TMenuItem has the ordinal number associated with a particular command stored in it.

TOleContainer, File IO, and Scaling

Another important functionality of the TOleContainer object is the capability to save an object to a file:

```
procedure TForm1.bSaveClick(Sender: TObject);
begin
  if SaveDialog1.Execute then
    OleContainer1.SaveToFile(SaveDialog1.Filename);
end;
```

If you inserted a bitmap file into a TOleContainer object using the InsertObject dialog, you can save that object to disk using the preceding code. The filename you use is totally up to your particular tastes, though in the example found on disk I chose to save all the sample OLE objects with the letters "OLE" as an extension.

To read one of these files back in, all you need to do is call the LoadFromFile method of TOleContainer, as follows:

```
procedure TForm1.bOpenClick(Sender: TObject);
begin
  OpenDialog1.Filter := 'OleObject¦*.ole';
  if OpenDialog1.Execute then begin
    OleContainer1.LoadFromFile(OpenDialog1.FileName);
    ListBox1.Items := OleContainer1.ObjectVerbs;
    ListBox1.Items.Insert(0, 'Items added to Options Menu');
    ListBox1.Items.Insert(1, '------');
    FillMenu;
  end;
end;
```

This code goes a little further than it needs to, in that it not only reads the file into the TOleContainer, but it also shows the available verbs in a listbox to the user. It then calls the FillMenu method, shown previously, to add these verbs to the menu. You do not have to add code that shows the verbs to the user, but it is a nice touch for most applications. The ability to access the object's verbs through a right-click on the object is part of the default behavior of the TOleContainer object.

I should also mention the SizeMode property. You can set this property to the following values: smAutoSize, smCenter, smClip, smScale, and smStretch. Each of these values changes the way the object appears on your form before it is activated.

As I said previously, the TOleContainer object has been vastly improved in this version of Delphi. You will find that the object differs in many respects from the TOleContainer object found in the first version of the product. This is one of the very few places where there are differences between components that appear in both the first and second versions of Delphi. However, the changes to TOleContainer are so overwhelmingly positive that complaining about this major revitalization of a previously rather unimportant component would be hard.

This overview of Delphi and OLE has touched on the key methods and properties of TOleContainer. I have not, however, discussed a number of TOleContainer methods and properties at all. In particular, if you are interested in the inner workings of OLE, you should spend time viewing the OLECNTRS.PAS file, which ships with Delphi. It contains the source for the TOleContainer object, as well as implementations of the IOleClientSite, IOleInplaceSite, and IAdviseSink.

> **NOTE**
>
> One of the most important aspects of Delphi 2.0's OLE implementation is that the COM objects used to build it are on display in the Delphi RTL source. Most of these objects are almost unbelievably small when considering the complexity of the subject involved. Reading the key Delphi OLE source files such as OLE2.PAS, OLECNTRS.PAS, OLEAUTO.PAS, and OLECTRLS.PAS offers one of the most enlightening tutorials on OLE that I have seen anywhere. This body of objects and routines represents the best and most readable implementation of OLE that I have seen in any language, and also represents one of the most sophisticated and well-designed pieces of Object Pascal code in existence.

In the following chapters, you see more technical explanations of OLE functionality such as automation, structured storage, the Component Object Model, and the Games SDK. However, the material shown so far in this chapter should help to introduce you to Delphi 2.0's sophisticated implementation of OLE technology. The DDE code shown in the following sections of this chapter is not nearly as important as the OLE code by which it is surrounded. However, this material is still worth examining, particularly if you think you will be using DDE in your own programs.

Using DDE

In the rest of this chapter, you see two paired projects: one called CLIENT1.DPR and the second called SERVER1.DPR. The first application requests data; the second application supplies data. The technical terms for these two types of applications are, respectively, *client applications* and *server applications*.

> **NOTE**
>
> You should check the Unleashed CD for additional DDE examples that were discussed in some depth in the original edition of this book. You also find introductory material on DDE that I cut from this edition of the book. The text is stored in a Word 7.0 file called DDECUT.DOC. I made the cut on the grounds that the material's length alone

put too much emphasis on a technology, DDE, that does not play a very important role in the strategic vision of Delphi 2.0.

Simple DDE Servers

To create a DDE server, start a new project and then drop a TDDEServerConv and a TDDEServerItem on to the default form. Other than playing with the Object Inspector for a moment, that's all you need to do to build the simplest possible Delphi DDE server.

> **NOTE**
>
> The SIMPSERV and SIMPCLI example programs discussed in this section are on the CD in the SIMPDDE directory. Neither of them need to contain any code, so I won't provide the traditional listings in this section. In this case and in the programs shown in the next section, I have broken a convention and placed two projects in a single directory. I have done this because you want to be able to load the server automatically from the client application. To do that, the server needs to be in the current directory or on the path. The former of these two options was more convenient in this case. To make this system work, I named the form for the SIMPSERV application MAINS and the form for the SIMPCLI application MAINC. I follow the same convention in the Client1 and Server1 example. The programs I am about to describe, however, are so simple that I wouldn't bother with the disk versions unless you are having trouble creating the connection due to the general quirkiness of DDE technology.

A server application needs to publish three pieces of information:

- A service name
- A topic name
- An item name

In Delphi, it's easy to specify this information:

- To publish a service name, give your project a name and save it to disk. The name of your application automatically becomes the service name.
- To create a topic name, just assign a name to your TDDEServerConv component, or keep the default.
- The item names that your application uses are the names you assign to the TDDEServerItem components on the server form. Set the name property of the TDDEServerItem component to a meaningful string of your own choice, or keep the default name. Set the ServerConv property to the name of the DDEServerConv that's on the same form.

To try this system out, drop a TDDEServerConv and a TDDEServerItem on a form and save the application under the name SIMPSERV. To send information to a client application, you need to do nothing more than assign a string to the TDDEServerItem's Text property. For instance, you might write this:

```
DDEServerItem1.Text := '25';
```

If you want, you can simply fill in the Text field in the Object Inspector. If you follow this latter path, you will complete the server application after writing zero lines of code!

Because there is no code for this program, I instead show you the text for the DFM file. Remember that you can open any Delphi form in the code editor by right-clicking on the form and choosing View as Text from the pop-up menu that appears. In the SIMPSERV program, the resulting file looks like this:

```
object SimpleServer: TSimpleServer
  Left = 200
  Top = 99
  Width = 278
  Height = 97
  Caption = 'SimpleServer'
  Color = clLime
  Font.Color = clWindowText
  Font.Height = -13
  Font.Name = 'System'
  Font.Style = []
  OnCreate = FormCreate
  PixelsPerInch = 96
  TextHeight = 16
  object Edit1: TEdit
    Left = 120
    Top = 24
    Width = 121
    Height = 24
    TabOrder = 0
    Text = 'Edit1'
    OnChange = Edit1Change
  end
  object DdeServerItem1: TDdeServerItem
    ServerConv = DdeServerConv1
    Text = '25'
    Lines.Strings = (
      '25')
    Left = 56
    Top = 16
  end
  object DdeServerConv1: TDdeServerConv
    Left = 16
    Top = 16
  end
end
```

You don't have to spend a lot of time studying the DFM text translations shown in this section. I have included them because the Windows DDE technology can be a bit quirky at times and I don't want you wasting a lot of time wondering whether you have filled in the values correctly. If you are having trouble connecting, you can turn to these listings to be sure you have set everything up right; otherwise, I wouldn't bother with them unless you find them inherently interesting.

Any client that connects to the simple server shown previously can easily access the string you have assigned to DDEServerItem1.Text. You can begin creating a client that connects to this server by starting a new project and dropping a TDDEClientConv and TDDEClientItem onto a form along with a button labeled Connect. You can then associate the button with the following routine or else manipulate the proper fields in the Object Inspector:

```
procedure TForm1.ConnectClick(Sender: TObject);
begin
  DDEClientConv1.SetLink('SimpServ', 'DdeServerConv1');
  DDEClientItem1.DDEConv := DDEClientConv1;
  DDEClientItem1.DDEItem := 'DdeServerItem1';
  Label1.Caption := DDEClientItem1.Text;
end;
```

If you are unclear how to use the DDEService and DDETopic properties in the Object Inspector, you can read the DDECUT.DOC file found on disc for further information.

If you then place a label on the form for the client program, you can read values from the server by making the following assignments in a method:

```
Label1.Caption := DDEClient1Item1.Text;
```

That's all there is to it. Just follow those simple steps, either by writing code or by filling in the appropriate sections in the Object Inspector.

To test these programs, first launch the SimpServ project using the Windows Explorer. Then launch the SimpCli program either from the Windows Explorer or from inside Delphi. If you click the Connect button in the SimpCli program, the number specified in the server appears on the main form of the client. You can then use the edit control on the server to change this number, and it will be updated in the client each time you click the Connect button.

Another DDE Client and Server Example

The DDE client and server example shown in the preceding section is extremely simple. This section of the chapter provides a second example that has a little more substance to it.

To get started, create a new project and save it under the name SERVER1.DPR. Drop a TDDEServerConv and three TDDEServerItems onto the main form of the project. The name of the TDDEServerConv component should be set to BigServer, and the TDDEServerItem components are called Item1, Item2, and Item3. The code for the program is shown in Listing 28.2.

Listing 28.2. Server1 assigns strings from its edit controls to its DDEClientItem.Text field.

```
unit Mains;

{ Program copyright (c) 1996 by Charles Calvert }
{ Project Name: CLI-SERV }

interface

uses
  SysUtils, WinTypes, WinProcs,
  Messages, Classes, Graphics,
  Controls, Forms, Dialogs,
  DdeMan, StdCtrls;

type
  TServe1 = class(TForm)
    BigServer: TDdeServerConv;
    DDEItem1: TDdeServerItem;
    DDEItem2: TDdeServerItem;
    DDEItem3: TDdeServerItem;
    Label1: TLabel;
    Edit1: TEdit;
    Edit2: TEdit;
    Edit3: TEdit;
    Memo1: TMemo;
    procedure DDEItem1PokeData(Sender: TObject);
    procedure BigServerExecuteMacro(Sender: TObject; Msg: TStrings);
    procedure Edit1Change(Sender: TObject);
    procedure FormCreate(Sender: TObject);
  end;

var
  Serve1: TServe1;

implementation

{$R *.DFM}

procedure TServe1.DDEItem1PokeData(Sender: TObject);
begin
  case TDDEServerItem(Sender).Tag of
    0: Edit1.Text := DDEItem1.Text;
    1: Edit2.Text := DDEItem2.Text;
    2: Memo1.Lines := DDEItem3.Lines;
  end;
end;
```

```
procedure TServe1.BigServerExecuteMacro(Sender: TObject; Msg: TStrings);
var
  i: Integer;
  S: string;
begin
  S := Msg.Strings[0];
  if S = 'Clear' then begin
    for i := 0 to ComponentCount - 1 do
      if (Components[i] is TEdit) or (Components[i] is TMemo) then
        TEdit(Components[i]).Clear;
    PostMessage(Edit1.Handle, wm_KeyDown, 32, 0);
    PostMessage(Edit1.Handle, wm_KeyDown, vk_Back, 0);
  end else
    Close;
end;

procedure TServe1.Edit1Change(Sender: TObject);
begin
  DDEItem1.Text := Edit1.Text;
  DDEItem2.Text := Edit2.Text;
  DDEItem3.Text := Edit3.Text;
end;

procedure TServe1.FormCreate(Sender: TObject);
begin
  MoveWindow(Handle, 1, 1, Width, Height, False);
end;

end.
```

I talk about the DDE code in Server1 later in this chapter. However, you should notice the call to MoveWindow in the FormCreate method. MoveWindow is a Windows API call that moves a window from one place on the screen to another. You can simultaneously move the upper-left corner of the window and change the window's width and height. In this case, I don't want to change the dimensions of the window, so I simply pass in the existing Height and Width properties. However, I specify 1,1 as the coordinates for the upper-left corner. This moves the window to the top of the monitor so that you can have enough screen real estate to display both the Server1 and Client1 applications at the same time.

The Server1 application is meant to work in conjunction with the Client1 program. Both programs are saved in the CLI-SERV subdirectory. The code for the Client1 program is shown in Listings 28.4 through 28.9.

Client1 has three labels that correspond to the edit controls in Server1. Whenever the user types in any of Server1's edit controls, the keystrokes are sent immediately to Client1 and displayed in its labels.

Listing 28.3. The Client1 application has means for receiving information from the server and for sending information back.

```
unit Mainc1;

interface

{ Program copyright (c) 1995 by Charles Calvert }
{ Project Name: CLI-SERV }

{
  Every call to LoadResource needs to be followed
  by a call to FreeResource. Also, LockResource is
  paired with UnLockResource. I provide examples
  below that demonstrate how this works.
}

uses
  Windows, Messages, SysUtils,
  Classes, Graphics, Controls,
  Forms, Dialogs, DdeMan,
  StdCtrls, Buttons, ExtCtrls,
  Menus;

type
  TForm1 = class(TForm)
    MainMenu1: TMainMenu;
    Options1: TMenuItem;
    Clear1: TMenuItem;
    Close1: TMenuItem;
    Panel1: TPanel;
    Label1: TLabel;
    Label2: TLabel;
    Label3: TLabel;
    Label4: TLabel;
    Label5: TLabel;
    Label6: TLabel;
    Poke1: TBitBtn;
    Poke2: TBitBtn;
    Poke3: TBitBtn;
    Conv1: TDdeClientConv;
    Client1: TDdeClientItem;
    Client2: TDdeClientItem;
    Client3: TDdeClientItem;
    procedure FormCreate(Sender: TObject);
    procedure FormDestroy(Sender: TObject);
    procedure Poke1Click(Sender: TObject);
    procedure Poke2Click(Sender: TObject);
    procedure Poke3Click(Sender: TObject);
    procedure Clear1Click(Sender: TObject);
    procedure Close1Click(Sender: TObject);
    procedure Client1Change(Sender: TObject);
  private
    { Private declarations }
    Resource: THandle;
  public
    { Public declarations }
  end;
```

```
var
  Form1: TForm1;

implementation

{$R *.DFM}
{$R MILTON1.RES}

procedure TForm1.FormCreate(Sender: TObject);
begin
  Conv1.SetLink('Server1', 'BigServer');
  Client1.DDEItem := 'DDEItem1';
  Client2.DDEItem := 'DDEItem2';
  Client3.DDEItem := 'DDEItem3';
  Resource := LoadResource(hInstance,
              FindResource(hInstance, 'Milton', 'TEXT'));
end;

procedure TForm1.FormDestroy(Sender: TObject);
begin
  FreeResource(Resource);
end;

procedure TForm1.Poke1Click(Sender: TObject);
begin
  Conv1.PokeData('DDEItem1', 'Sammy Swim''s back!');
end;

procedure TForm1.Poke2Click(Sender: TObject);
var
  S: string;
begin
  S := '';
  InputQuery('Talk to a DDE Server', 'Enter Data to Poke', S);
  Conv1.PokeData('DDEItem2', PChar(S));
end;

procedure TForm1.Poke3Click(Sender: TObject);
var
  Poem: PChar;
begin
  Poem := PChar(LockResource(Resource));
  Conv1.PokeData('DDEItem3', Poem);
  UnLockResource(Resource);
end;

procedure TForm1.Clear1Click(Sender: TObject);
begin
  Conv1.ExecuteMacro('Clear', True);
end;

procedure TForm1.Close1Click(Sender: TObject);
begin
  Conv1.ExecuteMacro('Close', True);
end;

procedure TForm1.Client1Change(Sender: TObject);
begin
```

continues

Listing 28.3. continued

```
  Label1.Caption := Client1.Text;
  Label4.Caption := Client2.Text;
  Label6.Caption := Client3.Text;
end;

end.
```

Listing 28.4 shows a text file called MILTON.TXT.

Listing 28.4. Client1 has a second custom resource made up of a single long string stored in text file called MILTON.TXT.

```
From Paradise Lost
by John Milton

From Book I
===========
Of man's first disobedience, and the fruit
Of that forbidden tree, whose mortal taste
Brought death into the world, and all our woe,
With loss of Eden, till one greater Man
Restore us, and regain the blissful seat,
Sing Heav'nly Muse, that on the secret top
Of Oreb, or of Sinai, didst inspire
That shepherd who first taught the chosen seed
In the beginning how the heav'ns and earth
Rose out of Chaos; or if Sion hill
Delight thee more, and Siloa's brook that flowed
Fast by the oracle of God, I thence
Invoke thy aid to my advent'rous song,
That with no middle flight intends to soar
Above th' Aonian mount, while it pursues
Things unattempted yet in prose or rhyme.

From Book IX
============
To whom the Tempter guilefully replied:
"Indeed? Hath God then said that of the fruit
Of all these garden trees ye shall not eat,
Yet lords declared of all in earth or air?"
To whom thus Eve yet sinless: "Of the fruit
Of each tree in the garden we may eat,
But of the fruit of this fair tree amidst
The garden, God hath said, 'Ye shall not eat
Thereof, nor shall ye touch it, lest ye die.'"
...
The Tempter all impassioned thus began:
"O sacred, wise, and wisdom giving Plant,
Mother of Science, now I feel thy power
Within me clear, not only to discern
Things in their causes, but to trace the ways
Of highest agents, deemed however wise.
```

```
... If they all things, who enclosed
Knowledge of good and evil in this tree,
That whoso eats thereof, forthwith attains
Wisdom without their leave? And wherein lies
Th' offense, that man should thus attain to know?
What can your knowledge hurt him, or this tree
Impart against his will, if all be his?
Or is it envy, and can envy dwell
In heav'nly breasts? These, these and many more
Causes import your need of this fair fruit.
Goddess humane, reach then, and freely taste!"
```

Listing 28.5 shows the RC file for MILTON.TXT.

Listing 28.5. Here is the RC file that holds the resource stored in MILTON.TXT.

```
/*    From Paradise Lost    */
Milton TEXT milton.txt
```

Listing 28.6. Here is the RC file for creating CLIENT1.RES.

```
/*    Client1 Icon    */
Icon ICON "client1.ico"
```

Listing 28.7. Here is a batch file for creating the Client1 and Server1 programs from the command line.

```
@echo off
echo *********************************
echo You must create and properly edit
echo a DCC.CFG file before running this
echo macro. Search in this directory
echo for an example DCC.CFG file.
echo *********************************
brcc32 -r client1.rc
brcc32 -r milton1.rc
dcc32 /b server1.dpr
dcc32 /b client1.dpr
```

Listing 28.8. Here is a sample configuration file for the command-line compiler. It is called DCC.CFG.

```
/Uc:\delphi32\lib
/Rc:\delphi32\lib
```

The Client1 program has two parts to it. The first part shows off DDE techniques such as exchanging data, poking data, and sending macros. The second part shows how to use a RES file with Delphi and how to compile from the command line. I treat these two parts in two different sections, with the DDE code handled first.

The Server1 form sports three edit controls. The OnChange event for these controls looks like this:

```
procedure TForm1.Edit1Change(Sender: TObject);
begin
  Item1.Text := Edit1.Text;
  Item2.Text := Edit2.Text;
  Item3.Text := Edit3.Text;
end;
```

Whenever the user types anything in these edit controls, the DDEServItem components, called Item1, Item2, and Item3, reflect these changes in their Text property.

At the other end, the Client1 program has three labels. Whenever any of the DDEClientItems record an OnChange event, the following method gets called:

```
procedure TForm1.DdeClientItem1Change(Sender: TObject);
begin
  Label1.Caption := DDEClientItem1.Text;
  Label4.Caption := DDEClientItem2.Text;
  Label6.Caption := DDEClientItem3.Text;
end;
```

This code transfers the information from the server into the labels on the form of the client program. The changes take place letter by letter as you type them, so it appears that you are typing in two places at once.

When you want to send data from a client back to a server, you can do so through two different means: by poking and by executing a macro. The Client1 program has three different methods that poke data into the Server1 application:

```
procedure TClientOne.Poke1Click(Sender: TObject);
begin
  Conv1.PokeData('DDEItem1', 'Finny Fun');
end;

procedure TClientOne.Poke2Click(Sender: TObject);
var
  S: string;
begin
  S := '';
  InputQuery('Talk to a DDE Server', 'Enter Data to Poke', S);
  Conv1.PokeData('DDEItem2', PChar(S));
end;
procedure TClientOne.Poke3Click(Sender: TObject);
var
  Poem: PChar;
begin
  Poem := PChar(LockResource(Resource));
  Conv1.PokeData('DDEItem3', Poem);
end;
```

The `Poke1Click` method is the classic and simplest means of sending data from a client to a server. It calls a method of `TDDEClientConv` called `PokeData`. `PokeData` takes a string in the first parameter. This string specifies the name of the server item to which you want to send information. The second parameter is a `PChar` that holds the information you want to send. Delphi uses a `PChar` here rather than a string because you might need to send information longer than 256 characters, and because `PChar`s are the standard when you are passing information between an application and Windows.

The `Poke2Click` method follows the same pattern as `Poke1Click` except that it first asks the user for the string to send. Once the string is captured, it is translated into a `PChar` and sent to the second edit control in the Server1 program.

`Poke3Click` again uses `PokeData` to send information to Server1, but this time the information is the entire poem shown in Listing 28.5. The poem is first retrieved from the MILTON1.RES file via a mechanism to be explained in the next section, and then it is sent to Server1 and displayed in a memo.

> **NOTE**
>
> You can poke information to a server via either the `PokeData` method or the `PokeDataLines` method. `PokeDataLines` takes a `TStringList` or `TStrings` object as a parameter. You can use `PokeDataLines` if you want to send information from a memo, list box, or other `TStrings`-based component. Remember, however, that both `PokeData` and `PokeDataLines` can handle large chunks of data. Furthermore, recall that if you want to create the whole list on the fly, without the aid of a Delphi component, you should use a `TStringList`, not an instance of the abstract `TStrings` class.

On the server end, all this poking of information is handled by a single method, which is attached to the `OnPokeData` event of the `DDEServerItem` controls:

```
procedure TServe1.DDEItem1PokeData(Sender: TObject);
begin
  case TDDEServerItem(Sender).Tag of
    0: Edit1.Text := DDEItem1.Text;
    1: Edit2.Text := DDEItem2.Text;
    2: Memo1.Lines := DDEItem3.Lines;
  end;
end;
```

Note that the long poem sent by Client1 is automatically hung on a `TStrings` object so that it can be easily transferred to a memo or list box. I have set the `Tag` properties of the `DDEServerItems` to 0, 1, and 2.

To send a macro from the Client1 program to Server1, just call the `ExecuteMacro` function:

```
procedure TClientOne.Clear1Click(Sender: TObject);
begin
  Conv1.ExecuteMacro('Clear', True);
end;
```

```
procedure TClientOne.Close1Click(Sender: TObject);
begin
  Conv1.ExecuteMacro('Close', True);
end;
```

ExecuteMacro takes two parameters. The first is a string specifying the command you want to send. The second is a Boolean flag stating whether DDE should wait for the result of this macro to return before executing any more pokes or macros. It can be a mess if too many signals are flying back and forth between a server and a client at the same time, so it is generally best to set this flag to True.

> **NOTE**
>
> The commands used in the first parameter of the ExecuteMacro function are just strings that you can make up to suit your own sense of aesthetics. In other words, these aren't predefined commands—they are just strings you create to identify the various commands you might want to give to a server. If you create a server and then publish a list of commands that it obeys, you can go far toward creating a very easy-to-implement form of DDE Automation. Of course, if you are serious about this kind of functionality, and you are not tied to any legacy code, you should use OLE automation.

The following method appears in Server1 and is meant to handle the macro once it is sent. Note that this event occurs in response to the OnExecuteMarco event of the TDDEServerConv component:

```
procedure TServe1.BigServerExecuteMacro(Sender: TObject;
                                        Msg: TStrings);
var
  i: Integer;
  S: string;
begin
  S := Msg.Strings[0];
  if S = 'Clear' then begin
    for i := 0 to ComponentCount - 1 do
      if (Components[i] is TEdit) or (Components[i] is TMemo) then
        TEdit(Components[i]).Clear;
    PostMessage(Edit1.Handle, wm_KeyDown, 32, 0);
    PostMessage(Edit1.Handle, wm_KeyDown, vk_Back, 0);
  end else
    Close;
end;
```

There are two commands that Client1 can send to Server1. The first command is called 'Close', and Server1 responds to it by calling the VCL Close method. The second command comes in the form of the string 'Clear', and Server1 responds to it by clearing the text of any component of type TEdit or TMemo. I then notify the client that this event has occurred by creating a fake keyboard event: I insert a space character (#32) into Edit1 and then immediately delete the character. This latter move is a rather extreme kluge, but it does work. In fact, it works even in a different type of program where there might be text in one of the controls that needs to be preserved.

In this section, I have given a very brief overview of how to create DDE client and server applications. This discussion has made no attempt to be all-inclusive, and I have ignored material on using multiple Clipboard formats to transfer data. Some Clipboard concepts are demonstrated in the DDE demos that ship with Delphi. After seeing the brief examples in this chapter, you should have little trouble deciphering the extra material in the Delphi demos.

Compiling from the Command Line

In this section, I add a few notes on compiling from the command line using DCC32.EXE. This can be useful in examples such as this one, where you need to compile two separate projects before you can fully test the code in an example program.

Two important parameters that you can pass to DCC32.EXE tell whether to perform a make or a build:

```
/b: Rebuild all units.
/m: make sure all units are up to date.
```

To actually perform a compilation at the command line, you can enter a command that looks like this:

```
dcc32 /b MYPROG.DPR
```

MYPROG is the name of your application, and /b says you want to compile all the units in the project. Here are the commands for compiling Server1 and Client1:

```
dcc32 /b server1.dpr
dcc32 /b client1.dpr
```

Just passing in these lines doesn't always work. Delphi also needs to know where the units are that are listed in the program's uses clause. You can pass this information into DCC32 with special parameters like those shown, or you can place it in a separate text file labeled DCC32.CFG. On my system, a typical DCC32.CFG file looks like this:

```
/Uc:\delphi32\lib
/Rc:\delphi32\lib
```

/U marks the beginning of the line where I show the path to the main Delphi units, and /R shows the path to the main Delphi resources. If you have an additional location where you save files such as STRBOX.PAS or MATHBOX.PAS, you can add those to the preceding code using the same syntax used to build a DOS path:

```
/Uc:\delphi\lib;c:\delcode\units
/Rc:\delphi\lib;c:\delcode\resfiles
```

I keep my DCC32.CFG file in my DELPHI32\BIN subdirectory and also save a copy to a place where I store backup files.

> **NOTE**
>
> There are other options available for use as parameters to DCC32 and also for use inside DCC32.CFG files. If you want to pursue these valuable resources, just type DCC32 at the command line with no parameters. You can place any parameters you pass to DCC32 inside a CFG file and therefore have them implemented automatically. On the DCC32 command line, you can also specify the directory in which you keep the CFG file you want to use. As a result, you can specify different parameters in various CFG files and then pass only the directory of the CFG file to DCC32 (using the -T option).

Besides the options shown previously, other important parameters are as follows:

```
/v : Include debug info for the stand alone debugger
/gd : Create a detailed map file
/D : Define a conditional directive
/$R+ : Range checking on
```

You can use the $ syntax to define any of the compiler switches found in the Options | Project | Compiler page.

Working with Resources

It's important to remember why I have placed two resource files inside Client1. There is absolutely no reason why you can't put all your resources in one RES file. In other words, CLIENT1.RES can be expanded to store all the resources that you want to add to the Client1 program. However, Delphi has full claim to the CLIENT1.RES file, so it is necessary for you to have a second RES file that you alone manage. In short, I am showing you how to add a second RES file to a Delphi project so that you can have one that is created and managed by Delphi and a second that is defined only by the programmer.

To build this custom resource, place MILTON.TXT (included on the CD) in the same directory as the following small text file, which is called MILTON1.RC:

```
/*   From Paradise Lost    */
Milton TEXT milton.txt
```

This file compiles MILTON.TXT into an RES file. The type of resource being used here is labeled more or less at random as TEXT, and it is given the word Milton as an identifier so you can access it easily from inside Delphi.

The following code shows a simple DOS batch file you can run. It compiles the resources used by the Client1 program, as well as both the Server1 and Client1 executables:

```
Brcc32 -r client1.rc
brcc32 -r milton1.rc
```

```
dcc32 /b server1.dpr
dcc32 /b client1.dpr
```

Note that CLIENT1.RC will not compile successfully unless you have an icon called CLIENT1.ICO in the same directory. There is not really any need to build the CLIENT1.RES file, but I threw it in here just to remind you that you can control all parts of Delphi programs through code, if you so desire.

The CLIENT1.RES file is automatically linked into your program because of the `$R *.RES` line found in CLIENT1.DPR. However, you have to take special steps to link MILTON1.RES into your program. Specifically, you should add the following lines to MAINC.PAS:

```
{$R *.DFM}
{$R MILTON1.RES}
```

The line in question is the second of the two shown, where the first is merely meant as a clue as to where in the file the reference to MILTON1.RES should occur.

Working with the *LoadResource* API Call

Client1 declares a variable called `Resource` as type `THandle`. Variables of this type can be used to point to a resource loaded into a Windows program. To retrieve a resource, you need to call the `LoadResource` Windows API function, passing in the `HInstance` of your program in the first parameter and the handle of the resource you want to snag in the second parameter. `HInstance` is a predeclared variable filled out by Delphi and available to you at any time. To get the handle to the resource itself you need to call `FindResource`, passing in the name of the resource in the second parameter and its type in the third:

```
Resource := LoadResource(hInstance,
            FindResource(hInstance, 'Milton', 'TEXT'));
```

In the Client1 program I make the call to `LoadResource` in the `FormCreate` method. Notice that if you were trying to load a bitmap, you would call `LoadBitmap` rather than `LoadResource`.

Once you have loaded a resource into a program, you can retrieve the specific data you want by calling `LockResource`:

```
Poem := PChar(LockResource(Resource));
```

In this case, the resource is just a long string, so it is safe to typecast it as a `PChar` and then assign it to a variable called `poem`, which is declared to be of type `PChar`. Note, however, that nothing dictates that the resource in question has to be a string. Because this is a custom resource, you can load any kind of binary data this way, including a PCX file or an encrypted file.

I suppose the main theme of the last section is that Delphi can handle any of the resources that you would normally associate with a C++ or BP7 program. However, Delphi tries to stream-line this system by providing simple ways to handle most resources. For instance, remember that the Image Editor enables you to open RES files and store icons and bitmaps inside them.

Summary

In this chapter, you saw some of the basic features of OLE and DDE programming. In particular, you learned that both techniques enable you to link one process to another so they can interact dynamically at runtime. You have seen that DDE is really only a nascent part of a larger project that is reaching fruition in OLE. DDE is, however, still useful, in part because it enables you to support a wide range of legacy applications. You should not, however, decide on DDE as your core technology until you have first had a good hard look at OLE automation. Using DDE in any new application you are starting today would be very unusual. It is legacy code, meant to support legacy applications.

If DDE looks to the past, OLE and COM look to the future. Microsoft has hinted that they hold the seeds for future operating systems that will be based on an object-oriented architecture. Specifically, the various parts of the operating system will offer a COM interface that is similar to that offered by a Delphi object. Programmers will interact with these objects by gaining access to an interface and then calling the object's functions, as shown in Chapter 30, "COM Object Basics," and 31, "COM, Automation and Structured Storage." Microsoft has claimed that these new object-based operating systems will be more flexible and more configurable than DOS, Windows 3.1, or Windows 95.

As you have seen, the goal of the Delphi OLE implementation is to find practical ways to encapsulate complex technologies inside an easy-to-use interface. The code in this chapter covers powerful but easy-to-use Delphi objects that show the capabilities of OLE, but it teaches you little about how OLE actually works. The next few chapters, however, dig continually deeper into this technology, and end up laying a foundation on which you can build a deep understanding of OLE.

OLE Automation Basics

OLE automation enables you to control objects that reside in other applications and in DLLs. It works not only across application boundaries, but also across language boundaries. An OLE automation object written in Delphi can be used in C++ or in Visual Basic, and Visual Basic or C++ automation objects can be used in Delphi.

Many people feel that OLE automation and other key OLE technologies, such as OCXs, represent some of the most important developments in contemporary computing. This rapidly growing technology is only just starting to unfold. For instance, Microsoft promises that in the near future Distributed OLE will allow applications to control objects that reside on other computers. This means that you can access applications and individual objects that reside not only on your computer, not only on your network, but on any part of the Internet. It's at least conceivable to me that this change, or one similar to it, is likely to have the same overwhelming impact on computing that occurred with the introduction of the first PCs. In short, it's likely to change everything.

In this chapter you use high-level Delphi objects to create automation servers and clients. The actual act of creating automation servers and clients is not difficult. However, this technology has a number of implications that make the subject more complicated than it at first appears. As a result, this chapter also attempts to explain some of the key architectural guidelines needed to make this technological work on a large scale.

In particular, the following subjects are covered:

- Creating OLE objects with the `CreateOleObject` function
- Using variants to encapsulate OLE objects
- OLE servers, clients, in-process servers, and local servers
- Variant arrays
- Working with Word and Excel as automation servers
- The `Null` and `UnAssigned` global variables
- The `TAutomation`, `TAutoDispatch`, and `TAutoObject` Delphi objects
- Registering and unregistering servers

The subject matter for this chapter is so large that it carries over into Chapter 30, which features an explanation and example of an in-process server, as well as additional information on local servers.

This is a relatively challenging chapter, but it contains some of the most important material in the entire book. As a result, I have done my best to become the Hubble telescope of the technical writing world, struggling to make each issue as clear as possible, regardless of its distance from the mind's eye of the reader!

What Is OLE Automation?

OLE automation is a simple concept to grasp, and it's easy to implement in Delphi. It enables you to access objects that reside not in only your own program, but in other programs that reside on your system. In particular, you can access methods and properties of these objects, but not their raw data. The advent of distributed OLE will allow programmers to extend this same functionality so that it works across networked machines.

There are two major types of automation:

- Automation servers
- Automation clients

Automation servers provide functionality that can be accessed by automation clients. In other words, the application or DLL that hosts an object is called a *server*, and the application or DLL that accesses it is called a *client*. A single application or DLL can be both a server and a client.

Classic examples of OLE automation servers are Word for Windows and Excel. Both of these applications can be controlled by Delphi applications, or by other automation clients.

There are two types of OLE automation servers:

- In-process servers
- Local servers

In-process servers are DLLs that are loaded into your program's address space. *Local servers* are stand-alone executables that contain automation servers. Word for Windows is a classic example of a local server.

NOTE

You may have heard other names for automation clients, servers, in-process servers, and local servers. I've chosen to use these particular names because they seem to me to be the clearest of the terms I've heard. The one possible exception would be the use of the term "out-of-process server" instead of local server. Once Distributed OLE is released, however, there may be a need to distinguish between in-process servers, local servers, and remote servers. The term "out-of-process server," which seems clear now, might become ambiguous at that point.

In general, I consider the "Creating OLE Servers" section of the *Professional Features* manual for Visual Basic to be the closest thing we have to an OLE automation bible. I don't follow it slavishly, but I have read it carefully and try to follow its (usually well-thought-out and well-presented) viewpoint whenever possible. *Inside OLE* by Kraig

> Brockschmidt (Microsoft Press) also is valuable from a purely technical point of view, but it's hindered by one of the more peculiar and idiosyncratic writing styles I've ever encountered. It's an intelligent and spirited book, and a "must have" for serious OLE programmers, but it's not a good place to turn when you want plain talk about a complicated subject, or when you want to find clearly stated standards.

The main reason for creating an in-process server is to share an object written in one language with an application written in a second language. For instance, you can share Delphi objects with C++ and Visual Basic applications using this method.

OLE automation objects are not necessarily better than standard Delphi objects. For instance, if you did not need to move across language barriers, your DLL would be faster and easier to implement if you used straight Object Pascal code that did not use OLE services.

A Simple OLE Automation Client

The classic example of OLE automation involves controlling Word for Windows. If you have Word 6.x or Word 7.x on your system, you can access it from a Delphi application by entering the following code:

```
uses
  OleAuto;

procedure TForm1.Button1Click(Sender: TObject);
var
  V: Variant;
begin
  V := CreateOleObject('Word.Basic');
  V.Insert('Hello from Delphi');
end;
```

This code inserts the words "Hello from Delphi" into an existing Word document. You can find the code as OLEWord1 on the CD-ROM included with this book.

You must have Word up and running with a document open for this code to work. In a moment I show how to handle the situation where Word is not already up and running, but at first it's best to stick with the simplest possible case.

There are three key elements to the code shown above. The first is the OleAuto unit listed in the uses clause. This unit has all the key code for handling automation inside Delphi applications. If you want to get good at this subject, you should know that unit like the back of your hand.

The use of the variant V is one of the more important code fragments in Delphi 2.0 programming. Variants were introduced into Delphi because Microsoft uses them extensively in automation-based code. They are not a necessity for automation, but they make it much easier, given the OLE implementation provided by Microsoft. In other words, variants are important in Delphi not primarily as a technique for accessing strings or integers, but explicitly because OLE objects can be assigned to them:

```
V := CreateOleObject('Word.Basic');
```

The code shown above assigns the OLE object to variant V. The OLE object in question resides inside Word for Windows. In particular, it is an OLE automation server that resides inside Word. I discuss the assignment statement shown above in more depth in just one moment.

The third key element in the code is the call to the Word Basic Insert method:

```
V.Insert('Hello from Delphi');
```

This simple line of code is one of the most radical innovations in recent programming. Insert is not an Object Pascal method or function, nor is it part of the Windows API. It's part of Word for Windows, and you are able to call it directly from inside of a Delphi application due to the technology called OLE automation. In short, the closest you can get to the heart of OLE automation is the moment when you call a method or access a property by using a line of code like the insert statement shown above. This is what automation is all about, and the ability to make these calls is what is important in this technology.

NOTE

There currently is no way for Delphi to perform syntax checking on a call to an OLE method or property. Therefore, you could successfully compile code that looks like this, even though it will not perform correctly at runtime:

```
var
V: Variant;
begin
V := CreateOleObject('Word.Basic');
V.FormatDriveC;
end;
```

It happens that there is no FormatDriveC function in Word Basic. However, there is no way for Delphi to discern this fact at compile time, and so you will not get an error until you run the application. The whole issue of raising and handling errors in an OLE automation server or client is approached later in this chapter and in the next chapter.

Variants as OLE Objects

Creating an OLE automation client is not quite as simple as creating a "Hello World" application, but it's close. However, this simplicity hides a good deal of complexity. In particular, savvy programmers are bound to raise a collective eyebrow when they see the line that assigns a Variant to the return value of CreateOleObject. The next few paragraphs are dedicated to exploring this line of code.

Here is the record, found in SYSTEM.PAS, used to describe a Variant:

```
TVarData = record
  VType: Word;
  Reserved1, Reserved2, Reserved3: Word;
  case Integer of
    varSmallint: (VSmallint: Smallint);
    varInteger:  (VInteger: Integer);
    varSingle:   (VSingle: Single);
    varDouble:   (VDouble: Double);
    varCurrency: (VCurrency: Currency);
    varDate:     (VDate: Double);
    varOleStr:   (VOleStr: PWideChar);
    varDispatch: (VDispatch: Pointer);
    varError:    (VError: Integer);
    varBoolean:  (VBoolean: WordBool);
    varUnknown:  (VUnknown: Pointer);
    varByte:     (VByte: Byte);
    varString:   (VString: Pointer);
    varArray:    (VArray: PVarArray);
    varByRef:    (VPointer: Pointer);
end;
```

As I explained earlier, this variant record defines the possible types that can be expressed by a Variant.

NOTE

Remember that variant records and the Variant have nothing to do with one another, and the similarity in their names is just a coincidence.

Just for sake of clarity, let me spell out a few important points here. Variant records have nothing to do with the TVarData type. Instead, they are Object Pascal's take on the Unions you find in the C programming language. Here is an example of a commonly used variant record found in WINDOWS.PAS:

```
PRect = ^TRect;
TRect = record
case Integer of
0: (Left, Top, Right, Bottom: Integer);
1: (TopLeft, BottomRight: TPoint);
end;
```

This record can be interpreted as containing four integers or two TPoint records. The choice is yours, depending on the needs of the moment.

The issue here is that the record can have *varying* interpretations, depending on your whims. It is called, therefore, a variant record. This has absolutely nothing to do with the Variant type or the TVarData record. If you are confused about variant records, look them up in the online help under the subject "record types."

You can find out what kind of Variant you have by either typecasting the Variant as a TVarData and checking its VType field, or by calling the VarType function. In particular, if a Variant is fronting for an OLE object, its VType field is set to VarDispatch.

The following code fragment creates a pop-up message box containing the word "Yes":

```
V := CreateOleObject('Word.Basic');
If VarType(V) = VarDispatch then
  ShowMessage('Yes')
else
  ShowMessage('No');
```

It would display the word No if you tried to compare the VType field from TVarData with varByte, varString, and so on. In particular, what you are getting back is an oblique reference to an object of type IDispatch. If you want to get the IDispatch object itself, which is not recommended, here is how to proceed:

```
A := VarToInterface(V);
A.AddRef;
A.GetTypeInfoCount(i);
ShowMessage(IntToStr(i));
A.Release;
```

VarToInterface is implemented in the OleAuto unit. In particular, this function first checks to see if the Variant does, in fact, contain a valid IDispatch interface. If it does, it returns the interface by executing the following line of code:

```
Result := TVarData(V).VDispatch;
```

The code then goes on to call GetTypeInfoCount, a method of IDispatch, which usually returns the value 1.

Another function closely related to VarToInterface is VarToAutoObject. This routine returns, not an IDispatch interface, but the Delphi object used for manipulating IDispatch objects. In short, it returns the Delphi wrapper that is built around IDispatch. This wrapper is called TAutoObject, and you learn about it later in this chapter. When possible, you should use TAutoObject rather than raw IDispatch objects, because TAutoObject is much easier to use and much less likely to lead you down the dark path that leads to the Land of Embarrassing Programming Errors.

It is possible for a Variant to be set to the value UnAssigned or to Null. For instance, the following code is valid:

```
var
  MyVariant: Variant;
begin
  MyVariant := CreateOleObject('Word.Basic');
  // User defined code added here
  MyVariant := UnAssigned;
end;
```

The code shown here first obtains an OLE object and then releases it. You might use code like this to free an OLE object if you find that it is in an error state, or if you no longer need its services.

UnAssigned is a variable of type Variant that is preset to varEmpty during the initialization for the System unit:

```
TVarData(Unassigned).VType := varEmpty;
TVarData(Null).VType := varNull;
```

As you can see, Null also is a globally declared Variant that gets initialized to varNull before any of the code in your program is executed. A null Variant is used primarily in database applications to signify that there is no data associated with a particular field.

A null Variant has been initialized but is set to Null. An unassigned Variant has been set to varEmpty, which is one way of explicitly stating that it has not been initialized.

This matter is confusing enough to warrant a few explicit examples. Consider the following code fragment:

```
procedure TForm1.Button1Click(Sender: TObject);
var
  V: Variant;
begin
  if varType(V) = varNull then
    ShowMessage('Null');
  if varType(V) = varEmpty then
    ShowMessage('Unassigned');
end;
```

This example pops up a message box containing the word "Unassigned". It's guaranteed to do that, even though V is a local variable. In other words, Variants are automatically set to varEmpty when they first come in scope.

Consider the following example:

```
procedure TForm1.Button1Click(Sender: TObject);
var
  V: Variant;
begin
  V := Null;
  if varType(V) = varNull then
    ShowMessage('Null');
  V := Unassigned;
```

```
    if varType(V) = varEmpty then
       ShowMessage('Unassigned');
end;
```

This code pops up the word Null and then the word Unassigned. Notice that an unassigned Variant is actually set to varEmpty. There is no such thing as varUnassigned.

To add one final complication to this issue, you should remember that a Variant can also be set to varUnknown. VarUnknown is distinct from either varEmpty or varNull.

Automation and the Registry

When you call CreateOleObject, you pass it a string. This string contains something called a program ID, or ProgID. Word.Basic is the ProgID for the OLE automation server in Word for Windows. A ProgID is a string that can be looked up in the registry, and which references a CLSID. CLSIDs are statistically unique numbers that can be used by the operating system to reference an OLE object.

In this case, it's probably best if you visit the actual perpetrator in its native habitat, which is the registry. To get started, use the Run menu on the Windows Taskbar to launch the RegEdit program that ships with Windows 95 in the Windows subdirectory. Search through the HKEY_CLASSES_ROOT for the Word.Basic entry. When you find it, you can see that it's associated with the following CLSID:

```
{000209FE-0000-0000-C000-000000000046}
```

This is a unique class ID that is inserted into the registry of all machines that contain a valid, and properly installed, copy of Word for Windows. The only application that uses this ID is Word for Windows. It belongs uniquely to that application.

Now go further up HKEY_CLASSES_ROOT and look for the CLSID branch. Open it up and search for the CLSID shown above. When you find it, you can see two entries associated with it: one is called LocalServer, or LocalServer32, and the other is called ProgID. The ProgID is set to word.basic. The LocalServer entry looks something like this:

```
C:\WINWORD\WINWORD.EXE /Automation
```

If you take a look at this command, you can begin to grasp how Windows can translate the ProgID passed to CreateOleObject into the name of an executable.

Having these kinds of entries in the registration database does not mean that the applications in question are necessarily automation servers. For instance, there are many applications with LocalServer and ProgID entries that are not automation servers. However, all automation servers do have these two entries. Note, further, that this is a reference to the automation server in Word, and not a reference to Word as a generic application. It references an automation object inside of Word, and not Word itself.

When you call `CreateOleObject`, a number of complex things happen, some of which are explained in detail in this book. But from the 25,000-foot perspective, what happens is that Windows looks to see whether Word is loaded in memory. If Word is not loaded, `CreateOleObject` launches it, passing the command line shown above. `CreateOleObject`, however, automatically opens an empty document when it launches Word. Windows then finds an interface pointer to the OLE automation object requested, and returns that pointer in the form of the result of the call to `CreateOleObject`. Once again, you are not being returned a pointer to Word itself, but only a pointer to an object that resides in Word.

Once you have an interface (an `IDispatch` VMT) to the OLE automation object in Word, you can start calling the functions made available by the OLE automation object. In particular, any of the Word Basic functions found in the Word online Help are available to you. There are some 200 of these functions, and they include commands for opening documents, saving documents, formatting documents, printing documents, and so on. This means that if you have a Delphi 2.0 application and a copy of Word on your target systems, you need never implement any code for handling documents. You can let Word carry the whole burden. After all, Word is great at word processing, and now the entire application is in effect an extension of your Delphi application. This is, to put it mildly, what programmers mean when they talk about code reuse.

NOTE

There is some hope, but no certainty, that this system will spell the end of gargantuan applications such as Word. In the future, applications could consist of a series of OLE automation servers and OCXs, each linked together dynamically according to the needs of the moment.

In particular, you might find that your application needs the services of an editing kernel. Using OLE automation and type libraries, you could search the system for available editors, choose the one you want, and use it. You might then need the services of a printer object, and you could once again search for one and use it. There might be 10 or 15 different printer objects on the market, all supporting the same low-level automation API, but all implementing the API differently. Furthermore, with Distributed OLE, there may be no need for these objects to reside on your current system.

The whole idea of trying to copyright an interface to an application, *a la* Lotus/IBM, will become even more absurd than it is at this time. Part of the definition of a spreadsheet will be the standardized automation interface that it presents to other programs. It is not, however, even remotely clear as to whether or not the lawyers who have been arguing these cases have a clue as to the nature of the technology they are attempting to regulate. Nor is it clear at this time whether some influential companies might try to copyright their automation interfaces rather than presenting them as a standard to which all entries in a particular market should adhere.

Running an Automation Server in the Background

`CreateOleObject` will start Word, but it won't open a blank document for you. The first example of using Word as an automation server assumed that Word was already running, and that it contained an open document into which text could be inserted. But what if Word isn't running? What if you want to start a new document? How should you proceed?

If you want to insert something into a document when Word is shut down, you could use the following code (which features a quote from the Tao te Ching):

```
procedure TForm1.Button1Click(Sender: TObject);
begin
  V := CreateOleObject('Word.Basic');
  V.FileNew('Normal');
  V.Insert('The mark of a healthy mind' + #13);
  V.Insert('is freedom from its own ideas.');
  V.FileSaveAs('C:\SEMPERFI.DOC');
end;
```

This code is part of an application called OleWord2. The application is available on the book's CD-ROM.

The interesting thing about this code is that it never causes Word to appear on the screen. Instead, Word is launched temporarily into memory, but stays invisible. The moment the variable `v` goes out of scope, or the moment it is set to `varNothing`, Word is shut down again. Besides the sound of your hard disk drive churning, the only way to tell that the above code works is to actually launch Word after a run of your application, then attempt to open SEMPERFI.DOC and see if it has the proper contents.

The above code starts by calling `CreateOleObject`. This line launches Word into memory if it is not already started. If Word is not started, `CreateOleObject` launches it, but passes the `/Automation` parameter to Word. Word knows that when it's started with this parameter it should run quietly in the background, without ever becoming visible. It closes itself down as soon as it no longer has an OLE automation client to service.

It's no mere coincidence that Word runs in the background when called into memory by an OLE automation client. In fact, it is part of the usual definition of a server that it should run in the background unless specifically invoked by a user, rather than by an automation client. If it is merely started by an automation client, it should remain hidden. This way the client can use the services provided by Word without ever disturbing the user with the sordid technical details of how an operation might be performed.

OLE Parameters: Named and Positional

The FileNew and FileSaveAs commands are standard Word Basic procedures that you can look up in the Word online Help (if you have Word Basic Help installed). The basic functionality of these commands is self-explanatory. However, if you look up FileSaveAs in the Word online Help, you find the following listing for it:

```
FileSaveAs [.Name = text] [, .Format = number] [, .LockAnnot = number]
[, .Password = text] [, .AddToMru = number] [, .WritePassword = text]
[, .RecommendReadOnly = number] [, .EmbedFonts = number]
[, .NativePictureFormat = number] [, .FormsData = number]
[, .SaveAsAOCELetter = number]
```

As you can see, FileSaveAs takes a total of 11 parameters. These parameters are called, respectively, Name, Format, LockAnnot, Password, AddToMru, WritePassword, RecommendReadOnly, EmbedFonts, NativePictureFormat, FormsData, and SaveAsAOCELetter. If FileSaveAs takes 11 parameters, how come our call to this function passes in only one parameter?

The issue here is that Word supports optional parameters. In the case shown in the last section, I am passing only one parameter to the object. I could, if I wanted, pass two:

```
V.FileSaveAs('C:\SEMPERFI.TXT', 3);
```

The code shown here takes advantage of the fact that FileSaveAs takes a Format specification in the second parameter. The Format parameter can have one of the following values:

```
0       Word document
1       Document template
2       Text Only
3       Text Only with Line Breaks
4       MS-DOS Text (extended characters saved in IBM® PC character set)
5       MS-DOS Text with Line Breaks
6       Rich-Text Format
```

It is not necessary for you to define parameters in a particular order. For instance, you could write:

```
V.FileSaveAs('C:\SEMPERFI.DOC', Password := 'Sam');
```

This saves SEMPERFI.DOC in Word format, and assigns it a password called Sam. The next time you try to open this document, you must supply a password.

> **NOTE**
>
> I'm sure you have noticed that the second parameter of the call to FileSaveAs includes an assignment statement! This BASIC-like syntax is such anathema to veteran Object Pascal programmers that I am tempted to simply mutter a few imprecations and then move on as quickly as possible. Perhaps I should, however, take a moment to clarify the situation. The issue here is that you need to state simultaneously the name of the

parameter you want to reference, as well as its value. The code shown above performs this task. Other than these few basic hints, I don't want to chance any more in-depth explanations of this syntax. This book is on Delphi, not BASIC.

You should remember, however, that the parameters you pass to OLE automation objects are not necessarily part of the Object Pascal language. All Delphi does is pass the parameters onto Word, where your code can be ground up by the exceedingly fine teeth of a BASIC interpreter. Delphi performs little syntax checking on these parameters. If Word does not like your syntax, it will raise an exception.

OLE automation is a powerful technology that is likely to have enormous impact on the programming world. It does, however, expose the unwary to a host of foreign syntaxes, much as the introduction of intercontinental travel brought the ways of heathens into the refined courts of Europe!

This line of code is an example of using a named parameter. In particular, you are naming the Password parameter. Password normally is the fourth parameter passed to this function, but you can place it in the second position if you call it by name. The following line of code has the same effect:

```
V.FileSaveAs(Password := 'Sam', Name := 'C:\SEMPERFI.DOC');
```

This code demonstrates that named parameters enable you not only to skip parameters, but actually to reverse the order in which you call them.

Besides named parameters, Word also supports positional parameters.

```
V.FileSaveAs('C:\SEMPERFI.DOC',,,'Sammy');
```

In the code shown above, the password Sammy is added to SEMPERFI.DOC. Word knows that you want Sammy to be a password because it resides in the fourth position. In this case the second and third parameters use default values because they are left blank.

Note that I can add a carriage return to these lines from the Tao te Ching by inserting a line-feed character (#13) into the text.

You can look up the use of carriage returns, and information on Word Basic methods shown in this example, in the Word online Help. Here, for example, is an excerpt from the Word Help describing what various characters mean when embedded in the text of a Word document:

```
Chr$(9)     Tab character
Chr$(11)    Newline character (SHIFT+ENTER)
Chr$(13)    Paragraph mark
Chr$(30)    Nonbreaking hyphen
Chr$(31)    Optional hyphen
Chr$(32)    Space character
Chr$(34)    Quotation mark
```

```
Chr$(160)     Nonbreaking space (Windows)
Chr$(202)     Nonbreaking space (Macintosh)
```

This code is specific to BASIC. In Object Pascal you would write, for example, #30 or Chr(30) rather than Chr$(30).

One of the interesting implications of OLE automation is that it brings even more APIs knocking at your door, requesting to be mastered. Many Delphi users, for instance, have copies of Word, Visio, and Excel on their systems. All of these applications have powerful OLE-automation capabilities. Once you have mastered a few thousand Windows and Delphi API commands, you can further exercise your mind by learning additional commands in Word, Excel, and Visio.

This is progress, right?

If you think about this situation for a moment, you can see that there is clear need to establish standards for certain commands. For instance, nearly all document-centered Windows application respond to the Alt+F+O keystrokes by letting you open a document. It doesn't take too much foresight to see that there should probably be similar standards for performing the same steps in an automation server! In fact, there are some standards currently being established, and I show a few of them to you later in this chapter.

Variant Arrays

Delphi enables you to create variant arrays, which are the Delphi version of the safe arrays used in OLE Automation. Variant arrays (and safe arrays) are costly in terms of memory and CPU cycles, so you would not normally use them except in automation code, or in special cases where they provide obvious benefits over standard arrays. For instance, the database code makes some use of variant arrays.

The most important calls for manipulating variant arrays are VarArrayCreate and VarArrayOf. In particular, these functions are both used to create variant arrays.

The declaration for VarArrayCreate looks like this:

```
function VarArrayCreate(const Bounds: array of Integer;
  VarType: Integer): Variant;
```

The Bounds parameter defines the dimensions of the array. The VarType parameter defines the type of variable stored in the array. A one-dimensional array of variants would be allocated like this:

```
MyVariant := VarArrayCreate([0, 5], varVariant);
```

This array has six elements in it, where each element is a variant. You can assign a variant array to one or more of the elements in this array. That way you can have arrays within arrays within arrays, if you so desire.

If you know the type of the elements to be used in an array, you can set the VarType parameter to that type. For instance, if you knew you were going to be working with integers, you could write:

```
MyVariant := VarArrayCreate([0, 5], varInteger);
```

You cannot use varString in the second parameter; instead, use varOleStr. Remember that an array of Variant takes up 16 bytes for each member of the array, whereas other types might take up less space.

Arrays of Variant can be resized with the VarArrayRedim function:

```
procedure VarArrayRedim(var A: Variant; HighBound: Integer);
```

The variable to be resized is passed in the first parameter, and the number of elements to be contained in the resized array is held in the second parameter.

A two-dimensional array would be declared like this:

```
MyVariant := VarArrayCreate([0, 5, 0, 5], varVariant);
```

This array has two dimensions, each with six elements. To access a member of this array you would write code that looks like this:

```
procedure TForm1.GridClick(Sender: TObject);
var
  MyVariant: Variant;
begin
  MyVariant := VarArrayCreate([0, 5, 0, 5], varVariant);
  MyVariant[0, 1] := 42;
  Form1.Caption := MyVariant[0, 1];
end;
```

Notice that the array performs type conversions for you, as it is an array of variants and not, for instance, an array of integer.

You can use the VarArrayOf routine to quickly construct a one-dimensional variant array:

```
function VarArrayOf(const Values: array of Variant): Variant;
```

The function internally calls VarArrayCreate, passing an array of Variant in the first parameter and varVariant in the second parameter. Here is a typical call to VarArrayOf:

```
V := VarArrayOf([1, 2, 3, 'Total', 5]);
```

The following code fragment shows how to use the VarArrayOf function:

```
procedure TForm1.ShowInfo(V: Variant);
begin
  Caption := V[3];
end;

procedure TForm1.Button1Click(Sender: TObject);
var
  V: Variant;
```

```
begin
  V := VarArrayOf([1, 2, 3, 'Total', 5]);
  ShowInfo(V);
end;
```

This code prints the word Total in the caption of Form1.

The ShowInfo methods demonstrates how to work with a variant array passed as a parameter. Notice that you don't have to do anything special to access a variant as an array. The type travels with the variable.

If you tried to pass a variant with a VType of varInteger to this function, Delphi would raise an exception when you tried to treat the variant as an array. In short, the Variant must have a VType of VarArray or the call to ShowInfo will fail. You can use the VarType function to check the current setting for the VType of a Variant, or you can call VarIsArray, which returns a Boolean value.

You can use the VarArrayHighBound, VarArrayLowBound, and VarArrayDimCount functions to find out about the number of dimensions in your array, and about the bounds of each dimension. The following function creates a pop-up message box showing the number of dimensions in a variant array, as well as the high and low values for each dimension:

```
procedure TForm1.ShowInfo(V: Variant);
var
  Count, HighBound, LowBound, i: Integer;
  S: string;
begin
  Count := VarArrayDimCount(V);
  S := #13 + 'DimCount: ' + IntToStr(Count) + #13;
  for i := 1 to Count do begin
    HighBound := VarArrayHighBound(V, i);
    LowBound := VarArrayLowBound(V, i);
    S := S + 'HighBound: ' + IntToStr(HighBound) + #13;
    S := S + 'LowBound: ' + IntToStr(LowBound) + #13;
  end;
  ShowMessage(S);
end;
```

This routine starts by getting the number of dimensions in the array. It then iterates through each dimension, retrieving its high and low values. If you created an array with the following call:

```
MyVariant := VarArrayCreate([0, 5, 1, 3], varVariant);
```

the ShowInfo function would produce the following output if passed MyVariant:

```
DimCount: 2
HighBound: 5
LowBound: 0
HighBound: 3
LowBound: 1
```

ShowInfo would raise an exception if you passed in a variant that would cause VarIsArray to return False.

There is a certain amount of overhead in working with variant arrays. If you want to process the arrays quickly, you can use two functions called VarArrayLock and VarArrayUnlock. The first of these routines returns a pointer to the data stored in an array. In particular, VarArrayLock takes a variant array and returns a standard Pascal array. For this to work, the array must be explicitly declared with one of the standard types, such as Integer, Bool, string, Byte, or Float. The type used in the variant array and the type used in the Pascal array must be identical.

Here is an example of using VarArrayLock and VarArrayUnlock:

```
const
  HighVal = 12;

function GetArray: Variant;
var
  V: Variant;
  i, j: Integer;
begin
  V := VarArrayCreate([0, HighVal, 0, HighVal], varInteger);
  for i := 0 to HighVal do
    for j := 0 to HighVal do
      V[j, i] := i * j;
  Result := V;
end;

procedure TForm1.LockedArray1Click(Sender: TObject);
type
  TData = array[0..HighVal, 0..HighVal] of Integer;
var
  i, j: Integer;
  V: Variant;
  Data: ^TData;
begin
  V := GetArray;
  Data := VarArrayLock(V);
  for i := 0 to HighVal do
    for j := 0 to HighVal do
      Grid.Cells[i, j] := IntToStr(Data^[i, j]);
  VarArrayUnLock(V);
end;
```

Notice that this code first locks down the array, then accesses it as a pointer to a standard array. Finally, it releases the array when the operation is finished. You must remember to call VarArrayUnlock when you are finished working with the data from the array:

```
  Data := VarArrayLock(V);
  for i := 0 to HighVal do
    for j := 0 to HighVal do
      Grid.Cells[i, j] := IntToStr(Data^[i, j]);
  VarArrayUnLock(V);
```

Remember that the point of using VarArrayLock and VarArrayUnlock is that it speeds access to the array. The actual code you write is more complex and verbose, but the performance is faster.

One of the most useful reasons for using a variant array is to transfer binary data to and from a server. If you have a binary file, say a WAV file or AVI file, you can pass it back and forth between your program and an OLE server using variant arrays. Such a situation would present an ideal time for using VarArrayLock and VarArrayUnlock. You would, of course, use VarByte as the second parameter to VarArrayCreate when you were creating the array. That is, you would be working with an array of Byte, and accessing it directly by locking down the array before moving data in and out of the structure. Such arrays are not subject to translation while being marshaled across boundaries.

Listing 29.1 contains a single example program that encapsulates most of the ideas that you have seen in this section on variant arrays. The program from which this code is excerpted is called VarArray.

Listing 29.1. The VarArray program shows how to use variant arrays.

```
unit main;

interface

uses
  Windows, Messages, SysUtils,
  Classes, Graphics, Controls,
  Forms, Dialogs, StdCtrls,
  Menus, Grids;

type
  TForm1 = class(TForm)
    Grid: TStringGrid;
    MainMenu1: TMainMenu;
    Info1: TMenuItem;
    OneDimension1: TMenuItem;
    TwoDimension1: TMenuItem;
    Show1: TMenuItem;
    Normal1: TMenuItem;
    LockedArray1: TMenuItem;
    procedure bOneDimClick(Sender: TObject);
    procedure bTwoDimClick(Sender: TObject);
    procedure Normal1Click(Sender: TObject);
    procedure LockedArray1Click(Sender: TObject);
  private
    procedure ShowInfo(V: Variant);
  end;

var
  Form1: TForm1;

implementation

{$R *.DFM}

procedure TForm1.ShowInfo(V: Variant);
var
  Count, HighBound, LowBound, i: Integer;
  S: string;
begin
  Count := VarArrayDimCount(V);
  S := #13 + 'DimCount: ' + IntToStr(Count) + #13;
```

```
  for i := 1 to Count do begin
    HighBound := VarArrayHighBound(V, i);
    LowBound := VarArrayLowBound(V, i);
    S := S + 'HighBound: ' + IntToStr(HighBound) + #13;
    S := S + 'LowBound: ' + IntToStr(LowBound) + #13;
  end;
  ShowMessage(S);
end;

procedure TForm1.bOneDimClick(Sender: TObject);
var
  V: Variant;
begin
  V := VarArrayOf(['Variant Info', 12, 15, 23, 25]);
  ShowInfo(V);
end;

procedure TForm1.bTwoDimClick(Sender: TObject);
var
  V: Variant;
begin
  V := VarArrayCreate([0, 5, 1, 5], varVariant);
  ShowInfo(V);
end;

function GetArray: Variant;
var
  V: Variant;
  i, j: Integer;
begin
  V := VarArrayCreate([0, 12, 0, 12], varInteger);
  for i := 0 to 12 do
    for j := 0 to 12 do
      V[j, i] := i * j;
  Result := V;
end;

procedure TForm1.Normal1Click(Sender: TObject);
var
  i, j: Integer;
  V: Variant;
begin
  V := GetArray;
  for i := 0 to VarArrayHighBound(V, 1) do
    for j := 0 to VarArrayHighBound(V, 2) do
      Grid.Cells[i, j] := V[i, j];
end;

procedure TForm1.LockedArray1Click(Sender: TObject);
type
  TData = array[0..12, 0..12] of Integer;
var
  i, j: Integer;
  V: Variant;
  Data: ^TData;
begin
  V := GetArray;
  Data := VarArrayLock(V);
```

continues

Listing 29.1. continued

```
  for i := 0 to 12 do
    for j := 0 to 12 do
      Grid.Cells[i, j] := IntToStr(Data^[i, j]);
  VarArrayUnLock(V);
end;

end.
```

This program has two menu items:

■ One enables you to look at the dimensions and bounds of two different variant arrays. The first array has one dimension and the second has two.

■ The second pop-up menu enables you to display an array in a string grid using two different methods. The first method accesses the array through standard techniques, and the second lets you lock down the data before accessing it.

Remember that variant arrays are of use only in special circumstances. They are useful tools, especially when making calls to OLE automation objects. However, they are slower and bulkier than standard Delphi arrays, and should be used only when necessary.

Getting Started with Excel Automation

Excel is another large and popular automation server. You can access the features of Excel easily from a Delphi application. However, the internal structure of Excel's objects are much more complex than the structure of the objects in Word.

To get started, first open a copy of Excel. Next, create a Delphi application containing the following code:

```
var
  V: Variant;

procedure TForm1.Button1Click(Sender: TObject);
begin
  V := CreateOleObject('Excel.Sheet');
  V.Range('A1:D8').Formula := '=RAND()';
end;
```

This code creates a new worksheet in Excel, then fills a range of cells in the worksheet with random values.

The following example starts a new worksheet in Excel. It then fills part of the sheet with random data and adds a second sheet to the worksheet. Finally, it counts the number of sheets in the worksheet and displays the result in the caption of the Delphi application.

```
procedure TForm1.Button1Click(Sender: TObject);
begin
  V := CreateOleObject('Excel.Sheet');
```

```
    V.Range('A1:D8').Formula := '=RAND()';
    V.Application.Sheets.Add;
    Caption := 'Num Sheets = ' + IntToStr(V.Application.Sheets.Count);
end;
```

Here is a second example that demonstrates a slight variation on the code in the Button1Click method:

```
procedure TForm1.Button2Click(Sender: TObject);
begin
  V := CreateOleObject('Excel.Application'); // Start a new copy of Excel
  V.Visible := True;
  V.WorkBooks.Add;
  V.Sheets.Add;
  Caption := 'Num Sheets = ' + IntToStr(V.Sheets.Count);
end;
```

This code makes sure the application object is visible before adding to the workbook. In particular, the first two lines of the code start a new version of Excel and launch it without any open spreadsheets. The call to WorkBooks.Add opens up a workbook with a number of spreadsheets in it, and so on.

The Button1Click method shown starts a new worksheet in an already running copy of Excel, if one is available; if Excel is not already running, this method starts it. The Button2Click method always starts a new copy of Excel, even if one is already running.

To understand automation with Excel, you have to grasp a few of its OLE automation objects. In particular, Excel has an Application object, a WorkBook object, a Range object, and a Sheets object. For instance, in the Button1Click and Button2Click methods you are accessing, among other things, both the Range and Sheets objects that reside inside Excel. You should read the Excel online Help to get a better feeling for how these objects work.

Assuming you have created an Excel OLE object by using something similar to these code fragments, you can access the individual cells of a spreadsheet like this:

```
procedure TForm1.bFancyAryClick(Sender: TObject);
var
  i, j: Integer;
  Ch: Char;
begin
  for i := 1 to 10 do
    for j := 1 to 10 do
      SimpAry.Cells[j, i].Value := i * j;
  for i := 1 to 10 do begin
    Ch := Chr(64 + i);
    SimpAry.Cells[11, i].Value := Format('=Sum(%s1:%s10)', [Ch, Ch]);
  end;
end;
```

Notice that the code shown here accesses the cells both as an array of Integer and an array of String. In particular, it fills out a 10×10 grid with the multiplication table, and then adds formulas into the 11th row, which lies directly beneath the times table. The formulas calculate the sum of each column in the table.

The code shown in the `FancyAryClick` method is a classic example of how variants are integrated into the heart of OLE automation. If Delphi did not support variants, writing code like that in this section would be considerably more complicated. In particular, `Cells.Value` must be treated as both an array of `Integer` and an array of `String`. Variants make these easy to express and easy to access.

Simple OLE Automation Servers

In this section you learn how to create a simple OLE automation server using the built-in Delphi classes. In other parts of this book you get an in-depth look at creating OLE automation servers from scratch. Doing things the hard way gives you the maximum amount of freedom, as well as providing you with the knowledge you need to judge just what can and can't be done through automation. However, before showing you the in-depth techniques, I want to start by showing you the easy way.

Here is a quick overview of the basic steps involved:

1. Start a new application and save it into its own directory.
2. Choose File | New and, in the New page of the New Items dialog box, select Automation Object.
3. In the dialog box that appears when you choose Automation Object, give the object a class name, such as `TMyAuto`. Leave Instancing at Multiple Instance, and give the object a short description. Click OK.
4. Save the new unit under its own name, such as MYAUTO.PAS.

The following step is needed in the beta versions of Delphi:

After performing these steps you need to run the application once in order to register the object in the registration database. In early versions of Delphi 2.0, you sometimes needed to

5. Select Run | Parameters from the menu and enter:

```
/regserver
```

Then run the application. It would return immediately, without the main form appearing. You could then remove the `/regserver` line from the Parameters dialog. This step should not be required in any of the shipping versions of Delphi 2.0.

As you might have surmised, this step was needed to register the object in the registration database. If you want to remove the object, you can run your application with the parameter `/unregserver`.

In the shipping version of Delphi, if you look in the code for the `MyAuto` unit, you should find the following declaration:

```
AutoClassInfo: TAutoClassInfo = (
    AutoClass: TMyAuto;
```

```
ProgID: 'AUTOPROJ.MyAuto';
ClassID: '{FE67CF61-2EDD-11CF-B536-0080C72EFD43}';
Description: 'Sam';
Instancing: acMultiInstance);
```

The key elements here are the ProgID and the ClassID. When you ran the program with the /regserver parameter, these keys were added to the registration database. ProgID is an alpha-numeric alias for the ClassID. The alias is needed because it would be awkward for programmers to refer to the class by its lengthy, opaque-looking number. As a result, a relatively easy-to-manage program ID is created. To confirm the existence of these keys, run REGEDIT.EXE from its home in the Windows directory.

After starting RegEdit, expand HKEY_CLASSES_ROOT and search for the CLSID key. Expand the CLSID node and search for your ClassID. In the example above, that number begins with FE67F61..., though the number will almost certainly be different if you created the application from scratch on your system. The whole point of creating a ClassID is that it should prove to be unique if generated by an internal Microsoft algorithm called automatically for you by Delphi.

> **NOTE**
>
> The idea that a number such as CLSID is said to be statistically unique is the source of considerable humor in the computer world. However, a CLSID has a fairly large number of significant digits, and Microsoft does, in fact, have the resources and intelligence to implement an algorithm that can generate something at least potentially worthy of the name "random number." I am not, however, qualified to take a stand on this matter. I simply state that this concept is key to the entire implementation of OLE, and therefore I at least choose to assume that Microsoft's algorithm is well-designed. After distributed OLE is released, this issue is bound to receive a certain amount of public attention, at which time various numerical experts will weigh in with their opinions on the matter.

As explained a moment ago, underneath the CLSID for your program are two entries: LocalServer32 and ProgID. The ProgID is the same as the similar entry in the AutoClassInfo structure shown above. The LocalServer32 entry is the path and name of your executable.

If your program compiles, and if you have added the entry successfully in the registration database, then you have successfully completed a Delphi automation server.

Needless to say, the steps for constructing an OLE server outlined in this section are relatively easy to master. However, as you are about to see, some of the implications of this technology can become rather complex.

Instancing Issues: Multiple or Single?

The AutoClassInfo structure shown in the last section states that the AutoProj.MyAuto server is MultiInstance. A server can be designated acMultiInstance, acSingle, or acInternal.

If multiple clients can safely access your server at the same time, you should declare it to be of type acMultiInstance. If you need to ensure that only one client at a time can access your server, you should set its type to acSingle. If you want to declare an object that will be used only internally by your application, you should declare it as acInternal.

Adding Methods and Properties to Automation Servers

Ambitious programmers will probably want to not only produce automation servers, but to actually have them do something useful! To start adding functions to your server, you can place code in the Automated section of the object declaration:

```
TMyAuto = class(TAutoObject)
private
  { Private declarations }
automated
  { Automated declarations }
end;
```

For instance, you could add a method that creates a pop-up dialog box:

```
TMyAuto = class(TAutoObject)
private
  { Private declarations }
automated
  { Automated declarations }
  procedure ShowDialog;
end;
implementation

uses
  Dialogs;

procedure TMyAuto.ShowDialog;
begin
  ShowMessage('hi');
end;
```

The ShowDialog procedure now is available to other applications, just as the Insert routine in Word and the Add routine in Excel are available to other applications. The act of placing a property or method in the automated section is all that's needed to make it part of your object's public interface.

The following types are legal to use in the declarations for the methods or properties in the Automated section:

```
Currency
Double
Integer
LongInt
Single
SmallInt
String
TDateTime
Variant
WordBool
```

The following types are illegal to use in the declarations for the methods or properties in the Automated section:

```
Arrays
Boolean
Byte
Cardinal
Comp
Pointer
POleStr
Records
ShortInt
Word
```

There is no need for you to memorize these list of types, as the compiler will report an error if you try to use an illegal type in an automation server.

NOTE

When you change the interface of an existing automation server, you should always make sure the interface is backward-compatible. That is, don't remove properties or methods already included, as that will cause errors in existing clients. You should only add to existing interfaces. If you modify an existing interface in ways that are not backward-compatible, you should change the object's name as well.

Here is a list of further rules, stolen from the Delphi online Help, that you must follow inside the automated section of a TAutoObject declaration:

■ Property declarations can include only access specifiers (Read and Write). No other specifiers (Index, Stored, Default, NoDefault) are allowed.

- Access specifiers must list a method identifier. Field identifiers are not allowed.
- Property-access methods must use register calling conventions.
- Array properties are supported.
- Property overrides (property declarations that don't include the property type) are not allowed.
- Method declarations must use register-calling conventions. Methods can be virtual, but not dynamic. Method overrides are allowed.
- A property or method declaration can include an optional dispid directive, which must be followed by an integer constant expression that gives the dispatch ID of the property or method. If a dispid clause is not present, the compiler automatically picks a number one larger than the largest dispatch ID used by any property or method in the class and its ancestors. Specifying an already-used dispatch ID in a dispid clause causes an error.

It's now time to take a look at the code for the entire application, which is called AutoProj. Listing 29.2 contains the code for the automation unit. Listing 29.3 contains the DPR file for the automation server.

Listing 29.2. The code for the MyAuto unit shows how to create a simple automation server.

```
unit MyAuto;

{ Copyright (c) 1996 by Charlie Calvert

  This object has one method and one property that
  are available via OLE automation. The property
  allows you to set the value of a string, and
  the method shows the string in a dialog.

  For this example to work, you need to run the TestAp
  program, stored in this same directory. Before running
  TestAp, you should run this program once, passing in
  /regserver as the program's sole parameter.

  Open up the DPR file to see the call to
  Automation.ServerRegistration. }

interface

uses
  OleAuto;

type
  TMyAuto = class(TAutoObject)
  private
    FMyProp: string;
```

```
    function GetMyProp: string;
    procedure SetMyProp(S: string);
  public
    constructor Create; override;
  automated
    procedure ShowDialog;
    property MyProp: string read GetMyProp write SetMyProp;
  end;

implementation

uses
  Dialogs;

constructor TMyAuto.Create;
begin
  inherited Create;
end;

procedure TMyAuto.ShowDialog;
begin
  if FMyProp = '' then
    FMyProp := 'This object has a property called MyProp';
  ShowMessage(FMyProp);
end;

procedure TMyAuto.SetMyProp(S: string);
begin
  FMyProp := S;
end;

function TMyAuto.GetMyProp: string;
begin
  Result := FMyProp;
end;

procedure RegisterMyAuto;
const
  AutoClassInfo: TAutoClassInfo = (
    AutoClass: TMyAuto;
    ProgID: 'AUTOPROJ.MyAuto';
    ClassID: '{FE67CF61-2EDD-11CF-B536-0080C72EFD43}';
    Description: 'Sam';
    Instancing: acMultiInstance);
begin
  Automation.RegisterClass(AutoClassInfo);
end;

initialization
  RegisterMyAuto;
end.
```

Listing 29.3. The DPR file for the automation server.

```
program AutoProj;

uses
  OleAuto,
  Forms,
  MAIN in 'MAIN.pas' {Form1},
  myauto in 'myauto.pas';

{$R *.RES}

begin
  if Automation.ServerRegistration then Exit;
  Application.CreateForm(TForm1, Form1);
  Application.Run;
end.
```

In these declarations, take special notice of the call to the TAutomation object's ServerRegistration method. This code updates the registry if you passed /regserver or /unregserver as a parameter to your application. Remember that you must pass /regserver to it at least once, so as to enter the proper items in the registration database.

Now that you have a complete (and functional) automation server, you can easily test it by creating a separate application that references the OleAuto unit and which contains a few additional lines of code:

```
uses
  OleAuto;

procedure TForm1.Button1Click(Sender: TObject);
var
  V: variant;
begin
  V := CreateOleObject('AutoProj.MyAuto');
  V.ShowDialog;
end;
```

When you run this second application and press the button that calls the Button1Click method, the automation server is automatically launched, and the ShowDialog procedure called. An example program, called TestDA, is available on the book's CD-ROM.

> **NOTE**
>
> OLE automation controls can be publicized to the outside world through something called a type library. Delphi does not support type libraries, and there are no tools for building them in the package. Instead, you should just provide the interface to your object—which will, of course, provide all the information found in a type library.

Furthermore, as explained above, the call to ShowDialog is not resolved at compile time. By reading type information, it's at least theoretically possible to resolve this call at compile time, or at least to check the syntax of the call, but this version of Delphi makes no forays in that direction.

In the last two sections you learned the basics about making an OLE automation server. The rest of this chapter is dedicated to explaining some of the implications of this capability.

Local Automation Servers In Depth

The MemoEdit application found in the Delphi 2.0\Demos\OleAuto subdirectory shows how to create a more complex server. The first time you run this application, pass /regserver as a parameter in the Run | Parameters menu from the IDE. This places the MemoEdit.Application ProgID in the registration database. If you wish, run RegEdit to confirm that the registration occurred properly.

To control the MemoEdit application, you should run the AutoDemo program found in the same directory. The moment you launch the AutoDemo program, you find that the MemoEdit application also is loaded into memory.

The AutoDemo application lets you control the MemoEdit server in several different ways. In particular, you can open up three MDI child windows in the server, insert text into them, tile them, cascade them, and then close them again. In short, the MemoEdit application is a small and very limited word processor that enables you to edit multiple documents at the same time.

The first thing to grasp about this pair of applications is that the MemoEdit application contains, not one, but two automation objects. The first is called TMemoApp and the second is called TMemoDoc.

TMemoApp is the object with a ProgID of MemoEdit.Application. A copy of this object can be obtained through a call to CreateOleObject. The TMemoDoc object has no ProgID, no ClassID, and no AutoClassInfo record, and cannot be created through a call to CreateOleObject or to any other OLE function. Instead, you must access this second object using a copy of the TMemoApp object.

TMemoApp is called an *externally creatable object*. TMemoDoc is called a *dependent*, or *nested*, *object*.

From the point of view of the AutoDemo application, the automation objects in the MemoEdit application look like this:

```
TMemoApp
   TMemoDoc
```

This diagram does not imply that TMemoDoc is a descendant of TMemoApp, only that it is contained by TMemoApp. Containment implies that you can create or access copies of TMemoDoc using a copy of TMemoApp. This type of diagram is used widely in OLE automation documentation; for instance, look up "Application Object" in the Excel online Help. There you will find the following excerpt from the Excel "hierarchy" of objects:

```
Application
  WorkBook
    WorkSheet
      Button
```

Once again, this is not an object hierarchy in the traditional sense, but only a way of diagramming the relationship between objects, where the word "relationship" designates which object contains another. An Application object can contain WorkBook, WorkSheet, and Button objects.

Application and WorkSheet objects are creatable objects, while button objects are dependent objects. Note that from inside of Excel or MemoEdit, all of the objects belonging to those applications are creatable. The idea of creatability versus dependence is only valid from the OLE client's point of view.

WorkBook is not a descendant of the Excel Application object, but you can obtain or reference copies of it once you have a copy of the Application object. TMemoDoc is not a descendant of TMemoApp; however, it can be obtained or referenced from TMemoApp. In short, TMemoApp contains TMemoDoc.

In the MemoEdit application, the TMemoApp object handles high-level functions involving the entire user interface, while the TMemoDoc object handles tasks specific to a single document. In particular, TMemoApp gives you access to the following methods:

```
function NewMemo: Variant;
Creates a new editor window and returns the window's automation object.

function OpenMemo(const FileName: string): Variant;
Loads an existing file into a new editor window and returns the window's
automation object.

procedure TileWindows;
Tiles all open editor windows.

procedure CascadeWindows;
Cascades all open editor windows.

property MemoCount: Integer;
Number of open editor windows.

property Memos[Index: Integer]: Variant;
Array of automation objects for the currently open editor windows. }
```

The TMemoDoc object, on the other hand, has the following interface:

```
procedure Clear;
Clears the contents of the memo.

procedure Insert(const Text: string);
Inserts the given string at the current cursor position.
```

```
procedure Save;
Saves the contents of the memo.

procedure Close;
Closes the memo.

property FileName: string;
The name of the file associated with the memo. The memo can be renamed
by assigning to this property.

property Modified: WordBool;
True if the memo has been modified since it was loaded or last saved.
```

As you can see, all the methods in TMemoDoc involve handling a single document. TMemoApp, on the other hand, creates new instances of TMemoDoc, and enables you to manipulate the program's user interface.

All of the methods of TMemoApp manipulate a single instance of the TMainForm object, which is the main object for the entire application:

```
procedure TMemoApp.CascadeWindows;
begin
  MainForm.Cascade;
end;
```

Take a moment to consider the implications of this code. TMemoApp doesn't do anything in and of itself. Instead, it is just a wrapper around the TMainForm object.

In practice, this means you can design an entire application using standard Delphi objects. Then, if you want to turn it into an OLE automation server, you can add additional TAutoObject descendants that provide an interface, allowing you to manipulate one or more of the objects inside your application.

You cannot simply add an automated section on to an existing TForm object because TForm is not a descendant of TAutoObject. Instead, you must create separate objects, such as the TMemoApp and TMemoDoc objects shown here. TMemoApp controls the TMainForm object, and TMemoDoc controls the TEditForm object found in EDITFRM.PAS.

> **NOTE**
>
> It's interesting to speculate whether the developers of Delphi ever considered adding the functionality of TAutoObject to one of the root objects in the Delphi hierarchy. This would be a powerful step from a syntactical point of view, but it would undoubtedly also entail a penalty in terms of performance.

Containment in Detail

The most interesting lines of code in the TMemoApp object are the ones that retrieve copies of the TMemoDoc object. These are the methods that allow the container, TMemoApp, to return its dependent object, which is called TMemoDoc. Here are the implementations of the three methods that give you access to a TMemoDoc instance:

```
function TMemoApp.GetMemo(Index: Integer): Variant;
begin
  Result := TEditForm(MainForm.MDIChildren[Index]).OleObject;
end;

function TMemoApp.NewMemo: Variant;
begin
  Result := MainForm.CreateMemo('').OleObject;
end;

function TMemoApp.OpenMemo(const FileName: string): Variant;
begin
  Result := MainForm.CreateMemo(FileName).OleObject;
end;
```

Notice that all of these methods return a Variant, not an instance of TMemoDoc. The issue here is that a Variant can contain an OLE object, as you saw earlier when you learned how to call CreateOleObject. In particular, the most common way to pass an OLE object across boundaries in an automation application is to first wrap it in a Variant.

To understand the call to the OleObject property, you must refer back to the declaration for TAutoObject that appears in OLEAUTO.PAS:

```
TAutoObject = class(TObject)
  private
    FAutoDispatch: TAutoDispatch;
    ...
  protected
    procedure GetExceptionInfo(ExceptObject: TObject;
      var ExcepInfo: TExcepInfo); virtual;
  public
    constructor Create; virtual;
    destructor Destroy; override;
    function AddRef: Integer;
    function Release: Integer;
    property AutoDispatch: TAutoDispatch read FAutoDispatch;
    property OleObject: Variant read GetOleObject;
    property RefCount: Integer read FRefCount;
  end;
end;
```

All Delphi OLE objects are descendants of TAutoObject. TAutoObject exists so that you don't have to call messy IDispatch methods such as GetIDsOfNames and Invoke. The primary job of TAutoObject is to hide that kind of complexity from Delphi programmers so that automation presents a friendly easy-to-use face to the programmer.

NOTE

The IDispatch object is used by OLE to implement automation. When you call CreateOleObject, what you get back is an IDispatch interface.

When looking at the TAutoObject declaration, take special notice of the two properties called AutoDispatch and OleObject. TAutoObject and another object, called TAutoDispatch, reference each other internally and work together to make automation easy for you to implement. TAutoDispatch is Delphi's implementation of the IDispatch interface.

A call to CreateOleObject returns an instance of TAutoDispatch, not an instance of your descendant of TAutoObject. However, the TAutoDispatch object that is returned contains a reference to your TAutoObject descendant, and TAutoDispatch frequently does nothing more than call TAutoObject's methods. In a sense, the TAutoDispatch object is like a Trojan horse that is smuggled across process boundaries under the guise of a simple IDispatch interface. However, once you have a copy of it, you can use it to access your descendant of TAutoObject and other fancy Delphi features that make automation simple.

However, there are times when you may want (either consciously or unconsciously) to access the IDispatch implementation directly. One such occasion is when you need to return a copy of an OLE object across application boundaries, which is what happens in the MemoEdit application when you call NewMemo, GetMemo, or OpenMemo.

To pass an IDispatch object across application boundaries you usually need to wrap it in a Variant, which is the job of the OleObject property. Alternatively, if you don't want to access a Variant but want the raw IDispatch interface, you can use the AutoDispatch property. The only difference between AutoDispatch and OleObject is that one returns the IDispatch implementation directly, while the other wraps it inside a Variant.

NOTE

Never call the Free or Destroy methods of an automation object. OLE objects are reference-counted, because they might be in use by more than one client. When you are finished using an OLE object, call its Release method. Release decrements the reference count. If the reference count reaches zero, the object automatically destroys itself.

The Automation Object

The OLEAUTO unit contains a simple object called TAutomation. This object is used solely by automation servers. It's not important to automation clients.

The following three properties of the TAutomation object might be useful to you on occasion:

```
property IsInprocServer: Boolean;
    property StartMode: TStartMode;
    property OnLastRelease: TLastReleaseEvent;
```

The IsInprocServer states whether your automation object is an InProcServer or a Local server.

The StartMode property returns one of the values smStandAlone, smAutomation, smRegServer, or smUnregServer. The following table describes these four possible values:

Value	Meaning
smStandAlone	A user started the application.
smAutomation	Windows started the application for the purpose of creating an OLE object.
smRegServer	The application was started solely to register one or more OLE objects.
smUnregServer	The application was started solely to unregister one or more OLE objects.

The OnLastRelease is triggered when a server started by the system for automation purposes no longer is needed. This occurs when all clients have released all OLE objects created by the server. Delphi usually automatically shuts the server down once it is no longer needed, although you can override this behavior if you wish.

OnLastRelease gets a Boolean var parameter called ShutDown, which is True by default. Setting ShutDown to True overrides Delphi's default behavior, and keeps the server in memory even though it no longer is needed.

Summary

OLE Automation is a protocol by which one application can access an object that resides inside another application or DLL. Access to this object enables you to:

- Control the actions of an application or DLL.
- Access the features of an application or DLL.

An application that can be automated is called an automation server. An application that automates another is an automation client. An application can be simultaneously both a server and a client.

Delphi supports easily building both automation clients and servers. That is, you can use an application written with Delphi to automate another application, or you can set up your application so that it can be automated by other applications.

In the next chapter you learn about in-process automation servers and more about local servers. The discussion then moves on to take an in-depth look at how automation servers work behind the scenes.

COM Object Basics

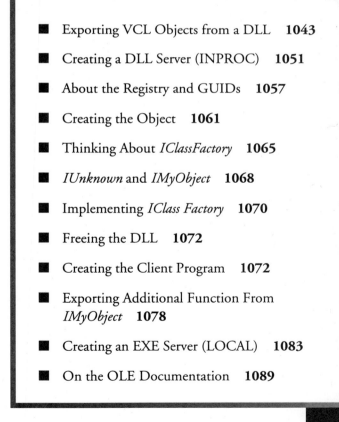

30

In this chapter you learn how to create classes based on the Component Object Model (COM). COM is the technology that underlies OLE, but is not itself part of OLE. It's a more fundamental layer of the operating system, implementing objects that can be used across address spaces and across languages. Someday it will work across operating systems, and across machines that are connected to a network.

At the time of this writing the only major non-OLE architecture implemented using COM is the Microsoft Games SDK. The games SDK is fun, and I discuss it in Chapter 32, "Games SDK." However, it is not enough of a force to create a compelling argument for COM as a major technology. Why, then, should I bother to include this chapter in this book?

Here are three reasons to suppose that the COM architecture may be of importance to the general programmer:

- COM is the architecture upon which OLE is based. OLE automation, OCXs, and (to a much lesser degree) object linking and embedding all are major forces, or potentially major forces, in the computer industry. As developers we owe it to ourselves to understand the technology upon which they are based.

- COM represents a way to implement objects on the level of the operating system. This means that objects need no longer be created as a layer that lies on top of the linear code base, which forms that core of the operating system. Instead, objects can be integrated into the operating system itself, and can act as natural extensions to that operating system.

  It's likely that future operating systems will themselves be object-oriented; more specifically, they could be based on COM. This means that COM technology would not only be tightly integrated with the operating system, but would be a part of its warp and woof.

  (When you find yourself asking, no doubt repeatedly, "Why is COM so complicated?", the answer is that Microsoft has grandiose plans for this system and wants to make it as flexible as possible. It's arguable that that flexibility is coming at too high a price in terms of complexity. However, an object-oriented operating system could well prove to be a significant boon to all computer users.)

- COM objects are designed to cross natural boundaries, such as those that exist between programs, between languages, between machines, and between operating systems. If you create a COM object in Delphi, you can instantiated it in a C++ or BASIC program. Furthermore, a C++ programmer could create "descendants" of your object; that is, they could extend the object by adding additional interfaces.

  COM objects also can cross the boundaries between programs. That is, they can reside in one program and be instantiated in another program. (I merely hint at this technique in this chapter. You can, after all, use OLE automation to achieve the same end.)

Finally, at the time of this writing Microsoft is planning to roll out extensions to the COM model that will allow it to communicate across machine- and operating-system boundaries. This means that you could instantiate an instance of an object that existed on another machine, even if that machine was running on a different operating system, such as UNIX or the Mac.

Having said all this, I need to stress that right now all we have is OLE and the Games SDK. Whether everything that I have described above actually will become true is still a matter of conjecture. We will have object-oriented operating systems based on COM technology on the day when such a creature is actually released into the world and physically sold in stores or mail-order houses, and not a moment before. Even networked OLE is not yet a reality, although Visual Basic 4.0 offers some technology that mimics portions of its behavior. In other words, nothing of this nature actually exists until it ships, and that casts a somewhat problematic pall over this entire discussion.

There's also the issue of whether you believe in Microsoft's vision of the future, or whether you are more inclined toward competing technologies (such as CORBA and SOM). But these are religious issues (and, despite its pro-Delphi bias, this text refuses to give in to its weakest impulses and become an overtly religious book. Our motto: "No language or OS bigots allowed!")

If you work in both C++ and Delphi, it is arguable that it would be foolish to use anything but COM for most of your serious work. After all, why create objects that are bound to Delphi or bound to C++? Why not create objects on the operating-system level, and then use them in both your C++ and Delphi projects? This is a completely realistic goal, fully realizable at the time of this writing. Indeed, the MS Games SDK shows that it can be done, and that the resulting code can be very fast. It's the hard evidence. Furthermore, OLE promises to be one of the major technologies of the next few years, and it is based on COM objects. If you want to understand OLE, then, you have to understand COM objects.

This chapter shows you how to create COM objects that reside in DLLs. You can share these COM objects between Delphi, C++, and other languages. This chapter also hints at how to create COM objects that reside in executables; although, as I suggested above, this is a more complex subject and one that is perhaps always going to play second fiddle to OLE automation.

Exporting VCL Objects from a DLL

A couple of potential sources of confusion will be cleared up if I start this chapter by showing you a Delphi application that does something that looks a lot like a COM object, but that is not actually a COM object. Specifically, this first example shows you how to create a DLL, put a Delphi object in it, and then access all the methods of that object. Once again, this is not a

COM object example. It's just a simple Pascal object. However, it's doing something that you might think Delphi objects can't do: it's letting you call the methods of this object even though it resides in a DLL. Furthermore, the techniques used to access this object form a sort of miniature introduction to the COM object model.

The point here is that COM objects also let you do this. However, you can also instantiate an instance of a COM object that resides in another executable, which is something you can't do with a VCL object. (OK, "can't" probably is too strong a word. But it would be difficult.)

There are three reasons why I'm showing you this example:

- This is a useful general programming technique that can help you write small, flexible programs. Specifically, you can place large object hierarchies in DLLs, then load these DLLs dynamically by calling `LoadLibrary` and `FreeLibrary`. That way you can load your main program without having to simultaneously load all its modules. Furthermore, objects that are kept in DLLs can be shared by multiple applications. The point here is that even if there were no COM object model, and no need for a COM object model, this technique still would be useful.

- It's simple to do this kind of thing using Delphi objects, while it's relatively hard to do it using COM objects. Therefore, one of the reasons for showing you this example is to let you know that there is simple way to accomplish these ends. If all you want is to put objects in DLLs and call them, there's no need to use COM objects. Just use the simple technique shown here. COM objects buy you cross-language capabilities that extend beyond Borland C++ and Delphi.

- The third reason for showing you this code is that it serves as the perfect lead-in for using COM objects. Many of the principles shown here surface again when using COM objects. However, these Object Pascal-based examples are fairly easy to understand, while the COM material can be a bit confusing, especially the first time you see it. In a sense, then, this is COM objects with training wheels. It introduces, in simplified form, some concepts that reappear in more complex form later in this chapter.

It will perhaps be simplest to start by showing you the DLL you must create. Once you have that down, the next step is to see how to call the DLL from an executable. There's nothing at all unusual about the DLL. It's just a standard DLL that contains a few unusual-looking code constructions. The tricky code appears in the executable; although, once again, this is a simple trick, and one that's easy to utilize. Listings 30.1 and 30.2 show the code for the DNOOLE.DLL. Listing 30.3, presented later in this section, shows the code for the executable.

Listing 30.1. The DPR file for the DNOOLE.DLL.

```
library dnoole;

uses
  Forms,
  myvclobj in 'myvclobj.pas';
```

```
{$R *.RES}

exports
  CreateObject name 'CreateObject';

begin

end.
```

Listing 30.2. This module contains the object that is exported from the DNOOLE.DLL.

```
unit myvclobj;

interface

const
  ID_MyObject = 1;

type
  TMyObject = class
    function AddOne(i: Integer): Integer; virtual;
    function AddTwo(i: Integer): Integer; virtual;
  end;

function CreateObject(ID: Integer; var Obj): Boolean; export;

implementation

function TMyObject.AddOne(i: Integer): Integer;
begin
  Result := i + 1;
end;

function TMyObject.AddTwo(i: Integer): Integer;
begin
  Result := i + 2;
end;

function CreateObject(ID: Integer; var Obj): Boolean;
var
  M: TMyObject;
begin
  if ID = ID_MyObject then begin
    M := TMyObject.Create;
    Pointer(Obj) := M;
    Result := True
  end else begin
    M := nil;
    Result := False
  end;
end;

end.
```

This DLL exports a simple object called TMyObject. You can pass a number to the methods of this object and it increments that number by either one or two. In short, the methods don't do anything at all interesting. I include them simply so you have something to test, and because they produce predictable return values that make it easy to tell whether or not your calls to the DLL actually are succeeding.

It's time now to look at the code. Of course, the DPR file for the DLL uses the word library rather than program:

```
library dnoole;
```

It exports a single method called CreateObject:

```
exports
  CreateObject name 'CreateObject';
```

The actual object exported by the DLL is called TMyObject:

```
TMyObject = class
  function AddOne(i: Integer): Integer; virtual;
  function AddTwo(i: Integer): Integer; virtual;
end;
```

Notice that both of these methods are declared as virtual. It is important that all the methods in your object are declared this way.

When you want to export the object from the DLL, you call the CreateObject method:

```
function CreateObject(ID: Integer; var Obj): Boolean;
var
  M: TMyObject;
begin
  if ID = ID_MyObject then begin
    M := TMyObject.Create;
    Pointer(Obj) := M;
    Result := True
  end else begin
    M := nil;
    Result := False
  end;
end;
```

This is the method that looks so much like the COM code you see later in this chapter. In particular, you should compare this method with the QueryInterface method that is part of every COM object, and also with the IClassFactory.CreateInstance method. But I'm getting ahead of myself.

The CreateObject method expects to be passed both an ID and a typeless variable that is assigned to an instance of TMyObject. In this particular case, there's no need for you to pass in an ID. It would be useful only if you had multiple objects that you wanted to export, and you wanted some simple method to designate which object it was that you wanted to retrieve. For instance, you could assign the number 1 to your first object and the number 2 to your second object. Then, if you passed in ID 1 you would get the first object back, and if you passed in ID

2 you would get the second object back. I'm implementing this method here because it might be useful to you in your own code, and because it exactly parallels a technique used in COM code.

The second parameter of CreateObject is a typeless parameter. If I were implementing this code from scratch, with no guidelines, I would probably make this variable a pointer, or else assign it type TObject. However, COM code uses these typeless types in similar situations, so I have mirrored that style in this example.

The code checks first to see if it is being passed a valid ID. If the ID is not valid, the method returns nil in the second parameter. If the ID is valid, the method returns an instance of TMyObject:

```
if ID = ID_MyObject then begin
  M := TMyObject.Create;
  Pointer(Obj) := M;
  ...
end;
```

Notice that I typecast the typeless parameter to be a pointer. I do this merely to please the compiler, which uses its valuable type-checking skills to be sure that I'm writing code that at least makes some kind of nominal sense.

As I said earlier, the DLL is simple and contains only a small amount of fairly easy-to-read code. There are a few tricky lines in the CreateObject method, but the code in that method is easy enough to understand once you grasp its purpose.

The next step, of course, is to call this DLL from an executable. The ENoOle example program in Listing 30.3 demonstrates how to proceed.

Listing 30.3. The ENoOle program calls the DNOOLE.DLL.

```
unit main;

interface

uses
  SysUtils, Windows, Messages,
  Classes, Graphics, Controls,
  Forms, Dialogs, StdCtrls;

type
  TMyObject = class
    function AddOne(i: Integer): Integer; virtual; abstract;
    function AddTwo(i: Integer): Integer; virtual; abstract;
  end;

  TForm1 = class(TForm)
    AddOne: TButton;
    AddTwo: TButton;
```

continues

Listing 30.3. continued

```
    procedure AddOneClick(Sender: TObject);
    procedure AddTwoClick(Sender: TObject);
  private
    { Private declarations }
  public
    { Public declarations }
  end;

var
  Form1: TForm1;

implementation

{$R *.DFM}

function CreateObject(id: Integer; var Obj): Boolean;
  external 'DNOOLE' name 'CreateObject';

procedure TForm1.AddOneClick(Sender: TObject);
var
  AObj: TMyObject;
begin
  if CreateObject(1, AObj) then begin
    Caption := IntToStr(AObj.AddOne(5));
    AObj.Free;
  end;
end;

procedure TForm1.AddTwoClick(Sender: TObject);
var
  AObj: TMyObject;
begin
  if CreateObject(1, AObj) then begin
    Caption := IntToStr(AObj.AddTwo(5));
    AObj.Free;
  end;
end;

end.
```

This program enables you to call the two methods stored in the DLL. It posts the results of the method in the caption of the ENoOle application, as shown in Figure 30.1.

FIGURE 30.1.

The ENoOle application calls methods from an object stored in a DLL, then prints the results of those calls in its caption.

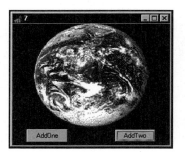

NOTE

Yes, it's a little strange to use an application's caption to display data. However, I find myself doing this kind of thing quite often when I'm experimenting with new ideas, so I thought I might add some verisimilitude to this example by presenting it in this fashion! It also has the benefit of helping me keep the code as simple as possible.

Under normal circumstances, you could not export TMyObject from a DLL because there's no way to get at the type information and variables declared in the interface of the DLL. DLLs simply don't know how to export that kind of information. As a result, Pascal objects declared in DLLs typically have been out of reach of the application that wanted to call them. The point of the ENoOle example is that it shows a trick demonstrating how to get at those DLLs. As far as I know, this is not a documented trick, so there is no guarantee that it will work in future versions of Delphi. However, I have reason to believe that this particular technique will not disappear any time soon. I might also add that you can use this same technique to import a C++ object into your program!

Here's how it works. This program imports the sole exported function from the DNOOLE.DLL:

```
function CreateObject(id: Integer; var Obj): Boolean;
  external 'DNOOLE' name 'CreateObject';
```

This is the standard technique for importing a routine from a DLL, and there's absolutely nothing unusual here. You simply declare the method and its parameters, then tell the compiler that it is defined externally. To wrap up, you give the explicit name of the external module in which it is defined, and then state the name under which it is exported.

Once again, there is nothing tricky about importing the CreateObject method into the executable. What is tricky, however, is both the fact that TMyObject must be redeclared in the executable and, more specifically, the way it is redeclared:

```
TMyObject = class
  function AddOne(i: Integer): Integer; virtual; abstract;
  function AddTwo(i: Integer): Integer; virtual; abstract;
end;
```

This may look like nonsense at first blush. After all, the keyword abstract is used to designate a method that is not implemented. Furthermore, calling an abstract method terminates your application. So what good does it do you to declare these abstract methods? What you need is something you can call, not a method that's explicitly declared in a manner that prevents you from calling it!

> **NOTE**
>
> Abstract methods exist because there are times when you want to define base classes that are not meant to be instantiated. For examples of this technique, see the TStrings and TStream class, both of which are declared in CLASSES.PAS. Of course, there are descendants of both TStrings and TStream that are used all the time in Delphi, but you would not normally ever see an instance of either of these classes. If you tried to create an instance of one of these classes you would succeed, but the act of calling certain methods in the class would result in an exception being raised, and your application summarily closing.
>
> The point here is that a call to an abstract method is an error, and Delphi has to provide some way of letting your know that things have gone wrong. Terminating your application is certainly one effective means of letting your know that all is not well!

By now it should be clear that calls to abstract methods usually result in an error. So why are the methods in TMyObject declared as abstract?

Well, the trick here is that redeclaring TMyObject as shown above is a valid way to access the methods of the real TMyObject under certain circumstances. In particular, it works as long as you can get at the virtual method table for a valid instance of the object! In other words, if you can ask the DLL for a pointer to a fully initialized instance of TMyObject, you can use the abstract method declaration to call its methods:

```
var
  AObj: TMyObject;
begin
  if CreateObject(1, AObj) then begin
    Caption := IntToStr(AObj.AddTwo(5));
    AObj.Free;
  end;
end;
```

The CreateObject call shown here retrieves a pointer to the virtual method table for a fully implemented instance of TMyObject. If you like, you can think of it as retrieving a pointer to TMyObject. Given that pointer, and an abstract declaration of TMyObject, you can call the methods of TMyObject in the normal manner.

As I just stated, an abstract method normally terminates your application when it executes. The point here is that it's not the compiler that forces your application to close when you call an abstract method. Instead, an actual call to a method called Abstract is made. The purpose of that call is to raise an exception that closes your application. In the previous example, however, the compiler jumps not to an instance of the abstract method, but instead jumps to the valid methods exported from the DLL. In short, this technique tricks the compiler into calling your method instead of the abstract routine defined by the creators of Delphi. The end result is that you can call the methods of an object that resides in a DLL as long as all of those methods are declared as virtual.

Once again, this entire example represents a useful trick that happens to mimic some of the standard behaviors of certain COM objects. Use this technique when you need it, and study its implementation so you can recycle this knowledge when you are working with the COM examples shown below.

Creating a DLL Server (INPROC)

It's time now to look at a real COM object. I show three interrelated examples over the next few pages:

- One example shows how to put a simple COM object called TMyObject in a DLL. This example is in two phases: the first phase is a minimal example of such an object, and the second shows how to build on that minimal example. In particular, I first show how to create the object, and then how to start adding your own methods to it.

- A second example shows how to put the same object in an executable. I do not, however, implement all the details required to successfully handle a COM object inside an executable. That would require creating an IMarshal interface, which is beyond the scope of this book. I do, however, present a working example that will get you started creating this type of code. (If you want to learn more about IMarshal, you should get *Inside OLE*, by Kraig Brockschmidt, and published by the Microsoft Press.)

- A third example shows how to write a client executable program that uses these other two objects.

I first create the DLL-based COM object, then create the client program, then later create the COM object that resides in an executable. That way you won't have to create two objects before you get a chance to test the first one. By the time you've had a look at all three binaries, you should have a good feeling for the way COM objects are put together.

COM objects can reside in either DLLs or executables—or, eventually, on remote machines. When they reside in DLLs they are known as *in-process servers*. When they reside in executables they are known as *local servers*. At the time of this writing Microsoft has not yet released the specification for creating *distributed objects* that reside on remote machines.

The first COM object example resides in a DLL called SimpObj. Later in this chapter you see a client program, called MakeCom1, that instantiates an instance of this object and calls some of its methods. The code for SIMPOBJ.DLL is shown in Listing 30.4. Listing 30.5 shows the code for MYOBJ.PAS, which contains the COM object to be exported from the DLL. Listing 30.6 contains the registration file for SIMPOBJ.DLL. All the source files for this example are found on the *Unleashed* CD-ROM in the SIMPDLL directory.

Listing 30.4. The code for SIMPOBJ.DLL, the DPR file controlling the COM object that resides in a DLL.

```
library SimpObj;

  { This DLL is designed to be run with the MAKEOLE1.DPR project
    that ships with Delphi Unleashed. It could also be used with
    other properly constructed client programs.

    You must use REGEDIT.EXE to register SIMPOBJ.DLL before you
    access it from MakeOle1. To register this DLL with the system,
    choose Registry | Import Registry from REGEDIT.EXE and import the
    WIN32.REG file found in the directory where SimpObj is stored.
    You can also register this DLL by simply double clicking on
    its REG files from inside the Windows Explorer.

    Note that there is a DOS path included in SimpObj's REG files.
    The REG file itself is just ASCII text. You may have to edit it
    with Notepad so that the path points to the place on your
    system where SIMPOBJ.DLL is stored. }

uses
  Ole2, OleAuto, SysUtils,
  myobj in 'myobj.pas';

{$R *.RES}

function DllGetClassObject(const rclsid: TCLSID; const riid: TGUID;
                           var ppv): hResult; stdcall export;
var
  HR:  HRESULT;
  MyClassFactory: IMyClassFactory;
begin
  if not IsEqualIID(CLSID_MyObject, rclsid) then begin
    result := E_FAIL;
    Exit;
  end;

  try
    MyClassFactory := IMyClassFactory.Create;
  except
```

```
    Result := E_OUTOFMEMORY;
    Exit;
  end;

  hr := MyClassFactory.QueryInterface(riid, ppv);

  if (FAILED(hr)) then begin
    MyClassFactory.Free;
    Result := hr;
    Exit;
  end;

  Result := hr;
end;

function DllCanUnloadNow: hResult;
begin
  if (LockCount = 0) and (ObjCount = 0) then
    Result := S_Ok
  else
    Result := S_False;
end;

exports
  DllGetClassObject name 'DllGetClassObject',
  DllCanUnloadNow name 'DllCanUnloadNow';

begin
end.
```

Listing 30.5. MYOBJ.PAS contains the COM object to be exported from the DLL.

```
unit myobj;

{
  There are three things you need to keep track of:
    1) How many objects have been created
    2) How many references each object has
    3) How many locks are on each object
  If all three are zero, then DllCanUnloadNow will return true.
}

interface

uses
  Ole2, Windows, SysUtils;

const
  { I've lost track of my block of GUID's, so this one might be dup on
    your system! Kind of unlikely, though... Best to use GENGUID.EXE. }

  CLSID_MyObject: TGUID = (
    D1:$C9B0B160;D2:$1308;D3:$11cf;D4:($AB,$35,$00,$00,$C0,$7E,$BA,$2B));
```

continues

Listing 30.5. continued

```pascal
type
  TObjectDestroyed = procedure;

  IMyObject = class(IUnknown)
  private
    FRefCount: LongInt;
    FObjectDestroyed: TObjectDestroyed;
  public
    constructor Create(ObjectDestroyed: TObjectDestroyed);
    function QueryInterface(const iid: TIID; var obj): HResult; override;
    function AddRef: Longint; override;
    function Release: Longint; override;
    function GetTwelve: Integer; virtual;
  end;

  IMyClassFactory = class(IClassFactory)
  private
    FRefCount: LongInt;
  public
    constructor Create;
    function QueryInterface(const iid: TIID; var obj): HResult; override;
    function AddRef: Longint; override;
    function Release: Longint; override;
    function CreateInstance(unkOuter: IUnknown; const iid: TIID;
      var obj): HResult; override;
    function LockServer(fLock: BOOL): HResult; override;
  end;

var
  LockCount: Integer;
  ObjCount: Integer;
{ F: TextFile; }

implementation

constructor IMyObject.Create(ObjectDestroyed: TObjectDestroyed);
begin
  inherited Create;
  FObjectDestroyed := ObjectDestroyed;
  FRefCount := 0;
end;

function IMyObject.QueryInterface(const iid: TIID; var obj): HResult;
begin
  if IsEqualIID(iid, IID_IUnknown) or
    IsEqualIID(iid, CLSID_MyObject) then begin
    Pointer(obj) := Self;
    AddRef;
    Result := S_OK;
  end else begin
    Pointer(obj) := nil;
    Result := E_NOINTERFACE;
  end;
end;

function IMyObject.AddRef: Longint;
begin
```

```
    Inc(FRefCount);
    Result := FRefCount;
end;

function IMyObject.Release: Longint;
begin
  Dec(FRefCount);
  if FRefCount = 0 then begin
    FObjectDestroyed;
    Free;
    Result := 0;
  end else
    Result := FRefCount;
end;

function IMyObject.GetTwelve: Integer;
begin
  Result := 12;
end;

{ -- IMyClassFactory -- }

{ This routine is passed as a parameter to TMyObject }
procedure ObjectDestroyed;
begin
  Dec(ObjCount)
end;

constructor IMyClassFactory.Create;
begin
  inherited Create;
  FRefCount := 0;
end;

function IMyClassFactory.QueryInterface(const iid: TIID; var obj): HResult;
begin
  if IsEqualIID(iid, IID_IClassFactory) or
     IsEqualIID(iid, IID_IUnknown) then begin
    Pointer(obj) := Self;
    AddRef;
    Result := S_OK;
  end else begin
    Pointer(obj) := nil;
    Result := E_NOINTERFACE;
  end;
end;

function IMyClassFactory.AddRef: Longint;
begin
  Inc(FRefCount);
  Result := FRefCount;
end;

function IMyClassFactory.Release: Longint;
begin
  Dec(FRefCount);
  if FRefCount = 0 then begin
```

continues

Listing 30.5. continued

```
    Destroy;
    Result := 0;
  end else
    Result := FRefCount;
end;

function IMyClassFactory.CreateInstance(UnkOuter: IUnknown;
                                        const iid: Tiid;
                                        var Obj): hResult;
var
  hr: HResult;
  MyObject: IMyObject;
begin
  if UnkOuter <> nil then begin
    Result := E_Fail;
    Exit;
  end;
  if (not isEqualIID(iid, IID_IUnknown)) and
     (not isEqualIID(iid, CLSID_MyObject)) then begin
    Result := E_Fail;
    Exit;
  end;

  MyObject := IMyObject.Create(ObjectDestroyed);

  if MyObject = nil then begin
    Pointer(Obj) := nil;
    Result := E_OutOfMemory;
    Exit;
  end;

  hr := MyObject.QueryInterface(iid, Obj);
  if Failed(hr) then
    MyObject.Free
  else
    Inc(ObjCount);

  Result := hr;
end;

function IMyClassFactory.LockServer(fLock: BOOL): HResult;
begin
  if fLock then
    Inc(LockCount)
  else
    Dec(LockCount);
  Result := S_Ok;
end;


initialization
{ AssignFile(F, 'c:\info.txt');
  ReWrite(F);
  WriteLn(F, 'Initialization'); }
  LockCount := 0;
  ObjCount := 0;
```

```
finalization
  {  CloseFile(F); }
end.
```

Listing 30.6. The registration file for SIMPOBJ.DLL.

```
REGEDIT
HKEY_CLASSES_ROOT\MyObject1.0 = MyObject Test 1
HKEY_CLASSES_ROOT\MyObject1.0\CLSID = {C9B0B160-1308-11cf-AB35-0000C07EBA2B}
HKEY_CLASSES_ROOT\MyObject = MyObject Test 1
HKEY_CLASSES_ROOT\MyObject\CurVer = MyObject1.0
HKEY_CLASSES_ROOT\MyObject\CLSID = {C9B0B160-1308-11cf-AB35-0000C07EBA2B}

HKEY_CLASSES_ROOT\CLSID\{C9B0B160-1308-11cf-AB35-0000C07EBA2B} =
  MyObject Test 1
HKEY_CLASSES_ROOT\CLSID\
  {C9B0B160-1308-11cf-AB35-0000C07EBA2B}\ProgID = MyObject1.0
HKEY_CLASSES_ROOT\CLSID\{C9B0B160-1308-11cf-AB35-
0000C07EBA2B}\VersionIndependentProgID = MyObject
HKEY_CLASSES_ROOT\CLSID\{C9B0B160-1308-11cf-AB35-0000C07EBA2B}\InProcServer32 =
  c:\src\unleash\chap30\simpdll\simpobj.dll
HKEY_CLASSES_ROOT\CLSID\{C9B0B160-1308-11cf-AB35-0000C07EBA2B}\NotInsertable
```

This DLL, of course, cannot be run on its own. Before you can test it you first must create a client, or *container*, program called MakeOle1. As a writer I normally try to get readers up and running with working example programs as quickly as possible. However, in this case, I'm going to ask you to wait awhile before viewing the MakeOle1 program. The issue here is that there is so much material to cover that I can't imagine throwing more code at you before explaining at least something about the code you have seen so far.

The last paragraph implies that there is considerable complexity in creating even the simplest COM objects. On the whole, I would have to agree that this is a fairly complex subject. However, this material is not as complex as it's often rumored to be in the computer press. Take your time with it; study it carefully, and you'll find that it yields up its secrets in a fairly short period of time. There is some complexity here, perhaps more than there needs to be, but it is not insurmountable.

All About the Registry and GUIDs

You worked with the registry a little in Chapter 29, "OLE Automation Basics." Here I review key aspects of it, particularly as the apply to COM objects. The registry is not really that complicated, but I don't want it to become a stumbling block for anyone trying to become familiar with this technology.

As far as COM objects are concerned, the registry is a simple database that has one primary task: it associates a numerical value with each of the COM objects available on the system. This is not a complete definition of the registry, but it's what you need to know about it for now.

To work with the registry, open up REGEDIT.EXE. You will see something that looks like the screen shot in Figure 30.2.

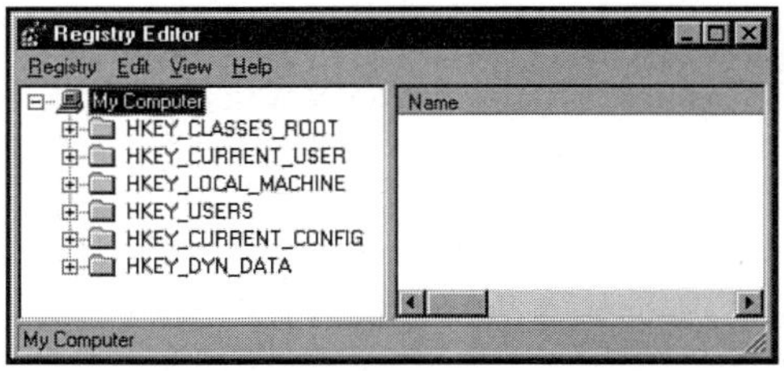

FIGURE 30.2.

The Registry Editor displays this screen when it first opens.

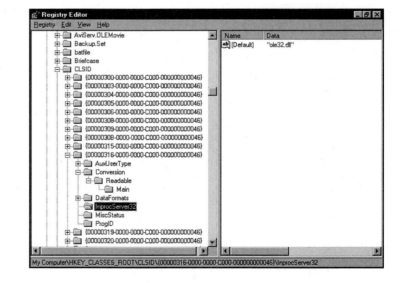

Open up the tree called HKEY_CLASSES_ROOT. Scroll down the list of entries until you come to one called CLSID. Open up the CLSID tree and scroll down the entries, as shown in Figure 30.3.

FIGURE 30.3.

The CLSID section of HKEY_CLASSES_ROOT in the RegEdit program. The CLSIDs are on the left; the associated program, class, or file type is on the right.

You might notice that, as you scroll down the list, various familiar names appear on the right side of the RegEdit screen. For instance, the CLSID {0003000C-0000-0000-C000-000000000046} is associated with the Package program. Scroll down even further in HKEY_CLASSES_ROOT, and you come to an entry on the left side that reads Package. If you open up the tree for the Package entry, as shown in Figure 30.4, you see a CLSID entry identical to the one you found earlier.

FIGURE 30.4.

The Package entry in REGEDIT.EXE has leaves called CLSID, Protocol, Server, and Verb.

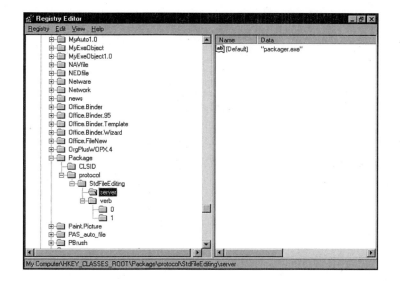

The point here is that you can find the CLSID of the Package program by looking it up by name in the registry. Conversely, if you have the CLSID of an object, you can find out its name. Figure 30.4 suggests that there also are other important pieces of information stored in RegEdit and associated with the Package program, but for now all you need to know is that it's a place to store CLSIDs.

If you want to insert an entry, or set of entries, in the registry, you can do so by preparing text like the WIN32.REG file shown in Listing 30.6. Consider the following entry in that file:

```
HKEY_CLASSES_ROOT\MyObject\CLSID =
    {C9B0B160-1308-11cf-AB35-0000C07EBA2B}
```

I have divided this into two lines because of space considerations. You, however, should type this in as a single line. The code shown here tells the registry to create an entry called MyObject\CLSID in the registry, and to associate a particular CLSID with that entry.

Besides associating a CLSID with a name, and a name with a CLSID, the registry also associates a CLSID with a path to an executable or DLL:

```
HKEY_CLASSES_ROOT\
  CLSID\
    {C9B0B160-1308-11cf-AB35-0000C07EBA2B}\InProcServer32 =
        c:\src\unleash\chap30\simpdll\simpobj.dll
```

Given an entry like this in the registry database, it's easy to see how you can give the COM services a CLSID, and then have COM in turn load a DLL or executable that is associated with the CLSID. It should also be obvious that you can easily create an error condition by specifying the wrong path in your REG file. If you are having trouble with one of the programs in this chapter, look carefully at the REG file and make sure that it points at the file you want to launch. You should also make sure this information is listed correctly in the registry itself.

So what is a CLSID? Well, a CLSID is very much like an IID, and both CLSIDs and IIDs are forms of GUIDs (pronounced Goo ID). In particular, a GUID is generic name for a *globally unique identifier*. A CLSID is a GUID that identifies a class, and an IID is a GUID that identifies an interface. From a purely structural point of view, IIDs, GUIDs, and CLSIDs are identical. They differ only in what they represent; that is, in what they are meant to designate.

The basic fact to understand about them is that they are guaranteed to be statistically unique; which means, I suppose, that it's unlikely that any two of them will be identical. It's probable that in the future there will be thousands of COM objects on our machines. Furthermore, we'll have simultaneous access to thousands of other machines, which all have thousands of COM objects on them. Given these kinds of numbers, it would not be possible to uniquely identify objects by giving them names. (For instance, there seem to be many different programs called EDIT.EXE, or EXPLORER.EXE. These are not unique names.) CLSIDs, and the closely related group of numbers called GUIDs, are meant to be statistically unique. Therefore, they should help to meet the needs foreseen by the developers of the Component object model.

For now, you don't need to know a great deal else about CLSIDs other than that they follow, in Object Pascal terms, this record structure:

```
TGUID = record
  D1: Longint;
  D2: Word;
  D3: Word;
  D4: array[0..7] of Byte;
end;
```

When creating instances of these GUIDs for you to use, Microsoft's code generates random numbers based on the current date and time, and on the supposedly unique numeric properties of certain pieces of hardware, such as network cards. In particular, you can run a program called GUIDGEN.EXE (Borland) or UUIDGEN (Microsoft) that generates these numbers for you There are also Windows API calls you can make to generate these numbers on the fly.

For now, I am not going to spend any more time discussing the Registry. The key point to remember is that the Registry is just a database. This database serves a wide range of purposes, but one of the most important is that it associates CLSIDs with the names of programs and with other associated bits of information, such as version numbers and the location at which binaries are stored.

> **NOTE**
>
> Most of the fundamental routines used in COM are declared in OLE2.PAS. Here are some routines that you can use to explore the Registry:
>
> ```
> OleRegGetUserType
> OleRegGetMiscStatus
> OleRegEnumFormatEtc
> OleRegEnumVerbs
> ```

Here are some functions for use with CLSIDs:

```
StringFromCLSID(const clsid: TCLSID; var psz: POleStr): HResult; stdcall;
CLSIDFromString(psz: POleStr; var clsid: TCLSID): HResult; stdcall;
StringFromIID(const iid: TIID; var psz: POleStr): HResult; stdcall;
IIDFromString(psz: POleStr; var iid: TIID): HResult; stdcall;
CoIsOle1Class(const clsid: TCLSID): BOOL; stdcall;
ProgIDFromCLSID(const clsid: TCLSID; var pszProgID: POleStr): HResult;
stdcall;
CLSIDFromProgID(pszProgID: POleStr; var clsid: TCLSID): HResult; stdcall;
StringFromGUID2(const guid: TGUID; psz: POleStr; cbMax: Integer): Integer;
```

This is not meant to be an exhaustive discussion of either OLE or COM, so I do not attempt to explain each of these functions. Instead, I refer you instead to the Delphi online Help or to other books on this subject. Note, however, that `POleStr`s are `WideChar`s, and that you should use the `MultiByteToWideChar` and `WideCharToMultiByte` functions for conversions between `PChar`s and `WideChar`s.

Creating the Object

Now that you've had a brief look at the registry, it's time to move on to the actual code that makes up an in-process server. I divide this code into parts:

- One part is the code representing the actual object to be exported; that is, `TMyObject` and its implementation.
- The other part is the code that facilitates or makes possible the exporting of the object; that is, `TMyClassFactory` and `DllGetClassObject`.

The client program that seeks a reference to `TMyObject` can obtain it by calling either `CoGetClassObject` or `CoCreateInstance`. Both of these functions cause a call to be made to a function inside SIMPOBJ.DPR called `DllGetClassObject`.

NOTE

As a rule, you can consider any function that begins with the letters `Co` to be part of the COM API. For instance, both `CoGetClassObject` and `CoCreateInstance` are part of the Windows API, and are listed in books that discuss OLE 2.*x*. These are functions that belong to the operating system, just as `CreateWindow` and `MessageBox` are Windows API functions.

When writing the type of code shown in this chapter, you should try to stick to COM functions because of memory and performance considerations. For instance, don't call `OleInitiailize` if `CoInitialize` will do. COM is a subset of OLE. It's smaller and more compact.

1062

The COM API is fairly large, and the OLE API as a whole is huge. You should do anything you can to obtain Microsoft SDKs, documents, and Help files that will enable you to sort out some of these functions. Joining the Microsoft Developer Network is one way to get this information. Buying third-party books is another way to get information. You also should study OLE2.PAS, OLECTL.PAS, OLEAUTO.PAS, and OLECTRLS.PAS. All of these files ship with the Delphi RTL, and they provide hundreds of examples of how to write COM-based code.

The signature for DllGetClassObject is defined in the COM specification, but it is not implemented there. Instead, it is up to you to implement the method. In other words, COM gives you a particular function header, and then promises to call this function at the appropriate time if you export it from a DLL. (This is similar to the process seen when you create a dialog box or implement a callback. Of course, there are significant differences, but a parallel does exit.)

Here is the declaration for DllGetClassObject:

```
function DllGetClassObject(
  const rclsid: TCLSID;       // Class you ultimately after
  const riid: TGUID;          // Usually IClassFactory
  var ppv                     // Usually returns pointer to IClassFactory
): hResult; stdcall export; // S_OK on success
```

The first parameter passed to this function is the CLSID of the object you want to retrieve from the DLL. However, DllGetClassObject does not return an instance of the object specified by the CLSID. It just checks to see if the class you want is supported by the current DLL and by the IClassFactory object specified in the second parameter. Don't be fooled into thinking that DllGetClassObject returns the class object you are seeking to instantiate. That would be the logical thing for a function with this name to do—but this is OLE code, and nothing in OLE is quite so obvious as all that!

The second parameter is the ID of an intermediate class used to communicate with the object you want to retrieve. This intermediate class is usually IClassFactory. I explain both the details of this communication and the reason for the existence of this intermediate class in just a few moments.

The final parameter passed to DllGetClassObject holds the pointer to the object specified in the second parameter. In particular, the third parameter usually returns an instance of IClassFactory. This is what you are after when you call this function.

Note also that the object returns an hResult. This hResult is passed back to the calling application so that you can see if the call succeeded. In other words, when you call CoGetClassObject, it in turn calls DllGetClassObject, and CoGetClassObject returns the result of the call to DllGetClassObject.

> **NOTE**
>
> The strange thing about this process is that you call `CoGetClassObject`, which is a Windows API function that really only ends up calling another function you implemented. This kind of indirection can be confusing at first. For instance, if your call to `CoGetClassObject` fails, you're likely to say, "Hey, that call can't fail. I know I've called it correctly. I'm sure of it!" And, indeed, you may be calling the function correctly. However, even if it's called correctly, it still can return an error if you have incorrectly implemented `DllGetClassObject` or any of the routines that `DllGetClassObject` calls.

It is perhaps worth reiterating that you probably will never directly call `DllGetClassObject`. Instead, this routine is called by OLE after you first call `CoGetClassObject` or `CoCreateInstance`. Needless to say, when you call either of these functions, you pass them the CLSID you want to retrieve, the ID of the interface you want to use to communicate with the object, and a pointer variable that usually references an instance of `IClassFactory`.

`CoGetClassObject` usually returns an instance of `IClassFactory`, while `CoCreateInstance` returns the object that you seek. For instance, in this case it would return `IMyObject`.

As I stated earlier, `CoGetClassObject` and `CoCreateInstance` are vaguely analogous to calls such as `DialogBox` or `EnumFontFamilies`. `DllGetClassObject` is vaguely analogous to a dialog procedure, a window procedure, or a `TFNFontEnumProc`. You call `CoGetClassObject` and `EnumFontFamilies` directly, but you would never call `DllGetClassObject` or a dialog procedure directly. Once again, this analogy is meant to help you understand the concepts involved; it's not meant to draw a direct parallel between blatantly disparate technologies.

> **NOTE**
>
> I'm aware that all this complexity can be a bit overwhelming. Remember, however, that this book ships with working examples of COM technology. Once you have implemented it correctly a first time, you can reuse the code simply by cutting and pasting. The first time is hard, but once you have an example up and running, you can go on to create your own COM-based programs with relatively little work.

The implementation for `DllGetClassObject` begins by checking to be sure that the object you requested is supported by this DLL and by `IMyClassFactory`:

```
if not IsEqualIID(CLSID_MyObject, rclsid) then begin
  result := E_FAIL;
  Exit;
end;
```

The reason it performs this check is just to make sure that the whole process is not a waste of time. `DllGetClassObject` is not going to return the object specified in the CLSID. However, it knows what objects are supported by the DLL and by its implementation of `IClassFactory`. It therefore checks the CLSID to see if the calling process is off on some kind of wild goose chase. I could, if I wanted, ask `IMyClassFactory` directly if it supports this interface. After all, I implemented `IMyClassFactory, so` I can figure out which CLSIDs it supports and which it doesn't. In this case, I know it supports only `CLSID_MyObject`, so I give the okay.

It should come as no surprise to learn that the COM function called `IsEqualIID` enables you to compare two GUIDs to see if they are equivalent. You will use this function over and over again in COM code to ensure that the objects being requested actually are supported by your server.

> **NOTE**
>
> You can find a whole series of return codes specified in OLE2.PAS. Many of these constants begin with either S or E. S stands for success and E stands for error.
>
> The code fragment shown above returns E_FAIL if the two GUIDs being compared are not equal. Two other, entirely self-explanatory, error codes include E_ACCESSDENIED and E_ABORT. The two primary success codes are S_OK and S_FALSE, both of which also are self-explanatory.
>
> Often you don't really care exactly what happened when a function executes, but are concerned only with whether it succeeded or failed. Most OLE functions return something called an HResult, and you can use the Succeeded and Failed functions to determine whether or not an HResult is a success or failure code. For instance, if a function returns S_FALSE, Succeeded returns True. If a functions returns E_ABORT, Succeeded returns False. Here are some of the routines used to examine the return values from COM and OLE functions:
>
> ```
> function Succeeded(Res: HResult): Boolean;
> function Failed(Res: HResult): Boolean;
> function ResultCode(Res: HResult): Integer;
> function ResultFacility(Res: HResult): Integer;
> function ResultSeverity(Res: HResult): Integer;
> function MakeResult(Severity, Facility, Code: Integer): HResult;
> ```

In most cases, `DllGetClassObject` is a tool for retrieving class factories from a DLL. That is, `DllGetClassObject` instantiates an instance of `IClassFactory` and returns it to the calling process. That's what it does.

There is, in fact, no written rule saying that `DllGetClassObject` has to return an instance of `IClassFactory`, but that is, in fact, what it usually does. One possible variation you could run on this scenario would be to have several `IClassFactorys` stored in a single DLL or set of DLLs. Then you could return a particular class factory in one circumstance, and another class factory in a different circumstance. Once again, the point is that Microsoft designed this architecture to be flexible. That flexibility comes with a price, however, and the price you pay is an increase in complexity, and a resultant potential ambiguity.

> **NOTE**
>
> It might be worth noting that the developers of Delphi appear to have a formula they follow when designing their product. In particular, they seek to find the best way to do something, and to then make it as easy as possible for you to use that method. This technique stands in contrast to architectures that seek to find the most flexible way to do things. A third alternative is represented by a language like BASIC, which seeks to find not the the best, not the most flexible, but the easiest way to do something. OLE and C++ are flexible but difficult. BASIC is inflexible but easy to use. Delphi seeks to find the middle ground. It's developers look for the best way to do something, and then make it as easy as possible without sacrificing preformance.

Thinking About *IClassFactory*

Just for the sake of clarity, let me reiterate that when you call DllGetClassObject, you pass in three parameters. The first is the name of the object you really want to get. DllGetClassObject, however, doesn't really care much about this parameter. It only checks to see if this parameter is, in fact, the CLSID of an object supported by the DLL. (I'm intentionally repeating myself here. I want to state these complex ideas in several different ways in the hopes that they will finally come clear to all readers of this book!)

The first parameter is relatively easy to understand. However, the second parameter, the one called riid, appears to serve a rather mysterious and elusive purpose. I said above that this GUID is used to designate the object that is used to communicate with the object you want to retrieve. Furthermore, I said that it usually is set to the GUID of IClassFactory. Well, what does this mean? What's it all about?

It turns out that most servers are able to export a wide range of objects. The SimpObj project in Listing 30.4 exports only one object, called TMyObject. But the DLL itself is capable of hosting many objects. In fact, this is a trait of most servers, whether they are DLLs, executables, or some other type of entity. All of these servers can host multiple objects, just as the DNoOle example in Listings 30.1 and 30.2 could have exported many objects.

COM defines a particular type of class, called an IClassFactory, which is meant to churn out pointers to the interfaces that reside in a DLL or other server. A class factory instantiates objects and passes them on to the user.

Turn, for a moment, to the DNoOle program in Listings 30.1 and 30.2. The DLL in that program had a single function called CreateObject. That function was something of a miniature class factory. You passed in to it an ID and a pointer; it did some hand waving, and then set your pointer equal to a valid instance of the type of class identified by the ID you passed in. The function was, in effect, a tiny factory that manufactured valid instances of classes. IClassFactory performs the same task.

Consider the following code from DllGetClassObject:

```
try
  pObj := IMyClassFactory.Create;
except
  Result := E_OUTOFMEMORY;
  Exit;
end;
```

This code attempts to create an instance of IMyClassFactory. If the code fails, DllGetClassObject is terminated and the function returns an error message stating that the system is out of memory. It is unlikely that this call would ever fail. (You're seeing very conservative code here.)

If the attempt to call IMyClassFactory succeeds, the IClassFactory method called QueryInterface is called. This routine has an implementation almost identical to the CreateObject method shown in the ENoOle and DNoOle examples:

```
  hr := pObj.QueryInterface(riid, ppv);
```

The following code checks the result of the call to QueryInterface:

```
if (FAILED(hr)) then begin
  pObj.Free;
  Result := hr;
  Exit;
end;
```

```
Result := hr;
```
If the call fails, the class factory is freed and the function returns an error. If the call succeeds, the function returns a success code and a valid pointer to IMyClassFactory.

To help you understand this, I want to show you the implementation of IClassFactory.QueryInterface:

```
function IMyClassFactory.QueryInterface(const iid: TIID; var obj): HResult;

begin
  if IsEqualIID(iid, IID_IClassFactory) or
    IsEqualIID(iid, IID_IUnknown) then begin
    Pointer(obj) := Self;
    AddRef;
    Result := S_OK;
  end else begin
    Pointer(obj) := nil;
    Result := E_NOINTERFACE;
  end;
end;
```

This code checks to see whether iid is equal to IID_IClassFactory or IID_IUnknown. If either of these things are true, it returns a pointer to Self! From the OOP programmer's point of view, this is ridiculous. We had to have a pointer to IMyClassFactory or we wouldn't have been able to call QueryInterface. It's as if the OOP programmer is being forced to jump through a hoop in order to obtain something already in that programmer's hands. The advantage of this type of code, however, is that it makes sure you really are getting a pointer to the object you requested. It's performing type checking!

Once you have a pointer to an object, you call QueryInterface to retrieve a particular interface. If the call to QueryInterface does not return the object you wish to retrieve, QueryInterface is telling you that the current object does not support the desired interface. In this sense, QueryInterface enables you to query an object and ask it what it can and cannot do. It's a means of building type checking into COM technology.

> **NOTE**
>
> Remember, when using COM you often don't have access to the object's source code, and you don't have a way for the compiler to perform careful type checking. As a result, some other system has to be implemented that ensures that you really are obtaining a pointer to the specific object you requested. This QueryInterface business is a way to implement type checking, even if you are working across process or language boundaries!

Because COM is so peculiar, it is perhaps worth going over the import of DllGetClassObject one last time:

- The first parameter is the object you want to ultimately retrieve. However, DllGetClassObject doesn't actually retrieve an object of this type. It just checks to make sure it's supported by the DLL. In some cases, it may even be a case of whether the value specified in the second parameter supports the requested interface. That is, the DLL may support the CLSID in the first parameter, but the GUID in the second paramater may not be the proper means of accessing it!

- The second parameter usually is set to IID_IClassFactory. IClassFactory is used to retrieve the desired object. It is possible that the DLL supports the class specified in the first parameter, but the instance of IClassFactory requested in the second parameter does not. However, for now, you don't need to worry about that kind of situation.

- The third parameter usually is used to return an instance of IClassFactory, or of whatever interface is being used to communicate with the desired class.

IUnknown and IMyObject

Now that you have seen DllGetClassObject, the next step is to look at the code for IMyObject and IMyClassFactory. It's arguable that the two most fundamental objects in COM are IUnknown and IClassFactory. It's now time for you to get a close look at these objects, and to see exactly why they exist and what they do!

IMyObject is a direct descendant of IUnknown. In fact, it is merely an implementation of IUnknown, although it could be made to do more, as I will show in a moment.

COM objects implement something called *reference counting*. Each time an instance of an object is created, a function called AddRef is called:

```
function IMyObject.AddRef: Longint;
begin
  Inc(FRefCount);
  Result := FRefCount;
end;
```

This code increments a field of IMyObject called FRefCount. FRefCount is set to zero in the object's constructor.

This same variable is decremented whenever the object is released:

```
function IMyObject.Release: Longint;
begin
  Dec(FRefCount);
  if FRefCount = 0 then begin
    FObjectDestroyed;
    Free;
    Result := 0;
  end else
    Result := FRefCount;
end;
```

As you can see, if this variable reaches zero, the entire object is automatically destroyed. This is called reference counting. It guarantees that the object is not destroyed until all the processes or objects that have attached to it have called Release.

> **NOTE**
>
> Delphi uses referencing counting internally when it works with long strings. If you have two variables that point to the same string, Delphi doesn't create two copies of the string; it merely increments its reference count.

ObjectDestroyed is a simple, stand-alone routine that keeps track of the total number of objects in a DLL or executable. If that number reaches zero, the entire DLL or executable can be unloaded from memory. You therefore track two reference counts: one that is internal to an object, and one that is global to the whole DLL. Here is the very simple implementation of

ObjectDestroyed:

```
procedure ObjectDestroyed;
begin
  Dec(ObjCount)
end;
```

Reference counting is not the main job of a direct descendant of IUnknown. Rather, its key job is creating, and perhaps implementing, interfaces. From the point of view of Object Pascal, an object is created when its constructor is called. From the point of view of COM, the creation of an object is relatively unimportant. What is key is the moment when QueryInterface returns a pointer to an interface.

The issue here is that COM must perform some type checking to ensure that you really are getting the object that you requested. Because there is no way to do type checking in the traditional sense, the next best thing is to use this system of GUIDs and CLSIDs. You could, therefore, say that COM enforces a kind of type checking by insisting that you go through QueryInterface if you want to retrieve a pointer to an object.Getting hold of what a Delphi programmer would call an object is, therefore a multi-step process. First, the container application calls into the DLL, usually asking for an instance of IClassFactory. The DLL then creates an instance of the requested object; that is, it calls the constructor for IClassFactory. The DLL then calls IClassFactory's QueryInterface method, asking for a valid, "type checked" instance of IClassFactory. If that succeeds, it returns the object. From the OOP programmer's point of view, this call to QueryInterface is a spurious and absurd process; however, it's the way things are done in COM land!

When you retrieve an instance if IMyObject, the same process that occurred with IClassFactory must be repeated. That is, first you call the constructor, then you call IMyObject.QueryInterface to see if the specific requested interface is, in fact, supported:

```
function IMyObject.QueryInterface(const iid: TIID; var obj): HResult;
begin
   if IsEqualIID(iid, IID_IUnknown) or
     IsEqualIID(iid, CLSID_MyObject) then begin
    Pointer(obj) := Self;
    AddRef;
    Result := S_OK;
  end else begin
    Pointer(obj) := nil;
    Result := E_NOINTERFACE;
  end;
end;
```

IMyObject returns a pointer to Self if iid is set to either IID_IUnknown or CLSID_MyObject. IID_IUnknown is an object that supports three methods, as shown from its declaration in OLE2.PAS:

```
IUnknown = class
public
  function QueryInterface(const iid: TIID; var obj): HResult;
    virtual; stdcall; abstract;
```

```
    function AddRef: Longint; virtual; stdcall; abstract;
    function Release: Longint; virtual; stdcall; abstract;
end;
```

As you can see, IMyObject implements all three of these methods, so it can be said to implement the interface to IUnknown. Therefore, it returns a pointer to Self if the requested ID is IUnknown.

The point here is that IMyObject might implement 30 methods in addition to the interface to IUnknown. However, if it does in fact support IUnknown, it's safe to return an instance of itself when IUnknown is requested. The user may then end up calling only 3 of the 30 available methods, but the calls to these methods will in fact succeed, and will behave as you would expect the methods of IUnknown to behave. This is what is meant when programmers say that IMyObject supports the IUnknown interface!

Obviously, the specific example shown here leaves a little bit to be desired. The problem is that this instance of IMyObject only supports the interface to IUnknown. It does not expland its reach beyond the minimal capabilities of IUnknown, It is, in fact, a bland and rather unappatizing example, but it has the virtue of being relatively easy to understand. When you are working with OLE, things that are easy to understand are always virtuous!

Later in this chapter I show how you can add additional methods to IMyObject, and then access them from an executable. This is the technique used in the Games SDK, and you are only a few pieces of information away from understanding how it works. Before I can show it to you, however, I must first talk about IClassFactory and freeing up DLLs, and then about accessing IMyObject from an executable. When you understand this additional material, you can see how to go back and extend the functionality of IMyObject so that it implements a little something more than the IUnknown interface.

Implementing *IClassFactory*

After all this talk, it turns out that it is quite easy to implement IClassFactory:

```
IMyClassFactory = class(IClassFactory)
  private
    FRefCount: LongInt;
  public
    constructor Create;
    function QueryInterface(const iid: TIID; var obj): HResult; override;
    function AddRef: Longint; override;
    function Release: Longint; override;
    function CreateInstance(unkOuter: IUnknown; const iid: TIID;
      var obj): HResult; override;
    function LockServer(fLock: BOOL): HResult; override;
  end;
```

As you can see, all but two of these methods also are implemented in IUnknown, so there is no need to discuss them further.

The key new method is `CreateInstance`, which is the method used to retrieve an instance of `IMyObject`:

```
function IMyClassFactory.CreateInstance(UnkOuter: IUnknown;
                                        const iid: Tiid;
                                        var Obj): hResult;
var
  hr: HResult;
  MyObject: IMyObject;
begin
  if UnkOuter <> nil then begin
    Result := E_Fail;
    Exit;
  end;
  if (not isEqualIID(iid, IID_IUnknown)) and
     (not isEqualIID(iid, CLSID_MyObject)) then begin
    Result := E_Fail;
    Exit;
  end;

  MyObject := IMyObject.Create(ObjectDestroyed);

  if MyObject = nil then begin
    Pointer(Obj) := nil;
    Result := E_OutOfMemory;
    Exit;
  end;

  hr := MyObject.QueryInterface(iid, Obj);
  if Failed(hr) then
    MyObject.Free
  else
    Inc(ObjCount);

  Result := hr;
end;
```

`ClassFactory.CreateInstance` is very like `ClassFactory.QueryInterface`. The difference, of course, is that it does not return a pointer to `Self`. Instead, it returns the long-sought-after pointer to `IMyObject`!

The function first checks to make sure the first parameter is set to `nil`. If it is not, it exits, as this object does not support aggregation. (Aggregation is a topic that is beyond the scope of this book.) It's up to you decide what errors you want to return under what circumstances. You could, for instance, simply return `E_FAIL` rather than `CLASS_E_NOAGGREGATION`. Either way, the container is going to get the information.

Code to check the requested CLSID is then executed. Finally, the routine creates an instance of `IMyObject`, calls it `QueryInterface`, and returns a pointer to the requested object!

The call to `LockServer` is meant only to keep the server in memory if someone is accessing the object. It's a bookkeeping routine that is not part of the main show.

Freeing the DLL

Calls to `CoGetClassObject` or `CoCreateInstance` force a DLL to be loaded into memory, if it is not already in memory. Calls to `CoUnintialize` cause the DLL to be unloaded, along with any other OLE-related files. However, there are times when you want to merely unload a specific COM-related DLL. To do this, you can call the OLE API function `DLLCanUnloadNow`.

The key point to grasp here is that the SimpObj DLL keeps track of the number of objects it hosts and the number of calls to `LockServer` that it experiences. If the user calls `CoFreeUnusedLibraries`, a call is made to `DLLCanUnloadNow`. In its turn, the `DLLCanUnloadNow` routine checks to see if the number of objects created in the DLL and the number of locks on its server both are set to zero. If this is the case, it returns `S_OK`, and OLE in its turn unloads the library.

> **NOTE**
>
> Remember that you must call `CoInitialize` before you can use COM. `CoInitialize` usually takes `nil` in its sole parameter. When you are done using COM, you should call `CoUninitialize`. Internally, these are reference counted objects, and only the first call `CoInitialize` does anything useful.

For this system to work, you must keep track of the number of objects created in your DLL and the number of locks placed on your server. Notice that both of these numbers are different than the internal `FRefCount` variable manipulated in `AddRef` and `Release`.

Creating the Client Program

This section shows how to create an executable called MakeOle1 that can use the COM objects defined in the last section. You have already created the object. Now all you have to do is see how to use it!

Listing 30.7 shows the source code for the MakeOle1 program.

Listing 30.7. The code for the MakeOle1 program shows how to call COM objects residing in either DLLs or executables.

```
unit main;

{ Copyright (c) 1996 by Charlie Calvert

  This program is designed to run with the SIMPEXE.EXE program and
  SIMPOBJ.DLL file, both of which ship with Delphi Unleashed. You
  must use REGEDIT.EXE to register SIMPEXE and SIMPOBJ before you
  run this program. To register these binary files with the system,
```

choose Registry ¦ Import Registry from REGEDIT.EXE and then select the
WIN32.REG file found in the directories where SimpExe and SimpObj
are stored. You can also register these programs by simply double
clicking on their REG files from inside the Windows Explorer.

Note that there is a DOS path included in these REG files. The REG
files themselves are just ASCII text. You may have to edit them
with Notepad so that the path points at the appropriate file. If you
are registering SIMPOBJ.DLL, then the path in the REG file should
point to the place on your system where SIMPOBJ.DLL is stored.

I list a few additional CLASSIDs below, in case you want to experiment
with this program. CLSID_KOALA is from the classic example progarm
that ships with Inside OLE. }

```
interface

uses
  SysUtils, Windows, Messages,
  Classes, Graphics, Controls,
  Forms, Dialogs, StdCtrls,
  Ole2, OleAuto, Menus,
  ExtCtrls;

type

  TForm1 = class(TForm)
    MainMenu1: TMainMenu;
    File1: TMenuItem;
    Exit1: TMenuItem;
    Exes1: TMenuItem;
    Dlls1: TMenuItem;
    ExeGetObject: TMenuItem;
    ExeCreateInstance: TMenuItem;
    DllGetObject: TMenuItem;
    DLLCreateInstance: TMenuItem;
    Panel1: TPanel;
    N2: TMenuItem;
    ClearText1: TMenuItem;
    N1: TMenuItem;
    FreeLibrary1: TMenuItem;
    procedure FormCreate(Sender: TObject);
    procedure ExeGetObjectClick(Sender: TObject);
    procedure ExeCreateInstanceClick(Sender: TObject);
    procedure DllGetObjectClick(Sender: TObject);
    procedure DLLCreateInstanceClick(Sender: TObject);
    procedure ClearText1Click(Sender: TObject);
    procedure Exit1Click(Sender: TObject);
    procedure FreeLibrary1Click(Sender: TObject);
    procedure FormDestroy(Sender: TObject);
  private
    procedure GetClass(CLSID: TGUID; ClassContext: DWord);
    procedure CreateInstance(CLSID: TGUID; ClassContext: DWord);
    procedure MessageOut(S: string);
  end;
```

continues

Listing 30.7. continued

```
  IFooObject = class(IUnknown)
  public
    function GetTwelve: Integer; virtual; stdcall; abstract;
  end;

var
  Form1: TForm1;

implementation

{$R *.DFM}

uses
  OleBox;

const
  CLSID_MyDllObject: TGUID = (
    D1:$C9B0B160;D2:$1308;D3:$11cf;D4:($AB,$35,$00,$00,$C0,$7E,$BA,$2B));
  CLSID_MyExeObject: TGUID = (
    D1:$C9B0B161;D2:$1307;D3:$11cf;D4:($AB,$35,$00,$00,$C0,$7E,$BA,$2B));
  CLSID_Koala: TGUID = (
    D1:$00021146;D2:$0000;D3:$0000;D4:($C0,$00,$00,$00,$00,$00,$00,$46));
  CLSID_WordBasic: TGUID = (
    D1:$000209FE;D2:$0000;D3:$0000;D4:($C0,$00,$00,$00,$00,$00,$00,$46));
  CLSID_MyAuto: TGUID = (
    D1:$C9B0B162;D2:$1307;D3:$11cf;D4:($AB,$35,$00,$00,$C0,$7E,$BA,$2B));


procedure TForm1.MessageOut(S: string);
begin
  Panel1.Caption := S;
  Panel1.UpDate;
end;

procedure TForm1.FormCreate(Sender: TObject);
begin
  OleCheck(CoInitialize(nil));
  Left := 0;
  Top := 0;
end;

procedure TForm1.FormDestroy(Sender: TObject);
begin
  CoUninitialize;
end;


procedure TForm1.Exit1Click(Sender: TObject);
begin
  Close;
end;

procedure TForm1.FreeLibrary1Click(Sender: TObject);
begin
  CoFreeUnusedLibraries;
end;
```

```
procedure TForm1.CreateInstance(CLSID: TGUID; ClassContext: DWord);
var
  hr: hResult;
  P: IFooObject;
begin
  hr := CoCreateInstance(CLSID, nil, ClassContext, IID_IUnknown, P);
  if Succeeded(hr) then
    MessageOut('Object Exists')
  else
    MessageOut('No Object');

  if IsEqualIID(CLSID, CLSID_MyDllObject) then begin
    ShowMessage((P.ClassName));         // Since IMarshal is not implemented
    ShowMessage(IntToStr(P.GetTwelve)); // do this thing for inprocess objs only
  end;

  OleCheck(P.Release);
end;

procedure TForm1.GetClass(CLSID: TGUID; ClassContext: DWord);
var
  hr: HResult;
  ClassFactory: IClassFactory;
  P: IFooObject;
begin
  hr := CoGetClassObject(CLSID, ClassContext, nil,
                         IID_IClassFactory, ClassFactory);
  OleCheck(hr);
  hr := ClassFactory.CreateInstance(nil, IID_IUnknown, P);

  if Succeeded(hr) then
    MessageOut('Object Exists')
  else begin
    MessageOut(GetOleError(hr));
    Exit;
  end;

  if IsEqualIID(CLSID, CLSID_MyDllObject) then begin
    ShowMessage((P.ClassName));         // Since IMarshal is not implemented
    ShowMessage(IntToStr(P.GetTwelve)); // do this thing for inprocess objs only
  end;

  OleCheck(ClassFactory.Release);
  OleCheck(P.Release);
end;


procedure TForm1.ExeGetObjectClick(Sender: TObject);
begin
  MessageOut('Opening Exe');
  GetClass(CLSID_MyExeObject, CLSCTX_LOCAL_SERVER);
end;

procedure TForm1.ExeCreateInstanceClick(Sender: TObject);
begin
  MessageOut('Opening Exe');
  CreateInstance(CLSID_MyExeObject, CLSCTX_LOCAL_SERVER);
end;
```

continues

Listing 30.7. continued

```
procedure TForm1.DllGetObjectClick(Sender: TObject);
begin
  MessageOut('Opening DLL');
  GetClass(CLSID_MyDLLObject, CLSCTX_INPROC_SERVER);
end;

procedure TForm1.DLLCreateInstanceClick(Sender: TObject);
begin
  MessageOut('Creating Instance');
  CreateInstance(CLSID_MyDLLObject, CLSCTX_INPROC_SERVER);
end;

procedure TForm1.ClearText1Click(Sender: TObject);
begin
  MessageOut('');
end;

end.
```

The MakeOle1 program shown in Listing 30.7 enables you to call the DLL server created above. This program has a file menu and two separate pop-up menus called DLLs and EXEs. The DLLs pop-up menu is for launching objects that reside in-process. The EXEs pop-up menu is for launching COM objects that reside in executables.

The code starts in the OnCreate method by making sure that COM is initialized. No OLE code runs unless either COM or OLE is initialized:

```
procedure TForm1.FormCreate(Sender: TObject);
begin
  OleCheck(CoInitialize(nil));
  Left := 0;
  Top := 0;
end;
```

The code shown here initializes only COM. If you want to initialize both COM and OLE, call OleInitialize. Both CoInitialize and OleInitialize take a single parameter, which usually is set to nil.

After initializing OLE, you can call either CoCreateInstance or CoGetGetClassObject in order to retrieve your COM object from the DLL or executable. It's easiest to call CoCreateInstance, so that's the way to proceed in most circumstances:

```
procedure TForm1.CreateInstance(CLSID: TGUID; ClassContext: DWord);
var
  hr: hResult;
  P: IUnknown;
begin
  hr := CoCreateInstance(CLSID, nil, ClassContext, IID_IUnknown, P);
  if Succeeded(hr) then
    MessageOut('Object Exists')
  else
```

```
    MessageOut('No Object');
  OleCheck(P.Release);
end;
```

The code shown here retrieves either an in-process server or a local server, depending on the value you pass in the third parameter to CoCreateInstance. If you pass in CLSCTX_INPROC_SERVER, you're stating that you want to work with an in-process server. If you pass in CLSCTX_LOCAL_SERVER, you're stating that you want to work with a local server. Remember that an in-process server is a DLL and a local server is an executable. There are, of course, excellent reasons why the jolly boys and girls in Redmond didn't call these variables CLSCTX_DLL_SERVER and CLSCTX_EXE_SERVER! Excellent reasons I'm sure!

Here are the parameters, laid out one by one:

```
function CoCreateInstance(
  const clsid: TCLSID;    // The ID of the class you are after
  unkOuter: IUnknown;     // Controling unknown of agregate, usually nil
  dwClsContext: Longint;  // The context of the class.
  const iid: TIID;        // Interface to use when talking to the object
  var pv                  // On success, returned object is placed here.
): HResult; stdcall;      // Returns S_OK on success
```

CoCreateInstance is a wrapper around the CoGetClassObject and ClassFactory.CreateInstance routines mentioned earlier, and described next in more depth.

Here are the possible values that can be returned by the function:

S_OK	An instance of the specified object class was successfully created.
REGDB_E_CLASSNOTREG	The specified class was not registered in the registration database.
E_OUTOFMEMORY	The system is out of memory.
E_INVALIDARG	One or more arguments are invalid.
E_UNEXPECTED	An unexpected error occurred.
CLASS_E_NOAGGREGATION	This class cannot be created as part of an aggregate.

Here, from OLE2.PAS, are the possible values that can be passed in the dwClsContext field:

```
CLSCTX_INPROC_SERVER    = 1;
CLSCTX_INPROC_HANDLER   = 2;
CLSCTX_LOCAL_SERVER     = 4;
CLSCTX_INPROC_SERVER16  = 8;

CLSCTX_ALL    = CLSCTX_INPROC_SERVER or CLSCTX_INPROC_HANDLER or
                CLSCTX_LOCAL_SERVER;
CLSCTX_INPROC = CLSCTX_INPROC_SERVER or CLSCTX_INPROC_HANDLER;
CLSCTX_SERVER = CLSCTX_INPROC_SERVER or CLSCTX_LOCAL_SERVER;
```

As I stated earlier, the CoCreateInstance function is a wrapper around CoGetClassObject. Here is how to call CoGetClassObject:

```
procedure TForm1.GetClass(CLSID: TGUID; ClassContext: DWord);
var
```

```
  hr: HResult;
  ClassFactory: IClassFactory;
  P: IUnKnown;
begin
  hr := CoGetClassObject(CLSID, ClassContext, nil,
                         IID_IClassFactory, ClassFactory);
  OleCheck(hr);
  hr := ClassFactory.CreateInstance(nil, CLSID, P);

  if Succeeded(hr) then
    MessageOut('Object Exists')
  else begin
    MessageOut('No object');
    Exit;
  end;

  OleCheck(ClassFactory.Release);
  OleCheck(P.Release);
end;
```

The issue here is that you first call `CoGetClassObject` in order to retrieve an instance of `IClassFactory`. You then use the `ClassFactory` from the DLL or executable to retrieve an instance of your object:

```
function CoGetClassObject(
  const clsid: TCLSID;       // The class you want to retrieve
  dwClsContext: Longint;     // In processes or local server?
  pvReserved: Pointer;       // Reserved, must be nil
  const iid:                 // Communication interface (IClassFactory)
  TIID; var pv               // Returned Communication Object.
): HResult; stdcall;         // Returns S_OK on success
```

`CoGetClassObject` usually requests an instance of `IClassFactory`. It then uses the `CreateInstance` function in `IClassFactory` to retrieve the sought-after object. Contrast this with `CoCreateInstance`, which automatically loads `IClassFactory` for you and automatically calls its `CreateInstance` method. As I stated earlier, `CoCreateInstance` is a wrapper around calls to `CoGetClassObject` and `IClassFactory.CreateInstance`.

Exporting Additional Function From *IMyObject*

In the code shown earlier in this chapter, `IMyObject` does nothing more than implement `IUnknown`. However, it could do more:

```
IMyObject = class(IUnknown)
  private
    FRefCount: LongInt;
    FObjectDestroyed: TObjectDestroyed;
public
    constructor Create(ObjectDestroyed: TObjectDestroyed);
    function QueryInterface(const iid: TIID; var obj): HResult; override;
    function AddRef: Longint; override;
```

```
    function Release: Longint; override;
    function GetTwelve: Integer; virtual;
  end;
```

In this case, IMyObject also supports a virtual function called GetTwelve. The implementation for GetTwelve is trivial:

```
function IMyObject.GetTwelve: Integer;
begin
  Result := 12;
end;
```

To access this function from an executable you must declare an object that supports the GetTwelve method:

```
IFooObject = class(IUnknown)
public
  function GetTwelve: variant; virtual; stdcall; abstract;
end;
```

This object has its methods declared as virtual abstract, as described in the DNoOle example. Notice that you don't redeclare Release, AddRef, and QueryInterface, as they already are declared for you in IUnknown. IFooObject is a descendant of IUnknown, so it inherits virtual abstract declarations from its parents. (In the C++ world, virtual abstract methods are sometimes called pure virtual methods.)

When you want to call the method, you change the way you implement CoCreateInstance or CoGetClassObject:

```
procedure TForm1.CreateInstance(CLSID: TGUID; ClassContext: DWord);
var
  hr: hResult;
  P: IFooObject;
begin
  hr := CoCreateInstance(CLSID, nil, ClassContext, IID_IUnknown, P);
  if Succeeded(hr) then
    MessageOut('Object Exists')
  else
    MessageOut('No Object');
  ShowMessage(IntToStr(P.GetTwelve));
  OleCheck(P.Release);
end;
```

And here is CoGetClassObject, replete with a call to the GetTwelve method:

```
procedure TForm1.GetClass(CLSID: TGUID; ClassContext: DWord);
var
  hr: HResult;
  ClassFactory: IClassFactory;
  P: IFooObject;
begin
  hr := CoGetClassObject(CLSID, ClassContext, nil,
                         IID_IClassFactory, ClassFactory);
  OleCheck(hr);
  hr := ClassFactory.CreateInstance(nil, IID_IUnknown, P);
```

```
if Succeeded(hr) then
  MessageOut('Object Exists')
else begin
  MessageOut(GetOleError(hr));
  Exit;
end;

ShowMessage((P.ClassName));  // Since IMarshal is not implemented
ShowMessage((P.GetTwelve));  // try this with in-process objs only
OleCheck(ClassFactory.Release);
OleCheck(P.Release);
end;
```

In this second example, notice that you can call other standard TObject VCL routines, such as ClassName.

The technique shown here is close to the technique used in the Microsoft Games SDK. In other words, it is a powerful technique that is used by many professional programmers.

Why would you use this technique rather than the technique used in the DNoOle example? Well, DNoOle works with Delphi and Borland C++, but it doesn't work with any other tools. COM, however, works with Delphi, Borland C++, Visual C++, Visual Basic, Symantec C++, and any other tool that supports COM.

The final point to make here is that you cannot use this technique to export an object from an executable. At least, you can't do it through the relatively simple techniques shown in this chapter. The issue is that you need to expand the capability of IMyObject and IMyClassFactory by adding support for marshaling. Marshaling is a subject that is beyond the scope of this book.

Debugging the DLL

Because a COM object resides in a DLL or a local server, it becomes difficult to find the proper method for debugging it. As it turns out, there are two good techniques that you can use. The first involves the simple (and often unfairly maligned) WriteLn debugging method. The second utilizes the stand-alone Turbo Debugger.

Before debuggers were commonplace, the WriteLn method of debugging was commonly used. Because debuggers are so much more powerful than WriteLn, there is a tendency to disparage WriteLn as a tool for debugging. However, in the case of the COM objects shown here, this can be an effective tool, particularly when you write your output to a file.

To get started, declare a variable F as a file of Text in the interface of the MYOBJ.PAS file:

```
var
  F: Text;
```

Notice that in this case you don't have to write System.Text; this is a outside of any VCL object. Next, add the following code at the bottom of the MYOBJ.PAS:

```
initialization
  NumLocks := 0;
```

```
  NumObjs := 0;
  Assign(F, 'c:\oletest.txt');
  ReWrite(F);
  WriteLn(F, 'Initialization');
finalization
  WriteLn(F, 'Finalization');
  Close(F);
end.
```

This code takes care of opening and closing the file to which you want to write. It also keeps a written record of the moment when your DLL is loaded and unloaded from memory.

> **NOTE**
>
> The code above uses the reserved word finalization, which has been added to Delphi 2.0. The initialization section of a unit will execute before any other part of the unit is called, and the finalization section will execute just before the unit is shut down. This means that the initialization section is usually called at program launch, and the finalization section is called just before the program closes. If your unit is inside a DLL, then the initialization section will be called just as the DLL is loaded into memory, and the finalization section will be called when the DLL is freed. Besides the example shown above, another classic use of the initialization and finalization section appears in the OleAuto unit that ships with the Delphi RTL. That unit calls OleInitialize in the initialization section and OleUninitialize in the finalization section.

Now that you have a file set up, you can write to it as needed. For instance, if you are concerned that your AddRef and Release pairs are not being matched up evenly, you can add WriteLn statements to all of them:

```
function IMyObject.AddRef: Longint;
begin
  Inc(FRefCount);
  WriteLn(F, 'MyAddRef: ' + IntToStr(FRefCount));
  Result := FRefCount;
end;

function IMyObject.Release: Longint;
begin
  Dec(FRefCount);
  WriteLn(F, 'MyRelease: ' + IntToStr(FRefCount));
  if FRefCount = 0 then begin
    FObjectDestroyed;
    Free;
    Result := 0;
  end else
    Result := FRefCount;
end;

function IMyClassFactory.AddRef: Longint;
begin
```

```
  Inc(FRefCount);
  WriteLn(F, 'AddRef: ' + IntToStr(FRefCount));
  Result := FRefCount;
end;

function IMyClassFactory.Release: Longint;
begin
  Dec(FRefCount);
  WriteLn(F, 'Release: ' + IntToStr(FRefCount));
  if FRefCount = 0 then begin
    Destroy;
    Result := 0;
  end else
    Result := FRefCount;
end;
```

Given the presence of these statements, you can produce a text file that looks like this:

```
Initialization
AddRef: 1
MyAddRef: 1
Release: 0
MyRelease: 0
Finalization
```

This gives an orderly, easy-to-read report on the progress of your program. You can see that the AddRefs and Releases are all properly paired, and you can see that the DLL is properly unloaded when you're through with it.

Here, for instance, is a report that illustrates what happens when something goes wrong:

```
Initialization
AddRef: 1
MyAddRef: 1
Release: 0
DllCanUnloadNow
Finalization
```

As you can see, there are two calls to AddRef but only one call to Release. The call to DLLCanUnloadNow should have failed, but the finalization immediately after it correctly suggests that it succeeded.

NOTE

If you use the technique described here on a local server, you may find that you get additional, unexpected calls to QueryInterface, AddRef, and Release. These additional entries in your text file are due to internal OLE calls to your object involving IMarshal and other interfaces.

Creating an EXE Server (LOCAL)

I now briefly discuss using COM in an executable. I want to make clear that the code here is far less valuable that it might at first appear. The issue is that you cannot port function return values and parameters across application boundaries without implementing IMarshal. I don't have room to explore that subject in this book, so this code will not be of use in a working program. It will, however, compile and run successfully. Its shortcoming is that it's not very useful.

All the calls shown in this example succeed. As a result, it serves as a starting point for you if you want to explore this complicated subject. The point, however, is that you will have to do additional work if you wanted to add other routines to your code, such as the GetTwelve method I discussed earlier.

This example program, shown in Listings 30.8 through 30.10, is called SimpExe. It's nearly identical to SimpObj (Listing 30.4), but it houses its object in an executable, not in a DLL.

Listing 30.8. The source code for the main module of the SimpExe program.

```
unit main;

{ This EXE is designed to be run with the MAKEOLE1.DPR project
  that ships with Delphi Unleashed. It could also be used with
  other properly constructed client programs.

  You must use REGEDIT.EXE to register SIMPEXE.EXE before you
  access it from MakeOle1. To register this executable with the system,
  choose Registry | Import Registry from REGEDIT.EXE and import the
  WIN32.REG file found in the directory where SimpExe is stored.
  You can also register this program by simply double clicking on
  its REG files from inside the Windows Explorer.

  Note that there is a DOS path included in SimpExe's REG files.
  The REG file itself is just ASCII text. You may have to edit it
  with Notepad so that the path points to the place on your
  system where SIMPEXE.EXE is stored. }

interface

uses
  SysUtils, Windows, Messages,
  Classes, Graphics, Controls,
  Forms, Dialogs, StdCtrls,
  Ole2, ExeObj, OleAuto;

type
  TForm1 = class(TForm)
    Button1: TButton;
    procedure FormCreate(Sender: TObject);
  private
    RegCo: LongInt;
```

continues

Listing 30.8. continued

```pascal
  public
    { Public declarations }
  end;

var
  Form1: TForm1;

implementation

{$R *.DFM}

function Embedding: Boolean;
var
  i: Integer;
begin
  Result := False;
  for i := 0 to ParamCount do
    if Pos('Embedding', ParamStr(i)) > 0 then
      Result := True;
end;

procedure TForm1.FormCreate(Sender: TObject);
var
  hr: hResult;
  MyClassFactory: IMyClassFactory;
begin
{  if not Embedding then Exit; }

  ExeObj.AHandle := Handle;
  RegCo := 0;

  try
    MyClassFactory := IMyClassFactory.Create;
  except
    Close;
    Exit;
  end;

  hr := CoRegisterClassObject(CLSID_MyExeObject, MyClassFactory,
          CLSCTX_LOCAL_SERVER, REGCLS_MULTIPLEUSE, RegCO);

  if Succeeded(hr) then
    Caption := 'Success';
end;

end
```

Listing 30.9. The source code for the object implementation in the SimpExe program.

```pascal
unit exeobj;

interface
```

```
uses
  Ole2, Windows, SysUtils;

const
  CLSID_MyExeObject: TGUID = (
    D1:$C9B0B161;D2:$1307;D3:$11cf;D4:($AB,$35,$00,$00,$C0,$7E,$BA,$2B));

type
  IExeObject = class(IUnknown)
  private
    FRefCount: LongInt;
  public
    constructor Create;
    function QueryInterface(const iid: TIID; var obj): HResult; override;
    function AddRef: Longint; override;
    function Release: Longint; override;
  end;

  IMyClassFactory = class(IClassFactory)
  private
    FRefCount: LongInt;
  public
    constructor Create;
    function QueryInterface(const iid: TIID; var obj): HResult; override;
    function AddRef: Longint; override;
    function Release: Longint; override;
    function CreateInstance(unkOuter: IUnknown; const iid: TIID;
      var obj): HResult; override;
    function LockServer(fLock: BOOL): HResult; override;
  end;

var
  LockCount: Integer;
  AHandle: hwnd;

implementation

constructor IExeObject.Create;
begin
  inherited Create;
  FRefCount := 0;
end;

function IExeObject.QueryInterface(const iid: TIID; var obj): HResult;
begin
  if IsEqualIID(iid, IID_IUnknown) or
     IsEqualIID(iid, CLSID_MyExeObject) then begin
    Pointer(obj) := Self;
    AddRef;
    Result := S_OK;
  end else begin
    Pointer(obj) := nil;
    Result := E_NOINTERFACE;
  end;
end;
```

continues

Listing 30.9. continued

```
function IExeObject.AddRef: Longint;
begin
  Inc(FRefCount);
  Result := FRefCount;
end;

function IExeObject.Release: Longint;
begin
  Dec(FRefCount);
  Result := FRefCount;
  if FRefCount = 0 then Free
end;


{ -- IMyClassFactory -- }

constructor IMyClassFactory.Create;
begin
  inherited Create;
  FRefCount := 0;
end;

{ Windows may call this function several times, besides the occasions
  when you explicitly ask it to do so. It may call asking to see if
  this interface supports IMarshall, IUnknown, etc. Remember, though,
  AddRef will only get called if iid equals IID_IUnknown or
  IID_IClassFactory }

function IMyClassFactory.QueryInterface(const iid: TIID; var obj): HResult;
begin
  if IsEqualIID(iid, IID_IUnknown) or IsEqualIID(iid, IID_IClassFactory) then begin
    Pointer(obj) := Self;
    AddRef;
    Result := S_OK;
  end else begin
    Pointer(obj) := nil;
    Result := E_NOINTERFACE;
  end;
end;

function IMyClassFactory.AddRef: Longint;
begin
  Inc(FRefCount);
  Result := FRefCount;
end;

function IMyClassFactory.Release: Longint;
begin
  Dec(FRefCount);
  Result := FRefCount;
  if FRefCount = 0 then Free;
end;


function IMyClassFactory.CreateInstance(UnkOuter: IUnknown; const iid: Tiid;
                                        var Obj): hResult;
```

```
var
  hr: HResult;
  ExeObject: IExeObject;
begin
  Result := E_OutOfMemory;
  if UnkOuter <> nil then begin
    Result := CLASS_E_NOAGGREGATION;
    Exit;
  end;

  if not IsEqualIID(iid, IID_IUnknown) and
     not IsEqualIID(iid, CLSID_MyExeObject) then begin
    Result := E_Fail;
    Exit;
  end;
  ExeObject := IExeObject.Create;
  if ExeObject = nil then begin
    Pointer(Obj) := nil;
    Result := E_OutOfMemory;
    Exit;
  end;

  hr := ExeObject.QueryInterface(iid, Obj);
  if Failed(hr) then begin
    ExeObject.Release;
    Exit;
  end;
  Result := hr;
end;

{ LockServer:
    This function can be used to tell the whole EXE that it
    ought to stay in memory. The exe should not exit until
    this LockCount is zero and the RefCount for all objects
    is zero. Its up to the programmer to track this information;
    there is nothing magic about LockServer! You use these tools
    to decide when its okay to unload the EXE! When everything
    is equal to zero, then you unload. I don't check for these
    contingencies in this example. }

function IMyClassFactory.LockServer(fLock: BOOL): HResult;
begin
  if fLock then
    Inc(LockCount)
  else
    Dec(LockCount);
  Result := S_Ok;
end;

initialization
  CoInitialize(nil);
  LockCount := 0;
finalization
  CoUninitialize;
end.
```

Listing 30.10. The registration file for the SimpExe program.

```
REGEDIT
HKEY_CLASSES_ROOT\MyExeObject1.0 = MyExeObject Test 1
HKEY_CLASSES_ROOT\MyExeObject1.0\CLSID = {C9B0B161-1307-11cf-AB35-0000C07EBA2B}
HKEY_CLASSES_ROOT\MyExeObject = MyExeObject Test 1
HKEY_CLASSES_ROOT\MyExeObject\CurVer = MyExeObject1.0
HKEY_CLASSES_ROOT\MyExeObject\CLSID = {C9B0B161-1307-11cf-AB35-0000C07EBA2B}

HKEY_CLASSES_ROOT\CLSID\{C9B0B161-1307-11cf-AB35-0000C07EBA2B} =
   MyExeObject Test 1
HKEY_CLASSES_ROOT\CLSID\{C9B0B161-1307-11cf-AB35-0000C07EBA2B}\ProgID =
   MyExeObject1.0
HKEY_CLASSES_ROOT\CLSID\
   {C9B0B161-1307-11cf-AB35-0000C07EBA2B}\VersionIndependentProgID = MyExeObject
HKEY_CLASSES_ROOT\CLSID\{C9B0B161-1307-11cf-AB35-0000C07EBA2B}\LocalServer32 =
   c:\src\unleash\Chap30\simpexe\simpexe.exe
HKEY_CLASSES_ROOT\CLSID\{C9B0B161-1307-11cf-AB35-0000C07EBA2B}\NotInsertable
```

The implementation of the ExeObject is basically identical to the implementation of IMyObject. The instance of IMyClassFactory also is essentially unchanged. What is different, however, is how this object talks to the outside world.

In the DLL example, DllGetClassObject is the main interface with the outside world. When working with an executable, however, you have to take a difference tack. In particular, instead of DllGetClassObject, the following FormCreate method is implemented:

```
procedure TForm1.FormCreate(Sender: TObject);
var
  hr: hResult;
  MyClassFactory: IMyClassFactory;
begin
{  if not Embedding then Exit; }

  ExeObj.AHandle := Handle;
  RegCo := 0;

  try
    MyClassFactory := IMyClassFactory.Create;
  except
    Close;
    Exit;
  end;

  hr := CoRegisterClassObject(CLSID_MyExeObject, MyClassFactory,
          CLSCTX_LOCAL_SERVER, REGCLS_MULTIPLEUSE, RegCO);

  if Succeeded(hr) then
    Caption := 'Success';
end;
```

This code creates an instance of IMyClassFactory. It then passes this object to CoRegisterClassObject, which publishes it so that it can be reached by container objects.

The issue here is that the FormCreate method can't directly return a pointer to IClassFactory, as is the case with DllGetClassObject. DllGetClassObject succeeds because it does not need to return the pointer across a process boundary. An executable does not reside inside another applications address space, and so it can't directly pass a pointer to it. Instead, it registers the object with the system, and then the system can pass the object on to CoGetClassObject or CoCreateInstance.

Here is the call to CoRegisterClassObject:

```
function CoRegisterClassObject(
  const clsid: TCLSID;    // The object the user will want to retrieve
  unk: IUnknown;          // The intermediate communicator object
  dwClsContext: Longint;  // The class context: Local server?
  flags: Longint;         // Single or multiple use?
  var dwRegister: Longint // The function returns a unique identifier
): HResult; stdcall;      // S_OK on success.
```

The fourth parameter specifies whether the object is multiple- or single-use. Objects that are multiple-use can service requests for many containers at the same time. Objects that are single-use can serve only one container at a time. If an object is single-use, a new instance of the executable is created for each new container that wants to access it.

Here are the possible result codes returned by a call to CoRegisterClassObject:

S_OK	The object was registered successfully.
CO_E_OBJISREG	The object class already was registered in the class object table.
E_OUTOFMEMORY	The system is out of memory.
E_INVALIDARG	One or more arguments are invalid.
E_UNEXPECTED	An unexpected error occurred.

On the OLE Documentation

Here, from the official Microsoft documentation, is the description of the first two parameters passed to CoRegisterClassObject:

rclsid: Specifies the object class being registered.

pUnk: Points to the class object whose availability is being published.

Any programmer wrestling with this documentation must overcome two difficulties:

- Variable names, such as rclsid and pUnk, and their accompanying capitalization schemes, are not very intuitive.
- The explanation of these variables rests on a dicey differentiation between an "object class" and a "class object."

Having faults of my own, I refrain from commenting on the quality of this type of code and documentation. However, I will state that anyone who attempts to wrestle with COM and OLE has to be prepared to contend with some formidable obstacles.

I personally find myself continually weighing the obvious significance of COM and OLE against the seemingly inexplicable complexity of its implementation. Overall, the subjective weight of this chapters adds up to a heavy recommendation of COM. However, I would be remiss as a writer if I did not temper that enthusiasm with a few words of warning about the complexity of the COM implementation, and the relative opaqueness of its documentation.

Summary

In this chapter you had a look at the Component Object Model (COM). This technique enables you to write objects that can be placed in DLLs and shared across various language boundaries. It is also the ground in which all OLE technologies are rooted.

Once you understand how it's implemented, this code can prove to be a relatively easy way for you to create objects that can be used by multiple languages. One of the key factors to keep in mind is that the Games SDK is implemented using techniques similar to those shown in this chapter. The whole point of the Games SDK is that it's fast—faster even than the graphics code written in DOS. With its speed and flexibility, COM provides an excellent means for you to create objects that can be used by multiple parts of your development team, or that can be sold to many different types of programmers who use many different languages.

I do not explore this issue here, but COM is designed so that it can be accessed even by procedural languages that do not support objects. This gives COM an extraordinary flexibility that is almost unheard of in today's programming world.

Finally, there is the fact that COM is the basis for OLE, and is the likely basis for the future object-oriented operating systems that Microsoft should be rolling out in the next few years. Quite simply, this means that all of our programming could become COM-based in the next five to ten years. That gives this technology a tremendous significance that is hard to ignore under any circumstances.

COM, Automation, and Structured Storage

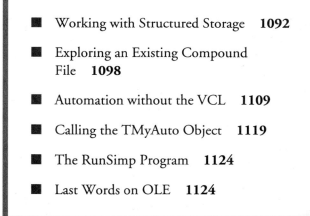

CHAPTER

31

In this chapter, you get a look at two more architectures rooted in the COM technology you learned about in the last chapter. In particular, you will learn about structured storage and the technical details of how to implement OLE automation.

You have already heard quite a bit about automation, but now you are going to take a step behind the facade of the Delphi TAutoObject class and see how to implement the technology out of the raw elements of the OLE API. I'm exploring this subject in depth because I believe automation is one of the key building blocks of the monolithic OLE edifice. If you want to understand OLE, automation is one of the technologies you need to master.

Structured storage is a new technique for writing objects or data to disk. This technique provides all the services you are used to seeing in standard file I/O. You can write files to disk, you can create subdirectories, and you can read and write data to and from these files and directories through a wide variety of techniques. The difference between structured storage and standard file I/O is that each set of structured storage directories and files resides inside a single larger file, much as a set of InterBase tables resides inside a single GDB file.

A structured storage file is called a compound file. The "directories" inside these compound files are called storages, and the "files" inside these compound files are called streams. Other types of objects can be stored in a compound file, but that subject will only be hinted at in this chapter.

Structured storage sounds a bit esoteric when you first hear about it. However, it is a very common technology that could become ubiquitous in the near future. For instance, you will see in this chapter that all the .DOC files you use in WordPad or Word for Windows are actually structured storage files. When you open them up with the right tools, you will find that they actually consist of a series of smaller files and directories embedded inside a single large .DOC file.

Microsoft has hinted that structured storage will probably be the standard form of file I/O under future versions of Windows. This means that if you begin using structured storage today, you will be able to port your code more readily to the advanced object-oriented operating systems that loom on the horizon.

Working with Structured Storage

A simple structured storage example is not nearly as difficult to implement as the COM objects you saw in the last chapter. However, this is OLE, so if you dig deep enough, you can count on the technology becoming relatively complicated. The examples in this chapter will take you in far enough to show you how the core technology works, but they will skirt around some of the more complex issues.

The first structured storage example is called MakeStg, and it shows how to create a simple structured storage file and how to read back its contents. This is a stripped-down, simplest-possible-case example. The chapter then goes on to explore a somewhat more complex example that enables the user to explore any structured storage file found on his or her system.

The code for the MakeStg program is found in Listing 31.1. A picture of the simple form for the program is shown in Figure 31.1.

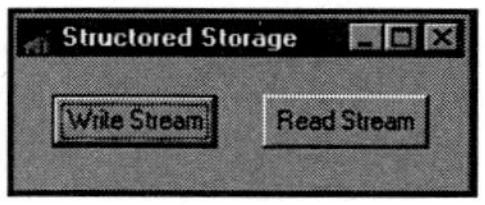

FIGURE 31.1.

The MakeStg program has two buttons. The first creates a simple file, and the second reads back its contents.

Listing 31.1. The MakeStg program shows how to create and read a simple structured storage file.

```
unit main;

interface

uses
  Windows, Messages, SysUtils,
  Classes, Graphics, Controls,
  Forms, Dialogs, StdCtrls,
  Ole2;

type
  TForm1 = class(TForm)
    bWriteStream: TButton;
    bReadStream: TButton;
    procedure FormCreate(Sender: TObject);
    procedure FormClose(Sender: TObject; var Action: TCloseAction);
    procedure bWriteStreamClick(Sender: TObject);
    procedure bReadStreamClick(Sender: TObject);
  end;

var
  Form1: TForm1;

implementation

uses
  OleAuto;

{$R *.DFM}

procedure TForm1.FormCreate(Sender: TObject);
begin
  OleInitialize(nil);
end;

procedure TForm1.FormClose(Sender: TObject; var Action: TCloseAction);
begin
```

continues

Listing 31.1. continued

```
  OleUninitialize;
end;

procedure TForm1.bWriteStreamClick(Sender: TObject);
var
  Hr: HResult;
  Storage: IStorage;
  Stream: IStream;
  Size: LongInt;
  S: string;
begin
  Hr := StgCreateDocFile('C:\SAM.STG',
    STGM_DIRECT or STGM_CREATE or STGM_WRITE or STGM_SHARE_EXCLUSIVE,
    0, Storage);
  if Hr <> S_OK then
    ShowMessage('Err');
  Hr := Storage.CreateStream('MyStream', STGM_DIRECT or STGM_CREATE or
        STGM_WRITE or STGM_SHARE_EXCLUSIVE, 0, 0, Stream);
  OleCheck(HR);
  S := 'Sam';
  Stream.Write(PChar(S), 4, @Size);
  if Size <> 4 then ShowMessage('Wrong size written');
  Stream.Release;
  Storage.Release;
end;

procedure TForm1.bReadStreamClick(Sender: TObject);
var
  Storage: IStorage;
  Stream: IStream;
  hr: HResult;
  S: PChar;
  Size: LongInt;
begin
  hr := StgOpenStorage('C:\SAM.STG', nil,
    STGM_DIRECT or STGM_READ or STGM_SHARE_EXCLUSIVE,
    nil, 0, Storage);
  OleCheck(hr);

  hr := Storage.OpenStream('MyStream', nil,
    STGM_DIRECT or STGM_READ or STGM_SHARE_EXCLUSIVE,
    0, Stream);
  OleCheck(hr);

  GetMem(S, 4);
  Stream.Read(S, 4, @Size);
  ShowMessage(S);
  Stream.Release;
  Storage.Release;
end;

end.
```

The first thing to notice about this program is that it calls OleInitialize in its OnCreate handler and OleUninitialize in its OnClose handler:

```
procedure TForm1.FormCreate(Sender: TObject);
begin
  OleInitialize(nil);
end;

procedure TForm1.FormClose(Sender: TObject; var Action: TCloseAction);
begin
  OleUninitialize;
end;
```

Structured storage is part of OLE proper, so you must call `OleInitialize` rather than `CoInitialize`. The parameter passed to `OleInitialize` is an instance of `IMalloc` that can usually be set to `nil`. (As civilized Object Pascal programmers, we will overlook the indiscretion of naming a class after a now relatively obsolete C programming language function.)

The code to create a compound file looks like this:

```
procedure TForm1.bWriteStreamClick(Sender: TObject);
var
  Hr: HResult;
  Storage: IStorage;
  Stream: IStream;
  Size: LongInt;
  S: string;
begin
  Hr := StgCreateDocFile('C:\SAM.STG',
    STGM_DIRECT or STGM_CREATE or STGM_WRITE or STGM_SHARE_EXCLUSIVE,
    0, Storage);
  if Hr <> S_OK then
    ShowMessage('Err');
  Hr := Storage.CreateStream('MyStream', STGM_DIRECT or STGM_CREATE or
        STGM_WRITE or STGM_SHARE_EXCLUSIVE, 0, 0, Stream);
  OleCheck(HR);
  S := 'Sam';
  Stream.Write(PChar(S), 4, @Size);
  if Size <> 4 then ShowMessage('Wrong size written');
  Stream.Release;
  Storage.Release;
end;
```

The two key functions in this method are `StgCreateDocFile` and `IStorage.CreateStream`. The first is used to retrieve an initialized IStorage object, and the second is used to retrieve an initialized IStream object. Both IStream and IStorage are OLE objects declared in OLE2.PAS.

Here is the declaration for `StgCreateDocFile`:

```
function StgCreateDocfile(
  pwcsName: POleStr;    // Name of file, nil if you want a temp file.
  grfMode: Longint;     // Access mode. Direct or Transacted?
  reserved: Longint;    // Must be zero
  var stgOpen: IStorage // The IStorage object is returned here.
): HResult; stdcall;    // S_OK on success
```

This is an OLE function, declared in OLE2.PAS, and so it takes a `POleStr`, in the first parameter, and not a long string. A `POleStr` is declared to be a `PWideChar`, which means it is a Unicode string. This is not an issue in the simple code shown here, but if you want to pass a variable to this function, you will probably end up having to wrestle with `MultiByteToWideChar` and `WideCharToMultiByte`. For help with these functions, see the following routine in OLEAUTO.PAS:

```
procedure WideCharToShortString(P: PWideChar; var S: ShortString);
```

See also the following routines in SYSUTILS.PAS:

```
function WideCharToString(Source: PWideChar): string;
function WideCharLenToString(Source: PWideChar; SourceLen: Integer): string;
procedure WideCharToStrVar(Source: PWideChar; var Dest: string);
procedure WideCharLenToStrVar(Source: PWideChar; SourceLen: Integer;
  var Dest: string);
function StringToWideChar(const Source: string; Dest: PWideChar;
  DestSize: Integer): PWideChar;
```

There is also some code in OLEBOX.PAS, which ships with this book. However, the routines in SYSUTILS.PAS are the core source of help when you need to translate strings to WideChars and back.

The access mode you use when working with compound files is relatively important. The key point here is that you can open a file in direct mode or in transacted mode. Transacted mode is like using transactions with a database: it enables you to roll back your work if you decide you have made a mistake. You can, in fact, make huge changes to a compound file and then undo them all if you are working in transacted mode.

When working with IStorage objects, you should always use `STGM_DIRECT`, which is the flag designating direct mode. Here are three possible combinations of flags for use with root IStorage objects:

```
STGM_READ OR STGM_SHARE_EXCLUSIVE OR STGM_READWRITE OR STGM_SHARE_DENY_WRITE

STGM_PRIORITY OR STGM_READ

STGM_READ OR STGM_SHARE_DENY_WRITE OR
  STGM_READWRITE OR STGM_SHARE_EXCLUSIVE OR
  STGM_READ OR STGM_PRIORITY OR STGM_SHARE_DENY_NONE
```

Here are the routines available in the IStorage object:

```
CreateStream
OpenStream
CreateStorage
OpenStorage
CopyTo
MoveElementTo
Commit
Revert
EnumElements
DestroyElement
SetElementTimes
SetClass
SetStateBits
Stat
```

The call to CreateStream looks like this:

```
Hr := Storage.CreateStream('MyStream',
      STGM_DIRECT or STGM_CREATE or
      STGM_WRITE or STGM_SHARE_EXCLUSIVE,
      0, 0, Stream);
```

CreateStream creates a file inside a storage object. It's as if the storage created by StgCreateDocFile were a new hard drive, and the stream returned by IStorage.CreateStream is the first file on the hard drive:

```
function CreateStream(
  pwcsName: POleStr;    // Unicode name of stream
  grfMode: Longint;     // Access mode
  reserved1: Longint;   // Must be zero
  reserved2: Longint;   // Must be zero
  var stm: IStream      // Stream is returned here
): HResult; virtual; stdcall; abstract; // S_OK on success
```

Here are the values that can be returned by this function:

S_OK	The stream was created successfully.
STG_E_ACCESSDENIED	Insufficient permissions to create stream.
STG_E_FILEALREADYEXISTS	The stream with the specified name already exists and grfMode is set to STGM_FAILIFTHERE.
STG_TOOMANYOPENFILES	There are too many open files.
STG_E_INSUFFICIENTMEMORY	Out of memory.
STG_E_INVALIDFLAG	Unsupported value(s) specified in grfMode.
STG_E_INVALIDPOINTER	A bad pointer was passed in.
STG_E_INVALIDPARAMETER	Invalid parameter.
STG_E_REVERTED	The object has been invalidated by a revert operation above it in the transaction tree.
STG_E_INVALIDNAME	Invalid value for pwcsName.

Here are the functions in the IStream object:

```
Read
Write
Seek
SetSize
CopyTo
Commit
Revert
LockRegion
UnlockRegion
Stat
Clone
```

You can see that stream can be written to, read from, and copied. You can also seek to a particular point in the stream. If you used the STGM_TRANSACTED flag, then you can commit your work or revert to a previous state.

Once a stream is open, then you can write to it using `IStream.Write`:

```
function Write(
  pv: Pointer;          // Data to be written to stream
  cb: Longint;          // Number of bytes you want to write
  pcbWritten: Plongint  // Number of bytes actually written, can pass nil.
): HResult; virtual; stdcall; abstract;
```

There is no particular need to comment in depth on the act of reading the information back from the file. The core of that code looks like this:

```
hr := StgOpenStorage('C:\SAM.STG', nil,
    STGM_DIRECT or STGM_READ or STGM_SHARE_EXCLUSIVE,
    nil, 0, Storage);
OleCheck(hr);

hr := Storage.OpenStream('MyStream', nil,
    STGM_DIRECT or STGM_READ or STGM_SHARE_EXCLUSIVE,
    0, Stream);
OleCheck(hr);

GetMem(S, 4);
Stream.Read(S, 4, @Size);
```

`StgOpenStorage` opens an existing compound file, and `Storage.OpenStream` opens a particular stream in that file. Remember, most compound objects will have multiple streams in them, so you need to specify which stream you want to use. In a sense, these two calls are equivalent to the following standard Object Pascal calls:

```
StgOpenStorage     Û ChDir;            // Change directory
Storage.OpenStream Û AssignFile, ReSet // open a file
```

Exploring an Existing Compound File

The following program, called Storage, shows how to open up a compound file and examine its contents. The program makes heavy use of an object I created called `TOpenStorage`. This object iterates through a compound file, examining each stream that it finds, and exploring each substorage that it locates. A substorage is like a subdirectory: it's a storage found within a compound file. You can nest storages as deeply as you like.

> **NOTE**
>
> Some of the code in the Storage program is derived from an article by John Lam that appeared in *PC Magazine*.

Figure 31.2 shows the interface for the Storage program. In the TMemo control on the program's main window, you can see an open compound file containing various streams and substorages. Notice also the `SummaryInformation` property. This is an instance of a standard summary page found in most Microsoft products such as Word, Excel, or PowerPoint. It contains information about the title, subject, and author of a document. The code for the Storage program is found in Listings 31.2 and 31.3.

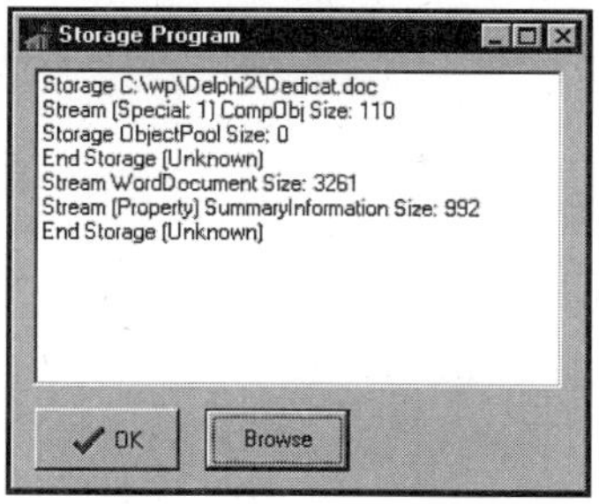

FIGURE 31.2.

The Storage program iterates through the objects in compound file.

Listing 31.2. The simple main module for the Storage program.

```
unit main;

{ Copyright © 1996 Charlie Calvert }

interface

uses
  Windows, Messages, SysUtils,
  Classes, Graphics, Controls,
  Forms, Dialogs, StdCtrls,
  Ole2, OleStg, Buttons;

type
  TForm1 = class(TForm)
    bBrowse: TButton;
    OpenDialog1: TOpenDialog;
    ListBox1: TListBox;
    bOk: TBitBtn;
    procedure FormCreate(Sender: TObject);
    procedure FormClose(Sender: TObject; var Action: TCloseAction);
    procedure bBrowseClick(Sender: TObject);
    procedure bOkClick(Sender: TObject);
  end;

var
  Form1: TForm1;

implementation

uses
  StrBox, OleAuto;

{$R *.DFM}

procedure TForm1.FormCreate(Sender: TObject);
begin
  OleInitialize(nil);
end;
```

continues

Listing 31.2. continued

```pascal
procedure TForm1.FormClose(Sender: TObject; var Action: TCloseAction);
begin
  OleUninitialize;
end;

procedure TForm1.bBrowseClick(Sender: TObject);
var
  OpenStorage: TOpenStorage;
begin
  if not OpenDialog1.Execute then Exit;
  OpenStorage := TOpenStorage.Create(OpenDialog1.FileName);
  ListBox1.Items := OpenStorage.StgStrings;
  OpenStorage.Free;
end;

procedure TForm1.bOkClick(Sender: TObject);
begin
  Close;
end;

end.
```

Listing 31.3. The object that performs all the grunt work for the Storage program.

```pascal
unit olestg;

{ Copyright © 1996 Charlie Calvert }

{ An article by John Lam in the PC Magazine Vol 14 No 22
  helped with the development of this unit }

interface

uses
  Windows, Classes, Ole2,
  OleAuto, StrBox, Dialogs,
  SysUtils;

type
  TOpenStorage = class(TObject)
  private
    FStgStrings: TStringList;
    procedure OpenStorage(FileName: string);
    function ShowStorageElement(S: string; StatStg: TStatStg): Integer;
    procedure EnumStorageElements(var Storage: IStorage);
    procedure HandleProperty(Storage: IStorage);
    procedure HandleSubStorage(var Storage: IStorage; StatStg: TStatStg);
    destructor Destroy; override;
  public
    constructor Create(FileName: string); virtual;
    property StgStrings: TStringList read FStgStrings;
  end;
```

```
implementation

uses
  OleBox;

constructor TOpenStorage.Create(FileName: string);
begin
  inherited Create;
  FStgStrings := TStringList.Create;
  OpenStorage(FileName);
end;

destructor TOpenStorage.Destroy;
begin
  FStgStrings.Free;
  inherited Destroy;
end;

function Test(hr: HResult): Boolean;
begin
  if Succeeded(hr) then
    Result := True
  else begin
    ShowMessage('Enum Failed');
    Result := False;
  end;
end;


{-------------------------------------------------------
        Name: HandleProperty
Declaration:
        Unit: Main
Description: Show Summary Info
----------------------------------------------------}
procedure TOpenStorage.HandleProperty(Storage: IStorage);
begin
  { Not Implemented }
end;

{-------------------------------------------------------
        Name: ShowStorageElement
Declaration: ShowStringType(S: string; StatStg: TStatStg);
        Unit: Main
Description: Nonroot storage elements may have a first
             character between #1 and #6 that has a special meaning.
             We deal with that here.
----------------------------------------------------}
function TOpenStorage.ShowStorageElement(S: string; StatStg: TStatStg): Integer;
var
  Temp: string;
begin
  if S = 'Unknown' then begin
    StgStrings.Add('End Storage (Unknown)');
    Result := -1;
    Exit;
  end;
```

continues

Listing 31.3. continued

```
  Temp := UnicodeToAnsi(StatStg.pwcsName) + ' Size: ' +
IntToStr(Round(StatStg.cbSize)));
    case Temp[1] of
      #1,#2,#3,#4,#6: Temp := '(Special: ' +
                          IntToStr(Ord(Temp[1])) + ') ' +
                          StripFromFront(Temp, 1);

      #5: begin
        Temp := StripFromFront(Temp, 1);
        Temp := '(Property) ' + Temp;
      end;
  end;
  StgStrings.Add(S + ' ' + Temp);
  Result := Ord(Temp[1]);
end;

procedure TOpenStorage.HandleSubStorage(var Storage: IStorage; StatStg: TStatStg);
var
  hr: HResult;
  SubStorage: IStorage;
begin
  hr := Storage.OpenStorage(StatStg.pwcsName, nil,
          Stgm_Read or Stgm_Share_Exclusive,
          nil, LongInt(nil), SubStorage);
  if Succeeded(hr) then
    EnumStorageElements(SubStorage)
  else
    ShowMessage('Count not open subStorage');
end;

{------------------------------------------------------
        Name: EnumStorageElements
 Declaration: EnumStorageElements(var Storage: IStorage);
        Unit: Main
 Description: Enumerate the elements inside a storage.
              This is a recursive routine, but the
              recursion occurs in the HandleSubStorage routine.
--------------------------------------------------}

procedure TOpenStorage.EnumStorageElements(var Storage: IStorage);
var
  Enum: IEnumStatStg;
  hr: hResult;
  StatStg: TStatStg;
  Count: LongInt;
  S: string;
begin
  if not Test(Storage.EnumElements(0, nil, 0, Enum)) then Exit;

  repeat
    hr := Enum.Next(1, StatStg, @Count);
    OleCheck(hr);
    case StatStg.dwType of
      STGTY_STREAM: S := 'Stream';
      STGTY_STORAGE: S := 'Storage';
      STGTY_LOCKBYTES: S := 'LockBytes';
```

```
      STGTY_PROPERTY: S := 'Property';
    else
      S := 'Unknown';
    end;

    if ShowStorageElement(S, StatStg) = 5 then
      HandleProperty(Storage);

    if S = 'Storage' then HandleSubStorage(Storage, StatStg);
  until HR <> S_OK;
  Enum.Release;
end;


{------------------------------------------------------
        Name: OpenStorage
 Declaration: OpenStorage(FileName: string);
        Unit: Main
 Description: Given a filename, try to open it as a storage
             file.
--------------------------------------------------------}
procedure TOpenStorage.OpenStorage(FileName: string);
var
  hr: HResult;
  S: PWideChar;
  Size: Integer;
  Storage: IStorage;
  Failed: Boolean;
begin
  Failed := False;
  S := nil;
  try
    try
      S := AnsiToUnicode(FileName, Size);
      hr := StgIsStorageFile(S);
      if hr <> NoError then
        raise Exception.Create('Not a valid storage file.');
      StgStrings.Add('Storage ' + FileName);
      hr := StgOpenStorage(S, nil,
              Stgm_Direct or Stgm_ReadWrite or Stgm_Share_Exclusive,
              nil, LongInt(nil), Storage);
      if Ole2.Failed(hr) then
        raise Exception.Create('Call to StgOpenStorage failed');
    except
      Failed := True;
      raise;
    end; { try..except }
  finally
    VirtualFree(S, Size, Mem_Release);
  end; { try..finally }

  if not Failed then begin
    EnumStorageElements(Storage);
    Storage.Release;
  end;
end;

end.
```

Listing 31.4. The OleBox unit contains some simple routines that might be helpful when you are working with OLE code.

```pascal
unit olebox;

interface

uses
  Ole2, SysUtils, Windows;

const
  SOleError = 62211;

type
  EOleError = class(Exception);


function AnsiToUnicode(S: string; var NewSize: Integer): PWideChar;
function GetCLSIDName(iid: TCLSID): string;
procedure OleError(ErrorCode: HResult);
procedure OleSucceeded(hr: HResult);
function GetOleError(ErrorCode: HResult): ShortString;
function CLSIDToStr(ID: TCLSID): string;
function UnicodeToAnsi(S: PWideChar): string;


implementation

{ This function returns the size of the allocated string in NewSize.
  You have to free up this memory yourself. }
function AnsiToUnicode(S: string; var NewSize: Integer): PWideChar;
var
  Size: Integer;
  P: PWideChar;
begin
  Size := Length(S);
  NewSize := Size * 2;
  P := VirtualAlloc(nil, Size, Mem_Commit, Page_ReadWrite);
  MultiByteToWideChar(CP_ACP, 0, PChar(S), Size, P, NewSize);
  Result := P;
end;

function CLSIDToStr(ID: TCLSID): string;
var
  hr: hResult;
  WideString: PWideChar;
begin
  hr := StringFromCLSID(ID, WideString);
  if hr < 0 then OleError(hr);
  Result := UnicodeToAnsi(WideString);
end;

function GetCLSIDName(iid: TCLSID): string;
var
  S: string;
begin
  if IsEqualIID(iid, IID_IUnknown) then
    S := 'IID_IUnknown'
  else if IsEqualIID(iid, IID_IClassFactory) then
    S := 'IID_IClassFactory'
```

```
    else if IsEqualIID(iid, IID_IMarshal) then
      S := 'IID_IMarshal'
    else if IsEqualIID(iid, IID_IStdMarshalInfo) then
      S := 'IID_IStdMarshalInfo'
    else if IsEqualIID(iid, IID_IExternalConnection) then
      S := 'IID_IExternalConnection'
    else
      S := CLSIDToStr(iid);
    Result := S;
end;


procedure OleError(ErrorCode: HResult);
var
  Message: string;
begin
  Message := SysErrorMessage(ErrorCode);
  if Message = '' then FmtStr(Message, LoadStr(SOleError), [ErrorCode]);
  raise EOleError.Create(Message);
end;

procedure OleSucceeded(hr: HResult);
begin
  if not Succeeded(hr) then
    OleError(hr);
end;

function GetOleError(ErrorCode: HResult): ShortString;
var
  AMessage: string;
begin
  AMessage := SysErrorMessage(ErrorCode);
  if AMessage = '' then FmtStr(AMessage, LoadStr(SOleError), [ErrorCode]);
  Result := AMessage;
end;

function UnicodeToAnsi(S: PWideChar): string;
var
  S1: PChar;
  i: Integer;
begin
  i := lstrlenw(S) + 1;
  GetMem(S1, 500);
  WideCharToMultiByte(CP_ACP, 0, S, i, S1, i * 2, nil, nil);
  Result := S1;
  FreeMem(S1, 500);
end;

initialization
finalization
end.
```

The core of the main module for this program contains one simple routine:

```
procedure TForm1.bBrowseClick(Sender: TObject);
var
  OpenStorage: TOpenStorage;
```

continues

Listing 31.4. continued

```
begin
  if not OpenDialog1.Execute then Exit;
  OpenStorage := TOpenStorage.Create(OpenDialog1.FileName);
  ListBox1.Items := OpenStorage.StgStrings;
  OpenStorage.Free;
end;
```

This code pops up an open dialog. You can then browse around looking for compound files. In most cases, you can just select a Word or .DOC file like the ones that ship on the CD.

Assuming that the user chooses a file, the next step is to create an instance of TOpenStorage. The Create method for TOpenStorage first creates a TStringList object called FStgStrings and then calls an internal method called OpenStorage:

```
procedure TOpenStorage.OpenStorage(FileName: string);
var
  hr: HResult;
  P: IUnknown;
  S: PWideChar;
  Size: Integer;
  Storage: IStorage;
  Failed: Boolean;
begin
  Failed := False;
  try
    try
      S := AnsiToUnicode(FileName, Size);
      hr := StgIsStorageFile(S);
      if hr <> NoError then
        raise Exception.Create('Not a valid storage file.');
      StgStrings.Add('Storage ' + FileName);
      hr := StgOpenStorage(S, nil,
              Stgm_Direct or Stgm_ReadWrite or Stgm_Share_Exclusive,
              nil, LongInt(nil), Storage);
      if Ole2.Failed(hr) then
        raise Exception.Create('Call to StgOpenStorage failed');
    except
      Failed := True;
      raise;
    end; { try..except }
  finally
    VirtualFree(S, Size, Mem_Release);
  end; { try..finally }

  if not Failed then begin
    EnumStorageElements(Storage);
    Storage.Release;
  end;
end;
```

OpenStorage contains a try..except and try..finally block. The code begins by calling AnsiToUnicode, which is a function found in the OleBox unit that ships with this book:

```
function AnsiToUnicode(S: string; var NewSize: Integer): PWideChar;
var
  Size: Integer;
  P: PWideChar;
begin
  Size := Length(S);
  NewSize := Size * 2;
  P := VirtualAlloc(nil, Size, Mem_Commit, Page_ReadWrite);
  MultiByteToWideChar(CP_ACP, 0, PChar(S), Size, P, NewSize);
  Result := P;
end;
```

AnsiToUnicode calls VirtualAlloc to get memory for a PWideChar. This is necessary because a call to GetMem did not work in this situation with the copy of Delphi I had at the time of this writing. The code then calls the MultiByteToWideChar function, which converts a long string into a Unicode string. This function leaves it up to the user to dispose of the memory allocated by the call to VirtualAlloc. As a result, you might consider calling one of the functions in SysUtils as shown rather than this routine.

StgIsStorageFile is one of the core OLE routines declared in OLE2.PAS. It takes the name of the file in a parameter called pwcsName, and it returns one of the following values:

```
S_OK    The file contains an IStorage.
S_FALSE    The file does not contain an IStorage object.
STG_E_INVALIDFILENAME    A bad name was passed in.
STG_E_FILENOTFOUND    The pwcsName parameter could not be determined.
```

The function is called because the user might have chosen a file that was not a real structured storage file. In that case, the code just raises an exception:

```
if hr <> NoError then
  raise Exception.Create('Not a valid storage file.');
```

Notice that I don't bother creating an exception class for this particular error. This is not recommended programming practice, but it works well enough.

Assuming that the user chose a valid structured storage file, the next step is to call StgOpenStorage so as to retrieve an instance of an IStorage object. If the call succeeds, then the following method is called, with the IStorage object passed as a parameter:

```
procedure TOpenStorage.EnumStorageElements(var Storage: IStorage);
var
  Enum: IEnumStatStg;
  hr: hResult;
  StatStg: TStatStg;
  Count: LongInt;
  S: string;
begin
  if not Test(Storage.EnumElements(0, nil, 0, Enum)) then Exit;

  repeat
    hr := Enum.Next(1, StatStg, @Count);
    OleCheck(hr);
```

```
      case StatStg.dwType of
        STGTY_STREAM: S := 'Stream';
        STGTY_STORAGE: S := 'Storage';
        STGTY_LOCKBYTES: S := 'LockBytes';
        STGTY_PROPERTY: S := 'Property';
      else
        S := 'Unknown';
      end;

      if ShowStorageElement(S, StatStg) = 5 then
        HandleProperty(Storage);

      if S = 'Storage' then HandleSubStorage(Storage, StatStg);
    until HR <> S_OK;
    Enum.Release;
end;
```

This routine calls IStorage.EnumElements, which is a bit like entering the DIR command in a subdirectory at the DOS prompt. Perhaps another, more apt analogy would be to the FindFirst and FindNext commands shown in the TFileIterator component used by the DelAllDb program. At any rate, the call first retrieves an instance of IEnumStatStorage, which is an enumerator that retrieves each of the elements in the current storage:

```
var
  Enum: IEnumStatStg;
begin
  if not Test(Storage.EnumElements(0, nil, 0, Enum)) then Exit;
  ...
```

IEnumStatStg is a very simple OLE class that enables you to iterate over a series of elements:

```
IEnumStatStg = class(IUnknown)
public
  function Next(celt: Longint; var elt;
    pceltFetched: PLongint): HResult; virtual; stdcall; abstract;
  function Skip(celt: Longint): HResult; virtual; stdcall; abstract;
  function Reset: HResult; virtual; stdcall; abstract;
  function Clone(var enm: IEnumStatStg): HResult; virtual; stdcall; abstract;
end;
```

> **NOTE**
>
> Remember that OLE classes such as IEnumStatStg are declared by Microsoft and implemented originally in C++. It takes a while to get used to the idea that OLE objects are language-independent!

Each call to Enum.Next retrieves a record of type TStatStg:

```
TStatStg = record
  pwcsName: POleStr;
  dwType: Longint;
  cbSize: Largeint;
```

```
    mtime: TFileTime;
    ctime: TFileTime;
    atime: TFileTime;
    grfMode: Longint;
    grfLocksSupported: Longint;
    clsid: TCLSID;
    grfStateBits: Longint;
    reserved: Longint;
  end;
```

The fields of this record track the name, time, and type of one of the streams, substorages, or properties stored in the compound file. In particular, here are the possible types stored in a compound file:

```
case StatStg.dwType of
    STGTY_STREAM: S := 'Stream';
    STGTY_STORAGE: S := 'Storage';
    STGTY_LOCKBYTES: S := 'LockBytes';
    STGTY_PROPERTY: S := 'Property';
  else
    S := 'Unknown';
  end;
```

Because it is possible that this code can stumble across a substorage, the code that iterates over the elements in the stream recursively calls a method of TOpenStorage called HandleSubStorage, which in turn recalls EnumStorageElements. I usually try to avoid recursion in my code, but here the solution it offers is too simple to pass up.

That is all I'm going to say for now about the technical aspects of structured storage. This system is widely used in OLE. If you embed an object, then it will be stored to disk using structured storage. Many OCXs also make heavy use of structured storage.

To me, the technology is also intriguing because it represents a means of storing many small files inside one larger file. There are several occasions in programming where you need to save a series of small files to disk. If you haven't created such a program yourself, then you have almost certainly used one. When you enter the program directory and type DIR, some one or two hundred odd files may scroll by. It's intriguing to think of the possibility of storing all these small utility files inside one large compound file.

Automation without the VCL

In the last chapter, you learned a great deal about COM objects. In the rest of this chapter, you will see how to implement OLE automation without any help from the VCL. You will find that this process involves code that looks very much like the simple COM objects created in the last chapter.

To get started, you need to look at the executable that will export an OLE automation object. The executable, shown in Figure 31.3, is called AUTO1.EXE.

FIGURE 31.3.

The Auto1 program exports an OLE automation object.

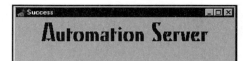

The object exported from the executable should be a descendant of IDispatch, which is declared like this in OLE2.PAS:

```
IDispatch = class(IUnknown)
public
  function GetTypeInfoCount(var ctinfo: Integer): HResult;
    virtual; stdcall; abstract;
  function GetTypeInfo(itinfo: Integer; lcid: TLCID;
    var tinfo: ITypeInfo): HResult; virtual; stdcall; abstract;
  function GetIDsOfNames(const iid: TIID; rgszNames: POleStrList;
    cNames: Integer; lcid: TLCID; rgdispid: PDispIDList): HResult;
    virtual; stdcall; abstract;
  function Invoke(dispIDMember: TDispID; const iid: TIID; lcid: TLCID;
    flags: Word; var dispParams: TDispParams; varResult: PVariant;
    excepInfo: PExcepInfo; argErr: PInteger): HResult;
    virtual; stdcall; abstract;
end;
```

You will need to implement an instance of this class. That is, you cannot leave this as an abstract object, but must instead implement each of its methods.

In the COM object programs from the last chapter, you saw objects called IMyObject and IExeObject. Those objects played the same role in the SimpDll and SimpExe that this object plays in the Auto1 project. The difference, of course, is that this object knows how to transmit information across process boundaries. That, as you recall, was a problem with the SimpExe program!

In the Auto1 program, the instance of IDispatch that you will be working with is called TMyAuto. The other key object in the program is called TMyClassFactory, and it is nearly identical to the TMyClassFactory instances seen in the last chapter. The code in question is shown in Listing 31.5, with Listing 31.6 featuring the same calls to CoRegisterClassObject seen in the last chapter. Listing 31.7 contains the REG file you need to pass to REGEDIT.EXE.

Listing 31.5. The Automat unit implements IDispatch and IClassFactory.

```
unit automat;

{ Copyright (c) 1996 by Charlie Calvert
  Big thanks to Danny Thorpe for some
  direction on this code! }

interface

uses
  Ole2, Windows, SysUtils,
  Dialogs;
```

```
const
  CLSID_MyAuto: TGUID = (
    D1:$C9B0B162;D2:$1307;D3:$11cf;D4:($AB,$35,$00,$00,$C0,$7E,$BA,$2B));

type
  TMyAuto = class(IDispatch)
  private
    RefCount: Integer;
  public
    constructor Create;
    function QueryInterface(const iid: TIID; var Obj): HResult;
      override;
    function AddRef: Longint; override;
    function Release: Longint; override;
    function GetTypeInfoCount(var ctinfo: Integer): HResult; override;
    function GetTypeInfo(itinfo: Integer; lcid: TLCID;
                         var tinfo: ITypeInfo): HResult; override;
function GetIDsOfNames(const iid: TIID; rgszNames: POleStrList;
      cNames: Integer; lcid: TLCID; rgdispid: PDispIDList): HResult; override;
    function Invoke(dispIDMember: TDispID; const iid: TIID; lcid: TLCID;
      flags: Word; var dispParams: TDispParams; varResult: PVariant;
      excepInfo: PExcepInfo; argErr: PInteger): HResult; override;
  end;

  TMyClassFactory = class(IClassFactory)
  private
    FRefCount: Integer;
  public
    constructor Create;
    function QueryInterface(const iid: TIID; var obj): HResult; override;
    function AddRef: Longint; override;
    function Release: Longint; override;
    function CreateInstance(unkOuter: IUnknown; const iid: TIID;
      var obj): HResult; override;
    function LockServer(fLock: BOOL): HResult; override;
  end;

var
  RegCo: LongInt;

implementation

uses
  OleBox;

/////////////////////////////
////////// TMyAuto //////////
/////////////////////////////

constructor TMyAuto.Create;
begin
  inherited Create;
  RefCount := 0;
end;

function TMyAuto.QueryInterface(const iid: TIID;
                               var Obj): HResult;
```

continues

Listing 31.5. continued

```
begin
  if IsEqualGUID(iid, IID_IUNKNOWN) or
    IsEqualGUID(iid, IID_IDispatch) or
    IsEqualGUID(iid, CLSID_MyAuto) then begin
    TObject(Obj) := Self;
    AddRef;
    Result := NOERROR;
    if IsEqualGUID(iid, CLSID_MyAuto) then ;
  end else
    Result := E_NOINTERFACE;
end;

function TMyAuto.AddRef: Longint;
begin
  Inc(RefCount);
  Result := RefCount;
end;

function TMyAuto.Release: Longint;
begin
  Dec(RefCount);
  Result := RefCount;
  if RefCount = 0 then Free;
end;

function TMyAuto.GetTypeInfoCount(var ctinfo: Integer): HResult;
begin
  ctinfo := 0;
  Result := E_NOTIMPL;
end;

function TMyAuto.GetTypeInfo(itinfo: Integer; lcid: TLCID;
                            var tinfo: ITypeInfo): HResult;
begin
  Result := E_NOTIMPL;
end;

function TMyAuto.GetIDsOfNames(const iid: TIID; rgszNames: POleStrList;
      cNames: Integer; lcid: TLCID; rgdispid: PDispIDList): HResult;
var
  S: string;
begin
  if not IsEqualGUID(iid, GUID_NULL) then begin
    Result := E_NOINTERFACE;
    Exit;
  end;
  Result := DISP_E_UNKNOWNNAME;
  S := UnicodeToAnsi(rgszNames[0]);
  if cNames <> 1 then Exit;
  if S = 'Sam' then
    rgDispID^[0] := 1
  else if S = 'Mike' then
    rgDispID^[0] := 2
  else if S = 'ChangeCaption' then
    rgDispID^[0] := 3;

  Result := S_OK;
end;
```

```
function TMyAuto.Invoke(dispIDMember: TDispID; const iid: TIID; lcid: TLCID;
      flags: Word; var dispParams: TDispParams; varResult: PVariant;
      excepInfo: PExcepInfo; argErr: PInteger): HResult;
begin
  if not IsEqualGUID(iid, GUID_NULL) then begin
    Result := E_NOINTERFACE;
    Exit;
  end;
  Result := E_NOTIMPL;

  if flags and DISPATCH_METHOD <> 0 then begin
    if dispIdMember = 3 then
      ShowMessage('Groovy AutoTalk Jive');
    Result := NOERROR;
  end;

  if flags and DISPATCH_PROPERTYGET <> 0 then begin
    case dispIdMember of
      1: varResult^ := 7;
      2: varResult^ := 11;
    else
      varResult^ := -1;
    end;
    Result := NOERROR;
    Exit;
  end;
end;

///////////////////////////
/////  TMyClassFactory /////
///////////////////////////

constructor TMyClassFactory.Create;
begin
  inherited Create;
  FRefCount := 0;
end;

function TMyClassFactory.QueryInterface(const iid: TIID; var obj): HResult;
begin
  if IsEqualIID(iid, IID_IUnknown) or
     IsEqualIID(iid, IID_IClassFactory) or
     IsEqualIID(iid, CLSID_MyAuto) then begin
    Pointer(obj) := Self;
    AddRef;
    Result := S_OK;
  end else begin
    Pointer(obj) := nil;
    Result := E_NOINTERFACE;
  end;
end;

function TMyClassFactory.AddRef: Longint;
begin
  Inc(FRefCount);
  Result := FRefCount;
end;
```

continues

Listing 31.5. continued

```pascal
function TMyClassFactory.Release: Longint;
begin
  Dec(FRefCount);
  Result := FRefCount;
  if FRefCount = 0 then Free;
end;

function TMyClassFactory.CreateInstance(unkOuter: IUnknown; const iid: TIID;
                          var obj): HResult;
var
  Auto: TMyAuto;
  hr: HResult;
begin
  Result := E_OutOfMemory;
  if UnkOuter <> nil then Exit;
  if not IsEqualIID(iid, IID_IUnknown) then Exit;

  Auto := TMyAuto.Create;
  if Auto = nil then begin
    Pointer(Obj) := nil;
    Result := E_OutOfMemory;
    Exit;
  end;

  hr := Auto.QueryInterface(iid, Obj);
  if Failed(hr) then Auto.Release;
  Result := hr;
end;

function TMyClassFactory.LockServer(fLock: BOOL): HResult;
begin
  Result := S_Ok;
end;

var
  Inithr: hResult;

initialization
  Inithr := OleInitialize(nil);
finalization
  CoRevokeClassObject(RegCo);
  if Inithr = S_OK then OleUnInitialize;
end.
```

Listing 31.6. The code for the main module of the Auto1 program.

```pascal
unit main;

interface

uses
  Windows, Messages, SysUtils,
  Classes, Graphics, Controls,
  Forms, Dialogs, StdCtrls;
```

```
type
  TForm1 = class(TForm)
    Label1: TLabel;
    procedure FormCreate(Sender: TObject);
  private
    { Private declarations }
  public
    { Public declarations }
  end;

var
  Form1: TForm1;

  implementation

  uses
    AutoMat, Ole2, OleBox;


{$R *.DFM}


procedure TForm1.FormCreate(Sender: TObject);
var
  MyClassFactory: TMyClassFactory;
  hr: HResult;
begin
  RegCo := 0;

  try
    MyClassFactory := TMyClassFactory.Create;
  except
    Close;
    Exit;
  end;

  hr := CoRegisterClassObject(CLSID_MyAuto, MyClassFactory,
          CLSCTX_LOCAL_SERVER, REGCLS_MULTIPLEUSE, RegCO);

  if Succeeded(hr) then
    Caption := 'Success'
  else
    Caption := GetOleError(hr);
end;

end.
```

Listing 31.7. The REG file for the Auto1 program.

```
REGEDIT
HKEY_CLASSES_ROOT\MyAuto1.0 = MyAuto 1
HKEY_CLASSES_ROOT\MyAuto1.0\CLSID = {C9B0B162-1307-11cf-AB35-0000C07EBA2B}
HKEY_CLASSES_ROOT\MyAuto = MyAuto 1
HKEY_CLASSES_ROOT\MyAuto\CurVer = MyAuto1.0
HKEY_CLASSES_ROOT\MyAuto\CLSID = {C9B0B162-1307-11cf-AB35-0000C07EBA2B}
```

continues

Listing 31.7. continued

```
HKEY_CLASSES_ROOT\CLSID\{C9B0B162-1307-11cf-AB35-0000C07EBA2B} = MyAuto 1
HKEY_CLASSES_ROOT\CLSID\{C9B0B162-1307-11cf-AB35-0000C07EBA2B}\ProgID =
  MyAuto1.0
HKEY_CLASSES_ROOT\CLSID\{C9B0B162-1307-11cf-AB35-0000C07EBA2B}\
  VersionIndependentProgID = MyAuto
HKEY_CLASSES_ROOT\CLSID\{C9B0B162-1307-11cf-AB35-0000C07EBA2B}\LocalServer32 =
  c:\src\unleash\chap31\auto1\auto1.exe
HKEY_CLASSES_ROOT\CLSID\{C9B0B162-1307-11cf-AB35-0000C07EBA2B}\NotInsertable
```

Given the lengthy explanation of COM objects presented in the last chapter, I am going to assume that most of the code in these units makes sense to you. If you don't understand how IClassFactory works, or how QueryInterface works, then you should return to the last chapter, which explains these things in some detail.

There are, however, two key methods in the Automat unit that need to be explained. Both of these methods are part of the IDispatch implementation called TMyAuto. The first call is GetIDsOfNames, and the second is called Invoke.

Remember that the idea of an automation object is to enable the user to call functions or access properties located inside an executable. In this case, the executable in question is called AUTO1.EXE. To call a function or use a property, you need to call the InvokeMethod of TMyAuto. However, you can't pass the name of a function directly to TMyAuto; instead, you need to first call GetIDsOfNames, which provides a set of IDs that serve as aliases for the names and parameters by which you know the functions and properties supported by the object. Once you know which ID is associated with which name, then you can call Invoke.

This process is a bit confusing at first blush, so I will take a moment to restate the matter in slightly different terms. To get started, you pass GetIDsOfNames an array of strings. In response, it passes back to you an array of IDs. The array of IDs define not only the individual functions or properties supported by the object, but also the parameters passed to the function. You can then pass these ideas to Invoke, and in turn Invoke will actually call the methods or properties you specified when calling GetIDsOfNames.

GetIDsOfNames will translate a string name into a number that can be passed to Invoke:

```
function TMyAuto.GetIDsOfNames(const iid: TIID; rgszNames: POleStrList;
      cNames: Integer; lcid: TLCID; rgdispid: PDispIDList): HResult;
var
  S: string;
begin
  if not IsEqualGUID(iid, GUID_NULL) then begin
    Result := E_NOINTERFACE;
    Exit;
  end;
  Result := DISP_E_UNKNOWNNAME;
  S := UnicodeToAnsi(rgszNames[0]);
  if cNames <> 1 then Exit;
  if S = 'Sam' then
    rgDispID^[0] := 1
```

```
  else if S = 'Mike' then
    rgDispID^[0] := 2
  else if S = 'ChangeCaption' then
    rgDispID^[0] := 3;

  Result := S_OK;
end;
```

In this case, the only element of interest is the first member of the array of strings passed in. The code shown here uses a routine called UnicodeToAnsi from the OleBox unit to translate the first member of the array to a string. It then sets the first element of the array of IDs to the appropriate value associated with a particular string.

Here is a look at the parameters passed to GetIDsOfNames:

```
function TMyAuto.GetIDsOfNames(
  const iid: TIID;          // Reserved for future use, set to GUID_NULL
  rgszNames: POleStrList;   // Array of names to be mapped
  cNames: Integer;          // Number of names in array
  lcid: TLCID;              // Context used to interpret names
  rgdispid: PDispIDList      // Returned list of IDS
): HResult;
```

When considering this function, it's important to remember that you will typically be calling it from another executable. In particular, you will first call CoCreateInstance or CoGetClassName as explained in the last chapter. Once you have a pointer to an instance of TMyAuto, then you can call GetIDsOfNames or Invoke. This whole process will be explained in more depth later in this section, but the general idea should be starting to make sense by this time.

Once you know the ID associated with the function or property that you want to access, then you can pass that number to Invoke:

```
function TMyAuto.Invoke(dispIDMember: TDispID; const iid: TIID; lcid: TLCID;
    flags: Word; var dispParams: TDispParams; varResult: PVariant;
    excepInfo: PExcepInfo; argErr: PInteger): HResult;
begin
  if not IsEqualGUID(iid, GUID_NULL) then begin
    Result := E_NOINTERFACE;
    Exit;
  end;
  Result := E_NOTIMPL;

  if flags and DISPATCH_METHOD <> 0 then begin
    if dispIdMember = 3 then
      ShowMessage('Groovy AutoTalk Jive');
    Result := NOERROR;
  end;

  if flags and DISPATCH_PROPERTYGET <> 0 then begin
    case dispIdMember of
      1: varResult^ := 7;
      2: varResult^ := 11;
    else
      varResult^ := -1;
    end;
```

```
    Result := NOERROR;
    Exit;
  end;
end;
```

Invoke checks to see whether you want to call a function (DISPATCH_METHOD), or whether you want to access a property (DISPATCH_PROPERTYGET). If the former, then a method is called, and if the latter, then a property is accessed. In this particular implementation, the code is extremely simple, with the method being nothing more than a call to ShowMessage, and the two properties simply returning integer values of either 7 or 11.

Here are the parameters passed to Invoke:

```
function TMyAuto.Invoke(
  dispIDMember: TDispID;      // ID obtained from GetIDsOfNames
  const iid: TIID;            // Reserved, must be GUID_NULL
  lcid: TLCID;                // Multi-lingual apps only: French, German, etc
  flags: Word;                // Is it a property, a method, a put or a get?
  var dispParams: TDispParams;// Arguments to calls placed here
  varResult: PVariant;        // Return value placed here by Invoke
  excepInfo: PExcepInfo;      // Exception info placed here on error
  argErr: Pinteger            // If parameters are wrong error here
): HResult;                   // S_OK on success
```

The first parameter is the ID you got when you called GetIDsOfNames. The second should be set to nil. The third parameter is for multi-lingual applications that need to be concerned about which national language is being used. These are not computer languages, but national languages such as French, Spanish, German, and so on.

The flags parameter can be set to one of the following values:

DISPATCH_METHOD	Method call in process
DISPATCH_PROPERTYGET	Retrieving property value
DISPATCH_PROPERTYPUT	Setting property value
DISPATCH_PROPERTYPUTREF	Property is being changed by reference, not by value. In short, is it a var parameter?

If there are any arguments to the call, they are placed in the dispParams parameter. If a result is returned from the call, then it is placed in pvarResult; otherwise, this parameter is set to nil. The last two parameters involve error-reporting if something goes wrong.

Here are the possible return values from Invoke. I won't bother to explain them, as they are well declared:

```
S_OK
DISP_E_BADPARAMCOUNT
DISP_E_BADVARTYPE
DISP_E_EXCEPTION
DISP_E_MEMBERNOTFOUND
DISP_E_NONAMEDARGS
DISP_E_OVERFLOW
DISP_E_PARAMNOTFOUND
```

```
DISP_E_TYPEMISMATCH
DISP_E_UNKNOWNINTERFACE
DISP_E_UNKNOWNLCID
DISP_E_PARAMNOTOPTIONAL
```

I'm not going to dig any further into this function. You should, however, have enough information now to see the way the basic process operates. For additional information, see the relevant Microsoft documentation. For instance, it is instructive to look this function up in the MSDN, if you have a copy available.

Calling the TMyAuto Object

The RunAuto program, shown in Figure 31.4, is able to access the TMyAuto object. This program will be very familiar after reading the last chapter. However, I will still discuss it briefly so as to explain the calls to GetIDsOfNames and Invoke. The code for the program is found in Listing 31.8.

FIGURE 31.4.

The RunAuto program is similar to the MakeOle1 project seen in the last chapter.

Listing 31.8. The code for the RunAuto program shows how to call an automation object without the aid of the VCL.

```
unit main;

interface

uses
  SysUtils, Windows, Messages,
  Classes, Graphics, Controls,
  Forms, Dialogs, StdCtrls,
  Ole2, OleAuto, Menus,
  ExtCtrls;

type

  TForm1 = class(TForm)
    MainMenu1: TMainMenu;
    File1: TMenuItem;
    Exit1: TMenuItem;
    Exes1: TMenuItem;
    ExeGetObject: TMenuItem;
```

continues

Listing 31.8. continued

```
    ExeCreateInstance: TMenuItem;
    Panel1: TPanel;
    N2: TMenuItem;
    ClearText1: TMenuItem;
    procedure FormCreate(Sender: TObject);
    procedure ExeGetObjectClick(Sender: TObject);
    procedure ExeCreateInstanceClick(Sender: TObject);
    procedure ClearText1Click(Sender: TObject);
    procedure Exit1Click(Sender: TObject);
    procedure FormDestroy(Sender: TObject);
  private
    procedure GetClass(CLSID: TGUID; ClassContext: DWord);
    procedure CreateInstance(CLSID: TGUID; ClassContext: DWord);
    procedure MessageOut(S: string);
  end;

var
  Form1: TForm1;

implementation

{$R *.DFM}

uses
  OleBox;

const
  CLSID_WordBasic: TGUID = (
    D1:$000209FE;D2:$0000;D3:$0000;D4:($C0,$00,$00,$00,$00,$00,$00,$46));
  CLSID_MyAuto: TGUID = (
    D1:$C9B0B162;D2:$1307;D3:$11cf;D4:($AB,$35,$00,$00,$C0,$7E,$BA,$2B));


procedure TForm1.MessageOut(S: string);
begin
  Panel1.Caption := S;
  Panel1.UpDate;
end;

procedure TForm1.FormCreate(Sender: TObject);
begin
  OleCheck(CoInitialize(nil));
  Left := 0;
  Top := 0;
end;

procedure TForm1.FormDestroy(Sender: TObject);
begin
  CoUninitialize;
end;


procedure TForm1.Exit1Click(Sender: TObject);
begin
  Close;
end;
```

```
procedure TForm1.CreateInstance(CLSID: TGUID; ClassContext: DWord);
var
  hr: hResult;
  P: IUnknown;
  P1: IDispatch;
  Disp: TDispIDList;
  S: TOleStrList;
  Size: Integer;
  V: Variant;
  DispP: TDispParams;
begin
  hr := CoCreateInstance(CLSID, nil, ClassContext, IID_IUnknown, P);
  if Succeeded(hr) then
    MessageOut('Object Exists')
  else begin
    MessageOut('No Object');
    Exit;
  end;
  hr := P.QueryInterface(IID_IDispatch, P1);
  if not Succeeded(hr) then Exit;
  S[0] := AnsiToUnicode('Sam', Size);
  hr := P1.GetIdsOfNames(GUID_NULL, @S, 1, 0, @Disp);
  OleCheck(hr);
  VirtualFree(S[0], Size, Mem_Release);
  P1.Invoke(Disp[0], GUID_NULL, 0, Dispatch_PropertyGet, DispP, @V, nil, nil);

  S[0] := AnsiToUnicode('ChangeCaption', Size);
  hr := P1.GetIdsOfNames(GUID_NULL, @S, 1, 0, @Disp);
  OleCheck(hr);
  VirtualFree(S[0], Size, Mem_Release);
  P1.Invoke(Disp[0], GUID_NULL, 0, Dispatch_Method, DispP, @V, nil, nil);
  ShowMessage(V);
  OleCheck(P1.Release);
  OleCheck(P.Release);
end;

procedure TForm1.GetClass(CLSID: TGUID; ClassContext: DWord);
var
  hr: HResult;
  ClassFactory: IClassFactory;
  P: IUnKnown;
begin
  hr := CoGetClassObject(CLSID, ClassContext, nil,
                         IID_IClassFactory, ClassFactory);
  OleCheck(hr);
  hr := ClassFactory.CreateInstance(nil, IID_IUnknown, P);

  if Succeeded(hr) then
    MessageOut('Object Exists')
  else begin
    MessageOut(GetOleError(hr));
    Exit;
  end;

  OleCheck(ClassFactory.Release);
  OleCheck(P.Release);
end;
```

continues

Listing 31.8. continued

```
procedure TForm1.ExeGetObjectClick(Sender: TObject);
begin
  MessageOut('Opening Exe');
  GetClass(CLSID_MyAuto, CLSCTX_LOCAL_SERVER);
end;

procedure TForm1.ExeCreateInstanceClick(Sender: TObject);
begin
  MessageOut('Opening Exe');
  CreateInstance(CLSID_MyAuto, CLSCTX_LOCAL_SERVER);
end;

procedure TForm1.ClearText1Click(Sender: TObject);
begin
  MessageOut('');
end;

end.
```

The key method in this program is the one to TForm1.CreateInstance. The call to TForm1.GetClass also invokes the TMyAuto object, but it does not do anything interesting with the object once it has hold of it. As a result, it's the CreateInstance method that forms the center of the program's intellectual life.

The call to CoCreateInstance should be self-explanatory after reading the last chapter:

```
hr := CoCreateInstance(CLSID, nil, ClassContext, IID_IUnknown, P);
```

This function retrieves a pointer, P, which is an instance of IUnknown. You can then ask IUnknown if it supports IDispatch:

```
hr := P.QueryInterface(IID_IDispatch, P1);
```

If it does, then you know you have hold of a copy of TMyObject, and you can begin calling the method and properties that it supports.

Here is the code to access a property called Sam that is supported by TMyObject:

```
S[0] := AnsiToUnicode('Sam', Size);
hr := P1.GetIDsOfNames(GUID_NULL, @S, 1, 0, @Disp);
OleCheck(hr);
VirtualFree(S[0], Size, Mem_Release);
P1.Invoke(Disp[0], GUID_NULL, 0, Dispatch_PropertyGet, DispP, @V, nil, nil);
ShowMessage(V);
```

S is an array of WideChars, and I use the AnsiToUnicode function from the OleBox unit to fill its first member. Remember that there are similar routines in the SysUtils unit that are a bit easier to use. In particular, they don't require that you call VirtualFree.

Once you have filled out the array, you can pass it to GetIDsOfNames, which returns an array of IDs in its last parameter. In this particular case, there will only be one ID in the array, and you can pass it to Invoke in that method's first parameter. This is a property, so Dispatch_PropertyGet is passed in the fourth parameter.

The address of the value returned by the function is passed in the sixth parameter. This variable is called V, and it is declared to be of type variant. You will almost always pass variants in this parameter when working with OLE automation.

Once V has been successfully retrieved, the only task left is to show the value to the user. This is simple enough because the variant can convert the integer associated with property Sam into a string:

```
ShowMessage(V);
```

Once you understand how this process works, it's easy enough to see how to call a method, rather than accessing a property:

```
S[0] := AnsiToUnicode('ChangeCaption', Size);
hr := P1.GetIDsOfNames(GUID_NULL, @S, 1, 0, @Disp);
OleCheck(hr);
VirtualFree(S[0], Size, Mem_Release);
P1.Invoke(Disp[0], GUID_NULL, 0, Dispatch_Method, DispP, @V, nil, nil);
```

The method in question here is called ChangeCaption. The first step is to place this name into an array of WideChars, and to pass it in to GetIDsOfNames. This function returns the appropriate ID in the variable called Disp, which is in turn passed to Invoke.

In this case, there is no need to worry about a return value, as the method will simply be invoked and will have no side effects. As you recall, the method does little more than pop up a message box, as shown in this code fragment from the TMyAuto object:

```
if flags and DISPATCH_METHOD <> 0 then begin
  if dispIdMember = 3 then
    ShowMessage('Groovy AutoTalk Jive');
  Result := NOERROR;
end;
```

Here you can see that the code first checks to see if it is indeed a method that's being called, that is, whether the flag is set to DISPATCH_METHOD. If it is a method and the ID associated with that method is 3, the method is called. In this particular case the method is nothing more than a call to ShowMessage, but there is no reason why a separate routine of considerable complexity could not be invoked in its stead.

That's all I'm going to say about the RunAuto program. Clearly this is a subject that could be dwelled on in greater depth, but hopefully the information presented here will be enough to get you started with this fascinating technology.

The RunSimp Program

The RUNSIMP.DPR project found on the *Unleashed* CD-ROM provides a very simple method for running the Auto1 project. The only handcrafted code in the program looks like this:

```
procedure TForm1.Button1Click(Sender: TObject);
var
  V: Variant;
begin
  V := CreateOleObject('MyAuto1.0');
  Memo1.Lines.Add(V.Sam);
  Memo1.Lines.Add(V.Mike);
  V.ChangeCaption;
end;
```

This code takes advantage of the simple routines in the OLEAUTO.PAS unit that ships with Delphi. In many ways this technique is simpler and more intuitive to use the methods shown in the RunAuto program. However practical it might be, this kind of code also protects you from fundamental OLE routines that you ought to understand.

Last Words on OLE

One of the themes of this book is that it is always helpful to understand how a technology works. For instance, in the last chapter you saw how the COM object model is put together. In this chapter, you saw that the knowledge you gained about COM makes it relatively easy for you to implement your own OLE automation calls. As it turns out, there are other technologies in OLE that depend on OLE automation. For instance, it plays a role in OCX development.

OLE is a huge, complex technology. Despite its apparent opaqueness, OLE turns out to be nothing more than an assemblage of objects. In the last two chapters you have been introduced to IUnknown, IClassFactory, IStorage, IStream, IEnumStatStg, and one or two other objects. This is a humble start, but nonetheless it is a true beginning. If you understand what has been said so far, you are now free to continue your exploration of OLE.

The point here is not that RunAuto and Auto1 represent something better than the VCL TAutoObject. In fact, it's obviously much easier to use the VCL than to risk calls to GetIDsOfNames and Invoke. No, the point is obviously not that you should avoid the VCL. Instead, the point is that this code shows you how OLE works. If you can start to understand OLE, then you can use and extend the technology in any way you desire.

Already OLE technologies such as Object Linking and Embedding, automation, and OCXs are starting to have a major impact on our programming styles. In the future, OLE may form the basis for our operating system and for the distributed objects that we create and manipulate on a day-to-day basis. If this turns out to be the case, then an in-depth knowledge of OLE will become a necessity for most serious programmers. The last two chapters have attempted to prepare the ground for the foundation on which that knowledge can be built.

Summary

In this chapter, you got a look at structured storage and the technology behind OLE automation. In particular, you learned how to create compound files with these two calls:

```
StgCreateDocFile,
Storage.CreateStream,
```

You also learned how to open a compound file with these two calls:

```
StgOpenStream
Storage.OpenStream
```

The section on automation introduced you to the IDispatch interface, which is one of the most important in OLE. The example code gave specific examples of how to implement `GetIDsOfNames` and `Invoke`, and how to call these functions from inside an executable.

There is little doubt but that OLE deserves its reputation for complexity. However, you have seen that it is not an unapproachable subject, and that it can be mastered if you have the time and the will to set your mind to the task. No one can say for sure where the computer world is headed, but there is at least a possibility that code of this type will come to dominate the computer world over the next five years.

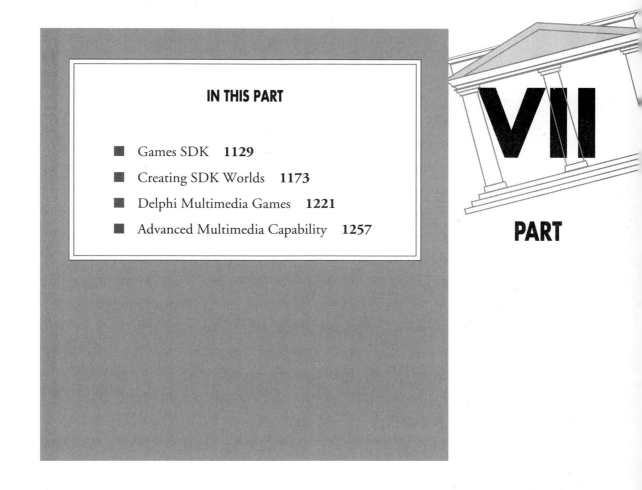

PART

VII

Multimedia and Games

The chapter on the Games SDK was written by multimedia expert Mike Scott. One of Delphi's earliest adopters, Mike has proven his expertise in a number of settings, including construction of a popular Delphi WinG add-on. Creating multimedia programs with visual tools is the subject matter of this section. The first multimedia chapter probably contains the easiest-to-understand material in this book. The second chapter in this section, about advanced multimedia, takes an in-depth look at the MCI interface to the Windows multimedia services.

Games SDK

32

by Mike Scott

1996 marks a turning point in the computer games industry. Microsoft has just introduced the Windows 95 Game Software Development Kit (Game SDK) to great critical acclaim from game developers and users alike. This is pivotal to the Windows game market. In this chapter, you learn how you can program the graphical part of the Game SDK using Delphi 2.0.

> **NOTE**
>
> The Game SDK is available from Microsoft on CD-ROM. This must be installed on your system before you can run any of the examples in this chapter. In particular, you need the freely redistributable portion of the games SDK found on the CD for this book. Once you have those DLLs, the Object Pascal files distributed with this book will allow you to access them and use them in your own programs.

Historical Perspective

Microsoft Windows never really has been able to compete with DOS as a game platform. This is a pity, because it has some great characteristics that game writers could use: device independence, a large protected-mode memory space, and so on. But it's the device independence that also has proven to be the stumbling block. The developer has been shielded from the eccentricities of the specific hardware by a layer of software device drivers. This has been great for writing code that works on all kinds of devices, but something had to give—and that was speed.

Not only that, but Windows even stopped the programmers from getting their hands dirty by preventing direct access to bit-map surfaces. This generally was a good thing, because the bit-map format is defined by the driver and graphics card, and is therefore proprietary. True, often the format is obvious—but it's not guaranteed to not change. Of course, the graphics-card hardware itself also was taboo. Windows applications have to be sociable and conform to strict rules. There was no way you could be allowed to get at the screen directly, because other programs would be sharing it with you.

You had to make display requests through the Windows Graphical Device Interface (GDI) API. This (along with its cousin, the user interface, which lives in USER.DLL) manages the screen and arbitrates contentions by overlapping windows and clipping output to regions inside these windows. The GDI is reasonably rich, but it was born as part of an operating system designed for business computing. This fact is betrayed by the glaring omission of one of the most essential functions for game programming: a function that overlays images with transparent areas. Almost all games require this feature somewhere.

The advent of Windows 3.0 helped slightly with the introduction of the device-independent bitmap, or DIB for short. This has a defined format so you can access it with confidence. New API functions were added to allow conversion from DIBs to device-dependent bitmaps (DDBs) and vice versa. Because the DIB format is open, you could easily get at the pixel data yourself and, for example, write your own high-performance routines for transparent overlays, if necessary. The only problem was that the performance of the DIB conversion and display routines was awful. So no matter how brilliant your 32-bit, hand-crafted assembler was, the bottleneck was getting the final image to the screen.

In the last couple of years, we've seen the growth in popularity of the Windows graphics accelerator to the extent that it now has become ubiquitous. Even the most basic PC has some form of acceleration these days. However, once again, DIBs could not take advantage of this. Of course, the same is true of DOS, where games still are not able to use the silicon processing power languishing on modern graphics cards. One reason why game writers never took to using this power is the proliferation of proprietary chip sets and standards. Windows is such a huge market, and every player offers a driver for that environment, so your Windows graphics code looks the same no matter whose card it's running on. But there ain't no such thing as a generic game driver that lets the game developer get at the accelerator.

Over the past few years, Microsoft has gradually been waking up to this situation. It has openly recognized the growing need for Windows to provide better support for game writers. The first move toward this was the release of DIB.DRV, which was a device driver that used DIBs as its native format. This gave you a DIB that you could paint on using the standard GDI calls, and you could get at it directly with your own code. But it still wasn't any good at getting the image onto the screen quickly.

In the middle of 1993, Microsoft made its next stab at a solution in the form of WinG. This was a development of DIB.DRV, but had optimized routines for copying the DIB onto the graphics card. In most cases, the performance of this operation was nearly as good as the native BitBlt code in the driver, which was optimized by the manufacturers for specific cards. A great achievement, but you still had to compose your image on an off-screen DIB buffer and then move all that data to the display. This was a real waste of time. What's more, it couldn't be synchronized with the vertical retrace, making screen updates "tear" as the raster caught them in mid-step.

Meanwhile, the DOS games had it all their own way. Their trump card is undoubtedly the ability to page-flip between two or more display memory areas. This technique is simple, and all modern (and even not-so-modern) home computers and consoles use it. Basically, you compose the next frame in the memory buffer that's not currently visible. When you're finished, you set some registers on the graphics card, telling the card to display this second buffer instead. Then you do it all over again with the first buffer, and so on. You can easily synchronize this process with the vertical retrace, so when the next raster scan starts, it's displaying a whole new, different image. There's no moving around of memory blocks, so the technique is efficient.

The other advantage, of course, is that you can't see the frames being drawn. You see them only when they're complete. Of course, this flipping occurs quickly, with rates of 25 frames per second now common. At such speeds, it's too quick for your eye to see. The motion becomes apparently continuous, just as it is with television and movies.

But there was a crunch coming. Microsoft realized that their future was in Windows. DOS is an ancient relic, and has become obsolete in virtually all areas except one. Yes, those darned games! And with the massive drop in prices and the subsequent huge take-up of PCs as home computers, the game market is important. In fact, it's so important in the home sector that unless Microsoft could offer a viable, or even better, alternative to DOS, the old operating system would hang around forever just so people could play their games using it. It was out of this necessity that the Microsoft Game SDK was born.

The Windows 95 Game SDK

The Game SDK consists of several interfaces grouped into five broad categories. These categories all begin with the word Direct, and you'll often hear people talk of the Game SDK as DirectX. The two terms are synonymous. Here are the five groupings:

- **DirectDraw**

  This is the graphical part of the Game SDK. It is by far the largest and most significant part, answering the concerns raised a moment ago. It gives transparent access to hardware acceleration, provides direct access to bitmaps in off-screen video memory and supports the page-flipping capabilities of the hardware.

- **DirectSound**

  This supplies sound-playing and real-time mixing capabilities, implemented in sound card hardware if the appropriate drivers are available, or in software if not.

- **DirectPlay**

  This provides a set of functions to help build multi-player games, either over a modem or on a network.

- **DirectInput**

  This supplies a set of joystick-input functions.

- **DirectSetup**

  This is a simple API function that installs the other DirectX components on a user's system, making it easier to write an installation program.

As you can see from the list, the Game SDK is a large and sophisticated development platform. To cover all the DirectX components would require several chapters, maybe even a whole book. Here I explore the most innovative and ground-breaking of these: the DirectDraw graphics system.

As you work through the chapter, you build a DirectDraw page-flipping application from scratch. Each stage in the tutorial illustrates a specific feature or function, and how to implement it in Delphi 2.0. You'll be able to use the code here as a basis for your own DirectX applications. I cover:

- The IDirectDraw object
- Switching into full-screen, page-flipping mode
- Creating and using IDirectDrawSurface objects
- Loading bitmaps and palettes
- Transparent bit blitting
- Handling keyboard input
- Handling exceptions in a full-screen DirectDraw application

In addition, several utilities, object classes, and components are supplied on the CD-ROM, which you can use royalty-free in your own programs. I also cover this in this chapter. They include:

- Functions for loading graphics from BMP files and resources
- Functions for loading palettes
- A custom DirectDraw Canvas class for Delphi 2.0
- A simple animation class
- A DirectDraw sprite component

Component Object Model (COM)

Before launching into the gory details of DirectDraw, first a few words about the Component Object Model—COM for short. Delphi uses an object-oriented programming language, Object Pascal. The Delphi designers chose to make the native Delphi objects fully compatible with COM and OLE. This is great news for us because DirectDraw uses a COM interface, and so it's easy to access it in Delphi.

COM objects are covered in detail in Chapter 30, "COM Object Basics." But to save you having to turn there, here's a quick overview.

In Delphi, you treat a COM object more or less as you would any other object. COM objects look like ordinary Delphi objects, in fact. They have methods, which you call to access their services. They have no fields or properties, however. The main difference is that you call the Release method rather than the Free method when you want to dispose of them.

You never create a COM object by calling a constructor, either. Instead, you call a function in DirectDraw to create the main DirectDraw object. This object has further methods that you use to create the other objects.

Apart from these two issues, you really can think of them as Delphi objects.

The DirectDraw COM objects are defined in a rather complicated C header file supplied with the Game SDK. However, I have translated these into an import unit that you can use in Delphi. This is file DDraw.pas on the companion CD. To access DirectDraw, you simply add DDraw to your unit's uses clause.

DirectDraw

DirectDraw can be a fairly tricky API to use. It seems simple enough at first glance; there are only a few COM classes, and they don't have that many methods. However, DirectDraw uses records to specify all kinds of different parameters when creating its objects. At first sight, these look really daunting. You can find them in the Game SDK Help file starting with the letters DD, such as DDSurfaceDesc. Being a relatively low-level API, there are many options and settings that allow for differences in hardware specifications and capabilities. Fortunately, in the vast majority of cases, we can ignore most of these options. The biggest problem at the time of this writing is the lack of information in the GDK documentation, which describes what combinations of options are allowed.

So to help you find your way through the minefield, this chapter goes through all the stages in building a DirectDraw application in incremental steps. I present the code that's added at each stage and use that to explain an aspect of DirectDraw, as well as to give you a working example on which to build your own programs.

The *IDirectDraw* Object

The DirectDraw DLL actually has the simplest of interfaces. It exports only a single function: DirectDrawCreate. You use this function to create an IDirectDraw COM object, which opens up the rest of the API. So the first thing the example must do is create one of these. You create it in the form's OnCreate event handler and destroy it in OnDestroy. The best place to store the object is in a private field of the main form. Listing 32.1 contains the basic code to do that.

Listing 32.1. Creating an IDirectDraw object.

```
{\DDemo1\unit1.pas}

unit Unit1;

interface

uses
  Windows, Messages, SysUtils, Classes, Graphics, Controls, Forms, Dialogs,
  DDraw ;

type
  TForm1 = class(TForm)
    procedure FormCreate(Sender: TObject);
    procedure FormDestroy(Sender: TObject);
  private
    DirectDraw : IDirectDraw ;  // the main DirectDraw object
  end;

var
  Form1: TForm1;
```

```
implementation

{$R *.DFM}

procedure TForm1.FormCreate(Sender: TObject);
begin
  { create the DirectDraw COM object }
  if DirectDrawCreate( NIL, DirectDraw, NIL ) <> DD_OK then
    Raise Exception.Create( 'Failed to create IDirectDraw object' ) ;
end;

procedure TForm1.FormDestroy(Sender: TObject);
begin
  { free the DirectDraw COM object by calling its Release method }
  if Assigned( DirectDraw ) then DirectDraw.Release ;
end;

end.
```

You can find this trivial example in the DDDemo1 directory on the companion CD. It doesn't do anything obvious when you run it, so don't expect too much! I include it to show you how little code is required to create and free a DirectDraw COM object. It really is that simple.

DirectDraw Result Codes and Delphi Exceptions

The vast majority of the DirectDraw functions return an integer result code called an HResult, which you can think of as an integer. The file DDraw.pas has all the possible error constants listed, and the Game SDK Help file specifies the possible error codes returned by each function. You must check the results of these functions and, in most cases, raise an exception if the result is anything other than DD_OK.

However, there are problems with using exceptions because you're switching to a special screen mode. This means you aren't able to see the Delphi IDE when it breaks on an exception and your program seems to freeze. Setting a breakpoint usually results in the same problem: the application stops at the breakpoint all right, but you aren't able to see Delphi. Welcome to Windows game programming! I discuss this in more detail a little later.

Switching to a Full-Screen Mode

The next thing to do is switch the display into a page-flipping mode. When you do this, only your application is visible. It takes over the whole screen. Any other Windows applications that are running, such as Windows Explorer, continue to run and may write output to what it thinks is the screen. You don't see that output appear because these other applications still use the Windows Graphics Device Interface (GDI) for output, and the GDI is unaware of DirectDraw. But you don't need to worry about that. The GDI will continue happily writing to the display memory, even though you can't actually see its output.

By switching into a special display mode, you take over the whole display. Normally, you can run many regular Windows applications at the same time; their windows overlap and everything is handled nicely for you by the GDI. But what happens if you try to run two or more full-screen DirectDraw applications at the same time? The answer is that only one is allowed full-screen access. DirectDraw controls this by requiring that you have exclusive access to the display card before you change modes. You do this by setting the DirectDraw object's *cooperative level* to exclusive. DirectDraw allows only one application to hold exclusive level at a time. If you try to get exclusive access and some other application has it, the call fails. Similarly, if you try to change display modes without obtaining exclusive access, that call fails. So you try to get exclusive access and then switch display modes.

One thing to note here is that you must supply a window handle to SetCooperativeLevel. DirectDraw resizes this window automatically so that it fills the screen in the new display mode. You must pass the handle of a form to SetCooperativeLevel. Because the window handle has not been created by the time OnCreate is called, you must do all this in the OnShow event. Listing 32.2 shows how to do this.

Listing 32.2. Switching to full-screen mode in OnShow.

```
procedure TForm1.FormShow(Sender: TObject);
begin
  { try to set exclusive cooperative level so we can change display mode }
  if DirectDraw.SetCooperativeLevel( Handle,
                                     DDSCL_EXCLUSIVE or
                                     DDSCL_FULLSCREEN ) <> DD_OK then
    Raise Exception.Create( 'Unable to acquire exclusive full-screen access' ) ;

  { change to 640x480x8 display mode }
  if DirectDraw.SetDisplayMode( 640, 480, 8 ) <> DD_OK then
    Raise Exception.Create( 'Unable to set new display mode' ) ;
end;
```

So far so good—nothing complicated here. If you run the example now, your application switches modes and you see your form filling the screen. If you move it or resize it, you see Delphi behind it. You're still looking at the GDI output surface. GDI can output happily in these different modes, so you'll see your ordinary Windows applications as long as this surface is at the front. But because you're creating a page-flipping application, that will not always necessarily be the case.

The DDDemo2 directory contains the example so far.

Adding an Application Exception Handler

As I mentioned earlier, the fact that DirectDraw takes over the entire display can cause a problem with exception handling. When an exception is raised, by default the Delphi IDE will drop into the debugger and pause program execution, positioning the code window on the offending line. The problem is that when page-flipping, you will probably not be able to see the IDE and your application will appear to freeze. Even worse, if you manage to continue execution, or have the Break on exception IDE option switched off, you may not see the message box that comes up giving the exception message.

One way to avoid this scenario is to uncheck the Break on exception checkbox in the IDE (Tools | Options menu) and install a special application-exception handler in your application. This exception handler should switch to the GDI surface before showing the exception message. This is a lot easier than it may sound. All you have to do is create a private method in your form and assign it to `Application.OnException` in the form's `OnCreate`. Remember to set it back to `nil` in `OnDestroy`. The new handler can use the `IDirectDraw` object's `SwitchToGDISurface` method before calling `MessageDlg`. Listing 32.3 shows the exception handler.

Listing 32.3. An application exception handler.

```
procedure TForm1.ExceptionHandler( Sender : TObject ;
                                   E      : Exception ) ;

begin
  if Assigned( DirectDraw ) then DirectDraw.FlipToGDISurface ;
  MessageDlg( E.Message, mtError, [ mbOK ], 0 ) ;
end ;
```

To install the exception handler, we add this line to `OnCreate`:

```
Application.OnException := ExceptionHandler ;
```

Remember to switch off Break on exception (in Tools | Options). Once you get a bit more experienced, you can try switching it on again for specific debugging tasks. However, if your application raises an exception while the GDI surface is not visible, the IDE will take over, and you won't see anything. Pressing F9 should restart execution, or press Ctrl-F2 to reset the application and return you to Delphi.

Display Surfaces

Now you're ready to create the display surfaces. In `DirectDraw`, a display surface represents a linear region of display memory that can be directly accessed and manipulated. The display surface that you see on the screen is called the *primary surface*. It represents the visible frame buffer memory on the display card. You also can have nonvisible surfaces, which are termed *off-screen*, or *overlay, surfaces*. These may exist either in regular system memory or in an off-screen area of memory on the graphics card itself. To create a page-flipping situation, you need the primary surface and at least one off-screen surface to flip with it. In order for the off-screen surface to be flippable, it must reside in video memory. However, `DirectDraw` tries to create surfaces in video memory by default, so you don't have to do anything special.

There's a way to create the primary surface and one or more flipping surfaces at the same time: by creating a *complex surface*. Another useful aspect of creating a complex surface is that you can free all surfaces in a complex flipping chain by freeing the complex surface. You're about to create a complex surface with one back-buffer surface for the example.

> **NOTE**
>
> Any background surfaces that are created as part of a complex surface are known as *implicit surfaces*. There are a number of things you cannot do with implicit surfaces, such as detach them from the primary surface or free them independently of the primary surface. However, complex surfaces are much easier to create because DirectDraw creates the back buffers for you and links them to the primary surface.

At this point I must touch on the complexity of DirectDraw, because you must fill in fields in a TDDSurfaceDesc record. If you look this up in the DirectDraw Help file, you can see that it looks rather daunting! But, as I said before, you can happily ignore most of these fields. Listing 32.4 shows the code you need to add to the OnShow handler to create the complex surface.

Listing 32.4. Creating a complex flipping surface.

```
{ fill in the DirectDrawSurface descriptor prior to creating the surface }
FillChar( DDSurfaceDesc, SizeOf( DDSurfaceDesc ), 0 ) ;
with DDSurfaceDesc do begin
  dwSize := SizeOf( DDSurfaceDesc ) ;
  dwFlags := DDSD_CAPS or DDSD_BACKBUFFERCOUNT ;
  ddSCaps.dwCaps := DDSCAPS_COMPLEX or DDSCAPS_FLIP or
                    DDSCAPS_PRIMARYSURFACE ;
  dwBackBufferCount := 1 ;
end ;

{ create the complex flipping surface }
if DirectDraw.CreateSurface( DDSurfaceDesc,
                             PrimarySurface, NIL ) <> DD_OK then
  Raise Exception.Create( 'CreateSurface failed' ) ;
```

DDSurface is a local variable. The dwFlags field tells DirectDraw which of the other fields are valid. This is what enables you to ignore most of them. In this case, you're only using ddSCaps and the dwBackBufferCount. (ddSCaps must always be filled in and valid.) Note how the record has a dwSize field that must be filled in with its own size. If you don't do this, the call to CreateSurface will fail immediately. If you have a call failing and seem to be filling everything in correctly, check to be sure that you're doing dwSize. It's easy to forget. PrimarySurface is a private IDirectDrawSurface object that I've added to the form's declaration after the DirectDraw object.

You also must remember to free the surfaces, which you can do in the FormDestroy handler by adding the following code before the DirectDraw object is freed:

```
if Assigned( PrimarySurface ) then PrimarySurface.Release ;
```

Remember, freeing a complex surface frees all implicit surfaces that were originally created with it.

Flipping the Pages

Now you're almost ready to start page flipping. However, you need some way to tell the primary surface to flip. Add a TTimer component and call the IDirectDrawSurface's Flip method, as shown in listing 32.5.

Listing 32.5. Flipping display surfaces in a timer event handler.

```
procedure TForm1.Timer1Timer(Sender: TObject);
begin
  { flip the display surfaces }
  if Assigned( PrimarySurface ) then
    PrimarySurface.Flip( NIL, DDFLIP_WAIT ) ;
end;
```

The first parameter to Flip is the surface to which you want to flip. Passing nil means flip to the next surface. Flip always synchronizes with the vertical retrace. However, it returns an error if the retrace is not occurring when called. To avoid this, pass DDFLIP_WAIT to cause the method to not return until the flip has happened. There are times when you'll want to do other processing while waiting for the flip to occur. In this case, call Flip repeatedly in your loop, passing 0 as the second parameter and checking the result to see if it's DD_OK.

If you create more than one background flipping surface, each call to Flip cycles to the next surface in the cycle. What actually happens when you call Flip is that the display memory associated with each surface is cycled to the next surface. The IDirectDrawSurface objects don't change order. The primary surface always remains the primary surface, and the display memory changes "underneath it." Similarly, the next surface to be flipped to always is the surface immediately after the primary surface, even when there are many back buffers. The only exception to this is when you call Flip and pass it a specific surface to which you want to flip.

You also must modify the exception-handler method to disable the timer while the exception message is being displayed. If you don't do this, page flipping will continue merrily, making the message box difficult to read! This is pretty straightforward, as shown in Listing 32.6.

Listing 32.6. Making sure exception messages are visible.

```
procedure TForm1.ExceptionHandler( Sender : TObject ;
                                    E      : Exception ) ;
var TimerEnabled : boolean ;
begin
  // make sure the GDI surface is visible before displaying exception message
  TimerEnabled := Timer1.Enabled ;
  Timer1.Enabled := false ;        // stop any page-flipping for a moment
  if Assigned( DirectDraw ) then DirectDraw.FlipToGDISurface ;
  MessageDlg( E.Message, mtError, [ mbOK ], 0 ) ;
  Timer1.Enabled := TimerEnabled ; // restart any page-flipping activity
end ;
```

Adding an Escape Breakout

Now, one more thing to do. Because your application may have flipped away from the GDI surface, you won't be able to see your form's close button or system menu. It's therefore a good idea to be able to close the application with a single keystroke during testing. An easy way to do this is to add an OnKeyDown handler to the form and check for an Esc or F12 key press, which is shown in Listing 32.7.

Listing 32.7. Testing for the Escape and F12 keys.

```
procedure TForm1.FormKeyDown(Sender: TObject; var Key: Word;
  Shift: TShiftState);
begin
  // if Escape or F12 pressed then close app
  case Key of
    VK_ESCAPE, VK_F12 : Close ;
  end ;
end;
```

And that's it! You'll find the example so far in DDDemo3. If you run it you see the display flipping between the GDI surface, containing the form sized to fill the screen, and the back buffer, which probably is filled with various bits of display "remnants." Remember, press Esc or F12 (or Alt+F4, of course) to exit.

Getting at the Back Buffer

Now that you've got the basics of the page-flipping application, you probably want to do something with it. You need to be able to draw on the back-buffer surface. However, in the last section you created a complex surface, which created the back buffer for us automatically. The problem is that the CreateSurface function filled in the PrimarySurface field, and you must get at the back buffer. You can call the GetAttachedSurface method to do this. Add a BackBuffer field to the form, and the code in Listing 32.8 to OnShow:

Listing 32.8. Getting at the back buffer surface.

```
{ get the back buffer surface object }
DDSCaps.dwCaps := DDSCAPS_BACKBUFFER ;
if PrimarySurface.GetAttachedSurface( DDSCaps,
                                      BackBuffer ) <> DD_OK then
  Raise Exception.Create( 'Failed to get back buffer surface' ) ;
```

DDSCaps is a local variable of type TDDSCaps, which you add to the FormShow handler. You fill in the flags for the attached surface you want and call GetAttachedSurface. In this case, you want the back buffer. The method can return only a single surface. The call fails if more than one attached surface matches the passed DDSCaps flags. However, no matter how many background surfaces you created, there's always only one with the back-buffer flag, and that's the first one in the flipping chain after the primary surface. If you need to get all the attached surfaces, you can call the EnumAttachedSurfaces function.

Restoring Surfaces

One of the many idiosyncrasies of DirectDraw is that surfaces may lose their memory for various reasons; for example, when the display mode changes. When this happens, you have to call the Restore method of the surface to get your memory back. You also have to redraw the surface. It's a bit like having to paint your window in regular Windows programming when it becomes uncovered and needs updating. Most of the IDirectDrawSurface functions can return the DDERR_SURFACELOST result. When this happens, you must restore the surface and redraw it. Many of those functions also can return DDERR_WASSTILLDRAWING, which basically means that the hardware is busy and you have to repeat the request until it succeeds, or until you get a different error.

Here's the basic logic, using the Flip method. This is a bare-bones example just to give you the idea. It doesn't redraw the surfaces. See listing 32.9.

Listing 32.9. "Traditional" code to check and restore a surface.

```
repeat
  DDResult := PrimarySurface.Flip( NIL, 0 ) ;
  case DDResult of
    DD_OK : break ;
    DDERR_SURFACELOST : begin
      DDResult := PrimarySurface.Restore() ;
      if DDResult <> DD_OK then break ;
    end ;
    else if DDResult <> DDERR_WASSTILLDRAWING then break ;
  end ;
until false ;
```

The annoying thing is that you need code like this for almost every call to an `IDirectDrawSurface` method. Any time the call specification in the Game SDK Help file has `DDERR_SURFACELOST` as a possible result, it's necessary. But Pascal is a structured, high-level language, right? So why not write a little utility method to help us? Here's just such a method, with the name borrowed from one of my favorite shows. (It helps me remember what I called it!) It's shown in Listing 32.10.

Listing 32.10. The `MakeItSo` function to assist surface restoration.

```
function  TForm1.MakeItSo( DDResult : HResult ) : boolean ;
begin
  { utility function to help restore surfaces }
  case DDResult of
    DD_OK : Result := true ;
    DDERR_SURFACELOST : Result := RestoreSurfaces <> DD_OK ;
    else Result := DDResult <> DDERR_WASSTILLDRAWING ;
  end ;
end ;
```

This method restores the surface if necessary, and then calls the form's `RestoreSurfaces` function, which I show you in a moment. But first, here's how you use it, using `Flip` as in the first example:

```
repeat
until MakeItSo( PrimarySurface.Flip( NIL, DDFLIP_WAIT ) ) ;
```

Now, I'm sure you'll agree that's a lot neater and nicer than having to keep duplicating the code I showed you first. `Flip` (or whatever other method you have to call) is called repeatedly until either it succeeds or a serious problem occurs. I could have raised an exception in `MakeItSo` if an unrecoverable problem occurred, but I decided to ignore the failure this time. There's no hard and fast rule in this case. For example, the Game SDK samples, being written in C without exception handling, just ignore error results.

However, if you want to use exceptions, change `MakeItSo` as shown in Listing 32.11.

Listing 32.11. Optional `MakeItSo`, which raises exceptions.

```
function  TForm1.MakeItSo( DDResult : HResult ) : boolean ;
begin
  { utility function to help restore surfaces - exception version }
  Result := false ;
  case DDResult of
    DD_OK : Result := true ;
    DDERR_SURFACELOST : if RestoreSurfaces <> DD_OK then
      Raise Exception.Create( 'MakeItSo failed' ) ;
    else if DDResult <> DDERR_WASSTILLDRAWING then
      Raise Exception.Create( 'MakeItSo failed' ) ;
  end ;
end ;
```

OK, now for the `RestoreSurfaces` method, called by `MakeItSo` when necessary. Listing 32.12 shows the `RestoreSurfaces` method.

Listing 32.12. Restoring and redrawing a `DirectDraw` surface.

```
function  TForm1.RestoreSurfaces : HResult ;
begin
  { called by MakeItSo if surfaces are lost - restore and redraw them }
  Result := PrimarySurface.Restore ;
  if Result = DD_OK then DrawSurfaces ;
end ;
```

No surprises there. The `Restore` method of the primary surface object is called. Because you created it as a complex object, it restores any implicit surfaces automatically. Therefore, you don't have to call `Restore` for the back buffer. If `Restore` successfully restored the surface memory, you call `DrawSurfaces`, which I discuss in detail next.

Drawing on *DirectDraw* Surfaces

There are two ways to draw on a `DirectDraw` surface. You can obtain a pointer directly to the memory area of the surface and manipulate that directly yourself. This is a very powerful option, but requires you to write specialized code, often in assembler for speed. You will seldom have to do this, however, because `DirectDraw` can create a device context (DC) that's compatible with GDI. This means you can draw on it using standard GDI calls, as you would do with any DC. However, GDI calls are tedious, and Delphi already wraps a DC in its `TCanvas` class. So, in the example, I create a `TCanvas` and use that to make life easy. Don't you just love Delphi!

All you have to do is create a `TCanvas` object and call the surface's `GetDC` method. You then assign the DC to `Canvas.Handle`, being careful to reset the `Handle` to zero when you're done. Also, creating canvases and allocating device contexts uses memory and resources. Device contexts are an especially scarce resource. It's essential that you free them when you're finished. To make the code bomb-proof, use `try...finally` blocks. Listing 32.13 shows the code. It simply fills the primary surface with blue and outputs the text "Primary surface" at center left. The back buffer is colored red and has the text "Back buffer" at center right.

Listing 32.13. Drawing on the `DirectDraw` surfaces.

```
procedure TForm1.DrawSurfaces ;
var DC      : HDC ;
    ARect    : TRect ;
    DDCanvas : TCanvas ;
    ATopPos  : integer ;
begin
  // fill the primary surface with red and the back buffer with blue
  // and put some text on each. Using a canvas makes this trivial.
```

continues

Listing 32.13. continued

```
DDCanvas := TCanvas.Create ;
try
  // first output to the primary surface
  if PrimarySurface.GetDC( DC ) = DD_OK then
  try
    ARect := Rect( 0, 0, 640, 480 ) ;
    with DDCanvas do begin
      Handle := DC ;              // make the canvas output to the DC
      Brush.Color := clRed ;
      FillRect( ARect ) ;
      Brush.Style := bsClear ;  // transparent text background
      Font.Name := 'Arial' ;
      Font.Size := 24 ;
      Font.Color := clWhite ;
      ATopPos := ( 480 - TextHeight( 'A' ) ) div 2 ;
      TextOut( 10, ATopPos, 'Primary surface' ) ;
    end ;
  finally
    // make sure we tidy up and release the DC
    DDCanvas.Handle := 0 ;
    PrimarySurface.ReleaseDC( DC ) ;
  end ;

  // now do back buffer
  if BackBuffer.GetDC( DC ) = DD_OK then
  try
    with DDCanvas do begin
      Handle := DC ;              // make the canvas output to the DC
      Brush.Color := clBlue ;
      FillRect( ARect ) ;
      Brush.Style := bsClear ;  // transparent text background
      Font.Name := 'Arial' ;
      Font.Size := 24 ;
      Font.Color := clWhite ;
      TextOut( 630 - TextWidth( 'Back buffer' ), ATopPos, 'Back buffer' ) ;
    end ;
  finally
    // make sure we tidy up and release the DC
    DDCanvas.Handle := 0 ;
    BackBuffer.ReleaseDC( DC ) ;
  end ;
finally
  // make sure the canvas is freed
  DDCanvas.Free ;
end ;
end ;
```

Notice that I don't use MakeItSo here when I call GetDC. There are two reasons:

■ First, the surfaces should have been restored just before DrawSurfaces is called.

■ Second, DrawSurfaces usually is called by MakeItSo, and you want to avoid infinite recursion. If the GetDC call fails, Windows just doesn't create any output. And it's extremely unlikely that GetDC would fail. If you do want to get an error message should this occur, you can check for success and raise an exception.

Freezing Up Windows

Windows 95 uses a lot of 16-bit legacy code from Windows 3.1. Because of this, calling certain GDI code that obtains the Win16 mutex effectively stops preemptive multitasking because it suspends any other task that tries to output to the display using GDI. For example, this happens when you call `IDirectDrawSurface.GetDC`. It's therefore essential that you keep the DC for as short a time as possible, and then relinquish it immediately using the `ReleaseDC` method. Failure to do this will bring Windows 95 to its knees. That is another reason why I protected the allocation of the DC with `try...finally` blocks.

Incapacitating the Main Form

In the previous examples, the form was clearly visible filling the primary surface. However, you don't really want the user to see a form. This is a page-flipping application, and it draws on the whole screen. So you must prevent the form from displaying. Also, you must get rid of the system menu and the nonclient buttons. This can all be achieved simply by setting the form's `BorderStyle` to bsNone in the FormCreate method. You don't want a cursor, either, so set it to crNone. Add these three lines to FormCreate:

```
BorderStyle := bsNone ;
Color := clBlack ;
Cursor := crNone ;
```

The only remaining thing you must do is make sure the surfaces get drawn properly at the start. Do this by calling `DrawSurfaces` in the form's `OnPaint` event handler. If you don't do this, the primary surface initially would display the form; that is, the screen would be completely black. Listing 32.14 shows the form's `OnPaint` event handler.

Listing 32.14. `OnPaint` event handler simply calls `DrawSurfaces`.

```
procedure TForm1.FormPaint(Sender: TObject);
begin
  // draw something on the primary surface and back buffer
  DrawSurfaces ;
end;
```

That's it! You can find the updated code in DDDemo4.

Leveraging Delphi: A Custom Canvas Class

Earlier, you saw how to take advantage of Delphi's excellent `TCanvas` to access device context that lets you draw on a `DirectDraw` surface. However, we can really simplify things by making use of object orientation. You now create a specialized `TCanvas` subclass to make drawing on a surface even easier. It's pretty simple; the code is shown in Listing 32.15.

Listing 32.15. A Delphi `DirectDraw` canvas object.

```
unit DDCanvas;

interface

uses Windows, SysUtils, Graphics, DDraw ;

type
  TDDCanvas = class( TCanvas )
  private
    FSurface      : IDirectDrawSurface ;
    FDeviceContext : HDC ;
  protected
    procedure CreateHandle ; override ;
  public
    constructor Create( ASurface : IDirectDrawSurface ) ;
    destructor Destroy ; override ;
    procedure Release ;
  end;

implementation

constructor TDDCanvas.Create( ASurface : IDirectDrawSurface ) ;
begin
  inherited Create ;
  if ASurface = NIL then
    Raise Exception.Create( 'Cannot create canvas for NIL surface' ) ;
  FSurface := ASurface ;
end ;

destructor TDDCanvas.Destroy ;
begin
  Release ;
  inherited Destroy ;
end ;

procedure TDDCanvas.CreateHandle ;
begin
  if FDeviceContext = 0 then begin
    FSurface.GetDC( FDeviceContext ) ;
    Handle := FDeviceContext ;
  end ;
end ;

procedure TDDCanvas.Release ;
begin
  if FDeviceContext <> 0 then begin
    Handle := 0 ;
    FSurface.ReleaseDC( FDeviceContext ) ;
    FDeviceContext := 0 ;
  end ;
end ;

end.
```

To use this class, you should copy the DDCanvas.pas unit into the Lib directory, which lives in your Delphi 2.0 directory, or to another directory that's on your library search path.

Remember the dreaded Win16 mutex that stops the multitasking? Well, once again I emphasize the necessity of releasing the DC. The TDDCanvas class has a Release method for this purpose. Always wrap any access to the canvas in a try...finally block, like this:

```
try
  DDCanvas.TextOut( 0, 0, 'Hello Flipping World!' ) ;
  { etc… }
finally
  DDCanvas.Release ;
end ;
```

Or, as I often do, use the with construct to save typing:

```
with DDCanvas do try
  TextOut( 0, 0, 'Hello Withering World!' ) ;
  { etc… }
finally
  Release ;
end ;
```

So now you can add a couple of such canvases to the form declaration, creating them in FormShow, like so:

```
{ create TDDCanvases for our two surfaces }
PrimaryCanvas := TDDCanvas.Create( PrimarySurface ) ;
BackCanvas := TDDCanvas.Create( BackBuffer ) ;
```

Free them in FormDestroy before freeing the surfaces:

```
{ free the TDDCanvas objects before the surfaces }
PrimaryCanvas.Free ;
BackCanvas.Free ;
```

Now you can output to either the primary surface or the back buffer just by using these canvases. So you change DrawSurfaces to use them, simplifying the code greatly, as shown in Listing 32.16.

Listing 32.16. DrawSurfaces using TDDCanvas objects.

```
procedure TForm1.DrawSurfaces ;
var ARect    : TRect ;
    ATopPos  : integer ;
begin
  // fill the primary surface with red and the back buffer with blue
  // and put some text on each. Using a canvas makes this trivial.

  // first output to the primary canvas.
  ARect := Rect( 0, 0, 640, 480 ) ;
  with PrimaryCanvas do try
    Brush.Color := clRed ;
    FillRect( ARect ) ;
```

continues

Listing 32.16. continued

```
    Brush.Style := bsClear ;
    Font.Name := 'Arial' ;
    Font.Size := 24 ;
    Font.Color := clWhite ;
    ATopPos := ( 480 - TextHeight( 'A' ) ) div 2 ;
    TextOut( 10, ATopPos, 'Primary surface' ) ;
  finally
    // make sure we release the DC as soon as possible
    // because Windows freezes as long as we have it.
    Release ;
  end ;

  // now do back buffer
  with BackCanvas do try
    Brush.Color := clBlue ;
    FillRect( ARect ) ;
    Brush.Style := bsClear ;
    Font.Name := 'Arial' ;
    Font.Size := 24 ;
    Font.Color := clWhite ;
    TextOut( 630 - TextWidth( 'Back buffer' ), ATopPos, 'Back buffer' ) ;
  finally
    // make sure we release the DC
    Release ;
  end ;
end ;
```

Note the try...finally blocks with the call to Release. Apart from that, you've now gotten to the stage of being able to draw on the DirectDraw surfaces without any nasty DirectDraw code—just nice Delphi canvas methods!

Improving Our Image

Now that you have the page-flipping working nicely, it's time to see how to load a bitmap image into a display surface. The process of loading a bitmap is greatly simplified from how it was with Windows 3.x by the addition of the LoadImage and CreateDIBSection functions in the WIN32 API. In Windows 95 you can use LoadImage to load a bitmap from either a disk file or a resource. In the production application, you'll almost certainly bind your images into the EXE file as resources. However, it's useful to be able to load them from a file during development.

I've written a set of utility routines for handling bitmaps. They are in the file DDUtils\DDUtils.pas. The one to look at first is DDReloadBitmap. You can go right ahead and use it without understanding what it does, but it's educational to have a little peek at the code. There are times when you may need to write specialized bitmap-handling code yourself. This should give you some idea of how to do that. Listing 32.17 shows the procedure.

Listing 32.17. DDReLoadBitmap utility for loading images.

```
procedure DDReLoadBitmap( Surface          : IDirectDrawSurface ;
                          const BitmapName : string ) ;

var Bitmap : HBitmap ;

begin
   //  try to load the bitmap as a resource, if that fails, try it as a file
   Bitmap := LoadImage( GetModuleHandle( NIL ), PChar( BitmapName ),
                     IMAGE_BITMAP, 0, 0, LR_CREATEDIBSECTION ) ;
   try
     if Bitmap = 0 then
       Bitmap := LoadImage( 0, PChar( BitmapName ), IMAGE_BITMAP,
                          0, 0, LR_LOADFROMFILE or LR_CREATEDIBSECTION ) ;
     if Bitmap = 0 then
       Raise Exception.CreateFmt( 'Unable to load bitmap %s', [ BitmapName ] ) ;

     DDCopyBitmap( Surface, Bitmap, 0, 0, 0, 0 ) ;
   finally
     DeleteObject( Bitmap ) ;
   end ;
end ;
```

You pass DDReLoadBitmap a DirectDraw surface and the name of the bitmap you want to load into the surface. The procedure first tries to load from a resource, assuming BitmapName is a resource name. If that fails, it assumes you passed a file name and tries to load it from there. What actually is created by LoadImage in this case is a DIB section. This is a Windows Hbitmap with the format of a device-independent bitmap (DIB). You can use such a DIB section as if it were a regular Hbitmap; for example, selecting it into a DC and calling GDI's BitBlt standard function.

DDReLoadBitmap calls another utility routine, DDCopyBitmap, which copies the DIB section image on to the DirectDraw surface. The try...finally block then disposes of the DIB section because it's no longer needed. Unlike Windows 3.x bit-map handling code, this procedure is pretty trivial.

Now, how about DDCopyBitmap? It's not much more difficult, as shown in Listing 32.18.

Listing 32.18. Utility procedure to copy a bitmap to a surface.

```
procedure DDCopyBitmap( Surface : IDirectDrawSurface ;
                        Bitmap  : HBITMAP ;
                        x, y, Width, Height : integer ) ;

var ImageDC     : HDC ;
    DC          : HDC ;
    BM          : Windows.TBitmap ;
    SurfaceDesc : TDDSurfaceDesc ;
```

continues

Listing 32.18. continued

```
begin
  if ( Surface = NIL ) or ( Bitmap = 0 ) then
    Raise Exception.Create( 'Invalid parameters for DDCopyBitmap' ) ;

  // make sure this surface is restored.
  Surface.Restore ;

  //  select bitmap into a memoryDC so we can use it.
  ImageDC := CreateCompatibleDC( 0 ) ;
  try
    SelectObject( ImageDC, Bitmap ) ;

    // get size of the bitmap
    GetObject( Bitmap, SizeOf( BM ), @BM ) ;
    if Width = 0 then Width := BM.bmWidth ;
    if Height = 0 then Height := BM.bmHeight ;

    // get size of surface.
    SurfaceDesc.dwSize := SizeOf( SurfaceDesc ) ;
    SurfaceDesc.dwFlags := DDSD_HEIGHT or DDSD_WIDTH ;
    Surface.GetSurfaceDesc( SurfaceDesc ) ;

    if Surface.GetDC( DC ) <> DD_OK then
      Raise Exception.Create( 'GetDC failed for DirectDraw surface' ) ;
    try
      StretchBlt( DC, 0, 0, SurfaceDesc.dwWidth, SurfaceDesc.dwHeight,
                  ImageDC, x, y, Width, Height, SRCCOPY ) ;
    finally
      Surface.ReleaseDC( DC ) ;
    end ;
  finally
    DeleteDC( ImageDC ) ;
  end ;
end ;
```

After doing some parameter checking, DDCopyBitmap calls Restore to make sure the surface memory is valid. It then goes through the normal Windows routine for copying a bitmap from one DC to another. The source bitmap is selected into the first DC, a standard memory DC obtained by a call to CreateCompatibleDC. Passing a width or height of zero to the routine tells the routine to use the actual width and height of the bitmap. To get this information, the routine uses the GetObject function.

Next, a SurfaceDesc record is prepared by switching on the DDSD_HEIGHT and DDSD_WIDTH flags. This is passed to GetSurfaceDesc, which responds by filling in the dwHeight and dwWidth fields of the descriptor. The routine obtains the second DC from the surface by calling GetDC and doing a simple StretchBlt. As usual, try..finally blocks are used to ensure that the DCs are released. All pretty simple stuff. It dispels the old reputation that Windows bit-map code was hard to write. Hopefully, you'll now be able to jump into writing code like this without feeling daunted by the prospect!

The DrawSurfaces code has been further simplified because the back buffer is now loaded elsewhere using DDReloadBitmap. The simplified DrawSurfaces is shown in Listing 32.19.

Listing 32.19. DrawSurfaces without code to draw the back surface.

```
procedure TForm1.DrawSurfaces ;
var ARect    : TRect ;
    ATopPos  : integer ;
begin
  // output to the primary canvas.
  ARect := Rect( 0, 0, 640, 480 ) ;
  with PrimaryCanvas do try
    Brush.Color := clBlue ;
    FillRect( ARect ) ;
    Brush.Style := bsClear ;
    Font.Name := 'Arial' ;
    Font.Size := 24 ;
    Font.Color := clWhite ;
    ATopPos := ( 480 - TextHeight( 'A' ) ) div 2 ;
    TextOut( 10, ATopPos, 'Primary surface' ) ;
  finally
    // make sure we release the DC as soon as possible
    // because Windows freezes as long as we have it.
    Release ;
  end ;

  { load the bitmap into the back buffer }
  DDReloadBitmap( BackBuffer, GetBitmapName ) ;
end ;
```

What About Palettes?

I knew you were going to ask that! OK, we still have to deal with palettes. Time to introduce another DirectDraw COM object. This time it's IDirectDrawPalette. This is a useful little object that looks after most of the palette stuff for us. To use IDirectDrawPalette, you create it with IDirectDraw.CreatePalette, which takes a pointer to an array of palette entries that was used to initialize the palette object. You then attach it to a DirectDraw surface and it's used automatically for all subsequent operations. Quite nice, really.

So how do you go about getting these color values? Well, I've written another little function to load them from a bitmap, or create a default wash of colors, and create and return an IDirectDrawPalette object. It's in DDUtils.pas as well, and is called DDLoadPalette. You simply pass it your IDirectDraw object, with either the name of the bitmap or (if you want a default palette) an empty string. (Like the other routines, DDLoadPalette first tries to load the bitmap from the application's resource. If that fails, it tries loading the bitmap from a file. I don't repeat the code here as it's a bit longer than the other functions. It mainly deals with verifying that the DIB has a color table, and copying that into a palette-entry array.)

I've added a palette object to the form's declaration, loaded it in `FormShow`, and attached the palette object to the primary surface as follows:

```
{ load the palette from the bitmap and attach it to the primary surface }
DDPalette := DDLoadPalette( DirectDraw, GetBitmapName ) ;
PrimarySurface.SetPalette( DDPalette ) ;
```

Having created it, you must free it from the primary surface in `FormDestroy`:

```
{ free the DD palette }
if Assigned( DDPalette ) then DDPalette.Release ;
```

Having made all the changes, you're ready to try it. DDDemo5 has all the changes up to this point.

Putting It All Together

At this point you can set up a page-flipping `DirectDraw` application and load a bitmap and palette. You're all set to do some real page flipping, at full speed! To make this interesting, how about some animation? `DirectDraw` ships with a file called ALL.BMP in one of the demos. You'll also find it in the DDDemo5 directory. It contains a more interesting background image and a set of animation frames for a red, rotating, 3-D torus.

Before each page flip, you want to draw the background image and then the current animation frame of the torus. You create three toruses at different positions on the screen and rotating at different rates. Because the back buffer is repeatedly drawn on, you must store the source image, loaded from ALL.BMP, somewhere else. Therefore, create another `DirectDraw` surface for this. It's an off-screen surface and has nothing to do with the page-flipping; it's just somewhere to put the image.

The neat thing is that, by default, `DirectDraw` creates the source image in display memory. That means that when you use the image to update the back buffer, any bit blitting you do makes use of the hardware blitter, if there is one, on the graphics card. Pretty much all PCs ship with an accelerated graphics card these days, and this is how `DirectDraw` makes use of it. Because such hardware is much faster than the processor at doing bit-blitting, `DirectDraw` games should have a performance edge on DOS games, where the processor does everything.

> **NOTE**
>
> Bit-blitting is a term used to describe the transfer of areas of bitmaps to, from, or within other bitmaps. The term is sometimes written more accurately as *bitblting*, but this is difficult to read so you'll often find it split into the two words bit-blitting as it is here. BitBlt is short for the term *BITmap BLock Transfer*.

So, to work. Create this extra surface and call it `Image`. Add it to the form declaration. It's just an `IDirectDrawSurface`, so there's no need to show that trivial line of code here.

Next, add code to FormShow that creates the bitmap. Using DDLoadBitmap, this is only one line! Here it is:

```
Image := DDLoadBitmap( DirectDraw, GetBitmapName, 0, 0 ) ;
```

The other thing you must remember to do is add to the RestoreSurfaces method now that you have a new, explicit surface. If the primary surface memory restoration went OK, try to restore the Image surface memory. If both restorations work, call DrawSurfaces as shown in Listing 32.20.

Listing 32.20. Restoring all the surfaces.

```
function  TForm1.RestoreSurfaces : HResult ;
begin
  { called by MakeItSo if surfaces are lost - restore and redraw them }
  Result := PrimarySurface.Restore ;
  if Result = DD_OK then begin
    Result := Image.Restore ;
    if Result = DD_OK then DrawSurfaces ;
  end ;
end ;
```

Now let's look at an important facility in game programming: transparency.

Blitting with Transparency

Most games build their display frames by laying down a background and then adding irregularly shaped graphics on top. The usual name for such irregular graphics is *sprites*. Sprites normally move around and are animate, but not necessarily. They may just be static images drawn over the background.

Sprites usually have a complex, irregular border, and may also have holes in them within the region defined by that border. Drawing such an irregular image with code would be extremely tedious and far too slow. Instead, we create a bit-map image of the sprite. But a bitmap is always a filled, rectangular block, and sprites are rarely completely filled in, as I said. So we need a mechanism whereby you can define areas of the bit-map block as transparent. One way to do this is to define a color, or range of colors, that can be used to define transparent pixels. Any pixel with this color is not drawn during blitting, leaving the background pixel in place. This gives the effect of the background showing through. This technique is known as *source color keying*.

DirectDraw has rich support for other kinds of color keying, but for this demo (and probably for most of the code you'll write), source keying is fine. All you must do is tell DirectDraw the color that you want to be transparent. Because you're using a 256-color bitmap here, you actually specify the palette index of the color; that is, the index of the color in the DIB color table. To do this, fill in a TDDColorKey record, which is a simple record. It consists of the start and end colors for the color key. You're using only one color, so both start and end values are the same. At the time of this writing, it appears that DirectDraw supports only a single color source key in any case. Once the color values are filled in, call the SetColorKey method of IDirectDrawSurface, telling it that you want to use this as the source key when blitting. Add these lines to FormShow:

```
ColorKey.dwColorSpaceLowValue := 0 ;
ColorKey.dwColorSpaceHighValue := 0 ;
if Image.SetColorKey( DDCKEY_SRCBLT, ColorKey ) <> DD_OK then
  Raise Exception.Create( 'SetColorKey failed' ) ;
```

ColorKey is local variable of type TDDColorKey.

You must remember to free the Image surface, so add a line to FormDestroy to release it after releasing the primary surface.

Next, change DrawSurfaces once again. This time you must reload the bitmap. I've also added some explanatory text for anyone running the demo, as shown in Listing 32.21.

Listing 32.21. Adding some explanatory text to the background.

```
procedure TForm1.DrawSurfaces ;
begin
  // reload the background image
  DDReloadBitmap( Image, GetBitmapName ) ;

  // put some extra hints on about the cursor keys
  with TDDCanvas.Create( Image ) do try
    Font.Name := 'Arial' ;
    Font.Size := 14 ;
    Font.Color := clWhite ;
    Brush.Style := bsClear ;
    TextOut( 0, 0, 'Try cursor keys with and without Shift.' ) ;
    TextOut( 0, TextHeight( 'A' ),
             'Use combinations such as Left+Up for diagonal movement.' ) ;
    TextOut( 0, TextHeight( 'A' ) * 2,
             '1-3 selects the torus to move, 0 selects all.' ) ;
  finally
    Free ;
  end ;
end ;
```

Once again, note the try…finally around the TDDCanvas to make sure TDDCanvas gets freed.

A Simple Animation Class

I want the tori to be animate, displaying the appropriate frame to give the appearance of rotation. To make this easier, and reusable, I use object orientation by adding a simple animation class. This class stores the position of the sprite, the number of frames in its animation sequence, and the rate at which it is animated. It's a simple class, but makes changes to the code, such as adding or removing sprites, a lot easier. Listing 32.22 shows the simple animation class.

Listing 32.22. A simple animation class.

```
type
  TSimpleAnim = class
  private
    FFrameInterval   : integer ;
    FNumberOfFrames  : integer ;
    FLastTickCount   : integer ;
    FCurrentFrame    : integer ;
  protected
    function  GetCurrentFrame( TickCount : integer ) : integer ;
  public
    X : integer ;
    Y : integer ;
    constructor Create( AFrameInterval   : integer ;
                        ANumberOfFrames  : integer ;
                        Ax, Ay           : integer ) ;
    property CurrentFrame[ TickCount : integer ] : integer
             read GetCurrentFrame ;
  end ;

constructor TSimpleAnim.Create( AFrameInterval   : integer ;
                                ANumberOfFrames  : integer ;
                                Ax, Ay           : integer ) ;
begin
  FFrameInterval := AFrameInterval ;
  FNumberOfFrames := ANumberOfFrames ;
  X := Ax ;
  Y := Ay ;
end ;

function  TSimpleAnim.GetCurrentFrame( TickCount : integer ) : integer ;
begin
  if TickCount - FLastTickCount >= FFrameInterval then begin
    FLastTickCount := TickCount ;
    inc( FCurrentFrame ) ;
    if FCurrentFrame >= FNumberOfFrames then FCurrentFrame := 0 ;
  end ;
  Result := FCurrentFrame ;
end ;
```

As you can see, the Create constructor takes the parameters that define the sprite and stores them away in the object's fields. The property CurrentFrame tells us which frame of the sprite should be displayed, given the current TickCount. The TickCount is actually the number of milliseconds that have elapsed since Windows started up. You can obtain this simply by calling the GetTickCount function. The timer used has a high resolution, down to one millisecond. This is a lot better than using a TTimer component, which has a resolution of 55 milliseconds; it can't trigger faster than about 18 times a second, and that's too slow for game use. Also, a TTimer is not very accurate, and gives jerky results.

CurrentFrame is implemented by the GetCurrentFrame function. CurrentFrame uses a crude, but simple, technique of incrementing to the next frame in the sequence if the time in milliseconds since the last frame is greater than the frame interval. When this happens, CurrentFrame notes the time in FLastTickCount and wraps around to the start frame when the sequence goes past the last one.

You add this code straight into the main form unit. It's not a component, so it doesn't have to be added to the component palette. Instances are created only at runtime, with code. You do this by adding a TList called Animations to the form declaration. This list is created in FormShow, and you add three animation objects to it:

```
Animations := TList.Create ;
Animations.Add( TSimpleAnim.Create( 48, 60, 260, 120 ) ) ;
Animations.Add( TSimpleAnim.Create( 12, 60, 420, 248 ) ) ;
Animations.Add( TSimpleAnim.Create( 80, 60, 200, 320 ) ) ;
```

Note that the second parameter to Create, the number of frames in the animation sequence, is 60. What does this mean? Well, if you open ALL.BMP and scroll down, you see all the animation frames underneath the background image. There are 60 in all, arranged in six rows of 10. The main image is 640 by 480 pixels, to match the display resolution I'm using. Each frame is 64 pixels square, making 10 fit nicely across the bitmap.

Updating the Display

You're now ready to write the code to update the back buffer and do the flip. Add an UpdateDisplay method to do this, as shown in Listing 32.23.

Listing 32.23. Updating the display with some animation.

```
procedure TForm1.UpdateDisplay ;
var TickCount    : integer ;
    ARect        : TRect ;
    ACurrentFrame : integer ;
    i            : integer ;
begin
  // update and flip the surfaces - first blt the background
  ARect := Rect( 0, 0, 640, 480 ) ;
  repeat
  until MakeItSo( BackBuffer.BltFast( 0, 0, Image, ARect,
                                      DDBLTFAST_NOCOLORKEY ) ) ;

  // blt the animations
  TickCount := GetTickCount ;
  for i := 0 to Animations.Count - 1 do begin
    with TSimpleAnim( Animations[ i ] ) do begin
      ACurrentFrame := CurrentFrame[ TickCount ] ;
      ARect := Bounds( ( ACurrentFrame mod 10 ) * 64,
                       ( ACurrentFrame div 10 ) * 64 + 480, 64, 64 ) ;
      repeat
      until MakeItSo( BackBuffer.BltFast( X, Y, Image, ARect,
                                          DDBLTFAST_SRCCOLORKEY ) ) ;
    end ;
  end ;

  // now flip
  repeat
```

```
  until MakeItSo( PrimarySurface.Flip( NIL, DDFLIP_WAIT ) ) ;

  // update torus positions
  Move( XVelocity, YVelocity ) ;
end ;
```

The first thing this does is blit the background image to the back buffer. Remember that the top part of ALL.BMP is the background. `ARect` is created to define the rectangular area of that part of the bitmap and `BltFast`. `BltFast` functions more or less the same as `Blt`, but can't stretch the bitmap and doesn't do any clipping. You just give it the source surface to blit from, the rectangle on that surface that you want to blit, and the position on the destination where you want it to go. The last parameter tells `BltFast` to ignore the color key you set up, because this is the background and not one of the animation images. `BltFast` is quoted as being around 10 percent faster than `Blt` when done in software when there's no accelerator. Otherwise, there's no difference.

Now blit each of the animations. Get the `TickCount` and then loop through the `Animations` list. Obtain the current animation frame and then calculate the position of this frame in ALL.BMP. Calculate the x coordinate by doing a modulo (remainder) operation between the current frame and the number of frames per line. This works out to 10, which gives the index of the frame in the row. This is multiplied by the width of each frame, which is 64.

The y coordinate is calculated by dividing the frame number by 10 to get the row number; multiplying by the height of each row, which is 64; and adding 480. This is where the frames start in ALL.BMP: immediately under the 640×480 background image. All that's necessary now is to use `BltFast` again to blit the frame on to the back buffer, this time using the color key.

Once all animations have been drawn, the page flip is done. There is one vital thing to realize at this point: the page flip does not occur until the vertical retrace, so the application sits in the tight `MakeItSo` loop until this occurs. This sets the overall frame-per-second rate of the application. There's no need to control the animation with any timer. It simply goes as fast as it can, using `GetTickCount` to determine which animation frame to display.

> **NOTE**
>
> The image on a computer screen is created by an electron beam which starts at the top left of the picture and scans horizontal lines one under the other from left to right until it reaches the bottom-right corner. The beam then returns to the top-left to start again. The rate at which this scanning occurs is typically between 60Hz and 80Hz, although it can vary from 50Hz to well over 100Hz with the latest display cards and screens. The vertical retrace is the time when the electron beam is reset to the top-left in readiness for the next scan. Changing the image being displayed at this point, before the scan begins, results in perfectly smooth, flicker-free animation.

You may note an extra line at the end that calls a method to update the torus position. I decided to make the demo more interesting by letting you move the animation around with the keyboard. This is easy to do: the position is stored in the TSimpleAnim class. Listing 32.24 shows the code for the Move method.

Listing 32.24. The Move method moves the animations around the screen.

```
procedure TForm1.Move( dx, dy : integer ) ;
var i, nFrom, nTo : integer ;
begin
  // move the toruses
  if Assigned( Animations ) then begin
    if MoveOption = 0 then begin
      nFrom := 0 ;
      nTo := Animations.Count - 1 ;
    end else begin
      nFrom := MoveOption - 1;
      nTo := nFrom ;
    end ;
    for i := nFrom to nTo do begin
      with TSimpleAnim( Animations[ i ] ) do begin
        X := X + dx ;
        if X < 0 then X := 0 else
        if X > 640 - 64 then X := 640 - 64 ;
        Y := Y + dy ;
        if Y < 0 then Y := 0 else
        if Y > 480 - 64 then Y := 480 - 64 ;
      end ;
    end ;
  end ;
end;
```

The method takes two parameters, which represent the distance in pixels to move each of the animations in each axis. I added an extra field, called MoveOption, to the form. MoveOption takes a positive integer value: 0 means to move all the animation objects, and any other number means to move the corresponding animation object only. Having determined the range of animations to move (either all of them or a single one), you do a loop through the Animations array, adding dx and dy to each animation's position. Move also checks to make sure the animation objects don't move off the display.

Handling Keyboard Input

I've modified the OnKeyDown handler to process key presses of the cursor keys, which are used to move the animations around, as shown in Listing 32.25.

Listing 32.25. Moving the animations with the cursor keys.

```
procedure TForm1.FormKeyDown(Sender: TObject; var Key: Word;
  Shift: TShiftState);
var Speed : integer ;
    AnOption : integer ;
begin
  Speed := 4 ;
  if ssShift in Shift then Speed := 1 ;
  case Key of
    VK_ESCAPE, VK_F12 : Close ;
    VK_LEFT   : XVelocity := -Speed ;
    VK_RIGHT  : XVelocity := Speed ;
    VK_UP     : YVelocity := -Speed ;
    VK_DOWN   : YVelocity := Speed ;
    VK_SHIFT  : begin
      if Abs( XVelocity ) > 1 then XVelocity := XVelocity div 4 ;
      if Abs( YVelocity ) > 1 then YVelocity := YVelocity div 4 ;
    end ;
    byte( '0' )..byte( '9' ) : begin
      AnOption := Key - 48 ;
      if AnOption <= Animations.Count then MoveOption := AnOption ;
    end ;
  end ;
end;
```

If the Shift key is held down, the animations move four times slower, so the local variable Speed is set up accordingly. I've added XVelocity and YVelocity fields, which are set if one of the cursor keys is pressed. The Shift key, when pressed, slows the velocity down, if it's not already slow. The keys 0 through 9 set MoveOption, which controls which animations are moved. Note that monitoring the press of a specific key means that the animation can respond differently to different key combinations. In this case, you can move the sprites diagonally if you hold down two of the cursor keys.

There now has to be an OnKeyUp handler to counter these effects when the key is released. This is shown in Listing 32.26.

Listing 32.26. Noting when keys are released.

```
procedure TForm1.FormKeyUp(Sender: TObject; var Key: Word;
  Shift: TShiftState);
begin
  // check for release of movement keys
  case Key of
    VK_LEFT,
    VK_RIGHT : XVelocity := 0 ;
    VK_UP,
    VK_DOWN  : YVelocity := 0 ;
    VK_SHIFT : begin
      XVelocity := XVelocity * 4 ;
      YVelocity := YVelocity * 4 ;
    end ;
  end ;
end;
```

As you can see, movement is stopped in the horizontal or vertical direction when a cursor key is released, and the speed is increased by a factor of four when the Shift key is released.

Getting Into the Message Loop

Now that you've got all the main code in place, you must find a place from which to call UpdateDisplay. Basically, you call this as often as you can to get the fastest possible frame rate. In C or straight Pascal, you'd take over the message loop and call UpdateDisplay each time around the loop. You can do this in Delphi, but it's a little more tricky because Delphi has its own message loop. You must somehow transfer control to your own loop.

Instead of doing this, an alternative is to attach code to the Application variable's OnIdle and OnMessage events. You can look up the declaration of handlers for these events in the Delphi online Help, and add them as methods to your form. Here's what the declarations look like:

```
procedure HandleMessage( var Msg    : TMsg ;
                         var Handled : boolean ) ;
procedure IdleHandler( Sender   : TObject ;
                       var Done : boolean ) ;
```

These are added to the private section of the form declaration like any other method. The implementation is simple, mainly just calling UpdateDisplay. One crucial thing is to set Done to False in IdleHandler to make sure the VCL doesn't yield control awaiting a Windows message, which would stop screen updating. This is shown in Listing 32.27.

Listing 32.27. Updating the display as often as possible.

```
procedure TForm1.HandleMessage( var Msg    : TMsg ;
                                var Handled : boolean ) ;
begin
  UpdateDisplay ;
end ;

procedure TForm1.IdleHandler( Sender   : TObject ;
                              var Done : boolean ) ;
begin
  UpdateDisplay ;
  Done := false ;
end ;
```

Finally, add a FlippingEnabled property to the form, declaring it as shown in Listing 32.28.

Listing 32.28. Adding a FlippingEnabled property to the form.

```
type TForm1 = class( TForm )
  . . .
    FFlippingEnabled : boolean ;
```

```
  public
    property  FlippingEnabled : boolean read FFlippingEnabled
              write SetFlippingEnabled ;
  end ;
```

This works by plugging or unplugging the Application event handlers, which is implemented in the SetFlippingEnabled method, as shown in Listing 32.29.

Listing 32.29. Setting the FlippingEnabled property.

```
procedure TForm1.SetFlippingEnabled( Value : boolean ) ;
begin
  if Value <> FFlippingEnabled then begin
    FFlippingEnabled := Value ;
    if FFlippingEnabled then begin
      // plug in the Application event handlers
      Application.OnMessage := HandleMessage ;
      Application.OnIdle := IdleHandler ;
    end else begin
      // unplug the Application event handlers
      Application.OnMessage := NIL ;
      Application.OnIdle := NIL ;
    end ;
  end ;
end ;
```

FlippingEnabled is set to True at the end of FormShow once you've set everything up. It's set back to False temporarily in the exception handler to pause the application so you can see the message box, as Listing 32.30 shows.

Listing 32.30. Exception handler disables flipping.

```
procedure TForm1.ExceptionHandler( Sender : TObject ;
                                   E      : Exception ) ;
var WasEnabled : boolean ;
begin
  { make sure the GDI surface is visible before displaying exception message }
  WasEnabled := FlippingEnabled ;   // note if we were flipping or not
  FlippingEnabled := false ;        // stop any page-flipping for a moment
  if Assigned( DirectDraw ) then DirectDraw.FlipToGDISurface ;
  MessageDlg( E.Message, mtError, [ mbOK ], 0 ) ;
  FlippingEnabled := WasEnabled ;   // restart any page-flipping activity
end ;
```

Having done that, you're ready to run it. The code is in DDDemo6. If you play around with it, moving the tori around with the cursor keys, you'll see where we heading. We virtually have true sprites. With a little more work, that's exactly what we will have.

We Need Sprites!

You've seen how easy it is to manipulate animated objects with a simple animation class. Now we go whole hog and do a generic TDDSprite class. The TSimpleAnim class was a bit too simple, and was designed specifically for the last demo. Now let's start from scratch. (The sprite class I build here is a simplified version of the sprites from my commercial Game SDK Toolkit for Delphi 2.0. See the Author information for details.)

First of all, define some characteristics that you'd like these sprites to have. This generic sprite class should:

- Be self-contained and able to be subclassed to satisfy specific needs
- Be frame-based, supplying the frame number to display on demand
- Not do any rendering itself, leaving that responsibility to another class or a subclass
- Use fixed point coordinates on the display surface for fine control
- Have a fixed-point velocity vector, and be able to move along this vector automatically
- Have a fixed-point acceleration vector, and have this applied to the velocity automatically
- Have the option of being constrained within a rectangular area
- Have events that allow the position to be overridden, so that you can take manual control over sprite movement and constraints
- Be able to bounce off the edges of the constraining rectangle for test purposes

First, notice that I've specified fixed point for speed. You may ask, "Why not just use straight integers?" However, consider the velocity issue. If you express a velocity as two integer components, one horizontal and one vertical, you are severely limited in the number of possible angles your sprite can move in. For example, say you wanted to move slowly, at a rate of one pixel per time interval. You'd only be able to move in, at best, 45-degree steps. This is no good for a useful sprite. If you're going to have fixed-point velocity vectors, you also need a fixed-point position. Otherwise, the fractional part of the velocity is lost with each movement. Similar arguments apply to acceleration.

However, it's easy to implement simple, fixed-point using longints. You simply multiply the real number value by 65,536, and store the rounded result in an integer. You then can add similar integers together without conversion, giving no loss in performance over integers. For example, you can add the velocity and acceleration components using simple integer addition. If you're not too worried about the fractional part, you can even get the integer position by simply accessing the high word of the longint.

To make this easier, declare a simple variant record to hold any coordinate-style value. I've called this a TCoord, which you can see in Listing 32.31.

Listing 32.31. The `TCoord` type.

```
type
  TCoord = record
             case byte of
               0 : ( Value : longint ) ;
               1 : ( Frac  : word ;
                     Int   : SmallInt ) ;
           end ;
```

When you must do additions, you can access the full value by reading and writing the `Value` field. If you need just the integer part, you can get at that by accessing `Int`.

Now, let's see how to use this to build up the sprite class. First, let's look at the position, velocity, and acceleration properties, as shown in Listing 32.32.

Listing 32.32. Sprite position, velocity, and acceleration properties.

```
property X : SmallInt read GetX write SetX ;
property Y : SmallInt read GetY write SetY ;
property W : SmallInt read FW write FW ;
property H : SmallInt read FH write FH ;
property VelocityX : double read GetVelocityX write SetVelocityX ;
property VelocityY : double read GetVelocityY write SetVelocityY ;
property AccelerationX : double read GetAccelerationX write SetAccelerationX ;
property AccelerationY : double read GetAccelerationY write SetAccelerationY ;
```

Notice that the position and size properties are integral. In the case of position, the fixed-point value is rounded efficiently, without requiring any floating-point calculations, because the position properties are stored internally as `TCoord`s. Velocity and acceleration components are similarly stored as `TCoord`s, but are accessed as doubles. Conversion is required on read and write, but this happens infrequently, when you must change the speed or acceleration. On the other hand, the addition of these vectors occurs with every page flip, so it's essential that this function is efficient.

Next up is the animation-controlling properties. These are shown in Listing 32.33.

Listing 32.33. Sprite animation control properties.

```
property AnimationInterval : Cardinal read FAnimationInterval
                             write FAnimationInterval
                             default defAnimationInterval ;
property AnimationStart : Cardinal read FAnimationStart
                          write FAnimationStart ;
property AnimationStop : Cardinal read FAnimationStop write
                         FAnimationStop ;
property AnimationOffset : Cardinal read FAnimationOffset
                           write FAnimationOffset ;
```

`AnimationInterval` is the interval, in milliseconds, between subsequent animation frames. `AnimationStart` is the frame number where the current sequence starts, and `AnimationStop` is where it stops. `AnimationOffset` is added during the computation of the current frame number, enabling you to offset the position in the sequence in relation to the tick count.

There are a couple of methods that you can override in subclasses, and which also call corresponding events, as shown in Listing 32.34.

Listing 32.34. Methods to allow fine control of Sprite animation.

```
procedure GetFrameNumber( Ticks : longint ;
                          TicksSinceLastFrame : longint ;
                          var FrameNumber : Cardinal ) ; virtual ;
procedure CheckLimits ; virtual ;
```

`GetFrameNumber`, and it's event `OnGetFrameNumber`, enable you to override the current frame number in the animation sequence. This lets you take complete control over the animation of the sprite. `CheckLimits` and the `OnCheckLimits` event are called after the new sprite position has been computed, letting you override that position, if necessary; for example, to constrain the movement of the sprite. You also could set the position totally manually to make the sprite move along whatever path you like, or you may modify the velocity and acceleration. This flexibility lets you implement pretty much any kind of sprite movement and animation sequencing just by creating event handlers.

Finally, there are a couple of simple properties that control whether the sprite bounces around inside its `Limits` rectangle instead of being able to move without limit in any direction, and whether it is visible:

```
property AutoBounce : boolean read FAutoBounce write FAutoBounce ;
property Visible : boolean read FVisible write SetVisible default true ;
```

The implementation of the sprite class is pretty straightforward, and you can find it in the DDSprite.pas file. I don't go into the implementation details here because there's really not much to be gained, and it would take a lot of space. It's all pretty simple. More important is the way these sprites are used.

The *TDDSprite* Class

The sprite class actually is a generic class that can be used on pretty much any rendering platform. This is because it doesn't have anything to do with storing images or displaying itself. These functions are the responsibility of whatever is using the sprites. You can build up a simple sprite application to illustrate one way of using them. It's based on the example built so far, but with some of the code removed because it's been replaced by the new sprite functions. You remove the `Animations` list and replace it with a `Sprites` list.

It would be nice if any sprite added to the form, either at design time or runtime, was automatically added to this Sprites list. You can do this easily by overriding the form's Notification method, which is called whenever a component is added or removed. The Notification method also is called when a component is removed from the form, so you can delete any reference to a sprite in the Sprites array. Listing 32.35 shows the Notification method.

Listing 32.35. Notification method updates the Sprites list.

```
procedure TForm1.Notification( AComponent : TComponent ;
                               Operation  : TOperation ) ;

begin
  // watch for sprites being added or removed,
  // and update the Sprites list accordingly.
  inherited Notification( AComponent, Operation ) ;
  if AComponent is TDDSprite then begin
    if Operation = opInsert then begin
      // if the sprite has no limit set, set limit to the full screen
      with TDDSprite( AComponent ) do
        if IsRectEmpty( Limits ) then Limits := Rect( 0, 0, 640, 480 ) ;
      Sprites.Add( AComponent ) ;
    end else
      Sprites.Remove( AComponent ) ;
  end ;
end ;
```

This checks to see whether the component is a TDDSprite using the is operator. If so, if the component is being added, you add it to the Sprites list. If the component is not being added, it's being removed; you remove it from the list. I've added code here to set the Limits rect to the full screen if it's initially empty. An empty Limits rectangle means no limits; if a sprite is moving, it would disappear off the edge of the surface.

However, there is a potential pitfall here because Notification is called during the processing of TForm.Create. If any sprites are added to the form at design time, the Notification method tries to add them to the Sprites list. Therefore, the list has to be created before the inherited Create constructor is called. Fortunately, there is no problem doing this. You simply override the constructor and create the Sprites list before calling the inherited constructor, as shown in Listing 32.36.

Listing 32.36. Create constructor, which creates a Sprites list.

```
constructor TForm1.Create( AOwner : TComponent ) ;

begin
  Sprites := TList.Create ;
  inherited Create( AOwner ) ;
end ;
```

In FormShow, you call Randomize because you're going to be using the Random function. Add a single sprite to start with:

```
Randomize ;
AddSprites( 1 ) ;
```

The AddSprites function takes the number of sprites to add and creates them at random, adding them to the Sprites list, as shown in Listing 32.37.

Listing 32.37. Method to add a number of sprites.

```
procedure TForm1.AddSprites( n : integer ) ;
var Sprite : TDDSprite ;
    i      : integer ;
begin
  // simple routine to add n sprites with parameters set for demo bouncing
  for i := 1 to n do begin
    Sprite := TDDSprite.Create( Self ) ;
    with Sprite do begin
      AccelerationY := 1.6 ;
      AutoBounce := true ;
      X := Random( 640 - 74 ) ;
      W := 64 ;
      H := 64 ;
      AnimationStop := 59 ;
      AnimationOffset := Random( 60 ) ;
      Limits := Rect( 10, 10, 630, 470 ) ;
    end ;
  end ;
  UpdateStatsSurface ;
end ;
```

The code is self-explanatory. Notice the use of the fixed-point acceleration of 1.6 downward to simulate gravity. We are using the same ALL.BMP torus frames for this example, so the width and height are both 64 pixels and AnimationStop is 59 again. You would use similar code to add sprites such as missiles, enemies, or players to your game. To delete a sprite, you simply free it.

Having added the sprites, call UpdateStatsSurface, which updates statistical information displayed with each page flip.

Displaying Statistics

When writing DirectDraw applications, it's often helpful to be able to display information as the program is running. This is necessary because the program has taken over the whole screen, and you can't really use the IDE debugger effectively. I've done this in the sprite demo by creating another surface on which information, such as the frame rate, is drawn from time to time. This surface is overlaid on the back buffer just before flip is called.

I've added the surface to the form as field Stats of type IDirectDrawSurface. It's created in FormShow, as shown in Listing 32.37.

Listing 32.37. Creating a surface for displaying information.

```
with DDSurfaceDesc do begin
  with Canvas, Font do begin
    Name := 'Arial' ;
    Size := 16 ;
    // make it wide enough and tall enough for the stats string
    StatsRect := Rect( 0, 0,
                       TextWidth( '9999 sprites: 999 fps = 999.99MB/sec' ),
                       TextHeight( 'A' ) ) ;
    dwWidth := StatsRect.Right ;
    dwHeight := StatsRect.Bottom ;
  end ;
  dwFlags := DDSD_CAPS or DDSD_WIDTH or DDSD_HEIGHT ;
  ddSCaps.dwCaps := DDSCAPS_OFFSCREENPLAIN ;
end ;
if DirectDraw.CreateSurface( DDSurfaceDesc, Stats, NIL ) <> DD_OK then
  Raise Exception.Create( 'Unable to create Stats surface' ) ;

{ set the color key to black }
ColorKey.dwColorSpaceLowValue := 0 ;
ColorKey.dwColorSpaceHighValue := 0 ;
if Stats.SetColorKey( DDCKEY_SRCBLT, ColorKey ) <> DD_OK then
  Raise Exception.Create( 'Stats.SetColorKey failed' ) ;
```

You fill in the existing DDSurfaceDesc record. Use the form's own Canvas to calculate the width and height of the string you want to display, by calling TextWidth and TextHeight. This is used to initialize StatsRect, which is a TRect I've added to the form. I'm creating a simple, off-screen surface, so I just need to fill in the width and height fields, dwWidth and dwHeight, and then set the flags in dwFlags to say that these fields are valid. Set the type of the surface in DDSCaps.dwCaps, and then you're ready to call DirectDraw.CreateSurface.

Next, set the color key as you do with the Image surface, because you're going to be displaying the statistical information as text overlaid on the top of the background and sprites.

I've added a StatsCanvas to the other TDDCanvas objects already there. Create it and initialize it in FormShow so you don't have to do that every time you must update the Stats surface, as shown in Listing 32.38.

Listing 32.38. Creating and initializing the Stats surface.

```
StatsCanvas := TDDCanvas.Create( Stats ) ;
with StatsCanvas do try
  Font.Name := 'Arial' ;
  Font.Size := 16 ;
  Font.Color := clWhite ;
finally
  Release ;
end ;
```

Rendering the Sprites

I've said that the sprite implementation is generic because they don't know how to render themselves so they can be used with any display technology, including DirectDraw. Rendering is done in the modified UpdateDisplay method. This starts off exactly as in the previous example program, blitting the background image first. But now, instead of creating simple animation objects, you must draw the sprites, as shown in Listing 32.39.

Listing 32.39. Rendering the sprites.

```
TickCount := GetTickCount ;
TicksSinceLast := 0 ;
if LastTickCount <> 0 then
  TicksSinceLast := TickCount - LastTickCount ;

// limit the amount of time since the last update
if TicksSinceLast > MaxJump then TicksSinceLast := MaxJump ;
for i := 0 to Sprites.Count - 1 do begin
  with TDDSprite( Sprites[ i ] ) do if Visible then begin
    ACurrentFrame := 0 ;
    GetFrameNumber( TickCount, TicksSinceLast, ACurrentFrame ) ;
    if ACurrentFrame > 59 then ACurrentFrame := 59 ;
    ARect := Bounds( ( ACurrentFrame mod 10 ) * 64,
                     ( ACurrentFrame div 10 ) * 64 + 480, 64, 64 ) ;
    repeat
    until MakeItSo( BackBuffer.BltFast( X, Y, Image, ARect,
                                        DDBLTFAST_SRCCOLORKEY ) ) ;
  end ;
end ;
```

I need to know the number of milliseconds that have elapsed since the last sprite update, so I call GetTickCount and subtract the result from LastTickCount, noted the last time around as long as this is not the first time through (when LastTickCount will be zero). I also limit the number of milliseconds in case some other system activity has prevented updating for much longer than usual. This is quite common in Windows 95, and can be brought about by automated activity such as backups or disk scans. There may be several seconds' delay, and I don't want the sprites to go orbital when they do move.

The code loops through the Sprites list and, for every visible sprite, calls the GetFrameNumber method. This method returns the frame number that the sprite requests you to render. A quick check is made to ensure that this number is not higher than 59, the number of frames in ALL.BMP minus 1. You used the same calculation as last time to get the source rect for the specific frame. Use BltFast to do the business, as before.

Now that the background and sprites have been drawn, you must overlay the statistical information. This is simply a case of calling BltFast again with Stats as the source surface. Center the output and move it a quarter of the way down the display:

```
// blt the stats
repeat
until MakeItSo( BackBuffer.BltFast( ( 640 - StatsRect.Right ) div 2, 120,
                                    Stats, StatsRect,
                                    DDBLTFAST_SRCCOLORKEY ) ) ;
```

Now you're ready to do the page flip. This is the same as before, only this time you increment FlipCount, which I added to the form. It's an integer field used to keep a total of the number of page flips that have been displayed for the frames-per-second calculation. Here is the modified flipping code:

```
// now flip
repeat
until MakeItSo( PrimarySurface.Flip( NIL, DDFLIP_WAIT ) ) ;
inc( FlipCount ) ;
```

Finally, move the sprites. This is a simple case of calling their Move method and passing the number of ticks since the last move. The sprite class handles all of the details, calculating the sprite's new position based upon its velocity, updating that velocity by adding the acceleration, and calling the OnCheckLimits event to enable you to override if you wish to. Update LastTickCount before exiting the procedure. Listing 32.40 shows how you move the sprites.

Listing 32.40. Moving the sprites.

```
// move sprites
for i := 0 to Sprites.Count - 1 do
  TDDSprite( Sprites[ i ] ).Move( TicksSinceLast ) ;

// remember TickCount
LastTickCount := TickCount ;
end ;
```

Updating the Statistics

You don't update the statistics with each page flip. That would be inefficient, and the output would jitter like mad, being updated with slightly different values 60 times per second or more! Instead, add a TTimer with an interval of one second and update the Stats surface when the timer goes off. As you saw above, you keep a tally of the number of flips done in FlipCount. You use another field to keep a note of the TickCount value when the timer last went off, enabling you to get an accurate measurement of the interval between timer events. Set up the OnTimer event handler to call UpdateStatsData, which calculates the new frames per second and blit rate in megabytes per second, storing these in the form's FPS (short for Frames Per Second) and MBperSec (short for MegaBytes per Second) fields respectively. Listing 32.41 shows how to build the UpdateStatsData method.

Listing 32.41. The `UpdateStatsData` method updates statistical information.

```
procedure TForm1.UpdateStatsData ;
var TickCount : integer ;
begin
  // calculate frames per second (FPS) and blt speed in MB per second
  TickCount := GetTickCount ;
  if FlippingEnabled and ( LastTimerTick <> 0 ) and
    ( TickCount <> LastTimerTick ) then
  begin
    FPS := FlipCount * 1000 div ( TickCount - LastTimerTick ) ;
    MBperSec := ( ( 640 * 480 ) + Sprites.Count * ( 64 * 64 ) +
                  ( StatsRect.Right * StatsRect.Bottom ) ) * FPS /
                ( 1024 * 1024 )
  end ;
  LastTimerTick := TickCount ;
  FlipCount := 0 ;
end ;
```

Note that before each page flip, you blit the whole background area. This is 640 by 480 pixels, or 307,200 bytes, and this defines the minimum blitting rate. If our monitor is refreshing at 75 Hertz, this produces a basic blit rate of 75 * 307,200, or just a touch under 22 MB per second, even with no sprites! This kind of rate would be impossible over the old AT bus, and even with local buses it would soak up a significant chunk of the available bandwidth. But we're using DirectDraw, and the pixels are just being blasted around the memory on the display card by the display card's blitter hardware. That's why we can get such high blit rates.

You'll often be able to see the blit rate going up as you add sprites. On a modern graphics card, a rate of 40 MB per second is quite achievable. This is equal to around 60 of our sprites plus the background; a pretty impressive result, considering it's running at 75 frames per second. Even more impressive, at a quite acceptable 25 frames per second we can have over 340 64×64 sized sprites—quite a feat!

Back to the code. In the OnTimer event we then call UpdateStatsSurface to output the text, as shown in Listing 32.42.

Listing 32.42. Updating the Stats surface with statistics.

```
procedure TForm1.UpdateStatsSurface ;
var s : string[ 255 ] ;
    Plural : string[ 1 ] ;
begin
  // output statistical information to Stats surface
  if Assigned( StatsCanvas ) and StatsCanvas.DrawingAllowed then
    with StatsCanvas do try
      Brush.Color := clWhite ;
      FillRect( StatsRect ) ;
      Brush.Style := bsClear ;
      if Sprites.Count <> 1 then Plural := 's' else Plural := '' ;
      s := Format( '%d sprite%s: %d fps = %.2FMB/sec',
                   [ Sprites.Count, Plural, FPS, MBperSec ] ) ;
```

```
      TextOut( ( StatsRect.Right - TextWidth( s ) ) div 2, 0, s ) ;
    finally
      Release ;
    end ;
end ;
```

Note the check for StatsCanvas.DrawingAllowed. If you press Alt-Tab to switch away from your running application, DirectDraw minimizes its window and you lose your display surface memory until the application is restored. But the timer keeps ticking away, calling this event. If you attempt to draw on a TDDCanvas when the surface memory is unavailable, the canvas handle 0 is returned and the VCL raises an exception with the message "Canvas does not allow drawing." Checking the DrawingAllowed function before using a TDDCanvas safeguards against this.

The only other major change to the application is in the OnKeyDown handler. If you press up or down cursor keys, a sprite is added or deleted, respectively. If you press Page Up or Page Down, 10 sprites are added or deleted at a time. Pressing Delete or Backspace clears off all the sprites. Listing 32.43 shows the code for the FormKeyDown event handler.

Listing 23.43. The FormKeyDown handler with code to add and remove sprites.

```
procedure TForm1.FormKeyDown(Sender: TObject; var Key: Word;
  Shift: TShiftState);
begin
  // now handles keys for adding and deleting sprites.
  case Key of
    VK_ESCAPE, VK_F12 : Close ;
    VK_UP     : AddSprites( 1 ) ;
    VK_DOWN   : RemoveSprites( 1 ) ;
    VK_PRIOR  : AddSprites( 10 ) ;
    VK_NEXT   : RemoveSprites( 10 ) ;
    VK_DELETE,
    VK_BACK   : RemoveSprites( Sprites.Count ) ;
  end ;
end;
```

You can find the demo code in the DDDemo7 directory.

Creating Sprites at Design-Time

If you had a look at the DDSprite.pas source code file, you may have noticed that TDDSprite descends from TComponent and the unit has a Register procedure. This means you can add DDSprite.pas to your component palette. This adds TDDSprite to a Game SDK page. You now can add sprites to your form visually and set up the various properties with the Object Inspector.

The final `DirectDraw` example, DDDemo8, does exactly this. It does away with the sprite-adding and -removing code, the add/remove sprite key handling, and the instruction text. The sprites are sitting on the form in the designer, already set up. You can play around with them using the Object Inspector. You can make them invisible if you want to remove them temporarily from activity. The simple statistical code in the previous example just displays the total number of sprites on the surface. I've modified this by adding an integer field to the form to keep a tally of the number of visible sprites.

Summary

This brings us to the end of the `DirectDraw` section. There's a whole lot more stuff in `DirectDraw`, but it would need a whole book by itself to cover it all. But you now have enough information and samples to churn out a page-flipping application in Delphi 2.0!

Creating SDK Worlds

33

This chapter takes a look at the Games SDK as a tool for creating artificial worlds. You will see how to create overhead views of large colorful maps that scroll back and forth across the screen. You will also see how to plunge into a three-dimensional maze where you can wander about at will.

The code shown in this chapter is not a fully developed game, or a complete simulation. Instead, it's a framework out of which a game or artificial world could be built. This book is not about end users; it's about the people who program computers. My goal in this chapter is not to entertain, but to show how to construct artificial worlds.

The code shown here is not overly fancy by today's standards, but it would have turned more than few heads as recently as five years ago. I include it because it represents a relatively easy-to-understand example of how you can immerse the user in a computer-generated world. In other words, the simulation is technically sophisticated enough to give the user the sense that he or she is actually moving through a real world.

This is a realm of programming in which imagination is supreme, and what you do with this code is limited only by your own ability to engineer an environment of interest to others. This chapter is also meant to be more than a little fun, and you would perhaps not be remiss if you found yourself taking the time to play with this code merely for its own sake.

Fast Animation and the Games SDK

If you want to create a game, or if you want to create a simulation, you are likely to find the Games SDK to be very useful tool. The point here is that the Games SDK is useful whenever you need to write very quickly to the screen.

Though many are loathe to admit it, the standard Windows GDI functions are actually fairly fast when it comes to graphics performance. However, there are times when you will sacrifice almost anything to get just a little better graphics performance. In particular, when you are simulating real-world objects, you don't want the performance of the Windows blitting engine to come between you and a viable simulation. That's when the Games SDK can be useful.

Of course, another interesting aspect of the games SDK is that it is based on COM objects. In fact, a good deal of the discussion in this chapter will revolve around COM objects and their uses in typical post–Windows 3.1 programming environment.

The XFire Program

Below you will find a program called XFire. It presents the user with two possible views of the world. The first is the overhead view shown in Figures 33.1 and 33.2. This view allows you to scroll screen after screen of information across the desktop in either a horizontal or veritcal direction. Each screen is connected to the last in that it is a part of a huge map depicting a fictitious land. The total map is approximately 8 screens wide by 7 screens high, for a total of some 56 screens of information.

FIGURE 33.1.

An overhead view of the world in the XFire program.

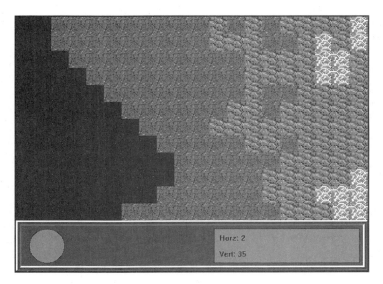

FIGURE 33.2.

Another look at the overhead view of the world found in the XFire program.

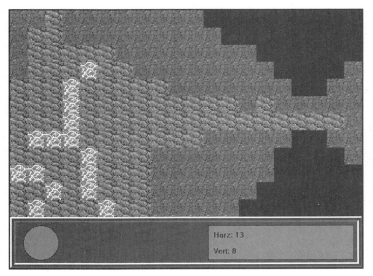

As I said earlier, all of the code in this book is free for you to use as you wish, so long as your goal is not to teach others how to use Delphi. However, the land depicted in the XFire program is copyrighted. I provide tools (MAKEWRLD.DPR) that would allow you to design your own land, but you cannot reuse the world shown here in your own programs!

The second view of the world presented by the XFire program is a maze view, as shown in Figures 33.3 and 33.4. This is a three-dimensional maze where you can wander about as you wish. The walls are solid, and you cannot walk through them. You can, however, strike out in various directions.

FIGURE 33.3.

A view of the maze found in the XFire program.

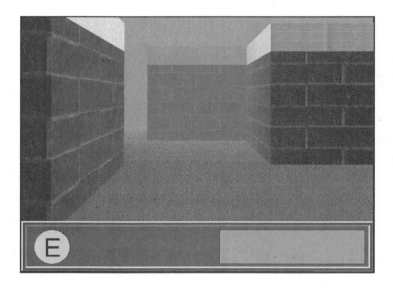

FIGURE 33.4.

A second view of the maze from the XFire program.

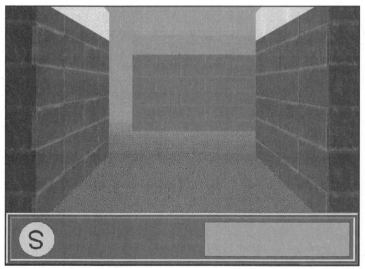

The code for XFire is shown in Listings 33.1 through 33.9. This is a large program, which has a number of dependencies to the *XXX*Box programs found in the UNITS directory that ships with this book. This dependency on units like StrBox and MathBox is typical of real-world programs. In other parts of this book I have tried to limit such dependencies, but in this chapter I have simply used whatever tools I needed to put this code together.

Listing 33.1. The main unit for the XFire program.

```
unit main;

{ ------------------------------------------
  Copyright (c) 1996 by Charlie Calvert

  There is an XUnits directory that holds
  some of the files used in this project.

  See overview in XFIRE.DPR and OBJS.DOC
  ------------------------------------------ }

interface

uses
  SysUtils, Windows, Messages,
  Classes, Graphics, Controls,
  Forms, Dialogs, StdCtrls,
  DDraw, PalBox, DrawBrd1,
  OleAuto, ExtCtrls, Menus,
  GameBrd1;

const
  AColor = 254;

type
  TGameModes = (gmWorld, gmCity, gmTest);

  TForm1 = class(TForm)
    MainMenu1: TMainMenu;
    File1: TMenuItem;
    Exit1: TMenuItem;
    Options1: TMenuItem;
    Dialog11: TMenuItem;
    StartGame1: TMenuItem;
    ReturntoGame1: TMenuItem;
    Timer1: TTimer;
    WorldMap1: TMenuItem;
    CityMap1: TMenuItem;
    NewTry1: TMenuItem;
    N2: TMenuItem;
    procedure StartWorldMode(Sender: TObject);
    procedure Dialog11Click(Sender: TObject);
    procedure ReturntoGame1Click(Sender: TObject);
    procedure FormKeyDown(Sender: TObject; var Key: Word;
      Shift: TShiftState);
    procedure Timer1Timer(Sender: TObject);
    procedure WorldMap1Click(Sender: TObject);
    procedure CityMap1Click(Sender: TObject);
    procedure NewTry1Click(Sender: TObject);
    procedure Exit1Click(Sender: TObject);
    procedure FormCreate(Sender: TObject);
```

continues

Listing 33.1. continued

```
  private
    FGameBoard: TDrawDirect;
    FGameMode: TGameModes;
    procedure Pause;
    procedure StartGame(Mode: TGameModes; BackGround: string);
    procedure HandleExcepts(Sender: TObject; E: Exception);
  end;

var
  Form1: TForm1;

implementation

uses
  Status, smallmp1;

{$R *.DFM}

procedure TForm1.StartGame(Mode: TGameModes; BackGround: string);
begin
  FGameBoard.Free;
  FGameMode := Mode;
  ReturntoGame1.Enabled := False;
  case FGameMode of
    gmWorld: FGameBoard := TWorldBoard.Create(Handle, BackGround, AColor);
    gmCity: FGameBoard := TCityBoard.Create(Handle, BackGround, AColor);
    gmTest: FGameBoard := TTestBoard.Create(Handle, BackGround, AColor);
  end;
  if not FGameBoard.InitObjects then Exit;
  FGameBoard.DoOneFlip;
  Timer1.Enabled := True;
end;

procedure TForm1.StartWorldMode(Sender: TObject);
begin
  StartGame(gmWorld, WorldBackground);
end;

procedure TForm1.CityMap1Click(Sender: TObject);
begin
  StartGame(gmCity, CityBackground);
end;

procedure TForm1.NewTry1Click(Sender: TObject);
begin
  StartGame(gmTest, CityBackground);
end;

procedure TForm1.Pause;
begin
  ReturntoGame1.Enabled := False;
  Timer1.Enabled := False;
  if FGameBoard.Pause then
    DrawMenuBar(Handle);
end;
```

```
procedure TForm1.FormKeyDown(Sender: TObject; var Key: Word;
➥Shift: TShiftState);
begin
  case Key of
    vk_F10: Pause;
  else
    FGameBoard.Move(Key);
  end;
end;

procedure TForm1.Exit1Click(Sender: TObject);
begin
  FGameBoard.Free;
  Close;
end;

procedure TForm1.WorldMap1Click(Sender: TObject);
begin
  WorldMap := TWorldMap.Create(Self);
  WorldMap.ShowModal;
  ReturnToGame1Click(nil);
  WorldMap.Free;
end;

procedure TForm1.Dialog11Click(Sender: TObject);
begin
  StatusDlg := TStatusDlg.Create(Self);
  StatusDlg.ShowModalPaint;
  ReturnToGame1Click(nil);
  StatusDlg.Free;
end;

procedure TForm1.ReturntoGame1Click(Sender: TObject);
begin
  FGameBoard.Restore;
  Timer1.Enabled := True;
end;

procedure TForm1.Timer1Timer(Sender: TObject);
begin
  FGameBoard.DoOneFlip
end;

procedure TForm1.HandleExcepts(Sender: TObject; E: Exception);
begin
  if FGameBoard <> nil then
    FGameBoard.ErrorEvent(0, E.Message)
  else
    ShowMessage(E.Message);
end;

procedure TForm1.FormCreate(Sender: TObject);
begin
  Application.OnException := HandleExcepts;
end;

end.
```

Listing 33.2. The `DrawBrd1` unit surfaces some of the key features of the Direct Draw interface.

```
unit DrawBrd1;

/////////////////////////////////////
// Copyright (c) 1996 by Charlie Calvert
// Base Object for use with DirectDraw
/////////////////////////////////////

interface

uses
  DDraw, Windows, Classes,
  OleAuto, DDUtils, Dialogs,
  SysUtils;

type
  EDDError = class(Exception);

  TDrawDirect = class
  private
    FActive: Boolean;
    FBackGroundMap: string;
    FDirectDraw: IDirectDraw;
    FBackSurface: IDirectDrawSurface;
    FDDSFront: IDirectDrawSurface;
    FWorkSurface: IDirectDrawSurface;
    FDDPal: IDirectDrawPalette;
    FHandle: HWnd;
    FTransColor: Integer;
    function CreateFront: Boolean;
    function SetUpBack: Boolean;
    function GetDib(Instance: THandle; S: string): THandle;
    function CreateSurface(Bitmap: THandle;
      DirectDraw: IDirectDraw): IDirectDrawSurface;
    function LoadPalette(Instance: THandle;
      DirectDraw: IDirectDraw; const BitmapName: string): IDirectDrawPalette;
    function MakeItSo(DDResult: HResult): Boolean;
  protected
    function BackGroundBlits: Boolean; virtual;
//  function ExtraBitmaps: Boolean; virtual;
    procedure DDTest(hr: HResult; S: string);
    function CreateDDSurface(var DDS: IDirectDrawSurface;
                            BitsName: string): Boolean;
  public
    procedure ErrorEvent(hr: HResult; S: string);
    constructor Create(Handle: Hwnd; BackGroundMapStr: string;
      TransColor: Integer); virtual;
    destructor Destroy; override;
    procedure DestroyObjects; virtual;
    procedure DoOneFlip; virtual;
    procedure InitFailed;
    function InitObjects: Boolean; virtual;
    procedure Move(Value: Integer); virtual;
    function Pause: Boolean; virtual;
    procedure Restore;
    property Active: Boolean read fActive write fActive;
```

```
    property BackGroundMap: string read FBackGroundMap write FBackGroundMap;
    property DirectDraw: IDirectDraw read FDirectDraw write FDirectDraw;
    property FrontSurface: IDirectDrawSurface read FDDSFront write FDDSFront;
    property BackSurface: IDirectDrawSurface read FBackSurface write FBackSurface;
    property WorkSurface: IDirectDrawSurface read FWorkSurface write FWorkSurface;
    property Palette: IDirectDrawPalette read FDDPal write FDDPal;
    property Handle: HWnd read FHandle;
  end;

implementation

uses
  OleBox;

constructor TDrawDirect.Create(Handle: hwnd; BackGroundMapStr: string;
                                    TransColor: Integer);
begin
  inherited Create;
  FHandle := Handle;
  FActive := False;
  FTransColor:= TransColor;              // Transparent color
  FBackGroundMap := BackGroundMapStr;    // Name of background bitmap
end;

destructor TDrawDirect.Destroy;
begin
  DestroyObjects;
  inherited Destroy;
end;

procedure TDrawDirect.ErrorEvent(hr: HResult; S: string);
begin
  FActive := False;
  FDirectDraw.FlipToGDISurface;
  FDirectDraw.SetCooperativeLevel(FHandle, DDSCL_Normal);
  // DestroyObjects;
  raise EDDError.Create(GetOleError(hr) + ' ' + S);
end;

procedure TDrawDirect.DDTest(hr: HResult; S: string);
begin
  if not Succeeded(hr) then
    ErrorEvent(hr, S);
end;

function TDrawDirect.BackGroundBlits: Boolean;
var
  R: TRect;
  hr: HResult;
begin
  R := Rect(0, 0, 639, 480);
  hr := BackSurface.BltFast(0, 0, WorkSurface, R,
    DDBLTFAST_WAIT or DDBLTFAST_SRCCOLORKEY);
  Result := Succeeded(hr);
  if not Result then
    ErrorEvent(hr, 'BackGround');
end;
```

continues

Listing 33.2. continued

```
procedure TDrawDirect.DestroyObjects;
begin
  FActive := False;
  FDirectDraw.SetCooperativeLevel(FHandle, DDSCL_Normal);
  if FDirectDraw <> nil then begin
    if FBackSurface <> nil then FBackSurface.Release;
    if FDDSFront <> nil then FDDSFront.Release;
    if FDDPal <> nil then FDDPal.Release;
    if FWorkSurface <> nil then FWorkSurface.Release;
    if FDirectDraw <> nil then FDirectDraw.Release;
  end;
  FDirectDraw := nil;
  FBackSurface := nil;
  FDDsFront := nil;
  FWorkSurface := nil;
  FDDPal := nil;
end;

{ utility function to help restore surfaces }
function TDrawDirect.MakeItSo(DDResult: HResult): Boolean;
begin
  case DDResult of
    DD_OK: Result := true;
//    DDERR_SURFACELOST: Result := RestoreSurfaces <> DD_OK;
  else
    Result := DDResult <> DDERR_WASSTILLDRAWING;
  end;
end;


// Description:  Draw image to background
//               Flip it to the front
//               Background blits is for special processing
procedure TDrawDirect.DoOneFlip;
begin
  try
    if FActive then begin
      BackGroundBlits;
      repeat until MakeItSo(FDDSFront.Flip(nil, DDFLIP_WAIT));
    end;
  except
    on Exception do
      ErrorEvent(0, 'Flipping');
  end;
end;

function TDrawDirect.CreateFront: Boolean;
var
  SurfaceDesc: TDDSurfaceDesc;
  hr: HResult;
begin
  Result := False;
  FillChar(SurfaceDesc, sizeOf(TDDSurfaceDesc), 0);
  SurfaceDesc.dwSize := sizeof(TDDSurfaceDesc);
  SurfaceDesc.dwFlags := DDSD_CAPS or DDSD_BACKBUFFERCOUNT;
```

```
    SurfaceDesc.ddsCaps.dwCaps := DDSCAPS_PRIMARYSURFACE or
                                  DDSCAPS_FLIP or
                                  DDSCAPS_COMPLEX;
    SurfaceDesc.dwBackBufferCount := 1;
    hr := FDirectDraw.CreateSurface(SurfaceDesc, FDDSFront, nil);
    if hr <> DD_OK then
      ErrorEvent(hr, 'CreateFront')
    else
      Result := True;
end;

function TDrawDirect.LoadPalette(Instance: THandle;
  DirectDraw: IDirectDraw; const BitmapName: string): IDirectDrawPalette;
type
  TRGB = array[ 0..255 ] of TRGBQuad;
  PRGB = ^TRGB;
var
  i, n: integer;
  h: HRsrc;
  BitmapInfo: PBitmapInfo;
  APE: array[ 0..255 ] of TPaletteEntry;
  RGB: PRGB;
  bfHeader: TBitmapFileHeader;
  biHeader: TBitmapInfoHeader;
  Temp: byte;
begin
  // build a 332 palette as the default.
  for i := 0 to 255 do with APE[ i ] do begin
    peRed := (((i SHR 5) and $07) * 255 div 7);
    peGreen := (((i SHR 2) and $07) * 255 div 7);
    peBlue := ((i and $03) * 255 div 3);
    peFlags := 0;
  end;

  // get a pointer to the bitmap resource.
  if BitmapName <> '' then begin
    h := FindResource(Instance, PChar(BitmapName), RT_BITMAP);
    if h <> 0 then begin
      BitmapInfo := PBitmapInfo(LockResource(LoadResource(0, h)));
      RGB := PRGB(@BitmapInfo^.bmiColors);
      if (BitmapInfo = NIL) or
         (BitmapInfo^.bmiHeader.biSize < sizeof(TBITMAPINFOHEADER)) then n := 0
      else
      if (BitmapInfo^.bmiHeader.biBitCount > 8) then n := 0
      else
      if (BitmapInfo^.bmiHeader.biClrUsed = 0) then
         n := 1 SHL BitmapInfo^.bmiHeader.biBitCount
      else
         n := BitmapInfo^.bmiHeader.biClrUsed;

      //  a DIB color table has its colors stored BGR not RGB
      //  so flip them around.
      for i := 0 to n - 1 do with APE[ i ], RGB^[ i ] do begin
        peRed := rgbRed;
        peGreen := rgbGreen;
        peBlue := rgbBlue;
        peFlags := 0;
      end;
```

continues

Listing 33.2. continued

```
    end else begin
      with TFileStream.Create(BitmapName, fmOpenRead) do try
        Read(bfHeader, SizeOf(bfHeader));
        Read(biHeader, SizeOf(biHeader));
        Read(APE, SizeOf(APE));
      finally
        Free;
      end;

      //  get the number of colors in the color table
      if biHeader.biSize <> SizeOf(TBitmapInfoHeader) then n := 0
      else
      if biHeader.biBitCount > 8 then n := 0
      else
      if biHeader.biClrUsed = 0 then n := 1 SHL biHeader.biBitCount else
        n := biHeader.biClrUsed;

      //  a DIB color table has its colors stored BGR not RGB
      //  so flip them around.
      for i := 0 to n - 1 do with APE[ i ] do begin
        Temp := peRed;
        peRed := peBlue;
        peBlue := Temp;
      end;
    end;
  end;

  // create the DD palette
  if DirectDraw.CreatePalette(DDPCAPS_8BIT, @APE[ 0 ], Result, NIL) <> DD_OK then
    raise Exception.Create('DirectDraw.CreatePalette failed');
end;

function TDrawDirect.GetDib(Instance: THandle; S: string): THandle;
begin
  Result := LoadImage(Instance, PChar(S), Image_Bitmap,
                      0, 0, LR_CREATEDIBSECTION);
  if Result = 0 then
    ErrorEvent(0, 'Could not load bitmap');
end;

function TDrawDirect.CreateSurface(Bitmap: THandle;
➥DirectDraw: IDirectDraw): IDirectDrawSurface;
var
  SurfaceDesc: TDDSurfaceDesc;
  BM: Windows.TBitmap;
begin
  try
    try
      GetObject(Bitmap, SizeOf(BM), @BM);

      FillChar(SurfaceDesc, SizeOf(SurfaceDesc), 0);
      with SurfaceDesc do begin
        dwSize := SizeOf(SurfaceDesc);
        dwFlags := DDSD_CAPS or DDSD_HEIGHT or DDSD_WIDTH;
        ddsCaps.dwCaps := DDSCAPS_OFFSCREENPLAIN;
        dwWidth := BM.bmWidth;
        dwHeight := BM.bmHeight;
      end;
```

```
        if DirectDraw.CreateSurface(SurfaceDesc, Result, NIL) <> DD_OK then
          raise Exception.Create('CreateSurface failed');

        DDCopyBitmap(Result, Bitmap, 0, 0, 0, 0);
    except
      on E: Exception do
        ErrorEvent(0, E.Message);
    end;
  finally
    if Bitmap <> 0 then DeleteObject(Bitmap);
  end;
end;

 function TDrawDirect.CreateDDSurface(var DDS: IDirectDrawSurface;
 ➥BitsName: string): Boolean;
 var
  ColorKey: TDDColorKey;
  hr: HResult;
  Lib: THandle;
begin
  Result := False;

  Lib := LoadLibrary('BitDll');
  if Lib < 32 then Exit;

  FDDPal := LoadPalette(Lib, FDirectDraw, PChar(FBackGroundMap));
  if FDDPal = nil then begin
     InitFailed;
     Exit;
  end;

  DDS := CreateSurface(GetDib(Lib, BitsName), DirectDraw);

  if DDS = nil then begin
    InitFailed;
    Exit;
  end;
  ColorKey.dwColorSpaceLowValue := FTransColor;
  ColorKey.dwColorSpaceHighValue := FTransColor;
  hr := DDS.SetColorKey(DDCKEY_SRCBLT, ColorKey);
  if hr <> DD_OK then
    ErrorEvent(hr, 'CreateSurfacePal')
  else
    Result := True;

  FreeLibrary(Lib);
end;

function TDrawDirect.SetUpBack: Boolean;
var
  hr: HResult;
  DDSCaps: TDDSCaps;
begin
  FillChar(DDSCaps, SizeOf(TDDSCaps), 0);
  Result := False;
  ddscaps.dwCaps := DDSCAPS_BACKBUFFER;
  hr := FDDSFront.GetAttachedSurface(ddscaps, FBackSurface);
  if hr <> DD_OK then
```

continues

1186

Listing 33.2. continued

```
      ErrorEvent(hr, 'InitObjects')
  else
    Result := True;
end;

function TDrawDirect.InitObjects: Boolean;
var
  hr: hResult;
begin
  Result := False;
  DDTest(DirectDrawCreate(nil, IDirectDraw(FDirectDraw), nil), 'InitObjects');
  DDTest(FDirectDraw.SetCooperativeLevel(FHandle, DDSCL_EXCLUSIVE or
➡DDSCL_FULLSCREEN), 'InitObjects');
  hr := FDirectDraw.SetDisplayMode(640, 480, 8);
  if(hr <> DD_OK) then
    ErrorEvent(hr, 'InitObjects');
  CreateFront;
  SetUpBack;
  if not CreateDDSurface(FWorkSurface, BackGroundMap) then Exit;
  FActive := True;
  Result := True;
end;

procedure TDrawDirect.InitFailed;
begin
  FActive := False;
  DestroyObjects;
  ShowMessage('Failed');
end;

procedure TDrawDirect.Move(Value: Integer);
begin
end;

function TDrawDirect.Pause: Boolean;
var
  ddrval: hResult;
begin
  Result := False;
  ddrval := FDirectDraw.FlipToGDISurface;
  if ddrval = DD_OK then
    Result := True;
end;

procedure TDrawDirect.Restore;
begin
  FDDSFront.Restore;
end;

end.
```

Listing 33.3. The `GameBrd1` unit defines the key Direct Draw objects used in the application.

```
unit GameBrd1;

{ Copyright (c) 1996 by Charlie Calvert }

{ Use 254 to initialize the color

  Here is sample code to initialize an instance of one
  of these objects:

  const
    BackGround = 'Back';
    AColor = 254;
  var
    Handle: THwnd;
    FGameBoard: TWorldBoard;
  begin
    FGameBoard := TWorldBoard.Create(Handle, BackGround, AColor);
    if not FGameBoard.InitObjects then Exit;
    FGameBoard.DoOneFlip;
  end;

  This code assumes that that bitmaps themselves are
  stored in the resources of a separate DLL called
  BITDLL.DLL. The code that implements this is in
  DRAWBRD1.PAS

  BackGroundBlits is a hook for descendant
  objects that want to do more in this area.

  Here are examples of the TCityBoard views:

            10
   1  4  7  11      10 11 12 13 14
   2  5  8  12       7  8  9
   3  6  9  13       4  5  6
            14       1  2  3
}
interface

uses
  DDraw, Windows, OleAuto,
  DDUtils, Dialogs, Classes,
  PalBox, MzTown, DrawBrd1,
  Entity;

const
  MaxMapRows = 12;
  MaxMapCols = 21;
  WorldBackGround = 'Back';
  CityBackGround = 'City';

type
  TCityWalls = array[1..14] of Byte;
```

continues

Listing 33.3. continued

```
  TSide = (ExtLeft, Left, Center, Right, ExtRight);

  TWorldBoard = class(TDrawDirect)
  private
    FCreatureList: TCreatureList;
    FHorzPos: Integer;
    FTimerOdd: Boolean;
    FVertPos: Integer;
    procedure DestroyObjects; override;
    procedure DrawText;
    function GetRect(Col, Row: Integer): TRect;
    procedure MoveGrid(Col, Row: Integer);
    function BackGroundBlits: Boolean; override;
  public
    constructor Create(Handle: hwnd; BackGroundMap: string;
      TransColor: Integer); override;
    procedure Move(Value: Integer); override;
    property CreatureList: TCreatureList
      read FCreatureList write FCreatureList;
  end;

  TCharacterDirection = (cdNorth, cdSouth, cdEast, cdWest);

  TCityBoard = class(TDrawDirect)
  private
    FDDSForeWall: IDirectDrawSurface;
    FDDSFrontWall: IDirectDrawSurface;
    FDDSMidWall: IDirectDrawSurface;
    mt: TMazeTown;
    function BackGroundBlits: Boolean; override;
    procedure DestroyObjects; override;
  public
    constructor Create(Handle: hwnd; BackGroundMap: string;
      TransColor: Integer); override;
    function InitObjects: Boolean; override;
    procedure Move(Value: Integer); override;
    procedure DrawScene;
    function HandlePanel: Boolean;
  end;

  TTestBoard = class(TDrawDirect)
    FrontWall: IDirectDrawSurface;
    FTimerOdd: Boolean;
    constructor Create(Handle: hwnd; BackGroundMap: string;
      TransColor: Integer); override;
    function BackGroundBlits: Boolean; override;
    function InitObjects: Boolean; override;
  end;

implementation

uses
  SysUtils;

{ -- TWorldBoard -- }
```

```
constructor TWorldBoard.Create(Handle: Hwnd; BackGroundMap: string;
  TransColor: Integer);
begin
  inherited Create(Handle, BackGroundMap, TransColor);
  FHorzPos := 0;
  FVertPos := 0;
  FCreatureList := TCreatureList.Create;
end;

procedure TWorldBoard.DrawText;
var
  S: string;
  DC: HDC;
// Font, OldFont: hFont;
begin
  BackSurface.GetDC(DC);
// Font := GetStockObject(Mono_Font);
// OldFont := SelectObject(DC, Font);
  SetBkMode(DC, Transparent);
  S := 'Horz: ' + IntToStr(FHorzPos);
  TextOut(DC, 370, 410, PChar(S), Length(S));
  S := 'Vert: ' + IntToStr(FVertPos);
  TextOut(DC, 370, 440, PChar(S), Length(S));
// SelectObject(DC, OldFont);
  BackSurface.ReleaseDC(DC);
end;

{ The back bitmap containst squares that are
  blitted to the screen to form a map }
function TWorldBoard.BackGroundBlits: Boolean;
var
  R: TRect;
  i, j, k: Integer;
begin
  inherited BackGroundBlits;
  k := 0;
  FTimerOdd := not FTimerOdd;
  DrawText;
  for j := 0 to (MaxMapRows - 1) do
    for i := 0 to (MaxMapCols - 1) do begin
      R := GetRect(i + FHorzPos, j + FVertPos);
      BackSurface.BltFast(32 * k, 32 * j, WorkSurface,
                          R, DDBLTFAST_SRCCOLORKEY);
      if i mod 20 = 0 then
        k := 0
      else
        Inc(k);
    end;
  Result := True;
end;

procedure TWorldBoard.DestroyObjects;
begin
  inherited DestroyObjects;
  FCreatureList.Free;
end;
```

continues

Listing 33.3. continued

```
function TWorldBoard.GetRect(Col, Row: Integer): TRect;
var
  X: Integer;
  MapType: TMapType;
begin
  MapType := TMapType(FCreatureList.Map[Col, Row + 1]);
  if ((FTimerOdd = True) and (MapType = mtWater)) then
    MapType := mtWater2;
  case MapType of
    mtGrass: X := 0;
    mtWater: X := 32;
    mtMountain: X := 64;
    mtFootHill: X := 160;
    mtWater2: X := 128;
  else
    X := 192;
  end;
  Result := Rect(X, 480, X + 32, 480 + 32);
end;

procedure TWorldBoard.Move(Value: Integer);
begin
  case Value of
    vk_Right: MoveGrid(1, 0);
    vk_Left: MoveGrid(-1, 0);
    vk_Down: MoveGrid(0, 1);
    vk_Up: MoveGrid(0, -1);
  end;
end;

procedure TWorldBoard.MoveGrid(Col, Row: Integer);
begin
  FHorzPos := FHorzPos + Col;
  FVertPos := FVertPos + Row;
  if FHorzPos < 0 then FHorzPos := 0;
  if FHorzPos > (MaxX - MaxMapCols) then FHorzPos := MaxX - MaxMapCols;
  if FVertPos < 0 then FVertPos := 0;
  if FVertPos > (MaxY - MaxMapRows) then FVertPos := MaxY - MaxMapRows;
  DoOneFlip;
end;

{ --- TCityBoard --- }

constructor TCityBoard.Create(Handle: Hwnd; BackGroundMap: string;
  TransColor: Integer);
begin
  inherited Create(Handle, BackGroundMap, TransColor);
  mt := TMazeTown.Create(1, 2, East);
end;

procedure TCityBoard.DestroyObjects;
begin
  if FDDSForeWall <> nil then FDDSForeWall.Release;
  if FDDSMidWall <> nil then FDDSMidWall.Release;
  inherited DestroyObjects;
end;
```

```
function TCityBoard.HandlePanel;
var
  R: TRect;
begin
  case mt.Direction of
    North: R := Rect(575, 480, 640, 545);
    South: R := Rect(575, 545, 640, 610);
    East:  R := Rect(575, 610, 640, 675);
    West:  R := Rect(575, 675, 640, 740);
  end;
  BackSurface.BltFast(23, 401, WorkSurface, R, DDBLTFAST_SRCCOLORKEY);
  Result := True;
end;

function GetForePos(Pos: TSide): TRect;
begin
  case Pos of
    Left: Result := Rect(0, 0, 54, 384);
    Right: Result := Rect(54, 0, 108, 384);
  end;
end;

function GetFrontPos(Pos: TSide): TRect;
begin
  case Pos of
    Left: Result := Rect(0, 0, 187, 384);
    Center: Result := Rect(1, 478, 533, 862);
    Right: Result := Rect(187, 0, 374, 382);
  end;
end;

function GetMidPos(Pos: TSide): TRect;
begin
  case Pos of
    Left: Result := Rect(0, 0, 231, 268);
    Center: Result := Rect(1, 268, 268, 536 );
    Right: Result := Rect(232, 0, 463, 268);
  end;
end;

function GetBackPos(Pos: TSide): TRect;
begin
  case Pos of
    ExtLeft: Result := Rect(108, 2, 229, 180);
    Left: Result := Rect(0, 385, 201, 563);
    Center: Result := Rect(272, 269, 453, 447); { 18? X 179 }
    Right: Result := Rect(202, 385, 402, 563);
    ExtRight: Result := Rect(109, 182, 229, 361);  { 121 * 179 }
  end;
end;

function TCityBoard.BackGroundBlits: Boolean;
var
  R: TRect;
begin
  inherited BackGroundBlits;
  HandlePanel;
```

continues

1192

Listing 33.3. continued

```
if mt.CurrentView[10].Value = 1 then begin
  R := GetBackPos(ExtLeft);
  BackSurface.BltFast(0, 54, FDDSForeWall, R, DDBLTFAST_SRCCOLORKEY);
end;

if mt.CurrentView[14].Value = 1 then begin
  R := GetBackPos(ExtRight);
  BackSurface.BltFast(519, 54, FDDSForeWall, R, DDBLTFAST_SRCCOLORKEY);
end;

if mt.CurrentView[11].Value = 1 then begin
  R := GetBackPos(Left);
  BackSurface.BltFast(51, 54, FDDSFrontWall, R, DDBLTFAST_SRCCOLORKEY);
end;

if mt.CurrentView[13].Value = 1 then begin
  R := GetBackPos(Right);
  BackSurface.BltFast(387, 54, FDDSFrontWall, R, DDBLTFAST_SRCCOLORKEY);
end;

if mt.CurrentView[12].Value = 1 then begin
  R := GetBackPos(Center);
  BackSurface.BltFast(229, 54, FDDSMidWall, R, DDBLTFAST_SRCCOLORKEY);
end;

if mt.CurrentView[7].Value = 1 then begin
  R := GetMidPos(Left);
  BackSurface.BltFast(0, 10, FDDSMidWall, R, DDBLTFAST_SRCCOLORKEY);
end;

if mt.CurrentView[9].Value = 1 then begin
  R := GetMidPos(Right);
  BackSurface.BltFast(409, 10, FDDSMidWall, R, DDBLTFAST_SRCCOLORKEY);
end;

if mt.CurrentView[8].Value = 1 then begin
  R := GetMidPos(Center);
  BackSurface.BltFast(186, 10, FDDSMidWall, R, DDBLTFAST_SRCCOLORKEY);
end;


if mt.CurrentView[4].Value = 1 then begin
  R := GetFrontPos(Left);
  BackSurface.BltFast(0, 0, FDDSFrontWall, R, DDBLTFAST_SRCCOLORKEY);
end;

if mt.CurrentView[6].Value = 1 then begin
  R := GetFrontPos(Right);
  BackSurface.BltFast(453, 0, FDDSFrontWall, R, DDBLTFAST_SRCCOLORKEY);
end;

if mt.CurrentView[5].Value = 1 then begin
  R := GetFrontPos(Center);
  BackSurface.BltFast(54, 0, WorkSurface, R, DDBLTFAST_SRCCOLORKEY);
end;
```

```
   if mt.CurrentView[1].Value = 1 then begin
     R := GetForePos(Left);
     BackSurface.BltFast(0, 0, FDDSForeWall, R, DDBLTFAST_SRCCOLORKEY);
   end;

   { Two is where you are standing, so you don't do that one. }

   if mt.CurrentView[3].Value = 1 then begin
     R := GetForePos(Right);
     BackSurface.BltFast(586, 0, FDDSForeWall, R, DDBLTFAST_SRCCOLORKEY);
   end;
   Result := True;
end;

function TCityBoard.InitObjects: Boolean;
begin
  inherited InitObjects;
  Result := False;
  if not Active then Exit;
  if not CreateDDSurface(FDDSFrontWall, 'FrontWall') then Exit;
  if not CreateDDSurface(FDDSForeWall, 'ForeWall') then Exit;
  if not CreateDDSurface(FDDSMidWall, 'MidWall') then Exit;
  Result := True;
end;

procedure TCityBoard.DrawScene;
var
  i: Integer;
begin
  for i := 14 downto 1 do begin
    with mt.CurrentView[i] do
      if Value <> - 1 then begin
{         DrawPlace(i, Value); }
      end;
  end;
end;

procedure TCityBoard.Move(Value: Integer);
begin
  case Value of
    vk_Right: mt.Key(vk_Right);
    vk_Left: mt.Key(vk_Left);
    vk_Down: mt.Key(vk_Down);
    vk_Up: mt.Key(vk_Up);
  end;
  DoOneFlip;
end;

{ --- TTestBoard ---}

constructor TTestBoard.Create(Handle: hwnd; BackGroundMap: string;
  TransColor: Integer);
begin
  inherited Create(Handle, CityBackGround, TransColor);
end;
```

continues

Listing 33.3. continued

```
function TTestBoard.BackGroundBlits: Boolean;
var
  R: TRect;
begin
  inherited BackGroundBlits;
  FTimerOdd := not FTimerOdd;
  if FTimerOdd then begin
    R := Rect(0, 0, 187, 384);
    BackSurface.BltFast(0, 0, FrontWall, R, DDBLTFAST_SRCCOLORKEY)
  end else begin
    R := Rect(24, 25, 187, 384);
    BackSurface.BltFast(0, 0, FrontWall, R, DDBLTFAST_SRCCOLORKEY)
  end;
  Result := True;
end;

function TTestBoard.InitObjects: Boolean;
begin
  Inherited InitObjects;
  CreateDDSurface(FrontWall, 'FrontWall');
  Result := True;
end;

end.
```

Listing 33.4. The MZTown unit defines the maze and its characteristics. It does the grunt work for working with a maze.

```
unit mztown;

{ Copyright (c) 1996 by Charlie Calvert }

{ This unit runs a city; }

{            10                    1  2  3
    1  4  7  11      10 11 12 13 14    4  5  6
    2  5  8  12          7  8  9       7  8  9
    3  6  9  13          4  5  6    10 11 12 13  14
             14          1  2  3
}

interface

uses
  Windows;

const
  XStreets = 12;
  YStreets = 10;

type
  TDirection = (North, East, South, West);
```

```
    TTownAry = array[0..XStreets  - 1, 0..YStreets - 1] of Integer;

    TCityPlace = record
      X, Y: Integer;
      Value: Integer;
    end;

    TCityPlaceAry = array[1..14] of TCityPlace;

    TMazeTown = class
    private
      FDirection: TDirection;
      FXSpot, FYSpot: Integer;
      FCurrentView: TCityPlaceAry;
      FViewChanged: Boolean;
      function CheckForwardMove: Boolean;
      procedure FillOutCurrentView;
      function GetNewDir(K: ShortInt): TDirection;
    public
      constructor Create(X, Y: Integer; Dir: TDirection);
      function GetWallSegment(X, Y: Integer): Integer;
      procedure Move(Direction: TDirection);
      procedure Key(vKey: Word);
      property CurrentView: TCityPlaceAry read FCurrentView write FCurrentView;
      property Direction: TDirection read FDirection write FDirection;
      property ViewChanged: Boolean read FViewChanged;
    end;

implementation

const
  FTownAry: TTownAry =
    ((1,1,1,1,1,1,1,1,1,1),
     (1,0,1,0,0,0,0,0,0,1),
     (1,0,0,0,1,1,0,1,1,1),
     (1,0,0,1,1,0,0,0,0,1),
     (1,1,1,1,1,1,1,0,1,1),
     (1,0,0,0,1,0,0,0,0,1),
     (1,1,1,1,0,1,0,1,0,1),
     (1,0,0,0,0,0,0,0,0,1),
     (1,1,1,1,1,1,1,1,0,1),
     (1,0,0,1,0,1,0,0,0,1),
     (1,1,0,0,0,0,0,1,0,1),
     (1,1,1,1,1,1,1,1,1,1)
     );


constructor TMazeTown.Create(X, Y: Integer; Dir: TDirection);
begin
  inherited Create;
  FXSpot := X;
  FYSpot := Y;
  FDirection := Dir;
  FillOutCurrentView;
end;
```

continues

Listing 33.4. continued

```
function TMazeTown.GetWallSegment(X, Y: Integer): Integer;
begin
  Result := FTownAry[X, Y];
end;

{ Fill out a record describing a location in a city. }
function GetCityPlace(X, Y: Integer): TCityPlace;
var
  C: TCityPlace;
begin
  C.X := X;
  C.Y := Y;
  if (X < 0) or (X > XStreets) or
     (Y < 0) or (Y > YStreets + 1) then
    C.Value := -1
  else
    C.Value := FTownAry[Y, X];
  Result := C;
end;

procedure TMazeTown.FillOutCurrentView;
begin
  case FDirection of
    North: begin
      FCurrentView[1] := GetCityPlace(FXSpot - 1, FYSpot);
      FCurrentView[2] := GetCityPlace(FXSpot, FYSpot);
      FCurrentView[3] := GetCityPlace(FXSpot + 1, FYSpot);
      FCurrentView[4] := GetCityPlace(FXSpot - 1, FYSpot - 1);
      FCurrentView[5] := GetCityPlace(FXSpot, FYSpot - 1);
      FCurrentView[6] := GetCityPlace(FXSpot + 1, FYSpot - 1);
      FCurrentView[7] := GetCityPlace(FXSpot - 1, FYSpot - 2);
      FCurrentView[8] := GetCityPlace(FXSpot, FYSpot - 2);
      FCurrentView[9] := GetCityPlace(FXSpot + 1, FYSpot - 2);
      FCurrentView[10] := GetCityPlace(FXSpot - 2, FYSpot - 3);
      FCurrentView[11] := GetCityPlace(FXSpot - 1, FYSpot - 3);
      FCurrentView[12] := GetCityPlace(FXSpot, FYSpot - 3);
      FCurrentView[13] := GetCityPlace(FXSpot + 1, FYSpot - 3);
      FCurrentView[14] := GetCityPlace(FXSpot + 2, FYSpot - 3);
    end;

    East: begin
      FCurrentView[1] := GetCityPlace(FXSpot, FYSpot - 1);
      FCurrentView[2] := GetCityPlace(FXSpot, FYSpot);
      FCurrentView[3] := GetCityPlace(FXSpot, FYSpot + 1);
      FCurrentView[4] := GetCityPlace(FXSpot + 1, FYSpot - 1);
      FCurrentView[5] := GetCityPlace(FXSpot + 1, FYSpot);
      FCurrentView[6] := GetCityPlace(FXSpot + 1, FYSpot + 1);
      FCurrentView[7] := GetCityPlace(FXSpot + 2, FYSpot - 1);
      FCurrentView[8] := GetCityPlace(FXSpot + 2, FYSpot);
      FCurrentView[9] := GetCityPlace(FXSpot + 2, FYSpot + 1);
      FCurrentView[10] := GetCityPlace(FXSpot + 3, FYSpot - 2);
      FCurrentView[11] := GetCityPlace(FXSpot + 3, FYSpot - 1);
      FCurrentView[12] := GetCityPlace(FXSpot + 3, FYSpot);
      FCurrentView[13] := GetCityPlace(FXSpot + 3, FYSpot + 1);
      FCurrentView[14] := GetCityPlace(FXSpot + 3, FYSpot + 2);
    end;
```

```
{$ifDef LookingFromAbove}
South: begin
  FCurrentView[1] := GetCityPlace(FXSpot - 1, FYSpot);
  FCurrentView[2] := GetCityPlace(FXSpot, FYSpot);
  FCurrentView[3] := GetCityPlace(FXSpot + 1, FYSpot);
  FCurrentView[4] := GetCityPlace(FXSpot - 1, FYSpot + 1);
  FCurrentView[5] := GetCityPlace(FXSpot, FYSpot + 1);
  FCurrentView[6] := GetCityPlace(FXSpot + 1, FYSpot + 1);
  FCurrentView[7] := GetCityPlace(FXSpot - 1, FYSpot + 2);
  FCurrentView[8] := GetCityPlace(FXSpot, FYSpot + 2);
  FCurrentView[9] := GetCityPlace(FXSpot + 1, FYSpot + 2);
  FCurrentView[10] := GetCityPlace(FXSpot - 2, FYSpot + 3);
  FCurrentView[11] := GetCityPlace(FXSpot - 1, FYSpot + 3);
  FCurrentView[12] := GetCityPlace(FXSpot, FYSpot + 3);
  FCurrentView[13] := GetCityPlace(FXSpot + 1, FYSpot + 3);
  FCurrentView[14] := GetCityPlace(FXSpot + 2, FYSpot + 3);
end;
West: begin
  FCurrentView[1] := GetCityPlace(FXSpot, FYSpot - 1);
  FCurrentView[2] := GetCityPlace(FXSpot, FYSpot);
  FCurrentView[3] := GetCityPlace(FXSpot, FYSpot + 1);
  FCurrentView[4] := GetCityPlace(FXSpot - 1, FYSpot - 1);
  FCurrentView[5] := GetCityPlace(FXSpot - 1, FYSpot);
  FCurrentView[6] := GetCityPlace(FXSpot - 1, FYSpot + 1);
  FCurrentView[7] := GetCityPlace(FXSpot - 2, FYSpot - 1);
  FCurrentView[8] := GetCityPlace(FXSpot - 2, FYSpot);
  FCurrentView[9] := GetCityPlace(FXSpot - 2, FYSpot + 1);
  FCurrentView[10] := GetCityPlace(FXSpot - 3, FYSpot - 2);
  FCurrentView[11] := GetCityPlace(FXSpot - 3, FYSpot - 1);
  FCurrentView[12] := GetCityPlace(FXSpot - 3, FYSpot);
  FCurrentView[13] := GetCityPlace(FXSpot - 3, FYSpot + 1);
  FCurrentView[14] := GetCityPlace(FXSpot - 3, FYSpot + 2);
end;
{$else}
South: begin
  FCurrentView[1] := GetCityPlace(FXSpot + 1, FYSpot);
  FCurrentView[2] := GetCityPlace(FXSpot, FYSpot);
  FCurrentView[3] := GetCityPlace(FXSpot - 1, FYSpot);
  FCurrentView[4] := GetCityPlace(FXSpot + 1, FYSpot + 1);
  FCurrentView[5] := GetCityPlace(FXSpot, FYSpot + 1);
  FCurrentView[6] := GetCityPlace(FXSpot - 1, FYSpot + 1);
  FCurrentView[7] := GetCityPlace(FXSpot + 1, FYSpot + 2);
  FCurrentView[8] := GetCityPlace(FXSpot, FYSpot + 2);
  FCurrentView[9] := GetCityPlace(FXSpot - 1, FYSpot + 2);
  FCurrentView[10] := GetCityPlace(FXSpot + 2, FYSpot + 3);
  FCurrentView[11] := GetCityPlace(FXSpot + 1, FYSpot + 3);
  FCurrentView[12] := GetCityPlace(FXSpot, FYSpot + 3);
  FCurrentView[13] := GetCityPlace(FXSpot - 1, FYSpot + 3);
  FCurrentView[14] := GetCityPlace(FXSpot - 2, FYSpot + 3);
end;

West: begin
  FCurrentView[1] := GetCityPlace(FXSpot, FYSpot + 1);
  FCurrentView[2] := GetCityPlace(FXSpot, FYSpot);
  FCurrentView[3] := GetCityPlace(FXSpot, FYSpot - 1);
  FCurrentView[4] := GetCityPlace(FXSpot - 1, FYSpot + 1);
```

continues

Listing 33.4. continued

```pascal
      FCurrentView[5] := GetCityPlace(FXSpot - 1, FYSpot);
      FCurrentView[6] := GetCityPlace(FXSpot - 1, FYSpot - 1);
      FCurrentView[7] := GetCityPlace(FXSpot - 2, FYSpot + 1);
      FCurrentView[8] := GetCityPlace(FXSpot - 2, FYSpot);
      FCurrentView[9] := GetCityPlace(FXSpot - 2, FYSpot - 1);
      FCurrentView[10] := GetCityPlace(FXSpot - 3, FYSpot + 2);
      FCurrentView[11] := GetCityPlace(FXSpot - 3, FYSpot + 1);
      FCurrentView[12] := GetCityPlace(FXSpot - 3, FYSpot);
      FCurrentView[13] := GetCityPlace(FXSpot - 3, FYSpot - 1);
      FCurrentView[14] := GetCityPlace(FXSpot - 3, FYSpot - 2);
    end;
   {$endif}
  end;
end;

function TMazeTown.CheckForwardMove: Boolean;
var
  X, Y: Integer;
begin
  X := FXSpot;
  Y := FYSpot;
  case FDirection of
    North: Dec(Y);
    South: Inc(Y);
    East: Inc(X);
    West: Dec(X);
  end;
  if FTownAry[Y, X] = 0 then begin
    FXSpot := X;
    FYSpot := Y;
    FViewChanged := True;
    Result := True
  end else begin
    FViewChanged := False;
    Result := False;
  end;
end;

function TMazeTown.GetNewDir(K: ShortInt): TDirection;
var
  NewDir: ShortInt;
begin
  NewDir := Ord(FDirection) + K;
  if NewDir = -1 then NewDir := 3;
  if NewDir = 4 then NewDir := 0;
  if NewDir = 5 then NewDir := 1;
  GetNewDir := TDirection(NewDir);
end;

procedure TMazeTown.Key(vKey: Word);
var
  NewDir: TDirection;
```

```
begin
  case vKey of
    vk_Up: NewDir := FDirection;
    vk_Left: NewDir := GetNewDir(-1);
    vk_Right: NewDir := GetNewDir(1);
    vk_Down: NewDir := GetNewDir(2);
  else
    NewDir := FDirection;
  end;
  Move(NewDir);
end;

procedure TMazeTown.Move(Direction: TDirection);
begin
  case Direction of

    North: begin
      if FDirection = North then
        CheckForwardMove
      else begin
        FDirection := North;
        FViewChanged := True;
      end;
    end;

    West: begin
      if FDirection = West then
        CheckForwardMove
      else begin
        FDirection := West;
        FViewChanged := True;
      end;
    end;

    East: begin
      if FDirection = East then
        CheckForwardMove
      else begin
        FDirection := East;
        FViewChanged := True;
      end;
    end;

    South: begin
      if FDirection = South then
        CheckForwardMove
      else begin
        FDirection := South;
        FViewChanged := True;
      end;
    end;
  end;
  if ViewChanged then
    FillOutCurrentView;
end;

end.
```

Listing 33.5. The Entity program helps the TWorldView object display an overhead view of the world.

```
unit Entity;

{ Copyright (c) 1996 by Charlie Calvert }

interface

uses
  Classes, dbList, SysUtils,
  Windows, Blini;

const
  MaxX = 255;
  MaxY = 252;
  ftSage = 100;
  ftSnake = 101;
  ftMonastery = 102;

const
  MaxCreatures = 3;
  CAry: array[0..(MaxCreatures - 1)] of string =
    ('Sage', 'Snake', 'Monastery');


type
  TMapType = (mtGrass, mtRoad, mtSwamp,
              mtWater, mtFootHill, mtMountain,
              mtWater2);

  { Its the job of this unit to make the user see it as Col, Row. So
    Even though its stored backwards in the disk file, this unit flips
    things around so that its users think its stored Col, Row. }
  TMap = array[1..MaxY,1..MaxX] of Byte;

  TCreature = class;

  TCreatureList = class(TList)
  private
    ScreenFile: string;
    CreatureFile: string;
    FMap: TMap;
  private
    function GetMapItem(Col, Row: Integer): Byte;
    procedure SetMapItem(Col, Row: Integer; Val: Byte);
  public
    constructor Create; virtual;
    destructor Destroy; override;
    function Load: Boolean;
    function Store: Boolean;
    procedure NewCreature(ID, Name: string;
                          AType, ACol, ARow, AChap, AQuest: Word);
{   procedure UpDate(Index: Integer; ID, Name: string;
                     AType, ACol, ARow, AChap, AQuest: Word); }
    procedure FreeAll;
    procedure FindCreatures;
    function GetColor(i: Byte): TColorRef;
```

```
    function GetMapType(Col, Row: Integer): string;
    function CordToName(Col: Integer; Row: Integer): string;
    function CordToType(Col: Integer; Row: Integer): string;
    function CordToCreature(Col: Integer; Row: Integer): TCreature;
  published
    property Map[Col, Row: Integer]: Byte read GetMapItem write SetMapItem;


  end;

  TCreature = class
  private
    FID: string;
    FName: string;
    FKind: Word;
    FCol, FRow: Word;
    FChapter, FQuestion: Word;
    function GetType: string;
  public
    procedure Store(Writer: TWriter);
    procedure Load(Reader: TReader);
    property ID: string read FID write FID;
    property Name: string read FName write FName;
    property TypeStr: string read GetType;
    property Kind: Word read FKind write FKind;
    property Col: Word read FCol write FCol;
    property Row: Word read FRow write FRow;
    property Question: Word read FQuestion write FQuestion;
    property Chapter: Word read FChapter write FChapter;
  end;

implementation

uses
  Binary, UtilBox, Dialogs;

constructor TCreatureList.Create;
begin
  inherited Create;
  ScreenFile := PathToExe + 'SCREEN.DTA';
  CreatureFile := PathToExe + 'CLIST.DTA';
  FindCreatures;
end;

destructor TCreatureList.Destroy;
begin
  inherited Destroy;
end;

function TCreatureList.Load: Boolean;
var
  FStream: TFileStream;
  FReader: TReader;
  C: TCreature;
  i: Word;
  FCreatureCount: Word;
```

continues

Listing 33.5. continued

```
begin
  Load := False;
  if not FileExists(CreatureFile) then
    Exit;
  FStream := TFileStream.Create(CreatureFile, fmOpenRead);
  FReader := TReader.Create(FStream, 4096);
  FCreatureCount := FReader.ReadInteger;
  for i := 0 to FCreatureCount - 1 do begin
    C := TCreature.Create;
    C.Load(FReader);
    Add(C);
  end;
  FReader.Free;
  FStream.Free;
  Load := True;
end;

function TCreatureList.Store: Boolean;
var
  FStream: TFileStream;
  FWriter: TWriter;
  i: Integer;
begin
  FStream := TFileStream.Create(CreatureFile, fmCreate);
  FWriter := TWriter.Create(FStream, 4096);
  FWriter.WriteInteger(Count);
  First;
  for i := 0 to Count - 1 do
    TCreature(Items[i]).Store(FWriter);
  FWriter.Free;
  FStream.Free;
  Store := True;
end;

procedure TCreatureList.FreeAll;
var
  i: Integer;
begin
  First;
  for i := 0 to Count - 1 do
    TCreature(Items[i]).Free;
  Clear;
end;

procedure TCreatureList.NewCreature(ID, Name: string;
                        AType, ACol, ARow, AChap, AQuest: Word);
var
  C: TCreature;
begin
  C := TCreature.Create;
  C.ID := ID;
  C.Name := Name;
  C.Kind := AType;
  C.Col := ACol;
  C.Row := ARow;
  C.Question := AQuest;
```

```
  C.Chapter := AChap;
  Add(C);
end;

{
procedure TCreatureList.UpDate(Index: Integer; ID, Name: string;
                              AType, ACol, ARow, AChap, AQuest: Word);
var
  C: TCreature;
begin
  C := Items[Index];
  C.ID := ID;
  C.Name := Name;
  C.Kind := AType;
  C.Col := ACol;
  C.Row := ARow;
  C.Chapter := AChap;
  C.Question := AQuest;
end;
 }

function TCreatureList.GetMapItem(Col, Row: Integer): Byte;
begin
  Result := FMap[Row, Col];
end;

procedure TCreatureList.SetMapItem(Col, Row: Integer; Val: Byte);
begin
  FMap[Row, Col] := Val;
end;

procedure TCreatureList.FindCreatures;
var
  i: Integer;
  C: TCreature;
  Temp: Byte;
  F: file of TMap;
begin
  System.Assign(F, ScreenFile);
  try
    System.Reset(F);
  except
    on E:EInOutError do begin
      E.Message := E.Message + ': ' + Screenfile;
      raise
    end;
  end;
  System.Read(F, FMap);
  System.Close(F);
  Load;
  for i := 0 to Count - 1 do begin
    C := Items[i];
    Temp := FMap[C.Row, C.Col];
    SetBit(7, 1, Temp);
    FMap[C.Row, C.Col] := Temp;
  end;
end;
```

continues

Listing 33.5. continued

```
function TCreatureList.GetColor(i: Byte): TColorRef;
{ GrassType, RoadType, SwampType,
  WaterType, FootHillType, MountainType }
var
  C: TColorRef;
begin
  if BitOn(7, i) then
    i := 50;
  case i of
    0: C := RGB(0, 255, 0);
    1: C := RGB(127, 127, 127);
    2: C := RGB(127, 0, 0);
    3: C := RGB(0, 0, 255);
    4: C := RGB(255, 255, 0);
    5: C := RGB(255, 255, 255);
   50: C := RGB(255, 0, 0);
  else
      C := RGB(0, 0, 0);
  end;
  GetColor := C;
end;

function TCreatureList.GetMapType(Col, Row: Integer): string;
{ GrassType, RoadType, SwampType,
  WaterType, FootHillType, MountainType }
var
  S: string;
  AType: Integer;
begin
  AType := Map[Col + 1, Row + 1];
  if BitOn(7, AType) then
    AType := 50;
  case AType of
    0: S := 'Grass';
    1: S := 'Road';
    2: S := 'Swamp';
    3: S := 'Water';
    4: S := 'FootHill';
    5: S := 'Mountain';
   50: S := CordToType(Col, Row);
  end;
  Result := S;
end;

function TCreatureList.CordToName(Col: Integer; Row: Integer): string;
var
  C: TCreature;
begin
  C := CordToCreature(Col, Row);
  if C <> nil then
    Result := C.Name
  else
    Result := 'Not Found';
end;
```

```
function TCreatureList.CordToType(Col: Integer; Row: Integer): string;
var
  C: TCreature;
begin
  C := CordToCreature(Col, Row);
  if C <> nil then
    Result := C.TypeStr
  else
    Result := 'Not Found';
end;

function TCreatureList.CordToCreature(Col: Integer; Row: Integer): TCreature;
var
  i: Integer;
  C: TCreature;
begin
  Inc(Col); Inc(Row);
  First;
  for i := 0 to Count - 1 do begin
    C := Items[i];
    if (Col = C.Col) and (Row = C.Row) then begin
      CordToCreature := C;
      Exit;
    end;
  end;
  CordToCreature := nil;
end;

{*** TCreature ***}

function TCreature.GetType: string;
begin
  GetType := CAry[FKind];
end;

procedure TCreature.Store(Writer: TWriter);
begin
  Writer.WriteStr(FID);
  Writer.WriteStr(FName);
  Writer.WriteInteger(FKind);
  Writer.WriteInteger(FRow);
  Writer.WriteInteger(FCol);
  Writer.WriteInteger(FQuestion);
  Writer.WriteInteger(FChapter);
end;

procedure TCreature.Load(Reader: TReader);
begin
  FID := Reader.ReadStr;
  FName := Reader.ReadStr;
  FKind := Reader.ReadInteger;
  FRow := Reader.ReadInteger;
  FCol := Reader.ReadInteger;
  FQuestion := Reader.ReadInteger;
  FChapter := Reader.ReadInteger;
end;

end.
```

Listing 33.6. The SMALLM1.PAS unit defines a high-level view of the world map.

```pascal
unit smallmp1;

{ Copyright (c) 1996 by Charlie Calvert }

{ See a relatively high level view of the world. In this view,
  you can see the whole world at once. }

interface

uses
  SysUtils, Windows, Messages,
  Classes, Graphics, Controls,
  Forms, Dialogs, ExtCtrls;

type
  TWorldMap = class(TForm)
    Image1: TImage;
  private
    procedure CreateParams(var Params: TCreateParams); override;
  end;

var
  WorldMap: TWorldMap;

implementation

{$R *.DFM}

procedure TWorldMap.CreateParams(var Params: TCreateParams);
begin
  inherited CreateParams(Params);
  Params.ExStyle := ws_ex_Topmost;
end;

end.
```

Listing 33.7. The Status dialog would allow the user to see the status of the characters in the game.

```pascal
unit status;

{ Copyright (c) 1996 by Charlie Calvert }

interface

uses
  SysUtils, Windows, Messages,
  Classes, Graphics, Controls,
  Forms, Dialogs, StdCtrls,
  Buttons, ExtCtrls, Gauges;
```

```
type
  TStatusDlg = class(TForm)
    Bevel1: TBevel;
    BitBtn1: TBitBtn;
    Gauge1: TGauge;
  private
    procedure CreateParams(var Params: TCreateParams); override;
  public
    procedure ShowModalPaint;
  end;

var
  StatusDlg: TStatusDlg;

implementation

{$R *.DFM}

procedure TStatusDlg.CreateParams(var Params: TCreateParams);
begin
  inherited CreateParams(Params);
  Params.ExStyle := ws_Ex_Topmost;
  Params.Style := Params.Style or ws_DlgFrame;
end;

procedure TStatusDlg.ShowModalPaint;
begin
  ShowModal;
end;

end.
```

Listing 33.8. The DLL that contains the bitmaps used by XFire program.

```
library BitDll;
{
  This library consists mostly of a huge Resource
  that contains all the bitmaps for the XFire or
  related programs.

  The goal is to call LoadLibrary and FreeLibrary
  when using this DLL. That way the huge resources in
  this DLL will only be in memory for a short time. This
  is better than loading the resource into your main
  program. }

{$R FIRES.RES}

begin
end.
```

Listing 33.9. The FIRES.RC file for the BitDll project.

```
Back BITMAP "PANEL.BMP"
City BITMAP "CITYPAN.BMP"
ForeWall BITMAP "FOREWALL.BMP"
MidWall BITMAP "MIDWALL.BMP"
FrontWall Bitmap "FRNTWALL.BMP"
```

When this program starts, you are presented with a small window with a menu on top. If you choose the Start Game menu option, you will get an overhead view of the scrolling world. You can move through this world by pressing the arrow keys.

If you select the F10 key, the menu will appear, allowing you to close the application or access certain of its features. You can use the menu to shift between the world view and the maze view. You can also pop up dialogs on top of the maze view or world view. The access to menus and dialogs shows how you can use standard Delphi features to enhance a Direct Draw program.

There is obviously more code here than could possibly be examined in one single chapter. So rather than stepping through the code line-by-line in my usual fashion, I will instead try to show you the structure of the program, and to focus on a few technical highlights.

An Overview of XFire

Below you will find a list of the main units used by the program, along with their classes, and a brief description of their purpose:

```
DPR File
XFire
Creates Form1.

UNITS
Main
   Form: Form1

GameBrd1 - GameBoard
  Form: None
  Classes: TWorldBoard, TCityBoard, TTestBoard
  Handles the drawing tasks for both the over head view and the maze view.

DrawBrd1 - DrawBoard
  Classes: TDrawDirect
  Contains a class from which TWorldBoard and TCityBoard descend

Entity
  Form none
  Classess: TCreatureList, TCreature
  Helper classes used by TWorldBoard when it draws an overhead view of the world.
```

MzTown - MazeTown
  Classes: TMazeTown
  Description: Helper calls that runs the city maze displayed by TCityBoard

Smallmp1 - SmallMap
  Form: WorldMap
  Classess: TWorldMap
  Description: Show a small map of the entire world

Status:
  Form: StatusDlg
  Classess: TStatusDlg
  Could display the status of the game and its characters or present other
information.

DIRECT DRAW UNITS
DDraw
DDUtils

HELPER UNITS
BLIini
Binary
DBList
OleBox
MathBox
PalBox
StrBox

OBJECTS
TObject
  TDrawDirect
    TWorldBoard
    TCityBoard
    TTestBoard

IUnknown
  IDirectDraw
  IDirectDrawPalette
  IDirectDrawClipper
  IDirectDrawSurface

TList
  TCreatureList

TObject
  TCreature

RESOURCE FILES
XFire.Res
Fires.Res
  Back BITMAP "PANEL.BMP"
  City BITMAP "CITYPAN.BMP"
  ForeWall BITMAP "FOREWALL.BMP"
  MidWall BITMAP "MIDWALL.BMP"
  FrontWall Bitmap "FRNTWALL.BMP"

The DrawBoard Unit

Perhaps the single most important piece of the XFire program is the reusable DrawBoard unit. This unit is kept in the XUNITS subdirectory, and not with the rest of the code for the XFire program. The reason for this is simply that it can be reused in multiple programs. In particular, it performs all the grunt work necessary to get Direct Draw up and running.

Take a look at this abbreviated version of the declaration for the TDrawDirect object:

```
TDrawDirect = class
  private
    FActive: Boolean;
    FBackGroundMap: string;
    FDirectDraw: IDirectDraw;
    FDDSBack: IDirectDrawSurface;
    FDDSFront: IDirectDrawSurface;
    FDDSWork: IDirectDrawSurface;
    FDDPal: IDirectDrawPalette;
    FHandle: HWnd;
    FTransColor: Integer;
  public
    constructor Create(Handle: Hwnd; BackGroundMapStr: string;
      TransColor: Integer); virtual;
    destructor Destroy; override;
    procedure DestroyObjects; virtual;
    procedure DoOneFlip; virtual;
    function InitObjects: Boolean; virtual;
    function Pause: Boolean; virtual;
    procedure Restore;
    property Active: Boolean read fActive write fActive;
    property BackGroundMap: string read FBackGroundMap write FBackGroundMap;
    property DirectDraw: IDirectDraw read FDirectDraw write FDirectDraw;
    property FrontSurface: IDirectDrawSurface read FDDSFront write FDDSFront;
    property BackSurface: IDirectDrawSurface read FDDSBack write FDDSBack;
    property WorkSurface: IDirectDrawSurface read FDDSWork write FDDSWork;
    property Palette: IDirectDrawPalette read FDDPal write FDDPal;
  end;
```

You can see that this object has methods for creating and initializing Direct Draw, as well as properties representing all the key fields in a Direct Draw program. All of these fields will be initialized for you automatically. In particular, notice the DirectDraw, FrontSurface, BackSurface, WorkSurface, and Palette properties. Here are the main Direct Draw objects ready for you to use as you wish.

> **NOTE**
>
> Mike Scott and I did not work together on our code, so there are some slight differences in naming conventions between this chapter and the last. What I call the FrontSurface Mike calls a PrimarySurface, and what I call the BackSurface Mike calls a BackBuffer. My WorkSurface is a place for you to draw into as you wish. This surface, or some portion thereof, can then be blitted into the BackSurface. The final step is to flip the BackSurface up to the front so that the user can see it.

The key method in the DrawBoard unit is InitObjects:

```
function TDrawDirect.InitObjects: Boolean;
var
  hr: hResult;
begin
  Result := False;
  DDTest(DirectDrawCreate(nil, IDirectDraw(FDirectDraw), nil), 'InitObjects');
  DDTest(FDirectDraw.SetCooperativeLevel(FHandle, DDSCL_EXCLUSIVE or
  ➥DDSCL_FULLSCREEN), 'InitObjects');
  hr := FDirectDraw.SetDisplayMode(640, 480, 8);
  if(hr <> DD_OK) then
    ErrorEvent(hr, 'InitObjects');
  CreateFront;
  SetUpBack;
  if not CreateDDSurface(FWorkSurface, BackGroundMap) then Exit;
  FActive := True;
  Result := True;
end;
```

This method is the rough equivalent of the FormShow methods that Mike showed you in the previous chapter. It initializes Direct Draw, sets up the screen, creates front, back, and work drawing surfaces, and sets up the palette.

Most of the key code found in the InitObjects method is split off into separate methods such as CreateFront:

```
function TDrawDirect.CreateFront: Boolean;
var
  SurfaceDesc: TDDSurfaceDesc;
  hr: HResult;
begin
  Result := False;
  FillChar(SurfaceDesc, sizeOf(TDDSurfaceDesc), 0);
  SurfaceDesc.dwSize := sizeof(TDDSurfaceDesc);
  SurfaceDesc.dwFlags := DDSD_CAPS or DDSD_BACKBUFFERCOUNT;
  SurfaceDesc.ddsCaps.dwCaps := DDSCAPS_PRIMARYSURFACE or
                                DDSCAPS_FLIP or
                                DDSCAPS_COMPLEX;
  SurfaceDesc.dwBackBufferCount := 1;
  hr := FDirectDraw.CreateSurface(SurfaceDesc, FDDSFront, nil);
  if hr <> DD_OK then
    ErrorEvent(hr, 'CreateFront')
  else
    Result := True;
end;
```

In short, I perform all the same steps that Mike showed you, and in the same order, but I prefer to handle each chore in its own routine.

After you initialize the object, you will usually start a timer, which will call the DoOneFlip method to flip the background surface to the front:

```
procedure TDrawDirect.DoOneFlip;
begin
  try
```

```
 if FActive then begin
    BackGroundBlits;
    repeat until MakeItSo(FDDSFront.Flip(nil, DDFLIP_WAIT));
  end;
except
  on Exception do
    ErrorEvent(0, 'Flipping');
end;
end;
```

Each time DoOneFlip is called, it ensures that a method called BackGroundBlits is called:

```
function TDrawDirect.BackGroundBlits: Boolean;
var
  R: TRect;
  hr: HResult;
begin
  R := Rect(0, 0, 639, 480);
  hr := BackSurface.BltFast(0, 0, WorkSurface, R,
    DDBLTFAST_WAIT or DDBLTFAST_SRCCOLORKEY);
  Result := Succeeded(hr);
  if not Result then
    ErrorEvent(hr, 'BackGround');
end;
```

This method provides you with your opportunity to draw to the back surface before it gets flipped up front.

BackGroundBlits is declared as virtual; in most cases you will override this method and perform your own special blitting operations. Had I been designing components, I might have made this an event rather than a method, but those kinds of changes could be made easily enough in your own code.

The GameBoard Unit

I designed the TDrawDirect object to be a base object for the classes that do the real work in your programs. The idea, once again, was to create a base object that would automatically initialize Direct Draw, asking only that you pass in the name of the bitmap to be displayed in the background, and the value of a transparent color.

The GameBoard unit shows how to implement objects that descend from TDrawDirect. In particular, there are two objects, one called TWorldBoard and the other called TCityBoard. As explained earlier, TWorldBoard is the object that lets you look down on a scrolling world from above. TCityBoard is the object that lets you walk through a maze.

I have also included a small object called TTestBoard that is close to a simplest possible case descended of TDrawDirect. TTestBoard creates its own InitObjects method:

```
function TTestBoard.InitObjects: Boolean;
begin
  Inherited InitObjects;
  CreateDDSurface(FrontWall, 'FrontWall');
  Result := True;
end;
```

This code first calls the inherited InitObjects, which ensures that Direct Draw is set up correctly, and that the front, back, and work surfaces are in place. The code then calls a method of TDrawDirect that creates a new IDirectDrawSurface object. In particular, the object to be created is called FrontWall, and the name of the bitmap to be displayed on the surface is FrontWall.

You can see that TDrawDirect makes it easy for you to work with Direct Draw. Instead of writing some 75 lines of ugly code, you can just call the inherited InitObjects. The CreateDDSurface method helps you perform a common task with a minimum of fuss.

The TDrawDirect object also overrides BackGroundBlits:

```
function TTestBoard.BackGroundBlits: Boolean;
var
  R: TRect;
begin
  inherited BackGroundBlits;
  FTimerOdd := not FTimerOdd;
  if FTimerOdd then begin
    R := Rect(0, 0, 187, 384);
    BackSurface.BltFast(0, 0, FrontWall, R, DDBLTFAST_SRCCOLORKEY)
  end else begin
    R := Rect(24, 25, 187, 384);
    BackSurface.BltFast(0, 0, FrontWall, R, DDBLTFAST_SRCCOLORKEY)
  end;
  Result := True;
end;
```

This method calls the inherited BackGroundBlits and then goes on to perform some additional processing. In particular, it manipulates a variable called FTimerOdd that flips back and forth between True and False each time DoOneFlip is called. In short, its value is usually swapped when a timer message is sent to the main window of the program. If FTimerOdd is True, then one image is blitted to the screen. If it is False, a slightly different image is blitted to the screen.

Taken together, the calls to InitObjects and BackGroundBlits represent the minimum amount of code that you need to write to do anything useful with the TDrawDirect object. Clearly, it is simpler to use TDrawDirect and these two methods than it is to write a Direct Draw program from scratch.

NOTE

You should note, however, that Mike Scott is creating, or has created, a more elaborate system for working with Direct Draw. If you think Direct Draw is going to play a big part in your life, you should consider getting his product, rather than working with the simple objects I show here.

Creating a Maze

The maze shown with the TCityBoard object is defined internally as a simple two-dimensional array found in MZTOWN.PAS:

```
FTownAry: TTownAry =
    ((1,1,1,1,1,1,1,1,1,1),
     (1,0,1,0,0,0,0,0,0,1),
     (1,0,0,0,1,1,0,1,1,1),
     (1,0,0,1,1,0,0,0,0,1),
     (1,1,1,1,1,1,1,0,1,1),
     (1,0,0,0,0,1,0,0,0,1),
     (1,1,1,1,0,1,0,1,0,1),
     (1,0,0,0,0,0,0,0,0,1),
     (1,1,1,1,1,1,1,1,0,1),
     (1,0,0,1,0,1,0,0,0,1),
     (1,1,0,0,0,0,1,0,1),
     (1,1,1,1,1,1,1,1,1,1)
    );
```

The 1s in this array represent the wall, and the 0s represent the open watery spaces in the maze. When you first enter the maze, you are located in row 3, column 2. Your goal, if there is one, might be to reach row 10, column 2. You should perhaps spend a few moments wandering through the maze, seeing if you can compare the places you go to the zeroes and ones shown above. You can change the shape of the maze by altering the patterns of ones and zeros shown above.

Wherever you are standing in the maze, you can see only the area directly in front of you. In particular, you can see part of the spaces immediately to your right and left, plus an additional 11 spaces out in front of you. When I say the word *space*, I am referring to a single element in the TTownAry shown above.

Here is a simple depiction of spaces you can see from any one particular spot:

```
            10
 1   4   7  11
 2   5   8  12
 3   6   9  13
            14
```

The user is always located on spot 2 in this scenario. The places to her immediate left or right are 1 and 3. The other visible areas appear directly in front of the person running the maze.

If the person were to turn to the right, the following array of numbers would represent her world view:

```
 1   2   3
     4   5   6
     7   8   9
10  11  12  13  14
```

In this case the maze runner is looking down the page toward number 5.

The key point to grasp here is that if position 5 is 0 in the TTownAry, the user will be able to see through to spot 8. If 8 is also a 0, the user can see to spot 12. If 12 is a 1, there will be a piece of the wall in that position.

Your goal as an artist is to draw shapes that fit each of the possibilities. The background should show the way things would look if all the visible areas are open. The next step is to draw pieces of the wall that fit in each of the numbered locations. If you look at the bitmaps that come in the directory for this application, you will find a series of 13 bitmaps, one depicting a wall in each of the possible locations shown above. The 14th location, of course, is occupied by the user.

To help you visualize the way this system works, I created a program called TestCoords that shows the view from above the maze, as shown in Figure 33.5. As you can tell, this is just a representation of a maze and does not give you the full three-dimensional sense that you get from the XFire program. For instance, the visible walls in this program are shown as 1s and the visible open spaces are shown as 0s. Anything outside the range of vision is simply blank.

FIGURE 33.5.

The view from above the maze, with the visible elements of the maze depicted as numbers.

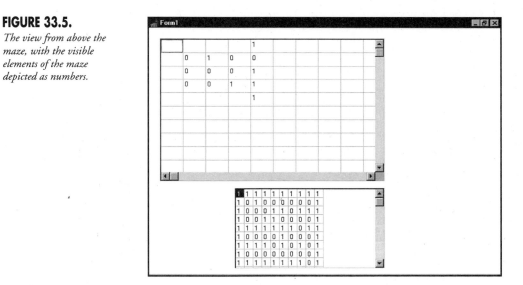

The TestCoords program (see Listing 33.10) is designed so that you cannot walk through walls nor see through walls. Therefore, it gives a sense of what the user experiences while moving through the maze. When you work with this program, you should have a picture of the TTownAry next to you, or you should use the visual representation of the array shown in the program. With its aid you should be able to navigate the maze. The point of this exercise, once again, is to help you visualize how the maze used by the TCityBoard object is put together.

Listing 33.10. The code for the TestCoords program.

```
unit main;

{ This program serves as a test pattern for drawing the walls
  of a city. It provides an easy to use test surface to check
  that the coordinates and values of the 14 visable wall squares
  are valid. The program draws the entire grid at the bottom
  of the screen, and then provides a way at the top of the
  screen to move the visible squares around on the screen.
}

interface

uses
  SysUtils, Windows, Messages,
  Classes, Graphics, Controls,
  Forms, Dialogs, StdCtrls,
  Grids, mzTown;

type
  TForm1 = class(TForm)
    sg: TStringGrid;
    StringGrid1: TStringGrid;
    procedure bNorthClick(Sender: TObject);
    procedure bWestClick(Sender: TObject);
    procedure bEastClick(Sender: TObject);
    procedure bSouthClick(Sender: TObject);
    procedure FormCreate(Sender: TObject);
    procedure FormDestroy(Sender: TObject);
    procedure FormKeyDown(Sender: TObject; var Key: Word;
      Shift: TShiftState);
  private
    mt: TMazeTown;
    procedure DrawAll;
    procedure DrawGrid;
  public
    { Public declarations }
  end;

var
  Form1: TForm1;

implementation

{$R *.DFM}


procedure TForm1.DrawAll;
var
  i, j: Integer;
begin
  for j := 0 to YStreets + 1 do
    for i := 0 to XStreets do
      SG.Cells[i, j] := '';
  for i := 1 to 14 do
    with mt.CurrentView[i] do
      if Value <> - 1 then
        SG.Cells[X, Y] := IntToStr(Value);
end;
```

```
procedure TForm1.bNorthClick(Sender: TObject);
begin
  mt.Move(North);
  if mt.ViewChanged then DrawAll;
end;

procedure TForm1.bWestClick(Sender: TObject);
begin
  Mt.Move(West);
  if mt.ViewChanged then DrawAll;
end;

procedure TForm1.bEastClick(Sender: TObject);
begin
  Mt.Move(East);
  if mt.ViewChanged then DrawAll;
end;

procedure TForm1.bSouthClick(Sender: TObject);
begin
  Mt.Move(South);
  if mt.ViewChanged then DrawAll;
end;

procedure TForm1.DrawGrid;
var
  i, j: Integer;
begin
  for j := 0 to YStreets - 1 do
    for i := 0 to XStreets - 1 do
      StringGrid1.Cells[j, i] := IntToStr(mt.GetWallSegment(i, j));
end;

procedure TForm1.FormCreate(Sender: TObject);
begin
  mt := TMazeTown.Create(1, 2, East);
  DrawGrid;
  DrawAll;
end;

procedure TForm1.FormDestroy(Sender: TObject);
begin
  mt.Free;
end;

procedure TForm1.FormKeyDown(Sender: TObject; var Key: Word;
  Shift: TShiftState);
begin
  case Key of
    vk_Left: mt.Key(vk_Left);
    vk_Right: mt.Key(vk_Right);
    vk_Up: mt.Key(vk_Up);
    vk_Down: mt.Key(vk_Down);
  end;
  if mt.ViewChanged then DrawAll;
end;

end.
```

The TMazeTown unit shown previously provides the methods necessary to aid the TCityBoard object when it draws the maze. In particular, all the calculations regarding the current location of the user, and her current view, are all performed inside TMazeTown. TCityBoard can then leave the navigation of the maze up to TMazeTown, and can instead concentrate on drawing the proper wall segments to the screen as necessary.

If you are interested in pursuing this subject further, you might want to see the book called *Dungeons of Discovery,* written by Clayton Walnum and published by Sams. It is written in C and uses WinG rather than the Games SDK, but it provides a more detailed explanation of the type of maze shown in the XFire program.

Scrolling Through a World

The TWorldBoard object works with an array similar to the one in the MZTown unit. However, the elements of this array are stored on disk in a file called SCREEN.DTA. The only logical manifestation of the array in the code is the following declaration from ENTITY.PAS:

```
const
  MaxX = 255;
  MaxY = 252;

type
  TMap = array[1..MaxY,1..MaxX] of Byte;
```

Rather than having just 1s and 0s in the array, TMap has up to 7 different values, defined by the following enumerated type:

```
TMapType = (mtGrass, mtRoad, mtSwamp,
            mtWater, mtFootHill, mtMountain,
            mtWater2);
```

In this array, the number 0 represents not an open watery place, but a grassy place. The number 1 represents a road, 2 is a swamp, 3 is water, 4 a foothill, 5 a mountain, and 6 an alternate shade of water. By using a variable like the FTimerOdd Boolean value shown above, you can switch back and forth between the two kinds of waters on each wm_Timer message, thereby at least theoretically creating the illusion of waves.

The TWorldMap object blits a series of tiny bitmaps to the screen. The actual bitmaps shown are dependent upon the values in the TMap array. For instance, if TMap says a particular location is grassy, TWorldMap blits a small chunk of grassy looking bitmap to the screen. By iterating through the array one element at a time, the code is able to blit a series of small watery, grassy or mountainous bitmaps to the screen, thereby creating a map like view of a fictitious country.

The bitmaps sent to the screen are stored inside large bitmaps found in the in a DLL called BITDLL.DLL. This DLL has a large resource file, called FIRE.RES. Notice that FIRE.RES has a number of bitmaps in it, and is over a megabyte in size. This large resources is the explanation for the large size of the BitDll. If you want to avoid working with such a large executable, you should store your bitmaps in a DLL, and load them into the executable only when they are needed, as shown in the XFire program. Or, if you prefer, you can store the Bitmaps in a RES file linked into the main program. It depends on where you want to keep all those large bitmaps.

Whenever the TWorldBoard object needs to know the value of a particular X and Y location on the map, it calls the `ReadMapItem` method from the TCreatureList object in the Entity unit:

```
function TCreatureList.ReadMapItem(Col, Row: Integer): Byte;
begin
  Result := FMap[Row, Col];
end;
```

This code is used to hide the `TMap` array from the outside world. As explained earlier, you should never allow one object to directly access the data of anther object. One of the reasons for doing this is shown here. The `TMap` array stores X and Y data in the opposite order from the one used by the TWorldBoard object. `ReadMapItem` therefore switches the value of the row and column information it stores. The act of reversing these values, however, is hidden from the consumers of this object. This will allow me to continue to present a consistent interface to the world, even if I later change the way I store this information.

If necessary, the TCreateList object can also convert the numerical values found at a particular location in the `TMap` array into a string which is meaningful to programmers:

```
function TCreatureList.GetMapType(Col, Row: Integer): string;
{ GrassType, RoadType, SwampType,
  WaterType, FootHillType, MountainType }
var
  S: string;
  AType: Integer;
begin
  AType := ReadMapItem(Col + 1, Row + 1);
  if BitOn(7, AType) then
    AType := 50;
  case AType of
    0: S := 'Grass';
    1: S := 'Road';
    2: S := 'Swamp';
    3: S := 'Water';
    4: S := 'FootHill';
    5: S := 'Mountain';
   50: S := CordToType(Col, Row);
  end;
  Result := S;
end;
```

Notice that a bit operation is performed on the values stored in the array. The first 7 bits of this value is used to depict the landscape, stating specifically whether it is grassy, mountainous, and so on. The eighth bit, however, is turned on if some kind of creature is living at a particular location on the map.

The actual type of creature is stored in a file called CLIST.DTA. You can look up information in CLIST.DTA by the coordinates of the creatures location in the TMap array. It would be difficult to store the actual record defining the creature in the TMap array because there is a wide range of information associated with these beasts. Some of that information, such as a name, could not be easily encoded using bit operations. As a result, the TCreature object in the Entity unit is used for tracking the details associated with a particular animal or person that you might find while wandering through the maze.

The code for creating CLIST.DTA is stored in the Entity unit. It's a bit more difficult to create the huge array stored in SCREEN.DTA. I did, however, write a program for creating such an array, and provide it on disc as MAKEWRLD.EXE, stored in the MAKEWRLD directory.

That is all I'm going to say about the XFire program. Clearly the explanation provided here is not complete. However, it should give you enough information to allow you to begin moving through the code of the program and finding out how specific parts of it work.

Summary

This chapter covered COM objects, fast graphics, and artificial environments. It's a fairly meaty chapter that would have been almost impossible to attempt in a book of this sort before the advent of several recent programming trends. With the advent of Delphi 2.0, the MCI interface, the Games SDK, and 3DR, it is now possible to accomplish a great deal with only a minimum of effort.

The degree to which computers simulate real world objects varies. For instance, the Notepad program has only a passing similarity to a real world notepad. In fact, one might say that it only makes use of a real world notepad as a metaphor, and does little else with the idea. The CALC.EXE program, on the other hand, looks and feels very much like a real world calculator.

Between these two extremes lies a whole world of possibilities. Some of the most interesting simulations performed by computers come from the game world. Programs such as SimCity, Heretic, or King's Quest VI allow us to enter an artificial environment that bares some faint resemblance to the world in which we actually live. The act of creating an artificial world or artificial environment is probably one of the most powerful tasks of which a computer is capable. It is also one of the most interesting for it weds the binary logic of a computer to the tidal swings of our imagination.

Until quite recently, the act of creating one of these artificial worlds required enormous effort on the part of skilled programmers. Now, however, we have programming environments, such as Windows, and programming tools, such as Delphi, which can be combined with high performance processors to give relatively easy access to the creation of artificial worlds.

Delphi Multimedia Programs

34

You can easily add multimedia features, such as sounds, movies, and music, to Delphi programs. This chapter shows how to achieve these ends using the multimedia control that is built into the Delphi environment.

When reading this chapter, you can expect to encounter five distinct sections. The first is a general discussion of multimedia. The remaining four sections explain:

- How to use the built-in Delphi multimedia control to play WAVE, MIDI, and AVI files. This section of the chapter also discusses accessing CD-ROM files.
- How to use Delphi to create presentation programs that utilize multimedia to explain a topic in clear and easy-to-understand terms.
- How to show an AVI file in a window on your form.
- How to know when the user starts playing a file; when the user stops playing a file; when a file reaches the end; when the user pauses a file; and, in general, how to track runtime information about the state of the multimedia player.

This chapter contains some rather detailed explanations of a few fundamental programming steps. I decided to include these programming basics because I wanted to be sure the relatively entertaining material in this chapter was accessible to a wide range of readers. The only challenging code in this chapter is found at the very end, when I discuss some low-level details of playing MIDI files.

As always, you can find the complete source code for all the programs on the *Unleashed* CD-ROM. MIDI, WAVE, and AVI files also are available in the MULTIMED subdirectory. You can use them to experiment with the sample code in this chapter.

Exploring Multimedia

Multimedia for Windows has developed over the last few years to the point where it is now commonplace. However, it's probably still worthwhile discussing the subject briefly in general terms, just to be sure that there is a common definition of the concepts involved.

Multimedia is a generic term. It refers to almost any form of animation, sound, or movie that is used on computers. Given this broad definition, it's possible to say that this chapter deals with a subset of multimedia that involves the following:

- Showing movies using Microsoft's Video for Windows files
- Playing music using MIDI and WAVE files
- Playing and recording sounds and voices using WAVE files

All of these formats can be handled by the Microsoft Multimedia Extensions to Windows, and are encapsulated in the TMediaPlayer control found on the Additional page in the Component Palette.

File Formats: How Much Disk Space Do I Need?

You learn about three different types of files while reading this chapter:

- Files that include an AVI extension produce video. Examples of these types of files might be ELEPHANT.AVI or FLOWERS.AVI.

- Files that include an MID extension produce music by using the Musical Instrument Digital Interface (or MIDI) format. Examples of these types of files might be JAZZ.MID or VIVALDI.MID.

- Files that include a WAV extension can be used to record sounds using Microsoft's WAVE technology. Examples of these types of files might be CRASH.WAV or SPEECH.WAV.

Of the three file formats discussed in this chapter, the AVI files usually are the largest. Even relatively short AVI films of one minute or less tend to take up five, or even 10, megabytes of disk space. It's possible to compress these files further, but the savings that result are usually fairly minimal.

AVI files come from video media of one sort or another. Usually they are short snippets of film transferred from a video camera. AVI can include sound, and can be shown in either black and white or color. The size of the window varies considerably, from 200×200 to full-screen. On the whole, however, these films typically are rather small; rarely more than a few inches in width or height, although Windows does support showing even these small files full-screen in 320×200 mode. There is distortion, however, when you blow a small file up to full-screen.

WAVE files also tend to be large, but not nearly as large as AVI files. A typical file ratio for a WAVE file is one minute of sound to one megabyte of disk space. One second of low-quality (8-bit mono, 11KHz sampling) sound can take up to 11,000 bytes of disk space. CD-quality sound (16-bit stereo, 44KHz sampling) can require up to 176,000 bytes of data per second. You can, however, record nearly anything on a WAVE file. For instance, the sound of glass breaking or the sound of someone singing could be handled inside a WAVE file. The quality of these files differs dramatically from instance to instance, but there's nothing preventing you from creating a high-quality sound file using the WAVE format. A lot of the quality is determined at digitization time. The same is true of AVI files: you can dial in the frame rate (the quality of motion) when digitizing. The basic formula is simple enough: the better the quality, the bigger file.

Unlike WAVE and AVI files, MIDI files can be extremely compact, yet offer superb sound quality. However, even good MIDI files often are ruined because they are played on systems with inadequate hardware, or hardware that has not been set up properly. In short, MIDI files offer excellent potential, but the art of playing them properly can be difficult to manage. Windows 95, however, has added some tools that make it much easier to get good sound out of MIDI files.

Every MIDI file is divided up into multiple tracks, and users generally record the sound one track at a time, with only one instrument on each track. If you play five or six of these tracks at the same time, the result can be the sound of an entire band. For instance, a typical MIDI file might feature the sound of drums on one track, bass on a second track, piano on a third track, and a horn on the fourth track. Depending on the hardware and software involved, you can record between three and 15 instruments on any one file. You can record the instruments using a MIDI connection, or you can literally write out the notes one at a time, as if you were composing sheet music. As a rule, MIDI records only instrumental notes, not vocal music. MIDI doesn't act like a tape recorder, capturing raw sound traveling through the air in waves. The sound is entirely synthesized by the hardware. MIDI captures the notes, the type of instrument to play the sound, and timing information; nothing more. It's extremely mathematical, and in that sense enables you to get very close to a pure musical form.

If you look at the same media from the point of view of the hardware, the formats appear in a quite different light. For instance, you can play AVI files on any machine that comes equipped with a functioning copy of Windows. The only requirements for playing AVI files are the Microsoft Video for Windows drivers, which are distributed free from a number of different sources. Decent reproduction of WAVE files, however, requires a sound card. Serious work with MIDI requires both a sound card and the presence of an instrument attached to your computer using a MIDI cable.

Hardware: What Kind of Machine Do I Need?

The two most important pieces of hardware required for multimedia are a sound card and a CD-ROM. CD-ROM disks are useful primarily because they give you a place to store large amounts of information. Sound cards, however, contain chips that make it possible to reproduce high-quality WAVE files, as well as any kind of MIDI file or the sound track for an AVI file. To make the sound from your card audible, you will want speakers, headphones, and possibly an amplifier. There is no reason that you can't plug the output jack from a sound card directly into your home stereo system.

When purchasing equipment, you might want to follow your general tastes when buying a stereo. If you are the type of person who wouldn't consider listening to music on anything less than a $1,000 stereo system, you should probably spend a similar sum of money to convert your computer into a multimedia machine. On the other hand, if you can get by listening to a $50 or $200 ghetto-blaster, you can probably convert your computer into a multimedia machine for a similar sum of money.

In general, high-quality machines have 16-bit sound cards, quad-speed CD-ROM drives, and speakers that range upwards of $200 in price. Low-end machines have 8-bit sound cards, double-speed CD-ROM drives, and speakers that cost in the range of $10 to $50 dollars. Of course, these are estimates, circa 1995, and by the time you read this any prices quoted here will almost certainly have dropped.

Why Bother with Multimedia?

The final topic in the general discussion section involves the whole question of why anyone would want to use multimedia.

Early attempts to utilize the technology involved tricks such as accompanying an error or the opening of a window with sounds produced by various WAVE files. In general, I've never found much use for any of the methods that attempt to jazz up standard computer applications such as spreadsheets or word processors. That kind of work requires efficiency and a quiet, distraction-free atmosphere. Though I may be proven wrong in the long term, I now believe that the working end of traditional applications aren't likely to become important outlets for multimedia programmers. Tutors and online help offer more possibilities, and probably will become a hunting ground for a small number of job-seeking multimedia programmers.

If standard computer applications aren't obvious outlets for multimedia, what's left? What good is this thing?

Well, the openings for multimedia right now are concentrated in three areas:

- Game programs
- Presentation programs
- Education

It doesn't take much imagination to see how multimedia can be used to enhance games. However, some people still fail to see the importance of using multimedia when presenting data.

If you combine music and graphics in effective ways, you can draw people's attention, thereby getting them to focus on information that you want to convey. This might not seem terribly important to some people—until they begin to realize that the information technology dominates the computer business, and plays an equally important role in large portions of the entire American economy. Information is wealth and power in this country, and if you can present information in the most effective and appealing manner possible, you will be providing an important and valuable service.

Education is another field where multimedia can play a huge role. Giving students easy access to film clips about historical personages is an obvious plus. Why just read about Nixon, Kennedy, Truman, Churchill, Hitler, Stalin, and Mao when you also can see film clips of them in action? Why just read Joyce, Ginsberg, Lowell, Mailer, Sexton, and other writers and poets if you can also watch interviews with them, and see and hear them reading their works? If you want to capture young mathematicians' interest, why not show them the relationship between math and music, between math and graphical images? There is no substitute for hands-on teaching, but there also is no reason to see the use of computers in an educational setting as an either/or proposition. We can have both hands-on teaching and multimedia computers. Clearly, education can be enhanced through multimedia; indeed, this process is already well under way.

If multimedia is part of your job, or if its potential interests you, then the next step is to learn how to manipulate the elements of multimedia programs. The remaining sections of this chapter are dedicated to showing you ways to achieve this end that are both simple to implement and powerful in their overall effect.

Delphi and Multimedia

Delphi has a TMediaPlayer component that gives you access to all the major features of multimedia programming. This control is extremely easy to use. In fact, it is so easy to use that many future programmers may find that their first program is not the classic "Hello World" application, but rather a simple one- or two-line effort that plays a movie or song.

Having a control this easy to use is a mixed blessing:

- On the positive side is the fact that Delphi can be used by nearly anyone to create multimedia applications or presentations.

- On the negative side, you will find that Delphi's multimedia control has somewhat limited capability. If you want more access to low-level functions, you will have to use the Delphi language to dig beneath the surface of the multimedia interface. In such cases, the TMediaPlayer component may actually stand between you and the knowledge you need to locate. Some channels to pursue in this regard are covered in Chapter 35, "Advanced Multimedia Capability." Having said this, I caution you not to sell the TMediaPlayer component short. It is more powerful than it might at first appear.

This chapter does not describe the internal workings of the Delphi control that you use to access multimedia functions. Instead, that material is covered in Chapter 35. For now, all you really need to know is that the Delphi multimedia component is called TMediaPlayer. It gives you access to a set of routines written by Microsoft called the Media Control Interface (MCI). These routines give programmers fairly easy access to a wide range of multimedia capabilities. The TMediaPlayer makes these routines extremely intuitive and easy to use.

> **NOTE**
>
> Before proceeding further, you should make sure that you are able to play multimedia files on your system. Use the MPLAYER.EXE tool that ships with Windows to test your ability to play WAVE, MIDI, and AVI files. In Windows 95, this is not likely to be a problem. As a result, I have cut out a section of this chapter included in the first edition that discusses the drivers and applets used to run and test your multimedia

system. If you can't play any of these files automatically, the issue is not a programming problem, but an operating system set-up issue. You should get on MSN, CompuServe, AOL, the Internet, or some other online service and see if you can find out what is wrong. Windows 95 should be able to play all three types of files automatically, so long as you have the hardware to support them.

The *TMediaPlayer* Component

To get started writing a multimedia application, create a new project and select the multimedia control (TMediaPlayer) from the System page of the Component Palette. Drop the tool in the middle of a form, as shown in Figure 34.1.

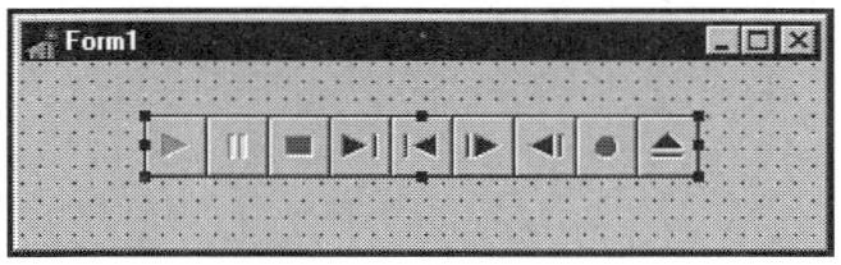

FIGURE 34.1.

The TMediaPlayer *control rests in the middle of a standard form.*

After you have placed the control on a form, you will find that the Object Inspector contains a FileName field, as shown in Figure 34.2. Fill in this field with the name of an AVI, MIDI, or WAVE file. For instance, on my system I can write E:\AVI\CLOUDS.AVI to indicate the name of a video file located on my CD-ROM. On some versions of Delphi, the ellipses icon ("...") on the right side of the property editor pops up a dialog box so that you can browse for files. In other versions you have to enter the name manually. After choosing a valid filename, be sure the AutoOpen property is set to True. This property ensures that Delphi automatically opens the MULTIMEDIA services when you start your program.

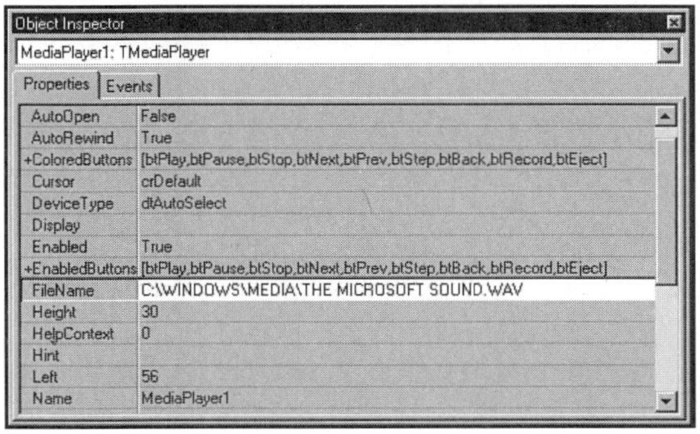

FIGURE 34.2.

The TMediaPlayer *component as seen through the Object Inspector.*

After completing these simple steps, you're ready to run the program. When it's launched, click the green button at the left of the TMediaPlayer to start the movie or sound file that you selected. If you get an error, there are three probable sources of the problem:

- You entered an invalid filename.
- You don't have multimedia set up correctly on your system. This means you either don't have the right hardware, or you have not installed the right drivers. Driver configuration occurs in the Control Panel, and hardware requirements are specified in detail in any good book on multimedia.
- You have AutoOpen set to true, but have left the FileName property blank. This produces the dreaded error message: "This command requires a parameter. Please supply one." What they mean to say, of course, is "The FileName property requires a parameter. Please supply one." As programmers, however, we love these kinds of puzzles and are grateful for the fun challenges they provide. Right? Of course.

An sample program is available on disk as MEDIA1.DPR. By default, it plays THE MICROSOFT SOUND.WAV, a file that ships with every copy of Windows 95. If you have deleted this file, if you run Windows NT, or if you do not store this file in a subdirectory called C:\WINDOWS\MEDIA, you must change the FileName property of this program.

If you experiment with the MEDIA1 program for a while, you find that you can play AVI, MIDI, and WAVE files simply by specifying the name of a file. This flexibility is the result of the control's capability to parse the filename, detect the file type from the extension, and apportion the act of actually playing the file to the appropriate internal routine.

Opening the *TMediaPlayer* at Runtime

If you place a TMediaPlayer component on a window, select a file, set AutoOpen to True, and run the program, you find that the media player starts out in operational mode (with most of its buttons lit up and ready for use). If you close the program, set the AutoOpen property to False, and restart the program, the media player will not be open. This can be useful under some circumstances, because it costs time and resources to open up the Windows multimedia drivers.

It takes only a few simple steps to gain control over the opening and closing of the TMediaPlayer. To get started, place a button on the form and name it Open. Double-click the button to create an OnClick method, and fill it in as follows:

```
procedure TForm1.Button1Click(Sender: TObject);
begin
  MediaPlayer.Open;
end;
```

When you run the program, you see a bar containing the universal symbols for playing a tape, CD, or video device. Click once on the button to open the appropriate MCI device. Wait a few moments for the buttons on the TMediaPlayer to change color, and then click once more on the green arrow at the left of the control. The file you specified in the FileName section now plays for you.

Two Varieties of Multimedia Programs

Programmers who work the TMediaPlayer are probably going to want to move in one of two directions:

■ Some programmers will want to give their users a simple way of playing the widest possible range of files. This means they will want to give the user access to the hard disk or CD-ROM, and allow them to select and play a wide range of individual files. This type of application is sometimes called a *media access program.*

■ Other programmers will want to hide the existence of the control from the user. They will want to play movie or sound files without the user ever being aware of how the selection was made. In particular, this type of activity would likely be part of a presentation. For instance, a MIDI or WAVE file might be played while a chart is on the screen that shows sales of a particular widget. The WAVE file could actually contain recorded speech explaining the graphs. Then, an AVI file might start that shows pictures of the plant where the widget is made. During this whole presentation, the user should not be aware of the existence of the TMediaPlayer. It should run entirely in the background. For now, let's call this type of application a *presentation program.*

The next few pages present two examples. The first shows how to give the user access to a wide range of files, and the second shows how to run the control in the background.

Media Access Programs

To create a media access application, start by dropping a TMediaPlayer and a button on a form. Name the button BSelectFile, and give it Select File as a caption. Then, choose the OpenDialog from the Dialogs page in the Component Palette, and place this control on the form. When you are done, your form should look like the one shown in Figure 34.3. This might be a good time to save this program under the name Access.

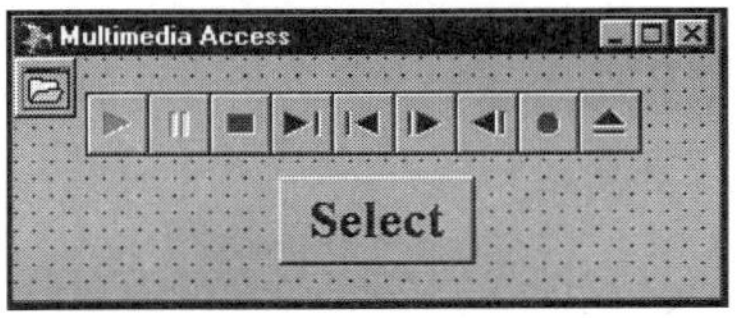

FIGURE 34.3.

The main form for the Access program.

Now create a `BSelectFileClick` method that looks like this:

```
procedure TForm1.BSelectFileClick(Sender: TObject);
begin
  MediaPlayer1.Close;
  if OpenDialog1.Execute then begin
    MediaPlayer1.FileName := OpenDialog1.FileName;
    MediaPlayer1.Open;
  end;
end;
```

The code shown here is going to be executed every time the user presses the Select File button. It has four purposes:

■ The first purpose is to close any MCI devices that might be currently open by calling `MediaPlayer1.Close`. When you first open the program, this line won't serve a useful purpose, but after you have opened a file and wish to open a second one, you will find that it helps clear the way. It is never an error to call `Close` on a `TMediaPlayer`.

■ The second purpose is to execute the `OpenDialog`. This allows users to roam at will across the hard drive, network, and any available CD-ROMs. If they find a file they wish to play, they can press the OK button to select it.

■ The third purpose only executes if the user selects a file. If the user chooses Cancel from the Open Dialog, nothing happens. If the user picks OK, the code assigns the filename selected by the user to the MCI control.

■ When an appropriate filename has been designated, the only step left is to open (or reopen) the MCI device by calling `MediaPlayer1.Open`. Now the user is free to click the green arrow to play the file.

You can make a few minor adjustments to this program to make it a bit more friendly for the user. For instance, you can automatically allow the user to select files with only a particular extension such as AVI, WAV, or MID. There are two different ways to achieve this end.

If you want to show all three types of files at once, enter the following string in the `Filter` section of the Object Inspector:

```
Multimedia Files(*.avi;*wav;*.mid)¦*.avi;*.wav;*.mid
```

Now the user can simultaneously select a WAVE, MIDI, or movie file.

Alternatively, you can change the `TOpenDialog`'s `Filter` property so that it contains the following string:

```
AVI File(*.avi)¦*.avi¦WAVE File(*.wav)¦*.wav¦ MIDI file(*.MID)¦*.mid
```

To make it easier for the reader to parse this string, break it up into three sections:

```
AVI File(*.avi)¦*.avi
WAVE File(*.wav)¦*.wav
MIDI file(*.MID)¦*.mid
```

Each of these sections contains one bar (¦) symbol and is divided from the next by another bar symbol. When the program is running and the Open Dialog is active, the first half of the string (up to the bar) is shown in the `List File Type` section of the Open Dialog, and the second half is shown in the `FileName` section. When shown this way, the user must select a different option in the File Type drop-down combo box in order to see files with a different extension.

> **NOTE**
>
> Delphi includes a special property editor, available in the Object Inspector, that makes it easier to input filters at design time. To use this dialog, simply enter the first half of the previous string in the left portion of the dialog, and place the portion shown after the bar in the right side of the dialog. Under most circumstances, you would use three lines that would look like those in the previous code example to complete the chore.
>
> If you want to assign values to the Filter field at runtime, you should use one of the first two coding examples in this chapter. For instance, you could assign the following string to the filter property at runtime:
>
> ```
> Multimedia Files(*.avi;*wav;*.mid)¦*.avi;*.wav;*.mid
> ```

Another field of `OpenDialog` that you might want to tweak is the `InitialDir` property. You can use this to designate the drive or directory that you want users to see first when they open the dialog. In my case, I prefer to enter the drive designating my CD-ROM:

```
g:
```

This allows the user to start the search for files on the drive most likely to contain a hit. Because I do not specify a particular directory, the user can select a particular directory and return to it over and over until he or she has seen all the files of interest in that location.

The few simple steps outlined here are the only ones you must take in order to give a user full access to all the media files on the system. Other additions you might consider making involve setting the background color of the form to black, or having the form start maximized. A program of this type is saved on disk as `access.dpr`, and the code for the program is shown below in Listing 34.1.

Listing 34.1. The Access program allows the user to play a wide range of multimedia files.

```
unit Main;

{ Program copyright (c) 1995 by Charles Calvert }
{ Project Name: ACCESS }

interface
```

continues

Listing 34.1. continued

```
uses
  WinTypes, WinProcs, Classes,
  Graphics, Forms, Controls,
  Dialogs, MPlayer, StdCtrls;

type
  TForm1 = class(TForm)
    Select: TButton;
    OpenDialog1: TOpenDialog;
    MediaPlayer1: TMediaPlayer;
    procedure SelectClick(Sender: TObject);
  private
    { Private declarations }
  public
    { Public declarations }
  end;

var
  Form1: TForm1;

implementation

{$R *.DFM}

procedure TForm1.SelectClick(Sender: TObject);
begin
  MediaPlayer1.Close;
  if OpenDialog1.Execute then begin
    MediaPlayer1.FileName := OpenDialog1.FileName;
    MediaPlayer1.Open;
  end;
end;

end.
```

A Closer Look at a Media Access Program

I have shown you one very simple media access program called Access, which nearly anyone can put together. This program is robust, and fits the needs of most programmers. However, there are occasions when you want a more in-depth look at what occurs when a multimedia file is being played. The next section of this chapter describes a program called Access2, which gives you all the information you need to gain full control over MCI multimedia capabilities.

Before plunging into this explanation, let me make two points:

- Although many programmers will find it useful, the information presented in this section is not essential to all multimedia programmers.

- Other readers might wish for even more control over multimedia files than is shown in this section. These readers should be aware that you can get down to a lower level of file control by entirely circumventing the TMediaPlayer and dealing directly with a set of low-level Windows commands found in the MMSYSTEM.PAS unit that ships with Delphi. You also can use the MCI commands described in Chapter 35.

With these two caveats fresh in your mind, you are ready to learn about some of the more subtle aspects of the TMediaPlayer.

You probably have noticed that the Events palette for the TMediaPlayer contains special capabilities that you can add to your program. These functions come in two categories:

- The first are the OnClick events that occur when the user presses part of the control. For instance, the OnPlay event, replete with a parameter called Button, is sent to your program whenever the user presses the green play arrow on the TMediaPlayer.

- The second are the OnNotify events containing the mm_MciNotify messages that are sent to your window when a file starts or stops playing, or when an error occurs.

I describe the first set of events in the next few paragraphs, and then move on to the second set.

There are eight major events generated by a direct click on the control, all of which are captured in the TMPBtnType:

- btPlay occurs when the user presses the green play arrow.
- btStop occurs when the user presses the square, red stop button.
- btBack occurs when the user presses the blue "back one frame" button.
- btStep occurs when the user presses the blue "forward one frame" button.
- btNext occurs when the user presses the blue fast-forward button.
- btPrev occurs when the user presses the blue rewind button.
- btPause occurs when the user presses the yellow pause button.
- btRecord occurs when the user presses the round, red record button.

If you want to see what it's like to capture one of these events, first place four edit controls on your form. Each of these edit controls will be used eventually, although they do not all play a role in the first parts of the program I describe here. Create an OnClick event for the TMediaPlayer, and fill it in so that it looks like this:

```
procedure TForm1.MediaPlayer1Click(Sender: TObject;
                                   Button: TMpBtnType;
                                   var DoDefault: Boolean);
begin
  Edit1.Text := 'Playing';
end;
```

When you understand how this system works, it should take you only a moment to be able to display an appropriate line of text whenever the user selects the TMediaPlayer. For instance, here is a method that can be called whenever the user presses a media player button:

```
procedure TForm1.MediaPlayer1Click(Sender: TObject;
                                   Button: TMPBtnType;
                                   var DoDefault: Boolean);
begin
  case Button of
    btPlay: Edit1.Text := 'Playing';
    btPause: Edit1.Text := 'Paused';
    btStop: Edit1.Text := 'Stop';
    btNext: Edit1.Text := 'Next';
    btPrev: Edit1.Text := 'Prev';
    btStep: Edit1.Text := 'Step';
    btBack: Edit1.Text := 'Back';
    btRecord: Edit1.Text := 'Record';
    btEject: Edit1.Text := 'Eject';
  end;
end;
```

The information provided here, though useful, is not enough to enable you to keep track of everything that occurs regarding the TMediaPlayer. For instance, to pause a file the user presses the pause button, which sends a btPause message to the TMediaPlayer. To start playing again, the user does not press the Play button but, instead, represses the pause button. In that case, the code here receives a second btPause message, and no btPlay message. This can result in confusion, and clearly additional information is needed to straighten the matter out. The next step, then, is to find out how to get additional information, and to see some of the things you can do with it.

To find out whether a piece has stopped playing, or whether an error has occurred, you can take a look at OnNotify messages. When working directly with the operating system, these messages come in four flavors:

```
mci_Notify_Successful: Sent when a command is completed
mci_Notify_Superseded: Command aborted by another function
mci_Notify_Aborted   : Current function is aborted
mci_Notify_Failure   : An error occurred
```

Delphi does not send these messages to you directly, but instead converts them into constants such as nvSuccessful, nvAborted, and so on. This system is adopted to provide consistency with other portions of the Delphi environment.

It's a bit tricky to understand exactly when each of these messages is sent by the Windows MCI device driver. As a rule, you get these messages in these cases:

- An nvSuccessful message comes when a piece finishes successfully.
- An nvSuperseded message might come if the system has been paused, and the user then presses the play button.
- An nvAborted message might come if the user presses the stop button, or causes the device to be closed.

Here's a function that responds to OnNotify messages by displaying a short descriptive string in an edit control:

```
procedure TForm1.MediaPlayer1Notify(Sender: TObject);
var
  S: String;
begin
  case MediaPlayer1.NotifyValue of
    nvSuccessful: begin
      Inc(Total);
      S := 'mci_Notify_Successful' + IntToStr(Total);
    end;
    nvSuperseded: S := 'mci_Notify_Superseded';
    nvAborted: S := 'mci_Notify_Aborted';
    nvFailure: S := 'mci_Notify_Failure';
  else
    S := 'Unknown notify message';
  end;

  Edit2.Text := S;

  if (MediaPlayer1.NotifyValue = nvSuccessful) and
    (MediaPlayer1.Mode = mpStopped) then
    Edit1.Text := 'File finished playing';

end;
```

This function is called automatically every time a significant event occurs that affects the MCI device. You never explicitly call this function yourself. Instead, you just set it up and wait for the function to be called by the system.

The heart of the `MediaPlayer1Notify` method is a case statement that hinges on the current state of the `NotifyValue` field of a `TMediaPlayer`. For instance, if the `NotifyValue` field is set to `mci_Notify_Successful`, a string specifying that fact is displayed in an edit control. Once again, you don't have to do anything to change the state of the `NotifyValue` field. It's changed for you automatically by the system. All you have to do is respond to an `OnNotify` event and then check the `NotifyValue` field.

To be sure that a file has finished playing, you can wait for the reception of an `mci_Notify_Successful` message, and then check to see the current mode.

The current mode of an MCI device is specified in the `Mode` property of a `TMediaPlayer`. Here is a listing of the common values designated in this field:

```
mci_Mode_Not_Ready
mci_Mode_Stop
mci_Mode_Play
mci_Mode_Record
mci_Mode_Seek
mci_Mode_Pause
mci_Mode_Open
```

Each of these modes is self-explanatory. If the Mode field is set to `mci_Mode_Stop`, the device is stopped. If it's set to `mci_Mode_Play`, the device is playing. Once again, Delphi does not send you these constants directly, but instead passes corresponding identifiers, such as `mpStopped`, `mpPlaying`, and so on. I believe the developers substituted these constants because they were easy to read, and also followed the style used by the rest of the Delphi objects.

If your application receives an mci_Notify_Successful message, and if the Mode field of the device is set to mci_Mode_Stop, you can be certain that the current file has finished playing. That is why the OnNotify method I showed you earlier checks for such a condition:

```
if (MediaPlayer1.NotifyValue = nvSuccessful) and
    (MediaPlayer1.Mode = mpStopped) then
    Edit1.Text := 'File finished playing';
```

The Access2 program also contains the following method, which can be used to track the current state of the media player:

```
procedure TForm1.SetMode;
begin
  case MediaPlayer1.Mode of
    mpNotReady: Edit3.Text := 'mci_Mode_Not_Ready';
    mpStopped: Edit3.Text := 'mci_Mode_Stop';
    mpPlaying: Edit3.Text := 'mci_Mode_Play';
    mpRecording: Edit3.Text := 'mci_Mode_Record';
    mpSeeking: Edit3.Text := 'mci_Mode_Seek';
    mpPaused: Edit3.Text := 'mci_Mode_Pause';
    mpOpen: Edit3.Text := 'mci_Mode_Open';
  else begin
      Edit1.Text := 'Device Inactive';
      Edit2.Text := 'No special messages';
      Edit3.Text := 'Unknown';
      Edit4.Text := 'No file selected';
    end;
  end;
end;
```

This routine gets called in response to an event generated by a TTimer that is placed on the form. To create a timer, simply select it from the System page of the Component Palette, drop it on a form, and create an OnTimer event handler. The method needs to do nothing more than call the SetMode procedure. The Interval property of a TTimer component defines how often OnTimer events are generated. If you leave Interval at the default 1000-millisecond level, SetMode is called once every second, thereby ensuring that the user is kept reasonably well informed of the current state of the TMediaPlayer.

The main form is shown in Figure 34.4.

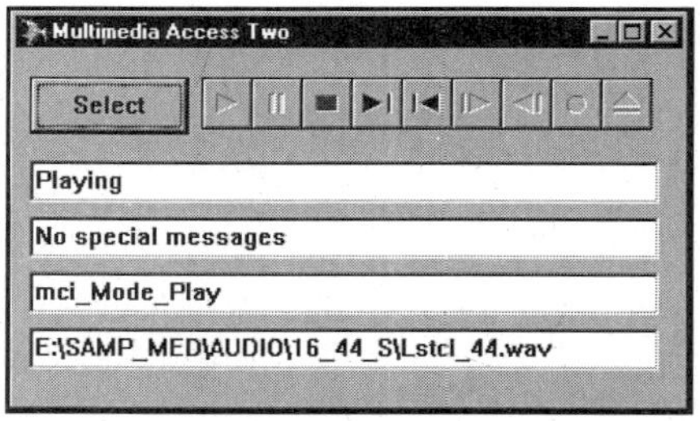

FIGURE 34.4.

The Access2 program displays the current state of the media player in a series of edit controls.

Listing 34.2. The Access2 program shows how to fine-tune the behavior of a TMediaPlayer.

```
unit Main;

{ Program copyright (c) 1995 by Charles Calvert }
{ Project Name: ACCESS2 }

interface

uses
  WinTypes, WinProcs, Classes,
  Graphics, SysUtils, Forms,
  Controls, StdCtrls, MPlayer,
  Dialogs, ExtCtrls;

type
  TForm1 = class(TForm)
    MediaPlayer1: TMediaPlayer;
    BSelect: TButton;
    Edit1: TEdit;
    Edit2: TEdit;
    Edit3: TEdit;
    Edit4: TEdit;
    OpenDialog1: TOpenDialog;
    Timer1: TTimer;
    procedure SetMode;
    procedure MediaPlayer1Notify(Sender: TObject);
    procedure BSelectClick(Sender: TObject);
    procedure Timer1Timer(Sender: TObject);
    procedure MediaPlayer1Click(Sender: TObject; Button: TMPBtnType;
      var DoDefault: Boolean);
  private
    { Private declarations }
    Total: Integer;
  public
    { Public declarations }
  end;

var
  Form1: TForm1;

implementation
uses
  MMSystem;

{$R *.DFM}

procedure TForm1.SetMode;
begin
  case MediaPlayer1.Mode of
    mpNotReady: Edit3.Text := 'mci_Mode_Not_Ready';
    mpStopped: Edit3.Text := 'mci_Mode_Stop';
    mpPlaying: Edit3.Text := 'mci_Mode_Play';
    mpRecording: Edit3.Text := 'mci_Mode_Record';
    mpSeeking: Edit3.Text := 'mci_Mode_Seek';
    mpPaused: Edit3.Text := 'mci_Mode_Pause';
    mpOpen: Edit3.Text := 'mci_Mode_Open';
```

continues

Listing 34.2. continued

```
  else begin
      Edit1.Text := 'Device Inactive';
      Edit2.Text := 'No special messages';
      Edit3.Text := 'Unknown';
      Edit4.Text := 'No file selected';
    end;
  end;
end;

procedure TForm1.MediaPlayer1Notify(Sender: TObject);
var
  S: String;
begin
  case MediaPlayer1.NotifyValue of
    nvSuccessful: begin
      Inc(Total);
      S := 'mci_Notify_Successful' + IntToStr(Total);
    end;
    nvSuperseded: S := 'mci_Notify_Superseded';
    nvAborted: S := 'mci_Notify_Aborted';
    nvFailure: S := 'mci_Notify_Failure';
  else
    S := 'Unknown notify message';
  end;
  Edit2.Text := S;

  if (MediaPlayer1.NotifyValue = nvSuccessful) and
     (MediaPlayer1.Mode = mpStopped) then
    Edit1.Text := 'File finished playing';
end;

procedure TForm1.BSelectClick(Sender: TObject);
begin
  MediaPlayer1.Close;
  if OpenDialog1.Execute then begin
    MediaPlayer1.FileName := OpenDialog1.FileName;
    Edit4.Text := OpenDialog1.FileName;
    MediaPlayer1.Open;
  end;
end;

procedure TForm1.Timer1Timer(Sender: TObject);
begin
  SetMode
end;

procedure TForm1.MediaPlayer1Click(Sender: TObject;
                                   Button: TMPBtnType;
                                   var DoDefault: Boolean);
begin
  case Button of
    btPlay: Edit1.Text := 'Playing';
    btPause: Edit1.Text := 'Paused';
    btStop: Edit1.Text := 'Stop';
    btNext: Edit1.Text := 'Next';
    btPrev: Edit1.Text := 'Prev';
```

```
      btStep: Edit1.Text := 'Step';
      btBack: Edit1.Text := 'Back';
      btRecord: Edit1.Text := 'Record';
      btEject: Edit1.Text := 'Eject';
   end;
end;

end.
```

When you are examining the Access2 program, you should look for code that demonstrates the following key points:

- Whenever the user clicks on the media player, an event is automatically generated. For instance, if the user clicks the green play arrow, a btPlay event is sent to your program. To respond to this event, just create an OnClick method by clicking on the appropriate part of the Object Inspector.

- mm_MciNotify messages are sent to your application after key events occur in the life-cycle of a multimedia file. For instance, if the file finishes playing, an mci_Notify_Successful message is sent to your application. You can respond to this event inside an OnNotify method.

- You can query the system to find out the current state of the selected multimedia device. To do this, simply see the value of the Mode property for the media player. For instance, if MediaPlayer1.Mode = mpPlaying, you know that the device is playing. This is part of one solution to the issue with the pause button discussed earlier in the chapter.

The TMediaPlayer control completely protects you from the need to work with the Microsoft MCI interface found in MMSYSTEM.PAS. However, if you want to become an expert in this field, you should begin by studying that source file, and seeing how it is called from MPLAYER.PAS. This subject is covered in Chapter 35.

Defining the Window in Which a Movie Plays

Sometimes you want an AVI file to play in a separate window, and sometimes you want it to play in a window that is part of your form. If you want a movie to be shown on your form, use the TMediaPlayer.Display property. For instance, you might drop a TPanel on the form and assign the Display property to it:

```
MediaPlayer1.Display := Panel1;
```

To further customize the view, you can use the DisplayRect property to define the rectangle in which you want the movie to play. For instance, if you want the movie to stretch to fit the entire surface of the panel, you write the following:

```
MediaPlayer1.DisplayRect := Rect(0, 0, Panel1.Width, Panel1.Height);
```

An example of this technique is found in the Windavi program shown in Listing 34.3. The form (shown in Figure 34.5) features two file-oriented listbox controls from the System page of the Object Inspector.

FIGURE 34.5.

The Windavi program shows members of the Visual Basic development team preparing to work on some pressing optimization issues.

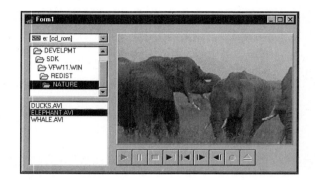

Listing 34.3. The Windavi program enables the user to play a movie in a predefined area.

```
unit main;

interface

uses
  Windows, Messages, SysUtils,
  Classes, Graphics, Controls,
  Forms, Dialogs, StdCtrls,
  FileCtrl, ExtCtrls, MPlayer;

type
  TForm1 = class(TForm)
    FileListBox1: TFileListBox;
    DirectoryListBox1: TDirectoryListBox;
    DriveComboBox1: TDriveComboBox;
    MediaPlayer1: TMediaPlayer;
    Panel1: TPanel;
    procedure FormCreate(Sender: TObject);
    procedure FileListBox1Click(Sender: TObject);
  private
    { Private declarations }
  public
    { Public declarations }
  end;

var
  Form1: TForm1;

implementation

{$R *.DFM}
```

```
procedure TForm1.FormCreate(Sender: TObject);
begin
  DirectoryListBox1.Directory := DriveComboBox1.Drive + ':\';
end;

procedure TForm1.FileListBox1Click(Sender: TObject);
begin
  MediaPlayer1.FileName := FileListbox1.fileName;
  MediaPlayer1.Open;
  Mediaplayer1.Display := Panel1;
  MediaPlayer1.DisplayRect :=
    Rect(2, 2, Panel1.Width - 4, Panel1.Height - 4);
end;

end.
```

This program is really a Windows AVI file viewer. It is custom made for that purpose, although it will, in fact, play other kinds of multimedia files. The basic flow of the program enables you to select AVI files from the directory tools on the left side of the form. When a valid file is selected, the TMediaPlayer is automatically activated and the user can press the green play arrow.

Whenever the user chooses a file from FileListBox1, the following code is called:

```
procedure TForm1.FileListBox1Click(Sender: TObject);
begin
  MediaPlayer1.FileName := FileListbox1.fileName;
  MediaPlayer1.Open;
  Mediaplayer1.Display := Panel1;
  MediaPlayer1.DisplayRect :=
    Rect(2, 2, Panel1.Width - 4, Panel1.Height - 4);
end;
```

The code assigns the proper filename, ensures that the media player is open, and finally displays output on the surface of Panel1. Notice that the program leaves the border around the panel open so that the 3-D effect of the panel is preserved. You can, if you wish, add a call to MediaPlayer1.Play at the end of this procedure, or you can let the user press the green play button.

The rest of the code in the program ensures that the three listbox controls on the left side of the form stay in sync. For instance, when you start the program, the following code is executed:

```
procedure TForm1.FormCreate(Sender: TObject);
begin
  DirectoryListBox1.Directory := DriveComboBox1.Drive + ':\';
end;
```

This just ensures that the directory listings start at the root of the current drive.

Note that in the Object Inspector the DirList property of the DriveComboBox is set to DirectoryListBox1, and the FileList property of DirectoryListBox1 is set to FileListBox1. The mask property of FileListBox1 is set to *.avi;*.wav;*.mid. Here is an alternate FormCreate method that performs all these actions for you in code:

```
procedure TForm1.FormCreate(Sender: TObject);
begin
  DriveComboBox1.DirList := DirectoryListBox1;
  DirectoryListBox1.FileList := FileListBox1;
  FileListBox1.Mask := '*.avi;*.wav;*.mid';
  DirectoryListBox1.Directory := DriveComboBox1.Drive + ':\';
end;
```

A more sophisticated version of this program might ask the user to specify startup directory information during setup, through the registration database or using an INI file.

Presentation Programs

From a programmer's perspective, a presentation program written in Delphi does not have to be a particularly demanding chore. The really complicated issues turn out not to be programming related, but design related.

The Present program discussed next provides a multimedia QuickStart for the previous Access2 program. Users of Access2 can run Present in order to learn how to use the Access2 program. (This is not really necessary, of course, but it gave me something on which to focus the presentation program.)

Present is written entirely in Delphi, and requires only a few very simple programming skills. I chose the Access2 program as a topic because it's easy to explain, and because it's familiar to all readers of this chapter. Clear, online explanation of how to run a program obviously is needed in the computer industry. A more sophisticated version of the Present program would belong to a family of multimedia applications for which there is an immediate and obvious market.

When running a presentation program, it's probably best to set the MediaPlayer1's Visible property to False inside the Object Inspector. That way, the user never sees the control itself. Of course, when you do this, you need to begin manipulating the control entirely through the program's code. In other words, you can't expect the user to press the green arrow that starts the sounds, nor can the user be responsible for closing one file and starting a second file. Everything has to be controlled through code.

The basic steps you need to take to run the multimedia control from behind the scenes are fourfold:

1. Assign a filename to the control.
2. Open the control.
3. Play the file.
4. Close the control.

The code required to perform these steps might look like this:

```
MediaPlayer1.FileName := Wave4;
MediaPlayer1.Open;
MediaPlayer1.Play;
MediaPlayer1.Close;
```

The trick here is to find the right way to arrange this code so that each method is called at the right time. The Present program in Listing 34.4 shows one simple way to achieve this end.

The first step is to choose a few key screen shots from the Access2 program. In this particular case, I've chosen three graphics:

Graphic One: A shot of the Access2 program's main screen
Graphic Two: A shot of the OpenDialog
Graphic Three: A close-up shot of the `TMediaPlayer`

I've chosen these shots because I feel that a user will know how to run the Access2 program when he or she understands what is on these screens and what they mean. After choosing the graphics, I used a screen capture program and the Windows PaintBrush program to create three BMPs: one for each shot.

When the graphics are secure, the next step is to create the text that accompanies each graphic. This part of the job is a bit like a movie director's work. For instance, I'll map this out in a series of four scenes. Each scene has a graphic associated with it, and a short paragraph of explanation:

Scene One:

- Visual: Graphic One
- Text: This is the main screen for the Access2 program. This program is designed to enable you to easily play a wide range of multimedia files. For instance, you can use this tool to play movies, music, or sound.

  The Access2 program uses the MCI interface to the Multimedia extensions to Windows. MCI stands for Multimedia Control Interface. This is a midlevel programmer's interface, which allows relatively easy access to the commands you need to play multimedia files.

  Using the Access2 program is easy. To get started, click on the Select File button with the mouse.

  (End Text of Part I)

Scene Two:

- Visual: Graphic Two
- Text: After you press the Select File button, the OpenDialog appears. You can use this dialog to select a WAVE file, MIDI file, or AVI file from your hard drive. To select a file, simply click on its name with the mouse and select the OK button.

  If you have the necessary hardware, you can then play any of these files via the MCI control.

  (End Text of Part II)

Scene Three:

- Visual: Graphic One
- Text: When the OpenDialog closes, you can then begin playing a file by pressing the green Start button. The other buttons each have a specific purpose, which should be intuitively obvious to most users.

    (End Text of Part III)

Scene Four:

- Visual: Graphic Three
- Text: This is an MCI control. You can use it to play multimedia files. This control works exactly like the similar button displays that you might see on a tape recorder or CD player. There are nine separate buttons on this control.

    When you want to begin playing a file, you can select the green arrow with the mouse. To pause the file, select the yellow pause buttons. To stop the file, press the red stop button.

    The four blue buttons enable you to move backward and forward through the file. The first two buttons enable you to move forward or backward to a particular frame. The second two buttons move one frame forward or one frame backward through a file.

    The last two buttons enable you to record to a file or eject a CD from a CD drive.

    (End Text of Part IV)

With this script to work from, you can use the TMediaPlayer to write a short program that enables you to record your voice in a WAVE file. You should record each of the previous scenes in a separate WAVE file, and save them to disk as MCINUM1.WAV, MCINUM2.WAV, and so on. Copies of these files come with this book, but you can create your own if you wish.

With the graphics and the sound files in your hands, all that's left to do is create the program. Experienced programmers should be able to make short work of this part of the task.

To get started, create a main form and place two labels and two buttons in it. Use the labels to write out the words Access Two and QuickStart. Name the first button BClose, and use it to close the application:

```
procedure TForm1.BCloseClick(Sender: TObject);
begin
  Close;
end;
```

Name the second button BStart. The response to this button is a few lines of code that drive the actual Quick Start presentation:

```
procedure TForm1.BStartClick(Sender: TObject);
begin
  FirstPic := TFirstPic.Create(Application);
  FirstPic.FileName := Wave1;
```

```
  FirstPic.ShowModal;
  FirstPic.Free;

  SecondPic := TSecondPic.Create(Application);
  SecondPic.ShowModal;
  SecondPic.Free;

  FirstPic := TFirstPic.Create(Application);
  FirstPic.FileName := Wave3;
  FirstPic.ShowModal;
  FirstPic.Free;

  ThirdPic := TThirdPic.Create(Application);
  ThirdPic.ShowModal;
  ThirdPic.Free;
end;
```

To understand this code, you must first grasp the structure of the Present program. Present has four separate forms, shown in Figures 34.6 through 34.9.

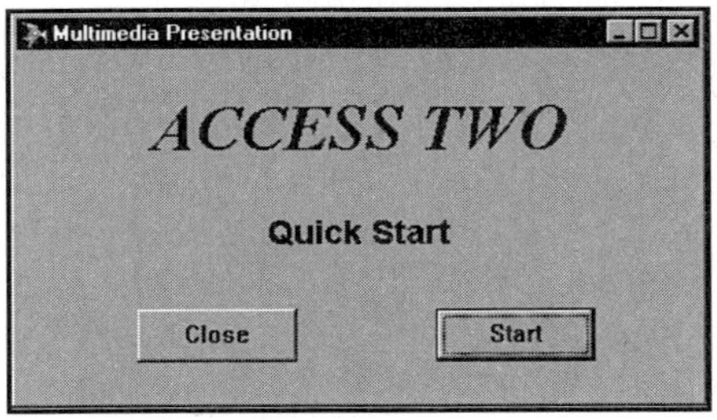

FIGURE 34.6.

The main screen of the Present program has two labels and two buttons.

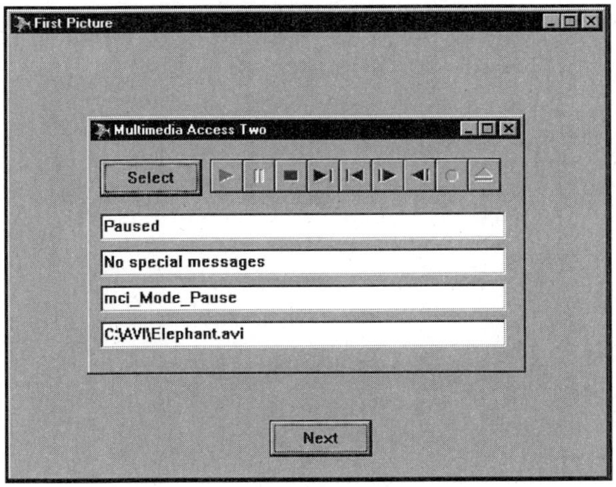

FIGURE 34.7.

The second form has a button on it labeled Next. Above the button is a TImage control.

FIGURE 34.8.

The third form also has a button labeled Next. Above the button is a TImage control and a common dialog box.

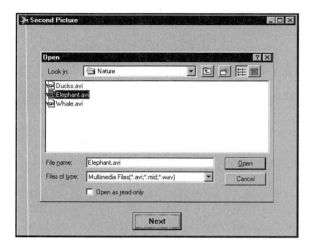

FIGURE 34.9.

The fourth form has a Next button and a TImage control with the close-up shot of the TMediaPlayer.

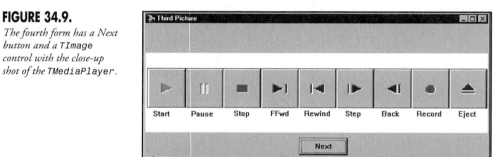

Because each graphic is shown on a separate form, it's easy to play the correct WAVE file at the correct time. For instance, there are four methods associated with the form containing the screen shot of the Access2 program. The first is called automatically by the system when the form is opened:

```
procedure TFirstPic.FormActivate(Sender: TObject);
begin
  MediaPlayer1.Visible := False;
  MediaPlayer1.FileName := FileName;
  MediaPlayer1.Open;
  MediaPlayer1.Notify := True;
  MediaPlayer1.Play;
  ActivateCalled := True;
end;
```

This method is used to assign the name of the file to the TMediaPlayer, and then to open and play the file. You can create the header for this file by double-clicking the space next to the OnActivate event in the Object Inspector.

When the form is closed, an `OnClose` message is automatically sent by the system:

```
procedure TFirstPic.FormClose(Sender: TObject;
                              var CloseWindow: Boolean);
begin
  MediaPlayer1.Close;
end;
```

To create a `FormClose` method, just click the space next to the `OnClose` event in the Object Inspector. As you can see, this method does nothing more than close the MCI device.

There are two other methods inside this form. The first method automatically closes the form when the associated WAVE file stops playing:

```
procedure TFirstPic.MediaPlayer1Notify(Sender: TObject);
begin
  with MediaPlayer1 do
    if ((NotifyValue = nvSuccessful) and
        (Mode = mpStopped)) then FirstPic.Close;
end;
```

The logic for the `if` statement shown here is explained earlier in this chapter, in the section called "A Closer Look at a Media Access Program."

The other method included in the form responds to a click on the next button:

```
procedure TFirstPic.BNextClick(Sender: TObject);
begin
  Close;
end;
```

Clearly, the only purpose of either of the last two methods is to close the form. The first method closes the form when the WAVE file stops playing. The second method closes the form if the user has grown impatient and has pressed the next button.

Returning now to the `BStartClick` method in the main form, you can see that after the first form has been shown, the Present program automatically disposes the first form and calls the next form:

```
FirstPic.ShowModal;
FirstPic.Free;

SecondPic := TSecondPic.Create(Application);
SecondPic.ShowModal;
SecondPic.Free;
```

Needless to say, the `SecondPic` form is structured exactly like the `FirstPic` form. It does the following:

- Responds to `OnActivate` by opening the MCI device and playing a WAVE file
- Responds to `OnClose` messages by closing the MCI device
- Responds to a click on the next button by closing the form
- Responds to the notification of the end of the WAVE file by closing the form

You now should have all the information you need to grasp the structure of the Present program. As you can see, it has a simple and robust architecture. The code for the program is shown in Listings 34.4 through 34.8.

Listing 34.4. Here is the unit behind the main form for the Present program.

```
unit Main;

{ Program copyright (c) 1995 by Charles Calvert }
{ Project Name: PRESENT }

interface

uses
  WinTypes, WinProcs,
  Classes, Graphics, StdCtrls,
  Controls, Printers, Forms;

type
  TForm1 = class(TForm)
    BStart: TButton;
    BClose: TButton;
    Label1: TLabel;
    Label2: TLabel;
    procedure BStartClick(Sender: TObject);
    procedure BCloseClick(Sender: TObject);
  end;

var
  Form1: TForm1;

implementation
uses
  Globals,
  Pict1,
  Pict2,
  Pict3;

{$R *.DFM}

procedure TForm1.BStartClick(Sender: TObject);
begin
  FirstPic := TFirstPic.Create(Application);
  FirstPic.FileName := Wave1;
  FirstPic.ShowModal;
  FirstPic.Free;

  SecondPic := TSecondPic.Create(Application);
  SecondPic.ShowModal;
  SecondPic.Free;

  FirstPic := TFirstPic.Create(Application);
  FirstPic.FileName := Wave3;
  FirstPic.ShowModal;
  FirstPic.Free;
```

```
    ThirdPic := TThirdPic.Create(Application);
    ThirdPic.ShowModal;
    ThirdPic.Free;
end;

procedure TForm1.BCloseClick(Sender: TObject);
begin
    Close;
end;

end.
```

Listing 34.5. The PICT1 dialog, which is the first to be shown after the user presses the Start button.

```
unit Pict1;

{ Program copyright (c) 1995 by Charles Calvert }
{ Project Name: PRESENT }

interface

uses
    WinTypes, WinProcs, Classes,
    Graphics, Forms, Controls,
    MPlayer, StdCtrls, ExtCtrls;

type
    TFirstPic = class(TForm)
        Next: TButton;
        MediaPlayer1: TMediaPlayer;
        Image1: TImage;
        procedure NextClick(Sender: TObject);
        procedure FormActivate(Sender: TObject);
        procedure MediaPlayer1Notify(Sender: TObject);
        procedure FormCreate(Sender: TObject);
        procedure FormClose(Sender: TObject; var Action: TCloseAction);
    private
        ActivateCalled: Boolean;
    public
        FileName: String;
    end;

var
    FirstPic: TFirstPic;

implementation
uses
    Globals,
    MmSystem;

{$R *.DFM}
```

continues

Listing 34.5. continued

```
procedure TFirstPic.NextClick(Sender: TObject);
begin
  Close;
end;

procedure TFirstPic.FormActivate(Sender: TObject);
begin
  if ActivateCalled then Exit;
  MediaPlayer1.Visible := False;
  MediaPlayer1.FileName := FileName;
  MediaPlayer1.Open;
  MediaPlayer1.Notify := True;
  MediaPlayer1.Play;
  ActivateCalled := True;
end;

procedure TFirstPic.MediaPlayer1Notify(Sender: TObject);
begin
  with MediaPlayer1 do
    if ((NotifyValue = nvSuccessful) and
        (Mode = mpStopped)) then
      FirstPic.Close;
end;

procedure TFirstPic.FormCreate(Sender: TObject);
begin
  ActivateCalled := False;
end;

procedure TFirstPic.FormClose(Sender: TObject; var Action: TCloseAction);
begin
  MediaPlayer1.Close;
  ActivateCalled := False;
end;

end.
```

Listing 34.6. The code for the PICT2 dialog.

```
unit Pict2;

{ Program copyright (c) 1995 by Charles Calvert }
{ Project Name: PRESENT }

interface

uses
  WinTypes, WinProcs, Classes,
  Graphics, Forms, Controls,
  MPlayer, StdCtrls, ExtCtrls;

type
  TSecondPic = class(TForm)
```

```
    Image1: TImage;
    MediaPlayer1: TMediaPlayer;
    Next: TButton;
    procedure NextClick(Sender: TObject);
    procedure MediaPlayer1Notify(Sender: TObject);
    procedure FormActivate(Sender: TObject);
    procedure FormCreate(Sender: TObject);
    procedure FormClose(Sender: TObject; var Action: TCloseAction);
  private
    ActivateCalled: Boolean;
  public
    { Public declarations }
  end;

var
  SecondPic: TSecondPic;

implementation
uses
  Globals,
  mmSystem;

{$R *.DFM}

procedure TSecondPic.NextClick(Sender: TObject);
begin
  MediaPlayer1.Close;
  Close;
end;

procedure TSecondPic.MediaPlayer1Notify(Sender: TObject);
begin
  if (MediaPlayer1.NotifyValue = nvSuccessful) and
     (MediaPlayer1.Mode = mpStopped) then SecondPic.Close;
end;

procedure TSecondPic.FormActivate(Sender: TObject);
begin
  if ActivateCalled then Exit;
  MediaPlayer1.Visible := False;
  MediaPlayer1.Close;
  MediaPlayer1.FileName := Wave2;
  MediaPlayer1.Open;
  MediaPlayer1.Notify := True;
  MediaPlayer1.Play;
  ActivateCalled := True;
end;

procedure TSecondPic.FormCreate(Sender: TObject);
begin
  ActivateCalled := False;
end;

procedure TSecondPic.FormClose(Sender: TObject; var Action: TCloseAction);
begin
  MediaPlayer1.Close;
end;

end.
```

Listing 34.7. The code for the PICT3 dialog.

```pascal
unit Pict3;

{ Program copyright (c) 1995 by Charles Calvert }
{ Project Name: PRESENT }

interface

uses
  WinTypes, WinProcs, Classes,
  Graphics, Forms, Controls,
  MPlayer, StdCtrls, ExtCtrls;

type
  TThirdPic = class(TForm)
    Next: TButton;
    MediaPlayer1: TMediaPlayer;
    Image1: TImage;
    procedure NextClick(Sender: TObject);
    procedure MediaPlayer1Notify(Sender: TObject);
    procedure FormCreate(Sender: TObject);
    procedure FormActivate(Sender: TObject);
    procedure FormClose(Sender: TObject; var Action: TCloseAction);
  private
    ActivateCalled: Boolean;
  public
    { Public declarations }
  end;

var
  ThirdPic: TThirdPic;

implementation
uses
  Globals,
  mmSystem;

{$R *.DFM}

procedure TThirdPic.NextClick(Sender: TObject);
begin
  Close;
end;

procedure TThirdPic.MediaPlayer1Notify(Sender: TObject);
begin
  if (MediaPlayer1.NotifyValue = nvSuccessful) and
     (MediaPlayer1.Mode = mpStopped) then
    Close;
end;

procedure TThirdPic.FormCreate(Sender: TObject);
begin
  ActivateCalled := False;
end;

procedure TThirdPic.FormActivate(Sender: TObject);
```

```
begin
  if ActivateCalled then Exit;
  MediaPlayer1.Visible := False;
  MediaPlayer1.FileName := Wave4;
  MediaPlayer1.Open;
  MediaPlayer1.Play;
  ActivateCalled := True;
end;

procedure TThirdPic.FormClose(Sender: TObject; var Action: TCloseAction);
begin
  MediaPlayer1.Close;
end;

end.
```

Listing 34.8. The `Globals` unit, which defines some constants used by all the units in the program.

```
unit Globals;

{ Program copyright (c) 1995 by Charles Calvert }
{ Project Name: PRESENT }

interface

var
  Wave1, Wave2,
  Wave3, Wave4: String;

implementation

uses
  StrBox;

var
  ThePath: String;

begin
  ThePath := StripLastToken(ParamStr(0), '\') + '\';
  Wave1 := ThePath + 'mcinum1.wav';
  Wave2 := ThePath + 'mcinum2.wav';
  Wave3 := ThePath + 'mcinum3.wav';
  Wave4 := ThePath + 'mcinum4.wav';
end.
```

The design of this program is too simple to merit much comment. However, experienced programmers will note that it would be possible to merge the PICT1, PICT2, and PICT3 forms into one unit. I kept them separate because most programs of this type need a separate object to manage each form shown to the user.

Notice also that I call the `StripLastToken` function from the `STRBOX` unit that ships with this book. This function effectively returns the directory from which the program was launched. It does this by parsing the `ParamStr` variable, which usually is used to record the parameters passed to a program. For instance, if you pass a single parameter to Present, you can retrieve the parameter with the following code:

```
S := ParamStr(1);
```

However, in this case I don't pass any parameters to the program. Nevertheless, I can retrieve the executable name and full path to where that executable is stored by writing the following:

```
S := ParamStr(0);
```

The `ParamCount` variable tells you how many parameters are passed to a program.

The Present program took about two hours to design and write. About half of that time was dedicated to composing the script for the WAVE files and then recording them through a microphone. The actual job of writing the code was trivial. One of the goals of Delphi is to simplify the mechanics of writing a Windows program. Certainly, the `TMediaPlayer` helps to achieve that goal.

MIDI Details

On the *Unleashed* CD-ROM you will find a console application called Sounder. This program uses low-level Windows multimedia calls to play MIDI notes. If a sound card and proper midi drivers are present, this code will allow you to designate:

- An instrument (such as piano, guitar, or drums)
- A note to play
- An approximate duration
- A volume

Before playing a note, you must open the MIDI device by calling `MidiOutOpen`. When doing so, you pass in a variable of type `phMidiOut`, which in Win32 resolves to a pointer to an integer, that is, a pointer to an unsigned 32-bit value. This latter value is the handle you use to identify your copy of the MIDI device, and you use it on all subsequent calls to MIDI services. In this program, a global variable called `hMidi` is used as the handle to the MIDI device.

Next you should initialize the device by selecting an instrument. To do this, pass `$C0` (ChangeInstrument) to the `MidiOutShortMsg` function.

`MidiOutShortMsg` takes two parameters. The first is the handle to the MIDI device (`hMidi`), and the second is a 32-bit integer represented here by a structure of type `TMidiMsg`:

```
TMidiMsg = Record
  Status,   The status field usually issues a command such as PlayNote
  Data1,    Additional information, such as the note to play
```

```
    Data2,    Additional information, such as the volume to play
    NoData: Byte;
end;
```

After you are set up, you can use the `MidiOutShortMsg` functions to play notes, setting the status field of the `TMidiMsg` structure to `$90` (`midiPlayNote`);

```
Msg.Status := midiNotePlay;
Msg.Data1 := Note;
Msg.Data2 := Volume;
Msg.NoData := 0;
Err := MidiOutShortMsg(hMidi^, LongInt(Msg));
if Err <> 0 then WriteLn(Err);
```

When you are done, call `MidiOutClose`, passing it the handle to the MIDI device (`hMidi^`).

Once again, the complete sample program is found on disc as SOUNDER.DPR and two related files. Remember that sounder is a console application. As a bonus, the program shows you a few tricks for handling keyboard input while in console applications.

Summary

In this chapter, you learned some of the basic facts about multimedia, and how to write two different types of multimedia programs.

The major types of multimedia files covered in this chapter were as follows:

- WAVE files for recording any type of sound
- MIDI files for recording music
- AVI files for recording movies

There were two types of multimedia applications covered:

- Access programs give the user the ability to play a wide range of programs.
- Presentation programs hide the internals of multimedia development from the user, and simply play sounds and films as a way of entertaining or informing the user.

Clearly, Delphi offers a simple and powerful way to create multimedia applications. When writing your own multimedia programs, use this chapter as a starting point, and your imagination as a guide.

Advanced Multimedia Capability

35

This chapter covers one fairly complicated subject: using the Multimedia Control Interface (MCI). In particular, these pages show how to play WAV files, MIDI files, AVI files, and the type of music CDs that you would buy at a record store.

The technique used in this chapter is the same used to create the TMediaPlayer component itself. Both this chapter and the TMediaPlayer base their technology on the MCI. This chapter therefore provides two services:

- It contains a commentary on the MCI and shows how to use it in your own programs. The MCI interface is quite powerful and, if you understand it, you can array your programs with a number of stunning multimedia features.

- The chapter also explains the technology used in the TMediaPlayer, giving you the ability to use the component to its capacity and to extend that when, or if, necessary.

The chapter starts off with some general comments about multimedia, then provides a few simple MCI examples and, finally, presents a large program custom designed to play AVI, WAV, and MIDI files, as well as standard CDs that you would buy in a music store. This program, called Media32, is a Delphi port of an old OWL program called Player, first shown in the first edition of this book. The code has been completely revamped to run under 32-bit Delphi.

Using OWL with Delphi

The Media32 program has something of a history in that it was originally written for Turbo Pascal using the OWL library. I converted that fairly lengthy program from Borland Pascal 7 to Delphi 1.0 in about 20 minutes. This was easy to do because Delphi 1.0 still recompiled OWL code. (OWL was the object-oriented library used in Borland Pascal.) However, the most recent version of Delphi does not work with OWL code, so I had to convert the program to the VCL. This was a more complicated process, although I don't think it took more than five or six hours total.

When making this conversion, I was again faced with the issue of whether to update certain aspects of the code. For instance, the code makes heavy use of PChars, as shown in this function:

```
const
  MsgLen: 128;

function GetErrorMessage(RC:LongInt; S: PChar): PChar;
begin
  if not mciGetErrorString(RC, S, MsgLen) then
    StrCopy(S, 'No message available');
  GetErrorMessage := S;
end;
```

When calling this routine, I ask the user to pass in a string with at least 128 bytes of memory allocated for it:

```
var
  S: array[0..128] of Char;
  RC: LongInt;
begin
  … // Additional code here
  GetErrorMessage(RC, S);
end;
```

In Delphi 2.0, I could easily upgrade this code to work with strings rather than PChars:

```
function GetErrorMessage(RC:LongInt; S: string): string;
begin
  SetLength(S, MsgLen);
  if not mciGetErrorString(RC, PChar(S), MsgLen) then
    S := 'No message available';
  Result := S;
end;
```

I could then call it like this:

```
var
  S: string;
  RC: Integer;
begin
  … // Additional code here.
  GetErrorMessage(RC, S);
end;
```

This might make the code somewhat easier for some programmers to read and use. However, to do so would require calling SetLength, and the SetLength function is not supported in Delphi 1.0 or in Turbo Pascal.

Which is better: maintaining compatibility with Delphi 1.0 and Borland Pascal or writing code that is slightly easier to read and use? For a beginner, the answer would be weighted in favor of the latter of these two options. This book, however, is not aimed at beginners, and so I decided to keep the code compatible with the widest possible range of tools.

In this context, it's important to note that this book is being written in the Winter of '95–'96. At this time most professional programmers will be targeting both Windows 3.1 and Win32, so compatibility with past versions of Delphi is a big issue. If you are reading this book in 1998 or 99, the need for backward compatibility will hopefully seem less pressing than it is at the time of this writing. Such is the nature of the rapidly changing world of computers.

At this time it seems best to make the code as flexible as possible, so long as it still runs smoothly in Win32, and so long as it is not extracting a price in terms of performance. Both of these criteria are met in this code, so I have left the core multimedia commands compatible with Delphi 1.0 wherever possible. Most of the interface code in this chapter will work only with Delphi 2.0, but it would not be hard to port it to Delphi 1.0.

The Tools and Definitions

I tested the programs in this chapter on PCs equipped with sound cards and CD-ROM drives. The first is a requirement for playing MIDI files; the second is a requirement for playing CDs.

If you don't have a sound card, you will not be able to run any of the code accompanying this chapter. Of course, if you don't have a CD-ROM drive, you will not be able to run the modules that work with CDs.

Some Notes on MIDI Files

The word MIDI stands for Musical Instrument Digital Interface. Put in the simplest possible terms, MIDI files can be thought of as containing a series of notes, such as C-sharp or an A-flat, which are sent to a synthesizer with instructions to play that note using the sounds associated with a particular instrument such as a piano, horn, or guitar.

The synthesizer chip I used when writing this chapter came as a standard part of the Sound Blaster Pro card, though I also used an AWE32 card. Most sound cards and MIDI files can play between six and 16 notes at once, and can imitate between three and nine instruments. MIDI files can store one minute of fairly high-quality musical sound in about 5 KB of disk space. This means that they are much more useful than WAV files for most computer users.

Coming to Terms with *mciSendCommand*

mciSendCommand provides an unusual interface to an API. As a result, it's possible that a few words of explanation are in order. The goal here is to totally encapsulate the multimedia API inside a message-based system that isolates multimedia programmers from the details of the code base's actual implementation. In other words, when using this mid-level interface, there is no point at which you or I would actually call a true, multimedia API function.

The reason for this is one that should be familiar to all object-oriented programmers: hardware and operating systems change over time. As a result, APIs are forced to change with them. When APIs change, existing code bases are rendered obsolete, and last year's work has to be done all over again.

The MCI command-message interface protects the programmer from any fluctuations in the API. For all practical purposes, all a programmer has to do is send a message into a dark hole. What goes on inside of that hole is of little concern to us. Five years from now CDs may have ten times their current capacity and have cut their access time down to a fifth of their current, snail-like pace. But none of that is going to affect your code. All you need to do is say that you want a particular track to be played. How it's played is of no concern to us.

Another crucial advantage of this style of programming is that it gives the user a common interface to a series of radically different pieces of hardware. For instance, at this time, the MCI command interface works with the following different types of devices, which are listed here opposite their official MCI names:

animation	Animation device
avivideo	Movie player
cdaudio	CD player
dat	Digital audio tape device
digitalvideo	Digital video device
scanner	Image scanner
sequencer	MIDI
vcr	Video tape player
videodisc	Videodisc device
waveaudio	A device that plays WAV files

What MCI has tried to do is to find the things that all these devices have in common, then use these similarities to bind them together. In particular, it makes sense to ask all of these devices to play something, to stop playing, to pause, to seek to a particular location in their media, and so on. In other words, they all respond to these commands as the primary MCI messages.

Talk about device independence! The Windows multimedia extensions not only protect you from the details of how a particular device might work, but they also frequently let you treat a CD and a WAV file in almost exactly the same manner. For that matter, you can come close to using the same code to play a WAV file as you would to play a MIDI. The only difference would be that one time you would tell MCI that you want to work with a waveaudio device, whereas the next time you would say that you want to work with a sequencer.

Narrowing the Focus

Now that you know something about the technology being discussed in this chapter, it's time to turn your attention to the programming techniques used to make a computer generate sounds.

As it happens, Microsoft provides three separate interfaces that can allow you to access multimedia devices. Two of these are part of MCI, whereas the third is a low-level API that tends to be quite rigorous and demanding.

Microsoft has stated publicly that it will not promise to support the low-level API in the future. Because few programmers can afford to spend time learning a standard that is fleeting at best, I can justify ignoring this rather challenging subject. (Phew!)

With the low-level API out of the way, that leaves only two remaining programming techniques. The first is a string-based interface designed primarily to provide support for high-level languages such as Visual BASIC. You can call these functions from Delphi, but I have opted to ignore them in favor of a third technique. The Media32 program has access to this third technique, which is a powerful, message-based interface.

The peculiar thing about this command-message interface is that it relies heavily on a single routine, called mciSendCommand, which takes four parameters. Though this might sound fairly limiting at first, in practice it turns out to be a reasonably flexible system.

Here is what a typical call to mciSendCommand might look like: '

```
Return := mciSendCommand(videoId, mci_Close, 0, LongInt(@mciClose));
```

The next few paragraphs introduce you to the four parameters passed to this function.

The first parameter passed to mciSendCommand is a handle or ID number used to identify the particular device in question. For instance, when you first open up a CD drive, you pass 0 in this parameter because you don't yet have an ID for the device. Thereafter, you pass in the ID returned to you when you opened the device.

The key to this entire interface is the second parameter, passed as a message to the function in order to specify a particular command. Here is a list of the 12 most common of these messages and their meanings:

mci_Capability	Queries the device's capabilities
mci_Close	Closes a device
mci_Info	Queries the of type hardware being used
mci_Open	Opens a device
mci_Play	Plays a song or piece on a device
mci_Record	Records to a device
mci_Resume	Resumes playing or recording
mci_Seek	Moves media forward or backward
mci_Set	Changes the settings on device
mci_Status	Queries about whether the device is paused, playing, and so on
mci_Stop	Stops playing or recording

To complement these commands, there is a set of flags and records available that can give programmers the kind of fine-tuning they need to get the job done right. For instance, the mci_Play message has four important flags that you can use together in an OR operation to form its third parameter:

```
mci_Notify              Post Mm_Notify message on completion
mci_Wait                Complete operation before returning
mci_From                Starting position is specified
mci_To                  Finish position is specified
```

You can use the last two flags here in an OR operation this way:

```
mci_From or mci_To
```

In this form, they inform MCI that a starting and finishing position will be specified in the last parameter:

```
RC := mciSendCommand(wDeviceId, MCI_PLAY, mci_From or mci_To, Longint(@Info));
```

The fourth parameter is a pointer to a record. The record passed by mciSendCommand differs, depending on the message being sent. In the preceding example, when an mci_Play message is used, the structure looks like this:

```
Pmci_Play_Parms = ^Tmci_Play_Parms;
Tmci_Play_Parms = Record
  dwCallback: LongInt;
  dwFrom: LongInt;
  dwTo: LongInt;
end;
```

Sometimes it's necessary to fill out all three fields of this structure. At other times, some or none of them can be filled out. For instance, if you set the mci_Notify flag in the second parameter of mciSendCommand, you probably will want to set dwCallback equal to the HWnd of the window you want MCI to notify. Specifically, if you were inside a TForm descendant at the time you started playing a WAV file, you would want to pass the dialog's HWnd in dwCallback, so that the dialog would be informed through an mm_Notify message when the WAV file stopped playing.

Of course, if you set both the mci_From and mci_To flags, you would want to fill out both the dwFrom and the dwTo fields of the Tmci_Play_Parms record (and so on). Remember that the Tmci_Play_Parms recorded is associated explicitly with the mci_Play message. Other messages have their own, unique record structures. For instance, the mci_Open message is associated with the Tmci_Open_Parms structure.

All of the multimedia structures or constants discussed in this chapter are listed in MMSYSTEM.PAS. Some versions of Delphi include an MMSYSTEM.HLP file. In some cases, the MMSYSTEM.HLP file may enable you to search for a structure using only the C language syntax; that is, without prefixing the name with a T. Therefore, you should search for MCI_OPEN_PARMS, not Tmci_Open_Parms.

The only major aspect of the mciSendCommand function not yet discussed is its return value, which happens to be an error number kept in the low-order word of a LongInt. Microsoft came through with a nice touch at this point by adding the mciGetErrorString function, which provides you with an explanation of any error in return for the result of mciSendCommand function. mciGetErrorString even sends you back a pleasant little message telling you that all has gone well, if that is indeed the case.

Playing a File

The first program I want to show you in this chapter provides the ability to play a WAV file. This is a console application, which takes a single WAV file as a parameter:

```
play vivaldi.wav
```

The code for the Play program is shown in Listing 35.1. Remember when you are working with console applications to go to the Project | Options | Linker menu choice and set Generate Console Application to TRUE. If you're working from the command prompt, you should enter the following:

```
dcc32 -CC play.pas
```

where the -CC directive tells the compiler to produce a console application.

Listing 35.1. The Play program is a small console application that enables you to play a single WAV file.

```pascal
program Play;

{ Program copyright (c) 1996 by Charles Calvert }
{ Project Name: Media32}

uses
  MMSystem;

const
  MaxStr = 200;

var
  DeviceID: LongInt;

function mciError(Return: LongInt; Caller: string): Boolean;
var
  S: array[0..MaxStr] of Char;
begin
  if Return <> 0 then begin
    mciGetErrorString(Return, S, MaxStr);
    WriteLn(S + ' ' + Caller);
    Halt;
  end;
  mciError := True;
end;

procedure PlaySound(FileName: PChar);
var
  mciOpen: Tmci_Open_Parms;
  mciPlay: Tmci_Play_Parms;
  Flags: Word;
begin
  mciOpen.lpstrDeviceType := 'waveaudio';
  mciOpen.lpstrElementName := FileName;
  Flags := mci_Open_Element or mci_Open_Type;
  mciError(MciSendCommand(0, mci_Open, Flags, LongInt(@mciOpen)), 'Open');
```

```
    DeviceID := mciOpen.wDeviceId;

    mciPlay.dwFrom := 0;
    Flags := mci_From or mci_Wait;
    mciError(MciSendCommand(DeviceId, mci_Play, Flags, LongInt(@mciPlay)), 'Play');

    mciError(MciSendCommand(DeviceID, mci_Close, 0, LongInt(nil)), 'Close');
end;

begin
  if ParamCount < 1 then Exit;
  PlaySound(PChar(ParamStr(1)));
end.
```

The core functionality in the program comes in two parts, both presented in the PlaySound function. In the Media32 program, these two steps are presented in two separate, reusable functions. The goal here is to create a single function that does all the work needed to play a WAV file: open the file, and then play it.

The following code opens the WAV file:

```
var
  mciOpen: Tmci_Open_Params;
begin  mciOpen.lpstrDeviceType := 'waveaudio';
  mciOpen.lpstrElementName := FileName;
  Flags := mci_Open_Element or mci_Open_Type;
  mciSendCommand(0, mci_Open, Flags, LongInt(@MciOpen));
  … // Additional code
end;
```

This code fragment appears a bit intimidating at first, but it should yield easily enough if you concentrate on it for a few moments.

The Tmci_Open_Params structure is the centerpiece of lines shown above:

```
  Tmci_Open_Parms = record
    dwCallback: DWORD;
    wDeviceID: MCIDEVICEID;
    lpstrDeviceType: PAnsiChar;
    lpstrElementName: PAnsiChar;
    lpstrAlias: PAnsiChar;
  end;
```

> **NOTE**
>
> If you're double-checking my work, you will find that the structure shown above actually is called Tmci_Open_ParmsA. The issue here, of course, is that there is an ANSI version of this record and also a Wide, or Unicode, version of this record. In Delphi 2.0, you want to use the ANSI version of the record, which is called Tmci_Open_ParmsA, in contrast to Tmci_Open_ParmsW. MMSYSTEM.PAS specifies this by making the following declaration:
>
> ```
> Tmci_Open_Parms := Tmci_Open_ParmsA;
> ```

> This type declaration means that Tmci_Open_Parms actually does resolve to the record shown above, even if it is not overtly declared that way.
>
> This system of having two declarations for a record is necessary only if the declaration has a string in one of its fields. If the types involved are not strings, there is no need for a separate Unicode declaration. Object Pascal supports Unicode, but the VCL controls are not Unicode ready. This means that Unicode is not practical in most Delphi applications, so the environment defaults to using the ANSI declarations.

To use the Tmci_Open_Parms structure, fill in the device type and element name and then pass in its address in the fourth parameter of mciSendCommand. A device ID identifying your handle to the multimedia WAV services is returned in the wDeviceID field if the function succeeds.

Because you are passing in the element name and its type, you should pass in the following flags when you call mciSendCommand:

```
Flags := mci_Open_Element or mci_Open_Type;
```

These constants inform Windows which parameters it should attempt to parse.

NOTE

For simple device types such as CD audio players, you don't need a device element. Compound device types require a device element. A compound device type requires you to specify an element name along with a device type. In most cases, an element name is just another way of referring to a file name. However, there are times when this second half of the compound device is not a file name, so some very literal folks at Microsoft called it an element, rather than a file. For all practical purposes, though, the element name is a file name.

Here's an example of opening a CD:

```
function OpenCD: Boolean;
var
  Info : Tmci_Open_Parms;
  ErrNo  : LongInt;
  Flags: LongInt;
  S1: array[0..MsgLen] of Char;
begin
  OpenCD := True;
  FillChar(Info, SizeOf(Tmci_Open_Parms), #0);
  Info.lpstrDeviceType := PChar(MCI_DEVTYPE_CD_AUDIO);
  Flags := MCI_OPEN_TYPE or MCI_OPEN_TYPE_ID;
  ErrNo := mciSendCommand(0, MCI_OPEN, Flags, Longint(@Info)); .
```

```
  wDeviceId := Info.wDeviceId;

  if ErrNo<>0 then begin
    ErrorMsg(ErrNo, S1);
    OpenCD := False;
  end;
end;
```

The ErrMsg function shown here is a generic routine for handling errors. It is discussed later in this chapter.

In this example there is no mci_Open_Element flag passed in. This is because you don't have to specify a file name when opening a simple device, such as a CD player. There is, however, another complication, in that I chose to specify that the device type is using an integer identifier called MCI_DEVTYPE_CD_AUDIO. Use of this identifier, rather than a string, requires that you pass in the MCI_OPEN_TYPE_ID flag. This latter flag informs windows that you are using an integer identifier and not a string, when you specify the device type.

There is, obviously enough, a somewhat maze-like quality to all these flags, parameters, and records. One of the major purposes of this chapter is to provide you with a series of functions that you can call with ease, rather than leaving you to always sort out all these flags on your own. In particular, this chapter presents functions like OpenCD, PlayCD, PlayTrackFromCD, and so on. These functions sort out the flags and records for you.

However, you also should understand how this business works, so that you can create your own functions or tweak the existing functions to serve your own purposes. To do this effectively, you must understand not only how the functions work, but how to look up all these parameters, flags, and so on. In particular, you should become familiar with MMSYSTEM.PAS and MMSYSTEM.HLP. You might also want to acquire some primary reference books, such as the *Microsoft Windows Multimedia Programmers Workbook* published by the Microsoft press.

The second parameter passed to mciSendCommand is the specific command that you want to invoke:

```
mciSendCommand(0, mci_Open, Flags, LongInt(@MciOpen));
```

In this case you're saying that you want to open a file, so you pass in mci_Open.

NOTE

There is a parallel between a command like mci_Open and the messages you use with SendMessage or PostMessage. For instance, if you pass wm_SetText to SendMessage, you are telling Windows that you want to set the text in some control. In the same way,

> when you pass in `mci_Open`, you are telling Windows that you want to open some device. Note also that `SendMessage` takes a window handle in the first parameter, just as `mciSendCommand` takes a device ID in the first parameter. In general, there is a great deal of similarity between `SendMessage` and `mciSendCommand`.

The first parameter is where you would normally pass in a device ID. Because the purpose of this particular call is to retrieve a device ID, it's natural that this parameter should be set to 0.

After opening up the WAV device, you should have a hold on the device ID:

```
DeviceID := mciOpen.wDeviceId;
```

However, there is some chance that something went wrong while opening the device. As a rule, the only things that can go wrong involve a user not having the system set up correctly, or else passing an invalid file name to Windows. In either case, the result returned by `mciSendCommand` would be set to a non-zero value.

You can pass the integer returned from `mciSendCommand` to the following error function:

```
function mciError(Return: LongInt; Caller: string): Boolean;
var
  S: array[0..MaxStr] of Char;
begin
  if Return <> 0 then begin
    mciGetErrorString(Return, S, MaxStr);
    WriteLn(S + ' ' + Caller);
    Halt;
  end;
  mciError := True;
end;
```

This function is tailor-made for the simple console application currently under discussion. In particular, it checks the value returned from `mciSendCommand`. If this value is non-zero, it prints a message and then terminates the application. Termination would be a bit too strong a reaction in a standard application, but it is the appropriate thing to do in this case.

Assuming that you have successfully opened the device, the next step is to play the file:

```
mciPlay.dwFrom := 0;
Flags := mci_From or mci_Wait;
MciSendCommand(DeviceId, mci_Play, Flags, LongInt(@mciPlay));
```

The code shown here works with `Tmci_Play_Parms` rather than `Tmci_Open_Parms`:

```
Tmci_Play_Parms = record
  dwCallback: DWORD;
  dwFrom: DWORD;
  dwTo: DWORD;
end;
```

The only way to know for sure which structure you should pass in is to look the information up in a book like this, or in the online Help.

In this case, the dwTo field of Tmci_PlayParms is ignored. To tell Windows of your intentions, you must leave out the mci_To flag when you call mciSendCommand:

```
Flags := mci_From or mci_Wait;
```

The mci_From flag states that you are going to designate where you want to start playing the file from; in this case, point 0. The mci_Wait flags tells Windows that you don't want this function to return until the file has finished playing.

The only other thing you need to know in order to call the function is which command causes a file to be played. Needless to say, mci_Play is the appropriate command to issue in this circumstance, so that parameter is passed in the second position.

The first parameter to mciSendCommand now is filled with the device ID retrieved during the call to open the device. Except for a call accompanying the mci_Open command, you should pass in a device ID when talking to the MCI a majority of the time.

Assuming that the code succeeded, and that the file played successfully, the only step left is to close the device:

```
mciError(MciSendCommand(DeviceID, mci_Close, 0, LongInt(nil)), 'Close');
```

Notice that this command does not take a special record in the fourth parameter, nor is there any need to pass in a special set of flags. As a result, the command is easy to issue, and you can close the device with little or no fuss. The line of code quoted here shows how to wrap mciSendCommand in a routine that checks for errors.

Recording Sound

The next program, called Records, is similar to the Play program. Once again, it contains only two functions: the first called RecordSound and the second called mciError. The RecordSound function enables you to first record a few words, and then to immediately play them back. The function takes a single parameter, which is the number of milliseconds you want the recording to last.

The code for the program is shown in Listing 35.2. Once again this is a console application, so you should either compile from the command prompt with the -CC switch, or else tell the IDE to Generate Console Applications, as described above.

You need a sound card and a microphone to use this program. Start the program from the command prompt. A single line of text appears stating that you should "record." Say whatever is on your mind, giving yourself a little less than 10 seconds to complete the task. The moment the 10 seconds are up, your words are repeated back to you. The program finishes by saving your words in a file called MYWAVE.WAV.

Listing 35.2. The code for the Records program shows how to record and play back sound from a WAV file.

```
program Records;

{ Program copyright (c) 1996 by Charles Calvert }
{ Project Name: Records }

uses
  MMSystem;

const
  MaxStr = 200;

var
  DeviceID: LongInt;

function mciError(Return: LongInt; Caller: string): Boolean;
var
  S: array[0..MaxStr] of Char;
begin
  if Return <> 0 then begin
    mciGetErrorString(Return, S, MaxStr);
    WriteLn(Strpas(S) + ' ' + Caller);
    Halt;
  end;
  mciError := True;
end;


function RecordSound(MMSecs: LongInt): LongInt;
var
  mciOpen: Tmci_Open_Parms;
  mciRecord: Tmci_Record_Parms;
  mciPlay: Tmci_Play_Parms;
  mciSave: Tmci_SaveParms;
  Flags: Word;
begin
  mciOpen.lpstrDeviceType := 'waveaudio';
  mciOpen.lpstrElementName := '';
  Flags := mci_Open_Element or mci_Open_Type;
  mciError(mciSendCommand(0, mci_Open, Flags, LongInt(@mciOpen)), 'Open');

  DeviceID := mciOpen.wDeviceId;

  WriteLn('Record');
  mciRecord.dwTo := MMSecs;
  Flags := mci_To or mci_Wait;
  mciError(mciSendCommand(DeviceID, mci_Record,
           Flags, LongInt(@mciRecord)), 'Record');

  WriteLn('Stop');
  mciPlay.dwFrom := 0;
  Flags := mci_From or mci_Wait;
  mciError(mciSendCommand(DeviceId, mci_Play, Flags, LongInt(@mciPlay)), 'Play');

  mciSave.lpfileName := 'MyWave.Wav';
  Flags := mci_Save_File or mci_Wait;
```

```
    mciError(mciSendCommand(DeviceID, mci_Save, Flags, LongInt(@mciSave)), 'Save');

    mciError(mciSendCommand(DeviceID, mci_Close, 0, LongInt(nil)), 'Close');
end;


begin
  RecordSound(10000);
end.
```

After the in-depth examination of the Play program, there's little need to go into much detail about Records. The program begins by opening the MCI WAV device. Notice that this time an empty element name is passed in, as you want to create a new file rather than play or modify an old one.

The next step is to record your voice:

```
    mciRecord.dwTo := MMSecs;
    Flags := mci_To or mci_Wait;
    mciError(mciSendCommand(DeviceID, mci_Record,
            Flags, LongInt(@mciRecord)), 'Record');
```

The mciRecord structure looks like this:

```
    Tmci_Record_Parms = record
      dwCallback: DWORD;
      dwFrom: DWORD;
      dwTo: DWORD;
    end;
```

You can ignore the dwCallback parameter, which is used to designate a callback window if you want to receive mm_mciNotify messages (such as the mci_Notify_Successful message I talked about in the last chapter).

The dwTo field is filled in with the amount of information you want to record, measured in milliseconds. If you don't fill in the dwTo field, the recording continues until you send an mci_Stop command, as shown later in this chapter, in the Media32 program. You can record from one point in a file to another point in a file using the dw_From and dw_To flags. That is, you can edit the middle of the file.

Once again, the mci_Wait command is passed in to designate that you don't want the function to return until the recording is completed:

```
Flags := mci_To or mci_Wait;
```

After recording the file, the program plays it back to the user:

```
    mciPlay.dwFrom := 0;
    Flags := mci_From or mci_Wait;
    mciSendCommand(DeviceId, mci_Play, Flags, LongInt(@mciPlay));
```

This is the same command given in the Play program, so there is no need for an explanation.

Before shutting down the device, the file is saved to disk:

```
mciSave.lpfileName := 'MyWave.Wav';
Flags := mci_Save_File or mci_Wait;
mciError(mciSendCommand(DeviceID, mci_Save, Flags, LongInt(@mciSave)), 'Save');
```

The `Tmci_SaveParms` structure looks like this:

```
Tmci_SaveParmsA = record
  dwCallback: DWORD;
  lpfilename: PAnsiChar;
end;
```

You can ignore the `dwCallback` field, but should designate the filename in the `lpFileName` field.

That's all I'm going to say about the Records program. Really, the basic theory behind the `mciSendCommand` interface is not that hard to understand. You have to spend some time wrestling with the flags, constants, and parameters, but the basic concepts involved are simple enough.

The Media32 Program

To illustrate the points made in this chapter, I have constructed a sample program called Media32 that works with CDs, WAV files, and MIDI files.

The Media32 program is divided into two major sections: a Delphi front and a set of utility files that do the grunt work. Specifically, there are five utility files:

- PLAYINFO.PAS contains general-purpose code for playing multimedia files.
- WAVEINFO.PAS contains code for playing WAV files.
- MIDIINFO.PAS contains code for playing MIDI files.
- AVIINFO.PAS contains code for playing AVI files.
- CDINFO.PAS contains code for playing music CDs.

Each of the four main types of files have a Delphi front end:

- WAVEPLAY.PAS is a Delphi front end for playing WAV files.
- MIDIPLAY.PAS is a Delphi front end for playing MIDI files.
- AVIPLAY.PAS is a Delphi front end for playing AVI files.
- CDPLAY.PAS is a Delphi front end for playing CDs.

There are three other files also used by the program:

- CAPABLE1.PAS contains the capability dialog showing what devices are supported on a particular system.
- TIMENAME.PAS is support dialog used by WAVEPLAY.PAS for recording WAV files.
- GLOBALS.PAS contains some global declarations.
- MAIN.PAS is the main file for the Media32 project.

This is a fairly large project but, as you can see, it's arranged in a sensible manner. All the files that contain raw MMSYSTEM.PAS-related code end with INFO: WAVEINFO, MIDIINFO, and so on. The Delphi front ends for these files all end in PLAY: WAVEPLAY, CDPLAY, and so on. Then there are a few other files used to glue the program together, or to report on the capabilities of the current system.

Listings 35.3 through 35.15 contain the code for the program. You can find the source on the CD-ROM, along with some WAV, MIDI, and AVI files that you can use for experimentation. Remember that the StrBox unit referenced in the uses clause for this program ships on the *Unleashed* CD-ROM, in a subdirectory called UNITS. To compile this program you need to go to the Project | Options | Directories/Conditionals menu page and specify this directory in the Search Path option, or else you should be sure this directory is listed in the Library Path found in the Tools | Options | Library menu page.

Listing 35.3. The code for playing AVI files. Note that I have ported portions of the Video for Windows headers from C to Pascal.

```
unit AviInfo;

{ Program copyright (c) 1995 by Charles Calvert }
{ Project Name: Media32}

interface

uses
  WinProcs, MMSystem, WinTypes,
  Classes;

const
  MCI_DGV_OPEN_PARENT         = $00020000;
  MCI_DGV_OPEN_WS             = $00010000;
  MCI_MCIAVI_PLAY_WINDOW      = $01000000;
  MCI_MCIAVI_PLAY_FULLSCREEN  = $02000000;
  MCI_MCIAVI_PLAY_FULLBY2     = $04000000;
  MCI_DGV_WHERE_SOURCE        = $00020000;
  MCI_DGV_STATUS_HWND         = $00004001;

type
  Tmci_Close_Parms = Tmci_Generic_Parms;

  Pmci_dgv_Set_Parms = ^Tmci_dgv_Set_Parms;
  Tmci_dgv_Set_Parms = record
    dwCallback: LongInt;
    dwTimeFormat: LongInt;
    dwAudio: LongInt;
    dwFileFormat: LongInt;
    dwSpeed: LongInt;
  end;

  TMainAviHeader = record
    dwMicroSecPerFrame: LongInt;
```

continues

Listing 35.3. continued

```
      dwMaxBytesPerSec: LongInt;
      dwPaddingGranularity: LongInt;
      dwFlags: LongInt;
      dwTotalFrames: LongInt;
      dwInitialFrames: LongInt;
      dwStreams: LongInt;
      dwSuggestedBufferSize: LongInt;
      dwWidth: LongInt;
      dwHeight: LongInt;
      dwScale: LongInt;
      dwRate: LongInt;
      dwStart: LongInt;
      dwLength: LongInt;
    end;

{ parameter block for MCI_OPEN command message }
  Pmci_dgv_Open_Parms = ^Tmci_dgv_Open_Parms;
  Tmci_dgv_Open_Parms = record
    dwCallback: LongInt;
    wDeviceID: Word;
    wReserved0: Word;
    lpstrDeviceType: PChar;
    lpstrElementName: PChar;
    lpstrAlias: PChar;
    dwStyle: LongInt;
    hWndParent: Hwnd;
    wReserved1: Word;
  end;

  pmci_dgv_Window_Parms = ^Tmci_dgv_Window_Parms;
  Tmci_dgv_Window_Parms = record
    dwCallback: LongInt;
    HWindow: HWnd;
    wReserved1: Word;
    nCmdShow: Word;
    wReserved2: Word;
    lpstrText: PChar;
  end;


  Pmci_dgv_status_parms = ^Tmci_dgv_status_Parms;_DGV_STATUS_PARMS;
  Tmci_dgv_status_parms = record
    dwCallback: LongInt;
    dwReturn: LongInt;
    dwItem: LongInt;
    dwTrack: LongInt;
    lpstrDrive: PChar;
    dwReference: LongInt;
  end;

  Pmci_dgv_Rect_Parms = ^Tmci_dgv_Rect_Parms;
  Tmci_Dgv_Rect_Parms = record
    dwCallback: LongInt;
  {$ifdef MCI_USE_OFFEXT}
    ptOffset: TPoint;
    ptExtent: TPoint;
```

```
    {$else}
    rc: TRect;
    {$endif}
  end;

function PlayFlick(ShowFullScreen: Boolean): Boolean;
function OpenFlick(Window: HWnd; Screen: HWnd; Path: PChar): Boolean;
function CloseFlick: Boolean;
procedure positionMovie;
function GetMovieRect(var R: TRect): Boolean;
function aviGetMode: Longint;
function GetCurrentFrame: LongInt;
procedure SetMoviePosition;
function SetDisplay: Boolean;
function SeekToStart: Boolean;

implementation

uses
  Globals;

var
  VideoID: LongInt;
  MovieOpen: Boolean;
  rcMovie: TRect;
  MovieWindow: HWnd; { The movie screen itself }
  OwnerWindow: Hwnd; { For Sending mm_Notify }


function CheckForError(Return: LongInt; CallerFunction: PChar): Boolean;
var
  S: array[0..MaxLen] of Char;
begin
  if Return <> 0 then begin
    mciGetErrorString(Return, S, MaxLen - 1);
    MessageBox(OwnerWindow, S, CallerFunction, mb_Ok);
    CheckForError := False;
    Exit;
  end;
  CheckForError := True;
end;

function GetCurrentFrame: LongInt;
var
  mciSet: Tmci_dgv_Set_Parms;
  mciStatus: Tmci_dgv_Status_Parms;
  ErrNo: LongInt;
begin
  Result := -1;
  { put in frame mode }
  FillChar(mciSet, SizeOf(mciSet), #0);
  mciSet.dwTimeFormat := mci_Format_Frames;
  mciSendCommand(videoID,
                 mci_Set,
                 mci_Set_Time_Format,
                 LongInt(@mciSet));
```

continues

Listing 35.3. continued

```
{ If device is playing get the position }
  if (aviGetMode = MCI_MODE_PLAY) then begin
    mciStatus.dwItem := MCI_STATUS_POSITION;
    ErrNo := mciSendCommand(videoID,
                 MCI_STATUS,
                 MCI_STATUS_ITEM,
                 LongInt(@mciStatus));
    if not CheckForError(ErrNo, 'GetCurrentFrame') then Exit;
  end;
  { Get the position from mciStatus.dwReturn }
  GetCurrentFrame := mciStatus.dwReturn;
end;

function GetMovieRect(var R: TRect): Boolean;
var
  ErrNo: LongInt;
  mciRect: Tmci_dgv_Rect_Parms;
begin
  GetMovieRect := False;
  FillChar(mciRect, SizeOf(mciRect), #0);
  ErrNo := mciSendCommand(VideoID,
                 mci_Where,
                 mci_dgv_Where_Source,
                 LongInt(@mciRect));

  if not CheckForError(ErrNo, 'GetMovieRect') then Exit;

  R := mciRect.rc;  { get it in the movie bounds rect }
  GetMovieRect := True;
end;

{ This function centers a movie in an existing window }
procedure CenterMovie;
var
  rcClient, rcMovieBounds: TRect;
begin
  if not MovieOpen then Exit;
  GetClientRect(MovieWindow, rcClient);
  GetMovieRect(rcMovieBounds);
  rcMovie.left := (rcClient.right div 2) - (rcMovieBounds.right div 2);
  rcMovie.top := (rcClient.bottom div 2) - (rcMovieBounds.bottom div 2);
  rcMovie.right := rcMovie.left + rcMovieBounds.right;
  rcMovie.bottom := rcMovie.top + rcMovieBounds.bottom;
  MoveWindow(MovieWindow, rcMovie.left, rcMovie.top,
             rcMovieBounds.right, rcMovieBounds.bottom, TRUE);
end;

{ This function wraps a window around a movie }
procedure positionMovie;
var
  rcClient, rcMovieBounds: TRect;
  Caption: Integer;
begin
  if not MovieOpen then Exit;
  GetMovieRect(rcMovieBounds);
  Caption := GetSystemMetrics(sm_cyCaption);
```

```
      GetWindowRect(MovieWindow, rcClient);
      MoveWindow(MovieWindow, rcClient.Left, rcClient.Top,
                 rcMovieBounds.Right, rcMovieBounds.bottom + Caption, TRUE);
      ShowWindow(MovieWindow, sw_ShowNormal);
end;

procedure SetMoviePosition;
var
  V: Tmci_Anim_rect_parms;
  R, R1: TRect;
  Flags: LongInt;
  ErrNo: LongInt;
begin
  GetClientRect(MovieWindow, R1);
  R := Rect(4, 4, R1.Right - 8, R1.Bottom - 8);
  Flags := mci_Anim_Rect or mci_Anim_Put_Destination;
  V.rc := R;
  ErrNo := mciSendCommand(VideoID, mci_Put, Flags, LongInt(@V));
  CheckForError(ErrNo, 'SetMoviePosition');
end;


function SetDisplay: Boolean;
var
  AnimWindow: Tmci_Anim_Window_Parms;
  Flags: LongInt;
  ErrNo: LongInt;
begin
  Flags := mci_Wait or mci_Anim_Window_Hwnd;
  AnimWindow.Wnd := MovieWindow;
  ErrNo := mciSendCommand(VideoID, mci_Window, Flags, LongInt(@AnimWindow));
  CheckForError(ErrNo, 'SetDisplay');
  Result := True;
end;

{--------------------------------------------------
  Window will get the mm_Notify messages.
  Screen is for showing them movie in another window.
 --------------------------------------------------}
function OpenFlick(Window: HWnd; Screen: HWnd; Path: PChar): Boolean;
var
  mciOpen: Tmci_dgv_Open_Parms;
  ErrNo: LongInt;
begin
  OpenFlick := False;
  OwnerWindow := Window;   { For mm_Notify }
  MovieWindow := Screen;   { For sizeing he screen }
  fillChar(mciOpen, SizeOf(mciOpen), #0);
  mciOpen.lpstrDeviceType := 'avivideo';
  mciOpen.lpstrElementName := Path;
  mciOpen.dwStyle := ws_Child;
  mciOpen.hWndParent := OwnerWindow;

  ErrNo := mciSendCommand(0,
                          mci_Open,
                          mci_dgv_Open_Parent or
                          mci_Open_Element or
```

continues

Listing 35.3. continued

```
                              mci_dgv_Open_ws,
                              LongInt(@mciOpen));

  if not CheckForError(ErrNo, 'OpenFlick') then Exit;

  videoID := mciOpen.wDeviceID;

  OpenFlick := True;
end;

function GetMovieWindow: hwnd;
var
  mciStatus: Tmci_dgv_Status_Parms;
begin
  mciStatus.dwItem := mci_DGV_Status_Hwnd;
  mciSendCommand(VideoID,
                 mci_Status,
                 mci_Status_Item,
                 LongInt(@mciStatus));
  OwnerWindow := mciStatus.dwReturn;
  GetMovieWindow := OwnerWindow;
end;

function PlayFlick(ShowFullScreen: Boolean): Boolean;
var
  mciPlay: Tmci_Play_Parms;
  ErrNo: LongInt;
  Flags: LongInt;
begin
  PlayFlick := False;

  FillChar(mciPlay, SizeOf(mciPlay), #0);
  mciPlay.dwCallback := OwnerWindow;
  if ShowFullScreen then
    Flags := mci_mciAvi_Play_FullScreen or mci_Notify
  else
    Flags := mci_Notify;

  ErrNo := mciSendCommand(videoID, mci_Play, Flags, LongInt(@mciPlay));

  if not CheckForError(ErrNo, 'PlayFlick') then Exit;

  MovieOpen := TRUE;
  PlayFlick := True;
end;

function CloseFlick: Boolean;
var
  mciClose: Tmci_Close_Parms;
  ErrNo: LongInt;
begin
  Result := False;
  if videoID = -1 then Exit;
  mciClose.dwCallBack := OwnerWindow;
  ErrNo := mciSendCommand(videoId, mci_Close, 0, LongInt(@mciClose));
```

```
  if not CheckForError(ErrNo, 'OpenFlick') then Exit;
  videoID := -1;
  CloseFlick := True;
end;

{ Totally identical to code in PLAYINFO.
  Can be removed once inside of DLLs }
function aviGetMode: Longint;
var
  Info: Tmci_Status_Parms;
  Flags,
  ErrNo: LongInt;
begin
  Result := -1;
  FillChar(Info, SizeOf(a_Status_Parms), 0);
  Info.dwItem := Mci_Status_Mode;
  Flags := mci_Status_Item;
  ErrNo := mciSendCommand(VideoId, Mci_Status, Flags, LongInt(@Info));
  if not CheckForError(ErrNo, 'GetMode') then Exit;
  aviGetMode := Info.dwReturn;
end;

function SeekToStart: Boolean;
var
  Parms: Tmci_Seek_Parms;
  Flags: LongInt;
  ErrNo: LongInt;
begin
  Result := False;
  Flags := mci_Wait or mci_Seek_To_Start;
  ErrNo := mciSendCommand(VideoID, mci_Seek, Flags, LongInt(@Parms));
  if not CheckForError(ErrNo, 'GetMode') then Exit;
  SeekToStart := True;
end;

initialization
  VideoID := -1;
finalization
  CloseFlick;
end.
```

Listing 35.4. The Delphi front end for playing AVI files.

```
unit AviPlay;

interface

uses
  SysUtils, Messages, Classes,
  Graphics, Controls, Forms,
  Dialogs, AviInfo, MMSystem,
  WinProcs, WinTypes, StdCtrls,
  ExtCtrls, Globals;
```

continues

Listing 35.4. continued

```
type
  THMMIO = Word;
  TMovieInfo = record
    PlayHandle: HWnd;
    Filename: TMaxString;
    Filesize: LongInt;
    Avi: TMainAviHeader;
    FullScreen: Boolean;
    FitInWindow: Boolean;
    DoRepeat: Boolean;
    UseScreen: Boolean;
  end;

  TAviDialog = class(TForm)
    Panel1: TPanel;
    OpenDialog1: TOpenDialog;
    Panel2: TPanel;
    cbFullScreen: TCheckBox;
    cbRepeat: TCheckBox;
    bBrowse: TButton;
    cbFitInWindow: TCheckBox;
    cbUseScreen: TCheckBox;
    bStop: TButton;
    bStart: TButton;
    procedure PlayFile(Sender: TObject);
    procedure FormResize(Sender: TObject);
    procedure bStartClick(Sender: TObject);
    procedure bStopClick(Sender: TObject);
  private
    AviInfo: TMovieInfo;
    FileName: String;
    Normal, FullScreen: HWnd;
    procedure Loaded; override;
    procedure CreateParams(var Params: TCreateParams); override;
    procedure SetInfoRecord(var AviInfo: TMovieInfo);
    function GetInfo(path: PChar): Boolean;
    function GetFullTitle: string;
    { Public declarations }
    procedure mciNotify(var Msg: TMessage);
      message mm_mciNotify;
    procedure PlayAviFile;
  end;

var
  AviDialog: TAviDialog;

implementation

{$R *.DFM}

procedure TAviDialog.Loaded;
begin
  inherited Loaded;
  Visible := false;
  Position := poDefault;
  BorderIcons := [];
```

```
    BorderStyle := bsNone;
    HandleNeeded;
    SetBounds(0,0,Width,Height);
end;

procedure TAviDialog.CreateParams(var Params: TCreateParams);
begin
  inherited CreateParams(Params);
  Params.WndParent := (Owner as TForm).Handle;
  Params.Style := WS_CHILD or WS_CLIPSIBLINGS;
  Params.X := 0;
  Params.Y := 0;
end;

function TAviDialog.GetFullTitle: string;
begin
  if OpenDialog1.Execute then
    Result := OpenDialog1.FileName
  else
    Result := '';
end;

procedure TAviDialog.SetInfoRecord(var AviInfo: TMovieInfo);
begin
  AviInfo.PlayHandle := Panel1.Handle;
  AviInfo.FullScreen := cbFullScreen.Checked;
  AviInfo.DoRepeat := cbRepeat.Checked;
  AviInfo.FitInWindow := cbFitInWindow.Checked;
  AviInfo.UseScreen := cbUseScreen.Checked;
end;


{The following sets the time format to frames and
 obtains the current position if the device is playing:}

function Min(x, y: LongInt): LongInt;
begin
  if X < Y then Min := X else Min := Y;
end;

function TAviDialog.GetInfo(Path: PChar): Boolean;
var
  SR: TSearchRec;
  h: THMMIO;
  mmParent, mmSub, mmSubSub: TMMCKINFO;
  n: Word;

begin
  GetInfo := False;
  FillChar(AviInfo, SizeOf(TMovieInfo), #0);
{ StrCopy(AviWindow.AviInfo.Filename, Path); }
  if findfirst(Filename, faArchive, SR) <> 0 then begin
    MessageBox(Handle,'Error finding file', nil, mb_Ok);
    Exit;
  end;
  AviInfo.Filesize := SR.Size;
```

continues

Listing 35.4. continued

```
  StrUpper(AviInfo.FileName);

  h := mmioOpen(path, nil, MMIO_READ);
  if h = 0 then begin
    MessageBox(Handle, 'Error opening file', nil, mb_Ok);
    Exit;
  end;

  mmParent.fccType := mmioStringToFOURCC('AVI ', mmio_ToUpper);
  if mmioDescend(h, @mmParent, nil, MMIO_FINDRIFF) <> 0 then begin
    mmioClose(h,0);
    MessageBox(Handle,'Error finding AVI chunk', nil, mb_Ok);
    Exit;
  end;

  mmSub.fccType := mmioStringToFOURCC('hdrl', 0);
  if mmioDescend(h,@mmSub,@mmParent, MMIO_FINDLIST) <> 0 then begin
    MessageBox(Handle,'Error finding hdrl chunk', nil, mb_Ok);
    mmioClose(h,0);
    Exit
  end;

  mmSubSub.ckid := mmioStringToFOURCC('avih', mb_Ok);
  if mmioDescend(h,@mmSubSub,@mmSub, MMIO_FINDCHUNK) <> 0then begin
    MessageBox(Handle, 'Error finding avih chunk', nil, mb_Ok);
    mmioClose(h,0);
    Exit;
  end;

  n := Min(mmSub.cksize, sizeof(TMainAviHeader));
  if(mmioRead(h, @AviInfo.Avi, n) <> n) then begin
    MessageBox(Handle, 'Error reading header chunk', nil, mb_Ok);
    mmioClose(h,0);
    Exit;
  end;

  mmioClose(h,0);
  GetInfo := True;
end;

procedure TAviDialog.PlayFile(Sender: TObject);
begin
  FileName := GetFullTitle;
end;

procedure TAviDialog.PlayAviFile;
var
  P: array[0..250] of Char;
begin
  CloseFlick;
  if not OpenFlick(Handle, Panel1.Handle, StrPCopy(P, FileName)) then Exit;
  if AviInfo.UseScreen then SetDisplay;
  if AviInfo.FitInWindow then SetMoviePosition;
  PlayFlick(aviInfo.FullScreen);
end;
```

```
procedure TAviDialog.mciNotify(var Msg: TMessage);
begin
  case Msg.WParam of
    MCI_NOTIFY_SUPERSEDED: ;
    MCI_NOTIFY_ABORTED: ;
    MCI_NOTIFY_SUCCESSFUL:
      if aviGetMode = mci_Mode_Stop then begin
        if AviInfo.DoRepeat then begin
          SeekToStart;
          PlayFlick(AviInfo.FullScreen)
        end else
          KillTimer(Handle, PlayTimer);
      end;
  end;
end;

procedure TAviDialog.FormResize(Sender: TObject);
const
  Space = 10;
begin
  Panel1.Left := Space;
  Panel1.Top := Space;
  Panel1.Width := ClientWidth - (2 * Space);
  Panel1.Height := ClientHeight - (Panel2.Height + (Space * 2));
end;

procedure TAviDialog.bStartClick(Sender: TObject);
begin
  CloseFlick;
  FullScreen := Panel1.Handle;
  SetInfoRecord(aviInfo);
  if Length(FileName) > 0 then
    PlayAviFile;
end;

procedure TAviDialog.bStopClick(Sender: TObject);
begin
  CloseFlick;
end;

end.
```

Listing 35.5. The PLAYINFO unit containing many generic calls relied on by all the devices.

```
unit PlayInfo;
{
  Routines shared by all the Play objects. These are things
  that everyone can do, or at least that can be done on more
  than one device.

  Copyright (c) 1996, by Charlie Calvert
}
```

continues

Listing 35.5. continued

```
interface

uses
  MMSystem, WinTypes, SysUtils,
  WinProcs;

const
  MsgLen = 200;

var
  wDeviceID: Word;
  PlayWindow: HWnd;
  ErrorState: Boolean;

function CloseMCI: Boolean;
function ErrorMsg(Error: LongInt; Msg: PChar): Boolean;
function GetDeviceID: Word;
function GetInfo(S: PChar): PChar;
function GetLen: Longint;
function GetLocation: LongInt;
function GetMode: Longint;
function OpenMCI(PWindow: HWnd; FileName, DeviceType: PChar): Boolean;
function PlayMCI: Boolean;
function SetTimeFormatMs: Boolean;
function StopMci: Boolean;

implementation

function CloseMci: Boolean;
var
  ErrNo: LongInt;
  S1: array[0..MsgLen] of Char;
begin
  CloseMci := True;
  ErrNo := mciSendCommand(wDeviceID, MCI_Close, 0, 0);
  if ErrNo <> 0 then begin
    CloseMci := False;
    ErrorMsg(ErrNo, S1);
    exit;
  end;
  wDeviceID := 0;
end;

function GetDeviceId: Word;
begin
  GetDeviceId := wDeviceId;
end;

function GetErrorMessage(RC:LongInt; S: PChar): PChar;
begin
  if not mciGetErrorString(RC, S, MsgLen) then
    StrCopy(S, 'No message available');
  GetErrorMessage := S;
end;
```

```
function ErrorMsg(Error: LongInt; Msg: PChar): Boolean;
var
  S, S1: array[0..MsgLen] of Char;
begin
  Result := False;
  if ErrorState then Exit;
  ErrorMsg := True;
  StrCopy(S, 'Return Code: ');
  Str(Error:5, S1);
  StrCat(S, S1);
  StrCat(S, Msg);
  StrCat(S, GetErrorMessage(Error, S1));
  if Error <> 0 then begin
    ErrorState := True;
    MessageBox(0, S1, 'Information', mb_OK);
    ErrorMsg := False;
  end;
end;

function GetInfo(S: PChar): PChar;
var
  Info: Tmci_Info_Parms;
  Flags: LongInt;
  S1: array[0..MsgLen] of Char;
  ErrNo: LongInt;
begin
  Info.dwCallBack := 0;
  Info.lpstrReturn := S;
  Info.dwRetSize := MsgLen;
  Flags := Mci_Info_Product;
  ErrNo := mciSendCommand(wDeviceID, Mci_Info, Flags, LongInt(@Info));
  ErrorMsg(ErrNo, S1);
  GetInfo := S;
end;

function GetLen: Longint;
var
  Info: Tmci_Status_Parms;
  Flags,
  ErrNo: LongInt;
  S1: array [0..MsgLen] of Char;
begin
  Result := -1;
  FillChar(Info, SizeOf(Tmci_Status_Parms), 0);
  Info.dwItem := Mci_Status_Length;
  Flags := Mci_Status_Item;
  ErrNo := MciSendCommand(wDeviceID, Mci_Status, Flags, LongInt(@Info));
  if ErrNo <> 0 then begin
    ErrorMsg(ErrNo, S1);
    exit;
  end;
  GetLen := Info.dwReturn;
end;

function GetLocation: LongInt;
var
```

continues

Listing 35.5. continued

```pascal
    Info: Tmci_Status_Parms;
    Flags: LongInt;
    ErrNo: LongInt;
    S: array[0..MsgLen] of Char;
begin
    Info.dwItem := Mci_Status_Position;
    Flags := Mci_Status_Item;
    ErrNo := MciSendCommand(wDeviceID, Mci_Status, Flags, LongInt(@Info));
    if ErrNo <> 0 then begin
      ErrorMsg(ErrNo, S);
      Result := -1;
      Exit;
    end;
    GetLocation := Info.dwReturn;
end;

function GetMode: Longint;
var
    Info: Tmci_Status_Parms;
    Flags,
    ErrNo: LongInt;
    S1: array [0..MsgLen] of Char;
begin
    FillChar(Info, SizeOf(Tmci_Status_Parms), 0);
    Info.dwItem := Mci_Status_Mode;
    Flags := Mci_Status_Item;
    ErrNo := MciSendCommand(wDeviceID, Mci_Status, Flags, LongInt(@Info));
    if ErrNo <> 0 then begin
      ErrorMsg(ErrNo, S1);
      Result := -1;
      exit;
    end;
    GetMode := Info.dwReturn;
end;

function OpenMCI(PWindow: HWnd; FileName, DeviceType: PChar): Boolean;
var
    OpenParms: Tmci_Open_Parms;
    Style: LongInt;
    ErrNo: LongInt;
    S1: array [0..MsgLen] of Char;
begin
    ErrorState := False;
    OpenMCI := True;
    PlayWindow := PWindow;
    OpenParms.lpstrDeviceType := DeviceType;
    OpenParms.lpstrElementName := FileName;
    Style := Mci_Open_Type or Mci_Open_Element;
    ErrNo := MciSendCommand(0, MCI_OPEN, Style, LongInt(@OpenParms));
    if ErrNo <> 0 then begin
      OpenMCI := False;
      ErrorMsg(ErrNo, S1);
      exit;
    end;
    wDeviceId := OpenParms.wDeviceID;
end;
```

```pascal
function PlayMCI: Boolean;
var
  ErrNo: LongInt;
  Info: Tmci_Play_Parms;
  S1: array[0..MsgLen] of Char;
begin
  PlayMci := True;
  Info.dwCallBack := PlayWindow;
  ErrNo := MciSendCommand(wDeviceID, Mci_Play, Mci_Notify, LongInt(@Info));
  if ErrNo <> 0 then begin
    PlayMci := False;
    ErrorMsg(ErrNo, S1);
    exit;
  end;
end;

function SetTimeFormatMS: Boolean;
var
  Info: Tmci_Set_Parms;
  Flags,
  ErrNo: LongInt;
  S1: array [0..MsgLen] of Char;
begin
  SetTimeFormatMS := True;
  Info.dwTimeFormat := Mci_Format_Milliseconds;
  Flags := Mci_Set_Time_Format;
  ErrNo := MciSendCommand(wDeviceID, MCI_Set, Flags, LongInt(@Info));
  if ErrNo <> 0 then begin
    ErrorMsg(ErrNo, S1);
    SetTimeFormatMS := False;
  end;
end;

function StopMci: Boolean;
var
  ErrNo: LongInt;
  Info: Tmci_Generic_Parms;
  S1: array[0..MsgLen] of Char;
begin
  StopMci := True;
  Info.dwCallBack := 0;
  ErrNo := MciSendCommand(wDeviceID, Mci_Stop, Mci_Notify, LongInt(@Info));
  if ErrNo <> 0 then begin
    StopMci := False;
    ErrorMsg(ErrNo, S1);
    exit;
  end;
end;

begin
  wDeviceId := 0;
end.
```

Listing 35.6. Code for playing WAV files.

```pascal
unit WaveInfo;
{
  Copyright (c) 1996, by Charlie Calvert
  Feel free to use this code as an adjunct to your own programs.
}

interface

uses
  MMSystem, PlayInfo, SysUtils,
  WinProcs, WinTypes;


function GetNumTracks: LongInt;
procedure PlayFromTo(Start, Finish: Byte);
function DoRecord(MMSecs: LongInt): LongInt;
function RecordToStop: LongInt;
function SaveFile(FileName: PChar): Boolean;

implementation

function GetNumTracks: LongInt;
Var
  Info   : Tmci_Status_Parms;
  ErrNo : LongInt;
  Flags  : LongInt;
  S1     : array [0..MsgLen] of Char;
begin
  FillChar(Info, SizeOf(Tmci_Status_Parms), 0);
  Info.dwItem     := mci_Status_Number_Of_Tracks;
  Flags := mci_Status_Item;
  ErrNo := mciSendCommand( wDeviceId, mci_Status, Flags, Longint(@Info));
  if ErrNo <> 0 then begin
    ErrorMsg(ErrNo, S1);
    GetNumTracks := -1;
    exit;
  end;
  GetNumTracks := Info.dwReturn;
end;

procedure PlayFromTo(Start, Finish: Byte);
Var
  Info         : Tmci_Play_Parms;
  Flags, ErrNo : LongInt;
  S1: array[0..MsgLen] of Char;
begin
  Info.dwCallBack := PlayWindow;
  Info.dwFrom := 600;
  Info.dwTo   := 1000;

  Flags := mci_From OR mci_To or mci_Notify;
  ErrNo := mciSendCommand(wDeviceId, mci_PLAY, Flags, Longint(@Info));

  if ErrNo <> 0 then ErrorMsg(ErrNo, S1);
end;
```

```
function DoRecord(MMSecs: LongInt): LongInt;
var
  Info: Tmci_Record_Parms;
  Flags: Word;
  ErrNo: LongInt;
  S1    : array [0..MsgLen] of Char;
begin
  Result := 0;
  Info.dwCallBack := PlayWindow;
  Info.dwTo := MMSecs;
  Flags := mci_To or mci_Notify;
  ErrNo := mciSendCommand(wDeviceID, mci_Record, Flags, LongInt(@Info));
  if ErrNo <> 0 then
    ErrorMsg(ErrNo, S1)
  else
    Result := 1;
end;

function RecordToStop: LongInt;
var
  Info: Tmci_Record_Parms;
  Flags: Word;
  ErrNo: LongInt;
  S1    : array [0..MsgLen] of Char;
begin
  Result := 0;
  Info.dwCallBack := PlayWindow;
  Flags := mci_Notify;
  ErrNo := mciSendCommand(wDeviceID, mci_Record, Flags, LongInt(@Info));
  if ErrNo <> 0 then
    ErrorMsg(ErrNo, S1)
  else
    Result := 1;
end;

function SaveFile(FileName: PChar): Boolean;
var
  mciSave: Tmci_SaveParms;
  Flags: Word;
  ErrNo: LongInt;
  S1    : array [0..MsgLen] of Char;
begin
  Result := False;
  mciSave.lpfileName := FileName;
  Flags := mci_Save_File or mci_Wait;
  ErrNo := mciSendCommand(wDeviceID, mci_Save, Flags, LongInt(@mciSave));
  if ErrNo <> 0 then
    ErrorMsg(ErrNo, S1)
  else
    Result := True;
end;

end.
```

Listing 35.7. The Delphi front endfor playing WAV files.

```
unit WavePlay;
{
  WavePlay
  Programmer: Charlie Calvert
  Date: March 1993
  UpDate: May 1994
  UpDate for 32 bits: August 1995

  Copyright (c) 1993-96 by Charlie Calvert
  Feel free to use this code as an adjunct to your own programs.
}

interface

uses
  Messages, MMSystem, WinProcs,
  TimeName, WaveInfo, WinTypes,
  SysUtils, Forms, StdCtrls,
  Controls, Classes, PlayInfo,
  FileCtrl, ExtCtrls, Dialogs;

const
  DevStr = 'WaveAudio';

type
  TWaveDlg = class(TForm)
    Play: TButton;
    bStop: TButton;
    FileListBox1: TFileListBox;
    Timer1: TTimer;
    Panel1: TPanel;
    Label1: TLabel;
    Label2: TLabel;
    Label3: TLabel;
    Label4: TLabel;
    DirectoryListBox1: TDirectoryListBox;
    DriveComboBox1: TDriveComboBox;
    StatInfo: TPanel;
    TimeLapsed: TPanel;
    DevInfo: TPanel;
    LenText: TPanel;
    bRecord: TButton;
    SaveDialog1: TSaveDialog;
    procedure SetUpWindow(Sender: TObject);
    procedure WaveAbort(Sender: TObject);
    procedure WavePlay(Sender: TObject);
    procedure WaveRecord(Sender: TObject);
    procedure Timer1Timer(Sender: TObject);
  private
    Recording: Boolean;
    Time: Word;
    procedure CreateParams(var Params: TCreateParams); override;
    procedure Loaded; override;
    procedure GetDetails;
    function GetTimeAndName: Boolean;
    procedure MciNotify(var Msg: TMessage);
```

```
      message mm_MciNotify;
    function GetMode: string;
  end;

var
  WaveDlg: TWaveDlg;

implementation

uses
  StrBox, Globals;

{$R *.dfm}

procedure TWaveDlg.Loaded;
begin
  inherited Loaded;
  Visible := false;
  Position := poDefault;
  BorderIcons := [];
  BorderStyle := bsNone;
  HandleNeeded;
  SetBounds(0,0,Width,Height);
end;

procedure TWaveDlg.CreateParams(var Params: TCreateParams);
begin
  inherited CreateParams(Params);
  Params.WndParent := (Owner as TForm).Handle;
  Params.Style := WS_CHILD or WS_CLIPSIBLINGS;
  Params.X := 0;
  Params.Y := 0;
end;

procedure TWaveDlg.SetUpWindow(Sender: TObject);
var
  S: array[0..MaxLen] of Char;
begin
  GetWindowsDirectory(S, MaxLen);
  DirectoryListBox1.Directory := S + '\media';
  Recording := False;
end;

function TWaveDlg.GetMode: string;
begin
  Result := GetModeString(PlayInfo.GetMode);
end;

procedure TWaveDlg.GetDetails;
var
  S: array[0..100] of Char;
  Result: LongInt;
begin
  Result := GetLen;
  StatInfo.Caption := GetMode;
  StrPCopy(S, Format('%d ms', [Result]));
  LenText.Caption := S;
```

continues

Listing 35.7. continued

```
    Str(GetLocation, S);
    TimeLapsed.Caption := S;
    DevInfo.Caption := StrPas(GetInfo(S));
end;

procedure TWaveDlg.MciNotify(var Msg: TMessage);
var
    S: array[0..100] of Char;
begin
    GetDetails;
    case PlayInfo.GetMode of
        mci_Mode_Stop: begin
            Timer1.Enabled := False;
            if Recording then begin
                Recording := False;
                bStop.Caption := 'Stop';
                if SaveDialog1.Execute then
                    SaveFile(StrPCopy(S, SaveDialog1.FileName));
            end;
            CloseMci;
            StatInfo.Caption := 'Stopped';
        end;
    end;
    Timer1.Enabled := False;
end;

procedure TWaveDlg.WaveAbort(Sender: TObject);
begin
    StopMci;
end;

procedure TWaveDlg.WavePlay(Sender: TObject);
var
    S1, Buf: string;
    Temp: array[0..100] of Char;
begin
    if (FileListBox1.ItemIndex < 0) then begin
        MessageBox(Handle, 'No file selected in listbox', '', mb_Ok);
        exit;
    end;
    Buf := FileListBox1.Items.Strings[FileListBox1.ItemIndex];
    S1 := FileListBox1.Directory + '\' + Buf;
    OpenMci(Handle, StrPCopy(Temp, S1), DevStr);
    SetTimeFormatMS;
    GetDetails;
    PlayMci;
    Timer1.Enabled := True;
end;

function TWaveDlg.GetTimeAndName: Boolean;
var
    D: TTimeNameDlg;
begin
    GetTimeAndName := True;
    D := TTimeNameDlg.Create(Self);
    if not D.Run(Time) then
        GetTimeAndName := False;
end;
```

```
procedure TWaveDlg.WaveRecord(Sender: TObject);
var
  Len: Word;
  S: string;
begin
  if not GetTimeAndName then Exit;
  if not OpenMci(Handle, '', DevStr) then Exit;
  StatInfo.Caption := 'Record';
  SetTimeFormatMS;
  Recording := True;
  if Time = -1 then begin
    bStop.Caption := 'Stop Record';
    RecordToStop
  end else begin
    Len := Time * 1000;
    S := Format('%d', [Len]);
    LenText.Caption := S;
    DoRecord(Len);
  end;
  Timer1.Enabled := True;
end;

procedure TWaveDlg.Timer1Timer(Sender: TObject);
begin
  GetDetails;
end;

end.
```

Listing 35.8. A dialog to designate settings when you are recording a file.

```
unit TimeName;

{ This one has to do with recording voice }

interface

uses
  SysUtils, WinProcs, Messages,
  Classes, Graphics, Controls,
  Forms, Dialogs, StdCtrls,
  WinTypes, Buttons, ExtCtrls;


type
  TTimeNameDlg = class(TForm)
    BitBtn1: TBitBtn;
    TimeSlicer: TRadioGroup;
    BitBtn2: TBitBtn;
    procedure OkPress(Sender: TObject);
  public
    Time: SmallInt;
    function Run(var ITime: Word): Boolean;
  end;
```

continues

Listing 35.8. continued

```
var
  TimeNameDlg: TTimeNameDlg;

implementation

{$R *.DFM}

function TTimeNameDlg.Run(var ITime: Word): Boolean;
begin
  Result := True;
  if ShowModal = mrCancel then
    Result := False;
  ITime := Time;
end;


procedure TTimeNameDlg.OkPress(Sender: TObject);
begin
  case TimeSlicer.ItemIndex of
    0: Time := 5;
    1: Time := 10;
    2: Time := 15;
    3: Time := 30;
    4: Time := 45;
    5: Time := 60;
    6: Time := -1;
  end;
end;

end.
```

Listing 35.9. Code for playing MIDI files.

```
unit MidiInfo;
{
  Copyright (c) June 1993, by Charlie Calvert
  Feel free to use this code as an adjunct to your own programs.
  Update for Delphi32: July, 1995
}

interface

uses
  MMSystem, PlayInfo, SysUtils,
  WinProcs, WinTypes;

procedure PauseMidi;
function GetMidiInfo(S: PChar): PChar;
function CheckForMapper: Boolean;

implementation

const
  MsgLen = 200;
```

```pascal
procedure PauseMidi;
var
  Info: Tmci_Generic_Parms;
  Flags: LongInt;
  S1: array[0..MsgLen] of Char;
  ErrNo: LongInt;
begin
  Info.dwCallBack := 0;
  Flags := 0;
  ErrNo := mciSendCommand(wDeviceID, Mci_Pause, Flags, LongInt(@Info));
  ErrorMsg(ErrNo, S1);
end;


function GetMidiInfo(S: PChar): PChar;
var
  Info: Tmci_Info_Parms;
  Flags: LongInt;
  S1: array[0..MsgLen] of Char;
  ErrNo: LongInt;
begin
  Info.dwCallBack := 0;
  Info.lpstrReturn := S;
  Info.dwRetSize := MsgLen;
  Flags := Mci_Notify or Mci_Info_Product;
  ErrNo := mciSendCommand(wDeviceID, Mci_Info, Flags, LongInt(@Info));
  ErrorMsg(ErrNo, S1);
  GetMidiInfo := S;
end;

function CheckForMapper: Boolean;
const
  S:PChar = ('Midi Mapper is not available, Continue?');
var
  Flags: LongInt;
  ErrNo: LongInt;
  StatusParms: Tmci_Status_Parms;
  Sti: Integer;
begin
  CheckForMapper := False;
  StatusParms.dwItem := Mci_Seq_Status_Port;
  Flags := Mci_Status_Item;
  ErrNo := MciSendCommand(wDeviceID, Mci_Status, Flags, LongInt(@StatusParms));
  if ErrNo <> 0 then begin
    CloseMci;
    Exit;
  end;

  StI := LoWord(StatusParms.dwReturn);
  if (Sti <> Midi_Mapper) then begin
    if(MessageBox(0, S, 'Query', mb_YesNo) <> IDYes) then begin
      CloseMci;
      exit;
    end;
  end;
  CheckForMapper := True;
end;

end.
```

Listing 35.10. The Delphi front end for playing MIDI files.

```
unit MidiPlay;

{
  MidiPlay
  Programmer: Charlie Calvert
  Copyright (c) 1996, by Charlie Calvert
  Feel free to use this code as an adjunct to your own programs.
}

interface

uses
  MidiInfo, Messages, MMSystem,
  SysUtils, WinProcs, Classes,
  Controls, StdCtrls, Forms,
  WinTypes, PlayInfo, FileCtrl,
  Buttons, ExtCtrls;

const
  DevType:PChar = 'Sequencer';

type
  TMidiDlg = class(TForm)
    FileListBox1: TFileListBox;
    bbAbort: TBitBtn;
    bbOpen: TBitBtn;
    bbPause: TBitBtn;
    bbPlay: TBitBtn;
    Panel1: TPanel;
    Label1: TLabel;
    Label2: TLabel;
    Label3: TLabel;
    pCurMode: TPanel;
    LenText: TPanel;
    DevInfo: TPanel;
    DirectoryListBox1: TDirectoryListBox;
    DriveComboBox1: TDriveComboBox;
    pCurTime: TPanel;
    Label4: TLabel;
    procedure MidiAbort(Sender: TObject);
    procedure MidiOpen(Sender: TObject);
    procedure MidiPause(Sender: TObject);
    procedure MidiPlay(Sender: TObject);
    procedure SetUpWindow(Sender: TObject);
  private
    FileName: string;
    Location: LongInt;
    DeviceIsOpen: Boolean;
    procedure Loaded; override;
    procedure CreateParams(var Params: TCreateParams); override;
    procedure StartTimer;
  public
    procedure wmDestroy(var M: TMessage); message wm_Destroy;
    procedure ReportStatus; virtual;
    procedure MciNotify(var Msg: TMessage);
```

```
      message mm_MciNotify;
    procedure WmTimer(var Msg: TMessage);
      message wm_Timer;
    function GetMode: LongInt; virtual;
  end;

var
  MidiDlg: TMidiDlg;

implementation

uses
  Globals;

{$R *.DFM}

procedure TMidiDlg.Loaded;
begin
   inherited Loaded;
   Visible := false;
   Position := poDefault;
   BorderIcons := [];
   BorderStyle := bsNone;
   HandleNeeded;
   SetBounds(0,0,Width,Height);
end;

procedure TMidiDlg.CreateParams(var Params: TCreateParams);
begin
  inherited CreateParams(Params);
  Params.WndParent := (Owner as TForm).Handle;
  Params.Style := WS_CHILD or WS_CLIPSIBLINGS;
  Params.X := 0;
  Params.Y := 0;
end;

procedure TMidiDlg.wmDestroy(var M: TMessage);
begin
  if GetDeviceId <> 0 then CloseMci;
  inherited;
end;

procedure TMidiDlg.SetUpWindow(Sender: TObject);
begin
  DeviceIsOpen := False;
  Location := 0;
  DirectoryListBox1.Directory := DriveComboBox1.Drive + ':\';
end;

procedure TMidiDlg.ReportStatus;
begin
  pCurMode.Caption := GetModeString(PlayInfo.GetMode);
  pCurTime.Caption := IntToStr(GetLocation);
end;

procedure TMidiDlg.MciNotify(var Msg: TMessage);
```

continues

Listing 35.10. continued

```
begin
  KillTimer(Handle, PlayTimer);
  ReportStatus;
  if GetMode = Mci_Mode_Stop then CloseMci;
end;

procedure TMidiDlg.MidiAbort(Sender: TObject);
begin
  StopMCI;
  DeviceIsOpen := False;
  ReportStatus;
end;

procedure TMidiDlg.MidiOpen(Sender: TObject);
begin
  if OpenMci(Handle, PChar(FileName), DevType) then
    DeviceIsOpen := True;
end;


function TMidiDlg.GetMode: LongInt;
begin
  if DeviceIsOpen then
    GetMode := PlayInfo.GetMode
  else
    GetMode := mci_Mode_Stop;
end;

procedure TMidiDlg.MidiPlay(Sender: TObject);
var
  S: PChar;
  Temp: string;
  Result: LongInt;
begin
  GetMem(S, 500);
  Location := 0;
  if GetMode <> Mci_Mode_Pause then begin
    if (FileListBox1.ItemIndex < 0) then begin
      MessageBox(Handle, 'No file selected in listbox', '', mb_Ok);
      exit;
    end;
    Temp := FileListBox1.Items.Strings[FileListBox1.ItemIndex];
    OpenMci(Handle, PChar(Temp), DevType);
    ReportStatus;
    if GetMode = MidiError then exit;
    CheckForMapper;
    StartTimer;
    SetTimeFormatMS;
    Result := GetLen;
    Temp := Format('%d ms', [Result]);
    LenText.Caption := Temp;
    DevInfo.Caption := StrPas(GetInfo(S));
  end;
  PlayMci;
  ReportStatus;
  FreeMem(S, 500);
end;
```

```
procedure TMidiDlg.MidiPause(Sender: TObject);
begin
  PauseMidi;
  ReportStatus;
end;

procedure TMidiDlg.StartTimer;
begin
  if (SetTimer(Handle, PlayTimer, 1000, nil) = 0) then
    MessageBox(Handle, 'No Timers!', 'Whoops!', mb_Ok + mb_IconExclamation);
end;

procedure TMidiDlg.WmTimer(var Msg: TMessage);
begin
  ReportStatus;
end;

end.
```

Listing 35.11. Code for playing musical CDs.

```
unit CDInfo;
{
  Programmer: Charlie Calvert

  Copyright (c) 1996, by Charlie Calvert
  Feel free to use this code as an adjunct to your own programs.
}

interface

uses
  MMSystem, PlayInfo, WinProcs,
  WinTypes;

function OpenCD(PWindow: HWnd): Boolean;
procedure SetMSFasFormat;
procedure SetTMSFasFormat;
procedure PlayMciCD(StartTrack,EndTrack:Byte);
function GetNumTracks: LongInt;
procedure GetTrackLength(TrackNum: LongInt;var Min, Sec, Frame: Byte);

function HasDiskInserted: Boolean;
procedure PlayCDOneTrack(StartTrack:Byte);
function GetCurrentCDTrack: LongInt;
function PauseCD: Boolean;
function ResumeCD: Boolean;

implementation

function OpenCD(PWindow: HWnd): Boolean;
```

continues

Listing 35.11. continued

```
var
  Info : Tmci_Open_Parms;
  ErrNo   : LongInt;
  Flags: LongInt;
  S1: array[0..MsgLen] of Char;
begin
  OpenCD := True;
  ErrorState := False;
  PlayWindow := PWindow;
  FillChar(Info, SizeOf(Tmci_Open_Parms), #0);
  Info.dwCallback := PlayWindow;
  Info.lpstrDeviceType:=PChar(MCI_DEVTYPE_CD_AUDIO);
  Flags := MCI_OPEN_TYPE or MCI_OPEN_TYPE_ID;
  ErrNo := mciSendCommand(0, MCI_OPEN, Flags, Longint(@Info));

  wDeviceId := Info.wDeviceId;

  if ErrNo<>0 then begin
    ErrorMsg(ErrNo, S1);
    OpenCD := False;
  end;
end;

procedure SetMSFasFormat;
var
  Info: Tmci_Set_Parms;
  ErrNo   : LongInt;
  S1   : array[0..MsgLen] of Char;

begin

  Info.dwCallback := 0;
  Info.dwTimeFormat := MCI_FORMAT_MSF;
  Info.dwAudio := 0;

  ErrNo:=mciSendCommand( wDeviceId,
                         MCI_SET,
                         MCI_SET_TIME_FORMAT,
                         Longint(@Info));

  if ErrNo<>0 then ErrorMsg(ErrNo, S1);
end;

procedure SetTMSFasFormat;
var
  Info: Tmci_Set_Parms;
  ErrNo   : LongInt;
  S1   : array[0..MsgLen] of Char;

begin
  Info.dwCallback := 0;
  Info.dwTimeFormat := MCI_FORMAT_TMSF;
  Info.dwAudio := 0;
```

```
      ErrNo:=mciSendCommand( wDeviceId, MCI_SET,
                       MCI_SET_TIME_FORMAT, Longint(@Info));

  if ErrNo<>0 then ErrorMsg(ErrNo, S1);
end;

procedure PlayCDOneTrack(StartTrack:Byte);
var
  Info    : Tmci_Play_Parms;
  Flags,
  ErrNo      : LongInt;
  S1      : array[0..MsgLen] of Char;
begin
  FillChar(Info, SizeOf(Tmci_Play_Parms), 0);
  Info.dwFrom := MCI_MAKE_TMSF(StartTrack,0,0,0);

  Flags := MCI_FROM or MCI_Notify;
  ErrNo := mciSendCommand( wDeviceId, MCI_PLAY, Flags, Longint(@Info));

  if ErrNo<>0 then ErrorMsg(ErrNo, S1);
end;

procedure PlayMciCD(StartTrack,EndTrack:Byte);
var
  Info    : Tmci_Play_Parms;
  Flags,
  ErrNo      : LongInt;
  S1      : array[0..MsgLen] of Char;

begin
  FillChar(Info, SizeOf(Tmci_Play_Parms), 0);
  Info.dwFrom := MCI_MAKE_TMSF(StartTrack,0,0,0);
  Info.dwTo   := MCI_MAKE_TMSF(EndTrack,  0,0,0);
  Info.dwCallBack := PlayWindow;

  Flags := MCI_FROM or MCI_TO or MCI_NOTIFY;
  ErrNo := mciSendCommand(wDeviceId, MCI_PLAY, Flags, Longint(@Info));

  if ErrNo<>0 then ErrorMsg(ErrNo, S1);
end;

function GetNumTracks: LongInt;
var
  Status: Tmci_Status_Parms;
  ErrNo    : LongInt;
  S1      : array[0..MsgLen] of Char;

begin
  Status.dwCallback := 0;
  Status.dwReturn    := 0;
  Status.dwItem      := MCI_STATUS_NUMBER_OF_TRACKS;
  Status.dwTrack     := 0;
  ErrNo := mciSendCommand(wDeviceId, MCI_STATUS,
                     MCI_STATUS_ITEM, Longint(@Status));
  if ErrNo<>0 then ErrorMsg(ErrNo, S1);
  GetNumTracks := Status.dwReturn;
end;
```

continues

Listing 35.11. continued

```
{------------------------------------------------------------
    Track information is stated in minutes and seconds relative
    to the beginning of the disc. The durations of each song can
    be constructed by subtracting the begin time of a song from the
    start time of the previous song.
------------------------------------------------------------}
procedure GetTrackLength(TrackNum: LongInt; var Min, Sec, Frame: Byte);
var
  Status           : Tmci_Status_Parms;
  ErrNo              : LongInt;
  MSF              : LongInt;
begin
  Status.dwTrack     := TrackNum;
  Status.dwCallback := 0;
  Status.dwReturn    := 0;
  Status.dwItem      := MCI_STATUS_LENGTH;

  ErrNo := mciSendCommand(wDeviceId, MCI_STATUS,
                  MCI_STATUS_ITEM or MCI_TRACK,
                  Longint(@Status));

  if ErrNo <> 0 then ErrorMsg(ErrNo, 'Could not get track length');

  MSF :=Status.dwReturn;
  Min := MCI_MSF_MINUTE(MSF);
  Sec := MCI_MSF_SECOND(MSF);
  Frame := MCI_MSF_FRAME(MSF);
end;

function GetCurrentCDTrack: LongInt;
var
  Status: Tmci_Status_Parms;
  ErrNo: LongInt;
  S1: array[0..MsgLen] of Char;
begin
  FillChar(Status, SizeOf(Status), #0);
  Status.dwItem := MCI_STATUS_CURRENT_TRACK;

  ErrNo := mciSendCommand(wDeviceId, MCI_STATUS,
                    MCI_STATUS_ITEM, Longint(@Status));

  if ErrNo <> 0 then ErrorMsg(ErrNo, S1);
  GetCurrentCDTrack := Status.dwReturn;
end;

function HasDiskInserted: Boolean;
var
  Status: Tmci_Status_Parms;
  ErrNo: LongInt;
  Flags: LongInt;
  S1: array[0..MsgLen] of Char;
begin
  FillChar(Status, SizeOf(Tmci_Status_Parms), 0);
  Status.dwItem := MCI_STATUS_MEDIA_PRESENT;
```

```pascal
    Flags := MCI_STATUS_ITEM;
    ErrNo:=mciSendCommand(wDeviceID, MCI_STATUS, Flags, Longint(@Status));

    if ErrNo<>0 then ErrorMsg(ErrNo, S1);
    HasDiskInserted := (Status.dwReturn > 0);
end;

procedure EjectCD;
var
  Info : Tmci_Set_Parms;
  Flags, ErrNo : LongInt;
  S1 : array[0..128] of Char;
begin
  FillChar(Info, SizeOf(Tmci_Set_Parms), 0);
  Flags := mci_Set_Door_Open;
  ErrNo:=mciSendCommand( wDeviceId, MCI_SET, Flags, Longint(@Info));
  if ErrNo <> 0 then ErrorMsg(ErrNo, S1);
end;

function PauseCD: Boolean;
var
  Info: Tmci_Generic_Parms;
  Flags: LongInt;
  S1: array[0..MsgLen] of Char;
  ErrNo: LongInt;
begin
  Info.dwCallBack := 0;
  Flags := 0;
  ErrNo := mciSendCommand(wDeviceID, Mci_Pause, Flags, LongInt(@Info));
  if ErrNo <> 0 then begin
    ErrorMsg(ErrNo, S1);
    Result := False;
    Exit;
  end;
  Result := True;
end;

function ResumeCD: Boolean;
var
  Info: Tmci_Generic_Parms;
  Flags: LongInt;
  S1: array[0..MsgLen] of Char;
  ErrNo: LongInt;
begin
  Info.dwCallBack := 0;
  Flags := 0;
  ErrNo := mciSendCommand(wDeviceID, Mci_Resume, Flags, LongInt(@Info));
  if ErrNo <> 0 then begin
    ErrorMsg(ErrNo, S1);
    Result := False;
    Exit;
  end;
  Result := True;
end;

end.
```

Listing 35.12. The Delphi Front End for Playing CDs.

```
unit CDPlay;
{
  First version June 1993, by Charlie Calvert
  Delphi Rewrite: Jan 1996, by Charlie Calvert

  This unit is the object oriented interface
  to the raw code that controls a CD player.
}

interface

uses
  Messages, MmSystem, CDInfo,
  SysUtils, Forms, Classes,
  PlayInfo, WinProcs, WinTypes,
  Controls, StdCtrls, Buttons,
  ExtCtrls;

type
  TCDDialog = class(TForm)
    TrackList: TListBox;
    Panel1: TPanel;
    Label1: TLabel;
    Label2: TLabel;
    Label3: TLabel;
    Label4: TLabel;
    pStatus: TPanel;
    pCurTime: TPanel;
    pCurTrack: TPanel;
    pNumTracks: TPanel;
    bbPlay: TBitBtn;
    bbPause: TBitBtn;
    bbPlayAll: TBitBtn;
    bAbort: TBitBtn;
    PlayList: TListBox;
    bbPlaySel: TBitBtn;
    Label5: TLabel;
    Label6: TLabel;
    procedure Abort(Sender: TObject);
    procedure Pause(Sender: TObject);
    procedure PlayAll(Sender: TObject);
    procedure BeginPlay(Sender: TObject);
    procedure SetUpWindow(Sender: TObject);
    procedure TrackListDblClick(Sender: TObject);
    procedure PlayListDblClick(Sender: TObject);
    procedure bbPlaySelClick(Sender: TObject);
  private
    procedure Loaded; override;
    procedure CreateParams(var Params: TCreateParams); override;
    procedure wmDestroy(var M: TMessage); message wm_Destroy;
    procedure FillTrackBox(HWindow: HWnd; NumTracks: LongInt);
    procedure MoveItem(A, B: TListBox);
    procedure SetAllTOPlayList;
  public
    NumTracks: LongInt;
    NumToPlay: LongInt;
```

```
      CurrentSelection: LongInt;
      Paused : Boolean;
    procedure StopNow; virtual;
    procedure GetInfoFiles;
    procedure ReportStatus; virtual;
    procedure PlayNext;
    function GetMode: LongInt; virtual;
    procedure MciNotify(var Msg: TMessage);
      message mm_MciNotify;
    procedure WMTimer(var Msg: TMessage);
      message wm_Timer;
    procedure StartTimer;
  end;

var
  CDDialog: TCDDialog;

implementation

uses
  Globals;

{$R *.DFM}

{-------------------------------------------------}
{ TCDPlayer's method implementations:             }
{-------------------------------------------------}

procedure TCDDialog.Loaded;
begin
   inherited Loaded;
   Visible := false;
   Position := poDefault;
   BorderIcons := [];
   BorderStyle := bsNone;
   HandleNeeded;
   SetBounds(0,0,Width,Height);
end;

procedure TCDDialog.CreateParams(var Params: TCreateParams);
begin
  inherited CreateParams(Params);
  Params.WndParent := (Owner as TForm).Handle;
  Params.Style := WS_CHILD or WS_CLIPSIBLINGS;
  Params.X := 0;
  Params.Y := 0;
end;

procedure TCDDialog.wmDestroy(var M: TMessage);
begin
  if GetDeviceID > 0 then begin
    StopMCI;
    CloseMci;
  end;
  inherited;
end;
```

continues

Listing 35.12. continued

```
function TCDDialog.GetMode: LongInt;
begin
  GetMode := PlayInfo.GetMode;
end;

procedure TCDDialog.StopNow;
begin
  KillTimer(Handle, PlayTimer);
  StopMCI;
end;

procedure TCDDialog.FillTrackBox(HWindow: HWnd; NumTracks: LongInt);
type
  TInfo = Record
    Track, Min, Sec, Frame: Word;
  end;
var
  i: Integer;
  Min,Sec,Frame: Byte;
  S: string;
begin
  for i := 1 to NumTracks do begin
    GetTrackLength(i, Min, Sec, Frame);
    if Sec < 9 then
      S := Format('%2d >> %d:0%d', [i, Min, Sec, Frame])
    else
      S := Format('%2d >> %d:%d', [i, Min, Sec, Frame]);
    TrackList.Items.Add(S);
  end;
end;

procedure TCDDialog.SetUpWindow(Sender: TObject);
begin
  if not OpenCD(Handle) then exit;
  while not HasDiskInserted do
    MessageBox(Handle, 'Insert Disk', 'Foo', mb_Ok);
  GetInfoFiles;
end;

procedure TCDDialog.ReportStatus;
type
  TTimeAry = Array[0..2] of Word;
var
  S: string;
  Track: LongInt;
  Time: LongInt;
  TimeAry: TTimeAry;
begin
  {$IfDef Debug}
  S := Format('CurrentSelection: %d', [CurrentSelection]);
  DC := GetDC(Handle);
  TextOut(DC, 1, 1, PChar(S), Length(S));
  ReleaseDC(Handle, DC);
  {$EndIf}
  PStatus.Caption := GetModeString(GetMode);
  Track := GetCurrentCDTrack;
```

```
  S := Format('%d', [Track]);
  pCurTrack.Caption := S;
  Time := GetLocation;
  TimeAry[2] := 0;
  TimeAry[1] := mci_tmsf_Second(Time);
  TimeAry[0] := mci_tmsf_Minute(Time);
  if TimeAry[1] > 9 then
    S := Format('%d:%d', [mci_tmsf_Minute(Time), mci_tmsf_Second(Time)])
  else
    S := Format('%d:%d%d', [mci_tmsf_Minute(Time), 0, mci_tmsf_Second(Time)]);
  PCurTime.Caption := S;
end;

procedure TCdDialog.GetInfoFiles;
var
  S: string;
begin
  SetTMSFasFormat;
  NumTracks := GetNumTracks;
  S := Format('%d', [NumTracks]);
  pNumTracks.Caption := S;
  FillTrackBox(Handle, NumTracks);
end;

procedure TCDDialog.Abort(Sender: TObject);
begin
  StopMci;
  ReportStatus;
end;

procedure TCDDialog.Pause(Sender: TObject);
begin
  if not Paused then begin
    PauseCD;
    Paused := True;
    pStatus.Caption := 'Resume';
  end else begin
    ResumeCD;
    Paused := False;
    pStatus.Caption := 'Pause';
  end;
end;

function Parse(S: PChar): Byte;
var
  S2: array[0..50] of Char;
  i,j: Integer;
begin
  i := 0;
  j := 0;
  while S[i] <> '>' do begin
    if S[i] <> ' ' then begin
      S2[j] := S[i];
      inc(j);
    end;
    inc(i);
  end;
```

continues

Listing 35.12. continued

```
  S2[j] := #0;
  Val(S2, i, j);
  Parse := i;
end;

procedure TCDDialog.PlayNext;
var
  S: string;
  Start: Byte;
begin
  if CurrentSelection = NumToPlay then begin
    StopNow;
    ReportStatus;
    Exit;
  end;

  PlayList.SetFocus;
  PlayList.ItemIndex := CurrentSelection;
  PlayList.UpDate;
  S := PlayList.Items.Strings[PlayList.ItemIndex];
  Inc(CurrentSelection);
  Start := Parse(PChar(S));
  StartTimer;
  if Start <> NumTracks then    { Don't pass in one more than total tracks }
    PlayMciCD(Start, Start + 1)
  else
    PlayCDOneTrack(Start);
  ReportStatus;
end;

procedure TCDDialog.SetAllTOPlayList;
begin
  while PlayList.Items.Count <> 0 do begin
    PlayList.SetFocus;
    PlayList.ItemIndex := 0;
    MoveItem(PlayList, TrackList);
  end;
  while TrackList.Items.Count <> 0 do begin
    TrackList.SetFocus;
    TrackList.ItemIndex := 0;
    MoveItem(TrackList, PlayList);
  end;
end;

procedure TCDDialog.PlayAll(Sender: TObject);
begin
  Paused := False;
  pStatus.Caption := 'Pause';
  SetAllToPlayList;
  PlayList.Sorted := True;
  PlayList.Sorted := False;
  NumToPlay := PlayList.Items.Count;
  CurrentSelection := 0;
  PlayNext;
end;
```

```
procedure TCDDialog.BeginPlay(Sender: TObject);
var
  S: string;
  Start: Byte;
begin
  Paused := False;
  pStatus.Caption := 'Pause';
  if PlayList.ItemIndex = - 1 then begin
    MessageBox(Handle, 'You must select a track first' , 'Info', Mb_Ok);
    Exit;
  end else
    S := PlayList.Items.Strings[PlayList.ItemIndex];
  Start := Parse(PChar(S));
  StartTimer;
  if Start <> NumTracks then
    PlayMciCD(Start, Start + 1)
  else
    PlayCDOneTrack(Start);
  ReportStatus;
end;

{ If you are playing multiple tracks, and one is
  completed, call StopNow so you don't let another
  mci_Notify_Successful message come in }
procedure TCDDialog.MciNotify(var Msg: TMessage);
begin
  case Msg.WPChar of
    mci_Notify_SuperSeded: StopNow;
    mci_Notify_Aborted: StopNow;
    mci_Notify_Successful: begin
      if GetMode = mci_Mode_Stop then begin
        StopNow;
        PlayNext;
      end;
    end;
  end;
end;

procedure TCDDialog.WMTimer(var Msg: TMessage);
begin
  ReportStatus;
end;

procedure TCDDialog.StartTimer;
begin
  if (SetTimer(Handle, PlayTimer, 1000, nil) = 0) then
    MessageBox(Handle, 'No Timers!', 'Whoops!', mb_Ok + mb_IconExclamation);
end;

procedure TCDDialog.MoveItem(A, B: TListBox);
var
  S: string;
begin
  if A.ItemIndex < 0 then Exit;
  S := A.Items.Strings[A.ItemIndex];
  A.Items.Delete(A.ItemIndex);
  B.Items.Add(S);
end;
```

continues

Listing 35.12. continued

```
procedure TCDDialog.TrackListDblClick(Sender: TObject);
begin
  MoveItem(TrackList, PlayList);
end;


procedure TCDDialog.PlayListDblClick(Sender: TObject);
begin
  MoveItem(PlayList, TrackList);
end;

procedure TCDDialog.bbPlaySelClick(Sender: TObject);
begin
  Paused := False;
  pStatus.Caption := 'Pause';
  NumToPlay := PlayList.Items.Count;
  CurrentSelection := 0;
  PlayNext;
end;

end.
```

Listing 35.13. The Capabilities unit that reports on the capability of a particular system in terms of what kind of multimedia files it can play.

```
unit Capable1;

interface

uses
  SysUtils, Messages, WinProcs,
  Classes, Graphics, Controls,
  Forms, Dialogs, MMSystem,
  StdCtrls, WinTypes, Globals;

type
  TCapableDlg = class(TForm)
    cbtcdAudio: TCheckBox;
    cbtdat: TCheckBox;
    cbtDigitalVideo: TCheckBox;
    cbtMMMovie: TCheckBox;
    cbtOther: TCheckBox;
    cbtOverLay: TCheckBox;
    cbtScanner: TCheckBox;
    cbtSequencer: TCheckBox;
    cbtVCR: TCheckBox;
    cbtVideoDisc: TCheckBox;
    cbtWaveAudio: TCheckBox;
    cbtAviVideo: TCheckBox;
    cbaNotSupported: TCheckBox;
    cbaCanEject: TCheckBox;
    cbaCanPlay: TCheckBox;
```

```
      cbaCanPause: TCheckBox;
      cbaCanStop: TCheckBox;
      cbaCanRecord: TCheckBox;
      cbaCanSave: TCheckBox;
      cbaIsCompound: TCheckBox;
      cbaHasAudio: TCheckBox;
      cbaHasVideo: TCheckBox;
      cbaUsesFiles: TCheckBox;
      bcdAudio: TButton;
      bDat: TButton;
      bDigitalVideo: TButton;
      bMMMovie: TButton;
      bOther: TButton;
      bOverLay: TButton;
      bScanner: TButton;
      bSequencer: TButton;
      bVCR: TButton;
      bVideoDisc: TButton;
      bWaveAudio: TButton;
      bAviVideo: TButton;
      procedure SetUpWindow(Sender: TObject);
      procedure TestAbilities(id: LongInt; OldResult: LongInt);
      function TestMCI(DeviceType: PChar; DoTest: Boolean): Boolean;
      procedure bcdAudioClick(Sender: TObject);
    private
      Box: TBox;
      BoxAble: TBox;
      { Private declarations }
      procedure ShowAbilities(var Msg: TMessage);
        message wm_ShowAble;
      procedure WmCommand(var Msg: TMessage);
        message wm_Command;
    public
      { Public declarations }
    end;

var
  CapableDlg: TCapableDlg;

implementation

uses
  StrBox;

{$R *.DFM}

procedure TCapableDlg.SetUpWindow(Sender: TObject);
var
  i: Integer;
begin
  for i:= 0 to 11 do begin
    Box[i] := TCheckBox(FindComponent('cbt' + StrPas(MMTypes[i]))).Handle;
    if i <> 11 then Boxable[i] := TCheckBox(FindComponent('cba' +
StrPas(MMAbles[i]))).Handle;
  end;
  PostMessage(Handle, wm_ShowAble, 0, 0);
end;
```

continues

Listing 35.13. continued

```pascal
procedure TCapableDlg.TestAbilities(id: LongInt; OldResult: LongInt);
var
  Info: Tmci_GetDevCaps_Parms;
  i: Integer;
  AFlags: LongInt;
begin
  for i := 0 to 10 do
    SendMessage(BoxAble[i], BM_SetCheck, 0, 0);
  if OldResult <> 0 then begin
    SendMessage(BoxAble[0], BM_SetCheck, 1, 0);
    Exit;
  end;
  for i := 1 to 10 do begin
    FillChar(Info, SizeOf(Info), #0);
    Info.dwItem := Tests[i];
    AFlags := Mci_GetDevCaps_Item or Mci_Notify;
    MciSendCommand(id, Mci_GetDevCaps, AFlags, LongInt(@Info));
    if Info.dwReturn > 0 then
      SendMessage(BoxAble[i], BM_SetCheck, 1, 0);
  end;
end;

function TCapableDlg.TestMCI(DeviceType: PChar; DoTest: Boolean): Boolean;
var
  OpenParms: Tmci_Open_Parms;
  Style: LongInt;
  AResult: LongInt;
begin
  TesTmci := True;
  OpenParms.lpstrDeviceType := DeviceType;
  Style := Mci_Open_Type;
  AResult := MciSendCommand(0, MCI_OPEN, Style, LongInt(@OpenParms));
  if DoTest then
    TestAbilities(OpenParms.wDeviceId, AResult);
  if AResult <> 0 then
    TesTmci := False
  else
    MciSendCommand(OpenParms.wdeviceId, MCI_CLOSE, 0, 0);
end;

procedure TCapableDlg.ShowAbilities(var Msg: TMessage);
var
  i: Integer;
begin
  for i := 0 to 11 do begin
    if TesTmci(MMTypes[i], False)then
      SendMessage(Box[i], BM_SetCheck, 1, 0);
  end;
end;

procedure TCapableDlg.WmCommand(var Msg: TMessage);
begin
  if (Msg.WParam > 100) and (Msg.WParam < 113) then
    TesTmci(MMTypes[Msg.WParam - 101], True);
  inherited;
end;
```

```
procedure TCapableDlg.bcdAudioClick(Sender: TObject);
var
  S: string;
  S1: array[0..MaxLen] of Char;
begin
  if Sender is TButton then begin
    S := TButton(Sender).Name;
    S := ReverseStr(S);
    S := Shorten(S, 1);
    S := ReverseStr(S);
    TesTmci(StrPCopy(S1,S), True);
  end;
end;

end.
```

Listing 35.14. The Globals units contains some generic code used by a number of units, especially CAPABLE1.PAS.

```
unit globals;

interface

uses
  mmSystem, Windows, Messages;

const
  MaxLen = 250;
  PlayTimer = 1;
  MidiError = - 251;

  MMTypes:array[0..11] of PChar = ('cdaudio', 'dat', 'digitalvideo',
                                   'MMMovie', 'other', 'overlay',
                                   'scanner', 'sequencer', 'vcr',
                                   'videodisc', 'waveaudio', 'avivideo');

  MMAbles:array[0..10] of PChar = ('NotSupported', 'CanEject', 'CanPlay',
                                   'CanPause', 'CanStop', 'CanRecord',
                                   'CanSave', 'IsCompound', 'HasAudio',
                                   'HasVideo', 'UsesFiles');

  Tests:array[1..10] of LongInt = (Mci_GetDevCaps_Can_Eject,
                                   Mci_GetDevCaps_Can_Play,
                                   Mci_GetDevCaps_Can_Play,
                                   Mci_GetDevCaps_Can_Play,
                                   Mci_GetDevCaps_Can_Record,
                                   Mci_GetDevCaps_Can_Save,
                                   Mci_GetDevCaps_Compound_Device,
                                   Mci_GetDevCaps_Has_Audio,
                                   Mci_GetDevCaps_Has_Video,
                                   Mci_GetDevCaps_Uses_Files);

  wm_ShowAble   = wm_User + 3;
```

continues

Listing 35.14. continued

```
type
  TMaxString = array[0..MaxLen] of Char;
  TBox = array[0..11] of HWnd;

function GetModeString(Mode: Integer): string;
implementation

function GetModeString(Mode: Integer): string;
var
  S: string;
begin
  case Mode of
    MCI_MODE_NOT_READY: S := 'Mode not ready';
    MCI_MODE_PAUSE: S := 'Mode pause';
    MCI_MODE_PLAY: S := 'Mode play';
    MCI_MODE_STOP: S := 'Mode stop';
    MCI_MODE_OPEN: S := 'Mode Open';
    MCI_MODE_RECORD: S := 'Record';
    MCI_MODE_SEEK: S := 'Seek';
  end;
  Result := S;
end;

end.
```

Listing 35.15. The main form for the Media32 program.

```
unit Main;

interface

uses
  SysUtils, WinTypes, WinProcs,
  Messages, Classes, Graphics,
  Controls, Forms, Dialogs,
  StdCtrls, Menus;

const
  MaxDlg = 3;
  dtAvi = 0;
  dtWave = 1;
  dtMidi = 2;
  dtCD = 3;

type
  TPlayMain = class(TForm)
    MainMenu1: TMainMenu;
    CD1: TMenuItem;
    CDMenu: TMenuItem;
    Midi1: TMenuItem;
    Wave1: TMenuItem;
    Avi1: TMenuItem;
    Other1: TMenuItem;
    Capability1: TMenuItem;
```

```
      Help1: TMenuItem;
      About1: TMenuItem;
      procedure CmWave(Sender: TObject);
      procedure CmCapability(Sender: TObject);
      procedure CmAbout(Sender: TObject);
      procedure FormResize(Sender: TObject);
      procedure FormCreate(Sender: TObject);
    private
      DlgAry: array[0..MaxDlg] of TForm;
      procedure FreeDlgs;
      procedure DoSize;
    end;

var
  PlayMain: TPlayMain;

implementation

uses
  CDPlay, MidiPlay, WavePlay,
  AviPlay, Capable1, About;

{$R *.DFM}

procedure TPlayMain.CmAbout(Sender: TObject);
begin
  AboutDlg.ShowModal;
end;

procedure TPlayMain.DoSize;
var
  i: Integer;
begin
  for i := 0 to MaxDlg do
    if  DlgAry[i] <> nil then begin
      DlgAry[i].Left := 0;
      DlgAry[i].Top := 0;
      DlgAry[i].Width := ClientWidth;
      DlgAry[i].Height := ClientHeight;
    end;
end;

procedure TPlayMain.FormResize(Sender: TObject);
begin
  DoSize;
end;

procedure TPlayMain.FormCreate(Sender: TObject);
begin
  DlgAry[dtAvi] := AviDialog;
  DlgAry[dtWave] := WaveDlg;
  DlgAry[dtMidi] := MidiDlg;
  DlgAry[dtCD] := CDDialog;
end;

procedure TPlayMain.FreeDlgs;
```

continues

Listing 35.15. continued

```
var
  i: Integer;
begin
  for i := 0 to MaxDlg do begin
    DlgAry[i].Free;
    DlgAry[i] := nil;
  end;
end;

procedure TPlayMain.CmWave(Sender: TObject);
begin
  FreeDlgs;
  case (Sender as TMenuItem).Tag of
    dtWave: begin
      WaveDlg := TWaveDlg.Create(Self);
      DlgAry[dtWave] := WaveDlg;
    end;
    dtAvi: begin
      AviDialog := TAviDialog.Create(Self);
      DlgAry[dtAvi] := AviDialog;
    end;
    dtMidi: begin
      MidiDlg := TMidiDlg.Create(Self);
      DlgAry[dtMidi] := MidiDlg;
    end;
    dtCD: begin
      CDDialog := TCDDialog.Create(Self);
      DlgAry[dtCD] := CDDialog;
    end;
  end;
  DoSize;
  DlgAry[(Sender as TMenuItem).Tag].Show;
end;

procedure TPlayMain.CmCapability(Sender: TObject);
begin
  CapableDlg := TCapableDlg.Create(Self);
  CapableDlg.ShowModal;
  CapableDlg.Free;
end;

end.
```

When you launch the Media32 program, you are presented with a blank form. You might want to start by pulling down the Capabilities dialog box, which you can use to find out what devices are supported on your current system. This dialog box lists the possible devices on the left and places a check mark in front of the ones that are supported. If you press the button in front of any item, the specific capabilities associated with that item are checked off in the far right column.

If you select any of the child windows listed in the File menu, you can play MIDI, WAV, or AVI files, as well as CDs. If you elect to play a CD, you are presented with a list box that shows the files available on the CD, as shown in Figure 35.1. To play a particular track for the CD, move it into the right-side list box, select it, then press the Play button. If you move several different files into the Selected list box, and then want to play them all in order, press the Play Selected button. If you want to play all the files on the CD, choose the Play All button.

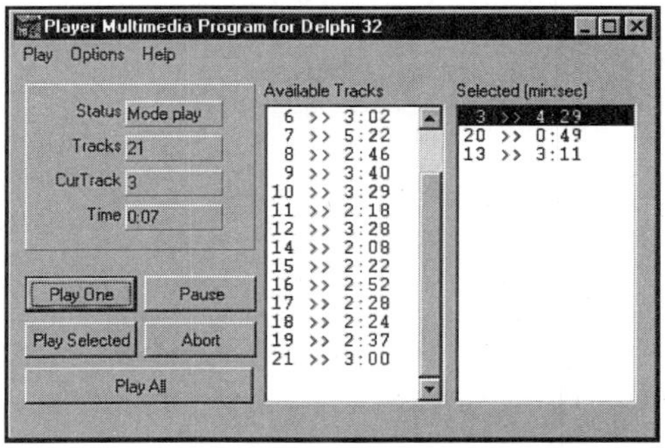

FIGURE 35.1.

The user selects three of the 21 tracks from a CD containing Vivaldi's Four Seasons.

The WavePlay child window is shown in Figure 35.2. You can select this form when you want to play or record WAV files. You can browse across the hard drive using the list boxes shown on the right side of the form. If you want to record a file, press the Record button. A dialog appears that enables you to select the time that you want your recording to last. For instance, you can say: "I want to record for 20 seconds." If you don't know how long your recording is going to last, choose the manual option. You can then record for as long as you want, and press the Stop button when you are through.

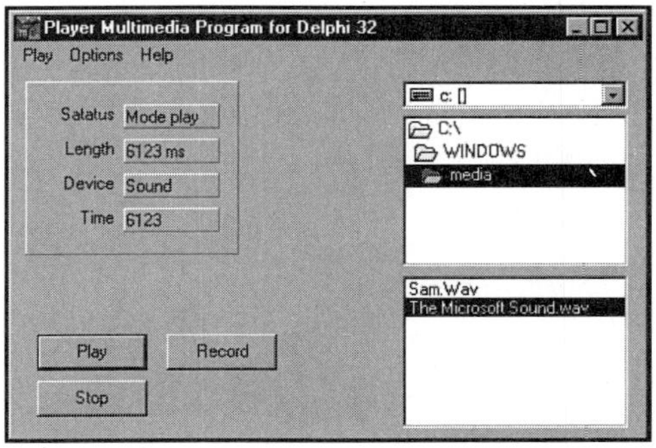

FIGURE 35.2.

You can press the Record button to start recording a file, and the Stop button to stop recording the file.

When you finish recording a file, a TSaveDialog appears. You can type a file name into this dialog, then press OK to save the file.

The Core Files for Accessing Multimedia Features

The MIDIINFO.PAS, WAVEINFO.PAS, and CDINFO.PAS units all rely to one degree or another on the routines in PLAYINFO.PAS. The reason all three units are able to share so much code is explained in the section called "Coming to Terms with `mciSendCommand`," where I describe the extreme device-independence of the MCI interface.

Here are the function headers from the interface to the PLAYINFO unit:

```
function CloseMCI: Boolean;
function ErrorMsg(Error: LongInt; Msg: PChar): Boolean;
function GetDeviceID: Word;
function GetInfo(S: PChar): PChar;
function GetLen: Longint;
function GetLocation: LongInt;
function GetMode: Longint;
function OpenMCI(PWindow: HWnd; FileName, DeviceType: PChar): Boolean;
function PlayMCI: Boolean;
function SetTimeFormatMs: Boolean;
function StopMci: Boolean;
```

Most of the time, all three devices can use the same code to play a file, close a file, stop a file, get the length (in milliseconds) of a file, and pause a file. There are few variations used by the AVI tools, so for now I am keeping it separate from the rest of this program.

> **NOTE**
>
> I put in a little additional work on this program from time to time, and will post the changes to CompuServe, the Internet, and the Borland BBS. If you are interested, you can check for updates. No promises, but I do tend to work on this thing every once in a while. The old Turbo Pascal version of the program, called Player, also is available online, and in the first edition of this book.

The `Open` command must be customized for each device. Its first parameter is the handle of the dialog, window, or control that is playing the file. The second parameter is the name of the file, and the third is the device type. Most of the major device types, such as sequencer, waveaudio, and videodisc, are listed in the section called "Coming to Terms with `mciSendCommand`." Obviously, the last parameter is in some ways the most important because it is the one that tells MCI whether you want to play a CD, a WAV file, or a MIDI file.

The Capability Dialog

The other half of the program, the part that makes up the front end, is written in standard VCL code. One of the most important parts of this program is the Capability menu item, which lets the user find out about the system's multimedia capabilities.

Media32 finds out about the capabilities of the current system by iterating through the following array of possible types of devices, to create a series of buttons and check boxes with the appropriate name as window text:

```
MMTypes:array[0..10] of PChar = ('cdaudio', 'dat',
                                 'digitalvideo', 'MMMovie', 'other',
                                 'overlay', 'scanner', 'sequencer',
                                 'vcr', 'videodisc', 'waveaudio');
```

Next to these controls is a second set of check boxes with window text made from the following array:

```
MMAbles:array[0..10] of PChar =
              ('Not Supported', 'Can Eject', 'Can Play',
              'Can Pause', 'Can Stop', 'Can_Record',
              'Can Save', 'Is Compound', 'Has Audio',
              'Has Video', 'Uses Files');
```

When Media32 starts, the check boxes associated with a particular device are marked if the current machine supports that device. If the user selects the button with that device's name on it, Media32 tells the user if the device can eject, play, pause, stop, and so on. It queries Windows to obtain this information by passing in one of the following flags in connection with the `mci_GetDevCaps` function:

```
Tests:array[1..10] of LongInt =
              (mci_GetDevCaps_Can_Eject,
              mci_GetDevCaps_Can_Play,
              mci_GetDevCaps_Can_Play,
              mci_GetDevCaps_Can_Play,
              mci_GetDevCaps_Can_Record,
              mci_GetDevCaps_Can_Save,
              mci_GetDevCaps_Compound_Device,
              mci_GetDevCaps_Has_Audio,
              mci_GetDevCaps_Has_Video,
              mci_GetDevCaps_Uses_Files);
```

Here is the way the code in question actually appears in the program:

```
Info.dwItem := Tests[i];
Flags := mci_GetDevCaps_Item or mci_Notify;
Result := mciSendCommand(id, mci_GetDevCaps, Flags,
                    LongInt(@Info));
if Info.dwReturn > 0 then
  SendMessage(BoxAble[i]^.HWindow, BM_SetCheck, 1, 0);
```

As you can see, the program sends a `BM_SetCheck` message to the appropriate check box if the capability is supported on the user's system. All of the preceding lines appear inside a loop that enables the code to check for each capability in turn.

The end result of these activities is to inform the user immediately of what devices are available on his or her system and what type of capabilities are associated with a particular device.

The Front End Proper

Along the top of the main window is a menu that enables the user to open one of four child windows; the first for running a CD player, the second for MIDI files, the third for WAV files, and the fourth for viewing movies.

Each of the child windows comes with buttons that let the user start, stop, and pause the relevant device. The rest of the window displays information about the device in question and about the current length and format of any file the user might choose to play.

> **NOTE**
>
> The child windows in the Media32 program are like the child windows used in the Music database program shown in Chapter 20, "Advanced InterBase Techniques." In particular, each child form is allocated memory explicitly by the main form, rather than autocreated by Delphi. The child forms then override the Loaded and CreateParams methods:
>
> ```
> procedure TWaveDlg.Loaded;
> begin
>    inherited Loaded;
>    Visible := false;
>    Position := poDefault;
>    BorderIcons := [];
>    BorderStyle := bsNone;
>    HandleNeeded;
>    SetBounds(0,0,Width,Height);
> end;
>
> procedure TWaveDlg.CreateParams(var Params: TCreateParams);
> begin
>   inherited CreateParams(Params);
>   Params.WndParent := (Owner as TForm).Handle;
>   Params.Style := WS_CHILD or WS_CLIPSIBLINGS;
>   Params.X := 0;
>   Params.Y := 0;
> end;
> ```
>
> Remember, these methods have been overridden. You must declare them with the override directive or the code will not work properly. You also must put in a little effort responding to wm_Size messages in the main form.

By now, the structure of this program should be fairly clear to you. The Media32 program consists of a main module called MAIN.PAS, which controls the main window and the four submodules, called WAVEPLAY, MIDIPALY, AVIPLAY, and CDPLAY, each of which controls a child form.

Working with Multimedia Files

In general, you should be aware of the steps that you must take whenever you open up a multimedia file. The first two steps are to find out if any existing hardware is available, and then to open the device itself. If either or both of these steps fail, you must exit as gracefully as possible. Because of the mciGetErrorMessage function, it's easy for you to post an appropriate error message for the user.

After opening up the file, the program reports on its length and format, and then begins to play it. While the user is listening to the file, Media32 reports on the file's progress, which is particularly important when playing CD or MIDI files—which can last for several minutes or more.

When the file has stopped playing, or if the user has aborted the play, the program closes the device before exiting. At all times, you should be checking the results of your calls so that you can be aware if an error occurs.

Overall, these steps are not as demanding as they might seem when you first learn about them. Certainly in some circumstances it might be appropriate for you to skip some of them. However, you should be aware of the general scheme and the way it fits together.

Setting the Time Format

At this point, all that remains to be covered are a few details that might cause you some confusion. In particular, you should notice the function called SetTimeFormatMS:

```
function SetTimeFormatMS: Boolean;
var
  Info: Tmci_Set_Parms;
  Flags,
  Result: LongInt;
  S1: array [0..MsgLen] of Char;
begin
  SetTimeFormatMS := True;
  Info.dwTimeFormat := mci_Format_Milliseconds;
  Flags := mci_Set_Time_Format;
  Result := mciSendCommand(wDeviceID, MCI_Set,
                           Flags, LongInt(@Info));
  if Result <> 0 then begin
    ErrorMsg(Result, S1);
    SetTimeFormatMS := False;
  end;
end;
```

This code is similar to the PlayWave procedure except that, instead of using a Tmci_Play_Parms record, it uses a Tmci_Set_Parms record:

```
Tmci_Set_Parms = record
  dwCallback: Longint;
  dwTimeFormat: Longint;
  dwAudio: Longint;
end;
```

The key member of this structure is dwTimeFormat, which you use to select a particular time format. The Media32 program uses milliseconds, although I could have chosen seconds and minutes, or even the number of tracks that have been played.

Notice that mciSendCommand receives mci_Set_Time_Format as the third parameter. Other messages I could have passed in instead include mci_Set_Door_Closed or mci_Set_Door_Open. This latter flag can be used to eject a CD from a CD player.

Some readers might not find it intuitively obvious to search out the mci_Set message as the place to issue the command to eject a cassette. This highlights one possible criticism of MCI: it lacks some of the intuitive feel of a more traditional API, which might feature a command such as EjectCD. Of course, once you know the trick, there is no reason why you cannot create your own EjectCD function. The key is to know the API well enough to find its hidden secrets.

Handling *mm_Notify* Message

One final point involves the posting of mm_Notify messages to the dialog objects in the main program. These messages are routed to standard Pascal dynamic message response functions, such as this one from MIDIPLAY.PAS:

```
procedure TMidiDlg.MciNotify(var Msg: TMessage);
begin
  KillTimer(HWindow, MidiTimer);
  ReportStatus;
  if Mode = mci_Mode_Stop then CloseMci;
end;
```

The preceding code implies the presence of a timer. The timer is used to check on the status of the device being played. For instance, if a MIDI file is being played, the timer enables you to check up on its progress at set intervals. In this particular program, the intervals are one-quarter second in duration.

NOTE

You won't get mm_Notify messages unless you specifically ask for them. The requests occur in the XXINFO.PAS units:

```
mciSendCommand(wDeviceID, mci_Stop, mci_Notify, LongInt(@Info));
```

The third parameter of this call to mciSendCommand specifies that you want to get mci_Notify messages that report on the program of the command. In particular, you want to be notified when the device is stopped.

By selecting the times when you use the mci_Notify flag, you can choose when you want to receive updates regarding the multimedia events that occur in your program. It often is difficult to find the right balance between getting a confusing flurry of messages and not getting enough messages. The goal is to be informed only when you really need to know that something has occurred.

To fully understand the `mci_Notify` method, you have to understand that Media32 can ask to receive a message whenever anything important happens to the file being played. For instance, if the file ends or if the user presses the Pause button, an `mm_Notify` message is posted. Here is the declaration for the `MciNotify` function:

```
procedure MciNotify(var Msg: TMessage);
    virtual wm_First + mm_MciNotify;
```

If the file currently being played is finished, or if the user has asked to abort the play, the proper response is to close the device. But this is not what you want to do if the user has simply paused the file. To distinguish between these two different events, you process an `mci_Status` message in the main program with the following code: ++++

```
function GetModeString(Mode: Integer): string;
var
  S: string;
begin
  case Mode of
    MCI_MODE_NOT_READY: S := 'Mode not ready';
    MCI_MODE_PAUSE: S := 'Mode pause';
    MCI_MODE_PLAY: S := 'Mode play';
    MCI_MODE_STOP: S := 'Mode stop';
    MCI_MODE_OPEN: S := 'Mode Open';
    MCI_MODE_RECORD: S := 'Record';
    MCI_MODE_SEEK: S := 'Seek';
  end;
  Result := S;
end;

procedure TMidiDlg.ReportStatus;
begin
  pCurMode.Caption := GetModeString(PlayInfo.GetMode);
  pCurTime.Caption := IntToStr(GetLocation);
end;
```

This procedure first gets the current mode of the device by calling the following procedure:

```
function GetMode: Longint;
var
  Info: Tmci_Status_Parms;
  Flags,
  ErrNo: LongInt;
  S1: array [0..MsgLen] of Char;
begin
  FillChar(Info, SizeOf(Tmci_Status_Parms), 0);
  Info.dwItem := Mci_Status_Mode;
  Flags := Mci_Status_Item;
  ErrNo := MciSendCommand(wDeviceID, Mci_Status, Flags, LongInt(@Info));
  if ErrNo <> 0 then begin
    ErrorMsg(ErrNo, S1);
```

```
   Result := -1;
   exit;
 end;
 GetMode := Info.dwReturn;
end;
```

In my opinion, the GetMode function highlights the opacity to which the MCI command interface can sometimes fall prey. Unless you actually looked up the mci_Status, mci_Status_Item, and mci_Status_Mode messages in the MCI reference books, it is unlikely that you would guess exactly what this function does just from looking at it.

Nevertheless, it does effectively meet the current needs. After calling it, you know whether the device is paused or stopped, so you can handle the mm_Notify message with the appropriate response. I set a variable called Mode to the value returned from GetMode, and then show the user a string that explains the result of the query. The string is displayed in a static text control that has been inserted in the object's dialog.

Summary

Although it has not been possible for me to explore all of the many aspects of the MCI interface in this chapter, I have given you enough information to get you up and running. If you want to learn more, the best thing you can do now is study the included example and MMSYSTEM.PAS interface. As soon as you have some feeling for how this code works, you should begin writing your own code for manipulating multimedia files. There also are several books out on this subject now, although most of them are based on the C language. With the information included in this chapter, you should have no trouble reading those books, even if the language is strange to you.

Overall, I think you'll find the MCI interface a flexible, well-structured tool that appears to be constructed so that it will withstand the ravages of time with a fair degree of aplomb. Certainly its weaknesses are more than made up for by the excitement of multimedia programming. So, go to it with a will and be sure to take the time to enjoy yourself.

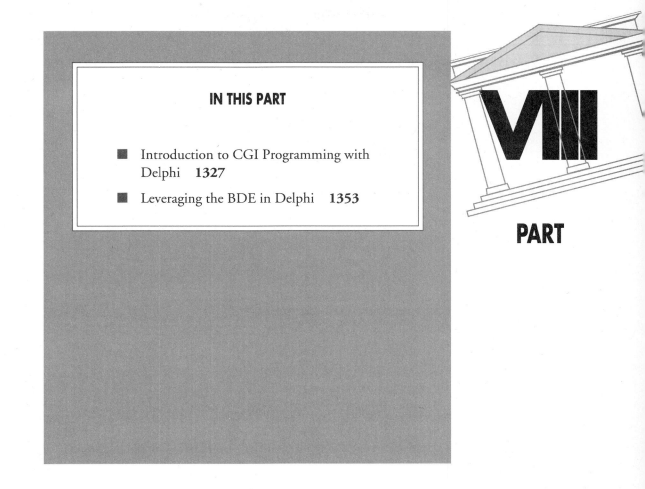

PART

VIII

The Internet

The final part of this book, by guest author Ann Lynnworth, explores the Internet. Ann and business partner Michael Ax have used Delphi to create a series of Web-based tools that gives the user powerful access to some of the most advanced features in contemporary programming. Ann shares many of her technical secrets and a working copy of her code so that you can see how the Internet tools that she presents are put together.

Introduction to CGI Programming with Delphi

by Ann
Lynnworth

36

IN THIS CHAPTER

In this part of the book, I'm going to show you Delphi's strengths as a platform for building interactive, database-driven applications on the World Wide Web. I'll give you a general introduction to the problem and then discuss the various aspects of the solution.

First, let me tell you about my background. I have been writing CGI applications for the Web since February 1995, which is a long time by Internet standards. Behind that, I have years of experience as a consultant, earning my way using everything from Basic 1.0 in 1983 to C language, Paradox, SQL, and now Delphi. I was lucky enough to stumble onto the Web ahead of the wave, and most fortunate to strike a deal with an Internet Service Provider (ISP) who let me set up an NT server early in the game. This led to my shipping a series of popular Delphi shareware components for doing simple CGI programming—all back in June 1995. Thereafter I set out to build something better: a solid, high-end CGI framework. I formed HREF Tools Corp. with Michael Ax; he wrote WebHub, and here we are.

In presenting this material to you, I'm doing my best to be objective and present issues rather than a sales pitch. Beyond that, all I can do is let you know my bias. So, without further ado...

> **NOTE**
>
> Delphi changed the way we write Windows applications in 1995, and it is now creating a revolution in Internet programming.

In this chapter, you'll begin to see how much Delphi offers in the context of the Web. Then in Chapter 37, "Leveraging the BDE in Delphi," we will look at specific "hot features" to prove the point concretely.

Where Do We Start?

Let's start with an experience that you've probably had by now. You're surfing the Web with a "browser" such as Netscape or Mosaic, and you're about to type in `http://` to go somewhere.

Have you wondered what http means? It stands for HyperText Transfer Protocol, the protocol for exchange of data between a Web browser and server over the Internet. (There's also SHTTP, which is the secure version thereof.)

The `http://` piece that you type to go somewhere on the Web is only the first of three strings that comprise the destination URL—Uniform Resource Locator.

More generally, a URL is comprised of three parts, as shown in Table 36.1.

FIGURE 36.1.

An HTTP request for a site on the World Wide Web.

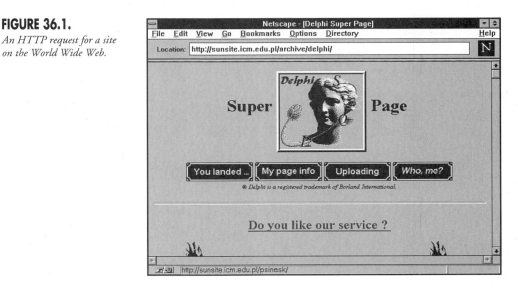

Table 36.1. URL string anatomy.

Component	For the Web	For E-mail	For FTP
Protocol/program/action	http	mailto	ftp
A separator	://	:	://
Name of resource	www.borland.com	info@href.com	FTP.sonic.net /pub/users/ann

When you ask your browser to go to a URL, it sends out a request (using TCP/IP as the networking protocol and http for the request itself). This request is generally for "a page" located on the indicated server. Often the URL that you type indicates only the name of a machine. In that case, it's the Web server's job to return the default page, which is generally named index.html.

The request can be for any type of file, including those shown in Table 36.2.

Table 36.2. File types available in requests.

File Type	File Extension	Where to get related software
HTML	.html	http://home.netscape.com/ and http://www.stars.com/
Graphics	.gif	everywhere!

continues

Table 36.2. continued

File Type	File Extension	Where to get related software
Audio, cross-platform	.au	`ftp://ftp.sonic.net/pub/mall/pcutil/old-technology`
Internet Wave	.vmd	`http://www.vocaltec.com`
RealAudio	.ra	`http://www.realaudio.com`
Java applets	.class	`http://java.sun.com`
True Speech	.tsp	`http://www.dspg.com/internet.htm`

The Web server's job is to respond to the http request by returning a file. When CGI is involved (see the following note), the server first runs a program which creates that file.

> **NOTE**
>
> CGI stands for Common Gateway Interface. A CGI program is any executable program that conforms to certain rules about how input and output are treated. The rules are discussed in detail below.
>
> CGI programs can be written in any language that can create an executable for the given operating system.

Figure 36.2 shows an overview of the interaction between a Web surfer, the server that responds to the request, a CGI program that can be written in Delphi, and a database engine.

FIGURE 36.2.

Suzie Surfer can use her browser to access information in a database.

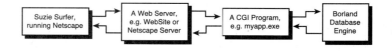

Keep this general overview in mind as we focus on the connection between surfer and Web server; soon we'll add the third and fourth pieces.

Web Documents are HTML Files

Most Web documents are HTML files, and most people get started on the Web by building their own personal "home page" using HTML. If you want to learn to write CGI programs that dynamically create Web pages, you need to learn HTML first.

A Five-Minute Introduction to HTML

HTML stands for HyperText Markup Language. The official specification site is at `http://www.ics.uci.edu/pub/ietf/html/`.

You can build HTML files using Notepad as your editor, or you can try any of the 100+ add-on editors that are available. To get started, just make an ASCII file and save it with an .html extension.

An excellent overview of HTML syntax is the *Bare Bones Guide,* available free online at `http://www.access.digex.net/~werbach/barebone.html`.

The great, searchable resource site for HTML authors is `http://www.stars.com`. You are also welcome to read my Infobahn Construction Workshop course notes at `http://super.sonic.net/ann/htmlsmnr.html`.

Table 36.3 lists the must-know HTML tags.

Table 36.3. Essential HTML tags.

HTML tag	Description
`<h1>`	Header on, largest size, level 1
`</h1>`	Header level 1, off
`<h2>`	Header level 2, on
`</h2>`	Header level 2, off
`<b>`	Bold on
`</b>`	Bold off (/ means off)
`<A HREF="other.html">` `Jump to Other Document</A>`	Hypertext link
`<A HREF="mailto:info@href.com">` `info@href.com</A>`	E-mail hot link
`<ul>`	Begin unordered list
`<li>`	List item starts here
`</ul>`	End unordered list
`<form method=post` `action=something>`	Begin data input form; `Something` = your program
`<input type=text name=x>`	Accept data entry; assign to x
`<input type=submit>`	An OK button for the form
`</form>`	End of the form

Of course there's more, but if you try out these commands and make them work, you'll be at least halfway along the HTML learning curve. (The form won't do any action without a CGI program.)

Netscape will let you open files that are stored on your local hard drive, so you can create *yourfile*.html and then just File | Open it.

The most popular way to learn HTML is to study other people's code. Go to a Web site and then ask your browser to show you the source code. With the Netscape browser, the command is View | Source. Of course, you can then copy the HTML to the Clipboard, or even do a File | Save command to capture the entire document.

If you feel guilty doing this, remember that once you publish something wonderful, other people will learn from your code in turn.

On the other hand, if you don't really like the idea of everyone in the world benefiting so quickly from your labors, read on—the source code behind CGI programs cannot be seen from a browser.

Why Bother Writing Web Applications?

Let's back up for a minute. There is so much hype about the Internet and the Web. What are the real reasons that individuals and corporations are rushing in?

- The Web is a relatively low-cost platform.
- Many important business applications can be made available instantly—around the globe.
- Applications written for the Web are cross-platform from the perspective of the "surfer"—they can be used by people with Windows, on a Mac, or running UNIX.
- Web applications can make and save money through sales, by supporting a public relations effort, and by automating customer service tasks.
- Publishing on the Web can be fun and offers individuals a new location-independent lifestyle.

Let's see what else you can notice about Web sites from your browser.

Comparing Web Sites

Looking at Web sites is like looking at a crowd of faces while walking down Madison Avenue in New York at 5 p.m. Every one is unique and interesting, and over time, patterns emerge.

Public Versus Private

Most of the media focus is naturally on public Web sites because they are easily accessible. However, there are a large and growing number of Intranet Web sites running on corporate, academic, and government networks. In many cases these networks are not connected to the public Internet. Therefore, Web sites on these networks are only accessible to people in the organization.

Such internal Web sites are ideal for publishing the organization's information to users on a wide range of hardware/software platforms. This is easy because there are HTML browsers for every situation. A further advantage to Intranet sites is that often the surfers have a high-speed network connection (not a 28.8 phone line). Because there are fewer bandwidth problems, the Intranet tends to enable more sophisticated, database-driven sites.

Although the purposes of these two types of sites are often quite different, the underlying techniques and challenges are the same.

What's the Server Platform?

As a surfer, you have few clues to determine this. Sometimes you can figure out at least what software is being used. In terms of software, the three questions are: (a) which operating system? (b) which Web server? and (c) which programming language is used for the CGI part? We'll discuss CGI in much more detail shortly.

Look closely at the URLs of interactive sites for a clue regarding (b). If the URL contains the phrase cgi-bin/, you are probably dealing with a flavor of UNIX; if it contains cgi-win/, you are definitely dealing with Windows.

> **NOTE**
>
> Where do I get my own Web server software?
>
> Web site: http://Website.ora.com
>
> Spry: http://server.spry.com
>
> Netscape: http://merchant.netscape.com/netstore/soft/serv/items/bud/146.html
>
> Purveyor: http://www.process.com/prod/purveyor.htp
>
> Quarterdeck: http://www.qdeck.com/qdeck/demosoft/WebServr/
>
> Spinnaker: http://www.searchlight.com/
>
> Novell: http://www.novell.com/

JBServer: `http://www.utm.edu:80/~bbradley/zbs/`

EMWACS: `http://emwac.ed.ac.uk/html/internet_toolchest/https/CONTENTS.HTM` (*free*)

WebCommander: `http://www.flicks.com/`

Static Versus Dynamic Pages

A key distinction to make when looking at Web sites is between *static* and *dynamic*.

Most public Web sites are simply set up to return static pages. Each time a surfer requests `http://super.sonic.net/ann/index.html`, literally the *same file* is returned by the Web server (and no custom .EXE is involved). Most large Internet Service Providers allow only this type of site.

See Figure 36.3 for a decision-tree to assist in choosing an ISP.

FIGURE 36.3.

Planning ahead can save you hundreds of dollars in Internet service fees.

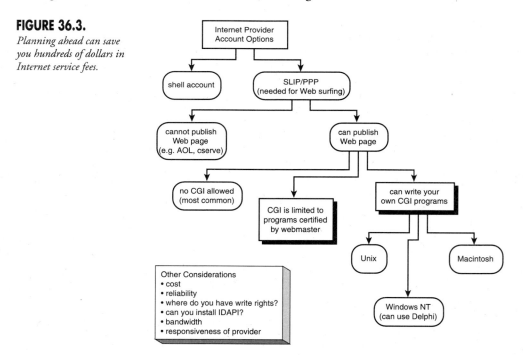

Let's move past the topic of static pages and discuss how one makes dynamically generated ones. If you're surfing the Web and you see a URL that contains the phrase CGI, you can assume that a program will be running to generate the requested HTML document on the fly.

Between the requirements of accepting the input and sending the output, the CGI program can do just about anything—that's where it gets interesting. A Delphi-based .EXE can run queries on local and remote databases, send e-mail and faxes, generate graphics, conduct electronic transactions over the Internet or other off-the-net connections, run other programs, move files around, and so on. When we talk about building a Web *application,* we are really talking about all these additional useful tasks.

Thus, the capability to run CGI applications on your Web server machine is a prerequisite to building interactive, database-driven Web sites. When evaluating Internet Service Providers, you should find out your options on this point. The larger the provider, the less likely that they will allow you to install and run custom CGI programs.

Interactive Web Sites

What does this phrase really mean? On one level, it means sites that sizzle and win awards. From the surfer's perspective, it means sites that let you "do something besides just read." From an implementation perspective, it means building search engines and chat rooms—Web pages that respond meaningfully to the user.

In a corporate setting, this might mean enabling data input, online reports, and graphs over the Web.

One state-of-the-art interactive site is `http://lanark.jf.intel.com/`, where the surfer can use Intel's Interactive Rendering Machine over the Web.

Database-Driven Web Sites

The cost of building a Web site can be deceptive. These could be the thoughts of a novice Web entrepreneur: "It's only $20/month for 10 MB of space; all I have to do is create .html files and overnight I'll have thousands of international customers. I'll create hundreds of pages describing my products and I'll never have to answer the phone. I'll move to the Colorado Rockies..."

But what does one do about data maintenance? Specifically, there are hidden costs associated with the following activities:

- Adding/changing/deleting catalog items
- Style changes, in terms of graphics, wallpaper, font size conventions
- Text changes, in terms of page headers, footers, and other items that tend to be repeated on every page

By using a database to store the catalog (or other) information and a CGI program to generate the pages on request, you suddenly reduce these tasks to a relatively standard data entry module on your database plus some custom programming for the style and text changes.

That is what I mean by database-driven Web sites.

Analyzing Web Sites

How do you determine what will be required to build a particular Web site? This section offers you a handy way to think about it.

Focus on Web Site Pages

Figure 36.4 shows the simple but powerful view of a Web site as a flow chart through a series of *pages*.

FIGURE 36.4.

A Web site is a collection of individual pages, with a suggested flow-through.

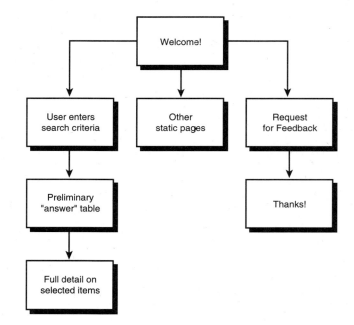

Once you have mapped the flow for a given Web site, you can identify which pages are basically static, and which ones need to be generated based on runtime information. In the diagram in Figure 36.4, the Preliminary "answer" table, "Full detail," and "Thanks" pages would be generated after running a CGI program.

Here's a quick summary of what each page would need to do:

- **Answer page:** Run a query based on the surfer's input criteria and generate the HTML to display that result in a convenient format. Make a "hot link" on each record so that the surfer can "drill down" to the next page. That hot link needs to communicate the primary key of the desired record. This can be done by putting the primary key in the URL, for example, /cgi-win/yourapp.exe?123 for item #123.

- **Detail page:** Access the CGI Environment Variable called "Query String" to determine the primary key and then locate the appropriate record. (The Query String would be "123" in our example.) Then generate the necessary HTML based on the fields in that record (and perhaps other linked tables).

- **Thanks page:** Collect all the inputs from the Feedback page and send them by e-mail to the site owner, and/or post them to a database for subsequent analysis. Then generate some simple HTML to say thanks.

Flowchart Pages as Placeholders

The flowchart gives a deceptively two-dimensional view of a Web site. There are two common features that add depth.

- **Conditional sections of pages:** Some pages will vary depending on what the user does. The Thanks page can be used as an example for this—what if the surfer didn't actually enter any feedback? Would you still send e-mail and say "Thanks" or would you say "Hey! Give me feedback!" The idea here is that the page in the flow chart is a placeholder for a couple of variations, both of which are feedback responses but which might look quite different.

- **Scrolling "answer" sets:** If you use Netscape and try Directory | Internet Search, you'll get to InfoSeek, one of the many search engines on the Web. They give you 10 matches at a time, and a button to click for the next 10. So their Answer page is again a placeholder where the text stays constant above and below a changing result set.

You can probably think of other situations in which the meaning of a page can be expanded.

Selecting Your Software Tools

If you want to build interactive, database-driven Web sites, you'll want to choose the best programming environment for your CGI work. It is very likely that you'll choose Delphi—here are the reasons at the top of my list:

- Delphi is fully *object-oriented*. In spite of Bruce Webster's warnings in *Pitfalls of Object-Oriented Development*, the appeal of building reusable components is extremely strong.

- Delphi has so *few limits*. You can express big ideas and make them run really fast.

- Delphi gives you an easy connection to most popular *database* file formats.

- Delphi code is relatively *self-documenting*, essential for team development.

- The integrated *debugger* lets you rapidly find most of your bugs.

- Delphi's *exception handling* is first-rate.

If you agree that Delphi is a great development environment, you must then embark on a quest for a Windows-based environment to use it in. (Yes, I hope it will ship for Linux and the Macintosh someday.) That means selecting Windows 95 or NT and finding a Web server for that platform.

The CGI Specification

Now we have to start talking about the CGI specification and a few of its variations.

The original CGI specification is available free on the Web at `http://hoohoo.ncsa.uiuc.edu/cgi/overview.html`. This is written for an audience using UNIX plus C or Perl as the programming language. (Perl is an interpreted scripting language and has been ported to NT.) The "hoohoo" files are a reasonable starting point for someone who wants a thorough understanding of CGI.

Robert Denny broke new ground by amending the CGI specification for use in the Windows environment.

> **NOTE**
>
> Bob Denny published one of the first Web servers for the Windows platform, Win-HTTPD, which ran on Windows 3.1x. It is still available as shareware from `http://www.city.net/win-httpd/`. He then went on to write a 32-bit version called WebSite, which is published by O'Reilly and Associates and available from `http://Website.ora.com/`. Bob's home computer is generally online with his latest achievements (and experiments) at `http://solo.dc3.com`.

Essentially, he stated that instead of using stdin and stdout to stream the data in and out of the CGI application, one would use a set of files in a temporary directory to hold the information. There would be a set of two or more files defining the HTTP request, and the CGI program would be responsible for creating a third output file before terminating.

> **NOTE**
>
> There are two ways to pass data to a CGI program:
>
> 1. **Pass one string** as a suffix after the .EXE filename, for example, `/cgi-win/yourprog.exe?hello` (sets the `CGIQueryString` to `'hello'`)
>
>   or
>
>   `/cgi-win/yourprog.exe/hello` (sets the `CGIPathInfo` to `'hello'`).
> 2. **Pass unlimited data** from fields on a form (this requires that the user enter the data, and it requires the use of `method=post` in the HTML FORM command).

If you are building a link from an overview page to a full-detail page, you could use technique #1 to pass the unique identifier of the item to the page that needs to display all the detail for that item. If you are building a scrolling grid, you might want to pass a command such as grid.next to indicate movement to the next set of records. In both these examples, only one string is passed to the CGI program. The string is used to signal the CGI program so that it knows what to do.

HTML forms are used in very different situations. Forms enable data entry, and all the surfer's data is passed to the CGI program.

Sometimes you might want to a combination of these two techniques so that you can post the user's data and signal the CGI program to do something special.

The temporary input files contain all the CGI environment data as defined on hoohoo, plus any data submitted by the surfer on an HTML form. (See Listing 36.1.)

Listing 36.1. Sample .INI file showing CGI environment data from a hit on a Classified Ads site.

```
[CGI]
Request Protocol=HTTP/1.0
Request Method=POST
Executable Path=/cgi-win/Webhub.exe
Query String=Fair:match:8257.5577
Server Software=WebSite/1.0k
Server Name=super.sonic.net
Server Port=80
Server Admin=ntsupport@sonic.net
CGI Version=CGI/1.2 (Win)
Remote Address=134.113.221.87
Referer=http://super.sonic.net/cgi-win/Webhub.exe
Authentication Method=Basic
Authentication Realm=Web Server
Content Type=application/x-www-form-urlencoded
Content Length=47

[System]
GMT Offset=-28800
Debug Mode=No
Output File=c:\temp\b37dws.out
Content File=c:\temp\b37dws.inp

[Form Literal]
Category=Computer Modems
city=
state=
shortzip=

[Accept]
*/*=Yes
image/gif=Yes
```

continues

Listing 36.1. continued

```
image/x-xbitmap=Yes
image/jpeg=Yes

[Extra Headers]
User-Agent=Mozilla/1.0N (Windows)
```

It's All in the .INI

Under the rules of win-cgi, the Web server and the CGI program communicate through temporary files.

The Web server creates

c:\temp*xxx*.ini	Shown previously, actual filename varies for each request
c:\temp*xxx*.inp	Raw input data for Form Literals
c:\temp*.*	external files if needed

The CGI program is responsible for creating

c:\temp*xxx*.out	Actual filename is defined in the .INI file, under [System] Output File

Take a minute and study the sample .INI file. The [CGI] section contains the "CGI Environment Data" as defined on hoohoo. At the risk of being a bit boring, here's a laundry list of the file contents and some insight into why they matter. (Some of the specifics are subject to change; see your Web server manual for current details.)

Request Protocol: Here you can look for the version of HTTP.

Request Method: This could be GET or POST.

Executable Path: The name of your program, which is the part of the URL after the server name.

Query String: This one is central to the communication between browser and CGI program. The query string is defined as those characters in the URL that follow a ?, which can follow the executable path. In this example, the request was /cgi-win/ Webhub.exe?Fair:match:8257.5577.

It is also possible to use the / separator instead of ?, and then the data is put into the PathInfo variable rather than QueryString.

Server Software: Simply reminds you whose software you're running.

Server Port: Generally 80 (can be changed within the server software).

Server Admin: E-mail address of administrator.

CGI Version: As stated.

Remote Address: This is what you can find out about the surfer—the IP address of their browser. You can run that through a reverse domain name lookup and determine the domain they are coming from (compuserve.com, aol.com, sonic.net, and so on).

Referer: The URL of the page they are "calling you from." The example here is deceptive because the query string portion of the URL has been stripped so that you cannot see enough to tell "which page." Often the Referer will be the name of a static .html page.

Authentication Method: Method used for authentication (for example, "Basic").

Authentication Realm: The name of the realm to which the authenticated user belongs. Blank if no authentication was needed. See `http://www.cis.ohio-state.edu/htbin/rfc/rfc931.html`.

Content Type: This refers to the content of the request; I have not yet seen it vary.

Content Length: In this case, 47 bytes, meaning the length of the strings sent under [Form Literals], as preserved in the temporary .INP file.

The [System] section is particular to win-cgi, and only the Web site server implements Debug Mode. The GMT Offset must be used by your CGI program to calculate the Greenwich Mean Time date, which goes on the response document back to the server. The Output File name must be used when creating the response document for the surfer.

The [Form Literal] section is particular to win-cgi and itemizes information about <INPUT> fields on the HTML form that called you (if applicable). All fields, radio buttons, and checkboxes will be listed. Checkboxes are an exception; they are listed only when checked. Text areas will show up under [Form Literal] if the surfer typed one line of text, and under [Form External] if they entered more.

The [Form External] section was not needed in this sample. It itemizes any data that the Web server does not want to put under [Form Literal], either because it is longer than 255 characters or because it appears that the data might be binary, not text. Thus even short form inputs that involve foreign languages generally end up under [Form External].

The [Accept] section enables the browser to tell the CGI program what type of data it can accept.

The [Extra Headers] section can vary, but you will generally be able to look at User-agent and find out what browser is in use.

Where's the user name? You don't generally find out the surfer's name. In some cases, you will get their e-mail address. If you request authentication, you will get their name and password.

The preceding apply to the Web site server. The concepts will apply to all servers, but the details may vary.

Working with HTML Forms

You will need to master HTML FORM syntax, because forms represent the only real way for a surfer to get data to your CGI program. Figure 36.5 shows one example, the form that led to the .INI file:

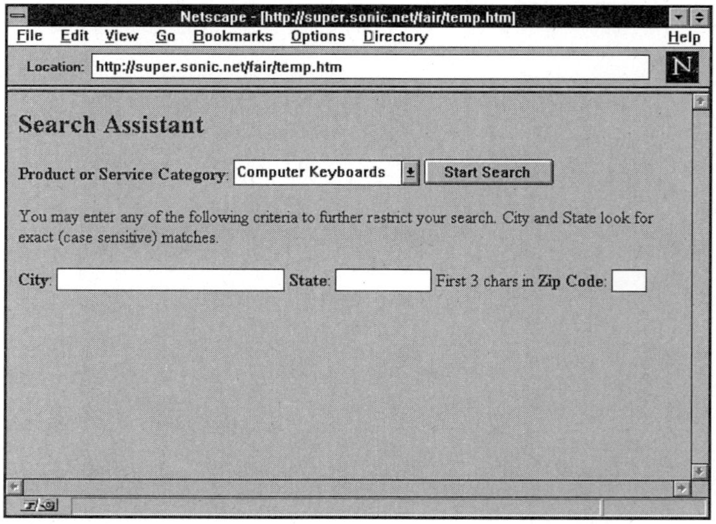

FIGURE 36.5.

An input form created using HTML FORM syntax.

You can check out the HTML source code with View | Source:

```
HTML source behind the form

<H2>Search Assistant</H2>

<FORM METHOD=POST ACTION="/cgi-win/Webhub.exe?fair:match:8257.5577">

<b>Product or Service Category</b>: <SELECT NAME="Category">
<OPTION>Computer Keyboards
<OPTION>Computer Laptops
<OPTION>Computer Modems
<OPTION>Computer Monitors
</SELECT>

<INPUT TYPE="submit" VALUE="Start Search"><p>

You may enter any of the following criteria to further
restrict your search.  City and State look for exact (case sensitive)
matches.<p>

<b>City</b>: <INPUT TYPE="TEXT" NAME="city" MAXSIZE=25 size=25>
<b>State</b>: <INPUT TYPE="TEXT" NAME="state" MAXSIZE=10 size=10>
First 3 chars in <b>Zip Code</b>: <INPUT TYPE="TEXT" NAME="shortzip" MAXSIZE=3
 SIZE=3> <br>

</FORM>
```

When analyzing an HTML form, look for the `<FORM>` tag and read the `ACTION=`part. The `ACTION` defines the name of the CGI program that will run.

The CGI Program's Job

The Web server will execute the CGI program. The CGI program needs to read the relevant parts of the input files and create an output file. The CGI program signals completion by terminating.

The output file needs to be in a certain format, which is basically a header section followed by HTML. The header is called the *Prologue* and is used to communicate status information back to the Web server and surfer, as shown in Listing 36.2.

Listing 36.2. Standard Prologue (including trailing blank line).

```
HTTP/1.0 200 OK
Server: server name here
Date: date/time in GMT format
Content-type: text/html
```

This would then be followed by whatever HTML was appropriate. Basically, the surfer's browser software reacts based on the Prologue and then displays the HTML.

Why Isn't This Trivially Easy?

So far it sounds easy, right? Just create a Delphi component to help read the .INI files and maybe to assist with the HTML syntax, and then have it run in response to each CGI request. Well, this is precisely what I did in June 1995—you can see my first round of components at `http://super.sonic.net/ann/delphi/cgicomp/`. The `TCGIEnvData` component was, and is, free.

> **NOTE**
>
> The `TCGIEnvData` component is included on the CD with this book, with source code so that you can compile it for 16- or 32-bit Delphi. Just install the CGI.PAS file into your component library.

Using that free component, you can create HTML documents on the fly. The Delphi source code to do this is quite simple:

```
procedure TForm1.formCreate( sender : TObject );
begin
  with CGIEnvData1 do begin
    { when this program runs under WebSite, parameter #1 will be the
      name of the ini file. }
    WebSiteINIFilename := paramstr(1);
    application.onException := cgiErrorHandler;
    application.processMessages;  { need to have this ! }
    createStdout;
    sendPrologue;
    send( '<HTML><HEAD>' );
    sendTitle( 'Sample HTML page' );
    send( '</HEAD><BODY>' );
    sendHdr( '1', 'Sample HTML page' );
    send( '...created by Delphi CGI Components...<p>' );
    send( 'Your IP address is: ' + CGIRemoteAddress^ );
    send( '<p>It <b>works</b>!!!' );
    sendHR;
    send( 'Generated on ' + Webdate(now) );
    send( '</BODY></HTML>' );
    closeStdout;
  end;
  closeApp( application );
end;
```

The Send() commands send a string to the correct output file; the rest is just initialization and shutdown.

Once this program is compiled, I can invoke it from my browser using http://127.0.0.1/cgi-win/demo1.exe, and, yes, it does work! You can see some of the sites built by Delphi developers around the world by going to the "Hall of Fame" at http://super.sonic.net/ann/delphi/cgicomp/hallfame.html.

What I found in building numerous Web applications with my components is that the larger and more popular the site, the less useful TCGIEnvData was. In this next section, I'll share the main challenges of Web site development, and the solutions.

Performance

The first challenge is really easy to understand: performance. If you have a 450,000-byte .EXE that needs to load and unload in response to each request, and maybe on top of that it needs to initialize IDAPI to use a database, it will take many seconds per execution, even on a dedicated Pentium 120 with 32 MB of RAM.

We really need a way to keep the program code in memory (a .DLL? an .EXE?) so that it doesn't need to reload each time. This would also solve the problem of keeping IDAPI initialized.

It does, however, create the problem of how to track "multiple threads" in that program.

Tracking Sessions

This is tied in with saving state—you need a way to uniquely identify each surfer and to store each surfer's data in a unique, structured, quickly accessible place. You want to do this in a non-invasive way (that is, without requiring login), and in a way that works regardless of whether the user comes in the "front door" or saves a bookmark to an unexpected page deeper in the flow chart.

Saving State

The second challenge is that of "saving state."

In general, in the world of CGI, each invocation of the executable program is a separate instance, with no knowledge of the surfer and the surfer's previous actions on the site.

As you saw from the [Form Literals] section of the .INI file in the previous section, it is possible to pass variables from any one page to the CGI program that runs directly off that page.

As you build larger sites, it will become necessary to have "global" variables that are available across many pages. Furthermore, it will be necessary to attribute that data to a given surfer.

In general, you need to "save state" whenever you need to carry variables from page n to somewhere other that page $n + 1$. (That is, going from page 1 to 2 is easy, but from 1 to 3 is not.) If you make a flowchart for your application, you should be able to quickly identify these situations.

Saving state lets you differentiate surfers and accumulate variable data about each one. Once you build in the generic ability to save state, you'll find lots of uses for it! Figure 36.6 provides a reminder that each page is processed separately, and that the "distance" between where you get the data to where you use it is crucial.

FIGURE 36.6.

You need to save state when there are one or more pages between "get" and "use."

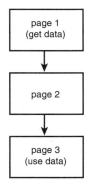

- **User preferences:** Perhaps you have a page where the surfer can set some preferences for the site, such as graphics file type (.GIF, .JPG, .PNG), use of wallpaper, font size, HTML table style, and so on. In this case, you would want to collect all that data on one page, but make use of it on all other generated pages.

- **Latent query results:** Perhaps on page one the surfer tells you about a general product category they are interested in and a price range. To help them narrow the search, the next screen gives them a table of possible product subcategories. After selecting a subcategory, they are then presented with the specific products that fit the price range entered on page 1. Here again, you need to remember information from page 1 and carry it through to page 3.

- **Shopping cart:** Figure 36.7 shows a flowchart for a Web site that allows order entry. As the surfer identifies likely items for purchase, the CGI program accumulates an order list and then makes that full list available on a checkout page.

FIGURE 36.7.

This cyberstore clearly requires "saving state."

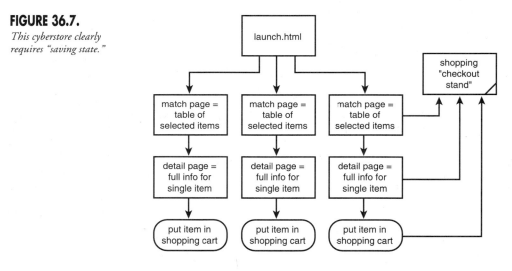

Typically the way that CGI applications save state is to assign each user a numeric ID and then pass that fact around the system through the URL. You can see this in action at many sites on the Net, including Virtual Vineyards (`http://www.virtualvin.com/`) and our Fish Store site at `http://www.href.com/fish/`.

I should emphasize that it's not enough to uniquely number each surfer; you also need a convenient way to track that surfer's *data*.

Separation of HTML Artist and Programmer

While we're longing for the ultimate CGI framework, let's also address the issue of site maintenance. Can't we put all the "static" HTML pieces *outside* the Delphi application in some sort of .INI file or something? Yes!

An excellent goal is to separate the tasks of the "HTML artist" (who deals with HTML, page layout, and graphics) from those of the "Delphi programmer" who should have the luxury of focusing on things that can't be done in HTML.

Let's add to this the requirement that these "pieces" (we ended up calling them "chunks") be reusable across pages and across Web applications.

This will also lend some structure to the programmer's dialog with the artist and the end-customer, which is why component *basics* are so important. People will be able to say "give me a grid with a default page height of 10, these two display sets, and these three index orders." The component structure provides a feature-set structure.

Business Rules

Once we get past all the annoyances of conforming to the CGI rules, we find ourselves facing fundamental issues that apply to any database-oriented application.

If you are building an application with some tables that are not read-only, the question arises, where should I define the "business rules?"

A simple, common example of such an application on the Web would be a "guest book" or "mailing list sign-up" page. Where do you define the required fields? How do you implement that requirement? (Many of you have probably built systems with much more sophisticated rules; the implementation suggestion here should still apply.)

With Delphi, you can define and implement the business rules in the events of the TTable object, such as BeforePost. You can make a custom table object for each relevant table, and then reuse that component in every application that uses that table, and be guaranteed consistent posting. This object-oriented strategy enables corporations to invest once in the Delphi technology and then reuse that in Web and non-Web applications.

In a client/server situation, for example with Interbase, you might have the code use stored procedures and triggers to implement certain business rules. You would use a different scheme for peer-to-peer access. Regardless, developers can maintain the implementation and the underlying assumptions about a system.

The Need for a Framework

"A framework is a set of prefabricated software building blocks that programmers can use, extend, or customize for specific computing solutions. With frameworks, software developers don't have to start from scratch each time they write an application. Frameworks are built from a collection of objects, so both the design and code of a framework may be reused."—From the *Taligent Glossary* at http://www.taligent.com/building-oofw.html#introducingoofw.

To summarize the points so far, you'd like a CGI framework that

- Keeps the program code loaded and the BDE connection open, yet satisfies the requirement that the application signal completion by terminating.
- Identifies and tracks user sessions.
- Saves state automatically, including "form literals" with compensation for checkboxes.
- Separates HTML from Pascal while giving you reusable HTML chunks.
- Doesn't restrict your business rule implementation options.

Let's add three more points:

- Is open "in the right places" so that component writers can add functionality.
- Is extremely reliable and easy to use.
- Is designed using state-of-the-art concepts to meet real business needs today.

With everything you've learned in this book, you might be able to develop such a framework.

You're also most welcome to download the free trial version of WebHub, the CGI framework developed by Michael Ax at HREF Tools Corp.—it meets or exceeds all these criteria (no surprise). Our URL is `http://www.href.com/`.

Electronic Commerce and Security

"The only way to make sure your credit card is not stolen on the Internet is to avoid typing it into any piece of software."—Nathaniel Borenstein, coauthor of MIME and Chief Scientist, First Virtual Holdings, Inc.

"May you live in interesting times..."—ancient curse.

We all want to play the consumer game on the Web. Shopping online can be so convenient; I would certainly rather telecommute than sit in my car on Route 101!

In the United States, there is little personal financial risk when using credit cards on the Internet because the banks pay the price of credit card fraud (indirectly passed back to us, of course). If someone steals my card, I just notify my bank and don't pay the bill. People in other countries don't necessarily have that luxury.

The competitive dance for market- and mind-share in the electronic commerce arena is perhaps entrancing. There are big name players—Microsoft, Visa, Mastercard, Intuit, Netscape, and RSA to name a few. They are all telling us that we can have secure transactions on the Internet. Given the various successful hackers who have broken through these limits, they really can't say "absolutely secure." So they say, "secure enough" and direct attention elsewhere.

NOTE

You can find more information at the following sites:

Cybercash: `http://www.cybercash.com/`

Digicash: `http://www.digicash.com/digicash/company.html`

First Virtual: `http://www.fv.cm/`

Intuit: `http://www.intuit.com/int-corp-press-release/120495.html`

Ziplock: `http://www.portsoft.com/`

Mark Twain Bank: `http://www.marktwain.com/`

ViaCheck: `http://TheYellowPages.com/Viacheck/index.htm`

ViaCrypt: `http://www.nha.com/vpgpwin.html`

In all fairness, sending a credit card number from a browser to a Web server when they both use encryption is more secure than calling PC Connection on your cellular phone. And some of the e-commerce options don't advocate putting the actual credit card number on the Internet (thereby moving the point of vulnerability but not eliminating it).

What we have here are millions of generally honest consumers and merchants who so desperately want to conduct Internet commerce that they are ignoring some painful facts. For example:

- If you store credit card numbers on your server, you have to give careful thought to security. You don't want to invite hackers to download your collection of 10,000 card numbers.

- If you don't store them on your server, but you want to accept them, you still run a risk on the channel between the browser and the server, plus you have to figure out a "secure" way to communicate them to your "off-the-Net" server.

- If instead of taking credit cards, you adopt a "pin-based" e-commerce strategy, you are then putting all your trust in that company's ability to maintain security. You will need to really read between the lines of their promotional material to find their vulnerabilities. Ask questions like: Who knows the one-and-only-private password and what if they were kidnapped? How many programmers worked on the one-and-only batch-transfer application, and are they still happily employed at the firm? How many years of security experience do they have? OK, it's unlikely, but *what if* someone did break through that firewall? Would one transaction be jeopardized, a batch, a day's, the whole company? How would merchants and consumers be treated fairly in such a case?

■ Here's a key point from Nathaniel Borenstein: "If you want it (encyrption keys) to work, you should only use an encryption mechanism that has a well-designed mechanism for specifying key lifetimes, so that encryption keys have a known and well-specified lifetime after which they need to be updated. That way, when it is time to use more bits for stronger encryption, it will be possible to gracefully and coherently upgrade the whole user base."

There are also important Big Brother questions such as: exactly who has access to all my financial transaction data? Systems like DigiCash are appealing because they maintain anonymity.

The implications for world commerce are staggering. On the optimistic side, the Web opens the playing field and makes global distribution an almost overnight reality.

> **NOTE**
>
> Computer crime in the news:
>
> Hack Netscape, win a T-Shirt: `http://www.c2.org/hacknetscape/`
>
> "Bank Robbers Go Electronic," *Byte Magazine*, Nov. 1995, p. 48

Security, piracy, and electronic commerce on the Internet are clearly an increasing part of our future. Today's confusion about encryption will settle as people realize that it's the virtual equivalent of a lock on the front door and that e-commerce will bequeath us all a new universal currency. The issues today are rooted in privacy and around "a constitutional right to anonymity."

What About Java?

Everyone wants to know what Java is, and where it fits in. Java is a C++-like language which runs on the client (surfer) machine. The programmer prepares "applet" files which are stored on the server and then sent to the surfer upon request. Unlike HTML, Java is a programming language and therefore enables a much richer user interface for surfers. Java can give us animated GIF files and a semi-interactive data-entry platform that can do more complex tasks than the browser usually can, and that is certainly important. I believe that Java's tremendous appeal really comes from its cross-platform nature.

However, Java has not yet matured. Right now, most people's first experience with it is somewhat jarring. The Java specs are still very much in flux, especially as regards the connections to the database back-ends.

WHERE TO LEARN MORE ABOUT JAVA

Borland is currently working on a Java compiler that should be released sometime during the summer of 1996. You can visit the Borland Web site, `www.borland.com`, to find out more about this project. The best way to find out what is state-of-the-art regarding Java is to do a search on the Web for something like `Java` and `demo`. That way you are sure to find people who are actually building Java applets.

EarthWeb is providing a directory of resources for Java programmers at `http://www.gamelan.com/`, in association with Sun Microsystems. Source code is available to some sample applets.

Right now, the framework we've discussed can easily serve up Java applets as *chunks*. More importantly, it can pass relevant data as parameters to the Java applet, making that key link between the server-side, surfer-aware application and the client-side, somewhat disconnected, Java applet. Listing 36.3 shows an HTML document with an embedded Java applet. Remember that the parameter values can be dynamically filled in by the CGI application.

Listing 36.3. HTML document with Java applet (contributed by Dan Dumbrill).

```
<title>Test For Ann</title>
<hr>
<applet code="TestForAnn.class" width=450 height=50>
<param name=text value="Fresh  from  the  Fish  Store">
</applet>
<p>
<applet code="Receipt.class" width=450 height=600>
<param name=Parameter1 value="Guppy                2.00">
<param name=Parameter2 value="Sunfish              3.00">
<param name=Parameter3 value="--------------------------">
<param name=Parameter4 value="Total                3.00">
</applet>
```

Summary

In this chapter, I've introduced the main concepts of Web site design and CGI programming—analyzing Web site requirements, the rules of CGI itself, the real need for a comprehensive framework, and how Java fits in as a surfer-side enhancement. The next chapter focuses on specific Web-application features and how to implement them with Delphi.

Leveraging the BDE in Delphi

37

by Ann Lynnworth

IN THIS CHAPTER

The previous chapter covered some general, theoretical aspects of building CGI programs for the World Wide Web. This chapter looks at what it really takes to build Web applications with Delphi and WebHub. This is a practical, do-it-yourself chapter. It's okay if it takes you more than an hour to read it and then experiment with the ideas presented here. You might find yourself in a new phase of your career.

> **NOTE**
>
> Where's the free code? To follow these examples, you will need a copy of the (free) WebHub System and Trial Components, which are available for download on the Web at `http://www.href.com/`. We typically ship a new release at least once a month, and the WebHub system has an expiration date (just to keep everyone honest). Therefore the components are not on the CD that accompanies this book.
>
> The source code (.PAS) files are on the CD, although for best results, just use the sample files that accompany the set of components you download from our Web site. That way you'll have the latest and greatest files.
>
> I thought long and hard about how to provide these files to you, and in the end it was clear that offering you state-of-the-art files was better than the short-term convenience of having them on the CD.

Life Is Uncertain; Have Dessert First

Here's a dessert buffet that I'd like you to try *before* you settle in for the full-course meal. This is an all-you-can-eat buffet, with ideas about Delphi component design and usage. These ideas won't spoil your appetite; in fact, they should make the rest of the chapter more palatable.

Components Live in the TForm Neighborhood

We all toss around the phrase "object-oriented" when talking about Delphi components. Bruce Webster writes: "You can think of an object as an entity that responds to a set of messages." For me, object-oriented means primarily "encapsulation" and "inheritance"—that the relevant data and methods are contained within the object, and that by designing a good class hierarchy, you gain maximum code re-use.

I'd like to extend your associations to "object-oriented" by saying that the ideal component is not only self-contained and self-reliant—it is also a "good neighbor" in the Delphi TForm neighborhood.

I'll define a good neighbor as a component that can communicate "I'm ready" versus "no, don't count on me yet" and that can adjust itself as other components are created and destroyed in the neighborhood.

> **NOTE**
>
> If you'd like to build "good neighbor" components, download Michael Ax's TPack and check out the TComponentExtension class.
>
> ```
> ftp://ftp.sonic.net/pub/users/ann/tpack16s.zip
> http://www.href.com/pascal/tshapes.html
> ```

Components Are Actors on a Stage

I would even extend this anthropomorphizing to say that components are like actors on a stage. If you want to have a good play, the characters need to be well defined and play their role consistently. Components likewise need a clear identity, a clear job to do. The larger the framework, the more important it is to have clear job descriptions.

Little Pieces Are More Versatile

If a class hierarchy has the class boundaries in the right places, you end up with a large set of "software Legos" that you can snap together to create delightful structures. (Remember Lego? It was one of my toys when I was growing up.) The littler pieces could be combined in many more ways than, say, the fancier large items that came out later in the toy's evolution. I remember my initial fascination with the prefabricated green plastic trees fading as I realized that I couldn't transform them into anything other than trees. The basic Legos were much simpler, and could become almost anything. It's the same with components. By making the pieces smaller, you enable a richer set of combinations. (No, I'm not advocating a return to assembler; just a recognition of the value of smaller pieces.)

Just Do It!

Some components have a simple job that they are expected to "execute." I call these "action components" and expect them to be able to do their job in the Delphi IDE as well as at runtime. If the job is sending e-mail, you'll want to be able to test that without compiling. If the job is creating a page of .html output, you'll want to see that, too.

Principles that are central to the extensibility of the WebHub development environment are (a) action components inside your Web application can be executed by "the hub" simply by "calling their name," and (b) if you create components descended from TtpAction, those components will be similarly cooperative and effective in the neighborhood. Delphi Run-Time Type Information (RTTI) makes this possible.

Back to the Main Course

Now we'll explore the identity and jobs of components such as TWebDataGrid, TWebMail, and TWebOutline, and how you snap them together to quickly create sophisticated Web applications. Most of the examples are from our sample cyberstore, called The Fish Store (`http://www.href.com/fish/`), which uses the biolife table that shipped with Delphi-16.

Getting Started with the Key Players

Before we get into writing any Pascal code, we have to build the neighborhood by inviting the key components.

TWebApp and Company

Make a new project and add in a TWebApp object (here we use TFishApp, which is a slightly customized descendant of TWebApp). Then right-click the component and choose Update from the menu. TFishApp is a descendent of TtpUpdate. As such it has a `tpUpdated` property, which lets you know whether it's ready, and a doUpdate method, which attempts to "achieve readiness" and reports back. You just activated the doUpdate method by choosing Update from the menu. (TPack introduced these ideas in March 1995; Delphi's `Updated` property is slightly different.)

Different components have different definitions of when they declare themselves "tpUpdated."

The TWebApp needs to be able to open its .INI file and initialize itself, and it needs to connect to many other WebHub components: TWebIniFileLink, TWebInfo, TWebAppOutput, TWebSession, TWebBrowser, and TStatusPanel. Rather than sit around depressed and lonely, TWebApp will create those components on the form if they don't already exist. Figure 37.1 shows all the components that appear after you right-click (I lined them up a bit; clicking TWebAppOutput brings in the TWebServer).

You won't even have to "snap them together" because TFishApp does that for you. (The status panel will immediately be active and will display messages from the components.)

A few other preliminary setup clicks are required.

TWebCommandLine

You'll need a connection out to the CGI command line, and this is accomplished by dropping in the TWebCommandLine component. You don't have to change any default settings.

FIGURE 37.1.

TWebApps and their descendants know how to create the components they depend on.

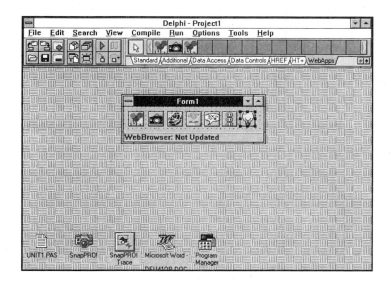

TWebHtmlMemo

This component is optional, but extremely useful during development. You can drop in this descendant of TMemo and connect it to the TWebAppOutput component. (Specifically, set the TWebAppOutput.showOutput property to True.) Later, when you test pages, the generated HTML will display in the memo field for your review. This will work in the Delphi IDE and at runtime. We advise deleting this component when you are ready to go into production mode.

TWebMenu

If you'd like a default menu for your application that will surface all the components' property editors and verbs, making them available for runtime customization—drop in a TWebApp menu component. It will survey the neighborhood and create a complete menu system for you in just a few seconds.

Let's See Some HTML Generated

If you want to test this a bit in the Delphi designer, you'll need to instantiate a TWebPage object. (This presupposes a bit more work in the .INI and .html files outside Delphi, which we won't go into here.)

On the TFishApp object, set the PageID property to ABOUT, which is the "About the Fish Store" page of the Web application. This will create a TWebPage object, which will appear just down and to the right of the TFishApp object.

Right-click the TWebPage object and select Test. Figure 37.2 shows how the generated HTML for that page will appear in the memo field. (You can also ask that the output be displayed in your Netscape browser using DDE.)

FIGURE 37.2.

*You can test page output
within the Delphi IDE.*

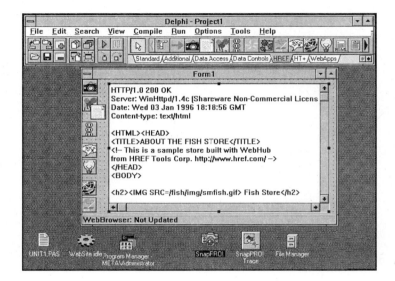

You can now compile your project to an .EXE. Invoke that from a browser (assuming you have an appropriate Web server installed, plus the WebHub system files), using this request:

```
http://127.0.0.1/cgi-win/Webhub.exe?fishapp:about
```

Then you will see the About page.

> **NOTE**
>
> 127.0.0.1 is an IP address that you can use to loop back onto your own machine (which is perfect when the Web server is installed there). You can substitute your real IP address, or a domain name, depending on your situation. With WebSite server, you can also use http://localhost/.

Leveraging the Delphi Database Components

Now that the preliminaries are out of the way, we can move on to adding "real features."

Probably the most common and well-grounded reason that someone will want to move from a static Web site to a dynamic one is to implement a search of some sort.

Delphi's database components (TDatabase, TTable, TQuery) give us a wonderful platform because they are by nature (fairly) file-format independent. You can add SQL statements to your TQuery component and expect it to work with Paradox, dBASE, Interbase, and so on.

So it is quite easy to make your Web application take the search criteria from the surfer and run a query. Then the question is, how do you return the result back to the surfer as HTML?

NOTE

What do I mean by "quite easy"? The surfer's criteria will be in the Literal[] property of the TWebApp component. For example, if you have an input field called MinimumFishLength, then TWebApp.Literal['MinimumFishLength'] would return the surfer's input.

You would then build the TQuery.SQL based on that value, for example:

```
with query1.sql do begin
  clear;
  add( 'select * from "biolife.db" ' );
  add( 'WHERE ("biolife.db"."Length (cm)" >= ' );
  add( WebAppCustom.Literal['MinimumFishLength'] + ') ' );
  end;
```

The HTML 3.0 specification includes "Tables," which are basically self-sizing grids; see Figure 37.3.

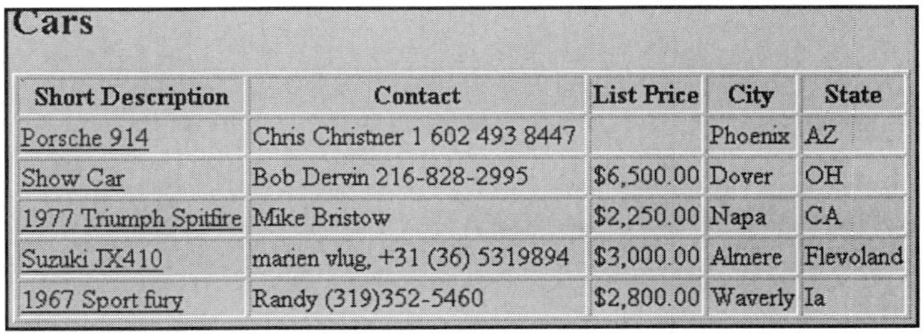

FIGURE 37.3.

HTML table syntax can easily accommodate a database table.

Cars					
Short Description	**Contact**	**List Price**	**City**	**State**	
Porsche 914	Chris Christner 1 602 493 8447		Phoenix	AZ	
Show Car	Bob Dervin 216-828-2995	$6,500.00	Dover	OH	
1977 Triumph Spitfire	Mike Bristow	$2,250.00	Napa	CA	
Suzuki JX410	marien vlug, +31 (36) 5319894	$3,000.00	Almere	Flevoland	
1967 Sport fury	Randy (319)352-5460	$2,800.00	Waverly	Ia	

In fact, HTML table syntax allows for cells that span multiple columns or rows, and even grids-within-grids, as shown in Figure 37.4.

The HTML to create a table is not that hard, but it's repetitive and bothersome to proof. Here's the HTML for the list of cars above:

```
<TABLE BORDER><TR><TH>Short Description<TH>Contact<TH>List Price<TH>City
➦<TH>State</TH></TR>

<TR><TD><A HREF="/cgi-win/Webhub.exe?Fair:Detail:3680.6188:228">Porsche 914</A>
➦<TD>Chris Christner 1 602 493 8447
<TD ALIGN=RIGHT> <TD>Phoenix<TD>AZ<br>
<TR><TD><A HREF="/cgi-win/Webhub.exe?Fair:Detail:3680.5815:230">Show Car</A>here
<TD>Bob Dervin 216-828-2995
<TD ALIGN=RIGHT>$6,500.00<TD>Dover<TD>OH<br>
<TR><TD><A HREF="/cgi-win/Webhub.exe?Fair:Detail:3680.7708:231">
1977 Triumph Spitfire</A><TD>Mike Bristow
<TD ALIGN=RIGHT>$2,250.00<TD>Napa<TD>CA<br>
<TR><TD><A HREF="/cgi-win/Webhub.exe?Fair:Detail:3680.1914:232">Suzuki JX410</A>
<TD>marien vlug, +31 (36) 5319894
<TD ALIGN=RIGHT>$3,000.00<TD>Almere<TD>Flevoland<br>
<TR><TD><A HREF="/cgi-win/Webhub.exe?Fair:Detail:3680.8947:243">1967 Sport fury</A>
<TD>Randy (319)352-5460
<TD ALIGN=RIGHT>$2,800.00<TD>Waverly<TD>Ia<br>
</TABLE>
```

The main tags are

`<TR>`	table row begins here
`<TH>`	table heading (will be bold)
`<TD>`	table detail (cell within the grid)

Introducing TWebDataGrid and TWebDataSource

To save you the trouble of generating this HTML on a row-by-row basis, we offer two components that work together with two standard Delphi components to create the necessary HTML table syntax (and do a few other tricks, too).

To set this up, you need to click the mouse and type a few things. Here's a quick summary:

Click This Component/Property	*And Type This*
`TTable.DatabaseName`	DBDEMOS
`TTable.Name`	TableBiolife
`TTable.TableName`	biolife.db
`TDataSource.DataSet`	TableBiolife ("snap together" here)
`TDataSource.Name`	DataSourceBiolife
`TWebDataSource.DataSource`	DataSourceBiolife ("snap together")
`TWebDataSource.Name`	WebDataSourceBiolife

TWebDataSource.DisplaySets	Set shortList = SpeciesNo,Category,Common_Name
TWebDataGrid.WebDataSource	WebDataSourceBiolife ("final snap")
TWebDataGrid.Name	gf (a short name worth remembering)
TWebDataGrid.PageHeight	Number of records to display at once, such as 3
TWebDataGrid.ButtonsWhere	dsbBelow

Your Web application can now create an HTML table.

How will this be called? In the page definition for the lookfish page, there is a section which names the gf component. When the WebHub system is creating that page and gets to that section, it will execute the action component named gf.

Your grid will include the scroll buttons (shown in Figure 37.4) due to the setting of ButtonsWhere to dsbBelow.

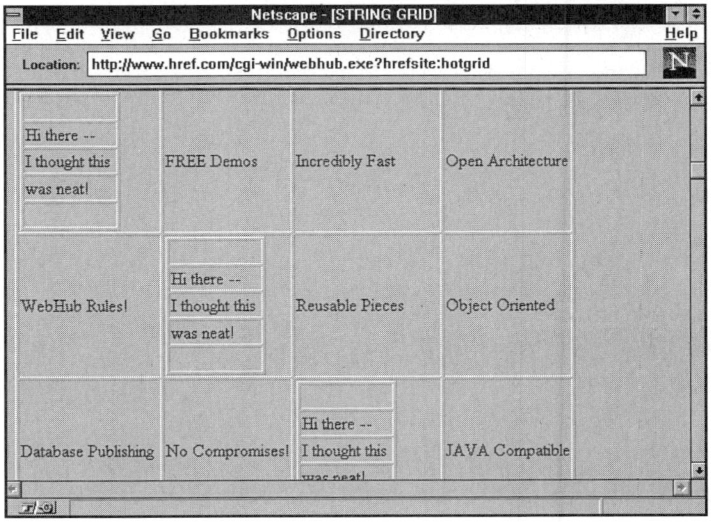

FIGURE 37.4.

Scroll buttons can be added to any grid by setting properties of the TWebDataGrid object.

The WebHub system takes care of scrolling the table, allowing for multiple users on the same table. (The TWebSession component encapsulates a camera snapshot of each surfer's unique data, including such things as their position in the table.)

The DisplaySet, which one enters on the TWebDataSource component, defines the columns to be displayed and their order. The column labels were customized by setting the DisplayLabel property of the fields, in the TTable's AfterOpen event handler:

```
procedure TForm1.TableBiolifeAfterOpen(DataSet: TDataset);
begin
```

```
  with TTable(DataSet) do begin
    fieldByName( 'Common_Name' ).displayLabel:='Fish Name';
    fieldByName( 'SpeciesNo' ).displayLabel:='Item ID';
  end;
end;
```

Drilling Down

Many, many database applications have a user interface where one proceeds through a series of queries, narrowing the search or "drilling down" through the data.

On the Web, you can create such a user interface by making hot links inside your table. In Figure 37.5, you can see the underlined <A HREF> links. This is done in two steps—identifying the hot field and customizing the event handler that defines the link.

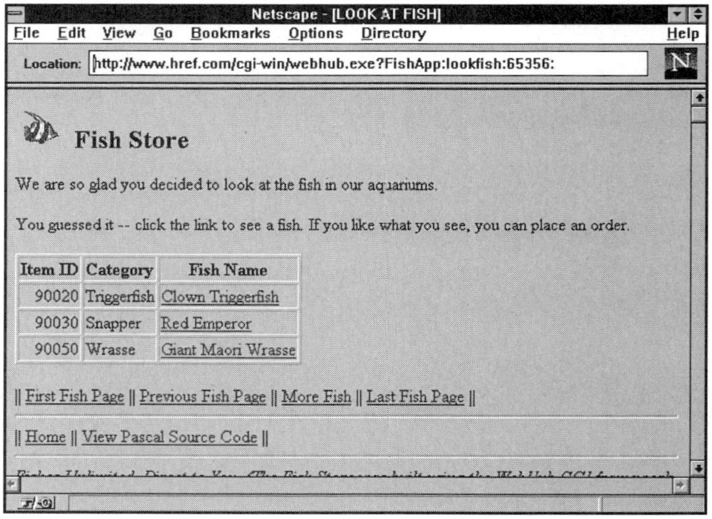

FIGURE 37.5.

Table with underlined links.

Hot fields are identified by setting the Tag property of the TField to a constant:

```
procedure TForm1.TableBiolifeAfterOpen(DataSet: TDataset);
begin
  with TTable(DataSet) do begin
    fieldByName( 'Common_Name' ).tag := HotFieldTag;
    end;
end;
```

The second step is customizing the OnHotField event handler of the TWebDataGrid component. It's helpful to keep in mind the HTML that you are trying to generate.

Hyperlink syntax: <A HREF="URL">visiblePhrase</A>

```
procedure TForm1.gfHotField(Sender: TWebDataScan; aField: TField;
  var s: OpenString);
```

```
var
  desc : string;
  id:String;
begin

  {note that fields[0] might not be the primary key due to display set changes}
  id:=aField.DataSet.fieldByName( 'SpeciesNo' ).asString;
  desc := aField.asString;

  { Here's the most important line to understand. This will expand to:
    <A HREF="/cgi-win/Webhub.exe?fishapp:detail:####:ItemID">fish name</A>
    See the Webhub.hlp file for more info on the %=macros=%. }
  s := '<TD><A HREF="%=cgiApp=%:detail:%=session=%:'
       + id + '">' + desc + '</A>';

end;
```

This event will be called for each row in the dataset, and for each hot field within that row. All you have to do is make sure that variable s is set to some valid HTML (which will lead the surfer to the next layer of your database/user interface).

Further Customizations

There are additional event handlers available: OnHotLabel, OnRowBegin, and OnRowEnd so that you can create all sorts of special effects within the basic grid template.

If you turn on the ControlsWhere property of the TWebDataGrid, you enable the surfer to set the grid page height, displayset, and indexorder. This is all handled by the WebHub system. If you want to customize that user interface, you can create variations yourself. The DropDown properties for DisplaySet and IndexOrder were surfaced to make this easy for you.

The DisplaySetDropDown property, for example, is basically a string list with this HTML content:

```
<b>Display Set</b>: <SELECT NAME="gf.DisplaySet">
<OPTION>ShortList
</SELECT>
```

You can access that HTML code from a "chunk" outside the Delphi application, thereby giving the user the ability to choose a DisplaySet. (Usually you'd have more than one defined!)

The same ideas apply for IndexOrder (which gives the surfer a choice of secondary index).

A New Cyber-Shopping Interface

Figure 37.6 demonstrates how you can put checkboxes (and input boxes) inside tables. This makes an elegant shopping interface (for small catalogs).

FIGURE 37.6.

Grids with checkboxes empower the surfer to order multiple items with minimal effort.

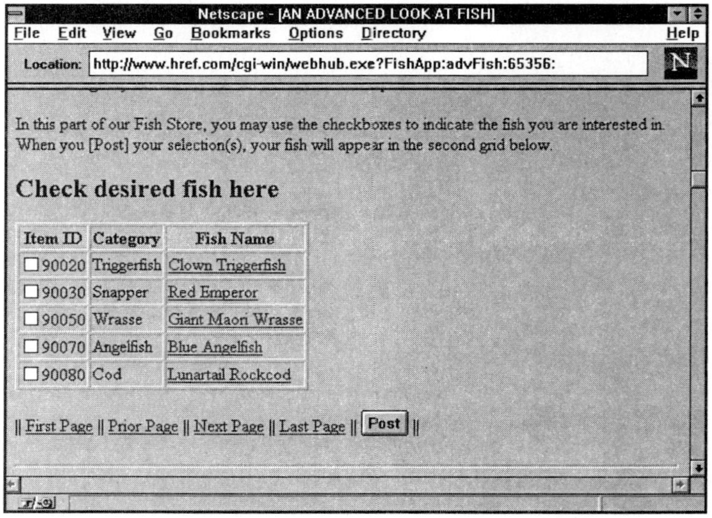

The biggest difficulty with using check boxes is that according to CGI rules, you only receive information about a check box when it is checked—there is no definitive False provided. This creates a bit of a mess when you want to save state—how do you differentiate "surfer hasn't answered this yet" from "surfer said no" when there is no False provided? In particular, how do you answer this about check boxes on a page other than the current one? (The current one is easy; you look in the .INI file and if the item is not found, of course it's False. But for noncurrent pages, you lose your reference guide.) The WebHub system compensates for this problem by keeping a list of "pending" checkboxes when a page is generated.

If you use the CKB command in your form action URL, it will then set all the pending items definitively to True or False. An example URL might look like this:

```
<A HREF="%=cgiApp=%:myPage:%=session=%:CKB">click me and remember</A>.
```

You also need to use the macro-on prefix to tell WebHub to pay attention, that is:

```
%=<INPUT TYPE=CHECKBOX NAME=SendInfo VALUE=YES> Send information
```

Check box values are accumulated in the Checked property of the TWebSession. When they are used in conjunction with a grid as shown above, you can then perform special processing on the "checked rows." Specifically, you can use a TWebDataGrid and set its ScanMode property to dsByChecked—and then when the grid is generated, only checked rows will be included.

Leveraging Delphi

This section explores the question, "What can Delphi and WebHub do together that other CGI frameworks cannot?" This is a key question, because you will have people trying to sell you a wide variety of "solutions" for building database-driven Web sites. Generally speaking, those other frameworks will be limited by the very nature of the programming environment. Often, all they can do is SQL.

Delphi can do SQL because that's part of the TQuery component. And Delphi can do much, much more—some of which is useful for Web applications. When you look at the Delphi palettes and wonder how much of that terrific technology can be used for a Web application, you begin to realize that most of it doesn't apply, because it's there to create a user interface under Windows. Web applications have a minimal user interface; they are meant to run unattended on the Web server! So we have minimal use for edit boxes, radio boxes, gauges, and so on.

Nonetheless, the component-based nature of Delphi makes it ideal for taking core functionality and extending it to other areas. This section will look at four such areas: string grids, e-mail, outlines, and graphics.

String Grid

Sometimes using a database table to store tabular data is overkill. This is especially true when the data rarely changes and is read-only from the surfer's perspective.

Figure 37.7 shows an HTML table that was generated from a TStringList, rather than from a TTable. Each string represents a row in the grid. The individual strings are formatted to indicate which items are headers (and thus should be sent with `<TH>` instead of `<TD>`, and appear bold in the figure) versus which items are regular cells. If you look at the sample .TXT file that is loaded into the string list, you'll see that ~ identifies headers, and ¦ separates cells:

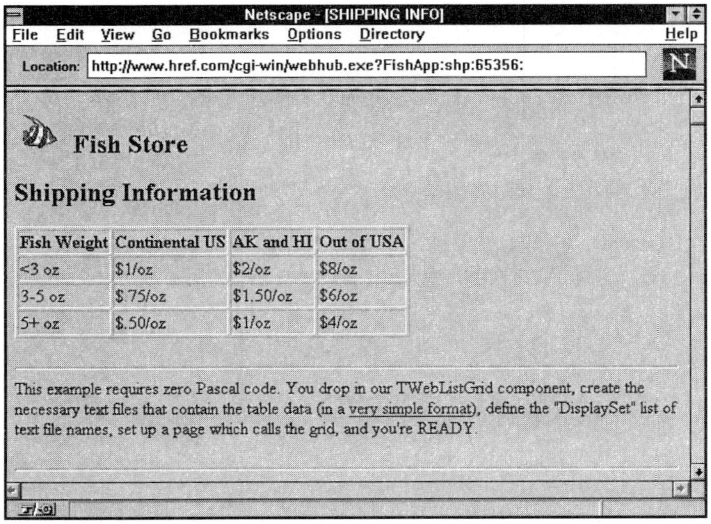
Netscape - [SHIPPING INFO]
File Edit View Go Bookmarks Options Directory Help
Location: http://www.href.com/cgi-win/webhub.exe?FishApp:shp:65356:
Fish Store
Shipping Information
Fish Weight | Continental US | AK and HI | Out of USA
<3 oz | $1/oz | $2/oz | $8/oz
3-5 oz | $.75/oz | $1.50/oz | $6/oz
5+ oz | $.50/oz | $1/oz | $4/oz
This example requires zero Pascal code. You drop in our TWebListGrid component, create the necessary text files that contain the table data (in a very simple format), define the "DisplaySet" list of text file names, set up a page which calls the grid, and you're READY.

FIGURE 37.7.
Behind the scenes, this table comes from a TStringList.

```
Fish Weight~Continental US~AK and HI~Out of USA
&lt3 oz¦$1/oz¦$2/oz¦$8/oz
3-5 oz¦$.75/oz¦$1.50/oz¦$6/oz
5+ oz¦$.50/oz¦$1/oz¦$4/oz
```

How do you code one of these? Well, it requires zero Pascal code! You do have to configure a few things:

- Drop a TWebListGrid component onto your form.
- Create the necessary text file that contains the table data (for example, fish weight info in preceding paragraph).
- Define the DisplaySet list of text filenames (this applies if you have multiple sets of data, for example, shipping by pound versus shipping by ounce).
- Set up a page that calls the grid (just invoke it by name using WebHub macro syntax—for example, %=WebListGrid1=%).

As with the TWebDataGrid, the DisplaySet controls are handled automatically by WebHub. You can turn them off and further customize the user interface if you want.

Electronic Mail

Thinking of the Internet brings electronic mail to mind pretty easily. Electronic communication underlies much of the technology and culture of the Net.

There are now several sets of components that will help you send e-mail from within a Delphi application. You can check out the components from StarTech at http://www.neosoft.com/~startech/delphi/delphi.htm, or Silverwave at http://rampages.onramp.net/~silver/, or our software at http://www.href.com/. There will probably be even more choices by the time you read this book.

Once you have your e-mail component(s) ready, sending electronic mail from a Web application is relatively easy. Here I'll show you how it can be done with our suite of three components: TWebSock, TWebMail, and TWebMailForm.

The context of this will be the extremely common goal of assembling all the inputs from an HTML form and e-mailing those values to the owner of the Web site. This is probably the most popular CGI program ever written, because it opens up so many possibilities for the Web site owner. You can use it for feedback pages, trivia contests, order entry, surveys, and more.

Figure 37.8 shows the Fish Store's sample feedback page.

The exact goal here is to e-mail the contents of the three fields: first name, e-mail address, and message, to info@href.com.

When Suzie clicks the [send] button, she "submits" her query to the Web server, which in turns passes the information on to the CGI program. If the CGI program was written with WebHub, all her data is automatically stored in the string list property, FormLiterals, of the TWebApp object.

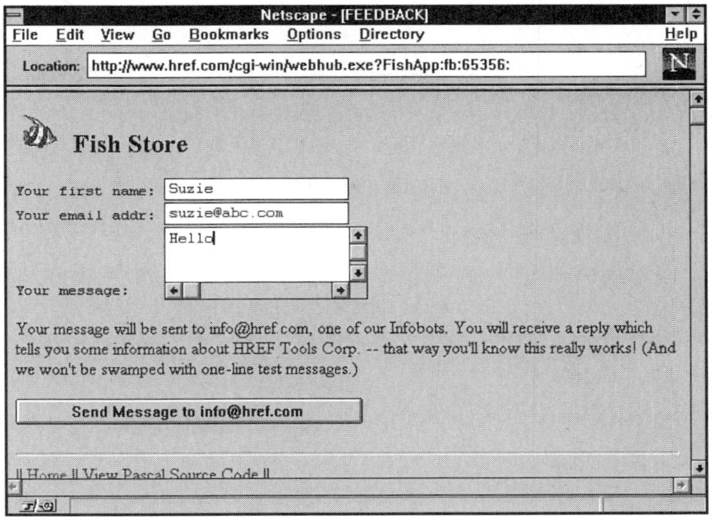

FIGURE 37.8.

Form-to-mail programs are extremely useful and common.

There are four general steps involved in setting this up within a WebHub application:

- Use four components.
- Initialize the unchanging e-mail settings.
- Define the variable e-mail setting (that is, the surfer's address, upon request).
- Execute the component so that mail is sent.

Drop in the Components

Drop in a TWebMailForm component, and as it updates, it will create the necessary linked TWebSockPanel and TWebMail components. Then right-click and update the TWebMail component, and it will take care of adding in the fourth required piece, TWebSock.

Define the Basic E-Mail Settings

There are many good ways of setting the e-mail component properties. This example does it in the FormCreate method using Pascal, so that you can see exactly what happens.

```
procedure TForm1.FormCreate(Sender: TObject);
begin
  { initialize the email components }
  { This could be done using the Object Inspector, but then you'd never
    see any Pascal! }
  { It would be best to load these settings from an .ini file, but this
    will do for now.}
  with WebMail1 do begin
    MailHost.Host:='mailhost.panix.com';
    MailHost.Port:=25;
```

```
    Sender.Name:='Someone at the Fish Store';
    MailTo.clear;
    MailTo.add( 'info@href.com' );
    Subject:='Test Message from The Fish Store';
  end;

  with WebMailForm1 do
    WebMailInclude:=[mfvFormLiterals];   {email all form input vars}
end;
```

Basically, the preceding code defines the mail server's hostname (which you find out from your Internet Service Provider), the port number (usually 25), plus the message sender, recipient, and subject. These values could also come from an .INI file, or from something in the runtime environment.

The TWebMailForm component has a property called WebMailInclude, which lets you toggle on various items for inclusion in the e-mail. Only one category is included here, the mfvLiterals. If this e-mail were going anywhere important, it would also be necessary to set the TextAreas property to FBAREA (the name of the HTML text area on the form).

All the setup is now complete. The next task is to customize the OnSection event handler for the fb (feedback) TWebPage object. This event handler is called whenever a new page section is sent to the surfer. Section 1 will be the page header, and this is a perfectly good time to finish setting up the message.

```
procedure TForm1.FishApp_FBPSection(Sender: TObject; Section: Integer;
  var Chunk, Options: OpenString);
var
  surferEMail:string[128];
begin
  if section>1 then exit;
  surferEMail:=WebAppFishApp.Literal['email'];
  if surferEMail='' then begin
    with WebAppFishApp.WebOutput do begin
      Send( 'You have to enter your email address!<p>' );
      Close;
    end;
    exit;
  end;
else begin
    Webmail1.Sender.EMail:=surferEMail;
  end;
end;
```

Most of the preceding code is just error-checking! The surfer's e-mail address is easily available as WebAppFishApp.Literal['email']. After determining that it is not blank, the following one line is all that's required to finish the e-mail settings:

```
Webmail1.Sender.EMail:=surferEMail;
```

The TWebMailForm component will do all the hard work of assembling the rest of the field inputs and creating the actual e-mail message.

You might be wondering what actually sends the message. The TWebMailForm component is invoked by name from the fbp (feedback post) chunk as follows:

```
%=pageBegin=%fbp=FeedBack Post%=endInfo=%
%=Webmailform1=%
<h2>Thanks!</h2>
Thank you for the feedback, %=Firstname=%.  Check your
email inbox — you should have a reply there soon.
```

TWebMailForm is an action component, and calling its name runs its Execute method.

If this were a survey page, or a mailing list signup page, rather than "feedback," it would be nice to additionally post the user's data to a table for later analysis. You can do this with standard Delphi techniques; insert a record into a TTable that you set up for this purpose.

Interactive Outlines

One of the issues that we all struggle with is information overload. This is true in the context of Web sites as well. Sites can have hundreds or thousands of pages, and surfers need some sort of navigation tool to help them both "see the forest for the trees" and "find that one special tree."

Various user interface solutions present themselves. Many sites use clickable image maps to let the surfer jump to a given area, but this interface breaks down as you increase the number of important sections. Other sites have a search engine, so that surfers can find items by keyword. That is very helpful, especially if the search is quick and reliable.

Another approach is to provide an outline of the site's pages. Delphi provides at least half the solution here with its TOutline component. This component knows how to manipulate strings, tracking indentation levels and the idea of expanded and collapsed nodes.

The TWebOutline component extends that functionality so that it's easy to generate HTML from the outline strings, and so that the outline is usable from the Web site. Figure 37.9 shows an example of this from the Table of Contents page at http://www.href.com/.

The icons are clickable, and they are set up to expand/collapse nodes so that the surfer can explore the outline interactively.

To implement this in your Web application, you need to load the strings into a Delphi TOutline component and drop in a TWebOutline component. Then invoke the TWebOutline component by name, from a chunk, exactly as you did with e-mail before.

The important point here is that a Delphi Web application can do much more than run SQL queries and generate grid responses! Furthermore, these features are easy to implement because Delphi gives you components and a terrific IDE. Compare this to programming in Perl, or C, or Visual Basic, and you'll see that there is really no comparison. Delphi is in its own league.

FIGURE 37.9.

*TWebOutline brings
Delphi's TOutline to
the Web.*

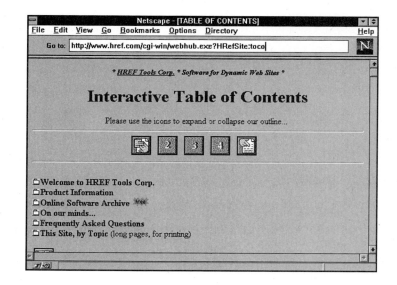

Custom Graphics

Graphics always make a good grand finale. There are so many fun features you can put in once you realize that you can build custom graphics on a Web site. This example is fairly simple:

- Accept some text
- Customize the text color and font and the frame
- Generate the bitmap
- Convert that to a .gif file
- Display the .gif for the surfer

Delphi takes care of the first three steps. The TWebPicture component includes .bmp to .gif conversion, and HTML makes it easy to display the .gif.

Figure 37.10 shows the HTML form that prompts the surfer for the parts of the graphic to be customized. (There is no other data input mechanism available.)

When the surfer clicks the [send] button, the request goes through the Web server and on to our Web application. We intervene in the onSection event for the page object:

```
procedure TForm1.FishApp_DRPSection(Sender: TObject; Section: Integer;
  var Chunk, Options: OpenString);
var
  aColor:String[128];
  shortFile:String[128];
begin
  if Section<>3 then exit;
  with WebLogo1, WebAppFishApp do begin
    Caption:=Literal['Caption'];
```

```
      Font.Name:=Literal['Font'];
      aColor:=Literal['BrushColor'];
      if aColor='White' then
        Font.Color:=clWhite
      else if aColor='Maroon' then
        Font.Color:=clMaroon
      else if aColor='Green' then
        Font.Color:=clGreen;
      aColor:=Literal['PenColor'];
      if aColor='Red' then
        Pen.Color:=clRed
      else if aColor='Teal' then
        Pen.Color:=clTeal
      else if aColor='Silver' then
        Pen.Color:=clSilver;
      FrameWidth:=StrToIntDef(Literal['FrameWidth'],5);
      shortFile:=getNextGifFilename;
      filename:=WebAppFishApp.pathForTempGifs + shortFile;
      Webpicture1.execute;
      WebOutput.Send( '<IMG SRC=%=ImageDir=%' + shortFile + '><P>' );
    end;

  end;
```

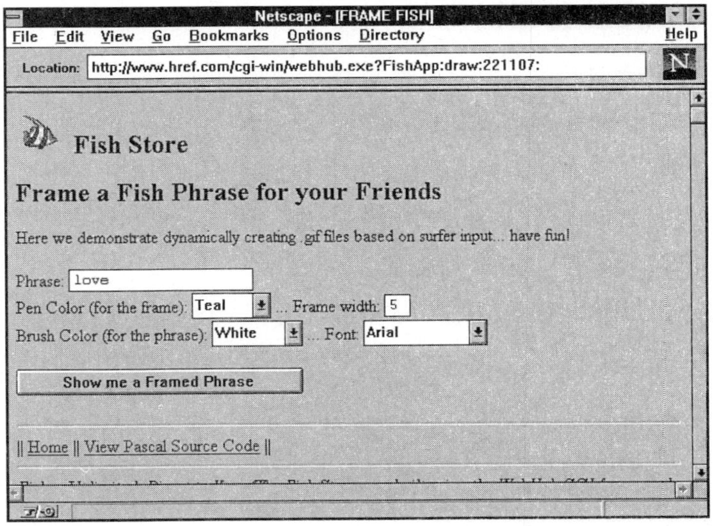

FIGURE 37.10.

*Delphi can create images
on the fly; why not display
them over the Web?*

Most of the preceding code just sets the indicated properties of the TWebPicture component. The .execute line makes the component create the bitmap and .gif file, and the .send line writes the necessary HTML out to the surfer. The result is shown in Figure 37.11.

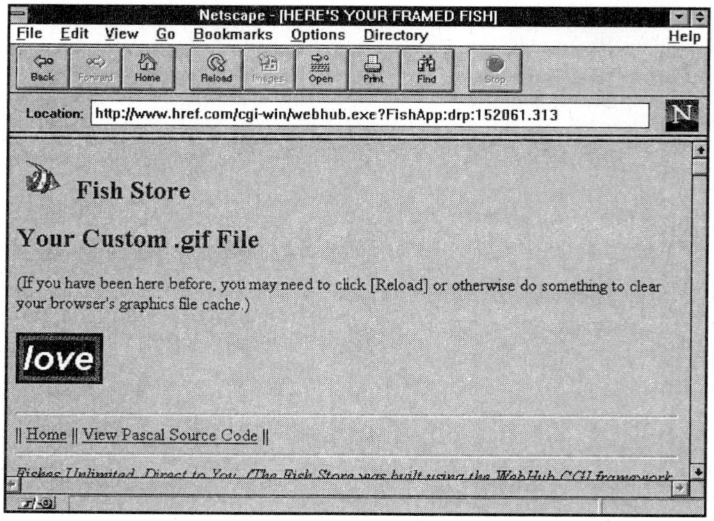

FIGURE 37.11.

This is the output from the TWebPicture component.

High-Traffic Issues

For sites that want to serve hundreds of surfers a minute rather than dozens per hour, additional care must be given to the overall Web application architecture. The WebHub framework enables you to dedicate separate .exes to pages that require special attention, and it lets you run those exe's on separate machines (connected by TCP/IP) for distributed processing.

Summary

It is my sincere hope that these two chapters have broken through some of the mystique that surrounds Web application building, transforming it into a domain that you feel comfortable exploring. I have had more fun programming Web applications with Delphi than using any other application framework to date.

See you on the Net....

INDEX

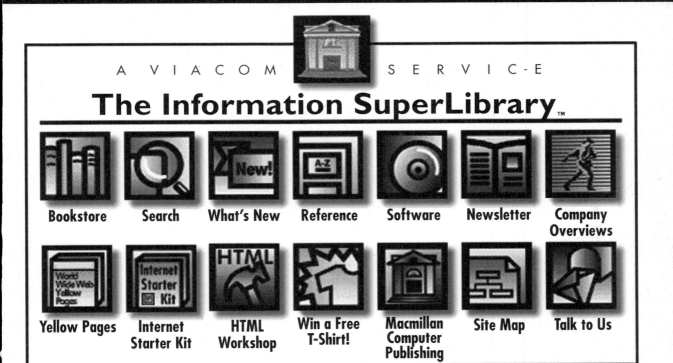

If you are a Developer looking for the best way to access Btrieve™ from Borland's Delphi™, look no further than...

TITAN
for Delphi

> "In thirty minutes time, (with no prior experience with the product) I was able to build a complete Btrieve file-browser! To reinforce the significance of this, it took me roughly two days of work to duplicate this effort with Visual Basic, calling WBTRCALL directly. I now have a fast, professional looking browser, and I didn't even have to miss my Star Trek re-run!"
> **Jim Barber,**
> **Btrieve Developer's Journal**
> **Autumn, 1995**

FEATURES & BENEFITS:

☒ Bypasses ODBC for high speed access to the Btrieve engine.

☒ Supports all Delphi data-aware components like DbGrid, DbEdit, etc.

☒ Supports "Live" display of Btrieve data at design time.

☒ Provides "low-level" access to Btrieve.

☒ Supports Delphi Master/Detail relations and Delphi Database experts.

☒ Supports Btrieve memo fields with Delphi DbMemo component.

☒ Works with 3rd Party components like InfoPower, Orpheus, & QuickReports.

☒ No need to distribute BDE runtime.

☒ No runtime license fees.

SCALABLE SQL SUPPORT:

☒ Supports Delphi TQuery component, allowing SQL statements.

☒ Mix & Match Delphi TTable & TQuery information.

☒ SQL Stored Procedures & Substitution variables fully supported.

PRICING:

☒ Titan Only:	$295.00
	- with Source:	$495.00
☒ Titan+SQL:	$395.00
	- with source:	$595.00
☒ Titan 32-Bit:	February

> "Titan has been instrumental in resolving reliability and performance concerns with Btrieve ODBC alternatives. Using Titan, we have been able to integrate our applications with other Btrieve applications without a single hitch."
> - Roy Kingsley, Lynk Soft-

TO ORDER TITAN CONTACT:

AmiSys, Inc.
1390 Willow Pass Rd
Suite 930
Concord, CA 94520

Phone: (510) 671-2103
Fax: (510) 671-2104
Cserve: 70441,3250
Email: amisys@amisysinc.com
Web: www.reggatta.com

© Copyright 1996 - Reggatta Systems.

ProtoView DataTable
The Fastest Grid Component Anywhere

DataTable is an industrial grid control. DataTable strength lies in its ability to handle massive amounts of data in an efficient manner. With a compact size, only 90K of memory, virtual memory, and advanced data cache scheme, DataTable is clearly designed for industrial, real-world applications.
Set colors, fonts, and picture formatting for cells. Has built-in column sorting. It's visual and easy. Supports the clipboard, hidden columns, row and column selection, and resizing. Cells may have drop-down combo boxes or check boxes. Full message and property set. MFC classes and message based programming interface. 16- and 32-bit DLL version, VBX and OCX available. Source code is available.
New features include bitmaps in cells, horizontal and vertical splitter window, numeric column totaling, column searching, cell overwriting, improved keyboard handling, auto row insert, region selection, European formatting for date, time, and numbers, and 3D effects. Windows 95-compatible look.

ProtoView Interactive Diagramming Object
The Visual Way to Add Diagramming To Your Application

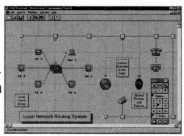

The Interactive Diagramming Object gives you advanced capabilities for creating easy-to-read diagrams. Choose from a wide assortment of shapes, pictures, lines, and arrows to design pleasing presentation visuals, outlines, process flows, hierarchy charts, floor plans, and much more.
With it you can: load and save diagrams, set colors, fonts and 3D effects, create custom design palettes, and respond to notifications and events for complete program control. It supports diagrams of any size with scrolling, zooming, printing, and the clipboard. Simply drop the IDO on a form and it's ready to go. It's easy to use and easy to program. Whether you want to explain a process or present a plan, the IDO helps you effectively communicate ideas and create applications that are more powerful, yet easier to use. Available as OCX or DLL. Source code is available.

ProtoView Interface Component Set
Polished User Interface Components

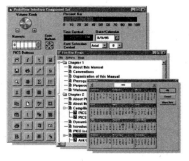

PICS offers sophisticated controls for calendar, date, time, and numeric input using your choice of odometer, LED readout, and normal display. Add to these a slick looking percent/gauge control, multi-directional spin button, a stereo volume control, and fancy icon buttons. You also get a font and point size selection control for your toolbars or dialogs. Also included are 21 PICS button controls with bitmap images.
You also get a powerful hierarchical list box that includes: setting unlimited number of bitmaps per list, lines between bitmaps and names, over 100 functions for complete control of subtrees, selection, display, search and item manipulation.
Complete on-line help, MFC classes, and message based programming interface. 16- and 32-bit DLL, VBX, and OCX available. Source code is available. Windows 95 compatible look. With PICS you can create the sharpest looking applications in no time at all.

ProtoView Visual Help Builder
The Fastest Way To Build Help Systems!

The ProtoView Visual Help Builder is the fastest way to author help systems. Developers can document an application, whether they have that application's "source" programs or not. With a few clicks of the mouse, ProtoView Visual Help Builder captures every dialog box, menu, and control field of an application and creates a full blown help system. Only ProtoView Visual Help Builder brings you these innovative features. Add multimedia support for video, sound, and high-res graphics. It provides the advanced features you need to create help systems, including macros, secondary windows, multiple hotspot graphics, help topics, hypertext links, jumps, browse sequences, and more.
Integrates into version control software. Includes help compiler. Requires Microsoft Word 2.0/6.0/7.0.

PROTOVIEW ®
The Visual Development Edge™

Add to Your Sams Library Today with the Best Books for Programming, Operating Systems, and New Technologies

The easiest way to order is to pick up the phone and call

1-800-428-5331

between 9:00 a.m. and 5:00 p.m. EST.
For faster service please have your credit card available.

ISBN	Quantity	Description of Item	Unit Cost	Total Cost
0-672-30704-9		Delphi Developer's Guide (book/CD-ROM)	$49.99	
0-672-30474-0		Windows 95 Unleashed (book/CD-ROM)	$39.99	
0-672-30602-6		Programming Windows 95 Unleashed (book/CD-ROM)	$49.99	
0-672-30745-6		HTML & CGI Unleashed (book/CD-ROM)	$49.99	
0-672-30837-1		Visual Basic 4 Unleashed (book/CD-ROM)	$45.00	
0-672-30851-7		Teach Yourself Database Programming with Delphi in 21 Days (book/CD-ROM)	$39.99	
0-672-30531-3		Teach Yourself Windows 95 Programming in 21 Days, Second Edition	$35.00	
0-672-30568-2		Teach Yourself OLE Programming in 21 Days (book/CD-ROM)	$39.99	
0-672-30855-X		Teach Yourself SQL in 14 Days	$29.99	
0-672-30620-4		Teach Yourself Visual Basic 4 in 21 Days, Third Edition	$35.00	
0-672-30736-7		Teach Yourself C in 21 Days, Premier Edition	$35.00	
0-672-30717-0		Tricks of the Doom-Programming Gurus (book/CD-ROM)	$39.99	
❏ 3 ½" Disk		Shipping and Handling: See information below.		
❏ 5 ¼" Disk		TOTAL		

Shipping and Handling: $4.00 for the first book, and $1.75 for each additional book. Floppy disk: add $1.75 for shipping and handling. If you need to have it NOW, we can ship product to you in 24 hours for an additional charge of approximately $18.00, and you will receive your item overnight or in two days. Overseas shipping and handling adds $2.00 per book and $8.00 for up to three disks. Prices subject to change. Call for availability and pricing information on latest editions.

201 W. 103rd Street, Indianapolis, Indiana 46290

1-800-428-5331 — Orders   1-800-835-3202 — FAX   1-800-858-7674 — Customer Service

Book ISBN 1-672-30858-4

Installing the
CD-ROM

The companion CD-ROM contains source code developed by the author, plus an assortment of third-party tools and product demos. The disc is designed to be explored using a browser program. Using Sams' Guide to the CD-ROM browser, you can view information concerning products and companies, and install programs with a single click of the mouse.

Windows 3.1 NT Installation Instructions

1. Insert the CD-ROM disc into your CD-ROM drive.

2. From File Manager or Program Manager, choose Run from the File menu.

3. Type `<drive>\setup` and press Enter, where `<drive>` corresponds to the drive letter of your CD-ROM. For example, if your CD-ROM is drive D:, type `D:\setup` and press Enter.

4. The installation creates a Program Manager group named *Delphi 2 Unleashed*. To browse the CD-ROM, double-click the Guide to the CD-ROM icon inside this Program Manager group.

Windows 95 Installation Instructions

1. Insert the CD-ROM disc into your CD-ROM drive. If the AutoPlay feature of your Windows 95 system is enabled, the Setup program will start automatically.

2. If the Setup program does not start automatically, double-click the My Computer icon.

3. Double-click the icon representing your CD-ROM drive.

4. Double-click the icon titled Setup.exe to run the installation program. Follow the onscreen instructions that appear. When Setup ends, the Guide to the CD-ROM program starts up, so that you can begin browsing immediately.

Following installation, you can restart the Guide to the CD-ROM program by pressing the Start button, and then selecting Programs, Delphi 2 Unleashed and Guide to the CD-ROM.

> **NOTE**
>
> The Guide to the CD-ROM program requires at least 256 colors. For best results, set your monitor to display between 256 and 64,000 colors. A screen resolution of 640×480 pixels is also recommended. If necessary, adjust your monitor settings before using the CD-ROM.